The Daily Prayer of the Church

edited by
Philip H. Pfatteicher

Lutheran University Press, Minneapolis, Minnesota
American Lutheran Publicity Bureau, Delhi, New York

Daily Prayer of the Church
Philip H. Pfatteicher, Editor

Library of Congress Cataloging-in-Publication Data

The daily prayer of the church / edited by Philip H. Pfatteicher.
p. cm.
Includes indexes.
ISBN 1-932688-10-2 (alk. paper)
1. Prayers. 2. Church year—Prayer-books and devotions—English. 3. Liturgies. I. Pfatteicher, Philip H.
BV245.D26 2005
264'.041015—dc22
2005045088

Lutheran University Press, PO Box 390759, Minneapolis, MN 55439
American Lutheran Publicity Bureau, PO Box 327, Delhi, New York 13753-0327

Manufactured in the United States of America

Contents

Sources

AC	*Ancient Collects and Other Prayers* tr. William Bright 5th ed. Oxford and London: James Parker, 1875.
APP	*A Procession of Passion Prayers* ed. Eric Milner-White London: SPCK, 1956.
Berg.	Bergamo sacramentary (Italy, ninth century)
BCP	The American *Book of Common Prayer* (1979)
BCPp	The English *Proposed Book of Common Prayer* (1928)
C&P	*Collects and Prayers for Use in Church* authorized by the United Lutheran Church in America. Philadelphia: Board of Publication of the United Lutheran Church in America, 1935.
CB	*The Church Book for the Use of Evangelical Lutheran Congregations* by Authority of the General Council of the Evangelical Lutheran Church in America. Philadelphia: Lutheran Book Store, 1868 ff.
CBB	*A Cambridge Bede Book* ed. Eric Milner-White. London, 1936.
Chain	*A Chain of Prayer across the Ages* ed. Selina Fitzherbert Fox. 5th ed. New York: E.P. Dutton, 1928.
COB	*Cuddesdon Office Book.* New York: Oxford University Press, 1961 [1940].
COO	*Cambridge Offices and Orisons* ed. Eric Milner-White and B.T.D. Smith. London: Mowbray, 1921.
CSB	*The Common Service Book of the Lutheran Church* Authorized by the United Lutheran Church in America. Philadelphia: Board of Publication of the United Lutheran Church in America, 1917, 1918. Text ed. 1919.
CSI	Church of South India, *Book of Common Worship*. London: Oxford University Press, 1963.

DFP — William Walsham How, *Daily Family Prayer* 24th ed. London: Wells, Gardner, Darton and Co. Ltd., 1907.

DO — *The Hours of the Divine Office in English and Latin.* 3 vols. Collegeville, MN: Liturgical Press, 1963.

DP — *Daily Prayer* ed. Eric Milner-White and George Wallace Briggs. London: Oxford University Press, Humphrey Milford, 1941.

DvD — The Revd Canon Dirk van Dissel

EA — *Euchologium Anglicanum. Prayers for Christian Faith and Practice*. ed. John E.W. Wallace and Leslie M. Stylar. London: SPCK, 1963.

EO — *The English Office Book* rev. ed. London: Church Literature Association, 1956.

FSB — *Family Service Book*, Philadelphia: Board of Publication of the United Lutheran Church in America, 1928.

Gebete — K.B. Ritter. *Gebete für das Jahr der Kirche* 2nd ed. Kassel, 1948.

Gel. — The Gelasian Sacramentary (Rome, mid-eighth century manuscript). L.C. Mohlberg ed. *Liber Sacramentorum Romanae Aeclesiae Ordinis Anni Circuli*. Rome: Herder, 1968.

Greg. — The Gregorian Sacramentary (Rome, late eighth century manuscript). J. Deschusses ed. *Le Sacramentaire Grégorien*. Fribourg, 1971.

HAM — *Hymns Ancient and Modern* (Anglican, 1861, 1867, rev. ed. 1904).

H33 — *The Hymnal as Authorized and Approved for Use by the General Convention of the Protestant Episcopal Church... MCMXVI.* New York: Church Pension Fund, 1933.

H40 — *The Hymnal of the Protestant Episcopal Church in the*

	United States of America 1940. New York: Church Pension Fund, 1940, 1943, 1961.
H82	*The Hymnal 1982* according to the Use of the Episcopal Church. New York: Church Hymnal Corporation, 1985.
ICEL	The International Commission on English in the Liturgy (Roman Catholic)
JWP	The Revd. Canon Joseph W. Poole
Leo.	The Leonine or Verona sacramentary (Rome, early seventh century). L.C. Mohlberg ed. *Sacramentum Veronese* rev. ed. Rome: Herder, 1966.
LBW	*The Lutheran Book of Worship*. Minneapolis: Augsburg and Philadelphia: Board of Publication of the Lutheran Church in America, 1978.
LDO	*The Daily Office* ed. Herbert F. Lindemann. St. Louis: Concordia, 1965.
LFF	*Lesser Feasts and Fasts 2003*. New York: Church Publishing Inc., 2003.
LH	*The Liturgy of the Hours* 4 vols. New York: Catholic Book Publishing Co., 1975-76.
LHd	Preliminary draft of the psalm prayers by ICEL for LH.
LSJC	The Liturgy of St. John Chrysostom, Pascha Kontakion
Lüneburg	The Lüneburg Church Order, 1564. Emil Sehling ed. *Die evangelische Kirchenordnungen des XVI Jahrhunderts*. vols 1-4 Leipzig:Reisland, 1902-1913; vols VI Tubingen: Mohr, 1955--.
Mat. Rit.	*Materia Ritualis* ed. William Reed Huntington. 1882.
Moz.	Mozarabic sacramentary (Spain, ca. 400). M. Ferotin, *Le Liber Mozarabicus Sacramentorum et les manuscrits Mozarabes*. Paris, 1912.
MG	*Missale Gothicum* (Gaul [France], ca. 700) ed. L.C. Mohlberg. Rome: Herder, 1961.

MGV	*Missale Gothicum vetus* ed. L.C. Mohlberg. Rome: Herder, 1958.
MIP	Richard Meux Benson, *The Manual of Intercessory Prayer*. London, 1914.
MPB	*The Minister's Prayer Book* ed. John W. Doberstein, rev. Philip H. Pfatteicher. Philadelphia: Fortress, 1986.
MPES	*Morning Praise and Evensong* ed. W.G. Storey, F.C. Quinn, D.F. Wright. Notre Dame, Indiana: Fides, 1973.
MR	*Missale Romanum* (Roman Catholic, 1570)
MSO	*Memorials upon Several Occasions* [later published as *After the Third Collect*] ed. Eric Milner-White. 3rd ed. London: Mowbray, 1952.
NEM	*New Every Morning*. London: BBC, 1937.
OAH	*Oxford American Hymnal* for Schools and Colleges ed. Carl F. Pfatteicher. New York: Oxford, 1930.
OPR	Eric Milner-White, *The Occasional Prayers in the 1928 Book Reconsidered*. London, 1930.
PBO	*The Prayer Book Office* ed. Howard Galley. New York: Seabury, 1980.
PHP	Philip H. Pfatteicher
Plummer	*Devotions from Ancient and Medieval Sources (Western)* tr. Charles Plummer. Oxford: Blackwell, 1916.
PP	*Parish Prayers* ed. Frank Colquhoun. London: Hodder and Stoughton, 1967.
PPB	*The Priest's Prayer Book* ed. Richard F. Littledale and J. Edward Vaux (Anglican, 7th ed. 1890).
RM	Roman Missal (Roman Catholic, 1952)
RS	*The Roman Sacramentary* (Roman Catholic, 1970)
Sarum	The Sarum rite (England, eleventh century). *The Sarum Missal in English* tr. Frederick E. Warren 2 vols. London: Moring, 1911.

Saxe-Coburg	The Saxe-Coburg Church Order, 1626.
Saxony	The Saxony (Duke Henry) Church Order, 1539.
SBH	*The Service Book and Hymnal*. Philadelphia: Board of Publication, Lutheran Church in America, 1958. Text ed. 1967.
Sw	The Church of Sweden, *Evangeliebok* (Lutheran, 1639).
TLH	*The Lutheran Hymnal*. St. Louis: Concordia, 1941.
WS	*Worship Supplement*. St. Louis: Concordia, 1969.
WTT	W.E. Scudamore, *Words To Take With Us*. 1850.

Acknowledgements

With gratitude I acknowledge the support and encouragement of many people who kept after me until at long last this book saw the light of day. Through the years a number of people have assisted with establishing the format and putting this complex and cumbersome manuscript in electronic form, the first of whom was Dorothy Zelenko, who did the initial work, completing more than half the book. I am grateful also to Fred Schumacher and the American Lutheran Publicity Bureau for their continuing interest in and support of the project, and to Leonard Flachman for agreeing to publish the book. Beyond these, I am indebted to a host of people, whom no one can number, living and dead, who by their writing, their lives, and their examples have taught me how to pray.

Prayers marked MPB are reprinted from *Minister's Prayer Book* by John W. Doberstein copyright © 1986 Fortress Press. Used by permission of Augsburg Fortress.

The translation of the Psalms and prayers marked [BCP] are from the 1979 American *Book of Common Prayer.*

The Collects for weekdays in Lent and Easter identified [LFF] are reprinted from *Lesser Feasts and Fasts 2003* copyright © 2003 The Church Pension Fund. All rights reserved. Used by permission of Church Publishing, Incorporated, New York, NY.

The text translations of "Alone thou goest forth, O Lord" (hymn 164), "Kind Maker of the world, O hear" (hymn 152), "O heavenly Word, eternal Light" (hymn 63, 64), "Sing, my tongue, the glorious battle" (hymn 165, 166), "The royal banners forward go" (hymn 162), are reprinted from the *Hymnal* 1982, copyright © 1985, The Church Pension Fund. Used by permission of Church Publishing, Incorporated, New York, NY.

The text translation of "O Savior, rend the heavens wide" from *Worship Supplement*, copyright © 1969 Concordia Publishing House. Used with permission. All rights reserved.

Scripture quotations (except from the Psalms) are from the New Revised Standard Version of the Bible copyright © 1989 by the Division of Christian Education of the National Council of the Churches of Christ in the U.S.A. Used by permission. All rights reserved.

The tune *Mighty Savior* by David Hurd, copyright © 1985 by G.I.A. Publications, Inc. All rights reserved. www.giamusic.com 800.442.1358

"A Christmas Hymn" ["A Stable lamp is lighted"] from *Advice to a Prophet and Other Poems*, copyright © 1961 and renewed 1989 by Richard Wilbur, is reprinted by permission of Harcourt Brace & Company.

The tune *Stable Lamp*, copyright © by Ana Hernandez, is used by permission of the composer.

The tune for the resurrection gospels in the Paschal Blessing for Advent, Christmas-Epiphany, Lent, Holy Week, and Easter, composed for this book and copyright © by Richard Hillert, are used by permission of the composer.

The tune *Abbott's Leigh* by Cyril V. Taylor, copyright © 1942 and renewed 1970 by Hope Publishing Co., Carol Stream, IL 60188. All rights reserved. Used by permission. The texts "For the fruit of all creation" by Fred Pratt Green, copyright © 1970 by Hope Publishing Company, and "God, who stretched the spangled heavens" by Catherine Cameron, copyright © 1967 by Hope Publishing Co. all rights reserved. Used by permission.

Antiphons, responsories, and prayers identified [LH] are from the English translation of *The Liturgy of the Hours* copyright © 1974, International Committee on English in the Liturgy, Inc. (ICEL). All rights reserved.

The text "Praise God for John, evangelist" from *Sing Glorias for all His Saints*, copyright © 1982 by F. Samuel Janzow, is used by the permission of the author.

The text translations "Christ, mighty Savior, Light of all creation" "Lord Jesus, Sun of Righteousness," "O blest Creator, source of light," copyright © 1982 by Anne LeCroy, are used by the permission of the author.

The text translation of "Oh, sing, my soul, your maker's praise" by Ernest E. Ryden and Tiovo Harjunpaa, alt. from *Laudamus*, copyright © 1970 by the Lutheran World Federation is used by permission of the LWF.

The text "Praise and thanksgiving" by Albert F. Bayly (1901-1984), copyright © Oxford University Press, is used by permission. All rights reserved. Photocopying this copyright material is ILLEGAL. The text "Father eternal, ruler of creation" by Laurence Housman (1865-1959), copyright © Oxford University Press, is used by

 The text translation of "The glory of these forty days" by Maurice F. Bell (1862-1947), copyright © Oxford University Press, is used by permission. The tune [illegible] arranged by Ralph Vaughan Williams (1872-1958) and the tune *Cornhill* by Harold Darke (1886-1976), copyright © Oxford University Press, are used by permission.

The translation and the tune of the thanksgiving for light from the *Apostolic Constitutions* and from the *Apostolic Tradition* from MORNING PRAISE AND EVENSONG are used by permission of Frank C. Quinn, O.P.

The text translation of "O Lord of light, who made the stars" by Melvin Farrell copyright © 1961 World Library Publications, 3708 River Road, Suite 400, Franklin Park, IL 60131-2158. www.wlpmusic.com. Used by permission.

The hymn text "Lord Christ, when first thou cam'st to earth" by Walter R. Bowie copyright © 1955 by Abingdon Press (Administered by The Copyright Company Nashville, TN). Used by permission.

The hymn text "Let all things now living" by Katherine K. Davis copyright © 1939, 1966, E. C. Schirmer Music Company, a division of ECS Publishing, Boston, MA. Used by permission.

The tune *Langham* by Geoffrey Shaw used by permission of the United Nations Association UK.

Introduction

The Daily Prayer of the Church is, as Martin Hauser observes, the treasure Christians took with them when they left the synagogue long ago. It is prayer designed for all the people of God, both clergy and laity, so that together they can join the perpetual praise of the choirs of heaven. This book is an expanded and enriched organization of the daily prayer offices in the *Lutheran Book of Worship*, which make use of modern understandings of daily prayer as it is received and practiced in the churches of Christendom today. The Roman Catholic Church has provided the *Liturgy of the Hours* (1975-1976) in four volumes; Howard Galley has edited *The Prayer Book Office* (1980) to enrich the offices in the *Book of Common Prayer* of the Episcopal Church. For the Lutheran Church in North America the Ministers Edition of the *Lutheran Book of Worship* (1978), like its predecessors the *Common Service Book* (1918) and the *Service Book and Hymnal* (1958), provides the necessary materials for praying Morning and Evening Prayer daily: the ordinary (basic text) of the services, invitatories for use with the Venite in Morning Prayer, versicles for use with the Service of Light in Evening Prayer, alternate thanksgivings for light, psalm antiphons, a table of psalms for daily use, lectionary citations for a two-year cycle of readings, an alphabetical list of office hymns, antiphons for use with Benedictus and Magnificat. The use of these riches, however, requires one to be not only knowledgeable, creative, and resourceful, but also to be not distracted from devotion by turning back and forth through many pages in the course of praying Morning or Evening Prayer. For those who want to pray in the ancient manner with a minimum of distraction, this book provides the materials necessary for the celebration of Morning and Evening Prayer arranged, it is hoped, in a clear and usable format to facilitate and encourage deepening daily devotion.

Using This Book

1. To allow for seasonal variation and to facilitate use, the ORDINARY (basic text) for each season of the church year is printed with the seasonal elements in place. The PROPER (variable psalms, antiphons, hymns, lessons) for the days of the week during that season follow.

2. Evening Prayer is given first to underscore the Christian continuity with Judaism which understands that the day both ends and begins with sundown, following the ancient account of creation in the first chapter of Genesis, "The evening and the morning were the first day…" Profound insight is preserved in that practice: we move from darkness to light, from closure to renewal, from death to life. Each day is a new creation as light drives out the darkness; the rising of the sun (Son) proclaims daily the resurrection which was bought by enduring the darkness. The Easter Vigil, the central liturgy of Christianity, is reflected, echoed, and recalled each day; and, conversely, the Great Vigil is an elaboration of what is experienced and celebrated each day of the year.

3. A full form of the office is provided for each day of the week. For many users of the office this may be too much; if so, the office may be shortened as desired by deleting the introductory portion, a psalm, the hymn. The basic core of each hour, however, should always be maintained: a psalm, a reading, the Gospel canticle, and the Lord's Prayer.

4. The order of the PSALMS is that of the *Lutheran Book of Worship*, slightly altered on the basis of the original plan submitted to the Liturgical Text Committee of the Inter-Lutheran Commission on Worship, in order to avoid repetition, to use a wider selection of psalms, and to avoid the use of Hallelujah during Lent. The psalms are printed so as to appear on the page like the poetry they are. Each psalm is identified by its Latin *incipit*, sometimes helpful in comparing various Catholic versions of the psalter and breviary. Moreover, each psalm is provided with a title that summarizes its significance to assist in praying

it. These titles are drawn from a variety of Bibles and breviaries. The psalms are pointed with bold-face syllables to encourage their being sung to the Psalm Tones (pp. 1590-1591).

The ANTIPHONS are usually taken from the psalms themselves and are often echoed in the psalm prayer; generally the antiphons are those used in the *Liturgy of the Hours* and in *The Prayer Book Office* so that there will be agreement in Roman Catholic, Episcopal, and Lutheran use. The antiphons are pointed so that they may be sung to the same tone as the psalm. An alternative practice, especially with brief antiphons, is the use of the antiphon melody for the particular psalm tone chosen.

The festival use of the office in the *Lutheran Book of Worship* includes an Old Testament canticle as a third psalm in Morning Prayer and a New Testament Canticle at Evening Prayer. In this book these additional elements are included in the Sunday office to emphasize the centrality of Sunday as the weekly commemoration of the resurrection; they are also included in the weekday office of Easter in keeping with the festive character of the great Fifty Days. The selection of canticles in large measure relies on that made in the *Liturgy of the Hours* and the plan originally submitted to the Liturgical Text Committee. Appropriate prayers are provided for each canticle.

5. An extra-biblical song, the HYMN, concludes the portion of poetic praise. Since the ninth or tenth century, the office hymns at Vespers have been connected with the days of creation, which began in the evening ("The evening and the morning were the first day"). Saturday evening (the beginning of the first day of the week) dealt with the creation of light; Sunday evening with the creation of the firmament or sky; Monday evening with the separation of earth from the seas and the creation of vegetation; Tuesday evening with the creation of sun, moon, and stars; Wednesday evening with the creation of fish and birds; Thursday evening with the creation of animals and humans; and Friday evening marked the beginning of the Sabbath rest. The office hymns in this book for the four-week "general" time after the Epiphany and after Pentecost follow that pattern. Some of the hymns are ancient office hymns, but many are more modern—and, to many, more familiar—compositions, but generally

following the pattern of the days of creation.

The hymns at Morning Prayer range from traditional office hymns for Matins and Lauds to more modern compositions appropriate to the beginning of the day. When the office is prayed privately, the hymn may be read as devotional poetry. Such use of hymn texts has a long history especially in Lutheran devotion.

6. The daily LECTIONARY in the *Book of Common Prayer* and the *Lutheran Book of Worship* provides three lessons for each day of the year. Matins has traditionally been the hour for more extended Scripture readings. This book honors that tradition by appointing two readings in the morning and one in the evening.

The rubrics in the *Book of Common Prayer* and in the Ministers Edition of the *Lutheran Book of Worship* allow other practices. If two readings are desired for both morning and evening, the Old Testament reading for the alternate year may be used. When more than one reading is used, the first should be from the Old Testament to counteract the tendency in some parts of the church to neglect the original covenant. (Ministers Edition, p. 15 #5; p. 16 #8; *Book of Common Prayer*, p. 934.)

The daily lectionary is arranged in a two-year system. YEAR ONE is used beginning on the First Sunday in Advent preceding odd-numbered years, and YEAR TWO is used beginning on the First Sunday in Advent preceding even-numbered years (Ministers Edition, p. 18); BCP p. 934.

The lessons are (unfortunately) not printed out in full in this book for to do so would require a very large work of several volumes. To avoid making the book of impossible size, and following the practice of certain German devotional books and Herbert Lindemann's *The Daily Office* (1965), a one or two verse portion of each lesson is provided. This brief lesson is not intended to replace the reading of the whole lesson, but it may be taken as a key for devotional meditation throughout the day. To read the lessons, therefore, one needs to have a Bible (with the Apocrypha) at hand. The virtue of this is that one is free to use any translation one chooses, indeed to move from translation to translation as the seasons and years go by.

The basic Bible translation for the antiphons, readings, and responsories of this book is the New Revised Standard Version.

7. The Roman Catholic and Lutheran tradition encourages the use of a RESPONSORY after each reading. This office book therefore gives such responsories, taken mostly from the *Liturgy of the Hours*. The classic responsory is a device that combines scriptural verses in such a way that scripture is made to comment on itself. The responsories in this book are at least based on scripture, sometimes being a quotation, sometimes an adaptation, sometimes a free composition—a technique familiar to those who know the work of Bach and Schütz.

Two responsories are provided in Morning Prayer for each day. One, whichever is more appropriate, may be used after the first lesson and the other after the second lesson, or only one may be used, whichever is more suitable, after the second reading. One may be used in Evening Prayer, although the responsory is not traditionally part of Vespers.

The responsories are pointed so that they may be sung to a psalm tone. They may be read responsively by a single voice, preferably not the same person as the reader of the lesson, with the congregation responding with the repeated refrain verse.

The final responsory is traditionally concluded with the ancient form of the Gloria Patri—"Glory to the Father, and to the Son, and to the Holy Spirit"—and the refrain verse is repeated. Thus the responsory after the second reading at Morning Prayer on the First Sunday in Advent (p.110) would take this form:

Wash yourselves; make yourselves clean; remove the
evil of your doings from before my eyes.*
Though your sins are like scarlet,
they shall be like snow.
Cease to do evil, learn to do good; seek justice.*
Though your sins are like scarlet,
they shall be like snow.
Glory to the Father, and to the Son, and to the
Holy Spirit.*
Though your sins are like scarlet,
they shall be like snow.

When it is necessary to divide the Gloria Patri, as for use with a double tone, it is done this way:

Glory to the Father, and to the Son, *
and to the Holy Spirit.
Though your sins are like scarlet,*
they shall be like snow.

That pattern may be followed throughout the office. It is given in place in Morning Prayer for the Fifty Days of Easter.

8. The form of PRAYER at the conclusion of each hour varies from season to season to provide variety and to make use of the riches of the Christian tradition. When one prays the office alone, litanies do not work well and may be replaced with the three-fold Kyrie (Lord, have mercy. Christ, have mercy. Lord, have mercy) and a series of collects or extempore prayer, concluded with the prayer provided and the Our Father.

The salutation and response "The Lord be with you. *And also with you.*" is traditionally not said when one prays the office alone but is replaced with "Lord, hear my prayer. And let my cry come before you". But, as Peter Damian, reflecting Pauline doctrine, taught, if we who are many are one in Christ, each of us possesses the whole. Indeed, the various members of the church of Christ being so united as to form a single body, the entire church may be regarded as mystically present in each individual. It is a useful reminder that no one, not even a hermit, prays alone.

A number of considerations have encouraged the rearrangement or replacement in this volume of many of the prayers (collects) of the day to bring the Lutheran series more in line with the Roman and Episcopal series and reestablish an ecumenical bond of common prayer that had been maintained through the Reformation to the later twentieth century.

A regular plan for prayers and intercessions is desirable. Such a plan might be:

Sunday (the Resurrection): the church
its unity, renewal, constant return to the source of its life, attention to scripture, the health of one's own parish.

Monday (creation and providence): the world
the leaders of the nations; justice, reconciliation, and peace; the isolated, the uncared-for, the forgotten; the unemployed; the responsible use of the earth and its resources.

Tuesday (the Holy Spirit): all learners
young people, inquirers, catechumens, all the people of God; deepened devotion and commitment; greater knowledge and love of God.

Wednesday (the Holy Trinity): missions
missions at home and abroad; missionaries and their families, the conversion of sinners, those outside the church; a more convincing witness by each member of the church.

Thursday (the Holy Communion): clergy and people
deeper commitment to the baptismal covenant; greater love for Christ in the Holy Communion; better prepared communions; those who minister at the font and altar, bishops and pastors.

Friday (redemption): family and friends
those we love, family and friends; our enemies.

Saturday (death and judgment): the sick and the aged
the sick and the sorrowful, the dying, those who have no one to pray for them; commemoration of the departed.

The collection of Prayers and Intercessions pp. 1539-1555 follows this pattern. During General Time two prayers may be used each day of the four-week cycle, indicated by the small Roman numerals.

9. For those times and occasions when a fuller cycle of prayer is desired, a simple form of PRAYER FOR MID-MORNING and another for NOON AND MID-AFTERNOON are provided.

10. Prayer at the Close of the Day, COMPLINE, is a fixed office, which does not employ seasonal variations. To prevent excessive repetition by those who pray this office frequently, daily variation in the psalms and brief lessons is provided on the basis of the Roman Catholic and Episcopal forms.

11. The CALENDAR in this book is a conflation of the calendar in the *Lutheran Book of Worship* and in *Lesser Feasts and Fasts* of the Episcopal Church, supplemented with certain other days suggested by the editor of this prayer book. ALL CAPITAL LETTERS indicate what are called Solemnities in the Roman Catholic Calendar, Principal Feasts in the *Book of Common Prayer*, and Greater Festivals in the *Lutheran Book of Worship*. SMALLER CAPITALS indicate what are classified as Feasts in the Roman Catholic Calendar, Holy Days in the *Book of Common Prayer* and Lesser Festivals in the *Lutheran Book of Worship*. Roman type indicates what are classified as Memorials in the Roman Catholic Calendar, Days of Optional Observance in the *Book of Common Prayer*, and Commemorations in the *Lutheran Book of Worship*. *Italic type* indicates what are called on the Roman Catholic Calendar Memorials. [*Italic type within square brackets*] indicates days of primarily denominational interest.

In praying the office, the daily cycle is primary; the seasonal theme is secondary. Saints' days and holy days are commemorated by use of the appropriate collect.

12. Gestures reinforce devotion by making dramatic explication of what is being said or sung. At the opening verse of Morning Prayer, "O Lord, open my lips," a cross is traditionally made over the mouth with the right thumb to enact what is being asked and to consecreate what is to be said to the glory of God. At the Name of the Holy Trinity in the Gloria Patri, "Glory to the Father, and to the Son, and to the Holy Spirit," and in doxologies at the conclusion of hymns, the head is bowed in reverence to the Triune God. At the beginning of the Gospel Canticles,

Benedictus in Morning Prayer, Magnificat in Evening Prayer, and Nunc Dimittis in Compline, the sign of the cross is made as an enacted prayer and a gesture of praise. At blessings and benedictions the sign of the cross is made as an affirmation of the reality of God's blessing. The ✠ in the text indicates where making the cross is appropriate.

Advent

The office for Advent begins with First Vespers (Saturday Evening Prayer) of the First Sunday in Advent and continues until Evening Prayer on December 24. In this book, the second part of Advent, which begins December 17, overlaps the Sunday office, suggesting that the Church has not simply reached a particular date—one week before Christmas Eve—but that a culminating week of preparation begins, looking with intense longing and expectation to the Christmas celebration. From December 17 until Christmas Eve the propers for the dated days are to be used, regardless of the day of the week on which they fall.

Christmas-Epiphany

The office for Christmas-Epiphany begins with Evening Prayer on December 24 (the First Vespers of Christmas) and continues through Second Vespers (Sunday Evening Prayer) on the Baptism of our Lord, the First Sunday after the Epiphany. In the interest of simplicity, since in this book the office is tied to the dated days between Christmas and the Baptism of our Lord, the Laudate Psalms (145-150) are not used. For those who wish nonetheless to maintain the practice of tying these psalms to particular days of the week, the second psalm may be the appropriate Laudate psalm according to the table in the *Lutheran Book of Worship* (p. 178). To emphasize the festive character of the season, a biblical canticle is added to the two Psalms for each office. The propers for the dated days after January 6, the Epiphany, are used only until the Baptism of Our Lord. Those not needed are omitted that year.

General Time after the Epiphany

General (ordinary or ordered) time begins with Morning Prayer for Monday of Week I on the day after The Baptism of Our Lord (Epiphany I) and runs until Ash Wednesday. The four weeks of General time run successively and repeat as necessary. Beginning with First Vespers of the Last Sunday after the Epiphany, Week I is used to conclude the time after the Epiphany.

Lent

The office for Lent begins with Morning Prayer on Ash Wednesday and continues until First Vespers (Saturday Evening Prayer) of the Sunday of the Passion. To avoid the use of Hallelujah (Alleluia) during this season, a practice of the Western church at least since the seventh century, the Laudate psalms are not used.

Holy Week

The office for Holy Week begins with First Vespers (Saturday Evening Prayer) of the Sunday of the Passion and continues through Evening Prayer on Holy Saturday, preceding the Easter Vigil. For Good Friday, in addition to Morning and Evening Prayer, offices for mid-morning, noon, and mid-afternoon are provided because many will wish to spend much of that most solemn day in prayer. The basic source of these offices is the *Liturgy of the Hours*. A simple noonday office is provided for Holy Saturday.

Easter

The office for Easter begins with Morning Prayer on Easter Day and continues through Second Vespers (Sunday Evening Prayer) of the Day of Pentecost. To emphasize the festive character of the entire Fifty Days, a biblical canticle is added to the two psalms for each day of the week so that each day of Easter is treated as if it were a Sunday.

General Time after Pentecost

General time resumes with Morning Prayer for Monday after Pentecost (for the Day of Pentecost is the fiftieth and last day, the culmination, of Easter) and continues until First Vespers of the First Sunday in Advent.

General Time begins with Monday of Week I. On the Monday after Trinity Sunday (Sunday of Week II) General Time continues with the appropriate Proper according to the date of Trinity Sunday that year. Thereafter the Propers are used consecutively. (For those who prefer to follow the pattern of the *Lutheran Book of Worship* and its predecessor books, General Time continues successively according to the numbered Sundays after Pentecost.)

The four weeks of general time run successively and repeat as necessary. Beginning with First Vespers of Christ the King (the Last Sunday after Pentecost) Week I is used to conclude the time after Pentecost.

The daily prayer of the Church, deriving from ancient Hebrew practice, is corporate prayer. Nonetheless, when one is alone, by making use of congregational prayer forms, one can move beyond merely private and introspective concerns to join the prayer and praise of the whole church on earth and in heaven and indeed the song of all creation as we and all creatures await the final manifestation of the will and purpose of God for the universe.

The Calendar

January

1 THE HOLY NAME OF JESUS
2 *Johann Konrad Wilhelm Löhe, Pastor, 1872*
3 *[Charles Porterfield Krauth, Teacher, 1883]*
4
5 Kai Munk, Martyr, 1944
6 THE EPIPHANY OF OUR LORD
7
8
9 *[Julia Chester Emery, 1922]*
10 *[William Laud, Archbishop of Canterbury, 1645]*
11
12 *Aelred, Abbott of Rievaulx, 1167*
13 Hilary, Bishop of Poitiers, 367
14 *Elvind Josef Berggrav, Bishop of Oslo, 1959*
15
16 George Fox, Renewer of Society, 1691 [d. January 13]
17 Antony, Abbot in Egypt, 356
18 THE CONFESSION OF ST. PETER. The week of prayer for Christian unity begins.
19 Henry, Bishop of Uppsala, Missionary to Finland, Martyr, 1156
Wulfstan, Bishop of Worcester, 1095
20 Fabian, Bishop of Rome, Martyr, 250
21 Agnes, Martyr at Rome, 304
22 Vincent, Deacon at Saragossa, Martyr, 304
23 *Phillips Brooks, Bishop of Massachusetts, 1893*
24 Francis de Sales, Bishop of Geneva, 1622
[Ordination, 1944, of Florence Li Tim-Oi,
First Woman Priest in the Anglican Communion]
25 THE CONVERSION OF ST. PAUL. The week of prayer for Christian unity ends.
26 Timothy, Titus, [and Silas], Companions of St. Paul
27 Lydia, Dorcas, Phoebe
28 Thomas Aquinas, Teacher, 1274 [LBW: March 7]
29
30
31

February

1 *Brigid (Bride), 253*
2 THE PRESENTATION OF OUR LORD
3 Ansgar, Archbishop of Hamburg, Missionary to Denmark and Sweden, 865
4 *Cornelius the Centurion*
5 Paul Miki and his comapnions, the Martyrs of Japan, 1597
6 *[Philipp Jacob Spener, Renewer of the Church, 1705]*
7
8
9
10
11
12
13 *[Absalom Jones, Priest, 1818]*
14 Cyril Monk, 865; Methodius, Bishop, 885; Missionaries to the Slavs
15 *[Thomas Bray, Priest and Missionary, 1730]*
16
17 *[Janani Luwum, Archbishop of Uganda, Martyr, 1977]*
18 Martin Luther, Renewer of the Church, 1546
19
20 *[Rasmus Jensen, First Lutheran Pastor in North America, 1620]*
21
22
23 Polycarp, Bishop of Smyrna, Martyr, 156
24 ST. MATTHIAS, APOSTLE, MARTYR [RC: MAY 14]
25 *[Elizabeth Fedde, Deaconess, 1921]*
26 *[Bartholomäus Ziegenbalg, Missionary to India, 1719 LBW: February 23]*
27
28

March

1 George Herbert, Priest, 1633 [BCP: February 27]
David Bishop of Menevia, Wales, ca. 544
2 John Wesley, 1791; Charles Wesley, 1788; Renewers of the Church [BCP: March3]
Chad, Bishop of Lichfield, 672
3
4
5
6
7 Perpetua and her companions, Martyrs at Carthage, 202
8
9
10
11
12 Gregory the Great, Bishop of Rome, 604 [RC: September 3]
13
14
15
16
17 Patrick, Bishop, Missionary to Ireland, 461
18 Cyril, Bishop of Jerusalem, 386
19 ST. JOSEPH, HUSBAND OF MARY AND GUARDIAN OF OUR LORD
20 *Cuthbert, Bishop of Lindisfarne, 687*
21 *Thomas Ken, Bishop of Bath and Wells, 1711*
22 Jonathan Edwards, Teacher, Missionary to the Native Americans, 1758
[James DeKoven, Priest, 1879]
23 Gregory the Illuminator, Bishop and Missionary of Armenia, *ca.* 332
24 Oscar Arnulfo Romero, Archbishop of San Salvador, Martyr, 1980
25 THE ANNUNICATION OF OUR LORD
26
27 *[Charles Henry Brent, Bishop of the Philippines and of Western New York, 1*
28
29 *[Hans Nielsen Hauge, Renewer of the Church, 1824]*
John Keble, Priest, 1866
30
31 John Donne, Priest, 1631

April

1 *Amalie Sieveking, Renewer of Society, 1859*
Frederick Denison Maurice, Priest, 1872
2 *[James Lloyd Breck, Priest, 1876]*
3 Richard, Bishop of Chichester, 1253
4 Martin Luther King, Jr., Renewer of Society, 1968
5
6 Albrecht Dürer, Painter, 1528; Michelangelo Buonarroti, Artist, 1564
7
8 *William Augustus Muhlenberg, Priest, 1877*
9 Dietrich Bonhöffer, Teacher, Martyr, 1945
10 *Mikael Agricola, Bishop of Turku, 1557; Renewer of the Church*
William Law, Priest, 1761
11 *[George Augustus Selwyn, Bishop of New Zealand and of Lichfield, 1878]*
12
13
14
15
16
17
18
19 *Alphege, Archbishop of Canterbury, 1012*
Olavus Petri, Priest, 1552; Laurentius Petri, Archbishop of Uppsala, 1573;
Renewers of the Church
20
21 Anselm, Archbishop of Canterbury, Theologian, 1109
22
23 Toyohiko Kagawa, Renewer of Society, 1960
24
25 ST. MARK, EVANGELIST
26
27
28
29 Catherine of Siena, Teacher, 1380
30

May

1 ST. PHILIP AND ST. JAMES, APOSTLES, MARTYRS [RC: MAY 3]
2 Athanasius, Bishop of Alexandria, 373
3
4
5
6
7
8 Dame Julian of Norwich, *ca.* 1417
9
10
11
12
13
14
15
16
17
18 *Erik, King of Sweden, Martyr, 1160*
19 Dunstan, Archbishop of Canterbury, 988
20 Alcuin, Deacon and Abbot of Tours, 804
21 John Eliot, Missionary to the Native Americans, 1690
22
23 *[Ludwig Nommensen, Missionary to Sumatra, 1918]*
24 *Nicolaus Copernicus, 1543; Leonhard Euler, 1783; Teachers*
[Jackson Kemper, First Missionary Bishop in the United States, 1870]
25 Bede, the Venerable, Priest and Monk of Jarrow, 735
26 Augustine, Archbishop of Canterbury, Missionary, 605
27 John Calvin, Renewer of the Church, 1564
28
29 *Jiri Tranovsky, Hymnwriter, 1637*
30
31 THE VISITATION

June

1 Justin, Martyr at Rome, *ca.* 165
2 Blandina and her companions, Martyrs at Lyons, 177
3 *The Martyrs of Uganda, 1886*
4 John XXIII, Bishop of Rome, Renewer of the Church, 1963
5 Boniface, Archbishop of Mainz, Missionary to Germany, Martyr, 754
6 *William A. Passavant, Renewer of Society, 1894*
7 Sealth [Seattle], Chief of the Duwamish Confederacy, 1866
8
9 Columba, Abbot of Iona, 597; Aidan, Bishop of Lindisfarne, 651 [BCP: August 31};
10 Ephrem of Edessa, Deacon, 373
11 ST. BARNABAS, APOSTLE
12
13
14 Macrina, Teacher and Monsastic, 379 [LFF: July 19];
Basil the Great, Bishop of Caesarea, 379 [RC: January 2];
Gregory of Nazianzus, Bishop of Constantinople, *ca.* 389 [RC: January 2;
BCP: May9];
Gregory, Bishop of Nyssa, *ca.* 385 [BCP: March 9]
15 Evelyn Underhill, 1941
16 *[Joseph Butler, Bishop of Durham, 1752]*
17
18 *[Bernard Mizeki, Catechist and Martyr in Rhodesia, 1896]*
19
20
21 *[Onesimos Nesib, Translator, Evangelist, 1931]*
22 *Alban, the First Martyr in Britain, ca. 304*
23
24 THE NATIVITY OF ST. JOHN THE BAPTIST
25 *Presentation of the Augsburg Confession, 1530*
Philipp Melanchthon, Renewer of the Church, 1560
26
27
28 Irenaeus, Bishop of Lyons, *ca.* 202
29 ST. PETER AND ST. PAUL, APOSTLES
30 *Johann Olof Wallin, Archbishop of Uppsala, Hymn Writer, 1839*

July

1 Catherine Winkworth, 1878;
John Mason Neale, 1866, [BCP: August 7] Hymn Writers
2
3
4
5
6 Jan Hus, Martyr, 1415
7
8
9
10
11 Benedict of Nursia, Abbot of Monte Cassino, ca. 540;
Scholastica *ca.* 542 [RC: February 10]
12 Nathan Söderblom, Archbishop of Uppsala, 1930
13 *[Johannes Flierl, Missionary to Papua New Guinea, 1947]*
14
15 Olga, Princess of Kiev, confessor, 969
Vladimir, first Christian ruler of Russia, 1015
16
17 Bartolome de Las Casas, Missionary to the Indes, 1566
[William White, Bishop of Pennsylvania, 1816]
18
19
20 *Elizabeth Cady Stanton, Amelia Bloom, Sojourner Truth, Harriet Ross Tubman*
21
22 ST. MARY MAGDALENE
23 Birgitta of Sweden, 1373
24 *Thomas a Kempis, Priest, 1471*
25 ST. JAMES THE ELDER, APOSTLE
26 The Parents of the Blessed Virgin Mary
27 *[William Reed Huntington, Priest, 1919]*
28 Johann Sebastian Bach, 1750;
Heinrich Schütz, 1672
George Frederick Handel, 1759, Musicians
29 Mary, Martha, and Lazarus of Bethany
Olaf, King of Norway, Martyr, 1030
30 *William Wilberforce, 1833*
31 Ignatius Loyola, 1556

August

1 *Joseph of Arimathea [LFF; BCP: July 31]*
2
3
4
5
6 THE TRANSFIGURATION OF OUR LORD
7
8 Dominic, Friar, 1221
9
10 St. Lawrence, Deacon, Martyr, 258
11 Clare, Abbess at Assisi, 1253
12
13 Florence Nightingale, 1910;
Clara Maas, 1901, Renewers of Society
Jeremy Taylor, Bishop of Down, Connor, and Dromore, 1667
14 *[Jonathan Myrick Daniels, 1965]*
15 ST. MARY THE VIRGIN, MOTHER OF OUR LORD
16 Stephen, King of Hungary, 1038
17
18 *[William Porcher DuBose, Priest, 1918]*
19
20 Bernard, Abbot of Clairvaux, 1153
21
22
23
24 ST. BARTHOLOMEW, APOSTLE
25 Louis, King of France, 1270
26
27 Monica, Mother of Augustine, 387 [BCP: May4]
Thomas Gallaudet, 1902, with Henry Winter Syle, 1890
28 Augustine, Bishop of Hippo, Teacher, 430
29 The Beheading of St. John the Baptist
30
31 John Bunyan, Teacher, 1688

September

1 *[David Pendleton Oakerhater, Deacon and Missionary, 1931]*
2 *Nikolai Frederik Severin Grundtvig, Bishop, Renewer of the Church, 1872*
[The Martyrs of New Guinea, 1942]
3
4 Albert Schweitzer, Missionary to Africa, 1965
5 *[Paul Jones, 1941]*
6
7
8 The Nativity of the Blessed Virgin Mary
9 Peter Claver, Priest, Missionary to Colombia, 1654
[Constance, Nun, and her companions, 1878]
10 *[Alexander Crummell, 1898]*
11
12 *[John Henry Hobart, Bishop of New York, 1830]*
13 John Chrysostom, Bishop of Constantinople, 407
14 HOLY CROSS DAY
15
16 *Cyprian, Bishop and Martyr at Carthage, 258*
Ninian, Bishop in Galloway, ca. 430
17 Hildegard of Bingen, Renewer of the Church, 1179
18 Dag Hammarskjold, Peacemaker, 1961
[Edward Bouverie Pusey, Priest, 1882]
19 *Theodore of Tarsus, Archbishop of Canterbury, 690*
20 *[John Coleridge Patteson, Bishop of Melanesia and his Companions, Martyrs, 1871]*
21 ST. MATTHEW, APOSTLE, EVANGELIST
22 *Justus Falckner, Pastor, 1723*
[Philander Chase, Bishop of Ohio, and of Illinois, 1852]
23
24
25 Sergius of Radonezh, Abbot of Holy Trinity, Moscow, 1392
26 *Lancelot Andrewes, Bishop of Winchester, 1626*
27 Vincent de Paul, Renewer of Church and Society, 1660
28
29 ST. MICHAEL AND ALL ANGELS
30 Jerome, Translator, Teacher, 420

October

1 *Remigius, Bishop of Rheims, ca. 530*
2
3
4 Francis of Assisi, Renewer of the Church, 1226
5 *Frederike Fliedner, 1842; Karoline Fliedner, 1892, Theodor Fliedner, 1864 [LBW:October 4]; Renewers of Society*
6 William Tyndale, Translator, Martyr, 1536
7 *[Henry Melchior Muhlenberg, Missionary to America, 1787]*
8
9 *Robert Grosseteste, Bishop of Lincoln, 1253*
10
11 *Philip, Deacon and Evangelist*
12
13 Elizabeth Fry, Renewer of Society, 1845
14 *[Samuel Isaac Joseph Schereschewsky, Bishop of Shanghai, 1906]*
15 Teresa of Avila, 1582 [LBW: December 14]
16 *[Hugh Latimer and Nicholas Ridley, Bishops, 1555]*
Thomas Cranmer, Archbishop of Canterbury, 1556
17 Ignatius, Bishop of Antioch, Martyr, *ca.* 115
18 ST. LUKE, EVANGELIST
19 *[Henry Martyn, Priest and Missionary to India and Persia, 1812]*
20
21
22
23 ST. JAMES OF JERUSALEM, BROTHER OF OUR LORD JESUS CHRIST, MARTYR, *CA.* 62
24 *[Jehu Jones, Pastor]*
25
26 *Philipp Nicolai, 1608; Johann Heermann, 1647; Paul Gerhart, 1676; Hymn Writers*
Alfred the Great, King of West Saxons, 899
27
28 ST. SIMON AND ST. JUDE, APOSTLES
29 *[James Hannington, Bishop of Eastern Equatorial Africa, and his Companions, 1885]*
30
31 Reformation Day

November

1 ALL SAINTS' DAY
2 Commemoration of All the Faithful Departed
3 *[Richard Hooker, Priest, 1600]*
4
5 Elizabeth and Zechariah, Parents of John the Baptist
6 *William Temple, Archbishop of Canterbury, 1944*
7 *Willibrord, Archbishop of Utrecht, Missionary to Frisia, 739*
8 *[John Christian Frederick Heyer, Missionary to India, 1873]*
9
10 Leo the Great, Bishop of Rome, 461
11 Martin, Bishop of Tours, 397
12 *[Charles Simeon, Priest, 1836]*
Soren Aabye Kierkegaard, Teacher, 1855
13
14 *[Consecration of Samuel Seabury, First American Bishop, 1784]*
15
16 Margaret, Queen of Scotland, 1093
17 Elizabeth of Thuringia, Princess of Hungary, 1231 [BCP: November 19]
Hugh, Bishop of Lincoln, 1200
18 Hilda, Abess of Whitby, 680
19 Mechtild of Hackeborn, 1298
Gertrude the Great of Helfta, 1302
Mechtild of Magdeburg, 1282, Renewers of the Church
20 *Edmund, King of East Anglia, 870*
21
22 Clive Staples Lewis, Teacher, 1963
23 Clement. Bishop of Rome, *ca.* 100
24 Miguel Agustin Pro, Priest, Martyr in Mexico, 1927
25 Isaac Watts, Hymn Writer, 1748
[James Otis Sargent Huntington, Priest and Monk, 1935]
26
27
28 *[Kamehameha and Emma, King and Queen of Hawaii, 1864, 1885]*
29
30 ST. ANDREW, APOSTLE

December

1 *Nicholas Ferrar, Deacon, 1637*
2 *[Channing Moore Williams, Missionary Bishop in China and Japan, 1910]*
3 Francis Xavier, Missionary to Asia, 1552
4 John of Damascus, Priest, ca. 760
5 *Clement of Alexandria, Priest, ca. 210*
6 Nicholas, Bishop of Myra, ca. 342
7 Ambrose, Bishop of Milan, 397
8
9
10
11 *[Lars Olsen Skrefsrud, Missionary to India, 1910]*
12
13 *Lucy [Lucia], Martyr at Syracuse, ca. 304*
14 John of the Cross, Renewer of the Church
15
16
17 *O Sapientia*
18
19
20
21 ST. THOMAS, APOSTLE [RC: JULY 31]
22
23 *Thorlak of Skalholt, 1193*
24
25 THE NATIVITY OF OUR LORD
26 ST. STEPHEN, DEACON, MARTYR
27 ST. JOHN, APOSTLE, EVANGELIST
28 THE HOLY INNOCENTS, MARTYRS
29 *Thomas Becket, Martyr, 1170*
30
31

Before Praying the Office

✠

O Lord, open our lips, that we may bless your holy Name;
cleanse our hearts from all vain, evil, and wandering thoughts;
enlighten our understanding;
enkindle our affections;
that we may worthily and devoutly offer our prayers and praises to you,
and be heard in the presence of your divine Majesty,
through Jesus Christ our Lord.

✠

✠

EVENING PRAYER

Vespers or Evensong during Advent

The SERVICE OF LIGHT may be used to begin Evening Prayer. The service may begin with a procession in which a large, lighted candle is carried to its stand in front of the congregation.

When the Service of Light is omitted, Evening Prayer begins on page 7.

Stand

Leader

The Spirit and the Church cry out:

Congregation

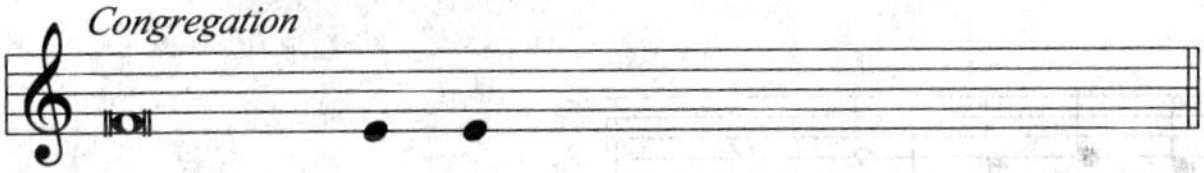

Come, Lord Je - sus.

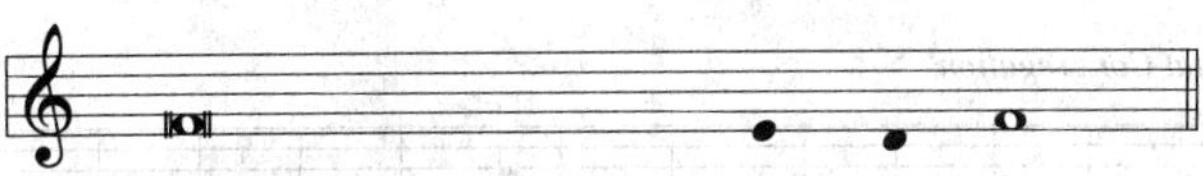

L All those who await his ap - pear - ance pray:

C Come, Lord Je - sus.

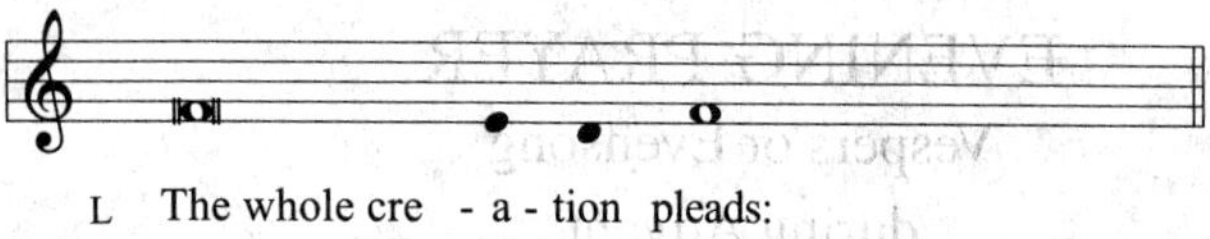

[Revelation 22:17, 20; 2 Timothy 4:8; Romans 8:22]

As this ancient hymn, Phos hilaron, *is sung, the candles on and near the altar are lighted. When the large candle is used, the candles are lighted from its flame.*

bless - ed Je - sus Christ. We have come to the
set - ting of the sun, and we look to the eve - ning light.
We sing to God, the Fa - ther, Son, and Ho - ly Spir - it:
You are wor - thy of be - ing praised with pure voic - es for
ev - er. O Son of God, O Giv - er of life:
The u - ni - verse pro - claims your glo - ry.

The thanksgiving from the Apostolic Constitutions *(ca. 380) concludes the Service of Light.*

with-out end; through Christ you are the Creator and Preserver of
the whole world, but above all you are his God and Fa - ther,
the Giver of the Spirit, and the ruler of all that is seen and un - seen.
You made the day for the works of light and the night for the refreshment
of our weak-ness. O loving Lord and Source of all that is good,
mercifully accept our evening sac - ri - fice of praise.
As you have conducted us through the day, and brought us to

night's be-gin-ning, keep us now in Christ, grant us a peaceful evening
and a night free from sin, and at the end bring us to ever - last - ing life
through Christ our Lord. Through him we offer glory, honor and worship
to you in the Ho - ly Spir - it, now and always and for ev - er
and ev - er. C A - men.

[MPES]

+

When the Service of Light is omitted, Evening Prayer may begin with these verses:

Stand

L Make haste, O God,✠ to deliver me.

C O Lord, make haste to help me.

[Ps. 70:1; LH; CB, CSB, SBH; BCP]

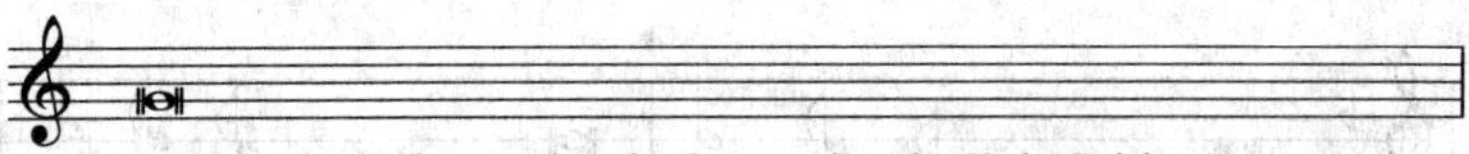

L Glory to the Father, and to the Son, and to the Holy Spirit:

C As it was in the beginning, is now, and will be for ev - er. A - men.

Al - le - lu - ia.

Kneel or Sit

The PSALMODY begins with this song for forgiveness and protection from Psalm 141, Domine clamavi

C 1 O Lord, I call to
you; come . . . . . . to me quickly; hear my voice when I cry to you.

3 Set a watch
before my . . . . . . mouth, O Lord; and guard the door of my lips.

6 Glory to the
Father, and . . . . . to the Son, and to the . . . . Ho - ly Spirit;

2 Let my prayer rise
before . . . . you as incense; the lifting up of my
hands as the evening sac - ri - fice.

4 Let not my heart
incline to any . . . . e - vil thing; let me not be occupied
in wickedness with e - vil - doers.

5 But my eyes are
turned to . . . . you, Lord God; in you I take refuge.
Strip me not . . . . of my life.

7 as it was in the
begin - ning, is now, and will be for ev - er. A - men.

Silence for meditation

Let the incense of our repentant prayer ascend before you, O Lord, and let your lovingkindness descend upon us, that with purified minds we may sing your praises with the Church on earth and the whole heavenly host, and may glorify you for ever and ever.

C Amen

Sit

A second psalm is sung or said; additional psalms and a New Testament canticle may be sung or said also. Silence for meditation follows each psalm or canticle. The psalm prayer appropriate to each psalm or canticle follows the silence.

C Amen

Stand

THE HYMN is sung.

Sit

One or two LESSONS are read. Silence for meditation follows each reading.

After this the leader continues:

L In many and various ways God spoke to his people of old by the prophets.

C But now in these last days he has spoken to us by his Son.

[Heb. 1:1-2]

Stand

The GOSPEL CANTICLE, Magnificat, *is sung or said. The proper Antiphon is given on pp. 33-83.*

The Antiphon is sung or said.

1 My soul proclaims
the greatness . . . of the Lord; my spirit
rejoices in . . . God my Savior.

3 From this day all gen - er - ations will . . . . . . call me blessed.

5 He has mercy on those who fear him in every . . . gen - er - ation.

2 for he has . . . looked with favor on his . . . low - ly servant.

4 The Almighty
has done great things for me, and holy . . . is his Name.

6 He has shown
the strength of his arm; he has scattered
the proud in their con - ceit.

7 He has cast down
the mighty . . . from their thrones, and has lifted up the lowly.

9 He has come to
the help of his . . . ser - vant Israel, for he has
remembered
his prom - ise of mercy,

11 Glory to the Father,
and . . . . to the Son, and to the . . . Ho - ly Spirit;

8 He has filled
the hungry . . with good things, and the rich
he has sent a - way empty.

10 the promise
he made . . . . to our fathers, to Abraham
and his chil - dren for ever.

12 as it was in the
begin - ing, is now, and will be
for ev - er. A - men

The Antiphon is repeated.

Kneel or stand

The GREAT LITANY is sung or said.

L Lord, have mercy. C Lord, have mer - cy.

L Christ, have mercy. C Christ, have mer - cy.

L Lord, have mercy. C Lord, have mer - cy.

L O Christ, hear us. C In mer - cy hear us.

L God the Father in . . . . heaven, C have mer - cy on us.
L God, the Son, redeemer of the world, C have mer - cy on us.
L God, the Holy . . . . Spirit, C have mer - cy on us.
L Holy Trinity, one . . . . God, C have mer - cy on us.

L Be gra - cious to us. C Spare us, good Lord.

L Be gra - cious to us. C Help us, good Lord.

L From all sin, from all error, from all evil;
from the cunning assaults of the devil;
from an unprepared and . . . . e - vil death: C Good Lord, de- liv- er us.

L From war, bloodshed, and violence;
from corrupt and unjust government;
from sedi - . . . . tion and treason: C Good Lord, de- liv- er us.

L From epidemic, drought, and famine,
from fire and flood, earthquake,
lightning and storm;
and from ever - . . . . last - ing death: C Good Lord, de- liv- er us.

L By the mystery of your incarnation; by your ho- ly birth: C Help us, good Lord.

L By your baptism, fasting, and temptation;
by your agony and bloody sweat;
by your cross and suffering;
by your precious . . . . death and burial: C Help us, good Lord.

L By your glorious resurrection and ascension;
by the gift of the . . . . Ho- ly Spirit: C Help us, good Lord.

L In all time of our tribulation;
in all time of our prosperity;
in the hour of death; and in the . . . . day of judgment: C Save us, good Lord.

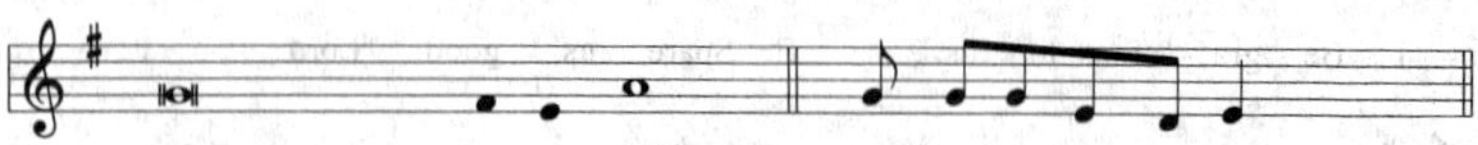

L Though unworthy, we im - plore you C to hear us, Lord our God.

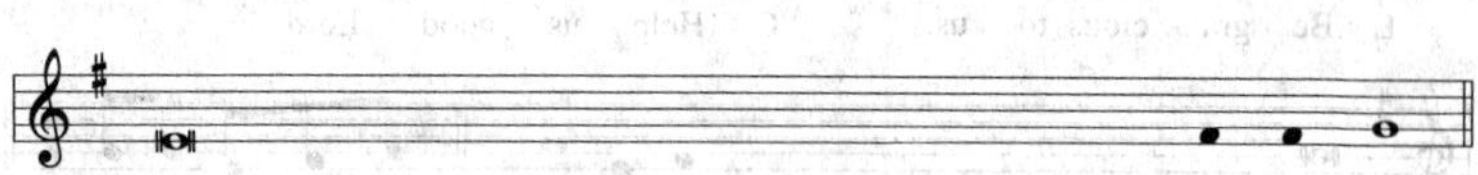

L To rule and govern your holy catholic Church;
to guide all servants of your Church in the true knowledge
and understanding of your Word and in holiness of life;
to put an end to all schisms
and causes of offense to those who would believe;
and to bring into the way of truth all who have erred and gone a - stray:

C We im - plore you to hear us, good Lord.

L To beat down Satan under our feet;
to send faithful workers into your harvest;
to accompany your Word with your Spirit and power;
to raise up those who fall and to strengthen those who stand;
and to comfort and help the fainthearted and . . . . the dis - tressed:

C We im - plore you to hear us, good Lord.

L To give to all nations justice and peace;
to preserve our country from discord and strife;
to direct and guard those who have civil authority;
and to bless and guide . . . . all our people:

C We im - plore you to hear us, good Lord.

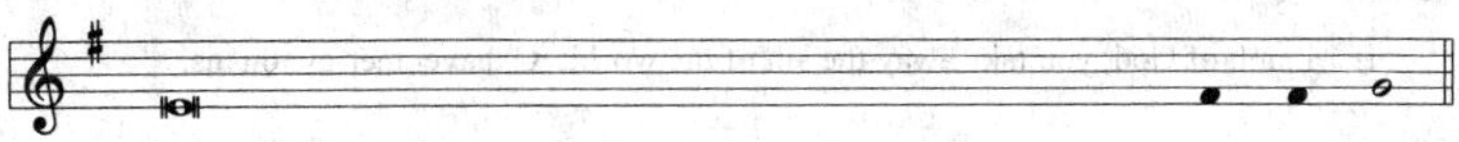

L To behold and help all who are in danger, need, or tribulation;
to protect and guide all who travel;
to preserve and provide for all women in childbirth;
to watch over children and to guide the young;
to heal the sick and to strengthen their families and friends;
to bring reconciliation to families in discord;
to provide for the unemployed and for all in need;
to be merciful to all who are imprisoned;
to support, comfort, and guide all orphans, widowers, and widows;
and to have mercy on . . . . all your people:

C We im - plore you to hear us, good Lord.

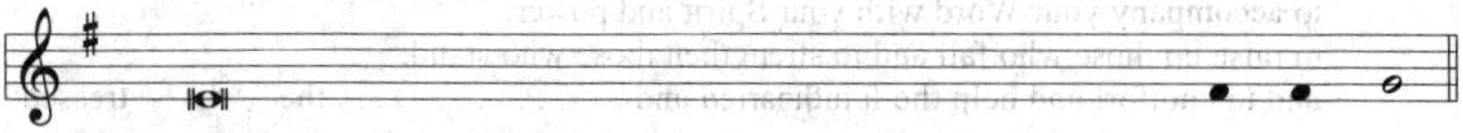

L To forgive our enemies, persecutors, and slanderers,
and to reconcile us to them;
to help us use wisely the fruits and treasures
of the earth, the sea, and the air;
and graciously to . . . . hear our prayers:

C We im - plore you to hear us, good Lord.

L Lord Jesus Christ, Son of God, C We im - plore you to hear us.

L Lamb of God, you take away the sin of the world; C have mer-cy on us.

L Lamb of God, you take away the sin of the world; C have mer-cy on us.

L Lamb of God, you take away the sin of the world; C give us peace. A- men.

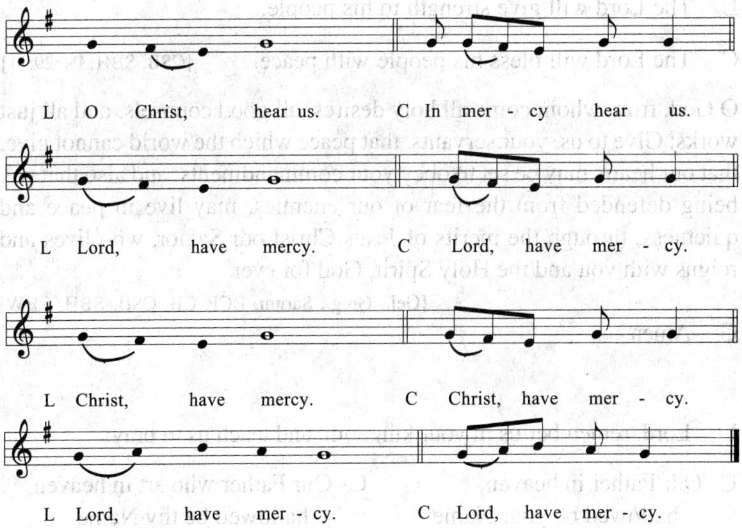

The Prayer of the Day may be said. Then:

L Rise up, O Lord, and help us;

C And save us for the sake of your steadfast love. [Ps. 44:26]

Hasten, O Father, the coming of your kingdom; and grant that we your servants, who now live by faith, may with joy behold your Son at his coming in glorious majesty; even Jesus Christ, our only Mediator and Advocate. [BCP]

C Amen

L The Lord will give strength to his people.

C The Lord will bless his people with peace. [CSB, SBH: Ps. 29:11]

O God, from whom come all holy desires, all good counsels, and all just works: Give to us, your servants, that peace which the world cannot give, that our hearts may be set to obey your commandments; and also that we, being defended from the fear of our enemies, may live in peace and quietness; through the merits of Jesus Christ our Savior, who lives and reigns with you and the Holy Spirit, God for ever.

[Gel., Greg., Sarum, BCP, CB, CSB, SBH, LBW]

C Amen

L Lord, remember us in your kingdom, and teach us to pray:

C Our Father in heaven,
hallowed be your Name
your kingdom come,
your will be done,
on earth as in heaven.
Give us today our daily bread.
Forgive us our sins
as we forgive those
who sin against us.
Save us from the time of trial
and deliver us from evil.
For the kingdom, the power,
and the glory are yours,
now and for ever. Amen.

C Our Father who art in heaven,
hallowed be thy Name
thy kingdom come,
thy will be done,
on earth as it is in heaven.
Give us this day our daily bread;
and forgive us our trespasses,
as we forgive those
who sin against us;
And lead us not into temptation
but deliver us from evil.
For thine is the kingdom,
and the power, and the glory,
for ever and ever. Amen.

Stand

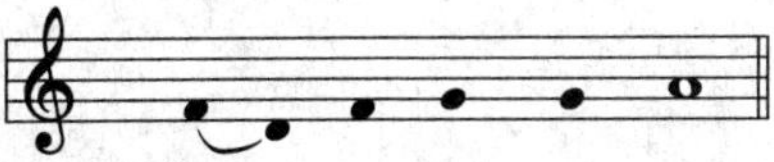

The BENEDICTION concludes the service when there is no sermon. A hymn may follow the benediction.

When there is a sermon, this benediction is omitted, and the order continues with the Offering and Hymn.

When there is a sermon

Sit

An OFFERING may be received during which a hymn, psalm, or anthem may be sung.

A HYMN is sung.

The SERMON. Following the sermon one of these prayers is said.

Stand

Almighty God, grant to your Church your Holy Spirit and the wisdom which comes down from heaven, that your Word may not be bound but have free course and be preached to the joy and edifying of Christ's holy people, that in steadfast faith we may serve you and in the confession of your Name may abide to the end; through Jesus Christ our Lord.

[Brandenburg-Nuremberg 1533, CSB, TLH, SBH, LBW]

or

Lord God, you have called your servants to ventures of which we cannot see the ending, by paths as yet untrodden, through perils unknown: Give us faith to go out with good courage, not knowing where we go, but only that your hand is leading us and your love supporting us; through Jesus Christ our Lord. [DP, SBH, LBW]

or

Lord, we thank you that you have taught us what you would have us believe and do. Help us by your Holy Spirit, for the sake of Jesus Christ, to keep your Word in pure hearts, that thereby we may be strengthened in faith, perfected in holiness, and comforted in life and death.

[*Lutheran Hymnary*, LBW]

C Amen

The minister blesses the congregation.

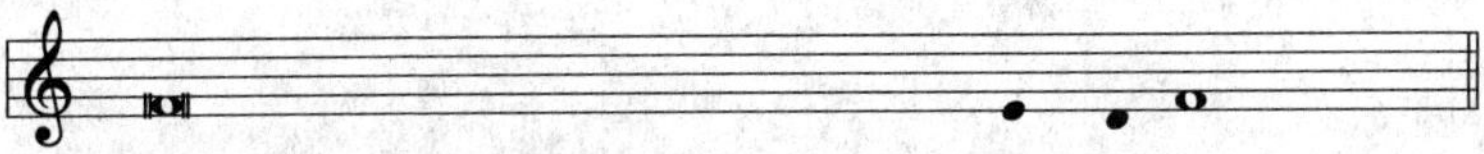

P The almighty and merciful Lord,
the Father, the Son, and the Holy Spirit, bless and pre-serve you.

C A - men

Saturdays in Advent and December 17

Antiphon to PSALM 80 *Qui regis Israel*

eve of Advent 1 Stir up your **strength**, O Lord, *
and **come** to help us. [LH, PBO]

eve of Advent 2 Restore us, O **God** of hosts;*
show us the light of your countenance,
and we **shall** be saved.

eve of Advent 3 Let the mountains break out with joy
and the hills with an**swer**ing gladness*
for the world's true light
comes with pow**er** and might.
[LH: see Isa. 49:13; 55:12]

December 17 The treasure of all na**tions** shall come*
his dwelling **shall** be glorious.
[LH: Hag. 2:7; Isa. 11:10]

80 *Plea for the return of God's favor*

1 Hear, O Shepherd of Israel, leading Joseph **like** a flock;*
shine forth, you that are enthroned up**on** the cherubim.

2 In the presence of Ephraim, Benjamin, **and** Manasseh,*
stir up your strength and **come** to help us.

3 Restore us, O **God** of hosts;*
show the light of your countenance, and we **shall** be saved.

4 O LORD **God** of hosts,*
how long will you be angered
despite the prayers **of** your people?

5 You have fed them with the **bread** of tears;*
you have given them bowls of **tears** to drink.

6 You have made us the derision **of** our neighbors,*
and our enemies laugh **us** to scorn.

7 Restore us, O **God** of hosts;*
show the light of your countenance, and we **shall** be saved.

8 You have brought a vine **out** of Egypt;*
you cast out the nations and **plant**ed it.

9 You prepared the **ground** for it;*
it took root and **filled** the land.

10 The mountains were covered **by** its shadow*
and the towering cedar trees **by** its boughs.

11 You stretched out its tendrils **to** the sea*
and its branches **to** the River.

12 Why have you broken **down** its wall,*
so that all who pass by pluck **off** its grapes?

13 The wild boar of the forest has **rav**aged it,*
and the beasts of the field have **grazed** upon it.

14 Turn now, O God of hosts, look down from heaven;
behold and **tend** this vine;*
preserve what your right **hand** has planted.

15 They burn it with **fire** like rubbish;*
at the rebuke of your countenance **let** them perish.

16 Let your hand be upon the man of **your** right hand,*
the son of man you have made so strong **for** yourself.

17 And so will we never turn a**way** from you;*
give us life, that we may call up**on** your Name.

18 Restore us, O LORD **God** of hosts;*
show the light of your countenance, and we **shall** be saved.

The Antiphon is repeated.

Silence for meditation

Lord God, you so tend the vine you planted that now it extends its branches even to the farthest shore: Keep us in your Son as branches on the vine, that, rooted firmly in your love, we may testify before the whole world to your great power working everywhere; through Jesus Christ our Lord.

[LH, LBW]

+

Antiphon to PSALM 72 *Deus, judicum*

eve of Advent 1 Rejoice greatly, O daugh**ter** of Zion!*
Shout aloud, O daughter Jer**u**salem.
[CSB, SBH, LH: Zech. 9:9]

eve of Advent 2 Proclaim the good news a**mong** the nations:*
our God will **come** to save us. [LH: see Isa. 35:4]

eve of Advent 3 I, the Lord, am coming to save you;
already **I** am near;*
soon I will free you **from** your sins. [LH]

December 17 May the Holy One from heaven come down
like **gen**tle rain;*
may the earth burst into blossom
and bear the **ten**der Savior.
[LH: see Isa. 45:8, Ps. 72:6]

72 *The kingdom of peace*

1 Give the king your jus**tice**, O God,*
and your righteousness to **the** King's Son;

2 That he may rule your **peo**ple righteously*
and the **poor** with justice;

3 That the mountains may bring prosperity **to** the people,*
and the little **hills** bring righteousness.

4 He shall defend the needy a**mong** the people;*
he shall rescue the poor and crush **the** oppressor.

5 He shall live as long as the sun and **moon** endure,*
from one generation **to** another.

6 He shall come down like rain upon **the** mown field,*
like showers that wa**ter** the earth.

7 In his time shall the **right**eous flourish;*
there shall be abundance of peace till the moon shall
be no more.

8 He shall rule from **sea** to sea,*
and from the River to the ends **of** the earth.

9 His foes shall bow **down** before him,*
and his enemies **lick** the dust.

10 The kings of Tarshish and of the isles **shall** pay tribute,*
and the kings of Arabia and Saba **o**ffer gifts.

11 All kings shall bow **down** before him,*
and all the nations **do** him service.

12 For he shall deliver the poor who cries out **in** distress,*
and the oppressed who **has** no helper.

13 He shall have pity on the low**ly** and poor;*
he shall preserve the lives **of** the needy.

14 He shall redeem their lives from oppres**sion** and violence,*
and dear shall their blood be **in** his sight.

15 Long may he live!
and may there be given to him gold **from** Arabia;*
may prayer be made for him always,
and may they bless him all **the** day long.

16 May there be abundance of grain on the earth,
growing thick even **on** the hilltops;*
may its fruit flourish like Lebanon,
and its grain like grass up**on** the earth.

17 May his Name remain for ever
and be established as long as the **sun** endures;*
may all the nations bless themselves in him and
call him blessed.

18 Blessed be the Lord GOD, the **God** of Israel,*
who alone does **won**drous deeds!

19 And blessed be his glorious **Name** for ever!*
and may all the earth be filled with his glory.
A**men**. Amen.

The Antiphon is repeated.

Silence for meditation

Almighty God, you gave the kingdom of justice and peace to David and his descendant, our Lord Jesus Christ: Extend this kingdom to every nation, so that through your Son the poor may receive justice, the destitute relief, and the people of the earth peace in the Name of him who lives and reigns with you and the Holy Spirit, one God, now and for ever.

[LHd, LBW]

+

Antiphon to the NEW TESTAMENT CANTICLE *Coram Deo*

eve of Advent 1 New city of Zion, let your heart **sing** for joy;*
see how humbly your king **comes** to you.

[LH: see Zech. 9:9]

eve of Advent 2 Know that the Lord is coming
and with him **all** his saints;*
that day will dawn with a won**der**ful light.

[LH, CSB, SBH: see Zech. 14:5-7]

eve of Advent 3 Our Lord will come to claim his **glor**ious throne*
in the assembly **of** the princes.

[LH: see Ps. 82:1]

December 17 The fullness of time has come upon **us** at last; *
God sends his Son in**to** the world. [LH: see Gal. 4:4]

A Song of the Advent of Christ 1 Timothy 6:13-16

In the presence of God who gives life **to** all things,*
keep the commandment without **spot** or blame,

watching for the Appearing of our Lord **Je**sus Christ,*
the blessed and only Sovereign,
the King of kings and **Lord** of lords,

who alone has immor**tal**ity,*
and dwells in unapproach**a**ble light,

whom no one has ever seen, whom no one is a**ble** to see:*
to him be honor and eter**nal** dominion

[PHP]

The Antiphon is repeated.

Silence for meditation

Most merciful God, you have given your eternal Word to take our human nature from the pure Virgin: Grant your people grace to put away the desires of the flesh so that they may be ready for your visitation; through your Son, Jesus Christ our Lord. [Thomas Münzer 1524, CB, CSB, SBH]

Stand

THE HYMN is sung. *Wie soll ich dich empfangen*

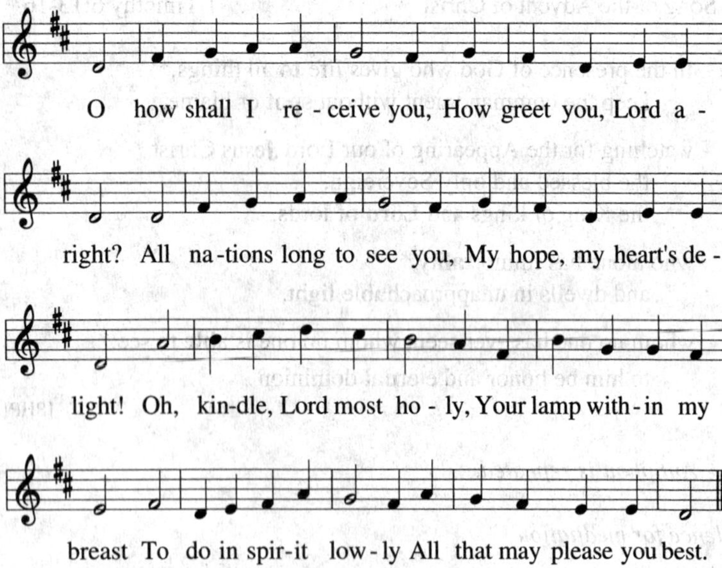

2 Your Zion palms is strewing
And branches fresh and fair;
My heart, its powers renewing,
An anthem shall prepare.
My soul puts off her sadness
Your glories to proclaim;
With all her strength and gladness
She fain would serve your Name.

3 I lay in fetters groaning,
You came to set me free.
I stood, my shame bemoaning,
You came to honor me.

A glorious crown you give me,
  A treasure safe on high,
That will not fail or leave me
  As earthly riches fly.

4 Love caused your incarnation,
  Love brought you down to me;
Your thirst for my salvation
  Procured my liberty.
O love beyond all telling
  That led you to embrace
In love, all loves excelling,
  Our lost and fallen race.

5 Rejoice, then, you sad-hearted,
  Who sit in deepest gloom,
Who mourn o'er joys departed
  And tremble at your doom.
He who alone can cheer you
  Is standing at the door;
He brings his pity near you
  And bids you weep no more.

6 He comes to judge the nations,
  A terror to his foes,
A light of consolations
  And blessed hope to those
Who love the Lord's appearing.
  O glorious sun, now come,
Send forth your beams most cheering
  And guide us safely home. [CSB 6; LBW 23]

Text: Paul Gerhardt, 1606-1676; st. 1-5 tr. Arthur Tozer Russell, 1806-1874, alt.;
st. 6 tr. Catherine Winkworth, 1829-1878

Tune: *Wie soll ich dich empfangen*, Johann Crüger, 1598-1662 76 76 D

Sit

A LESSON is read.

Year 1 (preceding odd-numbered years)	Year 2 (preceding even-numbered years)
eve of Advent 1 Matthew 20:24-34	Luke 19:41-48
Moved with compassion, Jesus touched their eyes. Immediately they regained their sight and followed him.	If you, even you, had only recognized on this day the things that make for peace! But now they are hidden from your eyes.
eve of Advent 2 Luke 21: 5-19	Matthew 22:15-22
You will be hated by all because of my name. But not a hair of your head will perish. By your endurance you will gain our souls.	Give therefore to the emperor the things that are the emperor's and to God the things that are God's.
eve of Advent 3 Luke 22: 31-38	Matthew 24: 1-14
I tell you, this scripture must be fulfilled in me, "And he was counted among the lawless"; and indeed what is written about me is being fulfilled.	This good news of the kingdom will be proclaimed throughout the world, as a testimony to all the nations; and then the end will come.

December 17

Luke 3:1-9

Every valley shall be filled, and every mountain and hill shall be made low, and the crooked shall be made straight, and the rough ways made smooth; and all flesh shall see the salvation of God.

Matthew 25:31-46

Come, you that are blessed by my Father, inherit the kingdom prepared for you from the foundation of the world; for I was hungry and you gave me food, I was thirsty and you gave me something to drink, I was a stranger and you welcomed me, I was naked and you gave me clothing, I was sick and you took care of me, I was in prison and you visited me.

Antiphon to the MAGNIFICAT

eve of Advent 1 See the Lord is coming **from** afar;*
his splendor **fills** the earth.
[LH, CSB, SBH, PBO; see Jer. 30:10]

eve of Advent 2 Come **to** us, Lord,*
and may your presence **be** our peace. [LH]

eve of Advent 3 Before me no god was formed,
nor shall there be any **af**ter me;*
before me every knee shall bow
and every **tongue** confess.
[LH, PBO; Isa. 43:10; see Phil. 2:10-11]

December 17 *O Sapientia*

O WISDOM, proceding from the mouth of the Most High,
pervading and permeating all creation,
mightily order**ing** all things:*
come and teach us the way of **un**derstanding.
[LH, PBO, LBW: Sirach 24:3, Wis. 8:1, Isa 40:14]

Sundays in Advent and December 18

Antiphon to PSALM 25 *Ad te, Domine, levavi*

Advent 1 — Daughter of Jerusalem, rejoice and be glad;
your king **comes** to you.*
Zion, do not fear:
your Savior hastens **on** his way.
[CSB, SBH, LH: see Zech. 9:9]

Advent 2 — Christ our king will **come** to us;*
the Lamb of God fore**told** by John.
[LH: see John 1:29, 36, 26]

Advent 3 — Rejoice, Jerusalem, let your joy **o**verflow;*
your Savior will **come** to you. [LH]

December 18 — The crooked shall be made straight
and the rough **ways** made smooth.*
Come, O Lord, do **not** delay.
[LH, LBW; Luke 3:5]

25 *Prayer for guidance and protection*

1 To you, O LORD, I lift up my soul;
my God, I put my **trust** in you;*
let me not be humiliated,
nor let my enemies triumph **o**ver me.

2 Let none who look to you be **put** to shame;*
let the treacherous be disappointed **in** their schemes.

3 Show me your **ways**, O LORD,*
and teach **me** your paths.

4 Lead me in your **truth** and teach me,*
for you are the God of my salvation;
in you have I trusted all **the** day long.

5 Remember, O LORD, your compass**sion** and love,*
for they are from **ev**erlasting.

6 Remember not the sins of my youth and **my** transgressions;*
remember me according to your love
and for the sake of your good**ness**, O LORD.

7 Gracious and upright **is** the LORD;*
therefore he teaches sinners **in** his way.

8 He guides the humble in **do**ing right*
and teaches his way **to** the lowly.

9 All the paths of the LORD are **love** and faithfulness*
to those who keep his covenant and his **test**imonies.

10 For your Name's **sake**, O LORD,*
forgive my sin, for **it** is great.

11 Who are they who **fear** the LORD?*
he will teach them the way that **they** should choose.

12 They shall dwell **in** prosperity,*
and their offspring shall inher**it** the land.

13 The LORD is a friend to **those** who fear him,*
and will show **them** his covenant.

14 My eyes are ever looking **to** the LORD,*
for he shall pluck my feet out **of** the net.

15 Turn to me and have pi**ty** on me,*
for I am left alone **and** in misery.

16 The sorrows of my heart **have** increased;*
bring me out **of** my troubles.

17 Look upon my adversi**ty** and misery*
and forgive me **all** my sin.

18 Look upon my enemies, for **they** are many,*
and they bear a violent ha**tred** against me.

19 Protect my life and de**liv**er me;*
let me not be put to shame, for I have trust**ed** in you.

20 Let integrity and upright**ness** preserve me,*
for my hope has **been** in you.

21 Deliver Isra**el**, O God,*
out of **all** his troubles.

The Antiphon is repeated.

Silence for meditation

Lord our God, you show us your ways of compassion and love, and you spare sinners. Remember not our sins; relieve our misery; satisfy the longing of your people; and fulfill all our hopes for eternal peace through your Son, Jesus Christ our Lord. [LH, LBW]

+

Antiphon to PSALM 110, *Dixit Dominus*

Advent 1 The Lord, our **king** and lawgiver,*
will **come** to save us. [LH: see Isa. 33:22]

Advent 2 Let us cleanse our hearts
that we may welcome **our** great king;*
he is coming and will **not** delay. [LH]

Advent 3 Behold, the Lord shall appear on the **clouds** of heaven*
with power **and** great glory.
[LH, PBO: see Matt. 24:30]

December 18 See how **glor**ious he is,*
coming forth as Savior **of** all peoples.
[LH: see Ps. 19:5]

110 *The Messiah, king and priest*

1 The LORD said to my Lord, "Sit **at** my right hand,*
until I make your ene**mies** your footstool."

2 The LORD will send the scepter of your power **out** of Zion,*
saying, "Rule over your enemies **round** about you.

3 Princely state has been yours from the day **of** your birth;*
in the beauty of holiness have I begotten you,
like dew from the womb **of** the morning."

4 The LORD has sworn and he will **not** recant:*
"You are a priest for ever after the order **of** Melchizedek."

5 The Lord who is at your right hand
will smite kings in the day **of** his wrath;*
he will rule o**ver** the nations.

6 He will heap **high** the corpses;*
he will smash heads over **the** wide earth.

7 He will drink from the brook be**side** the road;*
therefore he will lift **high** his head.

The Antiphon is repeated.

Silence for meditation

Almighty God, make known in every place the perfect offering of your Son, the eternal high priest of the new Jerusalem, and so consecrate all nations to be your holy people, that the kingdom of Christ, your anointed one, may come in its fullness; and to you, Father, Son, and Holy Spirit, be all honor and praise now and for ever. [LHd, LBW]

+

Antiphon to the NEW TESTAMENT CANTICLE *Coram Deo*

Advent 1 — The Lord will come with **migh**ty power;*
every **eye** will see him. [LH: see Rev. 1:7]

Advent 2 — Let us live in holiness and love
as we patiently await our **bless**ed hope,*
the coming **of** our Savior. [LH: see Titus 2:12-13]

Advent 3 — Let the mountains break out with joy
and the hills with an**swer**ing gladness,*
for the world's true light, the Lord,
comes with pow**er** and might. [LH: see Isa. 49:13, 55:12]

December 18 — Ever wider will his **king**dom spread,*
eternal**ly** at peace. [LH]

A Song of the Advent of Christ — 1 Timothy 6:13-16

In the presence of God who gives life **to** all things,*
keep the commandment without **spot** or blame,

watching for the Appearing of our Lord **Je**sus Christ,*
the blessed and only Sovereign,
the King of kings and **Lord** of lords,

who alone has immor**ta**lity,*
and dwells in unapproach**a**ble light,

whom no one has ever seen, whom no one is a**ble** to see:*
to him be honor and eter**nal** dominion [PHP]

The Antiphon is repeated.

Silence for meditation

Make us, we pray you, O Lord our God, watchful and heedful in awaiting the Advent of your Son; that when he shall come and knock, he may find us not asleep in our sins but awake and rejoicing in his praises; through Jesus Christ our Lord. [Gel., AC; RS Advent 1 Monday]

Stand

THE HYMN is sung. *Conditor alme siderum*

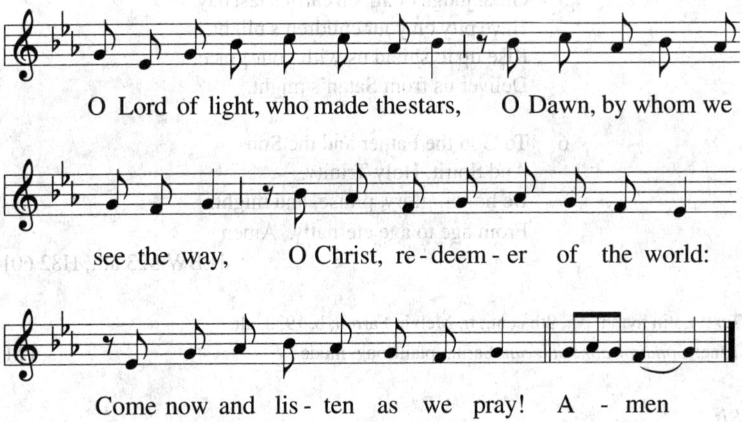

2 In lowliness you came on earth
To rescue us from Satan's snares;
Oh, wondrous love that healed our wounds
By taking on our mortal cares!

3 To pay the debt we owed for sin
Your painful cross was made the price;
From blessed Mary's womb you came,
A victim pure for sacrifice.

4 But now you reign, the King of kings,
Adorned in highest majesty;
Your very Name is held in awe
From pole to pole and sea to sea!

5 Great judge of all, on earth's last day
Have pity on your children's plight;
Rise up to shield us with your grace;
Deliver us from Satan's might.

6 To God the Father and the Son
And Spirit, Holy Trinity,
Be honor, glory, praise, and might,
From age to age eternally. Amen

[LBW 323 alt.; H82 60]

Text: Latin hymn, *ca.*, 9th cent.; tr. Melvin Farrell, b. 1930, alt.
Tune: *Conditor alme siderum* Sarum plainsong, mode IV LM

Sit

A LESSON is read.

Year 1	Year 2
Advent 1 Matthew 25:1-13	Luke 21:5-19
Keep awake therefore, for you know neither the day nor the hour.	You will be hated by all because of my name. But not a hair of your head will perish. By your endurance you will gain your souls.
Advent 2 Luke 7:28-35	Luke 1:57-68
I tell you, among those born of women no one is greater than John;	His father Zechariah was filled with the Holy Spirit and spoke this

yet the least in the kingdom of God is greater than he.

prophecy: "Blessed be the Lord God of Israel, for he has looked favorably on his people and redeemed them."

Advent 3

John 3:22-30

He who has the bride is the bridegroom. The friend of the bridegroom, who stands and hears him, rejoices greatly at the bridegroom's voice. For this reason my joy has been fulfilled.

John 5:30-47

John was a burning and shining lamp, and you were willing to rejoice for a while in his light.

December 18

John 3:16-21

God did not send his Son into the world to condemn the world, but in order that the world might be saved through him.

John 3:16-21

God did not send the Son into the world to condemn the world, but in order that the world might be saved through him.

Antiphon to the MAGNIFICAT

Advent 1

Do not be afraid, Mary,
for you have found fa**vor** with God.*
And now, you will conceive and **bear** a Son.
[LH, LBW: Luke 1:30]

Advent 2

The voice of one crying out in the wilderness,
Prepare the way **of** the Lord;*
make straight in the desert a highway **for** our God.
[PBO: Luke 3:4; Isa. 40:3]

Advent 3 The blind shall receive their sight,
the **dead** are raised,*
and the poor have good news **brought** to them.
[LH: Matt 11:5]

December 18 O ADONAI and ruler of the house of Israel,
who appeared to Moses in the burning bush
and gave him the **law** on Sinai:*
Come with an outstretched arm
and redeem us.
[LH, PBO, LBW: Exod. 6:2,3; 3:2; 19:20; 6:6]

Mondays in Advent and December 19

Antiphon to PSALM 40 *Expectans, expectavi Dominum*

The ransomed of the Lord shall return
and come to Zi**on** with singing;*
everlasting joy shall be up**on** their heads. [Isa. 51:1]

on December 19
You are my helper and **my** deliverer;*
do not tarry, **O** my God.

40 *Thanksgiving and plea for help*

1 I waited patiently up**on** the LORD;*
he stooped to me and **heard** my cry.

2 He lifted me out of the desolate pit, out of the **mire** and clay;*
he set my feet upon a high cliff and made my **foot**ing sure.

3 He put a new song in my mouth,
a song of praise **to** our God;*
many shall see, and stand in awe,
and put their trust **in** the LORD.

4 Happy are they who trust **in** the LORD!*
they do not resort to evil spirits or turn **to** false gods.

5 Great things are they that you have done, O LORD my God!
how great your wonders and your **plans** for us!*
there is none who can be com**pared** with you.

6 Oh, that I could make them **known** and tell them!*
but they are more than **I** can count.

7 In sacrifice and offering you **take** no pleasure;*
you have given me **ears** to hear you;

8 Burnt-offering and sin-offering you have **not** required,*
and so I said, "Be**hold**, I come.

9 In the roll of the book it is written con**cern**ing me:*
'I love to do your will, O my God;
your law is deep **in** my heart.'"

10 I proclaimed righteousness in the great **con**gregation;*
behold, I did not restrain my lips;
and that, O **Lord**, you know.

11 Your righteousness have I not hidden in my heart;
I have spoken of your faithfulness and **your** deliverance;*
I have not concealed your love and faithfulness from the great **con**gregation.

12 You are the LORD;
do not withhold your com**pas**sion from me;*
let your love and your faithfulness keep me **safe** for ever,

13 For innumerable troubles have crowded upon me;
my sins have overtaken me, and I **can**not see;*
they are more in number than the hairs of my head,
and **my** heart fails me.

14 Be pleased, O LORD, to de**liv**er me;*
O Lord, make **haste** to help me.

15 Let them be ashamed and altogether dismayed
who seek after my life **to** destroy it;*
let them draw back and be disgraced
who take pleasure in **my** misfortune.

16 Let those who say "Aha!" and gloat over me **be** confounded,*
because they **are** ashamed.

17 Let all who seek you rejoice in you **and** be glad;*
let those who love your salvation continually say,
"Great **is** the Lord!"

18 Though I am poor **and** afflicted,*
the Lord will have re**gard** for me.

19 You are my helper and **my** deliverer;*
do not tarry, **O** my God.

Antiphon The ransomed of the Lord shall return
and come to Zi**on** with singing;*
everlasting joy shall be up**on** their heads.

on December 19
You are my helper and **my** deliverer;*
do not tarry, **O** my God.

Silence for meditation

Lord Jesus Christ, you became obedient to death and your Name was exalted above all others: Teach us always to do the Father's will, so that, made holy by your obedience and united to your sacrifice, we can know your great love in times of sorrow and sing a new song to our God now and for ever. [LH, LBW]

Antiphon to PSALM 67 *Deus misereatur nostri*

Show us the light **of** your countenance*
and come to **us**, O Lord. [LH]

on December 19
Lord, let your ways be known **up**on earth,*
your saving health a**mong** all nations. [LH]

67 *Harvest song*

1 May God be merciful to **us** and bless us,*
show us the light of his countenance, and **come** to us.

2 Let your ways be known **up**on earth,*
your saving health a**mong** all nations.

3 Let the peoples praise **you**, O God;*
let all the **peo**ples praise you.

4 Let the nations be glad and **sing** for joy,*
for you judge the peoples with equity
and guide all the nations **up**on earth.

5 Let the peoples praise **you**, O God;*
let all the **peo**ples praise you.

6 The earth has brought **forth** her increase;*
may God, our own God, give **us** his blessing.

7 May God give **us** his blessing,*
and may all the ends of the earth stand in **awe** of him.

Antiphon Show us the light **of** your countenance*
and come to **us**, O Lord.

on December 19
Lord, let your ways be known **up**on earth,*
your saving health **among** all nations.

Silence for meditation

Father, through your power the earth has brought forth its noblest fruit, the tree of the cross: Unite all people in its embrace, and feed them with its fruit, everlasting life through Jesus Christ our Lord. [LHd, LBW]

+

Stand

THE HYMN is sung. *Instantis adventum Dei*

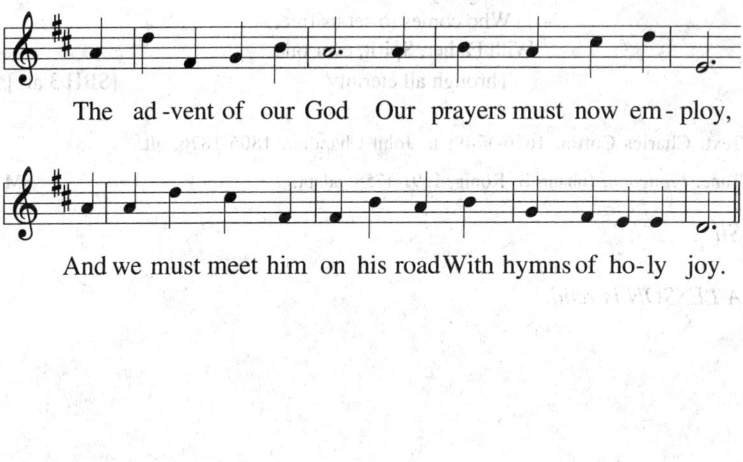

2 The everlasting Son
Incarnate deigns to be,
Himself a servant's form puts on
To set his people free.

3 Come, Zion's daughter, rise
To meet thy lowly king,
Nor let thy faithless heart despise
The peace he comes to bring.

4 As judge, on clouds of light,
He soon will come again,
And all his scattered saints unite
With him in heaven to reign.

5 Before the dawning day
Let sin's foul deeds be gone;
The old life all be put away,
The new life all put on.

6 All glory to the Son,
Who comes to set us free,
With Father, Spirit, ever one,
Through all eternity. [SBH 3 alt.]

Text: Charles Coffin, 1676-1749; tr. John Chandler, 1806-1876, alt.

Tune: *Franconia* Johann B. König, 1691-1758, adapt. SM

Sit

A LESSON is read.

Year 1

Year 2

First Monday in Advent

Luke 20:1-8

Tell us, by what authority are you doing these things? Who is it who gave you this authority?

Matthew 21:1-11

Tell the daughter of Zion, Look, your king is coming to you.

Second Monday in Advent

Luke 21:20-28

Now when these things began to take place, stand up and raise your heads, because your redemption is drawing near.

Matthew 22:23-33

And as for the resurrection of the dead, have you not read what was said to you by God, "I am the God of Abraham, the God of Isaac, and the God of Jacob?" He is God not of the dead, but of the living.

Third Monday in Advent

Luke 22:39-53

Pray that you may not come into the time of trial.

Matthew 24:15-31

Then the sign of the Son of Man will appear in heaven, and then all the tribes of the earth will mourn, and they will see 'the Son of Man coming on the clouds of heaven' with power and great glory.

December 19

John 5:30-47

John was a burning and shining lamp, and you were willing to rejoice for a while in his light.

Luke 1:1-25

With the spirit and power of Elijah, John will go before him, to turn the hearts of the parents to their children, and the disobedient to the wisdom of the righteous, to make ready a people prepared for the Lord.

Antiphon to the MAGNIFICAT

First Monday in Advent

Behold, your King comes, the Ruler **of** the earth;*
he will shatter the yoke **of** our slavery.

[LH: see Zech. 9:9; Isa. 9:4]

Second Monday in Advent

The angel of the Lord brought God's mes**sage** to Mary,*
and she conceived by the **Ho**ly Spirit.

[LH: see Luke 1:35]

Third Monday in Advent

All generations will **call** me blessed;*
the Lord has looked with favor
on the lowliness **of** his servant.

[LH: Luke 1:48]

December 19 *O radix Jesse*

O ROOT OF JESSE,
standing as an ensign before the peoples,
before whom all kings are mute,
to whom the nations **will** do homage:*
Come quickly **to** deliver us.

[LH, PBO: Isa. 11:10; Isa. 52:15; Ps. 22:27; Heb. 10:37]

Tuesdays in Advent and December 20

Antiphon to PSALM 85 *Benedixisti, Domine*

Shower, O heavens, **from** above,*
and let the skies **rain** down righteousness. [CSB: Isa. 45:8a]

on December 20
The Lord will come from his **ho**ly place*
to **save** his people. [LH]

85 *The coming age of justice and peace*

1 You have been gracious to your **land**, O LORD;*
you have restored the good for**tune** of Jacob.

2 You have forgiven the iniquity **of** your people*
and blotted out **all** their sins.

3 You have withdrawn **all** your fury*
and turned yourself from your wrathful **in**dignation.

4 Restore us then, O **God** our Savior;*
let your anger de**part** from us.

5 Will you be displeased with **us** for ever?*
Will you prolong your anger from **age** to age?

6 Will you not give us **life** again,*
that your people may re**joice** in you?

7 Show us your mer**cy**, O LORD,*
and grant us **your** salvation.

8 I will listen to what the LORD **God** is saying,*
for he is speaking peace to his faithful people
and to those who turn their **hearts** to him.

9 Truly, his salvation is very near to **those** who fear him,*
that his glory may dwell **in** our land.

10 Mercy and truth have **met** together;*
righteousness and peace have **kissed** each other.

11 Truth shall spring up **from** the earth,*
and righteousness shall look **down** from heaven.

12 The LORD will indeed **grant** prosperity,*
and our land will **yield** its increase.

13 Righteousness shall **go** before him,*
and peace shall be a pathway **for** his feet.

Antiphon Shower, O heavens, **from** above,*
and let the skies **rain** down righteousness.

on December 20
The Lord will come from his **ho**ly place*
to **save** his people.

Silence for meditation

God of love and faithfulness, you so loved the world that you gave your only Son to be our Savior: Help us to receive him as both Lord and brother and freely celebrate him as our gracious Redeemer now and for ever. [LH, LBW]

+

Antiphon to PSALM 94 *Deus ultionum*

God will grant justice to his **cho**sen ones*
who cry to him **day** and night. [Luke 18:7]

on December 20
Your God will **come** with vengeance,*
he will **come** to save you. [Isa. 35:4]

94 *God, the Judge and Vindicator*

1 O LORD **God** of vengeance,*
O God of vengeance, **show** yourself.

2 Rise up, O Judge **of** the world;*
give the arrogant their **just** deserts.

3 How long shall the wick**ed**, O LORD,*
how long shall the **wick**ed triumph?

4 They bluster **in** their insolence;*
all evildoers are **full** of boasting.

5 They crush your peo**ple**, O LORD,*
and afflict your **cho**sen nation.

6 They murder the widow **and** the stranger*
and put the or**phans** to death.

7 Yet they say, "The LORD **does** not see,*
the God of Jacob **takes** no notice."

8 Consider well, you dullards a**mong** the people;*
when will you fools **un**derstand?

9 He that planted the ear, does **he** not hear?*
he that formed the eye, does **he** not see?

10 He who admonishes the nations, will **he** not punish?*
he who teaches all the world, has **he** no knowledge?

11 The LORD knows our **hu**man thoughts;*
how like a puff of **wind** they are.

12 Happy are they whom you in**struct**, O Lord,*
whom you teach out **of** your law;

13 To give them rest in **evil** days,*
until a pit is dug **for** the wicked.

14 For the LORD will not aban**don** his people,*
nor will he for**sake** his own.

15 For judgment will a**gain** be just,*
and all the true of heart will **fol**low it.

16 Who rose up for me a**gainst** the wicked?*
who took my part against the **e**vildoers?

17 If the LORD had not come **to** my help,*
I should soon have dwelt in the **land** of silence.

18 As often as I said, "My **foot** has slipped,"*
your love, O **LORD**, upheld me.

19 When many cares **fill** my mind,*
your consolations **cheer** my soul.

20 Can a corrupt tribunal have any **part** with you,*
one which frames evil **in**to law?

21 They conspire against the life **of** the just*
and condemn the inno**cent** to death.

22 But the LORD has be**come** my stronghold,*
and my God the rock **of** my trust.

23 He will turn their wickedness back upon them
and destroy them in **their** own malice;*
the LORD our God **will** destroy them.

Antiphon God will grant justice to his **cho**sen ones*
who cry to him **day** and night.

on December 20
Your God will **come** with vengeance,*
he will **come** to save you.

Silence for meditation

Lord Jesus, do not abandon your people, nor ignore the power of the enemy against your Church. Grant that those who suffer for the sake of justice may find consolation in the cross and be filled with your joy now and for ever. [LH, LBW]

+

Stand

THE HYMN is sung. *O Heiland, reiss die Himmel auf*

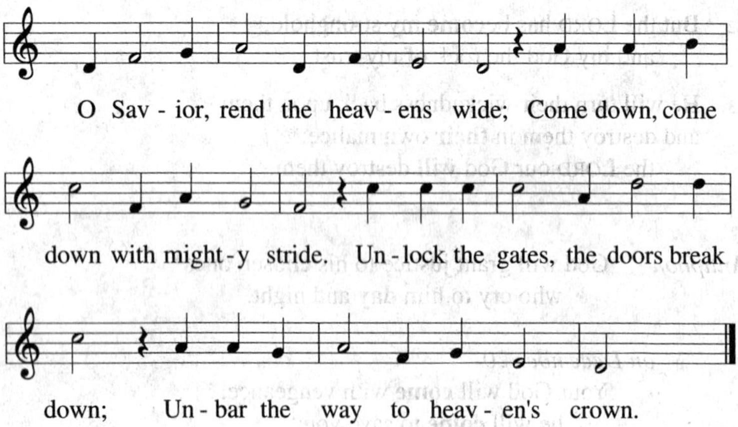

2 O Father, dew from heaven send;
As gentle dew, O Son, descend.
Drop down, you clouds, and torrents bring;
To Jacob's line rain down the King.

3 O earth, in flowering bud be seen;
Clothe hill and dale in garb of green.
O earth, bring forth this Blossom rare;
O Savior, rise from meadow fair.

4 O Fount of hope, how long, how long?
When will you come with comfort strong?
O come, O come, high heaven forego;
Console us in our vale of woe.

5 O Morning Star, O radiant Sun,
When will our hearts behold your dawn?
O Sun, arise; without your light
We grope in gloom and dark of night.

6 Sin's dreadful doom upon us lies;
Grim death looms fierce before our eyes.
O come, lead us with mighty hand
From exile to our promised land.

7 There shall we all our praises bring
Ever to you, our Savior King;
There shall we laud you and adore
For ever and for evermore. [LBW 38]

Text: Old German Catholic spiritual song, Cologne, 1623; trans. Martin L. Seltz (1909-67)
Tune: *O Heiland, reiss die Himmel auf,* Augsburg, 1666 LM

Sit

A LESSON is read.

Year 1	Year 2
First Tuesday in Advent Luke 20:9-18	Matthew 21:12-22
I will send my beloved Son; perhaps they will respect him.	Whatever you ask for in prayer with faith, you will receive.
Second Tuesday in Advent Luke 21:29-38	Matthew 22:34-46
Be alert at all times, praying that you may have the strength to escape all	You shall love the Lord your God with all your heart, and with all your

these things that will take place, and to stand before the Son of Man.	soul, and with all your mind. You shall love your neighbor as yourself.

Third Tuesday in Advent

Luke 22:54-69	Matthew 24:32-44
From now on the Son of Man will be seated at the right hand of the power of God.	You also must be ready, for the Son of Man is coming at an unexpected hour.

December 20

Luke 1:5-25	Luke 1:26-38
With the spirit and power of Elijah he will go before him, to turn the hearts of parents to their children, and the disobedient to the wisdom of the righteous, to make ready a people prepared for the Lord.	He will be great, and will be called the Son of the Most High, and the Lord God will give to him the throne of his ancestor David. He will reign over the house of Jacob for ever, and of his kingdom there will be no end.

Antiphon to the MAGNIFICAT

First Tuesday in Advent

Seek the Lord while he **may** be found;*
call upon him while **he** is near. [LH: Isa. 55:6]

Second Tuesday in Advent

The voice of one crying out in the **wil**derness:*
Prepare the way of the Lord,
make **his** paths straight. [LH: Matt. 3:3]

Third Tuesday in Advent

Before Mary and Joseph **lived** together,*
she was found to be with child from the **Hol**y Spirit.
[LH: Matt. 1:18]

December 20 *O clavis David*

O KEY OF DAVID,
and scepter of the house of Israel,
you open and no one can close,
you close and no **one** can open:*
Come and rescue the prisoners
who dwell in darkness and the sha**dow** of death.
[LH, PBO, LBW: Isa. 22:22; Numb. 24:17; Heb. 1:8; Rev. 3:7; Isa. 42:7; Ps 107:14; Luke 1:79]

Wednesdays in Advent and December 21

Antiphon to PSALM 53 *Dixit insipiens*

Oh, that Israel's de**liv**erance*
would come **out** of Zion!

on December 21
Say to daughter Zion, see your sal**va**tion comes;*
his reward is with him, and his recom**pense** before him.
[Isa. 62:11]

53 *The foolishness of sinners*

1 The fool has said in his heart, "There **is** no God."*
All are corrupt and commit abominable acts;
there is none who does **an**y good.

2 God looks down from heaven up**on** us all,*
to see if there is any who is wise,
if there is one who seeks **af**ter God.

3 Every one has proved faithless;
all alike **have** turned bad;*
there is none who does good; **no**, not one.

4 Have they no knowledge, those **e**vildoers*
who eat up my people like bread
and do not call **up**on God?

5 See how greatly they tremble,
such trembling as **ne**ver was;*
for God has scattered the bones of the enemy;
they are put to shame, because God has re**ject**ed them.

6 Oh, that Israel's deliverance would come **out** of Zion!*
when God restores the fortunes of his people,
Jacob will rejoice and Isra**el** be glad.

Antiphon Oh, that Israel's de**li**verance*
would come **out** of Zion!

on December 21
Say to daughter Zion, see, your sal**va**tion comes;*
his reward is with him, and his recom**pense**
before him.

Silence for meditation

Holy Father, apart from you nothing is true, nothing is holy: Eradicate our sins and give us strength in our weakness, so that all who believe in your Son may rejoice in his glory now and for ever. [LH, LBW]

+

Antiphon to PSALM 17, *Exaudi, Domine, justitiam*

Arise, O Lord;*
deliver me **by** your hand.

on December 21
A shoot shall come out of the **stump** of Jesse,*
and a branch shall grow out **of** his roots. [Isa. 11:1]

17 *An appeal of the innocent*

1 Hear my plea of innocence, O LORD;
give heed **to** my cry;*
listen to my prayer, which does not come from **ly**ing lips.

2 Let my vindication come forth **from** your presence;*
let your eyes be **fixed** on justice.

3 Weigh my heart, summon **me** by night,*
melt me down; you will find no impur**ity** in me.

4 I give no offense with my mouth as **oth**ers do;*
I have heeded the words **of** your lips.

5 My footsteps hold fast to the ways **of** your law;*
in your paths my feet **shall** not stumble.

6 I call upon you, O God, for you will **an**swer me;*
incline your ear to me and **hear** my words.

7 Show me your marvelous **lov**ing-kindness,*
O Savior of those who take refuge at your right hand
from those who rise **up** against them.

8 Keep me as the apple **of** your eye;*
hide me under the shadow **of** your wings,

9 From the wicked **who** assault me,*
from my deadly enemies **who** surround me.

10 They have closed their **heart** to pity,*
and their mouth **speaks** proud things.

11 They press me hard;
now **they** surround me,*
watching how they may cast me **to** the ground,

12 Like a lion, greedy **for** its prey,*
and like a young lion lurking in **se**cret places.

13 Arise, O LORD; confront them and **bring** them down;*
deliver me from the wicked **by** your sword.

14 Deliver me, O LORD, **by** your hand*
from those whose portion in life **is** this world;

15 Whose bellies you fill **with** your treasure,*
who are well supplied with children
and leave their wealth to their **lit**tle ones.

16 But at my vindication I shall **see** your face;*
when I awake, I shall be satisfied, behold**ing** your likeness.

Antiphon A**rise**, O Lord;*
deliver me **by** your hand.

on December 21
A shoot shall come out of the **stump** of Jesse,*
and a branch shall grow out **of** his roots.

Silence for meditation

Lord God, you vindicated your Son when he was unjustly condemned and surrounded by the wicked: Watch over your people as the apple of your eye, and guard our steps until we see your face; through your Son, Jesus Christ our Lord. [LHd, LBW]

+

Stand

THE HYMN is sung.

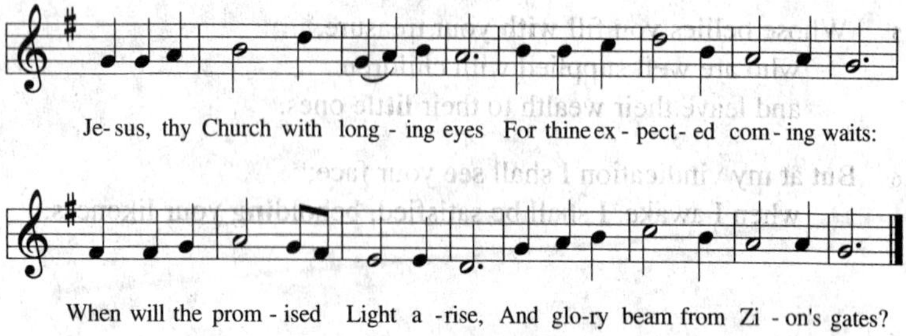

2 E'en now, when tempests round us fall,
And wintry clouds o'ercast the sky,
Thy words with pleasure we recall,
And deem that our redemption's nigh.

3 Come, gracious Lord, our hearts renew,
Our foes repel, our wrongs redress,
Our ancient enmity subdue,
And crown thy gospel with success.

4 O come and reign o'er every land;
Let Satan from his throne be hurled.
All nations bow to thy command
And grace revive a dying world.

5 Teach us in watchfulness and prayer
To wait for the appointed hour;
And fit us by thy grace to share
The triumphs of thy conquering power. [CSB 16]

Text: William Hiley Bathurst, 1796-1877, alt.
Tune: *Herr Jesu Christ, meins Lebens Licht,* from *Nürnberg Gesangbuch*, 1676 LM

Sit

A LESSON is read.

Year 1

First Wednesday in Advent
Luke 20:19-26

Give to the emperor the things that are the emperor's, and to God the things that are God's.

Second Wednesday in Advent
John 7:53-8:11

Let anyone among you who is without sin be the first to throw a stone at her.

Year 2

Matthew 21:23-32

John came to you in the way of righteousness and you did not believe him, but the tax collectors and the prostitutes believed him.

Matthew 23:1-12

The greatest among you will be your servant. All who exalt themselves will be humbled, and all who humble themselves will be exalted.

Third Wednesday in Advent

Mark 1:1-8

See, I am sending my messenger ahead of you, who will prepare your way; the voice of one crying in the wilderness: Prepare the way of the Lord, make his paths straight.

Matthew 24:45-51

Who then is the faithful and wise slave, whom his master has put in charge of his household, to give the other slaves their allowance of food at the proper time? Blessed is that slave whom his master will find at work when he arrives.

December 21

Luke 1:26-38

He will be great, and will be called the Son of the Most High, and the Lord God will give to him the throne of his ancestor David. He will reign over the house of Jacob forever, and of his kingdom there will be no end.

Luke 1:39-48a (48b-56)

Blessed are you among women, and blessed is the fruit of your womb.

Antiphon to the MAGNIFICAT

First Wednesday in Advent

Out of Zion shall go **forth** instruction;*
the word of the Lord from Jer**u**salem. [LH: Micah 4:2]

Second Wednesday in Advent

Zion, you will **be** renewed,*
and you will see the Righteous One who is com**ing** to you.
[LH: see Hos. 11:9]

Third Wednesday in Advent

You, O Lord, are the one whose coming **was** foretold:*
we long for you to come and set your **peo**ple free. [LH]

December 21 [Winter Solstice] *O Oriens*

O DAYSPRING,
splendor of light everlasting and sun of **right**eousness:*
come and give light to those who sit in darkness
and in the sha**dow** of death.
[LH, PBO, LBW: Mal. 4:2; Luke 1:78-79]

Thursdays in Advent and December 22

Antiphon to PSALM 126 *In convertendo*

Those who **sowed** with tears*
will reap with **songs** of joy. [LH]

on December 22
The Lord, the mighty God, will come **forth** from Zion*
to set his **peo**ple free. [LH: see Amos 1:2]

126 *Song of the returning exiles*

1 When the LORD restored the for**tunes** of Zion,*
then were we like **those** who dream.

2 Then was our mouth **filled** with laughter,*
and our tongue with **shouts** of joy.

3 Then they said a**mong** the nations,*
"The LORD has done great **things** for them."

4 The LORD has done great **things** for us,*
and we are **glad** indeed.

5 Restore our for**tunes**, O LORD,*
like the watercourses **of** the Negev.

6 Those who **sowed** with tears*
will reap with **songs** of joy.

7 Those who go out weeping, carry**ing** the seed,*
will come again with joy, shoulder**ing** their sheaves.

Antiphon Those who **sowed** with tears*
will reap with **songs** of joy.

on December 22
The Lord, the mighty God, will come **forth** from Zion*
to set his **peo**ple free.

Silence for meditation

Lord Jesus, our life and our resurrection, the tears you sowed in the sorrow of your Passion brought the earth to flower on Easter morning: Renew the wonders of your power in the Church, so that, after the sorrows of our exile, we may come home to you in gladness and praise you now and for ever. [LHd, LBW]

+

Antiphon to PSALM 62, *Nonne Deo*

For God alone my soul in **si**lence waits;*
truly, my hope **is** in him.

on December 22
We wait for the **bless**ed hope,*
and the manifestation of the glory **of** our Savior.
[LH, PBO: Titus 2:13]

62 *Confidence in God's protection*

1 For God alone my soul in **si**lence waits;*
from him comes **my** salvation.

2 He alone is my rock and **my** salvation,*
my stronghold, so that I shall not be **great**ly shaken.

3 How long will you assail me to crush me,
all of **you** together,*
as if you were a leaning fence, a **top**pling wall?

4 They seek only to bring me down from my **place** of honor;*
lies are their **chief** delight.

5 They bless **with** their lips,*
but in their **hearts** they curse.

6 For God alone my soul in **si**lence waits;*
truly, my hope **is** in him.

7 He alone is my rock and **my** salvation,*
my stronghold, so that I shall **not** be shaken.

8 In God is my safety **and** my honor;*
God is my strong rock **and** my refuge.

9 Put your trust in him al**ways**, O people,*
pour out your hearts before him, for God **is** our refuge.

10 Those of high degree are but a **fleet**ing breath,*
even those of low estate can**not** be trusted.

11 On the scales they are lighter **than** a breath,*
all of **them** together.

12 Put no trust in extortion;
in robbery take no **emp**ty pride;*
though wealth increase, set not your **heart** upon it.

13 God has spoken once, twice **have** I heard it,*
that power be**longs** to God.

14 Steadfast love is **yours**, O Lord,*
for you repay everyone according **to** his deeds.

Antiphon For God alone my soul in silence waits;*
truly, my hope is in him.

on December 22
We wait for the **bless**ed hope,*
and the manifestation of the glory **of** our Savior.

Silence for meditation

Lord God, in a constantly changing world we look to you as our rock of hope: Hear us as we pour out our hearts to you, and give us your grace and secure protection; through your Son, Jesus Christ our Lord.

[LH, LBW]

+

Stand

THE HYMN is sung. *Tröstet, tröstet, meine Lieben*

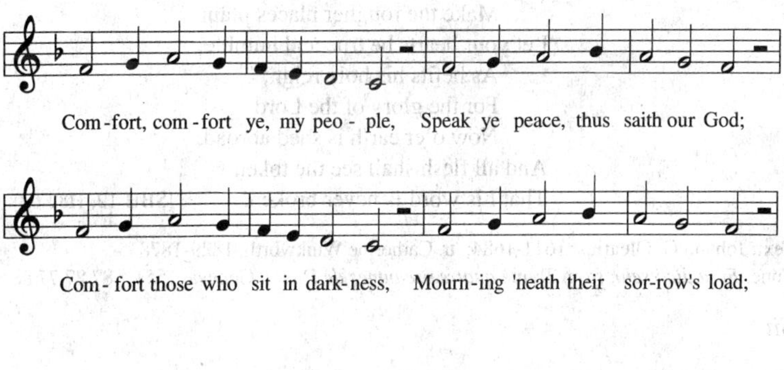

2 For the herald's voice is crying
In the desert far and near,
Bidding all hearts to repentance
Since the kingdom now is here.
O, that warning cry obey!
Now prepare for God a way;
Let the valleys rise to meet him,
And the hills bow down to greet him.

3 Make ye straight what long was crooked,
Make the rougher places plain;
Let your hearts be true and humble,
As befits his holy reign;
For the glory of the Lord
Now o'er earth is shed abroad,
And all flesh shall see the token
That his word is never broken. [SBH 12, H82 67]

Text: Johann G. Olearius, 1611-1684; tr. Catherine Winkworth, 1829-1878
Tune: *Freu dich sehr,* from *Trente quatre pseaumes de David*, Geneva, 1551 87 87 77 88

Sit

A LESSON is read.

Year 1	Year 2
First Thursday in Advent Luke 20:27-40	Matthew 21:33-46
Now he is God not of the dead, but of the living; for to him all of them are alive.	The stone that the builders rejected has become the cornerstone; this was the Lord's doing, and it is amazing in our eyes.
Second Thursday in Advent Luke 22:1-13	Matthew 23:13-26
The teacher asks you, "Where is the guest room, where I may eat the Passover with my disciples?"	You lock people out of the kingdom of heaven. For you do not go in yourselves, and when others are going in, you stop them.
Third Thursday in Advent Matthew 3:1-12	Matthew 25:1-13
The voice of one crying out in the wilderness: "Prepare the way of the Lord, make his paths straight."	Keep awake therefore, for you know neither the day nor the hour.
December 22 Luke 1:39-48a (48b-56)	Luke 1:57-66
Blessed are you among women, and blessed is the fruit of your womb.	Now the time came for Elizabeth to give birth, and she bore a son.

Antiphon to the MAGNIFICAT

First Thursday in Advent

Blessed are you **a**mong women,*

and blessed is the fruit **of** your womb.

[LH: Luke 1:42]

Second Thursday in Advent

The one who is coming after me exist**ed** before me;*

I am not worthy to un**tie** his sandals.

[LH: see John 1:30,27]

Third Thursday in Advent

Rejoice with Jer**u**salem,*

and be glad for her, all **you** who love her.

[LH: Isa. 66:10]

December 22 *O rex gentium*

O KING OF THE NATIONS,
the ruler they long for,
the cornerstone unit**ing** all people:*
Come and save us all,
whom you formed **out** of clay.

[LH, PBO, LBW: Jer. 10:7; Hag. 2:7 (AV); Isa. 28:16; Ephes. 2:14, 20-21; Gen. 2:7]

Fridays in Advent and December 23

Antiphon to PSALM 120 *Ad Dominum*

Have courage, all of you, **lost** and fearful;*
take heart and say, Our God will **come** to save us.

[LH: see Isa. 35:4]

on December 23

Our King will **come** from Zion;*
the Lord Emmanuel is his **mighty** Name.

[LH: see Rom. 11:26; Matt. 1:23]

120 *Longing for peace*

1 When I was in trouble, I called **to** the LORD;*
I called to the LORD, and he **an**swered me.

2 Deliver me, O LORD, from **ly**ing lips*
and from the de**ceit**ful tongue.

3 What shall be done to you, and what **more** besides,*
O you de**ceit**ful tongue?

4 The sharpened arrows **of** a warrior,*
along with hot **glow**ing coals.

5 How hateful it is that I must **lodge** in Meshech*
and dwell among the **tents** of Kedar!

6 Too long have I **had** to live*
among the ene**mies** of peace.

7 I am on the **side** of peace,*
but when I speak of it, they **are** for war.

Antiphon Have courage, all of you, **lost** and fearful;*
take heart and say, Our God will **come** to save us.

on December 23
Our King will **come** from Zion;*
the Lord Emmanuel is his **might**y Name.

Silence for meditation

Lord Jesus, you blessed the peacemakers and called them children of God: Give us that peace which the world cannot give, so that your Church may be freed from the schemes of the arrogant and, devoted to works of peace, may go forward joyfully to meet you, the Prince of Peace, our Savior and our Lord. [LH, LBW]

+

Antiphon to PSALM 130, *De profundis*

I wait for the Lord; my soul **waits** for him;*
in his word **is** my hope.

on December 23
Come, Lord, do **not** delay;*
free your people **from** their sin.
[CSB, SBH, LH: see Ps. 40:17, 70:5]

130 *A cry from the depths*

1 Out of the depths have I called to you, O LORD;
LORD, **hear** my voice;*
let your ears consider well the voice of my **sup**plication.

2 If you, LORD, were to note what is **done** amiss,*
O LORD, **who** could stand?

3 For there is forgive**ness** with you;*
therefore you **shall** be feared.

4 I wait for the LORD; my soul **waits** for him;*
in his word **is** my hope.

5 My soul waits for the LORD,
more than watchmen **for** the morning,*
more than watchmen **for** the morning.

6 O Israel, wait **for** the LORD,*
for with the LORD **there** is mercy;

7 With him there is plente**ous** redemption,*
and he shall redeem Israel from **all** their sins.

Antiphon I wait for the Lord; my soul **waits** for him;*
in his word **is** my hope.

on December 23
Come, Lord, do **not** delay;*
free your people **from** their sin.

Silence for meditation

God of might and compassion, you sent your Word into the world as a watchman to announce the dawn of salvation: Do not leave us in the depths of our sins, but listen to your Church pleading for the fullness of your redeeming grace; through Jesus Christ our Lord. [LHd, LBW]

+

Stand

THE HYMN is sung. *Komm, du wertes Lösegeld*

2 Enter now my waiting heart,
Glorious King and Lord most holy.
Dwell in me and ne'er depart
Though I am but poor and lowly.
What vast riches will be mine
When you are my guest divine.

3 My hosannas and my palms
Graciously receive, I pray you;
Evermore, as best I can,

Homage I will gladly pay you,
And in faith I will embrace
Life eternal by your grace.

4 Hail! Hosanna! David's Son!
Jesus, hear our supplication!
Let your kingdom, scepter, crown
Bring us blessing and salvation;
That for ever we may sing:
Hail, Hosanna! to our king.

[TLH 55, LBW 24]

Text: Johann G. Olearius, 1611-1684; tr. August Crull, 1846-1923, alt.
Tune: *Meinen Jesum lass ich nicht,* from *Neuverfertigtes Gesangbuch,* Darmstadt, 1699 78 78 77

Sit

A LESSON is read.

Year 1

First Friday in Advent
Luke 20:41-21:4

Truly I tell you, this poor widow has put in more than all of them; for all of them contributed out of their abundance, but she out of her poverty has put in all she had to live on.

Year 2

Matthew 21:1-14

Go therefore into the main streets, and invite everyone you find to the wedding banquet.

Second Friday in Advent
Luke 22:14-30

The greatest among you must become like the youngest, and the leader like one who serves.

Matthew 23:27-39

How often have I desired to gather your children together as a hen gathers her brood under her wings, and you were not willing! See, your house is left to you, desolate.

Third Friday in Advent
Matthew 11:2-15

For all the prophets and the law prophesied until John came; and if you are willing to accept it, he is Elijah who is to come.

Matthew 25:14-30

For to all those who have, more will be given, and they will have an abundance; but from those who have nothing, even what they have will be taken away.

December 23
Luke 1:57-66

Now the time came for Elizabeth to give birth, and she bore a son.

Luke 1:67-80

The child grew and became strong in spirit, and he was in the wilderness until the day he appeared publicly to Israel.
or Matthew 1:1-17

An account of the genealogy of Jesus the Messiah, the son of David, the son of Abraham.

Antiphon to the MAGNIFICAT

First Friday in Advent

Out of Egypt I have **called** my son;*
he will come to **save** his people.

[LH: see Matt. 2:15]

Second Friday in Advent

With joy will **you** draw water*
from the wells **of** salvation.

[LH: Isa. 12:3]

Third Friday in Advent

This was the testimony given by **John** the Baptist:*
the one who comes after me exist**ed** before me.

[LH: John 1:19,30]

December 23 *O Emmanuel*

O EMMANUEL, our king and lawgiver,
the desire of the nations **and** their Savior:*
come and save us, O **Lord** our God.

[LH, PBO, LBW: Isa. 7:14, 33:22; Hag. 2:7(AV)]

✠

MORNING PRAYER

Matins or Morning Praise during Advent

Stand

Leader

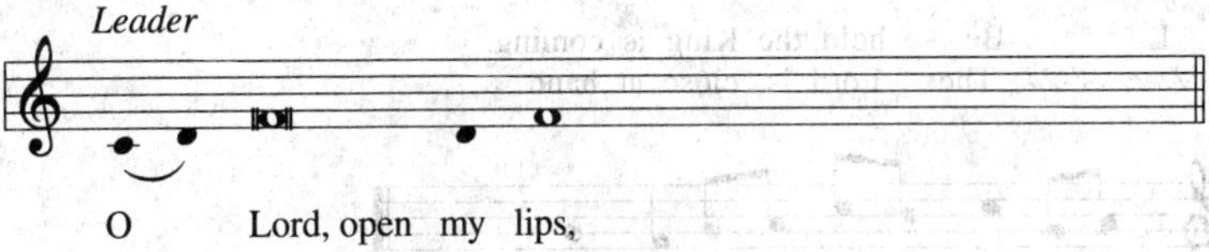

Congregation

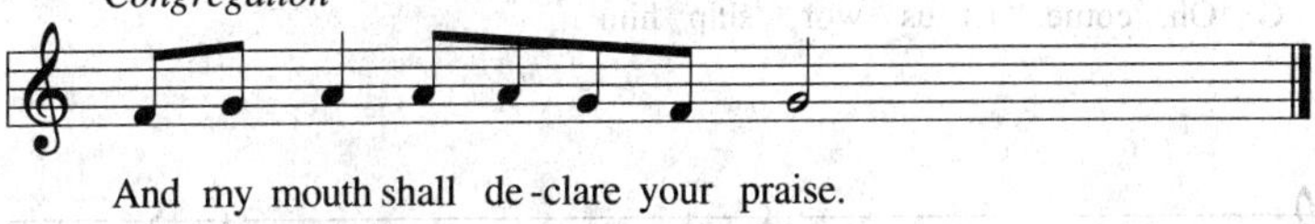

Leader and Congregation

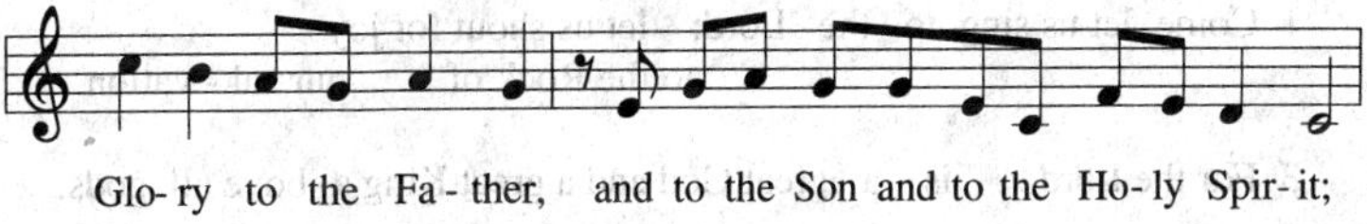

The PSALMODY begins with this song of praise, Venite exultemus.

L Be - hold, the King is coming.
Dec. 17-24: The Lord is close at hand.

C Oh, come, let us wor - ship him.

1 Come, let us sing to the Lord; let us shout for joy
to the Rock of . . . . our sal - vation.

3 For the Lord . . . is a great God and a great King a- bove all gods.

5 The sea is his, for he made it; and his hands
have mold - ed the dry land.

8 Glory to the
Father, and . . . . to the Son, and to the . . . . . . Ho - ly Spirit;

2 Let us come before
his presence . . . . with thanks-giving and raise a
loud shout to him with psalms.

4 In his hand are
the caverns . . . . . of the earth, and the heights
of the hills are al - so his.

6 Come, let us bow
down and . . . . . . bend the knee, and kneel
before the . . . . Lord, our Maker.

7 For he . . . . is our God; and we are
the people of
his pasture and
the sheep . . . . . . of his hand.

9 As it was in
the begin - ning, is now, and will be for ev- er. A-men.

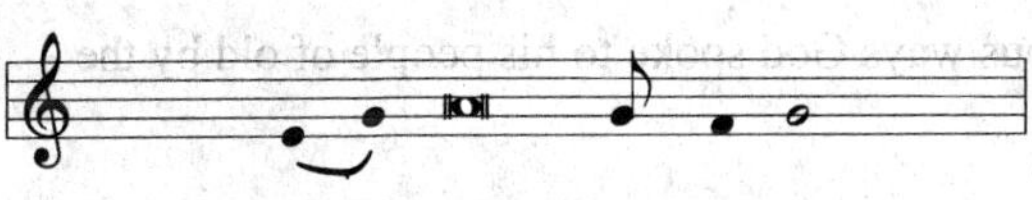

L Be - hold, the King is coming.
Dec. 17-24: The Lord is close at hand.

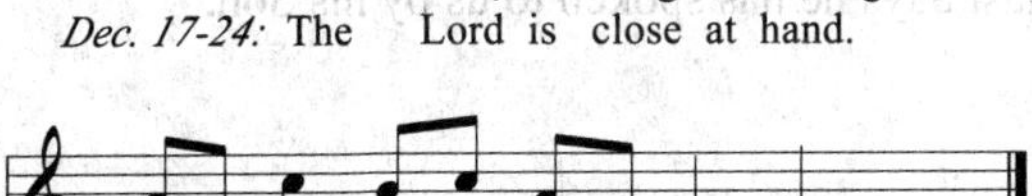

C Oh, come, let us wor - ship him.

Sit

A second psalm is sung or said; additional psalms and an Old Testament canticle may be sung or said also. Silence for meditation follows each psalm or canticle. The psalm prayer appropriate to each psalm or canticle follows the silence.

C Amen

Stand

THE HYMN is sung.

Sit

One or two LESSONS are read. Silence for meditation follows each reading.

The Responsory to the reading(s) follows the silence. After the Responsory the leader then continues:

L In many and various ways God spoke to his people of old by the prophets.

C But now in these last days he has spoken to us by his Son.

Stand

The GOSPEL CANTICLE, Benedictus Dominus Deus, *is sung or said. The proper Antiphon is given on pp. 113-181.*

The Antiphon is sung or said.

1 ✠ Blessed be the Lord,
the . . . . God of Israel; he has come
to his people and set them free.

3 Through his holy
prophets he promised
of old that he
would save us . . . . . . from our enemes, from the hands of all who hate us.

5 This was the oath
he swore to our . . . . fa - ther Abraham: to set us free
from the hands of our enemies,

2 He has raised up for
us a . . . . might - y Savior, born of the house of his ser -vant David.

4 He promised to show
mercy . . . . to our fathers and to remember his . . . ho - ly covenant.

6 free to worship him with - out fear, holy and righteous in
his sight all the days of our life.

7 You, my child, shall be
called the prophet of the most high, for you will
go before
the Lord to pre - pare his way,
9 In the tender
compassion . . . . of our God, the dawn
from on
high shall break up - on us.
11 Glory to the
Father and . . . . to the Son, and to the . . . . Ho - ly Spirit;

8 to give his people
knowledge . . . . of sal - vation by the forgiveness . . . . of their sins.

10 to shine on those
who dwell in darkness
and the shad - ow of death, and to guide
our feet into the . . . . . way of peace.
12 as it was in the
begin - ning, is now, and will be for ev - er. A - men.

The Antiphon is repeated.

Kneel or stand

The SUFFRAGES are said. [BCP, LBW]

L Show us your mercy, O Lord;
C And grant us your salvation. [Ps. 85:7]

L Clothe your ministers with righteousness;
C Let your people sing with joy. [Ps. 132:9]

L Give peace, O Lord, in all the world; [see Ps. 122:7]
C For only in you can we live in safety. [see Ps. 4:8]

L Lord, keep this nation under your care;
C And guide us in the way of justice and truth.

L Let your way be known upon earth;
C Your saving health among all nations. [Ps. 67:2]

L Let not the needy, O Lord, be forgotten;
C Nor the hope of the poor be taken away. [Ps. 9:18]

L Create in us clean hearts, O God; [Ps. 51:11a]
C And sustain us with your Holy Spirit. [Ps. 51:13b]

L Lord, hear my prayer;
C And let my cry come before you. [Ps. 102:1]

L The Lord be with you.
C And also with you.

L Let us pray.

The PRAYER OF THE DAY is said.

First Week in Advent

Stir up your power, O Lord, and come; that by your protection we may be rescued from the threatening perils of our sins and saved by your mighty deliverance; for you live and reign with the Father and the Holy Spirit, one God, now and for ever.

[Greg., MR, CB, CSB, SBH, LBW; RS Fri. of Adv. 1]

Second Week in Advent

Stir up our hearts, O Lord, to make ready the way of your only-begotten Son, so that by his advent we may be enabled to serve you with purified minds; through Jesus Christ our Lord who lives and reigns with you and the Holy Spirit, one God, now and for ever.

[Gel., MR, Sarum, AC, CB, CSB, SBH, LBW; RS Thurs. of Advent 2]

Third Week in Advent

Lord, we beseech you, give ear to our prayers, and enlighten the darkness of our hearts by your gracious visitation; for you live and reign with the Father and the Holy Spirit, one God, now and for ever.

[Greg., MR, Sarum, 1549 BCP, CB, CSB, SBH, LBW, RS Advent 3 Monday]

BCP: below, Advent 4

The prayers for December 17-23 are given with the propers for those days, pp. 113-181.

Fourth Sunday in Advent

Stir up, we beseech you, O Lord, your power and come; and with great might succor us, so that our deliverance, impeded by our sins, may be hastened by your gracious mercy; through your Son, Jesus

Christ our Lord, who lives and reigns with you and the Holy Spirit, one God now and for ever.

[Gel., MR, CB, CSB, SBH; RS Thurs. of Adv. 1, BCP Adv.3]

Other prayers may be said by the leader with the congregation responding Amen *to each. The leader then concludes:*

L Shower, O heavens, from above
and let the skies rain down righteousness.

C Let the earth open,
that salvation may spring up. [CSB, LH: Isa 45:8]

We give thanks to you, holy Lord, almighty Father, everlasting God, for you have protected us through the night and brought us safely to the morning. Give us grace, we implore you, to pass this day without sin, so that when evening comes we may once again give thanks to you; through Jesus Christ our Lord. [Gel., Greg., AC; tr. DvD and GA]

L Lord, remember us in your kingdom, and teach us to pray:

C Our Father in heaven,
hallowed be your Name
your kingdom come,
your will be done,
on earth as in heaven.
Give us today our daily bread.
Forgive us our sins
as we forgive those
who sin against us.
Save us from the time of trial
and deliver us from evil.
For the kingdom, the power,
and the glory are yours,
now and for ever. Amen.

C Our Father who art in heaven,
hallowed be thy Name
thy kingdom come,
thy will be done,
on earth as it is in heaven.
Give us this day our daily bread;
and forgive us our trespasses,
as we forgive those
who sin against us;
And lead us not into temptation
but deliver us from evil.
For thine is the kingdom,
and the power, and the glory,
for ever and ever. Amen.

Stand

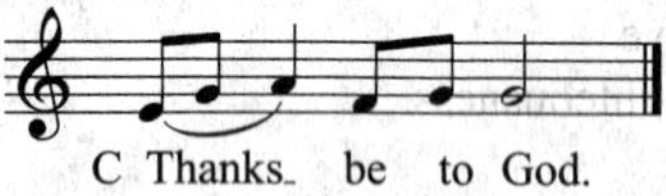

The BENEDICTION concludes the service when there is no sermon nor Paschal Blessing. On Sundays the Paschal Blessing may replace the benediction. A hymn may follow the benediction.

When there is a sermon, the order continues as on p. 20; on Sundays the Paschal Blessing may follow the prayer after the sermon.

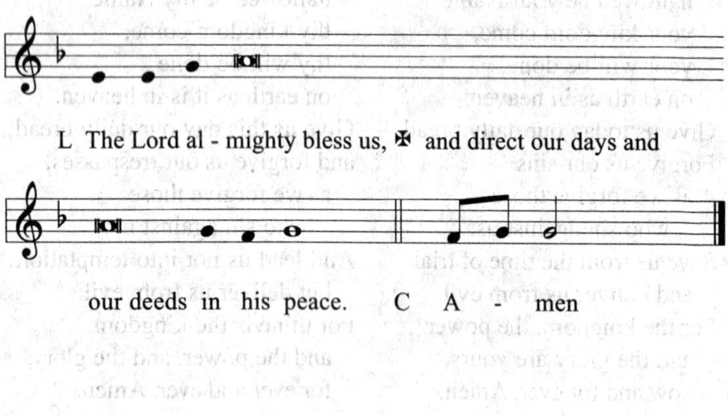

The PASCHAL BLESSING may be used on Sundays to conclude Morning Prayer. The service may be led from the font.

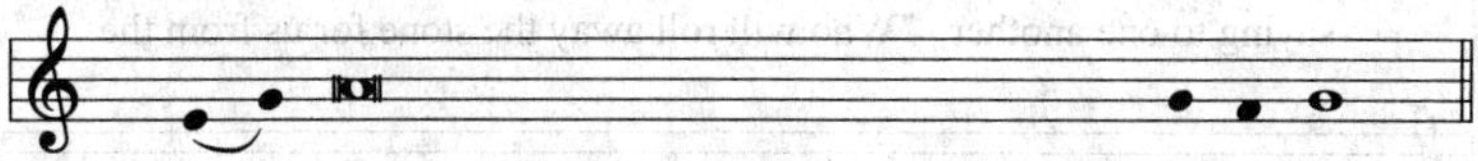

L As many as have been baptized into Christ have put on Christ.

C Al - le - lu - ia.

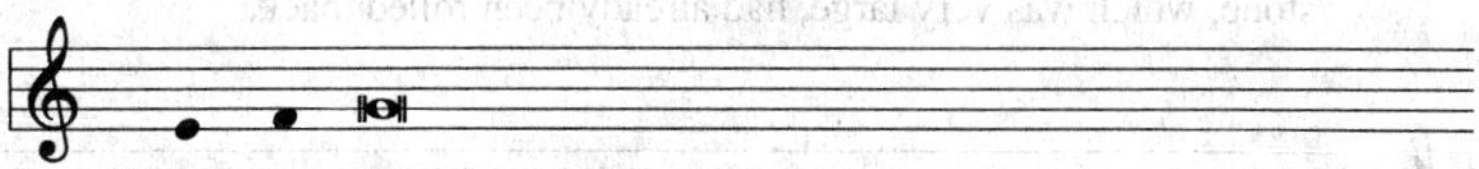

L When the Sabbath was over, Mary Magdalene, and Mary, the

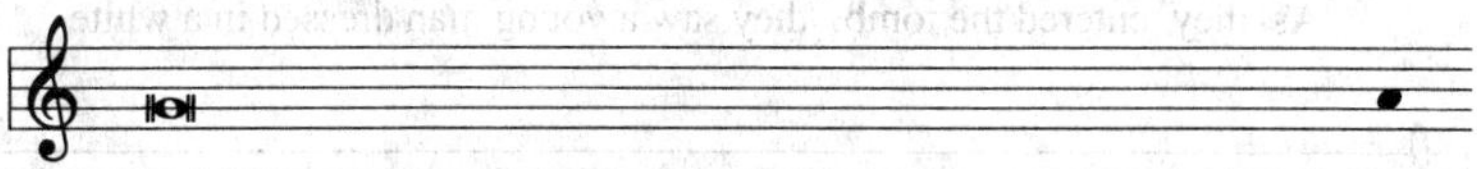

mother of James, and Salome, brought spices, so that they might go

and a - noint him. And ve - ry early on the first day of the week,

when the sun had risen, they went to the tomb. They had been

saying to one another, "Who will roll away the stone for us from the
en - trance to the tomb?" When they looked up, they saw that the
stone, which was very large, had already been rolled back.
As they entered the tomb, they saw a young man dressed in a white
robe sitting on the right side; and they were a - larmed. But he said to
them, "Do not be alarmed; you are looking for Jesus of Nazareth,
who was crucified. He has been raised; he is not here. Look, there is

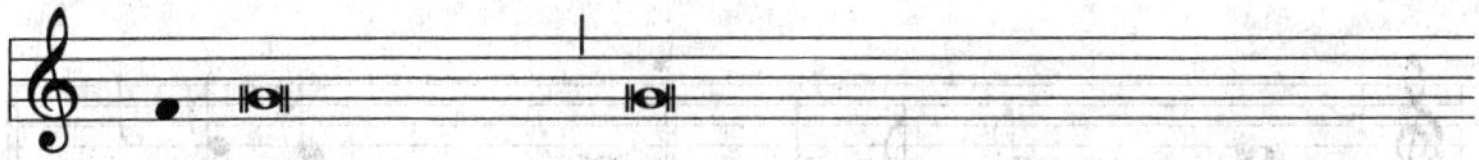

the place they laid him. But go, tell the disciples and Peter that he is

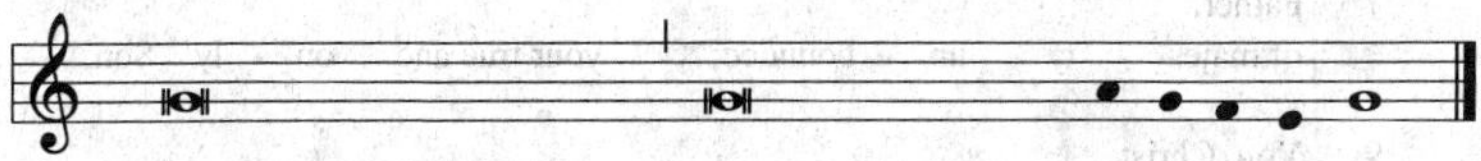

going ahead of you to Galilee; there you will see him, just as he told you."

[Mark 16:1-7. Setting © 1993 Richard Hillert]

The Te Deum Laudamus is sung.

1 You are . . . . . . God; we praise you. You are the Lord; we ac - claim you.

3 To you all angels, all the pow'rs of heaven, cherubim and seraphim sing in end - less praise:

5 The glorious company of the a - pos - tles praise you. The noble fellowship of pro - phets praise you.

2 You are the e - ter - nal Father; all creation . . . . wor - ships you.

4 Holy, holy, holy Lord, God of . . . pow'r and might, heaven and earth are full . . . . . . of your glory.

6 The white-robed army of . . . . mar - tyrs praise you. Throughout the world the holy Church ac - claims you:

7 Father,
of majes - ty un - bounded; your true and on - ly Son,

9 You, Christ
are the . . . . . king of glory, the eternal
Son . . . . of the Father.

11 You overcame
the . . . . sting of death, and opened
the kingdom
of heaven to all be - lievers.

13 Come, then,
Lord, and help your people, bought with
the price of your own blood.

8 worthy . . . . of all worship; and the Holy
Spirit, advo - cate and guide.

10 When you
became man to set us free, you did not
spurn the . . . . vir - gin's womb.

12 You are seated
at God's right hand in glory. We believe that
you will come and be our judge.

14 and bring us with your saints to glory . . . . ev - er - lasting.

L Save your people, Lord, and bless your in-her-i-tance;
C Govern them and uphold them, now and always.
L Day by day we bless you;
C We praise your Name for ev-er.
L Keep us today, Lord from all sin.
C Have mercy on us, Lord, have mercy.
L Lord, show us your love and mer cy;
C For we put our trust in you.

L In you, Lord, is our hope;
C And we shall never hope in vain.
L Almighty God, give us grace to cast away the works of darkness, and
put on the ar -mor of light, now in the time of this mortal life in which
your Son came to visit us in great hu - mility; that at the last day,
when he shall come again in his glorious majesty to judge both the living
and the dead, we may rise to life im-mortal; through him who lives
and reigns with you and the Holy Spirit, one God, now and for ever.

[BCP]

C A - men

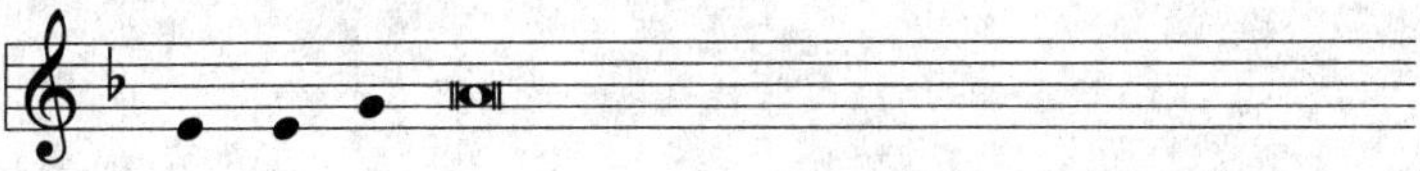

L The Lord al - mighty bless us, ✠ and direct our days and

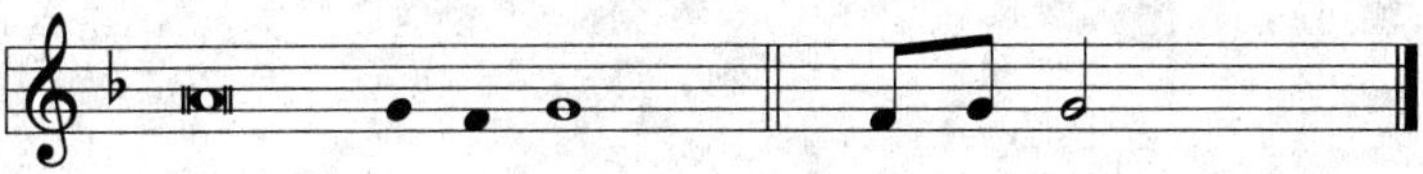

our deeds in his peace. C A - men

Sundays in Advent and December 17

Antiphon to PSALM 24 *Domini est terra*

Advent 1 — In that day the mountains shall **drip** sweet wine,*
and the hills shall flow with **milk** and honey.
[LH, LBW: Joel 3:18]

Advent 2 — Zion is our mighty citadel,
our saving Lord its wall **and** defense;*
throw open the gates, for our God is **here** among us.
[LH: see Isa. 26:1-2]

Advent 3 — The Lord is coming with**out** delay.*
He will reveal things kept hidden
and show himself to **all** the world.
[LH: see Isa. 48:6; Jer. 33:3]

December 17 — Blow the trumpet in Zion,
for the day of the **Lord** is near.*
Behold, he **comes** to save us.
[LH, PBO: see Joel 2:1]

24 *The Lord's entry into his temple*

1 The earth is the LORD's and all **that** is in it,*
the world and all who **dwell** therein.

2 For it is he who founded it up**on** the seas*
and made it firm upon the rivers **of** the deep.

3 "Who can ascend the hill **of** the LORD?*
and who can stand in his **ho**ly place?"

4 "Those who have clean hands and **a** pure heart,*
who have not pledged themselves to falsehood,
nor sworn by what **is** a fraud.

5 They shall receive a blessing **from** the LORD*
and a just reward from the God of **their** salvation."

6 Such is the generation of **those** who seek him,*
of those who seek your face, O **God** of Jacob.

7 Lift up your heads, O gates;
lift them high, O ever**last**ing doors;*
and the King of glory **shall** come in.

8 "Who is this **King** of glory?"*
"The LORD, strong and mighty,
the LORD, mighty in battle."

9 Lift up your heads, O gates;
lift them high, O ever**last**ing doors;*
and the King of glory **shall** come in.

10 "Who is he, this **King** of glory?"*
"The LORD of hosts,
he is the **King** of glory."

The Antiphon is repeated.

Silence for meditation

Lord God, ruler and guide of heaven and earth, you made your Son a priest for ever and brought him into your everlasting temple: Open our hearts that the King of glory may enter, and bring us rejoicing to your holy mountain, where you live and reign, one God, now and for ever.

[LHd, LBW]

+

Antiphon to the OLD TESTAMENT CANTICLE *Exultavit cor meum*

Advent 1 This is our heav**en**ly King;*
he comes with power and might to **save** the nations.
[LH]

Advent 2 Our God will come **with** great power*
to enlighten the eyes **of** his servants.
[LH: see Ezra 9:8]

Advent 3 I shall enfold Zion with **my** salvation*
and shed my glory a**round** Jerusalem.
[LH: see Isa. 46:13b]

December 17 Your all-powerful **word**, O Lord,*
will come to earth from his **throne** of glory.
[LH: see Wis. 18:15]

The Song of Hannah 1 Samuel 2:1-10

My heart exults **in** the Lord;*
my strength is exalted **in** my God.

My mouth de**rides** my enemies,*
exultant because **you** have saved me.

There is no Holy One **like** the Lord;*
there is no Rock **like** our God.

Stop **your** proud boasting;*
let not arrogance come **from** your mouth;

For the Lord is a **God** of knowledge,*
and by him ac**tions** are weighed.

The bows of the mighty are broken,*
but the feeble **gird** on strength.

Those who were full have hired themselves **out** for bread,*
but those who were hungry are **fat** with spoil.

The barren has borne **se**ven children,*
but she who has many children **is** forlorn.

The Lord kills and **brings** to life;*
he brings down to Sheol and **rais**es up.

The Lord makes poor **and** makes rich;*
he brings low, he al**so** exalts.

He raises up the poor **from** the dust;*
he lifts the needy **from** the ashes

To make them **sit** with princes*
 and inherit a **seat** of honor.

The pillars of the earth **are** the Lord's,*
 and on them he has **set** the world.

He will guard the feet of his **faith**ful ones;*
 but the wicked shall perish in darkness,
 for not by might does **one** prevail.

The Lord! His adversaries **shall** be shattered*
 when the High God will thunder **out** of heaven.

The Lord will judge the ends **of** the earth;*
 he will give strength to his king
 and exalt the power of **his** anointed. [CSB, SBH; NRSV, alt.]

The Antiphon is repeated.

Silence for meditation

Lord, we beseech you mercifully to hear the prayers of your people, that we, who for our sins are justly afflicted, may be consoled by your visitation; for you live and reign with the Father and the Holy Spirit, one God, now and for ever. [Gel., MR Ember Sat., CSB, SBH]

+

Antiphon to PSALM 150 *Laudate Dominum in sanctis ejus*

Advent 1 The mountains and hills will sing praise to God;
all the trees of the forest will **clap** their hands;*
 for he is coming,
 the Lord of a kingdom that **lasts** for ever.
[LH: see Ps. 96:12]

Advent 2 Ho, everyone who thirsts, come **to** the waters;*
 seek the Lord while he **may** be found.
[LH: Isa. 55:1,6]

Advent 3 Zion is our mighty citadel,
our saving Lord its wall and **its** defense;*
open wide the gates: our God is **here** among us.
[LH, PBO: see Ps. 48:1-2; Isa. 26:1-2]

December 17 The Lord is here; go out to **meet** him, saying,*
Great is his birth, eternal his kingdom,
strong God, Ruler of all, **Prince** of Peace.
[LH: see Matt. 25:6; Isa. 9:6]

150 *The great alleluia*

1 Hallelujah!
Praise God in his **ho**ly temple;*
praise him in the firmament **of** his power.

2 Praise him for his **migh**ty acts;*
praise him for his ex**cel**lent greatness.

3 Praise him with the blast **of** the ram's-horn;*
praise him with **lyre** and harp.

4 Praise him with tim**brel** and dance;*
praise him with **strings** and pipe.

5 Praise him with re**sound**ing cymbals;*
praise him with loud-**clang**ing cymbals.

6 Let everything **that** has breath*
praise the LORD.
Hallelujah!

The Antiphon is repeated.

Silence for meditation

God of surpassing greatness, enthroned upon the praises of your people, fill our hearts with your love and unite our voices with the praise of all creation so that you may be honored and glorified by everything that has breath; through Jesus Christ our Lord. [PHP]

Stand

THE HYMN is sung. *Verbum supernum prodiens*

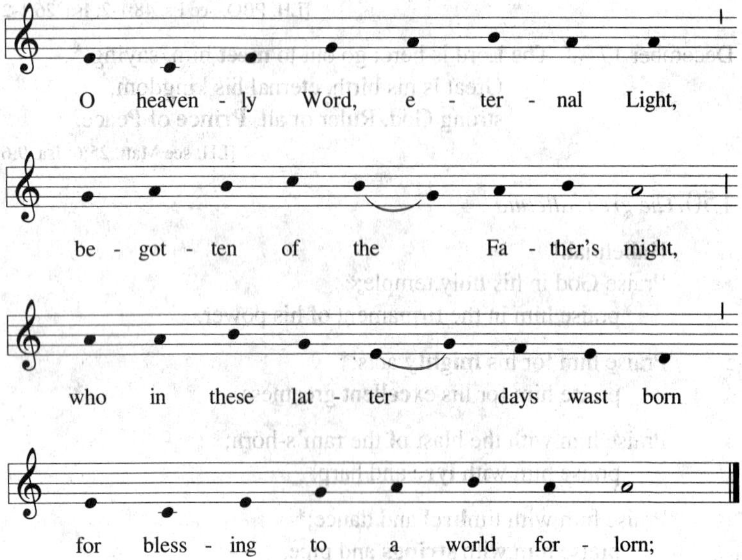

2 Pour light upon us from above,
And fire our hearts with ardent love,
That, as we hear thy truth today,
All wrong desires may burn away;

3 And when, as judge, thou drawest nigh
The secrets of our hearts to try,
To recompense each hidden sin
And bid the saints their reign begin;

4 O let us not, for evil past,
Be driven from thy face at last,
But with thy saints for evermore
Behold thee, love thee, and adore.

5 To God the Father, God the Son,
And God the Spirit, ever one,
Praise, honor, might, and glory be
From age to age eternally. [H82 63]

Text: Latin hymn, c. 7th cent.; tr. *Hymnal 1982*
Tune: *Verbum supernum prodiens,* Plainsong mode 2, Nevers MS, 13th cent. LM

Sit

One or two LESSONS are read.

Silence for meditation follows each reading.

Year 1	Year 2
Advent 1	
Isaiah 1:1-9	Amos 1:1-5,13-2:8
Why do you seek further beatings? Why do you continue to rebel? The whole head is sick, and the whole heart faint.	The LORD roars from Zion, and utters his voice from Jerusalem; the pastures of the shepherds wither, and the top of Camel dries up.

RESPONSORY

Watching **from** afar,*
I see the power of God coming,
and a cloud covering **the** whole earth.
Go out to meet **him** and say,*
Tell us if you are the one who is to reign over your **peo**ple Israel.

All peoples of the earth, all children of dust,
rich and **poor** alike,*
go out to meet **him** and say,
Shepherd of Israel, hear us,
you lead Joseph's race **like** a flock:*
Tell us if you **are** the one.

Open wide the **gates**, you princes,*
let the King of glory enter
who is to reign over your **peo**ple Israel.

Watching **from** afar,*
I see the power of God coming,
and a cloud covering **the** whole earth.
Go out to meet **him** and say,*
Tell us if you are the one who is to reign over your **peo**ple Israel.

[LH: see Job 36:25; Jer. 30:10; 46:27; Ezek. 38:9,16; Matt. 11:3; Micah 4:7; Ps. 49:2; 80:1; 24:7]

2 Peter 3:1-10

The Lord is not slow about his promise, as some think of slowness, but is patient with you, not wanting any to perish, but all to come to repentance.

1 Thessalonians 5:1-11

Encourage one another and build up each other, as indeed you are doing.

RESPONSORY

Wash yourselves, make yourselves clean;
remove the evil of your doings from be**fore** my eyes.*
Though your sins are like scarlet, they shall **be** like snow.
Cease to do evil, learn to do **good**; seek justice.*
Though your sins are like scarlet, they shall **be** like snow.

[LH: Isa. 1:16,18,17]

Advent 2

Isaiah 5:1-7

What more was there to do for my vineyard that I have not done in it?

Amos 6:1-14

Alas for those who are at ease in Zion, and for those who feel secure on Mount Samaria.

2 Peter 3:11-18

In accordance with his promise, we wait for new heavens and a

2 Thessalonians 1:5-12

The Lord comes to be glorified by his saints and to be marveled

new earth, where righteousness is at home.

RESPONSORY

The words of the holy one, the true one, who has the **key** of David:*

Behold I have set before you an open door, which no one is a**ble** to shut.

You have kept my word and have not de**nied** my name.*

Behold I have set before you an open door, which no one is a**ble** to shut.

[LH: Rev. 3:7-8]

at on that day among all who have believed.

The herald of the Lord approaches, of **whom** the Lord says:*

Among those born of women no one has arisen greater than **John** the Baptist.

Truly this is a great prophet, and more than a prophet, of **whom** the Lord says:*

Among those born of women no one has arisen greater than **John** the Baptist.

[LH: see Matt. 11:11,9]

Advent 3

Isaiah 13:1-13

Listen, a tumult on the mountains as of a great multitude! Listen, an uproar of kingdoms, of nations gathering together! The LORD of hosts is mustering an army for battle.

Amos 9:11-15

I will plant them upon their land, and they shall never again be plucked up out of the land that I have given them, says the LORD your God.

Hebrews 12:18-29

Since we are receiving a kingdom that cannot be shaken, let us give thanks, by which we offer to God an acceptable worship with reverence and awe; for indeed our God is a consuming fire.

2 Thessalonians 2:1-3,13-17

Now may our Lord Jesus Christ himself and God our Father, who loved us and through grace gave us eternal comfort and good hope, comfort your hearts and strengthen them in every good work and word.

RESPONSORY

In that day the deaf shall hear the words **of** a book,*
and out of their gloom and darkness the eyes of the **blind** shall see.

And the poor **shall** exult*
in the Holy **One** of Israel.

Go and tell John what you **hear** and see:*
the blind receive their sight and the lame walk, the deaf hear, and the poor have the good news **preached** to them.

And the poor **shall** exult*
in the Holy **One** of Israel.

[LH: Isa. 29:18,19; Matt. 11:4-5]

He must increase, but **I** must decrease;*
the one who comes after me exist**ed** before me;

and I **am** not worthy*
to untie the thong **of** his sandal.

I have baptized **you** with water,*
but he will baptize you with the **Ho**ly Spirit.

And I **am** not worthy*
to untie the thong **of** his sandal.

[LH: John 3:30; 1:27; Mark 1:8]

December 17

Isaiah 10:20-27

A remnant will return, the remnant of Jacob, to the mighty God.

Zechariah 8:9-17

Just as you have been a cursing among the nations, O house of Judah and house of Israel, so I will save you and you shall be a blessing.

Jude 17-25

To the only God our Savior, through Jesus Christ our Lord, be glory, majesty, power, and authority before all time and now and forever.

Revelation 6:1-17

The great day of their wrath has come, and who is able to stand?

RESPONSORY

Shower, O heavens, from above, and let the skies **rain** down righteousness;*
let the earth open that salvation **may** spring up.
Lord, send the Lamb, the ruler of the earth, from the rock in the desert to the daught**er** of Zion.*
Let the earth open that salvation **may** spring up.
[CSB, LH: Isa. 45:8; see Isa. 16:1]

Behold, the root of Jesse will come down to save the people,*
and his dwellings **shall** be glorious.
The Lord God will give to him the throne of his father David, and he will reign over the house of Ja**cob** forever.
And his dwellings **shall** be glorious.
[LH: see Isa. 11:10; Luke 1:32]

Antiphon to the BENEDICTUS

Advent 1 The Holy Spirit will oversha**dow** you, Mary:*
fear not; you will carry in your womb the **Son** of God.
[LH: see Luke 1:35]

Advent 2 I am sending my messen**ger** before me*
to prepare the way **for** my coming.
[LH: see Mal. 3:1]

Advent 3 Are you the one who **is** to come,*
or are we to wait **for** another?
[LH: Matt. 11:3]

December 17 Believe me, the kingdom of God **is** at hand;*
I tell you solemnly,
your Savior will not de**lay** his coming.
[LH: see Matt. 4:17]

PRAYER OF THE DAY for December 17

O God, creator and redeemer of the human race, it was your will that in the womb of the ever-virgin Mary your Word should take flesh: Mercifully hear our prayers, and grant that your only-begotten Son, who came to share our human nature, may lead us to share in his divine life; through the same Jesus Christ our Lord, who lives and reigns with you and the Holy Spirit, one God, now and for ever. [Leo., RS; tr. ICEL, DvD, PHP]

Mondays in Advent and December 18

Antiphon to PSALM 14 *Dixit insipiens in corde suo*

The treasure of all na**tions** shall come,*
and I will fill this house with splendor, **says** the Lord.
[LH: Hag. 2:7]

on December 18

Reward those who **wait** for you,*
and let your prophets **be** found trustworthy. [LH: Sirach 36:21]

14 *The foolishness of sinners*

1 The fool has said in his heart, "There **is** no God."*
All are corrupt and commit abominable acts;
there is none who does **an**y good.

2 The LORD looks down from heaven up**on** us all,*
to see if there is any who is wise,
if there is one who seeks **af**ter God.

3 Every one has proved faithless;
all alike **have** turned bad;*
there is none who does good; **no**, not one.

4 Have they no knowledge, all those **e**vildoers*
who eat up my people like bread
and do not call up**on** the LORD?

5 See how they trem**ble** with fear,*
because God is in the company **of** the righteous.

6 Their aim is to confound the plans of **the** afflicted,*
but the LORD **is** their refuge.

7 Oh, that Israel's deliverance would come **out** of Zion!*
when the LORD restores the fortunes of his people,
Jacob will rejoice and Isra**el** be glad.

Antiphon The treasure of all na**tions** shall come,*
and I will fill this house with splendor, **says** the Lord.

on December 18

Reward those who **wait** for you,*
and let your prophets **be** found trustworthy.

Silence for meditation

God of wisdom and truth, without you neither truth nor holiness can survive. Show your mighty presence among us, and make us glad in proclaiming your deliverance in Jesus Christ our Lord. [LH, LBW]

+

Antiphon to PSALM 145 *Exaltabo te, Deus*

This is our heav**en**ly King;*
he comes with power and might to **save** the nations. [LH]

on December 18

Daughter of Jerusalem, rejoice and be glad;
your King will **come** to you.*
Zion, do not fear; your Savior hastens **on** his way.
[LH: see Zech. 9:9]

145 *Praise of God's majesty*

1 I will exalt you, O **God** my King,*
and bless your Name for ev**er** and ever.

2 Every day **will** I bless you*
and praise your Name for ev**er** and ever.

3 Great is the LORD and greatly **to** be praised;*
there is no end **to** his greatness.

4 One generation shall praise your works **to** another*
and shall de**clare** your power.

5 I will ponder the glorious splendor **of** your majesty*
and all your **mar**velous works.

6 They shall speak of the might of your **won**drous acts,*
and I will tell **of** your greatness.

7 They shall publish the remembrance of **your** great goodness;*
they shall sing of your **right**eous deeds.

8 The LORD is gracious and full **of** compassion,*
slow to anger and **of** great kindness.

9 The LORD is loving to **ev**eryone*
and his compassion is over **all** his works.

10 All your works praise **you**, O LORD,*
and your faithful **ser**vants bless you.

11 They make known the glory **of** your kingdom*
and speak **of** your power;

12 That the peoples may know **of** your power*
and the glorious splendor **of** your kingdom.

13 Your kingdom is an ever**last**ing kingdom;*
your dominion endures through**out** all ages.

14 The LORD is faithful in **all** his words*
and merciful in **all** his deeds.

15 The LORD upholds all **those** who fall;*
he lifts up those who **are** bowed down.

16 The eyes of all wait upon **you**, O LORD,*
and you give them their food **in** due season.

17 You open **wide** your hand*
and satisfy the needs of every **liv**ing creature.

18 The LORD is righteous in **all** his ways*
and loving in **all** his works.

19 The LORD is near to those who **call** upon him,*
to all who call up**on** him faithfully.

20 He fulfills the desire of **those** who fear him;*
he hears their **cry** and helps them.

21 The LORD preserves all **those** who love him,*
but he destroys **all** the wicked.

22 My mouth shall speak the praise **of** the LORD;*
let all flesh bless his holy Name for ev**er** and ever.

Antiphon This is our heav**en**ly King;*
he comes with power and might to **save** the nations.

on December 18

Daughter of Jerusalem, rejoice and be glad;
your King will **come** to you.*
Zion, do not fear; your Savior hastens **on** his way.

Silence for meditation

Loving Father, you are faithful in your promises and tender in your compassion: Listen to our hymn of joy, and continue to satisfy the needs of all your creatures, that all flesh may bless your Name in your everlasting kingdom, where with your Son and the Holy Spirit you live and reign, now and for ever. [LBW]

+

Stand

THE HYMN is sung. *En clara vox redarguit*

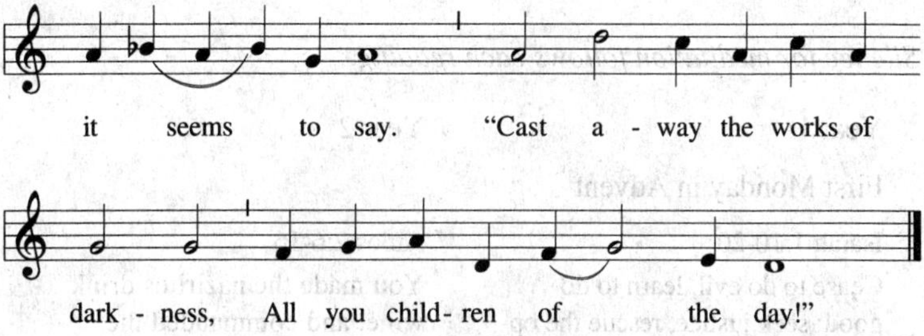

2 Startled at the solemn warning,
Let the earth-bound soul arise;
Christ her sun, all sloth dispelling,
Shines upon the morning skies.

3 See the Lamb, so long expected,
Comes with pardon down from heaven.
Let us haste, with tears of sorrow,
One and all, to be forgiven.

4 So, when next he comes in glory
And the world is wrapped in fear,
May he then as our defender
On the clouds of heaven appear.

5 Honor, glory, might, and blessing
To the Father and the Son
With the everlasting Spirit
While unending ages run! [CSB 3, LBW 37, alt., H82 59]

Text: Latin hymn, 1632; tr. Edward Caswall, 1814-1878
Tune: *Freuen wir uns all in ein,* Michael Weisse, c. 1480-1534 87 87
or *Merton*, SBH 1, H82 59

Sit

One or two LESSONS are read.

Silence for meditation follows each reading.

Year 1	Year 2
First Monday in Advent	
Isaiah 1:10-20	Amos 2:6-16
Cease to do evil, learn to do good; seek justice, rescue the oppressed, defend the orphan, plead for the widow.	You made the nazirites drink wine, and commanded the prophets, saying, "You shall not prophesy."
1 Thessalonians 1:1-10	2 Peter 1:1-11
Wait for his Son from heaven, whom he raised from the dead--Jesus, who rescues us from the wrath that is coming.	Be all the more eager to confirm your call and election, for if you do this, you will never stumble. For in this way, entry into the eternal kingdom of our Lord and Savior Jesus Christ will be richly provided for you.
Second Monday in Advent	
Isaiah 5:8-17	Amos 7:1-9
The LORD of hosts is exalted by justice, and the Holy God shows himself holy by righteousness. [BCP: 5:8-12, 18-23]	The high places of Isaac shall be made desolate, and the sanctuaries of Israel shall be laid waste, and I will rise against the house of Jeroboam with the sword.
1 Thessalonians 5:1-11	Revelation 1:1-8
God has destined us not for wrath but for obtaining salvation through our Lord Jesus Christ, who died for us, so that whether we are awake or asleep we may live with him.	Look! He is coming with the clouds; every eye will see him, even those who pierced him; and on his account all the tribes of the earth will wail.

Third Monday in Advent

Isaiah 8:16-9:1

I will wait for the LORD, who is hiding his face from the house of Jacob, and I will hope in him.

Zechariah 1:7-17

My cities shall again overflow with prosperity; the LORD will again comfort Zion and again choose Jerusalem.

2 Peter 1:1-11

Make every effort to support your faith with goodness, and goodness with knowledge, and knowledge with self-control, and self-control with endurance, and endurance with godliness, and godliness with mutual affection, and mutual affection with love.

Revelation 3:7-13

I am coming soon; hold fast what you have, so that no one may seize your crown.

RESPONSORY for Mondays

Come, let us go up to the mountain **of** the Lord,*
to the house of the **God** of Jacob;
that he may teach **us** his ways,*
and that we may walk **in** his paths.
The Messiah, who is called **Christ**, is coming.*
When he comes he will proclaim all **things** to us
that he may teach **us** his ways,*

Sound the trum**pets** in Zion,*
sum**mon** the nations.
Call the people together and tell **them** the good news:*
Our God and our Sav**ior** is coming.
Pro**claim** the good news,*
let **it** be heard.
Tell it to everyone,
shout **it** aloud:*
Our God and our Sav**ior** is coming. [LH: see Joel 2:15; see Isa. 62:11; see Jer. 4:5]

and that we may walk **in**
his paths.
[LH: Micah 4:2; John 4:25]

December 18

Isaiah 11:1-9

A shoot shall come out from the stump of Jesse, and a branch shall grow out of his roots.

Genesis 3:8-15

I will put enmity between you and the woman, and between your offspring and hers; he will strike your head, and you will strike his heel.

Ephesians 6:10-20

Be strong in the Lord and in the strength of his power.

Revelation 12:1-10

She gave birth to a son, a male child, who is to rule all the nations with a rod of iron.

RESPONSORY for December 18

Listen to me, you stub**born** of heart,*
You who are far **from** deliverance.
I will put salva**tion** in Zion,
for Isra**el** my glory.
I bring near my deliverance;
it is **not** far off,*
and my salvation **will** not tarry.
I will put salva**tion** in Zion,
for Isra**el** my glory.
[LH: Isa. 46:12,13]

There is salvation in **no** one else,*
for there is no other name under heaven given among mortals by which we **must** be saved.
He is named Wonderful Counselor, Mighty God, Everlasting Father, **Prince** of Peace;*
for there is no other name under heaven given among mortals by which we **must** be saved.
[LH: Acts 4:12; Isa. 9:6]

Antiphon to the BENEDICTUS

First Monday in Advent

Lift up your eyes, Jerusalem,
and see the great power **of** your King;*
your Savior comes to **set** you free. [LH]

Second Monday in Advent

Repent, **says** the Lord;*
for the kingdom of God **has** come near.
[LH: Matt. 3:2]

Third Monday in Advent

From heaven he comes, the **Lord** and Ruler;*
in his hand are honor and roy**al** authority.
[LH]

December 18

Let everything within you **watch** and wait,*
for the Lord our **God** draws near. [LH]

PRAYER OF THE DAY for December 18

Almighty God, grant that we who are oppressed and weighed down by the chains of our ancient slavery to sin may be set free by the long-awaited yet ever-new birth of your Son, Jesus Christ our Lord, who lives and reigns with you and the Holy Spirit, one God, now and for ever. [RS; tr. ICEL, DvD, PHP]

Tuesdays in Advent and December 19

Antiphon to PSALM 33 *Exultate, justi, in Domino*

Our soul waits **for** the Lord;*
he is our help **and** our shield.

on December 19

Wait **for** the Lord,*
and he will come to you with his **sav**ing power.

[LH]

33 *Praise of God's continual care*

1 Rejoice in the **Lord**, you righteous;*
it is good for the just **to** sing praises.

2 Praise the Lord **with** the harp;*
play to him upon the psalte**ry** and lyre.

3 Sing for him **a** new song;*
sound a fanfare with all your skill up**on** the trumpet.

4 For the word of the **Lord** is right,*
and all his **works** are sure.

5 He loves righteous**ness** and justice;*
the loving-kindness of the Lord fills **the** whole earth.

6 By the word of the Lord were the **hea**vens made,*
by the breath of his mouth all the heav**en**ly hosts.

7 He gathers up the waters of the ocean as **in** a water-skin*
and stores up the depths **of** the sea.

8 Let all the earth **fear** the Lord;*
let all who dwell in the world stand in **awe** of him.

9 For he spoke, and it **came** to pass;*
he commanded, and **it** stood fast.

10 The LORD brings the will of the na**tions** to naught;*
he thwarts the designs **of** the peoples.

11 But the LORD's will stands **fast** for ever,*
and the designs of his heart from **age** to age.

12 Happy is the nation whose God **is** the LORD!*
happy the people he has chosen to **be** his own!

13 The LORD looks **down** from heaven,*
and beholds all the people **in** the world.

14 From where he sits enthroned he **turns** his gaze*
on all who dwell **on** the earth.

15 He fashions all the **hearts** of them*
and understands **all** their works.

16 There is no king that can be saved by a **might**y army;*
a strong man is not delivered by **his** great strength.

17 The horse is a vain hope **for** deliverance;*
for all its strength it **can**not save.

18 Behold, the eye of the LORD is upon **those** who fear him,*
on those who wait up**on** his love,

19 To pluck their **lives** from death,*
and to feed them in **time** of famine.

20 Our soul waits **for** the LORD;*
he is our help **and** our shield.

21 Indeed, our heart rejoic**es** in him,*
for in his holy Name we **put** our trust.

22 Let your loving-kindness, O LORD, **be** upon us,*
as we have put our **trust** in you.

Antiphon Our soul waits **for** the Lord;*
he is our help **and** our shield.

on December 19

Wait **for** the Lord,*
and he will come to you with his **sav**ing power.

Silence for meditation

Lord God, through your Son you made the heavens and the earth; through him you continue to accomplish the intentions of your heart: Make your chosen people witnesses of your truth among the nations and heralds of your glory in the heavens; for the sake of your Son, Jesus Christ our Lord.
[LHd, LBW]

+

Antiphon to PSALM 146 *Lauda, anima mea*

Tell it out among the na**tions** and say,*
Behold, he comes, our **God** and Savior. [PBO]

on December 19

The Spirit of the Lord **is** upon me;*
because he has anointed me to bring good news **to** the poor.
[LH: Luke 4:18]

146 *Praise of God's faithfulness*

1 Hallelujah!
Praise the LORD, **O** my soul!*
I will praise the LORD as long as I live;
I will sing praises to my God while I **have** my being.

2 Put not your trust in rulers, nor in any **child** of earth,*
for there is no **help** in them.

3 When they breath their last, they re**turn** to earth,*
and in that day **their** thoughts perish.

4 Happy are they who have the God of Jacob **for** their help!*
whose hope is in the **LORD** their God;

5 Who made heaven and earth, the seas, and all that **is** in them;*
who keeps his prom**ise** for ever;

6 Who gives justice to those who **are** oppressed,*
and food to **those** who hunger.

7 The LORD sets the prisoners free;
the LORD opens the eyes **of** the blind;*
the LORD lifts up those who **are** bowed down;

8 The LORD loves the righteous;
the LORD cares **for** the stranger;*
he sustains the orphan and widow,
but frustrates the way **of** the wicked.

9 The LORD shall **reign** for ever,*
your God, O Zion, throughout all generations.
Hallelujah!

Antiphon Tell it out among the na**tions** and say,*
Behold, he comes, our **God** and Savior.

on December 19

The Spirit of the Lord **is** upon me;*
because he has anointed me to bring good news **to** the poor.

Silence for meditation

God of glory and power, happy indeed are those who have put their trust in you: Shine the brightness of your light upon us, that we may love you always with a pure heart and praise you for ever; through your Son Jesus Christ our Lord. [LH, LBW]

+

Stand

THE HYMN is sung. *Jordanis oras praevia*

2 E'en now the air, the sea, the land
Feel that their maker is at hand;
The very elements rejoice,
And welcome him with cheerful voice.

3 Then cleansed be every breast from sin;
Make straight the way for God within,
And let us each our hearts prepare
For Christ to come and enter there.

4 For you are our salvation, Lord,
Our refuge and our great reward;
Without your grace we waste away
Like flowers that wither and decay.

5 Stretch forth your hand, our health restore,
And make us rise to fall no more;
Once more upon your people shine
And fill the world with love divine.

6 To him who left the throne of heaven
To save the world high praise be given;
Whom with the Father we adore
And Holy Spirit, evermore. [H82 76, LBW 36]

Text: Charles Coffin, 1676-1749; tr. John Chandler, 1806-1876, alt
Tune: *Winchester New,* melody from *Musicalisches Hand-buch*, Hamburg, 1690 LM

Sit

One or two LESSONS are read.

Silence for meditation follows each reading.

Year 1

First Tuesday in Advent

Isaiah 1:21-31

Zion shall be redeemed by justice, and those in her who repent, by righteousness.

1 Thessalonians 2:1-12

We dealt with each one of you like a father with his children, urging and encouraging you and pleading that you lead a life worthy of God, who calls you into his own kingdom and glory.

Second Tuesday in Advent

Isaiah 5:18-25

The anger of the LORD was kindled against his people, and he stretched out his hand against

Year 2

Amos 3:1-11

You only have I known of all the families of the earth; therefore I will punish you for all your iniquities.

2 Peter 1:12-21

We have the prophetic message more fully confirmed. You will do well to be attentive to this as to a lamp shining in a dark place, until the day dawns and the morning star rises in your hearts.

Amos 7:10-17

I am no prophet, nor a prophet's son; but I am a herdsman, and a dresser of sycamore trees, and the

them and struck them; the mountains quaked.
[BCP: 5:13-17, 24-25]

LORD took me from following the flock, and the LORD said to me, "Go, prophesy to my people Israel."

1 Thessalonians 5:12-28
May the God of peace himself sanctify you entirely; and may your spirit and soul and body be kept sound and blameless at the coming of our Lord Jesus Christ.

Revelation 1:9-16
In his right hand he held seven stars, and from his mouth came a sharp, two-edged sword, and his face was like the sun shining with full force.

Third Tuesday in Advent

Isaiah 9:1-7
A child has been born for us, a son given to us; authority rests upon his shoulders.

Zechariah 2:1-13
Be silent, all people, before the LORD; for he has roused himself from his holy dwelling.

2 Peter 1:12-21
We have the prophetic message more fully confirmed. You will do well to be attentive to this as to a lamp shining in a dark place, until the day dawns and the morning star rises in your hearts.

Revelation 3:14-22
I reprove and discipline those whom I love. Be earnest, therefore, and repent.

RESPONSORY for Tuesdays

The haughty shall **be** brought low,*
and the pride of everyone **shall** be humbled.
    And the **Lord** alone*
    will be exalted **in** that day.
They will see the Son of Man coming on the **clouds** of heaven*

We are expecting a **Savior**, from heaven,*
Our Lord **Je**sus Christ.
    He will transform the body of your hu**mili**ation*
    that it may be conformed to the body **of** his glory.
In the present age live lives that

with power **and** great glory.
And the **Lord** alone*
will be exalted **in** that day.
[LH: Isa. 2:11; Matt. 24:30]

are **self**-controlled,*
while we wait for the
manifestation of the glory of
our great God and Savior, **Je**sus
Christ.
He will transform the body
of your hu**mil**iation*
that it may be conformed to
the body **of** his glory.
[LH: Phil. 3:20-21; Titus 2:12-13]

December 19

Isaiah 11:10-16

On that day the root of Jesse shall stand as a signal to the peoples; the nations shall inquire of him, and his dwelling shall be glorious.

Zephaniah 3:14-20

The LORD, your God, is in your midst, a warrior who gives victory; he will rejoice over you with gladness, he will renew you in his love.

Revelation 20:1-10

Then I saw thrones, and those seated on them were given authority to judge.

Titus 1:1-16

To the pure all things are pure, but to the corrupt and unbelieving nothing is pure. Their very minds and consciences are corrupted.

RESPONSORY for December 19

Hear the word of the **Lord**, O nations,*
and declare it to the ends **of** the earth.
Say to the **far**-off islands:*
our Sav**ior** is coming.
Proclaim the good news,
let **it** be heard;*

Sing for joy, O heavens,
and ex**ult**, O earth;*
break forth, O mountains **in**to singing!
The Lord has comfort**ed** his people,*
and will have compassion
on his **suffer**ing ones.

tell everyone,
shout **it** aloud;
  Say to the **far**-off islands:*
  our Sav**ior** is coming.
  [LH: see Jer. 31:10; see Jer. 4:5]

Our Redeemer—the Lord of
hosts **is** his name—*
is the Holy **One** of Israel.
  The Lord has comfort**ed**
  his people,*
  and will have compassion
  on his **suffer**ing ones.
  [LH: Isa. 49:13; 47:4]

Antiphon to the BENEDICTUS

First Tuesday in Advent

From the root of Jesse a flower will blossom,
the glory of the Lord will **fill** the earth,*
  and all creation shall see the saving
  pow**er** of God.
  [LH: see Isa. 11:1,10]

Second Tuesday in Advent

Rejoice and be glad, O daught**er** of Zion;*
  I will come and make my dwelling in
  you, **says** the Lord.
  [LH: see Zech. 9:9]

Third Tuesday in Advent

Arise, arise.
Wake from your slumber, Je**ru**salem;*
  shake the chain from your neck,
  captive daught**er** of Zion.
  [LH: see Isa. 52:1-2]

December 19

Like the sun in the morning sky,
the Savior of the **world** will dawn;*
  like rain on the meadows,
  he will descend to rest in the womb
  of the Virgin.
  [LH: see Sirach 24:30-32]

PRAYER OF THE DAY for December 19

O God, in the child-bearing of the holy virgin you revealed to the world the radiance of your glory: Grant that we may celebrate with full and reverent faith this great mystery of the Word made flesh, your Son, Jesus Christ our Lord, who lives and reigns with you and the Holy Spirit, one God, now and for ever. [Leo., RS; tr. ICEL, DvD, PHP]

Wednesdays in Advent and December 20

Antiphon to PSALM 50 *Deus deorum*

I desire steadfast love and not **sac**rifice,*
the knowledge of God rather **than** burnt offerings.

[PBO: Hos. 6:6]

on December 20

Out of Zion God reveals him**self** in glory;*
our God will come and will **not** keep silence. [CSB, LH, PBO]

50 *Worship in spirit and truth*

1 The LORD, the God of **gods**, has spoken;*
he has called the earth from the rising of the sun **to** its setting.

2 Out of Zion, perfect **in** its beauty,*
God reveals him**self** in glory.

3 Our God will come and will **not** keep silence;*
before him there is a consuming flame,
and round about him a **rag**ing storm.

4 He calls the heavens and the earth **from** above*
to witness the judgment **of** his people.

5 "Gather before me my **loy**al followers,*
those who have made a covenant with me
and sealed **it** with sacrifice."

6 Let the heavens declare the rightness **of** his cause;*
for God him**self** is judge.

7 Hear, O my people, and I will speak:
"O Israel, I will bear wit**ness** against you;*
for I am **God**, your God.

8 I do not accuse you because **of** your sacrifices;*
your offerings are al**ways** before me.

9 I will take no bull-calf **from** your stalls,*
nor he-goats out **of** your pens;

10 For all the beasts of the **forest** are mine,*
the herds in their thousands up**on** the hills.

11 I know every bird **in** the sky,*
and the creatures of the fields are **in** my sight.

12 If I were hungry, I **would** not tell you,*
for the whole world is mine and all **that** is in it.

13 Do you think I eat the **flesh** of bulls,*
or drink the **blood** of goats?

14 Offer to God a sacrifice **of** thanksgiving*
and make good your vows to **the** Most High.

15 Call upon me in the **day** of trouble;*
I will deliver you, and you shall **hon**or me."

16 But to the wick**ed** God says:*
"Why do you recite my statutes,
and take my covenant up**on** your lips;

17 Since you refuse **dis**cipline,*
and toss my words be**hind** your back?

18 When you see a thief, you make **him** your friend,*
and you cast in your lot **with** adulterers.

19 You have loosed your **lips** for evil,*
and harnessed your tongue **to** a lie.

20 You are always speaking evil **of** your brother*
and slandering your own **moth**er's son.

21 These things you have done, and **I** kept still,*
and you thought that I **am** like you.

22 I have made my **ac**cusation;*
I have put my case in order be**fore** your eyes.

23 Consider this well, you who **for**get God,*
lest I rend you and there be none to de**li**ver you.

24 Whoever offers me the sacrifice of thanksgiving **hon**ors me;*
but to those who keep in my way will I show the sal**va**tion of God."

Antiphon I desire steadfast love and not **sac**rifice,*
the knowledge of God rather **than** burnt offerings.

on December 20

Out of Zion God reveals him**self** in glory;*
our God will come and will **not** keep silence.

Silence for meditation

Heavenly Father, because Jesus your servant became obedient to death, his sacrifice was greater than all the holocausts of old: Accept the sacrifice of praise we offer you through him, and help us to show the effects of it in our lives by striving to do your will, until our whole life becomes adoration in spirit and truth; through your Son, Jesus Christ our Lord. [LHd, LBW]

+

Antiphon to PSALM 147:1-12 *Laudate Dominum*

The Lord has comfort**ed** his people,*
and will have compassion on his suf**fer**ing ones. [Isa. 49:3]

on December 20

Turn to **us**, O Lord,*
make haste to **help** your people. [LH]

147 *Praise of God, who maintains the world*

1 Hallelujah!
How good it is to sing praises **to** our God!*
how pleasant it is to honor **him** with praise!

2 The LORD re**builds** Jerusalem;*
he gathers the ex**iles** of Israel.

3 He heals the **bro**kenhearted*
and binds **up** their wounds.

4 He counts the number **of** the stars*
and calls them all **by** their names.

5 Great is our LORD and mighty in power;*
there is no limit **to** his wisdom.

6 The LORD lifts **up** the lowly,*
but casts the wicked **to** the ground.

7 Sing to the LORD **with** thanksgiving;*
make music to our God up**on** the harp.

8 He covers the heav**ens** with clouds*
and prepares rain **for** the earth;

9 He makes grass to grow up**on** the mountains*
and green plants to **serve** mankind.

10 He provides food for **flocks** and herds*
and for the young ravens **when** they cry.

11 He is not impressed by the might **of** a horse;*
he has no pleasure in the strength **of** a man;

12 But the LORD has pleasure in **those** who fear him,*
in those who await his **gra**cious favor.

Antiphon The Lord has comfort**ed** his people,*
and will have compassion on his suf**fer**ing ones.

on December 20

Turn to **us**, O Lord,*
make haste to **help** your people.

Silence for meditation

God our Father, great builder of the heavenly Jerusalem, you know the number of the stars and call each of them by name: Heal hearts that are broken, gather those who have been scattered, and enrich us all from the plenitude of your eternal wisdom, Jesus Christ our Lord. [LH, LBW]

+

Stand

THE HYMN is sung. *Veni Redemptor gentium*

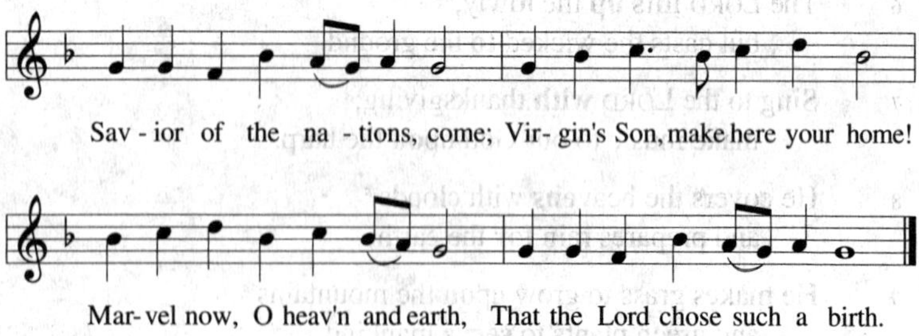

2 Not by human flesh and blood;
By the mystic breath of God
Was the Word divine made flesh—
Woman's offspring pure and fresh.

3 Wondrous birth! more wondrous Child
Of the virgin undefiled!
Human and divine in one,
Eager now his race to run.

4 Then stepped forth the Lord of all
From his pure and royal hall;
God of God, incarnate made,
In our mortal form arrayed.

5 God the Father is his source,
Back to God he runs his course;
Down to death and hell descends,
God's high throne he reascends.

6 Father's equal, you will win
Mighty triumph over sin:
Take on flesh to rout the wrong,
Make our flesh in frailty strong.

7 From the manger newborn light
Sends a glory through the night.
Darkness now must fade away;
Faith within the light shall stay.

8 Glory to the Father sing,
Glory to the Son, our King,
Glory to the Spirit be
Now and through eternity. [WS 701, LBW 28 alt.]

Text: attr. St. Ambrose, 340-397; tr. composite
Tune: *Nun komm, der heiden Heiland,* J. Walter, *Geistliche Gesangbüchlein*, 1524 77 77

Sit

One or two LESSONS are read.

Silence for meditation follows each reading.

Year 1

First Wednesday in Advent

Isaiah 2:1-4 (5-11)
In days to come the mountain of the LORD's house shall be established as the highest of the mountains, and shall be raised above the hills; and all the nations shall stream to it.

Year 2

Amos 3:12-4:5
Hear, and testify against the house of Jacob, says the Lord GOD, the God of hosts.

1 Thessalonians 2:13-20

What is our hope or joy or crown of boasting before our Lord Jesus at his coming? Is it not you? Yes, you are our glory and joy!

2 Peter 3:1-10

The Lord is not slow about his promise, as some think of slowness, but is patient with you, not wanting any to perish, but all to come to repentance.

Second Wednesday in Advent

Isaiah 6:1-13

I heard the voice of the Lord saying, "Whom shall I send, and who will go for us?" And I said, "Here am I: send me!"

Amos 8:1-14

The time is surely coming, says the Lord GOD, when I will send a famine on the land; not a famine of bread, or a thirst for water, but of hearing the words of the LORD.

2 Thessalonians 1:1-12

He comes to be glorified by his saints and to be marveled at on that day among all who have believed.

Revelation 1:17-2:7

To everyone who conquers, I will give permission to eat from the tree of life that is in the paradise of God.

Third Wednesday in Advent

Isaiah 9:8-17

For all this, his anger has not turned away; his hand is stretched out still.

Zechariah 3:1-10

See, I have taken your guilt away from you, and I will clothe you with festal apparel.

2 Peter 2:1-10a

The Lord knows how to rescue the godly from trial, and to keep the unrighteous under punishment until the day of judgment.

Revelation 4:1-8

Holy, holy, holy, the Lord God the Almighty, who was and is and is to come.

RESPONSORY for Wednesdays

The eyes of those who have sight will **not** be closed,*
and ears of those who have hear**ing** will listen.
The minds **of** the rash*
will **have** good judgment.
I will raise up for David a **right**eous Branch,*
and he shall reign as king **and** deal wisely.
The minds **of** the rash*
will **have** good judgment.
[LH: Isa. 32:3,4; Jer. 23:5]

The Lord will come **down** to us,*
radiant in his splendor, awesome **in** his power.
The Lord shall give strength **to** his people;*
the Lord shall give his people the bless**ing** of peace.
Our **God** will come,*
awesome **in** his power.
The Lord shall give strength **to** his people;*
the Lord shall give his people the bless**ing** of peace.
[LH: see Isa. 40:10; Ps. 29:11]

December 20

Isaiah 28:9-22

Thus says the Lord GOD, See I am laying in Zion a foundation stone, a tested stone, a precious cornerstone, a sure foundation.

1 Samuel 2:1b-10

The LORD will judge the ends of the earth; he will give strength to his king, and exalt the power of his anointed.

Revelation 20:11-21:8

See, the home of God is among mortals. He will dwell with them as their God; they will be his peoples, and God himself will be with them.

Titus 2:1-10

Show yourself in all respects a model of good works.

RESPONSORY for December 20

I have refined you, but **not** like silver;*
I have tried you in the furnace **of** adversity
For my own sake, I do it, for why should my Name **be** profaned?*
My glory I will not give **to** another.
In overflowing wrath for a moment I hid my **face** from you,*
but with everlasting love I will have compassion on you, says the Lord, **your** Redeemer,
For my own sake, I do it, for why should my Name **be** profaned?*
My glory I will not give **to** another.

[LH: Isa. 48:10,11; 54:8]

Receive, O **Vir**gin Mary,*
the word which the Lord has made known to you by the message **of** the angel:
you will conceive and **bear** a Son,*
both **God** and man.
Blessed are you **a**mong women,*
and blessed is the fruit **of** your womb.
A virgin, you will indeed **bear** a Son;*
ever chaste and holy,
you will be the mother **of** our Savior.
Blessed are you **a**mong women,*
and blessed is the fruit **of** your womb.

[LH: see Luke 1:31,42]

Antiphon to the BENEDICTUS

First Wednesday in Advent
One who is more powerful than I is coming **af**ter me;*
I am not worthy to car**ry** his sandals.

[LH: Matt. 3:11]

Second Wednesday in Advent
He will be enthroned in **Da**vid's place*
to be **king** for ever.

[LH: see Luke 1:32]

Third Wednesday in Advent — Comfort, O com**fort** my people,*
says the **Lord** your God.

[LH: Isa. 40:1]

December 20 — The angel Gabriel was sent by God
to the **Vir**gin Mary,*
who was engaged to a man
whose **name** was Joseph.

[LH: Luke 1:26]

The PRAYER OF THE DAY for December 20

O God, by accepting the message of the angel the pure virgin became the temple of your ineffable Word and was filled with the light of the Holy Spirit: Give us grace to follow her example and be always ready to do your will; through your Son, Jesus Christ our Lord, who lives and reigns with you and the Holy Spirit, one God, now and for ever. [Leo., RS; tr. ICEL, PHP]

Thursdays in Advent and December 21

Antiphon to PSALM 18 *Diligam te, Domine*

Who is this that comes from Edom,
from Bozrah in gar**ments** stained crimson?*
Who is this so splendidly robed,
marching in **his** great might?

[Isa. 63:1]

on December 21

Israel, prepare to **meet** your God,*
for **he** is coming. [LH: see Amos 4:12]

18 *David's thanksgiving for victory*
Part I *[until December 21]*

1 I love you, O **LORD** my strength,*
O LORD my stronghold, my crag, **and** my haven.

2 My God, my rock in whom I **put** my trust,*
my shield, the horn of my salvation, and my refuge;
you are wor**thy** of praise.

3 I will call up**on** the LORD,*
and so shall I be saved **from** my enemies.

4 The breakers of death rolled **o**ver me,*
and the torrents of oblivion made **me** afraid.

5 The cords of hell en**tangl**ed me,*
and the snares of death were **set** for me.

6 I called upon the LORD in **my** distress*
and cried out to my **God** for help.

7 He heard my voice from his heav**en**ly dwelling;*
my cry of anguish came **to** his ears.

8 The earth **reeled** and rocked;*
the roots of the mountains shook;
they reeled because **of** his anger.

9 Smoke rose from his nostrils
and a consuming fire out **of** his mouth;*
hot burning coals blazed **forth** from him.

10 He parted the heavens **and** came down*
with a storm cloud un**der** his feet.

11 He mounted on cheru**bim** and flew;*
he swooped on the wings **of** the wind.

12 He wrapped dark**ness** about him;*
he made dark waters and thick clouds **his** pavilion.

13 From the brightness of his presence, **through** the clouds,*
burst hailstones and **coals** of fire.

14 The LORD thundered **out** of heaven;*
the Most High ut**tered** his voice.

15 He loosed his arrows and **scat**tered them;*
he hurled thunderbolts and **rout**ed them.

16 The beds of the seas were uncovered,
and the foundations of the **world** laid bare,*
at your battle cry, O LORD,
at the blast of the breath **of** your nostrils.

17 He reached down from on **high** and grasped me;*
he drew me out **of** great waters.

18 He delivered me from my strong enemies
and from those who **hat**ed me;*
for they were too mighty for me.

19 They confronted me in the day of **my** disaster;*
but the LORD was **my** support.

20 He brought me out into an **op**en place;*
he rescued me because he delight**ed** in me.

Part II *Et retribuet mihi [on December 21]*

21 The LORD rewarded me because of my **right**eous dealing;*
because my hands were clean he re**ward**ed me;

22 For I have kept the ways **of** the LORD*
and have not offended **against** my God;

23 For all his judgments are be**fore** my eyes,*
and his decrees I have not put a**way** from me;

24 For I have been blame**less** with him*
and have kept myself **from** iniquity;

25 Therefore the LORD rewarded me according to my **right**eous dealing,*
because of the cleanness of my hands **in** his sight.

26 With the faithful you show yourself faith**ful**, O God;*
with the forthright you show **your**self forthright.

27 With the pure you show **your**self pure,*
but with the crooked **you** are wily.

28 You will save a **low**ly people,*
but you will humble the **haughty** eyes.

29 You, O LORD, **are** my lamp;*
my God, you make my **dark**ness bright.

30 With you I will break **down** an enclosure;*
with the help of my God I will scale **an**y wall.

31 As for God, his ways are perfect;
the words of the LORD are tried **in** the fire;*
he is a shield to all who **trust** in him.

32 For who is God, **but** the LORD?*
who is the Rock, ex**cept** our God?

33 It is God who girds me a**bout** with strength*
and makes my **way** secure.

34 He makes me sure-footed **like** a deer*
and lets me stand firm **on** the heights.

35 He trains my **hands** for battle*
and my arms for bending even a **bow** of bronze.

36 You have given me your **shield** of victory;*
your right hand also sustains me;
your loving care **makes** me great.

37 You lengthen my **stride** beneath me,*
and my ankles do **not** give way.

38 I pursue my enemies and **o**vertake them;*
I will not turn back till I **have** destroyed them.

39 I strike them down, and they **can**not rise;*
they fall defeated **at** my feet.

40 You have girded me with strength **for** the battle;*
you have cast down my adversaries beneath me;
you have put my ene**mies** to flight.

41 I destroy those who hate me;
they cry out, but there is **none** to help them;*
they cry to the LORD, but he **does** not answer.

42 I beat them small like dust be**fore** the wind;*
I trample them like mud **in** the streets.

43 You deliver me from the strife **of** the peoples;*
you put me at the head **of** the nations.

44 A people I have not known shall serve me;
no sooner shall they hear than they **shall** obey me;*
strangers will **cringe** before me.

45 The foreign peoples **will** lose heart;*
they shall come trembling out **of** their strongholds.

46 The LORD lives! Blessed **is** my Rock!*
Exalted is the God of **my** salvation!

47 He is the God who gave me **vic**tory*
and cast down the peo**ples** beneath me.

48 You rescued me from the fury of my enemies;
you exalted me above those who **rose** against me;*
you saved me from my **dead**ly foe.

49 Therefore will I extol you among the **nations**, O LORD,*
and sing praises **to** your Name.

50 He multiplies the victories **of** his king;*
he shows loving-kindness to his anointed,
to David and his descend**ants** for ever.

Antiphon Who is this that comes from Edom,
from Bozrah in gar**ments** stained crimson?*
Who is this so splendIdly robed,
marching in **his** great might?

on December 21

Israel, prepare to **meet** your God,*
for **he** is coming.

Silence for meditation

Mighty God, our stronghold and our salvation, when the very foundations of the earth are shaken and your people cringe in fear, gird on your strength and come down to save us who cry out to you, sustain us with your hand, and care for us in your love; for the sake of Jesus Christ our Lord. [PHP]

+

Antiphon to PSALM 147:13-21 *Lauda, Ierusalem, Dominum*

In that day the mountains shall **drip** sweet wine,*
and the hills shall flow with **milk** and honey.

[PBO, LBW: Joel 3:18]

on December 21

Eagerly I watch **for** the Lord;*
I wait in joyful hope
for the appearing of **God**, my Savior. [LH: see Titus 2:13]

147:13-21 *The restoration of Jerusalem*

13 Worship the LORD, **O** Jerusalem;*
praise your **God**, O Zion;

14 For he has strengthened the bars **of** your gates;*
he has blessed your child**ren** within you.

15 He has established peace **on** your borders;*
he satisfies you with the **fin**est wheat.

16 He sends out his command **to** the earth,*
and his word runs **ver**y swiftly.

17 He gives **snow** like wool;*
he scatters hoar**frost** like ashes.

18 He scatters his **hail** like bread crumbs;*
who can stand a**gainst** his cold?

19 He sends forth his **word** and melts them;*
he blows with his wind, and the **wat**ers flow.

20 He declares his **word** to Jacob,*
his statutes and his judg**ments** to Israel.

21 He has not done so to any **oth**er nation;*
to them he has not revealed his judgments.
Hallelujah!

Antiphon In that day the mountains shall **drip** sweet wine,*
and the hills shall flow with **milk** and honey.

on December 21

Eagerly I watch **for** the Lord;*
I wait in joyful hope
for the appearing of **God**, my Savior.

Silence for meditation

Lord God, you establish peace in Jerusalem: Grant that your faithful people, nourished with the bread of heaven, may abide in your peace now and through eternity, where what we now perceive but dimly we may enjoy in the clarity of your truth, Jesus Christ our Lord. [LH, PHP]

Stand

THE HYMN is sung. *Macht hoch die Tür*

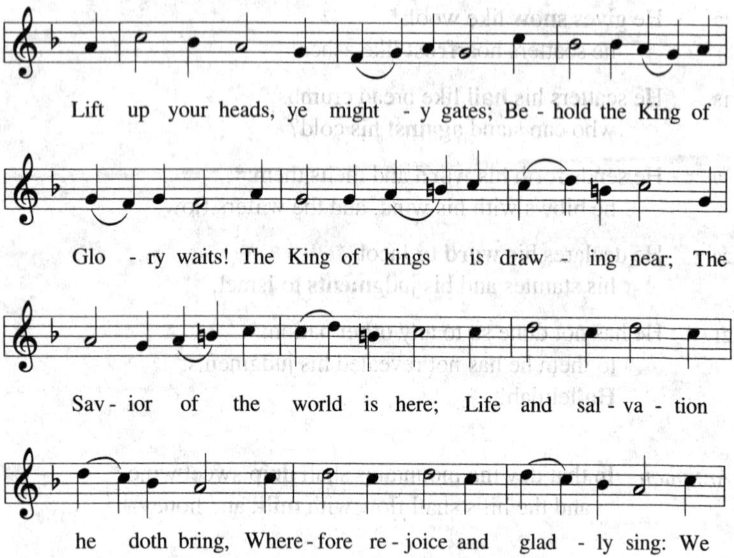

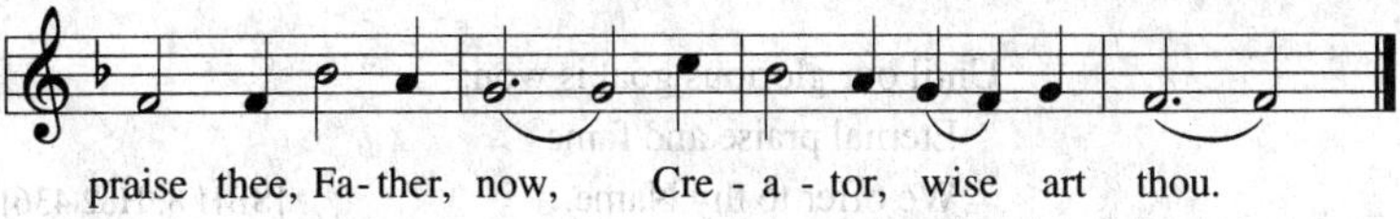

2 The Lord is just, a helper tried,
With mercy ever at his side;
His kingly crown is holiness,
His sceptre, pity in distress,
The end of all our woe he brings;
Wherefore the earth is glad and sings:
 We praise thee, Savior, now,
 Mighty in deed art thou.

3 O blest the land, the city blest,
Where Christ the Ruler is confest!
O happy hearts and happy homes
To whom this King in triumph comes!
The cloudless Sun of joy he is,
Who bringeth pure delight and bliss:
 O Comforter divine,
 What boundless grace is thine.

4 Fling wide the portals of your heart,
Make it a temple set apart
From earthly use for heaven's employ,
Adorned with prayer, and love, and joy;
So shall your Sovereign enter in,
And new and nobler life begin:
 To thee, O God, be praise,
 For word and deed and grace.

5 Redeemer, come! I open wide
My heart to thee; here, Lord, abide!
Let me thy inner presence feel:
Thy grace and love in me reveal.
Thy Holy Spirit guide us on,

Until our glorious goal is won:
Eternal praise and fame
We offer to thy Name. [SBH 8, H82 436]

Text: Georg Weissel, 1590-1635; tr. Catherine Winkworth, 1829-1878
Tune: *Macht hoch die Tür*, J. A. Freylinghausen, *Geistriches Gesang-Buch*, 1704 88 88 88 66

Sit

One or two LESSONS are read.

Silence for meditation follows each reading.

Year 1	Year 2
First Thursday in Advent	
Isaiah 2:5-22	Amos 4:6-13
O house of Jacob, come, let us walk in the light of the LORD!	Therefore thus I will do to you, O Israel; because I will do this to you, prepare to meet your God, O Israel!
1 Thessalonians 3:1-13	2 Peter 3:11-18
May the Lord so strengthen your hearts in holiness that you may be blameless before our God and Father at the coming of our Lord Jesus with all his saints.	In accordance with his promise, we wait for new heavens and a new earth, where righteousness is at home.
Second Thursday in Advent	
Isaiah 7:1-9	Amos 9:1-10
If you do not stand firm in faith, you shall not stand at all.	The Lord, GOD of hosts, he who touches the earth and it melts, and all who dwell in it mourn . . . the LORD is his name.

2 Thessalonians 2:1-12

Let no one deceive you in any way; for that day will not come unless the rebellion comes first, and the lawless one is revealed.

Revelation 2:8-17

Be faithful until death, and I will give you the crown of life.

Third Thursday in Advent

Isaiah 9:18-10:4

What will you do on the day of punishment, in the calamity that will come from far away? To whom will you flee for help?

Zechariah 4:1-14

Not by might, nor by power, but by my spirit, says the LORD of hosts.

2 Peter 2:10b-16

Bold and willful, they are not afraid to slander the glorious ones, whereas the angels, though greater in might and power, do not bring against them a slanderous judgment from the Lord.

Revelation 4:9-5:5

Do not weep. See, the Lion of the tribe of Judah, the Root of David, has conquered, so that he can open the scroll and its seven seals.

RESPONSORY for Thursdays

The days are surely coming, says the Lord, when I will raise up for David a **right**eous Branch,*
and he shall reign as king and deal wisely, and shall execute justice **in** the land.
> And this is the name by which he **will** be called:*
> "The Lord **is** our righteousness."

A throne shall be established in **stead**fast love*
I will make with you an ever**last**ing covenant,*
my steadfast, sure **love** for David.
> See, I have made him a witness **to** the people,*
> a leader and commander **for** the people.

This salvation of God has been sent **to** the Gentiles;*
the Gen**tiles** will listen.
> See, I have made him a witness **to** the people,*

and on it shall sit in faithfulness
a ruler who seeks justice and is
swift to do **what** is right.
    And this is the name by
    which he **will** be called:*
    "The Lord **is** our
    righteousness."
[CSB, SBH, LH: Jer. 23:5,6; Isa. 16:5]

a leader and commander
for the people.
[LH: Isa. 55:3-4; Acts 28:29 REB]

December 21

Isaiah 29:9-24

They will sanctify my name; they will sanctify the Holy One of Jacob, and will stand in awe of the God of Israel.

2 Samuel 7:1-17

Your house and your kingdom shall be made sure forever before me; your throne shall be established forever.

Revelation 21:9-21

In the spirit he carried me away to a great, high mountain, and showed me the holy city Jerusalem coming down out of heaven from God. It has the glory of God and a radiance like a very rare jewel, like jasper, clear as crystal.

Titus 2:11-3:8a

We wait for the blessed hope and manifestation of the glory of our great God and Savior, Jesus Christ. He it is who gave himself for us that he might redeem us from all iniquity and purify for himself a people of his own who are zealous for good deeds.

RESPONSORY for December 21

Let the heavens rejoice,
and let the **earth** be glad;*
let the sea thunder
and all **that** is in it.
Then shall all the trees of the
wood **shout** for joy*
when the Lord comes
to **judge** the earth.
    For the Lord has comfort**ed**

Blessed is she who believed that
there would be a fulfillment of
what was spoken to her **by** the
Lord.*
And **Mary** said:
    My soul proclaims the
    greatness **of** the Lord,*
    and my spirit rejoices
    in **God** my Savior.

his people,*
and will have compassion
on his suf**fer**ing ones.
In his time shall the **right**eous
flourish;*
there shall be abund**ance**
of peace.
For the Lord has comfort**ed**
his people,*
and will have compassion
on his suf**fer**ing ones.
[LH: Ps. 96:11-13; Isa. 49:13; Ps. 72:7]

Come and listen, all you
who fear God,*
and I will tell you
what he has **done** for me.
My soul proclaims the
greatness **of** the Lord,*
and my spirit rejoices in
God my Savior.
[LH: Luke 1:45 JB, 46; Ps. 66:16]

Antiphon to the BENEDICTUS

First Thursday in Advent — I shall wait for my **Lord** and Savior*
and point him out when **he** is near.
[LH]

Second Thursday in Advent — I will help you, **says** the Lord;*
I am your Savior, the Holy **One** of Israel.
[LH: see Isa. 43:3]

Third Thursday in Advent — Arise, a**rise**, O Lord;*
show us your pow**er** and might.
[LH: see Ps. 3:7; 44:26]

December 21 — There is no need to **be** afraid;*
in five days our Lord will **come** to us.
[LH: see Judith 7:30]

The PRAYER OF THE DAY for December 21

Lord, mercifully receive the prayers of your people, that as they rejoice in the advent of your only-begotten Son in human flesh, so when he comes a second time in his majesty they may receive the gift of eternal life; through the same Jesus Christ our Lord, who lives and reigns with you and the Holy Spirit, one God, now and for ever. [Gel., CSB, SBH, RS]

and for St. Thomas' Day

Almighty and everliving God, you strengthened your apostle Thomas with firm and certain faith in your Son's resurrection: Keep us, through all our days, steadfast in that same faith in Jesus Christ our Lord and our God; who lives and reigns with you and the Holy Spirit, one God, now and for ever. [PHP after BCP and TLH]

Fridays in Advent and December 22

Antiphon to PSALM 102 *Domine, exaudi orationem meum*

The Lord will **build** up Zion, *
and his glory **will** appear.

on December 22

You will arise and have compassion on Zion,
for it is time to have mer**cy** upon her;*
indeed, the appointed **time** has come.

102 *Prayer in misfortune*

1 LORD, hear my prayer, and let my cry **come** before you;*
hide not your face from me in the day **of** my trouble.

2 Incline your **ear** to me;*
when I call, make haste to **an**swer me,

3 For my days drift a**way** like smoke,*
and my bones are hot as **burn**ing coals.

4 My heart is smitten like **grass** and withered,*
so that I forget to **eat** my bread.

5 Because of the voice **of** my groaning*
I am but **skin** and bones.

6 I have become like a vulture **in** the wilderness,*
like an owl a**mong** the ruins.

7 I lie a**wake** and groan;*
I am like a sparrow, lonely **on** a house-top.

8 My enemies revile me **all** day long,*
and those who scoff at me have taken an **oath** against me.

9 For I have eaten ash**es** for bread*
and mingled my **drink** with weeping.

10 Because of your indignation and wrath*
you have lifted me up and thrown me away.

11 My days pass away like a shadow,*
and I wither like the grass.

12 But you, O LORD, endure for ever,*
and your Name from age to age.

13 You will arise and have compassion on Zion,
for it is time to have mercy upon her;*
indeed, the appointed time has come.

14 For your servants love her very rubble,*
and are moved to pity even for her dust.

15 The nations shall fear your Name, O LORD,*
and all the kings of the earth your glory.

16 For the LORD will build up Zion,*
and his glory will appear.

17 He will look with favor on the prayer of the homeless;*
he will not despise their plea.

18 Let this be written for a future generation,*
so that a people yet unborn may praise the LORD.

19 For the LORD looked down from his holy place on high;*
from the heavens he beheld the earth;

20 That he might hear the groan of the captive*
and set free those condemned to die.

21 That they may declare in Zion the Name of the LORD,*
and his praise in Jerusalem;

22 When the peoples are gathered together,*
and the kingdoms also, to serve the LORD.

23 He has brought down my strength before my time;*
he has shortened the number of my days;

24 And I said, "O my God,
do not take me away in the midst **of** my days;*
your years endure throughout all **gen**erations.

25 In the beginning, O LORD, you laid the foundations **of** the earth,*
and the heavens are the work **of** your hands;

26 They shall perish, but you will endure;
they all shall wear out **like** a garment;*
as clothing you will change them,
and they **shall** be changed;

27 But you are al**ways** the same,*
and your years will **nev**er end.

28 The children of your servants **shall** continue,*
and their offspring shall stand fast **in** your sight."

Antiphon The Lord will **build** up Zion, *
and his glory **will** appear.

on December 22

You will arise and have compassion on Zion,
for it is time to have mer**cy** upon her;*
indeed, the appointed **time** has come.

Silence for meditation

Lord, while our days vanish like shadows and our lives wear out like a garment, you remain undisturbed by change: Although our earthly lives come to an end, help us to live in Christ's endless life and at length attain our home, the heavenly Jerusalem, where he lives and reigns with you and the Holy Spirit, now and for ever. [LHd, LBW]

+

Antiphon to PSALM 148 *Laudate Dominum, de coelis*

I shall enfold Zion with **my** salvation*
and shed my glory a**round** Jerusalem.

[LH: see Isa. 24:23; see 46:13]

on December 22

I shall not cease to plead with **God** for Zion*
until he sends his Holy One in all his **ra**diant beauty.

[LH: see Dan. 4:13; Isa. 33:17]

148 *Cosmic praise*

1 Hallelujah!
Praise the LORD **from** the heavens;*
praise him **in** the heights.

2 Praise him, all you an**gels** of his;*
praise him, **all** his host.

3 Praise him, **sun** and moon;*
praise him, all you **shin**ing stars.

4 Praise him, heav**en** of heavens,*
and you waters a**bove** the heavens.

5 Let them praise the Name **of** the LORD;*
for he commanded, and they **were** created.

6 He made them stand fast for ev**er** and ever;*
he gave them a law which shall not **pass** away.

7 Praise the LORD **from** the earth,*
you sea-monsters **and** all deeps;

8 Fire and hail, **snow** and fog,*
tempestuous wind, do**ing** his will;

9 Mountains **and** all hills,*
fruit trees **and** all cedars;

10 Wild beasts **and** all cattle,*
creeping things and **wing**èd birds;

11 Kings of the earth **and** all peoples,*
princes and all rulers **of** the world;

12 Young **men** and maidens,*
old and **young** together.

13 Let them praise the Name **of** the LORD,*
for his Name only is exalted,
his splendor is over **earth** and heaven.

14 He has raised up strength for his people
and praise for all his **loy**al servants,*
the children of Israel, a people who are near him.
Hallelujah!

Antiphon I shall enfold Zion with **my** salvation*
and shed my glory a**round** Jerusalem.

on December 22

I shall not cease to plead with **God** for Zion*
until he sends his Holy One in all his **rad**iant beauty.

Silence for meditation

God Most High, by your Word you created a wondrous universe, and through your Spirit you breathed into it the breath of life: Accept creation's hymn of praise from our lips, and let the praise that is sung in heaven resound in the heart of every creature on earth, to the glory of the Father, and the Son, and the Holy Spirit, now and for ever. [LH, LBW]

Stand

THE HYMN is sung.

2 Every eye shall now behold him,
Robed in dreadful majesty;
Those who set at naught and sold him,
Pierced, and nailed him to the tree,
Deeply wailing,
Shall the true Messiah see.

3 Those dear tokens of his Passion
Still his dazzling body bears,
Cause of endless exaltation
To his ransomed worshipers.
With what rapture
Gaze we on those glorious scars.

4 Yea, amen, let all adore thee,
High on thine eternal throne;
Savior, take the power and glory,
Claim the kingdom for thine own.
Alleluia!
Everlasting God, come down. [H82 57, LBW 27]

Text: Charles Wesley, 1707-1788
Tune: *Helmsley*, Thomas Olivers, 1725-1799 87 87 12 7

Sit

One or two LESSONS are read.

Silence for meditation follows each reading.

Year 1	Year 2
First Friday in Advent	
Isaiah 3:1-4:1	Amos 5:1-17
The LORD rises to argue his case; he stands to judge the peoples.	Seek good and not evil, that you may live; and so the LORD, the God of hosts, will be with you.
1 Thessalonians 4:1-12	Jude 1-16
We ask and urge you in the Lord Jesus that, as you learned from us how you ought to live and to please God (as, in fact, you are doing), you should do so more and more.	Contend for the faith that was once for all entrusted to the saints.
Second Friday in Advent	
Isaiah 7:10-25	Haggai 1:1-15
Look, the young woman is with child and shall bear a son, and shall name him Immanuel.	Then Haggai, the messenger of the LORD, spoke to the people with the LORD's message, saying, "I am with you, says the LORD."

2 Thessalonians 2:13-3:5

The Lord is faithful; he will strengthen you and guard you from the evil one.

Revelation 2:18-29

Hold fast what you have, until I come.

Third Friday in Advent

Isaiah 10:5-19

The light of Israel will become a fire, and his Holy One a flame; and it will burn and devour his thorns and briers in one day.

Zechariah 7:8-8:8

Thus says the LORD: I will return to Zion, and will dwell in the midst of Jerusalem; Jerusalem shall be called the faithful city, and the mountain of the LORD of hosts shall be called the holy mountain.

2 Peter 2:17-22

It would have been better for them never to have known the way of righteousness than, after knowing it, to turn back from the holy commandment that was passed on to them.

Revelation 5:6-14

I heard every creature in heaven and on earth and under the earth and in the sea, and all that is in them singing, "To the one seated on the throne and to the Lamb be blessing and honor and glory and might forever and ever!"

RESPONSORY for Fridays

My people will abide in a peaceful **hab**itation,*
in secure dwellings, and in quiet **rest**ing places.
Then justice will dwell in the **wil**derness,*
and righteousness abide in the **fruit**ful field.
My peace I **give** to you;*
do not let your hearts be

As a mother com**forts** her child,*
so will I comfort you, **say**s the Lord.
You shall be comforted in Je**ru**salem,*
the city where I have chosen to **put** my name.
I will put salva**tion** in Zion,*
for Isra**el** my glory.

troubled, and do not let them **be** afraid.

Then justice will dwell in the **wil**derness,*
and righteousness abide in the **fruit**ful field.

[LH: Isa. 32:18,16; John 4:27]

You shall be comforted in Je**ru**salem,*
the city where I have chosen to **put** my name.

[LH: Isa. 66:13; 1 Kings 11:36; Isa. 46:13]

December 22

Isaiah 31:1-9
Like birds hovering overhead, so the LORD of hosts will protect Jerusalem; he will protect and deliver it, he will spare and rescue it.

2 Samuel 7:18-29
Who is like your people, like Israel? Is there another nation on earth whose God went to redeem it as a people, and to make a name for himself, doing great and awesome things for them?

Revelation 21:22-22:5
There will be no more night; they need no light of lamp or sun, for the Lord God will be their light, and they will reign forever and ever.

Galatians 3:1-14
In Christ Jesus the blessing of Abraham comes upon the Gentiles, so that we might receive the promise of the Spirit through faith.

RESPONSORY for December 22

Can a woman forget her **nurs**ing child,*
or show no compassion for the child **of** her womb?
Even these **may** forget,*
yet I will not forget you, **says** the Lord.
Though my father and my moth**er** forsake me,*
the Lord **will** sustain me.

The Lord has looked with favor on his **low**ly servant,*
From this day all generations will **call** me blessed.
The Almighty has done great **things** for me,*
and holy **is** his Name.
He has mercy on **those** who fear him*
in every **gen**eration.

Even these **may** forget,*
yet I will not forget you,
says the Lord.
[LH: Isa. 49:15; Ps. 27:10]

The Almighty has done
great **things** for me,*
and holy **is** his Name.
[LH: Luke 1:48-50]

Antiphon to the BENEDICTUS

First Friday in Advent — Our God comes, born of **Da**vid's line,*
enthroned as **king** for ever. [LH]

Second Friday in Advent — Say to the fainthearted, Take courage!*
The Lord our God is com**ing** to save us.
[LH: see Isa. 35:4]

Third Friday in Advent — Guard what is good and cherish **what** is true,*
for our Savior **is** at hand.
[LH: see Phil. 4:8]

December 22 — As soon as I heard the sound **of** your greeting,*
the child in my womb **leaped** for joy.
[Luke 1:44]

The PRAYER OF THE DAY for December 22

O God, when we had fallen into sin and death you turned toward us and rescued us by the advent of your only-begotten Son: Grant that we, who with reverent love acknowledge his incarnation, may also be found worthy to be counted as companions of him who is our Redeemer, Jesus Christ our Lord; who lives and reigns with you and the Holy Spirit, one God, now and for ever. [Berg., RS trans. PHP]

Saturdays in Advent and December 23

Antiphon to PSALM 90 *Domine, refugium*

Return, O Lord; how long **will** you tarry?*
Be gracious **to** your servants.

on December 23

The Lord, the ruler of the kings of the **earth**, will come;*
blessed are they who are ready to **wel**come him. [LH]

90 *The brevity of life*

1 Lord, you have **been** our refuge*
from one generation **to** another.

2 Before the mountains were brought forth,
or the land and the **earth** were born,*
from age to age **you** are God.

3 You turn us back to the **dust** and say,*
"Go back, O **child** of earth."

4 For a thousand years in your sight are like yesterday
when **it** is past*
and like a watch **in** the night.

5 You sweep us away **like** a dream;*
we fade away suddenly **like** the grass.

6 In the morning it is **green** and flourishes;*
in the evening it is dried **up** and withered.

7 For we consume away in **your** displeasure;*
we are afraid because of your wrathful **in**dignation.

8 Our iniquities you have **set** before you,*
and our secret sins in the light **of** your countenance.

9 When you are angry, all our **days** are gone;*
we bring our years to an end **like** a sigh.

10 The span of our life is seventy years,
perhaps in strength **e**ven eighty;*
yet the sum of them is but labor and sorrow,
for they pass away quickly and **we** are gone.

11 Who regards the power **of** your wrath?*
who rightly fears your **in**dignation?

12 So teach us to num**ber** our days*
that we may apply our **hearts** to wisdom.

13 Return, O LORD; how long **will** you tarry?*
be gracious **to** your servants.

14 Satisfy us by your loving-kindness **in** the morning;*
so shall we rejoice and be glad all the days **of** our life.

15 Make us glad by the measure of the days that you af**flict**ed us*
and the years in which we suf**fered** adversity.

16 Show your ser**vants** your works*
and your splendor **to** their children.

17 May the graciousness of the LORD our God **be** upon us;*
prosper the work of our hands;
pros**per** our handiwork.

Antiphon Return, O Lord; how long **will** you tarry?*
Be gracious **to** your servants.

on December 23

The Lord, the ruler of the kings of the **earth**, will come;*
blessed are they who are ready to **wel**come him.

Silence for meditation

Eternal Father of our mortal race, despite our sin you give us life and even add days and years to our lives to bring us to wisdom: Make us so to love and obey you that the works of our hands may show your graciousness to us until at last we behold the beauty of your face, shown to us in Jesus Christ our Lord. [LH, PHP]

+

Antiphon to PSALM 149 *Cantate Domino*

The LORD takes pleasure **in** his people*
and adorns the **poor** with victory.

on December 23

A great and trustworthy proph**et** will come;*
and he alone shall re**new** Jerusalem.

[LH, PBO: see Macc. 14:41]

149 *Praise to the God of victories*

1 Hallelujah!
Sing to the LORD **a** new song;*
sing his praise in the congregation **of** the faithful.

2 Let Israel rejoice **in** his Maker;*
let the children of Zion be joyful **in** their King.

3 Let them praise his Name **in** the dance;*
let them sing praise to him with tim**brel** and harp.

4 For the LORD takes pleasure **in** his people*
and adorns the **poor** with victory.

5 Let the faithful re**joice** in triumph;*
let them be joyful **on** their beds.

6 Let the praises of God be **in** their throat*
and a two-edged sword **in** their hand;

7 To wreak vengeance **on** the nations*
and punishment **on** the peoples;

8 To bind their **kings** in chains*
and their nobles with **links** of iron;

9 To inflict on them the judg**ment** decreed;*
this is glory for all his faithful people.
Hallelujah!

Antiphon The LORD takes pleasure **in** his people*
and adorns the **poor** with victory.

on December 23

A great and trustworthy proph**et** will come;*
and he alone shall re**new** Jerusalem.

Silence for meditation

Lord, let Israel rejoice in you and acknowledge you as creator and redeemer. In your lovingkindness embrace us now, that we may proclaim the wonderful truths of salvation with your saints in glory; through your Son, Jesus Christ our Lord. [LH, LBW]

Stand

THE HYMN is sung. *Wachet auf, ruft uns die Stimme*

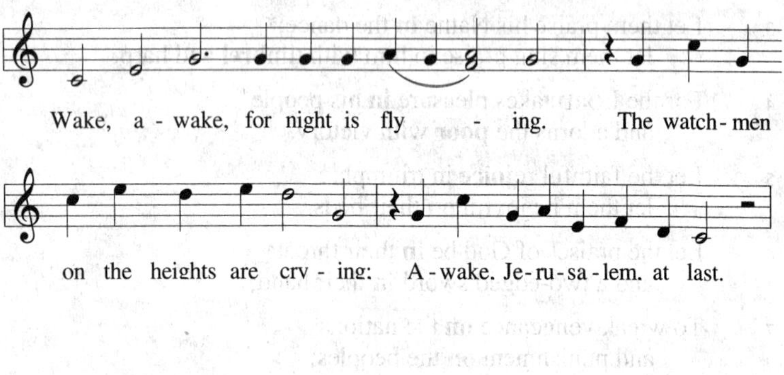

2 Zion hears the watchmen singing,
And all her heart with joy is springing.
She wakes, she rises from her gloom,
For her Lord comes down all glorious,
The strong in grace, in truth victorious.
Her star is risen, her light is come.
Oh come, awaited One,
Lord Jesus, God's own Son.
Alleluia!
We follow 'til the halls we view
Where you have bid us dine with you.

3 Now let all the heavens adore you,
And saints and angels sing before you.
The harps and cymbals all unite.
Of one pearl each shining portal,
Where, dwelling with the choir immortal,
We gather round your dazzling light.
No eye has seen, no ear
Has yet attained to hear.
What joy is ours!
Crescendos rise; your halls resound;
Hosannas blend in cosmic sound. [SBH 7, LBW 31 alt.]

Text: Philipp Nicolai, 1556-1608; tr. Catherine Winkworth, 1829-1878, alt.

Tune: *Wachet auf*, Philipp Nicolai, 1506-1608 PM

Sit

One or two LESSONS are read.

Silence for meditation follows each reading.

Year 1	Year 2
First Saturday in Advent	
Isaiah 4:2-6 The LORD will create over the whole site of Mount Zion and over its places of assembly a cloud by day and smoke and the shining of a flaming fire by night. Indeed over all the glory there will be a canopy. It will serve as a pavilion, a shade by day from the heat, and a refuge and a shelter from the storm and rain.	Amos 5:18-27 Let justice roll down like waters, and righteousness like an ever-flowing stream.

1 Thessalonians 4:13-18

The Lord himself with a cry of command, with the archangel's call and with the sound of God's trumpet, will descend from heaven.

Jude 17-25

To the only God our Savior, through Jesus Christ our Lord, be glory, majesty, power, and authority, before all time and now and forever.

Second Saturday in Advent

Isaiah 8:1-15

The LORD of hosts, him you shall regard as holy; let him be your fear, and let him be your dread.

Haggai 2:1-9

Once again, in a little while, I will shake the heavens and the earth and the sea and the dry land; and I will shake all the nations, so that the treasure of all nations shall come, and I will fill this house with splendor, says the LORD of hosts.

2 Thessalonians 3:6-18

Now may the Lord of peace himself give you peace at all times and in all ways.

Revelation 3:1-6

Remember then what you received and heard; obey it, and repent.

RESPONSORY for Saturdays in Advent

Do not fear, Jerusalem, for you will not **be** ashamed;*
    You will be visited by the **Lord** of hosts.
And the multitude of all the nations that fight against you shall be like a **dream** of dust;*
    You will be visited by the **Lord** of hosts.

[LH: see Isa. 54:4; 29:5,6,7]

I will place my dwelling **in** your midst,*
and I shall **not** abhor you;
    I will walk among you,
    and will **be** your God,*
    and you shall **be** my people.
For we are the temple of the **liv**ing God,*
as God him**self** has said.
    I will walk among you,
    and will **be** your God,*

and you shall **be** my people.
[LH: Lev. 26:11-12; 2 Cor. 6:16]

December 23

Isaiah 33:17-22
Your eyes will see the king in his beauty; they will behold a land that stretches far away.

Jeremiah 31:10-14
He who scattered Israel will gather him, and will keep him as a shepherd a flock.
[BCP: Baruch 4:21-29]

Revelation 22:6-11,18-20
"Surely I am coming soon." Amen. Come, Lord Jesus!

Galatians 3:15-22
The scripture has imprisoned all things under the power of sin, so that what was promised through faith in Jesus Christ might be given to those who believe.

RESPONSORY for December 23

Listen to **me**, my people,*
and give heed to **me**, my nation.
My salvation **has** gone out;*
I will bring near my
deliv**er**ance swiftly.
The ransomed of the Lord **shall** return,*
and come to Zi**on** with singing.
My salvation **has** gone out;*
I will bring near my
deliv**er**ance swiftly.
[LH: Isa. 51:4,5; 35:10]

A child has been **born** for us,*
and he is named **Might**y God.
His authority shall **grow** continually,*
and there shall be
endless peace for the throne
of David **and** his kingdom.
In **him** was life,*
and the life was the light **of** the world.
His authority shall **grow** continually,*
and there shall be
endless peace for the throne
of David **and** his kingdom.
[LH: Isa. 9:6,7; John 1:4; 8:12]

Antiphon to the BENEDICTUS

First Saturday in Advent	Banish your fears, O peo**ple** of Zion;* God, your own God, is com**ing** to you. [LH: see Isa. 35:4; 40:9-10]
Second Saturday in Advent	The Lord will raise a signal **for** the nations* and will assemble the out**casts** of Israel. [LH: Isa. 11:12]
December 23	All that God promised to the Virgin through the message **of** the angel* has **been** accomplished. [LH]

The PRAYER OF THE DAY for December 23

Almighty and everlasting God, as the feast of the nativity of your Son draws near, grant that we may know the mercy of the eternal Word who took flesh of the Virgin Mary and came to dwell among us, Jesus Christ our Lord, who lives and reigns with you and the Holy Spirit, one God, now and for ever. [Leo., RS; trans. ICEL, PHP]

December 24

Antiphon to PSALM 24 *Domini est terra*

Stand up and **raise** your heads,*
because your redemption is **draw**ing near.

[LH: Luke 21:28]

24 *The Lord's entry into his temple*

1 The earth is the LORD's and all **that** is in it,*
the world and all who **dwell** therein.

2 For it is he who founded it up**on** the seas*
and made it firm upon the rivers **of** the deep.

3 "Who can ascend the hill **of** the LORD?*
and who can stand in his **ho**ly place?"

4 "Those who have clean hands **and** a pure heart,*
who have not pledged themselves to falsehood,
nor sworn by what **is** a fraud.

5 They shall receive a blessing **from** the LORD*
and a just reward from the God of **their** salvation."

6 Such is the generation of **those** who seek him,*
of those who seek your face, O **God** of Jacob.

7 Lift up your heads,O gates;
lift them high, O ever**last**ing doors;*
and the King of glory **shall** come in.

8 "Who is this **King** of glory?"*
"The LORD, strong and mighty,
the LORD, mighty in battle."

9 Lift up your heads, O gates;
lift them high, O ever**last**ing doors;*
and the King of glory **shall** come in.

10 “Who is this **King** of glory?”*
“The LORD of hosts,
he is the **King** of glory.”

Antiphon Stand up and **raise** your heads,*
because your redemption is **draw**ing near.

Silence for meditation

Lord God, ruler and guide of heaven and earth, you made your Son a priest and brought him into your everlasting temple: Open our hearts that the King of glory may enter, and bring us rejoicing to your holy mountain, where you live and reign, one God, now and for ever. [LHd, LBW]

+

Antiphon to PSALM 150 *Laudate Dominum in sanctis ejus*

You, O Bethlehem in the **land** of Judah,*
from you shall come forth for me
one who is to **rule** in Israel.

[LH: Matt. 2:6; Micah 5:2]

150 *The great Alleluia*

1 Hallelujah!
Praise God in his **ho**ly temple;*
praise him in the firmament **of** his power.

2 Praise him for his **might**y acts;*
praise him for his ex**cel**lent greatness.

3 Praise him with the blast **of** the ram’s-horn;*
praise him with **lyre** and harp.

4 Praise him with tim**brel** and dance;*
praise him with **strings** and pipe.

5 Praise him with re**sound**ing cymbals;*
praise him with loud-**clang**ing cymbals.

6 Let everything **that** has breath*
praise the Lord.
Hallelujah!

Antiphon You, O Bethlehem in the **land** of Judah,*
from you shall come forth for me
one who is to **rule** in Israel.

Silence for meditation

God of surpassing greatness, enthroned upon the praises of your people, fill our hearts with your love and unite our voices with the praise of all creation so that you may be honored and glorified by everything that has breath; through Jesus Christ our Lord. [PHP]

+

Stand

THE HYMN is sung.

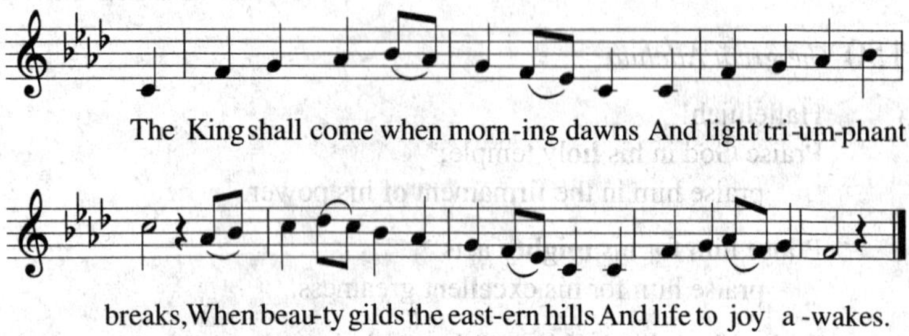

2 Not as of old a little child,
To bear and fight and die,
But crowned with glory like the sun
That lights the morning sky.

3 O brighter than the rising morn
When he, victorious, rose
And left the lonesome place of death,
Despite the rage of foes;

4 O brighter than that glorious morn
Shall this fair morning be
When Christ our King in beauty comes,
And we his face shall see.

5 The King shall come when morning dawns,
And earth's dark night is past
O haste the rising of that morn,
The day that aye shall last.

6 And let the endless bliss begin,
By weary saints foretold
When right shall triumph over wrong,
And truth shall be extolled.

7 The King shall come when morning dawns
And light and beauty brings.
Hail, Christ the Lord! Your people pray:
Come quickly, King of kings.

[CSB 14, H33 70; SBH 10, H 82 73, LBW 33]

Text: John Brownlie, 1859-1925, cento
Tune: *Consolation,* melody from *Kentucky Harmony*, 1816 CM

Sit

One or two LESSONS are read.

Silence for meditation follows each reading.

Year 1

Isaiah 35:1-10
They shall see the glory of the LORD, the majesty of our God.

or Isaiah 59:15b-21 [BCP]
He will come to Zion as Redeemer.

Year 2

Baruch 4:36-5:9 [BCP]
Look toward the east, O Jerusalem, and see the joy that is coming to you from God.

or Isaiah 59:15b-21 [BCP]
He will come to Zion as Redeemer.

RESPONSORY

Cleanse yourselves, people of Israel, **says** the Lord;*
for tomorrow the Lord **will** come down.
He will turn away from you **ev**ery illness*
and bring in ever**last**ing righteousness.
Tomorrow the wickedness of the earth will **be** destroyed,
and the Savior of the world will rule **o**ver us,*
He will turn away from you **ev**ery illness*
and bring in ever**last**ing righteousness.

[LH: see Exod. 19:10-11; Deut. 7:15; see Dan. 9:24]

Year 1

Revelation 22:12-17, 21
The Spirit and the bride say, "Come." And let everyone who hears say, "Come."

or Philippians 2:5-11 [BCP]
Christ Jesus emptied himself, taking the form of a slave, being born in human likeness.

Year 2

Galatians 3:23-4:7
When the fullness of time had come, God sent his Son, born of a woman, born under the law, so that we might receive adoption as children.

or Philippians 2:5-11 [BCP]
Christ Jesus emptied himself, taking the form of a slave, being born in human likeness.

RESPONSORY

A shoot shall come out from the **stump** of Jesse,*
and a Branch shall grow out **of** his roots.
Righteousness shall be the belt a**round** his waist*
and faithfulness the belt a**round** his loins.

The Spirit of the Lord shall **rest** on him,*
the Spirit of wisdom and understanding,
the spirit of coun**sel** and might.
Righteousness shall be the belt a**round** his waist*
and faithfulness the belt a**round** his loins.

[LH: Isa. 11:1,5,2]

Antiphon to the BENEDICTUS

The **time** has come*
for Mary to give birth to her **first**born Son.

[LH: see Luke 2:6-7]

The PRAYER OF THE DAY for December 24

O God, you gladden us with the yearly expectation of our redemption: Grant that we, who now joyfully receive your only-begotten Son as our Redeemer, may also behold him without fear when he comes to be our Judge; who lives and reigns with you and the Holy Spirit, one God, now and for ever. [Gel., Greg., Sarum, CB, RS, BCP]

Daily Prayer for Christmas begins with Evening Prayer on December 24, the first Vespers of Christmas.

✠

EVENING PRAYER

Vespers or Evensong from Christmas Eve through the Sunday of the Baptism of our Lord

The SERVICE OF LIGHT is appropriate every day of this season. The service may begin with a procession in which a large, lighted candle is carried to its stand in front of the congregation.

When the Service of Light is omitted, Evening Prayer begins with the verses on page 7.

Stand

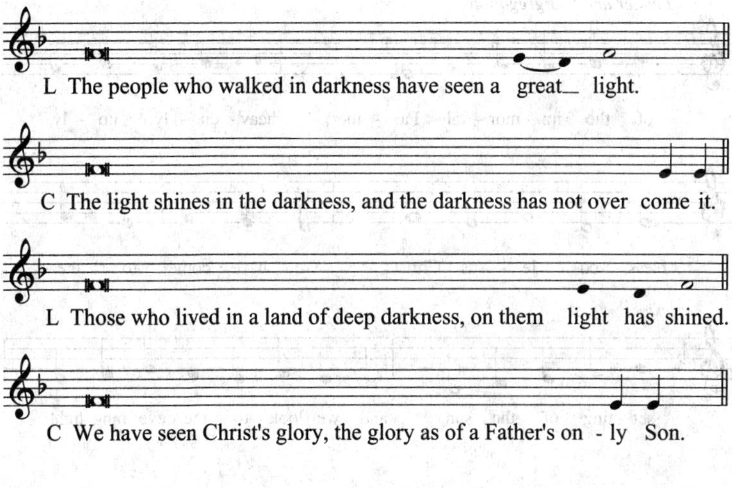

L For a child has been born born for us, a Son giv - en to us.

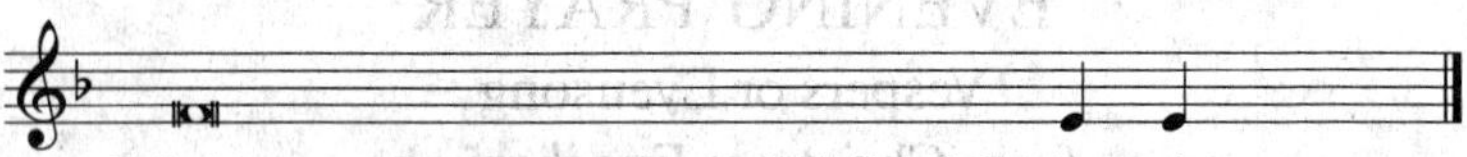

C In him was life, and the life was the light of all peo - ple.

[Isa. 9:2a + John 1:5; Isa. 9:2b + John 1:14b; Isa 9:6 + John 1:4]

As this ancient hymn, Phos hilaron, *is sung, the candles on and near the altar are lighted. When the large candle is used, the candles are lighted from its flame.*

Leader

Joy - ous Light of glo - ry:

Leader and Congregation

of the im - mor - tal Fa - ther; heav - en - ly, ho - ly,

bless - ed Je - sus Christ. We have come to the

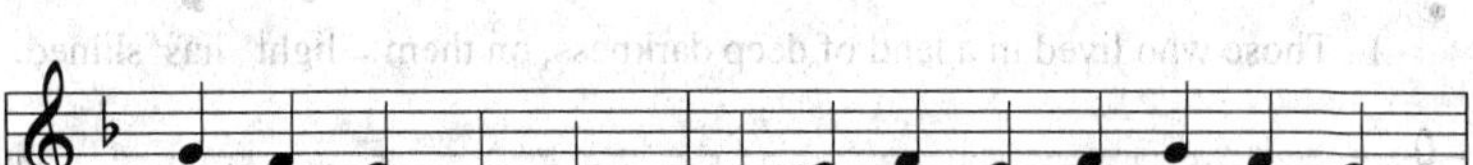

set - ting of the sun, and we look to the eve - ning light.

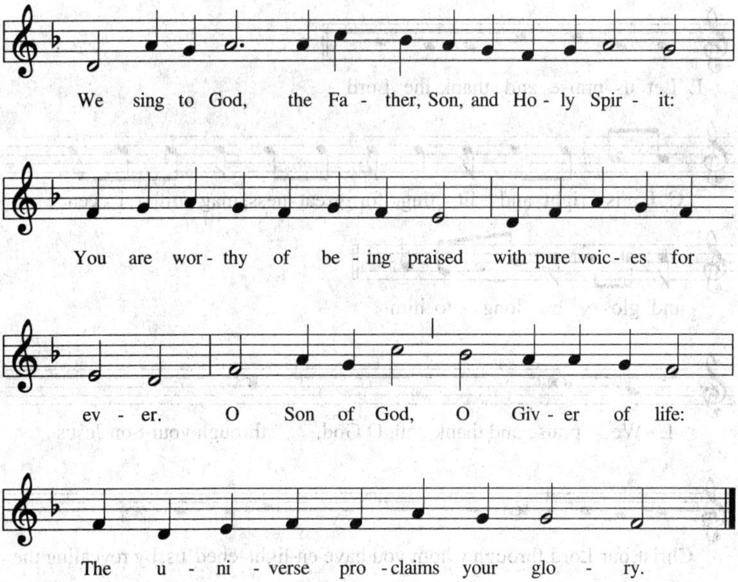

The thanksgiving from the Apostolic Tradition *(ca. 215) concludes the Service of Light.*

L Let us praise and thank the Lord.
C It is right and fit-ting, for great-ness, mag-nif-i-cence
and glo-ry be-long to him.
L We praise and thank you, O God, through your Son Jesus
Christ, our Lord, through whom you have en-light-ened us, by revealing the
light that nev-er fades. Night is fall-ing, and day's allotted span
draws to a close. The daylight which you created for our pleasure
has ful-ly sat-is-fied us, and yet, of your free gift, now the evening

The PSALMODY begins with this song for forgiveness and protection, from Psalm 141, Domine clamavi.

Kneel or sit

I cry to you. [II] Let my prayer rise be- fore_ you as in - cense;
the lift-ing up of my hands as the eve - ning sac - ri -fice.
[I] Set a watch be -fore my mouth, O Lord, and guard the door of my lips.
[II] Let not my heart in-cline to an - y e - vil thing; let me
not be oc - cu-pied in wick-ed-ness with e - vil do - ers.
[I] But my eyes are turned to you, Lord God; in you I take ref-uge.
Strip me not of my life. [II] Glo - ry to the Fa - ther, and to the
Son, and to the Ho-ly Spir- it; [I] as it was in the be- gin-

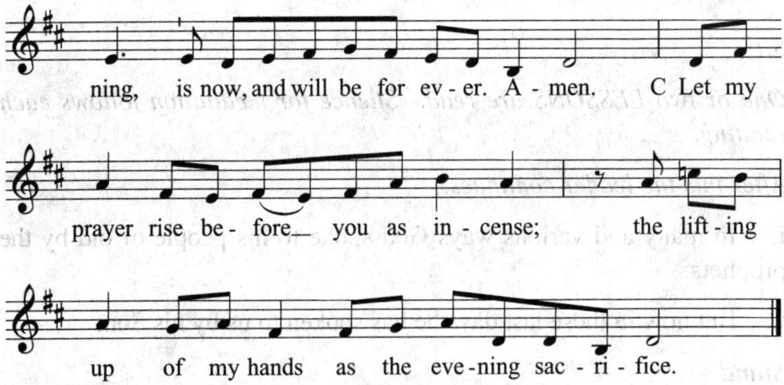

Silence for meditation.

L Let the incense of our repentant prayer ascend before you, O Lord, and let your lovingkindness descend upon us, that with purified minds we may sing your praises with the Church on earth and the whole heavenly host, and may glorify you for ever and ever.

C Amen

Sit

A second psalm is sung or said; additional psalms and a New Testament canticle may be sung or said also. Silence for meditation follows each psalm or canticle.

The psalm prayer appropriate to each psalm or canticle follows the silence.

C Amen

Stand

THE HYMN is sung.

Sit

One or two LESSONS are read. Silence for meditation follows each reading.

After this the leader continues:

L In many and various ways God spoke to his people of old by the prophets.

C But now in these last days he has spoken to us by his Son.

Stand

The GOSPEL CANTICLE, Magnificat, *is sung or said. The proper Antiphon is given on pp.208-258.*

The Antiphon is sung or said.

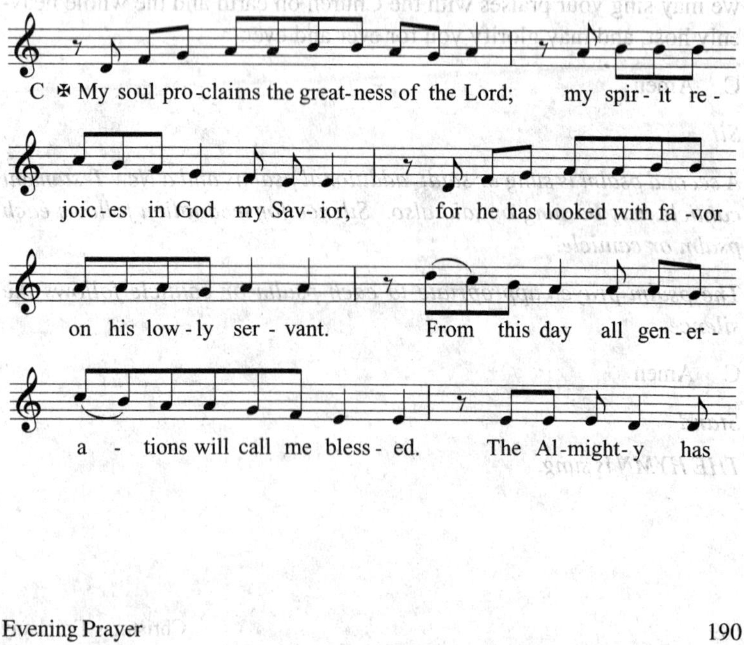

done great things for me, and ho - ly is his Name. He has
mer-cy on those who fear_ him in ev - 'ry gen - er - a - tion.
He has shown the strength of his arm; he has scat- tered the
proud in their con - ceit. He has cast down the might-y from their thrones,
and has lift - ed up the low - ly. He has filled the
hun-gry with good things, and the rich he has sent a-way emp - ty.
He has come to the help of his ser-vant Is - ra - el,
for he has re-mem-bered his pro-mise of mer-cy, the prom-ise he

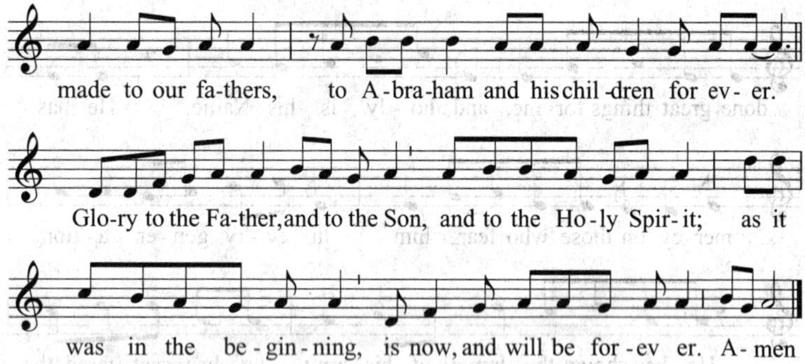

The Antiphon is repeated.

The Litany is sung or said. Kneel or stand.

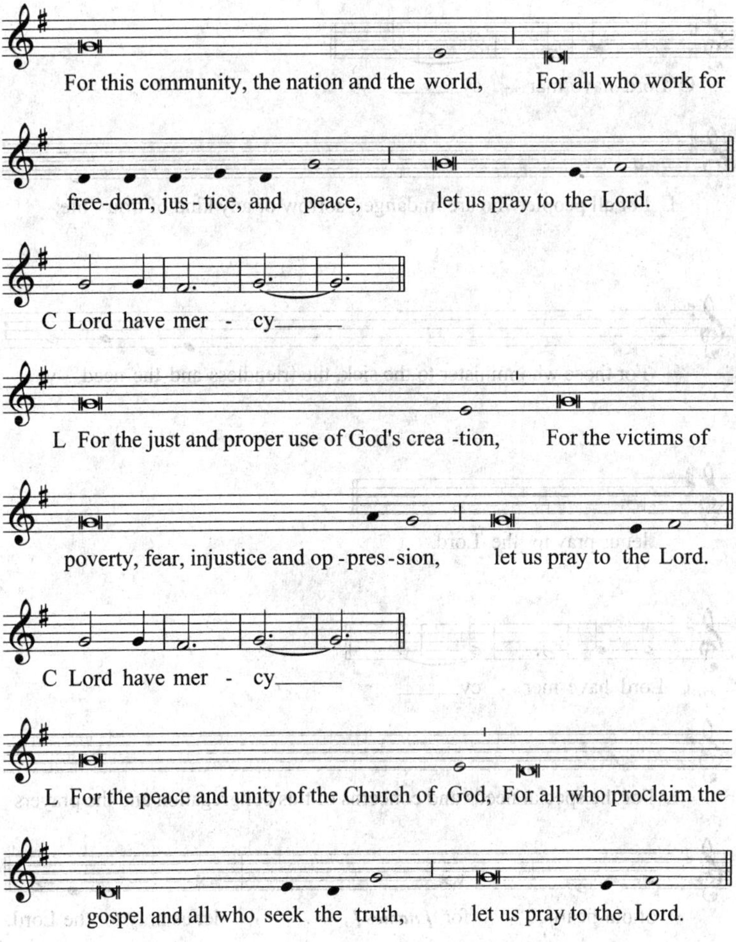
For this community, the nation and the world, For all who work for
free-dom, jus - tice, and peace, let us pray to the Lord.
C Lord have mer - cy
L For the just and proper use of God's crea -tion, For the victims of
poverty, fear, injustice and op - pres - sion, let us pray to the Lord.
C Lord have mer - cy
L For the peace and unity of the Church of God, For all who proclaim the
gospel and all who seek the truth, let us pray to the Lord.

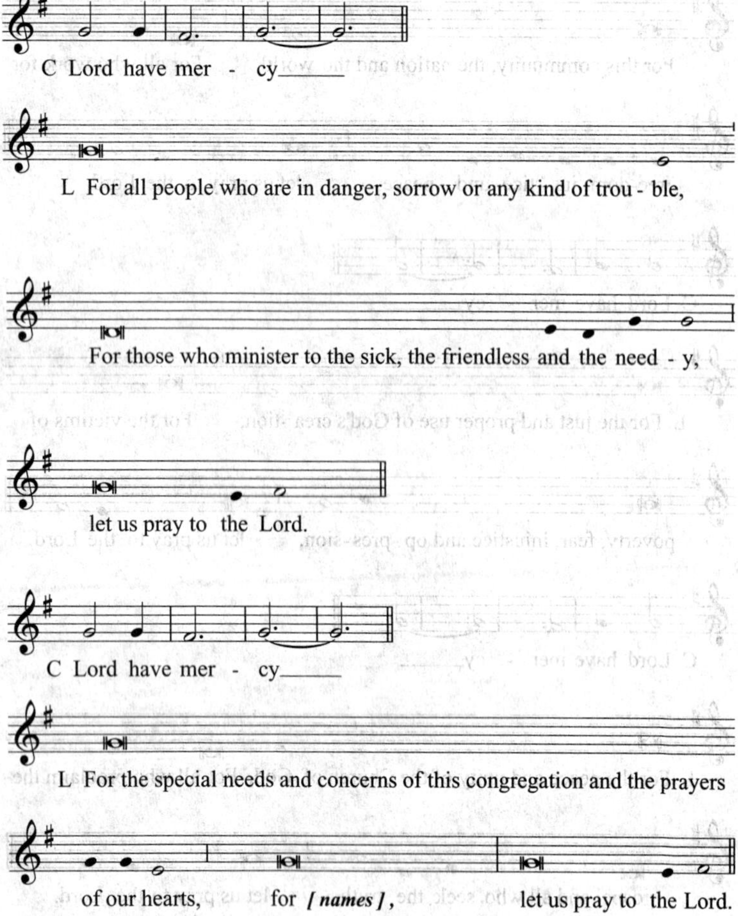
C Lord have mer - cy
L For all people who are in danger, sorrow or any kind of trou - ble,
For those who minister to the sick, the friendless and the need - y,
let us pray to the Lord.
C Lord have mer - cy
L For the special needs and concerns of this congregation and the prayers
of our hearts, for *[names]*, let us pray to the Lord.

[BCP adapt.; setting copyright © 2004 John W. Becker]

The appropriate collect concludes the litany.

On December 24:

O God, you gladden us with the yearly expectation of our redemption: Grant that we, who now joyfully receive your only-begotten Son as our Redeemer, may also behold him without fear when he comes to be our judge; who lives and reigns with you and the Holy Spirit, one God, now and for ever. [Gel., RS, CB, BCP]

December 25 and December 28 through January 1

O God, you wonderfully created, and yet more wonderfully restored, the dignity of human nature: Grant that we may share the divine life of him who humbled himself to share our humanity, your Son Jesus Christ; who lives and reigns with you and the Holy Spirit, one God, now and for ever.

[Leo., LH; BCP Christmas 2; LBW Christmas 1]

December 26 and January 2-5

Grant, we implore you, almighty God, that the new birth of your only-begotten Son in the flesh may set us free who are held in the old bondage under the yoke of sin; through Jesus Christ our Lord, who lives and reigns with you and the Holy Spirit, one God, now and for ever.

[Gel., MR, CB, CSB. SBH, LBW Christmas; RS December 30]

December 27 and January 6 through the Sunday of the Baptism of our Lord

Almighty and everlasting God, the glory of those who believe in you: Fill the world with your splendor, and show every nation the radiance of your light; through your Son Jesus Christ our Lord, who lives and reigns with you and the Holy Spirit, one God, now and for ever.

[Greg., LH; RS Christmas 2]

L Lord, remember us in your kingdom, and teach us to pray:

C Our Father in heaven, hallowed be your Name your kingdom come, your will be done, on earth as in heaven. Give us this day our daily bread; Forgive us our sins as we forgive those who sin against us. Save us from the time of trial and deliver us from evil. For the kingdom, the power, and the glory are yours, now and for ever. Amen.	C Our Father who art in heaven, hallowed be thy Name thy kingdom come, thy will be done, on earth as it is in heaven. Give us today our daily bread. and forgive us our trespasses, as we forgive those who sin against us; And lead us not into temptation but deliver us from evil. For thine is the kingdom, and the power, and the glory, for ever and ever. Amen.

Stand

L Let us bless the Lord.

C Thanks be to God.

The BENEDICTION concludes the service when there is no sermon. A hymn may follow the benediction.

When there is a sermon, this benediction is omitted, and the service *continues on p. 20.*

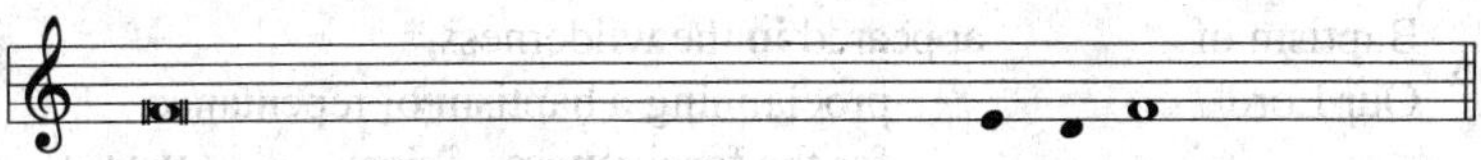

L The almighty and merciful Lord,
the Father, the Son, and the Holy Spirit, bless and pre-serve us.

C A - men

December 24, 31, January 5, and Eve of the Baptism of Our Lord

When the Epiphany falls on Saturday, Evening Prayer is of the Epiphany and Vespers of the Eve of the Baptism of Our Lord is omitted that year.

Antiphon to PSALM 114 *In exitu Israel*

December 24 Christmas Eve	The Lord comes forth like a bridegroom out **of** his chamber;* he rejoices like a champion to **run** his course. [LH: see Ps. 19:5]
December 31 Eve of the Holy Name of Jesus	The Lord sends out his command **to** the earth,* and his word runs very swiftly **through** the land. [LH: see Ps. 147:16]
January 5 Eve of the Epiphany	Begotten of the Father before the daystar shone or **time** began,* the Lord our Savior appeared on **earth** today. [LH]
Eve of the Baptism of Our Lord	John the baptizer appeared **in** the wilderness,* proclaiming a baptism of repentance for the forgive**ness** of sins. [LH: Mark 1:4]

114 *The wonders of the Exodus*

1 Hallelujah!
When Israel came **out** of Egypt,*
the house of Jacob from a people **of** strange speech,

2 Judah became God's **sanc**tuary*
and Israel **his** dominion.

3 The sea beheld **it** and fled;*
Jordan turned **and** went back.

4 The mountains **skipped** like rams,*
and the little hills **like** young sheep.

5 What ailed you, O sea, **that** you fled?*
O Jordan, that **you** turned back?

6 You mountains, that you **skipped** like rams?*
you little hills **like** young sheep?

7 Tremble, O earth, at the presence **of** the Lord,*
at the presence of the **God** of Jacob,

8 Who turned the hard rock into a **pool** of water*
and flint-stone into a **flow**ing spring.

The Antiphon is repeated.

Silence for meditation

Almighty God, you gave life to the new Israel by birth from water and the Spirit. Make all those whom you have called to walk in the splendor of the new light render you fitting service and adoration, through your Son, Jesus Christ our Lord. [LH, LBW]

+

Antiphon to PSALM 45 *Eructavit cor meum*

December 24 Christmas Eve	Tomorrow the iniquity of the earth shall be **blot**ted out,* and the Savior of the world shall rule **o**ver us. [LH]
December 31 Eve of the Holy Name of Jesus	He comes in splendor, the King who **is** our peace;* the whole world **longs** to see him. [LH: see Eph. 2:14; Heb. 7:2]

January 5 Eve of the Epiphany	Your throne, O God, endures for ev**er** and ever,* a scepter of righteousness is the scepter **of** your kingdom.
Eve of the Baptism of Our Lord	When Jesus had been baptized, just as he came up **from** the water,* suddenly the heavens were o**pened** to him. [Matt. 3:16; LH]

45 *Royal wedding song*

1 My heart is stirring with a noble song;
let me recite what I have fashioned **for** the king;*
my tongue shall be the pen of **a** skilled writer.

2 You are the fair**est** of men;*
grace flows from your lips,
because God has blessed **you** for ever.

3 Strap your sword upon your thigh, O **might**y warrior,*
in your pride and **in** your majesty.

4 Ride out and conquer in the **cause** of truth*
and for the **sake** of justice.

5 Your right hand will show you **marvel**ous things;*
your arrows are very sharp, O **might**y warrior.

6 The peoples are falling **at** your feet,*
and the king's enemies are **los**ing heart.

7 Your throne, O God, endures for ev**er** and ever,*
a scepter of righteousness is the scepter of your kingdom;
you love righteousness and **hate** iniquity.

8 Therefore God, your God, has a**noint**ed you*
with the oil of gladness a**bove** your fellows.

9 All your garments are fragrant with myrrh, a**loes**, and cassia,*
and the music of strings from ivory palaces **makes** you glad.

10 Kings' daughters stand among the ladies **of** the court;*
on your right hand is the queen,
adorned with the **gold** of Ophir.

11 "Hear, O daughter; consider and **list**en closely;*
forget your people and your **fath**er's house.

12 The king will have pleasure **in** your beauty;*
he is your master; therefore **do** him honor.

13 The people of Tyre are here **with** a gift;*
the rich among the people **seek** your favor."

14 All glorious is the princess **as** she enters;*
her gown is **cloth**-of-gold.

15 In embroidered apparel she is brought **to** the king;*
after her the bridesmaids follow **in** procession.

16 With joy and gladness **they** are brought,*
and enter into the palace **of** the king.

17 "In place of fathers, O king, you **shall** have sons;*
you shall make them princes over **all** the earth.

18 I will make your name to be remembered
from one generation **to** another;*
therefore nations will praise you for ev**er** and ever."

The Antiphon is repeated.

Silence for meditation

Lord God, you have formed the holy Church to be the bride of Christ. Grant to your Church the faith and peace she will need to do your will and to show your glory, through your Son, Jesus Christ our Lord. [LBW]

+

Antiphon to the NEW TESTAMENT CANTICLE

Qui cum in forma Dei esset

December 24 Christmas Eve	The eternal Word, born of the Father before **time** began,* today emptied himself for our sake and **be**came man. [LH]
December 31 Eve of the Holy Name of Jesus	O wondrous exchange! The Creator of the human race, having assumed a living body, deigned to be born **of** a virgin,* and, having become flesh without human aid, enriched us with **his** divinity. [LH]
January 5 Eve of the Epiphany	The star burned like a flame, pointing the way to the **King** of kings;* the Wise Men saw the sign and brought their gifts in homage to **the** great King. [LH]
Eve of the Baptism of Our Lord	I baptize **you** with water,* but one who is coming will baptize you with the Holy Spir**it** and fire. [LH: Luke 3:16]

A Song of Christ's Humiliation and Exaltation Phil. 2:6-11

Christ Jesus, being in the form of God,
did not cling to his equali**ty** with God*
but emptied himself, taking the form **of** a slave.

Bearing the human likeness, revealed in **hu**man shape,*
he humbled himself, in obedience accepting death,
even death **on** a cross.

Therefore God has raised him **to** the heights*
and bestowed on him the Name a**bove** all names,

that at the Name of JESUS every knee should bow —
in heaven, on earth, and **in** the depths —*

and every tongue confess to the glory of God the Father
that Jesus **Christ** is Lord. [LBW 20]

The Antiphon is repeated.

Silence for meditation

O God, your only-begotten Son appeared in the substance of our human flesh: Grant that he, whose outward form is like our own, may reshape us inwardly by his grace; through the same Jesus Christ our Lord.
[Gel., RS Tues. after Epiphany]

+

Stand

THE HYMN is sung.
on December 24, Christmas Eve *O Oriens*

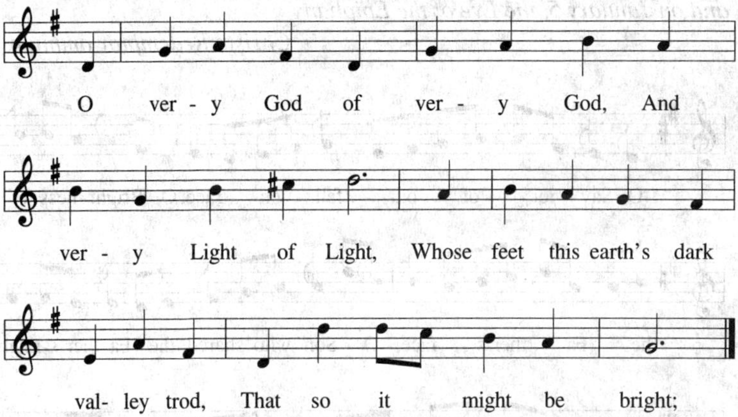

2 Our hopes are weak, our foes are strong,
Thick darkness blinds our eyes;
Cold is the night, and O, we long
That thou, our Sun, wouldst rise.

3 And even now, though dull and gray,
The east is brightening fast,
And kindling to the perfect day
That never shall be past.

4 O guide us till our path be done,
And we have reached the shore
Where thou, our everlasting Sun,
Art shining evermore!

5 We wait in faith, and turn our face
To where the daylight springs,
Till thou shalt come our gloom to chase,
With healing on thy wings. [CSB 11, H82 672]

Text: John Mason Neale, 1818-1866
Tune: *Nottingham*, Jeremiah Clarke (1670-1707) CM

on December 31, the Eve of the Holy Name of Jesus,
and on January 5, the Eve of the Epiphany

Christe Redemptor omnium

2 O Jesus, very Light of light,
Our constant star in sin's deep night:
Now hear the prayers your people pray
Throughout the world this holy day.

3 Remember, Lord of life and grace,
How once, to save our fallen race,
You put our human vesture on
And came to us as Mary's son.

4 Today, as year by year its light
Bathes all the world in radiance bright,
One precious truth outshines the sun:
Salvation comes from you alone.

5 For from the Father's throne you came,
His banished children to reclaim;
And earth and sea and sky revere
The love of him who sent you here.

6 And we are jubilant today,
For you have washed our guilt away.
Oh, hear the glad new song we sing
On this, the birthday of our king!

7 O Christ, redeemer virgin-born,
Let songs of praise your Name adorn,
Whom with the Father we adore
And Holy Spirit evermore. Amen. [LBW 49, H82 85]

Text: Latin office hymn, c. 6th cent.; tr. Gilbert E. Doan, Jr., b. 1930
Tune: *Christe redemptor omnium*, medieval plainsong, Mode I LM

on the Eve of the Baptism of Our Lord

A Patre unigenitus

2 Beginning from his home on high,
In human flesh he came to die;
Creation by his death restored,
And shed new joys of life abroad.

3 Glide on, O glorious Sun, and bring
The gift of healing on your wing;
To every dull and clouded sense
The clearness of your light dispense.

4 Abide with us, O Lord, we pray;
The gloom of darkness chase away;
Your work of healing, Lord, begin,
And take away the stain of sin.

5 Lord, once you came to earth's domain
And, we believe, shall come again;
Be with us on the battlefield,
From every harm your people shield.

6 To you, O Lord, all glory be
For this your blest Epiphany;
To God whom all his hosts adore,
And Holy Spirit evermore. [LBW 83]

Text: Latin office hymn, c. 11th cent.; tr. John Mason Neale, 1818-1866 alt.
Tune: *Deus tuorum militum*, from *Antiphoner*, Grenoble, 1753 LM

Sit

A LESSON is read.

Year 1	Year 2
December 24 [BCP: Isa. 59:15b-21 and Phil. 2:5-11]	
Luke 1:67-80	Matthew 1:18-25
Blessed be the Lord God of Israel, for he has looked favorably on his people and redeemed them.	Joseph, son of David, do not be afraid to take Mary as your wife, for the child conceived in her is from the Holy Spirit.
December 31 [BCP: Isa. 65:15b-25 and Revelation 21:1-6]	
John 8:12-19	John 5:1-15
I am the light of the world. Whoever follows me will never walk in darkness but will have the light of life.	At once the man was made well, and he took up his mat and began to walk.
January 5 [BCP: Isa. 66:18-23 and Rom. 15:7-13]	
John 15:1-16	John 11:17-27,38-44
I have said these things to you so that my joy may be in you, and that your joy may be complete.	Yes, Lord, I believe that you are the Messiah, the Son of God, the one coming into the world.
Eve of the Baptism of Our Lord	[BCP: Isa. 61:1-9 and Gal. 3:23-29; 4:4-7]
John 9:1-12,35-38	John 15:1-16
As long as I am in the world, I am the light of the world.	As the Father has loved me, so I loved you; abide in my love.

Silence for meditation follows the reading.

Antiphon to the MAGNIFICAT

December 24 Christmas Eve	When the sun rises in the **morn**ing sky,* you will see the King of kings coming forth from the Father like a radiant bridegroom from the **brid**al chamber. [LH]
December 31 Eve of the Holy Name of Jesus	In his great **love** for us,* God sent his Son into the world, born of a woman, born un**der** the law. [LH: see Gal. 4:4]
January 5 Eve of the Epiphany	Seeing the star, the **Wise** Men said,* This must signify the birth of **some** great king. Let us search for him and lay our treasures **at** his feet:* gold and frankin**cense** and myrrh. [LH]
Eve of the Baptism of Our Lord	Our Savior came to **be** baptized,* so that through the cleansing waters of baptism he might restore the old self to new life, heal our sinful nature, and clothe us with un**fail**ing holiness. [LH]

December 25, January 1, 6, and Baptism of Our Lord

Antiphon to PSALM 96 *Cantate Domino*

December 25 Christmas Day	In the beginning, before time began, the **Word** was God;* today he is born, the Savior **of** the world. [LH: see John 1:1]
January 1 The Holy Name of Jesus	Let the heavens rejoice, and let the earth be glad be**fore** the Lord,* for **he** has come. [PBO]
January 6 The Epiphany	He comes in splendor, the King who **is** our peace;* he is supreme over all the **kings** of earth. [LH: see Heb. 7:2]
The Baptism of Our Lord	The Father's voice resounded **from** the heavens,* This is my Son, the beloved, with whom I am well pleased; list**en** to him. [LH: Matt. 3:17; 17:5]

96 *The Lord, King and Judge of the world*

1 Sing to the LORD **a** new song;*
sing to the LORD, all **the** whole earth.

2 Sing to the LORD and **bless** his Name;*
proclaim the good news of his salvation from **day** to day.

3 Declare his glory a**mong** the nations*
and his wonders a**mong** all peoples.

4 For great is the LORD and greatly **to** be praised;*
he is more to be feared **than** all gods.

5 As for all the gods of the nations, they **are** but idols;*
but it is the LORD who **made** the heavens.

6 Oh, the majesty and magnificence **of** his presence!*
Oh, the power and the splendor of his **sanc**tuary!

7 Ascribe to the LORD, you families **of** the peoples;*
ascribe to the LORD hon**or** and power.

8 Ascribe to the LORD honor **due** his Name;*
bring offerings and come in**to** his courts.

9 Worship the LORD in the beau**ty** of holiness;*
let the whole earth trem**ble** before him.

10 Tell it out among the nations: "The **LORD** is King!*
he has made the world so firm that it cannot be moved;
he will judge the peo**ples** with equity."

11 Let the heavens rejoice, and let the earth be glad;
let the sea thunder and all **that** is in it;*
let the field be joyful and all that **is** therein.

12 Then shall all the trees of the wood shout for joy
before the LORD **when** he comes,*
when he comes to **judge** the earth.

13 He will judge the **world** with righteousness*
and the peoples **with** his truth.

The Antiphon is repeated.

Silence for meditation

Lord Jesus, the incarnate Word, when you consented to dwell with us, the heavens were glad and the earth rejoiced. In hope and love we await your return. Help us to proclaim your glory to those who do not know you, until the whole earth sings a new song to you and the Father and the Holy Spirit, one God, now and for ever. [LHd, LBW]

+

Antiphon to PSALM 100 *Jubilate Deo*

December 25 Christmas Day	Glory to God **in** the highest,* and peace to his peo**ple** on earth. [Luke 2:14]
January 1 The Holy Name of Jesus	The virgin has given birth to the Savior, a flower has sprung from Jesse's stock, and a star has ris**en** from Jacob:* O **God**, we praise you. [LH: see Isa. 7:14; 11:1; Numb. 24:17]
January 6 The Epiphany	All the people whom you have **made**, O Lord,* will come and wor**ship** before you. [LH]
The Baptism of Our Lord	In the Jordan river our Savior crushed the **ser**pent's head* and wrested us free **from** his grasp. [LH]

100 *Praise to God, Creator and Shepherd*

1 Be joyful in the LORD, **all** you lands;*
serve the LORD with gladness
and come before his presence **with** a song.

2 Know this: The LORD him**self** is God;*
he himself has made us, and we are his;
we are his people and the sheep **of** his pasture.

3 Enter his gates with thanksgiving;
go into his **courts** with praise;*
give thanks to him and call up**on** his Name.

4 For the LORD is good;
his mercy is **ev**erlasting;*
and his faithfulness endures from **age** to age,

The Antiphon is repeated.

Silence for meditation

God of goodness and might, by your power you created us and in your mercy you chose us as your own. Accept the praise we offer, and grant that the people of all lands may enter your courts with songs of praise; through Jesus Christ our Lord. [PHP, LH]

+

Antiphon to the NEW TESTAMENT CANTICLE *Gloria in excelsis*

December 25 Christmas Day	The people who **walk**ed in darkness* have seen **a** great light. [LH: Isa. 9:2]
January 1 The Holy Name of Jesus	By your miraculous birth from the virgin you have ful**fill**ed the Scriptures:* like a gentle rain falling upon earth you have come down to **save** your people. [LH: see Isa. 45:8; Ps. 72:6]
January 6 The Epiphany	He who was from the beginning, God from God, **Light** from Light,* is **born** for us. [LH]
The Baptism of Our Lord	A wondrous mystery is declared for **us** today:* the creator of the universe has washed away our sins in the waters **of** the Jordan. [LH]

The Song of the Angels see Luke 2:14

Glory to God **in** the highest,*
and peace to his peo**ple** on earth.

Lord God, heavenly King,
almighty **God** and Father*
we worship you, we give you thanks,
we praise you **for** your glory.

Lord Jesus Christ, only Son of the Father,
Lord God, Lamb of God,
you take away the sin **of** the world:*
have mer**cy** on us.

You are seated at the right hand **of** the Father;*
receive our prayer.

For you alone are the Holy One,
you alone are the Lord,
you alone **are** the Most High,*
Jesus Christ, with the Holy Spirit,
in the glory of **God** the Father.

The Antiphon is repeated.

Almighty and eternal God, through the advent of your only-begotten Son you filled the world with new radiance: Grant that, as he shares our human nature through his birth from the Virgin Mary, so we may share his new life in the kingdom of grace; where he lives and reigns with you and the Holy Spirit, one God, now and for ever. [Berg., RS Sat. before Epiphany]

+

Stand

THE HYMN is sung.

on December 25 *Christe Redemptor omnium*

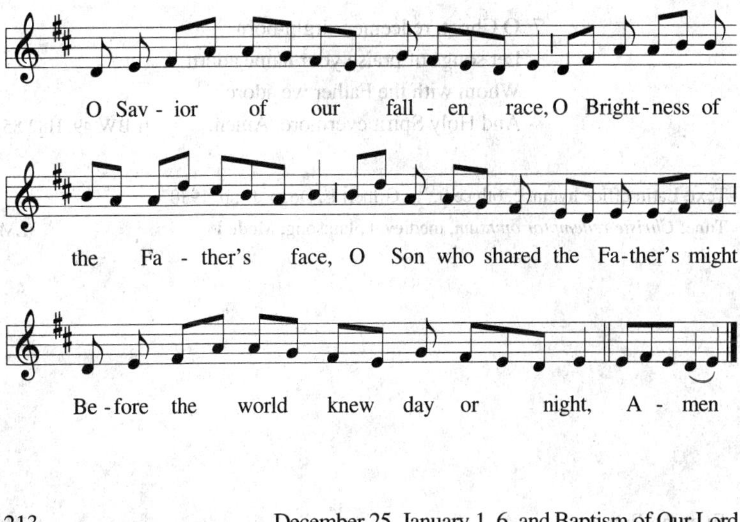

2 O Jesus, very Light of light,
Our constant star in sin's deep night:
Now hear the prayers your people pray
Throughout the world this holy day.

3 Remember, Lord of life and grace,
How once, to save our fallen race,
You put our human vesture on
And came to us as Mary's son.

4 Today, as year by year its light
Bathes all the world in radiance bright,
One precious truth outshines the sun:
Salvation comes from you alone.

5 For from the Father's throne you came,
His banished children to reclaim;
And earth and sea and sky revere
The love of him who sent you here.

6 And we are jubilant today,
For you have washed our guilt away.
Oh, hear the glad new song we sing
On this, the birthday of our king!

7 O Christ, redeemer virgin-born,
Let songs of praise your name adorn,
Whom with the Father we adore
And Holy Spirit evermore. Amen. [LBW 49, H82 85]

Text: Latin office hymn, c. 6th cent.; tr. Gilbert E. Doan, Jr., b. 1930
Tune: *Christe redemptor omnium*, medieval plainsong, Mode I LM

on January 1 *Gloriosi Salvatoris*

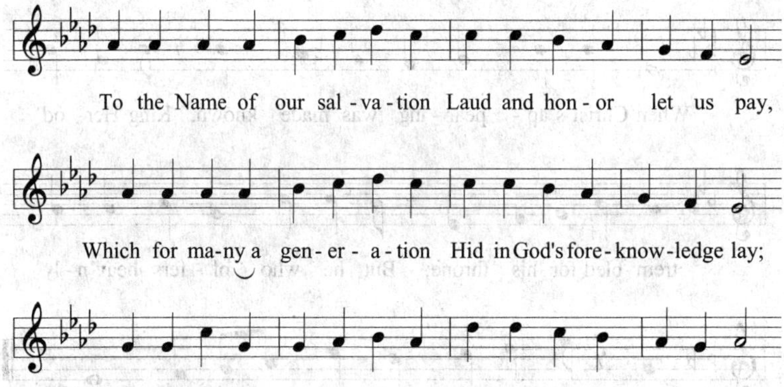

2 Jesus is the Name we treasure;
Name beyond what words can tell;
Name of gladness, Name of pleasure,
Ear and heart delighting well;
Name of sweetness, passing measure,
Saving us from sin and hell.

3 'Tis the Name that whoso preacheth
Speaks like music to the ear;
Who in prayer this Name beseecheth
Sweetest comfort findeth near;
Who its perfect wisdom reacheth,
Heavenly joy posesseth here.

4 Therefore we, in love adoring,
This most blessed Name revere,
Holy Jesus, thee imploring,
So to write it in us here
That hereafter, heavenward soaring,
We may sing with angels there. [CSB 36, H82 248]

Text: Latin, 15th Century; tr. *Hymns Ancient and Modern*, 1861
Tune: Oriel, Caspar Ett, 1788-1847 87 87 87

on January 6 and the Baptism of our Lord *Hostis Herodes impie*

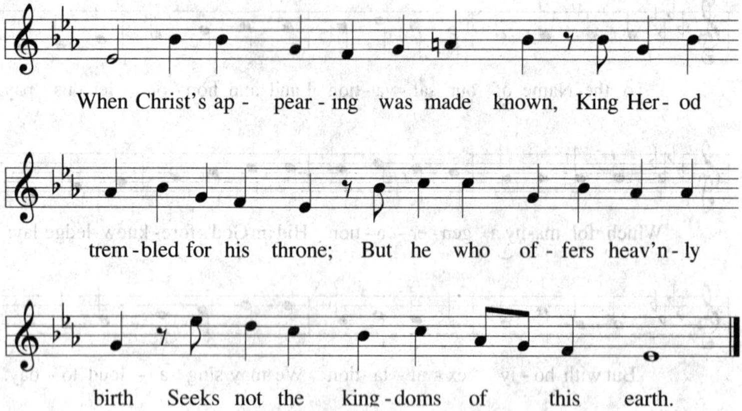

2 The eastern sages saw from far
And followed on his guiding star;
By light their way to Light they trod,
And by their gifts confessed their God.

3 Within the Jordan's sacred flood
The heavenly Lamb in meekness stood,
That he, of whom no sin was known,
Might cleanse his people from their own.

4 And oh, what miracle divine,
When water reddened into wine!
He spoke the word and forth it flowed
In streams that nature ne'er bestowed.

5 For this his glad Epiphany,
All glory unto Jesus be;
Whom with the Father we adore,
And Holy Ghost for evermore. [LBW 85, H82 131]

Text: Coelius Sedulius, c. 5th cent.; tr. composite

Tune: *Wo Gott zum Haus*, J. Klug, *Geistliche Lieder*, 1533 LM

Sit

A LESSON is read.

Year 1	Year 2
December 25	
John 3:31-36	John 3:31-36
The one who comes from above is above all.	The one who comes from above is above all.
January 1	
John 16:23b-30	Matthew 1:18-25
Very truly, I tell you, if you ask anything of the Father in my name, he will give it to you.	Joseph, son of David, do not be afraid to take Mary as your wife, for the child conceived in her is from the Holy Spirit.
January 6	
Matthew 12:14-21	Matthew 12:14-21
I will put my Spirit upon him, and he will proclaim justice to the Gentiles.	I will put my Spirit upon him, and he will proclaim justice to the Gentiles.
The Baptism of Our Lord	
John 1:1-7,19-20,29-34	John 1:19-34
John testified, "I saw the Spirit descending from heaven like a dove, and it remained on him."	I myself have seen and have testified that this is the Son of God.

Silence for mediation follows each reading.

Antiphon to the MAGNIFICAT

December 25 Christmas Day	Today Christ is born, today the Savior has appeared, today angels sing on earth, archangels exult, today the righteous re**joice** and sing,* Glory to God **in** the highest. [LH, PBO, LBW: see Ps. 68:3]

January 1
The Holy Name
of Jesus
	Marvelous is the mystery
	pro**claim**ed today:*
	    human nature is made new
	    as God **be**comes flesh;
	he remains what he was
	and becomes what **he** was not;*
	    yet each nature remains distinct
	    and for ever **un**divided. [LH]

January 6
The Epiphany
of our Lord
	Three mysteries mark this **ho**ly day;*
	    today the star leads the Magi
	    to the **in**fant Christ;
	today water is changed into wine
	for the **wed**ding feast;*
	    today Christ wills to be baptized
	    by John in the river Jordan
	    to bring **us** salvation. [LH]

The Baptism of Our Lord	Christ Jesus loved us, poured out his blood to wash away our sins, and made us a kingdom of priests to **serve** our God.* To him be glory and hon**or** for ever. [LH: see Rev. 5:10]

General or ordinary [ordered] time, the green season after the Epiphany, begins the day following the Baptism of Our Lord with Morning Prayer for Monday of General Week I, pp. 599ff, 647.

December 26, January 2, 7

NOTE: The propers for the dated days after January 6, the Epiphany, are used only until the Sunday of the Baptism of Our Lord. Those not needed are omitted that year.

Antiphon to PSALM 27 *Dominus illuminatio*

The LORD is my light and **my** salvation:*
whom then **shall** I fear? [LH, PBO]

27 *Triumphant trust in God*

1 The LORD is my light and my salvation;
whom then **shall** I fear?*
the LORD is the strength of my life;
of whom then shall I **be** afraid?

2 When evildoers came upon me to eat **up** my flesh,*
it was they, my foes and my adversaries, who stum**bled** and fell.

3 Though an army should en**camp** against me,*
yet my heart shall not **be** afraid;

4 And though war should rise **up** against me,*
yet will I put my **trust** in him.

5 One thing have I asked of the LORD;
one **thing** I seek;*
that I may dwell in the house of the LORD all the days **of** my life;

6 To behold the fair beauty **of** the LORD*
and to seek him **in** his temple.

7 For in the day of trouble he shall keep me safe **in** his shelter;*
he shall hide me in the secrecy of his dwelling
and set me high up**on** a rock.

8 Even now he lifts **up** my head*
above my enemies **round** about me.

9 Therefore I will offer in his dwelling an oblation
with sounds **of** great gladness;*
I will sing and make music **to** the LORD.

10 Hearken to my voice, O LORD, **when** I call;*
have mercy on me and **an**swer me.

11 You speak in my heart and say, "**Seek** my face."*
Your face, LORD, **will** I seek.

12 Hide not your **face** from me,*
nor turn away your servant **in** displeasure.

13 You have been my helper;
cast me **not** away;*
do not forsake me, O God of **my** salvation.

14 Though my father and my moth**er** forsake me,*
the LORD **will** sustain me.

15 Show me your **way**, O LORD;*
lead me on a level path, because **of** my enemies.

16 Deliver me not into the hand of my **ad**versaries,*
for false witnesses have risen up against me,
and also those **who** speak malice.

17 What if I had not believed
that I should see the goodness **of** the LORD*
in the land **of** the living!

18 O tarry and await the LORD's pleasure;
be strong, and he shall com**fort** your heart;*
wait patiently **for** the LORD.

Antiphon The LORD is my light and **my** salvation:*
whom **then** shall I fear?

Silence for meditation

Gracious Father, protector of those who hope in you, you heard the cry of your Son and kept him safe in your shelter in the day of evil: Grant that your servants who seek your face in times of trouble may see your goodness in the land of the living, through your Son, Jesus Christ our Lord. [LH, LBW]

+

Antiphon to PSALM 29 *Afferte Domino*

Worship the LORD in the beauty of holiness. [LH]

29 *The voice of the Lord in the storm*

1 Ascribe to the **LORD**, you gods,*
ascribe to the LORD glo**ry** and strength.

2 Ascribe to the LORD the glory **due** his Name;*
worship the LORD in the beau**ty** of holiness.

3 The voice of the LORD is upon the waters;
the God of **glo**ry thunders;*
the LORD is upon the **might**y waters.

4 The voice of the LORD is a pow**er**ful voice;*
the voice of the LORD is a **voice** of splendor.

5 The voice of the LORD breaks the **ce**dar trees;*
the LORD breaks the ce**dars** of Lebanon;

6 He makes Lebanon skip **like** a calf,*
and Mount Hermon like a **young** wild ox.

7 The voice of the LORD splits the flames of fire;
the voice of the LORD **shakes** the wilderness;*
the LORD shakes the wilder**ness** of Kadesh.

8 The voice of the LORD makes the **oak** trees writhe*
and strips the **for**ests bare.

9 And in the temple **of** the LORD*
all are **cry**ing, "Glory!"

10 The LORD sits enthroned a**bove** the flood;*
the LORD sits enthroned as King for **ever**more.

11 The LORD shall give strength **to** his people;*
The LORD shall give his people the bless**ing** of peace.

Antiphon Worship the LORD in the beauty of holiness.

Silence for meditation

Lord our King, your voice sounds over the waters as you reign above the flood: Help us, who are born again by water and the Holy Spirit, to praise your wonderful deeds in your holy temple; through your Son, Jesus Christ our Lord. [LHd, LBW]

+

Antiphon to the NEW TESTAMENT CANTICLE

Benedictus Deus et Pater

God planned to restore all **things** in Christ*
in the full**ness** of time. [LH]

A Song of God's Blessings in Christ Ephesians 1:3-12

Blessed be the God and Father
of our Lord **Je**sus Christ;*
who has bestowed on us in Christ
every spiritual blessing **in** the heavens.

Before the world began God chose us in him
to be holy **in** his sight,*
without blemish and **full** of love.

He destined us to be adopted as his children
through **Je**sus Christ*
according to the purpose **of** his will,

that the glory of God's gracious gift,
freely bestowed on us in **the** Beloved,*
might redound **to** his praise.

In Christ we have redemption **through** his blood:*
the forgiveness of our trespasses
according to the riches of grace
that he lav**ished** upon us.

He has made known to us the mystery **of** his will,*
the plan he was pleased to de**cree** in Christ,

a plan for the full**ness** of time,*
that all things in heaven and earth
might be unit**ed** in Christ,

in whom we have been given our share **in** the heritage,*
so that we might live for the praise **of** his glory. [PHP]

Antiphon God planned to restore all **things** in Christ*
in the full**ness** of time.

Silence for meditation

Almighty God, you have given your only-begotten Son to take our nature upon him, and to be born of a pure virgin: Grant that we, who have been born again and made your children by adoption and grace, may daily be renewed by your Holy Spirit; through our Lord Jesus Christ, to whom with you and the same Spirit be honor and glory, now and for ever. [BCP]

+

Stand

THE HYMN is sung. *A Patre unigenitus*

2 Beginning from his home on high,
In human flesh he came to die;
Creation by his death restored,
And shed new joys of life abroad.

3 Glide on, O glorious Sun, and bring
The gift of healing on your wing;
To every dull and clouded sense
The clearness of your light dispense.

4 Abide with us, O Lord, we pray;
The gloom of darkness chase away;
Your work of healing, Lord, begin,
And take away the stain of sin.

5 Lord, once you came to earth's domain
And, we believe, shall come again;
Be with us on the battlefield,
From every harm your people shield.

6 To you, O Lord, all glory be
For this your blest Epiphany;
To God whom all his hosts adore,
And Holy Spirit evermore. [LBW 83]

Text: Latin office hymn, c. 11th cent.; tr. John Mason Neale, 1818-1866 alt.
Tune: *Deus tuorum militum,* from *Antiphoner*, Grenoble, 1753 LM

Sit

A LESSON is read.

Year 1

December 26
Acts 7:59-8:8
Stephen prayed, "Lord Jesus, receive my Spirit." Then he knelt down and cried out in a loud voice, "Lord, do not hold this sin against them." When he had said this, he died.

January 2
John 6:35-42,48-51
I am the living bread which came down from heaven. Whoever eats of this bread will live forever; and the bread that I will give for the life of the world is my flesh.

January 7
John 2:1-11
Jesus did this, the first of his signs, in Cana of Galilee, and revealed his glory; and his disciples believed in him.

Year 2

Acts 7:59-8:8
Stephen prayed, "Lord Jesus, receive my Spirit." Then he knelt down and cried out in a loud voice, "Lord, do not hold this sin against them." When he had said this, he died.

John 6:1-14
When the people saw the sign that Jesus had done, they began to say, "This is indeed the prophet who is to come into the world."

John 6:30-33,48-51
The bread of God is that which comes down from heaven and gives life to the world.

Silence for meditation follows each reading.

Antiphon to the MAGNIFICAT

December 26 While gentle silence enveloped all things,
and night in its swift course was **now** half gone,*
your all-powerful Word leaped down from heaven,
from the **ro**yal throne. [LH, PBO:Wisdom 18:14-15]

January 2 O **ra**diant Child!*
You brought healing to human life as you
came forth from the womb of Mary, your mother,
like the bridegroom from the **mar**riage chamber.
[LH]

January 7 When they saw the star, the Magi were over**whelmed** with joy;*
they offered to the Lord their gifts of gold and
frankin**cense** and myrrh. [LH: Matt. 2:10-11]

December 27, January 3, 8

Antiphon to PSALM 107 *Confitemini Domino*

Give thanks to the LORD **for** his mercy*
and the wonders he does **for** his children. [LH, PBO]

107 *God's inexhaustible love*

1 Give thanks to the LORD, for **he** is good,*
and his mercy en**dures** for ever.

2 Let all those whom the LORD has re**deemed** proclaim*
that he redeemed them from the hand **of** the foe.

3 He gathered them out **of** the lands;*
from the east and from the west,
from the north and **from** the south.

4 Some wandered in **de**sert wastes;*
they found no way to a city where **they** might dwell.

5 They were hun**gry** and thirsty;*
their spirits lan**guished** within them.

6 Then they cried to the LORD **in** their trouble,*
and he delivered them from **their** distress.

7 He put their feet **on** a straight path*
to go to a city where **they** might dwell.

8 Let them give thanks to the LORD **for** his mercy*
and the wonders he does **for** his children.

9 For he satis**fies** the thirsty*
and fills the hungry **with** good things.

10 Some sat in darkness **and** deep gloom,*
bound fast in mise**ry** and iron;

11 Because they rebelled against the **words** of God*
and despised the counsel of **the** Most High.

12 So he humbled their spirits **with** hard labor;*
they stumbled, and there was **none** to help.

13 Then they cried to the LORD **in** their trouble,*
and he delivered them from **their** distress.

14 He led them out of darkness **and** deep gloom*
and broke their **bonds** asunder.

15 Let them give thanks to the LORD **for** his mercy*
and the wonders he does **for** his children.

16 For he shatters the **doors** of bronze*
and breaks in two the **iron** bars.

17 Some were fools and took to re**bel**lious ways;*
they were afflicted because **of** their sins.

18 They abhorred all man**ner** of food*
and drew near **to** death's door.

19 Then they cried to the LORD **in** their trouble,*
and he delivered them from **their** distress.

20 He sent forth his **word** and healed them*
and saved them **from** the grave.

21 Let them give thanks to the LORD **for** his mercy*
and the wonders he does **for** his children.

22 Let them offer a sacrifice **of** thanksgiving*
and tell of his acts with **shouts** of joy.

23 Some went down to the **sea** in ships*
and plied their trade **in** deep waters;

24 They beheld the works **of** the LORD*
and his wonders **in** the deep.

25 Then he spoke, and a stormy **wind** arose,*
which tossed high the waves **of** the sea.

26 They mounted up to the heavens and fell back **to** the depths;*
their hearts melted because **of** their peril.

27 They reeled and stag**gered** like drunkards*
and were at **their** wits' end.

28 Then they cried to the LORD **in** their trouble,*
and he delivered them from **their** distress.

29 He stilled the storm **to** a whisper*
and quieted the waves **of** the sea.

30 Then were they glad because **of** the calm,*
and he brought them to the harbor **they** were bound for.

31 Let them give thanks to the LORD **for** his mercy*
and the wonders he does **for** his children.

32 Let them exalt him in the congregation **of** the people*
and praise him in the counsel **of** the elders.

33 The LORD changed rivers **in**to deserts,*
and water-springs into **thirst**y ground,

34 A fruitful land **in**to salt flats,*
because of the wickedness of **those** who dwell there.

35 He changed deserts into **pools** of water*
and dry land into **wa**ter-springs.

36 He settled the **hun**gry there,*
and they founded a ci**ty** to dwell in.

37 They sowed fields, and **plant**ed vineyards,*
and brought in a **fruit**ful harvest.

38 He blessed them, so that they **in**creased greatly;*
he did not let their **herds** decrease.

39 Yet when they were diminished **and** brought low,*
through stress of adversi**ty** and sorrow,

40 (He pours con**tempt** on princes*
and makes them wander in **track**less wastes)

41 He lifted up the poor **out** of misery*
and multiplied their families like **flocks** of sheep.

42 The upright will see this **and** rejoice,*
but all wickedness will **shut** its mouth.

43 Whoever is wise will pon**der** these things,*
and consider well the mercies **of** the LORD.

Antiphon Give thanks to the LORD **for** his mercy*
and the wonders he does **for** his children.

Silence for meditation

Lord God, you fill the hungry with good things and break the sinner's chains. Hear your people who call to you in their need, and lead your Church from the shadows of death. Gather us from sunset to sunrise, that we may grow together in faith and love, and may give thanks for your kindness in Jesus Christ our Lord. [LH, LBW]

+

Antiphon to PSALM 15 *Domine, quis habitabit?*

Blessed are the **pure** in heart,*
for they **will** see God. [LH, PBO, Matt. 5:8]

15 *What God requires*

1 LORD, who may dwell in your **tab**ernacle?*
who may abide upon your **ho**ly hill?

2 Whoever leads a blameless life and does **what** is right,*
who speaks the truth **from** his heart.

3 There is no guile upon his tongue;
he does no evil **to** his friend;*
he does not heap contempt up**on** his neighbor.

4 In his sight the wicked **is** rejected,*
but he honors those who **fear** the LORD.

5 He has sworn to **do** no wrong*
and does not take **back** his word.

6 He does not give his money in **hope** of gain,*
nor does he take a bribe a**gainst** the innocent.

7 Whoever **does** these things*
shall never be **o**verthrown.

Antiphon Blessed are the **pure** in heart,*
for they **will** see God.

Silence for meditation

Lord Jesus, you first chose to live among us, and in returning to your Father you made an eternal home for us: Help us walk blameless in your ways and bring us at last to your holy mountain, where you live and reign with the Father and the Holy Spirit, one God, now and for ever. [LHd, LBW]

+

Antiphon to the NEW TESTAMENT CANTICLE *Dignus es*

God has spoken to us by a Son,
whom he appointed **heir** of all things,*
through whom he also creat**ed** the worlds. [Heb. 1:2]

A Song to the Lamb Revelation 4:11; 5:9-10,13

Splendor and honor and **king**ly power*
are yours by right, O **Lord** our God,
For you created every**thing** that is,*
and by your will they were created and **have** their being;

And yours by right, O Lamb **that** was slain,*
for with your blood you have re**deemed** for God,
From every family, language, peo**ple**, and nation,*
a kingdom of priests to **serve** our God.

And so, to him who sits up**on** the throne,*
and to **Christ** the Lamb,

Be worship and praise, domin**ion** and splendor,*
for ever and for **ev**ermore. [BCP]

Antiphon God has spoken to us by a Son,
whom he appointed **heir** of all things,*
through whom he also creat**ed** the worlds.

Silence for meditation

Merciful God, in your Son Jesus Christ you have raised up an unfailing light for all the nations: Grant that your people may know and confess the full splendor of their Redeemer and, by his grace, enter into light everlasting; through the same Jesus Christ our Lord. [Gel., RS Thurs. after Epiph.]

+

Stand

THE HYMN is sung. *Corde natus ex parentis*

2 Oh, that birth for ever blessèd,
When the virgin, full of grace,
By the Holy Ghost conceiving,
Bore the Savior of our race,
And the babe, the world's redeemer,
First revealed his sacred face,
Evermore and evermore.

3 This is he whom seers in old time
Chanted of with one accord,
Whom the voices of the prophets
Promised in their faithful word;
Now he shines, the long-expected;
Let creation praise its Lord
Evermore and evermore.

4 Let the heights of heaven adore him;
Angel hosts, his praises sing;
Powers, dominions, bow before him
And extol our God and King;
Let no tongue on earth be silent,
Every voice in concert ring
Evermore and evermore.

5 Christ, to thee, with God the Father,
And, O Holy Ghost, to thee,
Hymn and chant and high thanksgiving
And unwearied praises be:
Honor, glory, and dominion,
And eternal victory
Evermore and evermore! Amen. [LBW 42, H82 82]

Text: Marcus Aurelius Clemens Prudentius, 348-413; tr. composite
Tune: *Divinum mysterium*, plainsong, Mode V, 13th cent. 87 87 877

Sit

A LESSON is read.

Year 1	Year 2
December 27	
John 13:20-35	John 13:20-35
I give you a new commandment, that you love one another. Just as I have loved you, you also should love one another.	I give you a new commandment, that you love one another. Just as I have loved you, you also should love one another.
January 3	
John 10:7-17	John 6:15-27
I came that they may have life, and have it abundantly.	Do not work for the food that perishes, but for the food that endures for eternal life, which the Son of Man will give you.
January 8	
John 4:46-54	John 7:37-52
The father realized that this was the hour when Jesus had said to him, "Your son will live." So he himself believed, along with his whole household.	On the last day of the festival, the great day, while Jesus was standing there, he cried out, "Let anyone who is thirsty come to me, and let the one who believes in me drink."

Silence for meditation follows each reading.

Antiphon to the MAGNIFICAT

December 27 This is the message we have heard **and** proclaim:*
God is light and in him there is no dark**ness** at all.

[1 John 1:5]

January 3 Let us dance with delight in the Lord
and let our hearts be filled **with** rejoicing,*
for eternal salvation has ap**peared** on earth. [LH]

January 8 You, O Christ, are **Light** from Light;*
when you appeared on the earth,
the Wise Men offered their **gifts** to you. [LH]

December 28, January 4, 9

Antiphon to PSALM 110 *Dixit Dominus*

Princely state has been yours from the day **of** your birth,*
in the beauty of holiness have I be**got**ten you.

[LH, PBO, LBW]

110 *The Messiah, King and Priest*

1 The LORD said to my Lord, "Sit at **my** right hand,*
until I make your ene**mies** your footstool."

2 The LORD will send the scepter of your power **out** of Zion,*
saying, "Rule over your enemies **round** about you.

3 Princely state has been yours from the day **of** your birth;*
in the beauty of holiness have I begotten you,
like dew from the womb **of** the morning."

4 The LORD has sworn and he will **not** recant:*
"You are a priest for ever after the order **of** Melchizedek."

5 The Lord who is at your right hand
will smite kings in the day **of** his wrath;*
he will rule o**ver** the nations.

6 He will heap **high** the corpses;*
he will smash heads over **the** wide earth.

7 He will drink from the brook be**side** the road;*
therefore he will **lift** high his head.

Antiphon Princely state has been yours from the day **of** your birth,*
in the beauty of holiness have I be**got**ten you.

Silence for meditation

Almighty God, make known in every place the perfect offering of your Son, the eternal high priest of the new Jerusalem, and so consecrate all nations to be your holy people, that the kingdom of Christ, your anointed one, may come in its fullness; and to you, Father, Son, and Holy Spirit, be all honor and praise now and for ever. [LHd, LBW]

+

Antiphon to PSALM 111 *Confitebor tibi*

Let the mountains break out with joy
and the hills with an**swer**ing gladness,*
  for the world's true light, the Lord,
  comes with pow**er** and might. [LH]

111 *God's marvelous works*

1 Hallelujah!
I will give thanks to the LORD with **my** whole heart,*
  in the assembly of the upright, in the **con**gregation.

2 Great are the deeds **of** the LORD!*
  they are studied by all who de**light** in them.

3 His work is full of majes**ty** and splendor,*
  and his righteousness en**dures** for ever.

4 He makes his marvelous works to **be** remembered;*
  the LORD is gracious and full **of** compassion.

5 He gives food to **those** who fear him;*
  he is ever mindful **of** his covenant.

6 He has shown his people the power **of** his works*
  in giving them the lands **of** the nations.

7 The works of his hands are faithful**ness** and justice;*
  all his command**ments** are sure.

8 They stand fast for ev**er** and ever,*
  because they are done in **truth** and equity.

9 He sent redemption to his people;
he commanded his cove**nant** for ever;*
holy and awesome **is** his Name.

10 The fear of the LORD is the beginn**ing** of wisdom;*
those who act accordingly have a good understanding;
his praise en**dures** for ever.

Antiphon Let the mountains break out with joy
and the hills with an**swer**ing gladness,*
for the world's true light, the Lord,
comes with pow**er** and might.

Silence for meditation

Merciful and gentle Lord, the crowning glory of all the saints, give us, your children, the gift of obedience, which is the beginning of wisdom, so that we may be filled with your mercy and that what you command we may do by the might of Jesus Christ our Lord. [LH, LBW]

+

Antiphon to the NEW TESTAMENT CANTICLE

Gratias agentes Deo Patri

Through him everything **was** created;*
in him the whole universe is **held** together. [LH]

A Song of the Supremacy of Christ Colossians 1:12-20

Let us give thanks to **God** the Father,*
who has called us to share the inheritance
of the saints in the **realm** of light.

He rescued us from the do**main** of darkness*
and brought us into the kingdom of his beloved Son,
by whom we are set free and our **sins** forgiven.

He is the first-born of **all** creation;*
in him everything in heaven and on earth was created,
visible **and** invisible.

The whole universe has been created through him
and for him;*
he exists before all else that is;
in him everything is **held** together.

He is the head of the **Church**, his body;*
he is its origin, the first-born of the dead,
su**preme** in all things.

In him the fullness of God **came** to dwell;*
through him God chose to reconcile
the whole universe to himself,
making peace by the blood **of** his cross. [PHP]

Antiphon Through him everything **was** created;*
in him the whole universe is **held** together.

Silence for meditation

O Lord, our Creator and Redeemer, you have delivered us from the domain of darkness and have brought us into your kingdom of everlasting light. Fill us with your peace, and make us instruments of reconciliation in the world; through Jesus Christ our Lord. [PHP]

+

Stand

THE HYMN is sung. *Μεγα καi παραδοξον θαυμα*

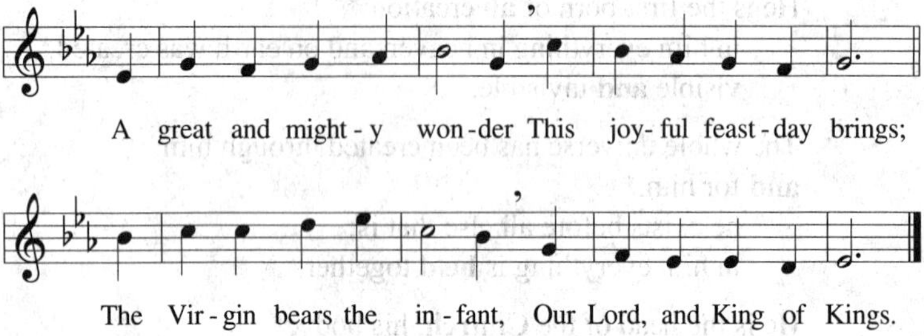

2 The Word becomes incarnate,
Descending from on high;
And shepherds hear glad anthems
Of angels from the sky.

3 We join their song triumphant
To praise the wondrous birth,
"To God on high be glory
And peace to those on earth."

4 While thus they sing your monarch,
Those bright angelic bands,
Rejoice, you vales and mountains!
You oceans, clap your hands!

5 Since all he comes to ransom,
By all be he adored,
The infant born in Bethlehem,
The Savior and the Lord!

6 All idol forms shall perish,
And error shall decay,
And Christ shall wield his scepter,
Our Lord and God for aye.

7 To Father, Son, and Spirit,
Eternal One in Three,
As was, and is for ever,
All praise and glory be. [SBH 18]

Text: St. Germanus, c. 634-734; tr. John Mason Neale, 1818-1866 alt.
Tune: *Ach bleib mit deiner Gnade*, Melchior Vulpius, c. 1560-1615 76 76

Sit

A LESSON is read.

Year 1

December 28

Isaiah 54:1-13

The mountains may depart and the hills be removed, but my steadfast love shall not depart from you, and my covenant of peace shall not be removed, says the LORD, who has compassion on you.

Year 2

Mark 10:13-16 [BCP]

Let the little children come to me; do not stop them; for it is to such as these that the kingdom of God belongs.

or Isaiah 54:1-13

January 4

John 14:6-14

Whoever has seen me has seen the Father.

John 9:1-12, 35-38

As long as I am in the world, I am the light of the world.

January 9

John 5:1-15

Jesus said to him, "Stand up, take up your mat and walk." At once the man was made well, and he took up his mat and began to walk.

John 8:12-19

I am the light of the world. Whoever follows me will never walk in darkness but will have the light of life.

Silence for meditation follows each reading.

Antiphon to the MAGNIFICAT

December 28 The holy virgin gave birth to God,
who became for us the frail, tender child she nursed **at** her breast.*
Let us worship the Lord who **comes** to save us. [LH]

January 4 I have come forth from God in**to** the world;*
I have not come of myself, but the **Fa**ther sent me.
[LH: see John 6:38]

January 9 Herod questioned the Magi:
What is this sign of which you speak, the sign of a **new**born king?*
We saw a brilliant star in the heavens;
its splendor **filled** the world. [LH]

December 29, January 10

Antiphon to PSALM 132 *Memento, Domine*

A son, the fruit **of** your body*
will I set up**on** your throne. [CSB, SBH, PBO]

132 *God's promises to the house of David*

1 LORD, re**mem**ber David,*
and all the hardships **he** endured;

2 How he swore an oath **to** the LORD*
and vowed a vow to the Mighty **One** of Jacob:

3 "I will not come under the roof **of** my house,*
nor climb up in**to** my bed;

4 I will not allow my **eyes** to sleep,*
nor let my **eye**lids slumber;

5 Until I find a place **for** the LORD,*
a dwelling for the Mighty **One** of Jacob."

6 "The ark! We heard it **was** in Ephratah;*
we found it in the **fields** of Jearim.

7 Let us go to God's **dwel**ling place;*
let us fall upon our knees be**fore** his footstool."

8 Arise, O LORD, into your **rest**ing-place,*
you and the ark **of** your strength.

9 Let your priests be **clothed** with righteousness;*
let your faithful people **sing** with joy.

10 For your servant **Da**vid's sake,*
do not turn away the face of **your** Anointed.

11 The LORD has sworn an **oath** to David;*
in truth, he **will** not break it:

12 “A son, the fruit **of** your body*
will I set up**on** your throne.

13 If your children keep my covenant
and my testimonies that **I** shall teach them,*
their children will sit upon your throne for **ev**ermore.”

14 For the LORD has **cho**sen Zion;*
he has desired her for his **hab**itation:

15 “This shall be my resting-**place** for ever;*
here will I dwell, for I de**light** in her.

16 I will surely bless **her** provisions,*
and satisfy her **poor** with bread.

17 I will clothe her priests **with** salvation,*
and her faithful people will re**joice** and sing.

18 There will I make the horn of **Da**vid flourish;*
I have prepared a lamp for **my** Anointed.

19 As for his enemies, I will clothe **them** with shame;*
but as for him, his **crown** will shine.”

Antiphon A son, the fruit **of** your body*
will I set up**on** your throne.

Silence for meditation

Lord God our King, you have chosen the new Zion as your dwelling place, the Church as your place of rest; you have kindled in it a lamp that will burn brightly for ever before Christ, your anointed one. Make our hearts your tabernacle, clothe your people with holiness, and give bread to the poor, that we may rejoice and sing to you now and for ever. [LHd, LBW]

+

Antiphon to PSALM 97 *Dominus regnavit, exultet*

Light has sprung up **for** the righteous,*
and joyful gladness for those who **are** truehearted. [LH]

97 *Earth rejoices in its king*

1 The LORD is king;
let the **earth** rejoice;*
let the multitude of the **isles** be glad.

2 Clouds and darkness are **round** about him,*
righteousness and justice are the foundations **of** his throne.

3 A fire **goes** before him*
and burns up his enemies on **ev**ery side.

4 His lightnings light **up** the world;*
the earth sees it and **is** afraid.

5 The mountains melt like wax at the presence **of** the LORD,*
at the presence of the Lord of **the** whole earth.

6 The heavens de**clare** his righteousness,*
and all the peoples **see** his glory.

7 Confounded be all who worship carved images
and delight **in** false gods!*
Bow down before him, **all** you gods.

8 Zion hears and is glad, and the cities of Ju**dah** rejoice,*
because of your judg**ments**, O LORD.

9 For you are the LORD,
most high over **all** the earth;*
you are exalted far a**bove** all gods.

10 The LORD loves those **who** hate evil;*
he preserves the lives of his saints
and delivers them from the hand **of** the wicked.

11 Light has sprung up **for** the righteous,*
and joyful gladness for those who **are** truehearted.

12 Rejoice in the **Lord**, you righteous,*
and give thanks to his **ho**ly Name.

Light has sprung up **for** the righteous,*
and joyful gladness for those who **are** truehearted.

Silence for meditation

God our king, you clothe the sky with light and the depths of the ocean with darkness. Among the peoples you work wonders, and rain terror upon your enemies. Do not try your servants by fire, but bring us rejoicing to the shelter of your home, where with your Son and the Holy Spirit you live and reign, now and for ever. [LH, LBW]

+

Antiphon to the NEW TESTAMENT CANTICLE *Gratias agimus tibi*

Now salvation and pow**er** have come,*
the kingdom of our God
and the authority of **his** Messiah. [LH]

A Song of the Judgment of God Revelation 11:17-18; 12:10b-12a

We give you thanks, Lord God almighty,
who are **and** who were,*
for you have taken your great power
and have be**gun** to reign.

The **na**tions raged,*
but your wrath has come and the time to **judge** the dead,

The time to reward your servants, the prophets,
and the holy ones and all who **fear** your Name,*
great and **small** alike.

Now salvation and pow**er** have come,*
the kingdom of our God
and the authority of **his** Messiah.

For the accuser of our companions
has **been** thrown down,*
who night and day accuses them **be**fore God.

They have conquered him by the sacrifice of the Lamb
and by the word **of** their testimony,*
for they did not cling to life
even in the **face** of death.

Rejoice **then**, you heavens,*
and all who **dwell** in them. [PHP]

Antiphon Now salvation and pow**er** have come,*
the kingdom of our God
and the authority of **his** Messiah.

Silence for meditation

Almighty Lord and God, bring us into your kingdom and rule us as Sovereign of righteousness, life, and salvation. Give us the Holy Spirit, that by his grace we may believe your holy word and live the new life to your praise through Jesus Christ our Lord now and for ever. [PHP]

+

Stand

THE HYMN is sung.

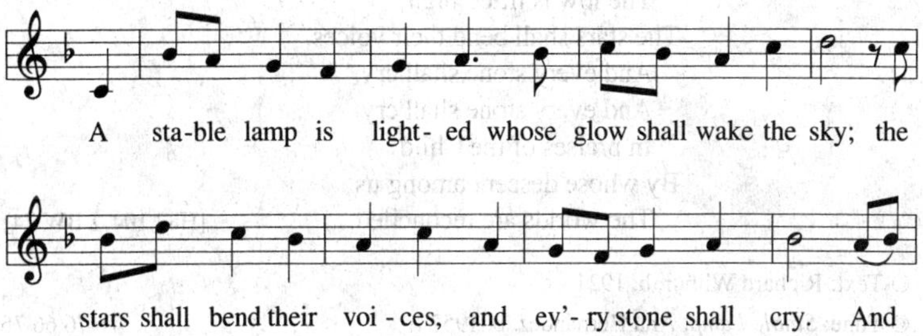

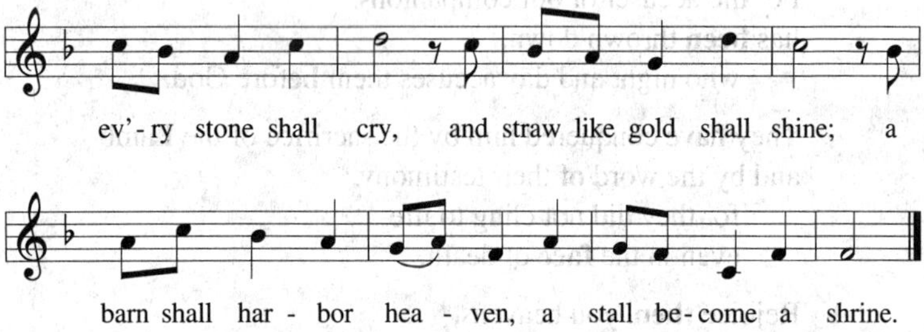

2 This child through David's city
Shall ride in triumph by;
The palm shall strew its branches,
And every stone shall cry.
And every stone shall cry,
Though heavy, dull, and dumb,
And lie within the roadway
To pave his kingdom come.

3 Yet he shall be forsaken
And yielded up to die;
The sky shall groan and darken,
And every stone shall cry.
And every stone shall cry
For stony hearts of men:
God's blood upon the spearhead,
God's love refused again.

4 But now, as at the ending,
The low is lifted high;
The stars shall bend their voices,
And every stone shall cry.
And every stone shall cry
In praises of the Child
By whose descent among us
The worlds are reconciled. [H82 104, LBW 74]

 76 76 66 76

Sit

A LESSON is read.

Year 1	Year 2
December 29	
John 7:37-52	John 2:1-11
On the last day of the festival, the great day, while Jesus was standing there, he cried out. "Let anyone who is thirsty come to me, and let the one who believes in me drink."	Jesus did this, the first of his signs, in Cana of Galilee, and revealed his glory; and his disciples believed in him.
January 10	
John 6:1-14	John 10:7-17
When the people saw the sign which Jesus had done, they began to say, "This is indeed the prophet who is to come into the world."	I came that they may have life, and have it abundantly.

Silence for meditation follows each reading.

Antiphon to the MAGNIFICAT

December 29 — The king of heaven humbled himself
to be born **of** a virgin,*
that he might restore humanity
to the kingdom **they** had lost. [LH]

January 10 — The people shall come **from** afar,*
bringing gold, frankin**cense**, and myrrh.
[LH: see Isa. 60:6; see Ps. 72:10; see Tobit 13:11]

December 30, January 11

Antiphon to PSALM 89:1-18 *Misericordias Domini*

Happy are the people who know the **fest**al shout!*
They walk, O Lord, in the light **of** your presence.

89 Part I *Hymn to God's faithfulness*

1 Your love, O LORD, for ever **will** I sing;*
from age to age my mouth will pro**claim** your faithfulness.

2 For I am persuaded that your love is estab**lished** for ever;*
you have set your faithfulness firmly **in** the heavens.

3 "I have made a covenant with my **cho**sen one;*
I have sworn an oath to Da**vid** my servant:

4 'I will establish your **line** for ever,*
and preserve your throne for all **gen**erations.'"

5 The heavens bear witness to your won**ders**, O LORD,*
and to your faithfulness in the assembly of the **ho**ly ones;

6 For who in the skies can be compared **to** the LORD?*
who is like the LORD a**mong** the gods?

7 God is much to be feared in the counsel of the **ho**ly ones,*
great and terrible to all those **round** about him.

8 Who is like you, LORD **God** of Hosts?*
O mighty LORD, your faithfulness is **all** around you.

9 You rule the raging **of** the sea*
and still the surging **of** its waves.

10 You have crushed Rahab of the deep with a **dead**ly wound;*
you have scattered your enemies with your **migh**ty arm.

11 Yours are the heavens; the earth al**so** is yours;*
you laid the foundations of the world and all **that** is in it.

12 You have made the north **and** the south;*
Tabor and Hermon rejoice **in** your Name.

13 You have a **might**y arm;*
strong is your hand and high is **your** right hand.

14 Righteousness and justice are the foundations **of** your throne;*
love and truth go be**fore** your face.

15 Happy are the people who know the **fest**al shout!*
they walk, O LORD, in the light **of** your presence.

16 They rejoice daily **in** your Name;*
they are jubilant **in** your righteousness.

17 For you are the glory **of** their strength,*
and by your favor our might **is** exalted.

18 Truly, the LORD **is** our ruler;*
the Holy One of Israel **is** our King.

Antiphon Happy are the people who know the **fest**al shout!*
They walk, O Lord, in the light **of** your presence.

Silence for meditation

Mighty God, in fulfillment of the promise made to David's descendants you established a lasting covenant through your firstborn Son. You anointed your servant Jesus with holy oil and raised him higher than all kings on earth. Remember your covenant, so that we who are signed with the blood of your Son may sing of your mercies for ever; through your Son, Jesus Christ our Lord. [LH, LBW]

+

Antiphon to PSALM 89:19-52 *Tunc locutus es*

I will establish his **line** for ever*
and his throne as the **days** of heaven.

89 Part II *Lament for the fall of David's dynasty*

19 You spoke once in a vision and said to your **faith**ful people:*
"I have set the crown upon a warrior
and have exalted one chosen out **of** the people.

20 I have found Da**vid** my servant;*
with my holy oil have I **anoint**ed him.

21 My hand will **hold** him fast*
and my arm will **make** him strong.

22 No enemy **shall** deceive him,*
nor any wicked man **bring** him down.

23 I will crush his **foes** before him*
and strike down **those** who hate him.

24 My faithfulness and love shall **be** with him,*
and he shall be victorious **through** my Name.

25 I shall make his domin**ion** extend*
from the Great Sea **to** the River.

26 He will say to me, 'You **are** my Father,*
my God, and the rock of **my** salvation.'

27 I will make **him** my firstborn*
and higher than the kings **of** the earth.

28 I will keep my love for **him** for ever,*
and my covenant will stand **firm** for him.

29 I will establish his **line** for ever*
and his throne as the **days** of heaven.

30 If his children for**sake** my law*
and do not walk according **to** my judgments;

31 If they **break** my statutes*
and do not keep **my** commandments;

32 I will punish their transgressions **with** a rod*
and their iniquities **with** the lash;

33 But I will not take my **love** from him,*
nor let my faithful**ness** prove false.

34 I will not **break** my covenant,*
nor change what has gone out **of** my lips.

35 Once for all I have sworn **by** my holiness:*
'I will not **lie** to David.

36 His line shall en**dure** for ever*
and his throne as the **sun** before me;

37 It shall stand fast for evermore **like** the moon,*
the abiding witness **in** the sky.'"

38 But you have cast off and rejected **your** anointed;*
you have become en**raged** at him.

39 You have broken your covenant **with** your servant,*
defiled his crown, and hurled it **to** the ground.

40 You have breached **all** his walls*
and laid his strong**holds** in ruins.

41 All who pass **by** despoil him;*
he has become the scorn **of** his neighbors.

42 You have exalted the right hand **of** his foes*
and made all his ene**mies** rejoice.

43 You have turned back the edge **of** his sword*
and have not sustained **him** in battle.

44 You have put an end **to** his splendor*
and cast his throne **to** the ground.

45 You have cut short the days **of** his youth*
and have covered **him** with shame.

46 How long will you hide yourself, O LORD?
will you hide your**self** for ever?*
  how long will your anger **burn** like fire?

47 Remember, LORD, how **short** life is,*
  how frail you have **made** all flesh.

48 Who can live and **not** see death?*
  who can save himself from the power **of** the grave?

49 Where, Lord, are your loving-kindness**es** of old,*
  which you promised David **in** your faithfulness?

50 Remember, Lord, how your ser**vant** is mocked,*
  how I carry in my bosom the taunts of **man**y peoples,

51 The taunts your enemies have **hurled**, O LORD,*
  which they hurled at the heels of **your** anointed.

52 Blessed be the LORD for **ev**ermore!*
  Amen, I **say**, Amen.

Antiphon I will establish his **line** for ever*
  and his throne as the **days** of heaven.

Silence for meditation

Lord God of mercy and faithfulness, you made a new and lasting covenant with humanity and sealed it with the blood of your Son. Forgive the folly of our unfaithfulness and strengthen us to keep your commandments, so that we may proclaim on earth your steadfast love and in heaven share your glory; through Jesus Christ our Lord. [LH, PHP]

+

Antiphon to the NEW TESTAMENT CANTICLE *Magna et mirabilia*

Your ways are ways of righteous**ness** and truth,*
  O King of **all** the ages. [LH]

O ruler of the uni**verse**, Lord God,*
great are the deeds that you have done,
surpassing human **un**derstanding.

Your ways are ways of righteous**ness** and truth,*
O King of all the nations,
O King of **all** the ages.

Who can fail to do you homage, Lord,
and sing the praises **of** your name?*
For you alone are the **Ho**ly One.

All nations will draw near and bow **down** before you,*
because your just and holy works have **been** revealed.

[BCP alt. LBW]

Antiphon Your ways are ways of righteous**ness** and truth,*
O King of **all** the ages.

Silence for meditation

O God, by the birth of your only-begotten Son you have begun the wondrous work of our redemption: Strengthen the faith of your people so that by his guidance we may attain the promised gift of glory; through the same Jesus Christ our Lord. [Gel.; RS Thurs. before Epiphany, trans. PHP]

+

Stand

THE HYMN is sung. *Frölich soll mein Herze springen*

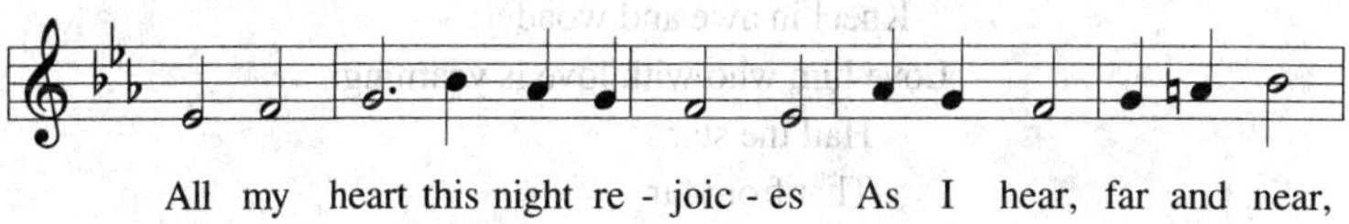

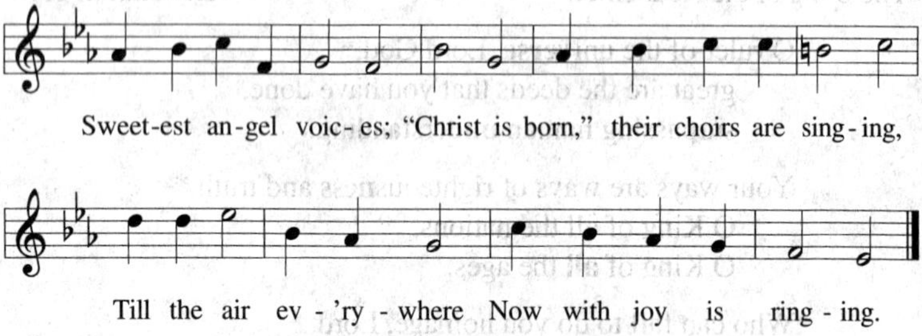

2 For it dawns—the promised morrow
Of his birth
Who the earth
Rescues from her sorrow.
God to wear our form descendeth,
Of his grace
To our race
Here his Son he lendeth.

3 Hark! A voice from yonder manger,
Soft and sweet,
Doth entreat,
"Flee from woe and danger;
Brethren, come; from all that grieves you
You are freed;
All you need
I will surely give you."

4 Come, then, let us hasten yonder;
Here let all,
Great and small,
Kneel in awe and wonder;
Love him who with love is yearning;
Hail the star
That from far
Bright with hope is burning.

5 Hither come, you poor and wretched;
Know his will
Is to fill
Every hand outstretchèd
Here are riches without measure,
Here forget
All regret,
Fill your hearts with treasure.

6 Thee, dear Lord, with heed I'll cherish,
Live to thee
And with thee
Dying shall not perish;
But shall dwell with thee for ever,
Far on high
In the joy
That can alter never. [SBH 26; LBW 46]

Text: Paul Gerhardt, 1607-1676; tr. Catherine Winkworth, 1829-1878
Tune: *Frölich soll mein Herze springen*, Johann Crüger, 1598-1662 866 866

Sit

A LESSON is read.

Year 1

December 30.
John 7:53-8:11
Let anyone among you who is without sin be the first to throw a stone at her.

Year 2

John 4:46-54
The father realized that this was the hour when Jesus had said to him, "Your son will live." So he himself believed, along with his whole household.

January 11	
John 6:15-27	John 14:6-14
Do not work for the food that perishes, but for the food that endures for eternal life, which the Son of Man will give you. For it is on him that God the Father has set his seal.	Whoever has seen me has seen the Father.

Silence for meditation follows each reading.

Antiphon to the MAGNIFICAT

December 30 — We honor you, O holy moth**er** of God,*
for you gave birth to our Savior **Je**sus Christ

[LH]

January 11 — The Wise Men, having been warned in a dream
not to re**turn** to Herod,*
left for their own country by an**oth**er road.

[LH: Matt. 2:12]

✠

MORNING PRAYER

Matins or Morning Praise from Christmas Day through The Baptism of our Lord

Stand

Leader

O Lord, open my lips,

Congregation

And my mouth shall de-clare your praise.

Leader and Congregation

Glo-ry to the Fa-ther, and to the Son and to the Ho-ly Spir-it;

as it was in the be-gin-ning, is now, and will be for ev-er. A-men

Al-le-lu-ia. Al-le-lu-ia.

The PSALMODY begins with this song of praise, Venite exultemus.

[II] The sea is his, for he made it;
and his hands have mold - ed the dry land.
[I] Oh, come, let us bow down and bend the knee,
and kneel be - fore the Lord, our Mak - er.
[II] For he is our God, and we are the peo-ple of his pas-ture
and the sheep of his hand.
C Glo - ry to the Fa - ther
and to the Son, and to the Ho - ly Spir - it;
As it was in the be - gin - ning is now, and will be for ev - er. A - men

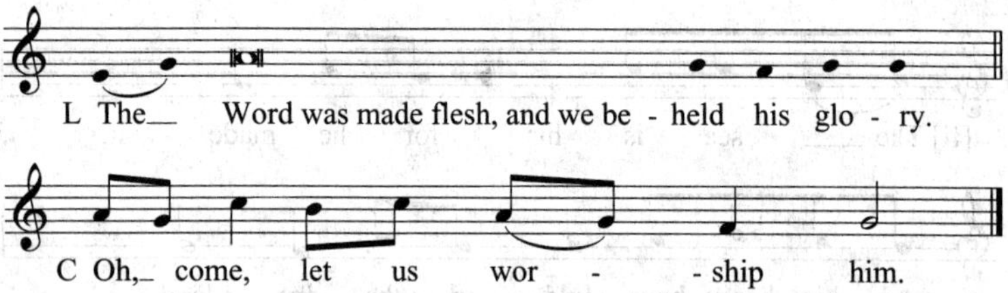

Sit

A second psalm is sung or said; additional psalms and an Old Testament canticle may be sung or said also. Silence for meditation follows each psalm or canticle.

The psalm prayer appropriate to each psalm or canticle follows the silence.

C Amen

Stand

THE HYMN is sung.

Sit

One or two LESSONS are read. Silence for meditation follows each reading.

The Responsory to the reading(s) follows the silence. After the Responsory the leader then continues:

L In many and various ways God spoke to his people of old by the prophets.

C But now in these last days he has spoken to us by his son.

The GOSPEL CANTICLE, Benedictus Dominus Deus, *is sung or said.*

The proper Antiphon is given on pp. 299-366.

The Antiphon is sung or said.

This was the oath he swore to our fa - ther A - bra - ham:
to set us free from the hands of our en - e - mies,
free to wor - ship him with - out fear, ho - ly and
right - eous in his sight all the days of our life.
L You, my child shall be called the pro - phet of the Most High,
for you will go be - fore the Lord to pre - pare his way,
to give his peo - ple know ledge of sal - va - tion by the for - give ness
of their sins. In the ten - der com - pas - sion of our God,

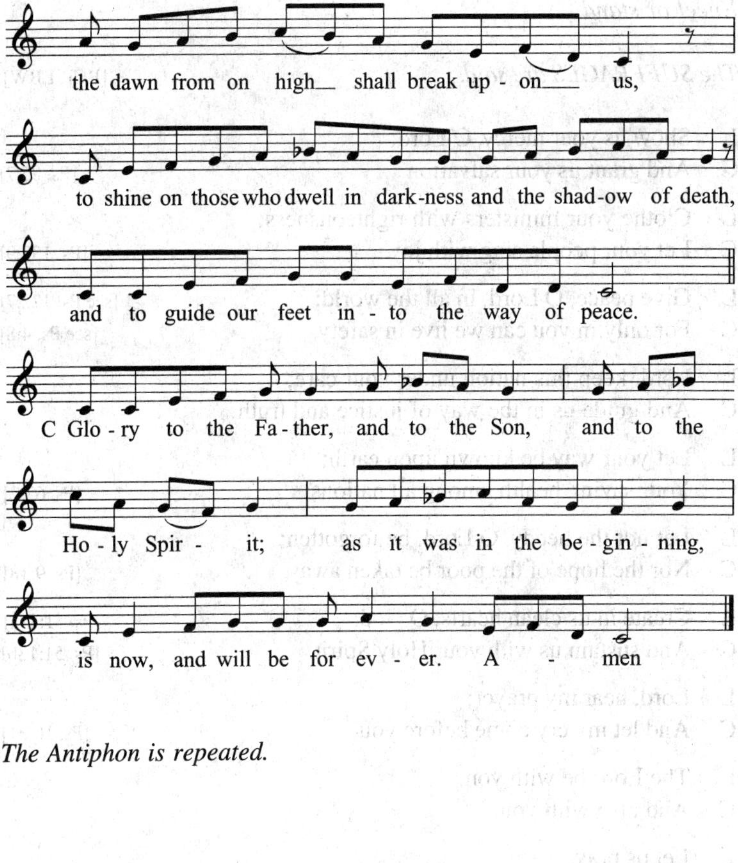

The Antiphon is repeated.

Kneel or stand

The SUFFRAGES are said. [BCP, LBW]

L Show us your mercy, O Lord;
C And grant us your salvation. [Ps. 85:7]

L Clothe your ministers with righteousness;
C Let your people sing with joy. [Ps. 132:9]

L Give peace, O Lord, in all the world; [see Ps. 122:7]
C For only in you can we live in safety. [see Ps. 4:8]

L Lord, keep this nation under your care;
C And guide us in the way of justice and truth.

L Let your way be known upon earth;
C Your saving health among all nations. [Ps. 67:2]

L Let not the needy, O Lord, be forgotten;
C Nor the hope of the poor be taken away. [Ps. 9:18]

L Create in us clean hearts, O God; [Ps. 51:11a]
C And sustain us with your Holy Spirit. [Ps. 51:13b]

L Lord, hear my prayer;
C And let my cry come before you. [Ps. 102:1]

L The Lord be with you.
C And also with you.

L Let us pray.

The PRAYER OF THE DAY is said.

December 25. The Nativity of Our Lord [and on the First Sunday after Christmas Day]

Almighty God, you have poured upon us the new light of your incarnate Word: Grant that this light, enkindled in our hearts, may shine forth in our lives; through your Son, Jesus Christ our Lord, who lives and reigns with you and the Holy Spirit, one God, now and for ever.

[Greg., Sarum, LH Christmas Lauds; BCP Christmas 1; LBW Christmas 2]

December 26. St. Stephen, Deacon and Martyr

We give you thanks, O Lord of glory, for the example of the first martyr St. Stephen, who died praying for those who killed him: Strengthen us to imitate his goodness and to love even our enemies; through Jesus Christ our Lord, who stands at your right hand and who lives and reigns with you and the Holy Spirit, one God, now and for ever.

[Acts 7:55, 60; Greg., RS, BCP, LBW, rev. PHP]

December 27. St. John the Divine, Apostle, Evangelist

Shed upon your Church, O Lord, the brightness of your light, that we, being illumined by the teaching of your apostle and evangelist John, may so walk in the light of your truth, that at length we may attain to the fullness of eternal life; through Jesus Christ our Lord, who lives and reigns with you and the Holy Spirit, one God, now and for ever.

[Leo., MR, BCP, CSB, SBH, LBW]

December 28. The Holy Innocents, Martyrs

O God, the Holy Innocents this day bore witness to you not by speaking words but by dying in the place of your infant Son: Grant, we pray, that the faith we profess with our lips we may proclaim with our lives; through

Jesus Christ our Lord, who lives and reigns with you and the Holy Spirit, one God, now and for ever. [Gel., RS trans. DvD]

We remember today, O God, the slaughter of the Holy Innocents of Bethlehem by order of King Herod: Receive, we pray, into the arms of your mercy all innocent victims, and by your great might frustrate the designs of evil tyrants and establish your reign of justice, love, and peace; through Jesus Christ our Lord, who lives and reigns with you and the Holy Spirit, one God, now and for ever. [BCP, LBW]

December 29. The Fifth Day of Christmas

Mighty God, beyond the reach of mortal eyes, the light which you have sent into the world has banished darkness from the earth: Turn your gentle face toward us, that we may worthily declare the praise of the glorious birth of your only-begotten Son Jesus Christ our Lord; who lives and reigns with you and the Holy Spirit, one God, now and for ever.

[Leo., RS, trans. PHP]

Commemoration of Thomas Becket. Martyrs (3)

December 30. The Sixth Day of Christmas

Grant, we implore you, almighty God, that the new birth of your only-begotten Son in the flesh may set us free who are held in the old bondage under the yoke of sin; through Jesus Christ our Lord, who lives and reigns with you and the Holy Spirit, one God, now and for ever.

[Isa. 9:4, Gal. 5:1; Gel., MR, RS, CB, CSB, SBH, LBW]

December 31. The Seventh Day of Christmas

Almighty and everlasting God, by the birth of your Son you established the source and fulfillment of all religion: Number us, we pray, among those who belong to Christ, in whom alone salvation is complete; through the same Jesus Christ our Lord, who lives and reigns with you and the Holy Spirit, one God, now and for ever. [Leo., AC; RS]

January 1. THE HOLY NAME OF JESUS. The Octave [Eighth Day] of Christmas

Eternal Father, you gave to your incarnate Son the holy Name of Jesus to be a sign of our salvation: Plant in every heart, we pray, the love of him who is the Savior of the world, our Lord Jesus Christ; who lives and reigns with you and the Holy Spirit, one God, now and for ever.

[CBB, BCP, LBW]

On the Second Sunday after Christmas Day

O God, you wonderfully created, and yet more wonderfully restored, the dignity of human nature: Grant that we may share the divine life of him who came to share our humanity, your Son, Jesus Christ; who lives and reigns with you and the Holy Spirit, one God, now and for ever.

[Leo., BCP Christmas 2; LBW Christmas 1; RS Christmas Day]

January 2. The Ninth Day of Christmas

O God, you willed that the humanity of your Son, who was born of the holy virgin, should not be subject to the sentence of death incurred by our race: Grant that, fashioned into a new creation in Christ, we may be set free from the old ways of sin; through Jesus Christ our Lord, who lives and reigns with you and the Holy Spirit, one God, now and for ever.

[Leo., RS Tuesday before Epiphany; trans. RS and PHP]

Commemoration of Wilhelm Löhe. Renewers of the Church (1)

January 3. The Tenth Day of Christmas

Grant to us, almighty God, that as your salvation, wondrous with a new and heavenly light, went forth at this time to redeem the world, so it may ever shine forth in the renewal of our hearts; through the same Jesus Christ our Lord, who lives and reigns with you and the Holy Spirit, one God, now and for ever. [Greg., AC; RS Wednesday before Epiphany]

[Commemoration of Charles Porterfield Krauth. Theologians (2)*]*

January 4. The Eleventh Day of Christmas

O God, by the birth of your only-begotten Son you have begun the wondrous work of our redemption: Strengthen the faith of your people so that by his guidance we may attain the promised gift of glory; through the same Jesus Christ our Lord, who lives and reigns with you and the Holy Spirit, one God, now and for ever.

[Gel., RS Thursday before Epiphany; trans. PHP]

January 5. The Twelfth Day of Christmas

Enlighten your people, we pray you, O Lord, and set their minds always on fire with the brightness of your glory; that they may unceasingly acknowledge him who is their Savior, and hold fast in truth to him who is their Lord; who lives and reigns with you and the Holy Spirit, one God, now and for ever. [Greg., AC, RS Friday before Epiphany; trans. PHP]

Commemoration of Kaj Munk. Martyrs (2)

January 6. THE EPIPHANY OF OUR LORD

O God, by the leading of a star you manifested your only-begotten Son to the peoples of the earth: Lead us, who know you now by faith, to your presence, where we may see your glory face to face; through Jesus Christ our Lord, who lives and reigns with you and the Holy Spirit, one God, now and for ever. [Greg., MR, RS, BCP, CB, CSB, SBH, LBW]

NOTE: The following prayers are used only until the Baptism of Our Lord.

January 7

We pray you, O Lord, mercifully to correct our wanderings, and by the guiding radiance of your compassion to bring us to the saving vision of your truth; through your Son Jesus Christ our Lord, who lives and reigns with you and the Holy Spirit, one God, now and for ever.

[Gothic Missal, AC]

[RS: see December 26, prayer to OT Canticle, p. 303]

January 8

O God, your only-begotten Son has appeared in the substance of our human flesh: Grant that he, whose outward form is like our own, may reshape us inwardly by his grace; through the same Jesus Christ our Lord, who lives and reigns with you and the Holy Spirit, one God, now and for ever. [Gel., MR Octave of Epiphany; RS Tuesday after Epiphany; AC]

January 9

O God, the light of all the nations, bless the peoples of the earth with perpetual peace, and pour into our hearts that radiant light by which you guided the Magi to Jesus Christ our Lord; who lives and reigns with you and the Holy Spirit, one God, now and for ever.

[Gel., RS Wednesday after Epiphany; AC]

[Commemoration of Julia Chester Emery. Saints(3)]

January 10

Everlasting God, in your Son Jesus Christ you have raised up an unfailing light for all the nations: Grant that your people may know and confess the full splendor of their Redeemer, and, by his grace, enter into light everlasting; through Jesus Christ our Lord, who lives and reigns with you and the Holy Spirit, one God, now and for ever.

[Greg., RS Thursday after Epiphany, trans. RS and PHP]

[Commemoration of William Laud. Pastors and Bishops (2)*]*

January 11

Almighty God, by the guidance of a star you made known the birth of Christ, the Savior of the world: Reveal to our hearts more fully each day the mystery of the coming of the same Jesus Christ our Lord; who lives and reigns with you and the Holy Spirit, one God, now and for ever.

[Greg., RS Friday after Epiphany, trans. RS and PHP]

January 12

Almighty and everlasting God, by your only-begotten Son you have made us a new creation for yourself: Preserve the works of your mercy and cleanse us from all our ancient stains, that by the assistance of your grace we may be found in the form of him in whom our substance dwells with you, Jesus Christ our Lord; who lives and reigns with you and the Holy Spirit, one God, now and for ever. [Gel., AC; RS Saturday after Epiphany]

Commemoration of Aelred. Monastics

The Sunday of the Baptism of Our Lord

Father in heaven, at the baptism of Jesus in the River Jordan you proclaimed him your beloved Son and anointed him with the Holy Spirit:

Make all who are baptized into Christ faithful in their calling to be your children and inheritors with him of everlasting life; through your Son Jesus Christ our Lord, who lives and reigns with you and the Holy Spirit, one God, now and for ever. [RS, BCP, LBW]

Other prayers may be said by the leader with the congregation responding Amen *to each. In concluding the prayers the leader says:*

L The Lord has remembered his promise of mercy;
C He has kept faith with his people Israel {LH: see Luke 1:54-55]

We give thanks to you, holy Lord, almighty Father, everlasting God, for you have protected us and brought us safely to the morning: Give us grace, we implore you, to pass this day without sin, so that when evening comes we may once again give thanks to you; through Jesus Christ our Lord, who lives and reigns with you and the Holy Spirit, one God, now and for ever. [Gel., Greg., AC; trans. DvD and GA]

C Amen.

L Lord, remember us in your kingdom, and teach us to pray:

C Our Father in heaven,
hallowed be your Name
your kingdom come,
your will be done,
on earth as in heaven.
Give us today our daily bread.
Forgive us our sins
as we forgive those
who sin against us.
Save us from the time of trial
and deliver us from evil.

C Our Father who art in heaven,
hallowed be thy Name
thy kingdom come,
thy will be done,
on earth as it is in heaven.
Give us this day our daily bread;
and forgive us our trespasses,
as we forgive those
who sin against us;
And lead us not into temptation
but deliver us from evil.

For the kingdom, the power, and the glory are yours, now and for ever. Amen.	For thine is the kingdom, and the power, and the glory, for ever and ever. Amen.

Stand

L Let us bless the_ Lord.

C Thanks_ be to God.

The BENEDICTION concludes the service when there is no sermon nor Paschal Blessing. On Sundays the Paschal Blessing may replace the benediction. A hymn may follow the benediction.

When there is a sermon, the order continues as on *p. 20**; On Sundays the Paschal Blessing may follow the prayer after the sermon.*

L The Lord al - mighty bless us, ✠ and direct our days and

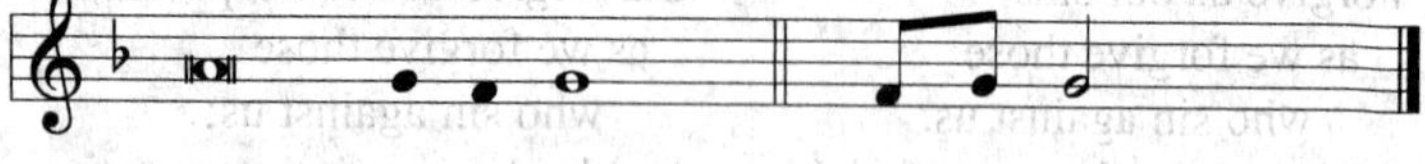

our deeds in his peace. C A - men

The PASCHAL BLESSING may be used on Sundays to conclude Morning Prayer. The service may be led from the font.

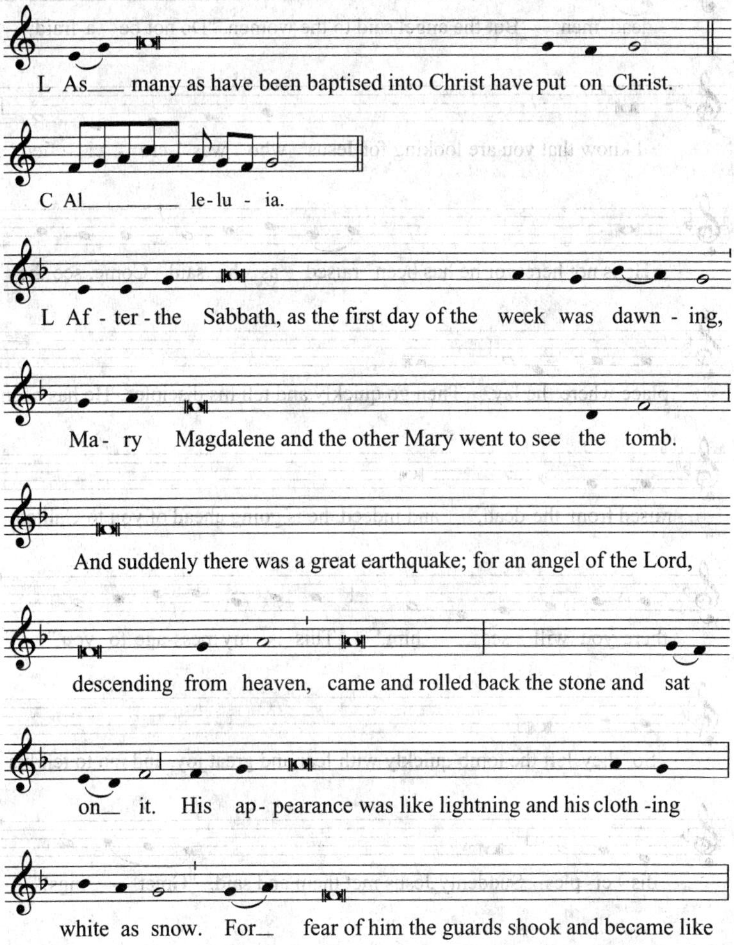

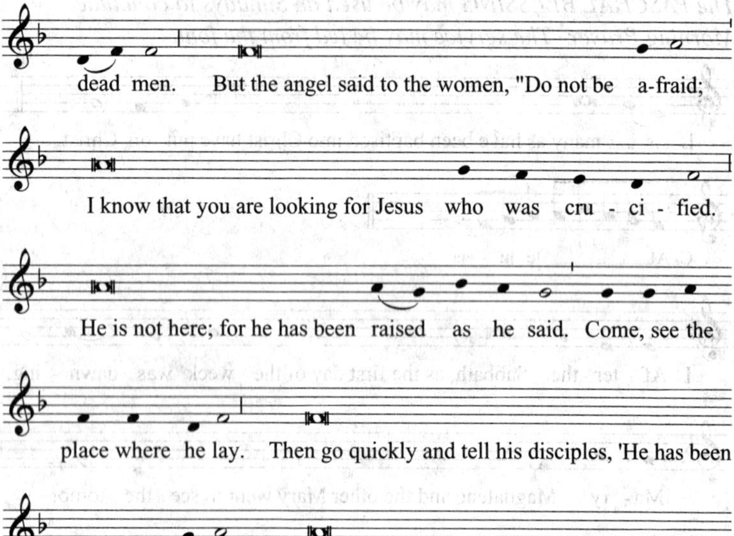
dead men. But the angel said to the women, "Do not be a-fraid;
I know that you are looking for Jesus who was cru - ci - fied.
He is not here; for he has been raised as he said. Come, see the
place where he lay. Then go quickly and tell his disciples, 'He has been
raised from the dead, and indeed, he is going ahead of you to Galilee;
there you will see him.' This is my mess-age to you."
So they left the tomb quickly with fear and great joy, and ran to tell his
dis - ci - ples. Suddenly Jesus met them and said, "Greet - ings!"

And they came to him, took hold of his feet, and wor-shiped him.

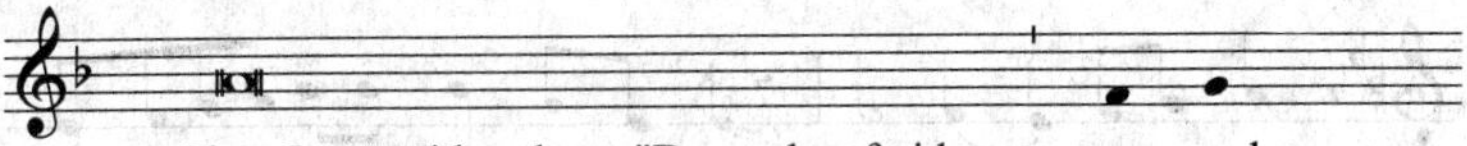

Then Jesus said to them, "Do not be afraid; go and

tell my brothers to go to Galilee; there they will see__ me."

[Matthew 28:1-10; setting © 1993 Richard Hillert]

The Te Deum Laudamus is sung.

C You are God; we_praise you. You are the Lord; we ac-claim you.

You are the e-ter-nal Fa-ther; all cre-a-tion wor-ships you.

[I] To you all an-gels, all the pow'rs of heav-en, cheru-bim and ser a-phim,

sing in end-less praise: C Ho-ly, ho-ly,

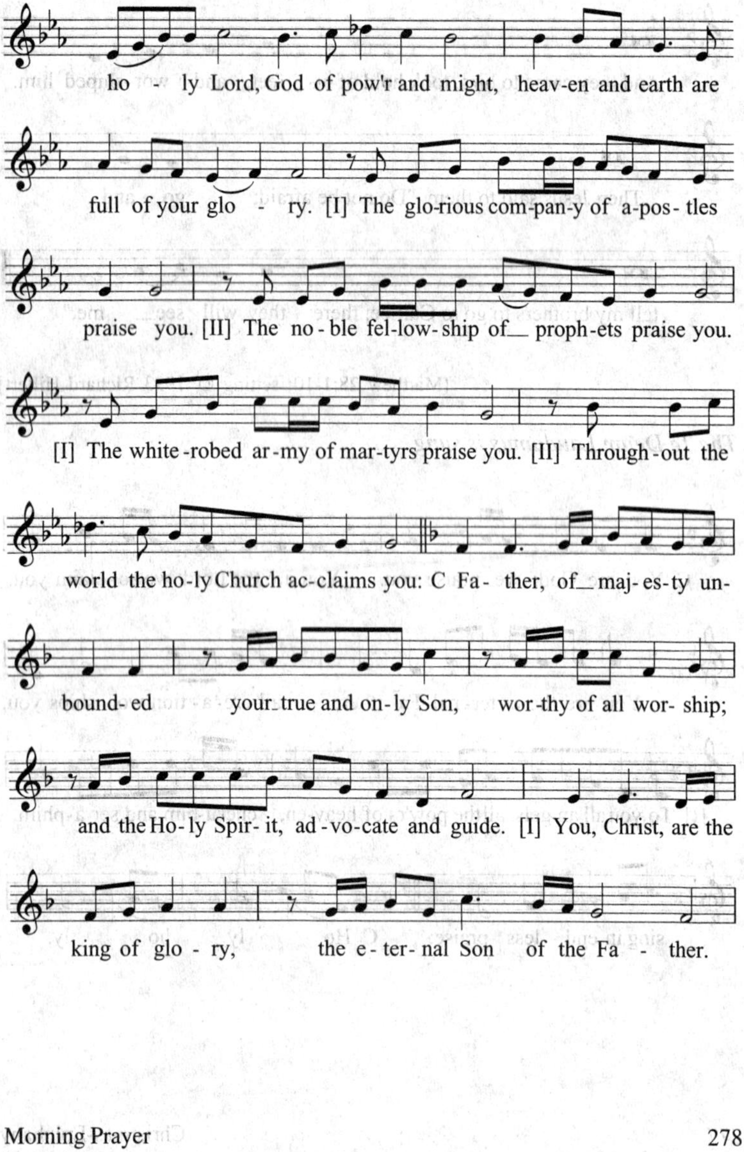
ho - ly Lord, God of pow'r and might, heav-en and earth are
full of your glo - ry. [I] The glo-rious com-pan-y of a-pos- tles
praise you. [II] The no - ble fel-low- ship of__ proph-ets praise you.
[I] The white -robed ar-my of mar-tyrs praise you. [II] Through-out the
world the ho-ly Church ac-claims you: C Fa- ther, of__maj- es-ty un-
bound- ed your_true and on-ly Son, wor-thy of all wor- ship;
and the Ho- ly Spir- it, ad -vo-cate and guide. [I] You, Christ, are the
king of glo - ry, the e - ter- nal Son of the Fa - ther.

[II] When you be- came man to_set us free, you did not spurn the
vir - gin's womb. [I] You o - ver came the_sting of death,
and_ o -pened the king-dom of heav-en to_ all be - liev - ers.
[II] You are seat - ed at_God's right hand in_ glo - ry.
We be- lieve that you will come and be our judge. C Come, then,
Lord, and_help your peo- ple, bought with the price of_your own blood,
and_bring us with your saints to glo - ry_ ev - er- last - ing.

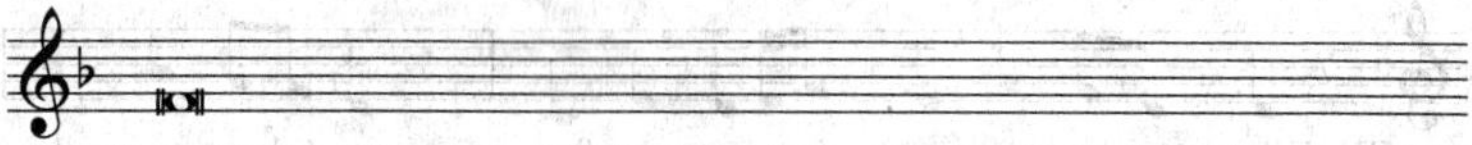

L Almighty God, grant that as he who was born the Savior of the world is

to us the Author of our heaven - ly birth, so he may also himself be

the Giver of our immortal - i - ty; who lives and reigns with you and

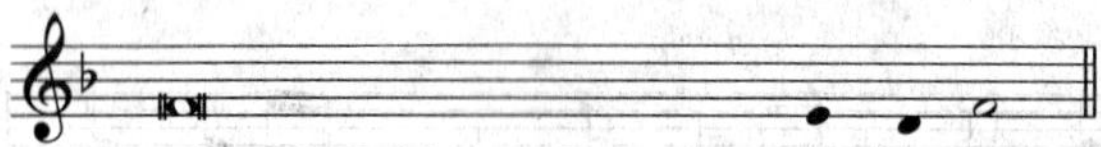

the Holy Spirit, one God, now and for- ever.

C A - men

[Leo., MR, RS, AC]

L The Lord al - mighty bless us, ✠ and direct our days and

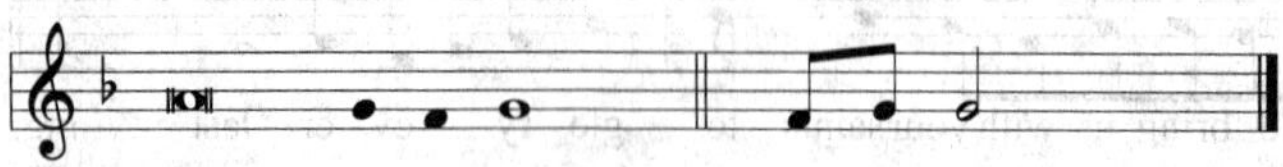

our deeds in his peace. C A - men

December 25, January 1, 6
and
The Baptism of our Lord

Antiphon to PSALM 2 *Quare fremuerunt gentes?*

December 25 Christmas Day	The Lord said to me, "**You** are my son;* this day have I be**got**ten you." [CSB, SBH, PBO]
January 1 The Holy Name of Jesus	At the Name of JESUS every **knee** should bend* and every tongue should confess that Jesus **Christ** is Lord. [Phil. 2:10,11]
January 6 The Epiphany	The Wise Men opened their **trea**sure chests* and offered to the Lord gifts of gold, frankin**cense**, and myrrh. [LH: Matt. 2:11]
The Baptism of Our Lord	The soldier baptizes his king; the servant his Lord, **John** his Savior;* the waters of the Jordan tremble, a dove hovers as a sign of witness, and the voice of the Father is heard, This **is** my Son. [LH]

2 *The Messiah, King and Conqueror*

1 Why are the nations **in** an uproar?*
Why do the peoples mutter **emp**ty threats?

2 Why do the kings of the earth rise up in revolt,
and the princes **plot** together,*
against the LORD and against **his** Anointed?

3 "Let us break their **yoke**," they say;*
"let us cast off their **bonds** from us."

4 He whose throne is in heav**en** is laughing;*
the Lord has them **in** derision.

5 Then he speaks to them **in** his wrath,*
and his rage fills **them** with terror.

6 "I myself have **set** my king*
upon my holy **hill** of Zion."

7 Let me announce the decree **of** the LORD:*
he said to me, "You are my Son;
this day have I be**got**ten you.

8 Ask of me, and I will give you the nations for **your** inheritance*
and the ends of the earth for **your** possession.

9 You shall crush them with an **i**ron rod*
and shatter them like a **piece** of pottery."

10 And now, you **kings**, be wise;*
be warned, you rulers **of** the earth.

11 Submit to the **LORD** with fear,*
and with trembling **bow** before him;

12 Lest he be angry **and** you perish;*
for his wrath is **quick**ly kindled.

13 Happy **are** they all*
who take ref**uge** in him!

The Antiphon is repeated.

Silence for meditation

Lord God, you gave the peoples of the world to be the inheritance of your Son; you crowned him as king of Zion, your holy city, and gave him your Church as his bride. As he proclaims the way of your eternal kingdom, grant that we may serve him faithfully, and so know the royal power of the same Jesus Christ our Lord. [LH, LBW]

+

Antiphon to the OLD TESTAMENT CANTICLE

Benedicite, omnia opera

December 25 Christmas Day	Tell us, shepherds, what have you seen? Who has ap**peared** on earth?* We have seen a newborn infant and a choir of angels prais**ing** the Lord. [LH]
January 1 The Holy Name of Jesus	A child is born for **us** today;* an infant and yet called the **might**y God. [LH]
January 6 The Epiphany	You wells and springs, **bless** the Lord,* you rivers and seas, praise **him** for ever. [LH]
The Baptism of Our Lord	Springs of water were made holy as Christ revealed his glory **to** the world.* Draw water from the fountain of the Savior, for Christ our God has hallowed **all** creation. [LH: see PBO, LBW]

A Song of Creation — Song of the Three Young Men 35-65

All you works of the Lord, **bless** the Lord–*
praise him and magnify **him** for ever.

You angels of the Lord, **bless** the Lord;*
you heavens, **bless** the Lord;
all you powers of the Lord, **bless** the Lord–*
praise him and magnify **him** for ever.

You sun and moon, **bless** the Lord;*
you stars of heaven, **bless** the Lord;
you showers and dew, **bless** the Lord–*
praise him and magnify **him** for ever.

You winds of God, **bless** the Lord;*
you fire and heat **bless** the Lord;
you winter and summer, **bless** the Lord–*
praise him and magnify **him** for ever.

You dews and frost, **bless** the Lord;*
you frost and cold, **bless** the Lord;
you ice and snow, **bless** the Lord–*
praise him and magnify **him** for ever.

You nights and days, **bless** the Lord;*
you light and darkness, **bless** the Lord;
you lightnings and clouds, **bless** the Lord–*
praise him and magnify **him** for ever.

Let the earth **bless** the Lord;*
you mountains and hills, **bless** the Lord;

all you green things that grow on the earth, **bless** the Lord–*
praise him and magnify **him** for ever.

You wells and springs, **bless** the Lord;*
you rivers and seas, **bless** the Lord;
you whales and all who move in the waters, **bless** the Lord–*
praise him and magnify **him** for ever.

All you birds of the air, **bless** the Lord;*
all you beasts and cattle, **bless** the Lord;
all you children of mortals, **bless** the Lord–*
praise him and magnify **him** for ever.

You people of God, **bless** the Lord;*
you priests of the Lord, **bless** the Lord;
you servants of the Lord, **bless** the Lord–*
praise him and magnify **him** for ever.

You spirits and souls of righteous, **bless** the Lord;*
you pure and humble of heart, **bless** the Lord;
let us bless the Father and the Son and the **Ho**ly Spirit–*
praise him and magnify **him** for ever. [LBW 18]

The Antiphon is repeated.

Silence for meditation

Most mighty and eternal Lord, at your coming to the world all creation danced for joy: Help us eagerly to join our praises with the songs of your servants and give voice to the exultation felt throughout the universe when you came to set your people free; through Jesus Christ our Lord. [PHP]

+

Antiphon to PSALM 98 *Cantate Domino*

December 25 Christmas Day	The angel said to the shepherds, I am bringing you good news of great joy for **all** the people:* To you is born today the Savior **of** the world. [LH: see Luke 2:10-11]
January 1 The Holy Name of Jesus	Let the rivers **clap** their hands,* and let the hills ring out with joy be**fore** the Lord.
January 6 The Epiphany	Jerusalem, your **light** has come;* the glory of the Lord has ris**en** upon you. [LH: Isa. 60:1,3]
The Baptism of Our Lord	You burned away our guilt by fire and the **Ho**ly Spirit;* we praise you, O God **our** Redeemer. [LH: see Luke 3:16b, Matt. 3:11c]

98 *God, the Ruler of the world*

1 Sing to the LORD **a** new song,*
for he has done **mar**velous things.

2 With his right hand and his **ho**ly arm*
has he won for him**self** the victory.

3 The LORD has made **known** his victory;*
his righteousness has he openly shown in the sight **of** the nations.

4 He remembers his mercy and faithfulness to the **house** of Israel,*
and all the ends of the earth have seen the victory **of** our God.

5 Shout with joy to the LORD, **all** you lands;*
lift up your voice, re**joice**, and sing.

6 Sing to the LORD **with** the harp,*
with the harp and the **voice** of song.

7 With trumpets and the sound **of** the horn*
shout with joy before the **king**, the LORD.

8 Let the sea make a noise and all **that** is in it,*
the lands and those who **dwell** therein.

9 Let the rivers **clap** their hands,*
and let the hills ring out with joy before the LORD,
when he comes to **judge** the earth.

10 In righteousness shall he **judge** the world*
and the peo**ples** with equity.

The Antiphon is repeated.

Silence for meditation

Lord, we sing to you a new song, for your victory is ever new. In the empty tomb you have given us a glimpse of your future, and in your victory over death you have shown us how we shall overcome the last enemy. As the seas roar and the hills sing together, we too will praise you for your great triumph, Father, Son, and Holy Spirit, now and for ever.

[LBW]

+

Stand

THE HYMN is sung.

on December 25 *A solis ortus cardine*

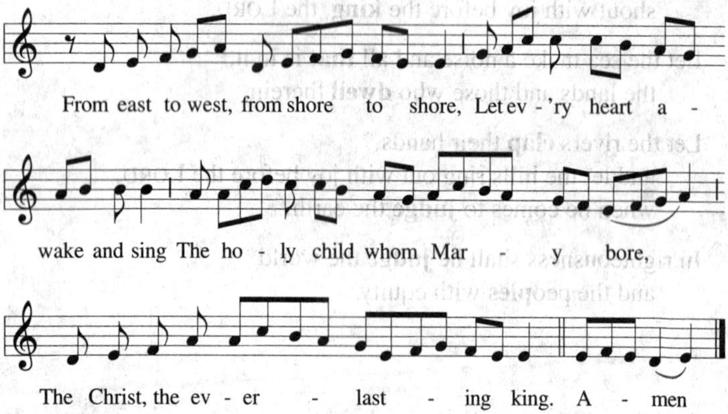

2 Behold, the world's creator wears
The form and fashion of a slave;
Our very flesh our maker shares,
The fallen human race to save.

3 For this how wondrously he wrought!
A maiden in her lowly place,
Became, in ways beyond all thought,
The chosen vessel of his grace.

4 And while the angels in the sky
Sang praise above the silent field,
To shepherds poor the Lord most high,
The one great Shepherd, was revealed.

5 All glory for this blessèd morn
To God the Father ever be;
All praise to you, O Virgin-born,
And Holy Ghost, eternally. Amen. [LBW64, H82 77]

Text: Coelius Sedulius, d. c. 450; tr. John Ellerton, 1826-1893, alt.
Tune: *A solis ortus cardine,* Sarum plainsong, mode III LM

on January 1, The Holy Name of Jesus *Gloriosi Salvatoris*

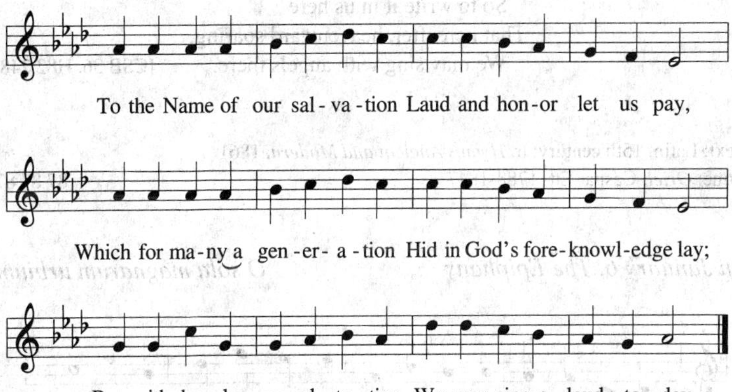

2 Jesus is the Name we treasure;
Name beyond what words can tell;
Name of gladness, Name of pleasure,
Ear and heart delighting well;
Name of sweetness, passing measure,
Saving us from sin and hell.

3 'Tis the Name that whoso preacheth
Speaks like music to the ear;
Who in prayer this Name beseecheth
Sweetest comfort findeth near;
Who its perfect wisdom reacheth,
Heavenly joy posesseth here.

4 Therefore we, in love adoring,
This most blessed Name revere,
Holy Jesus, thee imploring,
So to write it in us here
That hereafter, heavenward soaring,
We may sing with angels there. [CSB 36, H82 248]

Text: Latin, 15th century; tr. *Hymns Ancient and Modern*, 1861
Tune: *Oriel,* Caspar Ett, 1788-1847 87 87 87

on January 6, The Epiphany *O sola magnarum urbium*

2 Fairer than the sun at morning
Was the star that told his birth,
To the world its God announcing
Seen in fleshly form on earth.

3 Eastern sages at his cradle
Make oblations rich and rare;
See them give, in deep devotion,
Gold and frankincense and myrrh.

4 Sacred gifts of mystic meaning:
Incense doth their God disclose,
Gold the King of kings proclaimeth,
Myrrh his sepulcher foreshows.

5 Jesus, whom the Gentiles worshipped
At thy glad Epiphany,
Unto thee with God the Father
And the Spirit, glory be. [SBH 51, H82 127]

Text: Marcus Aurelius Clemens Prudentius, 348-413; tr. *Hymns Ancient and Modern*, 1861, alt.

Tune: *Stuttgart*, Christian Friedrich Witt, 1660-1716 87 87

on the Baptism of our Lord *Christ, unser Herr zum Jordan kamm*

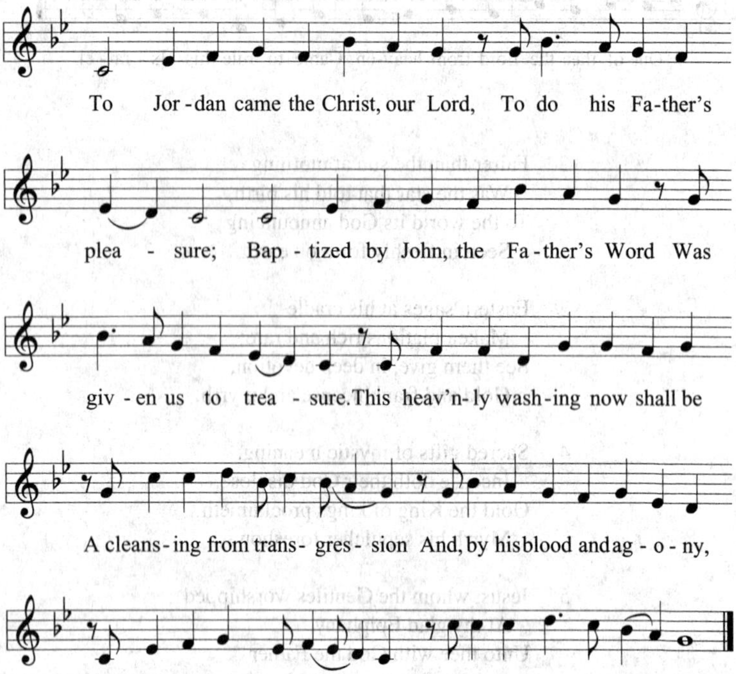

2 O hear and mark the message well,
For God himself has spoken.
Let faith, not doubt among us dwell
And so receive this token.
Our Lord here with his Word endows

Pure water, freely flowing.
God's Holy Spirit here avows
Our kinship while bestowing
The baptism of his blessing.

3 These truths on Jordan's banks were shown
By mighty word and wonder.
The Father's voice from heaven came down,
Which we do well to ponder:
"This man is my beloved Son,
In whom my heart has pleasure.
Him you must hear, and him alone,
And trust in fullest measure
The word that he has spoken."

4 There stood the Son of God in love,
His grace to us extending;
The Holy Spirit like a dove
Upon the scene descending;
The triune God assuring us,
With promises compelling,
That in our baptism he will thus
Among us find a dwelling
To comfort and sustain us.

5 To his disciples spoke the Lord,
"Go out to every nation,
And bring to them the living Word
And this my invitation:
Let everyone abondon sin
And come in true contrition
To be baptized and thereby win
Full pardon and remission,
And heavenly bliss inherit."

6 But woe to those who cast aside
This grace so freely given;
They shall in sin and shame abide
And to despair be driven.
For born in sin, their works must fail,
Their striving saves them never;
Their pious acts do not avail,
And they are lost for ever,
Eternal death their portion.

7 All that the mortal eye beholds
Is water as we pour it.
Before the eye of faith unfolds
The power of Jesus' merit.
For here it sees the crimson flood
To all our ills bring healing;
The wonders of his precious blood
The love of God revealing,
Assuring his own pardon. [LBW 79]

Text: Martin Luther, 1483-1546; tr. Elizabeth Quitmeyer, 1911-1988 alt.

Tune: *Christ, unser Herr,* J. Walther, *Geistliche Gesangbüchlein, 1524* 87 87 87 877

Sit

One or two LESSONS are read.

Silence for meditation follows each reading.

Year 1

December 25. Christmas Day
Zechariah 2:10-13

Sing and rejoice, O daughter of Zion! For lo, I will come and dwell in your midst, says the LORD.

1 John 4:7-16

God's love was revealed among us in this way: God sent his only Son into the world so that we might live through him.

RESPONSORY for Christmas Day

Today true peace came down to **us** from heaven.*
  Today the whole earth was filled with **hea**ven's sweetness.
Today a new day dawns, the day of our redemption, prepared by God from ages past, the beginning of our never-**end**ing gladness.*
  Today the whole earth was filled with **hea**ven's sweetness.
[LH]

Year 2

Micah 4:1-5; 5:2-4

But you, O Bethlehem of Ephrathah, who are one of the little clans of Judah, from you shall come forth for me one who is to rule in Israel, whose origin is from old, from ancient days.

1 John 4:7-16

God's love was revealed among us in this way: God sent his only Son into the world so that we might live through him.

Today for our sake the King of heaven chose to be born of his **vir**gin mother*
to reclaim the lost for his heav**en**ly kingdom.
  All the angels cry **aloud** with joy*
  for God has come himself to **save** humanity.
Glory to God **in** the highest,*
and peace to his peo**ple** on earth.
  All the angels cry **aloud** with joy*
  for God has come himself to **save** humanity. [LH]

January 1. The Holy Name of Jesus

Genesis 17:1-12a, 15-16

I will make you exceedingly fruitful; and I will make nations of you, and kings shall come from you.

Isaiah 62:1-5, 10-12

For Zion's sake I will not keep silent, and for Jerusalem's sake I will not rest, until her vindication shines out like the dawn, and her salvation like a burning torch.

Colossians 2:6-12

For in Christ the whole fullness of deity dwells bodily, and you have come to fullness in him, who is the head of every ruler and authority.

Revelation 19:11-16

On his robe and on his thigh he has a name inscribed, "King of kings and Lord of lords."

RESPONSORY for the Holy Name of Jesus

You will conceive in your womb
and bear a son, and you will
name him Jesus,*
 for he will save his people
 from their sins.
He was called Jesus, the Name
given by the angel before he was
conceived **in** the womb,*
 for he will save his people
 from their sins.
 [LH: Luke 1:31; Matt. 1:21; Luke 2:21]

O pure and **ho**ly virgin,*
how can I find words to **praise**
your beauty?
 The highest heavens can**not**
 contain God,*
 whom you carried in your womb.
Blessed are you **a**mong women,*
and blessed is the fruit **of** your
womb.
 The highest heavens can**not**
 contain God,*
 whom you carried **in** your womb.
 [LH: Luke 1:42]

January 6. The Epiphany of Our Lord

Isaiah 52:7-10

The LORD has bared his holy arm before the eyes of all the nations; and all the ends of the earth shall see the salvation of God.

Isaiah 49:1-7

I will give you as a light to the nations, that my salvation may reach to the end of the earth.

Revelation 21:22-27

The city has no need of sun or moon to shine on it, for the glory of God is its light, and its lamp is the Lamb. The nations will walk by its light, and the kings of the earth will bring their glory into it.

Revelation 21:22-27

The city has no need of sun or moon to shine on it, for the glory of God is its light, and its lamp is the Lamb. The nations will walk by its light, and the kings of the earth will bring their glory into it.

RESPONSORY for the Epiphany of our Lord

The Wise Men opened their **treas**ure chests*
and offered three precious gifts **to** the Lord:
Gold signifies the power **of** a king,*
frankincense signifies the office of high priest, and myrrh **the** Lord's burial.
The Wise Men entered the house to worship the author of **our** salvation,*
and from their treasures they offered these sym**bol**ic gifts:

This is the glorious day on which Christ himself, the Savior of the **world**, appeared;*
the prophets fotetold him, the angels **wor**shiped him.
The Magi **saw** his star and rejoiced to lay their treasures **at** his feet.
God's holy day has dawned for **us** at last:*
come, all you peoples, and wor**ship** the Lord.
The Magi **saw** his star and

Gold signifies the power **of** a king,*
frankincense signifies the
office of high priest, and myrrh
the Lord's burial.

[LH: see Matt 2:11, Heb. 5:9]

rejoiced to lay their treasures
at his feet.

[LH: see Matt. 2:10,11]

The Baptism of Our Lord

Isaiah 40:1-11

The glory of the LORD shall be revealed, and all people shall see it together.

Hebrews 1:1-12

He is the reflection of God's glory and the exact imprint of God's very being, and he susteains all things by his powerful word.

Genesis 1:1-2:3

A wind from God swept over the face of the waters.

Ephesians 1:3-14

God has made known to us the mystery of his will, according to his good pleasure that he set forth in Christ, as a plan for the fullness of time, to gather up all things in him, things in heaven and things on earth.

RESPONSORY for the Baptism of our Lord

Today in the Jordan as the **Lord**
was baptized,*
the heavens were opened and he
saw the Spirit of God descending
like a dove and alight**ing** on him;
And a voice from **hea**ven said,*
This is my Son, the Beloved,
with whom I **am** well pleased.
The Holy Spirit descend**ed**

Today the **hea**vens opened*
and the waters of the sea became
sweet and fragrant.
The earth rejoiced, the mountains
and **hills** exulted*
because Christ was baptized by
John **in** the Jordan.
What ailed you, O sea, that you fled?
O Jordan, that **you** turned back?*

upon him*
in bodily form **like** a dove.
And a voice from **heav**en said,*
This is my Son, the Beloved,
with whom I **am** well pleased.
[LH: Matt 3:16,17; Luke 3:22]

because Christ was baptized by
John **in** the Jordan.
[LH: Psalm 114:5]

Antiphon to the BENEDICTUS

December 25. Christmas Day

Glory to God **in** the highest,*
and peace to his peo**ple** on earth. [LH, PBO: Luke 2:14]

January 1. The Holy Name of Jesus

You are to **name** him Jesus,*
for he will save his people **from** their sins. [Matt. 1:21]

January 6. The Epiphany

Today the Bridegroom claims his **bride**, the Church,*
since Christ has washed her sins away in **Jor**dan's waters;
the Magi hasten with their gifts to the **roy**al wedding;*
and the wedding guests rejoice,
for Christ has changed water **in**to wine. [LH]

The Baptism of Our Lord

Christ is baptized, the world is made holy;
he has taken a**way** our sins.*
We shall be purified by water and the **Ho**ly Spirit. [LH]

December 26, January 2, and January 7

Antiphon to PSALM 116 *Dilexi, quoniam*

December 26 St. Stephen's Day	I see the **hea**vens opened,* and the Son of Man standing at the right **hand** of God. [LH:Acts 7:56]
January 2, 7	Come, you peoples **of** the earth;* drink from the wells **of** salvation. [LBW, PBO]

116 *Thanksgiving for deliverance from death*

1 I love the LORD, because he has heard the voice
of my **sup**plication,*
because he has inclined his ear to me whenever I
called upon him.

2 The cords of death entangled me;
the grip of the grave took **hold** of me;*
I came to **grief** and sorrow.

3 Then I called upon the Name **of** the LORD:*
"O LORD, I pray you, **save** my life."

4 Gracious is the **LORD** and righteous;*
our God is full **of** compassion.

5 The LORD watches o**ver** the innocent;*
I was brought very low, **and** he helped me.

6 Turn again to your rest, **O** my soul.*
for the LORD has treat**ed** you well.

7 For you have rescued my **life** from death,*
my eyes from tears, and my **feet** from stumbling.

8 I will walk in the presence **of** the LORD*
in the land **of** the living.

9 I believed, even when I said,
"I have been brought **very** low."*
In my distress I said, "No one **can** be trusted."

10 How shall I re**pay** the LORD*
for all the good things he has **done** for me?

11 I will lift up the cup **of** salvation*
and call upon the Name **of** the LORD.

12 I will fulfill my vows **to** the LORD*
in the presence of **all** his people.

13 Precious in the sight **of** the LORD*
is the death **of** his servants.

14 O LORD, I **am** your servant;*
I am your servant and the child of your handmaid;
you have freed me **from** my bonds.

15 I will offer you the sacrifice **of** thanksgiving*
and call upon the Name **of** the LORD.

16 I will fulfill my vows **to** the LORD*
in the presence of **all** his people,

17 In the courts of **the** LORD's house,*
in the midst of you, O Jerusalem.
Hallelujah!

Antiphon

December 26 St. Stephen's Day	I see the **hea**vens opened,* and the Son of Man standing at the right **hand** of God. [LH:Acts 7:56]
January 2, 7	Come, you peoples **of** the earth;* drink from the wells **of** salvation. [LBW, PBO]

Silence for meditation

God of power and mercy, through the Passion and resurrection of your Son you have freed us from the bonds of death and the anguish of separation from you: Be with us on our pilgrimage, and help us offer you a sacrifice of praise, fulfill our vows, and glorify you in the presence of all your people; through Jesus Christ our Lord. [LH, LBW]

+

Antiphon to the OLD TESTAMENT CANTICLE

Benedictus es, Domine

The Lord God will give to him
the throne of his an**ces**tor David,*
and he will reign for ev**er** and ever. [PBO: see Luke 1:32]

A Song of Praise — Song of the Three Young Men 29-34

Blessed are you, O Lord, God **of** our ancestors:*
praised and exalt**ed** for ever.

Blessed are you for the radiance of your **ho**ly Name:*
praised and exalt**ed** for ever.

Blessed are you in the temple **of** your holiness:*
praised and exalt**ed** for ever.

Blessed are you, beholding the depths
from your throne between the **cher**ubim:*
praised and exalt**ed** for ever.

Blessed are you on the glorious throne **of** your kingdom:*
praised and exalt**ed** for ever.

Blessed are you in the firma**ment** of heaven:*
praised and exalt**ed** for ever. [BCP, NRSV alt.]

Antiphon The Lord God will give to him
the throne of his an**ces**tor David,*
and he will reign for ev**er** and ever.

Silence for meditation

Illumine our hearts, we ask you, O Lord, with the splendor of your majesty, that we may pass beyond the darkness of this world and come at last to the radiance of our eternal home; through Jesus Christ our Lord.

[Gel., Sarum; AC; RS Mon. after Epiph.]

+

Antiphon to PSALM 48 *Magnus Dominus*

Let Mount Zion be glad,
and let the cities of Ju**dah** rejoice,*
for the **Lord** has come. [PBO]

48 *Zion, the city of God*

1 Great is the LORD, and highly **to** be praised;*
in the city of our God is his **ho**ly hill.

2 Beautiful and lofty, the joy of all the earth, is the **hill** of Zion,*
the very center of the world and the city of **the** great king.

3 God is **in** her citadels;*
he is known to be **her** sure refuge.

4 Behold, the kings of the **earth** assembled*
and marched for**ward** together.

5 They looked and **were** astounded;*
they retreated and **fled** in terror.

6 Trembling **seized** them there;*
they writhed like a woman in childbirth,
like ships of the sea when the **east** wind shatters them.

7 As we have heard, so have we seen,
in the city of the LORD of hosts, in the city **of** our God;*
God has established **her** for ever.

8 We have waited in silence on your loving-kind**ness**, O God,*
in the midst **of** your temple.

9 Your praise, like your Name, O God, reaches **to** the world's end;*
your right hand is **full** of justice.

10 Let Mount Zion be glad
and the cities of Ju**dah** rejoice,*
because **of** your judgments.

11 Make the circuit of Zion;
walk **round** about her;*
count the number **of** her towers.

12 Consider well her bulwarks;
exam**ine** her strongholds;*
that you may tell those **who** come after.

13 This God is our God for ev**er** and ever;*
he shall be our guide for **ev**ermore.

Antiphon Let Mount Zion be glad,
and let the cities of **Judah** rejoice,*
for the **Lord** has come.

Silence for meditation

Father, the body of your risen Son is the temple not made by human hands and the bulwark of the new Jerusalem: Make this holy city, built of living stones, so shine with spiritual radiance that it may show your greatness in the sight of all nations; for the sake of your Son, Jesus Christ our Lord. [LH, LBW]

Stand

THE HYMN is sung.

on December 26, St. Stephen's Day *Τῶν ἱερῶν αθλοφορον*

2 Never flinched they from the flame,
From the torment never;
Vain the tyrant's sharpest aim,
Vain each fierce endeavor:
For by faith they saw the land
Decked in all its glory,
Where triumphant now they stand
With the victor's story.

3 Up and follow, Christians all!
Press through toil and sorrow;
Turn from fear and heed the call
To a glorious morrow!
Who will venture on the strife;
Who will first begin it?
Who will grasp the land of life?
Christians up and win it! [SBH 546, H82 237]

Text: St. Joseph the hymnographer, d. 883; tr. John Mason Neale, 1818-1866, alt.
Tune: *Tempus adest floridum* from *Piae Cantiones,* 1582 76 76 D

on January 2 and 7

2 Cold on his cradle the dewdrops are shining;
   Low lies his head with the beasts of the stall;
Angels adore him in slumber reclining,
   Maker and Monarch and Savior of all.

3 Shall we then yield him, in costly devotion,
   Fragrance of Edom and offerings divine,
Gems of the mountain and pearls of the ocean,
   Myrrh from the forest or gold from the mine?

4 Vainly we offer each ample oblation,
   Vainly with gifts would his favor secure;
Richer by far is the heart's adoration,
   Dearer to God are the prayers of the poor.

5 Brightest and best of the stars of the morning,
   Dawn on our darkness and lend us your aid.
Star of the East, the horizon adorning,
   Guide where our infant redeemer is laid.

[H82 117, LBW 84]

Text: Reginald Heber, 1783-1826, alt.
Tune: *Morning star*, James Proctor Harding, 1850-1911 11 10 11 10

Sit

One or two LESSONS are read.

Silence for meditation follows each reading

Year 1

December 26. St. Stephen's Day

Wisdom 4:7-15

The righteous, though they die early, will be at rest.

or 2 Chronicles 24:17-22

Acts 6:1-7

The disciples chose Stephen, a man full of faith and the Holy Spirit, together with Philip, Prochorus, Nicanor, Timon, Parmenas, and Nicolaus, a proselyte of Antioch.

Year 2

Wisdom 4:7-15

The righteous, though they die early, will be at rest.

or 2 Chronicles 24:17-22

Acts 6:1-7

The disciples chose Stephen, a man full of faith and the Holy Spirit, together with Philip, Prochorus, Nicanor, Timon, Parmenas, and Nicolaus, a proselyte of Antioch.

RESPONSORY for St. Stephen's Day

A day made holy has dawned for us. Come, you nations, and wor**ship** the Lord.*
For a great light has come down up**on** the earth.
On this day the Lord has acted; we will rejoice and be **glad** in it.
For a great light has come down up**on** the earth.

[LH, Ps. 118:24]

Yesterday the Lord was **born** on earth* so that Stephen might be **born** in heaven.
The Lord entered in**to** our world*
so that Stephen might enter **in**to heaven.
Yesterday our King, clothed **in** our flesh,*
came forth from the virgin's womb to **dwell** among us.
The Lord entered in**to** our

world*
so that Stephen might enter
into heaven. [LH]

January 2
Genesis 12:1-7

Go from your country and your kindred and your father's house to the land I will show you.

1 Kings 19:1-8

Elijah got up and ate and drank; then he went in the strength of that food forty days and forty nights to Horeb the mount of God.

Hebrews 11:1-12

Now faith is the assurance of things hoped for, the conviction of things not seen.

Ephesians 4:1-16

Each of us was given grace according to the measure of Christ's gift.

January 7
Isaiah 52:3-6

You were sold for nothing, and you shall be redeemed without money.

Deuteronomy 8:1-3

One does not live by bread alone, buy by every word that comes from the mouth of the LORD.

Revelation 2:1-7

To everyone who conquers, I will give permission to eat from the tree of life that is in the paradise of God.

Colossians 1:1-14

Give thanks to the Father, who has enabled you to share in the inheritance of the saints in the light.

RESPONSORY for January 2 and 7

Arise, shine, Jerusalem, for your
light has come;*

The Spirit of the Lord God
is upon me,*

the glory of the Lord has ris**en**
upon you.
Nations shall come to your light,
and kings to the brightness **of**
your dawn.*
The glory of the Lord has ris**en**
upon you.
[CSB, SBH, LH: Isa. 60:1,3]

because the Lord has anointed
me to bring good news to **the**
oppressed,
to bind up the **bro**kenhearted,*
to proclaim liberty to the
captives, and release **to** the
prisoners.
I came from God, and now
I am here.*
I did not come on my own, **but**
he sent me
to bind up the **bro**kenhearted,*
to proclaim liberty to the
captives and release **to** the
prisoners.
[LH: Isa 61:1; John 8:42]

Antiphon to the BENEDICTUS

December 26 St. Stephen's Day

The gates of heaven opened out to **bless**ed Stephen,*
and he was crowned the **first** of martyrs. [LH: see Acts 7:56]

January 2

Helpless, he lay **in** a manger;*
glorious, he shines **in** the heavens.
Humbled, he lived **a**mong mortals,*
eternal, he dwells **with** the Father. [LH]

January 7

The Wise Men came **from** the East*
  to worship the **Lord** in Bethlehem.
Opening their treasures,
they offered him three **pre**cious gifts:*
  gold for the great king,
  frankincense for the true God,
  and **myrrh** for burial. [LH]

December 27, January 3, and January 8

Antiphon to PSALM 34 *Benedicam Dominum*

The pledge of new redemption and promise of eternal joy,
prepared through **ag**es past,*
has dawned for **us** today. [LH]

34 *In praise of God's goodness*

1 I will bless the LORD **at** all times;*
his praise shall ever be **in** my mouth.

2 I will glory **in** the LORD;*
let the humble hear **and** rejoice.

3 Proclaim with me the greatness **of** the LORD;*
let us exalt his **Name** together.

4 I sought the LORD, and he **an**swered me*
and delivered me out of **all** my terror.

5 Look upon him **and** be radiant,*
and let not your faces **be** ashamed.

6 I called in my affliction, and **the** LORD heard me*
and saved me from **all** my troubles.

7 The angel of the LORD encompasses **those** who fear him,*
and he will de**liv**er them.

8 Taste and see that the **LORD** is good;*
happy are they who **trust** in him!

9 Fear the LORD, you that **are** his saints,*
for those who fear **him** lack nothing.

10 The young lions lack and **suf**fer hunger,*
but those who seek the LORD lack nothing **that** is good.

11 Come, children, and lis**ten** to me;*
I will teach you the fear **of** the LORD.

12 Who among **you** loves life*
and desires long life to en**joy** prosperity?

13 Keep your tongue from **e**vil-speaking*
and your lips from **ly**ing words.

14 Turn from evil **and** do good;*
seek peace **and** pursue it.

15 The eyes of the LORD are up**on** the righteous,*
and his ears are open **to** their cry.

16 The face of the LORD is against those **who** do evil,*
to root out the remembrance of them **from** the earth.

17 The righteous cry, and **the** LORD hears them*
and delivers them from **all** their troubles.

18 The LORD is near to the **bro**kenhearted*
and will save those whose **spir**its are crushed.

19 Many are the troubles **of** the righteous,*
but the LORD will deliver him out **of** them all.

20 He will keep safe **all** his bones;*
not one of them **shall** be broken.

21 Evil shall **slay** the wicked,*
and those who hate the righteous **will** be punished.

22 The LORD ransoms the life **of** his servants,*
and none will be punished who **trust** in him.

Antiphon
The pledge of new redemption and promise of eternal joy,
prepared through **ag**es past,*
has dawned for **us** today. [LH]

Silence for meditation

Lord, graciously hear us, for we seek you alone. Calm our bodies and minds with the peace which passes understanding, and make us radiant with joy; through your Son, Jesus Christ our Lord. [LH, LBW]

+

Antiphon to the OLD TESTAMENT CANTICLE *Surge, illuminare*

The Lord will be your ever**last**ing light,*
and your God will **be** your glory. [PBO]

A Song of Isaiah Isaiah 60:1-3, 11a, 14c, 18-19

Arise, shine, for your **light** has come,*
and the glory of the Lord has **dawned** upon you.

For behold, darkness cov**ers** the land;*
deep gloom en**shrouds** the peoples.

But over you the **Lord** will rise,*
and his glory will ap**pear** upon you.

Nations will stream **to** your light,*
and kings to the brightness **of** your dawning.

Your gates will al**ways** be open;*
by day or night they will nev**er** be shut.

They will call you The City **of** the Lord,*
The Zion of the Holy **One** of Israel.

Violence will no more be heard **in** your land,*
ruin or destruction with**in** your borders.

You will call your **walls**, Salvation,*
and all your **por**tals, Praise.

The sun will no more be your **light** by day;*
by night you will not need the brightness **of** the moon.

The Lord will be your ever**last**ing light,*
and your God will **be** your glory. [BCP]

Antiphon The Lord will be your ever**last**ing light,*
and your God will **be** your glory.

Silence for meditation

God of light and glory, into the darkness of the world you have poured the brightness of your presence: Grant that all the peoples of the earth may come to worship you, walk by your light, and rejoice in your glory; through Jesus Christ our Lord. [PHP]

+

Antiphon to PSALM 108 *Paratum cor meum*

Lord, send out your light **and** your truth*
that **they** may lead me. [LH: Ps. 43:3]

108 *Prayer for victory*

1 My heart is firmly fixed, O God, my **heart** is fixed;*
I will sing **and** make melody.

2 Wake up, my spirit;
awake, **lute** and harp;*
I myself will wak**en** the dawn.

3 I will confess you among the peo**ples**, O LORD;*
I will sing praises to you a**mong** the nations.

4 For your lovingkindness is greater **than** the heavens,*
and your faithfulness reaches **to** the clouds.

5 Exalt yourself above the heav**ens**, O God,*
and your glory over **all** the earth.

6 So that those who are dear to you may **be** delivered,*
save with your right hand and **an**swer me.

7 God spoke from his holy **place** and said,*
"I will exult and parcel out Shechem;
I will divide the val**ley** of Succoth.

8 Gilead is mine and Manas**seh** is mine;*
Ephraim is my helmet and Ju**dah** my scepter.

9 Moab is my washbasin,
on Edom I throw down my san**dal** to claim it,*
and over Philistia will I **shout** in triumph."

10 Who will lead me into **the** strong city?*
Who will bring me **in**to Edom?

11 Have you not cast us **off**, O God?*
you no longer go out, O God, **with** our armies.

12 Grant us your help a**gainst** the enemy,*
for vain is the **help** of man.

13 With God we will do **val**iant deeds,*
and he shall tread our enemies **un**der foot.

Antiphon Lord, send out your light **and** your truth,*
that **they** may lead me.

Silence for meditation

Lord, accept the prayers of your servants, and prepare our hearts to praise your holy Name. Come to our aid in times of trouble, that we may sing you songs of thanksgiving; through Jesus Christ our Lord. [LH, LBW]

Stand

THE HYMN is sung.

on December 27, St. John's Day

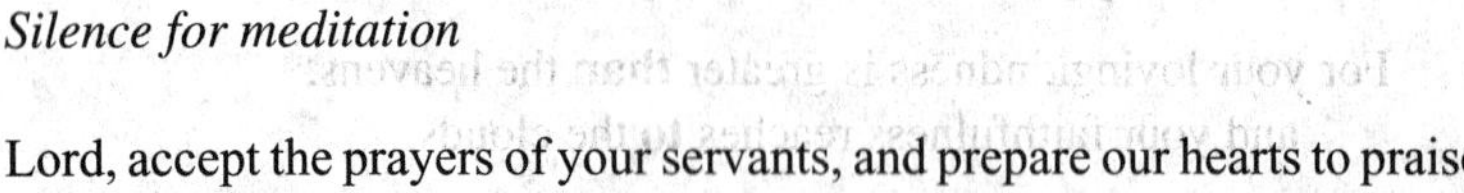

2 Your great I AM's Saint John records,
Signs of your grace divine:
"I am the way, the truth, the life;
The light; the living vine;
Your soul's true bread; thirst quenching stream.
All these I am, and more;
The faithful shepherd of the flock,
The sheepfold's only door."

3 O Word made flesh, your deeds and words
Refresh our hearts like dew.
Our thanks we raise that all John wrote
Bears witness, Lord, to you.

We praise you that John's voice still lives
Your glory to proclaim
Whereby your Spirit gives us life,
The faith to bear your Name. [H82 245]

Text: F. Samuel Janzow, 1913-2001
Tune: *Noel,* English melody, adapt. Arthur Seymour Sullivan, 1842-1900 CMD

on January 3 and 8

2 Worship we the Godhead,
Love incarnate, love divine;
Worship we our Jesus:
But wherewith for sacred sign?

3 Love shall be our token,
Love be yours and love be mine,
Love to God and neighbor,
Love for plea and gift and sign. [H82 84, SBH 37]

Text: Christina Georgina Rossetti, 1830-1894
Tune: *Gartan*, Traditional Irish Air 67 67

Sit

One or two LESSONS are read.

Silence for meditation follows each reading.

Year 1

December 27 St. John's Day
Proverbs 8:22-30

The LORD created me at the beginning of his work, the first of his acts of long ago.

1 John 5:1-12

Everyone who believes that Jesus is the Christ has been born of God, and everyone who loves the parent loves the child. [BCP: John 13:20-35]

Year 2

Proverbs 8:22-30

The LORD created me at the beginning of his work, the first of his acts of long ago.
or Isaiah 44:1-8 [BCP]

1 John 5:1-12

Everyone who believes that Jesus is the Christ has been born of God, and everyone who loves the parent loves the child. [BCP: John 13:20-35]

RESPONSORY for St. John's Day

We declare to you the eternal life
that was **with** the Father*
and was re**veal**ed to us
We are **writ**ing these things*
so that your joy may **be** complete.

The life was revealed and we have seen it, and declare to you
the e**ter**nal life*
that was with the Father and was re**veal**ed to us.
We know that the Son of God has

These **things** are written*
so that you may come to believe
that Jesus is the **Son** of God,
and that through believing you
may have life **in** his Name*
so that your joy may **be**
complete.
[LH: 1 John 1:2,4; John 16:24; 20:31]

come and has given us understanding so that we may know
him **who** is true;*
and we are in his Son **Je**sus
Christ.
He is the true God and e**ter**nal
life,*
that was with the Father and
was re**veal**ed to us.
[LH: 1 John 1:2; 5:20]

January 3
Genesis 28:10-22

I will not leave you until I have done what I have promised you.

1 Kings 19:9-18

Now there was a great wind, so strong that it was splitting the mountains and breaking the rocks in pieces before the LORD, but the LORD was not in the wind; and after the wind an earthquake but the LORD was not in the earthquake; and after the earthquake a fire, but the LORD was not in the fire; and after the fire, a sound of sheer silence.

Hebrews 11:13-22

They desire a better country, that is, a heavenly one.

Ephesians 4:17-32

Clothe yourselves with the new self, created according to the likeness of God in true righteousness and holiness.

January 8

Isaiah 59:15-21

Those in the west shall fear the name of the LORD, and those in the east, his glory.

Revelation 2:8-17

Be faithful unto death, and I will give you the crown of life.

Exodus 17:1-7

Strike the rock, and water will come out of it, so that the people may drink.

Colossians 1:15-23

Christ is before all things, and in him all things hold together.

RESPONSORY for January 3 and 8

The nations shall see your **vin**dication,*
and all the **kings** your glory.
  And you shall be called by **a** new name*
  that the mouth of the **Lord** will give.
You shall be a crown of beauty in the hand **of** the Lord,*
and a royal diadem in the hand **of** your God.
  And you shall be called by **a** new name*
  that the mouth of the **Lord** will give. [LH: Isa 62:2-3]

I saw the Spirit descending from heaven **like** a dove,*
and it re**main**ed on him.
  I myself have seen and have **test**ified*
  that this is the **Son** of God.
The one who sent me to baptize with water **said** to me,*
"He on whom you see the Spirit descend and remain is the one who baptizes with the **Ho**ly Spirit."*
  I myself have seen and have **test**ified*
  that this is the **Son** of God.
[LH: John 1:32, 34, 33]

Antiphon to the BENEDICTUS

December 27. St. John's Day

The Word became flesh and **lived** among us,*
and we have **seen** his glory. [LH: John 1:14]

January 3

The Word became flesh and lived among us,
full of **grace** and truth.*
And from his fullness we have all received,
grace **up**on grace. [LH: John 1:14, 16]

January 8

The Wise Men offered gifts of gold, frankincense,
and myrrh **to** the Lord,*
the Son of God and **King** most high. [LH]

December 28, January 4, and January 9

Antiphon to PSALM 2 *Quare fremuerunt gentes?*

December 28 Holy Innocents' Day	Out of the mouths of in**fants** and children* you have found praise to **foil** your enemies. [LH:Ps. 8:2-3]
January 4, 9	The Lord said to me "You **are** my Son;* this day have I be**got**ten you." [CSB, SBH, LH, PBO]

2 *The Messiah, King and Conqueror*

1 Why are the nations **in** an uproar?*
Why do the peoples mutter **emp**ty threats?

2 Why do the kings of the earth rise up in revolt,
and the princes **plot** together,*
against the LORD and against **his** Anointed?

3 "Let us break their **yoke**," they say;*
"let us cast off their **bonds** from us."

4 He whose throne is in heav**en** is laughing;*
the Lord has them **in** derision.

5 Then he speaks to them **in** his wrath,*
and his rage fills **them** with terror.

6 "I myself have **set** my king*
upon my holy **hill** of Zion."

7 Let me announce the decree **of** the LORD:*
he said to me, "You are my Son;
this day have I be**got**ten you.

8 Ask of me, and I will give you the nations for **your** inheritance*
and the ends of the earth for **your** possession.

9 You shall crush them with an **i**ron rod*
and shatter them like a **piece** of pottery."

10 And now, you **kings**, be wise;*
be warned, you rulers **of** the earth.

11 Submit to the LORD with fear,*
and with trembling **bow** before him;

12 Lest he be angry, **and** you perish;*
for his wrath is **quick**ly kindled.

13 Happy **are** they all*
who take ref**uge** in him!

Antiphon

December 28 Holy Innocents' Day	Out of the mouths of in**fants** and children* you have found praise to **foil** your enemies.
January 4, 9	The Lord said to me "You **are** my Son;* this day have I be**got**ten you."

Silence for meditation

Lord God, you gave the peoples of the world to be the inheritance of your Son; you crowned him as king of Zion, your holy city, and gave him your Church as his bride. As he proclaims the way of your eternal kingdom, grant that we may serve him faithfully, and so know the royal power of the same Jesus Christ our Lord. [LH, LBW]

+

Antiphon to the OLD TESTAMENT CANTICLE *Exultavit cor meum*

My heart exults **in** the Lord;*
he brings low, he al**so** exalts. [LH]

The Song of Hannah 1 Samuel 2:1-10

My heart exults **in** the LORD;*
my strength is exalted **in** my God.

My mouth de**rides** my enemies,*
exultant because **you** have saved me.

There is no Holy One **like** the LORD;*
there is no Rock **like** our God.

Stop **your** proud boasting;*
let not arrogance come **from** your mouth;

For the LORD is a **God** of knowledge,*
and by him ac**tions** are weighed.

The bows of the mighty are broken,*
but the feeble **gird** on strength.

Those who were full have hired themselves **out** for bread,*
but those who were hungry are **fat** with spoil.

The barren has borne **se**ven children,*
but she who has many children **is** forlorn.

The LORD kills and **brings** to life;*
he brings down to Sheol and **rais**es up.

The LORD makes poor **and** makes rich;*
he brings low, he al**so** exalts.

He raises up the poor **from** the dust;*
he lifts the needy **from** the ashes

To make them **sit** with princes*
and inherit a **seat** of honor.

The pillars of the earth **are** the LORD's,*
and on them he has **set** the world.

He will guard the feet of his **faith**ful ones;*
but the wicked shall perish in darkness,
for not by might does **one** prevail.

The LORD! His adversaries **shall** be shattered*
when the High God will thunder **out** of heaven.

The LORD will judge the ends **of** the earth;*
he will give strength to his king
and exalt the power of **his** annointed. [NRSV, PHP]

Antiphon My heart exults **in** the Lord;*
he brings low, he al**so** exalts.

Silence for meditation

Grant to your people, we pray you, O Lord, such an unshakable steadfastness of faith that, confessing that your only-begotten Son took flesh like ours and was born of the Virgin Mary, we may be set free from the evil that besets us and be confident of a share in his eternal glory; through the same Jesus Christ our Lord. [Leo., Gel.; AC; RS Mon. before Epiph.]

+

Antiphon to PSALM 20 *Exaudiat te Dominus*

December 28 Holy Innocents' Day	Lord, these little ones praise you and skip with **joy** like lambs,* for you have **set** them free. [LH]
January 4, 9	We will **shout** for joy* at the victory **of** our God. [PBO]

20 *A prayer for the king's victory*

1 May the LORD answer you in the **day** of trouble,*
the Name of the God of Ja**cob** defend you;

2 Send you help from his **ho**ly place*
and strengthen you **out** of Zion;

3 Remember **all** your offerings*
and accept **your** burnt sacrifice;

4 Grant you your **heart's** desire*
and prosper **all** your plans.

5 We will shout for joy at your victory
and triumph in the Name **of** our God;*
may the LORD grant all **your** requests.

6 Now I know that the LORD gives victory to **his** anointed;*
he will answer him out of his holy heaven,
with the victorious strength of **his** right hand.

7 Some put their trust in chariots and **some** in horses,*
but we will call upon the Name of the **LORD** our God.

8 They collapse **and** fall down,*
but we will arise **and** stand upright.

9 O LORD, give victory **to** the king*
and answer us **when** we call.

Antiphon

December 28 Holy Innocents' Day	Lord, these little ones praise you and skip with **joy** like lambs,* for you have **set** them free.
January 4, 9	We will **shout** for joy* at the victory **of** our God.

Silence for meditation

Lord God, you accepted the perfect sacrifice of your Son upon the cross: Hear us during times of trouble and protect us by the power of his Name, that we who share his struggle on earth may share in his victory in heaven, where he lives and reigns with you and the Holy Spirit, one God, now and for ever. [LH, LBW]

Stand

THE HYMN is sung.

on December 28 *Salvete, flores martyrum*

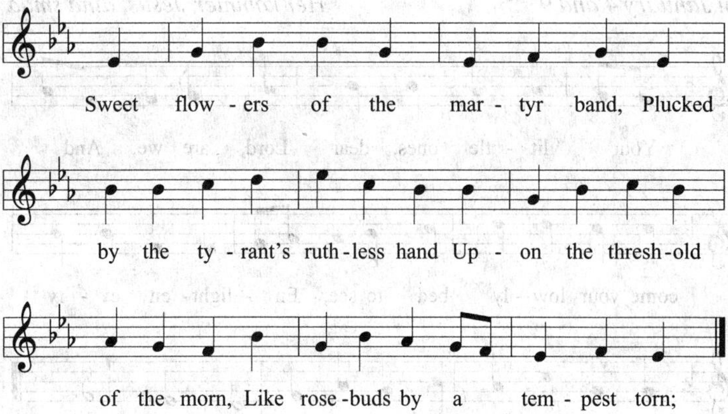

2 You, tender flock of lambs, we sing,
First victims slain for Christ your King;
Beneath the altar's heavenly ray
With martyr-palms and crowns you play.

3 O mothers, dry your tears; no more
These pledges of your love deplore;
They follow, fair and joyful train,
The Lamb for their salvation slain.

4 O Jesus, virgin-born to you
Eternal praise is ever due,
Whom with the Father we adore
And Holy Spirit evermore. [TLH 273 alt., H82 246, 247]

Text: Marcus Aurelius Clemens Prudentius, 348-412; tr. Henry Williams Baker, 1821-1877 and John Mason Neale, 1818-1866

Tune: *Das walt' Gott Vater,* Daniel Vetter, d. 1721 LM

on January 4 and 9 *Her kommer, Jesus, dina smaa*

2 With songs we hasten you to greet,
And kiss the ground before your feet.
O blessed hour, O sweetest night
That gave you birth, our soul's delight.

3 O draw us wholly to you, Lord,
And to us all your grace accord;
True faith and love to us impart,
That we may hold you in our heart.

4 Until at last we too proclaim,
With all your saints, your glorious Name;
In paradise our songs renew,
And praise you as the angels do. [SBH 49, LBW 52]

Text: Hans Adolph Brorson, 1694 - 1764;
tr. Harriet Reynolds Krauth Spaeth, 1845-1925, alt.
Tune: *Her kommer dine arme smaa,* Johann A.P. Schultz, 1747-1800 LM

Sit

One or two LESSONS are read.

Silence for meditation follows each reading.

Year 1

December 28 Holy Innocents' Day
Isaiah 49:13-23

Sing for joy, O heavens, and exult, O earth; break forth, O mountains, into singing! For the LORD has comforted his people, and will have compassion on his suffering ones.

Matthew 18:1-14

Tale care that you do not despise one of these little ones; for, I tell you, in heaven their angels continually see the face of my Father in heaven.

Year 2

Isaiah 49:13-23

Sing for joy, O heavens, and exult, O earth; break forth, O mountains, into singing! For the LORD has comforted his people, and will have compassion on his suffering ones.

Matthew 18:1-14

Tale care that you do not despise one of these little ones; for, I tell you, in heaven their angels continually see the face of my Father in heaven.

RESPONSORY for Holy Innocents' Day

The Word became flesh and **lived** among us.*
  We have seen his glory, the
  glory as of a father's only son,
  full of **grace** and truth.
In the beginning was the Word,

I will rejoice **in** Jerusalem,*
and delight **in** my people.
  No more shall the sound of
  weep**ing** be heard*
  or the cry **of** distress.
Death will **be** no more;*

and the Word was with God, and the **Word** was God.*
We have seen his glory, the
glory as of a father's only son,
full of **grace** and truth.
[CSB, SBH, LH: John 1:14,1]

January 4
Exodus 3:1-15

I have observed the misery of my people . . . I have heard their cry . . . ; I know their sufferings, and I have come down to deliver them.

Hebrews 11:23-31

By faith Moses, when he was grown up, refused to be called a son of Pharoah's daughter, choosing rather to share ill-treatment with the people of God.

January 9
Isaiah 63:1-5

It is I, announcing vindication, mighty to save.

mourning and crying and pain will be no more, for behold, I am making **all** things new.
No more shall the sound of
weep**ing** be heard*
or the cry **of** distress.
[LH: Isa. 65:19; Rev. 21:4,5]

Joshua 3:14-4:7

While all Israel were crossing over on dry ground, the priests who bore the ark of the covenant of the LORD stood on dry ground in the middle of the Jordan.

Ephesians 5:1-20

Once you were in darkness, but now in the Lord you are light. Live as children of light.

Isaiah 45:14-19

The wealth of Egypt and the merchandise of Ethiopia, and the Sabeans, tall of stature, shall come over to you and be yours, they shall follow you.

Revelation 2:18-29

To everyone who conquers and continues to do my works to the end, I will give authority over the nations, to rule them with an iron rod. I will also give the morning star.

Colossians 1:24-2:7

To his saints God chose to make known how great among the Gentiles are the riches of the glory of this mystery, which is Christ in you, the hope of glory.

RESPONSORY for January 4 and 9

From **all** eternity,*
God destined us for adoption **as** his children*
according to the good pleasure **of** his will,*
to the praise of his **glor**ious grace.
Long a**go** he knew us*
and chose to make us in the image of **his** own Son
according to the good pleasure **of** his will,*
to the praise of his **glor**ious grace.
[LH: Ephes. 1:5; see Rom. 8:29]

Jesus Christ, Light from Light, whom John baptized in the Jordan has ap**pear**ed to us:*
we believe that he was born of the **Vir**gin Mary.
The heavens opened above him, and the voice of the Fa**ther** was heard.*
We believe that he was born of the **Vir**gin Mary. [LH]

Antiphon to the BENEDICTUS

December 28. Holy Innocents' Day

At the king's command these children were **put** to death;*
they **died** for Christ.
And now in the glory of heaven as they follow him,
the sinless Lamb, they **sing** for ever:*
Glory to **you**, O Lord. [LH]

January 4

Christ our God, in whom the fullness of de**i**ty dwells,*
took upon himself our wounded nature
and became the first-born of **all** creation. [LH: see Col. 2:9, 1:15]

January 9

We observed his star **at** its rising*
and have come with gifts to wor**ship** the Lord.
[CSB, SBH, LH: see Matt. 2:2]

December 29, January 5, and January 10

Antiphon to PSALM 96 *Cantate Domino*

Let the heavens rejoice,
and let the earth be glad be**fore** the Lord;*
for **he** has come. [LH, PBO]

96 *The Lord, King, and Judge of the world*

1 Sing to the LORD **a** new song;*
sing to the LORD, all **the** whole earth.

2 Sing to the LORD and **bless** his Name;*
proclaim the good news of his salvation from **day** to day.

3 Declare his glory a**mong** the nations*
and his wonders a**mong** all peoples.

4 For great is the LORD and greatly **to** be praised;*
he is more to be feared **than** all gods.

5 As for all the gods of the nations, they **are** but idols;*
but it is the LORD who **made** the heavens.

6 Oh, the majesty and magnificence **of** his presence!*
Oh, the power and the splendor of his **sanc**tuary!

7 Ascribe to the LORD, you families **of** the peoples;*
ascribe to the LORD hon**or** and power.

8 Ascribe to the LORD the honor **due** his Name;*
bring offerings and come in**to** his courts.

9 Worship the LORD in the beau**ty** of holiness;*
let the whole earth trem**ble** before him.

10 Tell it out among the nations: "The **LORD** is king!*
he has made the world so firm that it cannot be moved;
he will judge the peo**ples** with equity."

11 Let the heavens rejoice, and let the earth be glad;
let the sea thunder and all **that** is in it;*
let the field be joyful and all that **is** therein.

12 Then shall all the trees of the wood shout for joy
before the LORD **when** he comes,*
when he comes to **judge** the earth.

13 He will judge the **world** with righteousness*
and the peoples **with** his truth.

Antiphon

Let the heavens rejoice,
and let the earth be glad be**fore** the Lord;*
for **he** has come.

Silence for meditation

Lord Jesus, the incarnate Word, when you consented to dwell with us, the heavens were glad and the earth rejoiced. In hope and love we await your return. Help us to proclaim your glory to those who do not know you, until the whole earth sings a new song to you and the Father and the Holy Spirit, one God, now and for ever. [LHd, LBW]

+

Antiphon to the OLD TESTAMENT CANTICLE *Attende caelum*

[CSB, SBH: *Audite Coeli*]

Extol the greatness of our God. [LH]

The Song of Moses Deuteronomy 32:1-4, 7, 36a, 43

Give ear, you heavens, to **what** I say,*
let the earth hearken to the words **of** my mouth.

May my teaching fall like **drops** of rain;*
my words distill **like** the dew,
Like gentle rain up**on** the grass,*
like showers on **grow**ing plants.

I will sing of the **LORD's** renown,*
extoll the greatness **of** our God,
The Rock whose **work** is perfect,*
for all his **ways** are just;
A faithful God, who **does** no wrong,*
righteous and **true** is he.

Remember the **days** of old;*
consider the **years** long past;
Ask your parents **to** recount it*
and your elders to tell **you** the tale.

The LORD will vindi**cate** his people*
and have compassion **on** his servants.
Rejoice with **him** you heavens;*
all you gods, bow **down** before him. [NSRV, REB, LH]

Antiphon Extol the greatness of our God.

Silence for meditation

O God, exaltation of the humble and strength of the righteous, you taught your people through Moses to sing your praise, that the law which he delivered to them might be helpful to us: Show your power among all nations that, in the forgiveness of sins, terror may turn to joy, and fear of retribution to salvation; through your Son, Jesus Christ our Lord.

[Gel., MR, LBW]

+

Antiphon to PSALM 72 *Deus, judicium*

Begotten of the Father before the daystar shone or **time** began,*
the Lord and Savior has humbled himself to be **born** for us.

[LH]

72 *The kingdom of peace*

1 Give the king your jus**tice**, O God,*
and your righteousness to **the** King's Son;

2 That he may rule your **peo**ple righteously*
and the **poor** with justice;

3 That the mountains may bring prosperity **to** the people,*
and the little **hills** bring righteousness.

4 He shall defend the needy a**mong** the people;*
he shall rescue the poor and crush **the** oppressor.

5 He shall live as long as the sun and **moon** endure,*
from one generation **to** another.

6 He shall come down like rain upon **the** mown field,*
like showers that wa**ter** the earth.

7 In his time shall the **right**eous flourish;*
there shall be abundance of peace till the moon shall **be** no more.

8 He shall rule from **sea** to sea,*
and from the River to the ends **of** the earth.

9 His foes shall bow **down** before him,*
and his enemies **lick** the dust.

10 The kings of Tarshish and of the isles **shall** pay tribute,*
and the kings of Arabia and Saba **of**fer gifts.

11 All kings shall bow **down** before him,*
and all the nations **do** him service.

12 For he shall deliver the poor who cries out **in** distress,*
and the oppressed who **has** no helper.

13 He shall have pity on the low**ly** and poor;*
he shall preserve the lives **of** the needy.

14 He shall redeem their lives from oppres**sion** and violence,*
and dear shall their blood be **in** his sight.

15 Long may he live!
and may there be given to him gold **from** Arabia;*
may prayer be made for him always,
and may they bless him all **the** day long.

16 May there be abundance of grain on the earth,
growing thick even **on** the hilltops;*
may its fruit flourish like Lebanon,
and its grain like grass up**on** the earth.

17 May his Name remain for ever
and be established as long as the **sun** endures;*
may all the nations bless themselves in him and
call him blessed.

18 Blessed be the Lord GOD, the **God** of Israel,*
who alone does **won**drous deeds!

19 And blessed be his glorious **Name** for ever,*
and may all the earth be filled with his glory.
A**men**. Amen.

Antiphon Begotten of the Father before the daystar shone
or **time** began,*
the Lord and Savior has humbled himself
to be **born** for us.

Silence for meditation

Almighty God, you gave the kingdom of justice and peace to David and his descendant, our Lord Jesus Christ: Extend this kingdom to every nation, so that through your Son the poor may receive justice, the destitute relief, and the people of the earth peace in the Name of him who lives and reigns with you and the Holy Spirit, one God, now and for ever.

[LHd, LBW]

+

Stand

THE HYMN is sung. *Heu quid iaces stabulo [Eya mea anima]*

2 “For the world a love supreme
Brought me to this stable;
All creation to redeem
I alone am able
By this lowly birth of mine,
Sinner, riches shall be thine,
Matchless gifts and free;
Willingly this yoke I take,
And this sacrifice I make,
Heaping joys for thee.”

3 Christ we praise with voices bold,
Laud and honor raising;
For these mercies manifold
Join the hosts in praising:
Father, glory be to thee
For the wondrous charity
Of thy Son our Lord.
Better witness to thy worth,
Purer praise than ours on earth,
Angels songs afford. [H82 97]

Text: Jean Mauburn, 1460-1503; tr. Elizabeth Rundle Charles, 1828-1896, and others
Tune: *Dies est laetitiae* from *Piae Cantiones*, 1582 76 76 775 775

Sit

One or two LESSONS are read.

Silence for meditation follows each reading.

Year 1

December 29
Isaiah 12:1-6

Shout aloud and sing for joy, O royal Zion, for great in your midst is the Holy One of Israel.

Revelation 1:1-8

I am the Alpha and the Omega, says the Lord God, who is and who was and who is to come, the Almighty.

January 5
Joshua 1:1-9

Be strong and courageous; do not be frightened or dismayed, for the LORD your God is with you wherever you go.
or Isa 66:18-23 [BCP]

Hebrews 11:32-12:2

Let us lay aside every weight and sin that clings so closely, and let us run with perseverance the race that is set before us.
or Rom. 15:7-13 [BCP]

Year 2

2 Samuel 23:13-17b

David said longingly, "O that someone would give me water to drink from the well of Bethlehem that is by the gate!"

2 John 1-13

But now, dear lady, I ask you, not as though I were writing you a new commandment, but one we have had from the beginning, let us love one another.

Jonah 2:2-9

Deliverance belongs to the LORD!
or Isa 66:18-23 [BCP]

Ephesians 6:10-20

Finally, be strong in the Lord and in the strength of his power.
or Rom. 15:7-13 [BCP]

January 10

Isaiah 65:1-9

I was ready to be sought by those who did not ask, to be found by those who did not seek me.

Jeremiah 23:1-8

The days are surely coming, says the LORD, when I will raise up for David a righteous Branch, and he shall reign as king and deal wisely, and shall execute justice and righteousness in the land.

Revelation 3:1-6

Wake up, and strengthen what remains and is on the point of death, for I have not found your works perfect in the sight of my God.

Colossians 2:8-23

In Christ the whole fullness of deity dwells bodily, and you have come to fullness in him, who is the head of every ruler and authority.

RESPONSORY

I will be their God, and they shall **be** my people.*
  The nations shall know that I the Lord sanctify **Is**rael.
When my sanctuary is in the midst of them for evermore, I will make a new covenant with the house of Israel, and the **house** of Judah.*
  The nations shall know that I the Lord sanctify **Is**rael.

[LH: Ezek. 37:27-28; Jer. 31:31]

Let us give thanks to **God** our Father,*
  he has rescued us from the power of darkness and transferred us into the kingdom of his be**lo**ved Son.
Every generous act of giving, with every perfect gift is from above, coming down from the Fa**ther** of lights;*
  he has rescued us from the power of darkness and transferred us into the kingdom of his be**lo**ved Son.

[LH: Col. 1:12,13; James 1:17]

Antiphon to the BENEDICTUS

December 29

The shepherds said to **one** another:*
Let us go now to Bethlehem and see this thing which the Lord has made **known** to us. [LH: Luke 2:15]

January 5

The Lord has come **to** his people*
and **set** them free. [LH:Luke 1:68]

January 10

All peoples, **bear**ing gifts,*
will come from afar to wor**ship** the Lord. [LH]

December 30 and January 11

Antiphon to PSALM 93 *Dominus regnavit*

Ever since the **world** began,*
your throne, O Lord, has **been** established. [PBO]

93 *Splendor of God the Creator*

1 The LORD is king;
he has put on splen**did** apparel;*
the LORD has put on his apparel
and girded him**self** with strength.

2 He has made the whole **world** so sure*
that it can**not** be moved;

3 Ever since the world began, your throne has **been** established;*
you are from **ev**erlasting.

4 The waters have lifted up, O LORD,
the waters have lifted **up** their voice;*
the waters have lifted up their **pound**ing waves.

5 Mightier than the sound of many waters,
mightier than the breakers **of** the sea,*
mightier is the LORD who **dwells** on high.

6 Your testimonies are **ver**y sure,*
and holiness adorns your house, O LORD,
for ever and for **ev**ermore

Antiphon

Ever since the **world** began,*
your throne, O Lord, has **been** established.

Silence for meditation

Lord Jesus, king of glory, when you rose from the grave in the power of the Spirit, you firmly established your kingdom, never to be shaken or destroyed by death: May your will be done on earth as in heaven until the Church is made holy by your embrace, our Redeemer and our Lord.

[LHd, LBW]

+

Antiphon to the OLD TESTAMENT CANTICLE *Domine, audivi*

His radiance spreads o**ver** the skies,*
and his splendor **fills** the earth.

A Song of Habakkuk Habakkuk 3:1-4, 6-10, 12-13, 15-16, 18-19

O LORD, I have heard of **your** renown;*
I am in awe, O LORD, **of** your work.
In our own **time** revive it;*
in our own time make it known,
in wrath re**mem**ber mercy.

God **came** from Teman,*
the Holy One **from** Mount Paran;
His radiance cov**ered** the skies,*
and his splendor **filled** the earth.
His brightness is **like** the dawn,*
rays flash from his hand where his pow**er** lay hidden.

He stopped and **shook** the earth,*
he looked and made the **na**tions tremble;
The eternal moun**tains** were shattered,*
along his ancient pathways
the everlasting **hills** sank low.
I saw the tents of Cush**an** collapse,*
the tent curtains of Midian flutter.
Was your wrath against the rivers, O LORD,
or your rage a**gainst** the sea*
when you drove your horses and chari**ots** to victory?
You brandished your **na**ked bow;*
sated were the arrows at **your** command.

You split the **earth** with rivers;*
the mountains saw you and **writhed** in fear.
A torrent of wat**er** swept by,*
and the deep sea thun**dered** aloud.
In fury you **trod** the earth;*
in anger you trampled **down** the nations.
You came forth to **save** your people;*
to save **your** annointed.

You trampled the sea **with** your horses,*
churning the **might**y waters.

I hear, and my **bod**y quakes;*
    my lips quiver **at** the sound;
Trembling comes o**ver** my bones,*
    and my feet tot**ter** beneath me.
Yet I will exult **in** the LORD*
    and rejoice in the **God** who saves me.
God the LORD **is** my strength:*
    he makes my feet nimble as the deer
    and sets me up**on** the heights. [PHP]

Antiphon His radiance spreads o**ver** the skies,*
    and his splendor **fills** the earth. [CSB, LH, NSRV alt.]

Silence for meditation

God of majesty and power, when you came forth to save your people the earth rose with joy to greet you: In your mercy renew in us the fruit of your love, fill the world with your splendor, and show the nations the light of your truth; through Jesus Christ our Lord. [PHP]

+

Antiphon to PSALM 21 *Domine, in virtute tua*

He asked you for life, and you **gave** it to him:*
    length of days, for ev**er** and ever. [PBO]

21 *Thanksgiving for the king's victory*

1 The king rejoices in your **strength**, O LORD;*
how greatly he exults **in** your victory!

2 You have given him his **heart's** desire;*
you have not denied him the request **of** his lips.

3 For you meet him with blessings **of** prosperity,*
and set a crown of fine gold up**on** his head.

4 He asked you for life, and you **gave** it to him:*
length of days, for ev**er** and ever.

5 His honor is great, because **of** your victory;*
splendor and majesty have you be**stowed** upon him.

6 For you will give him everlast**ing** felicity*
and will make him glad with the joy **of** your presence.

7 For the king puts his trust **in** the LORD;*
because of the loving-kindness of the Most High,
he **will** not fall.

8 Your hand will lay hold upon **all** your enemies;*
your right hand will seize all **those** who hate you.

9 You will make them like a **fier**y furnace*
at the time of your appear**ing**, O LORD;

10 You will swallow them up **in** your wrath,*
and fire **shall** consume them.

11 You will destroy their offspring **from** the land*
and their descendants from among the peoples **of** the earth.

12 Though they intend evil against you
and devise **wick**ed schemes,*
yet they shall **not** prevail.

13 For you will put **them** to flight*
and aim your ar**rows** at them.

14 Be exalted, O LORD, **in** your might;*
we will sing and **praise** your power.

Antiphon He asked you for life, and you **gave** it to him:*
length of days, for ev**er** and ever.

Silence for meditation

Father, you have given us life on this earth and have met us with the richness of your grace: Bestow on us your greatest blessing, the fullness of eternal life in Jesus Christ our Lord. [LH, LBW]

Stand

THE HYMN is sung. *Brich an, O schönes Morgenlicht*
[Ermuntre dich, mein schwacher Geist]

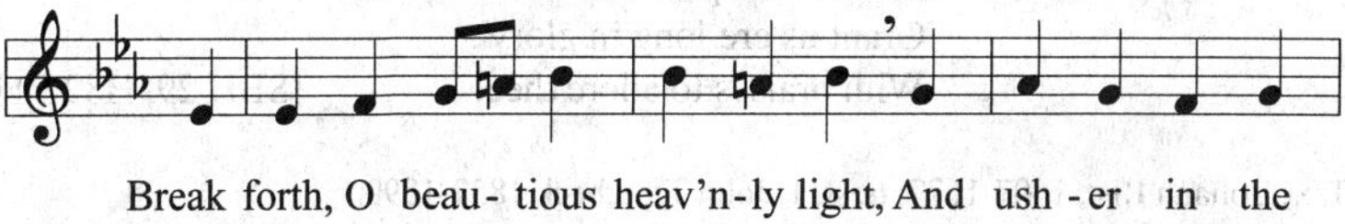

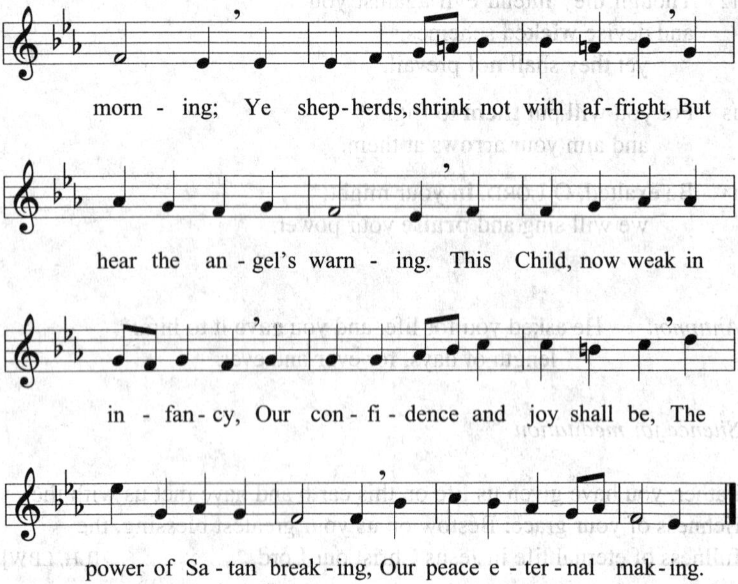

2 All blessing, thanks and praise to thee,
Lord Jesus Christ, be given:
Thou hast our brother deigned to be,
Our foes in sunder riven.
O grant us through our day of grace
With constant priase to seek thy face;
Grant us ere long in glory
With praises to adore thee. [SBH 29, H82 91]

Text: Johann Rist, 1607-1677; tr. st. 1, John Troutbeck 1832-1899,
st. 2 Arthur Tozer Russell, 1806-1874
Tune: *Schop*, Johann Schop, c. 1600-1665 87 87 88 77

Sit

One or two LESSONS are read.

Silence for meditation follows each reading.

Year 1

December 30

Isaiah 25:1-9

Lo, this is our God; we have waited for him, so that he might save us.

Revelation 1:9-20

Do not be afraid; I am the first and the last, and the living one.

Year 2

1 Kings 17:17-24

Elijah took the child, brought him down from the upper chamber into the house, and gave him to his mother; then Elijah said, "See your son is alive."

3 John 1-15

Beloved, you do faithfully whatever you do for the friends, even though they are strangers to you. They have testified to your love before the church.

Year 1

January 11

Isaiah 65:13-16

The former troubles are forgotten and are hidden from my sight.

Year 2

Isaiah 55:3-9

Nations that do not know you shall run to you, because of the LORD your God, the Holy One of Israel, for he has glorified you.

Revelation 3:7-13

I am coming soon; hold fast what you have, so that no one may seize your crown.

Colossians 3:1-17

When Christ who is your life is revealed, then you also will be revealed with him in glory.

RESPONSORY

The Word became flesh and **lived** among us.*
  We have seen his glory,
  glory as of a father's only son,
  full of **grace** and truth.
He appeared on earth and lived with **hu**mankind.*
  We have seen his glory,
  glory as of a father's only son,
  full of **grace** and truth.

[LH: John 1:14; see Baruch 3:37]

I saw a new heaven and **a** new earth,*
and I heard a loud voice from **the** throne saying:
  The home of God is **a**mong mortals;*
  he will **dwell** with them.
The Lord will wipe every tear **from** their eyes.*
Death will be no more; for the first things have **passed** away.
  The home of God is **a**mong mortals;*
  he will **dwell** with them.

[LH: Revelation 21:1, 3, 4]

Antiphon to the BENEDICTUS

December 30

At the Lord's birth choirs of **an**gels sang:*
  Blessed be our God enthroned as King
  and blessed **be** the Lamb. [LH]

January 11

All those **who** despised you*
shall bow down **at** your feet. [LH: Isaiah 60:14]

December 31, January 12

Antiphon to PSALM 99 *Dominus regnavit, irascantur*

On that day the root of Jesse shall stand as a signal **to** the peoples;*
the nations shall inquire of him,
and his dwelling **shall** be glorious. [Isaiah 11:10]

99 *The power and holiness of God*

1 The LORD is King;
let the **peo**ple tremble.*
he is enthroned upon the cherubim;
let **the** earth shake.

2 The LORD is **great** in Zion;*
he is high a**bove** all peoples.

3 Let them confess his Name, which is **great** and awesome;*
he is the **Ho**ly One.

4 "O mighty King, lover of justice,
you have es**tab**lished equity;*
you have executed justice and righteous**ness** in Jacob."

5 Proclaim the greatness of the LORD our God
and fall down be**fore** his footstool;*
he is the **Ho**ly One.

6 Moses and Aaron among his priests,
and Samuel among those who call up**on** his Name,*
they called upon the LORD, and he **an**swered them.

7 He spoke to them out of the pil**lar** of cloud;*
they kept his testimonies and the decree **that** he gave them.

8 O LORD our God, you answered **them** indeed;*
you were a God who forgave them,
yet punished them for their **e**vil deeds.

9 Proclaim the greatness of the LORD our God
and worship him upon his **ho**ly hill;*
for the LORD our God is the **Ho**ly One.

Antiphon

On that day the root of Jesse shall stand as a signal **to** the peoples;*
the nations shall inquire of him,
and his dwelling **shall** be glorious.

Silence for meditation

Most holy God, enthroned upon the cherubim, no one can look upon you and live: In your mercy, forgive us our sins and sanctify us through your life-giving Word, that we may live to proclaim your praise; through Jesus Christ our Lord. [PHP]

+

Antiphon to the OLD TESTAMENT CANTICLE *Ecce, Deus*

Cry a**loud**, O Zion;*
the Holy One of Israel is in the **midst** of you. [PBO]

A Song of Isaiah Isaiah 12:2-6

Surely it is **God** who saves me;*
    I will trust in him and not **be** afraid.
For the Lord is my stronghold and my **sure** defense,*
    and he will **be** my Savior.
Therefore you shall draw water **with** rejoicing*
    from the springs **of** salvation.
And on that day **you** shall say,*
    Give thanks to the Lord and call up**on** his Name;
Make his deeds known a**mong** the peoples;*
    see that they remember that his Name **is** exalted.
Sing the praises of the Lord, for he has **done** great things,*
    and this is known in **all** the world.
Cry aloud, inhabitants of Zion, ring **out** your joy,*
    for the great one in the midst of you is the Holy **One** of Israel.

[BCP]

Antiphon Cry a**loud**, O Zion;*
    the Holy One of Israel is in the **midst** of you.

Silence for meditation

Most holy God, our stronghold and our sure defense, so fill us with your mighty presence that by the newness of our life we may make known the great things that you have done for all the world; through Jesus Christ our Lord. [PHP]

+

Antiphon to PSALM 46 *Deus noster refugium*

They shall name him Em**man**uel:*
which means **God** is with us. [PBO: Matt. 1:23]

46 *A mighty fortress is our God*

1 God is our ref**uge** and strength,*
a very present **help** in trouble.

2 Therefore we will not fear, though the **earth** be moved,*
and though the mountains be toppled into the depths
of the sea;

3 Though its waters **rage** and foam,*
and though the mountains tremble **at** its tumult.

4 The LORD of **hosts** is with us;*
the God of Jacob **is** our stronghold.

5 There is a river whose streams make glad the cit**y** of God,*
the holy habitation of **the** Most High.

6 God is in the midst of her;
she shall not be **o**verthrown;*
God shall help her at the **break** of day.

7 The nations make much ado, and the king**doms** are shaken;*
God has spoken, and the earth shall **melt** away.

8 The LORD of **hosts** is with us;*
the God of Jacob **is** our stronghold.

9 Come now and look upon the works **of** the LORD,*
what awesome things he has **done** on earth.

10 It is he who makes war to cease in **all** the world;*
he breaks the bow, and shatters the spear,
and burns the **shields** with fire.

11 "Be still, then, and know that **I** am God;*
I will be exalted among the nations;
I will be exalted **in** the earth."

12 The LORD of **hosts** is with us;*
the God of Jacob **is** our stronghold.

Antiphon They shall name him Em**man**uel:*
which means **God** is with us.

Silence for meditation

Lord God, our refuge and strength, when the restless powers of this world and the waters of hell rise up against your holy city, watch over it and keep it safe. By the river that flows from the throne of the Lamb, purify this new Jerusalem as your chosen dwelling, for you are with us, our stronghold now and for ever. [LHd, LBW]

Stand

THE HYMN is sung. *Es ist ein Ros entsprungen*

2 Isaiah hath foretold it,
The Rose I have in mind,
And Mary's arms enfold it,
The Virgin mother kind.
Through God's eternal will
This Child to her is given
At midnight calm and still.

3 The shepherds heard the story
Proclaimed by angels bright,
How Christ, the Lord of glory,
Was born on earth this night.
To Bethlehem they sped,
And in the manger found him
As angel heralds said.

4 This Flower, whose fragrance tender
With sweetness fills the air,
Dispels with glorious splendor
The darkness everywhere.
True Man yet very God,
From sin and death he saves us
And lightens every load.

5 O Savior, child of Mary,
Who felt our human woe;
O Savior, king of glory,
Who dost our weakness know,
Bring us at length, we pray,
To the bright courts of heaven,
And to the endless day. [CSB 533; SBH 38, H82 81]

Text: German, 15th cent.; tr. st. 1 Theodore Baker (1851-1934),
st. 2-4 Harriet Reynolds Krauth Spaeth (1845-1925), st. 5 John Caspar Mattes (1876-1948)

Tune: *Es ist ein Ros* from *Alte Katholische Geistliche Kirchengesäng,* Cologne, 1599
76 76 676

Sit

One or two LESSONS are read.

Silence for meditation follows each reading.

Year 1

December 31
Isaiah 26:1-6 (7-9)

We have a strong city; he sets up victory like walls and bulwarks.

Year 2

1 Kings 3:5-14

Give your servant therefore an understanding mind to govern your people, able to discern between good and evil.

2 Corinthians 5:16-6:2

If anyone is in Christ, there is a new creation: everything old has passed away; see, everything has become new!
or Revelation 21:1-6 [BCP]

James 4:13-17; 5:7-11

You also must be patient. Strengthen your hearts, for the coming of the Lord is near.
or Revelation 21:1-6 [BCP]

January 12
Isaiah 66:1-2, 22-23

From new moon to new moon, and from sabbath to sabbath, all flesh shall come to worship before me, says the LORD.

Genesis 49:1-2, 8-12

The scepter shall not depart from Judah, nor the ruler's staff from between his feet, until tribute comes to him; and the obedience of the peoples is his.

Revelation 3:14-22

To the one who conquers I will give a place with me on my throne, just as I myself conquered and sat down with my Father on his throne.

Colossians 3:18-4:6

Whatever your task, put yourselves into it, as done for the Lord and not for your masters, since you know that from the Lord you will receive the inheritance as your reward; you serve the Lord Christ.

RESPONSORY

City of God, you will shine with **won**drous light;*
all the ends of the earth will see your light and a**dore** the Lord.

You who once were far off have been brought near through the **blood** of Christ;*
for he is our peace who has

Many nations will come to you from **far** away*
bearing gifts in their hands for the **King** of heaven.
They will come from east and west, from **north** and south,*
bearing gifts in their hands for the **King** of heaven.
[LH: see Tobit 13:9, 11; Luke 13:29]

made us one.
Christ came and proclaimed peace to you who were far off and peace to those **who** were near,*
for he is our peace who has **made** us one.
[LH: Ephes. 2:13-14, 17]

Antiphon to the BENEDICTUS

December 31

Suddenly there was with the angel a multitude of the heavenly host, praising **God** and saying,*
Glory to God in highest heaven,
and peace to his peo**ple** on earth. [LH: Luke 2:13]

January 12

He is the one of whom it has been written:
Christ is born in **Israel**;*
his kingdom will **last** for ever. [LH: see Micah 5:2; Luke 1:33]

EVENING PRAYER

Vespers or Evensong during General Time

The SERVICE OF LIGHT may be used to begin Evening Prayer. The service may begin with a procession in which a large, lighted candle is carried to its stand in front of the congregation.

Stand

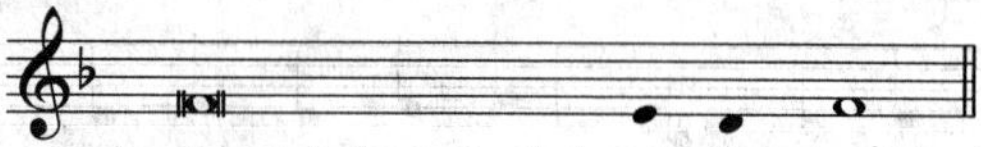

L Jesus Christ is the light of the world,

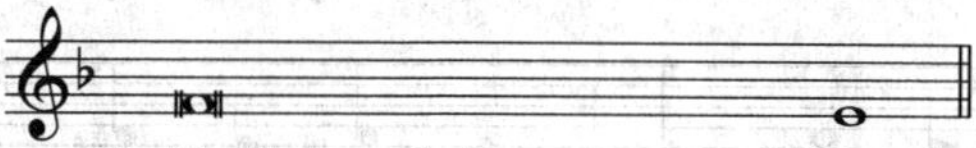

C The light no darkness can over - come.

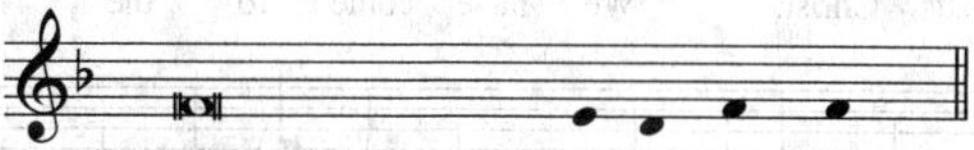

L Stay with us Lord, for it is eve - ning,

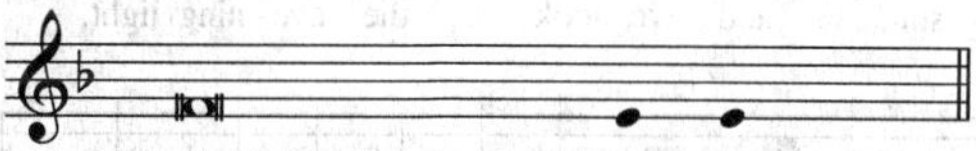

C And the day is almost o - ver.

L Let your light scat - ter the dark - ness,

C And illumine your Church.

[see John 1:14; Luke 24:29; 2 Cor. 4:6]

As this ancient hymn, Phos hilaron, *is sung, the candles on and near the altar are lighted. When the large candle is used, the candles are lighted from its flame. Paraphrases of the hymn "O gladsome light, O grace" (H82 36, SBH 220), "O gladsome light of the Father immortal" (LBW 279), "O brightness of the immortal Father's face" (H82 37) may on occasion replace this translation.*

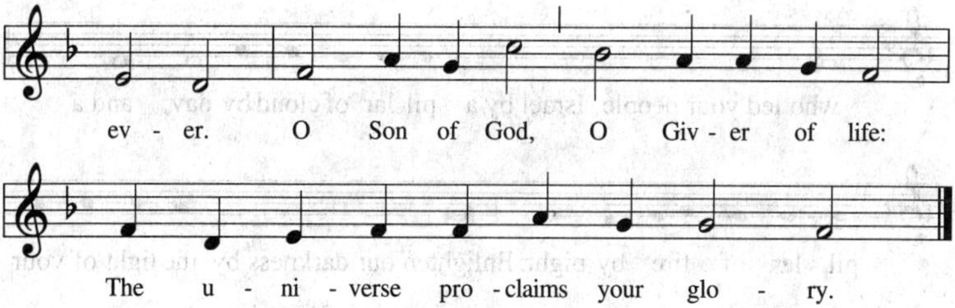

The thanksgiving concludes the Service of Light.

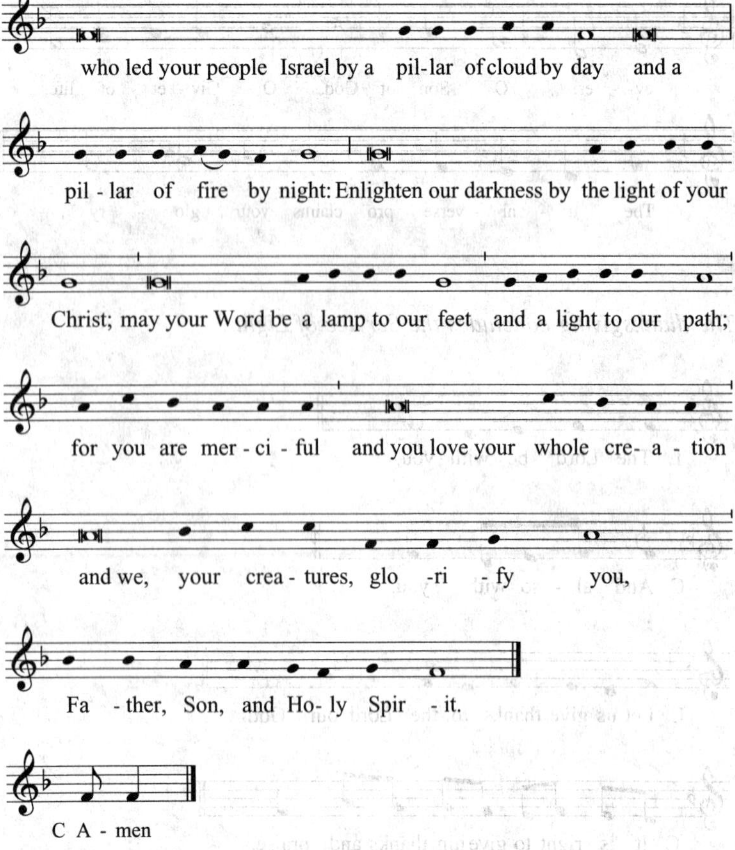

If the Service of Light is omitted, the service begins with the verses given on page 7.

Kneel or sit

The PSALMODY begins with this song for forgiveness and protection, from Psalm 141.

Silence for meditation

L Let the incense of our repentant prayer ascend before you, O Lord, and let your lovingkindness descend upon us, that with purified minds we may sing your praises with the Church on earth and the whole heavenly host, and may glorify you for ever and ever.

C Amen

Sit

A second psalm is sung or said: additional psalms and a New Testament canticle may be sung or said also. Silence for meditation follows each psalm or canticle.

The psalm prayer appropriate to each psalm or canticle follows the silence.

C Amen

Stand

THE HYMN is sung.

Sit

One or two LESSONS are read. Silence for meditation follows each reading.

After this the leader continues:

L In many and various ways God spoke to his people of old by the prophets.

C But now in these last days he has spoken to us by his Son.

Stand

The GOSPEL CANTICLE, Magnificat, *is sung or said, beginning with the antiphon.*

Saturday Here am I, the Servant of the Lord;*
let it be with me according to your word. [Luke 1:38; LH]

On the Transfiguration

First Vespers

Christ Jesus, the reflection of God's glory
and the exact imprint of God's very being,
who sustains all things with his powerful Word
and cleanses us of **all** our sins,*
on this day was exalted in glory upon **the**
high mountain. [LH; see Hebrews 1:3]

On Trinity Sunday

First Vespers

We give you thanks, O God, we **give** you thanks,*
Trinity one and true,
Divinity one and most high,
Unity **one** and holy [LH]

On Christ the King

First Vespers

The Lord God will give to him the throne
of his an**ces**tor David;*
and he will reign over the house of Jacob for ever,
and of his kingdom there will **be** no end.
[Luke 1:32-33; LH]

Sunday The Almighty has done great **things** for me;*
and holy **is** his Name.

On the Transfiguration

Second Vespers

When they heard the voice from the cloud,
the disciples fell to the ground
and were over**come** by fear.*
But Jesus came and touched them, saying,
"Get up and do not **be** afraid." [Matthew 17:6-7; LH]

On Trinity Sunday

Second Vespers

With our whole **heart** and voice*
we ac**claim** you, God;
We offer you our **praise** and worship,*
Unbegotten Father,
Only-begotten Son,
Holy Spirit, advo**cate** and guide;
Most holy and undi**vid**ed Trinity,*
To you be glo**ry** for ever. [LH]

On Christ the King

Second Vespers

All authority in heaven and on earth
has been giv**en** to me,*
says our Lord, the **King** of kings.
[LH; see Matthew 28:18, see Revelation 19:16]

Monday My soul proclaims the greatness of the Lord.

Tuesday My spirit rejoices in God my Savior.

Wednesday God has filled the hungry **with** good things,*
and the rich he has sent **a**way empty.

Thursday God has cast down the mighty **from** their thrones*
and has lifted **up** the lowly.

Friday The Lord has come to the help of his servant **Is**rael,*
For he has remembered his prom**ise** of mercy.

C ✠ My soul pro-claims the great-ness of the Lord; my spir - it re -
joic-es in God my Sav- ior, for he has looked with fa -vor
on his low-ly ser - vant. From this day all gen-er -
a - tions will call me bless - ed. The Al-might- y has
done great things for me, and ho - ly is his Name. He has
mer-cy on those who fear_ him in ev-'ry gen-er - a - tion.
He has shown the strength of his arm; he has scat- tered the
proud in their con-ceit. He has cast down the might-y from their thrones,

The Antiphon is repeated.

Saturday Here am I, the Servant of the Lord;*
let it be with me according to your word. [Luke 1:38; LH]

On the Transfiguration

First Vespers

Christ Jesus, the reflection of God's glory
and the exact imprint of God's very being,
who sustains all things with his powerful Word
and cleanses us of **all** our sins,*
on this day was exalted in glory upon **the** high mountain.

On Trinity Sunday

First Vespers

We give you thanks, O God, we **give** you thanks,*
Trinity one and true,
Divinity one and most high,
Unity **one** and holy

On Christ the King

First Vespers

The Lord God will give to him the throne
of his an**ces**tor David;*
and he will reign over the house of Jacob for ever,
and of his kingdom there will **be** no end.

Sunday The Almighty has done great **things** for me;*
and holy **is** his Name.

On the Transfiguration

Second Vespers

When they heard the voice from the cloud,
the disciples fell to the ground
and were over**come** by fear.*
But Jesus came and touched them, saying,
"Get up and do not **be** afraid."

On Trinity Sunday

Second Vespers

With our whole **heart** and voice*
we ac**claim** you, God;
We offer you our **praise** and worship,*
Unbegotten Father,
Only-begotten Son,
Holy Spirit, advo**cate** and guide;
Most holy and undi**vid**ed Trinity,*
To you be glo**ry** for ever.

On Christ the King

Second Vespers

All authority in heaven and on earth
has been giv**en** to me,*
says our Lord, the **King** of kings.

Monday My soul proclaims the greatness of the Lord.

Tuesday My spirit rejoices in God my Savior.

Wednesday God has filled the hungry **with** good things,*
and the rich he has sent **a**way empty.

Thursday God has cast down the mighty **from** their thrones*
and has lifted **up** the lowly.

Friday The Lord has come to the help of his servant **Is**rael,*
For he has remembered his prom**ise** of mercy.

Kneel or stand

The LITANY is sung or said. The complete Litany may be sung to the alternative musical form.

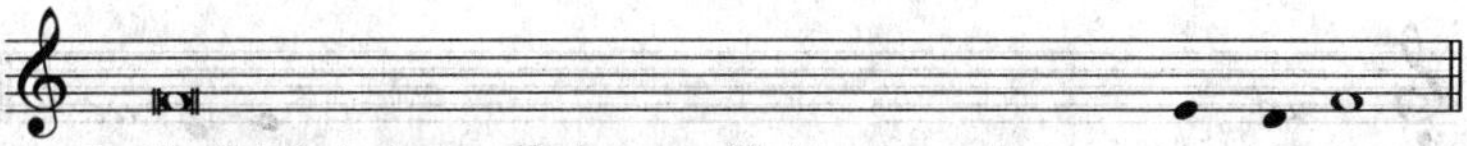

L For this holy house, [holy assembly],
and for all who offer here their worship and praise,
let us pray - - to the Lord.

C Lord, have mer - cy.

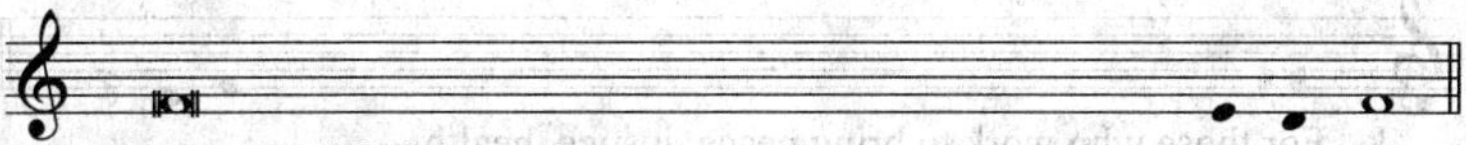

L For ——names——, for our *pastor /pastors* in Christ,
for all servants of the Church,
and for all the people, let us pray - - to the Lord.

C Lord, have mer - cy.

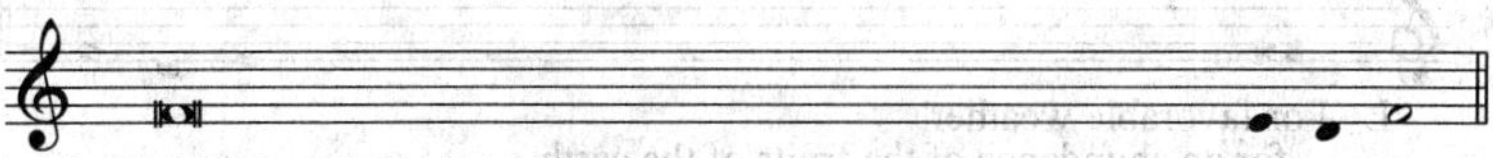

L For those who bring offerings,
those who do good works in this congregation,
those who toil, those who sing, and all the people
here present who await from the Lord
great and abundant mercy, let us pray - - to the Lord.

C Lord_ have mer- cy.

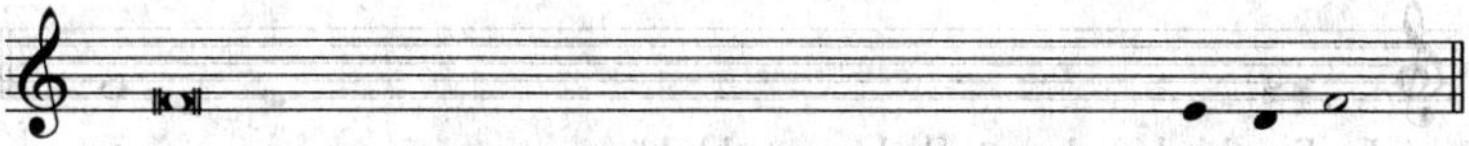

L For our public servants, for the government
and those who protect us, that they may be upheld
and strengthened in every good deed, let us pray to the Lord.

C Lord have mer- cy.

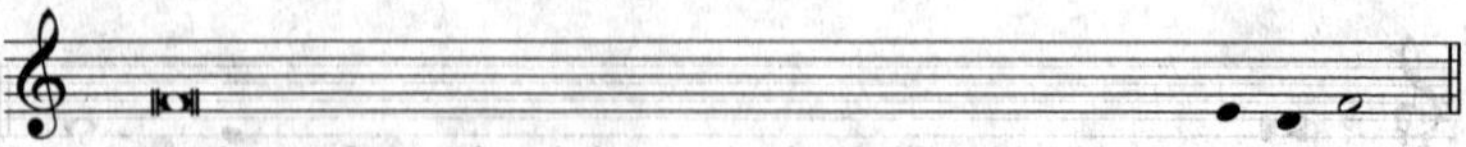

L For those who work to bring peace, justice, health,
and protection in this and every place, let us pray - to the Lord.

C Lord have mer - cy.

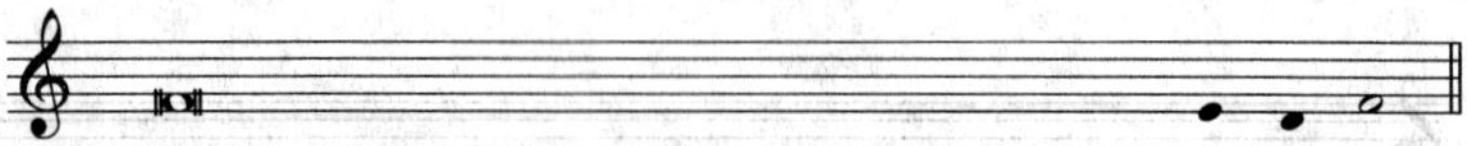

L For favorable weather,
for an abundance of the fruits of the earth,
and for peaceful times, let us pray - - to the Lord.

C Lord have mer- cy.

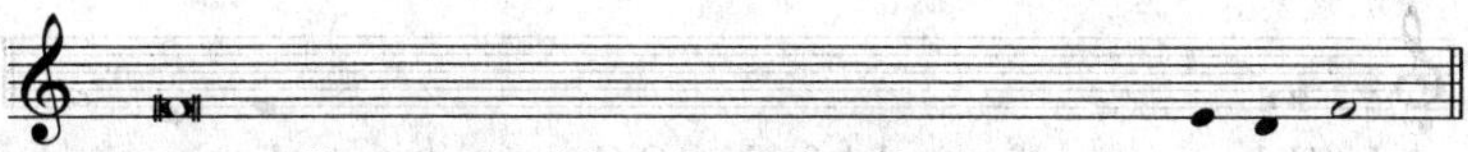

L For travellers, for the sick and suffering, for captives,
and for all who need our prayers, let us pray - to the Lord.

C Lord_ have mer - cy.

L For our deliverance from all affliction,
wrath, danger, and need, let us pray - to the Lord.

C Lord_ have mer - cy.

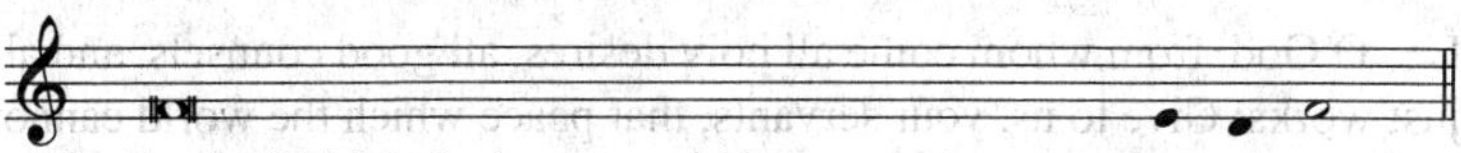

L For the faithful who have gone before us
and are at rest, let us pray [or give thanks] - to the Lord.

C Lord_ have mer - cy.

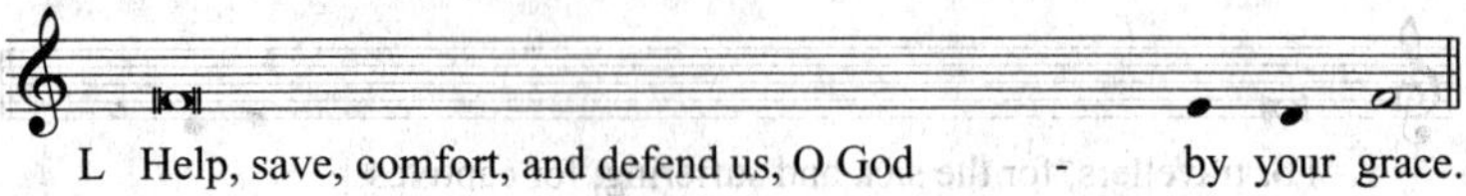

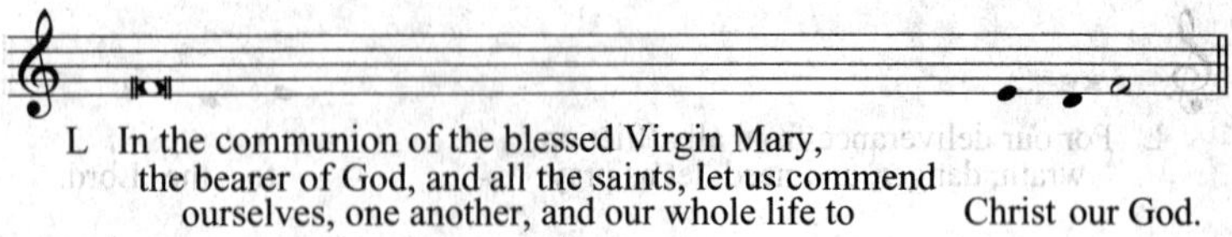

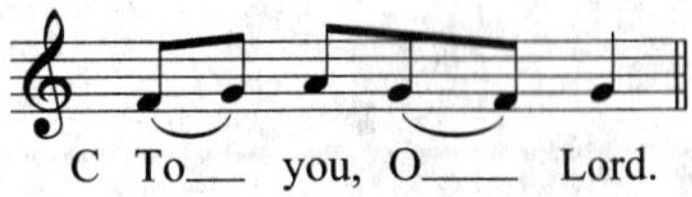

L O God, from whom come all holy desires, all good counsels, and all just works: Give to us, your servants, that peace which the world cannot give, that our hearts may be set to obey your commandments; and also that we, being defended from the fear of our enemies, may live in peace and quietness; through the merits of Jesus Christ our Savior, who lives and reigns with you and the Holy Spirit, God for ever.

[Gel., Greg., Sarum, BCP, CB, CSB, SBH, LBW]

C Amen

On Sundays and Festivals the proper Prayer of the Day may be said.

The appropriate prayer for the day of the week may follow.

Saturday

O God, the Source of eternal light: Shed forth your unending day upon us who wait for you, that our lips may praise you, our lives may bless you, and our worship on the morrow give you glory; through Jesus Christ our Lord.

[Psalm 130:5-6; *Chain*, BCP (1979)]

Sunday

Lord God, whose Son our Savior triumphed over the powers of death and prepared for us a place in the new Jerusalem: Grant that we, who have this day given thanks for his resurrection, may praise you in that City of which he is the light, and where he lives and reigns for ever and ever.

[Rev. 21; William Bright AC, BCP (1979)]

Monday

Hear, O Lord, your servants, who offer to your Name their evening prayer; and as you have preserved them through each moment of the day, so continue to guard them through the hours of the night; through Jesus Christ our Lord. [Greg. trans. Plummer]

Tuesday

Almighty God, we give you thanks for surrounding us, as daylight fades, with the brightness of the vesper light; and we implore you of your great mercy that, as you enfold us with the radiance of this light, so you would shine into our hearts the brightness of your Holy Spirit; through Jesus Christ our Lord.

[Ambrosian *Manuale* (11th cent.); BCP (1979)]

Wednesday

We give you thanks, O Lord, for you have guarded us through the day; we give thanks for you will be our guardian through the night: Bring us safely, we pray, to the morning that you may receive our praise at all times; through Jesus Christ our Lord.

[Gel., Greg., AC, DP rev.]

Thursday

O Lord, as the shadows lenghen, let Christ the Daystar rise in holiness and righteousness within our hearts, so that you may look with favor on us while we give you thanks now as daylight departs and again in the morning when we make our prayers to you; through Jesus Christ our Lord.

[Gel., Greg., Löhe, trans. DvD *et al*]

Friday

Lord Jesus Christ, by your death you took away the sting of death: Grant us your servants so to follow in faith where you have led the way, that we may at length fall asleep peacefully in you and wake in your likeness; for your tender mercies' sake.

[PPB, BCP (1892), CSB, SBH, LBW]

L Lord, remember us in your kingdom, and teach us to pray:

C Our Father in heaven, hallowed be your Name your kingdom come, your will be done, on earth as in heaven. Give us today our daily bread. Forgive us our sins as we forgive those who sin against us.	C Our Father who art in heaven, hallowed be thy Name thy kingdom come, thy will be done, on earth as it is in heaven. Give us this day our daily bread; and forgive us our trespasses, as we forgive those who sin against us;

Save us from the time of trial
and deliver us from evil.
For the kingdom, the power,
and the glory are yours,
now and for ever. Amen.

And lead us not into temptation
but deliver us from evil.
For thine is the kingdom,
and the power, and the glory,
for ever and ever. Amen.

Stand

The BENEDICTION concludes the service when there is no sermon. A hymn may follow the benediction.

When there is a sermon, this benediction is omitted, and the service continues as on p. 20.

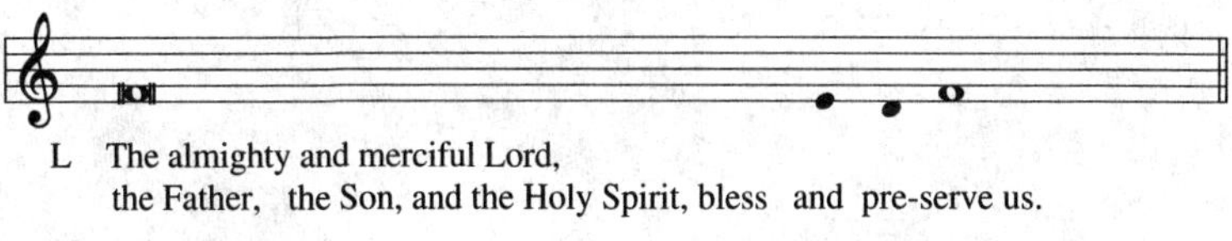

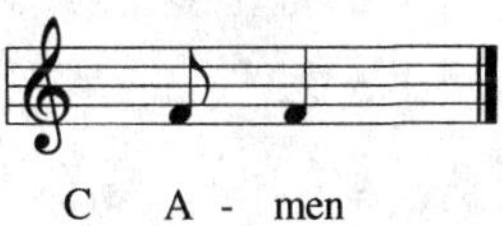

Saturday of Week I

Antiphon to PSALM 42 *Quemadmodum desiderat cervus*

My soul is athirst for God, athirst for the **li**ving God;*
when shall I come to appear before the pres**ence** of God?

[LH, PBO]

42 *The exile's nostalgia for God's temple*

1 As the deer longs **for** the water-brooks,*
so longs my soul for **you**, O God.

2 My soul is athirst for God, athirst for the **li**ving God;*
when shall I come to appear before the pres**ence** of God?

3 My tears have been my food **day** and night,*
while all day long they say to me,
"Where now **is** your God?"

4 I pour out my soul when I think **on** these things:*
how I went with the multitude and led them into the **house** of God,

5 With the voice of praise **and** thanksgiving,*
among those **who** keep holy-day.

6 Why are you so full of heaviness, **O** my soul?*
and why are you so disquiet**ed** within me?

7 Put your **trust** in God;*
for I will yet give thanks to him,
who is the help of my countenance, **and** my God.

8 My soul is heavy within me;*
therefore I will remember you from the land of Jordan,
and from the peak of Mizar among the **heights** of Hermon.

9 One deep calls to another in the noise **of** your cataracts;*
all your rapids and floods have gone **o**ver me.

10 The LORD grants his loving-kindness **in** the daytime;*
in the night season his song is with me,
a prayer to the God **of** my life.

11 I will say to the God of my strength,
"Why have you for**got**ten me?*
and why do I go so heavily while the enemy op**press**es me?"

12 While my bones are **be**ing broken,*
my enemies mock me **to** my face;

13 All day **long** they mock me*
and say to me, "Where now **is** your God?"

14 Why are you so full of heaviness, **O** my soul?*
and why are you so disquiet**ed** within me?

15 Put your **trust** in God;*
for I will yet give thanks to him,
who is the help of my countenance, **and** my God.

Antiphon My soul is athirst for God, athirst for the **li**ving God;*
when shall I come to appear before the pres**ence** of God?

Silence for meditation

Lord God never failing fountain of life, through the saving waters of baptism you called us from the depth of sin to the depths of mercy: Do not forget the trials of our exile, but from the wellspring of the Word satisfy our thirst for you, so that we may come rejoicing to your holy mountain, where you live and reign now and for ever. [LHd, LBW]

+

Antiphon to PSALM 43 *Judica me, Deus*

Send out your light **and** your truth,*
that **they** may lead me. [LH, PBO]

43 *Longing for the temple*

1 Give judgment for me, O God,
and defend my cause against an un**god**ly people;*
deliver me from the deceitful **and** the wicked.

2 For you are the God of my strength;
why have you put **me** from you?*
and why do I go so heavily while the enemy op**press**es me?

3 Send out your light and your truth, that **they** may lead me,*
and bring me to your holy hill
and **to** your dwelling;

4 That I may go to the altar of God,
to the God of my **joy** and gladness;*
and on the harp I will give thanks to you, O **God** my God.

5 Why are you so full of heaviness, **O** my soul?*
and why are you so disquiet**ed** within me?

6 Put your **trust** in God;*
for I will yet give thanks to him,
who is the help of my countenance, **and** my God.

Antiphon Send out your light **and** your truth,*
that **they** may lead me.

Silence for meditation

Almighty Father, source of everlasting light, send forth your truth into our hearts and pour over us the brightness of your light to bring us, through our joyful participation at your altar, to your eternal dwelling on high, where you live and reign now and for ever. [LHd, LBW]

+

Antiphon to the NEW TESTAMENT CANTICLE

Qui cum forma Dei esset

Christ Jesus hum**bled** himself,*
and God raised him **to** the heights. [LH]

A Song of Christ's Humiliation and Exaltation Philippians 2:6-11

Christ Jesus, being in the form of God,
did not cling to equali**ty** with God*
but emptied himself, taking the form **of** a slave.

Bearing the human likeness, revealed in **hu**man shape,*
he humbled himself, in obedience accepting death,
even death **on** a cross.

Therefore God has raised him **to** the heights*
and bestowed on him the Name a**bove** all names,

That at the Name of Jesus every knee should bow--
in heaven, on earth, and **in** the depths--*
and every tongue confess to the glory of God the Father
that Jesus **Christ** is Lord. [LH, LBW]

Antiphon Christ Jesus hum**bled** himself,*
and God raised him **to** the heights.

Silence for meditation

O everliving God, let this mind be in us which was also in Christ Jesus; that as he from his loftiness stooped to the death of the cross, so we in our lowliness may humble ourselves, believing, obeying, living, and dying to the glory of the Father; for the same Jesus Christ's sake.

[Christina Rossetti, PP]

+

Stand

THE HYMN is sung. *Christe, Lux mundi*

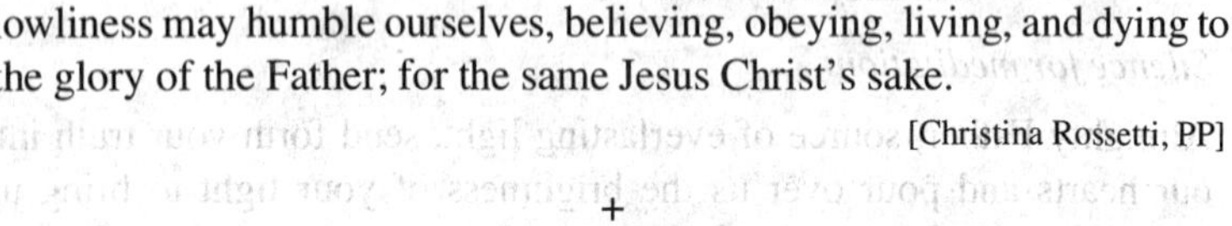

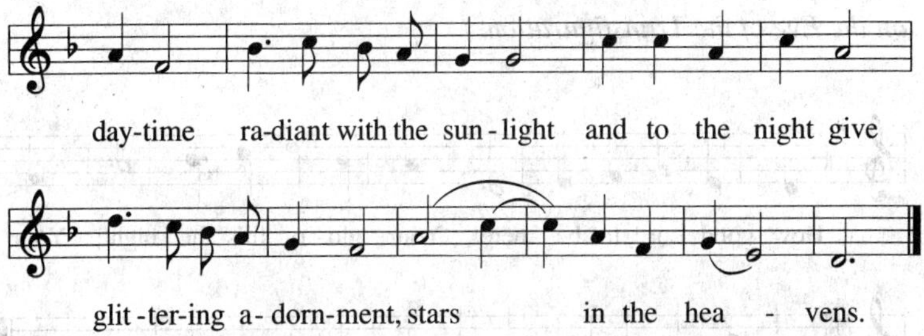

2 Now comes the day's end as the sun is setting:
Mirror of daybreak, pledge of resurrection;
While in the heavens choirs of stars appearing
Hallow the nightfall.

3 Therefore we come now evening rites to offer,
Joyfully chanting holy hymns to praise you,
With all creation joining hearts and voices
Singing your glory.

4 Give heed, we pray you, to our supplication:
That you may grant us pardon for offenses,
Strength for our weak hearts, rest for aching bodies,
Soothing the weary.

5 Though bodies slumber, hearts shall keep their vigil,
For ever resting in the peace of Jesus,
In light or darkness worshiping our Savior
Now and for ever. [H82 35]

Text: Mozarabic, 10th cent.; tr. Alan G. McDougall, 1895-1964, rev. Anne K. LeCroy, b. 1930
Tune: *Mighty Savior,* David Hurd, b. 1950 11 11 11 5

on the Eve of the Transfiguration

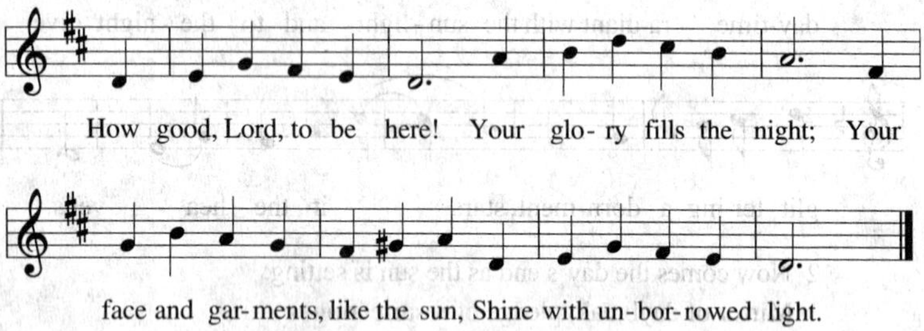

2 How good, Lord, to be here!
Your beauty to behold
Where Moses and Elijah stand,
Your messengers of old.

3 Fulfiller of the past,
Promise of things to be,
We hail your body glorified
And our redemption see.

4 Before we taste of death,
We see your kingdom come;
We long to hold the vision bright
And make this hill our home.

5 How good, Lord, to be here!
Yet we may not remain;
But since you bid us leave the mount,
Come with us to the plain. [CSB 49, LBW 89, alt.]

Text: Joseph Armitage Robinson, 1858-1933, alt.
Tune: *Potsdam*, Mercer, *Church Psalter*, 1854 SM

on the eve of Christ the King:

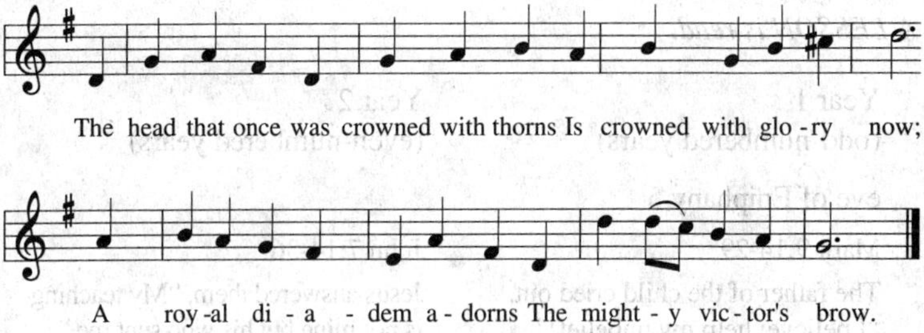

2 The highest place that heaven affords
Is his by sovereign right,
The King of kings, and Lord of lords,
And heaven's eternal Light.

3 The joy of all who dwell above,
The joy of all below,
To whom he manifests his love
And grants his Name to know;

4 To them the cross, with all its shame,
With all its grace, is given;
Their name, an everlasting name;
Their joy, the joy of heaven.

5 They suffer with their Lord below;
They reign with him above;
Their profit and their joy to know
The mystery of his love.

6 The cross he bore is life and health,
Though shame and death to him;
His people's hope, his people's wealth,
Their everlasting theme. [LBW 173, H82 483]

Text: Thomas Kelly, 1769-1855
Tune: *St. Magnus,* Jeremiah Clarke, c. 1669-1707 CM

Sit

A LESSON is read.

Year 1 (odd-numbered years)	Year 2 (even-numbered years)
eve of Epiphany 5	
Mark 9:14-29	John 7:14-36
The father of the child cried out, "I believe; help my unbelief!"	Jesus answered them, "My teaching is not mine but his who sent me."
eve of the Transfiguration, the Last Sunday after the Epiphany	
Matthew 7:22-29	John 18:1-14
The crowds were astonished at Jesus' teaching, for he taught them as one having authority, and not as their scribes.	When Jesus said to them, "I am he," they stepped back and fell to the ground.
eve of Proper 5 (Sunday between June 5 and 11) / Pentecost 4	
Luke 18:15-30	Matthew 15:1-20
Truly I tell you, whoever does not receive the kingdom of God as a little child will never enter it.	Listen and understand: it is not what goes into the mouth that defiles a person, but it is what comes out of the mouth that defiles.
eve of Proper 9 (Sunday between July 3 and 9) / Pentecost 8	
Luke 23:32-43	Matthew 22:23-40
Jesus, remember me when you come into your kingdom.	"You shall love the Lord your God with all your heart, and with all your soul, and with all your mind." This is the greatest and first commandment. And a second is like it: "You shall love your neighbor as yourself." On

these two commandments hang all the law and the prophets.

eve of Proper 13 (Sunday between July 31and August 6) / Pentecost 12

Mark 8:1-10

They ate and were filled; and they took up the broken pieces left over, seven baskets full.

Matthew 28:11-20

Remember, I am with you always, to the end of the age.

eve of Proper 17 (Sunday between August 28 and September 3) / Pentecost 16

Mark 14:43-52

Judas went up to Jesus at once and said, "Rabbi!" and kissed him. Then they laid hands on him and arrested him.

John 8:12-20

I am the light of the world. Whoever follows me will never walk in darkness but will have the light of life.

eve of Proper 21 (Sunday between September 25 and October 1) / Pentecost 20

Matthew 6:19-24

Where your treasure is, there your heart will be also.

Luke 4:38-44

As the sun was setting, all those who had any who were sick with various kinds of diseases brought them to Jesus; and he laid his hands on each of them and cured them.

eve of Proper 25 (Sunday between October 23 and 29) / Pentecost 24

Matthew 12:33-42

For just as Jonah was three days and three nights in the belly of the sea monster, so for three days and three nights the Son of Man will be in the heart of the earth.

Luke 11:1-13

Ask, and it will be given you; search, and you will find; knock, and the door will be opened for you.

eve of Christ the King

Matthew 18:21-35

I forgave you all that debt because you pleaded with me. Should you not have had mercy on your fellow slave, as I had mercy on you?

Luke 18:9-14

God, be merciful to me, a sinner!

Silence for meditation follows the reading.

Sunday of Week I

Antiphon to PSALM 117 *Laudate Dominum*

The faithfulness of the LORD endures for ever. [LH, PBO]

117 *Praise for God's compassion*

1 Praise the LORD, **all** you nations;*
laud him, **all** you peoples.

2 For his loving-kindness toward **us** is great,*
and the faithfulness of the LORD endures for ever.
Hallelujah!

Antiphon The faithfulness of the LORD endures for ever.

Silence for meditation

Lord God, you have revealed your kingdom to all people: Gather the nations into your Church, that in all the various tongues of this world one hymn of praise may be offered to you; through your Son, Jesus Christ our Lord. [LHd, LBW]

+

Antiphon to PSALM 139 *Domine, probasti me*

Search me out, O God, and **know** my heart;*
lead me in the way that is **ev**erlasting. [PBO]

139 *God's complete knowledge and care*

1 LORD, you have searched me **out** and known me;*
you know my sitting down and my rising up;
you discern my thoughts **from** afar.

2 You trace my journeys and my **rest**ing-places*
and are acquainted with **all** my ways.

3 Indeed, there is not a word **on** my lips,*
but you, O LORD, know it **al**together.

4 You press upon me behind **and** before*
and lay your **hand** upon me.

5 Such knowledge is too wonder**ful** for me;*
it is so high that I cannot at**tain** to it.

6 Where can I go then **from** your Spirit?*
where can I flee **from** your presence?

7 If I climb up to heaven, **you** are there;*
if I make the grave my bed, you **are** there also.

8 If I take the wings **of** the morning*
and dwell in the uttermost parts **of** the sea,

9 Even there your **hand** will lead me*
and your right hand **hold** me fast.

10 If I say, "Surely the darkness will **cov**er me,*
and the light around me **turn** to night,"

11 Darkness is not dark to you;
the night is as bright **as** the day;*
darkness and light to you are **both** alike.

12 For you yourself created my **in**most parts;*
you knit me together in my **moth**er's womb.

13 I will thank you because I am marvel**ous**ly made;*
your works are wonderful, and I **know** it well.

14 My body was not hid**den** from you,*
while I was being made in secret
and woven in the depths **of** the earth.

15 Your eyes beheld my limbs, yet unfinished in the womb;
all of them were written **in** your book;*
they were fashioned day by day,
when as yet there was **none** of them.

16 How deep I find your **thoughts**, O God!*
how great is the **sum** of them!

17 If I were to count them, they would be more in number **than** the sand;*
to count them all, my life span would need to **be** like yours.

18 Oh, that you would slay the wick**ed**, O God!*
You that thirst for blood, de**part** from me.

19 They speak despiteful**ly** against you;*
your enemies take your **Name** in vain.

20 Do I not hate those, O **LORD**, who hate you?*
and do I not loathe those who rise **up** against you?

21 I hate them with a **per**fect hatred;*
they have become **my** own enemies.

22 Search me out, O God, and **know** my heart;*
try me and know my **rest**less thoughts.

23 Look well whether there be any wicked**ness** in me*
and lead me in the way that is **ev**erlasting.

Antiphon Search me out, O God, and **know** my heart;*
lead me in the way that is **ev**erlasting.

Silence for meditation

Lord Jesus Christ, when you descended among the dead, you brought them the light of day; when you ascended into heaven, you brought it new radiance: Remain with us and lead us along the paths of life until we come to rest with your saints in the holy dwelling place, where with the Father and the Holy Spirit you live and reign, now and for ever. [LHd, LBW]

+

Antiphon to the NEW TESTAMENT CANTICLE

Magna et mirabilia

Your ways are ways of righteous**ness** and truth,*
O King of **all** the ages. [LH, PBO]

The Song of the Redeemed Revelation 15:3-4

O Ruler of the uni**verse**, Lord God,*
great are the deeds that you have done,
surpassing human **un**derstanding.

Your ways are ways of righteous**ness** and truth,*
O King of all the nations,
O King of **all** the ages.

Who can fail to do you homage, Lord,
and sing the praises **of** your Name?*
For you alone are the **Ho**ly One.

All nations will draw near and bow **down** before you,*
because your just and holy works have **been** revealed.

[BCP alt. LBW]

Antiphon Your ways are ways of righteous**ness** and truth,*
O King of **all** the ages.

Silence for meditation

Holy God, Ruler of the universe, you have vindicated your truth by raising your Son from death and exalting him to your right hand in glory: By the power of this love draw the nations of the world to you in whom alone we find perfect peace; through Jesus Christ our Lord. [PHP]

+

Stand

THE HYMN is sung. *Creator lucis optime*

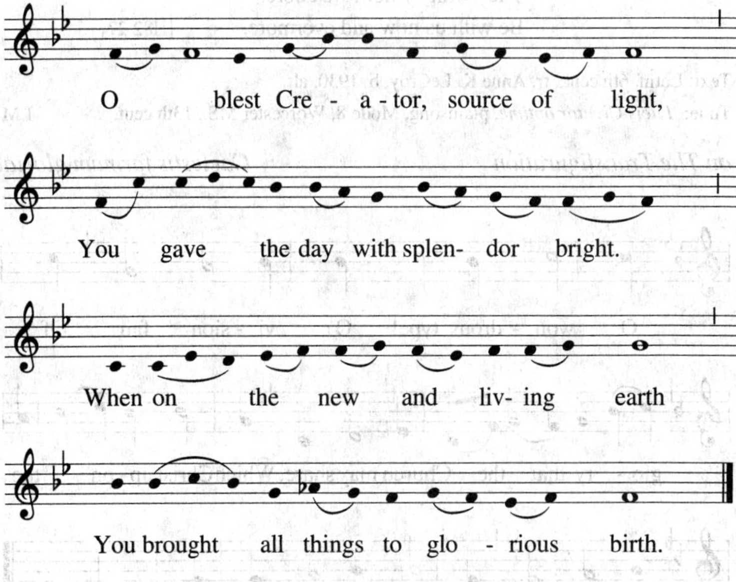

2 You joined the morn and evening ray;
You found it good and called it "day".
But now the threatening darkness nears
We pray you, Father, calm our fears.

3 Lest we, beset by doubt and strife,
Forget your blessed gift of life,
And anguished and in mind distressed,
Be crushed by guilt, by sin oppressed.

4 Eternal Father, help us rise
And strive to gain the heavenly prize;
For you alone can make us strong
To turn from sin and cease from wrong.

5 Defend us, Father, through the night,
And with your Son and Spirit bright,
The Trinity whom we adore,
Be with us now and evermore. [H82 27]

Text: Latin, 6th cent., tr. Anne K. LeCroy, b. 1930, alt.
Tune: *Lucis Creator optime*, plainsong, Mode 8, Worcester MS., 13th cent. LM

on The Transfiguration *Caelestis formam gloriae*

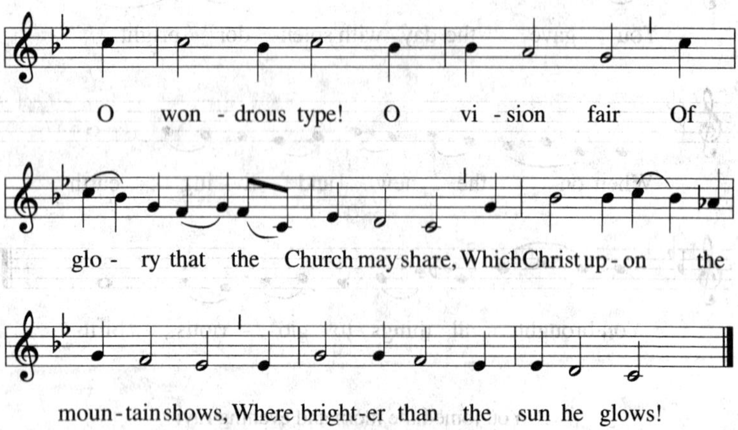

2 With Moses and Elijah nigh
The incarnate Lord holds converse high;
And from the cloud the Holy One
Bears record to the only Son.

3 With shining face and bright array,
Christ deigns to manifest today
What glory shall be theirs above
Who joy in God with perfect love.

4 And faithful hearts are raised on high
By this great vision's mystery;

For which in joyful strains we raise
The voice of prayer, the hymn of praise.

5 O Father, with th' eternal Son,
And Holy Spirit, ever one,
We pray you, bring us by your grace
To see your glory face to face. [LBW 80, H82 136, 137]

Text: Sarum, 15th cent. Office hymn, tr. John Mason Neale, 1818-1866, alt.
Tune: *Deo Gracias,* English, 15th cent. LM

on Christ the King:

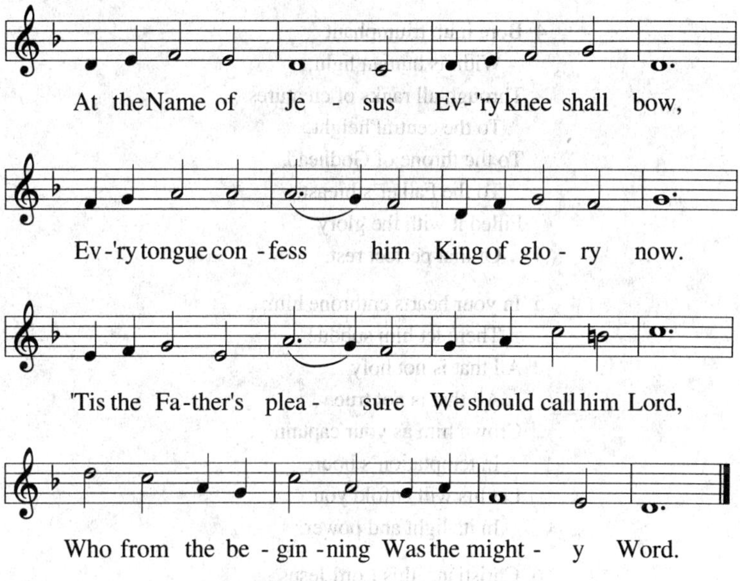

2 At his voice creation
Sprang at once to sight,
All the angel faces,
All the hosts of light,
Thrones and dominations,

Stars upon their way,
All the heavenly orders
In their great array.

3 Humbled for a season,
To receive a name
From the lips of sinners
Unto whom he came,
Faithfully he bore it
Spotless to the last;
Brought it back victorious
When from death he passed;

4 Bore it up triumphant
With its human light,
Through all ranks of creatures
To the central height,
To the throne of Godhead,
To the Father's breast;
Filled it with the glory
Of that perfect rest.

5 In your hearts enthrone him;
There let him subdue
All that is not holy
All that is not true.
Crown him as your captain
In temptation's hour;
Let his will enfold you
In its light and power.

6 Christians, this Lord Jesus
Shall return again
In his Father's glory,
With his angel train;
For all wreaths of empire
Meet upon his brow,

And our hearts confess him
King of glory now. [LBW 179, H82 435]

Text: Caroline Maria Noel, 1817-1877
Tune: *King's Weston*, Ralph Vaughan Williams, 1872-1958 65 65 D

Sit

A LESSON is read.

Year 1	Year 2
Epiphany 5	
John 7:37-46	Mark 10:13-22
Let anyone who is thirsty come to me, and let the one who believes in me drink.	Whoever does not receive the kingdom of God as a little child will never enter it.

The Transfiguration. The Last Sunday after the Epiphany

Year 1	Year 2
John 12:(24-26) 27-36a	Luke 9:18-27
Walk while you have the light, so that the darkness may not overtake you.	The Son of Man must undergo great suffering, and be rejected by the elders, chief priests, and scribes, and be killed, and on the third day be raised.

Proper 5 (Sunday between June 5 and 11) / Pentecost 4

Year 1	Year 2
Matthew 15:29-39	Luke 12:32-40
All of them ate and were filled.	Do not be afraid, little flock, for it is your Father's good pleasure to give you the kingdom.

Proper 9 (Sunday between July 3 and 9) / Pentecost 8

Matthew 22:1-14	Mark 1:14-20
Go therefore into the main streets, and invite everyone you find to the wedding banquet.	Repent, and believe in the good news.

Proper 13 (Sunday between July 31 and August 6) / Pentecost 12

John 1:43-51	Mark 3:20-30
Come and see.	Whoever blasphemes against the Holy Spirit can never have forgiveness.

Proper 17 (Sunday between August 28 and September 3) / Pentecost 16

John 8:47-59	Matthew 5:1-12
Very truly, I tell you, before Abraham was, I am.	Blessed are you when people revile you and persecute you and utter all kinds of evil against you falsely on my account.

Proper 21 (Sunday between September 25 and October 1) / Pentecost 20

Luke 5:1-11	Matthew 13:44-52
When they had brought their boats to shore, they left everything and followed him.	Every scribe who has been trained for the kingdom of heaven is like the master of a household who brings out of his treasure what is new and what is old.

Proper 25 (Sunday between October 23 and 29) / Pentecost 24

Luke 10:25-37	Matthew 18:15-20
Go and do likewise.	Where two or three are gathered in my name, I am there among them.

Christ the King

Luke 19:11-27

As for these enemies of mine who did not want me to be king over them—bring them here and slaughter them in my presence.

Matthew 21:1-13

Look, your king is coming to you.

Silence for meditation follows the reading.

Monday of Week I

Antiphon to PSALM 82 *Deus stetit*

Arise, O God, and rule the earth. [PBO]

82 *Judgment on corrupt authority*

1 God takes his stand in the coun**cil** of heaven;*
he gives judgment in the midst **of** the gods:

2 "How long will you **judge** unjustly,*
and show favor **to** the wicked?

3 Save the weak **and** the orphan;*
defend the hum**ble** and needy;

4 Rescue the weak **and** the poor;*
deliver them from the power **of** the wicked.

5 They do not know, neither do they understand;
they go a**bout** in darkness;*
all the foundations of the **earth** are shaken.

6 Now I say to you, '**You** are gods,*
and all of you children of **the** Most High;

7 Nevertheless, you shall **die** like mortals,*
and fall like **an**y prince.' "

8 Arise, O God, and **rule** the earth,*
for you shall take all nations **for** your own.

Antiphon Arise, O God, and rule the earth.

Silence for meditation

Jesus, our Lord and our God, by your death you give life to the dead; by your resurrection you give strength to the weak: Rise up to rule the earth, and at the end of the world, when the secrets of the heart are revealed, make us glad to celebrate your justice now and for ever. [LHd, LBW]

+

Antiphon to PSALM 29 *Afferte Domino*

Worship the Lord in the beauty of holiness. [LH, PBO]

29 *The voice of the Lord in the storm*

1 Ascribe to the **LORD**, you gods,*
ascribe to the LORD glo**ry** and strength.

2 Ascribe to the LORD the glory **due** his Name;*
worship the LORD in the beauty of **ho**liness.

3 The voice of the LORD is upon the waters;
the God of **glo**ry thunders;*
the LORD is upon the **might**y waters.

4 The voice of the LORD is a pow**er**ful voice;*
the voice of the LORD is a **voice** of splendor.

5 The voice of the LORD breaks the **ce**dar trees;*
the LORD breaks the ce**dars** of Lebanon;

6 He makes Lebanon skip **like** a calf,*
and Mount Hermon like a **young** wild ox.

7 The voice of the LORD splits the flames of fire;
the voice of the LORD shakes the **wil**derness;*
the LORD shakes the wilder**ness** of Kadesh.

8 The voice of the LORD makes the **oak** trees writhe*
and strips the **for**ests bare.

9 And in the temple **of** the LORD*
all are **cry**ing, "Glory!"

10 The LORD sits enthroned a**bove** the flood;*
the LORD sits enthroned as King for **ev**ermore.

11 The LORD shall give strength **to** his people;*
the LORD shall give his people the bless**ing** of peace.

Antiphon Worship the Lord in the beauty of holiness.

Silence for meditation

Lord our King, your voice sounds over the waters as you reign above the flood: Help us, who are born again by water and the Holy Spirit, to praise your wonderful deeds in your holy temple; through your Son, Jesus Christ our Lord. [LHd, LBW]

+

Stand

THE HYMN is sung. *Nun ruhen alle Wälder*

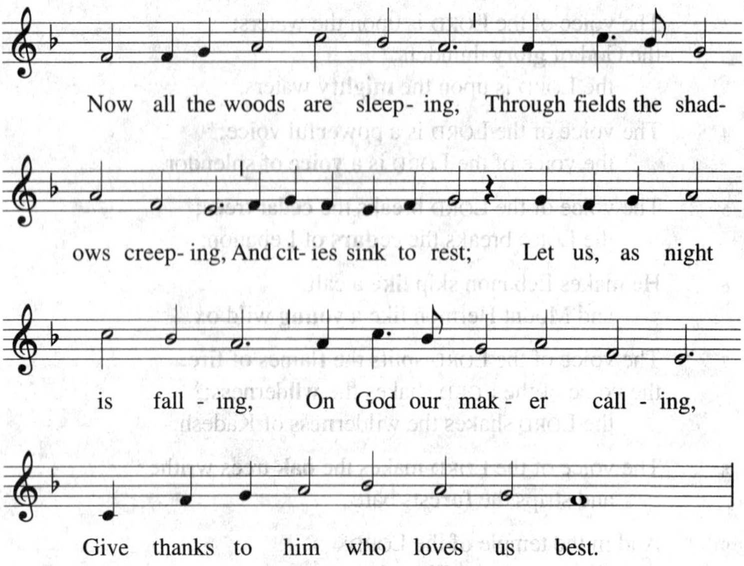

2 The radiant sun has vanished,
His golden rays are banished
From darkening skies of night;
But Christ, the sun of gladness,
Dispelling all our sadness,
Shines down on us in constant light.

3 Now all the heavenly splendor
Breaks forth in starlight tender
From myriad worlds unknown;
And we, this marvel seeing,
Forget our selfish being
For joy of beauty not our own.

4 Though long our mortal blindness
Has missed God's lovingkindness
And plunged us into strife;
Yet when life's day is over
Shall death's fair night discover
The fields of everlasting life. [LBW 276 alt., H82 46]

Text: Paul Gerhardt, 1607-1676; tr. composite

Tune: *O Welt, ich muss dich lassen*, Heinrich Isaac, c. 1450-1517 776 778

Sit

A LESSON is read.

Year 1	Year 2
after Epiphany 1	
Mark 1:1-13 You are my Son, the Beloved; with you I am well pleased.	John 1:1-18 The Word became flesh and lived among us, and we have seen his glory, the glory as of a father's only son, full of grace and truth.
after Epiphany 5	
Mark 9:30-41 The Son of Man is to be betrayed into human hands, and they will kill him, and three days after being killed, he will rise again.	John 7:37-52 Let anyone who is thirsty come to me, and let the one who believes in me drink.

Monday before Ash Wednesday

John 1:1-18
The Word became flesh and lived among us, and we have seen his glory, the glory as of a father's only son, full of grace and truth.

John 18:15-18,25-27
Again Peter denied it, and at that moment the cock crowed.

Proper 1 / after the Day of Pentecost

Luke 11:24-36
Blessed are those who hear the word of God and obey it!

Matthew 9:27-34
Have mercy on us, Son of David!

after Proper 5 / Pentecost 4

Luke 18:31-43
Jesus, Son of David, have mercy on me!

Matthew 15:21-28
Have mercy on me, Lord, Son of David; my daughter is tormented by a demon.

after Proper 9 / Pentecost 8

Luke 23:44-56a
Father, into your hands I commend my spirit.

Matthew 23:1-12
All who exalt themselves will be humbled, and all who humble themselves will be exalted.

after Proper 13 / Pentecost 12

Mark 8:11-21
Why does this generation ask for a sign? Truly I tell you, no sign will be given to this generation.

John 1:1-18
The Word became flesh and lived among us, and we have seen his glory, the glory as of a father's only son, full of grace and truth.

after Proper 17 / Pentecost 16

Mark 14:53-65

"You will see the Son of Man seated at the right hand of the power," and "coming with the clouds of heaven."

John 8:21-32

If you continue in my word, you are truly my disciples; and you will know the truth, and the truth will make you free.

after Proper 21 / Pentecost 20

Matthew 6:25-34

Strive first for the kingdom of God and his righteousness, and all these things will be given to you as well.

Luke 5:1-11

When they had brought their boats to shore, they left everything and followed him.

after Proper 25 / Pentecost 24

Matthew 12:43-50

Whoever does the will of my father in heaven is my brother and sister and mother.

Luke 11:14-26

If it is by the finger of God that I cast out the demons, then the kingdom of God has come to you.

after Christ the King

Matthew 19:1-12

There are eunuchs who have been so from birth, and there are eunuchs who have been made so by others, and there are eunuchs who have made themselves eunuchs for the sake of the kingdom of heaven. Let anyone accept this who can.

Luke 18:15-30

There is no one who has left house or wife or brothers or parents or children, for the sake of the kingdom of God, who will not get back very much more in this age, and in the age to come eternal life.

Silence for meditation follows the reading.

Tuesday of Week I

Antiphon to PSALM 71 *In te, Domine, speravi*

You have taught me since **I** was young,*
and now that I am old, do **not** forsake me. [LH]

71 *Prayer in old age*

1 In you, O LORD, have I **tak**en refuge;*
let me never **be** ashamed.

2 In your righteousness, deliver me and **set** me free;*
incline your ear to **me** and save me.

3 Be my strong rock, a castle to **keep** me safe;*
you are my crag **and** my stronghold.

4 Deliver me, my God, from the hand **of** the wicked,*
from the clutches of the evildoer and **the** oppressor.

5 For you are my hope, **O** Lord GOD,*
my confidence since **I** was young.

6 I have been sustained by you ever since I was born;
from my mother's womb you have **been** my strength;*
my praise shall be al**ways** of you.

7 I have become a por**tent** to many;*
but you are my refuge **and** my strength.

8 Let my mouth be full **of** your praise*
and your glory all **the** day long.

9 Do not cast me off in **my** old age;*
forsake me not when **my** strength fails.

10 For my enemies are talk**ing** against me,*
and those who lie in wait for my life take coun**sel** together.

11 They say, "God has forsaken him;
go after **him** and seize him;*
because there is none **who** will save."

12 O God, be not **far** from me;*
come quickly to help me, **O** my God.

13 Let those who set themselves against me be put to shame and **be** disgraced;*
let those who seek to do me evil be covered with scorn **and** reproach.

14 But I shall always **wait** in patience,*
and shall praise you **more** and more.

15 My mouth shall recount your mighty acts
and saving deeds **all** day long;*
though I cannot know the num**ber** of them.

16 I will begin with the mighty works of **the** Lord GOD;*
I will recall your righteousness, **yours** alone.

17 O God, you have taught me since **I** was young,*
and to this day I tell of your won**der**ful works.

18 And now that I am old and gray-headed, O GOD, do **not** forsake me,*
till I make known your strength to this generation
and your power to all who **are** to come.

19 Your righteousness, O God, reaches **to** the heavens;*
you have done great things;
who is like **you**, O God?

20 You have showed me great troubles **and** adversities,*
but you will restore my life
and bring me up again from the deep places **of** the earth.

21 You strengthen me **more** and more;*
you enfold and **com**fort me,

22 Therefore I will praise you upon the lyre for your faithfulness, **O** my God;*
I will sing to you with the harp, O Holy **One** of Israel.

23 My lips will sing with joy when I **play** to you,*
and so will my soul, which you **have** redeemed.

24 My tongue will proclaim your righteousness **all** day long,*
for they are ashamed and disgraced who sought to **do** me harm.

Antiphon You have taught me since **I** was young,*
and now that I am old, do **not** forsake me.

Silence for meditation

Lord God of the living, do not desert us in old age, but help us to follow your will in both good and bad times, so that for ever we may praise your faithfulness; through your Son, Jesus Christ our Lord. [LH, LBW]

+

Antiphon to PSALM 133 *Ecce, quam bonum!*

Oh, how good and **pleas**ant it is*
when brethren live togeth**er** in unity! [PBO]

133 *The blessings of unity*

1 Oh, how good and **pleas**ant it is,*
when brethren live togeth**er** in unity!

2 It is like fine oil up**on** the head*
that runs down up**on** the beard,

3 Upon the **beard** of Aaron,*
and runs down upon the collar **of** his robe.

4 It is like the **dew** of Hermon*
that falls upon the **hills** of Zion.

5 For there the LORD has or**dain**ed the blessing:*
life for **ev**ermore.

Antiphon Oh, how good and **pleas**ant it is*
when brethren live togeth**er** in unity!

Silence for meditation

Lord God, you have poured into our hearts the precious oil of your Spirit of love: Make us of one heart and of one will, so that we may be true members of the body of Jesus Christ, united as he has commanded us; and to you be the glory now and for ever. [LHd, LBW]

+

Stand

THE HYMN is sung.

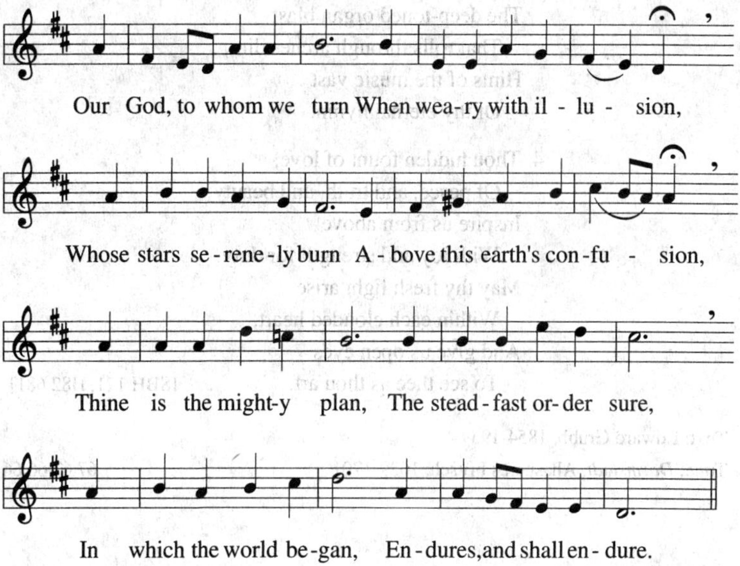

2 Thou art thyself the truth;
Though we, who fain would find thee,
Have tried, with thoughts uncouth,
In feeble words to bind thee,
It is because thou art
We're driven to the quest;
Till truth from falsehood part
Our souls can find no rest.

3 All beauty speaks of thee:
The mountains and the rivers,
The line of lifted sea,
Where spreading moonlight quivers,
The deep-toned organ blast
That rolls through arches dim,
Hints of the music vast
Of thy eternal hymn.

4 Thou hidden fount of love,
Of peace, and truth, and beauty,
Inspire us from above
With joy and strength for duty.
May thy fresh light arise
Within each clouded heart,
And give us open eyes
To see thee as thou art. [SBH 171, H82 681]

Text: Edward Grubb, 1854-1939

Tune: *Darmstadt*, Ahasuerus Fritsch, 1629-1701 67 67 66 66

on Shrove Tuesday, the day before Ash Wednesday

Alleluia dulce carmen

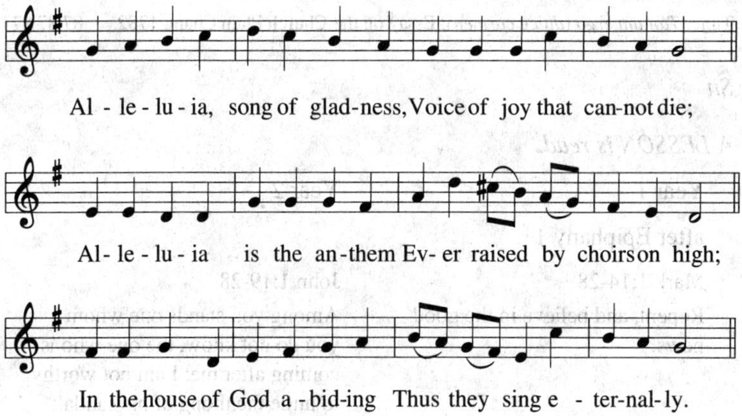

2 Alleluia thou resoundest,
True Jerusalem and free;
Alleluia, joyful mother,
All thy children sing with thee;
But by Babylon's sad waters
Mourning exiles now are we.

3 Alleluia cannot always
Be our song while here below;
Alleluia our transgressions
Make us for a while forego;
For the solemn time is coming
When our tears for sin must flow.

4 Therefore in our hymns we pray thee
Grant us, blessèd Trinity,
At the last to keep thine Easter
In our home beyond the sky,

There to thee for ever singing
Alleluia joyfully. [SBH 58; H82 122, 123]

Text: Latin hymn, 11th cent. tr. John Mason Neale, 1818-1866, alt.
Tune: *Tantum ergo* (*dulce carmen*), Essay on the Church Plain Chant, 1782 87 87 87

Sit

A LESSON is read.

Year 1	Year 2
after Epiphany 1	
Mark 1:14-28	John 1:19-28
Repent, and believe in the good news.	Among you stands one whom you do not know, the one who is coming after me; I am not worthy to untie the thong of his sandal.
after Epiphany 5	
Mark 9:42-50	John 7:53-8:11
Have salt in yourselves, and be at peace with one another.	Go your way, and from now on do not sin again.
Tuesday before Ash Wednesday	
John 1:19-28	John 18:28-38
Among you stands one whom you do not know, the one who is coming after me; I am not worthy to untie the thong of his sandal.	Everyone who belongs to the truth listens to my voice.
Proper 1 / after the Day of Pentecost	
Luke 11:37-52	Matthew 9:35-10:4
You neglect justice and the love of God.	Ask the Lord of the harvest to send out laborers into his harvest.

after Proper 5 / Pentecost 4

Luke 19:1-10
The Son of Man came to seek out and to save the lost.

Matthew 15:29-39
All of them ate and were filled.

after Proper 9 / Pentecost 8

Luke 23:56b-24:11 (12)
Why do you look for the living among the dead?

Matthew 23:13-26
Woe to you, blind guides.

after Proper 13 / Pentecost 12

Mark 8:22-33
Who do you say that I am?

John 1:19-28
Among you stands one whom you do not know, the one who is coming after me; I am not worthy to untie the thong of his sandal.

after Proper 17 / Pentecost 16

Mark 14:66-72
Peter remembered that Jesus had said to him, "Before the cock crows twice, you will deny me three times."

John 8:33-47
If the Son makes you free, you will be free indeed.

after Proper 21 / Pentecost 20

Matthew 7:1-12
Do not judge, so that you may not be judged.

Luke 5:12-26
Friend, your sins are forgiven you.

after Proper 25 / Pentecost 24

Matthew 13:1-9
Listen! A sower went out to sow.

Luke 11:27-36
Blessed are those who hear the word of God and obey it!

after Christ the King

Matthew 19:13-22

If you wish to be perfect, go, sell your possessions, and give the money to the poor, and you will have treasure in heaven; then come, follow me.

Luke 18:31-43

Jesus, Son of David, have mercy on me!

Silence for meditation follows each reading.

Wednesday of Week I

Antiphon to PSALM 89 part i *Misericordias Domini*

Righteousness and justice are the foundations **of** your throne;*
love and truth go be**fore** your face. [LH, PBO]

89 *Hymn to God's faithfulness*

1 Your love, O LORD, for ever **will** I sing;*
from age to age my mouth will pro**claim** your faithfulness.

2 For I am persuaded that your love is estab**lish**ed for ever;*
you have set your faithfulness firmly **in** the heavens.

3 "I have made a covenant with my **cho**sen one;*
I have sworn an oath to Dav**id** my servant:

4 'I will establish your **line** for ever,*
and preserve your throne for all **gen**erations.' "

5 The heavens bear witness to your won**ders,** O LORD *
and to your faithfulness in the assembly of the **ho**ly ones;

6 For who in the skies can be compared **to** the LORD?*
who is like the LORD a**mong** the gods?

7 God is much to be feared in the counsel of the **ho**ly ones,*
great and terrible to all those **round** about him.

8 Who is like you, LORD **God** of Hosts?*
O mighty LORD, your faithfulness is **all** around you.

9 You rule the raging **of** the sea*
and still the surging **of** its waves.

10 You have crushed Rahab of the deep with a **dead**ly wound;*
you have scattered your enemies with your **migh**ty arm.

11 Yours are the heavens; the earth al**so** is yours;*
you laid the foundations of the world and all **that** is in it.

12 You have made the north **and** the south;*
Tabor and Hermon rejoice **in** your Name.

13 You have a **might**y arm;*
strong is your hand and high is **your** right hand.

14 Righteousness and justice are the foundations **of** your throne;*
love and truth go be**fore** your face.

15 Happy are the people who know the **fes**tal shout!*
they walk, O LORD, in the light **of** your presence.

16 They rejoice daily **in** your Name;*
they are jubilant in your **right**eousness.

17 For you are the glory **of** their strength,*
and by your favor our might **is** exalted.

18 Truly, the LORD **is** our ruler;*
the Holy One of Israel **is** our King.

Antiphon Righteous and justice are the foundations **of** your throne;*
love and truth go be**fore** your face.

Silence for meditation

Mighty God, glorious in your creation and faithful in your promises, you have established David's line for ever: Remember your covenant, so that we who bear the name of David's greater son may rejoice in the light of your presence and sing of your mercies without end; through Jesus Christ our Lord. [PHP]

+

Antiphon to PSALM 89 part ii *Tunc locutus es*

His line shall en**dure** for ever*
and his throne as the **sun** before me. [PBO]

19 You spoke once in a vision and said to your **faith**ful people:*
"I have set the crown upon a warrior
and have exalted one chosen out **of** the people.

20 I have found Da**vid** my servant;*
with my holy oil have I a**noint**ed him.

21 My hand will **hold** him fast*
and my arm will **make** him strong.

22 No enemy **shall** deceive him,*
nor any wicked man **bring** him down.

23 I will crush his **foes** before him*
and strike down **those** who hate him.

24 My faithfulness and love shall **be** with him,*
and he shall be victorious **through** my Name.

25 I shall make his domin**ion** extend*
from the Great Sea **to** the River.

26 He will say to me, 'You **are** my Father,*
my God, and the rock of **my** salvation.'

27 I will make **him** my firstborn*
and higher than the kings **of** the earth.

28 I will keep my love for **him** for ever,*
and my covenant will stand **firm** for him.

29 I will establish his **line** for ever*
and his throne as the **days** of heaven.

30 If his children for**sake** my law*
and do not walk according **to** my judgments;

31 If they **break** my statutes*
and do not keep **my** commandments;

32 I will punish their transgressions **with** a rod*
and their iniquities **with** the lash;

33 But I will not take my **love** from him,*
nor let my faithful**ness** prove false.

34 I will not **break** my covenant,*
nor change what has gone out **of** my lips.

35 Once for all I have sworn **by** my holiness:*
'I will not **lie** to David.

36 His line shall en**dure** for ever*
and his throne as the **sun** before me;

37 It shall stand fast for evermore **like** the moon,*
the abiding witness **in** the sky.' "

38 But you have cast off and rejected **your** anointed;*
you have become en**raged** at him.

39 You have broken your covenant **with** your servant,*
defiled his crown, and hurled it **to** the ground.

40 You have breached **all** his walls*
and laid his strong**holds** in ruins.

41 All who pass **by** despoil him;*
he has become the scorn **of** his neighbors.

42 You have exalted the right hand **of** his foes*
and made all his ene**mies** rejoice.

43 You have turned back the edge **of** his sword*
and have not sustained **him** in battle.

44 You have put an end **to** his splendor*
and cast his throne **to** the ground.

45 You have cut short the days **of** his youth*
and have covered **him** with shame.

46 How long will you hide yourself, O LORD?
will you hide your**self** for ever?*
how long will your anger **burn** like fire?

47 Remember, LORD, how **short** life is,*
how frail you have **made** all flesh.

48 Who can live and **not** see death?*
who can save himself from the power **of** the grave?

49 Where, Lord, are your loving-kindness**es** of old,*
which you promised David **in** your faithfulness?

50 Remember, Lord, how your ser**vant** is mocked,*
how I carry in my bosom the taunts of **ma**ny peoples,

51 The taunts your enemies have **hurled**, O LORD,*
which they hurled at the heels of **your** anointed.

52 Blessed be the LORD for **e**vermore!*
Amen, I **say**, Amen.

Antiphon His line shall end**ure** for ever*
and his throne as the **sun** before me.

Silence for meditation

God of mercy and faithfulness, in fulfillment of the promise you made to David you anointed your servant Jesus with holy oil and raised him higher than all the kings of the earth: Forgive our faithlessness, help us keep your commandments, and give us a share in the victory of your Son, Jesus Christ our Lord. [LH and PHP]

+

Stand

THE HYMN is sung.

Let all things now liv - ing A song of thanks giv - ing To
God the cre - a - tor tri - um - phant - ly raise, Who fash - ioned and
made us, Pro - tect - ed and stayed us, Who still guides us
on to the end of our days. God's ban - ners are o'er us, His
light goes be - fore us, A pil - lar of fire shin - ing forth in the
night, Till shad - ows have van - ished And dark - ness is
ban - ished, As for - ward we trav - el from light in - to light.

2 His law he enforces,
The stars in their courses
And sun in its orbit obediently shine;
The hills and the mountains,
The rivers and fountains,
The deeps of the ocean proclaim him divine.
We too should be voicing
Our love and rejoicing;
With glad adoration a song let us raise
Till all things now living
Unite in thanksgiving:
"To God in the highest, hosanna and praise." [LBW 557]

Text: Katherine K. Davis, 1892-1980
Tune: *The Ash Grove,* Welsh folk tune 66 11 66 11 D

Sit

A LESSON is read.

Year 1	Year 2
after Epiphany 1	
Mark 1:29-45 That evening, at sundown, they brought to him all who were sick or possessed with demons.	John 1:(29-34) 35-42 Look, here is the Lamb of God!
after Epiphany 5	
Mark 10:1-16 Whoever does not receive the kingdom of God as a little child will never enter it.	John 8:12-20 Whoever follows me will never walk in darkness but will have the light of life.

Proper 1 / after the Day of Pentecost

Luke 11:53-12:12

Nothing is covered up that will not be uncovered, and nothing secret that will not become known.

Matthew 10:5-15

The kingdom of heaven has come near.

after Proper 5 / Pentecost 4

Luke 19:11-27

A nobleman went out to a distant country to get royal power for himself and then return.

Matthew 16:1-12

You know how to interpret the appearance of the sky, but you cannot interpret the signs of the times.

after Proper 9 / Pentecost 8

Luke 24:(12) 13-35

Were not our hearts burning within us while he was talking with us on the road, while he was opening the scriptures to us?

Matthew 23:27-39

How often have I desired to gather your children together as a hen gathers her brood under her wings, and you were not willing!

after Proper 13 / Pentecost 12

Mark 8:34-9:1

Those who want to save their life will lose it, and those who lose their life for my sake, and for the sake of the gospel, will save it.

John 1:29-42

Here is the Lamb of God who takes away the sin of the world!

after Proper 17 / Pentecost 16

Mark 15:1-11

"Are you the King of the Jews?" Jesus answered him, "You say so."

John 8:47-59

Very truly, I tell you, before Abraham was, I am.

after Proper 21 / Pentecost 20

Matthew 7:13-21

The gate is narrow and the road hard that leads to life, and there are few who find it.

Luke 5:27-39

I have come to call not the righteous but sinners to repentance.

after Proper 25 / Pentecost 24

Matthew 13:10-17

Many prophets and righteous people longed to see what you see, but did not see it, and to hear what you hear, but did not hear it.

Luke 11:37-52

Give for alms those things that are within; and see, everything will be clean for you.

after Christ the King

Matthew 19:23-30

Everyone who has left houses or brothers or sisters or father or mother or children or fields, for my name's sake, will receive a hundredfold, and will inherit eternal life.

Luke 19:1-10

The Son of Man came to seek out and to save the lost.

Silence for meditation follows each reading.

Thursday of Week I

Antiphon to PSALM 16 *Conserva me, Domine*

In your presence there is fullness of joy. [LH]

16 *The Lord is my heritage*

1 Protect me, O God, for I take ref**uge** in you;*
I have said to the LORD, "You are my Lord,
my good a**bove** all other."

2 All my delight is upon the godly that are **in** the land,*
upon those who are noble a**mong** the people.

3 But those who run after **oth**er gods*
shall have their troubles **mul**tiplied.

4 Their libations of blood I **will** not offer,*
nor take the names of their gods up**on** my lips.

5 O LORD, you are my portion **and** my cup;*
it is you who up**hold** my lot.

6 My boundaries enclose a **pleas**ant land;*
indeed, I have a **good**ly heritage.

7 I will bless the LORD who **gives** me counsel;*
my heart teaches me, night **af**ter night.

8 I have set the LORD al**ways** before me;*
because he is at my right hand I **shall** not fall.

9 My heart, therefore, is glad, and my spir**it** rejoices;*
my body also shall **rest** in hope.

10 For you will not abandon me **to** the grave,*
nor let your holy one **see** the Pit.

11 You will show me the **path** of life;*
in your presence there is fullness of joy,
and in your right hand are pleasures for **e**vermore.

Antiphon In your presence there is fullness of joy.

Silence for meditation

Lord Jesus, uphold those who hope in you, and give us your counsel, so that we may know the joy of your resurrection and share the pleasures of the saints at your right hand, where you live and reign with the Father and the Holy Spirit, one God, now and for ever. [LH, LBW]

+

Antiphon to PSALM 60 *Deus, repulisti nos*

Save us by your right **hand**, O God,*
that those who are dear to you may **be** delivered. [PBO]

60 *Prayer after disaster*

1 O God, you have cast us off and **bro**ken us;*
you have been angry;
oh, take us back to **you** again.

2 You have shaken the earth and **split** it open;*
repair the cracks in it, **for** it totters.

3 You have made your peo**ple** know hardship;*
you have given us wine that **makes** us stagger.

4 You have set up a banner for **those** who fear you,*
to be a refuge from the power **of** the bow.

5 Save us by your right hand and **an**swer us,*
that those who are dear to you may **be** delivered.

6 God spoke from his holy **place** and said:*
"I will exult and parcel out Shechem;
I will divide the val**ley** of Succoth.

7 Gilead is mine and Manas**seh** is mine;*
Ephraim is my helmet and Ju**dah** my scepter.

8 Moab is my wash-basin,
on Edom I throw down my san**dal** to claim it,*
and over Philistia will I **shout** in triumph."

9 Who will lead me into **the** strong city?*
who will bring me **in**to Edom?

10 Have you not cast us **off**, O God?*
you no longer go out, O God, **with** our armies.

11 Grant us your help a**gainst** the enemy,*
for vain is the **help** of man.

12 With God we will do **val**iant deeds,*
and he shall tread our enemies **un**der foot.

Antiphon Save us by your right **hand**, O God,*
that those who are dear to you may **be** delivered.

Silence for meditation

Lord Jesus, you have overcome the world, and all power and authority is yours. When evil seems to triumph, give us courage and faith, and help us never to forget that you are with us to the end of time. To you be glory now and for ever. [LH, LBW]

+

Stand

THE HYMN is sung.

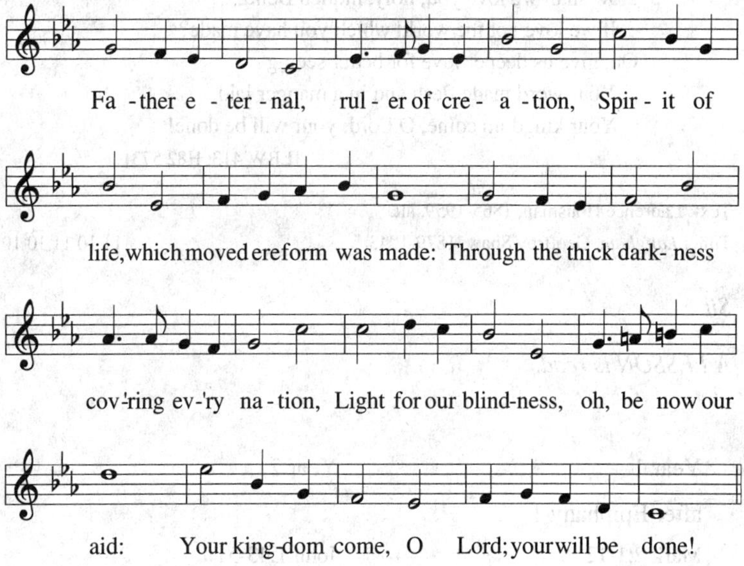

2 Races and peoples, lo, we stand divided,
And, sharing not our griefs, no joy can share;
By wars and tumults love is mocked, derided;
His conquering cross no nation wills to bear.
Your kingdom come, O Lord; your will be done!

3 Envious of heart, blind-eyed, with tongues confounded,
Nation by nation still goes unforgiven;
In wrath and fear, by jealousies surrounded,
Building proud towers which shall not reach to heaven.
Your kingdom come, O Lord; your will be done!

4 Lust of possession ends in desolations;
There is no meekness in the powers of earth;
Led by no star, the rulers of the nations
Still fail to bring us to the blissful birth.
Your kingdom come, O Lord; your will be done!

5 How shall we love you, holy, hidden Being,
If we love not the world which you have made?
Oh, give us deeper love for better seeing
Your word made flesh and in a manger laid.
Your kingdom come, O Lord; your will be done!

[LBW 413; H82 573]

Text: Laurence Housman, 1865-1959, alt.
Tune: *Langham*, Geoffrey Shaw, 1879-1943 11 10 11 10 10

Sit

A LESSON is read.

Year 1	Year 2
after Epiphany 1	
Mark 2:1-12 The Son of Man has authority on earth to forgive sins.	John 1:43-51 You will see heaven opened and the angels of God ascending and descending upon the Son of Man.
after Epiphany 5	
Mark 10:17-31 Children, how hard it is to enter the kingdom of God!	John 8:21-32 If you continue in my word, you are truly my disciples.
Proper 1 / after the Day of Pentecost	
Luke 12:13-21 Be on your guard against all kinds of greed; for one's life does not consist in the abundance of possessions.	Matthew 10:16-23 I am sending you out like sheep into the midst of wolves; so be wise as serpents and innocent as doves.

after Proper 5 / Pentecost 4

Luke 19:28-40

Blessed is the king who comes in the name of the Lord!

Matthew 16:13-20

You are the Messiah, the Son of the living God.

after Proper 9 / Pentecost 8

Luke 24:36-53

Stay here in the city until you have been clothed with power from on high.

Matthew 24:1-14.

This good news of the kingdom will be proclaimed throughout the world, as a testimony to all the nations; and then the end will come.

after Proper 13 / Pentecost 12

Mark 9:2-13

This is my Son, the Beloved; listen to him!

John 1:43-51

You will see heaven opened, and angels of God ascending and descending upon the Son of Man.

after Proper 17 / Pentecost 16

Mark 15:12-21

Crucify him!

John 9:1-17

We must work the works of him who sent me while it is day; night is coming when no one can work.

after Proper 21 / Pentecost 20

Matthew 7:22-29

The crowds were astounded at his teaching, for he taught as one having authority, and not as their scribes.

Luke 6:1-11

The Son of Man is lord of the sabbath.

after Proper 25 / Pentecost 24

Matthew 13:18-23

When anyone hears the word of the kingdom and does not understand it, the evil one comes and

Luke 11:53-12:12

Fear him who, after he has killed, has authority to cast into hell.

snatches away what is sown in the heart.

after Christ the King

Matthew 20:1-16

Am I not allowed to do what I choose with what belongs to me?

Luke 19:11-27

A nobleman went to a distant country to get royal power for himself and then return.

Silence for meditation follows the reading.

Friday of Week I

Antiphon to PSALM 70 *Deus, in adjutorium*

I am **poor** and needy;*
come to me speedi**ly**, O God. [LH, PBO]

70 *A cry of distress*

1 Be pleased, O God, to de**liv**er me;*
O LORD, make **haste** to help me.

2 Let those who seek my life be ashamed
and altogeth**er** dismayed;*
let those who take pleasure in my misfortune
draw back and **be** disgraced.

3 Let those who say to me "Aha!" and gloat over **me** turn back,*
because they **are** ashamed.

4 Let all who seek you rejoice and be **glad** in you;*
let those who love your salvation say for ever,
"Great **is** the LORD!"

5 But as for me, I am **poor** and needy;*
come to me speedi**ly**, O God.

6 You are my helper and **my** deliverer;*
O LORD, **do** not tarry.

Antiphon I am **poor** and needy;*
come to me speedi**ly**, O God.

Silence for meditation

Deliver us, O Lord, from every evil, and grant us peace in our day. In your mercy keep us free from sin and protect us from all anxiety, as we wait in joyful hope for the coming of your Son, Jesus Christ our Lord.
[RS, BCP, LBW]

+

Antiphon to PSALM 142 *Voce mea ad Dominum*

You are my **re**fuge, Lord;*
my portion in the land **of** the living. [LH, PBO]

142 *Prayer for help*

1 I cry to the LORD **with** my voice;*
to the LORD I make loud **sup**plication.

2 I pour out my com**plaint** before him*
and tell him **all** my trouble.

3 When my spirit languishes within me, you **know** my path;*
in the way wherein I walk they have hidden a **trap** for me.

4 I look to my right hand and find no **one** who knows me;*
I have no place to flee to, and no one **cares** for me.

5 I cry out to **you**, O LORD;*
I say, "You are my refuge,
my portion in the land **of** the living."

6 Listen to my cry for help, for I have been brought **ver**y low;*
save me from those who pursue me,
for they are too **strong** for me.

7 Bring me out of prison, that I may give thanks **to** your Name;*
when you have dealt bountifully with me,
the righteous will gath**er** around me.

Antiphon You are my **re**fuge, Lord;*
my portion in the land **of** the living.

Silence for meditation

Lord Jesus, hanging on the cross and left alone by your disciples, you called on your Father with a mighty cry as you gave up your spirit: Deliver us from the prison of affliction, and be yourself our inheritance in the land of the living, where with the Father and the Holy Spirit you are blessed now and for ever. [LHd, LBW]

+

Stand

THE HYMN is sung.

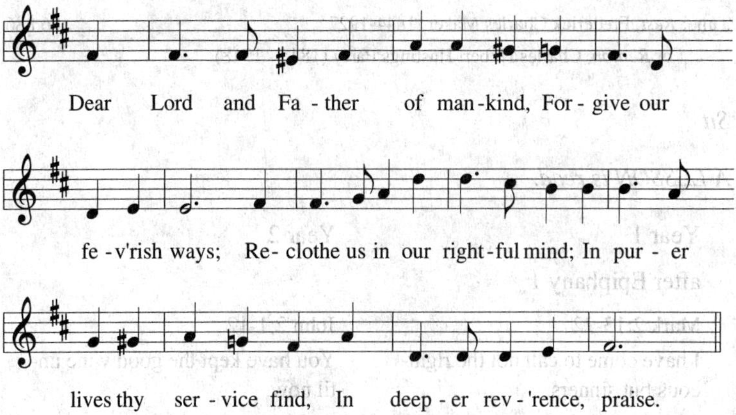

2 In simple trust like theirs who heard,
  Beside the Syrian sea,
The gracious calling of the Lord,
Let us, like them, without a word
  Rise up and follow thee.

3 O Sabbath rest by Galilee,
  O calm of hills above;
Where Jesus knelt to share with thee
The silence of eternity,
  Interpreted by love!

4 Drop thy still dews of quietness,
  Till all our strivings cease;
Take from our souls the strain and stress,
And let our ordered lives confess
  The beauty of thy peace.

5 Breathe through the heats of our desire
Thy coolness and thy balm;
Let sense be dumb, let flesh retire;
Speak through the earthquake, wind, and fire,
O still small voice of calm! [LBW 506; H82 652, 653]

Text: John Greenleaf Whittier, 1807-1892
Tune: *Rest*, Frederick Charles Maker, 1844-1927 86 886
or *Repton*, Charles Hubert Hastings Parry (1848 - 1918)

Sit

A LESSON is read.

Year 1	Year 2
after Epiphany 1	
Mark 2:13-22 I have come to call not the righteous but sinners.	John 2:1-12 You have kept the good wine until now.
after Epiphany 5	
Mark 10:32-45 Whoever wishes to become great among you must be your servant.	John 8:33-47 If the Son makes you free, you will be free indeed.
Proper 1 / after the Day of Pentecost	
Luke 12:32-48 Do not be afraid, little flock, for it is your Father's good pleasure to give you the kingdom.	Matthew 10:24-33 Do not fear those who kill the body but cannot kill the soul; rather fear him who can destroy both soul and body in hell.

after Proper 5 / Pentecost 4

Luke 19:41-48

If you, even you, had only recognized on this day the things that make for peace! But now they are hidden from your eyes.

Matthew 16:21-28

If any want to become my followers, let them deny themselves and take up their cross and follow me.

after Proper 9 / Pentecost 8

Mark 1:1-13

The beginning of the good news of Jesus Christ, the Son of God.

Matthew 24:15-31

Then the sign of the Son of Man will appear in heaven, and then all the tribes of the earth will mourn.

after Proper 13 / Pentecost 12

Mark 9:14-29

I believe; help my unbelief!

John 2:1-12

You have kept the good wine until now.

after Proper 17 / Pentecost 16

Mark 15:22-32

Those who were crucified with him also taunted him.

John 9:18-41

I came into this world for judgment so that those who do not see may see, and those who do see may become blind.

after Proper 21 / Pentecost 20

Matthew 8:1-17

"Go; let it be done for you according to your faith." And the servant was healed in that hour.

Luke 6:12-26

Jesus spent the night in prayer to God.

after Proper 25 / Pentecost 24

Matthew 13:24-30

Let both of them grow together until the harvest.

Luke 12:13-31

Be on your guard against all kinds of greed; for one's life does not consist in the abundance of possessions.

after Christ the King

Matthew 20:17-28

Whoever wishes to be great among you must be your servant.

Luke 19:28-40

Blessed is the king who comes in the name of the Lord!

Silence for meditation follows the reading.

Saturday of Week II

Antiphon to PSALM 118 *Confitemini Domino*

The Lord is my strength **and** my song,*
and he has become **my** salvation.

118 *Processional song of praise*

1 Give thanks to the LORD, for **he** is good;*
his mercy en**dures** for ever.

2 Let Israel **now** proclaim,*
"His mercy en**dures** for ever."

3 Let the house of Aaron **now** proclaim,
"His mercy en**dures** for ever."

4 Let those who fear the LORD **now** proclaim,
"His mercy en**dures** for ever."

5 I called to the LORD in **my** distress;*
the LORD answered by set**ting** me free.

6 The LORD is at my side, therefore I **will** not fear;*
what can anyone **do** to me?

7 The LORD is at my **side** to help me;*
I will triumph over **those** who hate me.

8 It is better to rely **on** the LORD*
than to put any **trust** in flesh.

9 It is better to rely **on** the LORD*
than to put any **trust** in rulers.

10 All the ungodly en**com**pass me:*
in the name of the LORD I **will** repel them.

11 They hem me in, they hem me in on **ev**ery side;*
in the name of the LORD I **will** repel them.

12 They swarm about me like bees;
they blaze like a **fire** of thorns;*
in the name of the LORD I **will** repel them.

13 I was pressed so hard that I **al**most fell,*
but the LORD came **to** my help.

14 The LORD is my strength **and** my song,*
and he has become **my** salvation.

15 There is a sound of exulta**tion** and victory*
in the tents **of** the righteous:

16 "The right hand of the **LORD** has triumphed!*
the right hand of the LORD is exalted!
the right hand of the **LORD** has triumphed!"

17 I shall not **die**, but live,*
and declare the works **of** the LORD.

18 The LORD has pun**ished** me sorely,*
but he did not hand me o**ver** to death.

19 Open for me the **gates** of righteousness;*
I will enter them;
I will offer thanks **to** the LORD.

20 "This is the gate **of** the LORD;*
he who is right**eous** may enter."

21 I will give thanks to you, for you **an**swered me*
and have become **my** salvation.

22 The same stone which the buil**ders** rejected*
has become the chief **cor**nerstone.

23 This is **the** LORD's doing,*
and it is marvelous **in** our eyes.

24 On this day the **LORD** has acted;*
we will rejoice and be **glad** in it.

25 Hosannah, **LORD**, hosannah!*
LORD, send us **now** success.

26 Blessed is he who comes in the name **of** the LORD;*
we bless you from the house **of** the LORD.

27 God is the LORD; he has **shined** upon us;*
form a procession with branches up to the horns **of** the altar.

28 "You are my God, and **I** will thank you;*
you are my God, and I **will** exalt you."

29 Give thanks to the LORD, for **he** is good;*
his mercy en**dures** for ever.

Antiphon The Lord is my strength **and** my song,*
and he has become **my** salvation.

Silence for meditation

Lord God, your Son, rejected by the builders, has become the cornerstone of the Church. Shed rays of your glory upon your Church, that it may be seen as the gate of salvation open to all nations. Let cries of joy celebrate the wonder of Christ's resurrection, now and for ever. [LH, LBW]

+

Antiphon to PSALM 111 *Confitebor tibi*

The Lord is gracious and full **of** compassion;*
he makes his marvelous works to **be** remembered.
[LH, PBO]

111 *God's marvelous works*

1 Hallelujah!
I will give thanks to the LORD with **my** whole heart,*
in the assembly of the upright, in the **con**gregation.

2 Great are the deeds **of** the LORD!*
they are studied by all who de**light** in them.

3 His work is full of majes**ty** and splendor,*
and his righteousness en**dures** for ever.

4 He makes his marvelous works to **be** remembered;*
the LORD is gracious and full **of** compassion.

5 He gives food to **those** who fear him;*
he is ever mindful **of** his covenant.

6 He has shown his people the power **of** his works*
in giving them the lands **of** the nations.

7 The works of his hands are faithful**ness** and justice;*
all his command**ments** are sure.

8 They stand fast for ev**er** and ever,*
because they are done in **truth** and equity.

9 He sent redemption to his people;
he commanded his cove**nant** for ever;*
holy and awesome **is** his Name.

10 The fear of the LORD is the begin**ning** of wisdom;*
those who act accordingly have a good understanding;
his praise end**ures** for ever.

Antiphon The Lord is gracious and full **of** compassion;*
he makes his marvelous works to **be** remembered.

Silence for meditation

Merciful and gentle Lord, the crowning glory of all the saints, give us, your children, the gift of obedience, which is the beginning of wisdom, so that we may be filled with your mercy and that what you command we may accomplish by the might of Jesus Christ our Lord. [LH, LBW]

+

Antiphon to the NEW TESTAMENT CANTICLE

Benedictus Deus et Pater

God planned to restore all **things** in Christ*
in the full**ness** of time. [LH]

A Song of God's Blessings in Christ Ephesians 1:3-12

Blessed be the God and Father
of our Lord **Je**sus Christ;*
who has bestowed on us in Christ
every spiritual blessing **in** the heavens.

Before the world began God chose us in him
to be holy **in** his sight,*
without blemish and **full** of love.

He destined us to be adopted as his children
through **Je**sus Christ*
according to the purpose **of** his will,

That the glory of God's gracious gift,
freely bestowed on us in **the** Beloved,*
might redound **to** his praise.

In Christ we have redemption **through** his blood:*
the forgiveness of our sins
according to the riches of grace that he la**vished** upon us.

He has made known to us the mystery **of** his will,*
the plan he was pleased to de**cree** in Christ,

A plan for the full**ness** of time,*
that all things in heaven and earth
might be unit**ed** in Christ,

In whom we have been given our share **in** the heritage,*
so that we might live for the praise **of** his glory. [LH, PHP]

Antiphon God planned to restore all **things** in Christ*
in the full**ness** of time.

Silence for meditation

Almighty and and eternal God, whom we dare to call our Father: Bring to perfection in us, we pray, the rebirth you have given us in Holy Baptism, by which we have been made your children and adopted into your family, that, rejoicing in our heritage, we may ever live for the praise of your glory; through Jesus Christ our Lord. [PHP]

On Trinity Sunday the Athanasian Creed, pp. 1585-1589, may be used as the Canticle.

+

Stand

THE HYMN is sung. *O lux beata Trinitas*

2 To thee our morning song of praise,
To thee our evening prayer we raise;
Thy glory suppliant we adore
For ever and for evermore.

3 All laud to God the Father be,
All praise, eternal Son, to thee,
All glory, as is ever meet,
To God the holy Paraclete.

[SBH 133; H82 29, 30]

Text: attr. St. Ambrose, 340-397; tr. John Mason Neale, 1818-1866
Tune: *O heilige Dreifaltigkeit*, Nikolaus Herman, c. 1480-1561 LM

Sit

A LESSON is read.

Year 1	Year 2

eve of Epiphany 2

Mark 2:23-3:6	John 2:13-22
The Son of Man is lord even of the sabbath.	Stop making my Father's house a marketplace!

eve of Epiphany 6

Mark 10:46-52	John 8:47-59
Jesus, Son of David, have mercy on me!	Very truly, I tell you, before Abraham was, I am.

eve of the Festival of the Holy Trinity

Luke 12:49-59	Matthew 10:34-42
I came to bring fire to the earth, and how I wish it were already kindled!	Do not think I have come to bring peace to the earth; I have not come to bring peace, but a sword.

[BCP: Sirach 42:15-25 Eph. 3:14-21]

eve of Proper 6 (Sunday between June 12 and 18) / Pentecost 5

Luke 20:1-8	Matthew 17:1-13
Tell us, by what authority are you doing these things?	This is my Son, the Beloved; with him I am well pleased; listen to him!

eve of Proper 10 (Sunday between July 10 and 16) / Pentecost 9

Mark 1:14-28	Matthew 24:32-51
The time is fulfilled, and the kingdom of God has come near; repent, and believe in the good news.	Heaven and earth will pass away, but my words will not pass away.

eve of Proper 14 (Sunday between August 7 and 13) / Pentecost 13

Mark 9:30-41

Whoever gives you a cup of water to drink because you bear the name of Christ will by no means lose the reward.

John 2:13-25

Destroy this temple, and in three days I will raise it up.

eve of Proper 18 (Sunday between September 4 and 10) / Pentecost 17

Mark 15:33-39

Truly, this man was God's Son!

John 10:1-18

I am the good shepherd.

eve of Proper 22 (Sunday between October 2 and 8) / Pentecost 21

Matthew 8:18-27

What sort of man is this, that even the winds and the sea obey him?

Luke 6:27-38

Love your enemies, do good to those who hate you.

eve of Proper 26 (Sunday between October 30 and November 5) / Pentecost 25

Matthew 13:31-35

Jesus told the crowds ask these things in parables; without a parable he told them nothing.

Luke 12:32-48

Do not be afraid, little flock, for it is your Father's good pleasure to give you the kingdom.

Silence for meditation follows the reading.

Antiphon to PSALM 77 *Voce mea ad Dominum clamavi*

Your way, O **God**, is holy;*
who is so great a god **as** our God? [LH, PBO]

77 *Meditation on Israel's past*

1 I will cry a**loud** to God;*
I will cry aloud, and **he** will hear me.

2 In the day of my trouble I **sought** the Lord;*
my hands were stretched out by night and did not tire;
I refused **to** be comforted.

3 I think of God, **I** am restless,*
I ponder, and my **spir**it faints.

4 You will not let my **eye**lids close;*
I am troubled and I **can**not speak.

5 I consider the **days** of old;*
I remember the **years** long past;

6 I commune with my heart **in** the night;*
I ponder and **search** my mind.

7 Will the Lord cast me **off** for ever?*
will he no more **show** his favor?

8 Has his loving-kindness come to an **end** for ever?
has his promise failed for **ev**ermore?

9 Has God forgotten **to** be gracious?*
has he, in his anger, withheld **his** compassion?

10 And I said, "My **grief** is this:*
the right hand of the Most High has **lost** its power."

11 I will remember the works **of** the LORD,*
and call to mind your wonders **of** old time.

12 I will meditate on **all** your acts*
and ponder your **migh**ty deeds.

13 Your way, O **God**, is holy;*
who is so great a god **as** our God?

14 You are the God **who** works wonders*
and have declared your power a**mong** the peoples.

15 By your strength you have re**deemed** your people,*
the children of Ja**cob** and Joseph.

16 The waters saw you, O God;
the waters saw **you** and trembled;*
the very **depths** were shaken.

17 The clouds poured out water;
the skies thundered;*
your arrows flashed **to** and fro;

18 The sound of your thunder was in the whirlwind;
your lightnings lit **up** the world;*
the earth trembl**ed** and shook.

19 Your way was in the sea,
and your paths in **the** great waters,*
yet your footsteps **were** not seen.

20 You led your people **like** a flock*
by the hand of **Moses** and Aaron.

Antiphon Your way, O **God**, is holy;*
who is so great a god **as** our God?

Silence for meditation

Heavenly Father, by signs and wonders you established your ancient covenant, and through the sacrifice of your Son you confirmed the new covenant yet more wondrously: Guide your Church to the land of promise, that there we may celebrate your Name with lasting praise through Jesus Christ our Lord. [LH, LBW]

+

Antiphon to PSALM 113 *Laudate, pueri*

From the rising of the sun to its **go**ing down*
let the Name of the **Lord** be praised. [LH, PBO]

113 *To the God of glory and compassion*

1 Hallelujah!
Give praise, you servants **of** the LORD;*
praise the Name **of** the LORD.

2 Let the Name of the **LORD** be blessed,*
from this time forth for **ev**ermore.

3 From the rising of the sun to its **go**ing down*
let the Name of the **LORD** be praised.

4 The LORD is high a**bove** all nations,*
and his glory a**bove** the heavens.

5 Who is like the LORD our God, who sits en**throned** on high,*
but stoops to behold the heavens **and** the earth?

6 He takes up the weak out **of** the dust*
and lifts up the poor **from** the ashes.

7 He sets them **with** the princes,*
with the princes **of** his people.

8 He makes the woman of a **child**less house*
to be a joyful moth**er** of children.

Antiphon From the rising of the sun to its **go**ing down*
let the Name of the **Lord** be praised.

Silence for meditation

Lord Jesus, surrendering the brightness of your glory, you become mortal so that we might be raised from the dust to share your very being: May the children of God always bless your Name from the rising of the sun to its going down, for you live and reign with the Father and the Holy Spirit, now and for ever. [LH, LBW]

+

Antiphon to the NEW TESTAMENT CANTICLE

Salus et gloria et virtus Deo

Al**le**luia.*
Al**le**luia. [LH]

A Song of Heaven Revelation 19:1,5,6,7

Victory and glory and power **to** our God,*
for true and just **are** his judgments.

Praise our God, all **you** his servants,*
and all who fear him, both **small** and great.

The Lord our God, the Almighty, has be**gun** his reign;*
let us rejoice and exult and give **him** the glory.

The marriage feast of the **Lamb** has come,*
and his bride is prepared to **wel**come him. [LH; PHP]

Antiphon Al**le**luia.*
Al**le**luia.

Silence for meditation

Mighty God, our Ruler, by the cross of your Son blot out our sins, sustain us in this world, and bring us to the house of life, where at last with all your saints we may praise and glorify the Father and the Son and the Holy Spirit for ever and ever. [PHP]

On Trinity Sunday the Athanasian Creed, pp. 1585-1589, may be used as the Canticle.

+

Stand

THE HYMN is sung.

2 We have ventured worlds undreamed of
Since the childhood of our race;
Known the ecstasy of winging
Through untravelled realms of space;
Probed the secrets of the atom,
Yielding unimagined power,
Facing us with life's destruction
Or our most triumphant hour.

3 As each far horizon beckons,
May it challenge us anew:
Children of creative purpose,
Serving others, honoring you.
May our dreams prove rich with promise;
Each endeavor well begun;
Great Creator, give us guidance
Till our goals and yours are one.
[LBW 463, H82 580]

Text: Catherine Cameron, b. 1927, alt., © Hope Publishing Co.
Tune: *Holy Manna,* W. Walker, *Southern Harmony*, 1835 87 87 D

Sit

A LESSON is read.

Year 1

Epiphany 2

John 4:27-42

Look around you, and see how the fields are ripe for harvesting.

Epiphany 6

John 8:12-19

Whoever follows me will never walk in darkness but will have the light of life.

The Festival of the Holy Trinity

John 1:1-18

No one has ever seen God. It is God the only Son, who is close to

Year 2

Epiphany 2

Mark 3:7-19

He appointed twelve, whom he also named apostles, to be with him, and to be sent out to proclaim the message, and to have authority to cast out demons.

Epiphany 6

Mark 10:23-31

How hard it will be for those who have wealth to enter the kingdom of God!

The Festival of the Holy Trinity

John 1:29-34

He on whom you see the Spirit descend and remain is the one who

the Father's heart, who has made him known.

baptizes with the Holy Spirit.

Proper 6 (Sunday between June 12 and 18) / Pentecost 5

Matthew 18:1-14

Unless you change and become like children, you will never enter the kingdom of heaven.

Luke 12:41-48

From everyone to whom much has been given, much will be required.

Proper 10 (Sunday between July 10 and 16) / Pentecost 9

Matthew 23:29-39

How often have I desired to gather your children together as a hen gathers her brood under her wings, and you were not willing!

Mark 1:21-27

They were astounded at his teaching, for he taught them as one having authority, and not as the scribes.

Proper 14 (Sunday between August 7 and 13) / Pentecost 13

John 3:22-36

The Father loves the Son and has placed all things in his hands.

Mark 4:35-41

Who then is this, that even the wind and the sea obey him?

Proper 18 (Sunday between September 4 and 10) / Pentecost 17

John 10:31-42

"Everything that John said about this man was true."

Matthew 5:13-20

You are the light of the world.

Proper 22 (Sunday between October 2 and 8) / Pentecost 21

Luke 7:11-17

"Young man, I say to you, rise!" The dead man sat up and began to speak, and Jesus gave him to his mother.

Matthew 14:1-12

His disciples came and took the body and buried it; then they went and told Jesus.

Proper 26 (Sunday between October 30 and November 5) / Pentecost 25

Luke 12:22-31

Strive for his kingdom, and all these things will be given to you as well.

Matthew 18:21-35

Should you not have had mercy on your fellow slave, as I had mercy on you?

Silence for meditation follows the reading.

Monday of Week II

Antiphon to PSALM 9 *Confitebor tibi*

I will tell of **all** your praises*
in the gates of the city of Zion. [LH]

9 *Thanksgiving for victory*

1 I will give thanks to you, O LORD, with **my** whole heart;*
I will tell of all your **marvel**ous works.

2 I will be glad and re**joice** in you;*
I will sing to your Name, **O** Most High.

3 When my enemies are **driv**en back,*
they will stumble and perish **at** your presence.

4 For you have maintained my right **and** my cause;*
you sit upon your throne **judg**ing right.

5 You have rebuked the ungodly and des**troyed** the wicked;*
you have blotted out their name for ev**er** and ever.

6 As for the enemy, they are finished, in per**pet**ual ruin,*
their cities ploughed under, the memory **of** them perished;

7 But the LORD is en**throned** for ever;*
he has set up his **throne** for judgment.

8 It is he who rules the **world** with righteousness;*
he judges the peo**ples** with equity.

9 The LORD will be a refuge for **the** oppressed,*
a refuge in **time** of trouble.

10 Those who know your Name will put their **trust** in you,*
for you never forsake those who seek **you**, O LORD.

11 Sing praise to the LORD who **dwells** in Zion;*
proclaim to the peoples the things **he** has done.

12 The Avenger of blood will re**mem**ber them;*
he will not forget the cry of **the** afflicted.

13 Have pity on **me**, O LORD;*
see the misery I suffer from those who hate me,
O you who lift me up from the **gate** of death;

14 So that I may tell of all your praises
and rejoice in **your** salvation*
in the gates of the city of Zion.

15 The ungodly have fallen into the **pit** they dug,*
and in the snare they set is their **own** foot caught.

16 The LORD is known by his **acts** of justice;*
the wicked are trapped in the works of **their** own hands.

17 The wicked shall be given over **to** the grave,*
and also all the peoples that **for**get God.

18 For the needy shall not always **be** forgotten,*
and the hope of the poor shall not per**ish** for ever.

19 Rise up, O LORD, let not the ungodly have the **up**per hand;*
let them be **judged** before you.

20 Put fear upon **them**, O LORD;*
let the ungodly know they **are** but mortal.

Antiphon I will tell of **all** your praises*
in the gates of the city of Zion.

Silence for meditation

Lord God, righteous judge, hear the cries of your oppressed people. Rescue them from their oppressors, and save them from the gates of death, so that we may always rejoice in your help and speak your praise in the gates of Zion; through your Son, Jesus Christ our Lord. [LH, LBW]

+

Antiphon to PSALM 10 *Ut quid, Domine?*

Surely, you behold troub**le** and misery;*
you see it and take it into **your** own hand. [LH, PBO]

10 *Prayer for help*

1 Why do you stand so far **off**, O LORD,*
and hide yourself in **time** of trouble?

2 The wicked arrogantly perse**cute** the poor,*
but they are trapped in the schemes they **have** devised.

3 The wicked boast of their **heart's** desire;*
the covetous curse and re**vile** the LORD.

4 The wicked are so proud that they care **not** for God;*
their only thought is, "God **does** not matter."

5 Their ways are devious at all times;
your judgments are far above out **of** their sight;*
they defy **all** their enemies.

6 They say in their heart, "I shall **not** be shaken;*
no harm shall happen **to** me ever."

7 Their mouth is full of cursing, deceit, **and** oppression;*
under their tongue are mis**chief** and wrong.

8 They lurk in ambush in public squares
and in secret places they mur**der** the innocent;*
they spy **out** the helpless.

9 They lie in wait, like a lion in a covert;
they lie in wait to seize up**on** the lowly;*
they seize the lowly and drag them away **in** their net.

10 The innocent are broken and hum**bled** before them;*
the helpless fall be**fore** their power.

11 They say in their heart, "God **has** forgotten;*
he hides his face; he will **nev**er notice."

12 Rise up, O LORD;
lift up your **hand**, O God;*
do not forget **the** afflicted.

13 Why should the wick**ed** revile God?*
why should they say in their heart, "You **do** not care"?

14 Surely, you behold troub**le** and misery;*
you see it and take it into **your** own hand.

15 The helpless commit them**selves** to you,*
for you are the help**er** of orphans.

16 Break the power of the wick**ed** and evil;*
search out their wickedness until **you** find none.

17 The LORD is King for ev**er** and ever;*
the ungodly shall perish **from** his land.

18 The LORD will hear the desire **of** the humble;*
you will strengthen their heart and your **ears** shall hear;

19 To give justice to the orphan **and** oppressed,*
so that mere mortals may strike ter**ror** no more.

Antiphon Surely, you behold troub**le** and misery;*
you see it and take it into **your** own hand.

Silence for meditation

Faithful Lord, remember your people; do not hide your face from our troubles. Father of orphans, wealth of the poor, give us comfort in times of pain, that we may proclaim the joyous news of freedom in your Son, Jesus Christ our Lord. [LH, LBW]

+

Stand

THE HYMN is sung.

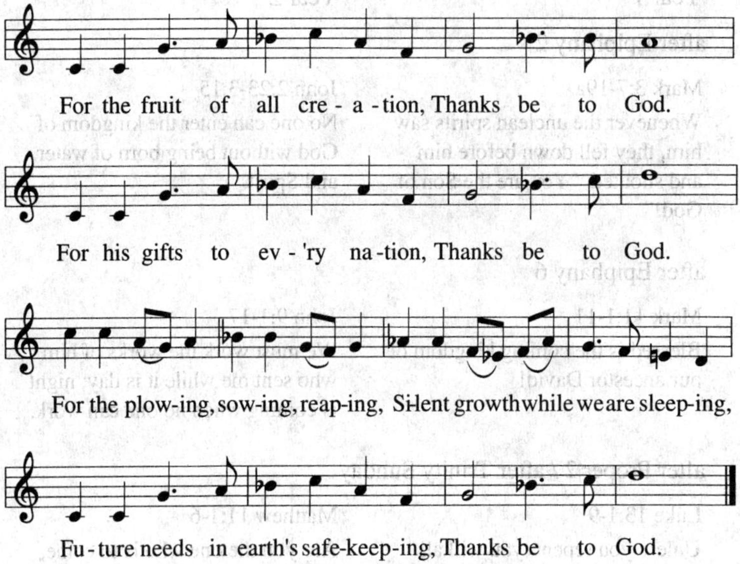

2 In the just reward of labor,
God's will is done.
In the help we give our neighbor,
God's will is done.
In the worldwide task of caring
For the hungry and despairing,
In the harvests we are sharing,
God's will be done.

3 For the harvests of the Spirit,
Thanks be to God.
For the good we all inherit,
Thanks be to God.
For the wonders that astound us,
For the truths that still confound us,
Most of all, that love has found us,
Thanks be to God.

[LBW 563, H82 424]

Text: F. Pratt Green, 1903-2000, © Hope Publishing Co.

Tune: *Santa Barbara* , Emma Lou Diemer, b. 1927 84 84 88 84

Sit

A LESSON is read.

Year 1	Year 2
after Epiphany 2	
Mark 3:7-19a Whenever the unclean spirits saw him, they fell down before him and shouted, "You are the Son of God!"	John 2:23-3:15 No one can enter the kingdom of God without being born of water and Spirit.
after Epiphany 6	
Mark 11:1-11 Blessed is the coming kingdom of our ancestor David!	John 9:1-17 We must work the works of him who sent me while it is day; night is coming when no one can work.
after Proper 2 / after Trinity Sunday	
Luke 13:1-9 Unless you repent, you will all perish as they did.	Matthew 11:1-6 Are you the one who is to come, or are we to wait for another?
after Proper 6 / Pentecost 5	
Luke 20:9-19 When the scribes and chief priests realized that he had told this parable against them, they wanted to lay hands on him at that very hour, but they feared the people.	Matthew 17:14-21 Jesus rebuked the demon, it came out of him, and the boy was cured instantly.
after Proper 10 / Pentecost 9	
Mark 1:29-45 He would not permit the demons to speak, because they knew him.	Matthew 25:1-13 Keep awake therefore, for you know nether the day nor the hour.

after Proper 14 / Pentecost 13

Mark 9:42-50

Have salt in yourselves, and be at peace with one another.

John 3:1-21

No one can enter the kingdom of God without being born of water and the Spirit.

after Proper 18 / Pentecost 17

Mark 15:40-47

Joseph of Arimathea, a respected member of the council, who was also himself waiting expectantly for the kingdom of God, went boldly to Pilate and asked for the body of Jesus.

John 10:19-30

My sheep hear my voice. I know them, and they follow me. I give them eternal life, and they will never perish.

after Proper 22 / Pentecost 21

Matthew 8:28-34

What have you to do with us, Son of God? Have you come here to torment us before the time?

Luke 6:39-49

Why do you call me, "Lord, Lord," and do not do what I tell you?

after Proper 26 / Pentecost 25

Matthew 13:36-43

Then the righteous will shine like the sun in the kingdom of their Father.

Luke 12:49-59

I came to bring fire to the earth, and how I wish it were already kindled!

Silence for meditation follows the reading.

Tuesday of Week II

Antiphon to PSALM 30 *Exaltabo te, Domine*

O Lord my God, I cried **out** to you,*
and you restored **me** to health. [LH, PBO]

30 *Thanksgiving after mortal danger*

1 I will exalt you, O LORD,
because you have lift**ed** me up*
and have not let my enemies triumph **o**ver me.

2 O LORD my God, I cried **out** to you,*
and you restored **me** to health.

3 You brought me up, O LORD, **from** the dead;*
you restored my life as I was going down **to** the grave.

4 Sing to the LORD, you ser**vants** of his;*
give thanks for the remembrance **of** his holiness.

5 For his wrath endures but the twinkling **of** an eye,*
his favor **for** a lifetime.

6 Weeping may **spend** the night,*
but joy comes **in** the morning.

7 While I felt secure, I said,
"I shall never **be** disturbed.*
You, LORD, with your favor, made me as strong **as**
the mountains.

8 Then you **hid** your face,*
and I was **filled** with fear.

9 I cried to **you**, O LORD;*
I pleaded with **the** Lord, saying,

10 "What profit is there in my blood, if I go down **to** the Pit?*
will the dust praise you or de**clare** your faithfulness?

11 Hear, O LORD, and have mer**cy** upon me;*
O LORD, **be** my helper."

12 You have turned my wailing **in**to dancing;*
you have put off my sack-cloth and clothed **me** with joy.

13 Therefore my heart sings to you **with**out ceasing;*
O LORD my God, I will give you **thanks** for ever.

Antiphon O Lord my God, I cried **out** to you,*
and you restored **me** to health.

Silence for meditation

God our Father, glorious in giving life and even more glorious in restoring it, in his last night on earth your Son knew anguish and deep sorrow. Do not turn away from us, or we shall fall back into dust; but rather turn our mourning into joy by raising us up with your Son, Jesus Christ our Lord.
[LH, LBW]

+

Antiphon to PSALM 86 *Inclina, Domine*

Gladden the soul **of** your servant,*
for to you, O LORD, I lift **up** my soul. [LH, PBO]

86 *Prayer in ordeal*

1 Bow down your ear, O LORD, and **an**swer me,*
for I am poor **and** in misery.

2 Keep watch over my life, for **I** am faithful;*
save your servant who puts his **trust** in you.

3 Be merciful to me, O LORD, for you **are** my God;*
I call upon you all **the** day long.

4 Gladden the soul **of** your servant,*
for to you, O LORD, I lift **up** my soul.

5 For you, O LORD, are good **and** forgiving,*
and great is your love toward all who **call** upon you.

6 Give ear, O LORD, **to** my prayer,*
and attend to the voice of my **supp**lications.

7 In the time of my trouble I will **call** upon you,*
for you will **an**swer me.

8 Among the gods there is none like **you**, O LORD,*
nor anything **like** your works.

9 All nations you have made will come and worship **you**, O LORD,*
and glori**fy** your Name.

10 For you are great;
you do **won**drous things;*
and you **alone** are God.

11 Teach me your way, O LORD,
and I will walk **in** your truth;*
knit my heart to you that I may **fear** your Name.

12 I will thank you, O LORD my God, with **all** my heart,*
and glorify your Name for **ev**ermore.

13 For great is your **love** toward me;
you have delivered me from the neth**er**most Pit.

14 The arrogant rise up against me, O God,
and a band of violent men **seeks** my life;*
they have not set you be**fore** their eyes.

15 But you, O LORD, are gracious and full **of** compassion,*
slow to anger, and full of kind**ness** and truth.

16 Turn to me and have mer**cy** upon me;*
give your strength to your servant;
and save the child **of** your handmaid.

17 Show me a sign of your favor,
so that those who hate me may see it and **be** ashamed,*
because you, O LORD have helped me and com**fort**ed me.

Antiphon Gladden the soul **of** your servant,*
for to you, O LORD, I lift **up** my soul.

Silence for meditation

God of mercy, when Christ called out to you in torment, you heard him and gave him victory over death: Fill us with the love of your Name and help us to proclaim you before the world, that all peoples may celebrate your glory in Christ our Lord. [LH, LBW]

+

Stand

THE HYMN is sung. *Hve dyrðlegur er drottinn*

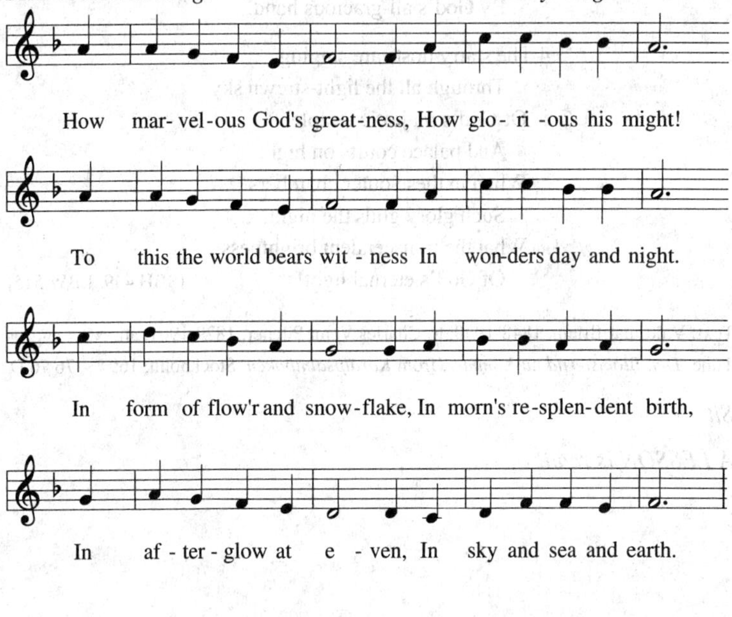

2 Each tiny floweret whispers
The great life-giver's Name;
The mighty mountain masses
His majesty proclaim;
The hollow vales are hymning
God's shelter for his own;
The snow-capped peaks are pointing
To God's almighty throne.

3 The ocean's vast abysses
In one grand psalm record
The deep mysterious counsels
And mercies of the Lord;
The icy waves of winter
Are thundering on the strand;
E'en grief's chill stream is guided
By God's all-gracious hand.

4 The starry hosts are singing
Through all the light-strewn sky
Of God's majestic temple
And palace courts on high;
When in these outer chambers
Such glory gilds the night,
What the transcendent brightness
Of God's eternal light! [SBH 449, LBW 515]

Text: Valdimar Briem, 1848-1930; tr. Charles Venn Pilcher, 1879-1961, alt.
Tune: *Den Blomstertid nu Kommer,* from *Koralpsalmboken*, Stockholm, 1697 76 76 D

Sit

A LESSON is read.

Year 1	Year 2

after Epiphany 2

Mark 3:19b-35	John 3:16-21
Whoever does the will of God is my brother and sister and mother.	Those who do what is true come to the light, so that it may be clearly seen that their deeds have been done in God.

after Epiphany 6

Mark 11:12-26	John 9:18-41
Whenever you stand praying, forgive, if you have anything against anyone.	If you were blind, you would not have sin. But now that you say, "We see," your sin remains.

after Proper 2 / after the Festival of the Holy Trinity

Luke 13:10-17	Matthew 11:7-15
The entire crowd was rejoicing at all the wonderful things that he was doing.	Among those born of women no one has arisen greater than John the Baptist; yet the least in the kingdom of heaven is greater than he.

after Proper 6 / Pentecost 5

Luke 20:19-26	Matthew 17:22-27
Give to the emperor the things that are the emperor's, and to God the things that are God's.	The Son of Man is going to be betrayed into human hands, and they will kill him, and on the third day he will be raised.

after Proper 10 / Pentecost 9

Mark 2:1-12	Matthew 25:14-30
Jesus said to the paralytic, "Son, your sins are forgiven."	To all those who have, more will be given, and they will have an abundance; but from those who have nothing, even what they have will be taken away.

after Proper 14 / Pentecost 13

Mark 10:1-16

Whoever does not receive the kingdom of God as a little child will never enter it.

John 3:22-36

Whoever believes in the Son has eternal life; whoever disobeys the Son will not see life, but must endure God's wrath.

after Proper 18 / Pentecost 17

Mark 16:1-8(9-20)

They went out and fled from the tomb, for terror and amazement had seized them; and they said nothing to anyone, for they were afraid.

John 10:31-42

"John performed no sign, but everything that John said about this man was true."

after Proper 22 / Pentecost 21

Matthew 9:1-8

The Son of Man has authority on earth to forgive sins.

Luke 7:1-17

"Young man, I say to you, rise!" The dead man sat up and began to speak, and Jesus gave him to his mother.

after Proper 26 / Pentecost 25

Matthew 13:44-52

Every scribe who has been trained for the kingdom of heaven is like a master of a household who brings out of his treasure what is new and what is old.

Luke13:1-9

Unless you repent, you will all perish as they did.

Silence for meditation follows the reading.

Wednesday of Week II

Antiphon to PSALM 48 *Magnus Dominus*

Great is the Lord, and highly **to** be praised;*
in the city of our God is his **ho**ly hill. [LH, PBO]

48 *Zion, the city of God*

1 Great is the LORD, and highly **to** be praised;*
in the city of our God is his **ho**ly hill.

2 Beautiful and lofty, the joy of all the earth, is the **hill** of Zion,*
the very center of the world and the city of **the** great King.

3 God is **in** her citadels;*
he is known to be **her** sure refuge.

4 Behold, the kings of the **earth** assembled*
and marched for**ward** together.

5 They looked and **were** astounded;*
they retreated and **fled** in terror.

6 Trembling **seized** them there;*
they writhed like a woman in childbirth,
like ships of the sea when the east wind **shat**ters them.

7 As we have heard, so have we seen,
in the city of the LORD of hosts, in the city **of** our God;*
God has established **her** for ever.

8 We have waited in silence on your loving-kind**ness**, O God,*
in the midst **of** your temple.

9 Your praise, like your Name, O God, reaches **to** the world's end;*
your right hand is **full** of justice.

10 Let Mount Zion be glad
and the cities of Ju**dah** rejoice,*
because **of** your judgments.

11 Make the circuit of Zion;
walk **round** about her;*
count the number **of** her towers.

12 Consider well her bulwarks;
ex**amine** her strongholds;*
that you may tell those **who** come after.

13 This God is our God for ev**er** and ever;*
he shall be our guide for **ev**ermore.

Antiphon Great is the Lord, and highly **to** be praised;*
in the city of our God is his **ho**ly hill.

Silence for meditation

Father, the body of your risen Son is the temple not made by human hands and the bulwark of the new Jerusalem: Make this holy city, built of living stones, so shine with spiritual radiance that it may show your greatness in the sight of all nations; for the sake of your Son, Jesus Christ our Lord.
[LH, LBW]

+

Antiphon to PSALM 59 *Eripe me de inimicis*

Protect **me**, O God,*
from those who rise **up** against me. [LH, PBO]

59 *Appeal to God, the stronghold*

1 Rescue me from my ene**mies**, O God;*
protect me from those who rise **up** against me.

2 Rescue me from **e**vildoers*
and save me from those who thirst **for** my blood.

3 See how they lie in wait for my life,
how the mighty gather togeth**er** against me;*
not for any offense or fault of **mine**, O LORD.

4 Not because of any **guilt** of mine*
they run and prepare them**selves** for battle.

5 Rouse yourself, come to my **side**, and see;*
for you, LORD God of hosts, are **Is**rael's God.

6 Awake, and punish all **the** ungodly;*
show no mercy to those who are faith**less** and evil.

7 They go to and fro **in** the evening;*
they snarl like dogs and run a**bout** the city.

8 Behold, they boast with their mouths,
and taunts are **on** their lips;*
"For who," they **say**, "will hear us?"

9 But you, O LORD, you **laugh** at them;*
you laugh all the ungod**ly** to scorn.

10 My eyes are fixed on you, **O** my Strength;*
for you, O God, **are** my stronghold.

11 My merciful God **comes** to meet me;*
God will let me look in triumph **on** my enemies.

12 Slay them, O God, lest my peo**ple** forget;*
send them reeling by your might
and put them down, O **LORD** our shield.

13 For the sins of their mouths, for the words of their lips,
for the cursing and lies **that** they utter,*
let them be caught **in** their pride.

14 Make an end of them **in** your wrath;*
make an end of them, and they shall **be** no more.

15 Let everyone know that God **rules** in Jacob,*
and to the ends **of** the earth.

16 They go to and fro **in** the evening;*
they snarl like dogs and run a**bout** the city.

17 They for**age** for food,*
and if they are not **filled**, they howl.

18 For my part, I will sing **of** your strength;*
I will celebrate your love **in** the morning;

19 For you have be**come** my stronghold,*
a refuge in the day **of** my trouble.

20 To you, O my Strength, **will** I sing;*
for you, O God, are my stronghold and my mer**ci**ful God.

Antiphon Protect **me**, O God,*
from those who rise **up** against me.

Silence for meditation

Lord God of power, you rescued your Son from the grasp of evil powers: Deliver us from evil and confirm our trust in you, so that with our rising we may sing of your power and at dawn exult in your mercy; through Jesus Christ our Lord. [LH, LBW]

+

Stand

THE HYMN is sung. *Sei Lob and Ehr dem höchsten Gut*

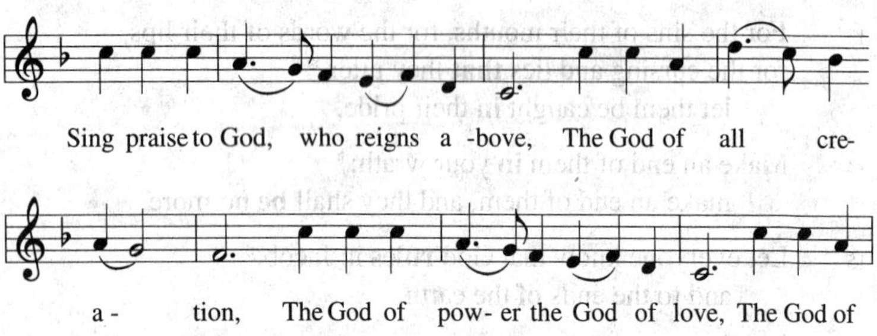

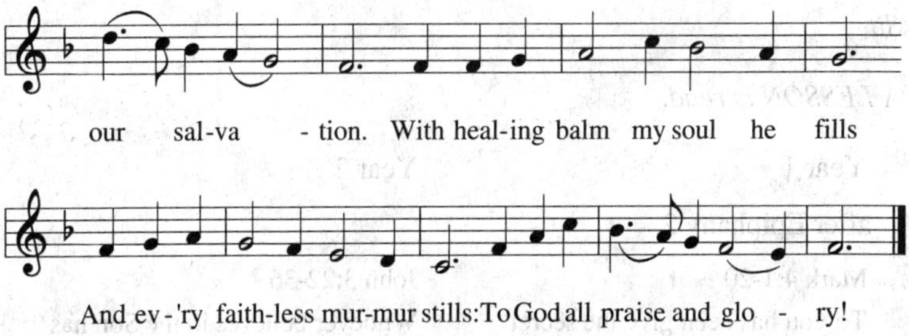

2 The angel host, O King of kings,
Thy praise for ever telling,
In earth and sky all living things
Beneath thy shadow dwelling,
Adore the wisdom which could span,
And power which formed creation's plan:
To God all praise and glory!

3 What God's almighty power hath made
His gracious mercy keepeth;
By morning glow or evening shade
His watchful eye ne'er sleepeth:
Within the kingdom of his might
Lo, all is just and all is right:
To God all praise and glory!

4 The Lord is never far away,
But through all grief distressing
An ever-present help and stay,
Our joy and peace and blessing.
As with a mother's tender hand
He leads his own, his chosen band;
To God all praise and glory.

5 Then all my gladsome way along
I sing aloud thy praises,
That all may hear the grateful song
My voice unwearied raises:
Be joyful in the Lord, my heart:
Both soul and body bear your part:
To God all praise and glory!

6 Let all who name Christ's holy Name
Give God the praise and glory.
Let all who know his power proclaim
Aloud the wondrous story.
Cast every idol from its throne,
For God is God, and he alone:
To God all praise and glory!

[CSB 285, TLH 19, SBH 422, LBW 542]

Text: Johann Jacob Schütz, 1640-1690; tr. Frances Elizabeth Cox, 1812-1897

Tune: *Lobet Gott den Herren, Ihr*, Melchior Vulpius, c. 1560-1615 87 87 887

Sit

A LESSON is read.

Year 1	Year 2
after Epiphany 2	
Mark 4:1-20	John 3:22-36
To you has been give the secret of the kingdom of God, but for those outside, everything comes in parables.	Whoever believes in the Son has eternal life; whoever disobeys the Son will not see life, but must endure God's wrath.
after Epiphany 6	
Mark 11:27-12:12	John 10:1-18
The stone that the builders rejected has become the cornerstone.	I am the good shepherd. The good shepherd lays down his life for the sheep.
after Proper 2 / after the Festival of the Holy Trinity	
Luke 13:18-30	Matthew 11:16-24
Some are last who will be first, and some are first who will be last.	He began to reproach the cities in which most of his deeds of power had been done, because they did not repent.
after Proper 6 / Pentecost 5	
Luke 20:27-40	Matthew 18:1-9
Now he is God not of the dead, but of the living; for to him all of them are alive.	Unless you change and become like children, you will never enter the kingdom of heaven.
after Proper 10 / Pentecost 9	
Mark 2:13-22	Matthew 25:31-46
I have come to call not the righteous but sinners.	Come, you that are blessed of my Father, inherit the kingdom pre-

pared for you from the foundation of the world.

after Proper 14 / Pentecost 13

Mark 10:17-31

Go, sell what you own, and give the money to the poor, and you will have treasure in heaven; then come, follow me.

John 4:1-26

Those who drink of the water that I will give them will never be thirsty.

after Proper 18 / Pentecost 17

Matthew 2:1-12

Opening their treasure chests, they offered him gifts of gold, frankincense, and myrrh.

John 11:1-16

Lazarus is dead. For your sake I am glad I was not there, so that you may believe.

after Proper 22 / Pentecost 21

Matthew 9:9-17

I have come to call not the righteous but sinners.

Luke 7:18-35

Among those born of women no one is greater than John; yet the least in the kingdom of God is greater than he.

after Proper 26 / Pentecost 25

Matthew 13:53-58

Where did this man get this wisdom and these deeds of power?

Luke 13:10-17

Ought not this woman, a daughter of Abraham whom Satan bound for eighteen long years, be set free from this bondage on the sabbath day?

Silence for meditation follows the reading.

Thursday of Week II

Antiphon to PSALM 80 *Qui regis Israel*

Stir up your **strength**, O Lord,*
and **come** to help us. [LH, PBO]

80 *Plea for the return of God's favor*

1 Hear, O Shepherd of Israel, leading Joseph **like** a flock;*
shine forth, you that are enthroned up**on** the cherubim.

2 In the presence of Ephraim, Benjamin, **and** Manasseh,*
stir up your strength and **come** to help us.

3 Restore us, O **God** of hosts;*
show the light of your countenance, and we **shall** be saved.

4 O LORD **God** of hosts,*
how long will you be angered
despite the prayers **of** your people?

5 You have fed them with the **bread** of tears;*
you have given them bowls of **tears** to drink.

6 You have made us the derision **of** our neighbors,*
and our enemies laugh **us** to scorn.

7 Restore us, O **God** of hosts;*
show the light of your countenance, and we **shall** be saved.

8 You have brought a vine **out** of Egypt;*
you cast out the nations and **plan**ted it.

9 You prepared the **ground** for it;*
it took root and **filled** the land.

10 The mountains were covered **by** its shadow*
and the towering cedar trees **by** its boughs.

11 You stretched out its tendrils **to** the Sea*
and its branches **to** the River.

12 Why have you broken **down** its wall,*
so that all who pass by pluck **off** its grapes?

13 The wild boar of the forest has **rav**aged it,*
and the beasts of the field have **grazed** upon it.

14 Turn now, O God of hosts, look down from heaven;
behold and **tend** this vine;*
preserve what your right **hand** has planted.

15 They burn it with **fire** like rubbish;*
at the rebuke of your countenance **let** them perish.

16 Let your hand be upon the man of **your** right hand,*
the son of man you have made so strong **for** yourself.

17 And so will we never turn a**way** from you;*
give us life, that we may call up**on** your Name.

18 Restore us, O LORD **God** of hosts;*
show the light of your countenance, and we **shall** be saved.

Antiphon Stir up your **strength**, O Lord,*
and **come** to help us.

Silence for meditation

Lord God, you so tend the vine you planted that now it extends its branches even to the farthest shore: Keep us in your Son as branches on the vine, that, rooted firmly in your love, we may testify before the whole world to your great power working everywhere; through Jesus Christ our Lord.

[LH, LBW]

+

Antiphon to PSALM 27 *Dominus illuminatio*

The Lord is my light and **my** salvation;*
whom then **shall** I fear? [LH]

27 *Triumphant trust in God*

1 The LORD is my light and my salvation;
whom then **shall** I fear?*
the LORD is the strength of my life;
of whom then shall I **be** afraid?

2 When evildoers came upon me to eat **up** my flesh,*
it was they, my foes and my adversaries, who stum**bled** and fell.

3 Though an army should en**camp** against me,*
yet my heart shall not **be** afraid;

4 And though war should rise **up** against me,*
yet will I put my **trust** in him.

5 One thing have I asked of the LORD;
one **thing** I seek;*
that I may dwell in the house of the LORD all the days **of** my life;

6 To behold the fair beauty **of** the LORD*
and to seek him **in** his temple.

7 For in the day of trouble he shall keep me safe **in** his shelter;*
he shall hide me in the secrecy of his dwelling
and set me high up**on** a rock.

8 Even now he lifts **up** my head*
above my enemies **round** about me.

9 Therefore I will offer in his dwelling an oblation
with sounds **of** great gladness;*
I will sing and make music **to** the LORD.

10 Hearken to my voice, O LORD, **when** I call;*
have mercy on me and **an**swer me.

11 You speak in my heart and say, "**Seek** my face."*
Your face, LORD, **will** I seek.

12 Hide not your **face** from me,*
nor turn away your servant **in** displeasure.

13 You have been my helper;
cast me **not** away;*
do not forsake me, O God of **my** salvation.

14 Though my father and my moth**er** forsake me,*
the LORD **will** sustain me.

15 Show me your **way**, O LORD;*
lead me on a level path, because **of** my enemies.

16 Deliver me not into the hand of my **ad**versaries,*
for false witnesses have risen up against me,
and also those **who** speak malice.

17 What if I had not believed
that I should see the goodness **of** the LORD*
in the land **of** the living!

18 O tarry and await the LORD's pleasure;
be strong, and he shall com**fort** your heart;*
wait patiently **for** the LORD.

Antiphon The Lord is my light and **my** salvation;*
whom then **shall** I fear?

Silence for meditation

Gracious Father, protector of those who hope in you, you heard the cry of your Son and kept him safe in your shelter in the day of evil. Grant that your servants who seek your face in times of trouble may see your goodness in the land of the living, through your Son, Jesus Christ our Lord.

[LH, LBW]

+

Stand

THE HYMN is sung. *Laudato sí, mi Signor, con tutte le tue creature*

2 Great rushing wind and breezes soft,
You clouds that ride the winds aloft:
  Oh, praise him! Alleluia!
O rising morn, in praise rejoice,
And lights of evening, find a voice.
  Oh, praise him! Oh, praise him! Alleluia, Alleluia, Alleluia!

3 O flowing water, pure and clear,
Make music for your Lord to hear.

Alleluia! Alleluia!
And fire so masterful and bright,
Providing us with warmth and light,
Oh, praise him! Oh, praise him! Alleluia, Alleluia, Alleluia!

4 Dear mother earth, you day by day
Unfold rich blessings on our way,
Oh, praise him! Alleluia!
The fruits and flowers that in you grow,
Let them his glory also show,
Oh, praise him! Oh, praise him! Alleluia, Alleluia, Alleluia!

5 O everyone of tender heart,
Forgiving others, take your part,
Oh, praise him! Alleluia!
All who long pain and sorrow bear,
Praise God and lay on him your care.
Oh, praise him! Oh, praise him! Alleluia, Alleluia, Alleluia!

6 And you, most kind and gentle death,
Waiting to hush our final breath,
Oh, praise him! Alleluia!
You lead to home the child of God,
Where Christ our Lord the way has trod,
Oh, praise him! Oh, praise him! Alleluia, Alleluia, Alleluia!

7 Let all things their Creator bless
And worship God in humbleness.
Oh, praise him! Alleluia!
Praise God the Father, praise the Son,
And praise the Spirit, Three in One,
Oh, praise him! Oh, praise him! Alleluia, Alleluia, Alleluia!
[LBW 527, H82 400]

Text: Francis of Assisi, 1182-1226; tr. William H. Draper, 1855-1933, alt.

Tune: *Lasst uns erfreuen, Geistliche Kirchengesänge*, Köln, 1623 88 44 88 and alleluias

Sit

A LESSON is read.

Year 1	Year 2

after Epiphany 2

Mark 4:21-34	John 4:1-15
There is nothing hidden, except to be disclosed; nor is anything secret, except to come to light.	The water that I will give will become in them a spring of water gushing up to eternal life.

after Epiphany 6

Mark 12:13-27	John 10:19-30
Give to the emperor the things that are the emperor's, and to God the things that are God's.	My sheep hear my voice. I know them, and they follow me. I give them eternal life.

after Proper 2 / after the Festival of the Holy Trinity

Luke 13:31-35	Matthew 11:25-30
Today, tomorrow, and the next day I must be on my way, because it is impossible for a prophet to be killed outside of Jerusalem.	Come to me, all you that are weary and are carrying heavy burdens, and I will give you rest.

after Proper 6 / Pentecost 5

Luke 20:41-21:4	Matthew 18:10-20
This poor widow has put in more than all of them; for all of them have contributed out of their abundance, but she out of her poverty has put in all she had to live on.	It is not the will of your Father in heaven that one of these little ones should be lost.

after Proper 10 / Pentecost 9

Mark 2:23-3:6

The Son of Man is Lord even of the sabbath.

Matthew 26:1-16

After two days the Passover is coming, and the Son of Man will be handed over to be crucified.

after Proper 14 / Pentecost 13

Mark 10:32-45

Whoever wishes to become great among you must be your servant.

John 4:27-42

It is no longer because of what you said that we believe, for we have heard for ourselves, and we know that this is truly the Savior of the world.

after Proper 18 / Pentecost 17

Matthew 2:13-23

Get up, take the child and his mother, and go to the land of Israel, for those who were seeking the child's life are dead.

John 11:17-29

Everyone who lives and believes in me will never die.

after Proper 22 / Pentecost 21

Matthew 9:18-26

Take heart, daughter; your faith has made you well.

Luke 7:36-50

The one to whom little is forgiven, loves little.

after Proper 26 / Pentecost 25

Matthew 14:1-12

His disciples came and took the body and buried it; then they went and told Jesus.

Luke 13:18-30

Strive to enter through the narrow door; for many, I tell you, will try to enter and will not be able.

Silence for meditation follows the reading.

Friday of Week II

Antiphon to PSALM 32 *Beati quorum*

Happy are they whose transgressions **are** forgiven,*
and whose sin is **put** away!

32 *The joy of being forgiven*

1 Happy are they whose transgressions **are** forgiven,*
and whose sin is **put** away!

2 Happy are they to whom the LORD im**putes** no guilt,*
and in whose spirit there **is** no guile!

3 While I held my tongue, my bones with**er**ed away,*
because of my groaning **all** day long.

4 For your hand was heavy upon me **day** and night;*
my moisture was dried up as in the **heat** of summer.

5 Then I acknowledged my **sin** to you,*
and did not con**ceal** my guilt.

6 I said, "I will confess my transgressions **to** the LORD."*
Then you forgave me the guilt **of** my sin.

7 Therefore all the faithful will make their prayers to you
in **time** of trouble;*
when the great waters overflow, they **shall** not reach them.

8 You are my hiding-place;
you preserve **me** from trouble;*
you surround me with shouts **of** deliverance.

9 "I will instruct you and teach you in the way that **you** should go;*
I will guide you **with** my eye.

10 Do not be like horse or mule, which have no **un**derstanding;*
who must be fitted with bit and bridle,
or else they will **not** stay near you."

11 Great are the tribulations **of** the wicked;*
but mercy embraces those who trust **in** the LORD.

12 Be glad, you righteous, and rejoice **in** the LORD;*
shout for joy, all who are **true** of heart.

Antiphon Happy are they whose transgressions **are** forgiven,*
and whose sin is **put** away!

Silence for meditation

Lord God, you desired to keep from us your wrath and so did not spare your holy servant Jesus Christ, who was wounded for our sins. We are your prodigal children, but we come back to you confessing our sins. Embrace us, that we may rejoice in your mercy together with your beloved Son, Jesus Christ our Lord. [LH, LBW]

+

Antiphon to PSALM 140 *Eripe me, Domine*

Keep me, O Lord, from the hands **of** the wicked,*
for you are the strength of **my** salvation. [LH]

140 *Prayer for protection*

1 Deliver me, O LORD, from evildoers;*
protect me **from** the violent,

2 Who devise evil **in** their hearts*
and stir up strife **all** day long.

3 They have sharpened their tongues **like** a serpent;*
adder's poison is **un**der their lips.

4 Keep me, O LORD, from the hands **of** the wicked;*
protect me from the violent,
who are determined to **trip** me up.

5 The proud have hidden a snare for me
and stretched out a **net** of cords;*
they have set traps for me a**long** the path.

6 I have said to the LORD, "You **are** my God;*
listen, O LORD, to my **sup**plication.

7 O Lord GOD, the strength of **my** salvation,*
you have covered my head in the **day** of battle.

8 Do not grant the desires of the wick**ed**, O LORD,*
nor let their e**vil** plans prosper.

9 Let not those who surround me lift **up** their heads;*
let the evil of their lips **o**verwhelm them.

10 Let hot burning coals **fall** upon them;*
let them be cast into the mire, never to rise **up** again."

11 A slanderer shall not be established **on** the earth,*
and evil shall hunt **down** the lawless.

12 I know that the LORD will maintain the cause **of** the poor*
and render justice **to** the needy.

13 Surely, the righteous will give thanks **to** your Name,*
and the upright shall continue **in** your sight.

Antiphon Keep me, O Lord, from the hands **of** the wicked,*
for you are the strength of **my** salvation.

Silence for meditation

Lord, you keep constant guard over your faithful people. Protect us from hidden snares, deliver us from those who would seek to do us harm, and make us holy; that we may praise and bless your Name and live in righteousness before you now and for ever. [LH, LBW]

+

Stand

THE HYMN is sung. *Herrasta veisaa kieleni*

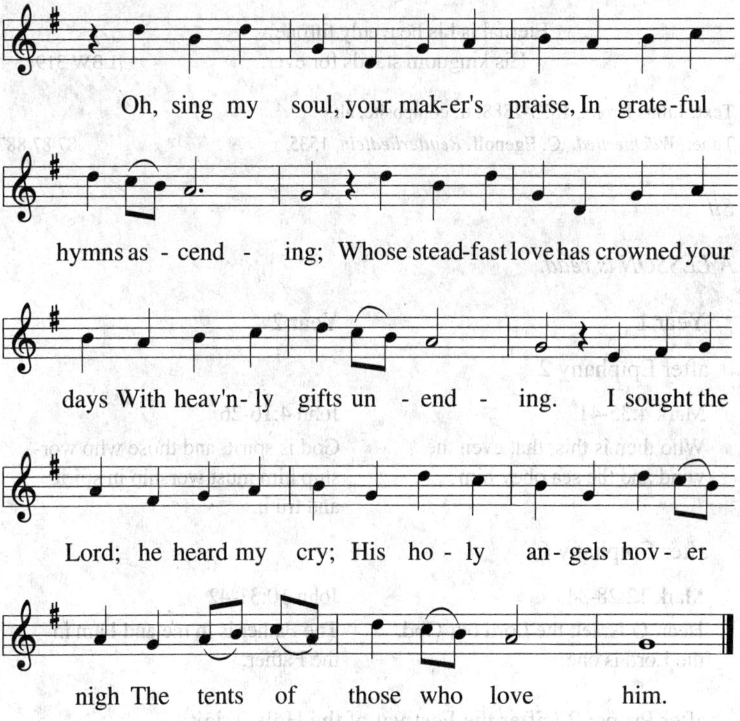

2 The Lord is good to those who seek
His face in time of sorrow,
Providing comfort to the weak
And grace for each tomorrow.
Though grief may tarry for the night,
The morn shall break in joy and light
With blessings from his presence.

3 The Lord will turn his face in peace
When troubled souls draw near him;
His lovingkindness shall not cease
To those who trust and fear him.
Our God will not forsake his own;

Eternal is his heavenly throne;
His kingdom stands for ever. [LBW 319]

Text: Julius Krohn, 1835-1888; tr. composite, alt.
Tune: *Wächterlied*, C. Egenolf, *Reutterliedlein*, 1535 87 87 887

Sit

A LESSON is read.

Year 1	Year 2
after Epiphany 2	
Mark 4:35-41	John 4:16-26
Who then is this, that even the wind and the sea obey him?	God is spirit, and those who worship him must worship in spirit and truth.
after Epiphany 6	
Mark 12:28-34	John 10:31-42
Hear, O Israel: the Lord our God, the Lord is one.	The Father is in me and I am in the Father.
after Proper 2 / after the Festival of the Holy Trinity	
Luke 14:1-11	Matthew 12:1-14
All who exalt themselves will be humbled, and those who humble themselves will be exalted.	The Son of Man is lord of the sabbath.
after Proper 6 / Pentecost 5	
Luke 21:5-19	Matthew 18:21-35
By your endurance you will gain your souls.	Should you not have had mercy on your fellow slave, as I had mercy on you?

after Proper 10 / Pentecost 9

Mark 3:7-19a

Whenever the unclean spirits saw him, they fell down before him and shouted, "You are the Son of God!"

Matthew 26:17-25

Woe to that one by whom the Son of Man is betrayed!

after Proper 14 / Pentecost 13

Mark 10:46-52

Jesus, Son of David, have mercy on me!

John 4:43-54

Go; your son will live.

after Proper 18 / Pentecost 17

Matthew 3:1-12

Repent, for the kingdom of heaven has come near.

John 11:30-44

Lazarus, come out!

after Proper 22 / Pentecost 21

Matthew 9:27-34

Have mercy on us, Son of David!

Luke 8:1-15

To you it has been given to know the secrets of the kingdom of God; but to others I speak in parables.

after Proper 26 / Pentecost 25

Matthew 14:13-21

All ate and were filled.

Luke 13:31-35

Yet today, tomorrow, and the next day I must be on my way, because it is impossible for a prophet to be killed outside of Jerusalem.

Silence for meditation follows the reading.

Saturday of Week III

Antiphon to PSALM 100 *Jubilate Deo*

Come before God's presence with a song. [LH, PBO]

100 *Praise to God, Creator and Shepherd*

1 Be joyful in the LORD, **all** you lands;*
serve the LORD with gladness
and come before his presence **with** a song.

2 Know this: The LORD him**self** is God;*
he himself has made us, and we are his;
we are his people and the sheep **of** his pasture.

3 Enter his gates with thanksgiving;
go into his **courts** with praise;*
give thanks to him and call up**on** his Name.

4 For the LORD is good;
his mercy is **ev**erlasting;*
and his faithfulness endures from **age** to age,

Antiphon Come before God's presence with a song.

Silence for meditation

God of goodness and might, by your power you created us and in your mercy you chose us as your own: Accept the praise we offer, and grant that the people of all lands may enter your courts with songs of praise; through Jesus Christ our Lord. [LH, PHP]

+

Antiphon to PSALM 138 *Confitebor tibi*

I will bow down toward your **ho**ly temple*
and **praise** your Name. [PBO]

138 *Hymn of thanksgiving*

1 I will give thanks to you, O LORD, with **my** whole heart;*
before the gods I will **sing** your praise.

2 I will bow down toward your holy temple
and **praise** your Name,*
because of your **love** and faithfulness;

3 For you have glori**fied** your Name*
and your word a**bove** all things.

4 When I called, you **an**swered me;*
you increased my **strength** within me.

5 All the kings of the earth will praise **you**, O LORD,*
when they have heard the words **of** your mouth.

6 They will sing of the ways **of** the LORD,*
that great is the glory **of** the LORD.

7 Though the LORD be high, he cares **for** the lowly;*
he perceives the haughty **from** afar.

8 Though I walk in the midst of trouble, you **keep** me safe;*
you stretch forth your hand against the fury of my enemies;
your right **hand** shall save me.

9 The LORD will make good his pur**pose** for me;*
O LORD, your love endures for ever;
do not abandon the works **of** your hands.

Antiphon I will bow down toward your **ho**ly temple*
and **praise** your Name.

Silence for meditation

Lord God, you keep the proud at a distance and look upon the lowly with favor: Stretch out your hand to us in our suffering, perfect in us the work of your love, and bring us to life in Jesus Christ our Lord. [LH, LBW]

+

Antiphon to the NEW TESTAMENT CANTICLE

Gratias agentes Deo Patri

Through him everything **was** created;*
in him the whole universe is **held** together. [LH]

A Song of the Supremacy of Christ Colossians 1:12-20

Let us give thanks to **God** the Father,*
who has called us to share the inheritance
of the saints in the **realm** of light.

He rescued us from the do**main** of darkness *
and brought us into the kingdom of his beloved Son,
by whom we are set free and our **sins** forgiven.

He is the first-born of **all** creation;*
in him everything in heaven and on earth
was created, visible **and** invisible.

The whole universe has been created through him
and for him;*
he exists before all else that is;
in him everything is **held** together.

He is the head of the **Church**, his body;*
he is its origin, the first-born of the dead,
su**preme** in all things.

In him the fullness of God **came** to dwell;*
through him God chose to reconcile
the whole universe to himself,
making peace by the blood **of** his cross. [LH, PHP]

Antiphon Through him everything **was** created;*
in him the whole universe is **held** together.

Silence for meditation

O Lord, our Creator and Redeemer, you have delivered us from the domain of darkness and have brought us into your kingdom of everlasting light: Fill us with your peace, and make us instruments of reconciliation in the world; through Jesus Christ our Lord. [PHP]

+

Stand

THE HYMN is sung.

2 Tell them I AM, the Lord God said,
To Moses while on earth in dread
And smitten to the heart,
At once above, beneath, around,
All nature without voice or sound
Replied, O Lord, thou art.

3 Glorious the sun in mid career;
Glorious the assembled fires appear;
  Glorious the comet's train;
Glorious the trumpet and alarm;
Glorious the almighty stretched-out arm;
  Glorious the enraptured main;

4 Glorious, most glorious, is the crown
Of him that brought salvation down
  By meekness, Mary's Son;
Seers that stupendous truth believed,
And now the matchless deed's achieved,
  Determined, dared, and done. [H82 387]

Text: Christopher Smart, 1722-1771, alt.
Tune: *Magdalen College,* William Hayes, 1706-1777 886 886

Sit

A LESSON is read.

Year 1	Year 2
eve of Epiphany 3	
Mark 5:1-20	John 4:27-42
Go home to your friends, and tell them how much the Lord has done for you, and what mercy he has shown you.	We have heard for ourselves, and we know that this is truly the Savior of the world.
eve of Epiphany 7	
Mark 12:35-44	John 11:1-16
The large crowd was listening to him with delight.	Having heard that Lazarus was ill, Jesus stayed two days longer in the place where he was.

eve of Proper 3 (Sunday between May 22 and 28) / Pentecost 2

Luke 14:12-24

When you give a banquet, invite the poor, the crippled, the lame, and the blind. And you will be blessed, because they cannot repay you.

Matthew 12:15-21

Many crowds followed him, and he cured all of them, and he ordered them not to make him known.

eve of Proper 7 (Sunday between June 19 and 25) / Pentecost 6

Luke 21:20-28

Jerusalem will be trampled on by the Gentiles, until the times of the Gentiles are fulfilled.

Matthew 19:1-12

What God has joined together, let no one separate.

eve of Proper 11 (Sunday between July 17 and 23) / Pentecost 10

Mark 3:19b-35

Whoever does the will of God is my brother and sister and mother.

Matthew 26:26-35

After I am raised up, I will go ahead of you to Galilee.

eve of Proper 15 (Sunday between August 14 and 20) / Pentecost 14

Mark 11:1-11

Blessed is the one who comes in the name of the Lord!

John 5:1-18

Stand up, take up your mat and walk.

eve of Proper 19 (Sunday between September 11 and 17) / Pentecost 18

Matthew 3:13-17

When Jesus had been baptized, just as he came up from the water, suddenly the heavens were opened to him and he saw the Spirit of God descending like a dove and alighting on him.

John 11:45-54

You do not understand that it is better for you to have one man die for the people than to have the whole nation destroyed.

eve of Proper 23 (Sunday between October 9 and 15) / Pentecost 22

Matthew 9:35-10:4

When Jesus saw the crowds, he had compassion for them, because they were harassed and helpless, like sheep without a shepherd.

Luke 8:16-25

Nothing is hidden that will not be disclosed, nor is anything secret that will not become known and come to light.

eve of Proper 27 (Sunday between November 6 and 12) / Pentecost 26

Matthew 14:22-36

Those in the boat worshiped him, saying, "Truly you are the Son of God."

Luke 14:1-11

All who exalt themselves will be humbled, and those who humble themselves will be exalted.

Silence for meditation follows the reading.

Sunday of Week III

Antiphon to PSALM 46 *Deus noster refugium*

The Lord of **hosts** is with us;*
the God of Jacob **is** our stronghold. [LH, PBO]

46 *A mighty fortress is our God*

1 God is our re**fuge** and strength,*
a very present **help** in trouble.

2 Therefore we will not fear, though the **earth** be moved,*
and though the mountains be toppled into the
depths **of** the sea;

3 Though its waters **rage** and foam,*
and though the mountains tremble **at** its tumult.

4 The LORD of **hosts** is with us;*
the God of Jacob **is** our stronghold.

5 There is a river whose streams make glad the city of God,*
the holy habitation of **the** Most High.

6 God is in the midst of her;
she shall not be **o**verthrown;*
God shall help her at the **break** of day.

7 The nations make much ado, and the king**doms** are shaken;*
God has spoken, and the earth shall **melt** away.

8 The LORD of **hosts** is with us;*
the God of Jacob **is** our stronghold.

9 Come now and look upon the works **of** the LORD,*
what awesome things he has **done** on earth.

10 It is he who makes war to cease in **all** the world;*
he breaks the bow, and shatters the spear,
and burns the **shields** with fire.

11 “Be still, then, and know that **I** am God;*
I will be exalted among the nations;
I will be exalted **in** the earth.”

12 The LORD of **hosts** is with us;*
The God of Jacob **is** our stronghold.

Antiphon The Lord of **hosts** is with us;*
the God of Jacob **is** our stronghold.

Silence for meditation

Lord God, our refuge and strength, when the restless powers of this world and the waters of hell rise up against your holy city, watch over it and keep it safe. By the river that flows from the throne of the Lamb, purify this new Jerusalem as your chosen dwelling, for you are with us, our stronghold now and for ever. [LHd, LBW]

+

Antiphon to PSALM 93 *Dominus regnavit*

Mighty is the Lord who dwells on high. [LH, PBO]

93 *The splendor of God the creator*

1 The LORD is King;
he has put on splen**did** apparel;*
the LORD has put on his apparel
and girded him**self** with strength.

2 He has made the whole **world** so sure*
that it can**not** be moved;

3 Ever since the world began, your throne has **been** established;*
you are from **ev**erlasting.

4 The waters have lifted up, O LORD,
the waters have lifted **up** their voice;*
the waters have lifted up their **pound**ing waves.

5 Mightier than the sound of many waters,
mightier than the breakers **of** the sea,*
mightier is the LORD who **dwells** on high.

6 Your testimonies are **ver**y sure,*
and holiness adorns your house, O LORD,
for ever and for **ev**ermore.

Antiphon Mighty is the Lord who dwells on high.

Silence for meditation

Lord Jesus, king of glory, when you rose from the grave in the power of the Spirit, you firmly established your kingdom, never to be shaken or destroyed by death: May your will be done on earth as in heaven until the world is made holy by your embrace, our Redeemer and our Lord. [LHd, LBW]

+

Antiphon to the NEW TESTAMENT CANTICLE *Dignus es*

You have made us a kingdom of **priests**, O Lord,*
to **serve** our God. [LH]

A Song to the Lamb Revelation 4:11; 5:9-10,13

Splendor and honor and **king**ly power*
are yours by right, O **Lord** our God,
For you created every**thing** that is,*
and by your will they were created and **have** their being;

And yours by right, O Lamb **that** was slain,*
for with your blood you have re**deemed** for God,
From every family, language, peo**ple,** and nation,*
a kingdom of priests to **serve** our God.

And so, to him who sits up**on** the throne,*
and to **Christ** the Lamb,
Be worship and praise, domin**ion** and splendor,*
for ever and for **ev**ermore. [BCP]

Antiphon You have made us a kingdom of **priests**, O Lord,*
to **serve** our God.

Silence for meditation

Mighty and loving God, by the cross and passion of your beloved Son you saved humanity from sin and death: In your mercy grant that by steadfast faith in his sacrifice we may triumph in the power of his enduring victory; through Jesus Christ our Lord. [PHP]

+

Stand

The HYMN is sung. *Die Nacht ist kommen, drin wir ruhen sollen*

2 Let evil thoughts and spirits flee before us;
Till morning comes, O Master, keep watch o'er us;
In soul and body from all harm defend us,
Your angels send us.

3 Let holy thoughts be ours when sleep o'ertakes us;
Our earliest thoughts be yours when morning wakes us;

All day serve you, in all that we are doing
Your praise pursuing.

4 As your beloved, soothe the sick and weeping,
And bid the prisoners lose their griefs in sleeping;
Widows and orphans to you we commend them;
Ever befriend them.

5 We have no refuge, none on earth to aid us,
Save you, O Father, who your own have made us;
But your dear presence will not leave them lonely
Who seek you only.

6 Father, your Name be praised, your kingdom given;
Your will be done on earth as 'tis in heaven;
Keep us in life, forgive our sins, deliver
Us now and ever. [CSB 459, OAH 39

Text: Petrus Herbert, d. 1571; tr. Catherine Winkworth, 1829-1878
Tune: *Lob den Herren, alle*, Johann Crüger, 1598-1662 11 11 11 5

Sit

A LESSON is read.

Year 1	Year 2
Epiphany 3	
John 5:2-18	Mark 7:31-37
"Stand up, take up your mat and walk." At once the man was made well, and he took up his mat and began to walk.	He has done everything well; he even makes the deaf to hear and the mute to speak.
Epiphany 7	
John 10:7-16	Mark 10:35-45
I am the good shepherd. I know my own and my own know me.	The Son of Man came not to be served but to serve, and to give his life as a ransom for many.

Proper 3 (Sunday between May 22 and 28) / Pentecost 2

Matthew 12:33-45	Luke 10:25-28,38-42
The tree is known by its fruit.	You shall love the Lord your God with all your heart, and with all your soul, and with all your strength, and with all your mind; and your neighbor as yourself.

Proper 7 (Sunday between June 19 and 25) / Pentecost 6

Matthew 19:23-30	Luke 12:49-56
It is easier for a camel to go through the eye of a needle than for someone who is rich to enter the kingdom of God.	Do you think that I have come to bring peace to the earth? No, I tell you, but rather division!

Proper 11 (Sunday between July 17 and 23) / Pentecost 10

Matthew 25:14-30	Mark 2:1-12
To all those who have, more will be given, and they will have an abundance; but from those who have nothing, even what they have will be taken away.	The Son of Man has authority on earth to forgive sins.

Proper 15 (Sunday between August 14 and 20) / Pentecost 14

John 5:30-47	Mark 5:25-34
The works that the Father has given me to complete, the very works that I am doing, testify on my behalf that the Father has sent me.	Daughter, your faith has made you well.

Proper 19 (Sunday between September 11 and 17) / Pentecost 18

John 11:45-57

You do not understand that it is better to have one man die for the people than to have the whole nation destroyed.

Matthew 5:21-26

First be reconciled to your brother or sister, and then come and offer your gift.

Proper 23 (Sunday between October 9 and 15) / Pentecost 22

Luke 7:36-50

The one to whom little is forgiven, loves little.

Matthew 15:21-28

Have mercy on me, Lord, Son of David.

Proper 27 (Sunday between November 6 and 12) / Pentecost 26

Luke 14:12-24

When you give a banquet, invite the poor, the crippled, the lame, and the blind. and you will be blessed, because they cannot repay you.

Matthew 20:1-16

I choose to give to this last the same as I give to you. Am I not allowed to do what I choose with what belongs to me?

Silence for meditation follows the reading.

Monday of Week III

Antiphon to PSALM 85 *Benedixisti, Domine*

You have been gracious to your **land**, O Lord,*
you have forgiven the iniquity **of** your people. [LH, PBO]

85 *The coming age of justice and peace*

1 You have been gracious to your **land**, O LORD,*
you have restored the good for**tune** of Jacob.

2 You have forgiven the iniquity **of** your people*
and blotted out **all** their sins.

3 You have withdrawn **all** your fury*
and turned yourself from your wrathful **in**dignation.

4 Restore us then, O **God** our Savior;*
let your anger de**part** from us.

5 Will you be displeased with **us** for ever?*
will you prolong your anger from **age** to age?

6 Will you not give us **life** again,*
that your people may re**joice** in you?

7 Show us your mer**cy**, O LORD,*
and grant us **your** salvation.

8 I will listen to what the LORD **God** is saying,*
for he is speaking peace to his faithful people
and to those who turn their **hearts** to him.

9 Truly, his salvation is very near to **those** who fear him,*
that his glory may dwell **in** our land.

10 Mercy and truth have **met** together;*
righteousness and peace have **kissed** each other.

11 Truth shall spring up **from** the earth,*
and righteousness shall look **down** from heaven.

12 The LORD will indeed **grant** prosperity,*
and our land will **yield** its increase.

13 Righteousness shall **go** before him,*
and peace shall be a pathway **for** his feet.

Antiphon You have been gracious to your **land**, O Lord,*
you have forgiven the iniquity **of** your people.

Silence for meditation

God of love and faithfulness, you so loved the world that you gave your only Son to be our Savior: Help us to receive him as both Lord and brother and freely celebrate him as our gracious Redeemer now and for ever.

[LHd, LBW]

+

Antiphon to PSALM 49 *Audite haec, omnes*

You cannot serve God and wealth. [LH: Matt. 6:24]

49 *Emptiness of riches*

1 Hear this, all you peoples;
hearken, all you who dwell **in** the world,*
you of high degree and low, rich and **poor** together.

2 My mouth shall **speak** of wisdom,*
and my heart shall meditate on **un**derstanding.

3 I will incline my ear **to** a proverb*
and set forth my riddle up**on** the harp.

4 Why should I be afraid in **e**vil days,*
when the wickedness of those at my **heels** surrounds me,

5 The wickedness of those who put their trust **in** their goods,*
and boast of **their** great riches?

6 We can never ran**som** ourselves,*
or deliver to God the price **of** our life;

7 For the ransom of our life **is** so great,*
that we should never have e**nough** to pay it,

8 In order to live for ev**er** and ever,*
and never **see** the grave.

9 For we see that the wise die also;
like the dull and stu**pid** they perish*
and leave their wealth to those who come **af**ter them.

10 Their graves shall be their homes for ever,
their dwelling places from generation to **gen**eration,*
though they call the lands after **their** own names.

11 Even though honored, they cannot **live** for ever;*
they are like the **beasts** that perish.

12 Such is the way of those who foolishly trust **in** themselves,*
and the end of those who delight in **their** own words.

13 Like a flock of sheep they are destined to die;
Death **is** their shepherd;*
they go down straightway **to** the grave.

14 Their form shall **waste** away,*
and the land of the dead shall **be** their home.

15 But God will ran**som** my life;*
he will snatch me from the **grasp** of death.

16 Do not be envious when **some** become rich,*
or when the grandeur of their **house** increases;

17 For they will carry nothing away **at** their death,*
nor will their grandeur **foll**ow them.

18 Though they thought highly of themselves **while** they lived,*
and were praised for **their** success,

19 They shall join the company **of** their forebears,*
who will never see the **light** again.

20 Those who are honored, but have no **un**derstanding,*
are like the **beasts** that perish.

Antiphon God has ransomed my life from the grasp of death.

Silence for meditation

Lord Jesus, you condemned the rich because they have already received their reward, and you proclaimed the poor blessed because the kingdom of heaven is theirs: Teach us to seek imperishable goods and to have confidence in your blood, poured out as the price of our redemption; and to you be the glory now and for ever. [LHd, LBW]

+

Stand

THE HYMN is sung.

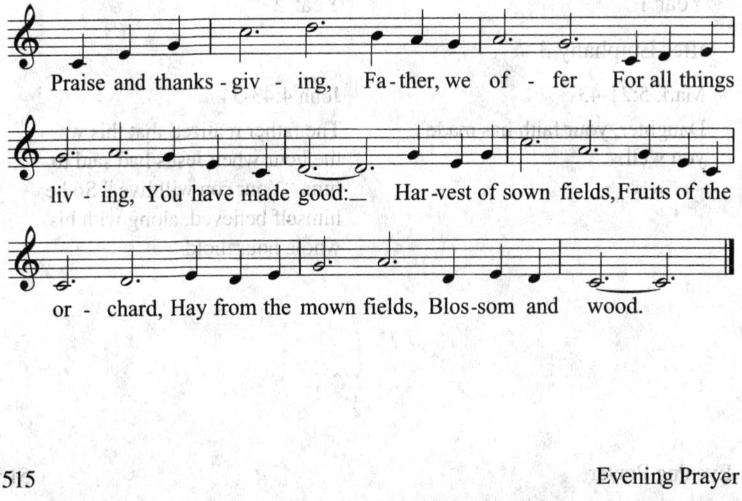

2 Bless, Lord, the labor
We bring to serve you,
That with our neighbor
We may be fed.
Sowing or tilling,
We would work with you
Harvesting, milling
For daily bread.

3 Father, providing
Food for your children,
Your wisdom guiding
Teaches us share
One with another,
So that, rejoicing
Others may know you
And praise your care.

4 Then will your blessing
Reach every people,
All lands confessing
Your gracious hand.
Where you are reigning,
No one will hunger;
Your love sustaining
Fruitful the land. [LBW 409 alt.]

Text: Albert F. Bayly, 1901-1984
Tune: *Bunessan,* Gaelic 55 54 D

Sit

A LESSON is read.

Year 1	Year 2
after Epiphany 3	
Mark 5:21-43	John 4:43-54
Daughter, your faith has made you well.	The father realized that this was the hour when Jesus had said to him, "Your son will live." So he himself believed, along with his whole household.

after Epiphany 7

Matthew 5:1-12

Blessed are you when people revile you and persecute you and utter all kinds of evil against you falsely on my account.

John 11:17-29

I am the resurrection and the life.

after Proper 3 / Pentecost 2

Luke 14:25-35

None of you can become my disciple if you do not give up all your possessions.

Matthew 12:22-32

Whoever speaks against the Holy Spirit will not be forgiven, either in this age or in the age to come.

after Proper 7 / Pentecost 6

Luke 21:29-36

Be alert at all times, praying that you may have the strength to escape all these things that will take place, and to stand before the Son of Man.

Matthew 19:13-22

Let the little children come to me, and do not stop them; for it is to such as these that the kingdom of heaven belongs.

after Proper 11 / Pentecost 10

Mark 4:1-20

These are the ones sown on the good soil: they hear the word and accept it and bear fruit.

Matthew 26:36-46

Stay awake and pray that you may not come into the time of trial.

after Proper 15 / Pentecost 14

Mark 11:12-26

Whenever you stand praying, forgive, if you have anything against anyone.

John 5:19-29

The hour is coming, and is now here, when the dead will hear the voice of the Son of God, and those who hear will live.

after Proper 19 / Pentecost 18

Matthew 4:1-11

Then Jesus was led up by the Spirit into the wilderness to be tempted by the devil.

John 11:55-12:8

You always have the poor with you, but you do not always have me.

after Proper 23 / Pentecost 22

Matthew 10:5-15

The kingdom of heaven has come near.

Luke 8:26-39

Return to your home, and declare how much God has done for you.

after Proper 27 / Pentecost 26

Matthew 15:1-20

Every plant that my Father has not planted will be uprooted.

Luke 14:12-24

When you give a banquet, invite the poor, the crippled, the lame, and the blind. And you will be blessed, because they cannot repay you.

Silence for meditation follows the reading.

Tuesday of Week III

Antiphon to PSALM 28 *Ad te, Domine, clamabo*

My heart trusts **in** the Lord,*
and I **have** been helped. [LH, PBO]

28 *Petition and thanksgiving*

1 O LORD, I call to you;
my Rock, do not be deaf **to** my cry;*
lest, if you do not hear me,
I become like those who go down **to** the Pit.

2 Hear the voice of my prayer when I cry **out** to you,*
when I lift up my hands to your ho**ly** of holies.

3 Do not snatch me away with the wicked or with the **ev**ildoers,*
who speak peaceably with their neighbors,
while strife is **in** their hearts.

4 Repay them according **to** their deeds,*
and according to the wickedness **of** their actions.

5 According to the work of their **hands** repay them,*
and give them their **just** deserts.

6 They have no understanding of the LORD's doings,
nor of the works **of** his hands;*
therefore he will break them down and not **build** them up.

7 Blessed **is** the LORD!*
for he has heard the voice **of** my prayer.

8 The LORD is my strength **and** my shield;*
my heart trusts in him, and I **have** been helped;

9 Therefore my heart dan**ces** for joy,*
and in my song **will** I praise him.

10 The LORD is the strength **of** his people,*
a safe refuge for **his** anointed:

11 Save your people and bless your in**her**itance;*
shepherd them and carry **them** for ever.

Antiphon My heart trusts **in** the Lord,*
and I **have** been helped.

Silence for meditation

Strong Shepherd of your people, when your Son stretched out his hands on the cross, you heard him and he did not become like those who go down into the pit: By his resurrection strengthen your people to offer you thanks for the mighty works that you have done, and make our hearts dance for joy; through your Son, Jesus Christ our Lord. [LHd, LBW]

+

Antiphon to PSALM 127 *Nisi Dominus aedificaverit*

Unless the Lord **builds** the house,*
their labor is in **vain** who build it. [LH, PBO]

127 *Success depends on God's blessing: a pilgrimage song*

1 Unless the LORD **builds** the house,*
their labor is in **vain** who built it.

2 Unless the LORD watches o**ver** the city,*
in vain the watchman **keeps** his vigil.

3 It is in vain that you rise so early and go to **bed** so late;*
vain, too, to eat the bread of toil,
for he gives to his be**lov**ed sleep.

4 Children are a heritage **from** the LORD,*
and the fruit of the womb **is** a gift.

5 Like arrows in the hand **of** a warrior*
are the children **of** one's youth.

6 Happy is the man who has his quiver **full** of them!*
he shall not be put to shame
when he contends with his enemies **in** the gate.

Antiphon Unless the Lord **builds** the house,*
their labor is in **vain** who build it.

Silence for meditation

Lord God, the land is brought to flower not with human tears but with the tears of your Son. Grant that those who labor for you may not trust in their own work but in your help, through Jesus Christ our Lord. [LH, LBW]

+

Stand

THE HYMN is sung. *Schönster Herr Jesu*

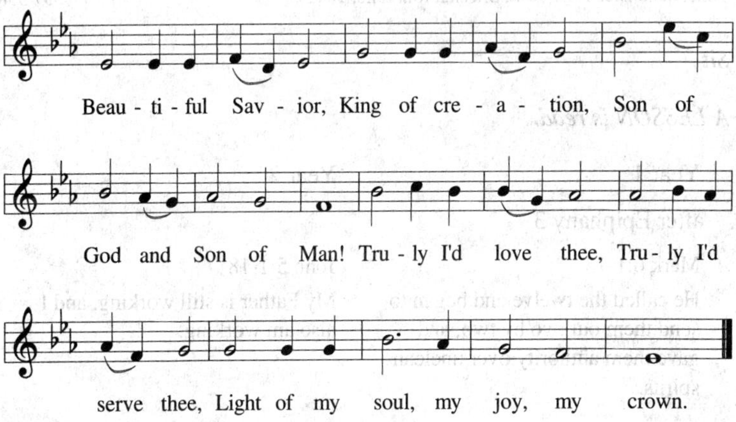

2 Fair are the meadows,
Fair are the woodlands,
Robed in flow'rs of blooming spring;
Jesus is fairer.

Jesus is purer,
He makes our sorrowing spirit sing.

3 Fair is the sunshine,
Fair is the moonlight,
Bright the sparkling stars on high;
Jesus shines brighter,
Jesus shines purer
Than all the angels in the sky.

4 Beautiful Savior,
Lord of the nations,
Son of God and Son of Man!
Glory and honor,
Praise, adoration,
Now and for evermore be thine. [LBW 518]

Text: *Gesangbuch*, Münster, 1677; tr. Joseph Augustus Seiss, 1823-1904
Tune: *Schönster Herr Jesu*, Silesian folk tune, 1842 557 558

Sit

A LESSON is read.

Year 1	Year 2
after Epiphany 3	
Mark 6:1-13	John 5:1-18
He called the twelve and began to send them out two by two, and gave them authority over unclean spirits.	My Father is still working, and I also am working.
after Epiphany 7	
Matthew 5:13-20	John 11:30-44
Unless your righteousness exceeds that of the scribes and Phari-	Lazarus, come out!

sees, you will never enter the kingdom of heaven.

after Proper 3 / Pentecost 2

Luke 15:1-10

There is joy in the presence of the angels of God over one sinner who repents.

Matthew 12:33-42

For three days and three nights the Son of Man will be in the heart of the earth.

after Proper 7 / Pentecost 6

Luke 21:37-22:13

Then came the day of Unleavened Bread, on which the Passover lamb had to be sacrificed.

Matthew 19:23-30

It is easier for a camel to go through the eye of a needle than for someone who is rich to enter the kingdom of God.

after Proper 11 / Pentecost 10

Mark 4:21-34

He did not speak to them except in parables, but he explained everything in private to his disciples.

Matthew 26:47-56

Then all the disciples deserted him and fled.

after Proper 15 / Pentecost 14

Mark 11:27-12:12

What then will the owner of the vineyard do? He will come and destroy the tenants and give the vineyard to others.

John 5:30-47

The works that my Father has given me to complete, the very works that I am doing, testify on my behalf that the Father has sent me.

after Proper 19 / Pentecost 18

Matthew 4:12-17

Repent, for the kingdom of heaven has come near.

John 12:9-19

Look, the world has gone after him!

after Proper 23 / Pentecost 22

Matthew 10:16-23

I am sending you out like sheep into the midst of wolves; so be wise as serpents and innocent as doves.

Luke 8:40-56

Daughter, your faith has made you well; go in peace.

after Proper 27 / Pentecost 26

Matthew 15:21-28

Have mercy on me, Lord, Son of David.

Luke 14:25-35

None of you can become my disciple if you do not give up all your possessions.

Silence for meditation follows the reading.

Wednesday of Week III

Antiphon to PSALM 125 *Qui confidunt in Domino*

The LORD stands round about his people. [LH, PBO]

125 *God protects the faithful*

1 Those who trust in the LORD are **like** Mount Zion,*
which cannot be moved, but stands **fast** for ever.

2 The hills stand a**bout** Jerusalem;*
so does the LORD stand round about his people,
from this time forth for **ev**ermore.

3 The scepter of the wicked shall not hold sway over the land allotted **to** the just,*
so that the just shall not put their **hands** to evil.

4 Show your goodness, O LORD, to those **who** are good*
and to those who are **true** of heart.

5 As for those who turn aside to crooked ways,
the LORD will lead them away with the **e**vildoers;*
but peace be **up**on Israel.

Antiphon The Lord stands round about his people.

Silence for meditation

Lord, surround your people with your presence: Do not let us stretch out our hands to evil deeds, nor be destroyed by the snares of the enemy, but bring us to share the land prepared for the saints in light, where you live and reign, God, now and for ever. [LH, LBW]

+

Antiphon to PSALM 91 *Qui habitat*

You shall not be afraid of any ter**ror** by night,*
and you shall find refuge un**der** his wings. [LH]

91 *God's sheltering care*

1 He who dwells in the shelter of **the** Most High,*
abides under the shadow of **the** Almighty.

2 He shall say to the LORD,
"You are my refuge **and** my stronghold,*
my God in whom I **put** my trust."

3 He shall deliver you from the snare **of** the hunter*
and from the **dead**ly pestilence.

4 He shall cover you with his pinions,
and you shall find refuge un**der** his wings;*
his faithfulness shall be a **shield** and buckler.

5 You shall not be afraid of any ter**ror** by night,*
nor of the arrow that **flies** by day;

6 Of the plague that stalks **in** the darkness,*
nor of the sickness that lays **waste** at mid-day.

7 A thousand shall fall at your side
and ten thousand at **your** right hand,*
but it shall **not** come near you.

8 Your eyes have only **to** behold*
to see the reward **of** the wicked.

9 Because you have made the **LORD** your refuge,*
and the Most High your **hab**itation,

10 There shall no evil hap**pen** to you,*
neither shall any plague come **near** your dwelling.

11 For he shall give his angels charge **o**ver you,*
to keep you in **all** your ways.

12 They shall bear you **in** their hands,*
lest you dash your foot a**gainst** a stone.

13 You shall tread upon the li**on** and adder;*
you shall trample the young lion and the serpent
un**der** your feet.

14 Because he is bound to me in love,
therefore will I de**li**ver him;*
I will protect him, because he **knows** my Name.

15 He shall call upon me, and I will **an**swer him;*
I am with him in trouble;
I will rescue him and bring **him** to honor.

16 With long life will I **sat**isfy him,*
and show him **my** salvation.

Antiphon You shall not be afraid of any ter**ror** by night,*
and you shall find refuge un**der** his wings.

Silence for meditation

Lord Jesus Christ, when tempted by the devil, you remained true to your Father, who commanded his angels to watch over you: Guard your Church from the plague of sin, so that we may remain faithful to you until the day when we enjoy the fullness of salvation; for you live and reign with the Father and the Holy Spirit, now and for ever. [LHd, LBW]

+

Stand

THE HYMN is sung. *Rerum Deus tenax vigor*

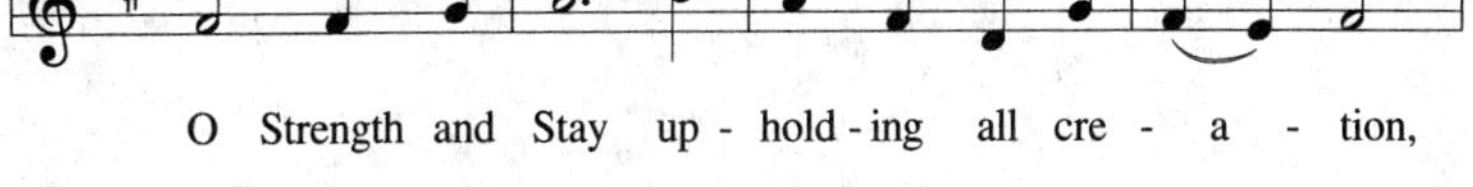

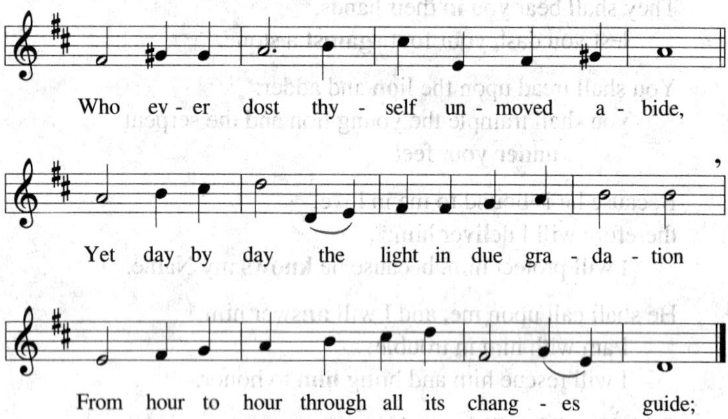

2 Grant to life's day a calm unclouded ending,
An eve untouched by shadows of decay,
The brightness of a holy deathbed blending
With dawning glories of the eternal day.

3 Hear us, O Father, gracious and forgiving,
Through Jesus Christ, thy co-eternal Word,
Who, with the Holy Ghost, by all things living,
Now and to endless ages art adored. [SBH 219]

Text: ascribed to St. Ambrose, 340-397; tr. John Ellerton, 1826-1893, and Fenton J. Hort, 1828-1892

Tune: *Strength and Stay,* John Bacchus Dykes, 1823-1876 11 10, 11 10

Sit

A LESSON is read.

Year 1	Year 2
after Epiphany 3	
Mark 6:13-29 When Herod heard of it, he said , "John, whom I beheaded, has been raised."	John 5:19-29 Anyone who hears my word and believes him who sent me has eternal life, and does not come under judgment, but has passed from death to life.
after Epiphany 7	
Matthew 5:21-26 First be reconciled to your brother or sister, and then come and offer your gift.	John 11:45-54 From that day on they planned to put him to death.
after Proper 3 / Pentecost 2	
Luke 15:1-2,11-32 We had to celebrate and rejoice, because this brother of yours was dead and has come to life; he was lost and has been found.	Matthew 12:43-50 Whoever does the will of my Father in heaven is my brother and sister and mother.
after Proper 7 / Pentecost 6	
Luke 22:14-23 I have eagerly desired to eat this Passover with you before I suffer.	Matthew 20:1-16 Take what belongs to you and go; I choose to give to this last the same as I give to you.
after Proper 11 / Pentecost 10	
Mark 4:35-41 Who then is this, that even the wind and the sea obey him?	Matthew 26:57-68 From now on you will see the Son of Man seated at the right hand of Power and coming on the clouds of heaven.

after Proper 15 / Pentecost 14

Mark 12:13-27

Give to the emperor the things that are the emperor's and to God the things that are God's.

John 6:1-15

This is indeed the prophet who is to come into the world.

after Proper 19 / Pentecost 18

Matthew 4:18-25

Jesus went throughout Galilee, teaching in their synagogues and proclaiming the good news of the kingdom and curing every disease and every sickness among the people.

John 12:20-26

Unless a grain of wheat falls into the earth and dies, it remains just a single grain; but if it dies, it bears much fruit.

after Proper 23 / Pentecost 22

Matthew 10:24-33

Do not fear those who kill the body but cannot kill the soul; rather fear him who can destroy both soul and body in hell.

Luke 9:1-17

Jesus called the twelve together and gave them power and authority over all demons and to cure diseases, and he sent them out to proclaim the kingdom of God and to heal.

after Proper 27 / Pentecost 26

Matthew 15:29-39

The crowd was amazed when they saw the mute speaking, the maimed whole, the lame walking, the blind seeing. And they praised the God of Israel.

Luke 15:1-10

There is joy in the presence of the angels of God over one sinner who repents.

Silence for meditation follows the readings.

Thursday of Week III

Antiphon to PSALM 81 *Exultate Deo*

Sing with joy to God our strength. [LH]

81 *Festal song in harvest time*

1 Sing with joy to **God** our strength*
and raise a loud shout to the **God** of Jacob.

2 Raise a song and **sound** the timbrel,*
the merry harp, **and** the lyre.

3 Blow the ram's-horn at **the** new moon,*
and at the full moon, the day **of** our feast.

4 For this is a stat**ute** for Israel,*
a law of the **God** of Jacob.

5 He laid it as a solemn charge **up**on Joseph,*
when he came out of the **land** of Egypt.

6 I heard an unfamil**iar** voice saying,*
"I eased his shoulder from the burden;
his hands were set free from bear**ing** the load."

7 You called on me in trouble, **and** I saved you;*
I answered you from the secret place of thunder
and tested you at the wa**ters** of Meribah.

8 Hear, O my people, and I will ad**mon**ish you:*
O Israel, if you would but list**en** to me!

9 There shall be no strange **god** among you;*
you shall not worship a **for**eign god.

10 I am the LORD your God,
who brought you out of the land of **Egypt** and said,*
"Open your mouth wide, and **I** will fill it."

11 And yet my people did not **hear** my voice,*
and Israel would **not** obey me.

12 So I gave them over to the stubbornness **of** their hearts,*
to follow their **own** devices.

13 Oh, that my people would **lis**ten to me!*
that Israel would walk **in** my ways!

14 I should soon sub**due** their enemies*
and turn my hand a**gainst** their foes.

15 Those who hate the LORD would **cringe** before him,*
and their punishment would **last** for ever.

16 But Israel would I feed with the **fin**est wheat*
and satisfy him with honey **from** the rock.

Antiphon Sing with joy to God our strength.

Silence for meditation

Almighty Father, you rescued your people from slavery and, through the Passion of your Son, acquired a new people united in his body and marked with the sign of his holiness: Feed us with your finest bread so that we may have food for this life and a foretaste of eternity, where you live and reign with your Son and the Holy Spirit, now and for ever. [LHd, LBW]

+

Antiphon to PSALM 116 *Dilexi, quoniam*

You, O Lord, have rescued my **life** from death,*
my eyes from tears, and my **feet** from stumbling. [LH]

116 *Thanksgiving for deliverance from death*

1 I love the LORD, because he has heard the voice of
my **sup**plication,*
because he has inclined his ear to me whenever
I **called** upon him.

2 The cords of death entangled me;
the grip of the grave took **hold** of me;*
I came to **grief** and sorrow.

3 Then I called upon the Name **of** the LORD:*
"O LORD, I pray you, **save** my life."

4 Gracious is the LORD and righteous;*
our God is full **of** compassion.

5 The LORD watches o**ver** the innocent;*
I was brought very low, **and** he helped me.

6 Turn again to your rest, **O** my soul,*
for the LORD has treat**ed** you well.

7 For you have rescued my **life** from death,*
my eyes from tears, and my **feet** from stumbling.

8 I will walk in the presence **of** the LORD*
in the land **of** the living.

9 I believed, even when I said,
"I have been brought **ver**y low."*
In my distress I said, "No one **can** be trusted."

10 How shall I re**pay** the LORD*
for all the good things he has **done** for me?

11 I will lift up the cup **of** salvation*
and call upon the Name **of** the LORD.

12 I will fulfill my vows **to** the LORD*
in the presence of **all** his people.

13 Precious in the sight **of** the LORD*
is the death **of** his servants.

14 O LORD, I **am** your servant;*
I am your servant and the child of your handmaid;
you have freed me **from** my bonds.

15 I will offer you the sacrifice **of** thanksgiving*
and call upon the Name **of** the LORD.

16 I will fulfill my vows **to** the LORD*
in the presence of **all** his people,

17 In the courts of **the** LORD's house,*
in the midst of you, O Jerusalem.
Hallelujah!

Antiphon You, O Lord, have rescued my **life** from death,*
my eyes from tears, and my **feet** from stumbling.

Silence for meditation

God of power and mercy, through the Passion and resurrection of your Son you have freed us from the bonds of death and the anguish of separation from you: Be with us on our pilgrimage, and help us offer you a sacrifice of praise, fulfill our vows, and glorify you in the presence of all your people; through Jesus Christ our Lord. [LH, LBW]

+

Stand

THE HYMN is sung. *Nun lob, mein Seel, den Herren*

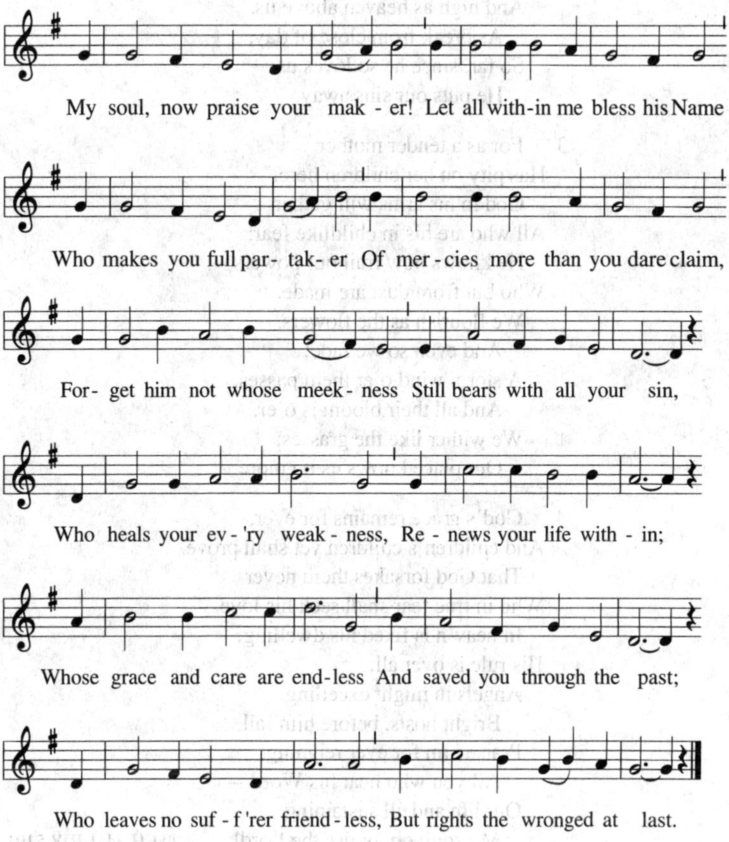

2 He offers all his treasure
Of justice, truth, and righteousness,
His love beyond all measure,
His yearning pity o'er distress;
Nor treats us as we merit,
But lays his anger by.
The humble contrite spirit
Finds his compassions nigh;

And high as heaven above us,
As break from close of day,
So far, since he so loves us,
He puts our sins away.

3 For as a tender mother
Has pity on her children here,
God in his arms will gather
All who are his in childlike fear;
He knows how frail our powers,
Who but from dust are made.
We flourish as the flowers,
And even so we fade;
A storm wind o'er them passes,
And all their bloom is o'er.
We wither like the grasses;
Our place knows us no more.

4 God's grace remains for ever,
And children's children yet shall prove
That God forsakes them never
Who in true fear shall seek his love.
In heav'n is fixed his dwelling,
His rule is over all;
Angels in might excelling,
Bright hosts, before him fall.
Praise him for ever reigning,
All you who hear his Word—
Our life and all sustaining.
My soul, oh, praise the Lord! [TLH 34, LBW 519]

Text: Johann Gramann, 1487-1541; tr. Catherine Winkworth, 1829-1878, alt.
Tune: *Nun lob, mein Seel,* Kugelmann, *Consentus Novi*, 1540 PM

Sit

A LESSON is read.

Year 1	Year 2
after Epiphany 3	
Mark 6:30-46 He had compassion for them, because they were like sheep without a shepherd; and he began to teach them many things.	John 5:30-47 The Father who sent me has himself testified on my behalf.
after Epiphany 7	
Matthew 5:27-37 If your right hand causes you to sin, cut it off and throw it away; it is better for you to lose one of your members than for your whole body to go into hell.	John 11:55-12:8 Mary took a pound of costly perfume made of pure nard, anointed Jesus' feet, and wiped them with her hair.
after Proper 3 / Pentecost 2	
Luke 16:1-9 His master commended the dishonest manager because he had acted shrewdly; for the children of this age are more shrewd in dealing with their own generation than are the children of light.	Matthew 13:24-30 Let both of them grow together until the harvest; and at harvest time I will tell the reapers, Collect the weeds first and bind them in bundles to be burned, but gather the wheat into my barn.
after Proper 7 / Pentecost 6	
Luke 22:24-30 The greatest among you must become like the youngest, and the leader like one who serves.	Matthew 20:17-28 Whoever wishes to be great among you must be your servant, and whoever wishes to be first among you must be your slave.

after Proper 11 / Pentecost 10

Mark 5:1-20

Go home to your friends, and tell them how much the Lord has done for you, and what mercy he has shown you.

Matthew 26:69-75

Peter remembered what Jesus had said, "Before the cock crows, you will deny me three times." And he went out and wept bitterly.

after Proper 15 / Pentecost 14

Mark 12:28-34

You shall love the Lord your God with all your heart, and with all your soul, and with all your mind, and with all your strength.

John 6:16-27

It is I; do not be afraid.

after Proper 19 / Pentecost 18

Matthew 5:1-10

Blessed are the poor in spirit, for theirs is the kingdom of heaven.

John 12:27-36a

While you have the light, believe in the light, so that you may become children of light.

after Proper 23 / Pentecost 22

Matthew 10:34-42

Do not think that I have come to bring peace to the earth; I have not come to bring peace, but a sword.

Luke 9:18-27

If any want to become my followers, let them deny themselves and take up their cross daily and follow me.

after Proper 27 / Pentecost 26

Matthew 16:1-12

You know how to interpret the appearance of the sky, but you cannot interpret the signs of the times.

Luke 15:1-2,11-32

We had to celebrate and rejoice, because this brother of yours was dead and has come to life; he was lost and has been found.

Silence for meditation follows the reading.

Friday of Week III

Antiphon to PSALM 11 *In Domino confido*

The **Lord** is righteous;*
and the just shall **see** his face. [LH, PBO]

11 *The confidence of the virtuous*

1 In the Lord have I **tak**en refuge;*
how then can you say to me,
"Fly away like a bird **to** the hilltop;

2 For see how the wicked bend the bow
and fit their arrows **to** the string,*
to shoot from ambush at the **true** of heart.

3 When the foundations are be**ing** destroyed,*
what can the **right**eous do?"

4 The Lord is in his **ho**ly temple;*
the Lord's throne **is** in heaven.

5 His eyes behold the inhab**it**ed world;*
his piercing eye **weighs** our worth.

6 The Lord weighs the righteous as well **as** the wicked,*
but those who delight in violence **he** abhors.

7 Upon the wicked he shall rain coals of fire and **burn**ing sulphur;*
a scorching wind shall **be** their lot.

8 For the Lord is righteous;
he delights in **right**eous deeds;*
and the just shall **see** his face.

Antiphon The **Lord** is righteous;*
and the just shall **see** his face.

Silence for meditation

Holy and righteous God, you search the hearts of all, the righteous as well as the wicked: Give strength to those who are now in danger because they love you, and in the day of judgment give them the joy of seeing you face to face; through Jesus Christ our Lord. [LH, PHP]

+

Antiphon to PSALM 21 *Domine, in virtute tua*

Be exalted, O LORD, **in** your might;*
we will sing and **praise** your power. [LH, PBO]

21 *Thanksgiving for the king's victory*

1 The king rejoices in your **strength**, O LORD;*
how greatly he exults **in** your victory!

2 You have given him his **heart's** desire;*
you have not denied him the request **of** his lips.

3 For you meet him with blessings **of** prosperity,*
and set a crown of fine gold up**on** his head.

4 He asked you for life, and you **gave** it to him:*
length of days, for ev**er** and ever.

5 His honor is great, because of your **vic**tory;*
splendor and majesty have you be**stowed** upon him.

6 For you will give him everlasting fe**li**city*
and will make him glad with the joy **of** your presence.

7 For the king puts his trust **in** the LORD;*
because of the loving-kindness of the Most High, he
will not fall.

8 Your hand will lay hold upon **all** your enemies;*
your right hand will seize all **those** who hate you.

9 You will make them like a fi**ery** furnace*
at the time of your appear**ing**, O LORD;

10 You will swallow them up **in** your wrath,*
and fire **shall** consume them.

11 You will destroy their offspring **from** the land*
and their descendants from among the peoples **of** the earth.

12 Though they intend evil against you
and devise **wick**ed schemes,*
yet they shall **not** prevail.

13 For you will put **them** to flight*
and aim your ar**rows** at them,

14 Be exalted, O LORD **in** your might;*
we will sing and **praise** your power.

Antiphon Be exalted, O LORD **in** your might;*
we will sing and **praise** your power.

Silence for meditation

Father, you have given us life on this earth and have met us with the richness of your grace: Bestow on us, we pray, your greatest blessing, the fullness of eternal life in Jesus Christ our Lord. [LH, LBW]

+

Stand

THE HYMN is sung. *Arglwydd, arwain trwy'r anialwch*

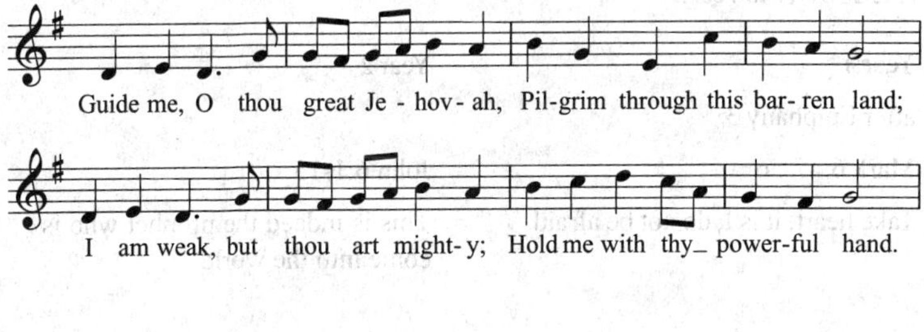

2 Open now the crystal fountain
Whence the healing stream doth flow,
Let the fire and cloudy pillar
Lead me all my journey through.
Strong deliv'rer, strong deliv'rer,
Be thou still my strength and shield.

3 When I tread the verge of Jordan,
Bid my anxious fears subside,
Death of death and hell's destruction
Land me safe on Canaan's side.
Songs of praises, songs of praises,
I will ever give to thee. [H82, 690, LBW 343]

Text: William Williams, 1717-1791; tr. Peter Williams, 1722-1796 alt.
Tune: Cwm rhonda John Hughes, 1873-1932 8787877

Sit

A LESSON is read.

Year 1	Year 2
after Epiphany 3	
Mark 6:47-56	John 6:1-15
Take heart, it is I, do not be afraid.	This is indeed the prophet who is come into the world

after Epiphany 7

Matthew 5:38-48

Be perfect, therefore, as your heavenly Father is perfect.

John 12:9-19

Blessed is the one who comes in the name of the Lord—the King of Israel!

after Proper 3 / Pentecost 2

Luke 16:10-17(18)

You cannot serve God and wealth.

Matthew 13:31-35

Jesus told the crowds all these things in parables; without a parable he told them nothing.

after Proper 7 / Pentecost 6

Luke 22:31-38

I tell you, Peter, the cock will not crow this day, until you have denied three times that you know me.

Matthew 20:29-34

Have mercy on us, Lord, Son of David!

after Proper 11 / Pentecost 10

Mark 5:21-43

Daughter, your faith has made you well; go in peace, and be healed of your disease.

Matthew 27:1-10

Throwing down the pieces of silver in the temple, Judas departed; and he went and hanged himself.

after Proper 15 / Pentecost 14

Mark 12:35-44

All of them have contributed out of their abundance; but she out of her poverty has put in everything she had, all she had to live on.

John 6:27-40

Do not work for the food that perishes, but for the food that endures for eternal life, which the Son of Man will give you.

after Proper 19 / Pentecost 18

Matthew 5:11-16

Let your light shine before others, so that they may see your good works and give glory to your Father in heaven.

John 12:36b-43

They loved human glory more than the glory that comes from God.

after Proper 23 / Pentecost 22

Matthew 11:1-6

Are you the one who is to come, or are we to wait for another?

Luke 9:28-36

This is my Son, my Chosen; listen to him!

after Proper 27 / Pentecost 26

Matthew 16:13-20

You are the Messiah, the Son of the living God.

Luke 16:1-9

His master commended the unjust manager because he had acted shrewdly; for the children of this age are more shrewd in dealing with their own generation than are the children of light.

Silence for meditation follows the reading.

Saturday of Week IV

Antiphon to PSALM 52 *Quid gloriaris?*

I trust in the mercy of God for ever and ever. [LH, PBO]

52 *The fate of the deceitful*

1 You tyrant, why do you **boast** of wickedness*
against the godly **all** day long?

2 You plot ruin;
your tongue is like a **sharp**ened razor,*
O worker **of** deception.

3 You love evil **more** than good*
and lying more than speak**ing** the truth.

4 You love all **words** that hurt,*
O you de**ceit**ful tongue.

5 Oh, that God would demol**ish** you utterly,*
topple you, and snatch you from your dwelling,
and root you out of the land **of** the living!

6 The righteous shall **see** and tremble,*
and they shall laugh **at** him, saying,

7 "This is the one who did not take God **for** a refuge,*
but trusted in great wealth
and relied **up**on wickedness."

8 But I am like a green olive tree in the **house** of God;*
I trust in the mercy of God for ev**er** and ever.

9 I will give you thanks for what **you** have done*
and declare the goodness of your Name in the
presence **of** the godly.

Antiphon I trust in the mercy of God for ever and ever.

Silence for meditation

Heavenly Father, you cut down the unfruitful branch for burning and prune the fertile to make it bear more fruit: Make us grow like rich olive trees in your kingdom, firmly rooted in the power and mercy of your Son, Jesus Christ our Lord. [LH, LBW]

+

Antiphon to PSALM 90 *Domine, refugium*

Our years wither a**way** like grass,*
but you, Lord, **are** eternal. [LH: Ps. 102:11-12]

90 *The brevity of life*

1 Lord, you have **been** our refuge*
from one generation **to** another.

2 Before the mountains were brought forth,
or the land and the **earth** were born,*
from age to age **you** are God.

3 You turn us back to the **dust** and say,*
"Go back, O **child** of earth."

4 For a thousand years in your sight are like yesterday
when **it** is past*
and like a watch **in** the night.

5 You sweep us away **like** a dream;*
we fade away suddenly **like** the grass.

6 In the morning it is **green** and flourishes;*
in the evening it is dried **up** and withered.

7 For we consume away in **your** displeasure;*
we are afraid because of your wrathful **in**dignation.

8 Our iniquities you have **set** before you,*
and our secret sins in the light **of** your countenance.

9 When you are angry, all our **days** are gone;*
 we bring our years to an end **like** a sigh.

10 The span of our life is seventy years,
perhaps in strength **e**ven eighty;*
 yet the sum of them is but labor and sorrow,
 for they pass away quickly and **we** are gone.

11 Who regards the power **of** your wrath?*
 who rightly fears your **in**dignation?

12 So teach us to num**ber** our days*
 that we may apply our **hearts** to wisdom.

13 Return, O LORD; how long **will** you tarry?*
 be gracious **to** your servants.

14 Satisfy us by your loving-kindness **in** the morning;*
 so shall we rejoice and be glad all the days **of** our life.

15 Make us glad by the measure of the days that you af**flic**ted us*
 and the years in which we suf**fered** adversity.

16 Show your ser**vants** your works*
 and your splendor **to** their children.

17 May the graciousness of the LORD our God **be** upon us;*
 prosper the work of our hands;
 pros**per** our handiwork.

Antiphon Our years wither a**way** like grass,*
 but you, Lord, **are** eternal.

Silence for meditation

Eternal Father of our mortal race, despite our sin you give us life and even add days and years to our lives to bring us to wisdom: Make us so to love and obey you that we may serve you all the days of our life, until at last we behold the beauty of your face, shown to us in Jesus Christ our Lord. [LH, PHP]

+

Antiphon to the NEW TESTAMENT CANTICLE *Gratias agimus tibi*

The victorious reign of our God **has** begun.*
Al**le**luia. [LH]

A Song of the Judgment of God Revelation 11:17-18; 12:10b-12a

We give you thanks, Lord God almighty,
who are **and** who were,*
for you have taken your great power
and have be**gun** to reign.

The **na**tions raged,*
but your wrath has come
and the time to **judge** the dead,

The time to reward your servants, the prophets,
and the holy ones and all who **fear** your Name,*
great and **small** alike.

Now salvation and pow**er** have come,*
the kingdom of our God
and the authority of **his** Messiah.

For the accuser of our companions has **been** thrown down,*
who night and day accuses them **be**fore God.

They have conquered him by the sacrifice of the Lamb
and by the word of their **tes**timony,*
for they did not cling to life
even in the **face** of death.

Rejoice **then**, you heavens,*
and all who **dwell** in them. [LH, PHP]

Antiphon The victorious reign of our God **has** begun.*
Al**le**luia.

Silence for meditation

Almighty Lord and God, bring us into your kingdom and rule us as Sovereign of righteousness, life, and salvation. Give us the Holy Spirit, that by his grace we may believe your holy Word and live the new life to your praise, through Jesus Christ our Lord, now and for ever. [PHP]

+

Stand

THE HYMN is sung. *Hora novissima, tempora pessima*

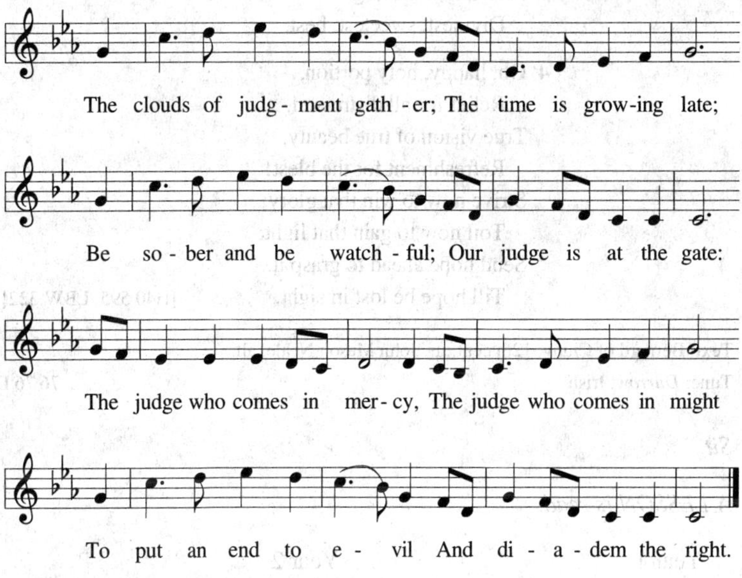

2 Arise, O true disciples;
Let wrong give way to right,
And penitential shadow
To Jesus' blessed light:
The light that has no evening,
That knows no moon or sun,

The light so new and golden,
The light that is but one.

3 The home of fadeless splendor,
Of blooms that bear no thorn,
Where they shall dwell as children
Who here as exiles mourn;
The peace of all the faithful,
The calm of all the blest,
Inviolate, unfading,
Divinest, sweetest, best.

4 Oh, happy, holy portion,
Relief for all distressed,
True vision of true beauty,
Refreshment for the blest!
Strive now to win that glory;
Toil now to gain that light;
Send hope ahead to grasp it,
Till hope be lost in sight. [H40 595, LBW 322]

Text: Bernard of Cluny, 12th cent.; tr. John Mason Neale, alt.
Tune: *Durrow*, Irish 76 76 D

Sit

A LESSON is read.

Year 1	Year 2
eve of Epiphany 4	
Mark 7:1-23	John 6:16-27
You abandon the commandment of God and hold to human tradition.	Do not work for the food that perishes, but for the food that endures for eternal life, which the Son of Man will give you.

eve of Epiphany 8

Matthew 6:1-6

Beware of practicing your piety before others in order to be seen by them; for then you have no reward from your Father in heaven.

John 12:20-26

Unless a grain of wheat falls into the earth and dies, it remains just a single grain; but if it dies, it bears much fruit.

eve of Proper 4 (Sunday between May 29 and June 4) / Pentecost 3

Luke 16:19-31

If they do not listen to Moses and the prophets, neither will they be convinced even if someone rises from the dead.

Matthew 13:36-43

Then the righteous will shine like the sun in the kingdom of their Father.

eve of Proper 8 (Sunday between June 26 and July 2) / Pentecost 7

Luke 22:39-51

Father, if you are willing, remove this cup from me; yet, not my will but yours be done.

Matthew 21:1-11

Blessed is the one who comes in the name of the Lord! Hosanna in the highest heaven!

eve of Proper 12 (Sunday between July 24 and 30) / Pentecost 11

Mark 6:1-13

Where did this man get all this? What is this wisdom that has been given to him? What deeds of power are being done by his hands!

Matthew 27:11-23

Let him be crucified!

eve of Proper 16 (Sunday between August 21 and 27) / Pentecost 15

Mark 13:1-13

Nation will rise against nation, and kingdom against kingdom; there will be earthquakes in various places; there will be famines. This is but the beginning of the birth-pangs.

John 6:41-51

Whoever eats of this bread will live forever; and the bread that I will give for the life of the world is my flesh.

eve of Proper 20 (Sunday between September 18 and 24) / Pentecost 19

Matthew 5:17-20

Do not think that I have come to abolish the law or the prophets; I have come not to abolish but to fulfill.

John 12:44-50

I am come as light into the world, so that everyone who believes in me should not remain in the darkness.

eve of Proper 24 (Sunday between October 16 and 22) / Pentecost 23

Matthew 11:7-15

Among those born of women no one has arisen greater than John the Baptist; yet the least in the kingdom of heaven is greater than he.

Luke 9:37-50

Let these words sink into your ears: The Son of Man is going to be betrayed into human hands.

eve of Proper 28 (Sunday between November 13 and 19) / Pentecost 27

Matthew 16:21-28

Those who want to save their life will lose it, and those who lose their life for my sake will find it.

Luke 16:10-17(18)

You cannot serve God and wealth.

Silence for meditation follows the reading.

Sunday of Week IV

Antiphon to PSALM 106 *Confitemini Domino*

Remember **us**, O Lord,*
and visit us with your **sa**ving help. [LH, PBO]

106 *The goodness of God; the faithlessness of God's people*

1 Hallelujah!
Give thanks to the LORD, for **he** is good,*
for his mercy en**dures** for ever.

2 Who can declare the mighty acts **of** the LORD*
or show forth **all** his praise?

3 Happy are those who **act** with justice*
and always do **what** is right!

4 Remember me, O LORD, with the favor you have
for your people,*
and visit me with your **sa**ving help;

5 That I may see the prosperity of your elect
and be glad with the gladness **of** your people,*
that I may glory with **your** inheritance.

6 We have sinned as our **fore**bears did;*
we have done wrong **and** dealt wickedly.

7 In Egypt they did not consider your marvelous works,
nor remember the abundance **of** your love;*
they defied the Most High **at** the Red Sea.

8 But he saved them for **his** Name's sake,*
to make his **pow**er known.

9 He rebuked the Red Sea, and **it** dried up,*
and he led them through the deep as **through** a desert.

10 He saved them from the hand of those who **hat**ed them*
and redeemed them from the hand **of** the enemy.

11 The waters covered **their** oppressors;*
not one of **them** was left.

12 Then they be**lieved** his words*
and sang him **songs** of praise.

13 But they soon for**got** his deeds*
and did not wait **for** his counsel.

14 A craving seized them **in** the wilderness,*
and they put God to the test **in** the desert.

15 He gave them **what** they asked,*
but sent leanness in**to** their soul.

16 They envied Moses **in** the camp,*
and Aaron, the holy one **of** the LORD.

17 The earth opened and **swal**lowed Dathan*
and covered the company **of** Abiram.

18 Fire blazed up a**gainst** their company,*
and flames de**voured** the wicked.

19 Israel made a bull-**calf** at Horeb*
and worshiped a **mol**ten image;

20 And so they ex**changed** their Glory*
for the image of an ox that **feeds** on grass.

21 They forgot **God** their Savior,*
who had done great **things** in Egypt,

22 Wonderful deeds in the **land** of Ham,*
and fearful things **at** the Red Sea.

23 So he would have destroyed them,
had not Moses his chosen stood before him **in** the breach,*
to turn away his wrath from con**sum**ing them.

24 They refused the **pleas**ant land*
and would not be**lieve** his promise.

25 They grumbled **in** their tents*
and would not listen to the voice **of** the LORD.

26 So he lifted his **hand** against them,*
to overthrow them **in** the wilderness,

27 To cast out their seed a**mong** the nations,*
and to scatter them through**out** the lands.

28 They joined themselves **to** Baal-Peor*
and ate sacrifices offered **to** the dead.

29 They provoked him to anger **with** their actions,*
and a plague broke **out** among them.

30 Then Phinehas stood up and **in**terceded,*
and the plague came **to** an end.

31 This was reckoned to **him** as righteousness*
throughout all genera**tions** for ever.

32 Again they provoked his anger at the wa**ters** of Meribah,*
so that he punished Moses be**cause** of them;

33 For they so embit**tered** his spirit*
that he spoke rash words **with** his lips.

34 They did not de**stroy** the peoples*
as the LORD had com**mand**ed them.

35 They intermingled **with** the heathen*
and learned their **pag**an ways.

36 So that they wor**shiped** their idols,*
which became a **snare** to them.

37 They sacri**ficed** their sons,*
and their daughters to **e**vil spirits.

38 They shed innocent blood,
the blood of their **sons** and daughters,*
which they offered to the idols of Canaan,
and the land was de**filed** with blood.

39 Thus they were polluted **by** their actions*
and went whoring in their **e**vil deeds.

40 Therefore the wrath of the LORD was kindled a**gainst** his people*
and he abhorred **his** inheritance.

41 He gave them over to the hand **of** the heathen,*
and those who hated them ruled **o**ver them.

42 Their ene**mies** oppressed them,*
and they were humbled un**der** their hand.

43 Many a time did he deliver them,
but they rebelled through their **own** devices,*
and were brought down in **their** iniquity.

44 Nevertheless, he saw **their** distress,*
when he heard their **lam**entation.

45 He remembered his cove**nant** with them*
and relented in accordance with **his** great mercy.

46 He caused them **to** be pitied*
by those who **held** them captive.

47 Save us, O LORD our God,
and gather us from a**mong** the nations,*
that we may give thanks to your holy Name
and glory **in** your praise.

48 Blessed be the LORD, the God of Israel,
from everlasting and to **ev**erlasting;*
and let all the people say, "Amen!"
Hallelujah!

Antiphon Remember **us**, O Lord,*
and visit us with your **sav**ing help.

Silence for meditation

God our Father, remembering your covenant, you graciously pardoned those who rebelled against you: Grant that, where sin abounds, grace may abound more; through Jesus Christ our Lord. [LH, LBW]

+

Antiphon to PSALM 131 *Domine, non est*

Whoever becomes humble **like** this child*
is the greatest in the king**dom** of heaven.
[LH, PBO: Matt. 18:4]

131 *Childlike trust in God*

1 O LORD, I **am** not proud;*
I have no **haugh**ty looks.

2 I do not occupy myself **with** great matters,*
or with things that are too **hard** for me.

3 But I still my soul and make it quiet,
like a child upon its **moth**er's breast;*
my soul is quiet**ed** within me.

4 O Israel, wait up**on** the LORD,*
from this time forth for **ev**ermore.

Antiphon Whoever becomes humble **like** this child*
is the greatest in the king**dom** of heaven.

Silence for meditation

Lord Jesus, gentle and humble of heart, you promised your kingdom to those who are like children: Never let pride reign in our hearts, but let the

Father's compassion embrace all who willingly bear your gentle yoke now and for ever. [LH, LBW]

+

Antiphon to the NEW TESTAMENT CANTICLE

Manifestatum est in carne

Praise the Lord, all you nations. [Ps. 117:1]

A Song of the Great Mystery of our Religion 1 Timothy 3:16

Christ the Lord—
manifested **in** the flesh,*
vindicated **in** the Spirit,

comtemplated **by** the angels,*
proclaimed **among** the nations,

believed in through**out** the world—*
is exalted in glory for **ev**ermore. [LH, PHP]

Antiphon Praise the Lord, all you nations.

Silence for meditation

God our Savior, you have revealed to us the great mystery of our religion: By your Spirit help us to receive your gifts with thanksgiving and teach us how to live as faithful members of your household, the Church; through your Son, Jesus Christ our Lord. [PHP]

+

Stand

THE HYMN is sung. *Primo dierum omnium*

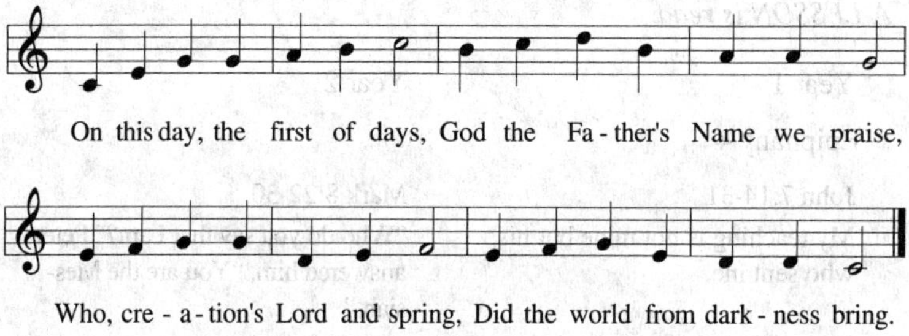

2 On this day the eternal Son
Over death his triumph won;
On this day the Spirit came
With his gifts of living flame.

3 Maker, who didst fashion me
Image of thyself to be,
Fill me with thy love divine,
Let my every thought be thine.

4 Holy Jesus, may I be
Dead and buried here with thee;
And, by love inflamed, arise
Unto thee a sacrifice.

5 Thou, who dost all gifts impart,
Shine, blest Spirit, in my heart;
Best of gifts, thyself bestow;
Make me burn thy love to know.

6 God, the blessed Three in One,
Dwell within my heart alone;
Thou dost give thyself to me:
Help me give myself to thee. [H82 47]

Text: Latin; tr. Henry Williams Baker, 1821-1877, alt.

Tune: *Gott sei dank,* melody from *Geistreiches Gesangbuch*, 1704; adapt. William Henry Havergal, 1793-1870, alt. 77 77

Sit

A LESSON is read.

Year 1	Year 2
Epiphany 4	
John 7:14-31	Mark 8:22-30
My teaching is not mine but his who sent me.	"Who do you say that I am?" Peter answered him, "You are the Messiah."
Epiphany 8	
John 12:1-8	Mark 10:46-52
Mary took a pound of costly perfume made of pure nard, anointed Jesus' feet, and wiped them with her hair. The house was filled with the fragrance of the perfume.	Jesus, Son of David, have mercy on me!
Proper 4 (Sunday between May 29 and June 4) / Pentecost 3	
Matthew 13:44-58	Luke 11:1-13
Every scribe who has been trained for the kingdom of heaven is like the master of a household who brings out of his treasure what is new and what is old.	Ask, and it will be given you; search, and you will find; knock, and the door will be opened for you.
Proper 8 (Sunday between June 26 and July 2) / Pentecost 7	
Matthew 21:23-32	Luke 13:10-17
John came to you in the way of righteousness and you did not believe him, but the tax collectors and prostitutes believed him; and even after you saw it, you did not change your minds and believe him.	All his opponents were put to shame; and the entire crowd was rejoicing at all the wonderful things that he was doing.

Proper 12 (Sunday between July 24 and 30) / Pentecost 11

Matthew 25:31-46

Come, you that are blessed by my Father, inherit the kingdom prepared for you from the foundation of the world.

Mark 2:23-28

The Son of Man is lord even of the sabbath.

Proper 16 (Sunday between August 21 and 27) / Pentecost 15

John 8:12-20

I am the light of the world. Whoever follows me will never walk in darkness but will have the light of life.

Mark 6:1-6a

Prophets are not without honor, except in their own hometown, and among their own kin, and in their own house.

Proper 20 (Sunday between September 18 and 24) / Pentecost 19

Luke 3:7-18

He will baptize you with the Holy Spirit and fire.

Matthew 6:1-6,16-18

Beware of practicing your piety before others in order to be seen by them.

Proper 24 (Sunday between October 16 and 22) / Pentecost 23

Luke 10:1-12,17-20

The harvest is plentiful, but the laborers are few; therefore ask the Lord of the harvest to send out laborers into his harvest.

Matthew 16:13-20

You are Peter, and on this rock I will build my church, and the gates of Hades will not prevail against it.

Proper 28 (Sunday between November 13 and 19) / Pentecost 27

Luke 16:1-13

The children of this age are more shrewd in dealing with their own generation than are the children of light.

Matthew 23:13-24

Woe to you, blind guides.

Silence for meditation follows the reading,

Monday of Week IV

Antiphon to PSALM 73 *Quam bonus Israel!*

You will guide me **by** your counsel,*
and afterwards receive **me** with glory. [PBO]

73 *The triumph of justice*

1 Truly, God is **good** to Israel,*
to those who are **pure** in heart.

2 But as for me, my feet had **near**ly slipped;*
I had almost **tripped** and fallen;

3 Because I en**vied** the proud*
and saw the prosperity **of** the wicked:

4 For they suf**fer** no pain,*
and their bodies are **sleek** and sound;

5 In the misfortunes of others they **have** no share;*
they are not afflicted as **oth**ers are;

6 Therefore they wear their pride **like** a necklace*
and wrap their violence about them **like** a cloak.

7 Their iniquity comes **from** gross minds,*
and their hearts overflow with **wick**ed thoughts.

8 They scoff and **speak** maliciously;*
out of their haughtiness they **plan** oppression.

9 They set their mouths a**gainst** the heavens,*
and their evil speech runs **through** the world.

10 And so the people **turn** to them*
and find in **them** no fault.

11 They say, "How **should** God know?*
is there knowledge in **the** Most High?"

12 So then, these **are** the wicked;*
always at ease, they in**crease** their wealth.

13 In vain have I kept **my** heart clean,*
and washed my **hands** in innocence.

14 I have been afflicted **all** day long,*
and punished **ev**ery morning.

15 Had I gone on speak**ing** this way,*
I should have betrayed the generation **of** your children.

16 When I tried to under**stand** these things,*
it was too **hard** for me;

17 Until I entered the sanctuar**y** of God*
and discerned the end **of** the wicked.

18 Surely, you set them in slip**per**y places;*
you cast them **down** in ruin.

19 Oh, how suddenly do they come **to** destruction,*
come to an end, and per**ish** from terror!

20 Like a dream when one awa**kens**, O Lord,*
when you arise you will make their **im**age vanish.

21 When my mind be**came** embittered,*
I was sorely wounded **in** my heart.

22 I was stupid and had no **un**derstanding;*
I was like a brute beast **in** your presence.

23 Yet I am **al**ways with you;*
you hold me by **my** right hand.

24 You will guide me **by** your counsel,*
and afterwards receive **me** with glory.

25 Whom have I in heav**en** but you?*
and having you I desire nothing **up**on earth.

26 Though my flesh and my heart should **waste** away,*
God is the strength of my heart and my por**tion** for ever.

27 Truly, those who forsake **you** will perish;*
you destroy all who **are** unfaithful.

28 But it is good for me to **be** near God;*
I have made the Lord **GOD** my refuge.

29 I will speak of **all** your works*
in the gates of the ci**ty** of Zion.

Antiphon You will guide me **by** your counsel,*
and afterwards receive **me** with glory.

Silence for meditation

Father, in your wisdom you allowed your Son to be dismayed by the prospect of his cross, but by his death the penalty of sin was changed into glory: Grant that, on our journey to you, the cross of your Son may not be a stumbling block but a beacon to guide us to that heavenly country where with your Son Jesus Christ and the Holy Spirit you live and reign, one God, now and for ever. [LHd, LBW]

+

Antiphon to PSALM 4 *Cum invocarem, exaudivit*

Have mercy on me and hear my prayer. [LH, PBO]

4 *Evening prayer of thanksgiving*

1 Answer me when I call, O God, defender **of** my cause;*
you set me free when I am hard-pressed;
have mercy on me and **hear** my prayer.

2 "You mortals, how long will you dishon**or** my glory;*
how long will you worship dumb idols
and run af**ter** false gods?"

3 Know that the LORD does wonders **for** the faithful;*
when I call upon the LORD, **he** will hear me.

4 Tremble, then, and **do** not sin;*
speak to your heart in silence up**on** your bed.

5 Offer the appointed **sac**rifices*
and put your trust **in** the LORD.

6 Many are saying, "Oh, that we might see **bet**ter times!"*
Lift up the light of your countenance upon **us**, O LORD.

7 You have put gladness **in** my heart,*
more than when grain and wine and **oil** increase.

8 I lie down in peace; at once I **fall** asleep;*
for only you, LORD, make me **dwell** in safety.

Antiphon Have mercy on me and hear my prayer.

Silence for meditation

Lord, you consoled your Son in his anguish and released him from the darkness of the grave: Turn your face toward us, that we may sleep in your peace and rise in your light; through your Son, Jesus Christ our Lord. [LHd, LBW]

+

Stand

THE HYMN is sung. *Wir pflügen und wir streuen*

We plow the fields and scat - ter The good seed on the land,
But it is fed and wa - tered By God's al - might - y hand.
He sends the snow in win - ter, The warmth to swell the grain,
The breez - es and the sun - shine, And soft re - fresh - ing rain.
Refrain
All good gifts a - round us Are sent from heav'n a - bove.
Then thank the Lord, oh, thank the Lord For all his love.

2 He only is the maker
Of all things near and far;
He paints the wayside flower,
He lights the evening star.
The winds and waves obey him;
By him the birds are fed.
Much more to us, his children,
He gives our daily bread.
All good gifts around us
Are sent from heaven above.
Then thank the Lord, oh thank the Lord,
For all his love.

3 We thank you, our creator,
For all things bright and good,
The seedtime and the harvest,
Our life, our health, our food.
No gifts have we to offer
For all your love imparts,
But what you most would treasure—
Our humble, thankful hearts.
All good gifts around us
Are sent from heaven above.
Then thank the Lord, O thank the Lord,
For all his love.

[LBW 362, H82 291]

Text: Matthias Claudius, 1740-1815; tr. Jane Montgomery Campell, 1817-1878, alt.
Tune: *Wir pflügen,* Johann A. P. Schulz, 1747-1800 76 76 D and refrain

Sit

A LESSON is read.

Year 1

after Epiphany 4

Mark 7:24-37
He has done everything well; he even makes the deaf to hear and the mute to speak.

after Epiphany 8

Matthew 6:7-15
If you forgive others their trespasses, your heavenly Father will also forgive you.

Year 2

John 6:27-40
The bread of God is that which comes down from heaven and gives life to the world.

John 12:27-36a
While you have the light, believe in the light, so that you may become children of light.

after Proper 4 / Pentecost 3

Luke 17:1-10

When you have done all that you were ordered to do, say, "We are worthless slaves; we have done only what we ought to have done!"

Matthew 13:44-52

Every scribe who has been trained for the kingdom of heaven is like the master of a household who brings out of his treasure what is new and what is old.

after Proper 8 / Pentecost 7

Luke 22:52-62

Peter remembered the word of the Lord, How he had said to him, "Before the cock crows today, you will deny me three times."

Matthew 21:12-22

Jesus entered the temple and drove out all who were selling and buying in the temple, and he overturned the tables of the money changers and the seats of those who sold doves.

after Proper 12 / Pentecost 11

Mark 6:14-29

Some were saying, "John the baptizer has been raised from the dead; and for this reason these powers are at work in him."

Matthew 27:24-31

So he released Barabbas for them; and after flogging Jesus, he handed him over to be crucified.

after Proper 16 / Pentecost 15

Mark 13:14-27

Then they will see "The Son of Man coming in clouds" with great power and glory.

John 6:52-59

The one who eats this bread will live forever.

after Proper 20 / Pentecost 19

Matthew 5:21-26

If you remember that your brother or sister has something against

Luke (1:1-4),3:1-14

John went into all the region around the Jordan, proclaiming a

you, leave your gift there before the altar and go; first be reconciled to your brother or sister, and then come and offer your gift.

baptism of repentance for the forgiveness of sins.

after Proper 24 / Pentecost 23

Matthew 11:16-24

John came neither eating nor drinking, and they say, "He has a demon"; the Son of Man came eating and drinking, and they say, "Look, a glutton and a drunkard, a friend of tax collectors and sinners!"

Luke 9:51-62

No one who puts a hand to the plow and looks back is fit for the kingdom of God.

after Proper 28 / Pentecost 27

Matthew 17:1-13

Elijah has already come, and they did not recognize him, but they did to him whatever they pleased. So also the Son of Man is about to suffer at their hands.

Luke 16:19-31

If they do not listen to Moses and the prophets, neither will they be convinced even if someone rises from the dead.

Silence for meditation follows the reading.

Tuesday of Week IV

Antiphon to PSALM 36 *Dixit injustus*

In your light, O Lord, we see light. [LH, PBO]

36 *The wickedness of the sinner; the goodness of God*

1 There is a voice of rebellion deep in the heart **of** the wicked;*
there is no fear of God be**fore** his eyes.

2 He flatters himself in **his** own eyes*
that his hateful sin will not **be** found out.

3 The words of his mouth are wicked **and** deceitful;*
he has left off acting wisely and **do**ing good.

4 He thinks up wickedness upon his bed
and has set himself in **no** good way;*
he does not abhor that **which** is evil.

5 Your love, O LORD, reaches **to** the heavens,*
and your faithfulness **to** the clouds.

6 Your righteousness is like the strong mountains,
your justice like **the** great deep;*
you save both man and **beast**, O LORD.

7 How priceless is your **love**, O God!*
your people take refuge under the shadow **of** your wings.

8 They feast upon the abundance **of** your house;*
you give them drink from the river of **your** delights.

9 For with you is the **well** of life,*
and in your light **we** see light.

10 Continue your loving-kindness to **those** who know you,*
and your favor to those who are **true** of heart.

11 Let not the foot of the **proud** come near me,*
nor the hand of the wicked push **me** aside.

12 See how they are fallen, those **who** work wickedness!*
they are cast down and shall not be a**ble** to rise.

Antiphon In your light, O Lord, we see light.

Silence for meditation

Lord God, source of light and life, by the light of your truth let the virtuous know your goodness and sinners feel your mercy, so that together they may drink from your river of delight and rejoice now and ever in your Son, Jesus Christ our Lord. [LHd, LBW]

+

Antiphon to PSALM 7 *Domine, Deus meus*

God is a **right**eous judge;*
he is the savior of the **true** in heart. [LH, PBO]

7 *A prayer for justice*

1 O LORD my God, I take ref**uge** in you;*
save and deliver me from all **who** pursue me;

2 Lest like a lion they tear **me** in pieces*
and snatch me away with none to de**liv**er me.

3 O LORD my God, if I have **done** these things:*
if there is any wickedness **in** my hands,

4 If I have repaid my **friend** with evil,*
or plundered him who without cause **is** my enemy;

5 Then let my enemy pursue and **o**vertake me,*
trample my life into the ground,
and lay my honor **in** the dust.

6 Stand up, O LORD, **in** your wrath;*
rise up against the fury **of** my enemies.

7 Awake, O my God, **de**cree justice;*
let the assembly of the peoples **gath**er round you.

8 Be seated on your lofty throne, **O** Most High;*
O LORD, **judge** the nations.

9 Give judgment for me according to my righteous**ness**, O LORD,*
and according to my innocence, **O** Most High.

10 Let the malice of the wicked come to an end,
but estab**lish** the righteous;*
for you test the mind and heart, O **right**eous God.

11 God is my shield **and** defense;*
he is the savior of the **true** in heart.

12 God is a **right**eous judge;*
God sits in judgment **ev**ery day.

13 If they will not repent, God will **whet** his sword;*
he will bend his bow and **make** it ready.

14 He has prepared his weap**ons** of death;*
he makes his arrows **shafts** of fire.

15 Look at those who are in la**bor** with wickedness,*
who conceive evil, and give birth **to** a lie.

16 They dig a pit and **make** it deep*
and fall into the hole that **they** have made.

17 Their malice turns back upon **their** own head;*
their violence falls on **their** own scalp.

18 I will bear witness that the **LORD** is righteous;*
I will praise the Name of the **LORD** Most High.

Antiphon God is a **right**eous judge;*
he is the savior of the **true** in heart.

Silence for meditation

God our Judge, you know what is in our hearts and yet you are slow to anger and merciful in judging: So direct our thoughts and actions that we may return good for evil and thus ourselves display the merciful justice you show toward us; through Jesus Christ our Lord. [LH, PHP]

Stand

THE HYMN is sung.

2 We are of thee, the children of thy love,
One fam'ly with thy well-belovèd Son;
Descend, O Holy Spirit, like a dove,
Into our hearts that we may be as one;
As one with thee, to whom we ever tend,
As one with him, our brother and our friend.

3 We would be one in hatred of all wrong,
One in the love of all things sweet and fair,
One with the joy that breaketh into song,
One with the grief that trembleth into prayer;
One in the power that makes thy children free
To follow truth, and thus to follow thee.

4 Oh, clothe us with thy heavenly armor, Lord,
Thy trusty shield, thy sword of love divine;
Our inspiration be thy constant Word,
We ask no victories that are not thine;
Give or withhold, let pain or pleasure be;
Enough to know that we are serving thee. [H82 617; SBH 350, alt.]

Text: John White Chadwick, 1840-1904, alt.
Tune: *Song 1*, Orlando Gibbons, 1583-1625 10 10, 10 10, 10 10

Sit

A LESSON is read.

Year 1	Year 2
after Epiphany 4	
Mark 8:1-10	John 6:41-51
They ate and were filled; and they took up the broken pieces left over, seven baskets full.	I am the living bread that came down from heaven. Whoever eats of this bread will live forever.

after Epiphany 8

Matthew 6:16-23

Where your treasure is, there your heart will be also.

John 12:36b-50

I have come as light into the world, so that everyone who believes in me should not remain in the darkness.

after Proper 4 / Pentecost 3

Luke 17:11-19

Was none of them found to return and give praise to God except this foreigner?

Matthew 13:53-58

Prophets are not without honor except in their own country and in their own house.

after Proper 8 / Pentecost 7

Luke 22:63-71

From now on the Son of Man will be seated at the right hand of the power of God.

Matthew 21:23-32

John came to you in the way of righteousness and you did not believe him, but the tax collectors and sinners believed him; and even after you saw it, you did not change your minds and believe him.

after Proper 12 / Pentecost 11

Mark 6:30-46

Come away to a deserted place all by yourselves and rest a while.

Matthew 27:32-44

He saved others; he cannot save himself.

after Proper 16 / Pentecost 15

Mark 13:28-37

Keep awake—for you do not know when the master of the house will come, in the evening,

John 6:60-71

Lord, to whom can we go? You have the words of eternal life.

or at midnight, or at cockcrow, or at dawn.

after Proper 20 / Pentecost 19

Matthew 5:27-37

But I say to you, that everyone who looks at a woman with lust has already committed adultery with her in his heart.

Luke 3:15-22

I baptize you with water; but one who is more powerful than I is coming; I am not worthy to untie the thong of his sandals. He will baptize you with the Holy Spirit and fire.

after Proper 24 / Pentecost 23

Matthew 11:25-30

Come to me, all you that are weary and are carrying heavy burdens, and I will give you rest.

Luke 10:1-16

The harvest is plentiful, but the laborers are few; therefore ask the Lord of the harvest to send out laborers into his harvest.

after Proper 28 / Pentecost 27

Matthew 17:14-21

If you have faith the size of a mustard seed, you will say to this mountain, "Move from here to there," and it will move; and nothing will be impossible for you.

Luke 17:1-10

When you have done all that you were ordered to do, say, "We are worthless slaves; we have done only what we ought to have done!"

Silence for meditation follows the reading.

Wednesday of Week IV

Antiphon to PSALM 132 *Memento, Domine*

The Lord has **cho**sen Zion;*
he has desired her for his **hab**itation. [LH, PBO]

132 *God's promises to the house of David*

1 LORD, re**mem**ber David,*
and all the hardships **he** endured;

2 How he swore an oath **to** the LORD*
and vowed a vow to the Mighty **One** of Jacob:

3 "I will not come under the roof **of** my house,*
nor climb up in**to** my bed;

4 I will not allow my **eyes** to sleep,*
nor let my **eye**lids slumber;

5 Until I find a place **for** the LORD,*
a dwelling for the Mighty **One** of Jacob."

6 "The ark! We heard it was in **Eph**ratah;*
we found it in the **fields** of Jearim.

7 Let us go to God's **dwell**ing place;*
let us fall upon our knees be**fore** his footstool."

8 Arise, O LORD, into your **rest**ing-place,*
you and the ark **of** your strength.

9 Let your priests be **clothed** with righteousness;*
let your faithful people **sing** with joy.

10 For your servant **Da**vid's sake,*
do not turn away the face of **your** Anointed.

11 The LORD has sworn an **oath** to David;*
in truth, he will **not** break it:

12 “A son, the fruit **of** your body*
will I set up**on** your throne.

13 If your children keep my covenant
and my testimonies that **I** shall teach them,*
their children will sit upon your throne for **ev**ermore.”

14 For the LORD has **cho**sen Zion;*
he has desired her for his **hab**itation:

15 “This shall be my resting-**place** for ever;*
here will I dwell, for I de**light** in her.

16 I will surely bless **her** provisions,*
and satisfy her **poor** with bread.

17 I will clothe her priests **with** salvation,*
and her faithful people will re**joice** and sing.

18 There will I make the horn of **Dav**id flourish;*
I have prepared a lamp for **my** Anointed.

19 As for his enemies, I will clothe **them** with shame;*
but as for him, his **crown** will shine.”

Antiphon The Lord has **cho**sen Zion;*
he has desired her for his **hab**itation.

Silence for meditation

Lord God, our King, you have chosen the new Zion as your dwelling-place, the Church as your place of rest; you have kindled in it a lamp that will burn brightly for ever before Christ, your anointed one: Make our hearts your tabernacle, clothe your people with holiness, and give bread to the poor, that we may rejoice and sing to you now and for ever. [LHd, LBW]

+

Antiphon to PSALM 134 *Ecce nunc*

Praise our God, all **you** his servants,*
and all who fear him, **small** and great. [LH: Rev. 19:5]

134 *Evening prayer in the temple*

1 Behold now, bless the LORD, all you servants **of** the LORD,*
you that stand by night in the house **of** the LORD.

2 Lift up your hands in the holy place and **bless** the LORD;*
the LORD who made heaven and earth bless you **out** of Zion.

Antiphon Praise our God, all **you** his servants,*
and all who fear him, **small** and great.

Silence for meditation

Lord, where two or three are gathered in your Name, you promised to be among them: Look down upon your family lifting our hands in thanksgiving to you and graciously pour out your blessing upon us; through Jesus Christ our Lord. [LHd, PHP]

+

Stand

THE HYMN is sung.

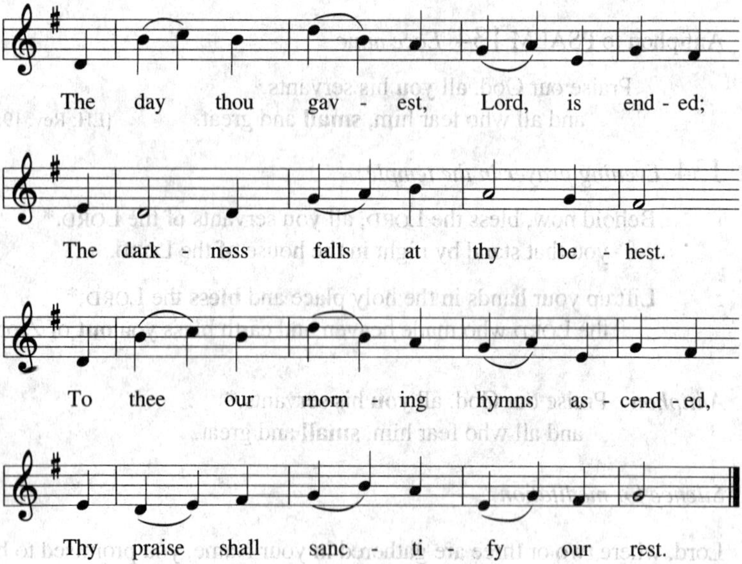

2 We thank thee that thy Church, unsleeping
While earth rolls onward into light,
Through all the world her watch is keeping,
And rests not now by day or night.

3 As o'er each continent and island
The dawn leads on another day,
The voice of prayer is never silent,
Nor dies the strain of praise away.

4 The sun, here having set, is waking
Thy children under western skies,
And hour by hour, as day is breaking,
Fresh hymns of thankful praise arise.

5 So be it, Lord; thy throne shall never,
Like earth's proud empires, pass away;
Thy kingdom stands and grows for ever,
Till all thy creatures own thy sway.
[SBH 227, H82 24, LBW 274]

Text: John Ellerton, 1826-1893, alt.

Tune: *St. Clement*, Clement C. Scholefield, 1839-1904 98 98

Sit

A LESSON is read.

Year 1	Year 2
after Epiphany 4	
Mark 8:11-26	John 6:52-59
Do you have eyes and fail to see? Do you have ears and fail to hear?	Those who eat my flesh and drink my blood abide in me, and I in them.
after Epiphany 8	
Matthew 6:24-34	John 13:1-20
Do not worry about tomorrow, for tomorrow will bring worries of its own. Today's trouble is enough for today.	Whoever receives one whom I send receives me; and whoever receives me receives him who sent me.
after Proper 4 / Pentecost 3	
Luke 17:20-37	Matthew 14:1-12
As the lightning flashes and lights up the sky from one side to the other, so will the Son of Man be in his day.	His disciples came and took the body and buried it; then they went and told Jesus.

after Proper 8 / Pentecost 7

Luke 23:1-12

That same day Herod and Pilate became friends with each other; before this they had been enemies.

Matthew 21:33-46

The kingdom of God will be taken away from you and given to a people that produces the fruits of the kingdom.

after Proper 12 / Pentecost 11

Mark 6:47-56

Take heart, it is I; do not be afraid.

Matthew 27:45-54

When the centurion and those with him, who were keeping watch over Jesus, saw the earthquake and what took place, they were terrified and said, "Truly this man was God's Son!"

after Proper 16 / Pentecost 15

Mark 14:1-11

She has done what she could; she has anointed my body beforehand for its burial.

John 7:1-13

The world cannot hate you, but it hates me because I testify against it that its works are evil.

after Proper 20 / Pentecost 19

Matthew 5:38-48

Love your enemies and pray for those who persecute you.

Luke 4:1-13

When the devil had finished every test, he departed from him until an opportune time.

after Proper 24 / Pentecost 23

Matthew 12:1-14

The Pharisees went out and conspired against him, how to destroy him.

Luke 10:17-24

Blessed are the eyes that see what you see!

after Proper 28 / Pentecost 27

Matthew 17:22-27

The Son of Man is going to be betrayed into human hands, and they will kill him, and on the third day he will be raised.

Luke 17:11-19

Was none of them found to return and give praise to God except this foreigner?

Silence for meditation follows the reading.

Thursday of Week IV

Antiphon to PSALM 26 *Judica me, Domine*

I have trusted in the Lord and have not faltered. [LH, PBO]

26 *Prayer of the blameless*

1 Give judgment for me, O LORD,
for I have lived **with** integrity;*
I have trusted in the Lord and **have** not faltered.

2 Test me, O **LORD**, and try me;*
examine my heart **and** my mind.

3 For your love is be**fore** my eyes;*
I have walked faithful**ly** with you.

4 I have not sat **with** the worthless,*
nor do I consort with **the** deceitful.

5 I have hated the company of **ev**ildoers;*
I will not sit down **with** the wicked.

6 I will wash my hands in inno**cence**, O LORD,*
that I may go in procession **round** your altar,

7 Singing aloud a song **of** thanksgiving*
and recounting all your won**der**ful deeds.

8 LORD, I love the house in **which** you dwell*
and the place where your glo**ry** abides.

9 Do not sweep me a**way** with sinners,*
nor my life with those who **thirst** for blood,

10 Whose hands are full of **e**vil plots,*
and their right hand **full** of bribes.

11 As for me, I will live with in**teg**rity;*
redeem me, O LORD, and have pi**ty** on me.

12 My foot stands on **le**vel ground;*
in the full assembly I will **bless** the LORD.

Antiphon I have trusted in the Lord and have not faltered.

Silence for meditation

Lord Jesus, Lamb without stain, image of the Father's glory: Give us the strength to avoid sin and be faithful to you always. Lead us to the place where God dwells in his glory, that we may praise him with joy among his saints now and for ever. [LHd, LBW]

+

Antiphon to PSALM 87 *Fundamenta ejus*

Glorious things are spo**ken** of you,*
O city **of** our God. [LH, PBO]

87 *Jerusalem, mother of all nations*

1 On the holy mountain stands the city **he** has founded;*
the LORD loves the gates of Zion
more than all the dwel**lings** of Jacob.

2 Glorious things are spo**ken** of you,
O city **of** our God.

3 I count Egypt and Babylon among **those** who know me;*
behold Philistia, Tyre, and Ethiopia:
in Zion **were** they born.

4 Of Zion it shall be said, "Everyone was **born** in her,*
and the Most High himself **shall** sustain her."

5 The LORD will record as he en**rolls** the peoples,*
"These **also** were born there."

6 The singers and the dan**cers** will say,*
"All my fresh springs **are** in you."

Antiphon Glorious things are spo**ken** of you,*
O city **of** our God.

Silence for meditation

Lord God, your Son wept over ancient Jerusalem, and he established the new Jerusalem firmly upon rock and made it the mother of the faithful: Make us rejoice in your Church, and grant that all people may be reborn into the freedom of your Spirit, through Jesus Christ our Lord. [LH, LBW

+

Stand

THE HYMN is sung.

2 By the toil of faithful workers
In some far outlying field,
By the courage where the radiance
Of the cross is still revealed,
By the victories of meekness,
Through reproach and suffering won:
Father, as in highest heaven,
So on earth your will be done.

3 Grant that knowledge, still increasing,
At your feet may lowly kneel;
With your grace our triumphs hallow,
With your charity our zeal;
Lift the nations from the shadows
To the gladness of the sun:
Father, as in highest heaven,
So on earth your will be done.

4 By the prayers of faithful watchers,
Never silent day or night;
By the cross of Jesus, bringing
Peace to all and healing light;
By the love that passes knowledge
Making all your children one:
Father, as in highest heaven,
So on earth your will be done. [LBW 405]

Text: Howell Elvet Lewis, 1860-1953, alt.

Tune: *Abbott's Leigh,* Cyril Vincent Taylor, 1907-1991, 87 87 D

Sit

A LESSON is read.

Year 1	Year 2
after Epiphany 4	
Mark 8:27-9:1	John 6:60-71
If any want to become my followers, let them deny themselves and take up their cross daily and follow me.	It is the spirit that gives life; the flesh is useless. The words that I have spoken to you are spirit and life.
after Epiphany 8	
Matthew 7:1-12	John 13:21-30
Do not judge, so that you may not be judged.	One of you will betray me.
after Proper 4 / Pentecost 3	
Luke 18:1-8	Matthew 14:13-21
Will not God grant justice to his chosen ones who cry to him day and night? Will he long delay in helping them? I tell you, he will quickly grant justice to them.	Taking the five loaves and the two fish, he looked up to heaven, and blessed and broke the loaves, and gave them to the disciples, and the disciples gave them to the crowds.
after Proper 8 / Pentecost 7	
Luke 23:13-25	Matthew 22:1-14
They kept urgently demanding with loud shouts that he should be crucified; and their voices prevailed.	The wedding is ready, but those invited were not worthy. Go therefore into the main streets, and invite everyone you find to the wedding banquet.
after Proper 12 / Pentecost 11	
Mark 7:1-23	Matthew 27:55-66
You have a fine way of rejecting the commandment of God in order to keep your tradition!	Joseph took the body and wrapped it in a clean linen cloth and laid it in his own new tomb.

after Proper 16 / Pentecost 15

Mark 14:12-26

I will never again drink of the fruit of the vine until that day when I drink it new in the kingdom of God.

John 7:14-36

I will be with you a little while longer, and then I am going to him who sent me.

after Proper 20 / Pentecost 19

Matthew 6:1-6,16-18

Beware of practicing your piety before others in order to be seen by them; for then you have no reward from your Father in heaven.

Luke 4:14-30

Then Jesus, filled with the power of the Spirit, returned to Galilee, and a report about him spread through all the surrounding country.

after Proper 24 / Pentecost 23

Matthew 12:15-21

Many crowds followed him, and he cured all of them, and he ordered them not to make him known.

Luke 10:25-37

He said, "The one who showed him mercy," Jesus said to him, "Go and do likewise."

after Proper 28 / Pentecost 27

Matthew 18:1-9

Unless you change and become like children, you will never enter the kingdom of heaven.

Luke 17:20-37

The kingdom of God is among you.

Silence for meditation follows the reading.

Friday of Week IV

Antiphon to PSALM 40 *Expectans, expectavi Dominum*

My food is to do the will of my Father. [LH, PBO: John 4:3]

40 *Thanksgiving and plea for help*

1 I waited patiently up**on** the LORD;*
he stooped to me and **heard** my cry.

2 He lifted me out of the desolate pit, out of the **mire** and clay;*
he set my feet upon a high cliff and made my **foot**ing sure.

3 He put a new song in my mouth,
a song of praise **to** our God;*
many shall see, and stand in awe,
and put their trust **in** the LORD.

4 Happy are they who trust **in** the LORD!*
they do not resort to evil spirits or turn **to** false gods.

5 Greater things are they that you have done, O LORD my God!
how great your wonders and your **plans** for us!*
there is none who can be com**pared** with you.

6 Oh, that I could make them **known** and tell them!*
but they are more than **I** can count.

7 In sacrifice and offering you **take** no pleasure*
(you have given me **ears** to hear you);

8 Burnt-offering and sin-offering you have **not** required,*
and so I said, "Be**hold**, I come.

9 In the roll of the book it is written con**cern**ing me:*
'I love to do your will, O my God;
your law is deep **in** my heart.'"

10 I proclaimed righteousness in the great **con**gregation;*
behold, I did not restrain my lips;
and that, **O LORD**, you know.

11 Your righteousness have I not hidden in my heart;
I have spoken of your faithfulness and **your** deliverance;*
I have not concealed your love and faithfulness from the
great **con**gregation.

12 You are the LORD;
do not withhold your com**pas**sion from me;*
let your love and your faithfulness keep me **safe** for ever,

13 For innumerable troubles have crowded upon me;
my sins have overtaken me, and I **can**not see;*
they are more in number than the hairs of my head,
and **my** heart fails me.

14 Be pleased, O LORD, to de**li**ver me;*
O LORD, make **haste** to help me.

15 Let them be ashamed and altogether dismayed
who seek after my life **to** destroy it;*
let them draw back and be disgraced
who take pleasure in **my** misfortune.

16 Let those who say, "Aha!" and gloat over me **be** confounded,*
because they **are** ashamed.

17 Let all who seek you rejoice in you **and** be glad;*
let those who love your salvation continually say,
"Great **is** the LORD!"

18 Though I am poor **and** afflicted,*
the Lord will have re**gard** for me.

19 You are my helper and **my** deliverer;*
do not tarry, **O** my God.

Antiphon My food is to do the will of my Father.

Silence for meditation

Lord Jesus Christ, you became obedient to death and your Name was exalted above all others: Teach us always to do the Father's will, so that, made holy by your obedience and united to your sacrifice, we can know your great love in times of sorrow and sing a new song to our God now and for ever. [LH, LBW]

+

Antiphon to PSALM 112 *Beatus vir qui timet*

Blessed are those who hunger and **thirst**
for righteousness,*
for they **shall** be filled. [LH, PBO: Matt. 5:6]

112 *The happiness of the virtuous*

1 Hallelujah!
Happy are they who **fear** the Lord*
and have great delight in **his** commandments!

2 Their descendants will be mighty **in** the land;*
the generation of the upright **will** be blessed.

3 Wealth and riches will be **in** their house,*
and their righteousness will **last** for ever.

4 Light shines in the darkness **for** the upright;*
the righteous are merciful and full **of** compassion.

5 It is good for them to be gener**ous** in lending*
and to manage their af**fairs** with justice.

6 For they will nev**er** be shaken;*
the righteous will be kept in everlast**ing** remembrance.

7 They will not be afraid of any **e**vil rumors;*
their heart is right;
they put their trust **in** the Lord.

8 Their heart is established and **will** not shrink,*
until they see their desire up**on** their enemies.

9 They have given freely **to** the poor,*
and their righteousness stands fast for ever;
they will hold up their **head** with honor.

10 The wicked will see it and be angry;
they will gnash their teeth and **pine** away;*
the desires of the wick**ed** will perish.

Antiphon Blessed are those who hunger and **thirst**
for righteousness,*
for they **shall** be filled.

Silence for meditation

Lord Jesus, you are the light shining in darkness for the upright: Teach us to love one another as you love us, that we might bring peace and joy to the world and find the happiness of your home, where you live and reign with the Father and the Holy Spirit, now and for ever. [LH, LBW]

+

Stand

THE HYMN is sung. *Es ist gewisslich an der Zeit*

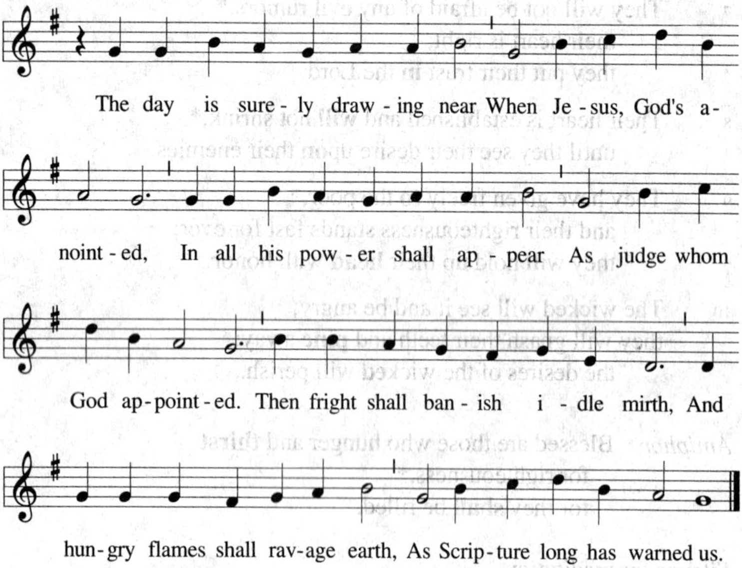

2 The final trumpet then shall sound,
  And all the earth be shaken,
And all who rest beneath the ground
  Shall from their sleep awaken.
But all who live will in that hour,
By God's almighty, boundless power,
  Be changed at his commanding.

3 May Christ our intercessor be
  And, through his blood and merit,
Read from his book that we are free
  With all who life inherit.
Then we shall see him face to face,
With all the saints in that blest place
  Which he has purchased for us.

4 O Jesus Christ, do not delay,
But hasten our salvation;
We often tremble on our way
In fear and tribulation.
Oh, hear and grant our fervent plea;
Come, mighty judge, and set us free
From death and every evil. [LBW 321]

Text: Bartholomäus Ringwaldt, 1532-c. 1600; tr. Philip A. Peter, 1832-1917, adapt.
Tune: *Es ist gewisslich,* melody from *Etlich christlich Lieder*, Wittenberg, 1524

87 87 887

Sit

A LESSON is read.

Year 1	Year 2
after Epiphany 4	
Mark 9:2-13	John 7:1-13
This is my Son, the Beloved; listen to him!	Not even his brothers believed him.
after Epiphany 8	
Matthew 7:13-21	John 13:31-38
Not everyone who says to me, "Lord, Lord, " will enter the kingdom of heaven, but only the one who does the will of my Father in heaven.	By this everyone will know that you are my disciples, if you have love for one another.
after Proper 4 / Pentecost 3	
Luke 18:9-14	Matthew 14:22-36
God, be merciful to me, a sinner!	Take heart, it is I; do not be afraid.

after Proper 8 / Pentecost 7

Luke 23:26-31

As they led him away, they seized a man, Simon of Cyrene, who was coming from the country, and they laid the cross on him, and made him carry it behind Jesus.

Matthew 22:15-22

Give therefore to the emperor the things that are the emperor's and to God the things that are God's.

after Proper 12 / Pentecost 11

Mark 7:24-37

He has done everything well; he even makes the deaf to hear and the mute to speak.

Matthew 28:1-10

They left the tomb quickly with fear and great joy, and ran to tell his disciples.

after Proper 16 / Pentecost 15

Mark 14:27-42

Abba, Father, for you all things are possible; remove this cup from me; yet, not what I want, but what you want.

John 7:37-52

Let anyone who is thirsty come to me, and let the one who believes in me drink.

after Proper 20 / Pentecost 19

Matthew 6:7-15

Your Father knows what you need before you ask him.

Luke 4:31-37

They were astounded at his teaching, because he spoke with authority.

after Proper 24 / Pentecost 23

Matthew 12:22-32

If it is by the Spirit of God that I cast out demons, then the kingdom of God has come to you.

Luke 10:38-42

There is need of only one thing. Mary has chosen the better part, which will not be taken away from her.

after Proper 28 / Pentecost 27

Matthew 18:10-20

It is not the will of your Father in heaven that one of these little ones should be lost.

Luke 18:1-8

When the Son of Man comes, will he find faith on earth?

Silence for meditation follows the reading.

✠

MORNING PRAYER

Matins or Morning Praise during General Time

Stand

Leader

Congregation

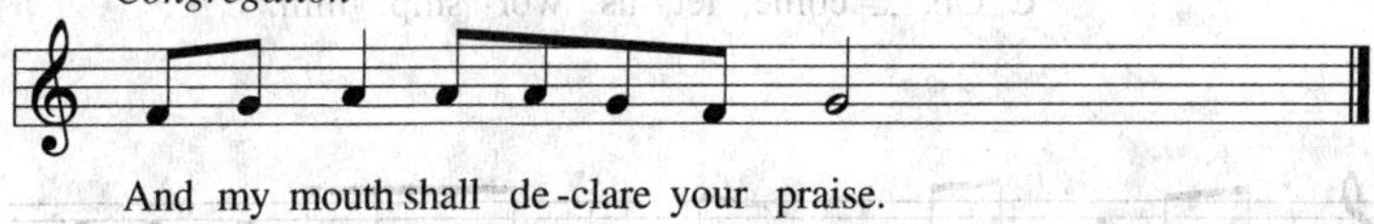

Leader and Congregation

The PSALMODY begins with this song of praise, Venite exultemus. *Psalm 24 (p. 103), Psalm 67 (p. 766), or Psalm 100 (p.498) may replace the* Venite exultemus.

[I] In his hand__ are the cav - erns of the earth;
the__ heights of the hills are__ al__ so his.
[II] The__ sea is his, for he made it;
and his hands have mold - ed the dry land.
[I] Oh,__ come,_ let us bow down and bend the knee,
and__ kneel be - fore the Lord, our__ Mak - er.
[II] For__ he is our God, and_ we are the peo-ple of his pas-ture
and the sheep of his hand.
C Glo - ry to the Fa - ther

Sit

A second psalm is sung or said; additional psalms and an Old Testament canticle may be sung or said also. Silence for meditation follows each psalm or canticle.

The psalm prayer appropriate to each psalm or canticle follows the silence.

C Amen

Stand

THE HYMN is sung.

Sit

One or two LESSONS are read. Silence for meditation follows each reading.

The Responsory to the reading(s) follows the silence. After the Responsory the leader then continues:

L In many and various ways God spoke to his people of old by the prophets.

C But now in these last days he has spoken to us by his Son.

Stand

The GOSPEL CANTICLE, Benedictus Dominus Deus, *is sung or said, beginning with the antiphon.*

Sunday The Lord has come **to** his people*
and **set** them free. [LH]

On the Transfiguration
From the cloud a voice said,
"This is my Son, the Beloved; with him I **am** well pleased;*
list**en** to him!" [LH: Matthew 17:5]

On Trinity Sunday
O holy and undivided Trinity,
creator and ruler of all **that** exists,*
all praise be yours now and through un**end**ing ages. [LH]

On Christ the King
He made us to be a kingdom,
priests serving his **God** and Father;*
he is the firstborn of the dead
and the ruler of the kings **of** the earth. [LH: Revelation 1:6, 5]

Monday Show us your **mer**cy, Lord;*
remem**ber** your covenant. [LH]

Tuesday Let us serve the **Lord** in holiness*
all the days **of** our life. [LH]

Wednesday Give your people knowledge of sal**va**tion, Lord,*
and forgive **us** our sins. [LH]

Thursday Through the tender compassion **of** our God*
the dawn from on high shall **break** upon us. [LH]

Friday Shine, O Lord, on those who **dwell** in darkness*
and in the sha**dow** of death. [LH]

Saturday Guide our **feet**, O Lord,*
into the **way** of peace. [LH]

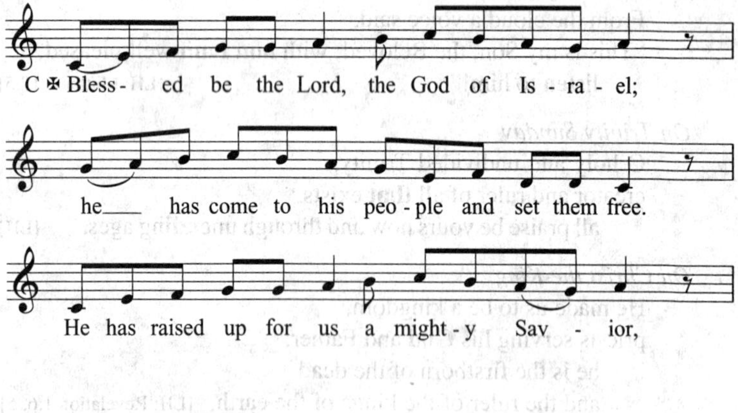

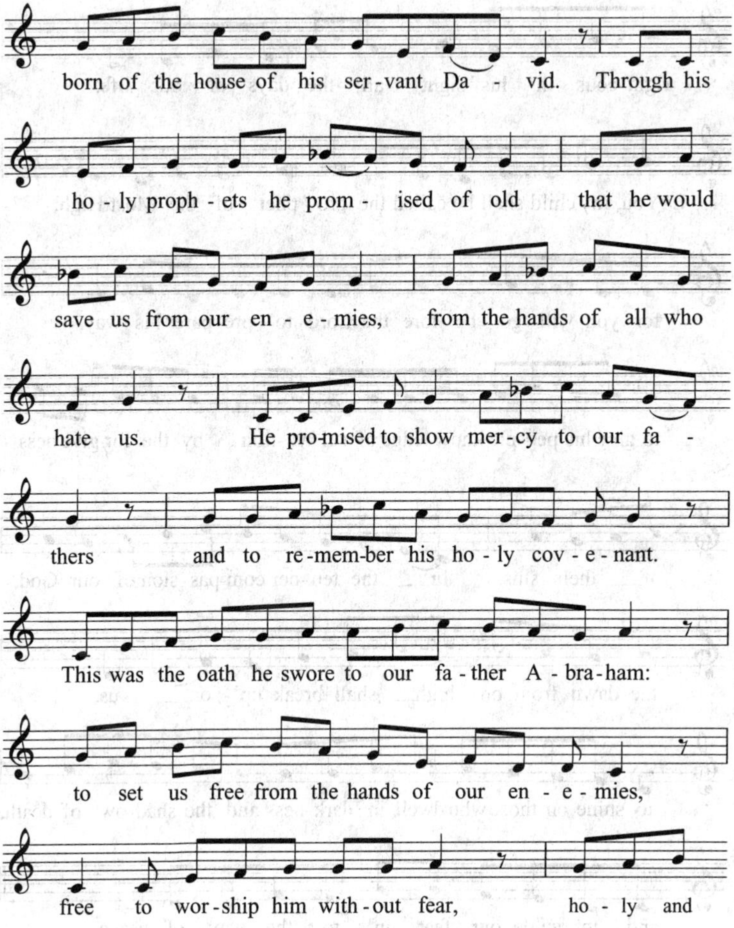
born of the house of his ser - vant Da - vid. Through his
ho - ly proph - ets he prom - ised of old that he would
save us from our en - e - mies, from the hands of all who
hate us. He pro-mised to show mer - cy to our fa -
thers and to re-mem-ber his ho - ly cov - e - nant.
This was the oath he swore to our fa - ther A - bra - ham:
to set us free from the hands of our en - e - mies,
free to wor - ship him with - out fear, ho - ly and

right-eous in his sight all the days of our life.
L You, my child shall be called the pro - phet of the Most High,
for you will go be - fore the Lord to pre-pare his way,
to give his peo-ple know ledge of sal - va-tion by the for-give ness
of their sins. In the ten-der com-pas- sion of our God,
the dawn from on high shall break up - on us,
to shine on those who dwell in dark-ness and the shad-ow of death,
and to guide our feet in - to the way of peace.

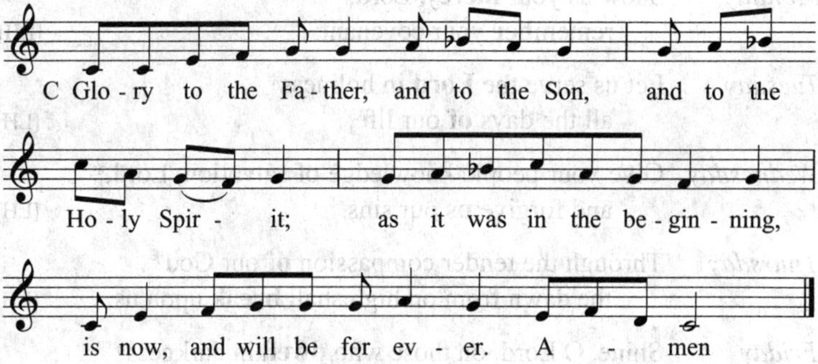

The Antiphon is repeated.

Sunday The Lord has come **to** his people*
and **set** them free. [LH]

On the Transfiguration
From the cloud a voice said,
"This is my Son, the Beloved; with him I **am** well pleased;*
list**en** to him!" [LH: Matthew 17:5]

On Trinity Sunday
O holy and undivided Trinity,
creator and ruler of all **that** exists,*
all praise be yours now through un**end**ing ages. [LH]

On Christ the King
He made us to be a kingdom,
priests serving his **God** and Father;*
he is the firstborn of the dead
and the ruler of the kings **of** the earth. [LH: Revelation 1:6, 5]

Monday	Show us your **mer**cy, Lord;* remem**ber** your covenant. [LH]
Tuesday	Let us serve the **Lord** in holiness* all the days **of** our life. [LH]
Wednesday	Give your people knowledge of sal**va**tion, Lord,* and forgive **us** our sins. [LH]
Thursday	Through the tender compassion **of** our God* the dawn from on high shall **break** upon us. [LH]
Friday	Shine, O Lord, on those who **dwell** in darkness* and in the shad**ow** of death. [LH]
Saturday	Guide our **feet**, O Lord,* into the **way** of peace. [LH]

Kneel or stand.

One of the following Daily Prayers may be said.

Sunday

Lord, you ask of your people love for love, and worship in return for life: Assist us to keep holy week by week the day of your Son's mighty rising from the dead, and bless us in the breaking of bread and the prayers; that other children of yours who behold our joy may seek your lovingkindness in the midst of your temple; through Jesus Christ our Lord. [OPR, SBH]

Monday

O God, the King eternal, whose light divides the day from the night and turns the shadow of death into the morning: Drive far from us all wrongful desires, incline our hearts to keep your law, and guide our feet into the way of peace; that, having done your will with cheerfulness during the day, we may, when night comes, rejoice to give you thanks; through Jesus Christ our Lord. [Mat. Rit., BCP (1979)]

Tuesday

Look mercifully, Lord God, on the morning prayers of your servants, and so enlighten the secrets of our hearts that no shameful desires may this day possess us who have been enlightened by your heavenly grace; through Jesus Christ our Lord. [Gel., Greg., AC rev. JWP, DvD, PHP]

Wednesday

Grant us, O Lord, to pass this day in gladness and peace, without stumbling and without stain, that reaching the eventide victorious over all temptation through your ever-present aid, we may praise you, the eternal God, Governor of all things and blessed for evermore; through Jesus Christ our Lord. [Moz. Breviary, AC, CSB, SBH]

Thursday

O God, the true light of believers, the eternal glory of the righteous, your light never sets and your brightness knows no bounds. As you have brought us through the night to the morning of a new day, so lead us at length to that blessed and everlasting day where night is no more; through Jesus Christ our Lord. [Ambrosian Breviary, trans. NEM]

Friday

Almighty God, your blessed Son willingly offered himself to endure the agony and shame of the cross for our redemption: Banish our cowardice, and give us courage to take up our cross and bear it patiently in his service; through Jesus Christ our Lord. [DP alt. JWP, PHP; see BCP]

Saturday

Almighty God, who after the creation of the world rested from all your works and sanctified a day of rest for all your creatures: Grant that we, putting away all earthly anxieties, may be duly prepared for the service of your sanctuary, and that our rest here upon earth may be a preparation for the eternal rest promised to your people in heaven; through Jesus Christ our Lord. [Edward Benson, *Chain*; BCP (1979)]

C Amen

The PRAYER OF THE DAY is said.

Weekdays following the Baptism of our Lord (the First Sunday after the Epiphany)/The First Week in Ordinary (Ordered) Time

O Lord, mercifully receive the prayers of your people who call upon you, and grant that they may know and understand what things they ought to do, and also may have grace and power to accomplish them; through your Son Jesus Christ our Lord, who lives and reigns with you and the Holy Spirit, one God, now and for ever.

[Greg., MR, CB, CSB, SBH, RS; LBW 8 Epiphany; BCP Proper 10]

The Second Week after the Epiphany
The Second Week in Ordinary (Ordered) Time

Almighty and everlasting God, you govern all things both in heaven and on earth: mercifully hear the supplications of your people, and in our time grant us your peace; through your Son, Jesus Christ our Lord, who lives and reigns with you and the Holy Spirit, one God, now and for ever.

[Greg., RS, MR, CB, CSB, SBH; BCP 4 Epiph., LBW 8 Epiph.]

The Third Week after the Epiphany
The Third Week in Ordinary (Ordered) Time

Almighty and everlasting God, direct our actions according to your gracious will, that we may abound in doing good in the Name of your beloved Son, Jesus Christ our Lord; who lives and reigns with you and the Holy Spirit, one God, now and for ever.

[Greg., RS; MR, CB, CSB, SBH 1 Christmas]

The Fourth Week after the Epiphany
The Fourth Week in Ordinary (Ordered) Time

Almighty God, you know that we are set in the midst of so many and great dangers, that by reason of the weakness of our nature we cannot always stand upright: Grant to us such strength and protection as may support us in all dangers and carry us through all temptations; through your Son Jesus Christ our Lord, who lives and reigns with you and the Holy Spirit, one God, now and for ever.

[Greg., MR, CB, CSB, SBH, LBW]

BCP: above, 2 Epiphany

The Fifth Week after the Epiphany
The Fifth Week in Ordinary (Ordered) Time

Lord God, we ask you to keep your Church and household continually in your true religion, that those who lean only on the hope of your heavenly grace may evermore be defended by your mighty power; through your Son, Jesus Christ our Lord, who lives and reigns with you and the Holy Spirit, one God, now and for ever.

[Greg, MR, RS, CB, CSB, SBH; LBW 7 Epiph.]

The Sixth Week after the Epiphany
The Sixth Week in Ordinary (Ordered) Time

O God, you have promised to dwell in true and upright hearts: Abide with us in your grace and mercy, and make us a dwelling worthy of you; through your Son, Jesus Christ our Lord, who lives and reigns with you and the Holy Spirit, one God, now and for ever.

[Leo., RS; tr. DvD]

BCP: below, Proper 6, p. 616
LBW: below, Proper 10, p. 617

The Seventh Week after the Epiphany
The Seventh Week in Ordinary (Ordered) Time

Almighty God, fix our hearts on what is right and true, that we may please you always by doing your will in word and deed; through your Son Jesus Christ our Lord, who lives and reigns with you and the Holy Spirit, one God, now and for ever.

[Gel., Greg., RS; MR 6 Epiphany]

BCP: below, p. 1549 no. 35
LBW: above, 5 Epiph.

The Eighth Week after the Epiphany
The Eighth Week in Ordinary (Ordered) Time

Almighty and everlasting God, in Christ you have revealed your glory among the nations: Preserve the works of your mercy, that your Church throughout the world may persevere with steadfast faith in the confession of your Name; through your Son, Jesus Christ our Lord, who lives and reigns with you and the Holy Spirit, one God, now and for ever. [Gel., Greg.; BCP Proper 24, LBW 22 Pent.]

RS: below, Proper 3
BCP: below p. 1544 no. 18
LBW: above, 2 Epiph.

The Last Sunday after the Epiphany. [The Transfiguration of our Lord]

Lord God, in the transfigured glory of Christ your Son you strengthen our faith by confirming the witness of Moses and Elijah and, in the voice that came from the bright cloud, foreshadowed in a wonderful manner our adoption as your children: In your mercy make us co-heirs with the King of his glory, and bring us at last to the fullness of eternal life in him, Jesus Christ our Lord; who lives and reigns with you and the Holy Spirit, one God, now and for ever.

[MR, RS, SBH Aug. 6; CB, CSB, SBH, LBW Last Sun. after Epiph.]

Monday and Tuesday before Ash Wednesday:

O God, who before the passion of your only-begotten Son revealed his glory upon the holy mountain: Grant to us that we, beholding by faith the light of his countenance, may be strengthened to bear our cross, and be changed into his likeness from glory to glory; through Jesus Christ our Lord, who lives and reigns with you and the Holy Spirit, one God, now and for ever.

[BCPp; BCP Last Sun. after Epiph.]

The prayers for Lent, Holy Week, and Easter are included in the proper Morning Prayer for those seasons.

Proper 1 (*week of the Sunday between May 10 and 14*)/Weekdays between the Day of Pentecost and Trinity Sunday/the sixth week in Ordinary (Ordered) Time)

Remember, O Lord, what you have wrought in us and not what we deserve; and, as you have called us to your service, make us worthy of our calling; through your Son, Jesus Christ our Lord, who lives and reigns with you and the Holy Spirit, one God, now and for ever.
[Leo., BCPp, SBH, BCP]

The Holy Trinity. The First Sunday after Pentecost

Almighty and everlasting God, you have given to us your servants grace, by the confession of a true faith, to acknowledge the glory of the eternal Trinity, and in the power of your divine Majesty to worship the Unity: Keep us steadfast in this faith and worship, and bring us at last to see you in your one and eternal glory, O Father; who with the Son and the Holy Spirit live and reign, one God, for ever and ever. [Greg.; MR, BCP, CB, CSB, SBH, LBW]

Proper 2 (*week of the Sunday between May 15 and 21*)/seventh week in Ordinary (Ordered) Time/weekdays between Trinity Sunday and the Second Sunday after Pentecost

Almighty and merciful God, in your goodness keep us, we pray, from all things that may hurt us, that we, being ready both in mind and body, may accomplish with free hearts those things which belong to your purpose; through your Son, Jesus Christ our Lord, who lives and reigns with you and the Holy Spirit, one God, now and for ever.
[Gel., Greg., BCP; MR 19 Pent.; CB, CSB, SBH 19 Trin., RS week 32]

RS: above, 7 Epiphany

Proper 3 (*the Sunday between May 22 and May 28*)/Eighth Week in Ordinary (Ordered) Time/The Second Sunday after Pentecost

Grant, O Lord, that the course of this world may be peaceably ordered by your providence; and that your Church may joyfully serve you in confidence and serenity; through Jesus Christ our Lord, who lives and reigns with you and the Holy Spirit, one God, now and for ever.

[Leo., RS, BCP; MR 4 Pent.; CB, CSB, SBH 4 Trin.]

Proper 4 (*the Sunday between May 29 and June 4*)/Ninth Week in Ordinary (Ordered) Time/the Third Sunday after Pentecost

O God, your never-failing providence sets in order all things both in heaven and on earth Put away from us, we entreat you, all hurtful things, and give us those things which are profitable for us; through your Son, Jesus Christ our Lord, who lives and reigns with you and the Holy Spirit, one God, now and for ever.

[Gel., RS, BCP; MR 7 Pent.; CB, CSB, SBH 7 Trin.]

LBW: below, Proper 6

Proper 5 (*the Sunday between June 5 and 11*)/Tenth Week in Ordinary (Ordered) Time/the Fourth Sunday after Pentecost

O God, from whom all good proceeds: Grant that by your inspiration we may think those things that are right, and by your merciful guiding may do them; through your Son, Jesus Christ our Lord, who lives and reigns with you and the Holy Spirit, one God, now and for ever.

[Gel., RS, BCP; MR, CB, CSB, SBH, LBW 5/6 Easter]

Proper 6 (*the Sunday between June 12 and 18*)/Eleventh Week in Ordinary (Ordered) Time/the Fifth Sunday after Pentecost

O God, the strength of all who put their trust in you: Mercifully accept our prayers; and because in our weakness we can do nothing good without you, give us the help of your grace, that in keeping your commandments we may please you both in will and deed; through your Son, Jesus Christ our Lord, who lives and reigns with you and the Holy Spirit, one God, now and for ever.

[Gel., Greg., RS; MR 1 Pent.; CB, CSB, SBH 1 Trin.; BCP 6 Epiph.; LBW 3 Pent.]

Proper 7 (*the Sunday between June 19 and 25*)/Twelfth Week in Ordinary (Ordered) Time/the Sixth Sunday after Pentecost

O Lord, make us have perpetual love and reverence for your holy Name, for you never fail to help and govern those whom you have set upon the sure foundation of your loving-kindness; through your Son, Jesus Christ our Lord, who lives and reigns with you and the Holy Spirit, one God, now and for ever.

[Gel., RS, BCP; MR 2 Pent.; CB, CSB, SBH 2 Trin.]

Proper 8 (*the Sunday between June 26 and July 2*)/Thirteenth Week in Ordinary (Ordered) Time/the Seventh Sunday after Pentecost

In your lovingkindness, O God, you have adopted us into your family as children of light: Grant that we may not become entangled in the darkness of error and lies, but may always live in the brightness of your truth; through your Son, Jesus Christ our Lord, who lives and reigns with you and the Holy Spirit, one God, now and for ever.

[Berg., RS; tr. DvD]

Proper 9 (*the Sunday between July 3 and 9*)/Fourteenth Week in Ordinary (Ordered) Time/the Eighth Sunday after Pentecost

O God, you have taught us to keep all your commandments by loving you and our neighbor: Grant us the grace of your Holy Spirit, that we may be devoted to you with our whole heart, and united to one another with pure affection; through your Son, Jesus Christ our Lord, who lives and reigns with you and the Holy Spirit, one God, now and for ever. [Leo., AC, *Chain*, PP, BCP]

RS: below, 3 Easter, p. 1332

Proper 10 (*the Sunday between July 10 and 16*)/Fifteenth Week in Ordinary (Ordered) Time/the Ninth Sunday after Pentecost

Grant to us, Lord, we pray, the spirit to think and do always those things that are right, that we, who cannot exist without you, may by you be enabled to live according to your will; through your Son Jesus Christ our Lord, who lives and reigns with you and the Holy Spirit, one God, now and for ever.
[Leo., CB, CSB, SBH, LBW 9 Pent.; BCP Proper 14; RS Thurs. after Ash Wed.]

RS: below, 4 Easter, p. 1334
BCP: above, weekdays after 1 Epiphany

Proper 11 (*the Sunday between July 17 and July 23*)/Sixteenth Week in Ordinary (Ordered) Time/the Tenth Sunday after Pentecost

Look in mercy, O Lord, upon your family and pour out upon us the gifts of your grace, so that, aflame with faith, hope, and love, we may always watch and pray, and walk in the path of your commandments; through your Son, Jesus Christ our Lord, who lives

and reigns with you and the Holy Spirit, one God, now and for ever.
[Berg., Amb., RS tr. DvD *et al.*]

BCP: below, p. 1557

Proper 12 (*the Sunday between July 24 and 30*)/Seventh Week in Ordinary (Ordered) Time/the Eleventh Sunday after Pentecost

O God, the protector of all who trust in you, without whom nothing is strong, nothing is holy: Increase and multiply upon us your mercy; that, with you as our ruler and guide, we may so pass through things temporal, that we lose not the things eternal; through your Son, Jesus Christ our Lord, who lives and reigns with you and the Holy Spirit, one God, now and for ever. [Greg., RS, BCP; MR 3 Pent.; SBH 3 Trin.]

Proper 13 (*the Sunday between July 31 and August 6*)/Eighteenth Week in Ordinary (Ordered) Time/the Twelfth Sunday after Pentecost

Let your continual mercy, O Lord, cleanse and defend your Church; and, because it cannot continue in safety without your help, protect and govern it always by your goodness; through Jesus Christ our Lord, who lives and reigns with you and the Holy Spirit, one God, now and for ever.
[Gel., BCP; MR 15 Pent.; CB, CSB,SBH 15 Trin.; RS Mon. of Lent 3]

LBW: below, Proper 22

Proper 14 (*the Sunday between August 7 and 13*)/Nineteenth Week in Ordinary (Ordered) Time/the Thirteenth Sunday after Pentecost

Almighty and everlasting God, with boldness and confidence we dare to call you Father: Fulfill and make perfect in our hearts the work of your Holy Spirit, through whom we have become your adopted children, so that we may be found worthy to enter upon the glorious inheritance you have promised to us in Jesus Christ our Lord; who lives and reigns with you and the Holy Spirit, one God, now and for ever. [Berg., Ambrosian Manuale, RS tr. DvD]

BCP: above, Proper 10

Proper 15 (*the Sunday between August 14 and 20*)/Twentieth Week in Ordinary (Ordered) Time/the Fourteenth Sunday after Pentecost

O God, you have prepared for those who love you such good things as surpass our understanding: Pour into our hearts such love towards you, that we, loving you in all things and above all things, may obtain your promises which exceed all that we can desire; through your Son, Jesus Christ our Lord, who lives and reigns with you and the Holy Spirit, one God, now and for ever.
[1 Cor. 2:9, 1 John 4:19; Gel., RS; BCP 6 Easter; SBH 5 Trin., LBW 6 Pent.]

BCP: below, p. 1550 no. 38

Proper 16 (*the Sunday between August 21 and 27*)/Twenty-first Week in Ordinary (Ordered) Time/The Fifteenth Sunday after Pentecost

O God, you make the minds of the faithful to be of one will: Grant that your people may love what you command and desire what you promise; that, among the manifold changes of this world, our hearts may there be fixed where true joys are to be found; through your Son Jesus Christ our Lord, who lives and reigns with you and the Holy Spirit, one God, now and for ever.
[Gel., RS; MR, CB, CSB, SBH 4 Easter, LBW 5 Easter, BCP 5 Lent]

Proper 17 (*the Sunday between August 28 and September 3*)/Twenty-second Week in Ordinary (Ordered) Time/the Sixteenth Sunday after Pentecost

Lord of all power and might, the author and giver of all good things: Graft in our hearts the love of your Name; increase in us true religion; nourish us with all goodness; and bring forth in us the fruit of good works; through your Son, Jesus Christ our Lord, who lives and reigns with you and the Holy Spirit, one God, now and for ever.

[Jas. 1:17; Gel., RS, BCP; MR 6 Pent.; CB, CSB, SBH 6 Trin.]

Proper 18 (*the Sunday between September 4 and 10*)/Twenty-third Week in Ordinary (Ordered) Time/the Seventeenth Sunday after Pentecost

Grant to us, O Lord, to trust in you with all our hearts; for, as you always resist the proud who confide in their own strength, so you never forsake those who make their boast of your mercy; through your Son, Jesus Christ our Lord, who lives and reigns with you and the Holy Spirit, one God, now and for ever.

[Jas. 4:6; Leo., AC, BCP]

RC:below, 5 Easter, p. 1336
LBW: below, Proper 21

Proper 19 (*the Sunday between September 11 and 17*)/Twenty-fourth Week in Ordinary (Ordered Time)/the Eighteenth Sunday after Pentecost

O God, because without you we are not able to please you, mercifully grant that your Holy Spirit may in all things direct and rule our hearts; through your Son, Jesus Christ our Lord, who lives and reigns with you and the Holy Spirit, one God, now and for ever.

[Gel., BCP; MR 18 Pent.; CB, CSB, SBH 18 Trin.]

Proper 20 (*the Sunday between September 18 and 24*)/Twenty-fifth Week in Ordinary (Ordered) Time/the Nineteenth Sunday after Pentecost

Grant us, Lord, not to be anxious about earthly things, but to love things heavenly; and even now, while we are placed among things that are passing away, to hold fast to those that shall endure; through your Son, Jesus Christ our Lord, who lives and reigns with you and the Holy Spirit, one God, now and for ever.

[Col. 3:2; Leo., AC, BCP]

LBW: above, Proper 3 revised

RS: see above, Proper 9

Proper 21 (*the Sunday between September 25 and October 1*)/Twenty-sixth Week in Ordinary (Ordered) Time/the Twentieth Sunday after Pentecost

O God, you declare your almighty power chiefly in showing mercy and pity: Grant us the fullness of your grace, that we, running to obtain your promises, may become partakers of your heavenly treasure; through your Son, Jesus Christ our Lord, who lives and reigns with you and the Holy Spirit, one God, now and for ever.

[Gel., RS, BCP; MR 10 Pent.; CS, CSB, SBH 10 Trin.; LBW 17 Pent.]

Proper 22 (*the Sunday between October 2 and 8*)/Twenty-seventh Week in Ordinary (Ordered) Time/the Twenty-first Sunday after Pentecost

Almighty and everlasting God, you are always more ready to hear than we to pray, and to give more than we either desire or deserve: Pour upon us the abundance of your mercy, forgiving us those things of which our conscience is afraid, and giving us those good things for which we are not worthy to ask, except through the merits and mediation of your Son, Jesus Christ our Lord; who lives and reigns with you and the Holy Spirit, one God, now and for ever.

[Leo., RS, BCP; MR 11 Pent.; CB, CSB, SBH 11 Trin.; LBW 12 Pent.]

Proper 23 (*the Sunday between October 9 and 15*)/Twenty-eighth Week in Ordinary (Ordered) Time/the Twenty-second Sunday after Pentecost

Lord, we pray that your grace may always precede and follow us, that we may be continually given to good works; through your Son, Jesus Christ our Lord, who lives and reigns with you and the Holy Spirit, one God, now and for ever.

[Greg., RS, BCP; MR 16 Pent.; CB, CSB, SBH 16 Trinity]
LBW: below, p. 1540 no. 4

Proper 24 (*the Sunday between October 16 and 22*)/Twenty-ninth Week in Ordinary (Ordered) Time/the Twenty-third Sunday after Pentecost

Almighty and everlasting God, make us always to have a will that is devoted to you and to serve your Majesty with a pure heart; through your Son, Jesus Christ our Lord, who lives and reigns with you and the Holy Spirit, one God, now and for ever.

[Gel., RS; MR, CB, CSB, SBH Sun. after Ascension]

LBW: below, Proper25
BCP: p. 1540 no. 4

Proper 25 (*the Sunday between October 23 and 29*)/Thirtieth Week in Ordinary (Ordered) Time/the Twenty-fourth Sunday after Pentecost

Almighty and everlasting God, increase in us the gifts of faith, hope, and charity; and, that we may obtain what you promise, make us love what you command; through your Son, Jesus Christ our Lord, who lives and reigns with you and the Holy Spirit, one God, now and for ever.

[Leo., RS, BCP; MR 13 Pent.; CB, CSB, SBH 13 Trin., LBW 23 Pent.]

Proper 26 (*the Sunday between October 30 and November 5*)/Thirty-first Week in Ordinary (Ordered) Time/the Twenty-fifth Sunday after Pentecost

Almighty and merciful God, it is only by your gift that your faithful people offer you true and laudable service: Grant that we may run without stumbling to obtain your heavenly promises; through your Son, Jesus Christ our Lord, who lives and reigns with you and the Holy Spirit, one God, now and for ever.

[Leo., RS, BCP; MR 12 Pent.; CB, CSB, SBH 12 Trin.]

LBW: below, weekdays after Christ the King

Proper 27 (*the Sunday between November 6 and 12*)/Thirty-second in Ordinary (Ordered) Time/the Twenty-sixth Sunday after Pentecost

O God, whose blessed Son came into the world that he might destroy the works of the devil and make us children of God and heirs of eternal life: Grant that, having this hope, we may purify ourselves as he is pure; that, when he comes again with power and great glory, we may be made like him in his eternal and glorious kingdom; where he lives and reigns with you and the Holy Spirit, one God, now and for ever. [1 John 1:3-9, John Cosin 1662, 6 Epiphany; BCP]

RS: above, Proper 2
LBW: below, Proper 28

Proper 28 (*the Sunday between November 13 and 19*)/Thirty-third Week in Ordinary (Ordered) Time/The Twenty-seventh Sunday after Pentecost

O God, so rule and govern our hearts and minds by your Holy Spirit, that being ever mindful of the end of all things and the day of your just judgment, we may be stirred up to holiness of living here, and dwell with you for ever hereafter; through your Son, Jesus Christ our Lord, who lives and reigns with you and the Holy Spirit, one God, now and for ever.

[Church of Sweden 1639, CB, CSB, SBH; LBW 26 Pent.]

BCP: below, p. 1540 no. 5

Christ the King. The Last Sunday after Pentecost

Almighty and everlasting God, whose will it is to restore all things in your well-beloved Son, the King of kings and Lord of lords: Mercifully grant that the peoples of the earth, divided and enslaved by sin, may be freed and brought together under his most gracious rule; who lives and reigns with you and the Holy Spirit, one God, now and for ever. [MR 1925, RS, BCP, LBW]

Weekdays between Christ the King and the First Sunday in Advent

Stir up, O Lord, the wills of your faithful people, that they, more earnestly seeking to do good, may receive more abundant help from your mercy; through your Son, Jesus Christ our Lord, who lives and reigns with you and the Holy Spirit, one God, now and for ever.
[Greg., RS; MR 24 Pent.; CB, CSB, SBH 24 Trin.]

C Amen

Other prayers may be said. *(See pp. 1539-1555)*

The prayers are concluded:

L Let my mouth be full of your praise
C And your glory all the day long. [CSB, SBH: Ps. 71:8]

O Lord, almighty and everlasting God, you have brought us in safety to this new day: Preserve us with your mighty power, that we may not fall into sin, nor be overcome by adversity; and in all we do, direct us to the fulfilling of your purpose; through Jesus Christ our Lord.
[Gel., Greg., Sarum, BCP, CB, CSB, SBH, LBW]

L Lord, remember us in your kingdom, and teach us to pray:

C Our Father in heaven,
hallowed be your Name
your kingdom come,
your will be done,
on earth as in heaven.

C Our Father who art in heaven,
hallowed be thy Name
thy kingdom come,
thy will be done,
on earth as it is in heaven.

Give us today our daily bread.
Forgive us our sins
as we forgive those
who sin against us.
Save us from the time of trial
and deliver us from evil.
For the kingdom, the power,
and the glory are yours,
now and for ever. Amen.

Give us this day our daily bread;
and forgive us our trespasses,
as we forgive those
who sin against us;
And lead us not into temptation
but deliver us from evil.
For thine is the kingdom,
and the power, and the glory,
for ever and ever. Amen.

Stand

The BENEDICTION concludes the service when there is no sermon. A hymn may follow. On Sundays the service may be concluded with the Paschal Blessing, page 628.

When there is a sermon, this benediction is omitted, and the service continues as on p. 20.

L The Lord al - mighty bless us, ✠ and direct our days and

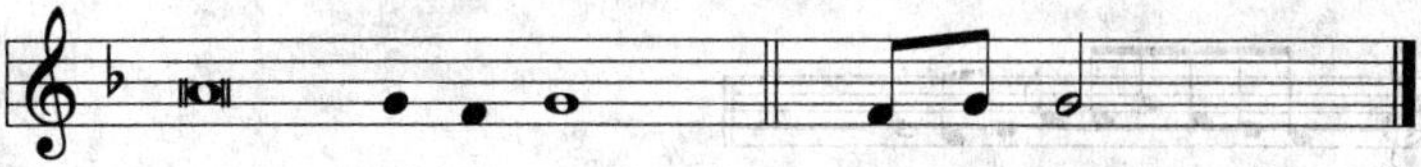

our deeds in his peace. C A - men

The PASCHAL BLESSING may be used on Sundays to conclude Morning Prayer. The service may be led from the font.

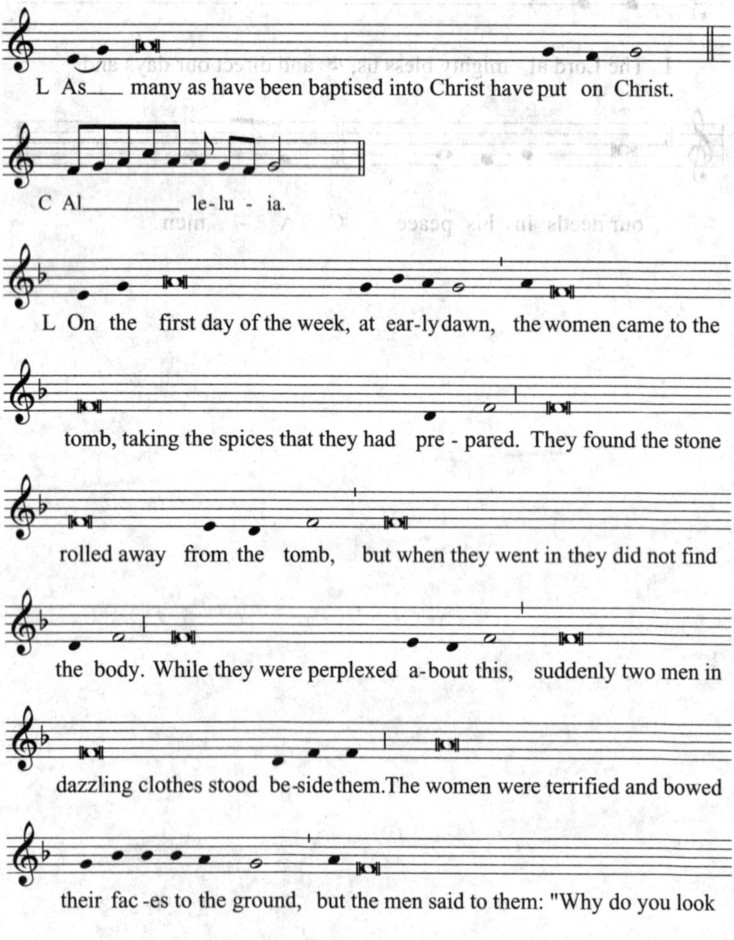

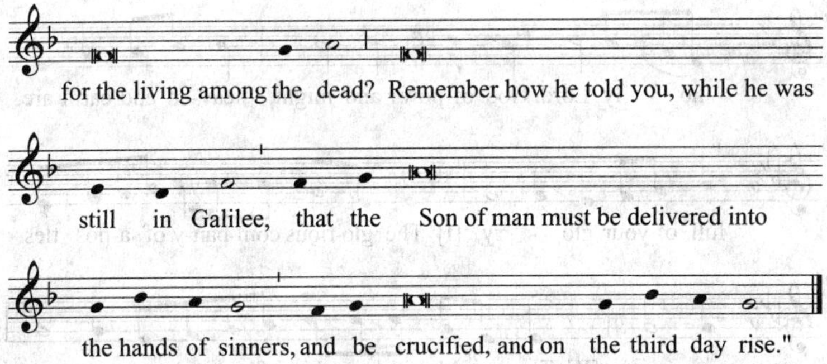

[Luke 24:1-7]

The TE DEUM is sung.

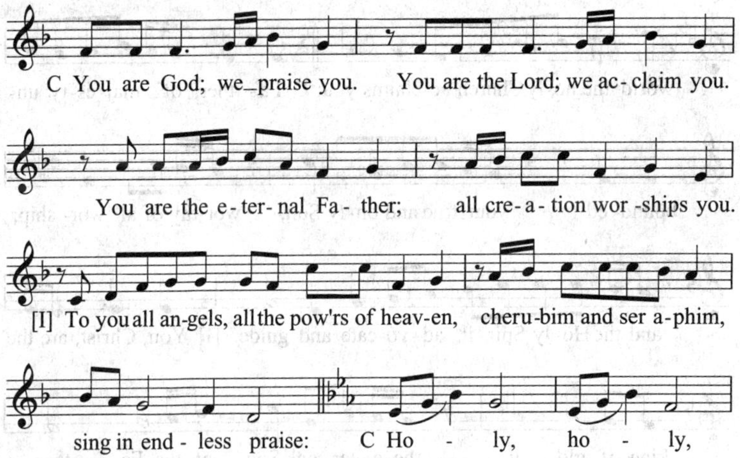

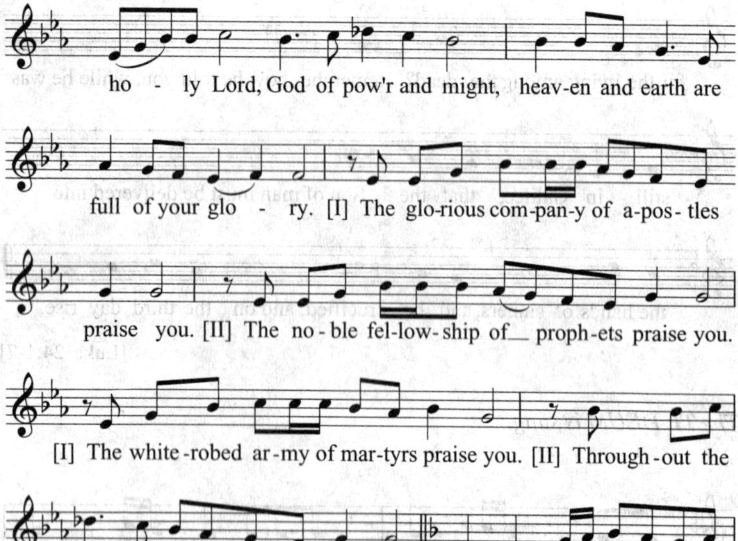
ho - ly Lord, God of pow'r and might, heav-en and earth are
full of your glo - ry. [I] The glo-rious com-pan-y of a-pos- tles
praise you. [II] The no - ble fel-low-ship of proph-ets praise you.
[I] The white-robed ar-my of mar-tyrs praise you. [II] Through-out the
world the ho-ly Church ac-claims you: C Fa- ther, of maj- es-ty un-
bound- ed your true and on-ly Son, wor-thy of all wor- ship;
and the Ho-ly Spir- it, ad-vo-cate and guide. [I] You, Christ, are the
king of glo - ry, the e-ter-nal Son of the Fa - ther.

[II] When you be-came man to_set us free, you did not spurn the
vir - gin's womb. [I] You o - ver came the_sting of death,
and_ o -pened the king-dom of heav-en to_ all be - liev - ers.
[II] You are seat - ed at_God's right hand in_ glo - ry.
We be- lieve that you will come and be our judge. C Come, then,
Lord, and help your peo- ple, bought with the price of_your own blood,
and_bring us with your saints to glo - ry_ ev - er- last - ing.

L Save your people, Lord, and bless your inheritance;

C Govern and uphold them now and always. [Ps. 29:10]

L Day by day we bless you;

C We praise your Name for ever. [Ps. 145:2]

L Keep us today, Lord, from all sin.

C Have mercy on us, Lord, have mercy. [Ps. 123:3]

L Lord, show us your love and mercy;

C For we put our trust in you. [Ps. 56:1,3]

L In you, Lord, is our hope:

C And we shall never hope in vain. [Ps. 31:1]

[ICET, BCP]

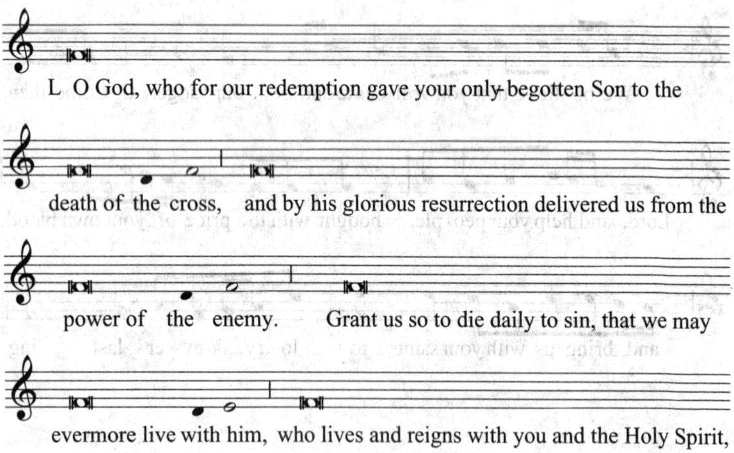

one God, now and for ever.

[BCP]

C A - men

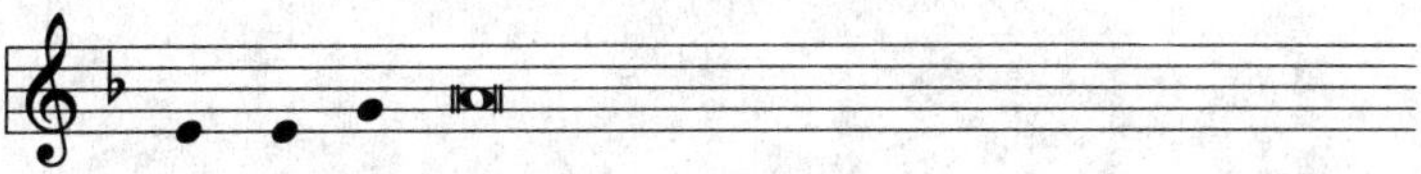
L The Lord al - mighty bless us, ✠ and direct our days and

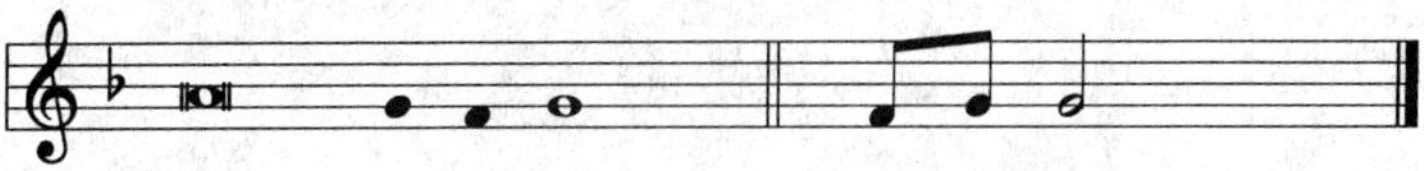
our deeds in his peace. C A - men

Sunday of Week I

Antiphon to PSALM 98 *Cantate Domino*

Shout with joy before the King, the LORD [LH, PBO]

98 *God, the ruler of the world*

1 Sing to the LORD **a** new song,*
for he has done **marvel**ous things.

2 With his right hand and his **ho**ly arm*
has he won for him**self** the victory.

3 The LORD has made **known** his victory;*
his righteousness has he openly shown
in the sight **of** the nations.

4 He remembers his mercy and faithfulness to
the **house** of Israel,*
and all the ends of the earth have seen the
victory **of** our God.

5 Shout with joy to the LORD, **all** you lands;*
lift up your voice, re**joice**, and sing.

6 Sing to the LORD **with** the harp,*
with the harp and the **voice** of song.

7 With trumpets and the sound **of** the horn*
shout with joy before the **King**, the LORD.

8 Let the sea make a noise and all **that** is in it,*
the lands and those who **dwell** therein.

9 Let the rivers **clap** their hands,*
and let the hills ring out with joy before the LORD,
when he comes to **judge** the earth.

10 In righteousness shall he **judge** the world*
and the peo**ples** with equity.

Antiphon Shout with joy before the King, the LORD.

Silence for meditation

Lord, we sing to you a new song, for your victory is ever new. In the empty tomb you have given us a glimpse of your future, and in your victory over death you have shown us how we shall overcome the last enemy. As the seas roar and the hills sing together, we too will praise you for your great triumph, Father, Son, and Holy Spirit, now and for ever. [LBW]

+

Antiphon to the OLD TESTAMENT CANTICLE *Cantemus Domino*

The Lord is my strength **and** my song;*
he has be**come** my Savior. [LH]

The Song of Miriam and Moses Exodus 15:1-2,6,11,13,17

I will sing to the Lord,
for he has **tri**umphed gloriously;*
horse and rider he has thrown in**to** the sea.

The Lord is my strength **and** my song;*
he has be**come** my Savior.

This is my God, and **I** will praise him,*
the God of my people, and I **will** exalt him.

Your right hand, O Lord, glori**ous** in power,*
your right hand, O Lord, shat**ters** the enemy.

Who among the gods is like **you**, O Lord?*
Who is like you, majestic in holiness,
awesome in splendor, **do**ing wonders?

With your constant love
you led forth the people whom **you** set free;*
you guided them in your strength
to your holy **hab**itation.

You will bring them **in** and plant them*
on the mount that is **your** possession,

The place, O Lord, which your hands **have** prepared.*
The Lord shall reign for ev**er** and ever. [BCP, RSV]

Antiphon The Lord is my strength **and** my song;*
he has be**come** my Savior.

Silence for meditation

O God, whose wonderful deeds of old shine forth even to our own day, by the power of your mighty arm you once delivered your chosen people from slavery under Pharoah, to be a sign for us of the salvation of all nations by the water of Baptism: Grant that all the peoples of the earth may be numbered among the offspring of Abraham, and rejoice in the inheritance of Israel; through Jesus Christ our Lord. [Gel., BCP, LBW]

+

Antiphon to PSALM 150 *Laudate Dominum in sanctis ejus*

Praise God for his **might**y acts;*
praise him for his ex**cel**lent greatness. [LH, PBO]

150 *The great alleluia*

1 Hallelujah!
Praise God in his **ho**ly temple;*
praise him in the firmament **of** his power.

2 Praise him for his **might**y acts;*
praise him for his ex**cel**lent greatness.

3 Praise him with the blast **of** the ram's-horn;*
praise him with **lyre** and harp.

4 Praise him with tim**brel** and dance;*
praise him with **strings** and pipe.

5 Praise him with re**sound**ing cymbals;*
praise him with loud-**clang**ing cymbals.

6 Let everything **that** has breath*
praise the LORD.
Hallelujah!

Antiphon Praise God for his **might**y acts;*
praise him for his ex**cel**lent greatness.

Silence for meditation

God of surpassing greatness, enthroned upon the praises of your people, fill our hearts with your love and unite our voices with the praise of all creation so that you may be honored and glorified by everything that has breath; through Jesus Christ our Lord. [PHP]

+

Stand

THE HYMN is sung.

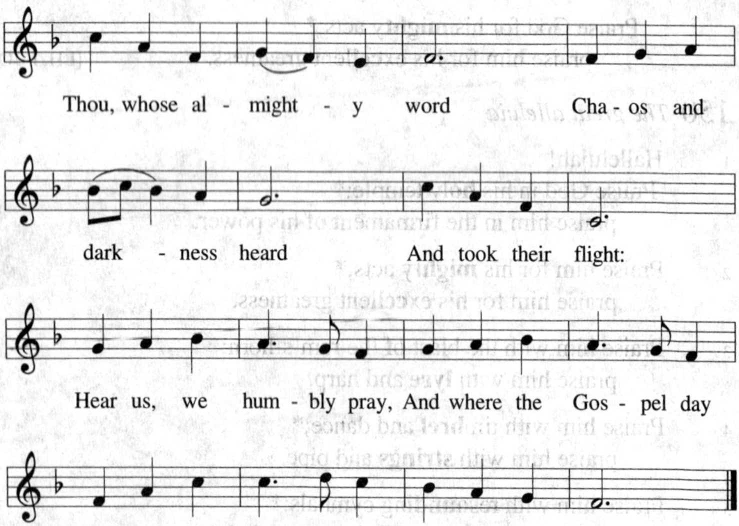

2 Thou, who didst come to bring
On thy redeeming wing
Healing and sight,
Health to the sick in mind,
Sight to the inly blind,
Now to all humankind
Let there be light!

3 Spirit of truth and love,
Life-giving holy Dove,
Speed forth thy flight!
Move on the water's face
Bearing the lamp of grace,
And in earth's darkest place
Let there be light!

4 Holy and blessèd Three,
Glorious Trinity,
Wisdom, love, might;
Boundless as ocean's tide
Rolling in fullest pride,
Through the world far and wide,
Let there be light!

[SBH 309, H82 371]

Text: John Marriott, 1780-1825, rev. Thomas Raffles, 1788-1863
Tune: *Italian Hymn*, Felice de Giardini, 1716-1796 — 664 6664

on The Transfiguration — *Caelestis formam gloriae*

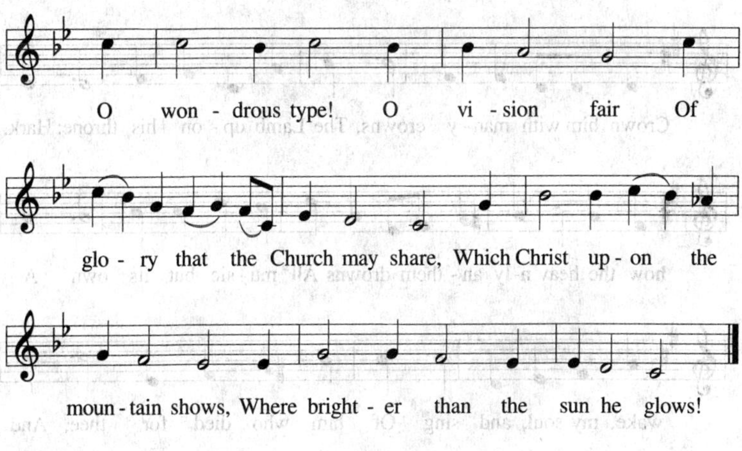

2 With Moses and Elijah nigh
Th'incarnate Lord holds converse high;
And from the cloud the Holy One
Bears record to the only Son.

3 With shining face and bright array,
Christ deigns to manifest today
What glory shall be theirs above
Who joy in God with perfect love.

4 And faithful hearts are raised on high
By this great vision's mystery;
For which in joyful strains we raise
The voice of prayer, the hymn of praise.

5 O Father, with the eternal Son,
And Holy Spirit, ever one,
We pray you, bring us by your grace
To see your glory face to face. [LBW 80; H82 136, 137]

Text: Sarum, 15th century office hymn, trans. John Mason Neale (1818-1866), alt.
Tune: *Deo Gracias*, English, 15th century LM

on Christ the King

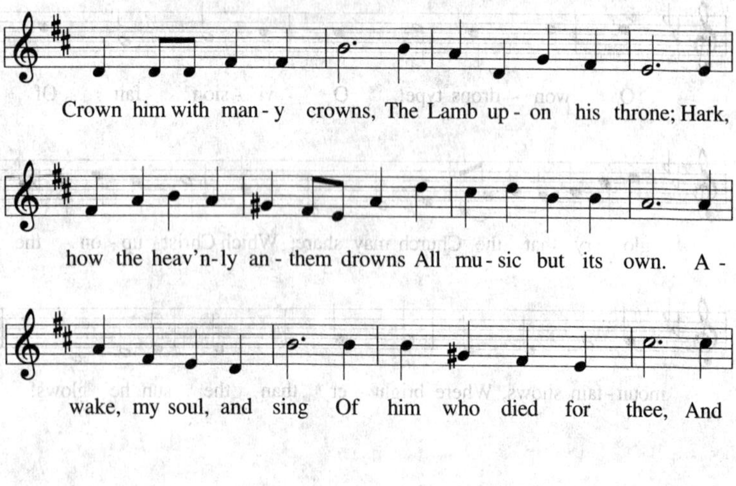

2 Crown him the virgin's Son,
The God incarnate born,
Whose arm those crimson trophies won
Which now his brow adorn;
Fruit of the mystic rose,
Yet of that rose the stem,
The root whence mercy ever flows,
The babe of Bethlehem.

3 Crown him the Lord of love —
Behold his hands and side,
Rich wounds, yet visible above,
In beauty glorified.
No angels in the sky
Can fully bear that sight,
But downward bend their burning eyes
At mysteries so bright.

4 Crown him the Lord of life,
Who triumphed o'er the grave,
And rose victorious in the strife
For those he came to save.
His glories now we sing,
Who died and rose on high,
Who died, eternal life to bring,
And lives that death may die.

5 Crown him the Lord of peace,
Whose power a scepter sways
From pole to pole, that wars may cease,
Absorbed in prayer and praise.
His reign shall know no end,
And round his piercèd feet
Fair flow'rs of paradise extend
Their fragrance ever sweet.

6 Crown him the Lord of years,
The potentate of time,
Creator of the rolling spheres,
Ineffably sublime.
All hail, Redeemer, hail!
For thou hast died for me;
Thy praise and glory shall not fail
Throughout eternity. [LBW 170]

Text: Matthew Bridges, 1800-1894; Godfrey Thring, 1823-1903
Tune: *Diademata*, George J. Elvey, 1816-1893 SMD

Sit

One or two LESSONS are read.

Year 1 [odd-numbered years]	Year 2 [even-numbered years]
Epiphany 5	
Isaiah 57:1-13	Genesis 24:50-67
Whoever takes refuge in me shall possess the land and inherit my holy mountain. [BCP: Isaiah 57:14-21]	Let Rebekah be the wife of your master's son, as the LORD has spoken.

Hebrews 12:1-6

Let us run with perseverance the race that is set before us.

2 Timothy 2:14-21

Do your best to present yourself to God as one approved by him, a worker who has no need to be ashamed, rightly explaining the word of truth.

The Transfiguration
The Last Sunday after the Epiphany

Daniel 7:9-10,13-14

I saw one like a human being coming with the clouds of heaven.

[BCP Deuteronomy 6:1-9]

Malachi 4:1-6

For you who revere my name the sun of righteousness shall rise, with healing in its wings.

[BCP: Sirach (Ecclesiasticus)] 48:1-11

2 Corinthians 3:1-9

If there was glory in the ministry of condemnation, much more does the ministry of justification abound in glory!

[BCP Heb. 12:18-29]

2 Corinthians 3:7-18

All of us, with unveiled faces, seeing the glory of the Lord as though reflected in a mirror, are being transformed into the same image from one degree of glory to another.

Proper 5 (Sunday between June 5 and 11) / Pentecost 4

Deuteronomy 29:16-29

The secret things belong to the LORD our God, but the revealed things belong to us and to our children forever, to observe all the words of this law.

Ecclesiastes 6:1-12

Who knows what is good for mortals while they live the few days of their vain life, which they pass like a shadow?

Revelation 12:1-12

Woe to the earth and the sea, for the devil has come down to you with great wrath, because he knows that his time is short!

Acts 10:9-23

What God has made clean, you must not call profane.

Proper 9 (Sunday between July 3 and 9) / Pentecost 8

1 Samuel 14:36-45

The people ransomed Jonathan, and he did not die.

Numbers 27:12-23

Take Joshua, son of Nun, a man in whom is the spirit, and lay your hand upon him.

Romans 5:1-11

Since we are justified by faith, we have peace with God through our Lord Jesus Christ.

Acts 19:11-20

God did extraordinary miracles through Paul.

Proper 13 (Sunday between July 31 and August 6) / Pentecost 12

2 Samuel 6:12-23

The LORD has blessed the household of Obed-edom and all that belongs to him, because of the ark of God.

Judges 6:1-24

The LORD is with you, you mighty warrior.

Romans 14:7-12

Whether we live or whether we die, we are the Lord's.

2 Corinthians 9:6-15

Thanks be to God for his indescribable gift!

Proper 17 (Sunday between August 28 and September 3) / Pentecost 16

1 Kings 8:22-30(31-40)

But will God indeed dwell on the earth? Even heaven and the highest heaven cannot contain you, much less this house that I have built!

Job 11:1-9,13-20

Know then that God exacts of you less than your guilt deserves.

1 Timothy 4:7b-16

We have our hope set on the living God, who is the Savior of all people, especially of those who believe.

Revelation 5:1-14

The lion of the tribe of Judah, the Root of David, has conquered.

Proper 21 (Sunday between September 25 and October 1) / Pentecost 20

2 Kings 17:1-18

The LORD was very angry with Israel and removed them out of his sight; none was left but the tribe of Judah alone.

Hosea 1:1-2:1

Go, take for yourself a wife of whoredom and have children of whoredom, for the land commits great whoredom by forsaking the LORD. [BCP: Hosea 2:2-14]

Acts 9:36-43

Calling the saints and widows, Peter showed Tabitha to be alive.

James 3:1-13

Show by your good life that your works are done with gentleness born of wisdom.

Proper 25 (Sunday between October 23 and 29) / Pentecost 24

Haggai 1:1-2:9

The latter splendor of this house shall be greater than the former, says the LORD of hosts.

or Jeremiah 44:15-30

Sirach[Ecclesiasticus] 18:19-33

Before judgment comes, examine yourself; and at the time of scrutiny you will find forgiveness.

or Jonah 1:1-17a

Acts 18:24-19:7

When Paul had laid his hands on them, the Holy Spirit came upon them, and they spoke in tongues and prophesied.

1 Corinthians 10:15-24

Because there is one bread, we who are many are one body, for we all partake of the one bread.

Christ the King
The Last Sunday after Pentecost

Isaiah 19:19-25

Blessed be Egypt my people, and Assyria the work of my hands, and Israel my heritage.

Zechariah 9:9-16

Lo, your king comes to you; triumphant and victorious is he.

Romans 15:5-13

May the God of hope fill you with all joy and peace in believing, so that you may abound in hope by the power of the Holy Spirit.

1 Peter 3:13-22

Jesus Christ has gone into heaven and is at the right hand of God, with angels, authorities, and powers made subject to him.

Silence for meditation follows each reading.

RESPONSORY

God has destined us not for wrath but for obtaining salvation through our Lord **Je**sus Christ*
so that we may **live** with him.
God, has rescued us from the domain of darkness and transferred us into the kingdom of his be**lo**ved Son,*
so that we may **live** with him.

[LH: 1 Thess. 5:9-10; Col. 1:3]

Our Savior Christ Jesus a**bol**ished death*
and brought immortality to light **through** the gospel;
from his fullness have we **all** received,*
grace **up**on grace.
All things have been created through **him** and for him.*
He himself is before all things and in him all things **hold** together.
From his fullness have we **all** received,*
grace **up**on grace.

[LH: 2 Tim. 1:10; John 1:16; Col. 1:16-17]

Monday of Week I

Antiphon to PSALM 83 *Deus, quis similis?*

Do not keep si**lent**, O God;*
for your enemies have lifted **up** their heads. [DO]

83 *Against the enemies of Israel*

1 O God, do **not** be silent;*
do not keep still nor hold your **peace**, O God;

2 For your enemies **are** in tumult,*
and those who hate you have lifted **up** their heads.

3 They take secret counsel a**gainst** your people*
and plot against those whom **you** protect.

4 They have said,"Come, let us wipe them out from a**mong**
the nations;*
let the name of Israel be remem**bered** no more."

5 They have con**spired** together;*
they have made an alli**ance** against you:

6 The tents of Edom **and** the Ishmaelites;*
the Moabites **and** the Hagarenes;

7 Gebal, and Am**mon**, and Amalek;*
the Philistines and those who **dwell** in Tyre.

8 The Assyrians al**so** have joined them,*
and have come to help the peo**ple** of Lot.

9 Do to them as you **did** to Midian,*
to Sisera, and Jabin at the riv**er** of Kishon:

10 They were de**stroyed** at Endor;*
they became like dung up**on** the ground.

11 Make their leaders like O**reb** and Zeëb,*
and all their commanders like Zebah **and** Zalmunna,

12 Who said, "Let us take **for** ourselves*
the fields of God as **our** possession."

13 O my God, make them like **whirl**ing dust*
and like chaff be**fore** the wind;

14 Like fire that burns **down** a forest,*
like the flame that sets moun**tains** ablaze.

15 Drive them **with** your tempest*
and terrify them **with** your storm;

16 Cover their faces with **shame**, O LORD,*
that they may **seek** your Name.

17 Let them be disgraced and terri**fied** for ever;*
let them be put to confus**ion** and perish.

18 Let them know that you, whose **Name** is YAHWEH,*
you alone are the Most High over **all** the earth.

Antiphon Do not keep si**lent**, O God;*
for your enemies have lifted **up** their heads.

Silence for meditation

Lord, dispel from us the error of pride and the illusions of greatness, and help us to abandon every vice and stand in awe of you, who alone are the Most High over all the world now and for ever. [LHd, LBW]

+

Antiphon to PSALM 145 *Exaltabo te, Deus*

Every day **will** I bless you*
and praise your Name for ev**er** and ever. [LH]

145 *Praise of God's majesty*

1 I will exalt you, O **God** my King,*
and bless your Name for ev**er** and ever.

2 Every day **will** I bless you*
and praise your Name for ev**er** and ever.

3 Great is the LORD and greatly **to** be praised;*
there is no end **to** his greatness.

4 One generation shall praise your works **to** another*
and shall de**clare** your power.

5 I will ponder the glorious splendor **of** your majesty*
and all your **mar**velous works.

6 They shall speak of the might of your **won**drous acts,*
and I will tell **of** your greatness.

7 They shall publish the remembrance of **your** great goodness;*
they shall sing of your **right**eous deeds.

8 The LORD is gracious and full **of** compassion,*
slow to anger and **of** great kindness.

9 The LORD is loving to **ev**eryone*
and his compassion is over **all** his works.

10 All your works praise **you**, O LORD,*
and your faithful **ser**vants bless you.

11 They make known the glory **of** your kingdom*
and speak **of** your power;

12 That the peoples may know **of** your power*
and the glorious splendor **of** your kingdom.

13 Your kingdom is an ever**last**ing kingdom;*
your dominion endures through**out** all ages.

14 The LORD is faithful in **all** his words*
and merciful in **all** his deeds.

15 The LORD upholds all **those** who fall;*
he lifts up those who **are** bowed down.

16 The eyes of all wait upon **you**, O LORD,*
and you give them their food **in** due season.

17 You open **wide** your hand*
and satisfy the needs of every **liv**ing creature.

18 The LORD is righteous in **all** his ways*
and loving in **all** his works.

19 The LORD is near to those who **call** upon him,*
to all who call up**on** him faithfully.

20 He fulfills the desire of **those** who fear him;*
he hears their **cry** and helps them.

21 The LORD preserves all **those** who love him,*
but destroys **all** the wicked.

22 My mouth shall speak the praise **of** the LORD;*
let all flesh bless his holy Name for ev**er** and ever.

Antiphon Every day **will** I bless you*
and praise your Name for ev**er** and ever.

Silence for meditation

Loving Father, you are faithful in your promises and tender in your compassion: Listen to our hymn of joy, and continue to satisfy the needs of all your creatures, that all flesh may bless your Name in your everlasting kingdom, where with your Son and the Holy Spirit you live and reign, now and for ever. [LBW]

+

Stand

THE HYMN is sung. *Nocte surgentes vigilemus omnes*

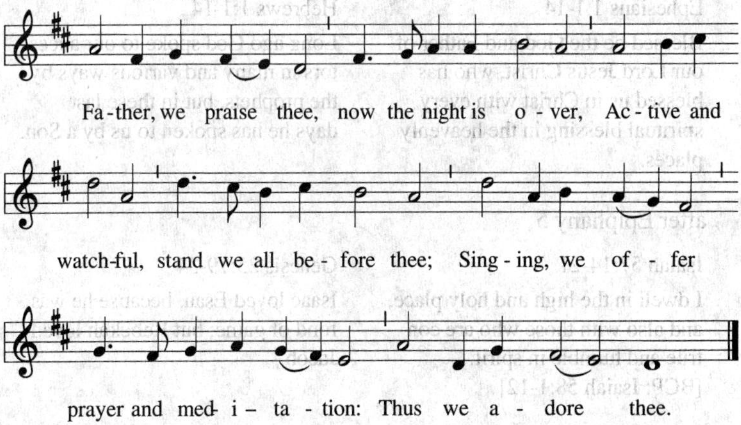

2 Monarch of all things, fit us for thy mansions;
Banish our weakness, health and wholeness sending;
Bring us to heaven, where thy saints united
Joy without ending.

3 All holy Father, Son, and equal Spirit,
Trinity blessèd, send us thy salvation;
Thine is the glory, gleaming and resounding
Through all creation. [LBW 267; H82 1]

Text: attr. Gregory I, 540-604; tr. Percy Dearmer, 1867-1936

Tune: *Christe sanctorum,* melody from *Antiphoner*, Paris, 1681 11 11 11 5

Sit

One or two LESSONS are read.

Year 1 | Year 2

after the Baptism of our Lord (Epiphany 1)

Isaiah 40:12-24
To whom then will you liken God, or what likeness compare with him?

Genesis 2:4-9(10-15)16-25
This at last is bone of my bones and flesh of my flesh.

Ephesians 1:1-14

Blessed be the God and Father of our Lord Jesus Christ, who has blessed us in Christ with every spiritual blessing in the heavenly places.

Hebrews 1:1-14

Long ago God spoke to our ancestors in many and various ways by the prophets, but in these last days he has spoken to us by a Son.

after Epiphany 5

Isaiah 57:14-21

I dwell in the high and holy place, and also with those who are contrite and humble in spirit.
[BCP: Isaiah 58:1-12]

Genesis 25:19-34

Isaac loved Esau, because he was fond of game; but Rebekah loved Jacob.

Galatians 6:11-18

May I never boast of anything except the cross of our Lord Jesus Christ, by which the world has been crucified to me, and I to the world.

Hebrews 13:1-16

Here we have no lasting city, but we are looking for the city that is to come.

Monday before Ash Wednesday

Deuteronomy 6:1-15

The LORD is our God, the LORD alone. You shall love the LORD your God with all your heart, and with all your soul, and with all your might.

Proverbs 27:1-6,10-12

Do not boast about tomorrow, for you do not know what a day may bring.

Hebrews 1:1-14

Long ago God spoke to our ancestors in many and various ways by the prophets, but in these last days he has spoken to us by a Son.

Philippians 2:1-13

It is God who is at work in you, enabling you both to will and to work for his good pleasure.

Proper 1/Monday after the Day of Pentecost

Isaiah 63:7-14
I will recount the gracious deeds of the LORD.

Ezekiel 33:1-11
I have no pleasure in the death of the wicked, but that the wicked turn from their ways and live.

2 Timothy 1:1-14
Guard the good treasure entrusted to you, with the help of the Holy Spirit living in us.

1 John 1:1-10
We declare to you what we have seen and heard so that you also may have fellowship with us.

after Proper 5 / Pentecost 4

Deuteronomy 30:1-10
Return to the LORD your God, and you and your children obey him with all your heart.

Ecclesiastes 7:1-14
The heart of the wise is in the house of the mourning; but the heart of fools is in the house of mirth.

2 Corinthians 10:1-18
Remind yourself of this, that just as you belong to Christ, so also do we.

Galatians 4:12-20
Have I now become your enemy by telling you the truth?

after Proper 9 / Pentecost 8

1 Samuel 15:1-3,7-23
I regret that I made Saul king, for he has turned back from following me.

Numbers 32:1-6,16-27
Shall your brothers go to war while you sit here?

Acts 9:19b-31
Immediately Paul began to proclaim Jesus in the synagogues, saying, "He is the Son of God."

Romans 8:26-30
We do not know how to pray as we ought, but that very Spirit intercedes with sighs too deep for words.

after Proper 13 / Pentecost 12

2 Samuel 7:1-17
The LORD declares to you that the LORD will make you a house.

Judges 6:25-40
The spirit of the LORD took possession of Gideon.

Acts 18:1-11

Do not be afraid, but speak and do not be silent; for I am with you, and no one will lay a hand on you to harm you.

Acts 2:37-47

They devoted themselves to the apostles' teaching and fellowship, to the breaking of bread and the prayers.

after Proper 17 / Pentecost 16

2 Chronicles 6:32-7:7

The glory of the LORD filled the temple.

Job 12:1-6,13-25

A just and blameless man, I am a laughingstock.

James 2:1-13

Do you with your acts of favoritism really believe in our glorious Lord Jesus Christ?

Acts 11:19-30

Those who were scattered because of the persecution that took place over Stephen traveled as far as Phoenicia, Cyprus, and Antioch.

after Proper 21 / Pentecost 20

2 Kings 17:24-41

The king of Assyria brought people from Babylon, Cuthah, Avva, Hamath, and Sepharvaim, and placed them in the cities of Samaria in place of the people of Israel.

Hosea 2:2-15

She shall pursue her lovers, but not overtake them; and she shall seek them, but shall not find them. Then she shall say, "I will go and return to my first husband."

[BCP: Hosea 2:14-23]

1 Corinthians 7:25-31

The present form of this world is passing away.

Acts 20:17-38

If only I may finish my course and the ministry that I received from the Lord Jesus, to testify to the good news of God's grace.

after Proper 25 / Pentecost 24

Zechariah 1:7-17

The LORD will again comfort Zion and choose Jerusalem.

or Jeremiah 45:1-5

Sirach [Ecclesiasticus] 19:4-17

One who trusts others too quickly has a shallow mind.

or Jonah 1:17-2:10

Revelation 1:4-20

He is coming with the clouds; every eye will see him, even those who pierced him.

Revelation 11:1-14

They went up to heaven in a cloud while their enemies watched them.

after Christ the King

Joel 3:1-2,9-17

The LORD roars from Zion, and utters his voice from Jerusalem, and the heavens and the earth shake.

Zechariah 10:1-12

I will make them strong in the LORD, and they shall walk in his name.

1 Peter 1:1-12

Blessed be the God and Father of our Lord Jesus Christ!

Galatians 6:1-10

Let us not grow weary in doing what is right.

Silence for meditation follows each reading.

RESPONSORY

The Lord has told you, O mortal, **what** is good;*
and what does the Lord require of you but to do justice, and to love kindness, and to walk humbly **with** your God?
Trust in the Lord and do good; so you will dwell **in** the land.*
and what does the Lord require of you but to do justice, and to love kindness, and to walk humbly **with** your God?

[LH: Micah 6:8; Ps. 37:3]

Be steadfast, immovable, always abounding in the work **of** the Lord,*
because you know that in the Lord your labor is **not** in vain.
Do not grow weary in doing **what** is right,*
because you know that in the Lord your labor is **not** in vain.

[LH: 1 Cor. 15:58; 2 Thess. 3:13]

Tuesday of Week I

PSALM 108 *Paratum cor meum*

I will sing praises to you among the peoples, O LORD. [PBO]

108 *Prayer for victory*

1 My heart is firmly fixed, O God, my **heart** is fixed;*
I will sing **and** make melody.

2 Wake up, my spirit;
awake, **lute** and harp;*
I myself will wak**en** the dawn.

3 I will confess you among the peo**ples**, O LORD;*
I will sing praises to you a**mong** the nations.

4 For your loving-kindness is greater **than** the heavens,*
and your faithfulness reaches **to** the clouds.

5 Exalt yourself above the heav**ens**, O God,*
and your glory over **all** the earth.

6 So that those who are dear to you may **be** delivered,*
save with your right hand and **an**swer me.

7 God spoke from his holy **place** and said,*
"I will exult and parcel out Shechem;
I will divide the val**ley** of Succoth.

8 Gilead is mine and Manas**seh** is mine;*
Ephraim is my helmet and Ju**dah** my scepter.

9 Moab is my washbasin,
on Edom I throw down my san**dal** to claim it,*
and over Philistia will I **shout** in triumph."

10 Who will lead me into **the** strong city?*
who will bring me **in**to Edom?

11 Have you not cast us **off**, O God?*
you no longer go out, O God, **with** our armies.

12 Grant us help a**gainst** the enemy,*
for vain is the **help** of man.

13 With God we will do **va**liant deeds,*
and he shall tread our enemies **un**der foot.

Antiphon I will sing praises to you among the peoples, O LORD.

Silence for meditation.

Lord, accept the prayers of your servants, and prepare our hearts to praise your holy Name. Come to our aid in times of trouble, that we may sing you songs of thanksgiving; through Jesus Christ our Lord. [LH, LBW]

+

Antiphon to PSALM 146 *Lauda, anima mea*

I will praise the LORD as long as I live. [LH]

146 *Praise of God's faithfulnes*

1 Hallelujah!
Praise the LORD, **O** my soul!*
I will praise the LORD as long as I live;
I will sing praises to my God while I **have** my being.

2 Put not your trust in rulers, nor in any **child** of earth,*
for there is no **help** in them.

3 When they breathe their last, they re**turn** to earth,*
and in that day **their** thoughts perish.

4 Happy are they who have the God of Jacob **for** their help!*
whose hope is in the **LORD** their God;

5 Who made heaven and earth, the seas, and all that **is** in them;*
who keeps his pro**mise** for ever;

6 Who gives justice to those who **are** oppressed,*
    and food to **those** who hunger.

7 The LORD sets the prisoners free;
the LORD opens the eyes **of** the blind;*
    the LORD lifts up those who **are** bowed down;

8 The LORD loves the righteous;
the LORD cares **for** the stranger;*
    he sustains the orphan and widow,
    but frustrates the way **of** the wicked.

9 The LORD shall **reign** for ever,*
    your God, O Zion, throughout all generations.
    Hallelujah!

Antiphon I will praise the LORD as long as I live.

Silence for meditation

God of glory and power, happy indeed are those who have put their trust in you: Shine the brightness of your light upon us, that we may love you always with a pure heart and praise you for ever; through your Son, Jesus Christ our Lord. [LH, LBW]

+

Stand

THE HYMN is sung.

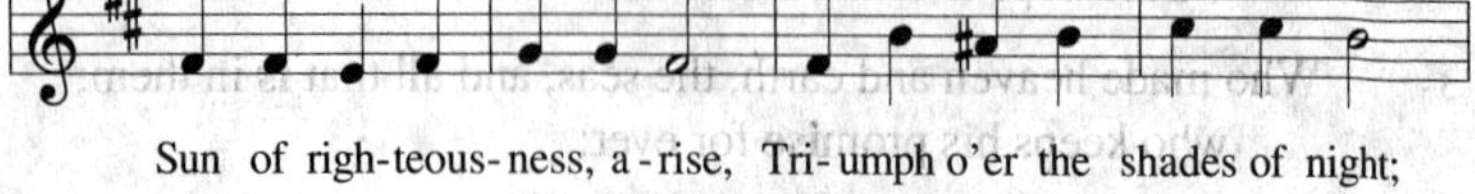

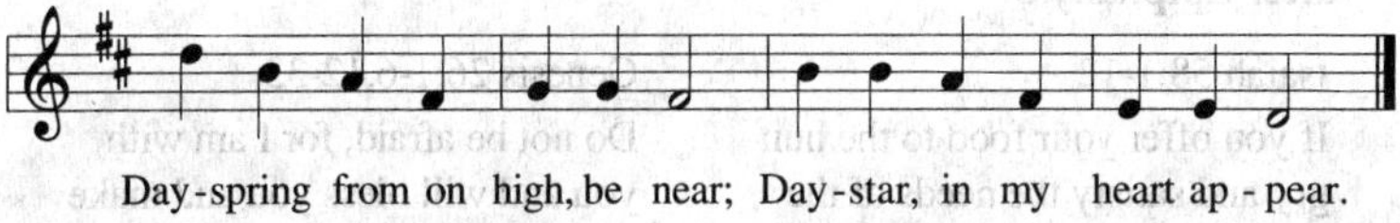

2 Dark and cheerless is the morn
Unaccompanied by thee;
Joyless is the day's return,
Till thy mercy's beams I see,
Till they inward light impart,
Glad my eyes and warm my heart.

3 Visit then this soul of mine,
Pierce the gloom of sin and grief;
Fill me, radiancy divine,
Scatter all my unbelief;
More and more thyself display,
Shining to the perfect day.

[LBW 265, H82 7]

Text: Charles Wesley, 1707-1788
Tune: *Ratisbon,* J.G. Werner, *Choral-Buch,* 1815 — 77 77 77

Sit

One or two LESSONS are read.

Year 1

after Epiphany 1

Isaiah 40:25-31

Those who wait for the LORD shall renew their strength, they shall mount up with wings like eagles, they shall run and not be weary, they shall walk and not faint.

Ephesians 1:15-23

I pray that the God of our Lord Jesus Christ, the Father of glory, may give you a spirit of wisdom and revelation as you come to know him.

Year 2

Genesis 3:1-24

He drove out the man; and at the east of the garden of Eden he placed the cherubim, and a sword flaming and turning to guard the way to the tree of life.

Hebrews 2:1-10

We see Jesus, who for a little while was made lower than the angels, now crowned with glory and honor because of the suffering of death, so that by the grace of God he might taste death for everyone.

after Epiphany 5

Isaiah 58:1-12

If you offer your food to the hungry and satisfy the needs of the afflicted, then your light shall rise in the darkness and your gloom be like the noonday.

[BCP: Isaiah 59:1-15a]

Genesis 26:1-6,12-33

Do not be afraid, for I am with you and will bless you and make your offspring numerous for my servant Abraham's sake.

2 Timothy 1:1-14

Guard the good treasure entrusted to you, with the help of the Holy Spirit living in us.

Hebrews 13:17-25

Now may the God of peace, who brought back from the dead our Lord Jesus, the great shepherd of the sheep, by the blood of the eternal covenant, make you complete in everything good so that you may do his will.

Tuesday before Ash Wednesday

Deuteronomy 6:16-25

Do what is right and good in the sight of the LORD, so that it may go well with you, and so that you may go in and occupy the good land.

Proverbs 30:1-4,24-33

Who has ascended to heaven and come down? Who has gathered the wind in the hollow of the hand?

Hebrews 2:1-10

We see Jesus, who for a little while was made lower than the angels, now crowned with glory and honor because of the suffering of death, so that by the grace of God he might taste death for everyone.

Philippians 3:1-11

I regard everything as loss because of the surpassing value of knowing Christ Jesus my Lord.

Proper 1 / Tuesday after the Day of Pentecost

Isaiah 63:15-64:9

O LORD, you are our Father; we are the clay, and you are our pot-

Ezekiel 33:21-33

To them you are like a singer of love songs, one who has a beau-ter; we are all the work of your hand.

tiful voice and plays well on an instrument; they hear what you say, but they will not do it.

2 Timothy 1:15-2:13

Be strong in the grace that is in Christ Jesus.

1 John 2:1-11

If anyone does sin, we have as advocate with the Father, Jesus Christ the righteous; and he is the atoning sacrifice for our sins, and not for ours only but also for the sins of the whole world.

after Proper 5 / Pentecost 4

Deuteronomy 30:11-20

The word is very near to you; it is in your mouth and in your heart for you to observe.

Ecclesiastes 8:14-9:10

There are righteous people who are treated according to the conduct of the wicked, and there are wicked people who are treated according to the conduct of the righteous. I said that this also is vanity.

2 Corinthians 11:1-21a

I am afraid that as the serpent deceived Eve by its cunning, your thoughts will be led astray from a sincere and pure devotion to Christ.

Galatians 4:21-31

We are children, not of the slave but of the free woman.

after Proper 9 / Pentecost 8

1 Samuel 15:24-35

Samuel grieved over Saul. And the LORD was sorry that he had made Saul king over Israel.

Numbers 35:1-3, 9-15, 30-34

You shall not defile the land in which you live, in which I also dwell; for I the LORD dwell among the Israelites.

Acts 9:32-43

Aeneas, Jesus Christ heals you; get up and make your bed!

Romans 8:31-39

We are more than conquerors through him who loved us.

after Proper 13 / Pentecost 12

2 Samuel 7:18-29

You, O Lord God, have spoken, and with your blessing shall the house of your servant be blessed forever.

Judges 7:1-18

Gideon returned to the camp of Israel and said, "Get up; for the Lord has given the army of Midian into your hand."

Acts 18:12-28

"I will return to you, if God wills". Then he set sail for Ephesus.

Acts 3:1-11

I have no silver or gold, but what I have I give you; in the name of Jesus Christ of Nazareth, stand up and walk.

after Proper 17 / Pentecost 16

1 Kings 8:65-9:9

I have consecrated this house that you have built, and put my name there forever; my eyes and my heart will be there for all time.

Job 12:1; 13:3-17, 21-27

I would speak to the Almighty, and I desire to argue my case with God.

James 2:14-26

Just as the body without the spirit is dead, so faith without works is also dead.

Acts 12:1-17

After Herod saw that it pleased the Jews, he proceeded to arrest Peter also.

after Proper 21 / Pentecost 20

2 Chronicles 29:1-3; 30:1(2-9)10-27

In the first year of his reign, in the first month, Hezekiah opened the

Hosea 2:16-23

I will take you for my wife in faithfulness; and you shall

doors of the house of the LORD and repaired them.

know the LORD.
[BCP: Hosea 4:1-10]

1 Corinthians 7:32-40
I want you to be free from anxieties.

Acts 21:1-14
I am ready not only to be bound but even to die in Jerusalem for the name of the Lord Jesus.

after Proper 25 / Pentecost 24

Ezra 5:1-17
Have a search made in the royal archives there in Babylon, to see whether a decree was issued by King Cyrus for the rebuilding of this house of God in Jerusalem.
or Lamentations 1:1-5 (6-9) 10-12

Sirach[Ecclesiasticus] 24:1-12
I came forth from the mouth of the Most High, and covered the earth like a mist.
or Jonah 3:1- 4:11

Revelation 4:1-11
You are worthy, our Lord and God, to receive glory and honor and power, for you created all things, and by your will they existed and were created.

Revelation 11:14-19
The kingdom of the world has become the kingdom of our Lord and of his Messiah.

after Christ the King

Nahum 1:1-13
The LORD is slow to anger but great in power, and the LORD will by no means clear the guilty.

Zechariah 11:4-17
Thus said the LORD my God: Be a shepherd of the flock doomed to slaughter.

1 Peter 1:13-25
Prepare your minds for action; discipline yourselves; set all your hope on the grace that Jesus

1 Corinthians 3:10-23
Do you not know you are God's temple and that God's Spirit dwells in you?

Christ will bring you when he is revealed.

Silence for meditation follows each reading.

RESPONSORY

You are a chosen race, a royal priesthood, a holy nation, **God's** own people.*
Once you were not a people but now you **are** God's people.
Once you were out**side** his mercy;*
but now you are out**side** no longer.
Because the **Lord** loves you*
the Lord your God has chosen you and brought you out from the **house** of slavery.
Once you were out**side** his mercy*
but now you are out**side** no longer.

[LH: 1 Peter 2:9-10 REB; Deut. 7:6, 8]

We have known and believe the love that **God** has for us.*
Those who abide in love abide in God and God **abides** in them.
Let us love one another,
because love **is** from God.
Those who abide in love abide in God and God **abides** in them.

[LH: 1 John 4:16,7]

Wednesday of Week I

Antiphon to PSALM 1 *Beatus vir qui non abiit*

Happy are they whose delight is in the law of the LORD.

[DO, PBO]

1 *The two ways*

1 Happy are they who have not walked in the counsel **of** the wicked,*
nor lingered in the way of sinners,
nor sat in the seats **of** the scornful!

2 Their delight is in the law **of** the LORD,*
and they meditate on his law **day** and night.

3 They are like trees planted by streams of water,
bearing fruit in due season, with leaves that **do** not wither;*
everything they **do** shall prosper.

4 It is not so **with** the wicked;*
they are like chaff which the wind **blows** away.

5 Therefore the wicked shall not stand upright when
judgment comes,*
nor the sinner in the council **of** the righteous.

6 For the LORD knows the way **of** the righteous,*
but the way of the wick**ed** is doomed.

Antiphon Happy are they whose delight is in the law of the LORD.

Silence for meditation

Lord God, in your loving wisdom you have set us beside the fountain of life, like a tree planted by running streams: Grant that the cross of your Son may become our tree of life in the paradise of your saints, through Jesus Christ our Lord. [LHd, LBW]

+

Antiphon to PSALM 147 part i *Laudate Dominum*

How pleasant it is to honor God with praise! [LH, PBO]

147 *Praise of God who maintains the world*

1 Hallelujah!
How good it is to sing praises **to** our God!*
how pleasant it is to honor **him** with praise!

2 The LORD re**builds** Jerusalem;*
he gathers the ex**iles** of Israel.

3 He heals the **bro**kenhearted*
and binds **up** their wounds.

4 He counts the number **of** the stars*
and calls them all **by** their names.

5 Great is our LORD and might**y** in power;*
there is no limit **to** his wisdom.

6 The LORD lifts **up** the lowly,*
but casts the wicked **to** the ground,

7 Sing to the LORD **with** thanksgiving;*
make music to our God up**on** the harp.

8 He covers the heav**ens** with clouds*
and prepares rain **for** the earth;

9 He makes grass to grow up**on** the mountains*
and green plants to **serve** mankind.

10 He provides food for **flocks** and herds*
and for the young ravens **when** they cry.

11 He is not impressed by the might **of** a horse;*
he has no pleasure in the strength **of** a man;

12 But the LORD has pleasure in **those** who fear him,*
in those who await his **gra**cious favor.

Antiphon How pleasant it is to honor God with praise!

Silence for meditation

God our Father, great builder of the heavenly Jerusalem, you know the number of the stars and call each of them by name: Heal hearts that are broken, gather those who have been scattered, and enrich us all from the plenitude of your eternal wisdom, Jesus Christ our Lord. [LH, LBW]

+

Stand

THE HYMN is sung. *Jam lucis orto sidere*

2 Would guard our hearts and tongues from strife;
From anger's din would shield our life;
From evil sights would turn our eyes,
And close our ears to vanities.

3 Would keep our inmost conscience pure;
Our souls from folly would secure;
Would bid us check the pride of sense
With due and holy abstinence.

4 So we, when this new day is gone
And night in turn is drawing on,
With conscience by the world unstained
Shall praise his Name for vict'ry gained.

5 "All praise to you, creator Lord!
All praise to you, eternal Word!
All praise to, O Spirit wise!"
We sing as daylight fills the skies.

[LBW 268, H40 st. 3; see H82 3, 4]

Text: Latin hymn, 7th or 8th cent.; tr. John Mason Neale, 1818-1866
Tune: *Laurel*, Dale Wood, b. 1934 LM

Sit

One or two LESSONS are read.

Year 1 | Year 2

after Epiphany 1

Isaiah 41:1-16

Do not fear, for I am with you, do not be afraid, for I am your God; I will strengthen you.

Ephesians 2:1-10

By grace you have been saved through faith, and this is not your own doing; it is the gift of God.

Genesis 4:1-16

Your brother's blood is crying out to me from the ground!

Hebrews 2:11-18

Because he himself was tested by what he suffered, he is able to help those who are being tested.

after Epiphany 5

Isaiah 59:1-21

Your iniquities have been barriers between you and your God, and your sins have hidden his face from you so that he does not hear.

2 Timothy 1:15-2:13

Be strong in the grace that is in Christ Jesus.

Genesis 27:1-29

The voice is Jacob's voice, but the hands are the hands of Esau.

Romans 12:1-8

Present your bodies as a living sacrifice, holy and acceptable to God, which is your spiritual worship.

Proper 1 / Wednesday after the Day of Pentecost

Isaiah 65:1-12

I was ready to be sought out by those who did not ask, to be found by those who did not seek me.

2 Timothy 2:14-26

God's firm foundation stands, bearing this inscription: "The Lord knows those who are his," and, "Let everyone who calls on

Ezekiel 34:1-16

I myself will search for my sheep, and will seek them out.

1 John 2:12-17

The world and its desire are passing away, but those who do the will of God live forever.

the name of the Lord turn away from wickedness."

after Proper 5 / Pentecost 4

Deuteronomy 31:30-32:14
The Rock, his work is perfect, and all his ways are just.

Ecclesiastes 9:11-18
I saw that under the sun the race is not to the swift, nor the battle to the strong, nor bread to the wise, nor riches to the intelligent, nor favor to the skillful; but time and chance happen to them all.

2 Corinthians 11:21b-33
If I must boast, I will boast of the things that show my weakness.

Galatians 5:1-15
The whole law is summed up in a single commandment, " You shall love your neighbor as yourself."

after Proper 9 / Pentecost 8

1 Samuel 16:1-13
Samuel took the horn of oil, and anointed him in the presence of his brothers; and the spirit of the LORD came mightily upon David from that day forward.

Deuteronomy 1:1-18
Go in and take possession of that land that I swore to your ancestors, to Abraham, to Isaac, and to Jacob, to give to them and to their descendants after them.

Acts 10:1-16
What God has made clean, you must not call profane.

Romans 9:1-18
So it depends not on human will or exertion, but on God who shows mercy.

after Proper 13 / Pentecost 12

2 Samuel 9:1-13
David asked, "Is there still anyone left of the house of Saul to whom I may show kindness for Jonathan's sake?"

Judges 7:19-8:12
A sword for the LORD and for Gideon!

Acts 19:1-10

When Paul had laid his hands on them, the Holy Spirit came upon them, and they spoke in tongues and prophesied.

Acts 3:12-26

Repent therefore, and turn to God so that your sins may be wiped out.

after Proper 17 / Pentecost 16

1 Kings 9:24-10:13

Because the LORD loved Israel forever, he has made you king to execute justice and righteousness.

Job 12:1;14:1-22

A mortal, born of woman, few of days and full of trouble, comes up like a flower and withers, flees like a shadow and does not last.

James 3:1-12

The tongue is a small member, yet it boasts of great exploits.

Acts 12:18-25

The word of God continued to advance and gain adherents.

after Proper 21 / Pentecost 20

2 Kings 18:9-25

The king of Assyria carried the Israelites away to Assyria, because they did not obey the voice of the Lord their God but transgressed his covenant.

Hosea 3:1-5

Go, love a woman who has a lover and is an adulteress, just as the LORD loves the people of Israel.
[BCP: Hosea 4:11-19]

1 Corinthians 8:1-13

Take care that this liberty of yours does not somehow become a stumbling block to the weak.

Acts 21:15-26

After greeting them, Paul related one by one the things that God had done among the Gentiles through his ministry.

after Proper 25 / Pentecost 24

Ezra 6:1-22

The LORD had made them joyful, and had turned the heart of the king of Assyria to them, so that he aided them in the work on the house of God, the God of Israel.

or Lamentations 2:8-15

Sirach [Ecclesiasticus] 28:(12-13) 14-26

Many have fallen by the edge of the sword, but not as many as have fallen because of the tongue.

or Nahum 1:1-14

Revelation 5:1-10

The Lion of the tribe of Judah, the Root of David, has conquered.

Revelation 12:1-6

A great portent appeared in heaven: a woman clothed with the sun, with the moon under her feet, and on her head a crown of twelve stars.

after Christ the King

Obadiah 15-21

On Mount Zion there shall be those that escape, and it shall be holy.

Zechariah 12:1-10

I will pour out a spirit of compassion and supplication on the house of David and the inhabitants of Jerusalem, so that, when they look on the one whom they have pierced, they shall mourn for him, as one mourns for an only child.

1 Peter 2:1-10

You are a chosen race, a royal priesthood, a holy nation, God's own people, in order that you may proclaim the mighty acts of him who called you out of darkness into his marvelous light.

Ephesians 1:3-14

He destined us for adoption as his children through Jesus Christ, according to the good pleasure of his will.

Silence for meditation follows each reading.

RESPONSORY

At all times bless the Lord God and ask him that your ways **may** be straight,*
that all your paths and **plans** may prosper.
Serve God faithfully and do what is pleasing **in** his sight,*
that all your paths and **plans** may prosper.
[LH: Tobit 4:19;14:8, 9]

God loved us and sent his Son to be the atoning sacrifice **for** our sins,*
so we have known and believe the love God **has** for us.
The Lord himself has become our Savior; in his love **he** redeemed us,*
so we have known and believe the love God **has** for us.
[LH:1 John 4:10, 16; see Isa. 63:8, 9]

Thursday of Week I

Antiphon to PSALM 97 *Dominus regnavit exultet*

The **LORD** is king;*
let the **earth** rejoice. [LH, PBO]

97 *Earth rejoices in its king*

1 The LORD is king;
let the **earth** rejoice;*
let the multitude of the **isles** be glad.

2 Clouds and darkness are **round** about him,*
righteousness and justice are the foundations **of** his throne.

3 A fire **goes** before him*
and burns up his enemies on **ev**ery side.

4 His lightnings light **up** the world;*
the earth sees it and **is** afraid.

5 The mountains melt like wax at the presence **of** the LORD,*
at the presence of the Lord of **the** whole earth.

6 The heavens de**clare** his righteousness,*
and all the peoples **see** his glory.

7 Confounded be all who worship carved images
and delight **in** false gods!*
Bow down before him, **all** you gods.

8 Zion hears and is glad, and the cities of Ju**dah** rejoice,*
because of your judg**ments**, O LORD.

9 For you are the LORD,
most high over **all** the earth;*
you are exalted far a**bove** all gods.

10 The LORD loves those **who** hate evil;*
he preserves the lives of his saints
and delivers them from the hand **of** the wicked.

11 Light has sprung up **for** the righteous,*
and joyful gladness for those who **are** truehearted.

12 Rejoice in the **LORD**, you righteous,*
and give thanks to his **ho**ly Name.

Antiphon The **LORD** is king;*
let the **earth** rejoice.

Silence for meditation

God our king, you clothe the sky with light and the depths of the ocean with darkness. Among the peoples you work wonders, and rain terror upon your enemies. Do not try your servants by fire, but bring us rejoicing to the shelter of your home, where with your Son and the Holy Spirit you live and reign, now and for ever. [LH, LBW]

+

Antiphon to PSALM 147 part ii *Lauda, Jerusalem, Dominum*
Praise the LORD, O Jerusalem. [LH]

147 *Praise of God's personal care of Israel*

13 Worship the LORD, **O** Jerusalem;*
praise your **God**, O Zion;

14 For he has strengthened the bars **of** your gates;*
he has blessed your chil**dren** within you.

15 He has established peace **on** your borders;*
he satisfies you with the **fin**est wheat.

16 He sends out his command **to** the earth,*
and his word runs **ver**y swiftly.

17 He gives **snow** like wool;*
he scatters hoar**frost** like ashes.

18 He scatters his **hail** like bread crumbs;*
who can stand a**gainst** his cold?

19 He sends forth his **word** and melts them;*
he blows with his wind, and the **wa**ters flow.

20 He declares his **word** to Jacob,*
his statutes and his judg**ments** to Israel.

21 He has not done so to any **oth**er nation;*
to them he has not revealed his judgments.
Hallelujah!

Antiphon Praise the LORD, O Jerusalem.

Silence for meditation

Almighty God, through your Church, generously endowed with gifts of grace and fortified by the Holy Spirit, you send out your Word to all nations: Strengthen your Church with heavenly food, make it dauntless in faith, and multiply its children, that with joy we may celebrate your love at the altar on high; through Jesus Christ our Lord. [LH, PHP]

+

Stand

THE HYMN is sung. *Jesu, meine Freude*

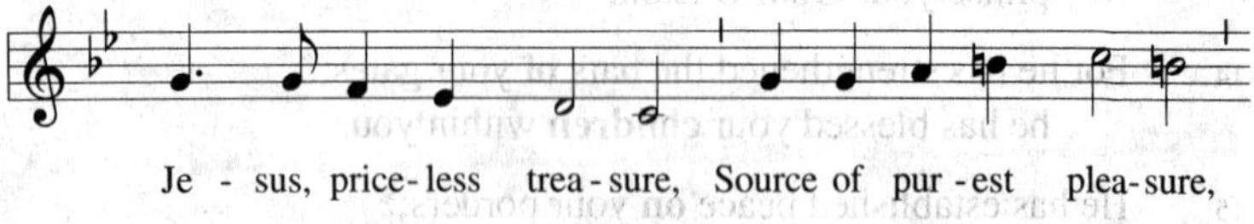

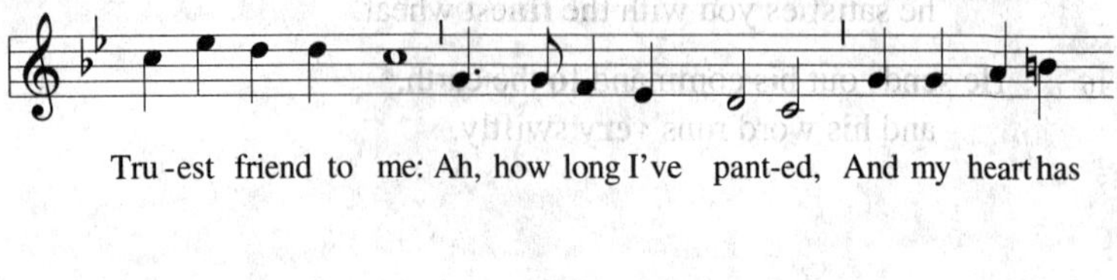

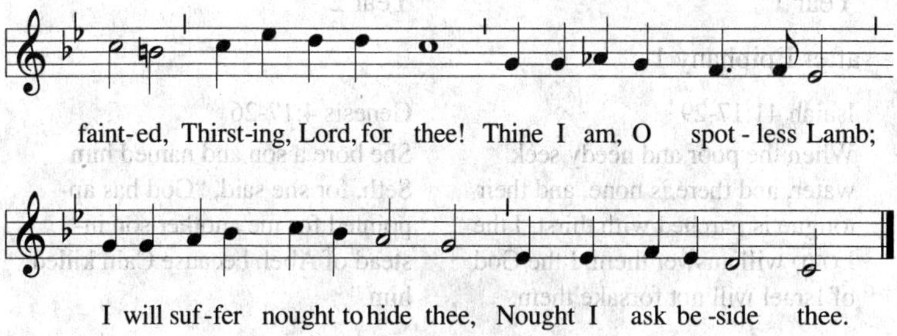

2 In thine arm I rest me;
Foes who would molest me
Cannot reach me here.
Though the earth be shaking,
Ev'ry heart be quaking,
Jesus calms my fear.
Sin and hell in conflict fell
With their bitter storms assail me,
Jesus will not fail me.

3 Hence, all fears and sadness,
For the Lord of gladness,
Jesus, enters in.
Those who love the Father,
Though the storms may gather,
Still have peace within.
Yea, whate'er I here must bear,
Still in thee lies purest pleasure,
Jesus, priceless treasure! [LBW 457]

Text: Johann Franck, 1618-1677; tr. Catherine Winkworth, 1829-1878

Tune: *Jesu, meine Freude,* Johann Crüger, 1598-1662 665 665 786

Sit

One or two LESSONS are read.

Year 1	Year 2
after Epiphany 1	
Isaiah 41:17-29 When the poor and needy seek water, and there is none, and their tongue is parched with thirst, I the LORD will answer them, I the God of Israel will not forsake them.	Genesis 4:17-26 She bore a son and named him Seth, for she said, "God has appointed for me another son instead of Abel, because Cain killed him."
Ephesians 2:11-22 Now in Christ Jesus you who were once far off have been brought near by the blood of Christ.	Hebrews 3:1-11 Brothers and sisters, holy partners in a heavenly calling, consider that Jesus, the apostle and high priest of our confession, was faithful to the one who appointed him.
after Epiphany 5	
Isaiah 60:1-22 The LORD will arise upon you, and his glory will appear over you.	Genesis 27:30-45 When Esau heard his father's words, he cried out with an exceedingly great and bitter cry, and said to his father, "Bless me, me also, father!"
2 Timothy 2:14-26 Shun youthful passions and pursue righteousness, faith, love, and peace, along with those who call on the Lord from a pure heart.	Romans 12:9-21 Let love be genuine; hate what is evil, hold fast to what is good.
Proper 1 / Thursday after the Day of Pentecost	
Isaiah 65:17-25 The wolf and the lamb shall feed together, the lion shall eat straw like the ox. They shall not hurt or destroy in all my holy mountain.	Ezekiel 37:21b-28 My dwelling place shall be with them; and I will be their God, and they shall be my people.

2 Timothy 3:1-17

All scripture is inspired by God and is useful for teaching, for repoof, for correction, and for training in righteousness.

1 John 2:18-29

And now, little children, abide in him, so that when he is revealed we may have confidence and not be put to shame before him at his coming.

after Proper 5 / Pentecost 4

Sirach [Ecclesiasticus] 44:19-45:5

Abraham certified the covenant in his flesh, and when he was tested he proved faithful.

or Song of Solomon 1:1-3, 9-11, 15-16a; 2:1-3a

Ecclesiastes 11:1-8

Just as you do not know how the breath comes to the bones in the mother's womb, so you do not know the work of God, who makes everything.

2 Corinthians 12:1-10

My grace is sufficient for you, for power is made perfect in weakness.

Galatians 5:16-24

Live by the Spirit, I say, and do not gratify the desires of the flesh.

after Proper 9 / Pentecost 8

1 Samuel 16:14-17:11

Whenever the evil spirit from God came upon Saul, David took the lyre and played it with his hand, and Saul would be relieved and feel better, and the evil spirit would depart from him.

Deuteronomy 3:18-28

Charge Joshua, and encourage and strengthen him, because it is he who shall cross over at the head of this people and who shall secure their possession of the land that you will see.

Acts 10:17-33

Cornelius, a centurion, an upright and God-fearing man, who is well spoken of by the whole Jewish nation, was directed by a holy angel to send for you to come to his house and to hear what you have to say.

Romans 9:19-33

Gentiles, who did not strive for righteousness, have attained it, that is, righteousness through faith.

after Proper 13 / Pentecost 12

2 Samuel 11:1-27

When the mourning was over, David sent and brought her to his house, and she became his wife, and bore him a son.

Judges 8:22-35

As soon as Gideon died, the Israelites relapsed and prostituted themselves with the Baals.

Acts 19:11-20

The word of the Lord grew mightily and prevailed.

Acts 4:1-12

There is salvation in no one else, for there is no other name under heaven given among mortals by which we must be saved.

after Proper 17 / Pentecost 16

1 Kings 11:1-13

When Solomon was old, his wives turned away his heart after other gods; and his heart was not true to the LORD his God.

Job 16:16-22;17:1,13-16

O earth, do not cover my blood; let my outcry find no resting place.

James 3:13-4:12

A harvest of righteousness is sown in peace for those who make peace.

Acts 13:1-12

While they were worshiping the Lord and fasting, the Holy Spirit said, "Set apart for me Barnabas and Saul for the work to which I have called them."

after Proper 21/ Pentecost 20

2 Kings 18:28-37

Has any of the gods of the nations ever delivered its land out of the hand of the king of Assyria?

Hosea 4:1-11a [NRSV]

Hear the word of the LORD, O people of Israel; for the LORD has an indictment against the inhabitants of the land.

[BCP: Hosea 5:8-6:6]

1 Corinthians 9:1-15

If we have sown spiritual good among you, is it too much if we reap your material benefits?

Acts 21:27-36

All the city was aroused, and the people rushed together. They seized Paul and dragged him out of the temple.

after Proper 25 / Pentecost 24

Nehemiah 1:1-11

O Lord, let your ear be attentive to the prayer of your servant.

or Lamentations 2:16-22

Revelation 5:11-6:11

To the one seated on the throne and to the Lamb be blessing and honor and glory and might forever and ever.

Sirach [Ecclesiasticus] 31:12-18, 25-32:2

Judge your neighbor's feelings by your own, and in every matter be thoughtful.

or Nahum 1:15-2:12

Revelation 12:7-17

Rejoice then, you heavens and all who dwell in them! But woe to the earth and the sea, for the devil has come down to you with great wrath, because he knows that his time is short!

after Christ the King

Zephaniah 3:1-13

Every morning he renders his judgment, each dawn without fail; but the unjust knows no shame.

1 Peter 2:11-25

Christ suffered for you, leaving you an example, so that you should follow in his steps.

Zechariah 13:1-9

On that day a fountain shall be opened for the house of David and the inhabitants of Jerusalem, to cleanse them from sin and impurity.

Ephesians 1:15-23

He has put all things under his feet and has made him the head of all things for the church.

Silence for meditation follows each reading.

RESPONSORY

You are worthy, our Lord and God, to receive glory and hon**or** and power,*
for you created all things
and by your will they
existed and **were** created.
You have made heaven and earth and every wonderful thing under heaven, and you are **Lord** of all;*
for you created all things
and by your will they
existed and **were** created.
[LH: Rev. 4:11; Esther 3:10]

God has made known to us the mystery of his will, as a plan for the full**ness** of time,*
to gather up all things in
Christ, things in heaven
and **things** on earth.
For in him all the fullness of God was **pleased** to dwell,*
to gather up all things in
Christ, things in heaven
and **things** on earth.
[LH: Eph. 1:9-10; Col. 1:19-20]

Friday of Week I

Antiphon to PSALM 51 *Miserere mei, Deus* [a penitential psalm]

Create in me a clean **heart**, O God,*
and renew a right spir**it** within me. [LH, PBO]

51 *Prayer for forgiveness*

1 Have mercy on me, O God, according to your
loving-kindness;*
in your great compassion blot out **my** offenses.

2 Wash me through and through from my **wick**edness*
and cleanse me **from** my sin.

3 For I know **my** transgressions,*
and my sin is ev**er** before me.

4 Against you only **have** I sinned*
and done what is evil **in** your sight.

5 And so you are justified **when** you speak*
and upright **in** your judgment.

6 Indeed, I have been wicked **from** my birth,*
a sinner from my **moth**er's womb.

7 For behold, you look for truth **deep** within me,*
and will make me understand **wis**dom secretly.

8 Purge me from my sin, and I **shall** be pure;*
wash me, and I shall be **clean** indeed.

9 Make me hear of **joy** and gladness,*
that the body you have broken **may** rejoice.

10 Hide your face **from** my sins*
and blot out all **my** iniquities.

11 Create in me a clean **heart**, O God,*
and renew a right spir**it** within me.

12 Cast me not away **from** your presence*
and take not your holy **Spir**it from me.

13 Give me the joy of your saving **help** again*
and sustain me with your boun**ti**ful Spirit.

14 I shall teach your ways **to** the wicked,*
and sinners shall re**turn** to you.

15 Deliver me from **death**, O God,*
and my tongue shall sing of your righteousness,
O God of **my** salvation.

16 Open my **lips**, O Lord,*
and my mouth shall pro**claim** your praise.

17 Had you desired it, I would have **of**fered sacrifice,*
but you take no delight **in** burnt-offerings.

18 The sacrifice of God is a **troub**led spirit;*
a broken and contrite heart, O God, you will **not** despise.

19 Be favorable and gra**cious** to Zion,*
and rebuild the walls **of** Jerusalem.

20 Then you will be pleased with the appointed sacrifices,
with burnt-offerings **and** oblations;*
then shall they offer young bullocks up**on** your altar.

Antiphon Create in me a clean **heart**, O God,*
and renew a right spir**it** within me.

Silence for meditation

Almighty and merciful Father, you freely forgive those who, as David of old, acknowledge and confess their sins. Create in us pure hearts, and wash away all our sins in the blood of your dear Son, Jesus Christ our Lord. [MPES, LBW]

+

Antiphon to PSALM 148 *Laudate Dominum de coelis*

Praise the LORD **from** the heavens;*
praise the LORD **from** the earth. [LH]

148 *Cosmic praise*

1 Hallelujah!
Praise the LORD **from** the heavens;*
praise him **in** the heights.

2 Praise him, all you an**gels** of his;*
praise him, **all** his host.

3 Praise him, **sun** and moon;*
praise him, all you **shin**ing stars.

4 Praise him, heav**en** of heavens,*
and you waters a**bove** the heavens.

5 Let them praise the Name **of** the LORD;*
for he commanded, and they **were** created.

6 He made them stand fast for ev**er** and ever;*
he gave them a law which shall not **pass** away.

7 Praise the LORD **from** the earth,*
you sea-monsters **and** all deeps;

8 Fire and hail, **snow** and fog,*
tempestuous wind, do**ing** his will;

9 Mountains **and** all hills,*
fruit trees **and** all cedars;

10 Wild beasts **and** all cattle,*
creeping things and **wingèd** birds;

11 Kings of the earth **and** all peoples,*
princes and all rulers **of** the world;

12 Young **men** and maidens,*
old and **young** together.

13 Let them praise the Name **of** the LORD,*
for his Name only is exalted,
his splendor is over **earth** and heaven.

14 He has raised up strength for his people
and praise for all his **loy**al servants,*
the children of Israel, a people who are near him.
Hallelujah!

Antiphon Praise the LORD **from** the heavens;*
praise the LORD **from** the earth.

Silence for meditation

God Most High, by your Word your created a wondrous universe, and through your Spirit you breathed into it the breath of life: Accept creation's hymn of praise from our lips, and let the praise that is sung in heaven resound in the heart of every creature on earth, to the glory of the Father, and the Son, and the Holy Spirit, now and for ever. [LH, LBW]

+

Stand

THE HYMN is sung. *Rex Christe, factor omnium*

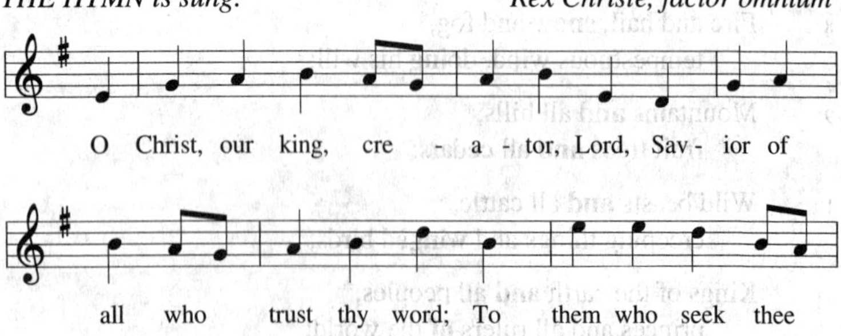

2 In thy dear cross a grace is found,
It flows from every streaming wound,
Whose power our inbred sin controls,
Breaks the firm bond and frees our souls.

3 Thou didst create the stars of night,
Yet thou hast veiled in flesh thy light,
Hast designed a mortal form to wear,
A mortal's painful lot to bear.

4 When thou didst hang upon the tree
The quaking earth acknowledged thee,
When thou didst there yield up thy breath
The earth grew dark as shades of death.

5 Now in the Father's glory high,
Great Conqueror, never more to die,
Us by thy mighty power defend,
And reign through ages without end. [SBH 62]

Text: Gregory I, 540-604; tr. Ray Palmer, 1808-1887
Tune: *Oakley,* R. Vaughan Williams, 1872-1958 LM

Sit

5. One or two LESSONS are read.

Year 1

after Epiphany 1

Isaiah 42:(1-9)10-17
Sing to the LORD a new song, his praise from the end of the earth!

Year 2

Genesis 6:1-8
I will blot out from the earth the human beings I have created–

people together with animals and creeping things and birds of the air, for I am sorry that I have made them.

Ephesians 3:1-13

Although I am the very least of all the saints, this grace was given to me to bring the Gentiles the news of the boundless riches of Christ.

Hebrews 3:12-19

We have become partners with Christ, if only we hold our first confidence firm to the end.

after Epiphany 5

Isaiah 61:1-9

The spirit of the Lord GOD is upon me, because the LORD has anointed me.

Genesis 27:46-28:4,10-22

How awesome is this place! This is none other than the house of God, and this is the gate of heaven.

2 Timothy 3:1-17

You must understand this, that in the last days distressing times will come.

Romans 13:1-14

Love does no wrong to a neighbor; therefore, love is the fulfilling of the law.

Proper 1 / Friday after the Day of Pentecost

Isaiah 66:1-6

Listen, an uproar from the city! A voice from the temple! The voice of the LORD, dealing retribution to his enemies!

Ezekiel 39:21-29

I will never again hide my face from them, when I pour out my spirit upon the house of Israel.

2 Timothy 4:1-8

I have fought the good fight, I have finished the race, I have kept the faith.

1 John 3:1-10

Beloved, we are God's children now; what we will be has not yet been revealed. What we do know is this: When he is revealed, we will be like him, for we will see him as he is.

after Proper 5 / Pentecost 4

Sirach [Ecclesiasticus] 45:6-16

He chose Aaron out of all the living to offer sacrifice to the Lord, incense and a pleasing odor as a memorial portion, to make atonement for the people.

or Song of Solomon 2:8-13;4:1-4a,5-7,9-11

Ecclesiastes 11:9-12:14

Fear God, and keep his commandments; for that is the whole duty of everyone.

2 Corinthians 12:11-21

The signs of a true apostle were performed among you with utmost patience, signs and wonders and mighty works.

Galatians 5:25-6:10

Let us not grow weary in doing what is right, for we will reap at harvest-time, if we do not give up.

after Proper 9 / Pentecost 8

1 Samuel 17:17-30

Who is this uncircumcised Philistine that he should defy the armies of the living God?

Deuteronomy 31:7-13, 24-32:4

Be strong and bold, for you are the one who will go with this people into the land that the LORD has sworn to their ancestors to give them.

Acts 10:34-48

God shows no partiality, but in every nation anyone who fears him and does what right is acceptable to him.

Romans 10:1-13

There is no distinction between Jew and Greek; the same Lord is Lord of all and is generous to all who call on him.

after Proper 13 / Pentecost 12

2 Samuel 12:1-14

Now therefore the sword shall never depart from your house, for you have despised me, and have taken the wife of Uriah the Hittite to be your wife.

Judges 9:1-16,19-21

Abimelech went to his father's house at Ophrah, and killed his brothers the sons Jerubbaal, seventy men, on one stone; but Jotham, the youngest son of Jerubbaal, survived, for he hid himself.

Acts 19:21-41

You also see and hear that not only in Ephesus but in almost the whole of Asia this Paul has persuaded and drawn away a considerable number of people by saying that gods made with hands are not gods.

Acts 4:13-31

Whether it is right in God's sight to listen to you rather than to God, you must judge; for we cannot keep from speaking about what we have seen and heard.

after Proper 17 / Pentecost 16

1 Kings 11:26-43

I will take the kingdom away from Solomon's son and give it to you — that is, the ten tribes. Yet to his son I will give one tribe, so that my servant David may always have a lamp before me in Jerusalem.

Job 19:1-7,14-27

I know that my Redeemer lives, and that at the last he will stand upon the earth.

James 4:13-5:6

You do not even know what tomorrow will bring. What is your life? For you are a mist that appears for a little while and then vanishes.

Acts 13:13-25

Of this man's posterity God has brought to Israel a Savior, Jesus, as he promised.

after Proper 21 / Pentecost 20

2 Kings 19:1-20

Incline your ear, O LORD, and hear; open your eyes, O LORD, and see; hear the words of Sennacherib, which he has sent to mock the living God.

Hosea 4:11b-19 [NRSV]

A spirit of whoredom has led them astray, and they have played the whore, forsaking their God. [BCP Hosea 10:1-15]

1 Corinthians 9:16-27

I punish my body and enslave it, so that after proclaiming to others I myself should not be disqualified.

Acts 21:37-22:16

The God of our ancestors has chosen you to know his will, to see the Righteous One and to hear his own voice.

after Proper 25 / Pentecost 24

Nehemiah 2:1-20

If it pleases the king, and if your servant has found favor with you, I ask that you send me to Judah, to the city of my ancestors' graves, so that I may rebuild it.

or Lamentations 4:1-22

Sirach[Ecclesiasticus] 34:1-8,21-27 [NRSV]

The eyes of the Lord are on those who love him, a mighty shield and strong support, a shelter from scorching wind and a shade from noonday sun.

or Nahum 2:13-3:7

Revelation 6:12-7:4

Do not damage the earth or the sea or the trees, until we have marked the servants of our God with a seal on their foreheads.

Revelation 13:1-10

Here is a call for the endurance and faith of the saints.

after Christ the King

Isaiah 24:14-23

The LORD of hosts will reign on Mount Zion and in Jerusalem, and before his elders he will manifest his glory.

Zechariah 14:1-11

The LORD will become king over all the earth; on that day the LORD will be one and his name one.

1 Peter 3:13-4:6

It is better to suffer for doing good, if suffering should be God's will, than to suffer for doing evil.

Romans 15:7-13

May the God of hope fill you with all joy and peace in believing, so that you may abound in hope by the power of the Holy Spirit.

Silence for meditation follows each reading.

RESPONSORY

The mountains shall drip sweet wine, the hills shall flow with milk, and all the stream beds of Judah shall **flow** with water;*
a fountain shall come forth from the house **of** the Lord.

Let everyone who is
thirsty come.*
Let anyone who wishes
take the water of life
as a gift.

The angel showed me the river of the wa**ter** of life,*
bright as crystal, flowing from the throne of God and **of** the Lamb.

Let everyone who is
thirsty come.*
Let anyone who wishes
take the water of life
as a gift.

[LH: Joel 3:18; Rev. 22:17,1]

To me living is Christ and dy**ing** is gain.*

May I never boast of any-
thing except the cross of
our Lord **Je**sus Christ,

By which the world has been crucified to me, and I **to** the world.*

May I never boast of any
thing except the cross of
our Lord **Je**sus Christ.

[LH: Phil. 1:21; Gal.6:14]

Saturday of Week I

Antiphon to PSALM 104 *Benedic, anima mea, Domine Deus meus*

O LORD my God,
you are clothed with majes**ty** and splendor;*
you wrap yourself with light as **with** a cloak. [LH, PBO]

104 *The glories of creation*

1 Bless the LORD, **O** my soul;*
O LORD my God, how excellent is your greatness!
you are clothed with majes**ty** and splendor.

2 You wrap yourself with light as **with** a cloak*
and spread out the heavens **like** a curtain.

3 You lay the beams of your chambers in the wa**ters** above;*
you make the clouds your chariot;
you ride the wings **of** the wind.

4 You make the **winds** your messengers*
and flames of **fire** your servants.

5 You have set the earth upon **its** foundations,*
so that it never shall move at **any** time.

6 You covered it with the Deep as **with** a mantle;*
the waters stood higher **than** the mountains.

7 At your re**buke** they fled;*
at the voice of your thunder they has**tened** away.

8 They went up into the hills and down to the val**leys** beneath,*
to the places you had appoint**ed** for them.

9 You set the limits that they **should** not pass;*
they shall not again cov**er** the earth.

10 You send the springs in**to** the valleys;*
they flow be**tween** the mountains.

11 All the beasts of the field drink their **fill** from them,*
and the wild asses **quench** their thirst.

12 Beside them the birds of the air **make** their nests*
and sing a**mong** the branches.

13 You water the mountains from your dwell**ing** on high;*
the earth is fully satisfied by the fruit **of** your works.

14 You make grass grow for **flocks** and herds*
and plants to **serve** mankind;

15 That they may bring forth food **from** the earth,*
and wine to glad**den** our hearts,

16 Oil to make a **cheer**ful countenance,*
and bread to strength**en** the heart.

17 The trees of the LORD are **full** of sap,*
the cedars of Lebanon **which** he planted,

18 In which the birds **build** their nests,*
and in whose tops the stork **makes** his dwelling.

19 The high hills are a refuge for the **moun**tain goats,*
and the stony cliffs for **the** rock badgers.

20 You appointed the moon to **mark** the seasons,*
and the sun knows the time **of** its setting.

21 You make darkness that it **may** be night,*
in which all the beasts of the **for**est prowl.

22 The lions roar af**ter** their prey*
and seek their **food** from God.

23 The sun rises, and they **slip** away*
and lay themselves down **in** their dens.

24 Man goes forth **to** his work*
and to his labor un**til** the evening.

25 O LORD, how manifold **are** your works!*
in wisdom you have made them all;
the earth is full **of** your creatures.

26 Yonder is the great and wide sea
with its living things too many to number,*
creatures both **small** and great.

27 There move the ships,
and there is **that** Leviathan,*
which you have made for the **sport** of it.

28 All of them **look** to you,*
to give them their food **in** due season.

29 You give it to them; they **gath**er it;*
you open your hand, and they are filled **with** good things.

30 You hide your face, and **they** are terrified;*
you take away their breath,
and they die and return **to** their dust.

31 You send forth your Spirit, and they **are** created;*
and so you renew the face **of** the earth.

32 May the glory of the LORD en**dure** for ever;*
may the LORD rejoice in **all** his works.

33 He looks at the earth **and** it trembles;*
he touches the mountains **and** they smoke.

34 I will sing to the LORD as long **as** I live;*
I will praise my God while I **have** my being.

35 May these words **of** mine please him;*
I will rejoice **in** the LORD.

36 Let sinners be consumed out **of** the earth,*
and the wicked **be** no more.

37 Bless the LORD, **O** my soul.*
Hallelujah!

Antiphon O LORD my God,
you are clothed with majes**ty** and splendor;*
you wrap yourself with light as **with** a cloak.

Silence for meditation

God of all light, life, and love, through the visible things of this world you raise our thoughts to things unseen, and you show us your power and your love: From your dwelling-place refresh our hearts and renew the face of the earth with the life-giving water of your Word, until the new heaven and new earth resound with the song of resurrection in Jesus Christ our Lord. [LHd, LBW]

+

Antiphon to PSALM 149 *Cantate Domino*

Let the children of Zion be joyful in their king. [LH, PBO]

149 *Praise to the God of victories*

1 Hallelujah!
Sing to the LORD **a** new song;*
sing his praise in the congregation **of** the faithful.

2 Let Israel rejoice **in** his Maker;*
let the children of Zion be joyful **in** their King.

3 Let them praise his Name **in** the dance;*
let them sing praise to him with tim**brel** and harp.

4 For the LORD takes pleasure **in** his people*
and adorns the **poor** with victory.

5 Let the faithful re**joice** in triumph;*
let them be joyful **on** their beds.

6 Let the praises of God be **in** their throat*
and a two-edged sword **in** their hand;

7 To wreak vengeance **on** the nations*
and punishment **on** the peoples;

8 To bind their **kings** in chains*
and their nobles with **links** of iron;

9 To inflict on them the judg**ment** decreed;*
this is glory for all his faithful people.
Hallelujah!

Antiphon Let the children of Zion be joyful in their king.

Silence for meditation

Lord, let Israel rejoice in you and acknowledge you as creator and redeemer. In your lovingkindness embrace us now, that we may proclaim the wonderful truths of salvation with your saints in glory; through your Son, Jesus Christ our Lord. [LH, LBW]

+

Stand

THE HYMN is sung. *O quanta qualia*

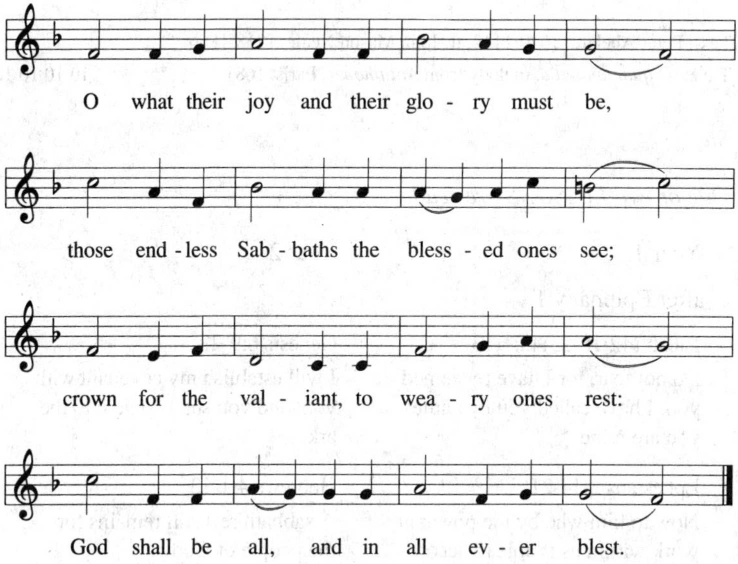

2 Truly, "Jerusalem" name we that shore,
City of peace that brings joy evermore;
Wish and fulfillment are not severed there,
Nor do things prayed for come short of the prayer.

3 There, where no troubles distraction can bring,
We the sweet anthems of Zion shall sing;
While for thy grace, Lord, their voices of praise
Thy blessèd people eternally raise.

4 Now, in the meanwhile, with hearts raised on high,
We for that country must yearn and must sigh,
Seeking Jerusalem, dear native land,
Through our long exile on Babylon's strand.

5 Low before him with our praises we fall;
Of whom and in whom and through whom are all;
Of whom, the Father; and in whom, the Son;
Through whom, the Spirit, with them ever one.

[H82 623, LBW 337 alt.]

Text: Peter Abelard, 1079-1142; tr. John Mason Neale, 1818-1866
Tune: *O quanta qualia,* melody from *Antiphoner*, Paris, 1681 10 10 10 10

Sit

One or two LESSONS are read.

Year 1	Year 2
after Epiphany 1	
Isaiah (42:18-25)43:1-13	Genesis 6:9-22
Do not fear, for I have redeemed you; I have called you by name, you are mine.	I will establish my covenant with you; and you shall come into the ark.
Ephesians 3:14-21	Hebrews 4:1-13
Now to him who by the power at work within us is able to accom-	A sabbath rest still remains for the people of God.

plish abundantly far more than all we can ask or imagine, to him be glory in the church and in Christ Jesus to all generations, forever and ever. Amen.

after Epiphany 5

Isaiah 61:10-62:5

The nations shall see your vindication, and all the kings your glory.

Genesis 29:1-20

So Jacob served seven years for Rachel, and they seemed to him but a few days because of the love he had for her.

2 Timothy 4:1-8

From now on there is reserved for me the crown of righteousness, which the Lord, the righteous judge, will give me.

Romans 14:1-23

Let us therefore no longer pass judgment on one another, but resolve instead never to put a stumbling block or hindrance in the way of another.

Proper 1 / Saturday after the Day of Pentecost

Isaiah 66:7-14

As a mother comforts her child, so I will comfort you.

Ezekiel 47:1-12

On the banks, on both sides of the river, there will grow all kinds of trees for food. Their leaves will not wither nor their fruit fail.

2 Timothy 4:9-22

The Lord will rescue me from every evil attack and save me for his heavenly kingdom.

1 John 3:11-18

This is the message you have heard from the beginning, that we should love one another.

after Proper 5 / Pentecost 4

Sirach [Ecclesiasticus] 46:1-10

Joshua called upon the Most High, the Mighty One, when

Numbers 3:1-13

You shall make a register of Aaron and his descendants; it is

enemies pressed him on every side,and the great Lord answered him with hailstones of mighty power.

or Song of Solomon 5:10-16; 7:1-2(3-5) 6-7a(9);8:6-7

they who shall attend to the priesthood.

2 Corinthians 13:1-14

The grace of the Lord Jesus Christ, the love of God, and the communion of the Holy Spirit be with all of you.

Galatians 6:11-18

May I never boast of anything except the cross of our Lord Jesus Christ, by which the world has been crucified to me and I to the world.

after Proper 9 / Pentecost 8

1 Samuel 17:31-49

You come to me with sword and spear and javelin; but I come to you in the name of the LORD of hosts, the God of the armies of Israel, whom you have defied.

Acts 11:1-18

God has given even to Gentiles the repentance that leads to life.

Deuteronomy 34:1-12

Then Moses, the servant of the LORD, died there in the land of Moab, at the LORD's command. He was buried in a valley in the land of Moab.

Romans 10:14-21

Faith comes from what is heard, and what is heard comes through the word of Christ.

after Proper 13 / Pentecost 12

2 Samuel 12:15-31

Then David consoled his wife Bathsheba, and went to her, and lay with her; and she bore him a son, and he named him Solomon.

Judges 9:22-25,50-57

God repaid Abimelech for the crime he committed against his father in killing his seventy brothers; and God also made all the wickedness of the people of Schechem fall back on their heads.

Acts 20:1-16

On the first day of the week, when we met to break bread, Paul was holding a discussion with them; since he intended to leave the next day, he continued speaking until midnight.

Acts 4:32-5:11

The whole group of those who believed were of one heart and soul, and no one claimed private ownership of any possessions, but everything they owned was held in common.

after Proper 17 / Pentecost 16

1 Kings 12:1-20

"What share do we have in David? We have no inheritance in the son of Jesse. To your tents, O Israel!"

Job 22:1-4,21-23:7

Oh, that I knew where I might find him, that I might come even to his dwelling! I would lay my case before him, and fill my mouth with arguments.

James 5:7-20

Be patient, therefore, beloved, until the coming of the Lord.
[BCP: James 7:1-12, 19-20]

Acts 13:26-43

Many Jews and devout converts to Judaism followed Paul and Barnabas, who spoke to them and urged them to continue in the grace of God.

after Proper 21 / Pentecost 20

2 Kings 19:21-36

I will defend this city to save it, for my own sake and for the sake of my servant David.

Hosea 5:1-7

Their deeds do not permit them to return to their God. For the spirit of whoredom is within them, and they do not know the LORD.
[BCP: Hosea 11:1-9]

1 Corinthians 10:1-13

God is faithful, and he will not let you be tested beyond your strength, but with the testing he will also provide the way out so that you may be able to endure it.

Acts 22:17-29

The tribune also was afraid, for he realized that Paul was a Roman citizen and that he had bound him.

after Proper 25 / Pentecost 24

Nehemiah 4:1-23

So we rebuilt the wall, and all the wall was joined together to half its height; for the people had a mind to work.

or Lamentations 5:1-22

Revelation 7:(4-8) 9-17

Salvation belongs to our God who is seated on the throne, and to the Lamb!

Sirach [Ecclesiasticus] 35:1-22a [NRSV]

Be generous when you worship the Lord, and do not stint the first fruits of your hands.

or Nahum 3:8-19

Revelation 13:11-18

Then I saw another beast that rose out of the earth; it had two horns like a lamb and it spoke like a dragon.

after Christ the King

Micah 7:11-20

He will again have compassion upon us; he will tread our iniquities under foot. You will cast all our sins into the depths of the sea.

1 Peter 4:7-19

Above all, maintain constant love for one another, for love covers a multitude of sins.

Zechariah 14:12-21

All who survive of the nations that have come against Jerusalem shall go up year after year to worship the King, the LORD of hosts.

Philippians 2:1-11

At the name of Jesus every knee should bend, in heaven and on earth and under the earth, and every tongue should confess that Jesus Christ is Lord, to the glory of God the Father.

Silence for meditation follows each reading.

RESPONSORY

Hear, O Israel, and keep the **Lord's** commandments.*
Know therefore that the Lord your God is God, the faithful God who

Proclaim with me the greatness **of** the Lord;*
let us exalt his **Name** together.*
Look upon him **and** be radiant,*

maintains covenant loyalty
with **those** who love him.

You shall love the Lord your God with all your heart, and with all your soul, and with **all** your might.*

Know therefore that the
Lord your God is God, the
faithful God who maintains
covenant loyalty with **those**
who love him.

[LH: Deut. 6:4, 2; 7:9; 6:5]

and let not your
faces **be** ashamed.

God has enabled you to share in the inheritance of the **saints** in light.*

He has rescued us from the pow**er** of darkness.

Look upon him **and** be
radiant,*
and let not your faces **be**
ashamed.

[LH: Ps. 34:4,6; Col. 1:12-13]

Antiphon to PSALM 84 *Quam dilecta tabernacula*

Happy are they who dwell in your house! [LH]

84 *Longing for God's temple*

1 How dear to me is your dwelling, O **LORD** of hosts!*
My soul has a desire and longing for the courts of the LORD;
my heart and my flesh rejoice in the **liv**ing God.

2 The sparrow has found her a house
and the swallow a nest where she may **lay** her young;*
by the side of your altars, O LORD of hosts,
my King **and** my God.

3 Happy are they who dwell **in** your house!*
they will always be **prais**ing you.

4 Happy are the people whose strength **is** in you!*
whose hearts are set on the **pil**grims' way.

5 Those who go through the desolate valley will find it a **pla**ce of springs,*
for the early rains have covered it with **pools** of water.

6 They climb from **height** to height,*
and the God of gods will reveal him**self** in Zion.

7 LORD God of hosts, **hear** my prayer;*
hearken, O **God** of Jacob.

8 Behold our defend**er**, O God;*
and look upon the face of **your** Anointed.

9 For one day in your courts is better than a thousand in **my** own room,*
and to stand at the threshold of the house of my God
than to dwell in the tents **of** the wicked.

10 For the LORD God is both **sun** and shield;*
he will give **grace** and glory;

11 No good thing will the **LORD** withhold*
from those who walk **with** integrity.

12 O **LORD** of hosts,*
happy are those who put their **trust** in you!

Antiphon Happy are they who dwell in your house!

Silence for meditation

Almighty God, you heard the prayer of Christ, your chosen one, and raised him to the lasting joy of your presence: Help us in our pilgrimage toward you to love your Church and to offer the sacrifice of praise at your altar, that we may hasten to your home and joyfully look upon your glorious splendor, which we have seen in your Son, Jesus Christ our Lord. [LHd, LBW]

+

On the Festival of the Holy Trinity, the canticle is the Athanasian Creed, pp. 0000-0000. It is used without an antiphon and is concluded by the prayer printed with it.

Antiphon to the OLD TESTAMENT CANTICLE *Attende caelum [Audite coeli]*

Extoll the greatness of our God. [LH]

A Song of Moses Deuteronomy 32:1-4 ,7, 36a ,43

Give ear, you heavens, to **what** I say,*
let the earth hearken to the words **of** my mouth.

May my teaching fall like **drops** of rain;*
my words distill **like** the dew,
Like gentle rain up**on** the grass*
like showers on **grow**ing plants.

I will sing of the **Lord's** renown,*
extoll the greatness **of** our God,
The Rock whose **work** is perfect,*
for all his **ways** are just;
A faithful God, who **does** no wrong,*
righteous and **true** is he.

Remember the **days** of old;*
consider the **years** long past;
Ask your parents **to** recount it*
and your elders to tell **you** the tale.

The Lord will vindi**cate** his people*
and have compassion **on** his servants.
Rejoice with **him**, you heavens;*
all you gods, bow **down** before him. [NRSV, REB, LH]

Antiphon Extoll the greatness of our God.

Silence for meditation

O God, exaltation of the humble and strength of the righteous, you taught your people through Moses to sing your praise, that the law which he delivered to them might be helpful to us: Show your power among all nations that, in the forgiveness of sins, terror may turn to joy, and fear of retribution to salvation; through your Son, Jesus Christ our Lord. [Gel., LBW]

+

Antiphon to PSALM 150 *Laudate Dominum in sanctis ejus*

Praise God for his **might**y acts;*
praise him for his ex**cel**lent greatness. [LH, PBO]

150 *The great alleluia*

1 Hallelujah!
Praise God in his **ho**ly temple;*
praise him in the firmament **of** his power.

2 Praise him for his **might**y acts;*
praise him for his ex**cel**lent greatness.

3 Praise him with the blast **of** the ram's-horn;*
praise him with **lyre** and harp.

4 Praise him with tim**brel** and dance;*
praise him with **strings** and pipe.

5 Praise him with re**sound**ing cymbals;*
praise him with loud-**clang**ing cymbals.

6 Let everything **that** has breath*
praise the LORD.
Hallelujah!

Antiphon Praise God for his **might**y acts;*
praise him for his ex**cel**lent greatness.

Silence for meditation

God of surpassing greatness, enthroned upon the praises of your people, fill our hearts with your love and unite our voices with the praise of all creation so that you may be honored and glorified by everything that has breath; through your Son, Jesus Christ our Lord. [PHP]

+

Stand

THE HYMN is sung. *O Pater sancte*

2 Trinity sacred, Unity unshaken;
Deity perfect, giving and forgiving,
Light of the angels, Life of the forsaken,
Hope of all living.

3 Maker of all things, all thy creatures praise thee;
Lo, all things serve thee through thy whole creation:
Hear us, Almighty, hear us as we raise thee
Heart's adoration.

4 To the all-ruling triune God be glory:
Highest and greatest, help thou our endeavor,
We too would praise thee, giving honor worthy,
Now and for ever. [SBH 134]

Text: Latin hymn, 10th cent.; tr. Percy Dearmer, 1867-1936
Tune: *Christe sanctorum,* melody from *Antiphoner*, Paris, 1681 11 11 11 5

Sit

One or two LESSONS are read.

Year 1	Year 2
Epiphany 2	
Isaiah 43:14-44:5	Genesis 7:1-10, 17-23
I am about to do a new thing; now it springs forth, do you not perceive it?	The waters swelled and increased greatly on the earth; and the ark floated on the face of the waters.

Hebrews 6:17-7:10

We have this hope, a sure and steadfast anchor of the soul, a hope that enters the inner shine behind the curtain, where Jesus, a forerunner on our behalf, has entered.

Ephesians 4:1-16

I therefore, a prisoner in the Lord, beg you to lead a life worthy of the calling to which you have been called.

Epiphany 6

Isaiah 62:6-12

Say to daughter Zion, "See, your salvation comes."

Genesis 29:20-35

When the LORD saw that Leah was unloved, he opened her womb; but Rachel was barren.

1 John 2:3-11

The true light is already shining.

1 Timothy 3:14-4:10

Train yourself in godliness.

The Festival of the Holy Trinity

Sirach [Ecclesiasticus] 43:1-12 (27-33)

We could say more but could never say enough; let the final word be: "He is the all."

or Deuteronomy 6:1-9 (10-15)

Job 38:1-11; 42:1-5

Where were you when I laid the foundation of the earth? Tell me, if you have understanding.

Ephesians 4:1-16

I therefore, a prisoner in the Lord, beg you to lead a life worthy of the calling to which you have been called.

Revelation 19:4-16

Hallelujah! For the Lord our God the Almighty reigns.

Proper 6 (Sunday between June 12 and 18) / Pentecost 5

Sirach [Ecclesiasticus] 46:11-20
Samuel was beloved by his Lord; a prophet of the Lord, he established the kingdom and anointed rulers over his people.

or Exodus 6:2-13; 7:1-6

Numbers 6:22-27
So shall they put my name on the Israelites, and I will bless them.

Revelation 15:1-8
The temple was filled with smoke from the glory of God and from his power.

Acts 13:1-12
Set apart for me Barnabas and Saul for the work to which I have called them.

Proper 10 (Sunday between July 10 and 16) / Pentecost 9

1 Samuel 17:50-18:4
The soul of Jonathan was bound to the soul of David; and Jonathan loved him as his own soul.

Joshua 1:1-18
As I was with Moses, so I will be with you; I will not fail or forsake you. Be strong and courageous.

Romans 10:4-17
Faith comes from what is heard, and what is heard comes through the word of Christ.

Acts 21:3-15
I am ready not only to be bound but even to die in Jerusalem for the name of the Lord Jesus.

Proper 14 (Sunday between August 7 and 13) / Pentecost 13

2 Samuel 13:1-22
He would not listen to her; and being stronger than she, he forced her and lay with her. Then Amnon was sized with a great loathing for her; indeed, his loathing was even greater than the lust he had felt for her.

Judges 11:1-11, 29-40
Jephthah made a vow to the LORD, and said, “If you will give the Ammonites into my hand, then whoever comes out of the doors of my house to meet me, when I return victorious from the Ammonites, shall be the LORD’s, to be offered up by me as a burnt offering.

Romans 15:1-13

May the God of hope fill you with all joy and peace in believing, so that you may abound in hope by the power of the Holy Spirit.

2 Corinthians 11:21b-31

If I must boast, I will boast of the things that show my weakness.

Proper 18 (Sunday between September 4 and 10) / Pentecost 17

1 Kings 12:21-33

"You have gone up to Jerusalem long enough. Here are your gods, O Israel, who brought you up out of the land of Egypt."

Job 25:1-6; 27:1-6

How then can a mortal be righteous before God?

Acts 4:18-31

Whether it is right in God's sight to listen to you rather than to God, you must judge; for we cannot keep from speaking about what we have seen and heard.

Revelation 14:1-7,13

Blessed are the dead who from now on die in the Lord. "Yes," says the Spirit, "they will rest from their labors, for their deeds follow them."

Proper 22 (Sunday between October 2 and 8) / Pentecost 21

2 Kings 20:1-21

Days are coming when all that is in your house, and that which your ancestors have stored up until this day, shall be carried to Babylon; nothing shall be left, says the LORD.

Hosea 5:8-6:6

Come, let us return to the LORD; for it is he who has torn, and he will heal us; he has struck down, and he will bind us up.
[BCP Hosea 13:4-14]

Acts 12:1-17

Herod lay violent hands upon some who belonged to the church. He had James, the brother of John, killed with the sword.

1 Corinthians 2:6-16

We speak God's wisdom, secret and hidden, which God decreed before the ages for our glory.

Nehemiah 5:1-19
Remember for my good, O my God, all that I have done for this people.

or Ezra 1:1-11

Acts 20:7-12
On the first day of the week, when we met to break bread, Paul was holding a discussion with them; since he intended to leave the next day, he continued speaking until midnight.

Sirach [Ecclesiasticus] 36:1-22 [NSRV]
Have mercy, O Lord, on the people called by your name, on Israel, whom you have named your firstborn.

or Zephaniah 1:1-6

1 Corinthians 12:27-13:13
And now faith, hope, and love abide, these three; and the greatest of these is love.

Silence for meditation follows each reading.

RESPONSORY

Holy, holy, holy, the Lord God the Almighty, who was and is, and **is** to come!*
the whole earth is full **of** his glory.
The seraphim called to one another and said, Holy, holy holy is the **Lord** of hosts;*
the whole earth is full **of** his glory.

[LH: Rev. 4:8; Isa. 6:3]

Above the dome there was something like a throne, in appear**ance** like sapphire; and seated above the likeness of a throne was something that seemed like a **hu**man form.
I heard behind me the sound of **a** loud rumbling.*
Blessed be the glory of the Lord in its **dwell**ing place.
To the one seated on the throne and to the Lamb be blessing and honor and glory and might for ev**er** and ever!*
Blessed be the glory of the Lord in its **dwell**ing place.

[LH: Ezek. 1:26; 3:12; Rev. 5:13]

Monday of Week II

Antiphon to PSALM 123 *Ad te levavi oculos meos*

Our eyes look to the **LORD** our God,*
until he show **us** his mercy. [LH, PBO]

123 *The Lord, unfailing help of his people*

1 To you I lift **up** my eyes,*
to you enthroned **in** the heavens.

2 As the eyes of servants look to the hand **of** their masters,*
and the eyes of a maid to the hand **of** her mistress,

3 So our eyes look to the **LORD** our God,
until he show **us** his mercy.

4 Have mercy upon us, O **LORD**, have mercy,*
for we have had more than enough **of** contempt,

5 Too much of the scorn of the in**do**lent rich,*
and of the derision **of** the proud.

Antiphon Our eyes look to the **LORD** our God,*
until he show **us** his mercy.

Silence for meditation

Father in heaven, we look to you for all that we need: Look with favor on us, confound the scorn of the proud, and graciously show us your mercy; through Jesus Christ our Lord. [LHd, PHP]

+

Antiphon to PSALM 145 *Exaltabo te, Deus*

The LORD is faithful in **all** his words*
and merciful in **all** his deeds. [LH]

145 *Praise of God's majesty*

1 I will exalt you, O **God** my King,*
and bless your Name for ev**er** and ever.

2 Every day **will** I bless you*
and praise your Name for ev**er** and ever.

3 Great is the LORD and greatly **to** be praised;*
there is no end **to** his greatness.

4 One generation shall praise your works **to** another*
and shall de**clare** your power.

5 I will ponder the glorious splendor **of** your majesty*
and all your **mar**velous works.

6 They shall speak of the might of your **won**drous acts,*
and I will tell **of** your greatness.

7 They shall publish the remembrance of **your** great goodness;*
they shall sing of your **right**eous deeds.

8 The LORD is gracious and full **of** compassion,*
slow to anger and **of** great kindness.

9 The LORD is loving to **ev**eryone*
and his compassion is over **all** his works.

10 All your works praise **you**, O LORD,*
and your faithful **ser**vants bless you.

11 They make known the glory **of** your kingdom*
and speak **of** your power;

12 That the peoples may know **of** your power*
and the glorious splendor **of** your kingdom.

13 Your kingdom is an ever**last**ing kingdom;*
your dominion endures through**out** all ages.

14 The LORD is faithful in **all** his words*
and merciful in **all** his deeds.

15 The LORD upholds all **those** who fall;*
he lifts up those who **are** bowed down.

16 The eyes of all wait upon **you**, O LORD,*
and you give them their food **in** due season.

17 You open **wide** your hand*
and satisfy the needs of every **liv**ing creature.

18 The LORD is righteous in **all** his ways*
and loving in **all** his works.

19 The LORD is near to those who **call** upon him,*
to all who call up**on** him faithfully.

20 He fulfills the desire of **those** who fear him;*
he hears their **cry** and helps them.

21 The LORD preserves all **those** who love him,*
but he destroys **all** the wicked.

22 My mouth shall speak the praise **of** the LORD;*
let all flesh bless his holy Name for ev**er** and ever.

Antiphon The LORD is faithful in **all** his words*
and merciful in **all** his deeds.

Silence for meditation

Loving Father, you are faithful in your promises and tender in your compassion: Listen to our hymn of joy, and continue to satisfy the needs of all your creatures, that all flesh may bless your Name in your everlasting kingdom, where with your Son and the Holy Spirit you live and reign, now and for ever. [LBW]

+

Stand

THE HYMN is sung.

2 Wake and lift up thyself, my heart,
And with the angels bear thy part,
Who all night long unwearied sing
High praise to the eternal king.

3 All praise to thee, who safe hast kept
And hast refreshed me while I slept:
Grant, Lord, when I from death shall wake
I may of endless light partake.

4 Lord, I my vows to thee renew;
Disperse my sins as morning dew;
Guard my first springs of thought and will,
And with thyself my spirit fill.

5 Direct, control, suggest, this day,
All I design, or do, or say,
That all my powers, with all their might,
In thy sole glory may unite.

6 Praise God, from whom all blessings flow;
Praise him, all creatures here below;
Praise him above, ye heavenly host;
Praise Father, Son, and Holy Ghost. [SBH 202, LBW 269]

Text: Thomas Ken, 1637-1711
Tune: *Morning Hymn,* François H. Barthélémon, 1741-1808 LM

Sit

One or two LESSONS are read.

Year 1	Year 2
after Epiphany 2	
Isaiah 44:6-8, 21-23 I am the first and I am the last; besides me there is no god.	Genesis 8:6-22 I will never again curse the ground because of humankind, for the inclination of the human heart is evil from youth; nor will I ever again destroy every living creature as I have done.
Ephesians 4:1-16 There is one body and one Spirit, just as you were called to the one hope of your calling, one Lord, one faith, one baptism.	Hebrews 4:14-5:6 Let us therefore approach the throne of grace with boldness, so that we may receive mercy and find grace to help in time of need.
after Epiphany 6	
Isaiah 63:1-6 Who is this who comes from Edom, from Bozrah in garments stained crimson? Who is this so splendidly robed, marching in his great might?	Genesis 30:1-24 Rachel conceived and bore a son, and said, "God has taken away my reproach"; and she named him Joseph.

1 Timothy 1:1-17

The saying is sure and worthy of full acceptance, that Christ Jesus came into the world to save sinners–of whom I am the foremost.

1 John 1:1-10

God is light and in him there is no darkness at all.

after Proper 2 / after the Festival of the Holy Trinity

Ruth 1:1-18

Where you go, I will go; where you lodge, I will lodge; your people shall be my people, and your God my God. Where you die, I will die–there will I be buried.

Proverbs 3:11-20

The Lord by wisdom founded the earth; by understanding he established the heavens.

1 Timothy 1:1-17

To the King of the ages, immortal, invisible, the only God, be honor and glory forever and ever. Amen.

1 John 3:18-4:6

Little children, let us love, not in words and speech, but in truth and action.

after Proper 6 / Pentecost 5

1 Samuel 1:1-20

In due time Hannah conceived and bore a son. She named him Samuel, for she said," I have asked him of the LORD."

Numbers 9:15-23; 10:29-36

At the command of the LORD they would camp, and at the command of the LORD they would set out.

Acts 1:1-14

All these were constantly devoting themselves to prayer, together with certain women, including Mary the mother of Jesus, as well as his brothers.

Romans 1:1-15

Grace to you and peace from God our Father and the Lord Jesus Christ.

after Proper 10 / Pentecost 9

1 Samuel 18:5-16 (17-27a) 27b-3

When Saul realized that the LORD was with David, and that Saul's daughter Michal loved him, Saul was still more afraid of David. So Saul was David's enemy from that time forward.

Joshua 2:1-14

Our life for yours! If you do not tell this business of ours, then we will deal kindly and faithfully with you when the LORD gives us the land.

Acts 11:19-30

For the entire year they met with the church and taught a great many people, and it was in Antioch that the disciples were first called "Christians."

Romans 11:1-12

So too at the present time there is a remnant, chosen by grace.

after Proper 14 / Pentecost 13

2 Samuel 13:23-39

Let not my lord suppose that they have killed all the young men the king's sons; Amnon alone is dead. This has been determined by Absalom from the day Amnon raped his sister Tamar.

Judges 12:1-7

Whenever one of the fugitives of Ephraim said, "Let me go over," the men of Gilead would say to him, "Are you an Ephraimite?" When he said,"No," they said to him, "Then say Shibboleth," and he said "Sibboleth," for he could not pronounce it right. Then they seized him and killed him.

Acts 20:17-38

Now, as a captive to the Spirit, I am on my way to Jerusalem, not knowing what will happen to me there, except that the Holy Spirit testifies to me in every city that imprisonment and persecutions are waiting for me.

Acts 5:12-26

Go, stand in the temple and tell the people the whole message about this life.

after Proper 18 / Pentecost 17

1 Kings 13:1-10

While Jeroboam was standing by the altar to offer incense, a man of God came out of Judah by the word of the LORD to Bethel and proclaimed against the altar by the word of the LORD.

Job 32:1-10, 19-33:1, 19-28

Truly it is the spirit in a mortal, the breath of the Almighty, that makes for understanding. It is not the old that are wise, nor the aged that understand what is right.

Philippians 1:1-11

I am confident of this, that the one who began a good work among you will bring it to completion by the day of Jesus Christ.

Acts 13:44-52

When the Gentiles heard this, they were glad and praised the word of the Lord; and as many as had been destined for eternal life became believers.

after Proper 22 / Pentecost 21

2 Kings 21:1-18

I will stretch over Jerusalem the measuring line for Samaria, and the plummet for the house of Ahab; I will wipe Jerusalem as one wipes a dish, wiping it and turning it upside down.

Hosea 6:7-7:7

They do not consider that I remember all their wickedness. Now their deeds surround them, they are before my face [BCP: Hosea 14:1-9].

1 Corinthians 10:14-11:1

Because there is one Lord, we who are many are one body, for we all partake of the one bread.

Acts 22:30-23:11

Keep up your courage! For just as you have testified for me in Jerusalem, so you must bear witness also in Rome.

after Proper 26 / Pentecost 25

Nehemiah 6:1-19

So the wall was finished, and when all our enemies heard of it, all the nations around us were afraid and fell greatly in their own esteem; for they perceived that this work had been accomplished with the help of our God.

or Ezra 3:1-13

Sirach [Ecclesiasticus] 38:24-34a

The wisdom of the scribe depends on the opportunity of leisure; only the one who has little business can become wise.

or Zephaniah 1:7-13

Revelation 10:1-11

In the days when the seventh angel is to blow his trumpet, the mystery of God will be fulfilled, as he announced to his servants the prophets.

Revelation 14:1-13

Here is a call for the endurance of the saints, those who keep the commandments of God and hold fast to the faith of Jesus.

Silence for meditation follows each lesson.

RESPONSORY

The Lord says, As I was with Moses, so I will **be** with you.*
Be strong **and** courageous.
Do not be frightened or dismayed; for the Lord your God is with you wherev**er** you go.*
Be strong **and** courageous.
[LH: Joshua 1:5,9]

Owe no one anything, except to love one another; for the one who loves another has ful**filled** the law:*
therefore love is the
fulfilling **of** the law.
The whole law is summed up in a single commandment, "You shall love your neighbor **as** yourself";
therefore love is the
fulfilling **of** the law.
[LH: Rom. 13:8,10; Gal. 5:14]

Tuesday of Week II

Antiphon to PSALM 135 *Laudate nomen Domini*

The **LORD** is great;*
our LORD is a**bove** all gods. [LH]

135 *Hymn of praise*

1 Hallelujah!
Praise the Name **of** the LORD;*
give praise, you servants **of** the LORD,

2 You who stand in the house **of** the LORD,*
in the courts of the house **of** our God.

3 Praise the LORD, for the **LORD** is good;*
sing praises to his Name, for **it** is lovely.

4 For the LORD has chosen Jacob **for** himself*
and Israel for his **own** possession.

5 For I know that the **LORD** is great,*
and that our LORD is a**bove** all gods.

6 The LORD does whatever pleases him, in heaven **and** on earth,*
in the seas and **all** the deeps.

7 He brings up rain clouds from the ends **of** the earth;*
he sends out lightning with the rain,
and brings the winds out **of** his storehouse.

8 It was he who struck down the first**born** of Egypt,*
the firstborn of both **man** and beast.

9 He sent signs and wonders into the midst of **you**, O Egypt,*
against Pharaoh and **all** his servants.

10 He overthrew **man**y nations*
and put mighty **kings** to death:

11 Sihon, king of the Amorites,
and Og, the **king** of Bashan,*
and all the king**doms** of Canaan.

12 He gave their land to be **an** inheritance,*
an inheritance for Isra**el** his people.

13 O LORD, your Name is **ev**erlasting;*
your renown, O LORD, endures from **age** to age.

14 For the LORD gives his **peo**ple justice*
and shows compassion **to** his servants.

15 The idols of the heathen are sil**ver** and gold,*
the work of **hu**man hands.

16 They have mouths, but they **can**not speak;*
eyes have they, but they **can**not see.

17 They have ears, but they **can**not hear;*
neither is there any breath **in** their mouth.

18 Those who make **them** are like them,*
and so are all who put their **trust** in them.

19 Bless the LORD, O **house** of Israel;*
O house of Aaron, **bless** the LORD.

20 Bless the LORD, O **house** of Levi;*
you who fear the LORD, **bless** the LORD.

21 Blessed be the LORD **out** of Zion,*
who dwells in Jerusalem.
Hallelujah!

Antiphon The **LORD** is great;*
our LORD is a**bove** all gods.

Silence for meditation

Lord our God, by signs and wonders you have shattered the powers of darkness and your renown endures from age to age: Strengthen us in our pilgrimage, keep us from being deceived by idols, and bring us safely to our eternal inheritance; through Jesus Christ our Lord. [LHd, PHP]

+

Antiphon to PSALM 146 *Lauda, anima mea*

I will praise the LORD as long as I live. [LH]

146 *Praise of God's faithfulnes*

1 Hallelujah!
Praise the LORD, **O** my soul!*
I will praise the LORD as long as I live;
I will sing praises to my God while I **have** my being.

2 Put not your trust in rulers, nor in any **child** of earth,*
for there is no **help** in them.

3 When they breathe their last, they re**turn** to earth,*
and in that day **their** thoughts perish.

4 Happy are they who have the God of Jacob **for** their help!*
whose hope is in the **LORD** their God;

5 Who made heaven and earth, the seas, and all that **is** in them;*
who keeps his prom**ise** for ever;

6 Who gives justice to those who **are** oppressed,*
and food to **those** who hunger.

7 The LORD sets the prisoners free;
the LORD opens the eyes **of** the blind;*
the LORD lifts up those who **are** bowed down;

8 The LORD loves the righteous;
the LORD cares **for** the stranger;*
he sustains the orphan and widow,
but frustrates the way **of** the wicked.

9 The LORD shall **reign** for ever,*
your God, O Zion, throughout all generations.
Hallelujah!

Antiphon I will praise the LORD as long as I live.

Silence for meditation

God of glory and power, happy indeed are those who have put their trust in you: Shine the brightness of your light upon us, that we may love you always with a pure heart and praise you for ever; through your Son, Jesus Christ our Lord. [LH, LBW]

+

Stand

THE HYMN is sung.

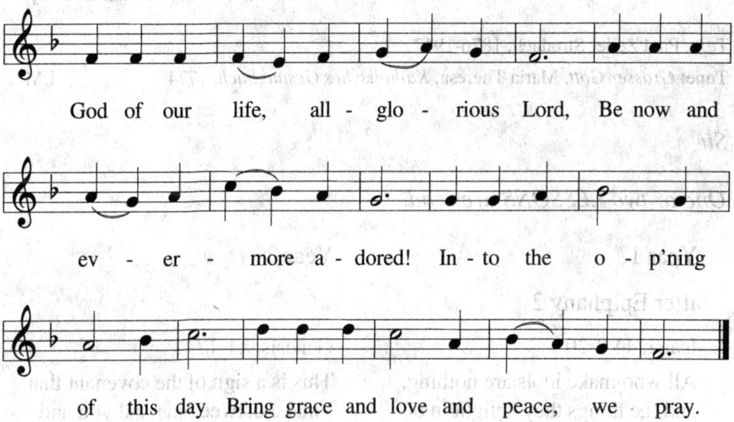

2 Make clear our path, that we may see
Where we must walk to be with thee,
And listen always for thy voice
That we may make thy way our choice.

3 Give help for doing every task,
Nor let us fail of thee to ask
For grace in speech, for love in deed,
From wrongful actions to be freed.

4 Inspire us now to do some deed
For other's good to help in need;
To rescue and to lead from shame;
To bless with comfort in thy Name.

5 Thus may we walk our way with thee,
Enabled by thy grace to be
A little less unworthy, Lord,
Of thee our friend, our Holy God.

6 At eventide then will we raise
A grateful heart in songs of praise;
And worship thee, and thy dear Son,
With God the Spirit, ever one. [SBH 209, LBW 270]

Text: Paul Zeller Strodach, 1876-1947
Tune: *Grosser Gott,* Maria Theresa, *Katholisches Gesangbuch,* 1774 LM

Sit

One or two LESSONS are read.

Year 1	Year 2
after Epiphany 2	
Isaiah 44:9-20	Genesis 9:1-17
All who make idols are nothing, and the things they delight in do not profit; their witnesses neither see nor know.	This is a sign of the covenant that I make between me and you and every living creature that is with you, for all future generations: I have set my bow in the clouds.

Ephesians 4:17-32

Do not grieve the Holy Spirit of God, with which you were marked with a seal for the day of redemption.

Hebrews 5:7-14

In the days of his flesh, Jesus offered up prayers and supplications, with loud cries and tears, to the one who was able to save him from death, and he was heard because of his reverent submission.

after Epiphany 6

Isaiah 63:7-14

I will recount the gracious deeds of the LORD, the praiseworthy acts of the LORD, because of all that the LORD has done for us.

Genesis 31:1-24

The LORD said to Jacob, "Return to the land of your ancestors and to your kindred, and I will be with you."

1 Timothy 1:18-2:8 (9-15)

I urge that supplications, prayers, intercessions, and thanksgivings be made for everyone.

1 John 2:1-11

If anyone does sin, we have an advocate with the Father, Jesus Christ the righteous; and he is the atoning sacrifice for our sins, and not for ours only but also for the sins of the whole world.

after Proper 2 / after the Festival of the Holy Trinity

Ruth 1:19-2:13

May the LORD reward you for your deeds, and may you have a full reward from the LORD, the God of Israel, under whose wings you have come for refuge!

Proverbs 4:1-27

Get wisdom; get insight: do not forget, nor turn away from the words of my mouth. Do not forsake her, and she will keep you; love her, and she will guard you.

1 Timothy 1:18-2:8

I urge that supplications, prayers, intercessions, and thanksgivings be made for everyone.

1 John 4:7-21

Since God loved us so much, we also ought to love one another.

after Proper 6 / Pentecost 5

1 Samuel 1:21-2:11

For this child I prayed; and the LORD has granted me the petition that I made to him. Therefore I have lent him to the LORD.

Numbers 11:1-23

Now our strength is dried up, and there is nothing at all but this manna to look at.

Acts 1:15-26

The lot fell on Matthias; and he was added to the eleven apostles.

Romans 1:16-25

I am not ashamed of the gospel; it is the power of God for salvation to everyone who has faith.

after Proper 10 / Pentecost 9

1 Samuel 19:1-18 (19-24)

Saul sent messengers to David's house to keep watch over him, planning to kill him in the morning.

Joshua 2:15-24

Truly the LORD has given all the land into our hands; moreover all the inhabitants of the land melt in fear before us.

Acts 12:1-17

He had James, the brother of John, killed with a sword. After he saw it pleased the Jews, he proceeded to arrest Peter also.

Romans 11:13-24

Note then the kindness and the severity of God: severity toward those who have fallen, but God's kindness toward you, provided you continue in his kindness.

after Proper 14 / Pentecost 13

2 Samuel 14:1-20

God will not take away a life; he will devise plans so as not to keep an outcast banished forever from his presence.

Judges 13:1-15

No razor is to come on his head, for the boy shall be a nazarite to God from birth. It is he who shall begin to deliver Israel from the hand of the Philistines.

Acts 21:1-14

I am ready not only to be bound but even to die in Jerusalem for the name of the Lord Jesus.

Acts 5:27-42

We must obey God rather than any human authority.

after Proper 18 / Pentecost 17

1 Kings 16:23-34

Hiel of Bethel built Jericho; he laid its foundation at the cost of Abiram his firstborn, and set up the gates at the cost of his youngest son.

Job 29:1-20

Oh, that I were as in the months of old, as in the days when God watched over me.

Philippians 1:12-30

To me living is Christ and dying is gain.

Acts 14:1-18

He has not left himself without a witness in doing good–giving you rains from heaven and fruitful seasons, and filling you with food and your hearts with joy.

after Proper 22 / Pentecost 21

2 Kings 22:1-13

Great is the wrath of the LORD that is kindled against us, because our ancestors did not obey the words of this book, to do according to all that is written concerning us.

Hosea 7:8-16

Destruction to them, for they have rebelled against me! I would redeem them, but they speak lies against me.
[BCP: Micah 1:1-9]

1 Corinthians 11:2 (3-16) 17-22

I commend you because you remember me in everything and maintain the traditions just as I handed them on to you.

Acts 23:12-24

"We have strictly bound ourselves by an oath to taste no food until we have killed Paul."

after Proper 26 / Pentecost 25

Nehemiah 12:27-31a, 42b-47

At the dedication of the wall of Jerusalem they sought out the Levites in all their places, to bring them to Jerusalem to celebrate the

Sirach [Ecclesiasticus] 43:1-22

The sun, when it appears, proclaims as it rises what a marvelous instrument it is, the work of the Most High.

dedication with rejoicing, with thanksgivings and with singing, with cymbals, harps, and lyres.
or Ezra 4:7, 11-24

Revelation 11:1-19
The kingdom of the world has become the kingdom of our Lord and of his Messiah.

or Zephaniah 1:14-18

Revelation 14:14-15:8
Just and true are your ways, King of the nations!

Silence for meditation follows each reading.

RESPONSORY

Be strong and bold because it is the Lord your God who **goes** with you.*
God goes before you;
do not fear or **be** dismayed.
The Lord will be your confidence and will keep your foot from **be**ing caught.*
God goes before you;
do not fear or **be** dismayed.
[LH: Deut. 31:6,8; Prov. 3:26]

God make you complete in everything good so that you may **do** his will,*
working among us that
which is pleasing in his
sight, through **Je**sus Christ.
May he open your heart to his law and his commandments, and may **he** bring peace,*
working among us that
which is pleasing in his
sight, through **Je**sus Christ.
[LH: Heb. 13:21; 2 Macc. 1:4]

Wednesday of Week II

Antiphon to PSALM 13 *Usquequo Domine oblivisceris*

My heart is joyful because of your saving help. [LH, PBO]

13 *A confident appeal in anxiety*

1 How long, O LORD?
will you forget **me** for ever?*
how long will you hide your **face** from me?

2 How long shall I have perplexity in my mind,
and grief in my heart, day **af**ter day?*
how long shall my enemy triumph **o**ver me?

3 Look upon me and answer me, **O LORD** my God;*
give light to my eyes, lest I **sleep** in death;

4 Lest my enemy say, "I have prevailed **o**ver him,"*
and my foes rejoice that **I** have fallen.

5 But I put my trust **in** your mercy;*
my heart is joyful because of your **sav**ing help.

6 I will sing to the LORD, for he has dealt **with** me richly;*
I will praise the Name of the **Lord** Most High.

Antiphon My heart is joyful because of your saving help.

Silence for meditation.

Lord our God, by the light of the resurrection of your Son you have helped us see that we shall not sleep in death for ever: Look upon the sufferings of your Church, so that our hearts may rejoice in your saving help and sing you songs of praise; through your Son, Jesus Christ our Lord. [LH, LBW]

+

Antiphon to PSALM 147 part i *Laudate Dominum*

How pleasant it is to honor God with praise! [LH, PBO]

147 *Praise of God who maintains the world*

1 Hallelujah!
How good it is to sing praises **to** our God!*
how pleasant it is to honor **him** with praise!

2 The LORD re**builds** Jerusalem;*
he gathers the ex**iles** of Israel.

3 He heals the **bro**kenhearted*
and binds **up** their wounds.

4 He counts the number **of** the stars*
and calls them all **by** their names.

5 Great is our LORD and migh**ty** in power;*
there is no limit **to** his wisdom.

6 The LORD lifts **up** the lowly,*
but casts the wicked **to** the ground,

7 Sing to the LORD **with** thanksgiving;*
make music to our God up**on** the harp.

8 He covers the heav**ens** with clouds*
and prepares rain **for** the earth;

9 He makes grass to grow up**on** the mountains*
and green plants to **serve** mankind.

10 He provides food for **flocks** and herds*
and for the young ravens **when** they cry.

11 He is not impressed by the might **of** a horse;*
he has no pleasure in the strength **of** a man;

12 But the LORD has pleasure in **those** who fear him,*
in those who await his **gra**cious favor.

Antiphon How pleasant it is to honor God with praise!

Silence for meditation

God our Father, great builder of the heavenly Jerusalem, you know the number of the stars and call each of them by name: Heal hearts that are broken, gather those who have been scattered, and enrich us all from the plenitude of your eternal wisdom, Jesus Christ our Lord. [LH, LBW]

+

Stand
THE HYMN is sung.

2 Sun of our life, thy quickening ray
Sheds on our path the glow of day;
Star of our hope, thy softened light
Cheers the long watches of the night.

3 Our midnight is thy smile withdrawn,
Our noontide is thy gracious dawn,
Our rainbow arch thy mercy's sign;
All, save the clouds of sin, are thine.

4 Lord of all life, below, above,
Whose light is truth, whose warmth is love,
Before thy ever-blazing throne
We ask no luster of our own.

5 Grant us thy truth to make us free,
And kindling hearts that yearn for thee,
Till all thy living altars claim
One holy light, one heavenly flame. [SBH 170; H82 419]

Text: Oliver Wendell Holmes, 1809-1894
Tune: *Louvain*, Virgil Corydon Taylor, 1817-1891 LM

Sit

One or two LESSONS are read.

Year 1	Year 2
after Epiphany 2	
Isaiah 44:24-45:7	Genesis 9:18-29
I form light and create darkness, I make weal and create woe; I the LORD do all these things.	Noah, a man of the soil, was the first to plant a vineyard.
Ephesians 5:1-14	Hebrews 6:1-12
Live in love, as Christ loved us and gave himself up for us, a fragrant offering and sacrifice to God.	We want each one of you to show the same diligence so as to realize the full assurance of hope to the very end.
after Epiphany 6	
Isaiah 63:15-64:9	Genesis 31:25-50
O that you would tear open the heavens and come down, so that the mountains would quake at your presence.	Remember that God is witness between you and me.

1 Timothy 3:1-16

Without any doubt, the mystery of our religion is great: He was revealed in the flesh, vindicated in the spirit, seen by angels, proclaimed among the Gentiles, believed in throughout the world, taken up in glory.

1 John 2:12-17

The world and its desire are passing away, but those who do the will of God live forever.

after Proper 2 / after the Festival of the Holy Trinity

Ruth 2:14-23

Stay close to my servants, until they have finished all my harvest.

Proverbs 6:1-19

Go to the ant, you lazybones; consider its ways, and be wise.

1 Timothy 3:1-16

Without any doubt, the mystery of our religion is great: He was revealed in the flesh, vindicated in the spirit, seen by angels, proclaimed among the Gentiles, believed in throughout the world, taken up in glory.

1 John 5:1-12

This is the victory that conquers the world, our faith.

after Proper 6 / Pentecost 5

1 Samuel 2:12-26

The boy Samuel grew up in the presence of the LORD.

Numbers 11:24-33 (34-35)

The LORD came down in a cloud and spoke to Moses, and took some of the spirit that was on him and put it on the seventy elders.

Acts 2:1-21

All of them were filled with the Holy Spirit and began to speak in other languages, as the Spirit gave them ability.

Romans 1:28-2:11

Do you not realize that God's kindness is meant to lead you to repentance?

after Proper 10 / Pentecost 9

1 Samuel 20:1-23

Jonathan made a covenant with the house of David, saying, "May the LORD seek out the enemies of David."

Joshua 3:1-13

When the soles of the feet of the priests who bear the ark of the LORD, the Lord of all the earth, rest in the waters of the Jordan, the waters of the Jordan flowing from above shall be cut off.

Acts 12:18-25

After completing the mission Barnabas and Saul returned to Jerusalem and brought with them John, whose other name was Mark.

Romans 11:25-36

The gifts and the calling of God are irrevocable.

after Proper 14 / Pentecost 13

2 Samuel 14:21-33

Absalom came to the king and prostrated himself with his face to the ground before the king; and the king kissed Absalom.

Judges 13:15-24

Manoah said to his wife, "We shall surely die, for we have seen God."

Acts 21:15-26

As for the Gentiles who have become believers, we have sent a letter with our judgment that they should abstain from what has been sacrificed to idols and from blood and from what is strangled and from fornication.

Acts 6:1-15

They could not withstand the wisdom and the spirit with which Stephen spoke.

after Proper 18 / Pentecost 17

1 Kings 17:1-24

The jar of meal was not emptied, neither did the jug of oil fail, according to the word of the LORD that he spoke by Elijah.

Job 29:1; 30:1-2, 16-31

My inward parts are in turmoil, and are never still; days of affliction come to meet me.

Philippians 2:1-11

Do nothing from selfish ambition or conceit, but in humility regard others as better than yourselves.

Acts 14:19-28

They called the church together and related all that God had done with them, and how he had opened the door of faith for the Gentiles.

after Proper 22 / Pentecost 21

2 Kings 22:14-23:3

The king went up to the house of the LORD, and with him went all the people of Judah, all the inhabitants of Jerusalem, the priests, the prophets, and all the people, both small and great; he read in their hearing all the words of the book of the covenant that had been found in the house of the LORD.

Hosea 8:1-14

Israel has forgotten his Maker, and built palaces; and Judah has multiplied fortified cities; but I will send a fire upon his cities, and it shall devour his strongholds.

[BCP: Micah 2:1-13]

1 Corinthians 11:23-34

As often as you eat this bread and drink the cup, you proclaim the Lord's death until he comes.

Acts 23:23-35

Provide mounts for Paul to ride, and take him safely to Felix the governor.

after Proper 26 / Pentecost 25

Nehemiah 13:4-22

I commanded the Levites that they should purify themselves and come and guard the gates, to keep the sabbath day holy. Remember this also in my favor, O my God, and spare me according to the greatness of your steadfast love.

or Haggai 1:1-2:9

Sirach [Ecclesiasticus] 43:23-33

Where can we find the strength to praise him? For he is greater than all his works.

or Zephaniah 2:1-15

Revelation 12:1-12

War broke out in heaven; Michael and his angels fought against the dragon.

Revelation 16:1-11

I heard a loud voice from the temple telling the seven angels, "Go and pour out on the earth the seven bowls of the wrath of God."

Silence for meditation follows each reading.

RESPONSORY

God chose what is weak in the world to shame the strong so that no one might boast in the presence **of** the Lord,*

for power is made per**fect** in weakness.

God chose what is low and despised in the world, things that are not, to reduce to nothing **things** that are,*

for power is made per**fect** in weakness.

[LH: 1 Cor. 1:27,29; 2 Cor. 12:9; 1 Cor. 1:28]

All of you, clothe yourselves with humility in your dealings with **one** another.*

Learn from me, says the Lord, for I am gentle and hum**ble** in heart.

For God opposes the proud, but gives grace **to** the humble.*

Learn from me, says the Lord, for I am gentle and hum**ble** in heart.

[LH: 1 Peter 5:5; Matt. 11:29]

Thursday of Week II

Antiphon to PSALM 128 *Beati omnes*

The LORD bless **you** from Zion*
all the days **of** your life. [LH, PBO]

128 *The blessings of home: a pilgrimage song*

1 Happy are they all who **fear** the LORD,*
and who follow **in** his ways!

2 You shall eat the fruit **of** your labor;*
happiness and prosperity **shall** be yours.

3 Your wife shall be like a fruitful vine with**in** your house,*
your children like olive shoots round a**bout** your table.

4 The man who **fears** the LORD*
shall thus in**deed** be blessed.

5 The LORD bless **you** from Zion,*
and may you see the prosperity of Jerusalem all the days
of your life.

6 May you live to see your **chil**dren's children;*
may peace be **up**on Israel.

Antiphon The LORD bless **you** from Zion*
all the days **of** your life.

Silence for meditation.

Lord Jesus, from your opened side your bride, the Church, was formed, and sanctified in your cleansing blood: Make your Church a fruitful vine, with many children who will rejoice with you at your table and celebrate your goodness now and for ever. [LHd, LBW]

+

Antiphon to PSALM 147 part ii *Lauda, Jerusalem, Dominum*

Praise the LORD, O Jerusalem. [LH]

147 *Praise of God's personal care of Israel*

13 Worship the LORD, **O** Jerusalem;*
praise your **God**, O Zion;

14 For he has strengthened the bars **of** your gates;*
he has blessed your chil**dren** within you.

15 He has established peace **on** your borders;*
he satisfies you with the **fin**est wheat.

16 He sends out his command **to** the earth,*
and his word runs **very** swiftly.

17 He gives **snow** like wool;*
he scatters hoar**frost** like ashes.

18 He scatters his **hail** like bread crumbs;*
who can stand a**gainst** his cold?

19 He sends forth his **word** and melts them;*
he blows with his wind, and the **wat**ers flow.

20 He declares his **word** to Jacob,*
his statutes and his judg**ments** to Israel.

21 He has not done so to any **oth**er nation;*
to them he has not revealed his judgments.
Hallelujah!

Antiphon Praise the LORD, O Jerusalem.

Silence for meditation

Almighty God, through your Church, generously endowed with gifts of grace and fortified by the Holy Spirit, you send out your Word to all nations: Strengthen your Church with heavenly food, make it dauntless in faith, and multiply its children, that with joy we may celebrate your love at the altar on high; through Jesus Christ our Lord. [LH]

+

Stand

THE HYMN is sung.

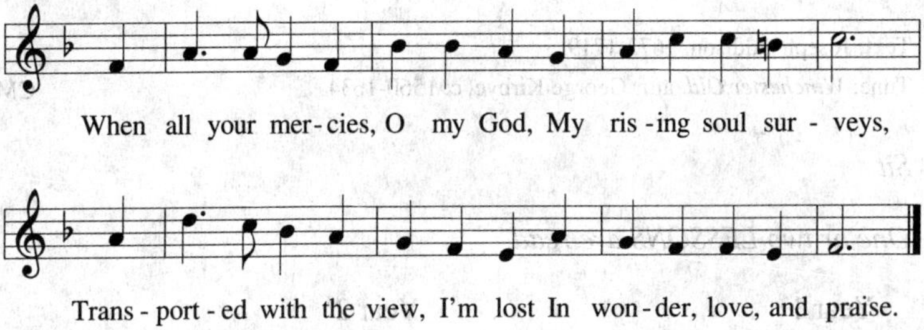

2 O how shall words with equal warmth
The gratitude declare
That glows within my fervent heart?
But you can read it there.

3 Unnumbered comforts to my soul
Your tender care bestowed,
Before my infant heart conceived
From whom these comforts flowed.

4 Ten thousand thousand precious gifts
My daily thanks employ;
Nor is the least a cheerful heart
That tastes those gifts with joy.

5 Through every period of my life
Your goodness I'll pursue,
And after death, in distant worlds,
The glorious theme renew.

6 When nature fails, and day and night
Divide your works no more,
My ever grateful heart, O Lord,
Your mercies shall adore.

7 Through all eternity, to you
A joyful song I'll raise;
But oh, eternity's too short
To utter all your praise! [LBW 264, SBH 440, H82 415]

Text: Joseph Addison, 1672-1719
Tune: *Winchester Old,* attr. George Kirbye, c. 1560-1634 CM

Sit

One or two LESSONS are read.

Year 1	Year 2
after Epiphany 2	
Isaiah 45:5-17	Genesis 11:1-9
Shower, O heavens, from above, and let the skies rain down righteousness; let the earth open, that salvation may spring up.	Come, let us build ourselves a city, and a tower with its top in the heavens, and let us make a name for ourselves.
Ephesians 5:15-33	Hebrews 6:13-20
Do not get drunk with wine, for that is debauchery; but be filled with the Spirit.	We have this hope, a sure and steadfast anchor of the soul, a hope that enters the inner shrine behind the curtain, where Jesus, a forerunner on our behalf, has entered.

after Epiphany 6

Isaiah 65:1-12
I was ready to be sought out by those who did not ask, to be found by those who did not seek me.

Genesis 32:3-21
Jacob thought, "I may appease him with the present that goes ahead of me, and afterwards I shall see his face; perhaps he will accept me."

1 Timothy 4:1-16
Everything created by God is good, and nothing is to be rejected, provided it is received with thanksgiving.

1 John 2:18-29
And now, little children, abide in him, so that when he is revealed we may have confidence and not be put to shame before him at his coming.

after Proper 2 / after the Festival of the Holy Trinity

Ruth 3:1-18
My daughter, do not be afraid, I will do for you all that you ask, for all the assembly of my people know that you are a worthy woman.

Proverbs 7:1-27
Say to wisdom, "You are my sister," and call insight your intimate friend.

1 Timothy 4:1-16
Everything created by God is good, and nothing is to be rejected, provided it is received with thanksgiving.

1 John 5:13-21
I write these things to you who believe in the name of the Son of God, so that you may know that you have eternal life.

after Proper 6 / Pentecost 5

1 Samuel 2:27-36
I will raise up for myself a faithful priest, who shall do according to what is in my heart and in my mind.

Numbers 12:1-16
With him I speak face to face–clearly, not in riddles; and he beholds the form of the LORD.

Acts 2:22-36

God raised him up, having freed him from death, because it was impossible for him to be held in its power.

Romans 2:12-24

When Gentiles, who do not possess the law, do instinctively what the law requires, these, though not having the law, are a law to themselves.

after Proper 10 / Pentecost 9

1 Samuel 20:24-42

Jonathan rose from the table in fierce anger and ate no food on the second day of the month, for he was grieved for David, and because his father had disgraced him.

Joshua 3:14-4:7

While all Israel were crossing over on dry ground, the priests who bore the ark of the covenant of the LORD stood on dry ground in the middle of the Jordan, until the entire nation finished crossing over the Jordan.

Acts 13:1-12

The Holy Spirit said, "Set apart for me Barnabas and Saul for the work to which I have called them."

Romans 12:1-8

We, who are many, are one body in Christ, and individually we are members one of another.

after Proper 14 / Pentecost 13

2 Samuel 15:1-18

The conspiracy grew in strength, and the people with Absalom kept increasing.

Judges 14:1-19

The spirit of the Lord rushed on Samson, and he went down to Ashkelon. He killed thirty men of the town, took their spoil, and gave the festal garments to those who had explained the riddle.

Acts 21:27-36

Then the tribune came, arrested Paul, and ordered him to be bound with two chains; he inquired who he was and what he had done.

Acts 6:15-7:16

All who sat in the council looked intently at Stephen, and they saw that his face was like the face of an angel.

after Proper 18 / Pentecost 17

1 Kings 18:1-19

I have not troubled Israel; but you have, and your father's house, because you have forsaken the commandments of the LORD and followed the Baals.

Job 29:1; 31:1-23

Does he not see my ways, and number all my steps?

Philippians 2:12-30

Work out your own salvation in fear and trembling; for it is God who is at work in you, enabling you both to will and to work for his good pleasure.

Acts 15:1-11

God, who knows the human heart, testified to them by giving them the Holy Spirit, just as he did to us.

after Proper 22 / Pentecost 21

2 Kings 23:4-25

Before Josiah there was no king like him, who turned to the LORD with all his heart, with all his soul, and with all his might, according to all the law of Moses; nor did any like him arise after him.

Hosea 9:1-9

The days of punishment have come, the days of recompense have come; Israel cries,"The prophet is a fool, the man of the spirit is mad!" Because of your great iniquity, your hostility is great.
[BCP Micah 3:1-8]

1 Corinthians 12:1-11

All these are activated by one and the same Spirit, who allots to each one individually just as the Spirit chooses.

Acts 24:1-23

This I admit to you, that according to the Way, which they call a sect, I worship the God of our ancestors, believing everything laid down according to the law or written in the prophets.

after Proper 26 / Pentecost 25

Ezra 7:(1-10) 11-26

Whatever is commanded by the God of heaven, let it be done with zeal for the house of the God of heaven, or wrath will come upon the realm of the king and his heirs.

or Zechariah 1:7-17

Sirach [Ecclesiasticus] 44:1-15

Their bodies are buried in peace, but their name lives on generation after generation.

or Zephaniah 3:1-7

Revelation 14:1-13

Here is a call for the endurance of the saints, those who keep the commandments of God and hold fast to the faith of Jesus.

Revelation 16:12-21

The cities of the nations fell. God remembered great Babylon and gave her the wine-cup of the fury of his wrath. And every island fled away, and no mountains were to be found.

Silence for meditation follows each reading.

RESPONSORY

When you search for me, **you** will find me,*
if you seek me with **all** your heart.
I will let you find me,
says the Lord,*
and I will bring you **back** from exile.
Search, and **you** will find;*
knock, and the door will be **opened** for you.
I will let you find me,
says the Lord,*
and I will bring you **back** from exile.

[LH: Jer. 29:13-14; Matt. 7:7]

Christ Jesus became for us wisdom from God and our righteousness and sanctification **and** redemption,*
in order that, as it is written,
let the one who boasts
boast **of** the Lord.
From his fullness we have all received, grace **up**on grace;*
in order that, as it is written,
let the one who boasts
boast **of** the Lord.

[LH: 1 Cor. 1:30-31; John 1:16]

Friday of Week II

Antiphon to PSALM 129 *Saepe expugnaverunt*

My oppressors will not prevail against me. [LH, PBO]

129 *Against the enemies of Zion: a pilgrimage song*

1 "Greatly have they oppressed me **since** my youth,"*
let Isra**el** now say;

2 "Greatly have they oppressed me **since** my youth,*
but they have not pre**vailed** against me."

3 The plowmen plowed up**on** my back*
and made their **fur**rows long.

4 The LORD, the **Right**eous One,*
has cut the cords **of** the wicked.

5 Let them be put to shame **and** thrown back,*
all those who are ene**mies** of Zion.

6 Let them be like grass up**on** the housetops,*
which withers before it **can** be plucked;

7 Which does not fill the hand **of** the reaper,*
nor the bosom of him who **binds** the sheaves;

8 So that those who go by say not so much as,
"The LORD **pros**per you.*
We wish you well in the Name **of** the LORD."

Antiphon My oppressors will not prevail against me.

Silence for meditation

Lord Jesus, when our sins had plowed long furrows on your back, your death broke the bonds of sin and Satan for ever: Bless your Church, wounded in its members, and strengthen it by your power and grace, that it may praise you now and for ever. [LH, LBW]

+

Antiphon to PSALM 148 *Laudate Dominum*

Praise the LORD **from** the heavens;*
praise the LORD **from** the earth. [LH]

148 *Cosmic praise*

1 Hallelujah!
Praise the LORD **from** the heavens;*
praise him **in** the heights.

2 Praise him, all you an**gels** of his;*
praise him, **all** his host.

3 Praise him, **sun** and moon;*
praise him, all you **shin**ing stars.

4 Praise him, heav**en** of heavens,*
and you waters a**bove** the heavens.

5 Let them praise the Name **of** the LORD;*
for he commanded, and they **were** created.

6 He made them stand fast for ev**er** and ever;*
he gave them a law which shall not **pass** away.

7 Praise the LORD **from** the earth,*
you sea-monsters **and** all deeps;

8 Fire and hail, **snow** and fog,*
tempestuous wind, do**ing** his will;

9 Mountains **and** all hills,*
fruit trees **and** all cedars;

10 Wild beasts **and** all cattle,*
creeping things and **wing**èd birds;

11 Kings of the earth **and** all peoples,*
princes and all rulers **of** the world;

12 Young **men** and maidens,*
old and **young** together.

13 Let them praise the Name **of** the LORD,*
for his Name only is exalted,
his splendor is over **earth** and heaven.

14 He has raised up strength for his people
and praise for all his **loy**al servants,*
the children of Israel, a people who are near him.
Hallelujah!

Antiphon Praise the LORD **from** the heavens;*
praise the LORD **from** the earth.

Silence for meditation

God Most High, by your Word your created a wondrous universe, and through your Spirit you breathed into it the breath of life: Accept creation's hymn of praise from our lips, and let the praise that is sung in heaven resound in the heart of every creature on earth, to the glory of the Father, and the Son, and the Holy Spirit, now and for ever. [LH, LBW]

+

Stand

THE HYMN is sung.

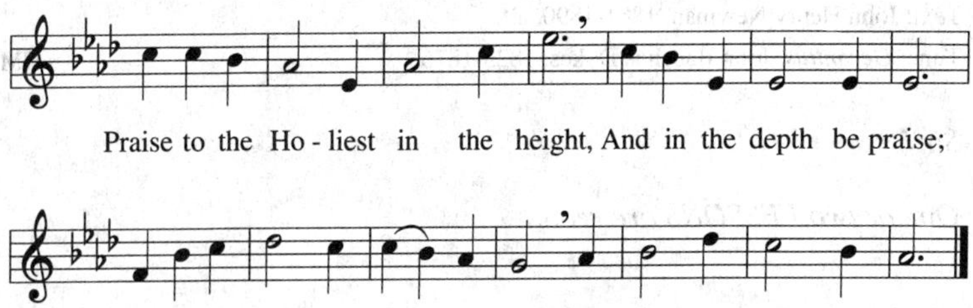

2 O loving wisdom of our God!
When all was sin and shame,
A second Adam to the fight
And to the rescue came.

3 O wisest love! that flesh and blood
Which did in Adam fail,
Should strive afresh against the foe,
Should strive, and should prevail;

4 And that a higher gift than grace
Should flesh and blood refine,
God's presence and God's very self
And essence all divine.

5 O generous love! that he who smote
For us our deadly foe,
The double agony in flesh
For us should undergo.

6 And in the garden secretly
And on the cross on high,
Should teach his kindred, and inspire
To suffer and to die.

7 Praise to the holiest in the height,
And in the depth be praise;
In all his words most wonderful,
Most sure in all his ways. [SBH 411; H82 445]

Text: John Henry Newman, 1801-1890, alt.
Tune: *Gerontius,* John Bacchus Dykes, 1823-1876 CM

Sit

One or two LESSONS are read.

Year 1

Year 2

after Epiphany 2

Isaiah 45:18-25
Turn to me and be saved, all the ends of the earth! For I am God, and there is no other.

Genesis 11:27-12:8
The LORD said to Abram, "Go from your country and your kindred and your father's house to the land that I will show you. I will make of you a great nation, and I will bless you, and make your name great."

Ephesians 6:1-9
Whatever good we do, we will receive the same again from the Lord, whether we are slaves or free.

Hebrews 7:1-17
You are a priest forever, according to the order of Melchizedek.

after Epiphany 6

Isaiah 65:17-25
I will rejoice in Jerusalem, and delight in my people; no more shall the sound of weeping be heard in it, or the cry of distress.

Genesis 32:22-33:17
Truly to see your face is like seeing the face of God–since you have received me with such favor.

1 Timothy 5:(1-16) 17-22 (23-25)
Let the elders who rule well be considered worthy of double honor, especially those who labor in preaching and teaching.

1 John 3:1-10
Beloved, we are God's children now; what we will be has not yet been revealed. What we do know is this: when he is revealed, we will be like him, for we will see him as he is.

after Proper 2 / after the Festival of the Holy Trinity

Ruth 4:1-22

May the LORD make the woman who is coming into your house like Rachel and Leah, who together built up the house of Israel. May you produce children in Ephrathah and bestow a name in Bethlehem.

Proverbs 8:1-21

Wisdom is better than jewels, and all that you desire cannot compare to her.

1 Timothy 5:17-22 (23-25)

Let the elders who rule well be considered worthy of double honor, especially those who labor in preaching and teaching.

2 John 1-13

This is love, that we walk according to his commandments.

after Proper 6 / Pentecost 5

1 Samuel 3:1-21

Go, lie down; and if he calls you, you shall say, "Speak, LORD, for your servant is listening."

Numbers 13:1-3, 21-30

We came to the land to which you sent us; it flows with milk and honey.

Acts 2:37-47

They devoted themselves to the apostles' teaching and fellowship, to the breaking of bread and the prayers.

Romans 2:25-3:8

A person is a Jew who is one inwardly, and real circumcision is a matter of the heart–it is spiritual and not literal.

after Proper 10 / Pentecost 9

1 Samuel 21:1-15

I did not bring my sword or my weapons with me, because the king's business required haste.

Joshua 4:19-5:1, 10-15

The manna ceased on the day they ate the produce of the land, and the Israelites no longer had manna; they ate the crops of the land of Canaan that year.

Acts 13:13-25

Of this man's posterity God has brought to Israel a savior, Jesus, as he promised.

Romans 12:9-21

Do not be overcome by evil, but overcome evil with good.

after Proper 14 / Pentecost 13

2 Samuel 15:19-37

As the LORD lives, and as my lord the king lives, wherever my lord the king may be, whether for death or for life, there also your servant will be.

Judges 14:20-15:20

Samson said to them, "If this is what you do, I swear I will not stop until I have taken revenge on you." He struck them down hip and thigh with great slaughter.

Acts 21:37-22:16

The God of our ancestors has chosen you to know his will, to see the Righteous One and to hear his own voice; for you will be his witness to all the world of what you have seen and heard.

Acts 7:17-29

As the time drew near for the fulfillment of the promise that God had made to Abraham, our people in Egypt increased and multiplied.

after Proper 18 / Pentecost 17

1 Kings 18:20-40

Answer me, O LORD, answer me, so that this people may know that you, O LORD, are God, and that you have turned their hearts back.

Job 29:1; 31:24-40

Oh, that I had one to hear me! (Here is my signature! let the Almighty answer me!) Oh, that I had the indictment written by my adversary!

Philippians 3:1-16

I regard everything as loss because of the surpassing value of knowing Christ Jesus my Lord.

Acts 15:12-21

In every city, for generations past, Moses has had those who proclaimed him, for he has been read aloud every sabbath in the synagogues.

after Proper 22 / Pentecost 21

2 Kings 23:36-24:17

Nebuchadnezzar carried off all the treasures of the house of the LORD, and the treasures of the king's house; he cut in pieces all the vessels of gold in the temple which King Solomon of Israel had made, all this as the LORD had foretold.

Hosea 9:10-17

Because of the wickedness of their deeds I will drive them out of my house. I will love them no more; all their officials are rebels. [BCP: Micah 3:9-4:5]

1 Corinthians 12:12-26

Just as the body is one and has many members, and all the members of the body, though many, are one body, so it is with Christ.

Acts 24:24-25:12

I appeal to the emperor.

after Proper 26 / Pentecost 25

Ezra 7:27-28; 8:21-36

At that time those who had come from captivity, the returned exiles, offered burnt offerings to the God of Israel.

or Ezra 5:1-17

Sirach [Ecclesiasticus] 50:1, 11-24

And now bless the God of all, who everywhere works great wonders, who fosters our growth from birth, and deals with us according to his mercy.

or Zephaniah 3:8-13

Revelation 15:1-8

Great and amazing are your deeds, Lord God the Almighty! Just and true are your ways, King of the nations!

Revelation 17:1-18

The Lamb will conquer them, for he is Lord of lords and King of kings, and those with him are called chosen and faithful.

Silence for meditation follows each reading.

RESPONSORY

God reconciled us to him**self** through Christ*
  and has given us the ministry of recon**cili**ation.
He did not withhold his own Son, but gave him up for **all** of us*
  and has given us the ministry of recon**cili**ation.

[LH: 2 Cor. 5:18; Rom. 8:32]

You know the generous act of our Lord Jesus Christ, that though he was rich, yet for your sakes he **be**came poor,*
  so that by his poverty you might **be**come rich.
He emptied himself, taking the form **of** a slave,*
  so that by his poverty you might **be**come rich.

[LH: 2 Cor. 8:9; Phil. 2:7]

Saturday of Week II

Antiphon to PSALM 19 *Coeli enarrant*

The statutes of the LORD re**joice** the heart*
and give light **to** the eyes. [LH]

19 *The Lord, creator and lawgiver*

1 The heavens declare the glo**ry** of God,*
and the firmament **shows** his handiwork.

2 One day tells its tale **to** another,*
and one night imparts knowledge **to** another.

3 Although they have no **words** or language,*
and their voices **are** not heard,

4 Their sound has gone out **in**to all lands,*
and their message to the ends **of** the world.

5 In the deep has he set a pavilion **for** the sun;*
it comes forth like a bridegroom out of his chamber;
it rejoices like a champion to **run** its course.

6 It goes forth from the uttermost edge of the heavens
and runs about to the end of **it** again;*
nothing is hidden from its **burn**ing heat.

7 The law of the LORD is perfect
and re**vives** the soul;*
the testimony of the LORD is sure
and gives wisdom **to** the innocent.

8 The statutes of the LORD are just
and re**joice** the heart;*
the commandment of the LORD is clear
and gives light **to** the eyes.

9 The fear of the LORD is clean
and en**dures** for ever;*
the judgments of the LORD are true
and righteous **al**together.

10 More to be desired are they than gold,
more than **much** fine gold,*
sweeter far than honey,
than honey **in** the comb.

11 By them also is your ser**vant** enlightened,*
and in keeping them there is **great** reward.

12 Who can tell how often **he** offends?*
cleanse me from my **se**cret faults.

13 Above all, keep your servant from presumptuous sins;
let them not get dominion **o**ver me;*
then shall I be whole and sound,
and innocent of a **great** offense.

14 Let the words of my mouth and the meditation of my
heart be acceptable **in** your sight,*
O LORD, my strength and **my** redeemer.

Antiphon The statutes of the LORD re**joice** the heart*
and give light **to** the eyes.

Silence for meditation

Heavenly Father, you have filled the world with beauty: Open our eyes to see your gracious hand in all your works, that rejoicing in your whole creation, we may learn to serve you with gladness, for the sake of him through whom all things were made, your Son, Jesus Christ our Lord. [BCP, LBW]

+

Antiphon to PSALM 149 *Cantate Domino*

Let the children of Zion be joyful in their king. [LH, PBO]

149 *Praise to the God of victories*

1 Hallelujah!
Sing to the LORD **a** new song;*
sing his praise in the congregation **of** the faithful.

2 Let Israel rejoice **in** his Maker;*
let the children of Zion be joyful **in** their King.

3 Let them praise his Name **in** the dance;*
let them sing praise to him with tim**brel** and harp.

4 For the LORD takes pleasure **in** his people*
and adorns the **poor** with victory.

5 Let the faithful re**joice** in triumph;*
let them be joyful **on** their beds.

6 Let the praises of God be **in** their throat*
and a two-edged sword **in** their hand;

7 To wreak vengeance **on** the nations*
and punishment **on** the peoples;

8 To bind their **kings** in chains*
and their nobles with **links** of iron;

9 To inflict on them the judg**ment** decreed;*
this is glory for all his faithful people.
Hallelujah!

Antiphon Let the children of Zion be joyful in their king.

Silence for meditation

Lord, let Israel rejoice in you and acknowledge you as creator and redeemer. In your lovingkindness embrace us now, that we may proclaim the wonderful truths of salvation with your saints in glory; through your Son, Jesus Christ our Lord. [LH, LBW]

+

Stand

THE HYMN is sung.

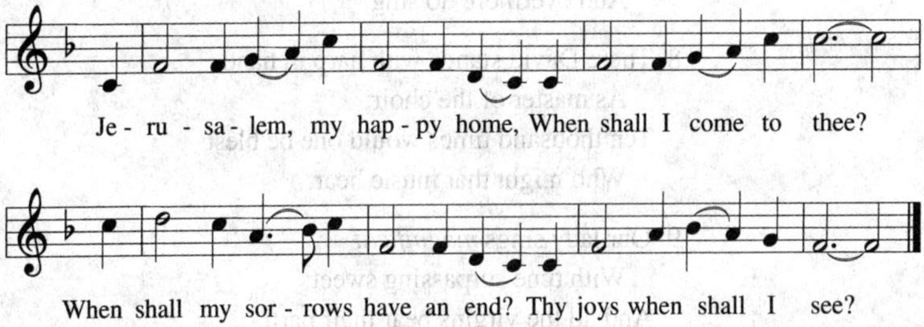

2 O happy harbor of the saints,
O sweet and pleasant soil!
In thee no sorrow may be found,
No grief, no care, no toil.

3 Thy saints are crowned with glory great:
They see God face to face,
They triumph still, they still rejoice:
Most happy is their case.

4 Thy vineyards and thy orchards are
Most beautiful and fair,
Full furnishèd with trees and fruits
Most wonderful and rare.

5 Thy gardens and thy gallant walks
Continually are green;
There grow such sweet and pleasant flowers
As nowhere else are seen.

6 Quite through the streets with silver sound
The flood of life doth flow,
Upon whose banks on every side
The wood of life doth grow.

7 There trees for evermore bear fruit
And evermore do spring;
There evermore the angels sit
And evermore do sing.

8 There David stands with harp in hand
As master of the choir;
Ten thousand times would one be blest
Who might that music hear.

9 Our lady sings *magnificat*
With tune surpassing sweet;
And all the virgins bear their part,
Sitting about her feet.

10 *Te Deum* doth Saint Ambrose sing;
Saint Augustine doth the like;
Old Simeon and Zachary
Have not their songs to seek.

11 There Magdalene hath left her moan
And cheerfully doth sing
With blessèd saints whose harmony
In every street doth ring.

12 Jerusalem, my happy home,
Would God I were in thee!
Would God my woes were at an end,
Thy joys that I might see!

[SBH 587, LBW 331, H82 620]

Text: F.B.P., 16th cent., [st. 8 alt. H82]
Tune: *Land of Rest*, American — CM

Sit

One or two LESSONS are read.

Year 1	Year 2
after Epiphany 2	
Isaiah 46:1-13	Genesis 12:9-13:1
I am God, and there is no one like me, declaring the end from the beginning and from ancient times things not yet done, saying, "My purpose shall stand."	Pharaoh called Abram and said, "What is this you have done to me? Why did you not tell me she was your wife? Why did you say, 'She is my sister'?"
Ephesians 6:10-24	Hebrews 7:18-28
Finally, be strong in the Lord and in the strength of his power.	He is able for all time to save those who approach God through him, since he always lives to make intercession for them.
after Epiphany 6	
Isaiah 66:1-6	Genesis 35:1-20
This is the one to whom I will look, to the humble and contrite in spirit, who trembles at my word.	I am God Almighty: be fruitful and multiply; a nation and a company of nations shall come from you, and kings shall spring from you.
1 Timothy 6:(1-5) 6-21	1 John 3:11-18
Fight the good fight of faith; take hold of the eternal life, to which you were called and for which you made the good confession in the presence of many witnesses.	This is the message you have heard from the beginning, that we should love one another.
after Proper 2 / after the Festival of the Holy Trinity	
Deuteronomy 1:1-8	Proverbs 8:22-36
See, I have set the land before you; go in and take possession of the land that I swore to your ancestors, to Abraham, to Isaac, and	The LORD created me at the beginning of his work, the first of his acts of long ago.

to Jacob, to give to them and to their descendants after them.

1 Timothy 6:6-21

There is great gain in godliness combined with contentment; for we brought nothing into the world, so that we can take nothing out of it.

3 John 1-15

Beloved, do not imitate what is evil but imitate what is good.

after Proper 6 / Pentecost 5

1 Samuel 4:1b-11

The ark of God was captured; and the two sons of Eli, Hophni and Phineas, died.

Numbers 13:31-14:25

Forgive the iniquity of this people according to the greatness of your steadfast love, just as you have pardoned this people, from Egypt even until now.

Acts 4:32-5:11

The whole group of those who believed were of one heart and soul, and no one claimed private ownership of any possessions, but everything they owned was held in common.

Romans 3:9-20

For "no human being will be justified in his sight" by deeds prescribed by the law, for through the law comes the knowledge of sin.

after Proper 10 / Pentecost 9

1 Samuel 22:1-23

Everyone who was in distress, and everyone who was in debt, and everyone who was discontented gathered to David; and he became captain over them.

Joshua 6:1-14

The LORD said to Joshua, "See, I have handed Jericho over to you, along with its king and soldiers."

Act 13:26-43

We bring you the good news that what God promised to our ancestors he has fulfilled for us, their children, by raising Jesus.

Romans 13:1-7

Let every person be subject to the governing authorities.

after Proper 14 / Pentecost 13

2 Samuel 16:1-23

It may be that the LORD will look on my distress, and the LORD will repay me with good for this cursing of me today.

Judges 16:1-14

Delilah said to Samson, "Please tell me what makes your strength so great, and how you could be bound, so that one could subdue you."

Acts 27:17-29

Go, for I will send you far away to the Gentiles.

Acts 7:30-43

Our ancestors were unwilling to obey Moses; instead, they pushed him aside, and in their hearts they turned back to Egypt.

after Proper 18 / Pentecost 17

1 Kings 18:41-19:8

Elijah got up, and ate and drank; then he went in the strength of that food forty days and forty nights to Horeb the mount of God.

Job 38:1-17

Where were you when I laid the foundation of the earth? Tell me, if you have understanding.

Philippians 3:17-4:7

The peace of God, which surpasses all understanding, will guard your hearts and your minds in Christ Jesus.

Acts 15:22-35

Judas and Silas, who were themselves prophets, said much to encourage and strengthen the believers.

after Proper 22 / Pentecost 21

Jeremiah 35:1-19

I am going to bring on Judah and on all the inhabitants of Jerusalem every disaster that I have pronounced against them; because I

Hosea 10:1-15

Sow for yourselves righteousness; reap steadfast love; break up your fallow ground; for it is time to seek the LORD, that he may come and

have spoken to them and they have not listened.

rain righteousness upon you.
[BCP: Micah 5:1-4, 10-15]

1 Corinthians 12:27-13:3
If I give away all my possessions, and if I hand over my body so that I may boast, but do not have love, I gain nothing.

Acts 25:13-27
Agrippa said to Festus, "I would like to hear the man myself." "Tomorrow," he said, "you will hear him."

after Proper 26 / Pentecost 25

Ezra 9:1-15
The holy seed has mixed itself with the peoples of the lands, and in this faithlessness the officials and leaders have led the way.
or Ezra 6:1-22

Sirach [Ecclesiasticus] 51:1-12
I give thanks to your name, for you have been my protector and helper and have delivered me from destruction.
or Zephaniah 3:14-20

Revelation 17:1-14
The Lamb will conquer them, for he is Lord of lords and King of kings, and those with him are called and chosen and faithful.

Revelation 18:1-14
Alas, alas, the great city Babylon, the mighty city! For in one hour your judgment has come.

Silence for meditation follows each reading.

RESPONSORY

You are a chosen race, a royal priesthood, a holy nation, **God's** own people,*
in order that you may proclaim the mighty acts of him who called you out of darkness into his **mar**velous light.

Listen to my appeal, agree with one another, **live** in peace,*
and the God of love
and peace will **be** with you.
And the peace of God which surpasses all understanding, will guard your hearts and your minds **in** Christ Jesus;*

Once you were not a people, but
now you **are** God's people,*
in order that you may
proclaim the mighty acts
of him who called you out
of darkness into his
marvelous light.

[LH: 1 Peter 2:9-10]

and the God of love
and peace will **be** with you.

[LH: 2 Cor. 13:11; Phil. 4:7]

Sunday of Week III

Antiphon to PSALM 67 *Deus misereatur nostri*

May God show us the light **of** his countenance*
and give **us** his blessing. [LH]

67 *Harvest song*

1 May God be merciful to **us** and bless us,*
show us the light of his countenance and **come** to us.

2 Let your ways be known **up**on earth,*
your saving health a**mong** all nations.

3 Let the peoples praise **you**, O God;*
let all the **peo**ples praise you.

4 Let the nations be glad and **sing** for joy,*
for you judge the peoples with equity
and guide all the nations **up**on earth.

5 Let the peoples praise **you**, O God;*
let all the **peo**ples praise you.

6 The earth has brought **forth** her increase;*
may God, our own God, give **us** his blessing.

7 May God give **us** his blessing,*
and may all the ends of the earth stand in **awe** of him.

Antiphon May God show us the light **of** his countenance*
and give **us** his blessing.

Silence for meditation

Father, through your power the earth has brought forth its noblest fruit, the tree of the cross: Unite all people in its embrace, and feed them with its fruit, everlasting life through Jesus Christ our Lord. [LHd, LBW]

+

Antiphon to the OLD TESTAMENT CANTICLE *Ecce, Deus*

Sing the praises **of** the Lord,*
for he has **done** great things. [LH, PBO]

A Song of Isaiah Isaiah 12:2-6

Surely, it is **God** who saves me;*
I will trust in him and not **be** afraid.

For the Lord is my stronghold and my **sure** defense,*
and he will **be** my Savior.

Therefore you shall draw water **with** rejoicing*
from the springs **of** salvation.

And on that day **you** shall say,*
Give thanks to the Lord and call up**on** his Name;*

Make his deeds known a**mong** the peoples;*
see that they remember that his Name **is** exalted.

Sing the praises of the Lord, for he **done** great things,*
and this is known in **all** the world.

Cry aloud, inhabitants of Zion, ring **out** your joy,*
for the great one in the midst of you is the Holy **One** of Israel.
[BCP]

Antiphon Sing the praises **of** the Lord,*
for he has **done** great things.

Silence for meditation

Lord God, our stronghold and sure defense, we praise you for the mighty acts you have done for your people but chiefly for the resurrection of your Son. By his victory bring us at last to share in the fullness of joy with all those who rejoice in your presence in the eternal city; through Jesus Christ our Lord. [PHP]

+

Antiphon to PSALM 150 *Laudate Dominum in sanctis ejus*

Praise God for his **might**y acts,*
praise him for his ex**cel**lent greatness. [LH, PBO]

150 *The great alleluia*

1 Hallelujah!
Praise God in his **ho**ly temple;*
praise him in the firmament **of** his power.

2 Praise him for his **might**y acts;*
praise him for his ex**cel**lent greatness.

3 Praise him with the blast **of** the ram's-horn;*
praise him with **lyre** and harp.

4 Praise him with tim**brel** and dance;*
praise him with **strings** and pipe.

5 Praise him with re**sound**ing cymbals;*
praise him with loud-**clang**ing cymbals.

6 Let everything **that** has breath*
praise the LORD.
Hallelujah!

Antiphon Praise God for his **might**y acts,*
praise him for his ex**cel**lent greatness.

Silence for meditation

God of surpassing greatness, enthroned upon the praises of your people, fill our hearts with your love and unite our voices with the praise of all creation so that you may be honored and glorified by everything that has breath; through Jesus Christ our Lord. [PHP]

+

Stand

THE HYMN is sung. *Splendor Paternae gloriae*

2 O thou true Sun, on us thy glance
Let fall in royal radiance;
The Spirit's sanctifying beam
Upon our earthly senses stream.

3 The Father, too, our prayers implore,
Father of glory evermore,
The Father of all grace and might,
To banish sin from our delight.

4 To guide whate'er we nobly do,
With love all envy to subdue,
To make ill-fortune turn to fair,
And give us grace our wrongs to bear,

5 Rejoicing may this day go hence;
Like virgin dawn our innocence,
Like fiery noon our faith appear,
Nor know the gloom of twilight drear.

6 Morn in her rosy car is borne;
Let him come forth, our perfect morn,
The Word in God the Father one,
The Father perfect in the Son.

7 All laud to God the Father be;
All praise, eternal Son, to thee;
All glory, as is ever meet,
To God the holy Paraclete. [SBH 206]

Text: St. Ambrose, 340-397; tr. Robert Bridges, 1844-1930
Tune: *Splendor Paternae*, mode 1; *Antiphoner*, Sarum LM

Sit

One or two LESSONS are read.

Year 1	Year 2
Epiphany 3	
Isaiah 47:1-15	Genesis 13:2-18
Our Redeemer--the LORD of hosts is his name--is the Holy One of Israel.	All the land that you see I will give to you and your offspring forever.
Hebrews 10:19-31	Galatians 2:1-10
Let us approach with a true heart in full assurance of faith, with our hearts sprinkled clean from an evil conscience and our bodies washed with pure water.	I had been entrusted with the gospel for the uncircumcised, just as Peter had been entrusted with the gospel for the circumcised.
Epiphany 7	
Isaiah 66:7-14	Proverbs 1:20-33
Rejoice with Jerusalem, and be glad for her, all you who love her.	Wisdom cries out in the street; in the squares she raises her voice. *or* Tobit 1:1-22

1 John 3:4-10

Those who have been born of God do not sin, because God's seed abides in them; they cannot sin, because they have been born of God.

2 Corinthians 5:11-21

Christ died for all, so that those who live might live no longer for themselves, but for him who died and was raised for them.

Proper 3 (Sunday between May 22 and 28) / Pentecost 2

Deuteronomy 4:1-9

Take care and watch yourselves closely, so as neither to forget the things that your eyes have seen nor to let them slip from your mind all the days of your life; make them known to your children and your children's children.

Proverbs 9:1-12

The fear of the Lord is the beginning of wisdom, and the knowledge of the Holy One is insight.

Revelation 7:1-4, 9-17

Salvation belongs to our God who is seated on the throne, and to the Lamb!

Acts 8:14-25

Then Peter and John laid their hands on them, and they received the Holy Spirit.

Proper 7 (Sunday between June 19 and 25) / Pentecost 6

1 Samuel 4:12-22

The glory has departed from Israel, for the ark of God has been captured.

Numbers 14:26-45

Not one of you shall come into the land in which I swore to settle you, except Caleb son of Jephunneh and Joshua the son of Nun. But your little ones, who you said would become booty, I will bring in, and they shall know the land that you have despised.

James 1:1-18

Whenever you face trials of any kind, consider it nothing but joy, because you know that the testing of your faith produces endurance.

Acts 15:1-12

The whole assembly kept silence, and listened to Barnabas and Paul as they told of all the signs and wonders that God had done through them among the Gentiles.

Proper 11 (Sunday between July 17 and 23) / Pentecost 10

1 Samuel 23:7-18

Do not be afraid; for the hand of my father Saul shall not find you; you shall be king over Israel, and I shall be second to you; my father Saul also knows that this is so.

Joshua 6:15-27

The LORD was with Joshua; and his fame was in all the land.

Romans 11:33-12:2

O the depth of the riches and wisdom and knowledge of God! How unsearchable are his judgments and how inscrutable his ways!

Acts 22:30-23:11

Keep up your courage! For just as you have testified for me in Jerusalem, so you must bear witness also in Rome.

Proper 15 (Sunday between August 14 and 20) / Pentecost 14

2 Samuel 17:1-23

The LORD had ordained to defeat the good counsel of Ahithophel, so that the LORD might bring ruin on Absalom.

Judges 16:15-31

Samson called out to the LORD and said, "Lord GOD, remember me and strengthen me only this once, O God, so that with this one act of revenge I may pay back the Philistines for my two eyes.

Galatians 3:6-14

Christ redeemed us from the curse of the law by becoming a curse for us.

2 Corinthians 13:1-11

Agree with one another, live in peace; and the God of love and peace will be with you.

Proper 19 (Sunday between September 11 and 17) / Pentecost 18

1 Kings 19:8-21

You shall anoint Jehu son of Nimshi as king over Israel; and you shall anoint Elisha son of Shaphat of Abel-Meholah as prophet in your place.

Job 38:1,18-41

Have you comprehended the expanse of the earth? Declare, if you know all this.

Acts 5:34-42

As they left the council, they rejoiced that they were considered worthy to suffer dishonor for the sake of the name.

Revelation 18:1-8

She will be burned with fire; for mighty is the Lord God who judges her.

Proper 23 (Sunday between October 9 and 15) / Pentecost 22

Jeremiah 36:1-10

It may be that when the house of Judah hears of all the disasters that I intend to do to them, all of them may turn from their evil ways, so that I may forgive their iniquity and their sin.

Hosea 11:1-11

When Israel was a child, I loved him, and out of Egypt I called my son.

[BCP Micah 6:1-8]

Acts 14:8-18

We are mortals just like you, and we bring you good news, that you should turn from all these worthless things to the living God, who made the heaven and the earth and the sea and all that is in them.

1 Corinthians 4:9-16

I think that God has exhibited us apostles as last of all, as though sentenced to death, because we have become a spectacle to the world, to angels and to mortals.

Proper 27 (Sunday between November 6 and 12) / Pentecost 26.

Ezra 10:1-17
Now make confession to the LORD the God of your ancestors, and do his will; separate yourselves from the peoples of the land.

or Nehemiah 1:1-11

Sirach [Ecclesiasticus] 51:13-22
I sought wisdom openly in my prayer. Before the temple I asked for her, and I will search for her until the end.

or Joel 1:1-13

Acts 24:10-21
This I admit to you, that according to the Way, which they call a sect, I worship the God of our ancestors, believing everything laid down according to the law or written in the prophets.

1 Corinthians 14:1-12
Since you are eager for spiritual gifts, strive to excel in them for building up the church.

Silence for meditation follows each reading.

RESPONSORY

I will pour water on the thirsty land, and streams **on** the dry ground;*
I will pour my Spirit upon your descendants and they shall spring up like willows by **flow**ing streams.
The water that I will give will become a spring of water gushing up to e**ter**nal life.*
I will pour my Spirit upon your descendants and they shall spring up like willows by **flow**ing streams.
[LH: Isa. 44:3,4; John 4:14]

The marriage of the Lamb has come, and his bride has made **her**self ready.*
Blessed are those who are invited to the marriage supper **of** the Lamb.
I will take you for my wife in faithfulness; and you shall **know** the Lord.*
Blessed are those who are invited to the marriage supper **of** the Lamb.
[LH: Rev. 19:7,9; Hosea 2:20]

Monday of Week III

Antiphon to PSALM 57 *Miserere mei, Deus, miserere*

Awake, **lute** and harp;*
I myself will wak**en** the dawn. [LH]

57 *In time of danger*

1 Be merciful to me, O God, be merciful,
for I have taken re**fuge** in you;*
in the shadow of your wings will I take refuge
until this time of trouble **has** gone by.

2 I will call upon the **Most** High God,*
the God who main**tains** my cause.

3 He will send from heaven and save me;
he will confound those who tramp**le** upon me;*
God will send forth his love **and** his faithfulness.

4 I lie in the midst of lions that de**vour** the people;*
their teeth are spears and arrows,
their tongue **a** sharp sword.

5 They have laid a net for my feet,
and **I** am bowed low;*
they have dug a pit before me,
but have fallen into **it** themselves.

6 Exalt yourself above the heav**ens**, O God,*
and your glory over **all** the earth.

7 My heart is firmly fixed, O God, my **heart** is fixed;*
I will sing **and** make melody.

8 Wake up, my spirit;
awake, **lute** and harp;*
I myself will wak**en** the dawn.

9 I will confess you among the peo**ples**, O LORD;*
I will sing praise to you a**mong** the nations.

10 For your loving-kindness is greater **than** the heavens,*
and your faithfulness reaches **to** the clouds.

11 Exalt yourself above the heav**ens**, O God,*
and your glory over **all** the earth.

Antiphon Awake, **lute** and harp;*
I myself will wak**en** the dawn.

Silence for meditation

Lord, send your mercy and your truth to rescue us from the snares of the devil, and we will praise you among the peoples and proclaim you to the nations, happy to be known as companions of your Son, Jesus Christ our Lord. [LH, LBW]

+

Antiphon to PSALM 145 *Exaltabo te, Deus*

Antiphon Every day **will** I bless you*
and praise your Name for ev**er** and ever. [LH]

145 *Praise of God's majesty*

1 I will exalt you, O **God** my King,*
and bless your Name for ev**er** and ever.

2 Every day **will** I bless you*
and praise your Name for **ever** and ever.

3 Great is the LORD and greatly **to** be praised;*
there is no end **to** his greatness.

4 One generation shall praise your works **to** another*
and shall de**clare** your power.

5 I will ponder the glorious splendor **of** your majesty*
and all your **mar**velous works.

6 They shall speak of the might of your **won**drous acts,*
and I will tell **of** your greatness.

7 They shall publish the remembrance of **your** great goodness;*
they shall sing of your **right**eous deeds.

8 The LORD is gracious and full **of** compassion,*
slow to anger and **of** great kindness.

9 The LORD is loving to **ev**eryone*
and his compassion is over **all** his works.

10 All your works praise **you**, O LORD,*
and your faithful **ser**vants bless you.

11 They make known the glory **of** your kingdom*
and speak **of** your power;

12 That the peoples may know **of** your power*
and the glorious splendor **of** your kingdom.

13 Your kingdom is an ever**last**ing kingdom;*
your dominion endures through**out** all ages.

14 The LORD is faithful in **all** his words*
and merciful in **all** his deeds.

15 The LORD upholds all **those** who fall;*
he lifts up those who **are** bowed down.

16 The eyes of all wait upon **you**, O LORD,*
and you give them their food **in** due season.

17 You open **wide** your hand*
and satisfy the needs of every **liv**ing creature.

18 The LORD is righteous in **all** his ways*
and loving in **all** his works.

19 The LORD is near to those who **call** upon him,*
to all who call up**on** him faithfully.

20 He fulfills the desire of **those** who fear him;*
he hears their **cry** and helps them.

21 The LORD preserves all **those** who love him,*
but he destroys **all** the wicked.

22 My mouth shall speak the praise **of** the LORD;*
let all flesh bless his holy Name for ev**er** and ever.

Antiphon Every day **will** I bless you*
and praise your Name for ev**er** and ever.

Silence for meditation

Loving Father, you are faithful in your promises and tender in your compassion: Listen to our hymn of joy, and continue to satisfy the needs of all your creatures, that all flesh may bless your Name in your everlasting kingdom, where with your Son and the Holy Spirit you live and reign, now and for ever. [LBW]

+

Stand

THE HYMN is sung. *I Himmelen, i Himmelen*

2 In heaven above, in heaven above,
What glory deep and bright!
The splendor of the noonday sun
Grows pale before its light;
That mighty sun that goes not down,
Before whose face clouds never frown,
Is God, the Lord of hosts.

3 In heaven above, in heaven above,
No tears of pain are shed;
For nothing there can fade or die;

Life's fullness round is spread,
And, like an ocean, joy o'erflows,
And with immortal mercy glows
Our God, the Lord of hosts.

4 In heaven above, in heaven above,
God has a joy prepared,
Which mortal ear has never heard,
Nor mortal vision shared,
Which never entered mortal thought,
In mortal dreams was never sought,
O God, the Lord of hosts! [LBW 330]

Text: Laurentius Laurentii Laurinus, 1573-1655, rev. Johan Astrom, 1767-1844; tr. William Mascall, 1812-1888, alt.
Tune: *I Himmelen, i Himmelen,* Norwegian folk tune 86 86 886

Sit

One or two LESSONS are read.

Year 1	Year 2
after Epiphany 3	
Isaiah 48:1-11 From this time forward I make you hear new things, hidden things that you have not known.	Genesis 14:(1-7) 8-24 King Melchizedek of Salem brought out bread and wine; he was priest of God Most High. He blessed him and said, "Blessed be Abram by God Most High, maker of heaven and earth."
Galatians 1:1-7 I am astonished that you are so quickly deserting the one who called you in the grace of Christ and are turning to a different gospel.	Hebrews 8:1-13 Jesus has now obtained a more excellent ministry, and to that degree he is the mediator of a better covenant, which has been enacted through better promises.

after Epiphany 7

Ruth 1:1-14

Go back each of you to your mother's house. May the LORD deal kindly with you, as you have dealt kindly with the dead and with me.

2 Corinthians 1:1-11

Grace to you and peace from God our Father and the Lord Jesus Christ.

Proverbs 3:11-20

Happy are those who find wisdom, and those who get understanding.

or Tobit 2:1-3:3, 6-15

1 John 3:18-4:6

Little children, let us love, not in word or speech, but in truth and action.

after Proper 3 / Pentecost 2

Deuteronomy 4:9-14

Take care and watch yourselves closely, so as neither to forget the things that your eyes have seen nor to let them slip from your mind all the days of your life; make them known to your children and to your children's children.

2 Corinthians 1:1-11

Just as the sufferings of Christ are abundant for us, so also our consolation is abundant through Christ.

Proverbs 10:1-12

Hatred stirs up strife, but love covers all offenses.

1 Timothy 1:1-17

The saying is sure and worthy of full acceptance, that Christ Jesus came into the world to save sinners—of whom I am the foremost.

after Proper 7 / Pentecost 6

1 Samuel 5:1-12

When the people of Ashdod rose early the next day, there was Dagon, fallen on his face before the ark of the LORD.

Numbers 16:1-19

Hear now, you Levites! Is it too little for you that the God of Israel has separated you from the congregation of Israel, to allow you to approach him in order to perform the duties of the LORD's

Acts 5:12-26

Go, stand in the temple and tell the people the whole message about this life.

after Proper 11 / Pentecost 10

1 Samuel 24:1-22

"He is the LORD's anointed." So David scolded his men severely and did not permit them to attack Saul.

Acts 13:44-52

When the Gentiles heard this, they were glad and praised the Lord; and as many as had been destined for eternal life became believers.

after Proper 15 / Pentecost 14

2 Samuel 17:24-18:8

Deal gently for my sake with the young man Absalom.

Acts 22:30-23:11

Keep up your courage! For just as you have testified for me in Jerusalem, so you must bear witness also in Rome.

tabernacle and to stand before the congregation and to serve them?

Romans 3:21-31

There is no distinction, since all have sinned and fall short of the glory of God; they are now justified by his grace as a gift.

Joshua 7:1-13

Israel has sinned; they have transgressed my covenant that I imposed on them. They have taken some of the devoted things; they have stolen, they have acted deceitfully, and they have put them among their own belongings.

Romans 13:8-14

Love does no wrong to a neighbor; therefore, love is the fulfilling of the law.

Judges 17:1-13

In those days there was no king in Israel; all the people did what was right in their own eyes.

Acts 7:44-8:1a

Stephen knelt down and cried out in a loud voice, "Lord, do not hold this sin against them." When he had said this, he died.

after Proper 19 / Pentecost 18

1 Kings 21:1-16

Go, take possession of the vineyard of Naboth the Jezreelite, which he refused to give you for money; for Naboth is not alive, but dead.

Job 40:1-24

Will you even put me in the wrong? Will you condemn me that you may be justified?

1 Corinthians 1:1-19

God is faithful; by him you were called into the fellowship of his Son, Jesus Christ our Lord.

Acts 15:36-16:5

Barnabas took Mark with him and sailed away to Cyprus. But Paul chose Silas and set out.

after Proper 23 / Pentecost 22

Jeremiah 36:11-26

As Jehudi read three or four columns, the king would cut them off with a penknife and throw them into the fire in the brazier, until the entire scroll was consumed.

Hosea 11:12-12:1

Ephraim has surrounded me with lies, and the house of Israel with deceit; but Judah still walks with God, and is faithful to the Holy One.
[BCP Micah 7:1-7]

1 Corinthians 13:(1-3)4-13

And now faith, hope, and love abide, these three; and the greatest of these is love.

Acts 26:1-23

To this day I have had help from God, and so I stand here, testifying to both small and great, saying nothing but what the prophets and Moses said would take place.

after Proper 27 / Pentecost 26

Nehemiah 9:1-15(16-25)

Stand up and bless the LORD your God from everlasting to everlasting. Blessed be your glorious name, which is exalted above all blessing and praise.

or Nehemiah 2:1-20

Joel 1:1-13

Put on sackcloth and lament, you priests; wail, you ministers of the altar.

or Joel 1:15-2:2

Revelation 18:1-8

Fallen, fallen is Babylon the great! It has become a dwelling place for demons, a haunt of every foul and hateful bird, a haunt of every foul and hateful beast.

Revelation 18:15-24

Alas, alas, the great city, clothed in fine linen, in purple and scarlet, adorned with gold, with jewels, and with pearls! For in one hour all this wealth has been laid waste!

Silence for meditation follows each reading.

RESPONSORY

Your body is a temple of the Holy Spirit within you, which you **have** from God.*

Therefore glorify God **in** your body.

Sanctify yourselves therefore, and be holy, for I am holy, **says** the Lord.*

Therefore glorify God **in** your body.

[LH: 1 Cor. 6:19; Lev. 11:44]

In Christ God has anointed us, by putting his **seal** on us*

giving us his Spirit in our hearts as a **guar**antee.

The Lord our God made a covenant with us and spoke with us **face** to face;*

giving us his Spirit in our hearts as a **guar**antee.

[LH: 2 Cor. 1:21-22; Deut. 5:2,4]

Tuesday of Week III

Antiphon to PSALM 54 *Deus, in nomine tuo*

God **is** my helper;*
it is the Lord who sus**tains** my life. [LH]

54 *Plea for God's help*

1 Save me, O God, **by** your Name;*
in your might, de**fend** my cause.

2 Hear my **prayer,** O God;*
give ear to the words **of** my mouth.

3 For the arrogant have risen up against me,
and the ruthless have **sought** my life,*
those who have no re**gard** for God.

4 Behold, God **is** my helper;*
it is the Lord who sus**tains** my life.

5 Render evil to those who **spy** on me;*
in your faithful**ness**, destroy them.

6 I will offer you a **free**will sacrifice*
and praise your Name, O LORD, for **it** is good.

7 For you have rescued me from **ev**ery trouble,*
and my eye has seen the ruin **of** my foes.

Antphon God **is** my helper;*
it is the Lord who sus**tains** my life.

Silence for meditation

Father, hear our prayer and come to the aid of your Church. Mercifully deliver us from evil, so that from the rising of the sun to its setting we may offer you a pure sacrifice of praise; through your Son, Jesus Christ our Lord. [LHd, LBW]

+

Antiphon to PSALM 146 *Lauda, anima mea*

I will praise the LORD as long as I live. [LH]

146 *Praise of God's faithfulnes*

1 Hallelujah!
Praise the LORD, **O** my soul!*
I will praise the LORD as long as I live;
I will sing praises to my God while I **have** my being.

2 Put not your trust in rulers, nor in any **child** of earth,*
for there is no **help** in them.

3 When they breathe their last, they re**turn** to earth,*
and in that day **their** thoughts perish.

4 Happy are they who have the God of Jacob **for** their help!*
whose hope is in the **LORD** their God;

5 Who made heaven and earth, the seas, and all that **is** in them;*
who keeps his prom**ise** for ever;

6 Who gives justice to those who **are** oppressed,*
and food to **those** who hunger.

7 The LORD sets the prisoners free;
the LORD opens the eyes **of** the blind;*
the LORD lifts up those who **are** bowed down;

8 The LORD loves the righteous;
the LORD cares **for** the stranger;*
he sustains the orphan and widow,
but frustrates the way **of** the wicked.

9 The LORD shall **reign** for ever,*
your God, O Zion, throughout all generations.
Hallelujah!

Antiphon I will praise the LORD as long as I live.

Silence for meditation

God of glory and power, happy indeed are those who have put their trust in you: Shine the brightness of your light upon us, that we may love you always with a pure heart and praise you for ever; through your Son, Jesus Christ our Lord. [LH, LBW]

+

Stand

THE HYMN is sung.

2 The task thy wisdom hath assigned,
O let me cheerfully fulfill;
In all thy works thy presence find,
And prove thy good and perfect will.

3 Thee may I set at my right hand,
Whose eyes my inmost substance see,
And labor on at thy command,
And offer all my works to thee.

4 Give me to bear thy easy yoke,
And every moment watch and pray,
And still to things eternal look,
And hasten to thy glorious day;

5 For thee delightfully employ
Whate'er thy bounteous grace hath given,
And run my course with even joy,
And closely walk with thee to heaven.

[SBH 214, LBW 505]

Text: Charles Wesley, 1707-1788
Tune: *Song 34,* Orlando Gibbons, 1583-1625 LM

Sit

One or two LESSONS are read.

Year 1	Year 2
after Epiphany 3	
Isaiah 48:12-21(22)	Genesis 15:1-11,17-21
My hand laid the foundation of the earth, and my right hand spread out the heavens; when I	Abram believed the LORD; and the LORD reckoned it to him as righteousness.

summon them, they stand at attention.

Galatians 1:18-2:10

The one who formerly was persecuting us is now proclaiming the faith he once tried to destroy.

Hebrews 9:1-14

He entered once for all into the Holy Place, not with the blood of goats and calves, but with his own blood, thus obtaining eternal redemption.

after Epiphany 7

Ruth 1:15-22

Where you go, I will go; where you lodge, I will lodge; your people shall be my people, and your God my God. Where you die, I will die–there will I be buried.

2 Corinthians 1:12-22

In Christ every one of God's promises is a "Yes." For this reason it is through him that we say the "Amen," to the glory of God.

Proverbs 4:1-27

Keep hold of instruction; do not let go; guard her, for she is your life.

or Tobit 3:16-4:5, 12-13a, 14b-16, 19b-21

1 John 4:7-21

Beloved, since God loved us so much, we also ought to love one another.

after Proper 3 / Pentecost 2

Deuteronomy 4:15-24

The LORD your God is a devouring fire, a jealous God.

2 Corinthians 1:12-22

It is God who establishes us with you in Christ and has anointed us, by putting his seal on us and giving us his Spirit in our hearts as a first installment.

Proverbs 15:16-33

The LORD is far from the wicked, but he hears the prayer of the righteous.

1 Timothy 1:18-2:15

I urge that supplications, prayers, intercessions, and thanksgivings be made for everyone.

after Proper 7 / Pentecost 6

1 Samuel 6:1-16

Take the ark of the LORD and place it on the cart, and put in a box at its side the figures of gold, which you are returning to him as a guilt offering.

Numbers 16:20-35

The earth opened its mouth and swallowed them up, along with their households–everyone who belonged to Korah and all their goods.

Acts 5:27-42

As they left the council, they rejoiced that they were considered worthy to suffer dishonor for the sake of the name.

Romans 4:1-12

Abraham received the sign of circumcision as a seal of the righteousness that he had by faith while he was still uncircumcised.

after Proper 11 / Pentecost 10

1 Samuel 25:1-22

Now Samuel died; and all Israel assembled and mourned for him. They buried him at his home in Ramah.

Joshua 8:1-22

As soon as Joshua stretched out his hand, the troops in ambush rose quickly out of their place and rushed forward. They entered the city, took it, and at once set the city on fire.

Acts 14:1-18

In past generations he allowed all the nations to follow their own ways; yet he has not left himself without a witness in doing good–giving you rains from heaven and fruitful seasons, and filling you with food and your hearts with joy.

Romans 14:1-12

Why do you pass judgment on your brother or sister? Or you, why do you despise your brother or sister? For we all stand before the judgment seat of God.

after Proper 15 / Pentecost 14

2 Samuel 18:9-18

Joab took three spears in his hand and thrust them into the heart of Absalom, while he was still alive in the oak.

Judges 18:1-15

The land is broad–God has indeed given it into your hands–a place where there is no lack of anything on earth.

Acts 23:12-24
More than forty of their men are lying in ambush for Paul. They have bound themselves by an oath neither to eat nor drink until they kill him.

Acts 8:1-13
When they believed Philip, who was proclaiming the good news about the kingdom of God and the name of Jesus Christ, they were baptized, both men and women.

after Proper 19 / Pentecost 18

1 Kings 21:17-29
You shall say to Ahab, "Thus says the LORD: Have you killed, and also taken possession?" You shall say to him, "Thus says the LORD: In the place where dogs licked up the blood of Naboth, dogs will also lick up your blood."

Job 40:1; 41:1-11
Can you draw out Leviathan with a fishhook, or press down its tongue with a cord?

1 Corinthians 1:20-31
We proclaim Christ crucified, a stumbling block to Jews and foolishness to Gentiles, but to those who are called, both Jews and Greeks, Christ the power of God and the wisdom of God.

Acts 16:6-15
During the night Paul had a vision: there stood a man of Macedonia pleading with him and saying, "Come over to Macedonia and help us."

after Proper 23 / Pentecost 22

Jeremiah 36:27-37:2
The word of the LORD came to Jeremiah: Take another scroll and write on it all the former words that were in the first scroll, which King Jehoiakim of Judah has burned.

Hosea 12:2-14
Return to your God, hold fast to love and justice, and wait continually for your God.
[BCP: Jonah 1:1-17a]

1 Corinthians 14:1-12

Pursue love and strive for the spiritual gifts.

Acts 26:24-27:8

Whether quickly or not, I pray to God that not only you but also all who are listening to me today might become such as I am.

after Proper 27 / Pentecost 26

Nehemiah 9:26-38

You warned them in order to turn them back to your law. Yet they acted presumptuously and did not obey your commandments.

or Nehemiah 4:1-23

Joel 1:15-2:2(3-11)

Let all the inhabitants of the land tremble, for the day of the LORD is coming, it is near–a day of darkness and gloom, a day of clouds and thick darkness!

or Joel 2:3-11

Revelation 18:9-20

Alas, alas, the great city, Babylon, the mighty city! For in one hour your judgment has come.

Revelation 19:1-10

Blessed are those who are invited to the marriage supper of the Lamb.

Silence for meditation follows each reading.

RESPONSORY

I will place my dwelling in your midst, and I shall **not** abhor you.*

I will walk among you, and will be your God, and you shall **be** my people.

We are the temple of the living God, **as** God said.*

I will walk among you, and will be your God, and you shall **be** my people.

[LH: Lev. 26:11-12; 2 Cor. 6:16]

I beg you to lead a life worthy of the calling to which you **have** been called,*

making every effort to maintain the unity of the Spirit in the **bond** of peace.

There is one body and one Spirit, just as you were called in one hope **of** your calling;*

making every effort to maintain the unity of the Spirit in the **bond** of peace.

[LH: Eph. 4:1,3,4]

Wednesday of Week III

Antiphon to PSALM 65 *Te decet hymnus, Deus*

You are to be praised, O **God** in Zion;*
you make the dawn and the dusk to **sing** for joy. [LH]

65 *Thanksgiving hymn*

1 You are to be praised, O **God** in Zion;*
to you shall vows be performed **in** Jerusalem.

2 To you that hear prayer shall **all** flesh come,*
because of **their** transgressions.

3 Our sins are stron**ger** than we are,*
but you will **blot** them out.

4 Happy are they whom you choose
and draw to your **courts** to dwell there!*
they will be satisfied by the beauty of your house,
by the holiness **of** your temple.

5 Awesome things will you show us in your righteousness,
O God of **our** salvation,*
O Hope of all the ends of the earth
and of the seas that are **far** away.

6 You make fast the mountains **by** your power;*
they are girded a**bout** with might.

7 You still the roaring **of** the seas,*
the roaring of their waves,
and the clamor **of** the peoples.

8 Those who dwell at the ends of the earth will tremble at your
marvelous signs;*
you make the dawn and the dusk to **sing** for joy.

9 You visit the earth and water it abundantly;
you make it **very** plenteous;*
the river of God is **full** of water.

10 You pre**pare** the grain,*
for so you provide **for** the earth.

11 You drench the furrows and smooth **out** the ridges;*
with heavy rain you soften the ground and **bless** its increase.

12 You crown the year **with** your goodness,*
and your paths over**flow** with plenty.

13 May the fields of the wilderness be **rich** for grazing,*
and the hills be **clothed** with joy.

14 May the meadows cover themselves with flocks,
and the valleys cloak them**selves** with grain;*
let them shout for **joy** and sing.

Antiphon You are to be praised, O **God** in Zion;*
you make the dawn and the dusk to **sing** for joy.

Silence for meditation

Lord God, joy marks your presence; beauty, abundance, and peace are the tokens of your work in all creation: Work also in our lives, that by these signs we may see the splendor of your love and may praise you through Jesus Christ our Lord. [LBW]

+

Antiphon to PSALM 147 part i *Laudate Dominum*

How pleas**ant** it is
to honor **God** with praise! [LH, PBO]

147 *Praise of God who maintains the world*

1 Hallelujah!
How good it is to sing praises **to** our God!*
how pleasant it is to honor **him** with praise!

2 The LORD re**builds** Jerusalem;*
he gathers the ex**iles** of Israel.

3 He heals the **bro**kenhearted*
and binds **up** their wounds.

4 He counts the number **of** the stars*
and calls them all **by** their names.

5 Great is our LORD and might**y** in power;*
there is no limit **to** his wisdom.

6 The LORD lifts **up** the lowly,*
but casts the wicked **to** the ground,

7 Sing to the LORD **with** thanksgiving;*
make music to our God up**on** the harp.

8 He covers the heav**ens** with clouds*
and prepares rain **for** the earth;

9 He makes grass to grow up**on** the mountains*
and green plants to **serve** mankind.

10 He provides food for **flocks** and herds*
and for the young ravens **when** they cry.

11 He is not impressed by the might **of** a horse;*
he has no pleasure in the strength **of** a man;

12 But the LORD has pleasure in **those** who fear him,*
in those who await his **gra**cious favor.

Antiphon How pleasant it is to honor God with praise!

Silence for meditation

God our Father, great builder of the heavenly Jerusalem, you know the number of the stars and call each of them by name: Heal hearts that are broken, gather those who have been scattered, and enrich us all from the plenitude of your eternal wisdom, Jesus Christ our Lord. [LH, LBW]

+

Stand

THE HYMN is sung. *Wie schön leuchtet der Morgenstern*

2 My treasured Pearl, my priceless Crown,
The Son of Mary, God come down
The high-born King of ages!
You are my heart's most beauteous Flower:
Your saving Gospel's sweetest power
My raptured soul engages.
What bliss is this!
Sing Hosanna!
Heavenly manna
Gladly eating:
Here we taste eternal feasting.

3 Come, heavenly brightness, light divine,
And deep within my heart now shine;
There light a flame undying!
Fill me with joy and strength, that I
Your member, know you ever nigh
Your life my life supplying.
Longings for you
All possess me.
Turn and bless me.
For your gladness
Eye and heart here pine in sadness.

4 But if you look on me in love,
There straightway falls from God above
A ray of purest pleasure.
Your Word and Spirit, flesh and blood
Refresh my soul with heavenly food;
You are my hidden treasure!
Let your mercy
Warm and cheer me,
Oh, draw near me.
You have taught us
In your Word, that you have sought us.

5 Almighty Father, in your Son
You loved me when not yet begun
Was this old earth's foundation.
Your Son has ransomed me in love
To live in him here and above:
This is your great salvation.
Alleluia!
Christ the living,
To us giving
Life for ever
Keeps us yours and fails us never.

6 Let harp and voice break forth in sound
And joy be all with music crowned,
In God's high praises blended.
For Christ goes with us all the way,
Today, tomorrow, every day
Till travelling days be ended.
Sing out, ring out
Triumph glorious
O victorious
Chosen nation;
Praise the God of your salvation.

7 Here will I rest and hold it fast,
The Lord of love is First and Last
The End as the Beginning.
Here I can calmly die; your grace
Will raise me to your blessed place
Beyond all tears and sinning.
Amen! Amen!
Come, Lord Jesus
Soon release us;
With deep yearning
Lord, we look for your returning.

[CB 405, TLH 343, LBW 76]

Text: Philipp Nicolai, 1556-1608; tr. stanzas 1, 3-4, 7 Catherine Winkworth, stanza 2 TLH, stanzas 5-6 TLH-LBW; rev. PHP

Tune: *Wie schön leuchtet,* Philipp Nicolai, 1556-1608 PM

Sit

One or two LESSONS are read.

Year 1

after Epiphany 3

Isaiah 49:1-12

You are my servant, Israel, in whom I will be glorified.

Galatians 2:11-21

It is no longer I who live, but it is Christ who lives in me. And the life I now live in the flesh I live by faith in the Son of God, who loved me and gave himself for me.

after Epiphany 7

Ruth 2:1-13

May the LORD reward you for your deeds, and may you have a full reward from the LORD, the God of Israel, under whose wings you have come for refuge!

2 Corinthians 1:23-2:17

Thanks be to God, who in Christ always leads us in triumphal procession, and through us spreads in

Year 2

after Epiphany 3

Genesis 16:1-14

Sarai said to Abram, "May the wrong done to me be on you! I gave my slave-girl to your embrace, and when she saw that she conceived, she looked on me with contempt. May the LORD judge between you and me!"

Hebrews 9:15-28

Christ, having been offered once to bear the sins of many, will appear a second time, not to deal with sin, but to save those who are eagerly waiting for him.

after Epiphany 7

Proverbs 6:1-19

Go to the ant, you lazybones; consider its ways and be wise.
or Tobit 5:1-13a, 14-16

1 John 5:1-12

By this we know that we love the children of God, when we love God and obey his commandments.

every place the fragrance that comes from knowing him.

after Proper 3 / Pentecost 2

Deuteronomy 4:25-31

Because the LORD your God is a merciful God, he will neither abandon you nor destroy you; he will not forget the covenant with your ancestors that he swore to them.

Proverbs 17:1-20

The beginning of strife is like letting out water; so stop before the quarrel breaks out.

2 Corinthians 1:23-2:17

Thanks be to God, who in Christ always leads us in triumphal procession, and through us spreads in every place the fragrance that comes from knowing him.

1 Timothy 3:1-16

The mystery of our religion is great: He was revealed in flesh, vindicated in spirit, seen by angels, proclaimed among Gentiles, believed in throughout the world, taken up in glory.

after Proper 7 / Pentecost 6

1 Samuel 7:2-17

Samuel took a stone and set it up between Mizpah and Jeshanah, and named it Ebenezer; for he said, "Thus far the LORD has helped us."

Numbers 16:36-50

Aaron put on the incense, and made atonement for the people. He stood between the dead and the living; and the plague was stopped.

Acts 6:1-15

It is not right that we should neglect the word of God in order to wait on tables. Therefore, friends, select from among yourselves seven men of good standing, full of the Spirit and of wisdom, whom we may appoint to this task, while we, for our part, will devote ourselves to prayer and to serving the word.

Romans 4:13-25

Therefore Abraham's faith "was reckoned to him as righteousness." Now the words, "it was reckoned to him," were written not for his sake alone, but for ours also.

after Proper 11 / Pentecost 10

1 Samuel 25:23-44

When David heard that Nabal was dead, he said, "Blessed be the LORD who has judged the case of Nabal's insult to me, and has kept back his servant from evil; the LORD has returned the evildoing of Nabal upon his own head.

Joshua 8:30-35

Then Joshua built on Mount Ebal an altar to the LORD, the God of Israel, just as Moses the servant of the LORD had commanded the Israelites, as it is written in the book of the law of Moses, " an altar of unhewn stones, on which no iron tool has been used."

Acts 14:19-28

When they arrived, they called the church together and related all that God had done with them, and how he had opened a door of faith for the Gentiles.

Romans 14:13-23

Let us then pursue what makes for peace and for mutual upbuilding.

after Proper 15 / Pentecost 14

2 Samuel 18:19-33

O my son Absalom, my son, my son Absalom! Would I had died instead of you, O Absalom, my son, my son!

Judges 18:16-31

Is it better for you to be priest to the house of one person, or to be priest to a tribe or clan in Israel?

Acts 23:23-35

This man was seized by the Jews and was about to be killed by them, but when I had learned that he was a Roman citizen, I came with the guard and rescued him.

Acts 8:14-25

Then Peter and John laid their hands on them, and they received the Holy Spirit.

after Proper 19 / Pentecost 18

1 Kings 22:1-28

I saw all Israel scattered on the mountains, like sheep that have

Job 42:1-17

I had heard of you by the hearing of the ear, but now my eye sees

no shepherd; and the LORD said, “These have no master; let each one go home in peace.”

1 Corinthians 2:1-13
We speak God’s wisdom, secret and hidden, which God decreed before the ages for our glory.

you; therefore I despise myself and repent in dust and ashes.

Acts 16:16-24
These men are disturbing our city; they are Jews and are advocating customs that are not lawful for us as Romans to adopt or observe.

after Proper 23 / Pentecost 22

Jeremiah 37:3-21
Thus says the LORD: Do not deceive yourselves, saying, “The Chaldeans will surely go away from us,” for they will not go away.

Hosea 13:1-3
Therefore they shall be like the morning mist or like the dew that goes away early, like chaff that swirls from the threshing floor or like smoke from a window.
[BCP: Jonah 1:17-2:10

1 Corinthians 14:13-25
One who speaks in a tongue should pray for the power to interpret.

Acts 27:9-26
Do not be afraid, Paul; you must stand before the emperor; and indeed, God has granted safety to all those who are sailing with you.

after Proper 27 / Pentecost 26

Nehemiah 7:73b-8:3,5-18
They read from the book, from the law of God, with interpretation. They gave the sense, so that the people understood the reading.
or Nehemiah 5:1-19

Joel 2:12-19
Return to the LORD your God, for he is gracious and merciful, slow to anger, and abounding in steadfast love, and relents from punishing.

Revelation 18:21-24
In you was found the blood of prophets and of saints, and of all

Revelation 19:11-21
Then I saw heaven opened, and there was a white horse! Its rider

who have been slaughtered on earth.

is called Faithful and True, and in righteousness he judges and makes war.

Silence for meditation follows each reading.

RESPONSORY

You shall go **out** in joy,*
and be led **back** in peace.
The mountains and the hills before you shall burst **in**to song,*
and all the trees of the field shall **clap** their hands.
And there will be a highway for the remnant that is left **of** his people,*
as there was for Israel when they came up from the **land** of Egypt.
The mountains and the hills before you shall burst **in**to song,*
and all the trees of the field shall **clap** their hands.
[LH: Isa. 55:12; 11:16]

God grant that Christ may dwell in your hearts through faith as you are being rooted and ground**ed** in love,*
so that you may be filled with all the full**ness** of God.
As therefore you received Christ Jesus the Lord, continue to live your lives in him, rooted and built up in him and established in the faith, just as you were taught, abounding **in** thanksgiving,*
so that you may be filled with all the full**ness** of God.
[LH: Eph. 3:16,17,19; Col. 2:6-7]

Thursday of Week III

Antiphon to PSALM 101 *Misericordiam et judicium*

To you, O LORD, will **I** sing praises;*
I will strive to follow a **blame**less course. [LH, PBO]

101 *The ideal ruler*

1 I will sing of mer**cy** and justice;*
to you, O LORD, will **I** sing praises.

2 I will strive to follow a blameless course;
oh, when will you **come** to me?*
I will walk with sincerity of heart with**in** my house.

3 I will set no worthless thing be**fore** my eyes;*
I hate the doers of evil deeds;
they shall not re**main** with me.

4 A crooked heart shall be **far** from me;*
I will **not** know evil.

5 Those who in secret slander their neighbors I **will** destroy;*
those who have a haughty look and a proud
heart I can**not** abide.

6 My eyes are upon the faithful in the land, that they may
dwell with me,*
and only those who lead a blameless life shall
be my servants.

7 Those who act deceitfully shall not dwell **in** my house,*
and those who tell lies shall not continue **in** my sight.

8 I will soon destroy all the wicked **in** the land,*
that I may root out all evildoers from the city **of** the LORD.

Antiphon To you, O LORD, will **I** sing praises;*
I will strive to follow a **blame**less course.

Silence for meditation

Lord Jesus, you came to us so that your people might walk in innocence, and you taught us to be holy as your Father is holy. Help us, your children, to love what is truly perfect, so that we may neither speak what is evil nor do what is wrong. Then let us stand in your sight and celebrate with you the Father's love and justice for ever. [LH, LBW]

+

Antiphon to PSALM 147 part ii *Lauda, Jerusalem, Dominum*

Antiphon Praise the LORD, O Jerusalem. [LH]

147 *Praise of God's personal care of Israel*

13 Worship the LORD, **O** Jerusalem;*
praise your **God**, O Zion;

14 For he has strengthened the bars **of** your gates;*
he has blessed your chil**dren** within you.

15 He has established peace **on** your borders;*
he satisfies you with the **fin**est wheat.

16 He sends out his command **to** the earth,*
and his word runs **ver**y swiftly.

17 He gives **snow** like wool;*
he scatters hoar**frost** like ashes.

18 He scatters his **hail** like bread crumbs;*
who can stand a**gainst** his cold?

19 He sends forth his **word** and melts them;*
he blows with his wind, and the **wat**ers flow.

20 He declares his **word** to Jacob,*
his statutes and his judg**ments** to Israel.

21 He has not done so to any **oth**er nation;*
to them he has not revealed his judgments.
Hallelujah!

Antiphon Praise the LORD, O Jerusalem.

Silence for meditation

Almighty God, through your Church, generously endowed with gifts of grace and fortified by the Holy Spirit, you send out your Word to all nations: Strengthen your Church with heavenly food, make it dauntless in faith, and multiply its children, that with joy we may celebrate your love at the altar on high; through Jesus Christ our Lord. [LH]

+

Stand

THE HYMN is sung. *The Song of the Lamb*

2 Light of the glory divine dwells with him,
Light of a glory that cannot grow dim,
Light in its silence and beauty and calm,
Light in its gladness and brightness and balm.

3 Heights of the heavens resound with his Name,
All the earth rings with his glory and fame,
Ocean and mountain, stream, forest, and flower
Echo his praises and tell of his power.

4 Ever ascending the song and the joy,
Ever descending the love from on high,
Blessing and honor and glory and praise,
This is the theme of the hymns that we raise.

5 Give we the glory and praise to the Lamb;
Take we the robe and the harp and the palm;
Sing we the song of the Lamb who was slain,
Dying in weakness, but rising to reign.

[CSB 295, SBH 166; LBW 525, alt.]

Text: Horatius Bonar, 1808-1889, alt.
Tune: *American Hymn*, Matthias Keller, 1813-1890 10 10 10 10 10

Sit

One or two LESSONS are read.

Year 1

after Epiphany 3

Isaiah 49:13-23(24-26)

Sing for joy, O heavens, and exult, O earth; break forth, O mountains, into singing! For the LORD has comforted his people, and will have compassion on his suffering ones.

Year 2

Genesis 16:15-17:14

I will establish my covenant between me and you, and your offspring after you throughout their generations, for an everlasting covenant, to be God to you and to your offspring after you.

Galatians 3:1-14

The scripture, foreseeing that God would justify the Gentiles by faith, declared the gospel beforehand to Abraham, saying, "All the Gentiles shall be blessed in you."

Hebrews 10:1-10

It is by God's will that we have been sanctified through the offering of the body of Jesus Christ once for all.

After Epiphany 7

Ruth 2:14-23

Naomi said to her daughter-in-law, "Blessed be he by the LORD, whose kindness has not forsaken the living or the dead!

Proverbs 7:1-27

Keep my commandments and live, keep my teachings as the apple of your eye; bind them on your fingers, write them on the tablet of your heart.
or Tobit 6:1-17

2 Corinthians 3:1-18

All of us, with unveiled faces, seeing the glory of the Lord as though reflected in a mirror, are being transformed into the same image from one degree of glory to another; for this comes from the Lord, the Spirit.

1 John 5:13-21

I write these things to you who believe in the name of the Son of God, so that you may know that you have eternal life.

after Proper 3 / Pentecost 2

Deuteronomy 4:32-40

Has any people ever heard the voice of a god speaking out of a fire, as you have heard, and lived?

Proverbs 21:30-22:6

The horse is made ready for the day of battle, but the victory belongs to the LORD.

2 Corinthians 3:1-18

All of us, with unveiled faces, seeing the glory of the Lord as though reflected in a mirror, are being transformed into the same image from

1 Timothy 4:1-16

Everything created by God is good, and nothing is to be rejected, provided it is received with thanksgiving; for it is sanc-

one degree of glory to another; for this comes from the Lord, the Spirit.

tified by God's word and by prayer.

after Proper 7 / Pentecost 6

1 Samuel 8:1-22

We are determined to have a king over us, so that we also may be like other nations, and that our king may govern us and go out before us and fight our battles.

Numbers 17:1-11

When Moses went into the tent of the covenant on the next day, the staff of Aaron for the house of Levi had sprouted. It put forth buds, produced blossoms, and bore ripe almonds.

Acts 6:15-7:16

All who sat in the council looked intently at Stephen, and they saw that his face was like the face of an angel.

Romans 5:1-11

Therefore, since we are justified by faith, we have peace with God through our Lord Jesus Christ.

after Proper 11 / Pentecost 10

1 Samuel 28:3-20

The LORD has done to you just as he spoke by me; for the LORD has torn the kingdom out of your hand and given it to your neighbor, David.

Joshua 9:3-21

Joshua made peace with them, guaranteeing their lives by a treaty; and the leaders of the congregation swore an oath to them.

Acts 15:1-11

Peter stood up and said to them, "My brothers, you know that in the early days God made a choice among you, that I should be the one through whom the Gentiles would hear the message of the good news and become believers."

Romans 15:1-13

May the God of hope fill you with all joy and peace in believing, so that you may abound in hope by the power of the Holy Spirit.

after Proper 15 / Pentecost 14

2 Samuel 19:1-23

So the victory that day was turned into mourning for all the troops; for the troops heard that day, "The king is grieving for his son."

Job 1:1-22

Naked I came from my mother's womb, and naked shall I return there; the LORD gave and the LORD has taken away; blessed be the name of the LORD.

Acts 24:1-23

This I admit to you, that according to the Way, which they call a sect, I worship the God of our ancestors, believing everything laid down according to the law or written in the prophets.

Acts 8:26-40

Then Philip began to speak, and starting with this scripture, he proclaimed to him the good news about Jesus.

after Proper 19 / Pentecost 18

1 Kings 22:29-45

He walked in all the way of his father Asa; he did not turn aside from it, doing what was right in the sight of the LORD; yet the high places were not taken away, and the people still sacrificed and offered incense on the high places.

Job 28:1-28

Truly, the fear of the Lord, that is wisdom; and to depart from evil is understanding.

1 Corinthians 2:14-3:15

So neither the one who plants nor the one who waters is anything, but only God who gives the growth.

Acts 16:25-40

Believe on the Lord Jesus, and you will be saved, you and your household.

after Proper 23 / Pentecost 22

Jeremiah 38:1-13

Thus says the LORD, Those who stay in this city shall die by the sword, by famine, and by pesti-

Hosea 13:4-8

I have been the LORD your God ever since the land of Egypt; you know no God but me, and besides

lence; but those who go out to the Chaldeans shall live.

1 Corinthians 14:26-33a (33b-36) 37-40

God is not a God of disorder but of peace.

me there is no savior.
[BCP: Jonah 3:1-4:11]

Acts 27:27-44

The soldiers' plan was to kill the prisoners, so that none might swim away and escape; but the centurion, wishing to save Paul, kept them from carrying out their plan.

after Proper 27 / Pentecost 26

1 Maccabees 1:1-28

Antiochus shed much blood, and spoke with great arrogance. Israel mourned deeply in every community, rulers and elders groaned, young women and young men became faint, the beauty of the women faded.

or Nehemiah 6:1-19

Revelation 19:1-10

Salvation and glory and power to our God, for his judgments are true and just.

Joel 2:21-27

You shall know that I am in the midst of Israel, and that I, the LORD, am your God and there is no other. And my people shall never again be put to shame.

James 1:1-15

Whenever you face trials of any kind, consider it nothing but joy, because you know that the testing of your faith produces endurance.

Silence for meditation follows each reading.

RESPONSORY

Your love, O Lord, reaches **to** the heavens,*
and your faithfulness **to** the clouds.
  Your righteousness is like **the** strong mountains,*

I am standing at the door, knocking; if you hear my voice and o**pen** the door,*
  I will come in to you and eat with you, and **you** with me.

your justice like **the** great deep.

O the depth of the riches and wisdom and knowl**edge** of God!*
How unsearchable are his judgments and inscruta**ble** his ways!

Your righteousness is like **the** strong mountains,*
your justice like **the** great deep.

[LH: Ps. 36:6-7 (BCP); Rom. 11:33]

Blessed is that slave whom his master will find at work when **he** arrives.*

I will come in to you and eat with you, and **you** with me.

[LH: Rev. 3:20; Matt. 24:46]

Friday of Week III

Antiphon to PSALM 88 *Domine, Deus*

O LORD, I cry to **you** for help;*
in the morning my prayer **comes** before you. [LH, PBO]

88 *Prayer in desolation*

1 O LORD, my **God**, my Savior,*
by day and night I **cry** to you.

2 Let my prayer enter in**to** your presence;*
incline your ear to my **lam**entation.

3 For I am **full** of trouble;*
my life is at the brink **of** the grave.

4 I am counted among those who go down **to** the Pit;*
I have become like one who **has** no strength;

5 Lost a**mong** the dead,*
like the slain who lie **in** the grave,

6 Whom you remem**ber** no more,*
for they are cut off **from** your hand.

7 You have laid me in the depths **of** the Pit,*
in dark places, and in **the** abyss.

8 Your anger weighs up**on** me heavily,*
and all your great waves **o**verwhelm me.

9 You have put my friends far from me;
you have made me to be ab**horred** by them;*
I am in prison and can**not** get free.

10 My sight has failed me be**cause** of trouble;*
LORD, I have called upon you daily;
I have stretched out my **hands** to you.

11 Do you work wonders **for** the dead?*
will those who have died stand up and **give** you thanks?

12 Will your loving-kindness be declared **in** the grave?*
your faithfulness in the land **of** destruction?

13 Will your wonders be known **in** the dark?*
or your righteousness in the country where all
is forgotten?

14 But as for me, O LORD, I cry to **you** for help;*
in the morning my prayer **comes** before you.

15 LORD, why have you re**ject**ed me?*
why have you hidden your **face** from me?

16 Ever since my youth, I have been wretched and at the
point of death;*
I have borne your terrors with a **troub**led mind.

17 Your blazing anger has swept **o**ver me;*
your terrors **have** destroyed me;

18 They surround me all day long **like** a flood;*
they encompass me on **ev**ery side.

19 My friend and my neighbor you have put a**way** from me,*
and darkness is my on**ly** companion.

Antiphon O LORD, I cry to **you** for help;*
in the morning my prayer **comes** before you.

Silence for meditation

Lord Jesus, author of our salvation and redeemer of all, for us you descended to the dead and broke the grip of death: Hear the prayers of your family, and lift us from our slavery in evil, that we may be set free to see your Father's glory now and for ever. [LH, LBW]

+

Antiphon to PSALM 148 *Laudate Dominum*

Praise the LORD **from** the heavens;*
praise the LORD **from** the earth. [LH]

148 *Cosmic praise*

1 Hallelujah!
Praise the LORD **from** the heavens;*
praise him **in** the heights.

2 Praise him, all you an**gels** of his;*
praise him, **all** his host.

3 Praise him, **sun** and moon;*
praise him, all you **shin**ing stars.

4 Praise him, hea**ven** of heavens,*
and you waters a**bove** the heavens.

5 Let them praise the Name **of** the LORD;*
for he commanded, and they **were** created.

6 He made them stand fast for ev**er** and ever;*
he gave them a law which shall not **pass** away.

7 Praise the LORD **from** the earth,*
you sea-monsters **and** all deeps;

8 Fire and hail, **snow** and fog,*
tempestuous wind, do**ing** his will;

9 Mountains **and** all hills,*
fruit trees **and** all cedars;

10 Wild beasts **and** all cattle,*
creeping things and **wing**èd birds;

11 Kings of the earth **and** all peoples,*
princes and all rulers **of** the world;

12 Young **men** and maidens,*
old and **young** together.

13 Let them praise the Name **of** the LORD,*
for his Name only is exalted,
his splendor is over **earth** and heaven.
14 He has raised up strength for his people
and praise for all his **loy**al servants,*
the children of Israel, a people who are near him.
Hallelujah!

Antiphon Praise the LORD **from** the heavens;*
praise the LORD **from** the earth.

Silence for meditation

God Most High, by your Word your created a wondrous universe, and through your Spirit you breathed into it the breath of life: Accept creation's hymn of praise from our lips, and let the praise that is sung in heaven resound in the heart of every creature on earth, to the glory of the Father, and the Son, and the Holy Spirit, now and for ever. [LH, LBW]

+

Stand

THE HYMN is sung.

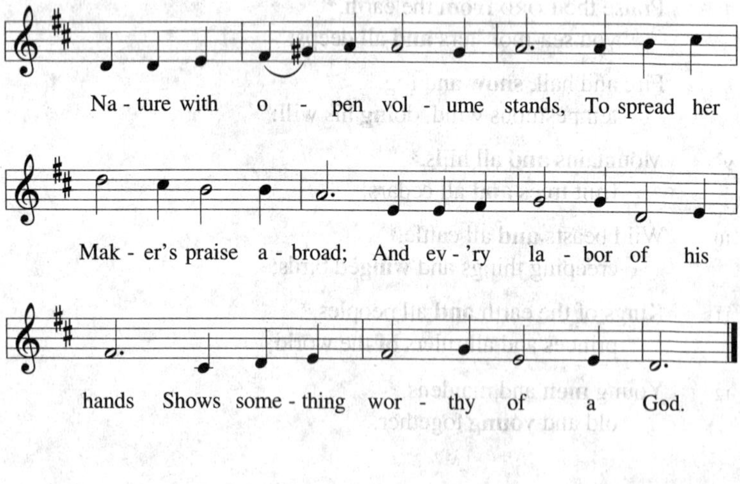

2 But in the grace that rescued us
His brightest form of glory shines;
Here on the cross 'tis fairest drawn
In precious blood and crimson lines.

3 Here his whole Name appears complete;
Nor wit can guess, nor reason prove
Which of the letters best is writ,
The power, the wisdom, or the love.

4 O, the sweet wonders of that cross,
Where Christ my Savior loved and died!
Her noblest life my spirit draws
From his dear wounds and bleeding side.

5 I would for ever speak his Name
In sounds to mortal ears unknown,
With angels join to praise the Lamb,
And worship at his Father's throne.

[H82 434; LBW 119 alt]

Text: Isaac Watts, 1674-1748
Tune: *Angelus,* Georg Joseph, 17th cent., adapt. LM

Sit

One or two LESSONS are read.

Year 1

after Epiphany 3

Isaiah 50:1-11
I gave my back to those who struck me, and my cheeks to those who pulled out the beard; I did not hide my face from insult and spitting.

Year 2

Genesis 17:15-27
Abraham fell on his face and laughed, and said to himself, "Can a child be born to a man who is a hundred years old? Can Sarah, who is ninety years old, bear a child?"

Galatians 3:15-22

The scripture has imprisoned all things under the power of sin, so that what was promised through faith in Jesus Christ might be given to those who believe.

Hebrews 10:11-25

Let us hold fast to the confession of our hope without wavering, for he who has promised is faithful.

after Epiphany 7

Ruth 3:1-18

I am Ruth, your servant; spread your cloak over your servant, for you are next-of-kin.

Proverbs 8:1-21

Does not wisdom call, and does not understanding raise her voice?
or Tobit 7:1-18

2 Corinthians 4:1-12

We have this treasure in clay jars, so that it may be clear that this extraordinary power belongs to God and does come from us.

Philemon 1-25

I pray that the sharing of your faith may become effective when you perceive all the good that we may do for Christ.

after Proper 3 / Pentecost 2

Deuteronomy 5:1-22

I am the LORD your God, who brought you out of the land of Egypt, out of the house of slavery; you shall have no other gods before me.

Proverbs 23:19-21, 29-24:2

The drunkard and the glutton will come to poverty, and drowsiness will clothe them with rags.

2 Corinthians 4:1-12

We have this treasure in clay jars, so that it may be clear that this extraordinary power belongs to God and does come from us.

1 Timothy 5:17-22 (23-25)

Let the elders who rule well be considered worthy of double honor, especially those who labor in preaching and teaching.

after Proper 7 / Pentecost 6

1 Samuel 9:1-14

There is a man of God in this town; he is a man held in honor. Whatever he says always comes true. Let us go there now; perhaps he will tell us about the journey on which we have set out.

Acts 7:17-29

Moses was instructed in all the wisdom of the Egyptians and was powerful in his words and deeds.

Numbers 20:1-13

Moses lifted up his hand and struck the rock twice with his staff; water came out abundantly, and the congregation and their livestock drank.

Romans 5:12-21

Where sin increased, grace abounded all the more.

after Proper 11 / Pentecost 10

1 Samuel 31:1-13

So Saul and his three sons and his armor-bearer and all his men died together on the same day.

Acts 15:12-21

The whole assembly kept silence, and listened to Barnabas and Paul as they told of all the signs and wonders that God had done through them among the Gentiles.

Joshua 9:22-10:15

The sun stood still, and the moon stopped, until the nation took vengeance on their enemies.

Romans 15:14-24

I myself feel confident about you, my brothers and sisters, that you yourselves are full of goodness, filled with all knowledge, and able to instruct one another.

after Proper 15 / Pentecost 14

2 Samuel 19:24-43

All the people of Judah, and also half the people of Israel, brought the king on his way.

Acts 24:24-25:12

I appeal to the emperor.

Job 2:1-13

Shall we receive the good at the hand of God, and not receive the bad?

Acts 9:1-9

He fell to the ground and heard a voice saying to him, "Saul, Saul, why do you persecute me?"

after Proper 19 / Pentecost 18

2 Kings 1:2-17

The angel of the Lord said to Elijah the Tishbite, "Get up, go to meet the messengers of the king of Samaria, and say to them, "Is it because there is no God in Israel that you are going to inquire of Baal-zebub, the god of Ekron?"

Esther 1:1-4,10-19

Queen Vashti refused to come at the king's command conveyed by the eunuchs. At this the king was enraged, and his anger burned within him.
[BCP: *or* Judith 4:1-15]

1 Corinthians 3:16-23

Do you not know that you are God's temple and that God's Spirit dwells in you?

Acts 17:1-15

These people who have been turning the world upside down have come here also.

after Proper 23 / Pentecost 22

Jeremiah 38:14-28

Thus says the LORD, the God of hosts, the God of Israel, If you will only surrender to the officials of the king of Babylon, then your life shall be spared, and this city shall not be burned with fire, and you and your house shall live.

Hosea 13:9-16

Shall I ransom them from the power of Sheol? Shall I redeem them from death? O Death, where are your plagues? O Sheol, where is your destruction? Compassion is hidden from my eyes.
[BCP: Sirach [Ecclesiasticus] 1:1-10,18-27]

1 Corinthians 15:1-11

Now I would remind you, brothers and sisters, of the good news that I proclaimed to you, which you in turn received, in which also you stand, through which also you are being saved, if you hold firmly to the message that I proclaimed to you.

Acts 28:1-16

When we came into Rome, Paul was allowed to live by himself, with the soldier who was guarding him.

after Proper 27 / Pentecost 26

1 Maccabees 1:41-63

The king wrote to his whole kingdom that all should be one people, and that all should give up their particular customs.

or Nehemiah 12:27-31a,42b-47

Joel 2:28-3:8

The sun shall be turned to darkness, and the moon to blood, before the great and terrible day of the LORD comes.

Revelation 19:11-16

Then I saw heaven opened and there was a white horse! Its rider is called Faithful and True, and in righteousness he judges and makes war.

James 1:16-27

Be doers of the word, and not merely hearers who deceive themselves.

Silence for meditation follows each reading.

RESPONSORY

I will seek **out** my sheep.*
I will rescue them from all the places to which they have scattered on a day of clouds **and** thick darkness.
I will bring them into **their** own land;*
    I will feed them **with** good pasture.
I came that they may have life, and have **it** abundantly.*
    I will feed them **with** good pasture.

[LH: Ezek. 34:12,13,14; John 10:10]

The love of Christ **urges** us on,*
because we are convinced that one has **died** for all,
    so that those who live might live no longer **for** themselves*
    but for him who died and was **raised** for them.
God did not withhold **his** own Son*
but gave him up for **all** of us,
    so that those who live might live no longer **for** themselves*
    but for him who died and was **raised** for them.

[LH: 2 Cor. 5:14,15; Rom. 8:32]

Saturday of Week III

Antiphon to PSALM 122 *Laetatus sum*

Pray for the peace of Jerusalem. [LH, PBO]

122 *Holy city of Jerusalem*

1 I was glad when they **said** to me,*
"Let us go to the house **of** the LORD."

2 Now our **feet** are standing*
within your gates, **O** Jerusalem.

3 Jerusalem is built **as** a city*
that is at unity **with** itself;

4 To which the tribes go up,
the tribes **of** the LORD,*
the assembly of Israel,
to praise the Name **of** the LORD.

5 For there are the **thrones** of judgment,*
the thrones of the **house** of David.

6 Pray for the peace of Je**ru**salem:*
"May they pros**per** who love you.

7 Peace be with**in** your walls*
and quietness with**in** your towers.

8 For my brethren and com**pan**ions' sake,*
I pray for **your** prosperity.

9 Because of the house of the **LORD** our God,*
I will seek to **do** you good."

Antiphon Pray for the peace of Jerusalem.

Silence for meditation

Lord Jesus, give us the peace of the new Jerusalem. Bring all nations into your kingdom to share your gifts, that they may render thanks to you without end and may come to your eternal city, where you live and reign with the Father and the Holy Spirit, now and for ever. [LH, LBW]

+

Antiphon to PSALM 149 *Cantate Domino*

Let the children of Zion be joyful in their king. [LH, PBO]

149 *Praise to the God of victories*

1 Hallelujah!
Sing to the LORD **a** new song;*
sing his praise in the congregation **of** the faithful.

2 Let Israel rejoice **in** his Maker;*
let the children of Zion be joyful **in** their King.

3 Let them praise his Name **in** the dance;*
let them sing praise to him with tim**brel** and harp.

4 For the LORD takes pleasure **in** his people*
and adorns the **poor** with victory.

5 Let the faithful re**joice** in triumph;*
let them be joyful **on** their beds.

6 Let the praises of God be **in** their throat*
and a two-edged sword **in** their hand;

7 To wreak vengeance **on** the nations*
and punishment **on** the peoples;

8 To bind their **kings** in chains*
and their nobles with **links** of iron;

9 To inflict on them the judg**ment** decreed;*
this is glory for all his faithful people.
Hallelujah!

Antiphon Let the children of Zion be joyful in their king.

Silence for meditation

Lord, let Israel rejoice in you and acknowledge you as creator and redeemer. In your lovingkindness embrace us now, that we may proclaim the wonderful truths of salvation with your saints in glory; through your Son, Jesus Christ our Lord. [LH, LBW]

+

Stand

THE HYMN is sung. *Urbs sion aurea, patria lactea*

2 They stand, those halls of Zion,
Conjubilant with song
And bright with many an angel
And all the martyr throng.
The Prince is ever in them;
The daylight is serene;
The pastures of the blessèd
Are decked with glorious sheen.

3 There is the throne of David,
And there, from care released,
The shout of those who triumph,
The song of those who feast.
And they, who with their leader
Have conquered in the fight,
For ever and for ever
Are clad in robes of white.

4 Oh, sweet and blessèd country,
The home of God's elect!
Oh, sweet and blessèd country,
That eager hearts expect!
In mercy, Jesus, bring us
To that dear land of rest!
You are, with God the Father,
And Spirit, ever blest. [LBW 347, H82 624]

Text: Bernard of Cluny, 12th cent.; tr. John Mason Neale, 1818-1866
Tune: *Complainer,* W. Walker, *Southern Harmony*, 1835
or Ewing, Alexander Ewing, 1830-1895 [H82, SBH] 76 76D

Sit

One or two LESSONS are read.

Year 1

after Epiphany 3

Isaiah 51:1-8
My deliverance will be forever, and my salvation to all generations.

Year 2

Genesis 18:1-16
Is anything too wonderful for the LORD? At the set time I will return to you, in due season, and Sarah shall have a son.

Galatians 3:23-29

There is no longer Jew or Greek, there is no longer slave or free, there is no longer male or female; for all of you are one in Christ Jesus.

Hebrews 10:26-39

You need endurance, so that when you have done the will of God, you may receive what was promised.

after Epiphany 7

Ruth 4:1-22

May the LORD make the woman who is coming into your house like Rachel and Leah, who together built up the house of Israel. May you produce children in Ephrathah and bestow a name in Bethlehem.

Proverbs 8:22-36

Hear instruction and be wise, and do not neglect it.
or Tobit 8:1-21

2 Corinthians 4:13-5:10

So we do not lose heart. Even though our outer nature is wasting away, our inner nature is being renewed day by day.

2 Timothy 1:1-14

God did not give us a spirit of cowardice, but rather a spirit of power and of love and of self-discipline.

after Proper 3 / Pentecost 2

Deuteronomy 5:22-33

You must follow exactly the path that the LORD your God has commanded you, so that you may live, and that it may go well with you, and that you may live long in the land that you are to possess.

Proverbs 25:15-28

If your enemies are hungry, give them bread to eat; and if they are thirsty, give them water to drink; for you will heap coals of fire on their heads, and the LORD will reward you.

2 Corinthians 4:13-5:10

So we do not lose heart. Even though our outer nature is wasting away, our inner nature is being renewed day by day.

1 Timothy 6:6-21

There is great gain in godliness combined with contentment; for we brought nothing into the world, so that we can take nothing out of it.

after Proper 7 / Pentecost 6

1 Samuel 9:15-10:1

Samuel took a vial of oil and poured it on Saul's head, and kissed him; he said, "The LORD has anointed you ruler over his people Israel. You shall reign over the people of the LORD and you will save them from the hand of their enemies all around."

Numbers 20:14-29

Moses stripped Aaron of his vestments, and put them on his son Eleazar; and Aaron died there on top of the mountain.

Acts 7:30-43

This is the Moses who said to the Israelites, "God will raise up a prophet for you from your own people as he raised me up."

Romans 6:1-11

We have been buried with him by baptism into death, so that, just as Christ was raised from the dead by the glory of the Father, so we too might walk in newness of life.

after Proper 11 / Pentecost 10

2 Samuel 1:1-16

David said to him, "Your blood be on your head; for your own mouth has testified against you, saying, 'I have killed the LORD's anointed'."

Joshua 23:1-16

Be very careful, therefore, to love the LORD your God.

Acts 15:22-35

It is has seemed good to the Holy Spirit and to us to impose on you no further burden than these essentials: that you abstain from what has been sacrificed to idols and from blood and from what is strangled and from fornication.

Romans 15:25-33

The peace of God be with all of you.

after Proper 15 / Pentecost 14

2 Samuel 23:1-7,13-17

Now these are the last words of David: The oracle of David, son of Jesse, the oracle of the man whom God exalted, the anointed of the God of Jacob, the favorite of the Strong One of Israel.

Job 3:1-26

Let the day perish in which I was born, and the night that said, "A man-child is conceived."

Acts 25:13-27

Agrippa and Bernice came with great pomp, and they entered the audience hall with the military tribunes and the prominent men of the city. Then Festus gave the order and Paul was brought in.

Acts 9:10-19a

Ananias laid his hands on Saul and said, "Brother Saul, the Lord Jesus, who appeared to you on your way here, has sent me so that you may regain your sight and be filled with the Holy Spirit.

after Proper 19 / Pentecost 18

2 Kings 2:1-18

As they continued walking and talking, a chariot of fire and horses of fire separated the two of them, and Elijah ascended in a whirlwind into heaven.

Esther 2:5-8,15-23

The king loved Esther more than all the other women; of all the virgins she won his favor and devotion, so that he set the royal crown on her head and made her queen instead of Vashti.
[BCP: *or* Judith 5:1-21]

1 Corinthians 4:1-7

Think of us this way, as servants of Christ and stewards of God's mysteries.

Acts 17:16-34

As I went through the city and looked carefully at the objects of your worship, I found among them an altar with the inscription, "To an unknown god." What therefore you worship as unknown, this I proclaim to you.

after Proper 23 / Pentecost 22

Jeremiah 52:1-34

Nebuzaradan the captain of the bodyguard who served the king of Babylon, entered Jerusalem. He burned the house of the LORD, the king's house, and all the houses of Jerusalem; every great house he burned down. [BCP 2 Kings 25:8-12, 22-26]

Hosea 14:1-9

I will heal their disloyalty; I will love them freely, for my anger has turned away from them. [BCP: Sirach [Ecclesiasticus] 3:17-31]

1 Corinthians 15:12-29

As all die in Adam, so all will be made alive in Christ.

Acts 28:17-31

He lived there two whole years at his own expense and welcomed all who came to him, proclaiming the kingdom of God and teaching about the Lord Jesus Christ with all boldness and without hindrance.

after Proper 27 / Pentecost 26

1 Maccabees 2:1-28

We will not obey the king's words by turning aside from our religion to the right hand or to the left.
or Nehemiah 13:4-22

Joel 3:9-17

The LORD roars from Zion, and utters his voice from Jerusalem, and the heavens and the earth shake. But the LORD is a refuge for his people, a stronghold for the people of Israel.

Revelation 20:1-6

I saw also the souls of those who had been beheaded for their testimony to Jesus and for the word of God. They had not worshiped the beast or its image and had not received its mark on their foreheads or their hands. They came to life and reigned with Christ a thousand years.

James 2:1-13

My brothers and sisters, do you with your acts of favoritism really believe in our glorious Lord Jesus Christ?

Silence for meditation follows each reading.

RESPONSORY

I will bring them back because I have compassion on them, for I am **the** Lord God.*
Their hearts shall exult **in** the Lord.
In that day the Lord of hosts will be a garland of glory, and a diadem of beauty, to the remnant **of** his people.*
Their hearts shall exult **in** the Lord.

[LH: Zech. 10:6,7; Isa. 28:5]

Sing for joy, O heavens, and ex**ult**, O earth;*
break forth, O mountains, into singing before the Lord **when** he comes.
For the Lord has comfort**ed** his people,*
and will have compassion on his **suf**fering ones.
In his time shall the **right**eous flourish;*
there shall be abun**dance** of peace.
For the Lord has comfort**ed** his people,*
and will have compassion on his **suf**fering ones.

[LH: Isa. 49:13; Ps. 96:12; 72:7]

Antiphon to PSALM 103 *Benedic, anima mea, Domino, et omnia*

Bless the LORD, **O** my soul,*
and forget not **all** his benefits. [LH, PBO]

103 *Praise of God's love*

1 Bless the LORD, **O** my soul,*
and all that is within me, bless his **ho**ly Name.

2 Bless the LORD, **O** my soul,*
and forget not **all** his benefits.

3 He forgives **all** your sins*
and heals all **your** infirmities;

4 He redeems your life **from** the grave*
and crowns you with mercy and **lov**ing-kindness;

5 He satisfies you **with** good things,*
and your youth is renewed **like** an eagle's.

6 The LORD executes **right**eousness*
and judgment for all who **are** oppressed.

7 He made his ways **known** to Moses*
and his works to the chil**dren** of Israel.

8 The LORD is full of compas**sion** and mercy,*
slow to anger and **of** great kindness.

9 He will not al**ways** accuse us,*
nor will he keep his an**ger** for ever.

10 He has not dealt with us according **to** our sins,*
nor rewarded us according **to** our wickedness.

11 For as the heavens are high a**bove** the earth,*
so is his mercy great upon **those** who fear him.

12 As far as the east is **from** the west,*
so far has he removed our **sins** from us.

13 As a father cares **for** his children,*
so does the LORD care for **those** who fear him.

14 For he himself knows whereof **we** are made;*
he remembers that we **are** but dust.

15 Our days are **like** the grass;*
we flourish like a flower **of** the field;

16 When the wind goes over it, **it** is gone,*
and its place shall know **it** no more.

17 But the merciful goodness of the LORD endures for ever
on **those** who fear him,*
and his righteousness on **chil**dren's children;

18 On those who **keep** his covenant*
and remember his command**ments** and do them.

19 The LORD has set his **throne** in heaven,*
and his kingship has dominion **o**ver all.

20 Bless the LORD, you angels of his,
you mighty ones who **do** his bidding,*
and hearken to the voice **of** his word.

21 Bless the LORD, all **you** his hosts,*
you ministers of his who **do** his will.

22 Bless the LORD, all you works of his,
in all places of **his** dominion;*
bless the LORD, **O** my soul.

Antiphon Bless the LORD, **O** my soul,*
and forget not **all** his benefits.

Silence for meditation

Lord, you have compassion for the sinner, as a father has compassion for his children: Heal the weakness of your people and save us from everlasting death, that with the saints we may praise and glorify you, Father, Son, and Holy Spirit, now and for ever. [LH, LBW]

+

Antiphon to the OLD TESTAMENT CANTICLE *Benedictus es, Domine*

Let us sing a hymn of praise **to** our God,*
alleluia. [LH]

A Song of Praise — Song of the Three Young Men 29-34

Blessed are you, O Lord, God **of** our ancestors:*
praised and exalt**ed** for ever.

Blessed are you for the radiance of your **ho**ly Name:*
praised and exalt**ed** for ever.

Blessed are you in the temple **of** your holiness:*
praised and exalt**ed** for ever.

Blessed are you beholding the depths
from your throne be**tween** the cherubim:*
praised and exalt**ed** for ever.

Blessed are you on the glorious throne **of** your kingdom:*
praised and exalt**ed** for ever.

Blessed are you in the firma**ment** of heaven:*
praised and exalt**ed** for ever. [BCP: NRSV alt.]

Antiphon Let us sing a hymn of praise **to** our God,*
al**le**luia.

Silence for meditation

Lord of all the generations and all the worlds, lift our eyes from the meanness of our lives toward your glorious majesty and out of discouragement and defeat bring us at last to praise you in your eternal kingdom, where with your Son and the Holy Spirit you live and reign one God, now and for ever. [PHP]

+

Antiphon to PSALM 150 *Laudate Dominum*

Praise God for his **might**y acts,*
praise him for his ex**cel**lent greatness. [LH, PBO]

150 *The great alleluia*

1 Hallelujah!
Praise God in his **ho**ly temple;*
praise him in the firmament **of** his power.

2 Praise him for his **might**y acts;*
praise him for his ex**cel**lent greatness.

3 Praise him with the blast **of** the ram's-horn;*
praise him with **lyre** and harp.

4 Praise him with tim**brel** and dance;*
praise him with **strings** and pipe.

5 Praise him with re**sound**ing cymbals;*
praise him with loud-**clang**ing cymbals.

6 Let everything **that** has breath*
praise the LORD.
Hallelujah!

Antiphon Praise God for his **might**y acts,*
praise him for his ex**cel**lent greatness.

Silence for meditation

God of surpassing greatness, enthroned upon the praises of your people, fill our hearts with your love and unite our voices with the praise of all creation so that you may be honored and glorified by everything that has breath; through Jesus Christ our Lord. [PHP]

+

Stand

THE HYMN is sung.

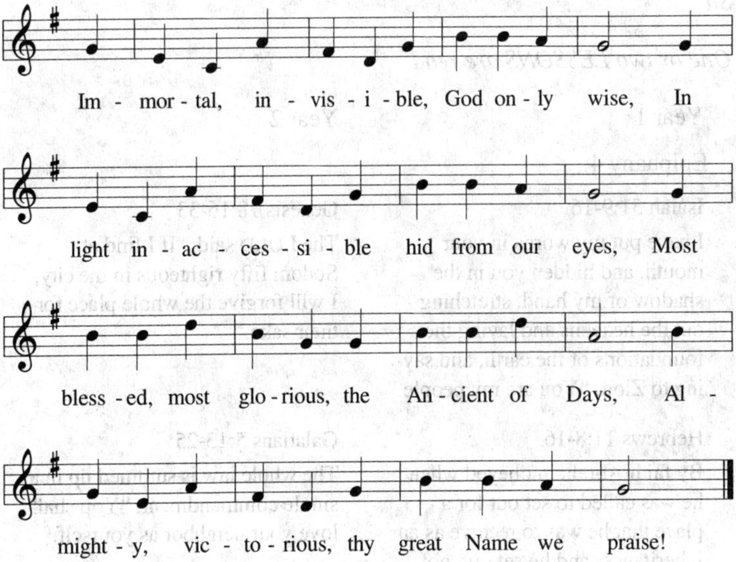

2 Unresting, unhasting, and silent as light,
Nor wanting, nor wasting, thou rulest in might;
Thy justice like mountains high soaring above
Thy clouds, which are fountains of goodness and love.

3 To all, life thou givest, to both great and small;
In all life thou livest, the true life of all;
We blossom and flourish like leaves on a tree,
Then wither and perish, but nought changeth thee.

4 Great Soverign of glory, pure fountain of light;
Thine angels adore thee, all veiling their sight;
All laud we would render; O help us to see
'Tis only the splendor of light hideth thee.

[SBH 172, H82 423, LBW 526]

Text: W. Chalmers Smith, 1824-1908, alt.
Tune: *St. Denio*, Welsh folk tune 11 11 11 11

Sit

One or two LESSONS are read.

Year 1	Year 2
Epiphany 4	
Isaiah 51:9-16	Genesis 18:16-33
I have put my words in your mouth, and hidden you in the shadow of my hand, stretching out the heavens and laying the foundations of the earth, and saying to Zion, "You are my people."	The LORD said, "If I find at Sodom fifty righteous in the city, I will forgive the whole place for their sake."
Hebrews 11:8-16	Galatians 5:13-25
By faith Abraham obeyed when he was called to set out for a place that he was to receive as an inheritance; and he set out, not knowing where he was going.	The whole law is summed up in a single commandment, "You shall love your neighbor as yourself."
Epiphany 8	
Deuteronomy 4:1-9	Proverbs 9:1-12
So now, Israel, give heed to the statutes and ordinances that I am teaching you to observe, so that you may live to enter and occupy the land that the LORD, the God of your ancestors, is giving you.	The fear of the LORD is the beginning of wisdom, and the knowledge of the Holy One is insight. *or* Tobit 9:1-10:7a; 11:1-4
2 Timothy 4:1-8	2 Corinthians 9:6b-15
From now on there is reserved for me the crown of righteousness, which the Lord, the righteous judge, will give me on that day, and not only to me but also to all who have longed for his appearing.	Thanks be to God for his indescribable gift!

Proper 4 (Sunday between May 29 and June 4) / Pentecost 3

Deuteronomy 11:1-12

You shall love the LORD your God, therefore, and keep his charge, his decrees, his ordinances, and his commandments always.

Ecclesiastes 1:1-11

Vanity of vanities, says the Teacher, vanity of vanities! All is vanity.

Revelation 10:1-11

I saw another mighty angel coming down from heaven, wrapped in a cloud, with a rainbow over his head; his face was like the sun, and his legs like pillars of fire.

Acts 8:26-40

Then Philip began to speak, and starting with this scripture, he proclaimed to him the good news about Jesus.

Proper 8 (Sunday between June 26 and July 2) / Pentecost 7

1 Samuel 10:1-16

A band of prophets met Saul; and the Spirit of God possessed him, and he fell into a prophetic frenzy along with them.

Numbers 21:4-9, 21-35

So Moses made a serpent of bronze, and put it upon a pole; and whenever a serpent bit someone, that person would look at the serpent of bronze and live.

Romans 4:13-25

No distrust made Abraham waver concerning the promise of God, but he grew strong in his faith as he gave glory to God, being fully convinced that God was able to do what he had promised.

Acts 17:(12-21) 22-34

He has fixed a day on which he will have the world judged in righteousness by a man whom he has appointed, and of this he has given full assurance to all by raising him from the dead.

Proper 12 (Sunday between July 24 and 30) / Pentecost 11

2 Samuel 1:17-27

How the mighty have fallen, and the weapons of war perished!

Joshua 24:1-15

Now therefore revere the LORD, and serve him in sincerity and in faithfulness; put away the gods that your ancestors served beyond the

Romans 12:9-21

Let love be genuine; hate what is evil, hold fast to what is good.

River and in Egypt, and serve the LORD.

Acts 28:23-31

He lived there two whole years at his own expense and welcomed all who came to him, proclaiming the kingdom of God and teaching about Jesus Christ with all boldness and without hindrance.

Proper 16 (Sunday between August 21 and 27) / Pentecost 15

2 Samuel 24:1-2,10-25

"I am in great distress; let us fall into the hand of the LORD, for his mercy is great; but let us not fall into human hands.

Job 4:1-6,12-21

Can mortals be righteous before God? Can humans be pure before their maker?

Galatians 3:23-4:7

There is no longer Jew or Greek, there is no longer slave or free, there is no longer male or female; for all of you are one in Christ Jesus.

Revelation 4:1-11

Holy, holy, holy, the Lord God the Almighty, who was and is and is to come.

Proper 20 (Sunday between September 18 and 24) / Pentecost 19

2 Kings 4:8-37

Elisha said, "At this season, in due time, you shall embrace a son."

Esther 3:1-4:3

All the king's servants who were at the king's gate bowed down and did obeisance to Haman; for the king so commanded concerning him. But Mordecai did not bow down or do obeisance.

[BCP: *or* Judith 5:22-6:4, 10-21]

Acts 9:10-31 (32)

Go, for he is an instrument whom I have chosen to bring my name before the Gentiles and kings and

James 1:19-27

Be doers of the word, and not merely hearers who deceive themselves.

before the people of Israel; I myself will show him how much he must suffer for the sake of my name.

Proper 24 (Sunday between October 16 and 22) / Pentecost 23.

Jeremiah 29:1,4-14

Seek the welfare of the city where I have sent you into exile, and pray to the LORD on its behalf, for in its welfare you will find your welfare.

or Jeremiah 39:11-40:6

Sirach [Ecclesiasticus] 4:1-10

My child, do not cheat the poor of their living, and do not keep needy eyes waiting.

or Micah 1:1-9

Acts 16:6-15

During the night Paul had a vision: there stood a man of Macedonia pleading with him and saying, "Come over to Macedonia and help us."

1 Corinthians 10:1-13

No testing has overtaken you that is not common to everyone. God is faithful, and he will not let you be tested beyond your strength, but with the testing he will also provide the way out so that you may be able to endure it.

Proper 28 (Sunday between November 13 and 19) / Pentecost 27.

1 Maccabees 2:29-43(44-50)

So they made this decision that day: "Let us fight against anyone who comes to attack us on the sabbath day; let us not all die as our kindred died in their hiding places."

or Ezra 7:(1-10) 11-26

Habakkuk 1:1-4(5-11)12-2:1

The law becomes slack and justice never prevails. The wicked surround the righteous–therefore judgment comes forth perverted.

Acts 28:14b-23

When we came to Rome, Paul was allowed to live by himself, with the soldier who was guarding him.

Philippians 3:13-4:1

But our citizenship is in heaven, and it is from there that we are expecting a Savior, the Lord Jesus Christ.

Silence for meditation follows each reading.

RESPONSORY

I am going to open your graves, says the Lord, and bring you up from your graves, **O** my people;*

and you shall know that I **am** the Lord.

I am the resurrection and the life; those who believe in me, even though they **die**, will live;*

and you shall know that I **am** the Lord.

[LH: Ezek. 37:12,13; John 11:25]

You are built upon the foundation of the apostles and prophets, with Christ Jesus himself as the **cor**nerstone.*

In him you are built together spiritually into a dwelling **place** of God.

In him the whole structure is joined together and grows into a holy temple **in** the Lord.*

In him you are built together spiritually into a dwelling **place** of God.

[LH: Eph. 2:20,22,21]

Monday of Week IV

Antiphon to PSALM 62 *Nonne Deo?*

We wait for the **bless**ed hope*
and the manifestation of the glory
of our great **God** and Savior. [LH: Titus 2:13]

62 *Confidence of God's protection*

1 For God alone my soul in **si**lence waits;*
from him comes **my** salvation.

2 He alone is my rock and **my** salvation,*
my stronghold, so that I shall not be **great**ly shaken.

3 How long will you assail me to crush me,
all of **you** together,*
as if you were a leaning fence, a **top**pling wall?

4 They seek only to bring me down from my **place** of honor;*
lies are their **chief** delight.

5 They bless **with** their lips,*
but in their **hearts** they curse.

6 For God alone my soul in **si**lence waits;*
truly, my hope **is** in him.

7 He alone is my rock and **my** salvation,*
my stronghold, so that I shall **not** be shaken.

8 In God is my safety **and** my honor;*
God is my strong rock **and** my refuge.

9 Put your trust in him al**ways**, O people,*
pour out your hearts before him, for God **is** our refuge.

10 Those of high degree are but a **fleet**ing breath,*
even those of low estate can**not** be trusted.

11 On the scales they are lighter **than** a breath,*
all of **them** together.

12 Put no trust in extortion;
in robbery take no **emp**ty pride;*
though wealth increase, set not your **heart** upon it.

13 God has spoken once, twice **have** I heard it,*
that power be**longs** to God.

14 Steadfast love is **yours**, O Lord,*
for you repay everyone according **to** his deeds.

Antiphon We wait for the **bless**ed hope*
and the manifestation of the glory
of our great **God** and Savior.

Silence for meditation

Lord God, in a constantly changing world we look to you as our rock of hope: Hear us as we pour out our hearts to you, and give us your grace and secure protection; through your Son, Jesus Christ our Lord. [LH, LBW]

+

Antiphon to PSALM 145 *Exaltabo te, Deus*

The LORD is faithful in **all** his words*
and merciful in **all** his deeds. [LH]

145 *Praise of God's majesty*

1 I will exalt you, O **God** my King,*
and bless your Name for ev**er** and ever.

2 Every day **will** I bless you*
and praise your Name for ev**er** and ever.

3 Great is the LORD and greatly **to** be praised;*
there is no end **to** his greatness.

4 One generation shall praise your works **to** another*
and shall de**clare** your power.

5 I will ponder the glorious splendor **of** your majesty*
and all your **mar**velous works.

6 They shall speak of the might of your **won**drous acts,*
and I will tell **of** your greatness.

7 They shall publish the remembrance of **your** great goodness;*
they shall sing of your **right**eous deeds.

8 The LORD is gracious and full **of** compassion,*
slow to anger and **of** great kindness.

9 The LORD is loving to **ev**eryone*
and his compassion is over **all** his works.

10 All your works praise **you**, O LORD,*
and your faithful **ser**vants bless you.

11 They make known the glory **of** your kingdom*
and speak **of** your power;

12 That the peoples may know **of** your power*
and the glorious splendor **of** your kingdom.

13 Your kingdom is an ever**last**ing kingdom;*
your dominion endures through**out** all ages.

14 The LORD is faithful in **all** his words*
and merciful in **all** his deeds.

15 The LORD upholds all **those** who fall;*
he lifts up those who **are** bowed down.

16 The eyes of all wait upon **you**, O LORD,*
and you give them their food **in** due season.

17 You open **wide** your hand*
and satisfy the needs of every **liv**ing creature.

18 The LORD is righteous in **all** his ways*
and loving in **all** his works.

19 The LORD is near to those who **call** upon him,*
to all who call up**on** him faithfully.

20 He fulfills the desire of **those** who fear him;*
he hears their **cry** and helps them.

21 The LORD preserves all **those** who love him,*
but destroys **all** the wicked.

22 My mouth shall speak the praise **of** the LORD;*
let all flesh bless his holy Name for ev**er** and ever.

Antiphon The LORD is faithful in **all** his words*
and merciful in **all** his deeds.

Silence for meditation

Loving Father, you are faithful in your promises and tender in your compassion: Listen to our hymn of joy, and continue to satisfy the needs of all your creatures, that all flesh may bless your Name in your everlasting kingdom, where with your Son and the Holy Spirit you live and reign, now and for ever. [LBW]

+

Stand

THE HYMN is sung. *O dass ich tausend Zungen hätte*

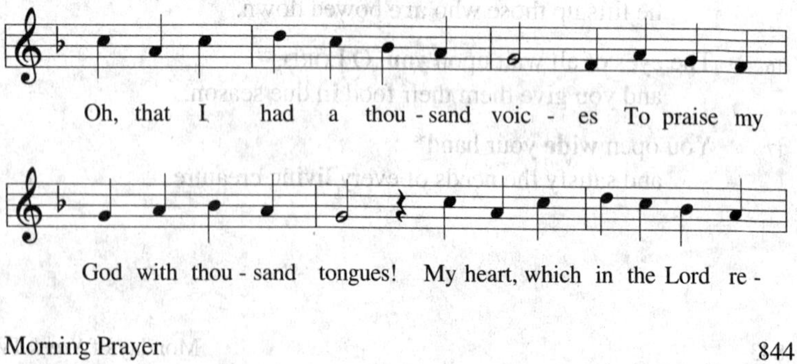

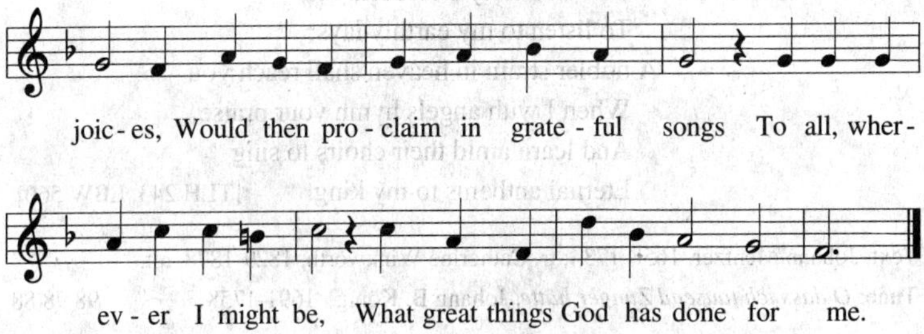

2 O all you powers that he implanted
Arise, keep silence now no more;
Put forth the strength that God has granted;
Your noblest work is to adore.
O soul and body, join to raise
With heartfelt joy our Maker's praise.

3 You forest leaves so green and tender
That dance for joy in summer air,
You meadow grasses, bright and slender,
You flowers so fragrant and so fair,
You live to show God's praise alone.
Help me to make his glory known.

4 All creatures that have breath and motion,
That throng the earth, the sea, the sky,
Now join me in my heart's devotion,
Help me to raise God's praises high.
My utmost powers can ne'er aright
Declare the wonders of his might.

5 But I will tell, while I am living,
His goodness forth with every breath,
And greet each morning with thanksgiving
Until my heart is stilled in death;
And, when at last my lips grow cold,
His praise shall in my sighs be told.

6 Creator, humbly I beseech you
To listen to my earthly lays;
A nobler strain in heaven shall reach you
When I with angels hymn your praise,
And learn amid their choirs to sing
Eternal anthems to my king. [TLH 243, LBW 560]

Text: Johann Mentzer, 1658-1734; tr. Catherine Winkworth, 1829-1878, alt.
Tune: *O dass ich tausend Zunger hätte,* Johann B. König, 1691-1758 98 98 88

Sit

One or two LESSONS are read.

Year 1	Year 2
after Epiphany 4	
Isaiah 51:17-23	Genesis 19:1-17(18-23)24-29
See, I have taken from your hand the cup of staggering; you shall drink no more from the bowl of my wrath.	Then the Lord rained on Sodom and Gomorrah sulfur and fire from the LORD out of heaven.
Galatians 4:1-11	Hebrews 11:1-12
When the fullness of time had come, God sent his Son, born of a woman, born under the law, in order to redeem those who were under the law, so that we might receive adoption as children.	Now faith is the assurance of things hoped for, the conviction of things not seen.
after Epiphany 8	
Deuteronomy 4:9-14	Proverbs 10:1-12
Take care and watch yourselves closely, so as neither to forget the things that your eyes have seen nor to let them slip from your	Hatred stirs up strife, but love covers all offenses. *or* Tobit 11:5-17; 12:1-22

mind all the days of your life; make them known to your children and your children's children.

2 Corinthians 10:1-18

If you are confident that you belong to Christ, remind yourself of this, that just as you belong to Christ, so also do we.

2 Timothy 1:15-2:13

Be strong in the grace that is in Christ Jesus.

after Proper 4 / Pentecost 3

Deuteronomy 11:13-19

You shall put these words of mine in your heart and soul, and you shall bind them as a sign on your hand, and fix them as an emblem on your forehead.

Ecclesiastes 2:1-15

Then I considered all that my hands had done and the toil I had spent in doing it, and again, all was vanity and a chasing after wind, and there was nothing to be gained under the sun.

2 Corinthians 5:11-6:2

Christ died for all, so that those who live might live no longer for themselves, but for him who died and was raised for them.

Galatians 1:1-17

Grace to you and peace from God our Father and the Lord Jesus Christ, who gave himself for our sins to set us free from the present evil age.

after Proper 8 / Pentecost 7

1 Samuel 10:17-27

Some worthless fellows said, "How can this man save us?" They despised Saul and brought him no present. But he held his peace.

Numbers 22:1-21

God said to Balaam, "You shall not go with them; you shall not curse the people, for they are blessed."

Acts 7:44-8:1a

While they were stoning Stephen, he prayed, "Lord Jesus, receive my spirit." Then he knelt down and cried out in a loud voice, "Lord, do not hold this sin against

Romans 6:12-23

The wages of sin is death, but the free gift of God is eternal life in Christ Jesus our Lord.

them." When he had said this, he died.

after Proper 12 / Pentecost 11

2 Samuel 2:1-11

May you be blessed by the LORD, because you showed this loyalty to Saul your lord, and buried him! Now may the LORD show steadfast love and faithfulness to you!

Joshua 24:16-33

Joshua said, "Then put away the foreign gods that are among you, and incline your hearts to the LORD, the God of Israel."

Acts 15:36-16:5

Paul said to Barnabas, "Come, let us return and visit the believers in every city where we proclaimed the word of the Lord and see how they are doing."

Romans 16:1-16

Greet one another with a holy kiss.

after Proper 16 / Pentecost 15

1 Kings 1:(1-4) 5-31

Your son Solomon shall succeed me as king, and he shall sit on my throne in my place.

Job 4:1; 5:1-11, 17-21, 26-27

Do not despise the discipline of the Almighty. For he wounds, but he binds up; he strikes, but his hands heal.

Acts 26:1-23

To this day I have had help from God, and so I stand here, testifying to both small and great, saying nothing but what the prophets and Moses said would take place: that the Messiah must suffer, and that, by being the first to rise from the dead, he would proclaim light both to our people and to the Gentiles.

Acts 9:19b-31

Saul began to proclaim Jesus in the synagogues, saying, "He is the Son of God."

After Proper 20 / Pentecost 19

2 Kings 5:1-19

Naaman went down and immersed himself seven times in the Jordan, according to the word of the man of God; his flesh was restored like the flesh of a young boy, and he was clean.

Esther 4:4-17

If you keep silence at such a time as this, relief and deliverance will rise from the Jews from another quarter, but you and your father's family will perish. Who knows? Perhaps you have come to royal dignity for just such a time as this. [BCP: or Judith 7:1-7, 19-32]

1 Corinthians 4:8-21

Indeed, in Christ Jesus I became your father through the gospel. I appeal to you, then, be imitators of me.

Acts 18:1-11

One night the Lord said to Paul in a vision, "Do not be afraid, but speak and do not be silent; for I am with you, and no one will lay a hand on you to harm you, for there are many in this city who are my people.

after Proper 24 / Pentecost 23

Jeremiah 44:1-14

None of the remnant of Judah who have come to settle in the land of Egypt shall escape or survive or return to the land of Judah. Although they long to go back and live there, they shall not go back, except some fugitives.

or Jeremiah 29:1,4-14

Sirach [Ecclesiasticus] 4:20-5:7

Do not delay to turn back to the Lord, and do not postpone it from day to day; for suddenly the wrath of the Lord will come upon you, and at the time of punishment you will perish.

or Micah 2:1-13

1 Corinthians 15:30-41

If the dead are not raised, "Let us eat and drink, for tomorrow we die."

Revelation 7:1-8

Do not damage the earth or the sea or the trees, until we have marked the servants of our God with a seal on their foreheads.

after Proper 28 / Pentecost 27

1 Maccabees 2:49-70

Now, my children, show zeal for the law, and give your lives for the covenant of our ancestors.
[BCP 1 Maccabees 3:1-24]
or Ezra 7:27-28; 8:21-36

Habakkuk 2:1-4, 9-20

For there is still a vision for the appointed time; it speaks of the end, and does not lie. If it seems to tarry, wait for it; it will surely come, it will not delay.

Revelation 20:7-15

The sea gave up the dead that were in it, Death and Hades gave up the dead that were in them, and all were judged according to what they had done.

James 2:14-26

So faith by itself, if it has no works, is dead.

Silence for meditation follows each reading

RESPONSORY

I will remove the heart of stone from their flesh and give them a **heart** of flesh,*
so that they may fol**low** my statutes.
They shall **be** my people, *
and I will **be** their God.
I will give them one heart, and put a new spir**it** within them.*
so that they may fol**low** my statutes.
They shall **be** my people, *
and I will **be** their God.
[LH: Ezek. 11:19-20,19]

Ask, and it will be **giv**en you;*
for everyone who asks receives, and everyone who searches finds, and for everyone who knocks the door **will** be opened.
The Lord is near to those who call upon him, to all who call up**on** him faithfully;*
for everyone who asks receives, and everyone who searches finds, and for everyone who knocks the door **will** be opened.
[LH: Matt. 7:7-8; Ps. 145:19]

Tuesday of Week IV

Antiphon to PSALM 12 *Salvum me fac*

The words of the **LORD** are pure words,*
like silver re**fined** from ore. [LH, PBO]

12 *A cry for God's help in a deceitful world*

1 Help me, LORD, for there is no god**ly** one left;*
the faithful have vanished **from** among us.

2 Everyone speaks falsely **with** his neighbor;*
with a smooth tongue they speak from a **doub**le heart.

3 Oh, that the LORD would cut off **all** smooth tongues,*
and close the lips that ut**ter** proud boasts!

4 Those who say, "With our tongue will **we** prevail;*
our lips are our own; who is lord **o**ver us?"

5 "Because the needy are oppressed,
and the poor cry **out** in misery,*
I will rise up," says the LORD,
"and give them the **help** they long for."

6 The words of the **LORD** are pure words,*
like silver refined from ore
and purified seven times **in** the fire.

7 O LORD, watch **o**ver us*
and save us from this genera**tion** for ever.

8 The wicked prowl on **ev**ery side,*
and that which is worthless is highly **prized** by everyone.

Antiphon The words of the **LORD** are pure words,*
like silver re**fined** from ore.

Silence for meditation

Lord God, protector of your people, your light is true light and your truth shines like the day: Through your pure and life-giving words direct us to salvation and give us the help we long for in Jesus Christ our Lord. [LH, LBW]

+

Antiphon to PSALM 146 *Lauda, anima mea*

I will praise the LORD as long as I live. [LH]

146 *Praise of God's faithfulnes*

1 Hallelujah!
Praise the LORD, **O** my soul!*
I will praise the LORD as long as I live;
I will sing praises to my God while I **have** my being.

2 Put not your trust in rulers, nor in any **child** of earth,*
for there is no **help** in them.

3 When they breathe their last, they re**turn** to earth,*
and in that day **their** thoughts perish.

4 Happy are they who have the God of Jacob **for** their help!*
whose hope is in the **LORD** their God;

5 Who made heaven and earth, the seas, and all **that** is in them;*
who keeps his prom**ise** for ever;

6 Who gives justice to those who **are** oppressed,*
and food to **those** who hunger.

7 The LORD sets the prisoners free;
the LORD opens the eyes **of** the blind;*
the LORD lifts up those who **are** bowed down;

8 The LORD loves the righteous;
the LORD cares **for** the stranger;*
he sustains the orphan and widow,
but frustrates the way **of** the wicked.

9 The LORD shall **reign** for ever,*
your God, O Zion, throughout all generations.
Hallelujah!

Antiphon I will praise the LORD as long as I live.

Silence for meditation

God of glory and power, happy indeed are those who have put their trust in you: Shine the brightness of your light upon us, that we may love you always with a pure heart and praise you for ever; through your Son, Jesus Christ our Lord. [LH, LBW]

+

Stand

THE HYMN is sung.

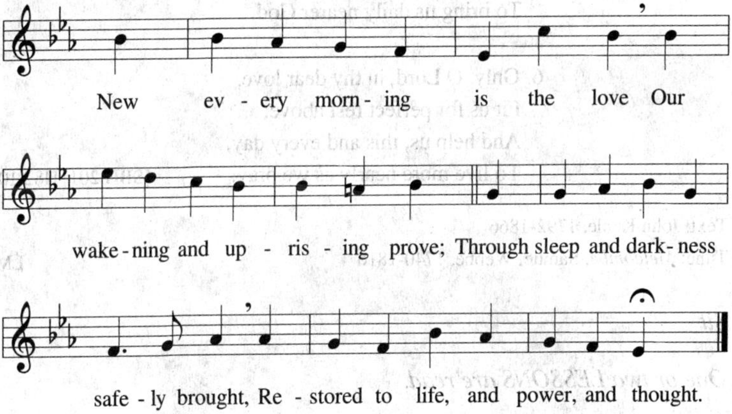

2 New mercies, each returning day,
Hover around us while we pray;
New perils past, new sins forgiven,
New thoughts of God, new hopes of heaven.

3 If on our daily course our mind
Be set to hallow all we find,
New treasures still, of countless price,
God will provide for sacrifice.

4 Old friends, old scenes, will lovelier be,
As more of heaven in each we see;
Some softening gleam of love and prayer
Shall dawn on every cross and care.

5 The trivial round, the common task,
Will furnish all we ought to ask,
Room to deny ourselves, a road
To bring us daily nearer God.

6 Only, O Lord, in thy dear love,
Fit us for perfect rest above;
And help us, this and every day,
To live more nearly as we pray. [SBH 201; H82 10]

Text: John Keble, 1792-1866
Tune: *Melcombe*, Samuel Webbe, 1740-1816 LM

Sit

One or two LESSONS are read.

Year 1

after Epiphany 4

Isaiah 52:1-12

Break forth together into singing, you ruins of Jerusalem; for the LORD has comforted his people, he has redeemed Jerusalem.

Galatians 4:12-20

Have I now become your enemy by telling you the truth?

after Epiphany 8

Deuteronomy 4:15-24

The LORD your God is a devouring fire, a jealous God.

2 Corinthians 11:1-21a

Even Satan disguises himself as an angel of light. So it is not strange if his ministers also disguise themselves as ministers of righteousness. Their end will match their deeds.

after Proper 4 / Pentecost 3

Deuteronomy 12:1-12

You shall not act as we are acting here today, all of us according to

Year 2

Genesis 21:1-21

The LORD did for Sarah as he had promised. Sarah conceived and bore Abraham a son in his old age, at the time of which he had spoken to him.

Hebrews 11:13-22

They desire a better country, that is, a heavenly one. Therefore God is not ashamed to be called their God; indeed, he has prepared a city for them.

Proverbs 15:16-33

Better is a little with the fear of the LORD than great treasure and trouble with it.

or Tobit 13:1-2, 8-14

2 Timothy 2:14-26

Do your best to present yourself to God as one approved by him, a worker who has no need to be ashamed, rightly explaining the word of truth.

Ecclesiastes 2:16-26

What do mortals get from all their toil and strain with which they toil

our own desires, for you have not yet come into the rest and the possession that the LORD your God is giving you.

2 Corinthians 6:3-13(14-7:1)
We are putting no obstacle in anyone's way, so that no fault may be found with our ministry.

under the sun? For all their days are full of pain, and their work is a vexation; even at night their minds do not rest. This also is vanity.

Galatians 1:18-2:10
The one who formerly was persecuting us is now proclaiming the faith he once tried to destroy.

after Proper 8 / Pentecost 7

1 Samuel 11:1-15
So all the people went to Gilgal, and there they made Saul king before the LORD in Gilgal. There they sacrificed offerings of well-being before the LORD, and there Saul and all the Israelites rejoiced greatly.

Numbers 22:21-38
The angel of the LORD said to Balaam, "Go with the men; but speak only what I tell you to speak."

Acts 8:1b-13
Devout men buried Stephen and made loud lamentation over him.

Romans 7:1-12
But now we are discharged from the law, dead to that which held us captive, so that we are slaves not under the old written code but in the new life of the Spirit.

after Proper 12 / Pentecost 11

2 Samuel 3:6-21
Abner said to David, "Let me go and rally all Israel to my lord the king, in order that they may make a covenant with you, and that you may reign over all that your heart desires."

Judges 2:1-5,11-23
Whenever the judge died, they would relapse and behave worse than their ancestors, following other gods, worshiping them and bowing down to them.

Acts 16:6-15
During the night Paul had a vision: there stood a man of

Romans 16:17-27
The God of peace will shortly crush Satan under your feet. The

Macedonia pleading with him and saying, "Come over to Macedonia and help us."

grace of our Lord Jesus Christ be with you.

after Proper 16 / Pentecost 15

1 Kings 1:32-2:4 (5-46a) 46b

As the LORD has been with my lord the king, so may he be with Solomon, and make his throne greater than the throne of my lord King David.

Acts 26:24-27:8

Agrippa said to Festus, "This man could have been set free if he had not appealed to the emperor."

Job 6:1-4,8-15,21

The arrows of the Almighty are in me; my spirit drinks their poison; the terrors of God are arrayed against me.

Acts 9:32-43

Peter kelt down and prayed. He turned to the body and said, "Tabitha, get up." Then she opened her eyes, and seeing Peter, she sat up.

after Proper 20 / Pentecost 19

2 Kings 5:19-27

Gehazi, the servant of Elisha the man of God, thought, "My master has let that Aramean Naaman off too lightly by not accepting from him what he offered. As the LORD lives, I will run after him and get something out of him."

1 Corinthians 5:1-8

Our paschal lamb, Christ, has been sacrificed. Therefore, let us celebrate the festival, not with the old yeast, the yeast of malice and evil, but with the unleavened bread of sincerity and truth.

Esther 5:1-14

Let a gallows fifty cubits high be made, and in the morning tell the king to have Mordecai hanged on it; then go with the king to the banquet in good spirits.
[BCP: *or* Judith 8:9-17; 9:1, 7-10]

Acts 18:12-28

Apollos had been instructed in the Way of the Lord; and he spoke with burning enthusiasm and taught accurately the things concerning Jesus, though he knew only the baptism of John.

after Proper 24 / Pentecost 23

Lamentations 1:1-5(6-9)10-12

How lonely sits the city that once was full of people!

or Jeremiah 40:7-41:3

Sirach [Ecclesiasticus] 6:5-17

Those who fear the Lord direct their friendship aright, for as they are, so are their neighbors also.

or Micah 3:1-8

1 Corinthians 15:41-50

Just as we have borne the image of the man of dust, we will also bear the image of the man of heaven.

Revelation 7:9-17

The Lamb at the center of the throne will be their shepherd, and he will guide them to springs of the water of life, and God will wipe away every tear from their eyes.

after Proper 28 / Pentecost 27

1 Maccabees 3:1-24

It is not on the size of the army that victory in battle depends, but strength comes from heaven.

[BCP: 1 Maccabees 3:25-41]

or Ezra 9:1-15

Habakkuk 3:1-10(11-15)16-18

O LORD, I have heard of your renown, and I stand in awe, O LORD, of your work.

Revelation 21:1-8

He will wipe away every tear from their eyes. Death will be no more; mourning and crying and pain will be no more, for the first things have passed away.

James 3:1-12

No one can tame the tongue—a restless evil, full of deadly poison. With it we bless the Lord and Father, and with it we curse those who are made in the likeness of God.

Silence for meditation follows each reading.

RESPONSORY

We are God's **child**ren now;*
what we will be has not yet **been**
revealed.
What we do **know** is this;*
when he is revealed we will
be like him, for we will see
him **as** he is.
And all those who have this
hope in him puri**fy** themselves,*
just as **he** is pure.
What we do **know** is this;*
when he is revealed we will
be like him, for we will see
him **as** he is.
[LH: 1 John 3:2-3]

You have died and your life is
hidden with **Christ** in God.*
When Christ who is your
life is revealed, then you
also will be revealed with
him in glory.
So you also must consider
yourselves dead to sin and alive
to God **in** Christ Jesus.*
When Christ who is your
life is revealed, then you
also will be revealed with
him in glory.
[LH: Col. 3:3-4; Rom. 6:11]

Wednesday of Week IV

Antiphon to PSALM 23 *Dominus regit me*

The LORD **is** my shepherd;*
I shall not **be** in want. [PBO]

23 *The good shepherd*

1 The LORD **is** my shepherd;*
I shall not **be** in want.

2 He makes me lie down **in** green pastures*
and leads me be**side** still waters.

3 He re**vives** my soul*
and guides me along right pathways for **his** Name's sake.

4 Though I walk through the valley of the shadow of death,
I shall **fear** no evil;*
for you are with me;
your rod and your staff, they **com**fort me.

5 You spread a table before me in the presence of **those**
who trouble me;*
you have anointed my head with oil,
and my cup is **run**ning over.

6 Surely your goodness and mercy shall follow me all the days
of my life,*
and I will dwell in the house of the **LORD** for ever.

Antiphon The LORD **is** my shepherd;*
I shall not **be** in want.

Silence for meditation

Lord Jesus Christ, shepherd of your Church, you give us new birth in the waters of baptism; you anoint us with oil, and call us to salvation at your table: Dispel the terrors of death and the darkness of error. Lead your people along safe paths, that they may rest securely in you and dwell in the house of the Lord now and for ever, for your Name's sake. [LH, LBW]

+

Antiphon to PSALM 147 part i *Laudate Dominum*

How pleasant it is to honor God with praise! [LH, PBO]

147 *Praise of God who maintains the world*

1 Hallelujah!
How good it is to sing praises **to** our God!*
how pleasant it is to honor **him** with praise!

2 The LORD re**builds** Jerusalem;*
he gathers the ex**iles** of Israel.

3 He heals the **bro**kenhearted*
and binds **up** their wounds.

4 He counts the number **of** the stars*
and calls them all **by** their names.

5 Great is our LORD and might**y** in power;*
there is no limit **to** his wisdom.

6 The LORD lifts **up** the lowly,*
but casts the wicked **to** the ground,

7 Sing to the LORD **with** thanksgiving;*
make music to our God up**on** the harp.

8 He covers the heav**ens** with clouds*
and prepares rain **for** the earth;

9 He makes grass to grow up**on** the mountains*
and green plants to **serve** mankind.

10 He provides food for **flocks** and herds*
and for the young ravens **when** they cry.

11 He is not impressed by the might **of** a horse;*
he has no pleasure in the strength **of** a man;

12 But the LORD has pleasure in **those** who fear him,*
in those who await his **gra**cious favor.

Antiphon How pleasant it is to honor God with praise!

Silence for meditation

God our Father, great builder of the heavenly Jerusalem, you know the number of the stars and call each of them by name: Heal hearts that are broken, gather those who have been scattered, and enrich us all from the plenitude of your eternal wisdom, Jesus Christ our Lord. [LH, LBW]

+

Stand

THE HYMN is sung. *Gott des Himmels und der Erde*

2 Thank you, God, for in your keeping
Safely have I slumbered here;
You have guarded me while sleeping
From all danger, pain, and fear,
And the cunning of my foe
Has not wrought my overthrow.

3 Let the night of sin that shrouded
All my life, with this depart;
Shine on me with beams unclouded,
Jesus! In your loving heart
Is my help and hope alone
From the evil I have done.

4 Help me as the morn is breaking
In the spirit to arise,
So from careless sloth awaking
That, when o'er the aged skies
Shall the morn of Doom appear,
I may see it without fear.

5 Lead me, and forsake me never
Guide my wanderings by your Word;
As you have been, so be ever
My defense, my refuge, Lord.
Never safe, except with you,
O my faithful guardian true.

6 O my God, I now commend me
Wholly to your mighty hand.
All the powers that you have lent me
Let me use at your command.
You, my glory, strength impart;
Hold me ever to your heart.

7 Thus afresh with each new morning
Save me from the power of sin;
Hourly let me feel your warning

Ruling, prompting me within,
Till my final rest has come
And your angels bear me home. [TLH 549, LBW 266]

Text: Heinrich Albert, 1604-1651; tr. Catherine Winkworth, 1829-1878, alt.
Tune: *Gott des Himmels,* Heinrich Albert, 1604-1651 87 87 77

Sit

One or two LESSONS are read.

Year 1	Year 2
after Epiphany 4	
Isaiah 52:13-53:12	Genesis 22:1-18
He shall startle many nations; kings shall shut their mouths because of him; for that which had not been told them they shall see, and that which they had not heard they shall contemplate. [BCP: Isaiah 54:1-10 (11-17)]	Abraham said, "God himself will provide the lamb for a burnt offering, my son." So the two of them walked on together.
Galatians 4:21-31	Hebrews 11:23-31
So then, friends, we are children, not of the slave but of the free woman.	By faith Moses, when he was grown up, refused to be called a son of Pharaoh's daughter, choosing rather to share ill-treatment with the people of God than to enjoy the fleeting pleasures of sin.
after Epiphany 8	
Deuteronomy 4:25-31	Proverbs 17:1-20
Because the LORD your God is a merciful God, he will neither abandon you nor destroy you; he will not forget the covenant with your ancestors that he swore to them.	The crucible is for silver, and the furnace is for gold, but the LORD tests the heart. *or* Susanna 1-33

2 Corinthians 11:21b-33

If I must boast, I will boast of the things that show my weakness.

after Proper 4 / Pentecost 3

Deuteronomy 13:1-11

The LORD your God is testing you, to know whether you indeed love the LORD your God with all your heart and soul.

2 Corinthians 7:2-16

Godly grief produces a repentance that leads to salvation and brings no regret, but worldly grief produces death.

after Proper 8 / Pentecost 7

1 Samuel 12:1-6 (7-15) 16-25

Only fear the LORD, and serve him faithfully with all your heart; for consider what great things he has done for you.

Acts 8:14-25

Then Peter and John laid their hands on them, and they received the Holy Spirit.

after Proper 12 / Pentecost 11

2 Samuel 3:22-39

David said, "I and my kingdom are forever guiltless before the Lord for the blood of Abner son

2 Timothy 3:1-17

Indeed, all who want to live a godly life in Christ Jesus will be persecuted.

Ecclesiastes 3:1-15

For everything there is a season, and a time for every matter under heaven.

Galatians 2:11-21

It is no longer I who live, but it is Christ who lives in me.

Numbers 22:41-23:12

From the top of the crags I see him, from the hills I behold him; here is a people living alone, and not reckoning itself among the nations! Who can count the dust of Jacob, or number the dust-cloud of Israel?

Romans 7:13-25

I do not do the good I want, but the evil I do not want is what I do.

Judges 3:12-30

When the Israelites cried out to the LORD, the LORD raised up for them a deliverer, Ehud son of

of Ner. May the guilt fall upon the head of Joab, and on all his father's house.

Acts 16:16-24

These men are disturbing our city; they are Jews and are advocating customs that are not lawful for us as Romans to adopt or observe.

after Proper 16 / Pentecost 15

1 Kings 3:1-15

I give you a wise and discerning mind; no one like you has been before you and no one like you shall arise after you. I give you also what you have not asked, both riches and honor all your life.

Acts 27:9-26

Do not be afraid, Paul; you must stand before the emperor; and indeed God has granted safety to all those who are sailing with you.

after Proper 20 / Pentecost 19

2 Kings 6:1-23

Elisha prayed: "O LORD, please open his eyes that he may see." So the LORD opened the eyes of the servant, and he saw; the mountain was full of horses and chariots of fire all around Elisha.

Gera, the Benjaminite, a left-handed man.

Acts 1:1-14

You will receive power when the Holy Spirit has come upon you; and you will be my witnesses in Jerusalem, and in all Judea and Samaria, and to the ends of the earth.

Job 6:1; 7:1-21

Remember that my life is a breath; my eye will never again see good.

Acts 10:1-16

The voice said to Peter again, a second time, "What God has made clean, you must not call profane."

Esther 6:1-14

His wife Zeresh said to him, "If Mordecai, before whom your downfall has begun, is of the Jewish people, you will not prevail against him, but will surely fall before him."

[BCP: *or* Judith 10:1-23]

1 Corinthians 5:9-6:11

You were washed, you were sanctified, you were justified in the name of the Lord Jesus Christ and in the Spirit of our God.

Acts 19:1-10

When Paul laid his hands on them, the Holy Spirit came upon them, and they spoke in tongues and prophesied.

after Proper 24 / Pentecost 23

Lamentations 2:8-15

They hiss and wag their heads at daughter Jerusalem; "Is this the city that was called the perfection of beauty, the joy of all the earth?"
or Jeremiah 41:4-18

1 Corinthians 15:51-58

Thanks be to God, who gives us the victory through our Lord Jesus Christ.

Sirach [Ecclesiasticus] 7:4-14

Do not grow weary when you pray; do not reglect to give alms.

or Micah 3:9-4:5

Revelation 8:1-13

Another angel with a golden censer came and stood at the altar; he was given a great quantity of incense to offer with the prayers of all the saints on the golden altar that is before the throne.

after Proper 28 / Pentecost 27

1 Maccabees 3:25-41

Lysias was to send a force against them to wipe out and destroy the strength of Israel and the remnant of Jerusalem; he was to banish the memory of them from the place, settle aliens in all their territory, and distribute their land by lot.
[BCP: 1 Maccabees 3:42-60]
or Ezra 10:1-17

Malachi 1:1,6-14

You bring what has been taken by violence or is lame or sick, and this you bring as your offering! Shall I accept that from your hand? says the LORD.

Revelation 21:9-21

In the spirit he carried me away to a great, high mountain and showed me the holy city Jerusalem coming down out of heaven from God.

James 3:13-4:12

A harvest of righteousness is sown in peace for those who make peace.

Silence for meditation follows each reading.

RESPONSORY

Yours, O Lord, are the greatness, the power, the glory, the victory, and the majesty; and you are exalted **a**bove all.*

Give to us peace in our **days**, O Lord.

O Lord, Lord God, Creator of all things, you are awe-inspiring and strong and **just** and merciful.*

Give to us peace in our **days**, O Lord.

[LH: 1 Chron. 29:11-12; see 2 Kings 20:19; 2 Maccabees 1:24]

May the God of peace make you complete in everything good so that you may **do** his will;*

working among us that which is pleasing in his sight, through **Je**sus Christ.

May he give you all a heart to worship him and to do his will with a strong heart and a **will**ing spirit,*

working among us that which is pleasing in his sight, through **Je**sus Christ.

[LH: Heb. 13:20, 21; 2 Macc. 1:3]

Thursday of Week IV

Antiphon to PSALM 58 *Si vere utique*

Surely, there is a reward **for** the righteous;*
surely, there is a God who rules **in** the earth. [PBO]

58 *Condemnation of injustice*

1 Do you indeed decree righteous**ness**, you rulers?*
do you judge the peo**ples** with equity?

2 No; you devise evil **in** your hearts,*
and your hands deal out violence **in** the land.

3 The wicked are perverse **from** the womb;*
liars go astray **from** their birth.

4 They are as venomous **as** a serpent,*
they are like the deaf adder which **stops** its ears,

5 Which does not heed the voice **of** the charmer,*
no matter how skill**ful** his charming.

6 O God, break their teeth **in** their mouths;*
pull the fangs of the young li**ons**, O LORD.

7 Let them vanish like water **that** runs off;*
let them wither like **trod**den grass.

8 Let them be like the snail that **melts** away,*
like a stillborn child that never **sees** the sun.

9 Before they bear fruit, let them be cut down **like** a brier;*
like thorns and thistles let them be **swept** away.

10 The righteous will be glad when they **see** the vengeance;*
they will bathe their feet in the blood **of** the wicked.

11 And they will say,
"Surely, there is a reward **for** the righteous;*
surely, there is a God who rules **in** the earth."

Antiphon Surely, there is a reward **for** the righteous;*
surely, there is a God who rules **in** the earth.

Silence for meditation

Merciful God, all judgment belongs to you: Give us the wisdom to perceive Christ in others, and to examine our own conduct; so that on the great and final day we may approach you not as severe judge, but as our Father, who loves us in Jesus Christ our Lord. [LHd, LBW]

+

Antiphon to PSALM 147 part ii *Lauda, Jerusalem, Dominum*

Praise the LORD, O Jerusalem. [LH]

147 *Praise of God's personal care of Israel*

13 Worship the LORD, **O** Jerusalem;*
praise your **God**, O Zion;

14 For he has strengthened the bars **of** your gates;*
he has blessed your chil**dren** within you.

15 He has established peace **on** your borders;*
he satisfies you with the **fin**est wheat.

16 He sends out his command **to** the earth,*
and his word runs **ver**y swiftly.

17 He gives **snow** like wool;*
he scatters hoar**frost** like ashes.

18 He scatters his **hail** like bread crumbs;*
who can stand a**gainst** his cold?

19 He sends forth his **word** and melts them;*
he blows with his wind, and the **wat**ers flow.

20 He declares his **word** to Jacob,*
his statutes and his judg**ments** to Israel.

21 He has not done so to any **oth**er nation;*
to them he has not revealed his judgments.
Hallelujah!

Antiphon Praise the LORD, O Jerusalem.

Silence for meditation

Almighty God, through your Church, generously endowed with gifts of grace and fortified by the Holy Spirit, you send out your Word to all nations: Strengthen your Church with heavenly food, make it dauntless in faith, and multiply its children, that with joy we may celebrate your love at the altar on high; through Jesus Christ our Lord. [LH]

+

Stand

THE HYMN is sung.

2 O tell of his might; O sing of his grace,
Whose robe is the light, whose canopy space;
His chariots of wrath the deep thunder-clouds form,
And dark is his path on the wings of the storm.

3 The earth with its store of wonders untold,
Almighty, thy power hath founded of old;
Hath stablished it fast by a changeless decree,
And round it hath cast, like a mantle, the sea.

4 Thy bountiful care what tongue can recite?
It breathes in the air, it shines in the light:
It streams from the hills, it descends to the plain,
And sweetly distills in the dew and the rain.

5 Frail children of dust, and feeble as frail,
In thee do we trust, nor find thee to fail;
Thy mercies, how tender, how firm to the end,
Our Maker, Defender, Redeemer, and Friend.

6 O measureless Might, ineffable Love,
While angels delight to hymn thee above,
The humbler creation, though feeble their lays,
With true adoration shall sing to thy praise.

[SBH 163, H82 388, LBW 548]

Text: Robert Grant, 1779-1838
Tune: *Hanover,* William Croft, 1678-1727 10 10 11 11

Sit

One or two LESSONS are read.

Year 1

after Epiphany 4

Isaiah 54:1-10 (11-17)

In overflowing wrath for a moment I hid my face from you, but with everlasting love I will have compassion on you, says the LORD, your Redeemer.
[BCP: Isaiah 55:1-13]

Galatians 5:1-15

The whole law is summed up in a single commandment, "You shall love your neighbor as yourself."

after Epiphany 8

Deuteronomy 4:32-40

Has any people ever heard the voice of a god speaking out of a fire, as you have heard, and lived?

2 Corinthians 12:1-10

He said to me, "My grace is sufficient for you, for power is made perfect in weakness."

Year 2

Genesis 23:1-20

Abraham buried Sarah his wife in the cave of the field of Machpelah facing Mamre (that is, Hebron) in the land of Canaan.

Hebrews 11:32-12:2

Therefore, since we are surrounded by so great a cloud of witnesses, let us also lay aside every weight and the sin that clings so closely, and let us run with perseverance the race that is set before us, looking to Jesus the pioneer and perfecter of our faith.

Proverbs 21:30-22:6

The rich and poor have this in common: the LORD is the maker of them all.
or Susanna 34-64

2 Timothy 4:1-8

From now on there is reserved for me the crown of righteousness, which the Lord, the righteous judge, will give me on that day, and not only to me but also to all who have longed for his appearing.

after Proper 4 / Pentecost 3

Deuteronomy 16:18-20; 17:14-20

Justice, only justice, you shall pursue, so that you may live and occupy the land that the LORD your God is giving you.

Ecclesiastes 3:16-4:3

Humans have no advantage over the animals; for all is vanity. All go to one place; all are from the dust, and all turn to dust again.

2 Corinthians 8:1-16

You know the generous act of our Lord Jesus Christ, that though he was rich, yet for your sakes he became poor, so that by his poverty you might become rich.

Galatians 3:1-14

Those who believe are blessed with Abraham who believed.

after Proper 8 / Pentecost 7

1 Samuel 13:5-18

But now your kingdom will not continue; the LORD has sought out a man after his own heart; and the LORD has appointed him to be ruler over his people, because you have not kept what the LORD commanded you.

Numbers 23:11-26

Then Balak said to Balaam, "What have you done to me? I brought you to curse my enemies, but now you have done nothing but bless them."

Acts 8:26-40

He commanded the chariot to stop, and both of them, Philip and the eunuch, went down into the water; and Philip baptized him.

Romans 8:1-11

There is therefore now no condemnation for those who are in Christ Jesus. For the law of the Spirit of life in Christ Jesus has set you free from the law of sin and death.

after Proper 12 / Pentecost 11

2 Samuel 4:1-12

When the one who told me, "See, Saul is dead," thought he was bringing good news, I seized him and killed him at Ziklag--this was the reward I gave him for his news. How much more then, when wicked men have killed a righteous man on his bed in his own house!

Acts 16:25-40

Believe on the Lord Jesus, and you will be saved, you and your household.

after Proper 16 / Pentecost 15

1 Kings 3:16-28

All Israel heard of the judgment that the king had rendered; and they stood in awe of the king, because they perceived that the wisdom of God was in him, to execute justice.

Acts 27:27-44

The soldiers' plan was to kill the prisoners, so that none might swim away and escape; but the centurion, wishing to save Paul, kept them from carrying out their plan.

after Proper 20 / Pentecost 19

2 Kings 9:1-16

Thus says the LORD the God of Israel: I anoint you king over the people of the LORD, over Israel.

Judges 4:4-23

The road on which you are going will not lead to glory, for the LORD will sell Sisera into the hand of a woman.

Acts 1:15-26

They cast lots for them and the lot fell on Matthias; and he was added to the eleven apostles.

Job 8:1-10, 20-22

Inquire now of bygone generations, and consider what their ancestors have found; for we are but of yesterday, and we know nothing, for our days on earth are but a shadow.

Acts 10:17-33

God has shown me that I should not call anyone profane or unclean.

Esther 7:1-10

They hanged Haman on the gallows that he had prepared for Mordecai. Then the anger of the king abated. [BCP: *or* Judith 12:1-20]

1 Corinthians 6:12-20

Do you not know that your body is a temple of the Holy Spirit within you, which you have from God, and that you are not your own? For you were bought with a price; therefore glorify God in your body.

Acts 19:11-20

The word of the Lord grew mightily and prevailed.

after Proper 24 / Pentecost 23

Ezra 1:1-11

Thus says King Cyrus of Persia: The LORD, the God of heaven, has given me all the kingdoms of the earth, and he has charged me to build him a house at Jerusalem in Judah.

or Jeremiah 42:1-22

Sirach [Ecclesiasticus] 10:1-18

The beginning of human pride is to forsake the Lord; the heart has withdrawn from its Maker.

or Micah 5:1-4,10-15

1 Corinthians 16:1-9

On the first day of every week, each of you is to put aside and save whatever extra you earn.

Revelation 9:1-12

The fifth angel blew his trumpet, and I saw a star that had fallen from heaven to earth, and he was given the key to the shaft of the bottomless pit.

after Proper 28 / Pentecost 27

1 Maccabees 3:42-60

It is better for us to die in battle than to see the misfortunes of our nation and of the sanctuary. But as his will in heaven may be, so shall he do.
[BCP: 1 Maccabees 4:1-25]
or Nehemiah 9:1-15(16-25)

Malachi 2:1-16

Take heed to yourselves and do not be faithless.

Revelation 21:22-22:5

There will be no more night; they need no light of lamp or sun, for the Lord God will be their light, and they will reign forever and ever.

James 4:13-5:6

You do not even know what tomorrow will bring. What is your life? For you are a mist that appears for a little while and then vanishes.

Silence for meditation follows each reading.

RESPONSORY

In returning and rest you **shall** be saved;*
In the quietness and in trust shall **be** your strength.
Therefore the Lord waits to be **gra**cious to you;*
to show mer**cy** to you.
Blessed are all those who **wait** for him:*
In the quietness and in trust shall **be** your strength.

[LH: Isa. 30:15,18]

Everyone who drinks of the water that I will give them will nev**er** be thirsty.*
The water that I will give will become in them a spring of water gushing up to e**ter**nal life.
Sir, give me this water, so that I may nev**er** be thirsty.*
The water that I will give will become in them a spring of water gushing up to e**ter**nal life.

[LH: John 4:13-15]

Friday of Week IV

Antiphon to PSALM 76 *Notus in Judaea*

The earth was afraid **and** was still*
when God rose **up** to judgment. [PBO]

76 *Thanksgiving for victory*

1 In Judah **is** God known;*
his Name is **great** in Israel.

2 At Salem is his **tab**ernacle,*
and his dwelling **is** in Zion.

3 There he broke the **flash**ing arrows,*
the shield, the sword, and the wea**pons** of battle.

4 How glori**ous** you are!*
more splendid than the ever**last**ing mountains!

5 The strong of heart have been despoiled;
they sink **in**to sleep;*
none of the warriors can **lift** a hand.

6 At your rebuke, O **God** of Jacob,*
both horse and rid**er** lie stunned.

7 What terror **you** inspire!*
who can stand before you when **you** are angry?

8 From heaven you **pro**nounced judgment;*
the earth was afraid **and** was still;

9 When God rose **up** to judgment*
and to save all the oppressed **of** the earth.

10 Truly, wrathful Edom will **give** you thanks,*
and the remnant of Hamath will **keep** your feasts.

11 Make a vow to the LORD your **God** and keep it;*
let all around him bring gifts to him who is worthy **to** be feared.

12 He breaks the spir**it** of princes,*
and strikes terror in the kings **of** the earth.

Antiphon The earth was afraid **and** was still*
when God rose **up** to judgment.

Silence for meditation

Mighty God, awesome in power and splendid in holiness, in your presence the earth both trembles and stands still, for by the cross you shattered the power of death. Rise to help your people; give the light of your salvation to the meek of the earth, that they may praise your Name for ever; through your Son, Jesus Christ our Lord. [LH, LBW]

+

Antiphon to PSALM 148 *Laudate Dominum*

Praise the LORD **from** the heavens;*
Praise the LORD **from** the earth. [LH]

148 *Cosmic praise*

1 Hallelujah!
Praise the LORD **from** the heavens;*
praise him **in** the heights.

2 Praise him, all you an**gels** of his;*
praise him, **all** his host.

3 Praise him, **sun** and moon;*
praise him, all you **shin**ing stars.

4 Praise him, heav**en** of heavens,*
and you waters a**bove** the heavens.

5 Let them praise the Name **of** the LORD;*
for he commanded, and they **were** created.

6 He made them stand fast for ev**er** and ever;*
he gave them a law which shall not **pass** away.

7 Praise the LORD **from** the earth,*
you sea-monsters **and** all deeps;

8 Fire and hail, **snow** and fog,*
tempestuous wind, do**ing** his will;

9 Mountains **and** all hills,*
fruit trees **and** all cedars;

10 Wild beasts **and** all cattle,*
creeping things and **wing**èd birds;

11 Kings of the earth **and** all peoples,*
princes and all rulers **of** the world;

12 Young **men** and maidens,*
old and **young** together.

13 Let them praise the Name **of** the LORD,*
for his Name only is exalted,
his splendor is over **earth** and heaven.

14 He has raised up strength for his people
and praise for all his **loy**al servants,*
the children of Israel, a people who are near him.
Hallelujah!

Antiphon Praise the LORD **from** the heavens;*
Praise the LORD **from** the earth.

Silence for meditation

God Most High, by your Word your created a wondrous universe, and through your Spirit you breathed into it the breath of life: Accept creation's hymn of praise from our lips, and let the praise that is sung in heaven resound in the heart of every creature on earth, to the glory of the Father, and the Son, and the Holy Spirit now and for ever. [LH, LBW]

+

Stand

THE HYMN is sung.

2 All thy works with joy surround thee,
Earth and heaven reflect thy rays,
Stars and angels sing around thee,
Center of unbroken praise.
Field and forest, vale and mountain,
Flowery meadow, flashing sea,

Chanting bird, and flowing fountain
 Call us to rejoice in thee.

3 Thou art giving and forgiving,
 Ever blessing, ever blest,
Well-spring of the joy of living,
 Ocean-depth of happy rest!
Thou our Father, Christ our brother,
 All who live in love are thine;
Teach us how to love each other,
 Lift us to the joy divine! [SBH 438, H82 376, LBW 551]

Text: Henry van Dyke, 1852-1933
Tune: *Hymn to Joy*, Ludwig van Beethoven, 1770-1827,
 adapt. Edward Hodges, 1796-1867, alt. 87 87 D

Sit

One or two LESSONS are read.

Year 1	Year 2
after Epiphany 4	
Isaiah 55:1-13	Genesis 24:1-27
Ho, everyone who thirsts, come to the waters; and you that have no money, come, buy and eat! Come, buy wine and milk without money and without price. [BCP: Isaiah 56:1-8]	The LORD has led me on the way to the house of my master's kin.
Galatians 5:16-24	Hebrews 12:3-11
Those who belong to Christ Jesus have crucified the flesh with its passions and desires.	Consider him who endured such hostility against himself from sinners, so that you may not grow weary or lose heart.

after Epiphany 8

Deuteronomy 5:1-22

You shall have no other gods before me.

Proverbs 23:19-21,29-24:2

Do not envy the wicked, nor desire to be with them.

or Song of Solomon 1:1-3, 9-11, 15-16a; 2:1-3a

2 Corinthians 12:11-21

The signs of a true apostle were performed among you with utmost patience, signs and wonders and mighty works.

2 Timothy 4:9-22

The Lord will rescue me from every evil attack and save me for his heavenly kingdom.

after Proper 4 / Pentecost 3

Deuteronomy 26:1-11

So now I bring the first of the fruit of the ground that you, O LORD, have given me.

Ecclesiastes 5:1-7

Guard your steps when you go the house of God; to draw near to listen is better than the sacrifice offered by fools.

2 Corinthians 8:16-24

Therefore openly before the churches, show them the proof of your love and of our reason for boasting about you.

Galatians 3:15-22

The scripture has imprisoned all things under the power of sin, so that what was promised through faith in Jesus Christ might be given to those who believe.

after Proper 8 / Pentecost 7

1 Samuel 13:19-14:15

It may be that the LORD will act for us; for nothing can hinder the LORD from saving by many or by few.

Numbers 24:1-13

If Balak should give me his house full of silver and gold, I would not be able to go beyond the word of the LORD, to do either good or bad of my own will; what the LORD says, that is what I will say.

Acts 9:1-9

He fell to the ground and heard a voice saying to him, "Saul, Saul, why do you persecute me?"

Romans 8:12-17

When we cry "Abba! Father!" it is that very Spirit bearing witness with our spirit that we are children of God.

after Proper 12 / Pentecost 11

2 Samuel 5:1-12

David then perceived that the LORD had established him king over Israel, and that he had exalted his kingdom for the sake of his people Israel.

Judges 5:1-18

The mountains quaked before the LORD, the One of Sinai, before the LORD, the God of Israel.

Acts 17:1-15

These people who have been turning the world upside down have come here also.

Acts 2:1-21

All of them were filled with the Holy Spirit and began to speak in other languages, as the Spirit gave them ability.

after Proper 16 / Pentecost 15

1 Kings 5:1-6:1,7

The house was built with stone finished at the quarry, so that neither hammer nor ax nor any tool of iron was heard in the temple while it was being built.

Job 9:1-15,32-35

How can a mortal be just before God?

Acts 28:1-16

And so we came to Rome. The believers from there, when they heard of us, came as far as the Forum of Appius and Three Taverns to meet us. On seeing them, Paul thanked God and took courage.

Acts 10:34-48

Then Peter began to speak to them: "I truly understand that God shows no partiality, but in every nation anyone who fears him and does what is right is acceptable to him."

after Proper 20 / Pentecost 19

2 Kings 9:17-37

"Is it peace, Jehu?" He answered, "What peace can there be, so long as the many whoredoms and sorceries of your mother Jezebel continue?"

Esther 8:1-8,15-17

In every province and in every city, wherever the king's command and his edict came, there was gladness and joy among the Jews, a festival and a holiday. Furthermore, many of the peoples of the country professed to be Jews, because the fear of the Jews had fallen upon them.

[BCP: *or* Judith 13:1-20]

1 Corinthians 7:1-9

I wish that all were as I myself am. But each has a particular gift from God, one having one kind and another a different kind.

Acts 19:21-41

Not only in Ephesus but in almost the whole of Asia this Paul has persuaded and drawn away a considerable number of people by saying that gods made with the hands are not gods.

after Proper 24 / Pentecost 23

Ezra 3:1-13

All the people responded with a great shout when they praised the LORD, because the foundation of the house of the LORD was laid.

or Jeremiah 43:1-13

1 Corinthians 16:10-24

Keep alert, stand firm in your faith, be courageous, be strong.

Sirach [Ecclesiasticus] 11:2-20

Good things and bad, life and death, poverty and wealth, come from the Lord.

or Micah 6:1-8

Revelation 9:13-21

The four angels were released, who had been held ready for the hour, the day, the month, and the year, to kill a third of humankind.

after Proper 28 / Pentecost 27

1 Maccabees 4:1-25

Do not fear their numbers or be afraid when they charge. Remember how our ancestors were saved at the Red Sea, when Pharaoh with his forces pursued them.
[BCP: 1 Maccabees 4:36-59]
or Nehemiah 9:26-38

Malachi 3:1-12

See, I am sending my messenger to prepare the way before me, and the Lord whom you seek will suddenly come to his temple.

Revelation 22:6-13

I am the Alpha and the Omega, the first and the last, the beginning and the end.

James 5:7-12

Be patient, therefore, beloved, until the coming of the Lord.

Silence for meditation follows each reading.

RESPONSORY

In holiness of spirit and genuine love let everyone re**turn**
to God;*
he erased the record that stood against us with its legal demands, nailing it **to** the cross.
Rend your hearts and not your clothing; return to the LORD your God:*
he erased the record that stood against us with its legal demands, nailing it **to** the cross.
[LH: see 2 Col. 6:6; Col. 2:14; Joel 2:13]

I regard everything as loss because of the surpassing value of knowing **Je**sus Christ,*
in order that I may know him and the power of his resurrection and sharing **of** his sufferings.
If we have died with Christ, we believe that we will also **live** with him,*
in order that I may know him and the power of his resurrection and sharing **of** his sufferings.
[LH: Phil. 3:8,10; Rom. 6:8]

Saturday of Week IV

Antiphon to PSALM 63 *Deus, Deus meus*

O God, **you** are my God;*
eager**ly** I seek you. [LH, PBO]

63 *Longing for God*

1 O God, you are my God; eager**ly** I seek you;*
my soul thirsts for you, my flesh faints for you,
as in a barren and dry land where there **is** no water.

2 Therefore I have gazed upon you in your **ho**ly place,*
that I might behold your power **and** your glory.

3 For your loving-kindness is better than **life** itself;*
my lips shall **give** you praise.

4 So will I bless you as long **as** I live*
and lift up my hands **in** your Name.

5 My soul is content, as with mar**row** and fatness,*
and my mouth praises you with **joy**ful lips,

6 When I remember you up**on** my bed,*
and meditate on you in **the** night watches.

7 For you have **been** my helper,*
and under the shadow of your wings I **will** rejoice.

8 My soul **clings** to you;*
your right hand **holds** me fast.

9 May those who seek my life **to** destroy it*
go down into the depths **of** the earth;

10 Let them fall upon the edge **of** the sword,*
and let them be **food** for jackals.

11 But the king will rejoice in God;
all those who swear by him **will** be glad;*
for the mouth of those who speak lies **shall** be stopped.

Antiphon O God, **you** are my God;*
eager**ly** I seek you.

Silence for meditation

Heavenly Father, creator of unfailing light, enlighten those who call to you that our lives may proclaim your goodness, our work give you honor, and our voices praise you for ever; for the sake of your Son, Jesus Christ our Lord. [LH, LBW]

+

Antiphon to PSALM 149 *Cantate Domino*

Let the children of Zion be joyful in their king. [LH, PBO]

149 *Praise to the God of victories*

1 Hallelujah!
Sing to the LORD **a** new song;*
sing his praise in the congregation **of** the faithful.

2 Let Israel rejoice **in** his Maker;*
let the children of Zion be joyful **in** their King.

3 Let them praise his Name **in** the dance;*
let them sing praise to him with tim**brel** and harp.

4 For the LORD takes pleasure **in** his people*
and adorns the **poor** with victory.

5 Let the faithful re**joice** in triumph;*
let them be joyful **on** their beds.

6 Let the praises of God be **in** their throat*
and a two-edged sword **in** their hand;

7 To wreak vengeance **on** the nations*
and punishment **on** the peoples;

8 To bind their **kings** in chains*
and their nobles with **links** of iron;

9 To inflict on them the judg**ment** decreed;*
this is glory for all his faithful people.
Hallelujah!

Antiphon Let the children of Zion be joyful in their king.

Silence for meditation

Lord, let Israel rejoice in you and acknowledge you as creator and redeemer. In your lovingkindness embrace us now, that we may proclaim the wonderful truths of salvation with your saints in glory; through your Son, Jesus Christ our Lord. [LH, LBW]

+

Stand

THE HYMN is sung. *Jerusalem, du hochgebaute Stadt*

2 O happy day, and yet far happier hour,
When will you come at last?
When fearless to my Father's love and power,
Whose Word continues fast,
My soul I gladly render;
For surely will his hand
Lead her, with guidance tender,
To heaven, her fatherland.

3 A moment's space, most wonderful to view,
Released from earthly ties,
Elijah's chariot bears her up to you,
Through all these lower skies
To yonder shining regions,
While down to meet her come
The blessed angel legions
And bid her welcome home.

4 O Zion, hail! Bright city, now unfold
The gates of grace to me.
How many times I longed for you of old
Ere yet I was set free
From yon grim life of sadness,
The world of shadowy nought,
And God had given the gladness,
The heritage, I sought.

5 What glorious throng and what resplendent host
Comes sweeping swiftly down?
The chosen ones, on earth who wrought the most,
The Church's brightest crown,
Our Lord has sent to meet me,
As in the far-off years
Their words oft came to greet me
In yonder land of tears.

6 The patriarchs' and prophets' noble train,
With all Christ's followers true,
Who bore the cross and could the worst disdain
That tyrants dared to do,
I see them shine for ever,
All-glorious as the sun,
'Mid light that fades not ever,
Their perfect freedom won.

7 And when, within that lovely paradise
At last I safely dwell,
From out my soul what songs of bliss shall rise
What joy my lips shall tell,
While holy saints are singing
Hosannas o'er and o'er,
Pure hallelujahs ringing
Around me evermore.

8 Unnumbered choirs before the shining throne
Their joyful anthems raise
Till heaven's glad halls are echoing with the tone
Of that great hymn of praise;
And all its host rejoices,
And all its blessèd throng
Unite their myriad voices
In one eternal song. [CSB 521; TLH 619; LBW 348]

Text: Johann M. Meyfart, 1590-1642; tr. Catherine Winkworth, 1829-1878, alt.
Tune: *Jerusalem, du hochgebaute Stadt,* Melchior Franck, c. 1573-1639 10 6 10 6 76 76

Sit

One or two LESSONS are read.

Year 1	Year 2
after Epiphany 4	
Isaiah 56:1-8 My house shall be called a house of prayer for all peoples. [BCP: Isaiah 57:3-13]	Genesis 24:28-38,49-51 Rebekah is before you, take her and go, and let her be the wife of your master's son, as the LORD has spoken.
Galatians 5:25-6:10 If we live by the Spirit, let us also be guided by the Spirit.	Hebrews 12:12-29 Since we are receiving a kingdom that cannot be shaken, let us give thanks, by which we offer to God an acceptable worship with reverence and awe.
after Epiphany 8	
Deuteronomy 5:22-33 The LORD our God has shown us his glory and greatness, and we have heard his voice out of the fire. Today we have seen that God may speak to someone and the person may still live.	Proverbs 25:15-28 If your enemies are hungry, give them bread to eat; and if they are thirsty, give them water to drink; for you will heap coals of fire on their heads, and the LORD will reward you. *or* Song of Solomon 2:8-13; 4:1-4a, 5-7, 9-11
2 Corinthians 13:1-14 Put things in order, listen to my appeal, agree with one another, live in peace; and the God of love and peace will be with you.	Philippians 1:1-11 Grace to you and peace from God our Father and the Lord Jesus Christ.
after Proper 4 / Pentecost 3	
Deuteronomy 29:2-15 You stand assembled today, all of you, before the LORD your God.	Ecclesiastes 5:8-20 This is what I have seen to be good: it is fitting to eat and drink and find enjoyment in all the toil with which one toils under the

2 Corinthians 9:1-15
Thanks be to God for his indescribable gift!

sun the few days of the life God gives us; for this is our lot.

Galatians 3:23-4:11
There is no longer Jew or Greek, there is no longer slave or free, there is no longer male or female; for all of you are one in Christ Jesus.

after Proper 8 / Pentecost 7

1 Samuel 14:16-30
Now Saul committed a very rash act on that day. He had laid an oath on the troops, saying, "Cursed be anyone who eats food before it is evening and I have been avenged on my enemies."

Numbers 24:12-25
I see him, but not now; I behold him but, not near–a star shall come out of Jacob, and a scepter shall rise out of Israel.

Acts 9:10-19a
Go, for he is an instrument whom I have chosen to bring my name to the Gentiles and kings and before the people of Israel; I myself will show him how much he must suffer for the sake of my name.

Romans 8:18-25
The creation waits with eager longing for the revealing of the children of God.

after Proper 12 / Pentecost 11

2 Samuel 5:22-6:11
David and all the house of Israel were dancing before the LORD with all their might, with songs and lyres and harps and tambourines and castinets and cymbals.

Judges 5:19-31
So perish all your enemies, O LORD! But may your friends be like the sun as it rises in its might.

Acts 17:16-34
He has fixed a day on which he will have the world judged in

Acts 2:22-36
This Jesus God raised up, and of that all of us are witnesses.

righteousness by a man whom he has appointed, and of this he has given assurance to all by raising him from the dead.

after Proper 16 / Pentecost 15

1 Kings 7:51-8:21

Now the LORD has upheld the promise that he made; for I have risen in the place of my father David; I sit on the throne of Israel, as the LORD promised, and have built a house for the name of the LORD, the God of Israel.

Job 9:1; 10:1-9,16-22

Remember that you fashioned me like clay; and will you turn me to dust again?

Acts 28:17-31

He lived there two whole years at his own expense and welcomed all who came to him, proclaiming the kingdom of God and teaching about the Lord Jesus Christ with all boldness and without hindrance.

Acts 11:1-18

They praised God, saying, "Then God has given even to the Gentiles the repentance that leads to life."

after Proper 20 / Pentecost 19

2 Kings 11:1-20a

Jehoiada brought out the king's son, put the crown on him, and gave him the covenant; they proclaimed him king, and anointed him; they clapped their hands and shouted, "Long live the king!"

Esther 9:1-32

The command of Queen Esther fixed these practices of Purim, and it was recorded in writing. [BCP: Hosea 1:1-2:1]

1 Corinthians 7:10-24

You were bought with a price; do not become slaves of human masters.

Acts 20:1-16

Paul was eager to be in Jerusalem, if possible, on the day of Pentecost.

after Proper 24 / Pentecost 23

Ezra 4:7,11-24

We make known to the king that, if this city is rebuilt and its walls finished, you will then have no possession in the province Beyond the River.

or Jeremiah 44:1-14

Sirach [Ecclesiasticus] 15:9-20

It was he who created humankind in the beginning, and he left them in the power of their own free choice.

or Micah 7:1-7

Philemon 1-25

When I remember you in my prayers, I always thank my God because I hear of your love for all the saints and your faith toward the Lord Jesus.

Revelation 10:1-11

In the days when the seventh angel is to blow his trumpet, the mystery of God will be fulfilled, as he announced to his servants the prophets.

after Proper 28 / Pentecost 27

1 Maccabees 4:36-59

See, our enemies are crushed; let us go up to cleanse the sanctuary and dedicate it.

[BCP: Isaiah 65:17-25]

or Nehemiah 7:73b-8:3,5-18

Malachi 3:13-4:6

For you who revere my name the sun of righteousness shall rise, with healing in its wings.

Revelation 22:14-21

"Surely I am coming soon." Amen. Come, Lord Jesus!

James 5:13-20

Whoever brings back a sinner from wandering will save the sinner's soul from death and will cover a multitude of sins.

Silence for meditation follows each reading.

RESPONSORY

The kingdom of the world has become the kingdom of our Lord and of **his** Messiah,*
and he will reign for ev**er** and ever.
For kingship belongs to the Lord; he rules o**ver** the nations,*
and he will reign for ev**er** and ever.
[LH: Rev. 11:17; Ps. 22:27]

Our citizenship is in heaven, and it is from there that we are expecting a Savior, the Lord **Je**sus Christ.*
He will transform the body of our humiliation that it may be conformed to the body **of** his glory.
When Christ who is your life is revealed, then you also will be revealed with **him** in glory.*
He will transform the body of our humiliation that it may be conformed to the body **of** his glory.
[LH: Phil. 3:20-21; Col. 3:4]

✠

EVENING PRAYER

Vespers or Evensong
during Lent
from Ash Wednesday until the Sunday of the Passion

When the Service of Light is omitted, Evening Prayer may begin with these verses:

Stand

L Make haste, O God,✠ to deliver me.

C O Lord, make haste to help me.

[Ps. 70:1; LH; CB, CSB, SBH; BCP]

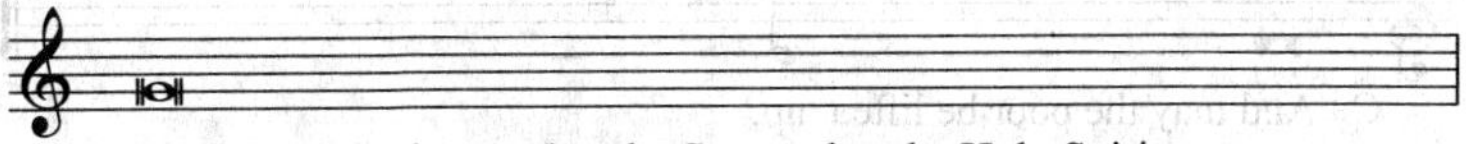

L Glory to the Father, and to the Son, and to the Holy Spirit:

C As it was in the beginning, is now, and will be for ev - er. A - men.

The PSALMODY follows, p. 903.

The SERVICE OF LIGHT may be used to begin Evening Prayer. The service may begin with a procession in which a large, lighted candle is carried to its stand in front of the congregation.

Stand

L Behold, now is the accept - a - ble time;

C Now is the day of sal - va - tion.

L Turn us again, O God of our sal - va - tion,

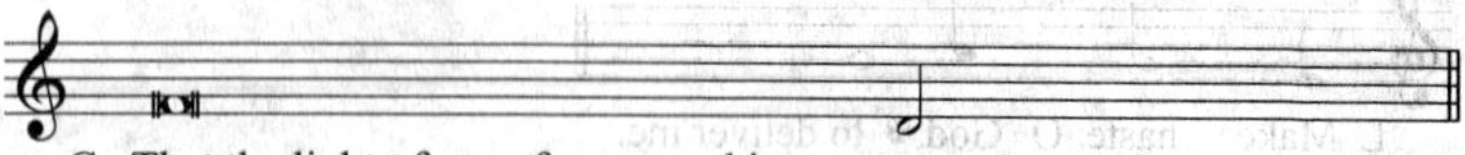

C That the light of your face may shine on us.

L May your justice shine like the sun;

C And may the poor be lifted up.

[2 Cor. 6:2; Ps. 85:4 + Ps. 4:6; see Mal. 4:2 + Ps. 113:7]

As this ancient hymn, Phos hilaron, *is sung, the candles on and near the altar are lighted. When the large candle is used, the candles are lighted from its flame.*

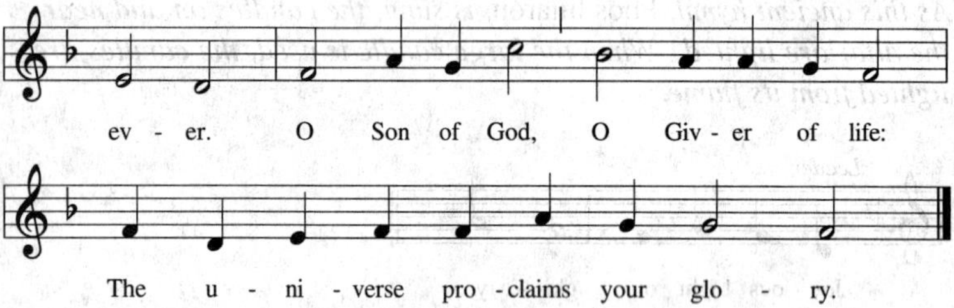

The thanksgiving from the Apostolic Constitutions *(ca. 380) concludes the Service of Light.*

and glo - ry be - long to him.
L We praise and thank you, O God, for you are without beginning and
with-out end; through Christ you are the Creator and Preserver of
the whole world, but above all you are his God and Fa - ther,
the Giver of the Spirit, and the ruler of all that is seen and un - seen.
You made the day for the works of light and the night for the refreshment

of our weak-ness. O loving Lord and Source of all that is good,
mercifully accept our evening sac - ri - fice of praise.
As you have conducted us through the day, and brought us to
night's be-gin-ning, keep us now in Christ, grant us a peaceful evening
and a night free from sin, and at the end bring us to ever - last - ing life
through Christ our Lord. Through him we offer glory, honor and worship

to you in the Ho - ly Spir - it, now and always and for ev - er

and ev - er. C A - men. [MPES]

Kneel or sit.

The PSALMODY begins with this song for forgiveness and protection from Psalm 141, Domine clamavi

L Let my prayer rise be - fore you as in -cense; the lift - ing

up of my hands as the eve - ning sac - ri - fice.

C 1 O Lord, I call to
you; come . . . . . to me quickly; hear my voice when I cry to you.

3 Set a watch
before my . . . . . . mouth, O Lord; and guard the door of my lips.

6 Glory to the
Father, and . . . . . to the Son, and to the . . . . Ho - ly Spirit;

2 Let my prayer rise
before . . . . you as incense; the lifting up of my
hands as the evening sac - ri - fice.

4 Let not my heart
incline to any . . . . e - vil thing; let me not be occupied
in wickedness with e - vil - doers.

5 But my eyes are
turned to . . . . you, Lord God; in you I take refuge.
Strip me not . . . . of my life.

7 as it was in the
begin - ning, is now, and will be for ev - er. A - men.

Silence for meditation

Let the incense of our repentant prayer ascend before you, O Lord, and let your lovingkindness descend upon us, that with purified minds we may sing your praises with the Church on earth and the whole heavenly host, and may glorify you for ever and ever.

C Amen

Sit

A second psalm is sung or said; additional psalms and a New Testament canticle may be sung or said also. Silence for meditation follows each psalm or canticle.

The psalm prayer appropriate to each psalm or canticle follows the silence.

C Amen

Stand

THE HYMN is sung.

Sit

One or two LESSONS are read. Silence for meditation follows each reading.

After this the leader continues:

L In many and various ways God spoke to his people of old by the prophets.

C But now in these last days he has spoken to us by his Son.

[Heb. 1:1-2]

Stand

The GOSPEL CANTICLE, Magnificat, *is sung or said. The proper Antiphon is given on pp. 924-968.*

The Antiphon is sung or said.

1 My soul proclaims
the greatness . . . of the Lord; my spirit
rejoices in . . . God my Savior.

3 From this day all gen - er - ations will . . . . . . call me blessed.

5 He has mercy on those who fear him in every . . . gen - er - ation.

2 for he has . . . looked with favor on his . . . low - ly servant.

4 The Almighty
has done great things for me, and holy . . . is his Name.

6 He has shown
the strength of his arm; he has scattered
the proud in their con - ceit.

7 He has cast down
the mighty . . . from their thrones, and has lifted up the lowly.

9 He has come to
the help of his . . . ser - vant Israel, for he has
remembered
his prom - ise of mercy,

11 Glory to the Father,
and . . . . to the Son, and to the . . . Ho - ly Spirit;

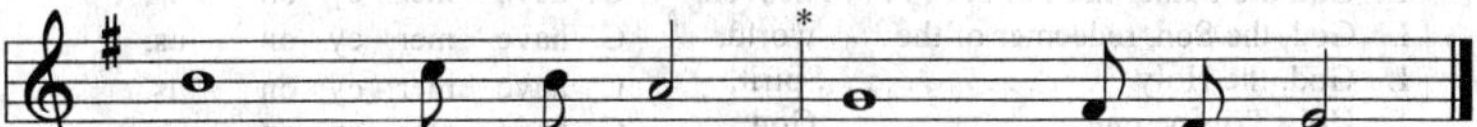

8 He has filled
the hungry . . with good things, and the rich
he has sent a - way empty.

10 the promise
he made . . . . to our fathers, to Abraham
and his chil - dren for ever.

12 as it was in the
begin - ing, is now, and will be
for ev - er. A - men

The Antiphon is repeated.

Kneel or Stand

The GREAT LITANY is sung or said.

L Lord, have mercy. C Lord, have mer - cy.

L Christ, have mercy. C Christ, have mer - cy.

L Lord, have mercy. C Lord, have mer - cy.

L O Christ, hear us. C In mer - cy hear us.

L God the Father in . . . . heaven, C have mer - cy on us.
L God, the Son, redeemer of the world, C have mer - cy on us.
L God, the Holy . . . . Spirit, C have mer - cy on us.
L Holy Trinity, one . . . . God, C have mer - cy on us.

L Be gra - cious to us. C Spare us, good Lord.

L Be gra - cious to us. C Help us, good Lord.

L From all sin, from all error, from all evil;
from the cunning assaults of the devil;
from an unprepared and . . . . e - vil death: C Good Lord, de- liv- er us.

L From war, bloodshed, and violence;
from corrupt and unjust government;
from sedi - . . . . tion and treason: C Good Lord, de- liv- er us.

L From epidemic, drought, and famine,
from fire and flood, earthquake,
lightning and storm;
and from ever - . . . . last - ing death: C Good Lord, de- liv- er us.

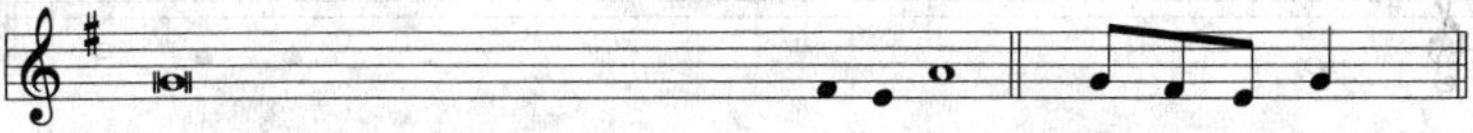

L By the mystery of your incarnation; by your ho- ly birth: C Help us, good Lord.

L By your baptism, fasting, and temptation;
by your agony and bloody sweat;
by your cross and suffering;
by your precious . . . . death and burial: C Help us, good Lord.

L By your glorious resurrection and ascension;
by the gift of the . . . . Ho- ly Spirit: C Help us, good Lord.

L In all time of our tribulation;
in all time of our prosperity;
in the hour of death; and in the . . . . day of judgment: C Save us, good Lord.

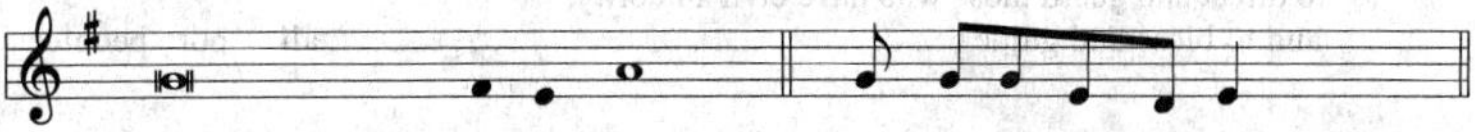

L Though unworthy, we im - plore you C to hear us, Lord our God.

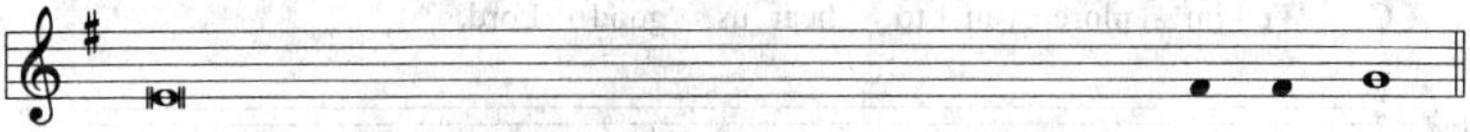

L To rule and govern your holy catholic Church;
to guide all servants of your Church in the true knowledge
and understanding of your Word and in holiness of life;
to put an end to all schisms
and causes of offense to those who would believe;
and to bring into the way of truth all who have erred and gone a - stray:

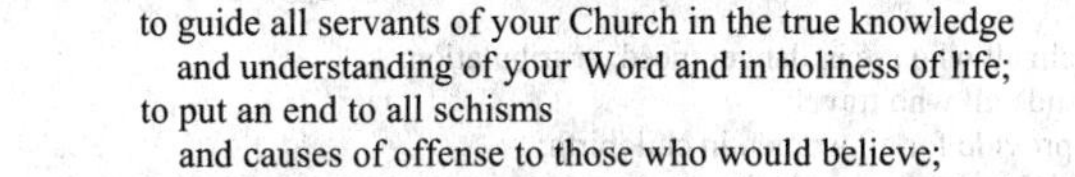

C We im - plore you to hear us, good Lord.

L To beat down Satan under our feet;
to send faithful workers into your harvest;
to accompany your Word with your Spirit and power;
to raise up those who fall and to strengthen those who stand;
and to comfort and help the fainthearted and . . . . the dis - tressed:

C We im - plore you to hear us, good Lord.

L To give to all nations justice and peace;
to preserve our country from discord and strife;
to direct and guard those who have civil authority;
and to bless and guide . . . . all our people:

C We im - plore you to hear us, good Lord.

L To behold and help all who are in danger, need, or tribulation;
to protect and guide all who travel;
to preserve and provide for all women in childbirth;
to watch over children and to guide the young;
to heal the sick and to strengthen their families and friends;
to bring reconciliation to families in discord;
to provide for the unemployed and for all in need;
to be merciful to all who are imprisoned;
to support, comfort, and guide all orphans, widowers, and widows;
and to have mercy on . . . . all your people:

C We im - plore you to hear us, good Lord.

L To forgive our enemies, persecutors, and slanderers,
and to reconcile us to them;
to help us use wisely the fruits and treasures
of the earth, the sea, and the air;
and graciously to . . . . hear our prayers:

C We im - plore you to hear us, good Lord.

L Lord Jesus Christ, Son of God, C We im - plore you to hear us.

L Lamb of God, you take away the sin of the world; C have mer-cy on us.

L Lamb of God, you take away the sin of the world; C have mer-cy on us.

L Lamb of God, you take away the sin of the world; C give us peace. A- men.

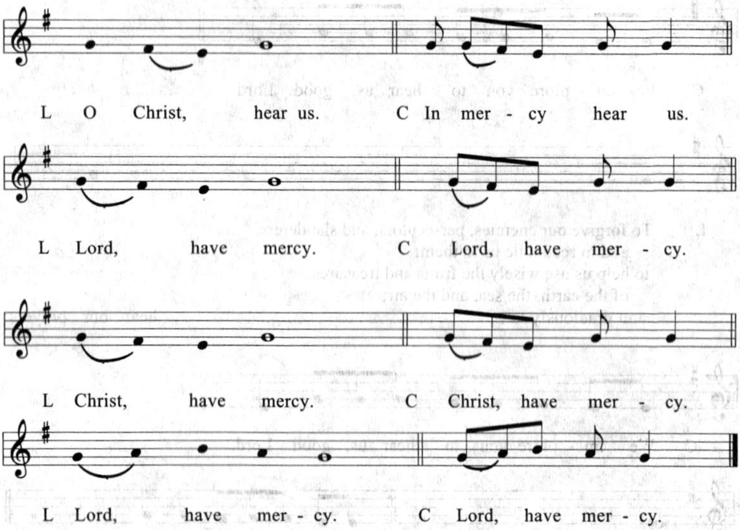

The Prayer of the Day may be said.

These versicles and prayers are said.

L O Lord, deal not with us according to our sins.

C Neither reward us according to our wickedness.

[CB, CSB, SBH; see Ps. 103:10]

Almighty God, our heavenly Father, you desire not the death of sinners, but rather that they should turn from their evil way and live: Graciously turn from those punishments which we by our sins have deserved, and grant us grace evermore to serve you in holiness and pureness of living; through Jesus Christ our Lord.

[Ezek. 18:23; Leo., Gel., Luther, CB, CSB, SBH]

L The Lord will give strength to his people.

C The Lord will bless his people with peace. [Ps. 29:11; CB, CSB, SBH]

O God, you commanded us to listen to your beloved Son: Nourish us inwardly with your Word of life, and purify the eyes of our spirit, so that we may at length rejoice in the sight of your glory; through Jesus Christ our Lord. [Moz., RS Lent 2]

C Amen

L Lord, remember us in your kingdom, and teach us to pray:

C Our Father in heaven,
hallowed be your Name
your kingdom come,
your will be done,
on earth as in heaven.
Give us today our daily bread.
Forgive us our sins
as we forgive those
who sin against us.
Save us from the time of trial
and deliver us from evil.
For the kingdom, the power,
and the glory are yours,
now and for ever. Amen.

C Our Father, who art in heaven,
hallowed be thy Name
thy kingdom come,
thy will be done,
on earth as it is in heaven.
Give us this day our daily bread;
and forgive us our trespasses,
as we forgive those
who sin against us;
And lead us not into temptation
but deliver us from evil.
For thine is the kingdom,
and the power, and the glory,
for ever and ever. Amen.

Stand

L Let us bless the Lord.

C Thanks be to God.

The BENEDICTION concludes the service when there is no sermon. A hymn may follow the benediction.

When there is a sermon, this benediction is omitted, and the service continues as on p. 20.

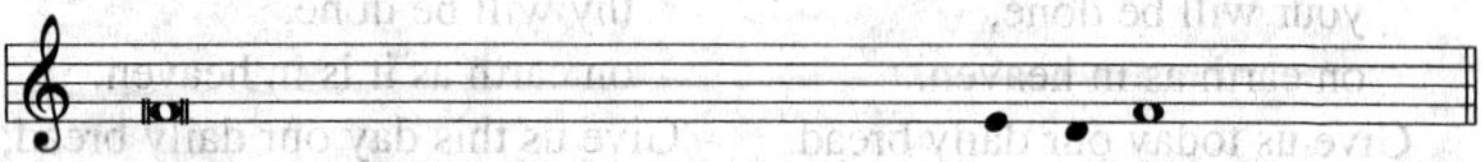

L The almighty and merciful Lord,
the Father, the Son, and the Holy Spirit, bless and pre-serve us.

C A - men

Saturdays in Lent

Antiphon to PSALM 31 *In te, Domine, speravi*

eve of Lent 1: Incline your **ear** to me;*
make haste to de**liv**er me. [LH, PBO]

eve of Lent 2: Make your face to shine up**on** your servant,*
and in your loving**kind**ness save me. [LH]

eve of Lent 3: Blessed **be** the Lord!*
for he shown me the wonders
of his love in a **be**sieged city. [LH]

eve of Lent 4: In returning and rest you **shall** be saved;*
in quietness and in trust
shall **be** your strength. [Isa. 30:15]

eve of Lent 5: Into your hands I com**mend** my spirit,*
for you have redeemed me, O Lord,
O **God** of truth.

31 *Confident prayer in distress*

1 In you, O LORD, have I taken refuge;
let me never be **put** to shame;*
deliver me **in** your righteousness.

2 Incline your **ear** to me;*
make haste to de**liv**er me.

3 Be my strong rock, a castle to keep me safe,
for you are my crag **and** my stronghold;*
for the sake of your Name, lead **me** and guide me.

4 Take me out of the net that they have secretly **set** for me,*
for you are my tow**er** of strength.

5 Into your hands I com**mend** my spirit,*
for you have redeemed me,
O LORD, O **God** of truth.

6 I hate those who cling to **worth**less idols,*
and I put my trust **in** the LORD.

7 I will rejoice and be glad because **of** your mercy;*
for you have seen my affliction;
you know **my** distress.

8 You have not shut me up in the power **of** the enemy;*
you have set my feet in an **o**pen place.

9 Have mercy on me, O LORD, for I **am** in trouble;*
my eye is consumed with sorrow,
and also my throat **and** my belly.

10 For my life is wasted with grief,
and my **years** with sighing;*
my strength fails me because of affliction,
and my bones **are** consumed.

11 I have become a reproach to all my enemies and
even to my neighbors,
a dismay to those of **my** acquaintance;*
when they see me in the street **they** avoid me.

12 I am forgotten like a dead man, **out** of mind;*
I am as useless as a **bro**ken pot.

13 For I have heard the whispering of the crowd;
fear is **all** around;*
they put their heads together against me;
they plot to **take** my life.

14 But as for me, I have trusted in **you**, O LORD.*
I have said, "You **are** my God.

15 My times are **in** your hand;*
rescue me from the hand of my enemies,
and from those who **per**secute me.

16 Make your face to shine up**on** your servant,*
and in your loving-**kind**ness save me."

17 LORD, let me not be ashamed for having **called** upon you;*
rather, let the wicked be put to shame;
let them be silent **in** the grave.

18 Let the lying lips be silenced which speak a**gainst**
the righteous,*
haughtily, disdainfully, and **with** contempt.

19 How great is your goodness, O LORD!
which you have laid up for **those** who fear you;*
which you have done in the sight of all
for those who put their **trust** in you.

20 You hide them in the covert of your presence from those
who **slan**der them;*
you keep them in your shelter from the **strife** of tongues.

21 Blessed **be** the LORD!*
for he has shown me the wonders of his love in a
besieged city.

22 Yet I said in my alarm,
"I have been cut off from the sight **of** your eyes."*
Nevertheless, you heard the sound of my entreaty
when I cried **out** to you.

23 Love the LORD, all you who **wor**ship him;*
the LORD protects the faithful,
but repays to the full those **who** act haughtily.

24 Be strong and let your **heart** take courage,*
all you who wait **for** the LORD.

The Antiphon is repeated.

Silence for meditation

God of kindness and truth, you saved your chosen one, Jesus Christ, and you give your martyrs strength: Watch over your people who come to you now, and strengthen the hearts of those who hope in you, that they may proclaim your saving acts of kindness in the eternal city; through your Son, Jesus Christ our Lord. [LH, LBW]

+

Antiphon to PSALM 143 *Domine, exaudi*

eve of Lent 1: I spread out my hands to **you**, O Lord;*
do not hide your **face** from me. [LH, PBO]

eve of Lent 2: Teach me to do what pleases you, for you **are** my God;*
let your good Spirit lead me on **lev**el ground.

eve of Lent 3: Revive me, O Lord, for **your** Name's sake;*
for your righteousness' sake bring me **out** of trouble.

eve of Lent 4: There will be a canopy as a pavilion,
a shade by day **from** the heat*
and a refuge and a shelter from the **storm** and rain. [Isa. 4:5-6]

eve of Lent 5: I regard every**thing** as loss*
because of the surpassing value of knowing Christ **Jesus** my Lord. [LH: Phil. 3:8]

143 *Prayer in distress: a penitential psalm*

1 LORD, hear my prayer,
and in your faithfulness heed my **sup**plications;*
answer me **in** your righteousness.

2 Enter not into judgment **with** your servant,*
for in your sight shall no one liv**ing** be justified.

3 For my enemy has sought my life;
he has crushed me **to** the ground;*
he has made me live in dark places like those who **are** long dead.

4 My spirit **faints** within me;*
my heart within **me** is desolate.

5 I remember the time past;
I muse upon **all** your deeds;*
I consider the works **of** your hands.

6 I spread out my **hands** to you;*
my soul gasps to you like a **thirst**y land.

7 O LORD, make haste to answer me; my **spir**it fails me;*
do not hide your face from me
or I shall be like those who go down **to** the Pit.

8 Let me hear of your loving-kindness in the morning,
for I put my **trust** in you;*
show me the road that I must walk,
for I lift up my **soul** to you.

9 Deliver me from my ene**mies**, O LORD,*
for I flee to **you** for refuge.

10 Teach me to do what pleases you, for you **are** my God;*
let your good Spirit lead me on **le**vel ground.

11 Revive me, O LORD, for **your** Name's sake;*
for your righteousness' sake, bring me **out** of trouble.

12 Of your goodness, destroy my enemies
and bring all my **foes** to naught,*
for truly I **am** your servant.

The Antiphon is repeated.

Silence for meditation

Lord Jesus, you bring the first light of dawn to those who dwell in darkness and make your love known to them. Enter not into judgment with your servants, but let your Spirit guide us into the land of justice, where with the Father and the Holy Spirit you live and reign, now and for ever. [LH, LBW]

+

Antiphon to the NEW TESTAMENT CANTICLE

Qui cum in forma Dei

eve of Lent 1: Christ suffered for sins once for all,
the righteous **for** the unrighteous,*
in order to bring **you** to God.
He was put to death **in** the flesh,*
but made alive **in** the spirit.
[LH: 1 Peter 3:18]

eve of Lent 2: Live in love, as Christ loved us and gave
himself **up** for us,*
a fragrant offering and sacri**fice**
to God. [Ephes. 5:2]

eve of Lent 3: No one takes my **life** from me;*
I lay it down of my own accord, and
I have power to take it **up** again.
[LH: John 10:18]

eve of Lent 4: So great was God's **love** for us*
that even when we were dead through our
trespasses, he made us alive togeth**er**
with Christ. [LH: see Ephes. 2:4]

eve of Lent 5: Although he **was** a Son,*
Christ learned obedience through **what**
he suffered. [LH: Heb. 5:8]

A Song of Christ's Humiliation and Exaltation   Philippians 2:6-11

Christ Jesus, being in the form of God,
did not cling to equali**ty** with God*
  but emptied himself, taking the form **of** a slave.

Bearing the human likeness, revealed in **hu**man shape,*
  he humbled himself, in obedience accepting death,
  even death **on** a cross.

Therefore God has raised him **to** the heights*
  and bestowed on him the Name a**bove** all names,

that at the Name of JESUS every knee should bow–
in heaven, on earth, and **in** the depths–*
  and every tongue confess to the glory of God the Father
  that Jesus **Christ** is LORD. [LBW]

The Antiphon is repeated.

Silence for meditation

Mighty God, grant that, chastened by Lenten discipline, we may find joy in serving you and that by relaxing our hold on things that are passing away we may grasp more firmly that which endures for ever; through Jesus Christ our Lord. [Gel., MR 4 Lent Thurs.]

+

Stand

THE HYMN is sung

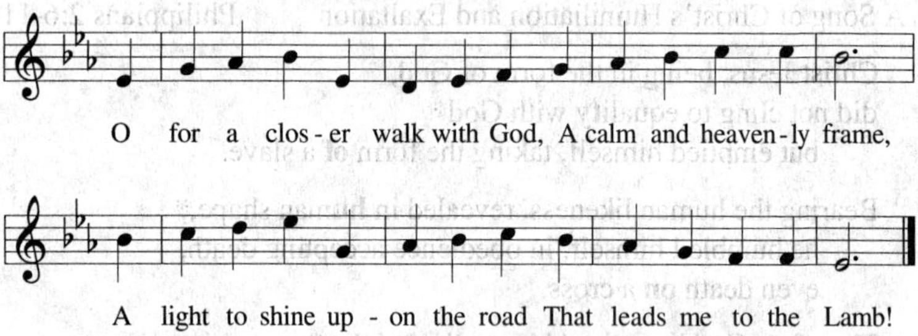

2 Where is the blessedness I knew
When first I saw the Lord?
Where is the soul-refreshing view
Of Jesus and his word?

3 What peaceful hours I once enjoyed!
How sweet their memory still!
But they have left an aching void
The world can never fill.

4 Return, O holy Dove, return,
Sweet messenger of rest!
I hate the sins that made thee mourn,
And drove thee from my breast.

5 The dearest idol I have known,
Whate'er that idol be,
Help me to tear it from thy throne,
And worship only thee.

6 So shall my walk be close with God,
Calm and serene my frame;
So purer light shall mark the road
That leads me to the Lamb. [H82 684; SBH 466]

Text: William Cowper, 1731-1800

Tune: *Caithness,* from *The Psalmes of David in Prose and Meter*, 1635 CM

Sit

A LESSON is read.

	Year 1	Year 2
eve of Lent 1	John 1:43-51 You will see heaven opened and the angels of God ascending and descending upon the Son of Man.	John 17:20-26 I in them and you in me, that they may become completely one, so that the world may know that you have sent me and have loved them even as you have loved me.
eve of Lent 2	John 4:1-26 God is spirit, and those who worship him must worship in spirit and truth.	Mark 2:23-3:6 The sabbath was made for humankind, not humankind for the sabbath; so the Son of Man is lord even of the sabbath.
eve of Lent 3	John 7:1-13 My time has not yet come, but your time is always here.	Mark 5:1-20 Go home to your friends, and tell them how much the Lord has done for you, and what mercy he has shown you.
eve of Lent 4	John 8:47-59 I do not seek my own glory; there is one who seeks it and he is the judge.	Mark 7:1-23 Whatever goes into a person from outside cannot defile; it is what comes out of a person that defiles.

eve of Lent 5

John 6:60-71	Mark 9:14-29
Many of Jesus' disciples turned back and no longer went about with him. So Jesus asked the twelve, "Do you also wish to go away?"	Jesus said, "All things can be done for the one who believes." Immediately the father of the child cried out, "I believe; help my unbelief!"

Silence for meditation follows the reading.

Antiphon to the MAGNIFICAT

eve of Lent 1 — One does not live by **bread** alone*
but by every word that comes from the **mouth** of God. [LH: Matt. 4:4]

eve of Lent 2 — I am going to bring Israel in**to** the wilderness*
and speak tender**ly** to her. [Hos. 2:14]

eve of Lent 3 — Justi**fied** by faith,*
we have peace with God through our Lord **Je**sus Christ. [LH: Rom. 5:1]

eve of Lent 4 — My presence will **go** with you,*
and I will **give** you rest. [Exod. 33:14]

eve of Lent 5 — Unless a grain of wheat falls into the earth and dies, it remains just a **sing**le grain;*
but if it dies, it **bears** much fruit. [LH: John 12:24]

Sundays in Lent

Antiphon to PSALM 42 *Quemadmodum desiderat cervus*

Lent 1: Elijah **ate** and drank;*
then he went in the strength of that food
forty days and forty nights to the **mount** of
God. [1 Kings 19:8]

Lent 2: My soul is a**thirst** for God,*
athirst for the **li**ving God [PBO]

Lent 3: My tears have been my food day and night.

Lent 4: Why are you so full of heaviness, O my soul?
[PBO]

Lent 5: Because Christ himself was tested by **what** he
suffered,*
he is able to help those who are **be**ing
tested. [Heb. 2:18]

42 *The exile's nostalgia for God's temple*

1 As the deer longs **for** the water-brooks,*
so longs my soul for **you**, O God.

2 My soul is athirst for God, athirst for the **li**ving God;*
when shall I come to appear before the pres**ence** of God?

3 My tears have been my food **day** and night,*
while all day long they say to me,
"Where now **is** your God?"

4 I pour out my soul when I think **on** these things:*
how I went with the multitude and led them into the
house of God,

5 With the voice of praise **and** thanksgiving,*
among those **who** keep holy-day.

6 Why are you so full of heaviness, **O** my soul?*
and why are you so disquiet**ed** within me?

7 Put your **trust** in God;*
for I will yet give thanks to him,
who is the help of my countenance, **and** my God.

8 My soul is heav**y** within me;*
therefore I will remember you from the land of Jordan,
and from the peak of Mizar among the **heights** of Hermon.

9 One deep calls to another in the noise **of** your cataracts;*
all your rapids and floods have gone **o**ver me.

10 The LORD grants his loving-kindness **in** the daytime;*
in the night season his song is with me,
a prayer to the God **of** my life.

11 I will say to the God of my strength,
"Why have you for**got**ten me?*
and why do I go so heavily while the enemy
op**press**es me?"

12 While my bones are **be**ing broken,*
my enemies mock me **to** my face;

13 All day **long** they mock me*
and say to me, "Where now **is** your God?"

14 Why are you so full of heaviness, **O** my soul?*
and why are you so disquiet**ed** within me?

15 Put your **trust** in God;*
for I will yet give thanks to him,
who is the help of my countenance, **and** my God.

The Antiphon is repeated.

Silence for meditation

Lord God, never-failing fountain of life, through the saving waters of baptism you called us from the depth of sin to the depths of mercy. Do not forget the trials of our exile, but from the wellspring of the Word satisfy our thirst for you, so that we may come rejoicing to your holy mountain, where you live and reign now and for ever. [LHd, LBW]

+

Antiphon to PSALM 32 *Beati quorum*

Lent 1: Worship the **Lord** your God,*
and serve **on**ly him. [LH: Matt. 4:10]

Lent 2: Happy are they to whom the Lord im**putes** no guilt,*
and whose sin is **put** away. [LH, PBO]

Lent 3: All the faithful will make their prayers to **you**, O Lord,*
in **time** of trouble.

Lent 4: You are my hiding **place**, O Lord;*
you preserve **me** from trouble.

Lent 5: Humble yourselves under the mighty **hand** of God,*
that he may exalt you **in** due time.
[1 Peter 5:6]

32 *The joy of being forgiven: a penitential psalm*

1 Happy are they whose transgressions **are** forgiven,*
and whose sin is **put** away!

2 Happy are they to whom the LORD im**putes** no guilt,*
and in whose spirit there **is** no guile!

3 While I held my tongue, my bones with**ered** away,*
because of my groaning **all** day long.

4 For your hand was heavy upon me **day** and night;*
my moisture was dried up as in the **heat** of summer.

5 Then I acknowledged my **sin** to you,*
and did not con**ceal** my guilt.

6 I said, "I will confess my transgressions **to** the LORD."*
Then you forgave me the guilt **of** my sin.

7 Therefore all the faithful will make their prayers to you in **time** of trouble;*
when the great waters overflow, they **shall** not reach them.

8 You are my hiding-place;
you preserve **me** from trouble;*
you surround me with shouts **of** deliverance.

9 "I will instruct you and teach you in the way that **you** should go;*
I will guide you **with** my eye.

10 Do not be like horse or mule, which have no **un**derstanding;*
who must be fitted with bit and bridle,
or else they will **not** stay near you."

11 Great are the tribulations **of** the wicked;*
but mercy embraces those who trust **in** the LORD.

12 Be glad, you righteous, and rejoice **in** the LORD;*
shout for joy, all who are **true** of heart.

The Antiphon is repeated.

Silence for meditation

Lord God, you desired to keep from us your wrath and so did not spare your holy servant Jesus Christ, who was wounded for our sins. We are your prodigal children, but we come back to you confessing our sins. Embrace us, that we may rejoice in your mercy together with your beloved Son, Jesus Christ our Lord. [LH, LBW]

+

Antiphon to the NEW TESTAMENT CANTICLE *Beati pauperes*

Lent 1 This is the one to whom **I** will look,*
to the humble and contrite in spirit
who trembles **at** my word. [Isaiah 66:26]

Lent 2 The lowly shall pos**sess** the land;*
they will delight in abun**dance** of peace. [Psalm 37:11]

Lent 3 Pursue peace with **ev**eryone,*
and holiness without which no one will **see** the Lord. [Hebrews 12:14]

Lent 4 Everyone who thirsts, come **to** the waters.*
Come, buy wine and milk **with**out price. [Isaiah 55:1]

Lent 5 Who can ascend the hill **of** the Lord?*
Those who have clean hands and **a** pure heart. [Psalm 24:3-4]

The Beatitudes Matthew 5:3-10

Blessed are the **poor** in spirit,*
for theirs is the king**dom** of heaven.

Blessed are **those** who mourn,*
for they **will** be comforted.

Blessed **are** the meek,*
for they will inher**it** the earth.

Blessed are those who hunger and **thirst** for righteousness,*
for they **will** be filled.

Blessed **are** the merciful,*
for they will **re**ceive mercy.

Blessed are the **pure** in heart,*
for they **will** see God.

Blessed **are** the peacemakers,*
for they will be called chil**dren** of God.

Blessed are those who are persecuted for right**eous**ness' sake,*
for theirs is the king**dom** of heaven.

Blessed are you when people revile you and persecute you and
utter all kinds of evil against you falsely on **my** account.*
Rejoice and be glad,
for great is your re**ward** in heaven. [CSB; chant, see H82 560]

The Antiphon is repeated.

Silence for meditation

Grant us, almighty God, that through this yearly observance of Lent we may enter more deeply into the mystery of Christ and follow his mind by conduct worthy of our calling; through Jesus Christ our Lord.

[Gel., AC, RS Lent 1]

+

Stand

THE HYMN is sung. *O sol salutis, intimis*

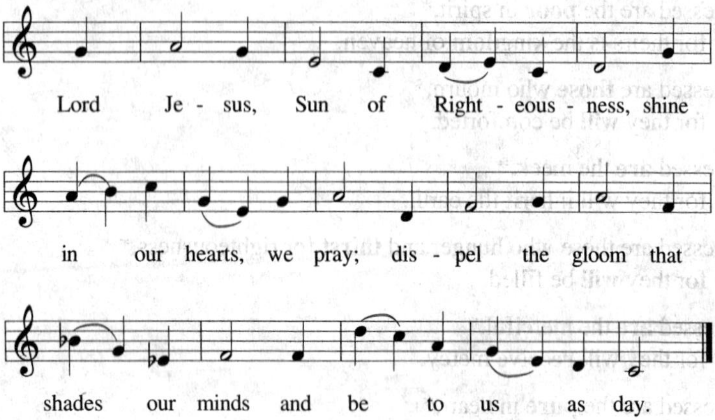

2 Give guidance to our wandering ways,
Forgive us, Lord, our sin;
Restore us by your loving care
To peace and joy within.

3 Lord, grant that we in penitence
May offer you our praise,
And through your saving sacrifice
Receive your gift of grace.

4 Now nearer draws the day of days
When paradise shall bloom,
When we shall be at one with you,
Lord, risen from the tomb.

5 The universe your glory shows,
Blest Father, Spirit, Son;
We shall acclaim your majesty,
Eternal Three in one. [H82 144]

Text: Latin; tr. Anne K. LeCroy, b. 1930
Tune: *Cornhill*, Harold Darke, 1888-1976, alt. CM

Sit

A LESSON is read.

Year 1

Lent 1

Mark 2:18-22

The days will come when the bridegroom is taken away from them, and then they will fast on that day.

Year 2

John 12:44-50

I have come as light into the world, so that everyone who believes in me should not remain in the darkness.

Year 1

Lent 2

Mark 3:31-4:9

Whoever does the will of God is my brother and sister and mother.

Year 2

John 5:19-24

Anyone who hears my word and believes him who sent me has eternal life, and does not come under judgment, but has passed from death to life.

Lent 3

Mark 5:1-20

Go home to your friends and tell them how much the Lord has done for you, and what mercy he has shown you.

John 5:25-29

The hour is coming, and is now here, when the dead will hear the voice of the Son of God, and those who hear will live.

Lent 4

Mark 8:11-21

Do you still not perceive or understand? Are your hearts hardened? Do you have eyes, and fail to see? Do you have ears, and fail to hear?

John 6:27-40

I am the bread of life. Whoever comes to me will never be hungry, and whoever believes in me will never be thirsty.

Lent 5

Mark 8:31-9:1

Jesus began to teach them that the Son of Man must undergo great suffering, and be rejected by the elders, the chief priests, and the scribes, and be killed, and after three days rise again.

John 8:46-59

I do not seek my own glory; there is one who seeks it and he is the judge.

Silence for meditation follows the reading.

Antiphon to the MAGNIFICAT

Lent 1 — Watch over us, eternal Savior; do not let the cunning **temp**ter seize us.*
We put all our trust in your un**fail**ing help.

[LH]

Lent 2 — Let justice roll **down** like waters,*
and righteousness like an ever**flow**ing stream.

[LBW: Amos 5:24]

Lent 3 Those who drink of the water that **I** will give them*
will nev**er** be thirsty. [LH: John 4:14]

Lent 4 You will guide me **by** your counsel*
and afterwards receive **me** with glory.
[Psalm 74:24]

Lent 5 When I am lifted up **from** the earth,*
I will draw all people **to** myself.
[LH: John 12:32]

Mondays in Lent

Antiphon to PSALM 121 *Levavi oculos*

My help comes **from** the LORD,*
the maker of heav**en** and earth. [LH, PBO]

121 *Guardian of his people*

1 I lift up my eyes **to** the hills;*
from where is my **help** to come?

2 My help comes **from** the LORD,*
the maker of heav**en** and earth.

3 He will not let your **foot** be moved*
and he who watches over you will not **fall** asleep.

4 Behold, he who keeps watch **o**ver Israel*
shall neither slum**ber** nor sleep;

5 The LORD himself watches **o**ver you;*
the LORD is your shade at **your** right hand,

6 So that the sun shall not strike **you** by day,*
nor the **moon** by night.

7 The LORD shall preserve you **from** all evil;*
it is he who shall **keep** you safe.

8 The LORD shall watch over your going out and
your **com**ing in,*
from this time forth for **ev**ermore.

Antiphon My help comes **from** the LORD,*
the maker of heav**en** and earth.

Silence for meditation

Lord Jesus Christ, you have prepared a quiet place for us in your Father's eternal home. Watch over our welfare on this perilous journey, shade us from the burning heat of the day, and keep our lives free of evil now and for ever. [LH, LBW]

+

Antiphon to PSALM 6 *Domine, ne in furore*

Turn, O LORD, and de**li**ver me;*
save me for your **mer**cy's sake. [LH, PBO]

6 *Prayer in time of distress: a penitential psalm*

1 LORD, do not rebuke me **in** your anger;*
do not punish me **in** your wrath.

2 Have pity on me, LORD, for **I** am weak;*
heal me, LORD, for my **bones** are racked.

3 My spirit **shakes** with terror;*
how long, O **LORD**, how long?

4 Turn, O LORD, and de**li**ver me;*
save me for your **mer**cy's sake.

5 For in death no one re**mem**bers you;*
and who will give you thanks **in** the grave?

6 I grow weary because **of** my groaning;*
every night I drench my bed
and flood my **couch** with tears.

7 My eyes are wast**ed** with grief*
and worn away because of **all** my enemies.

8 Depart from me, all **e**vildoers,*
for the LORD has heard the sound **of** my weeping.

9 The LORD has heard my **sup**plication;*
the LORD ac**cepts** my prayer.

10 All my enemies shall be confounded and **quake** with fear;*
they shall turn back and suddenly be **put** to shame.

Antiphon Turn, O LORD, and de**li**ver me;*
save me for your **mer**cy's sake.

Silence for meditation

Lord God, you love mercy and tenderness; you give life and overcome death. Look upon the weakness and grief of your Church; restore it to health by your risen Son, so that it may sing a new song in your praise; through your Son, Jesus Christ our Lord. [LH, LBW]

+

Stand

THE HYMN is sung. *Ου γαρ βλεπεις τους ταραττοντας*

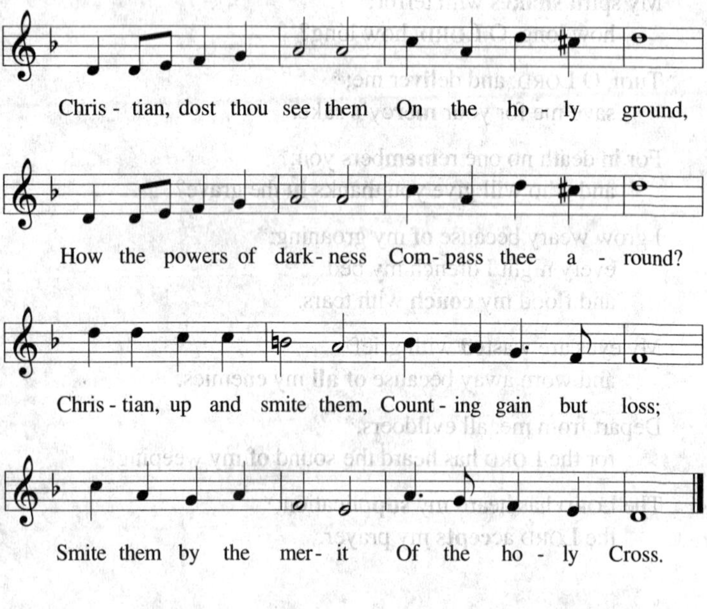

2 Christian, dost thou feel them,
How they work within,
Striving, tempting, luring,
Goading into sin?
Christian, never tremble,
Never be downcast;
Gird thee for the battle,
Watch and pray and fast.

3 Christian, dost thou hear them,
How they speak thee fair:
Always fast and vigil,
Always watch and prayer?
Christian, answer boldly,
"While I breathe I pray."
Peace shall follow battle,
Night shall end in day.

4 "Well I know thy trouble,
O my servant true,
Thou art very weary,
I was weary too;
But that toil shall make thee
Someday all my own,
And the end of sorrow
Shall be near my throne." [SBH 68; H40 556]

Text: attr. Andrew of Crete, c. 660-732; tr. John Mason Neale, 1818-1866 alt.
Tune: *Gute Bäume bringen,* from *Praxis Pietatis Melica,* Frankfurt, 1668 65 65 D

Sit

A LESSON is read.

Year 1	Year 2
Monday after Lent 1	
John 2:1-12	Mark 1:1-13
You have kept the good wine until now.	The Spirit immediately drove Jesus out into the wilderness. He was in the wilderness forty days, tempted by Satan; and he was with the wild beasts; and the angels waited on him.
Monday after Lent 2	
John 4:27-42	Mark 3:7-19a
It is no longer because of what you said that we believe, for we have heard for ourselves, and we know that this is truly the Savior of the world.	Whenever the unclean spirits saw him, they fell down before him and shouted, "You are the Son of God!"
Monday after Lent 3	
John 7:14-36	Mark 5:21-43
My teaching is not mine but his who sent me.	Your faith has made you well; go in peace, and be healed of your disease.
Monday after Lent 4	
John 6:1-15	Mark 7:24-37
When Jesus realized that they were about to come and take him by force to make him king, he withdrew again to the mountain by himself.	He has done everything well; he even makes the deaf to hear and the mute to speak.

Monday after Lent 5

John 9:1-17	Mark 9:30-41
We must work the works of him who sent me, while it is day; night is coming when no one can work.	The Son of Man is to be betrayed into human hands, and they will kill him, and three days after being killed, he will rise again.

Silence for meditation follows the reading.

Antiphon to the MAGNIFICAT

Monday after Lent 1 Whatever you do for the **least** of these,*
you **do** for me. [LH; see Matt. 25:40]

Monday after Lent 2 Do not judge, so that you may **not** be judged;*
for with the judgment you make,
God will judge you. [LH: Matt. 7:12]

Monday after Lent 3 The water that **I** will give*
will become a spring of water gushing up
to e**ter**nal life. [John 4:14]

Monday after Lent 4 Repent and **turn** to God*
so that times of refreshing may come from
the presence **of** the Lord. [Acts 3:19]

Monday after Lent 5 I am the light **of** the world.*
Whoever follows me will never walk in
darkness but will have the **light** of life.
[John 8:12]

Tuesdays in Lent

Antiphon to PSALM 25 *Ad te, Domine, levavi*

Lead me in your truth and teach me. [LH, PBO]

25 *Prayer for guidance and protection*

1 To you, O LORD, I lift up my soul;
my God, I put my **trust** in you;*
let me not be humiliated,
nor let my enemies triumph **o**ver me.

2 Let none who look to you be **put** to shame;*
let the treacherous be disappointed **in** their schemes.

3 Show me your **ways**, O LORD,*
and teach **me** your paths.

4 Lead me in your **truth** and teach me,*
for you are the God of my salvation;
in you have I trusted all **the** day long.

5 Remember, O LORD, your compass**ion** and love,*
for they are from **ev**erlasting.

6 Remember not the sins of my youth and **my** transgressions;*
remember me according to your love
and for the sake of your good**ness**, O LORD.

7 Gracious and upright **is** the LORD;*
therefore he teaches sinners **in** his way.

8 He guides the humble in **do**ing right*
and teaches his way **to** the lowly.

9 All the paths of the LORD are **love** and faithfulness*
to those who keep his covenant **and** his testimonies.

10 For your Name's **sake**, O LORD,*
forgive my sin, for **it** is great.

11 Who are they who **fear** the LORD?*
he will teach them the way that **they** should choose.

12 They shall dwell **in** prosperity,*
and their offspring shall inher**it** the land.

13 The LORD is a friend to **those** who fear him*
and will show **them** his covenant.

14 My eyes are ever looking **to** the LORD,*
for he shall pluck my feet out **of** the net.

15 Turn to me and have pi**ty** on me,*
for I am left alone **and** in misery.

16 The sorrows of my heart **have** increased;*
bring me out **of** my troubles.

17 Look upon my adversi**ty** and misery*
and forgive me **all** my sin.

18 Look upon my enemies, for **they** are many,*
and they bear a violent hat**red** against me.

19 Protect my life and de**liv**er me;*
let me not be put to shame, for I have trust**ed** in you.

20 Let integrity and upright**ness** preserve me,*
for my hope has **been** in you.

21 Deliver Isra**el**, O God,*
out of **all** his troubles.

Antiphon Lead me in your truth and teach me.

Silence for meditation

Lord our God, you show us your ways of compassion and love, and you spare sinners. Remember not our sins; relieve our misery; satisfy the longing of your people; and fulfill all our hopes for eternal peace through your Son, Jesus Christ our Lord. [LH, LBW]

+

Antiphon to PSALM 38 *Domine, ne in furore*

I will confess **my** iniquity;*
do not forsake me, O Lord of **my** salvation. [LH, PBO]

38 *Earnest prayer of one in danger: a penitential psalm*

1 O LORD, do not rebuke me **in** your anger;*
do not punish me **in** your wrath.

2 For your arrows have alr**ead**y pierced me,*
and your hand presses **hard** upon me.

3 There is no health in my flesh,
because of your **in**dignation;*
there is no soundness in my body, because **of** my sin.

4 For my iniquities **o**verwhelm me;*
like a heavy burden they are too much for **me** to bear.

5 My wounds **stink** and fester*
by reason **of** my foolishness.

6 I am utterly bowed **down** and prostrate;*
I go about in mourning all **the** day long.

7 My loins are filled with **sear**ing pain;*
there is no health **in** my body.

8 I am utterly **numb** and crushed;*
I wail, because of the groaning **of** my heart.

9 O LORD, you know all **my** desires,*
and my sighing is not hid**den** from you.

10 My heart is pounding, my **strength** has failed me,*
and the brightness of my eyes is **gone** from me.

11 My friends and companions draw back from **my** affliction;*
my neighbors stand **a**far off.

12 Those who seek after my life lay **snares** for me;*
those who strive to hurt me speak of my ruin
and plot treachery all **the** day long.

13 But I am like the deaf who **do** not hear,*
like those who are mute and do not o**pen** their mouth.

14 I have become like one who **does** not hear*
and from whose mouth comes **no** defense.

15 For in you, O LORD, have I **fixed** my hope;*
you will answer me, O **Lord** my God.

16 For I said, "Do not let them rejoice at **my** expense,"*
those who gloat over me when **my** foot slips.

17 Truly, I am on the **verge** of falling,*
and my pain is al**ways** with me.

18 I will confess **my** iniquity*
and be sorry **for** my sin.

19 Those who are my enemies without **cause** are mighty,*
and many in number are those who wrong**ful**ly hate me.

20 Those who repay evil for good **slan**der me,*
because I follow the course **that** is right.

21 O LORD, do **not** forsake me;*
be not far from me, **O** my God.

22 Make **haste** to help me,*
O Lord of **my** salvation.

Antiphon I will confess **my** iniquity;*
do not forsake me, O Lord of **my** salvation.

Silence for meditation

Lord our God, you did not forget the pierced body of your Son nor the mockery his love received. Do not abandon us, your children, weighed down with sins, but give us the fullness of your mercy in Jesus Christ our Lord. [LH, LBW]

+

Stand

THE HYMN is sung. Μνωεο Χριστε

2 Lord Jesus, think on me,
With care and woe oppressed;
Let me thy loving servant be,
And taste thy promised rest.

3 Lord Jesus, think on me,
Amid the battle's strife;
In all my pain and misery
Be thou my health and life.

4 Lord Jesus, think on me,
Nor let me go astray;
Through darkness and perplexity
Point thou the heavenly way.

5 Lord Jesus, think on me,
That, when the flood is past,
I may the eternal brightness see,
And share thy joy at last.

6 Lord Jesus, think on me,
That I may sing above
To Father, Spirit, and to thee,
The strains of praise and love. [SBH 365, H82 641]

Text: Synesius of Cyrene, c. 375- c. 414; tr. Allen William Chatfield, 1808-1896
Tune: *Southwell*, Daman, *Psalmes*, 1579 SM

Sit

A LESSON is read.

Year 1	Year 2
Tuesday after Lent 1	
John 2:13-22 Destroy this temple, and in three days I will raise it up.	Mark 1:14-28 The time is fulfilled, and the kingdom of God has come near; repent, and believe in the good news.
Tuesday after Lent 2	
John 4:43-54 The father realized that this was the hour when Jesus had said to him, “Your son will live.” So he himself believed, along with his whole household.	Mark 3:19b-35 Whoever does the will of God is my brother and sister and mother.
Tuesday after Lent 3	
John 7:37-52 Let anyone who is thirsty come to me, and let the one who believes in me drink. As the scripture has said, “Out of the believer’s heart shall flow rivers of living water.”	Mark 6:1-13 Prophets are not without honor, except in their hometown, and among their own kin, and in their own house.
Tuesday after Lent 4	
John 6:16-27 They saw Jesus walking on the sea and coming near the boat, and they were terrified. But he said to them, “It is I; do not be afraid.”	Mark 8:1-10 Jesus took the seven loaves, and after giving thanks he broke them and gave them to his disciples to distribute.

Tuesday after Lent 5

John 9:18-41

I came into this world for judgment so that those who do not see may see, and those who do see may become blind.

Mark 9:42-50

Salt is good; but if salt has lost its saltiness, how can you season it? Have salt in yourselves, and be at peace with one another.

Silence for meditation

Antiphon to the MAGNIFICAT

Tuesday after Lent — Whenever you pray, go into your room and **shut** the door*
and pray to your Fa**ther** in secret. [LH: Matt. 6:6]

Tuesday after Lent 2 — Call no one your fath**er** on earth, *
for you have one Father–the **one** in heaven.
Nor are you to be **called** instructors,
for you have one instructor, **the** Messiah. [LH: Matt. 23:9]

Tuesday after Lent 3 — Should you not have had mercy on your **fel**low slave*
as I had mer**cy** on you? [LH: Matt. 18:33]

Tuesday after Lent 4 — The Lord will **give** you rest*
from your pain and turmoil **and** hard service. [see Isa. 14:3]

Tuesday after Lent 5 — I do nothing **on** my own,*
but speak these things as the Father in**struct**ed me. [LH: John 8:28]

Wednesdays in Lent

Antiphon to PSALM 39 *Dixi, Custodiam*

Hear my **prayer**, O LORD;*
hold not your peace **at** my tears. [LH, PBO]

39 *Urgent prayer of a sick person*

1 I said, "I will keep watch up**on** my ways,*
so that I do not offend **with** my tongue.

2 I will put a muzzle **on** my mouth*
while the wicked are **in** my presence."

3 So I held my tongue **and** said nothing;*
I refrained from rash words;
but my pain be**came** unbearable.

4 My heart was hot within me;
while I pondered, the fire burst **in**to flame;*
I spoke out **with** my tongue:

5 LORD, let me know my end, and the number **of** my days,*
so that I may know how **short** my life is.

6 You have given me a mere handful of days,
and my lifetime is as nothing **in** your sight;*
truly, even those who stand erect are but a **puff** of wind.

7 We walk about like a shadow,
and in vain we **are** in turmoil;*
we heap up riches and cannot tell who will **gath**er them.

8 And now, what **is** my hope?*
O Lord, my hope **is** in you.

9 Deliver me from all **my** transgressions*
and do not make me the taunt **of** the fool.

10 I fell silent and did not **open** my mouth,*
for surely it was **you** that did it.

11 Take your af**flic**tion from me;*
I am worn down by the blows **of** your hand.

12 With rebukes for sin you punish us;
like a moth you eat away all that is **dear** to us;*
truly, everyone is but a **puff** of wind.

13 Hear my prayer, O LORD,
and give ear **to** my cry;*
hold not your peace **at** my tears.

14 For I am but a so**journ**er with you,*
a wayfarer, as all my **fore**bears were.

15 Turn your gaze from me, that I may be **glad** again,*
before I go my way and **am** no more.

Antiphon Hear my **prayer**, O LORD;*
hold not your peace **at** my tears.

Silence for meditation

Heavenly Father, through your Son you taught us not to fear tomorrow but to commit our lives to your care. Withhold not your Spirit from us, but help us find a life of peace after these days of trouble; for the sake of your Son, Jesus Christ our Lord. [LH, LBW]

+

Antiphon to PSALM 51 *Miserere mei, Deus secundum*

Create in me a clean **heart**, O God,*
and renew a right spir**it** within me. [LH, PBO]

51 *Prayer for forgiveness: a penitential psalm*

1 Have mercy on me, O God, according to your **lov**ing-kindness;*
in your great compassion blot out **my** offenses.

2 Wash me through and through **from** my wickedness*
and cleanse me **from** my sin.

3 For I know **my** transgressions,*
and my sin is ev**er** before me.

4 Against you only **have** I sinned*
and done what is evil **in** your sight.

5 And so you are justified **when** you speak*
and upright **in** your judgment.

6 Indeed, I have been wicked **from** my birth,*
a sinner from my **moth**er's womb.

7 For behold, you look for truth **deep** within me,*
and will make me understand **wis**dom secretly.

8 Purge me from my sin, and I **shall** be pure;*
wash me, and I shall be **clean** indeed.

9 Make me hear of **joy** and gladness,*
that the body you have broken **may** rejoice.

10 Hide your face **from** my sins*
and blot out all **my** iniquities.

11 Create in me a clean **heart**, O God,*
and renew a right spir**it** within me.

12 Cast me not away **from** your presence*
and take not your holy **Spir**it from me.

13 Give me the joy of your saving **help** again*
and sustain me with your boun**ti**ful Spirit.

14 I shall teach your ways **to** the wicked,*
and sinners shall re**turn** to you.

15 Deliver me from **death**, O God,*
and my tongue shall sing of your righteousness,
O God of **my** salvation.

16 Open my **lips**, O Lord,*
and my mouth shall pro**claim** your praise.

17 Had you desired it, I would have **of**fered sacrifice,*
but you take no delight **in** burnt-offerings.

18 The sacrifice of God is a **troub**led spirit;*
a broken and contrite heart, O God, you will **not** despise.

19 Be favorable and gra**cious** to Zion,*
and rebuild the walls **of** Jerusalem.

20 Then you will be pleased with the appointed sacrifices,
with burnt-offerings **and** oblations;*
then shall they offer young bullocks up**on** your altar.

Antiphon Create in me a clean **heart**, O God,*
and renew a right spir**it** within me.

Silence for meditation

Almighty and merciful Father, you freely forgive those who, as David of old, acknowledge and confess their sins. Create in us pure hearts, and wash away all our sins in the blood of your dear Son, Jesus Christ our Lord. [MPES, LBW]

+

Stand

THE HYMN is sung. *Audi benigne conditor*

2 Each heart is manifest to thee;
Thou knowest our infirmity;
Now we repent and seek thy face;
Grant unto us thy pardoning grace.

3 Spare us, O Lord, who now confess
Our sins and all our wickedness,
And, for the glory of thy Name,
Our weakened souls to health reclaim.

4 Give us the discipline that springs
From abstinence in outward things
With inward fasting, so that we
In heart and soul may dwell with thee.

5 Grant, O thou blessed Trinity;
Grant, O unchanging Unity;
That this our fast of forty days
May work our profit and thy praise! [H82 152]

Text: attr. Gregory the Great, 540-604; tr. *Hymnal 1940*, alt.
Tune: *A la venue de Noël,* from *Fleurs des noels*, 1535 LM

Sit

A LESSON is read.

Year 1	Year 2
Ash Wednesday	
Luke 18:9-14	Luke 18:9-14
The tax collector, standing far off, would not even look up to heaven, but was beating his breast and saying, "God be merciful to me, a sinner!"	The tax collector, standing far off, would not even look up to heaven, but was beating his breast and saying, "God be merciful to me, a sinner!"
Wednesday after Lent 1	
John 2:23-3:15	Mark 1:29-45
Just as Moses had lifted up the serpent in the wilderness, so must the Son of Man be lifted up, that whoever believes in him may have eternal life.	Jesus cured many who were sick with various diseases, and cast out many demons; and he would not permit the demons to speak, because they knew him.
Wednesday after Lent 2	
John 5:1-18	Mark 4:1-20
Jesus found him in the temple and said to him, "See, you have been made well! Do not sin any more, so that nothing worse happens to you."	Other seed fell into good soil and brought forth grain, growing up and increasing and yielding thirty and sixty and a hundredfold. And he said, "Let anyone with ears to hear, listen!"

Wednesday after Lent 3

John 8:12-20
I am the light of the world. Whoever follows me will never walk in darkness but will have the light of life.

Mark 6:13-29
When Jesus' disciples heard about it, they came and took John's body, and laid it in a tomb.

Wednesday after Lent 4

John 6:27-40
I am the bread of life. Whoever comes to me will never be hungry, and whoever believes in me will never be thirsty.

Mark 8:11-26
Do you still not perceive or understand? Are your hearts hardened? Do you have eyes, and fail to see? Do you have ears, and fail to hear?

Wednesday after Lent 5

John 10:1-18
I am the good shepherd. The good shepherd lays down his life for the sheep.

Mark 10:1-16
Whoever does not receive the kingdom of God as a little child will never enter it.

Silence for meditation follows the reading.

Antiphon to the MAGNIFICAT

Ash Wednesday

The grass withers, the **flow**er fades:*
but the word of our God will **stand** for ever. [Isa. 40:8]

Wednesday after Lent 1

The Spirit immediately drove Jesus out in**to** the wilderness.*
he was in the wilderness forty days, temp**ted** by Satan. [Mark 1:12-13a]

Wednesday after Lent 2

I am but a **so**journer,*
a wayfarer, as all my **fore**bears were. [Ps. 39:14]

Wednesday after Lent 3

Seek the **Lord** your God,*
and you will find him if you search
after him with all your **heart** and soul.
[Deut. 4:29]

Wednesday after Lent 4

Ask for the ancient paths,
where the **good** way lies,*
and walk in it, and find rest **for**
your souls. [Jer. 6:16]

Wednesday after Lent 5

I have no pleasure in the death of anyone,
says the Lord God.*
Turn, **then**, and live. [Ezek. 18:32]

Thursdays in Lent

Antiphon to PSALM 125 *Qui confidunt in Domino*

The Lord stands round about his people. [LH, PBO]

125 *God protects the faithful*

1 Those who trust in the LORD are **like** Mount Zion,*
which cannot be moved, but stands **fast** for ever.

2 The hills stand a**bout** Jerusalem;*
so does the LORD stand round about his people,
from this time forth for **ev**ermore.

3 The scepter of the wicked shall not hold sway over the land alloted **to** the just,*
so that the just shall not put their **hands** to evil.

4 Show your goodness, O LORD, to those **who** are good*
and to those who are **true** of heart.

5 As for those who turn aside to crooked ways,
the LORD will lead them away with the **ev**ildoers;*
but peace be **up**on Israel.

Antiphon The Lord stands round about his people.

Silence for meditation

Lord, surround your people with your presence. Do not let us stretch out our hands to evil deeds, nor be destroyed by the snares of the enemy, but bring us to share the land prepared for the saints in light, where you live and reign, God, now and for ever. [LH, LBW]

+

Antiphon to PSALM 102 *Domine, exaudi orationem meum*

My days pass away like a shadow, and I wither **like** the grass;*
but you, O LORD, en**dure** for ever.

102 *Prayer in misfortune: a penitential psalm*

1 LORD, hear my prayer, and let my cry **come** before you;*
hide not your face from me in the day **of** my trouble.

2 Incline your **ear** to me;*
when I call, make haste to **an**swer me,

3 For my days drift a**way** like smoke,*
and my bones are hot as **burn**ing coals.

4 My heart is smitten like **grass** and withered,*
so that I forget to **eat** my bread.

5 Because of the voice **of** my groaning*
I am but **skin** and bones.

6 I have become like a vulture **in** the wilderness,*
like an owl a**mong** the ruins.

7 I lie a**wake** and groan;*
I am like a sparrow, lonely **on** a house-top.

8 My enemies revile me **all** day long,*
and those who scoff at me have taken an **oath** against me.

9 For I have eaten ash**es** for bread*
and mingled my **drink** with weeping.

10 Because of your indigna**tion** and wrath*
you have lifted me up and thrown **me** away.

11 My days pass away **like** a shadow,*
and I wither **like** the grass.

12 But you, O LORD, en**dure** for ever,*
and your Name from **age** to age.

13 You will arise and have compassion on Zion,
for it is time to have mer**cy** upon her;*
indeed, the appointed **time** has come.

14 For your servants love her **very** rubble,*
and are moved to pity even **for** her dust.

15 The nations shall fear your **Name**, O LORD,*
and all the kings of the **earth** your glory.

16 For the LORD will **build** up Zion,*
and his glory **will** appear.

17 He will look with favor on the prayer **of** the homeless;*
he will not de**spise** their plea.

18 Let this be written for a future **gen**eration,*
so that a people yet unborn may **praise** the LORD.

19 For the LORD looked down from his holy **place** on high;*
from the heavens he be**held** the earth;

20 That he might hear the groan **of** the captive*
and set free those con**demned** to die;

21 That they may declare in Zion the Name **of** the LORD,*
and his praise **in** Jerusalem;

22 When the peoples are gath**ered** together,*
and the kingdoms also, to **serve** the LORD.

23 He has brought down my strength be**fore** my time;*
he has shortened the number **of** my days;

24 And I said, "O my God,
do not take me away in the midst **of** my days;*
your years endure throughout all **gen**erations.

25 In the beginning, O LORD, you laid the foundations **of** the earth,*
and the heavens are the work **of** your hands;

26 They shall perish, but you will endure;
they all shall wear out **like** a garment;*

as clothing you will change them,
and they **shall** be changed;

27 But you are al**ways** the same,*
and your years will **nev**er end.

28 The children of your servants **shall** continue,*
and their offspring shall stand fast **in** your sight."

Antiphon My days pass away like a shadow, and I wither **like** the grass;*
but you, O LORD, en**dure** for ever.

Silence for meditation

Lord, while our days vanish like shadows and our lives wear out like a garment, you remain undisturbed by change. Although our earthly lives come to an end, help us to live in Christ's endless life and at length attain our home, the heavenly Jerusalem, where he lives and reigns with you and the Holy Spirit, now and for ever. [LHd, LBW]

+

Stand

THE HYMN is sung. *Clarum decus jejunii*

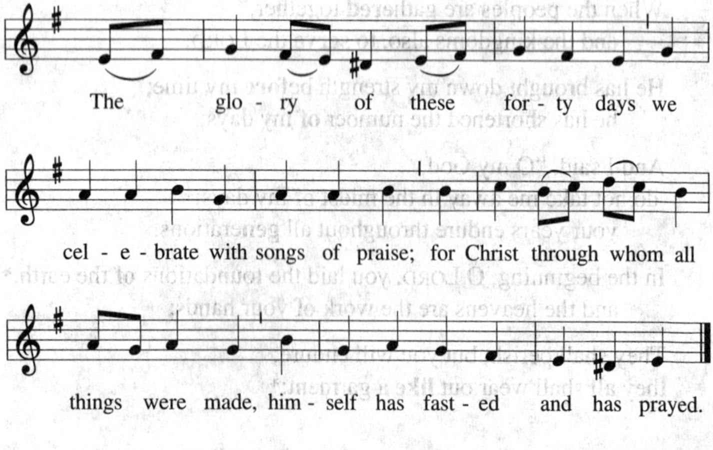

2 Alone and fasting Moses saw
The loving God who gave the law;
And to Elijah, fasting, came
The steeds and chariots of flame.

3 So Daniel trained his mystic sight,
Delivered from the lions' might;
And John, the Bridegroom's friend, became
The herald of Messiah's name.

4 Then grant us, Lord, like them to be
Full oft in fast and prayer with thee;
Our spirits strengthen with thy grace,
And give us joy to see thy face.

5 O Father, Son, and Spirit blest,
To thee be every prayer addressed,
Who art in threefold Name adored,
From age to age, the only Lord. [H82 143]

Text: Latin, 6th cent.; tr. Maurice F. Bell, 1862-1947

Tune: *Erhalt uns, Herr,* melody derived from *Geistliche Lieder*, 1543 LM

Sit

A LESSON is read.

Year 1

Thursday after Ash Wednesday

John 1:29-34
John saw Jesus coming toward him and declared, "Here is the Lamb of God who takes away the sin of the world!"

Year 2

John 17:1-8
This is eternal life, that they may know you, the only true God, and Jesus Christ whom you have sent.

Thursday after Lent 1

John 3:16-21

God did not send the Son into the world to condemn the world, but in order that the world might be saved through him.

Mark 2:1-12

He stood up, and immediately took the mat and went out before all of them; so that they were all amazed and glorified God, saying, "We have never seen anything like this!"

Thursday after Lent 2

John 5:19-29

Anyone who hears my word and believes him who sent me has eternal life, and does not come under judgment, but has passed from death to life.

Mark 4:21-34

With many such parables he spoke the word to them, as they were able to hear it; he did not speak to them except in parables, but he explained everything in private to his disciples.

Thursday after Lent 3

John 8:21-32

If you continue in my word, you are truly my disciples.

Mark 6:30-46

As Jesus went ashore he saw a great crowd; and he had compassion for them, because they were like sheep without a shepherd; and he began to teach them many things.

Thursday after Lent 4

John 6:41-51

I am the living bread that came down from heaven. Whoever eats of this bread will live for ever; and the bread that I will give for the life of the world is my flesh.

Mark 8:27-9:1

Jesus began to teach them that the Son of Man must undergo great suffering, and be rejected by the elders, the chief priests, and the scribes, and be killed, and after three days rise again.

Thursday after Lent 5

John 10:19-42

My sheep hear my voice. I know them, and they follow me. I give them eternal life, and they will never perish. No one will snatch them out of my hand.

Mark 10:17-31

There is no one who has left house or brothers or sisters or mother or father or children or fields, for my sake and for the sake of the good news, who will not receive a hundredfold now in this age–houses, brothers and sisters, mothers and children, and fields with persecutions–and in the age to come eternal life.

Silence for meditation follows the reading.

Antiphon to the MAGNIFICAT

Thursday after Ash Wednesday

Those who lose their life for my sake will get back
very much more **in** this age,*
and in the age to come eternal life, **says** the Lord.
[LH; see Luke 9:24; 18:29-30]

Thursday after Lent 1

Ask, and it will be given you; search, and **you** will find;*
knock, and the door will be o**pened** for you. [LH: Matt. 7:7]

Thursday after Lent 2

Return to me, says the **Lord** of hosts,*
and I will re**turn** to you. [Zech. 1:3b]

Thursday after Lent 3

Bless**ed** are those*
who hear the word of the **God** and keep it. [LH: Luke 11:27]

Thursday after Lent 4

Come to me, all you that are weary
and are carrying **hea**vy burdens,*
and I will **give** you rest. [Matt. 11:28]

Thursday after Lent 5

I will make with you an ever**last**ing covenant,*
my steadfast, sure **love** for David. [Isa. 55:3b]

Fridays in Lent

Antiphon to PSALM 119 *yodh* (:73-80) *Manus tuae fecerunt me*

Give me **un**derstanding,*
that I may learn **your** commandments.

119 *Meditation on God's law*

73 Your hands have made me and **fash**ioned me;*
give me understanding, that I may learn **your** commandments.

74 Those who fear you will be glad **when** they see me,*
because I trust **in** your word.

75 I know, O LORD, that your judg**ments** are right*
and that in faithfulness you have af**flict**ed me.

76 Let your loving-kindness **be** my comfort,*
as you have promised **to** your servant.

77 Let your compassion come to me, that **I** may live,*
for your law is **my** delight.

78 Let the arrogant be put to shame, for they wrong **me** with lies;*
but I will meditate on **your** commandments.

79 Let those who fear you **turn** to me,*
and also those who know **your** decrees.

80 Let my heart be sound **in** your statutes,*
that I may not be **put** to shame.

Antiphon Give me **un**derstanding,*
that I may learn **your** commandments.

Silence for meditation

Lord, you are just and your commandments are eternal. Teach us to love you with all our hearts and to love our neighbor as ourselves, for the sake of Jesus Christ our Lord. [LH, LBW]

+

Antiphon to PSALM 130 *De profundis*

With the LORD **there** is mercy;*
with him is plente**ous** redemption. [PBO]

130 *From the depths: a penitential psalm*

1 Out of the depths have I called you, O LORD;
LORD, **hear** my voice;*
let your ears consider well the voice of my **supp**lication.

2 If you, LORD, were to note what is **done** amiss,*
O Lord, **who** could stand?

3 For there is forgive**ness** with you;*
therefore you **shall** be feared.

4 I wait for the LORD; my soul **waits** for him;*
in his word **is** my hope.

5 My soul waits for the LORD,
more than watchmen **for** the morning,*
more than watchmen **for** the morning.

6 O Israel, wait **for** the LORD,*
for with the LORD **there** is mercy;

7 With him there is plente**ous** redemption,*
and he shall redeem Israel from **all** their sins.

Antiphon With the LORD **there** is mercy;*
with him is plente**ous** redemption.

Silence for meditation

God of might and compassion, you sent your Word into the world as a watchman to announce the dawn of salvation. Do not leave us in the depths of our sins, but listen to your Church pleading for the fullness of your redeeming grace; through Jesus Christ our Lord. [LHd, LBW]

+

Stand

THE HYMN is sung. *Giesu sommo conforto*

Je - sus, ref- uge of the wea - ry, ob - ject of the spir - it's love,

Foun-tain in life's des-ert drea-ry, Sav-ior from the world a - bove:

O how oft thine eyes, of-fend-ed, Gaze up-on the sin - ner's fall;

Yet up-on the Cross ex - tend-ed, Thou didst bear the pain of all.

2 Do we pass that Cross unheeding,
Breathing no repentant vow,
Though we see thee wounded, bleeding,
See thy thorn-encircled brow?
Yet thy sinless death hath brought us
Life eternal, peace, and rest;

Only what thy grace hath taught us
  Calms the sinner's stormy breast.

3 Jesus, may our hearts be burning
  With more fervent love for thee;
May our eyes be ever turning
  To thy Cross of agony;
Till in glory, parted never,
  From the blessèd Savior's side,
Graven in our hearts for ever,
  Dwell the Cross, the Crucified. [SBH 69, LBW 93]

Text: Girolamo Savanarola, 1452-1498; tr. Jane Francesca Wilde, 1826-1896
Tune: *O du Liebe meiner Liebe,* Herrenhut, c. 1735 87 87 D

Sit

A LESSON is read.

Year 1	Year 2
Friday after Ash Wednesday	
John 1:35-42	John 17:9-19
As John watched Jesus walk by, he exclaimed, "Look, here is the Lamb of God!"	Holy Father, protect them in your name that you have given me, so that they may be one, as we are one.
Friday after Lent 1	
John 3:22-36	Mark 2:13-22
The Father loves the Son and has placed all things in his hands.	The days will come when the bridegroom is taken away from them, and then they will fast on that day.

Friday after Lent 2

John 5:30-47

I can do nothing on my own. As I hear, I judge; and my judgment is just, because I seek to do not my will but the will of him who sent me.

Mark 4:35-41

They were filled with great awe and said to one another, "Who then is this, that even the wind and the sea obey him?"

Friday after Lent 3

John 8:33-47

If the Son makes you free, you will be free indeed.

Mark 6:47-56

Jesus spoke to them and said, "Take heart, it is I; do not be afraid."

Friday after Lent 4

John 6:52-59

This is the bread that came down from heaven, not like that which your ancestors ate, and they died. But the one who eats this bread will live forever.

Mark 9:2-13

As they were coming down the mountain, Jesus ordered them to tell no one about what they had seen, until after the Son of Man had risen from the dead.

Friday after Lent 5

John 11:1-27

I am the resurrection and the life. Those who believe in me, even though they die, will live, and everyone who lives and believes in me will never die.

or John 12:1-10

Six days before the Passover, Jesus came to Bethany, the home of Lazarus, whom he had raised from the dead.

Mark 10:32-45

Whoever wishes to become great among you must be your servant, and whoever wishes to be first among you must be slave to all. For the Son of Man came not to be served but to serve, and to give his life a ransom for many.

Silence for meditation follows the reading.

Antiphon to the MAGNIFICAT

Friday after Ash Wednesday

When the bridegroom is taken a**way** from them,*
then the wedding **guests** will fast. [LH: Matt. 9:15]

Friday after Lent 1

Let us approach the throne of **grace** with boldness,*
so that we may receive mercy and find grace to
help in **time** of need. [Heb. 4:16]

Friday after Lent 2

If you obey my voice and **keep** my covenant*
you shall be my treasured possession out of
all the peoples. [Exod. 19:5]

Friday after Lent 3

Go and learn **what** this means,*
"I desire mer**cy**, not sacrifice." [Matt. 9:13]

Friday after Lent 4

My **yoke** is easy,*
and my bur**den** is light. [Matt. 11:30]

Friday after Lent 5

Come, let us return to the Lord; for it is he who has torn,
and **he** will heal us;*
he was struck down, and he will **bind** us up. [Hos. 6:1]

MORNING PRAYER

Matins or Morning Praise during Lent from Ash Wednesday until the Sunday of the Passion

Stand

Leader

Congregation

Leader and Congregation

The PSALMODY begins with this Invitatory and Psalm.

The Lord is near to those who **call** on him.*
Oh, come, let us **wor**ship him. [Ps. 145:19a; LBW]

95 *A call to praise God*

1 Come let us sing **to** the LORD;*
let us shout for joy to the Rock of **our** salvation.

2 Let us come before his presence **with** thanksgiving*
and raise a loud shout to him with psalms.
The Lord is near to those who **call** on him.

3 For the LORD **is** a great God,*
and a great King a**bove** all gods.

4 In his hands are the caverns **of** the earth,*
and the heights of the hills **are** his also.

5 The sea is his, **for** he made it,*
and his hands have molded the dry land.
Oh, come let us **wor**ship him.

6 Come, let us bow down, and **bend** the knee,*
and kneel before the **LORD** our Maker.

7 For he is our God,
and we are the people of his pasture and the sheep **of** his hand.*
Oh, that today you would hearken to his voice!
The Lord is near to those who **call** on him.

8 Harden not your hearts,
as your forebears did **in** the wilderness,*
at Meribah, and on that day at Massah,
when they **tempt**ed me.

9 They put me **to** the test,*
though they had seen my works.
Oh, come, let us **wor**ship him.

10 Forty years long I detested that genera**tion** and said,*
"This people are wayward in their hearts;
they do not **know** my ways."

11 So I swore **in** my wrath,*
"They shall never enter in**to** my rest."
The Lord is near to those who **call** on him.*
Oh, come, let us **wor**ship him

Glory to the Father, and to the Son, and to the **Ho**ly Spirit;*
as it was in the beginning, is now, and will be for **e**ver. Amen.

The Lord is near to those who **call** on him.*
Oh, come, let us **wor**ship him

Sit

A second psalm is sung or said; additional psalms and an Old Testament canticle may be sung or said also. Silence for meditation follows each psalm or canticle. The psalm prayer appropriate to each psalm or canticle follows the silence.

C Amen

Stand

THE HYMN is sung.

Sit

One or two LESSONS are read. Silence for meditation follows each reading.

The Responsory to the reading(s) follows the silence. After the Responsory the leader then continues:

L In many and various ways God spoke to his people of old by the prophets.

C But now in these last days he has spoken to us by his Son.

Stand

The GOSPEL CANTICLE, Benedictus Dominus Deus, *is sung or said. The proper Antiphon is given on pp. 1006-1080.*

The Antiphon is sung or said.

1 ✠ Blessed be the Lord,
the . . . . God of Israel; he has come
to his people and set them free.

3 Through his holy
prophets he promised
of old that he
would save us . . . . . . from our enemes, from the hands of all who hate us.

5 This was the oath
he swore to our . . . . fa - ther Abraham: to set us free
from the hands of our enemies,

2 He has raised up for
us a . . . . might - y Savior, born of the house of his ser -vant David.

4 He promised to show
mercy . . . . to our fathers and to remember his . . . ho - ly covenant.

6 free to worship him with - out fear, holy and righteous in
his sight all the days of our life.

7 You, my child, shall be
called the prophet of the most high, for you will
go before
the Lord to pre - pare his way,

9 In the tender
compassion . . . . of our God, the dawn
from on
high shall break up - on us.

11 Glory to the
Father and . . . . to the Son, and to the . . . . Ho - ly Spirit;

8 to give his people
knowledge . . . . of sal - vation by the forgiveness . . . . of their sins.

10 to shine on those
who dwell in darkness
and the shad - ow of death, and to guide
our feet into the . . . . . way of peace.

12 as it was in the
begin - ning, is now, and will be for ev - er. A - men.

The Antiphon is repeated.

All say together

I believe in God, the Father almighty,
creator of heaven and earth.
I believe in Jesus Christ, his only Son, our Lord,
He was conceived by the power of the Holy Spirit
and born of the Virgin Mary.
He suffered under Pontius Pilate,
was crucified, died, and was buried.
He descended to the dead [*or* He descended into hell].
On the third day he rose again.
He ascended into heaven,
and is seated at the right hand of the Father.
He will come again to judge the living and the dead.
I believe in the Holy Spirit,
the holy catholic Church,
the communion of saints,
the forgiveness of sins,
the resurrection of the body,
and the life everlasting. Amen.

Kneel or stand

The GREAT SUFFRAGES are said. [BR, Löhe, CB, CSB, SBH]

L Kyrie eleison.
C Lord, have mercy.
L Christe, eleison.
C Christ, have mercy.
L Kyrie, eleison.
C Lord, have mercy.

L Our Father in heaven,
hallowed be your Name,
your kingdom come,
your will be done,
on earth as in heaven.
Give us today our daily bread.
Forgive us our sins
as we forgive those
who sin against us.
Save us from the time of trial,

C and deliver us from evil.

L Our Father, who art in heaven,
hallowed be thy Name,
thy kingdom come,
thy will be done,
on earth as it is in heaven.
Give us this day our daily bread;
and forgive us our trespasses,
as we forgive those
who trespass against us;
and lead us not into temptation,

C but deliver us from evil.

L I said, "Lord, be merciful to me;
C Heal me, for I have sinned against you." [Ps. 41:4]

L Return, O Lord; how long will you tarry?
C Be gracious to your servants. [Ps. 90:13]

L Let your loving-kindness, O Lord, be upon us,
C As we have put our trust in you. [Ps. 33:22]

L O Lord, save our nation.
C And answer us when we call. [see Ps. 20:9]

L Let your priests be clothed with righteousness;
C Let your faithful people sing with joy. [Ps. 132:9]

L Save your people and bless your inheritance;
C Shepherd them and carry them for ever. [Ps. 28:11]

L Remember your congregation
C That you purchased long ago. [Ps. 74:2]

L Peace be within your walls
C And quietness within your towers. [Ps. 122:7]

L Let us remember the faithful departed.
C Rest eternal grant to them, O Lord,
and let light perpetual shine upon them

L May they rest in peace.
C Amen

L Let us pray for our absent brothers and sisters.
C Save your servants who put their trust in you. [Ps. 86:2]

L Let us pray for the afflicted and captives.
C Send them help from your holy place,
and strengthen them out of Zion. [Ps. 20:2]

L Restore us, O God of hosts;
C Show the light of your countenance, and we shall be saved. [Ps. 80:7]

L Arise, O Christ, for our help;
C And save us, for the sake of your steadfast love. [Ps. 44:26]

L Lord, hear my prayer,
C And let my prayer come before you. [Ps. 102:1]

L The Lord be with you.
C And also with you.

L Let us pray.

The PRAYER OF THE DAY is said.

ASH WEDNESDAY

Almighty and everlasting God, you hate nothing you have made and forgive the sins of all who are penitent: Create and make in us new and contrite hearts, that we, worthily lamenting our sins and acknowledging our wretchedness, may obtain of you, the God of all mercy, perfect remission and forgiveness; through Jesus Christ our Lord, who lives and reigns with you and the Holy Spirit, one God, now and for ever.

[BCP, CB, CSB, SBH, LBW]

Thursday after Ash Wednesday

Direct us, O Lord, in all our doings with your most gracious favor and further us with your continual help, that in all our works, begun, continued, and ended in you, we may glorify your holy Name, and finally by your mercy obtain everlasting life; through your Son, Jesus Christ our Lord, who lives and reigns with you and the Holy Spirit, one God, now and for ever. [Greg., RS, LFF; BCP, CB, CSB, SBH, LBW]

Friday after Ash Wednesday

Support us, O Lord, with your gracious favor through the fast we have begun; that, as we observe it by bodily self denial, so we may fulfill it with inner sincerity of heart; through Jesus Christ our Lord, who lives and reigns with you and the Holy Spirit, one God, now and for ever.

[Gel., Greg., RS, AC, LFF]

Saturday after Ash Wednesday

Almighty and everlasting God, mercifully look upon our frailty, and in all our dangers and necessities, stretch forth the right hand of your maj-

esty to help and defend us; through Jesus Christ your Son our Lord, who lives and reigns with you and the Holy Spirit, one God, now and for ever.
[Greg., RS, LFF; MR, CB, CSB, SBH Epiphany 3]

THE FIRST SUNDAY IN LENT

O Lord God, you led your ancient people through the wilderness and brought them to the promised land: Bring us, your new Israel, safely through the wilderness of this world so that we may come at last to the glory of your heavenly kingdom; through your Son, Jesus Christ our Lord, who lives and reigns with you and the Holy Spirit, one God, now and for ever. [LBW rev. DvD, PHP]

Monday of the First Week in Lent

Turn our hearts back to you, O God of our salvation; grant us the grace of true conversion, and, that we may fully benefit from the Lenten fast, shape our minds with your heavenly teaching; through Jesus Christ our Lord, who lives and reigns with you and the Holy Spirit, one God, now and for ever. [Greg., MR, RS trans. DvD]

Tuesday of the First Week in Lent

Look mercifully, O Lord, upon your family, that as we discipline our desire for earthly things, a longing for you may grow in our hearts; through Jesus Christ our Lord, who lives and reigns with you and the Holy Spirit, one God, now and for ever. [MR, RS]

Wednesday of the First Week in Lent

Bless us, O God, in this holy season, in which our hearts seek your help and healing; and so purify us by your discipline that we may grow in grace and in the knowledge of our Lord and Savior Jesus Christ; who lives and reigns with you and the Holy Spirit, one God, now and for ever.

[Gel., AC rev. LFF;~RS]

Thursday of the First Week in Lent

Grant to us, Lord, we pray, the spirit to think and do always those things that are right; that we, who cannot exist without you, may by you be enabled to live according to your will; through Jesus Christ our Lord, who lives and reigns with you and the Holy Spirit, one God, now and for ever. [Leo., RS; BCP Proper 14; MR, CB, CSB, SBH Trinity 8]

Friday of the First Week in Lent

Lord Christ, our eternal Redeemer, grant us such fellowship in your sufferings, that, filled with your Holy Spirit, we may subdue the flesh to the spirit, and the spirit to you, and at the last attain to the glory of your resurrection; who live and reign with the Father and the Holy Spirit, one God, now and for ever. [LFF]

Saturday of the First Week in Lent

Eternal Father, turn our hearts back to you, that we may commit our lives to your praise and service, seeking always the one thing necessary, and providing for the needs of others; through Jesus Christ our Lord, who lives and reigns with you and the Holy Spirit, one God, now and for ever.

[Leo., RS]

THE SECOND SUNDAY IN LENT

O God, whose glory is always to have mercy: Be gracious to all who have gone astray from your ways, and bring them again with penitent hearts and steadfast faith to embrace and hold fast the unchangeable truth of your Word, Jesus Christ our Lord; who lives and reigns with you and the Holy Spirit, one God, now and for ever.

[Gel., Greg. Good Fri. Bidding Prayer; BCP, LBW]

Monday of the Second Week in Lent

Teach us, heavenly Father, to hold lightly to the things of this world, and enable us in this holy season gladly to forego some of the good things of your creation, so that we may attain the greater good of serving you with all our heart and mind and strength; through Jesus Christ our Lord, who lives and reigns with you and the Holy Spirit, one God, now and for ever.

[DvD]

Tuesday of the Second Week in Lent

Watch over your Church, O Lord, with your unfailing mercy, and, because human frailty without you will surely fall, protect us by your help from every harm, and lead us to all things that work for our good; through Jesus Christ our Lord, who lives and reigns with you and the Holy Spirit, one God, now and for ever.

[Gel., RS; MR Pentecost 14, CB, CSB, SBH Trinity 14; see LFF Lent 3 Thursday]

Wednesday of the Second Week in Lent

O God, you so loved the world that you gave your only-begotten Son to reconcile earth with heaven: Grant that we, loving you above all things, may love our friends in you, and our enemies for your sake; through Jesus Christ our Lord, who lives and reigns with you and the Holy Spirit, one God, now and for ever. [LFF]

Thursday of the Second Week in Lent

O Lord our God, you love innocence and you restore it in those who have sinned: Turn back to you our wayward hearts and inflame them with your Holy Spirit, that we may be steadfast in faith and fruitful in works of love; through Jesus Christ our Lord, who lives and reigns with you and the Holy Spirit, one God, now and for ever. [Greg., RS]

Friday of the Second Week of Lent

Grant, O Lord, that as your Son Jesus Christ on the cross prayed for his enemies, so we may have grace to forgive those who wrongfully or scornfully use us, that we ourselves may be able to receive your forgiveness; through Jesus Christ our Lord, who lives and reigns with you and the Holy Spirit, one God, now and for ever. [LFF rev.]

Saturday of the Second Week in Lent

O God, in your holy sacraments you have given us, while we are still on earth, a foretaste of the good things of heaven: Guide us, we beseech you, in this present life, and lead us to that everlasting light in which you yourself dwell; through Jesus Christ our Lord, who lives and reigns with you and the Holy Spirit, one God, now and for ever.

[Gel, RS trans. DvD; LFF Lent 4 Monday]

THE THIRD SUNDAY IN LENT

Almighty God, you know that we have no power in ourselves to help ourselves: Keep us both outwardly and inwardly that we may be defended from all adversities which may happen to the body and from all evil thoughts which may assault and hurt the soul; through your Son Jesus Christ our Lord, who lives and reigns with you and the Holy Spirit, one God, now and for ever. [Greg., BCP; MR, CB, CSB, SBH Lent 2]

Monday of the Third Week in Lent

Let your continual mercy, O Lord, cleanse and defend your Church; and, because it cannot continue in safety without your help, protect and govern it always by your goodness; through Jesus Christ our Lord, who lives and reigns with you and the Holy Spirit, one God, now and for ever.

[Gel., RS; BCP Proper 13; MR Pentecost 15; CB, CSB, SBH Trinity 15]

Tuesday of the Third Week in Lent

Do not forsake us, O Lord, in this time of penance, but by your grace confirm your power within us and renew our dedication to your service; through your Son Jesus Christ our Lord, who lives and reigns with you and the Holy Spirit, one God, now and for ever. [RM, RS]

Wednesday of the Third Week in Lent

God of wisdom, throughout these forty days you instruct your people and nourish them with your word of life: Teach us through self-denial to bind our hearts to your service, and make us one through constant prayer; through Jesus Christ our Lord, who lives and reigns with you and the Holy Spirit, one God, now and for ever.

[Sermon of Leo the Great+Gel., RS; AC, see LFF Lent 1 Saturday]

Thursday of the Third Week in Lent

We humbly implore your majesty, O Lord, that as the Paschal festival draws nearer, we may prepare ourselves with ever greater devotion to celebrate the mystery of the death and resurrection of our Lord; through the same Jesus Christ your Son, who lives and reigns with you and the Holy Spirit, one God, now and for ever. [Berg., RS trans. DvD]

Friday of the Third Week in Lent

Merciful Lord, pour your grace into our hearts that its power may restrain our unruly desires and keep us true to your words of eternal life; through Jesus Christ our Lord, who lives and reigns with you and the Holy Spirit, one God, now and for ever. [RM+Berg., RS]

Saturday of the Third Week in Lent

Grant, O Lord, that as we celebrate with joy this season of Lent, we may enter more deeply into the Paschal mystery and come to enjoy the fullness of its riches; through Jesus Christ our Lord, who lives and reigns with you and the Holy Spirit, one God, now and for ever. [Gel., RS]

THE FOURTH SUNDAY IN LENT

Grant, we beseech you, almighty God, that we, who for our evil deeds deserve to be punished, by the comfort of your grace may mercifully be set free; through your Son Jesus Christ our Lord, who lives and reigns with you and the Holy Spirit one God, now and for ever.

[Greg., MR, BCP pre-1979, CB, CSB, SBH]

Monday of the Fourth Week in Lent

O God, it is your will that the gate of mercy should stand open to your faithful people: Look upon us and be merciful to us; that we who by your grace are following the path of your will, may never turn aside from the way of life, even Jesus Christ our Lord; who lives and reigns with you and the Holy Spirit, one God, now and for ever. [Gel., trans. AC rev. DvD]

Tuesday of the Fourth Week in Lent

O Lord, by the reverent observance of this Lenten season prepare the hearts of your faithful people, that they may worthily enter upon the mystery of the death and resurrection of Christ, and proclaim the greatness of your salvation; through Jesus Christ our Lord, who lives and reigns with you and the Holy Spirit, one God, now and for ever.

[Gel., RS trans. HR rev. DvD]

Wednesday of the Fourth Week in Lent

God of mercy, you reward the just for the good they do and you forgive repentant sinners: Take pity on us and answer our prayer, that as we confess our guilt we may hear the voice of your pardon; through Jesus Christ our Lord, who lives and reigns with you and the Holy Spirit, one God, now and for ever. [MR, RS]

Thursday of the Fourth Week in Lent

Be gracious to your servants, we entreat you, O Lord, that, disciplined by penitence and trained in good works, we may in singleness of heart persevere in keeping your commandments and come unharmed by sin to the Paschal feast; through Jesus Christ our Lord, who lives and reigns with you and the Holy Spirit, one God, now and for ever.

[Berg., RS trans. DvD; see LFF Lent 5 Monday]

Friday of the Fourth Week in Lent

For our sake, O God, you willed that your Son should undergo the shame of the cross to deliver us from the power of the enemy: Grant that we may come to share the grace and power of the resurrection of the same Jesus Christ our Lord, who lives and reigns with you and the Holy Spirit, one God, now and for ever. [Greg., AC]

Saturday of the Fourth Week in Lent

Almighty God, let the working of your gentle mercy direct our hearts, for without your grace we cannot find favor in your sight; through your Son Jesus Christ our Lord, who lives and reigns with you and the Holy Spirit, one God, now and for ever. [RM, RS]

THE FIFTH SUNDAY IN LENT

Almighty God, you alone can bring into order the unruly wills and affections of sinners: Grant your people grace to love what you command and desire what you promise; that, among the swift and varied changes of the world, our hearts may surely there be fixed where true joys are to be found; through Jesus Christ our Lord, who lives and reigns with you and the Holy Spirit, one God, now and for ever.

[Gel., BCP; MR, CB, CSB, SBH Easter 4; LBW Easter 5]

Monday of the Fifth Week in Lent

O God, by whose amazing grace we are enriched with every blessing: Grant us so to pass from the old life of sin to the new life in Christ, that we may be made ready for the glory of your heavenly kingdom; through Jesus Christ our Lord, who lives and reigns with you and the Holy Spirit, one God, now and for ever. [Ambrosian, sermon of Leo, RS trans. DvD]

Tuesday of the Fifth Week in Lent

God of mercy and compassion, grant that your household the Church may persevere in obeying your will, so that in our own day those who offer you true service may increase in number and in holiness; through Jesus Christ our Lord, who lives and reigns with you and the Holy Spirit, one God, now and for ever. [RM, RS]

Wednesday of the Fifth Week in Lent

Almighty God, our heavenly Father, renew in us the gifts of your mercy; increase our faith, strengthen our hope, enlighten our understanding, widen our charity, and make us ready to serve you; through Jesus Christ our Lord, who lives and reigns with you and the Holy Spirit, one God, now and for ever. [LFF]

Thursday of the Fifth Week in Lent

O God, you have called us to be your children, and have promised that those who suffer with Christ will be heirs with him of your glory: Arm us with such trust in him that we may ask no rest from his demands and have no fear in his service; through Jesus Christ our Lord, who lives and reigns with you and the Holy Spirit, one God, now and for ever. [LFF]

Friday of the Fifth Week in Lent

Absolve, we beseech you, O Lord, your people from their offenses; that from the bonds of our sins, which by reason of our frailty we have brought upon ourselves, we may be delivered by your bountiful goodness; through Jesus Christ our Lord, who lives and reigns with you and the Holy Spirit, one God, now and for ever.

[Greg., RS; MR Pentecost 23, CB, CSB, SBH Trinity 23]

Saturday of the Fifth Week in Lent

O God, you ever work for the salvation of humanity, and in these Lenten days you gladden our hearts with yet more abundant grace: Mercifully look upon your chosen people and help and defend with your fatherly protection both those who are about to be baptized, and all who have already been born again in Holy Baptism; through Jesus Christ our Lord, who lives and reigns with you and the Holy Spirit, one God, now and for ever. [Gel., Ambrosian, RS trans. DvD; see LFF Lent 5 Tuesday]

Other prayers may be said by the Leader with the Congregation responding "Amen" to each. Members of the congregation may be invited to offer petitions and thanksgivings. In concluding the prayers, the Leader says:

We give thanks to you, heavenly Father, through Jesus Christ your dear Son, that you have protected us through the night from all danger and harm. We ask you to preserve and keep us, this day also, from all sin and evil, that in all our thoughts, words, and deeds we may serve and please you. Into your hands we commend our bodies and souls and all that is ours. Let your holy angels have charge concerning us, that the wicked one have no power over us. [Luther, CSB, SBH, LBW]

L Let my mouth be full of your praise.
C And your glory all the day long. [Ps. 71:8]

Grant, most merciful Lord, to your faithful people pardon and peace, that they may be cleansed from all their sins and serve you with a quiet mind; through Christ our Lord.

[Gel., MR Pentecost 20; BCP Trinity 21; CB, CSB, SBH Trinity 20; BCP, LBW Burial]

Stand

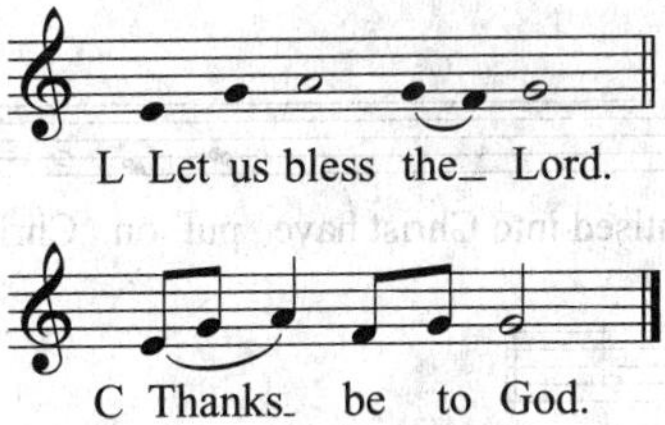

The BENEDICTION concludes the service when there is no sermon or Paschal Blessing. On Sundays the Paschal Blessing (p. 990) may replace the benediction. A hymn may follow the benediction.

When there is a sermon, this benediction is omitted, and the service continues as on p. 20; On Sundays the Paschal Blessing may follow the prayer after the sermon.

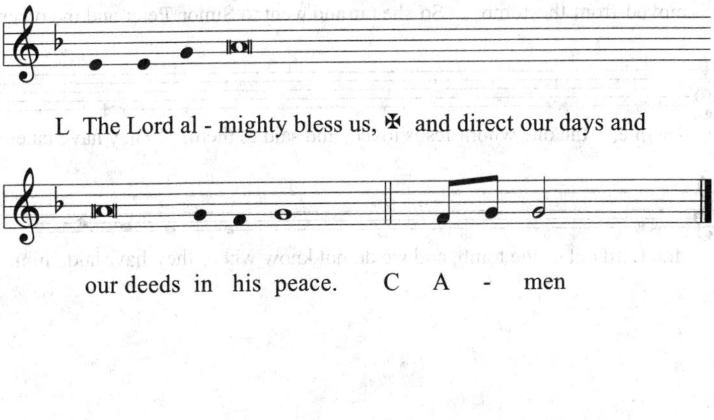

The PASCHAL BLESSING may be used on Sundays to conclude Morning Prayer. The service may be led from the font.

Stand

Then Pe-ter and the other disciple set out and went toward the tomb.
The two were running together, but the other disciple outran Peter and
reached the tomb_ first. He bent down to look in and saw the linen
wrappings lying there, but he did not go in. Then Si-mon Peter came,
following him, and went in - to the tomb. He saw the linen wrappings
lying there and the cloth that had been on Jesus' head, not lying with the
linen wrappings but rolled up in a place by it self. Then the oth-er dis-
ciple, who reached the tomb first, also went in, and he saw and be -lieved

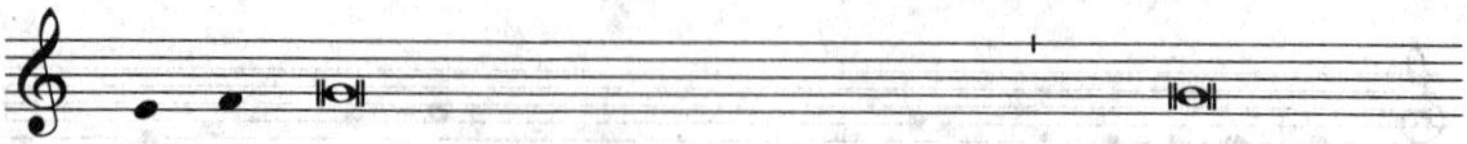

for as yet they did not understand the scripture, that he must

rise from the dead___.

The Te Deum Laudamus is sung.

1 You are . . . . . . God; we praise you. You are the Lord; we ac - claim you.

3 To you all
angels, all the pow'rs of heaven, cherubim and
seraphim sing in end - less praise:

5 The glorious
company
of the a - pos - tles praise you. The noble
fellowship of pro - phets praise you.

2 You are the e - ter - nal Father; all creation . . . . wor - ships you.

4 Holy, holy, holy
Lord, God of . . . pow'r and might, heaven and
earth are full . . . . . . of your glory.

6 The white-robed
army of . . . . mar - tyrs praise you. Throughout the
world the holy Church ac - claims
you:

7 Father,
of majes - ty un - bounded; your true and on - ly Son,

9 You, Christ
are the . . . . . king of glory, the eternal
Son . . . . of the Father.

11 You overcame
the . . . . sting of death, and opened
the kingdom
of heaven to all be - lievers.

13 Come, then,
Lord, and help your people, bought with
the price of your own blood.

8 worthy . . . . of all worship; and the Holy
Spirit, advo - cate and guide.

10 When you
became man to set us free, you did not
spurn the . . . . vir - gin's womb.

12 You are seated
at God's right hand in glory. We believe that
you will come and be our judge.

14 and bring us with your saints to glory . . . . ev - er - lasting.

L Almighty God, by our baptism into the death and resurrection of your
Son Jesus Christ, you turn us from the old life of sin: Grant that we,
being reborn to new life in him, may live in righteousness and holiness
all our days; through Jesus Christ our Lord, who lives and reigns
with you and the Holy Spirit, one God, now and for - ever.
C A - men
[BCP]
L The Lord al - mighty bless us, ✠ and direct our days and
our deeds in his peace. C A - men

Sundays in Lent

Antiphon to PSALM 84 *Quam dilecta tabernacula*

Lent 1 Happy are the people whose strength **is** in you,*
whose hearts are set on the **pil**grim's way. [LH, PBO]

Lent 2 No good thing will the **Lord** withold*
from those who walk **with** integrity.

Lent 3 Here we have no **last**ing city*
but are looking for the city that **is** to come.
[LH: Heb. 13:14]

Lent 4 Those who go through the des**o**late valley*
will find it a **place** of springs.

Lent 5 Behold our defend**er**, O God;*
and look upon the face of **your** Anointed.

84 *Longing for God's temple*

1 How dear to me is your dwelling, **O Lord** of hosts!*
My soul has a desire and longing for the courts of
the LORD;
my heart and my flesh rejoice in the **li**ving God.

2 The sparrow has found her a house
and the swallow a nest where she may **lay** her young,*
by the side of your altars, O LORD of hosts,
my King **and** my God.

3 Happy are they who dwell **in** your house!*
they will always be **prais**ing you.

4 Happy are the people whose strength **is** in you!*
whose hearts are set on the **pil**grims' way.

5 Those who go through the desolate valley will find
it a **place** of springs,*
for the early rains have covered it with **pools** of water.

6 They will climb from **height** to height,*
and the God of gods will reveal him**self** in Zion.

7 LORD God of hosts, **hear** my prayer;*
hearken, O **God** of Jacob.

8 Behold our defend**er**, O God;*
and look upon the face of **your** Anointed.

9 For one day in your courts is better than
a thousand in **my** own room,*
and to stand at the threshold of the house of my God
than to dwell in the tents **of** the wicked.

10 For the LORD God is both **sun** and shield;*
he will give **grace** and glory;

11 No good thing will the **LORD** withhold*
from those who walk **with** integrity.

12 O **LORD** of hosts,*
happy are they who put their **trust** in you!

The Antiphon is repeated.

Silence for meditation

Almighty God, you heard the prayer of Christ, your chosen one, and raised him to the lasting joy of your presence: Help us in our pilgrimage toward you to love your Church and to offer the sacrifice of praise at your altar, that we may hasten to your home and joyfully look upon your glorious splendor, which we have seen in your Son, Jesus Christ our Lord. [LHd, LBW]

+

Antiphon to THE OLD TESTAMENT CANTICLE *Quaerite Dominum*

Lent 1 Let the wicked aban**don** their ways*
and the evil **ones** their thoughts.

Lent 2 Return to the Lord, and he will **have** compassion,*
and to our God, who will **rich**ly pardon.

Lent 3 Return O faithless children, says the Lord [Jer. 3:14]

Lent 4 The rain and the snow fall **from** the heavens*
bringing forth life and **giv**ing growth.

Lent 5 My word that goes out **from** my mouth*
will not return **to** me empty.

The Second Song of Isaiah Isaiah 55:6-11

Seek the Lord while he **may** be found;*
call upon him when **he** draws near.

Let the wicked aban**don** their ways*
    and the evil **ones** their thoughts.
Let them return to the Lord,
and he will **have** compassion*
    and to our God, who will **rich**ly pardon.
For my thoughts **are** not your thoughts*
    and your ways are not my ways, **says** the Lord.
For as the heavens are higher **than** the earth,*
    so are my ways higher than your ways
    and my **thoughts** than your thoughts.
For as the rain and snow fall **from** the heavens*
    and return not again but wa**ter** the earth,
Bringing forth life and **giv**ing growth,*
    seed for sowing and **bread** for eating,
So is my word that goes out **from** my mouth:*
    it will not return **to** me empty;
But it will accomplish that which **I** have purposed*
    and prosper in that for **which** I sent it. [BCP alt. LBW 15]

The Antiphon is repeated.

Silence for meditation

God our Savior, in the unfolding year the fields are broken open to receive the seed of new life: By the discipline of the holy springtime of Lent, assist us to open our lives to your Word and thus to know within us the new life which you give to your creation; through your Son, Jesus Christ our Lord. [PHP]

+

Antiphon to the PSALM 61 *Exaudi, Deus, deprecationem*

Lent 1 You, O Lord, have **been** my refuge,*
a strong tower a**gainst** the enemy. [LH, PBO]

Lent 2 Your statutes have **been** my songs*
wherever I **live** in exile. [Ps. 119:54]

Lent 3 The Lord your God is **lead**ing you*
through the great and ter**ri**ble wilderness. [see Deut. 8:14-15]

Lent 4 We know that while we are at home **in** the body
we are away **from** the Lord. [LH: 2 Cor. 5:6]

Lent 5 We have a high priest who in every respect
has been tempted **as** we are,*
yet **with**out sin. [Heb. 4:15]

61 *Prayer of an exile*

1 Hear my **cry**, O God,*
and listen **to** my prayer.

2 I call upon you from the ends of the earth
with heaviness **in** my heart;*
set me upon the rock that is high**er** than I.

3 For you have **been** my refuge,*
a strong tower a**gainst** the enemy.

4 I will dwell in your **house** for ever;*
I will take refuge under the cover **of** your wings.

5 For you, O God, have **heard** my vows;*
you have granted me the heritage of those who **fear** your Name.

6 Add length of days **to** the king's life;*
let his years extend over many **gen**erations.

7 Let him sit enthroned before **God** for ever;*
bid love and faithfulness watch **o**ver him.

8 So will I always sing the praise **of** your Name,*
and day by day I will ful**fill** my vows.

The Antiphon is repeated.

Silence for meditation

Lord Jesus, love and truth of the Father, you came to earth to relieve the pain of our exile; you took our weakness as your own: When our hearts grow faint, uphold us until we stand with you before God and praise your Name for ever. [LH, LBW]

+

Stand

THE HYMN is sung. *Herzlich Lieb hab' ich dich, o Herr*

Lord, thee I love with all my heart; I pray thee, ne'er from
me de - part; With ten-der mer - cy cheer me. Earth
has no plea - sure I would share, Yea, heav'n it - self were
void and bare If thou, Lord, wert not near me. And should my
heart for sor - row break, My trust in thee can noth - ing shake.
Thou art the por - tion I have sought; Thy pre - cious
blood my soul has bought. Lord Je - sus Christ, My God and
Lord, my God and Lord, For - sake me not! I trust thy Word.

2 Yea, Lord, 'twas thy rich bounty gave
My body, soul, and all I have
In this poor life of labor.
Lord, grant that I in every place
May glorify thy lavish grace
And serve and help my neighbor.
Let no false doctrine me beguile,
Let Satan not my soul defile.
Give strength and patience unto me
To bear my cross and follow thee.
Lord Jesus Christ,
My God and Lord, my God and Lord,
In death thy comfort still afford.

3 Lord, let at last thine angels come,
To Abr'ham's bosom bear me home,
That I may die unfearing;
And in its narrow chamber keep
My body safe in peaceful sleep
Until thy reappearing.
And then from death awaken me,
That these mine eyes with joy may see,
O Son of God, thy glorious face,
My Savior and my fount of grace.
Lord Jesus Christ,
My prayer attend, my prayer attend,
And I will praise thee without end! [LBW 325]

Text: Martin Schalling, 1532-1608; tr. Catherine Winkworth, 1829-1878, alt. TLH
Tune: *Herzlich Lieb,* Bernhard Schmid, *Orgeltabulatur-Buch*, 1577 PM

Sit

One or two LESSONS are read.

Year 1

Lent 1
Jeremiah 9:23-24

Let those who boast boast in this, that they understand and know me, that I am the LORD.
[BCP Deut 8:1-10]

1 Corinthians 1:17-31

The message about the cross is foolishness to those who are perishing, but to us who are being saved it is the power of God.

Lent 2
Jeremiah 1:1-10

Today I appoint you over nations and over kingdoms, to pluck up and to pull down, to destroy and to overthrow, to build and to plant.

1 Corinthians 3:11-23

Do you not know that you are God's temple and that God's Spirit dwells in you?

Year 2

Daniel 9:3-10

I turned to the Lord God, to seek an answer by prayer and supplication with fasting and sackcloth and ashes.

Hebrews 2:10-18

Because Jesus himself was tested by what he suffered, he is able to help those who are being tested.

Genesis 41:14-45

Pharaoh said to Joseph, "See, I have set you over all the land of Egypt."

Romans 6:3-14

We have been buried with him by baptism into death, so that, just as Christ was raised from the dead by the glory of the Father, so we too might walk in newness of life.

Lent 3

Jeremiah 6:9-15

Thus says the LORD of hosts: Glean thoroughly as a vine the remnant of Israel; like a grape-gatherer, pass your hand again over its branches.

Genesis 44:1-17

Judah said, "What can we say to my lord? What can we speak? How can we clear ourselves? God has found out the guilt of your servants.

1 Corinthians 6:12-20

You were bought with a price; therefore glorify God in your body.

Romans 8:1-10

If Christ is in you, though the body is dead because of sin, the Spirit is life because of righteousness.

Lent 4

Jeremiah 14:1-9(10-16)17-22

You, O LORD, are in the midst of us, and we are called by your name; do not forsake us!

Genesis 48:8-22

Then Israel said to Joseph, "I am about to die, but God will be with you and will bring you again to the land of your ancestors."

Galatians 4:21-5:1

For freedom Christ has set us free. Stand firm, therefore, and do not submit again to a yoke of slavery.

Romans 8:11-25

When we cry, "Abba! Father!" it is that very Spirit bearing witness with our spirit that we are children of God.

Lent 5

Jeremiah 23:16-32

Look, the storm of the LORD! Wrath has gone forth, a whirling tempest; it will burst upon the head of the wicked.

Exodus 3:16-4:12

I will bring you up out of the misery of Egypt.

1 Corinthians 9:19-27

Do you not know that in a race the runners all compete but only one receives the prize? Run in such a way that you may win it.

Romans 12:1-21

Present your bodies as a living sacrifice, holy and acceptable to God, which is your spiritual worship.

Silence for meditation follows each reading.

RESPONSORY

Save the weak **and** the orphan,*
defend the hum**ble** and needy.
  Rescue the weak **and** the poor;*
  deliver them from the power **of**
  the wicked.
God chose the poor in the world
to be **rich** in faith*
and to be heirs of the kingdom
that he has promised to **those**
who love him.
  Rescue the weak **and** the poor;*
  deliver them from the power **of**
  the wicked.

[LH: Ps. 82:3-4; James 2:5]

You have come to Jesus,
the mediator of **a** new covenant.*
Do not re**fuse** to hear him.
  Oh, that today you would
  hearken **to** his voice!*
  Harden **not** your hearts.
If they did not escape when they
refused the one who warned
them on earth,*
how much less will we escape if
we reject the one who **warns**
from heaven!
  Oh, that today you would
  hearken **to** his voice!*
  Harden **not** your hearts.

[LH: Heb. 12:22,24,25; Ps. 95:8]

Antiphon to the BENEDICTUS

Lent 1 Jesus was led up by the Spirit into the wilderness to be
tempted **by** the devil.*
He fasted forty days and forty nights,
and afterward **he** was famished. [LH: Matt. 4:1-2]

Lent 2 Our Savior Jesus Christ a**bol**ished death,*
and brought life and immortality to light **through** the
gospel. [LH: 2 Timothy 1:10]

Lent 3 Destroy this temple, says the Lord,
and in three days I will **raise** it up.*
He was speaking of the temple **of** his body.
[LH: John 2:19,21]

Lent 4 Never since the world began has it been heard that anyone
opened the eyes of **one** born blind*
until the coming of Christ, the **Son** of God. [LH: see John 9:32]

Lent 5 Our friend Lazarus has fall**en** asleep,*
but I am going there to a**wak**en him. [LH: John 11:11]

Mondays in Lent

Antiphon to PSALM 78 Part i *Attendite, popule*

We will recount to generations to come,
the praiseworthy deeds and power **of** the LORD,*
and the wonderful works **he** has done. [LH, PBO]

78 Part I *The lessons of Israel's history*

1 Hear my teaching, **O** my people;*
incline your ears to the words **of** my mouth.

2 I will open my mouth **in** a parable;*
I will declare the mysteries of **an**cient times.

3 That which we have heard and known,
and what our forefa**thers** have told us,*
we will not hide **from** their children.

4 We will recount to generations to come
the praiseworthy deeds and the power **of** the LORD,*
and the wonderful works **he** has done.

5 He gave his decrees to Jacob
and established a **law** for Israel,*
which he commanded them to **teach** their children;

6 That the generations to come might know,
and the children **yet** unborn;*
that they in their turn might tell it **to** their children;

7 So that they might put their **trust** in God,*
and not forget the deeds of God,
but keep **his** commandments,

8 And not be like their forefathers,
a stubborn and rebellious **gen**eration,*
a generation whose heart was not steadfast,
and whose spirit was not faith**ful** to God.

9 The people of Ephraim, armed **with** the bow,*
turned back in the **day** of battle;

10 They did not keep the cove**nant** of God,*
and refused to walk **in** his law;

11 They forgot what **he** had done,*
and the wonders **he** had shown them.

12 He worked marvels in the sight **of** their forefathers,*
in the land of Egypt, in the **field** of Zoan.

13 He split open the sea and let **them** pass through;*
he made the waters stand **up** like walls.

14 He led them with a **cloud** by day,*
and all the night through with a **glow** of fire.

15 He split the hard rocks **in** the wilderness*
and gave them drink as from **the** great deep.

16 He brought streams out **of** the cliff,*
and the waters gushed **out** like rivers.

17 But they went on sin**ning** against him,*
rebelling in the desert against **the** Most High.

18 They tested God **in** their hearts,*
demanding food **for** their craving.

19 They railed against **God** and said,*
"Can God set a table **in** the wilderness?

20 True, he struck the rock, the waters gushed out, and the
gullies **o**verflowed;*
but is he able to give bread
or to provide meat **for** his people?"

21 When the LORD heard this, he was **full** of wrath;*
a fire was kindled against Jacob,
and his anger mounted **a**gainst Israel;

22 For they had no **faith** in God,*
nor did they put their trust in his **sav**ing power.

23 So he commanded the **clouds** above*
and opened the **doors** of heaven.

24 He rained down manna upon **them** to eat*
and gave them **grain** from heaven.

25 So mortals ate the **bread** of angels;*
he provided for them **food** enough.

26 He caused the east wind to blow **in** the heavens*
and led out the south wind **by** his might.

27 He rained down flesh upon **them** like dust*
and wingèd birds like the sand **of** the sea.

28 He let it fall in the midst **of** their camp*
and round a**bout** their dwellings.

29 So they ate and **were** well filled,*
for he gave them **what** they craved.

30 But they did not **stop** their craving,*
though the food was still **in** their mouths.

31 So God's anger mount**ed** against them;*
he slew their strongest men
and laid low the **youth** of Israel.

32 In spite of all this, they **went** on sinning*
and had no faith in his won**der**ful works.

33 So he brought their days to an end **like** a breath*
and their years in **sud**den terror.

34 Whenever he slew them, **they** would seek him,*
and repent, and diligently **search** for God.

35 They would remember that God **was** their rock,*
and the Most High God **their** redeemer.

36 But they flattered him **with** their mouths*
and lied to him **with** their tongues.

37 Their heart was not stead**fast** toward him,*
and they were not faithful **to** his covenant.

38 But he was so merciful that he forgave their sins
and did **not** destroy them;*
many times he held back his anger
and did not permit his wrath **to** be roused;

39 For he remembered that they **were** but flesh,*
a breath that goes forth and does **not** return.

Antiphon We will recount to generations to come,
the praiseworthy deeds and the power **of** the LORD,*
and the wonderful works **he** has done.

Silence for meditation

Lord Jesus, you bring water from the rock and rain bread from heaven for your people: Keep us from unfaithfulness, and grant that the covenant sealed with your blood may gain us a place with you in your kingdom, where you live and reign with the Father and the Holy Spirit, now and for ever. [LH, PHP]

+

Antiphon to PSALM 78 part ii *Quoties exacerbaverunt*

The Lord ransomed his people from the hand **of** the enemy*
and brought them into his **ho**ly land. [LH, PBO]

78 Part II *The lessons of Israel's history*

40 How often the people disobeyed him **in** the wilderness*
and offended him **in** the desert!

41 Again and again they **tempt**ed God*
and provoked the Holy **One** of Israel.

42 They did not remem**ber** his power*
in the day when he ransomed them **from** the enemy;

43 How he wrought his **signs** in Egypt*
and his omens in the **field** of Zoan.

44 He turned their rivers **in**to blood,*
so that they could not drink **of** their streams.

45 He sent swarms of flies among them, which **ate** them up,*
and frogs, **which** destroyed them.

46 He gave their crops to the **cat**erpillar,*
the fruit of their toil **to** the locust.

47 He killed their **vines** with hail*
and their syca**mores** with frost.

48 He delivered their cat**tle** to hailstones*
and their livestock **to** hot thunderbolts.

49 He poured out upon them his **blaz**ing anger:*
fury, indignation, and distress,
a troop of des**troy**ing angels.

50 He gave full rein to his anger;
he did not spare their **souls** from death;*
but delivered their lives **to** the plague.

51 He struck down all the first**born** of Egypt,*
the flower of manhood in the dwell**ings** of Ham.

52 He led out his peo**ple** like sheep*
and guided them in the wilderness **like** a flock.

53 He led them to safety, and they were **not** afraid;*
but the sea over**whelmed** their enemies.

54 He brought them to his **ho**ly land,*
the mountain his right **hand** had won.

55 He drove out the Canaanites before them
and apportioned an inheritance to **them** by lot;*
he made the tribes of Israel to dwell **in** their tents.

56 But they tested the Most High God, **and** defied him,*
and did not keep **his** commandments.

57 They turned away and were disloyal **like** their fathers;*
they were undependable like **a** warped bow.

58 They grieved him **with** their hill-altars*
and provoked his displeasure **with** their idols.

59 When God heard this, **he** was angry*
and utterly re**ject**ed Israel.

60 He forsook the **shrine** at Shiloh,*
the tabernacle where he had lived a**mong** his people.

61 He delivered the ark in**to** captivity,*
his glory into the adver**sar**y's hand.

62 He gave his people **to** the sword*
and was angered against **his** inheritance.

63 The fire consumed **their** young men;*
there were no wedding songs **for** their maidens.

64 Their priests fell **by** the sword,*
and their widows made no **la**mentation.

65 Then the LORD woke as **though** from sleep,*
like a warrior re**freshed** with wine.

66 He struck his enemies **on** the backside*
and put them to per**pet**ual shame.

67 He rejected the **tent** of Joseph*
and did not choose the **tribe** of Ephraim;

68 He chose instead the **tribe** of Judah*
and Mount Zion, **which** he loved.

69 He built his sanctuary like the **heights** of heaven,*
like the earth which he found**ed** for ever.

70 He chose Da**vid** his servant,*
and took him away **from** the sheepfolds.

71 He brought him from follow**ing** the ewes,*
to be a shepherd over Jacob his people
and over Israel **his** inheritance.

72 So he shepherded them with a faithful **and** true heart*
and guided them with the skillfulness **of** his hands.

Antiphon

The Lord ransomed his people from the hand **of** the enemy*
and brought them into his **ho**ly land.

Silence for meditation

Lord Jesus Christ, shepherd of your Church, to strengthen our faith and to lead us to the kingdom, you renewed and surpassed the marvels of the old covenant: Through the uncertainties of this earthly journey, lead us home to the everlasting pastures, where we may praise you now and for ever. [LH, LBW]

+

Stand

THE HYMN is sung. *O treuer Heiland Jesu Christ*

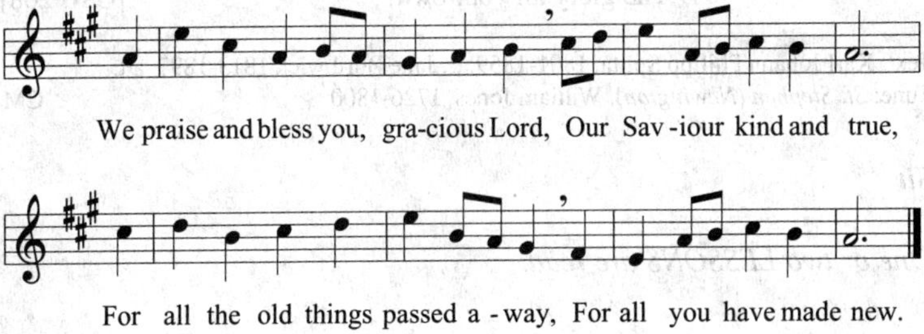

2 But yet how much must be destroyed
How much must be made new,
Ere we can fully stand complete
In likeness, Lord to you.

3 You, only you, must carry on
The work you have begun;
Of your own strength you must impart
In your own ways to run.

4 Lord, leave us not! From day to day
Revive, restore again;
Our weak, uncertain steps direct
Our enemies restrain.

5 So shall we faultless stand at last
Before your father's throne;
The blessedness for ever ours,
The glory all your own! [CSB 268]

Text: Karl Johann Philipp Spitta, 1801-1859; tr. Jane Borthwick 1813-1897, alt.
Tune: *St. Stephen (Newington),* William Jones, 1726-1800 CM

Sit

One or two LESSONS are read.

Year 1	Year 2
Monday after Lent 1 Deuteronomy 8:1-20	Genesis 37:1-11
Take care that you do not forget the LORD your God, by failing to keep his commandments, his ordinances, and his statutes, which I am commanding you today.	Israel loved Joseph more than any other of his children, because he was the son of his old age; and he had made him a long robe with sleeves.
Hebrews 2:11-18	1 Corinthians 1:1-19
Because Jesus himself was tested by what he suffered, he is able to help those who are being tested.	The message about the cross is foolishness to those who are perishing, but to us who are being saved it is the power of God.

Monday after Lent 2
Jeremiah 1:11-19

They will fight against you; but they shall not prevail against you, for I am with you, says the LORD, to deliver you.

Genesis 41:46-57

The seven years of plenty that prevailed in the land of Egypt came to an end; and the seven years of famine began to come, just as Joseph said.

Romans 1:1-15

Grace to you and peace from God our Father and the Lord Jesus Christ.

1 Corinthians 4:8-20(21)

The kingdom of God depends not on talk but on power.

Monday after Lent 3
Jeremiah 7:1-15

Thus says the LORD of hosts, the God of Israel: Amend your ways and your doings, and let me dwell with you in this place.

Genesis 44:18-34

Now therefore, please let your servant remain as a slave to my lord in place of the boy; and let the boy go back with his brothers.

Romans 4:1-12

Faith was reckoned to Abraham as righteousness.

1 Corinthians 7:25-31

The present form of this world is passing away.

Monday after Lent 4
Jeremiah 16:(1-9)10-21

My eyes are on all their ways; they are not hidden from my presence, nor is their iniquity concealed from my sight.

Genesis 49:1-28

Jacob called his sons, and said "Gather around, that I may tell you what will happen to you in days to come."

Romans 7:1-12

You have died to the law through the body of Christ, so that you may belong to another, to him who has been raised from the dead in order that we may bear fruit for God.

1 Corinthians 10:14-11:1

So, whether you eat or drink, or whatever you do, do everything for the glory of God.

Monday after Lent 5

Jeremiah 24:1-10

I will give them a heart to know that I am the LORD; and they shall be my people and I will be their God, for they shall return to me with their whole heart.

Romans 9:19-33

Who indeed are you, a human being, to argue with God? Will what is molded say to the one who molds it, "Why have you made me like this?"

Exodus 4:10-20(21-26)27-31

The people believed; and when they heard that the LORD had given heed to the Israelites and that they had seen their misery, they bowed down and worshiped.

1 Corinthians 14:1-19

Pursue love and strive for the spiritual gifts.

Silence for meditation follows each reading.

RESPONSORY

You are a chosen race, a royal priesthood, a **ho**ly nation.*
Once you were not a people but now you **are** God's people.
I will take you **as** my people,*
and I will **be** your God.
I am the Lord, and I free you from the bur**dens** of slavery,*
and I will deliver **you** from bondage.
I will take you **as** my people,*
and I will **be** your God.
[LH: 1 Peter 2:9,10; see Exod. 6:7,6]

Love your enemies, do **good**, and lend,*
expecting nothing **in** return.
Be **mer**ciful,*
just as your Fa**ther** is merciful.
Then you will be children of your Fa**ther** in heaven,*
who makes the sun rise on the evil and on the good, and sends rain on the righteous and **the** unrighteous.
Be **mer**ciful,*
just as your Fa**ther** is merciful.
[LH: Luke 6:35,36; Matt. 5:45]

Antiphon to the BENEDICTUS

Monday after Lent 1

The Lord your God has led you in the wilderness in order to **hum**ble you,*
testing you to know what was **in** your heart. [Deut. 8:2]

Monday after Lent 2

Be **mer**ciful*
just as your Fa**ther** is merciful. [LH: Luke 6:36]

Monday after Lent 3

Whoever follows me will never **walk** in darkness*
but will have the **light** of life. [John 8:12]

Monday after Lent 4

Return to the **LORD** your God,*
and live be**neath** my shadow. [Hos. 14:1,7]

Monday after Lent 5

While we live we are always being given up to death for **Je**sus' sake,*
so that the life of Jesus may be made visible in our **mor**tal flesh. [2 Cor. 4:11]

Tuesdays in Lent

Antiphon to PSALM 34 *Benedicam Dominum*

Those who **seek** the LORD*
lack nothing **that** is good. [LH]

34 *In praise of God's goodness*

1 I will bless the LORD **at** all times;*
his praise shall ever be **in** my mouth.

2 I will glory **in** the LORD;*
let the humble hear **and** rejoice.

3 Proclaim with me the greatness **of** the LORD;*
let us exalt his **Name** together.

4 I sought the LORD, and he **an**swered me*
and delivered me out of **all** my terror.

5 Look upon him **and** be radiant,*
and let not your faces **be** ashamed.

6 I called in my affliction, and **the** LORD heard me*
and saved me from **all** my troubles.

7 The angel of the LORD encompasses **those** who fear him,*
and he will de**liv**er them.

8 Taste and see that the **LORD** is good;*
happy are they who **trust** in him!

9 Fear the LORD, you that **are** his saints,*
for those who fear **him** lack nothing.

10 The young lions lack and **suf**fer hunger,*
but those who seek the LORD lack nothing **that** is good.

11 Come, children, and lis**ten** to me;*
I will teach you the fear **of** the LORD.

12 Who among **you** loves life*
and desires long life to en**joy** prosperity?

13 Keep your tongue from **e**vil-speaking*
and your lips from **ly**ing words.

14 Turn from evil **and** do good;*
seek peace **and** pursue it.

15 The eyes of the LORD are up**on** the righteous,*
and his ears are open **to** their cry.

16 The face of the LORD is against those **who** do evil,*
to root out the remembrance of them **from** the earth.

17 The righteous cry, and **the** LORD hears them*
and delivers them from **all** their troubles.

18 The LORD is near to the **bro**kenhearted*
and will save those whose spir**its** are crushed.

19 Many are the troubles **of** the righteous,*
but the LORD will deliver him out **of** them all.

20 He will keep safe **all** his bones;*
not one of them **shall** be broken.

21 Evil shall **slay** the wicked,*
and those who hate the righteous **will** be punished.

22 The LORD ransoms the life **of** his servants,*
and none will be punished who **trust** in him.

Antiphon Those who **seek** the LORD*
lack nothing **that** is good.

Silence for meditation

Lord, graciously hear us, for we seek you alone. Calm our bodies and minds with the peace which passes understanding, and make us radiant with joy; through your Son, Jesus Christ our Lord. [LH, LBW]

+

Antiphon to PSALM 41 *Beautus qui intelligit*

Lord be merci**ful** to me;*
heal me, for I have **sinned** against you. [LH, PBO]

41 *Prayer of a sick person*

1 Happy are they who consider the **poor** and needy!*
the LORD will deliver them in the **time** of trouble.

2 The LORD preserves them and keeps them alive,
so that they may be happy **in** the land;*
he does not hand them over to the will **of** their enemies.

3 The LORD sustains them **on** their sickbed*
and ministers to them **in** their illness.

4 I said, "LORD, be merci**ful** to me;*
heal me, for I have **sinned** against you."

5 My enemies are saying wicked **things** about me:*
"When will he die, and **his** name perish?"

6 Even if they come to see me, they speak **emp**ty words;*
their heart collects false rumors;
they go out**side** and spread them.

7 All my enemies whisper togeth**er** about me*
and devise e**vil** against me.

8 "A deadly thing," they say, "has fas**tened** on him;*
he has taken to his bed and will never get **up** again."

9 Even my best friend, whom I trusted,
who broke **bread** with me,*
has lifted up his heel and **turned** against me.

10 But you, O LORD, be merciful to me and **raise** me up,*
and I **shall** repay them.

11 By this I know you are **pleased** with me:*
that my enemy does not triumph **o**ver me.

12 In my integrity you **hold** me fast,*
and shall set me before your **face** for ever.

13 Blessed be the LORD **God** of Israel,*
from age to age. A**men**. Amen.

Antiphon Lord be merci**ful** to me;*
heal me, for I have **sinned** against you.

Silence for meditation

Lord Jesus, healer of soul and body, you said, "Blessed are the merciful, for they shall obtain mercy." Teach us to come to the aid of the needy in a spirit of love, as we have been received and strengthened by you; and to you be the glory and praise now and for ever. [LH, LBW]

+

Stand

THE HYMN is sung.

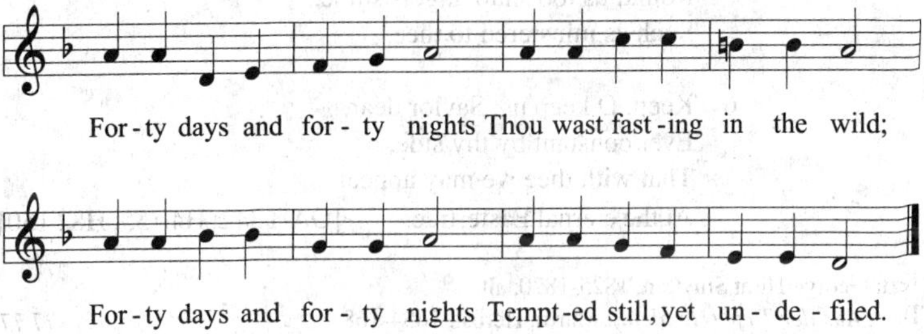

2 Sunbeams scorching all the day,
Chilly dew-drops nightly shed,
Prowling beasts about thy way,
Stones thy pillow, earth thy bed.

3 Should not we thy sorrow share
And from worldly joys abstain,
Fasting with unceasing prayer,
Strong with thee to suffer pain?

4 Then if Satan, vexing sore,
Flesh or spirit shall assail,
Thou, his vanquisher before,
Wilt not suffer us to fail.

5 So shall we have peace divine;
Holier gladness ours shall be;
Round us too shall angels shine,
Such as minstered to thee.

6 Keep, O keep us, Savior dear,
Ever constant by thy side,
That with thee we may appear
At the eternal Eastertide. [OAH 342; H40 55; H82 150]

Text: George Hunt Smyttan, 1825-1870, alt.
Tune: *Aus der Tiefe (Heinlein),* Martin Herbst, 1654-1681 77 77

Sit

One or two LESSONS are read.

Year 1

Tuesday after Lent 1
Deuteronomy 9:(1-3) 4-12

The LORD your God is not giving you this good land to occupy because of your righteousness; for you are a stubborn people.

Hebrews 3:1-11

Now Moses was faithful in all God's house as a servant, to testify to the things that would be spoken later. Christ, however, was faithful over God's house as a son, and we are his house if we hold firm the confidence and the pride that belongs to hope.

Year 2

Genesis 37:12-24

Here comes this dreamer. Come now, let us kill him and throw him into one of the pits; then we shall say that a wild animal has devoured him, and we shall see what will become of his dreams.

1 Corinthians 1:20-31

God chose what is foolish in the world to shame the wise; God chose what is weak in the world to shame the strong; God chose what is low and despised in the world, things that are not, to reduce to nothing things that are, so that no one might boast in the presence of God.

Year 1

Tuesday after Lent 2
Jeremiah 2:1-13, 29-32

My people have committed two evils: they have forsaken me, the fountain of living water, and dug out cisterns for themselves, cracked cisterns that can hold no water.

Year 2

Genesis 42:1-17

Joseph's brothers came and bowed themselves before him with their faces to the ground.

Romans 1:16-25

I am not ashamed of the gospel; it is the power of God for salvation to everyone who has faith, to the Jew first and also the Greek.

1 Corinthians 5:1-8

Therefore, let us celebrate the festival, not with the old yeast, the yeast of malice and evil, but with the unleavened bread of sincerity and truth.

Tuesday after Lent 3
Jeremiah 7:21-34

Obey my voice, and I will be your God, and you shall be my people; and walk only in the way that I command you, so that it may be well with you.

Genesis 45:1-15

I am your brother, Joseph, whom you sold into Egypt. And now do not be distressed, or angry with yourselves, because you sold me here; for God sent me before you to preserve life.

Romans 4:13-25

The promise that he would inherit the world did not come to Abraham or to his descendents through the law but through the righteousness of faith.

1 Corinthians 7:32-40

I say this for your own benefit, not to put any restraint upon you, but to promote good order and unhindered devotion to the Lord.

Tuesday after Lent 4
Jeremiah 17:19-27

Keep the sabbath day holy, as I commanded your ancestors. Yet they did not listen or incline their ear; they stiffened their necks and would not hear or receive instruction.

Genesis 49:29-50:14

After he had buried his father, Joseph returned to Egypt with his brothers and all who had gone up with him to bury his father.

Romans 7:13-25

I can will what is right, but I cannot do it. For I do not do the good I want, but the evil I do not want is what I do. Now if I do what I do not want, it is no longer I that do it, but sin that dwells within me.

1 Corinthians 11:2-34

As often as you eat this bread and drink the cup, you proclaim the Lord's death until he comes

Tuesday after Lent 5

Jeremiah 25:8-17

Thus the LORD, the God of Israel, said to me: Take from my hand this cup of the wine of wrath, and make all the nations to whom I send you drink it. They shall drink and stagger and go out of their minds because of the sword that I am sending among them.

Exodus 5:1-6:1

The LORD said to Moses, "Now you shall see what I will do to Pharaoh: Indeed, by a mighty hand he will let them go; by a mighty hand he will drive them out of his land.

Romans 10:1-13

The word is near you, on your lips and in your heart (that is, the word of faith that we proclaim); because if you confess with your lips that Jesus is Lord and believe in your heart that God raised him from the dead, you will be saved.

1 Corinthians 14:20-33a, 39-40

Do not be children in your thinking; rather, be infants in evil, but in thinking be adults.

Silence for meditation follows each reading.

RESPONSORY

This time of fasting opens the gates of **hea**ven to us;*
let us welcome **it** and pray,
that when **Eas**ter comes*
we may share the joy of the **ris**en Lord.
In **all** we do,*
let us show that we are the ser**vants** of God,
that when **Eas**ter comes*
we may share the joy of the **ris**en Lord. [LH]

The message about the cross is foolishness to those **who** are perishing,*
but to those who are being saved it is the pow**er** of God.
We proclaim Christ crucified, a stumbling block to Jews and foolish**ness** to Gentiles,*
but to those who are being saved it is the pow**er** of God.
[LH: 1 Cor. 1:18,23]

Antiphon to the BENEDICTUS

Tuesday after Lent 1

Lord, teach **us** to pray,*
as John taught **his** disciples. [LH: Luke 11:1]

Tuesday after Lent 2

You have one teacher, and he **is** in heaven:*
Jesus **Christ** your Lord. [LH: see Matt. 23:8-9]

Tuesday after Lent 3

I do not tell you to forgive only **se**ven times,*
but seventy-**se**ven times. [LH: see Matt 18:22]

Tuesday after Lent 4

For to me liv**ing** is Christ,*
and dy**ing** is gain. [Phil. 1:21]

Tuesday after Lent 5

When you have lifted up the **Son** of Man,*
then you will realize that **I** am he. [LH: John 8:28]

Wednesdays in Lent

Antiphon to PSALM 5 *Verba mea auribus*

Lead me, O LORD, in your **right**eousness;*
make your way **straight** before me.

5 *Morning prayer for protection*

1 Give ear to my **words**, O LORD;*
consider my **med**itation.

2 Hearken to my cry for help, my King **and** my God,*
for I make my **prayer** to you.

3 In the morning, LORD, you **hear** my voice;*
early in the morning I make my appeal and **watch** for you.

4 For you are not a God who takes pleas**ure** in wickedness,*
and evil cannot **dwell** with you.

5 Braggarts cannot stand **in** your sight;*
you hate all those **who** work wickedness.

6 You destroy those **who** speak lies;*
the bloodthirsty and deceitful, O LORD, **you** abhor.

7 But as for me, through the greatness of your mercy
I will go in**to** your house;*
I will bow down toward your holy temple in **awe** of you.

8 Lead me, O LORD, in your righteousness,
because of those who lie in **wait** for me;*
make your way **straight** before me.

9 For there is no truth **in** their mouth;*
there is destruction **in** their heart;

10 Their throat is an **o**pen grave;*
they flatter **with** their tongue.

11 Declare them guilt**y**, O God;*
let them fall, because **of** their schemes.

12 Because of their many transgressions **cast** them out,*
for they have re**belled** against you.

13 But all who take refuge in you **will** be glad;*
they will sing out their **joy** for ever.

14 You will **shel**ter them,*
so that those who love your Name may ex**ult** in you.

15 For you, O LORD, will **bless** the righteous;*
you will defend them with your favor as **with** a shield.

Antiphon Lead me, O LORD, in your **right**eousness;*
make your way **straight** before me.

Silence for meditation

Holy Lord, all justice and all goodness come from you; you hate evil and abhor lies: Lead us in the path of justice, so that all who hope in you may with the Church rejoice in your Son, Jesus Christ our Lord. [LH, LBW]

+

Antiphon to PSALM 137 *Super flumina*

If I forget you, **O** Jerusalem,*
let my right hand for**get** its skill. [LH, PBO]

137 *Lament of the exiles*

1 By the waters of Babylon we sat **down** and wept,*
when we remembered **you**, O Zion.

2 As for our harps, we **hung** them up*
on the trees in the midst **of** that land.

3 For those who led us away captive asked us for a song,
and our oppressors **called** for mirth:*
"Sing us one of the **songs** of Zion."

4 How shall we sing **the** LORD's song*
upon an **a**lien soil?

5 If I forget you, **O** Jerusalem,*
let my right hand for**get** its skill.

6 Let my tongue cleave to the roof of my mouth
if I do not re**mem**ber you,*
if I do not set Jerusalem above my **high**est joy.

7 Remember the day of Jerusalem, O LORD,
against the peo**ple** of Edom,*
who said, "Down with it! down with it!
even **to** the ground!"

8 O Daughter of Babylon, doomed **to** destruction,*
happy the one who pays you back
for what you have **done** to us!

9 Happy shall he be who takes your **lit**tle ones*
and dashes them a**gainst** the rock!

Antiphon If I forget you, **O** Jerusalem,*
let my right hand for**get** its skill.

Silence for meditation

Heavenly Father, you willed to make us citizens of your country and singers of your mercy: Do not abandon us in the land of exile, but bring us to the heavenly Jerusalem chanting your praise; through Jesus Christ our Lord. [LHd, LBW]

+

Stand

THE HYMN is sung. *Wer Gott vertraut, hat wohlgebaut*

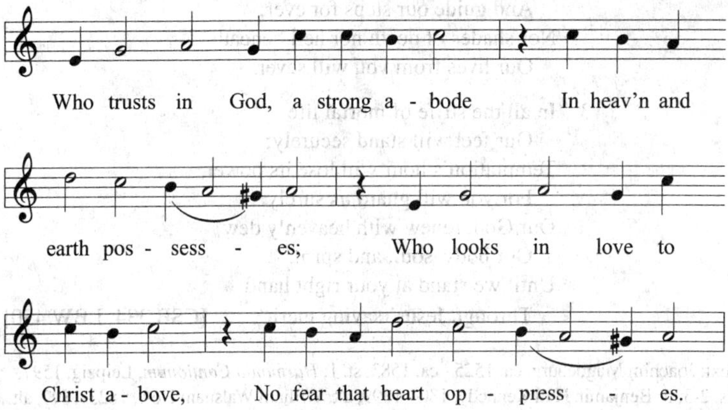

2 Though Satan's wrath beset our path
   And worldly scorn assail us,
While you are near, we shall not fear;
   Your strength will never fail us.
Your rod and staff will keep us safe
   And guide our steps for ever;
Nor shades of death nor hell beneath
   Our lives from you will sever.

3 In all the strife of mortal life
   Our feet will stand securely;
Temptation's hour will lose its power,
   For you will guard us surely.
Our God, renew with heavenly dew
   Our body, soul, and spirit,
Until we stand at your right hand
   Through Jesus' saving merit. [CSB 334, LBW 450]

Text: Joachim Magdeburg, ca. 1525 - ca. 1583, st. 1; *Harmonia Cantionum,* Leipzig, 1597, sts. 2-3; tr. Benjamin Hall Kennedy, 1804-1899, alt. William Walsham How, 1823-1897, alt.
Tune: *Was mein Gott will,* Claude de Sermisy, ca. 1490-1572 87 87 D

Sit

One or two LESSONS are read.

Year 1	Year 2
Ash Wednesday	
Jonah 3:1-4:11	Amos 5:6-15
When God saw what they did, how they turned from their evil ways, God changed his mind about the calamities that he had said he would bring upon them; and he did not do it.	Seek good and not evil, that you may live; and so the LORD, the God of hosts, will be with you.
Hebrews 12:1-14	Hebrews 12:1-14
Let us run with perseverence the race that is set before us, looking to Jesus the pioneer and perfecter of our faith, who for the sake of the joy that was set before him endured the cross, disregarding its shame, and has taken his seat at the right hand of the throne of God.	Let us run with perseverence the race that is set before us, looking to Jesus the pioneer and perfecter of faith, who for the sake of the joy that was set before him endured the cross, disregarding its shame, and has taken his seat at the right hand of the throne of God.
Wednesday after Lent 1	
Deuteronomy 9:13-21	Genesis 37:25-36
The LORD said to me, "I have seen that this people is indeed a stubborn people.	They drew Joseph up, lifting him out of the pit, and sold him to the Ishmaelites for twenty pieces of silver. And they took Joseph to Egypt.

Hebrews 3:12-19

Take care, brothers and sisters, that none of you may have an evil, unbelieving heart that turns away from the living God.

1 Corinthians 2:1-13

I decided to know nothing among you except Jesus Christ, and him crucified.

Wednesday after Lent 2

Jeremiah 3:6-18

I will not be angry forever. Only acknowledge your guilt, that you have rebelled against the LORD your God.

Genesis 42:18-28

"Alas, we are paying the penalty for what we did to our brother."

Romans 1:(26-27)28-2:11

Be your hard and impenitent heart you are storing up wrath for yourself on the day of wrath, when God's righteous judgment will be revealed.

1 Corinthians 5:9-6:11

You were washed, you were sanctified, you were justified in the name of the Lord Jesus Christ and in the Spirit of God.

Wednesday after Lent 3

Jeremiah 8:4-7,18-9:6

Why then has this people turned away in perpetual backsliding? They have held fast to deceit, they have refused to return.

Genesis 45:16-28

Israel said, "Enough! My son Joseph is still alive. I must go and see him before I die."

Romans 5:1-11

If while we were enemies, we were reconciled to God through the death

1 Corinthians 8:1-13

For us there is one God, the Father, from whom are all things and for

of his Son, much more surely, having been reconciled, will we be saved by his life.

whom we exist, and one Lord, Jesus Christ, through whom are all things and through whom we exist.

Wednesday after Lent 4

Jeremiah 18:1-11

Turn now, all of you from your evil way, and amend your ways and your doings.

Romans 8:1-11

If the Spirit of him who raised Jesus from the dead dwells in you, he who raised Christ from the dead will give life to your mortal bodies also through his Spirit that dwells in you.

Genesis 50:15-26

Even though you intended to do harm to me, God intended it for good.

1 Corinthians 12:1-11

Now there are varieties of gifts, but the same Spirit.

Wednesday after Lent 5

Jeremiah 25:30-38

The LORD will roar from on high, and from his holy habitation utter his voice; he will roar mightily against his fold, and shout, like those who tread grapes, against all the inhabitants of the earth.

Romans 10:14-21

I have been found by those who did not seek me; I have shown myself to those who did not ask for me.

Exodus 7:8-24

Moses and Aaron did just as the LORD commanded. In the sight of Pharaoh and of his officials he lifted up the staff and struck the water in the river, and all the water in the river was turned into blood.

2 Corinthians 2:14-3:6

Thanks be to God, who in Christ always leads us in triumphal procession, and through us spreads in every place the fragrance that comes from knowing him.

Silence for meditation follows each reading.

RESPONSORY

I will establish a new covenant with the **house** of Israel.
I will put my laws in their minds and write them **on** their hearts
  not with ink but with the Spirit of the **liv**ing God.
I will write my law not on tablets of stone but on tablets of **hu**man hearts*
  not with ink but with the Spirit of the **liv**ing God.
[LH: Heb 8:8,10; 2 Cor. 3:3]

The Lord says, This is the fast **that** I choose:*
to share your bread **with** the hungry.
  Then you shall call, and the **Lord** will answer;*
  you shall cry for help, and he will say, **Here** I am.
When the Son of Man comes in his glory, he will say to those at **his** right hand,*
Come, you that are blessed of my Father, inherit the kingdom, for I was hungry and you **gave** me food.
  Then you shall call, and the **Lord** will answer;*
  you shall cry for help, and he will say, **Here** I am.
[LH: Isa. 58:6,7,9; Matt. 25:31,34,35]

Antiphon to the BENEDICTUS

Ash Wednesday

Whenev**er** you fast,*
do not look dismal **like** the hypocrites. [LH: Matt. 6:16]

Wednesday after Lent 1

If any want to be**come** my followers,*
let them deny themselves and take up their cross
and **fol**low me. [Matt. 16:24]

Wednesday after Lent 2

The Son of Man came not to be served **but** to serve,*
and to give his life as a ran**som** for many. [LH: Matt. 20:28]

Wednesday after Lent 3

Do not think that I have come to abolish the law **and** the prophets;*
I have not come to abolish but **to** fulfill. [LH: Matt. 5:17]

Wednesday after Lent 4

Anyone who hears my word and believes **him** who sent me*
has e**ter**nal life. [LH: John 5:24]

Wednesday after Lent 5

Those who belong **to** Christ Jesus*
have crucified the flesh with its passions **and** desires.
[Gal. 5:24]

Thursdays in Lent

Antiphon to PSALM 35 *Judica, Domine*

O Lord, be not **far** from me;*
rise **up** to help me. [LH, PBO]

35 *Appeal for vindication*

1 Fight those who fight **me**, O LORD;*
attack those who are at**tack**ing me.

2 Take up **shield** and armor*
and rise **up** to help me.

3 Draw the sword and bar the way against those **who** pursue me;*
say to my soul, "I am **your** salvation."

4 Let those who seek after my life be **shamed** and humbled;*
let those who plot my ruin fall back and **be** dismayed.

5 Let them be like chaff be**fore** the wind,*
and let the angel of the LORD drive **them** away.

6 Let their way be **dark** and slippery,*
and let the angel of the **LORD** pursue them.

7 For they have secretly spread a net for me with**out** a cause;*
without a cause they have dug a pit to take **me** alive.

8 Let ruin come upon them **un**awares;*
let them be caught in the net they hid;
let them fall into the **pit** they dug.

9 Then I will be joyful **in** the LORD;*
I will glory **in** his victory.

10 My very bones will say, "LORD, **who** is like you?*
You deliver the poor from those who are too strong for them,
the poor and needy from **those** who rob them."

11 Malicious witnesses rise **up** against me;*
they charge me with matters I know noth**ing** about.

12 They pay me evil in ex**change** for good;*
my soul is full **of** despair.

13 But when they were sick I **dressed** in sack-cloth*
and humbled my**self** by fasting;

14 I prayed with my whole heart,
as one would for a friend **or** a brother;*
I behaved like one who mourns for his mother,
bowed **down** and grieving.

15 But when I stumbled, they were glad and gathered together;
they gath**ered** against me;*
strangers whom I did not know tore me to pieces and **would** not stop.

16 They put me to the **test** and mocked me;*
they gnashed at me **with** their teeth.

17 O Lord, how long will **you** look on?*
rescue me from the roaring beasts,
and my life from **the** young lions.

18 I will give you thanks in the great **con**gregation;*
I will praise you in the **might**y throng.

19 Do not let my treacherous foes rejoice **o**ver me,*
nor let those who hate me without a cause wink **at** each other.

20 For they do not **plan** for peace,*
but invent deceitful schemes against the quiet **in** the land.

21 They opened their mouths at **me** and said,*
"Aha! we saw it with **our** own eyes."

22 You saw it, O LORD; do **not** be silent;*
O Lord, be not **far** from me.

23 Awake, arise, **to** my cause!*
to my defense, my God **and** my Lord!

24 Give me justice, O LORD my God,
according **to** your righteousness;*
do not let them triumph **o**ver me.

25 Do not let them say in their hearts,
"Aha! just **what** we want!"*
Do not let them say, "We have swal**lowed** him up."

26 Let all who rejoice at my ruin be ashamed **and** disgraced;*
let those who boast against me be clothed with
dis**may** and shame.

27 Let those who favor my cause sing out with joy **and** be glad;*
let them say always, "Great is the LORD,
who desires the prosperity **of** his servant."

28 And my tongue shall be talking **of** your righteousness*
and of your praise all **the** day long.

Antiphon O Lord, be not **far** from me;*
rise **up** to help me.

Silence for meditation

Lord God, you rose to the aid of your beloved Son against those who unjustly sought his life: Look on your Church as we journey to you, and rescue the poor from their oppressors, that they may tell of your righteousness and your praise; through your Son, Jesus Christ our Lord.

[LH, LBW]

+

Antiphon to PSALM 44 *Deus, auribus*

Rise **up**, and help us,*
and save us, for the sake of your **stead**fast love. [LH, PBO]

44 *God's people in time of disaster*

1 We have heard with our ears, O God,
our forefa**thers** have told us,*
the deeds you did in their days,
in the **days** of old.

2 How with your hand you drove the peoples out
and planted our forefathers **in** the land;*
how you destroyed nations and made your **peo**ple flourish.

3 For they did not take the land by their sword,
nor did their arm win the victo**ry** for them;*

but your right hand, your arm, and the light of your countenance,
because you **fa**vored them.

4 You are my King **and** my God;*
you command victo**ries** for Jacob.

5 Through you we pushed back our **ad**versaries;*
through your Name we trampled on those who rose **up** against us.

6 For I do not rely **on** my bow,*
and my sword does not give **me** the victory.

7 Surely, you gave us victory over our **ad**versaries*
and put those who hate **us** to shame.

8 Every day we glo**ried** in God,*
and we will praise your **Name** for ever.

9 Nevertheless, you have rejected and **hum**bled us*
and do not go forth **with** our armies.

10 You have made us fall back before our **ad**versary,*
and our enemies have **plun**dered us.

11 You have made us like sheep **to** be eaten*
and have scattered us a**mong** the nations.

12 You are selling your people **for** a trifle*
and are making no profit on the **sale** of them.

13 You have made us the scorn **of** our neighbors,*
a mockery and derision to **those** around us.

14 You have made us a byword a**mong** the nations,*
a laughingstock a**mong** the peoples.

15 My humiliation is daily before me,*
and shame has covered my face;

16 Because of the taunts of the mockers **and** blasphemers,*
because of the enemy **and** avenger.

17 All this has **come** upon us;*
yet we have not forgotten you,
nor have we be**trayed** your covenant.

18 Our heart nev**er** turned back,*
nor did our footsteps stray **from** your path;

19 Though you thrust us down into a **place** of misery,*
and covered us over **with** deep darkness.

20 If we have forgotten the Name **of** our God,*
or stretched out our hands to **some** strange god,

21 Will not God **find** it out?*
for he knows the secrets **of** the heart.

22 Indeed, for your sake we are killed all **the** day long;*
we are accounted as sheep **for** the slaughter.

23 Awake, O Lord! Why **are** you sleeping?*
Arise! Do not reject **us** for ever.

24 Why have you hid**den** your face*
and forgotten our affliction **and** oppression?

25 We sink down in**to** the dust;*
our body cleaves **to** the ground.

26 Rise **up**, and help us,*
and save us, for the sake of your **stead**fast love.

Antiphon Rise **up** and help us,*
and save us, for the sake of your **stead**fast love.

Silence for meditation

Lord, rise up and come to our aid. You are the king who knows the secrets of our hearts; fill us with the light of truth, and with your strong arm lead us to freedom, as you mightily delivered our ancestors; for the sake of your Son, Jesus Christ our Lord. [LH, LBW]

+

Stand

THE HYMN is sung. *O Gott, du frommer Gott*

2 And grant me, Lord, to do
With ready heart and willing
Whatever you command
My calling here fulfilling,
And do it when I ought,
With all my strength, and bless
The work I thus have wrought,
For you must give success.

3 Keep me from saying words
That later need recalling;
Guard me lest idle speech
May from my lips be falling;
And grant, when in my place
I must and ought to speak,
My words due power and grace;
Nor let me wound the weak.

4 When dangers gather round,
Yet keep me calm and fearless;
And help me bear the cross
When life is dark and cheerless;
And overcome my foe
With words and actions kind;
When counsel I would know,
Good counsel let me find.

5 Let nothing that may chance,
Me from my Savior sever;
And dying, with him, take
My soul to you for ever;
And let my body have
A quiet resting place
Within a Christian grave,
And let it sleep in peace.

6 And when the day is come,
And all the dead are waking,
Reach down to me your hand,
Yourself my slumbers breaking;
Then let me hear your voice
And change this earthly frame,
And bid my eye rejoice
With those who love your Name. [LBW 504]

Text: Johann Heermann, 1585-1647; tr. Catherine Winkworth 1829-1878

Tune: *Was frag ich nach der Welt,* Ahasuerus Fritsch, 1629-1701 67 67 66 66

Sit

One or two LESSONS are read.

Year 1

Thursday after Ash Wednesday
Deuteronomy 7:6-11

You are a people holy to the LORD your God; the LORD your God has chosen you out of all the peoples on earth to be his people, his treasured possession.

Titus 1:1-16

To the pure all things are pure, but to the corrupt and unbelieving nothing is pure. Their very minds and consciences are corrupted.

Year 2

Habakkuk 3:1-10 (11-15) 16-18

O LORD, I have heard of your renown, and I stand in awe, O LORD, of your work. In our own time revive it; in our own time make it known; in wrath may you remember mercy.

Philippians 3:12-21

I press on toward the goal for the prize of the heavenly call of God in Christ Jesus.

Thursday after Lent 1
Deuteronomy 9:23-10:5

Lord GOD, do not destroy the people who are your very own possession, whom you redeemed in your greatness, whom you brought out of Egypt with a mighty hand.

Hebrews 4:1-10

While the promise of entering his rest is still open, let us take care that none of you should seem to have failed to reach it.

Genesis 39:1-23

The LORD was with Joseph, and he became a successful man. . . . His master saw that the LORD was with him, and that the LORD caused all that he did to prosper in his hands.

1 Corinthians 2:14-3:15

No one can lay any foundation other than the one that has been laid; that foundation is Jesus Christ

Thursday after Lent 2
Jeremiah 4:9-10, 19-28

I looked on the earth, and lo, it was waste and void; and to the heavens, and they had no light.

Romans 2:12-24

All who have sinned apart from the law will also perish apart from the law, and all who have sinned under the law will be judged by the law.

Genesis 42:18-28

Bring your youngest brother to me, and I shall know that you are not spies but honest men.

1 Corinthians 6:12-20

Do you not know that your body is a temple of the Holy Spirit within you, which you have from God and that you are not your own? For you were bought with a price.

Thursday after Lent 3
Jeremiah 10:11-24

Correct me, O LORD, but in just

Genesis 46:1-7, 28-34

I myself will go down with you to

measure; not in your anger, or you will bring me to nothing.

Egypt, and I will also bring you up again.

Romans 5:12-21

If the many died through the one man's trespass, much more surely have the grace of God and the free gift in the grace of the one man, Jesus Christ, abounded for the many.

1 Corinthians 9:1-15

If I am not an apostle to others, at least I am to you; for you are the seal of my apostleship in the Lord.

Thursday after Lent 4
Jeremiah 22:13-23

Woe to him who builds his house by unrighteousness, and his upper rooms by injustice; who makes his neighbors work for nothing, and does not give them their wages.

Exodus 1:6-22

Now a new king arose over Egypt, who did not know Joseph.

Romans 8:12-27

I consider that the sufferings of this present time are not worth comparing with the glory about to be revealed in us.

1 Corinthians 12:12-26

In the one Spirit we were all baptized into one body--Jews or Greeks, slaves or free--and we were all made to drink of one Spirit.

Thursday after Lent 5
Jeremiah 26:1-16 (17-24)

Stand in the court of the LORD's house, and speak to all the cities of Judah that come to worship in the house of the LORD; speak to them all the words that I command you; do not hold back a word.

Exodus 7:25-8:19

The magicians said to Pharaoh, "This is the finger of God!" But Pharaoh's heart was hardened, and he would not listen to them, just as the LORD had said.

Romans 11:1-12

So too at the present time there is a remnant, chosen by grace.

2 Corinthians 3:7-18

We, seeing the glory of the Lord as though reflected in a mirror, are being transformed into the same image from one degree of glory to another; for this comes from the Lord, the Spirit.

Silence for meditation follows each reading.

RESPONSORY

The whole law is summed up in a sin**gle** commandment,*
You shall love your neighbor **as** yourself.
Just as **I** have loved you,*
you also should love **one** another.
I give you a **new** commandment,*
that you love **one** another.
Just as **I** have loved you,*
you also should love **one** another.
[LH: Gal. 5:14; John 13:34]

You gave your people the **food** of angels,*
and from heaven supplied them with bread read**y** to eat,
providing **ev**ery pleasure*
and suited to **ev**ery taste.
It was not Moses who gave you the **bread** from heaven;*
my Father gives you the true **bread** from heaven,
providing **ev**ery pleasure*
and suited to **ev**ery taste.
[LH: Wisdom 16:20; John 6:32]

Antiphon to the BENEDICTUS

Thursday after Ash Wednesday

Store up for yourselves treas**ures** in heaven,*
where neither moth nor **rust** consumes [Matt. 6:20]

Thursday after Lent 1

You **need** endurance,*
so that when you have done the will of God,
you may receive **what** was promised. [Heb. 10:36]

Thursday after Lent 2

Do not be conformed to this world,
but be transformed by the renewing **of** your minds,*
so that you may discern what is the will of God—
what is good and accepta**ble** and perfect. [Rom. 12:2]

Thursday after Lent 3

As aliens and exiles, abstain from the desires **of** the flesh*
that wage war a**gainst** the soul. [1 Peter 2:11]

Thursday after Lent 4

In a dry place there will be **streams** of water*
and the shade of a great rock in a **wear**y land. [see Isa. 32:2]

Thursday after Lent 5

You were **sold** for nothing,*
and you will be redeemed **with**out money. [Isa. 52:3]

Fridays in Lent

Antiphon to PSALM 22 *Deus, Deus meus*

He was despised **and** rejected*
a man of suffering and acquainted **with** infirmity. [LH, PBO]

22 *God hears the suffering cry of his Holy One*

1 My God, my God, why have you for**sak**en me*
and are so far from my cry
and from the words of **my** distress?

2 O my God, I cry in the daytime, but you **do** not answer;*
by night as well, but I **find** no rest.

3 Yet you are the **Ho**ly One,*
enthroned upon the prais**es** of Israel.

4 Our forefathers put their **trust** in you;*
they trusted, and you de**liv**ered them.

5 They cried out to you and **were** delivered;*
they trusted in you and were not **put** to shame.

6 But as for me, I am a worm **and** no man,*
scorned by all and despised **by** the people.

7 All who see me laugh **me** to scorn;*
they curl their lips and wag **their** heads, saying,

8 “He trusted in the LORD; let him de**li**ver him;*
let him rescue him, if he de**lights** in him.”

9 Yet you are he who took me out **of** the womb,*
and kept me safe upon my **moth**er's breast.

10 I have been entrusted to you ever since **I** was born;*
you were my God when I was still in my **moth**er's womb.

11 Be not far from me, for trou**ble** is near,*
and there is **none** to help.

12 Many young bulls en**cir**cle me;*
strong bulls of Ba**shan** surround me.

13 They open wide their **jaws** at me,*
like a ravening and a **roar**ing lion.

14 I am poured out like water;
all my bones are **out** of joint;*
my heart within my breast is **melt**ing wax.

15 My mouth is dried out like a pot-sherd;
my tongue sticks to the roof **of** my mouth;*
and you have laid me in the dust **of** the grave.

16 Packs of dogs close me in,
and gangs of evildoers cir**cle** around me;*
they pierce my hands and my feet;
I can count **all** my bones.

17 They stare and gloat **o**ver me;*
they divide my garments among them;
they cast lots **for** my clothing.

18 Be not far a**way**, O LORD;*
you are my strength; hast**en** to help me.

19 Save me **from** the sword,*
my life from the power **of** the dog.

20 Save me from the **li**on's mouth,*
my wretched body from the horns **of** wild bulls.

21 I will declare your Name **to** my brethren;*
in the midst of the congregation **I** will praise you.

22 Praise the LORD, **you** that fear him;*
stand in awe of him, O offspring of Israel;
all you of Jacob's **line**, give glory.

23 For he does not despise nor abhor the poor in their poverty;
neither does he hide his **face** from them;*
but when they cry to **him** he hears them.

24 My praise is of him in the **great** assembly;*
I will perform my vows in the presence of those
who **wor**ship him.

25 The poor shall eat and be satisfied,
and those who seek the **LORD** shall praise him:*
"May your heart **live** for ever!"

26 All the ends of the earth shall remember and turn **to** the LORD,*
and all the families of the nations shall **bow** before him.

27 For kingship belongs **to** the LORD;*
he rules o**ver** the nations.

28 To him alone all who sleep in the earth bow **down** in worship;*
all who go down to the dust **fall** before him.

29 My soul shall live for him; my descend**ants** shall serve him;*
they shall be known as the **LORD's** for ever.

30 They shall come and make known to a people **yet** unborn*
the saving deeds that **he** has done.

Antiphon He was despised **and** rejected*
a man of suffering and acquainted **with** infirmity.

Silence for meditation

Father, when your Son was handed over to torture and felt abandoned by you, he cried out from the cross. Then death was destroyed, and life was restored. By his death and resurrection save the poor, lift up the downtrodden, break the chains of the oppressed, that your Church may sing your praises; through your Son, Jesus Christ our Lord. [LH, LBW]

+

Antiphon to PSALM 27 *Dominus illuminatio*

In the **day** of trouble*
he will keep me safe **in** his shelter.

27 *Triumphant trust in God*

1 The LORD is my light and my salvation;
whom then **shall** I fear?*
The LORD is the strength of my life;
of whom then shall I **be** afraid?

2 When evildoers came upon me to eat **up** my flesh,*
it was they, my foes and my adversaries, who
stumbled and fell.

3 Though an army should en**camp** against me,*
yet my heart shall not **be** afraid;

4 And though war should rise **up** against me,*
yet will I put my **trust** in him.

5 One thing have I asked of the LORD;
one **thing** I seek;*
that I may dwell in the house of the LORD all the days **of** my life;

6 To behold the fair beauty **of** the LORD*
and to seek him **in** his temple.

7 For in the day of trouble he shall keep me safe **in** his shelter;*
he shall hide me in the secrecy of his dwelling
and set me high up**on** a rock.

8 Even now he lifts **up** my head*
above my enemies **round** about me.

9 Therefore I will offer in his dwelling an oblation
with sounds **of** great gladness;*
I will sing and make music **to** the LORD.

10 Hearken to my voice, O LORD, **when** I call;*
have mercy on me and **an**swer me.

11 You speak in my heart and say, **"Seek** my face."*
Your face, LORD, **will** I seek.

12 Hide not your **face** from me,*
nor turn away your servant **in** displeasure.

13 You have been my helper;
cast me **not** away;*
do not forsake me, O God of **my** salvation.

14 Though my father and my moth**er** forsake me,*
the LORD **will** sustain me.

15 Show me your **way**, O LORD;*
lead me on a level path, because **of** my enemies.

16 Deliver me not into the hand of my **ad**versaries,*
for false witnesses have risen up against me,
and also those **who** speak malice.

17 What if I had not believed
that I should see the goodness **of** the LORD*
in the land **of** the living!

18 O tarry and await the LORD's pleasure;
be strong, and he shall com**fort** your heart;*
wait patiently **for** the LORD.

Antiphon In the **day** of trouble*
he will keep me safe **in** his shelter.

Silence for meditation

Gracious Father, protector of those who hope in you, you heard the cry of your Son and kept him safe in your shelter in the day of evil: Grant that your servants who seek your face in times of trouble may see your goodness in the land of the living, through your Son, Jesus Christ our Lord.

[LH, LBW]

+

Stand

THE HYMN is sung.

2 O aweful Love, which found no room
In life where sin denied thee
And, doomed to death, must bring to doom
The power which crucified thee.
Till not a stone was left on stone,
And all those nations' pride, o'erthrown,
Went down to dust beside thee!

3 New advent of the love of Christ,
Will we again refuse thee,
Till in the night of hate and war
We perish as we lose thee?
From old unfaith our souls release
To seek the kingdom of thy peace,
By which alone we choose thee.

4 O wounded hands of Jesus, build
In us thy new creation;
Our pride is dust, our vaunt is stilled;
We wait thy revelation.
O Love that triumphs over loss,
We bring our hearts before thy cross
To finish thy salvation. [H82 598, LBW421]

Text: Walter Russell Bowie, 1882-1969, alt.

Tune: *Mit Freuden zart,* from *Trente quatre pseaumes de David,* Geneva 1551 87 87 887

Sit

One or two LESSONS are read.

Year 1

Friday after Ash Wednesday
Deuteronomy 7:12-16

If you heed these ordinances, by diligently observing them, the LORD your God will maintain with you the covenant loyalty that he swore to your ancestors.

Titus 2:1-15

The grace of God has appeared, bringing salvation to all, training us to renouce impiety and worldly passions, and in the present age to live lives that are self-controlled, upright, and godly, while we wait for the blessed hope and the manifestation of the glory of our great God and Savior, Jesus Christ.

Friday after Lent 1
Deuteronomy 10:12-22

What does the LORD your God require of you? Only to fear the LORD your God, to walk in all his ways, to love him, to serve the LORD your God with all your heart and with all your soul, and to keep the commandments of the LORD your God.

Year 2

Ezekiel 18:1-4, 25-32

Cast away from you all the transgressions that you have committed against me, and get yourselves a new heart and a new spirit!

Philippians 4:1-9

Whatever is true, whatever is honorable, whatever is just, whatever is pure, whatever is pleasing, whatever is commendable, if there is any excellence and if there is anything worthy of praise, think about these things.

Genesis 40:1-23

"We have had dreams, and there is no one to interpret them." And Joseph said to them, "Do not interpretations belong to God? Please tell them to me."

Hebrews 4:11-16

We do not have a high priest who is unable to sympathize with our weaknesses, but we have one who in every respect has been tested as we are, yet without sin.

1 Corinthians 3:16-23

Do you not know that you are God's temple and that God's Spirit dwells in you?

Friday after Lent 2

Jeremiah 5:1-9

You have struck them, but they felt no anguish; you have consumed them, but they refused to take correction.

Genesis 43:1-15

The men took the present and they took double the money with them, as well as Benjamin. Then they went on their way down to Egypt, and stood before Joseph.

Romans 2:25-3:18

All have turned aside, together they have become worthless; there is no one who shows kindness, there is not even one.

1 Corinthians 7:1-9

Each has a particular gift from God, one having one kind and another a different kind.

Friday after Lent 3

Jeremiah 11:1-8,14-17(18-20)

I solemnly warned your ancestors when I brought them up out of the land of Egypt, warning them persistently, even to this day, saying, Obey my voice. Yet they did not obey or incline their ear.

Genesis 47:1-26

Joseph settled his father and his brothers, and granted them a holding in the land of Egypt, in the best part of the land.

Romans 6:1-11

We have been buried with him by baptism into death, so that, just as Christ was raised from the dead by the glory of the Father, so we too might walk in newness of life.

Friday after Lent 4
Jeremiah 23:1-8

I will raise up shepherds over them who will shepherd them, and they shall not fear any longer, or be dismayed, nor shall any be missing, says the LORD.

Romans 8:28-37

I am convinced that neither death, nor life, nor angels, nor rulers, nor things present, nor things to come, nor powers, nor height, nor depth, nor anything else in all creation, will be able to separate us from the love of God in Christ Jesus our Lord.

Friday after Lent 5
Jeremiah 29:1(2-3)4-14

I know the plans I have for you, says the LORD, plans for your welfare and not for harm, to give you a future with hope.

1 Corinthians 9:16-27

Do you not know that in a race the runners all compete, but only one receives the prize? Run in such a way you may win it.

Exodus 2:1-22

When the child grew up, she brought him to Pharaoh's daughter, and she took him as her son. She named him Moses, "Because," she said, "I drew him out of the water."

1 Corinthians 12:27-13:3

If I give away all my possessions, and if I hand over my body so that I may boast, but do not have love, I gain nothing.

Exodus 9:13-35

Thus says the LORD, the God of the Hebrews: Let my people go, so that they may worship me.

Romans 11:13-24

Note then the kindness and the severity of God: severity toward those who have fallen, but God's kindness toward you, provided you continue in his kindness.

2 Corinthians 4:1-12

While we live, we are always being given up to death for Jesus' sake, so that the life of Jesus may be made visible in our mortal flesh.

Silence for meditation follows each reading.

RESPONSORY

Why have you forgotten **us** completely?*
Why have you forsaken us these **man**y days?
Restore us to your**self**,
O Lord,*
that we may **be** restored.
O **Lord**, save us!*
We are perishing!
Restore us to your**self**,
O Lord,*
that we may **be** restored.

[LH: Lam. 5:20; Matt 8:25]

The Lord is full of compassion and mercy, slow to anger and **of** great kindness.*
He will not always accuse us nor will he keep his an**ger** for ever.
For he himself knows whereof **we** are made;*
he remembers that we **are** but dust.
As a father cares **for** his children,*
so does the Lord care for **those** who fear him.
For he himself knows whereof **we** are made;*
he remembers that we **are** but dust.

[LH:Ps. 103:8,9,14,13]

Antiphon to the BENEDICTUS

Friday after Ash Wednesday

We are aliens and transients before you, as were **all** our ancestors;*
our days on the earth are like a shadow, and there **is** no hope.
[1 Chron. 29:15]

Friday after Lent 1

Unless your righteousness exceeds that of the **scribes** and Pharisees,*
you will never enter the king**dom** of heaven. [LH: Matt. 5:20]

Friday after Lent 2

Do not neglect to do good and to share **what** you have,*
for such sacrifices are pleas**ing** to God. [Heb. 13:16]

Friday after Lent 3

Teacher, which commandment in the law **is** the greatest?*
You shall love the Lord your God with **all** your heart.
[LH: Matt. 22:36-37]

Friday after Lent 4

God will fully satisfy every **need** of yours*
according to his riches in glory **in** Christ Jesus. [Phil. 4:19]

Friday after Lent 5

Jesus died to gather **in**to one*
the dispersed child**ren** of God. [John 11:52]

Saturdays in Lent

Antiphon to PSALM 37 *Noli oemulari*

Commit your way **to** the LORD*
and put your **trust** in him. [LH, PBO]

37 *The destiny of the wicked and the good*

1 Do not fret yourself because of **e**vildoers;*
do not be jealous of those **who** do wrong.

2 For they shall soon wither **like** the grass,*
and like the green grass **fade** away.

3 Put your trust in the LORD **and** do good;*
dwell in the land and feed **on** its riches.

4 Take delight **in** the LORD,*
and he shall give you your **heart's** desire.

5 Commit your way to the LORD and put your **trust** in him,*
and he will bring **it** to pass.

6 He will make your righteousness as clear **as** the light*
and your just dealing **as** the noonday.

7 Be still be**fore** the LORD*
and wait patient**ly** for him.

8 Do not fret yourself over the **one** who prospers,*
the one who succeeds in **e**vil schemes.

9 Refrain from anger, leave **rage** alone;*
do not fret yourself; it leads on**ly** to evil.

10 For evildoers shall **be** cut off,*
but those who wait upon the LORD shall pos**sess** the land.

11 In a little while the wicked shall **be** no more;*
you shall search out their place, but they will **not** be there.

12 But the lowly shall pos**sess** the land;*
they will delight in abun**dance** of peace.

13 The wicked plot a**gainst** the righteous*
and gnash at them **with** their teeth.

14 The Lord laughs **at** the wicked,*
because he sees that their **day** will come.

15 The wicked draw their sword and bend their bow
to strike down the **poor** and needy,*
to slaughter those who are upright **in** their ways.

16 Their sword shall go through **their** own heart,*
and their bow **shall** be broken.

17 The little that the **right**eous has*
is better than great riches **of** the wicked.

18 For the power of the wicked **shall** be broken,*
but the LORD up**holds** the righteous.

19 The LORD cares for the lives **of** the godly,*
and their inheritance shall **last** for ever.

20 They shall not be ashamed **in** bad times,*
and in days of famine they shall **have** enough.

21 As for the wicked, **they** shall perish,*
and the enemies of the LORD, like the glory of
the meadows, shall vanish;
they shall van**ish** like smoke.

22 The wicked borrow and do **not** repay,*
but the righteous are gener**ous** in giving.

23 Those who are blessed by God shall pos**sess** the land,*
but those who are cursed by him shall **be** destroyed.

24 Our steps are directed **by** the LORD;*
he strengthens those in whose way **he** delights.

25 If they stumble, they shall **not** fall headlong,*
for the LORD holds them **by** the hand.

26 I have been young and now **I** am old,*
but never have I seen the righteous forsaken,
or their children **beg**ging bread.

27 The righteous are always generous **in** their lending,*
and their children shall **be** a blessing.

28 Turn from evil, **and** do good,*
and dwell in the **land** for ever.

29 For the **LORD** loves justice;*
he does not forsake his **faith**ful ones.

30 They shall be kept **safe** for ever,*
but the offspring of the wicked shall **be** destroyed.

31 The righteous shall pos**sess** the land*
and dwell in **it** for ever.

32 The mouth of the righteous **ut**ters wisdom,*
and their tongue speaks **what** is right.

33 The law of their God is **in** their heart,*
and their footsteps **shall** not falter.

34 The wicked spy **on** the righteous*
and seek occa**sion** to kill them.

35 The LORD will not abandon them **to** their hand,*
nor let them be found guilty when **brought** to trial.

36 Wait upon the LORD and **keep** his way;*
he will raise you up to possess the land,
and when the wicked are cut off, **you** will see it.

37 I have seen the wicked **in** their arrogance,*
flourishing like a tree **in** full leaf.

38 I went by, and behold, they **were** not there;*
I searched for them, but they could **not** be found.

39 Mark those who are honest;
ob**serve** the upright;*
for there is a future **for** the peaceable.

40 Transgressors shall be destroyed, **one** and all;*
the future of the wicked **is** cut off.

41 But the deliverance of the righteous comes **from** the LORD;*
he is their stronghold in **time** of trouble.

42 The LORD will help them and **res**cue them;*

he will rescue them from the wicked and deliver them,
because they seek ref**uge** in him.

Antiphon Commit your way **to** the LORD*
and put your **trust** in him.

Silence for meditation

Lord Jesus, you bless the poor with the kingdom of heaven: Teach us to put our trust in the Father and to seek his kingdom rather than to imitate the powerful or envy the rich; so may we serve you now and for ever.
[LH, LBW]

+

Antiphon to PSALM 56 *Miserere mei, Deus, quoniam*

In God I trust and will not **be** afraid,*
for what can mortals **do** to me? [LH, PBO]

56 *Unshakable confidence in God*

1 Have mercy on me, O God,
for my enemies are **hound**ing me;*
all day long they assault **and** oppress me.

2 They hound me all **the** day long;*
truly there are many who fight against me, **O** Most High.

3 Whenever I **am** afraid,*
I will put my **trust** in you.

4 In God, whose word I praise,
in God I trust and will not **be** afraid,*
for what can flesh **do** to me?

5 All day long they dam**age** my cause;*
their only thought is to **do** me evil.

6 They band together; they **lie** in wait;*
they spy upon my footsteps; because they **seek** my life.

7 Shall they escape de**spite** their wickedness?*
O God, in your anger, cast **down** the peoples.

8 You have noted my lamentation;
put my tears in**to** your bottle;*
are they not recorded **in** your book?

9 Whenever I call upon you, my enemies will be **put** to flight;*
this I know, for God is **on** my side.

10 In God the LORD, whose word I praise,
in God I trust and will not **be** afraid,*
for what can mortals **do** to me?

11 I am bound by the vow I made to **you**, O God;*
I will present to **you** thank-offerings;

12 For you have rescued my soul from death and my **feet** from stumbling,*
that I may walk before God in the light **of** the living.

Antiphon In God I trust and will not **be** afraid,*
for what can mortals **do** to me?

Silence for meditation

Lord Jesus Christ, victim for our sins, you trusted in your Father's protection and kept silent when you were tormented: Give us that same confidence, that we may gladly suffer with you and for you, offering the Father our sacrifice of praise and walking before him in the light of the living; and to you be the glory now and for ever. [LH, LBW]

+

Stand

THE HYMN is sung.

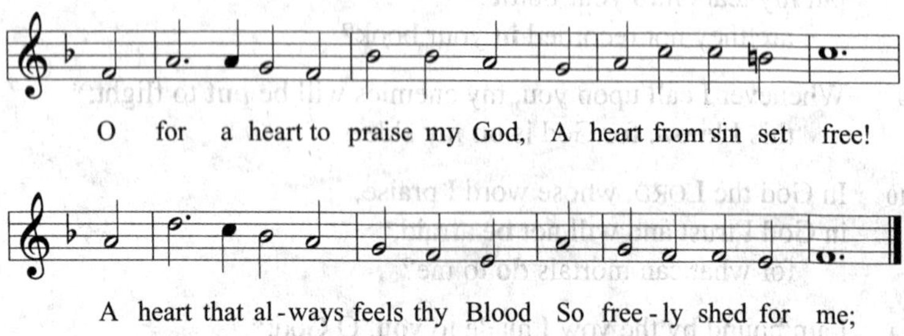

2 A heart resigned, submissive, meek,
  My great Redeemer's throne,
Where only Christ is heard to speak;
  Where Jesus reigns alone;

3 A humble, lowly, contrite heart,
  Believing, true, and clean,
Which neither life nor death can part
  From him that dwells within.

4 A heart in every thought renewed
And full of love divine;
Perfect, and right, and pure, and good,
A copy, Lord, of thine.

5 Thy nature, gracious Lord, impart.
Come quickly from above;
Write thy new name upon my heart,
Thy new, best name of love. [CSB 264, SBH 389, H40 414]

Text: Charles Wesley, 1707-1788
Tune: *Winchester,* Thomas Este's Psalter, 1592 CM

Sit

One or two LESSONS are read.

Year 1

Saturday after Ash Wednesday
Deuteronomy 7:17-26

Remember what the LORD your God did to Pharaoh and to all Egypt, the great trials that your eyes saw, the signs and wonders, the mighty hand and the outstretched arm by which the LORD your God brought you out.

Titus 3:1-15

When the goodness and lovingkindness of God our Savior

Year 2

Ezekiel 39:21-29

They shall know that I am the LORD their God because I sent them into exile among the nations, and then gathered them into their own land.

Philippians 4:10-20

I know what it is to have little, and I know what it is to have plenty. In

appeared, he saved us, not because of any works of righteousness that we had done, but according to his mercy.

any and all circumstances I have learned the secret of being well-fed and of going hungry, of having plenty and of being in need. I can do all things through him who strengthens me.

Saturday after Lent 1
Deuteronomy 11:18-28

You shall put these words of mine in your heart and soul, and you shall bind them as a sign on your hand, and fix them as an emblem on your forehead. Teach them to your children.

Genesis 41:1-13

A young Hebrew was there with us, a servant of the captain of the guard. When we told him, he interpreted our dreams to us, giving an interpretation to each according to his dream.

Hebrews 5:1-10

Although he was a Son, he learned obedience through what he suffered; and having been made perfect, he became the source of eternal salvation for all who obey him.

1 Corinthians 4:1-7

Do not pronounce judgment before the time, before the Lord comes, who will bring to light the things now hidden in darkness and will disclose the purposes of the heart.

Saturday after Lent 2
Jeremiah 5:20-31

This people has a stubborn and rebellious heart; they have turned aside and gone away.

Genesis 43:16-34

The men are to dine with me at noon.

Romans 3:19-31

For there is no distinction, since all

1 Corinthians 7:10-24

You were bought with a price; do not

have sinned and fall short of the glory of God; they are now justified by his grace as a gift.

Saturday after Lent 3
Jeremiah 13:1-11

This evil people, who refuse to hear my words, who stubbornly follow their own will and have gone after other gods to serve them and worship them, shall be like this loincloth, which is good for nothing

Romans 6:12-23

The wages of sin is death, but the free gift of God is eternal life in Christ Jesus our Lord.

Saturday after Lent 4
Jeremiah 23:9-15

Both prophet and priest are ungodly; even in my house I have found their wickedness, says the LORD.

Romans 9:1-18

He says to Moses, "I will have mercy on whom I have mercy, and I will have compassion on whom I have compassion."

become slaves of human masters.

Genesis 47:27-48:7

Thus Israel settled in the land of Egypt, in the region of Goshen; and they gained possessions in it, and were fruitful and multiplied exceedingly.

1 Corinthians 10:1-13

God is faithful, and he will not let you be tested beyond your strength, but with the testing he will also provide the way out so that you may be able to endure it.

Exodus 2:23-3:15

"I am the God of your father, the God of Abraham, the God of Isaac, and the God of Jacob." And Moses hid his face for he was afraid to look at God.

1 Corinthians 13:1-13

And now faith, hope, and love abide, these three; and the greatest of these is love.

Saturday after Lent 5

Jeremiah 31:27-34

Just as I have watched over them to pluck up and break down, to overthrow, destroy, and bring evil, so I will watch over them to build and to plant, says the LORD.

Romans 11:25-36

O the depth of the riches and wisdom and knowledge of God! How unsearchable are his judgments and how inscrutable his ways!

Exodus 10:21-11:8

Thus says the LORD: About midnight I will go out through Egypt. Every firstborn in the land of Egypt shall die.

2 Corinthians 4:13-18

This slight momentary afflication is preparing us for an eternal weight of glory beyond all measure.

Silence for meditation follows each reading.

RESPONSORY

You shall love the Lord your God will all your heart, and with all your soul, and with **all** your mind.*
  This is the greatest and **first** commandment.
What does the Lord your God require of you? Only to fear the Lord your God, to walk in all his ways, to love him, to serve the Lord your God with all your heart and with **all** your soul.*

I was hungry and you gave me food; I was thirsty and you gave me some**thing** to drink;*
I was a stranger and you **wel**comed me.
  This is **my** commandment,*
  that you love one another as I **have** loved you.
Just as you did it to one of the **least** of these,*
you did **it** to me.
  This is **my** commandment,*

This is the greatest and **first** commandment.
[LH: Matt. 22:37; Deut. 10:12]

that you love one another as I **have** loved you.
[LH: Matt. 25:35,40; John 15:12]

Antiphon to the BENEDICTUS

Saturday after Ash Wednesday

We are strangers and foreigners **on** the earth,*
seek**ing** a homeland [Heb. 11:13-14]

Saturday after Lent 1

If you want to be true children of your heav**en**ly Father,*
pray for those who persecute you and utter all kinds of evil against you falsely, **says** the Lord. [LH: Matt. 5:44-45,11]

Saturday after Lent 2

Let us hold fast to the confession of our hope **with**out wavering,*
for he who has prom**ised** is faithful. [Heb. 10:23]

Saturday after Lent 3

The tax collector, standing far off, would not even look up to heaven, but was beating his **breast** and saying,*
God be merciful to **me**, a sinner! [LH: Luke 18:13]

Saturday after Lent 4

The Lord, the God of Israel, has given rest **to** his people;*
and he resides in Jerusa**lem** for ever. [1 Chron. 23:25]

Saturday after Lent 5

An evil and adulterous generation asks **for** a sign,*
but no sign will be given to it except the sign
of the **pro**phet Jonah. [Matt. 12:39]

✠

EVENING PRAYER
Vespers or Evensong
during the Great and Holy Week
from the Sunday of the Passion until the Easter Vigil

The Service of Light is omitted during Holy Week.

Evening Prayer begins with this Psalm for forgiveness and protection.

Kneel or stand

Antiphon to PSALM 141 *Domine, clamavi*

Let my prayer rise before **you** as incense,*
the lifting up of my hands as the **eve**ning sacrifice.

141 *Evening prayer for protection*

1 O LORD, I call to you; come **to** me quickly;*
hear my voice when I **cry** to you.

2 Let my prayer be set forth in your **sight** as incense,*
the lifting up of my hands as the **e**vening sacrifice.

3 Set a watch before my mouth, O LORD,
and guard the door **of** my lips;*
let not my heart incline to any **e**vil thing.

4 Let me not be occupied in wickedness with **e**vildoers,*
nor eat of **their** choice foods.

5 Let the righteous smite me in friendly rebuke;
let not the oil of the unrighteous a**noint** my head;*
for my prayer is continually against their **wick**ed deeds.

6 Let their rulers be overthrown in **ston**y places,*
that they may know my **words** are true.

7 As when a plowman turns over the **earth** in furrows,*
let their bones be scattered at the mouth **of** the grave.

8 But my eyes are turned to **you**, Lord GOD;*
in you I take refuge;
do not strip me **of** my life.

9 Protect me from the snare which they have **laid** for me*
and from the traps of the **e**vildoers.

10 Let the wicked fall into **their** own nets,*
while I my**self** escape.

Antiphon Let my prayer rise before **you** as incense,*
the lifting up of my hands as the **eve**ning sacrifice.

Silence for meditation

Lord, from the rising of the sun to its setting your Name is worthy of all praise: Let our prayer rise before you as incense, and may the lifting up of our hands be as an evening sacrifice, acceptable to you, through your Son, Jesus Christ our Lord. [LH, LBW]

Sit

A second psalm is sung or said; additional psalms and a New Testament canticle may be sung or said also. Silence for meditation follows each psalm or canticle. The psalm prayer appropriate to each psalm or canticle follows the silence.

Stand

THE HYMN is sung.

Sit

A lesson is read. Silence for meditation follows the reading.

After the silence the leader continues:

L In many and various ways God spoke to his people of old by the prophets.

C But now in these last days he has spoken to us by his Son.

Stand

The GOSPEL CANTICLE, Magnificat, *is sung or said.*

The Antiphon is sung or said.

1 ✠ My soul proclaims the greatness . . . of the Lord; my spirit rejoices in . . . God my Savior.

3 From this day all gen - er - ations will . . . . . . call me blessed.

5 He has mercy on those who fear him in every . . . gen - er - ation.

2 for he has . . . looked with favor on his . . . low - ly servant.

4 The Almighty has done great things for me, and holy . . . is his Name.

6 He has shown the strength of his arm; he has scattered the proud in their con - ceit.

7 He has cast down
the mighty . . . from their thrones, and has lifted up the lowly.

9 He has come to
the help of his . . . ser - vant Israel, for he has
remembered
his prom - ise of mercy,

11 Glory to the Father,
and . . . . to the Son, and to the . . . Ho - ly Spirit;

8 He has filled
the hungry . . with good things, and the rich
he has sent a - way empty.

10 the promise
he made . . . . to our fathers, to Abraham
and his chil - dren for ever.

12 as it was in the
begin - ing, is now, and will be
for ev - er. A - men

The Antiphon is repeated.

I believe in God, the Father almighty,
creator of heaven and earth.
I believe in Jesus Christ, his only Son, our Lord,
he was conceived by the power of the Holy Spirit
and born of the virgin Mary.
He suffered under Pontius Pilate,
was crucified, died, and was buried.
He descended to the dead [*or* He descended into hell].
On the third day he rose again.
He ascended into heaven,
and is seated at the right hand of the Father.
He will come again to judge the living and the dead.
I believe in the Holy Spirit,
the holy catholic Church,
the communion of saints,
the forgiveness of sins,
the resurrection of the body,
and the life everlasting. Amen

Kneel or stand

The SUFFRAGES are said.

L Holy God,
Holy and Mighty,
Holy Immortal One,
C Have mercy on us.

L Our Father in heaven,
hallowed be your Name,
your kingdom come,
your will be done,
on earth as in heaven.

L Our Father, who art in heaven,
hallowed be thy Name,
thy kingdom come,
thy will be done,
on earth as it is in heaven.

Give us today our daily bread.
Forgive us our sins
as we forgive those
who sin against us.
Save us from the time of trial
C and deliver us from evil.

Give us this day our daily bread
and forgive us our trespasses,
as we forgive those
who trespass against us.
and lead us not into temptation
C but deliver us from evil.

L Turn away, O Lord, the fierceness of your wrath,
and in pity spare your people:
C And have mercy.

L Grant a favorable and speedy answer to the prayers of all,
we implore you:
C And have mercy.

L Look, O Christ, upon our groanings,
loose the bands of death, and grant us life:
C And have mercy.

L Behold our tears, consider our sighs,
and now at length in pity forgive our sins:
C And have mercy.

L Though none of us be worthy to be heard,
yet, O Christ, for your own self help us:
C And have mercy.

L We cry to you, O Lord; have mercy on us:
C And grant forgiveness.

L O King of heaven, everlasting Lord,
receive the prayers which we pour forth:
C And grant forgiveness.

L Visit the sick, bring forth the captives,
help the widow and the orphan:
C And grant forgiveness.

L We have sinned and have departed from you;
Redeemer of all, save us:
C And grant forgiveness.

L Have mercy on the penitent, and wash away the stains of sin:
C And grant forgiveness.

L Let us all with one voice cry:
C Lord, have mercy.

L Show us your mercy, O Lord, grant pardon, grant remission:
C And graciously have mercy. [Mozarabaic Breviary, *Chain*]

The PRAYER OF THE DAY is said.

The Sunday of the Passion

Almighty and everliving God, in your tender love for the human race you sent your Son our Savior Jesus Christ to take upon him our nature, and to suffer death upon the cross: Mercifully grant that we may walk in the way of his suffering, and also share in his resurrection; through your Son Jesus Christ our Lord, who lives and reigns with you and the Holy Spirit, one God, now and for ever. [Gel., RS, CB, CSB, SBH, LBW, BCP]

Monday in Holy Week

Almighty God, grant that we, who amid so many adversities fail through our own weakness, may be restored and strengthened by the passion and intercession of your only-begotten Son, who lives and reigns with you and the Holy Spirit, one God, now and for ever.

[Greg., MR, RS, LH, CB, CSB, SBH]

Tuesday in Holy Week

Almighty and everlasting God, grant us grace so to contemplate the passion of our Lord that we may find therein forgiveness for our sins; through your Son, Jesus Christ our Lord, who lives and reigns with you and the Holy Spirit, one God, now and for ever.

[Greg., MR, RS, CB, CSB, SBH]

Wednesday in Holy Week

Almighty and everlasting God, it was your will that your Son should bear for us the pains of the cross so that you might remove from us the power of the enemy: Help us so to remember and give thanks for our Lord's passion that we may obtain remission of sin and redemption from everlasting death; through your Son, Jesus Christ our Lord, who lives and reigns with you and the Holy Spirit, one God, now and for ever.

[Greg.,MR, RS, CB, CSB,SBH]

Maundy Thursday

Holy God, source of all love, on the night of his betrayal, Jesus gave his disciples a new commandment: To love one another as he had loved them. By your Holy Spirit write this commandment in our hearts; through your Son, Jesus Christ our Lord, who lives and reigns with you and the Holy Spirit, one God, now and for ever. [LBW]

Good Friday

Almighty God, we pray you graciously to behold this your family, for whom our Lord Jesus Christ was willing to be betrayed, and given into the hands of sinners, and to suffer death upon the cross; who now lives and reigns with you and the Holy Spirit, one God, now and for ever.

[Greg., Sarum, MG, LH, BCP CB, CSB, SBH, LBW]

Holy Saturday

Almighty and ever-living God, your only Son descended to the dead and rose again in glory: In your goodness raise up your faithful people, buried with him in baptism, to be one with him in the eternal life of heaven, where he lives and reigns with you and the Holy Spirit, one God, now and for ever. [LH~BCP 1662-1928]

Additional prayers may be said.

The prayers conclude:

L O Lord, deal not with us according to our sins,

C Neither reward us according to our wickedness.

[CB, CSB, SBH: see Ps. 103:10]

We give thanks to you, heavenly Father, through Jesus Christ your dear Son, that you have this day so graciously protected us. We beg you to forgive us all our sins and the wrong which we have done. By your great mercy defend us from all the perils and dangers of this night. Into your hands we commend our bodies and souls, and all that is ours. Let your holy angels have charge of us, that the wicked one have no power over us. [Luther, CSB, SBH, LBW]

L Enter not into judgment with your servants

C For in your sight shall no one living be justified.

[CB, CSB, SBH: see Psalm 143:2]

Lord Jesus Christ, Son of the living God, we pray you to set your passion, cross, and death between your judgment and our souls, now and in the hour of our death. Give mercy and grace to the living; pardon and rest to the dead; to your holy Church peace and concord; and to us sinners everlasting life and glory; for with the Father and the Holy Spirit you live and reign, one God, now and for ever. [medieval primers, PPP, BCP]

Stand

The BENEDICTION concludes the service when there is no sermon. A hymn may follow the benediction.

When there is a sermon, this benediction is omitted. The service continues as on p. 20.

L The Lord bless us, ✠ defend us from all evil, and bring us to everlasting life.

C Amen.

Eve of the Sunday of the Passion

Antiphon to PSALM 79 *Deus, venerunt*

Help us, O **God** our Savior,*
and forgive **us** our sins. [LH, PBO]

79 *Lament for Jerusalem*

1 O God, the heathen have come into your inheritance;
they have profaned your **ho**ly temple;*
they have made Jerusalem a **heap** of rubble.

2 They have given the bodies of your servants as food for the
birds **of** the air,*
and the flesh of your faithful ones to the beasts **of** the field.

3 They have shed their blood like water on every side **of** Jerusalem,*
and there was no one to **bur**y them.

4 We have become a reproach **to** our neighbors,*
an object of scorn and derision to **those** around us.

5 How long will you be an**gry**, O LORD?*
will your fury blaze like **fire** for ever?

6 Pour out your wrath upon the heathen who **have** not known you*
and upon the kingdoms that have not called up**on** your Name.

7 For they have de**vour**ed Jacob*
and made his dwel**ling** a ruin.

8 Remember not our past sins;
let your compassion be **swift** to meet us;*
for we have been brought **ver**y low.

9 Help us, O God our Savior, for the glory **of** your Name;*
deliver us and forgive us our sins, for **your** Name's sake.

10 Why should the heathen say, "Where **is** their God?"*
Let it be known among the heathen and in our sight
that you avenge the shedding of your **ser**vants' blood.

11 Let the sorrowful sighing of the prisoners **come** before you,*
and by your great might spare those who are con**dem**ned to die.

12 May the revilings with which they reviled **you**, O Lord,*
return seven-fold in**to** their bosoms.

13 For we are your people and the sheep **of** your pasture;*
we will give you thanks for ever
and show forth your praise from **age** to age.

Antiphon Help us, O **God** our Savior,*
and forgive **us** our sins.

Silence for meditation

Father of mercy, your Son told his enemies that, if they should destroy the temple of his body, you would raise it again in three days. By his death and resurrection demolish our pretensions of strength, and on the ruins build a temple worthy of your Name, so that all the world may know the glory of your transforming power, shown in Jesus Christ our Lord. [LH]

+

Antiphon to PSALM 143 *Domine, exaudi*

My spirit **faints** within me;*
my heart within **me** is desolate. [LH, PBO]

143 *Prayer in distress: a penitential psalm*

1 LORD, hear my prayer,
and in your faithfulness heed my **sup**plications;*
answer me **in** your righteousness.

2 Enter not into judgment **with** your servant,*
for in your sight shall no one liv**ing** be justified.

3 For my enemy has sought my life;
he has crushed me **to** the ground;*
he has made me live in dark places like those who
are long dead.

4 My spirit **faints** within me;*
my heart within **me** is desolate.

5 I remember the time past;
I muse upon **all** your deeds;*
I consider the works **of** your hands.

6 I spread out my **hands** to you;*
my soul gasps to you like a **thirst**y land.

7 O LORD, make haste to answer me; my **spir**it fails me;*
do not hide your face from me
or I shall be like those who go down **to** the Pit.

8 Let me hear of your loving-kindness in the morning,
for I put my **trust** in you;*
show me the road that I must walk,
for I lift up my **soul** to you.

9 Deliver me from my ene**mies**, O LORD,*
for I flee to **you** for refuge.

10 Teach me to do what pleases you, for you **are** my God;*
let your good Spirit lead me on **le**vel ground.

11 Revive me, O LORD, for **your** Name's sake;*
for your righteousness' sake, bring me **out** of trouble.

12 Of your goodness, destroy my enemies
and bring all my **foes** to naught,*
for truly I **am** your servant.

Antiphon My spirit **faints** within me;*
my heart within **me** is desolate.

Silence for meditation

Lord Jesus, you bring the first light of dawn to those who dwell in darkness and make your love known to them. Enter not into judgment against your servants, but let your Spirit guide us into the land of justice, where with the Father and the Holy Spirit you live and reign, now and for ever. [LH, LBW]

+

Antiphon to the NEW TESTAMENT CANTICLE *Qui cum in forma Dei*

The Lord Jesus humbled himself,
in obedience ac**cept**ing death,*
even death **on** a cross. [LH, LBW; see Philippians 2:8]

A Song of Christ's Humiliation and Exaltation Philippians 2:6-11

Christ Jesus, being in the form of God,
did not cling to equali**ty** with God*
but emptied himself, taking the form **of** a slave.

Bearing the human likeness, revealed in **hu**man shape,*
he humbled himself, in obedience accepting death,
even death **on** a cross.

Therefore God has raised him **to** the heights*
and bestowed on him the Name a**bove** all names,

that at the Name of JESUS every knee should bow—
in heaven, on earth, and **in** the depths—*
and every tongue confess to the glory of God the Father
that Jesus **Christ** is LORD. [LBW]

Antiphon The Lord Jesus humbled himself,
in obedience ac**cept**ing death,*
even death **on** a cross.

Silence for meditation

God of glory and compassion, by his willing embrace of the cross your Son revealed to us the way of life and peace. Grant that we, relaxing our hold on selfish desires, may boldly confess him as our Savior and gladly follow him as our Lord, who lives and reigns with you and the Holy Spirit, one God, now and forever. [PHP]

+

Stand

THE HYMN is sung.

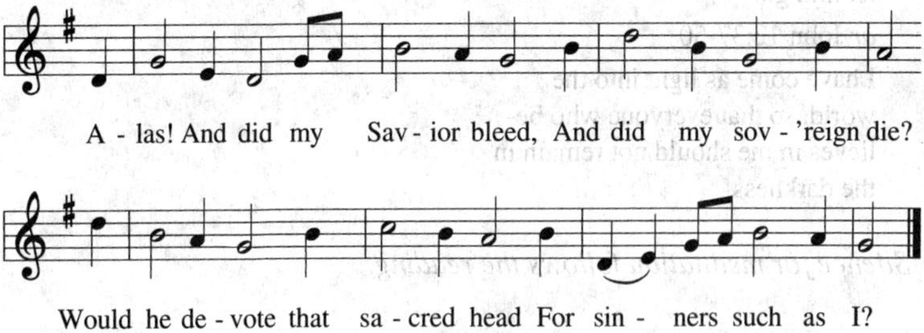

2 Was it for crimes that I had done
He groaned upon the tree?
Amazing pity, grace unknown,
And love beyond degree!

3 Well might the sun in darkness hide
And shut his glories in
When God, the mighty maker, died
For his own creatures' sin.

4 Thus might I hide my blushing face
While his dear cross appears,
Dissolve my heart in thankfulness,
And melt my eyes to tears.

5 But drops of grief can ne'er repay
The debt of love I owe;
Here Lord, I give myself away:
'Tis all that I can do.

[SBH 486, LBW 98]

Text: Isaac Watts, 1674-1748
Tune: *Martyrdom*, Hugh Wilson, 1764-1824 CM

Sit

A LESSON is read.

Year 1

John 11:28-44

Jesus cried with a loud voice, "Lazarus, come out!" The dead man came out, his hands and feet bound with strips of cloth, and his face wrapped in a cloth. Jesus said to them, "Unbind him, and let him go."

or John 12:37-50

I have come as light into the world, so that everyone who believes in me should not remain in the darkness.

Year 2

Mark 10:46-52

Jesus said to him, "Go; your faith has made you well." Immediately he regained his sight and followed him on the way.

Silence for meditation follows the reading.

Antiphon to the MAGNIFICAT

Glory to our King,
the Son of David and Redeemer **of** the world,*
whom the prophets foretold would come to the house of Israel to **be** their Savior. [LH, PBO]

The Sunday of the Passion

Antiphon to PSALM 75 *Confitebimur tibi*

Now is the judgment **of** this world,*
now the ruler of this world will be **driv**en out. [John 12:31]

75 *Judge of the world*

1 We give you thanks, O God, we **give** you thanks,*
calling upon your Name and declaring all your
won**der**ful deeds.

2 "I will appoint a **time**," says God;*
"I will **judge** with equity.

3 Though the earth and all its inhabi**tants** are quaking,*
I will make its **pil**lars fast.

4 I will say to the boasters, '**Boast** no more,'*
and to the wicked, 'Do not **toss** your horns;

5 Do not toss your **horns** so high,*
nor speak with **a** proud neck.' "

6 For judgment is neither from the east nor **from** the west,*
nor yet from the wilderness **or** the mountains.

7 It is **God** who judges;*
he puts down one and lifts **up** another.

8 For in the LORD's hand there is a cup,
full of spiced and foaming wine, which **he** pours out,*
and all the wicked of the earth shall drink and
drain the dregs.

9 But I will re**joice** for ever;*
I will sing praises to the **God** of Jacob.

10 He shall break off all the horns **of** the wicked;*
but the horns of the righteous shall **be** exalted.

Antiphon Now is the judgment **of** this world,*
now the ruler of this world will be **driv**en out.

Silence for meditation

Father, by the Passion of your Son you proclaimed the final judgment of the world; when you raised Christ upon the cross, you deposed the prince of darkness. Strike down the pride that rules our hearts, and raise us to the glory of the resurrection; through Jesus Christ our Lord. [LH, LBW]

+

Antiphon to PSALM 32 *Beati quorum*

Upon him was the punishment that **made** us whole,*
and by his bruises **we** are healed. [LBW: Isa. 53:5]

32 *The joy of being forgiven: a penitential psalm*

1 Happy are they whose transgressions **are** forgiven,*
and whose sin is **put** away!

2 Happy are they to whom the LORD im**putes** no guilt,*
and in whose spirit there **is** no guile!

3 While I held my tongue, my bones with**ered** away,*
because of my groaning **all** day long.

4 For your hand was heavy upon me **day** and night;*
my moisture was dried up as in the **heat** of summer.

5 Then I acknowledged my **sin** to you,*
and did not con**ceal** my guilt.

6 I said, "I will confess my transgressions **to** the LORD." *
Then you forgave me the guilt **of** my sin.

7 Therefore all the faithful will make their prayers to you in **time** of trouble;*
when the great waters overflow, they **shall** not reach them.

8 You are my hiding-place;
you preserve **me** from trouble;*
you surround me with shouts **of** deliverance.

9 "I will instruct you and teach you in the way that **you** should go;*
I will guide you **with** my eye.

10 Do not be like horse or mule, which have no **un**derstanding;*
who must be fitted with bit and bridle,
or else they will **not** stay near you."

11 Great are the tribulations **of** the wicked;*
but mercy embraces those who trust **in** the LORD.

12 Be glad, you righteous, and rejoice **in** the LORD;*
shout for joy, all who are **true** of heart.

Antiphon Upon him was the punishment that **made** us whole,*
and by his bruises **we** are healed.

Silence for meditation

Lord God, you desired to keep from us your wrath and so did not spare your holy servant Jesus Christ, who was wounded for our sins. We are your prodigal children, but we come back to you confessing our sins. Embrace us, that we may rejoice in your mercy together with your beloved Son, Jesus Christ our Lord. [LH, LBW]

+

Antiphon to the NEW TESTAMENT CANTICLE

Christus passus est pro nobis

He was wounded for **our** transgressions,*
crushed for **our** iniquities. [LH, LBW: Isa. 53:5]

Jesus' willing acceptance of his Passion 1 Peter 2:21-24

Christ suffered for you, leaving you **an** example,*
so that you should follow **in** his steps.

He committed no sin, and no deceit was found **in** his mouth.*
When he was abused, he did not re**turn** abuse.

When he suffered, he **did** not threaten;*
but he entrusted himself to the One who **judg**es justly.

He himself bore our sins in his body **on** the cross,*
so that, free from sins,
we might **live** for righteousness. [NRSV]

Antiphon He was wounded for **our** transgressions,*
crushed for **our** iniquities.

Silence for meditation

Merciful and everlasting God, you did not spare your only Son but delivered him up for us all, that he might bear our sins upon the cross: Grant that our hearts may be so fixed with steadfast faith in him that we may not fear the power of any adversaries; through Jesus Christ our Lord.

[Saxon Agenda, 1540; CB, CSB, SBH]

+

Stand

THE HYMN is sung. *Vexilla regis prodeunt*

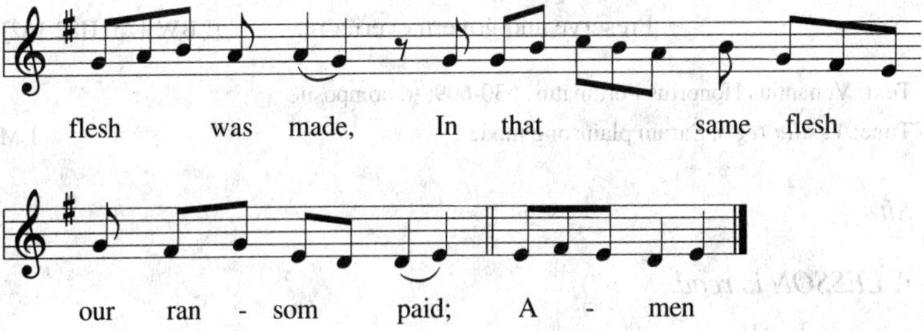

2 Where deep for us the spear was dyed,
Life's torrent rushing from his side,
To wash us in the precious flood
Where flowed the water and the blood.

3 Fulfilled is all that David told
In true prophetic song of old,
That God the nations' king should be
For God is reigning from the tree.

4 O tree of beauty, tree most fair,
Ordained those holy limbs to bear:
Gone is thy shame, each crimsoned bough
Proclaims the King of glory now.

5 Blest tree, whose chosen branches bore
The wealth that did the world restore,
The price of humankind to pay
And spoil the spoiler of his prey.

6 O cross, our one reliance, hail!
Still may thy power with us avail
To save us sinners from our sin,
God's righteousness for all to win.

7 To you, eternal Three in One,
Our songs shall rise in unison;

Those whom you ransom and restore
Preserve and govern evermore. [LBW 125; H82 162]

Text: Venantius Honorius Fortunatus, 530-609; tr. composite
Tune: *Vexilla regis,* Sarum plainsong mode I LM

Sit

A LESSON is read.

Year 1

Matthew 21:12-17

Jesus said to them, "It is written, 'My house shall be called a house of prayer'; but you are making it a den of robbers."

Year 2

Luke 19:41-48

Every day Jesus was teaching in the temple. The chief priests, the scribes, and the leaders of the people kept looking for a way to kill him; but they did not find anything they could do, for all the people were spellbound by what they heard.

Silence for meditation follows the reading.

Antiphon to the MAGNIFICAT

It is written, "I will strike the shepherd,
and the sheep **will** be scattered."*
But after I am raised up, I will go before **you** to Galilee.
[LH, PBO: Mark 14:27-28]

Monday in Holy Week

Antiphon to PSALM 94 *Deus ultionum*

They conspire against the life **of** the just*
and condemn the inno**cent** to death. [PBO]

94 *God: the judge and vindicator*

1 O LORD **God** of vengeance,*
O God of vengeance, **show** yourself.

2 Rise up, O Judge **of** the world;*
give the arrogant their **just** deserts.

3 How long shall the wick**ed**, O LORD,*
how long shall the wick**ed** triumph?

4 They bluster **in** their insolence;*
all evildoers are **full** of boasting.

5 They crush your peo**ple**, O LORD,*
and afflict your **chos**en nation.

6 They murder the widow **and** the stranger*
and put the or**phans** to death.

7 Yet they say, "The LORD **does** not see,*
the God of Jacob **takes** no notice."

8 Consider well, you dullards a**mong** the people:*
when will you fools **un**derstand?

9 He that planted the ear, does **he** not hear?*
he that formed the eye, does **he** not see?

10 He who admonishes the nations, will **he** not punish?*
he who teaches all the world, has **he** no knowledge?

11 The LORD knows our **hu**man thoughts;*
how like a puff of **wind** they are.

12 Happy are they whom you in**struct**, O Lord!*
whom you teach out **of** your law;

13 To give them rest in **e**vil days,*
until a pit is dug **for** the wicked.

14 For the LORD will not aban**don** his people,*
nor will he for**sake** his own.

15 For judgment will a**gain** be just,*
and all the true of heart will **fol**low it.

16 Who rose up for me a**gainst** the wicked?*
who took my part against the **e**vildoers?

17 If the LORD had not come **to** my help,*
I should soon have dwelt in the **land** of silence.

18 As often as I said, "My **foot** has slipped,"*
your love, O **LORD**, upheld me.

19 When many cares **fill** my mind,*
your consolations **cheer** my soul.

20 Can a corrupt tribunal have any **part** with you,*
one which frames evil **in**to law?

21 They conspire against the life **of** the just*
and condemn the inno**cent** to death.

22 But the LORD has be**come** my stronghold,*
and my God the rock **of** my trust.

23 He will turn their wickedness back upon them
and destroy them in **their** own malice;*
the LORD our God **will** destroy them.

Antiphon They conspire against the life **of** the just*
and condemn the inno**cent** to death.

Silence for meditation

Lord Jesus, do not abandon your people, nor ignore the power of the enemy against your Church. Grant that those who suffer for the sake of justice may find consolation in the cross and be filled with your joy now and for ever. [LH, LBW]

+

Antiphon to PSALM 6 *Domine, ne in furore*

Turn, O LORD, and de**li**ver me;*
save me for your **mer**cy's sake. [LH]

6 *Prayer in time of distress: a penitential psalm*

1 LORD, do not rebuke me **in** your anger;*
do not punish me **in** your wrath.

2 Have pity on me, LORD, for **I** am weak;*
heal me, LORD, for my **bones** are racked.

3 My spirit **shakes** with terror;*
how long, O **LORD**, how long?

4 Turn, O LORD, and de**li**ver me;*
save me for your **mer**cy's sake.

5 For in death no one re**mem**bers you;*
and who will give you thanks **in** the grave?

6 I grow weary because **of** my groaning;*
every night I drench my bed
and flood my **couch** with tears.

7 My eyes are wast**ed** with grief*
and worn away because of **all** my enemies.

8 Depart from me, all **e**vildoers,*
for the LORD has heard the sound **of** my weeping.

9 The LORD has heard my **sup**plication;*
the LORD ac**cepts** my prayer.

10 All my enemies shall be confounded and **quake** with fear;*
they shall turn back and suddenly be **put** to shame.

Antiphon Turn, O LORD, and de**liv**er me;*
save me for your **mer**cy's sake.

Silence for meditation

Lord God, you love mercy and tenderness; you give life and overcome death. Look upon the weakness and grief of your Church; restore it to health by your risen Son, so that it may sing a new song in your praise; through your Son, Jesus Christ our Lord. [LH, LBW]

+

Stand

THE HYMN is sung.

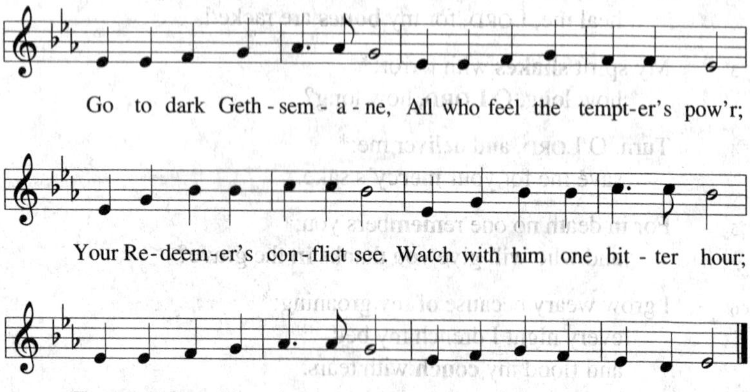

2 Follow to the judgment hall,
View the Lord of life arraigned;
Oh, the wormwood and the gall!
Oh, the pangs his soul sustained!
Shun not suffering, shame, or loss;
Learn from him to bear the cross.

3 Calvary's mournful mountain climb;
There, adoring at his feet,
Mark that miracle of time,
God's own sacrifice complete.
"It is finished!" hear him cry;
Learn from Jesus Christ to die.

4 Early hasten to the tomb
Where they laid his breathless clay;
All is solitude and gloom.
Who has taken him away?
Christ is risen! He meets our eyes.
Savior, teach us so to rise. [LBW 109, H82 171]

Text: James Montgomery, 1771-1854
Tune: *Gethsemane,* Richard Redhead, 1820-1901 77 77 77

Sit

A LESSON is read.

Year 1

John 12:9-19
The Pharisees then said to one another, "You see, you can do nothing. Look, the world has gone after him!"

Year 2

Mark 11:12-25
Whenever you stand praying, forgive, if you have anything against anyone; so that your Father in heaven may also forgive you your trespasses.

Silence for meditation follows the reading.

Antiphon to the MAGNIFICAT

Just as Moses lifted up the serpent in the wilderness,
so must the Son of Man be **lift**ed up,*
that whoever believes in him may have e**ter**nal life.
[LH: John 3:14]

Tuesday in Holy Week

Antiphon to PSALM 144 *Benedictus Dominus*

God is my help **and** my fortress,*
my shield in **whom** I trust. [LH]

144 *Prayer for victory and peace*

1 Blessed be the **LORD** my rock!*
who trains my hands to fight and my fin**gers** to battle;

2 My help and my fortress, my stronghold and **my** deliverer,*
my shield in whom I trust,
who subdues the peoples **un**der me.

3 O LORD, what are we that you should **care** for us?*
mere mortals that you should **think** of us?

4 We are like a **puff** of wind;*
our days are like a **pass**ing shadow.

5 Bow your heavens, O LORD, **and** come down;*
touch the mountains, and **they** shall smoke.

6 Hurl the lightning and **scat**ter them;*
shoot out your ar**rows** and rout them.

7 Stretch out your hand **from** on high;*
rescue me and deliver me from the great waters,
from the hand of **for**eign peoples,

8 Whose mouths **speak** deceitfully*
and whose right hand is **raised** in falsehood.

9 O God, I will sing to you **a** new song;*
I will play to you on a **ten**-stringed lyre.

10 You give victo**ry** to kings*
and have rescued **Da**vid your servant.

11 Rescue me from the **hurt**ful sword*
and deliver me from the hand of **for**eign peoples,

12 Whose mouths speak de**ceit**fully*
and whose right hand is **raised** in falsehood.

13 May our sons be like plants well nurtured **from** their youth,*
and our daughters like sculptured corners **of** a palace.

14 May our barns be filled to overflowing with all man**ner** of crops;*
may the flocks in our pastures increase by thousands
and tens of thousands;
may our cattle be **fat** and sleek.

15 May there be no breaching of the walls, no going **in**to exile,*
no wailing in the **pub**lic squares.

16 Happy are the people of whom **this** is so!*
happy are the people whose God **is** the LORD!

Antiphon God is my help **and** my fortress,*
my shield in **whom** I trust.

Silence for meditation

Lord God of strength, you gave your Son victory over death. Direct your Church's fight against evil in the world; clothe us with the weapons of light; and unite us under the banner of love, that after the battle of earthly life we may rejoice in your presence now and for ever. [LH, LBW]

+

Antiphon to PSALM 38 *Domine, ne in furore*

I will confess **my** iniquity;*
do not forsake me, O God of **my** salvation. [LH, PBO]

38 *Earnest prayer of one in danger: a penitential psalm*

1 O LORD, do not rebuke me **in** your anger;*
do not punish me **in** your wrath.

2 For your arrows have al**read**y pierced me,*
and your hand presses **hard** upon me.

3 There is no health in my flesh,
because of your **in**dignation;*
there is no soundness in my body, because **of** my sin.

4 For my iniquities **o**verwhelm me;*
like a heavy burden they are too much for **me** to bear.

5 My wounds **stink** and fester*
by reason **of** my foolishness.

6 I am utterly bowed **down** and prostrate;*
I go about in mourning all **the** day long.

7 My loins are filled with **sear**ing pain;*
there is no health **in** my body.

8 I am utterly **numb** and crushed;*
I wail, because of the groaning **of** my heart.

9 O Lord, you know all **my** desires,*
and my sighing is not hid**den** from you.

10 My heart is pounding, my **strength** has failed me,*
and the brightness of my eyes is **gone** from me.

11 My friends and companions draw back from **my** affliction;*
my neighbors stand **a**far off.

12 Those who seek after my life lay **snares** for me;*
those who strive to hurt me speak of my ruin
and plot treachery all **the** day long.

13 But I am like the deaf who **do** not hear,*
like those who are mute and do not **o**pen their mouth.

14 I have become like one who **does** not hear*
and from whose mouth comes **no** defense.

15 For in you, O LORD, have I **fixed** my hope;*
you will answer me, O **Lord** my God.

16 For I said, "Do not let them rejoice at **my** expense,*
those who gloat over me when **my** foot slips."

17 Truly, I am on the **verge** of falling,*
and my pain is al**ways** with me.

18 I will confess **my** iniquity*
and be sorry **for** my sin.

19 Those who are my enemies without **cause** are mighty,*
and many in number are those who wrong**ful**ly hate me.

20 Those who repay evil for good **slan**der me,*
because I follow the course **that** is right.

21 O LORD, do **not** forsake me;*
be not far from me, **O** my God.

22 Make **haste** to help me,*
O Lord of **my** salvation.

Antiphon I will confess **my** iniquity;*
do not forsake me, O God of **my** salvation.

Silence for meditation

Lord our God, you did not forget the pieced body of your Son nor the mockery his love received. Do not abandon us, your children, weighed down with sins, but give us the fullness of your mercy in Jesus Christ our Lord. [LH, LBW]

+

Stand

THE HYMN is sung. *Jesu, meines Lebens Leben*

2 You have suffered great affliction
And have borne it patiently,
Even death by crucifixion,
Fully to atone for me;
For you chose to be tormented
That my doom should be prevented.
Thousand, thousand thanks are due,
Dearest Jesus unto you.

3 Then, for all that wrought our pardon,
For the sorrows deep and sore,
For the anguish in the garden,
I will thank you evermore;
Thank you for the groaning, sighing,
For the bleeding and the dying,

For that last triumphant cry,
Praise you evermore on high. [SBH 79, LBW 97]

Text: Ernst Christoph Homburg, 1605-1681; tr. Catherine Winkworth, 1829-1878 alt.
Tune: *Jesu, meines Lebens Leben,* from *Das grosse Cantionale*, Darmstadt, 1687
87 87 88 77

Sit

A LESSON is read.

Year 1

John 12:20-26
Very truly, I tell you, unless a grain of wheat falls into the earth and dies, it remains just a single grain; but if it dies, it bears much fruit.

Year 2

Mark 11:27-33
They answered Jesus, "We do not know." And Jesus said to them, "Neither will I tell you by what authority I am doing these things."

Antiphon to the MAGNIFICAT

The **hour** has come*
for the Son of Man **to** be glorified. [PBO: John 12:23]

Wednesday in Holy Week

Antiphon to PSALM 55 *Exaudi, Deus*

Had it been an enemy who vaunted himself against me,
then I **could** have borne it;*
but it was you, my companion, my own fa**mil**iar friend.

[PBO]

55 *Distress of one betrayed by a friend*

1 Hear my **prayer**, O God;*
do not hide yourself from **my** petition.

2 Listen to me and **an**swer me;*
I have no peace, because **of** my cares.

3 I am shaken by the noise **of** the enemy*
and by the pressure **of** the wicked;

4 For they have cast an evil **spell** upon me*
and are set against **me** in fury.

5 My heart **quakes** within me,*
and the terrors of death have fal**len** upon me.

6 Fear and trembling have come **o**ver me,*
and horror **o**verwhelms me.

7 And I said, "Oh, that I had wings **like** a dove!*
I would fly away and **be** at rest.

8 I would flee to a **far**-off place*
and make my lodging **in** the wilderness.

9 I would hasten **to** escape*
from the stormy **wind** and tempest."

10 Swallow them up, O Lord;
con**found** their speech;*
for I have seen violence and strife **in** the city.

11 Day and night the watchmen make their rounds
upon her walls,*
but trouble and misery are in the **midst** of her.

12 There is corruption **at** her heart;*
her streets are never free of oppression **and** deceit.

13 For had it been an adversary who taunted me,
then I **could** have borne it;*
or had it been an enemy who vaunted himself against me,
then I could have hid**den** from him.

14 But it was you, a man after **my** own heart,*
my companion, my own fa**mil**iar friend.

15 We took sweet coun**sel** together,*
and walked with the throng in the **house** of God.

16 Let death come upon them suddenly;
let them go down alive in**to** the grave;*
for wickedness is in their dwellings, in their **ver**y midst.

17 But I will call **up**on God,*
and the LORD will de**liv**er me.

18 In the evening, in the morning, and at noonday,
I will complain **and** lament,*
and he will **hear** my voice.

19 He will bring me safely back from the battle **waged** against me;*
for there are many who fight me.

20 God, who is enthroned of old, will hear me
and **bring** them down;*
they never change; they do **not** fear God.

21 My companion stretched forth his hand a**gainst** his comrade;*
he has bro**ken** his covenant.

22 His speech is soft**er** than butter,*
but war is **in** his heart.

23 His words are smooth**er** than oil,*
but they **are** drawn swords.

24 Cast your burden upon the LORD,
and he **will** sustain you;*
he will never let the **right**eous stumble.

25 For you will bring the bloodthirsty **and** deceitful*
down to the pit of destruc**tion**, O God.

26 They shall not live out **half** their days,*
but I will put my **trust** in you.

Antiphon Had it been an enemy who vaunted himself against me,
then I **could** have borne it;*
but it was you, my companion, my own fa**mil**iar friend.

Silence for meditation

Lord Jesus, you were rejected by your people, betrayed by the kiss of a friend, and deserted by your disciples. In our trouble, give us the confidence that you had in the Father and the assurance of our salvation now and for ever. [LH, LBW]

+

Antiphon to PSALM 51 *Miserere mei, Deus, secundum*

A broken and a contrite **heart**, O God,*
you will **not** despise. [LH, PBO]

51 *Prayer for forgiveness: a penitential Psalm*

1 Have mercy on me, O God, according to your
loving-kindness;*
in your great compassion blot out **my** offenses.

2 Wash me through and through **from** my wickedness*
and cleanse me **from** my sin.

3 For I know **my** transgressions,*
and my sin is ev**er** before me.

4 Against you only **have** I sinned*
and done what is evil **in** your sight.

5 And so you are justified **when** you speak*
and upright **in** your judgment.

6 Indeed, I have been wicked **from** my birth,*
a sinner from my **moth**er's womb.

7 For behold, you look for truth **deep** within me,*
and will make me understand **wis**dom secretly.

8 Purge me from my sin, and I **shall** be pure;*
wash me, and I shall be **clean** indeed.

9 Make me hear of **joy** and gladness,*
that the body you have broken **may** rejoice.

10 Hide your face **from** my sins*
and blot out all **my** iniquities.

11 Create in me a clean **heart**, O God,*
and renew a right spir**it** within me.

12 Cast me not away **from** your presence*
and take not your holy **Spir**it from me.

13 Give me the joy of your saving **help** again*
and sustain me with your boun**ti**ful Spirit.

14 I shall teach your ways **to** the wicked,*
and sinners shall re**turn** to you.

15 Deliver me from **death**, O God,*
and my tongue shall sing of your righteousness,
O God of **my** salvation.

16 Open my **lips**, O Lord,*
and my mouth shall pro**claim** your praise.

17 Had you desired it, I would have offered **sac**rifice,*
but you take no delight **in** burnt-offerings.

18 The sacrifice of God is a **troub**led spirit;*
a broken and contrite heart, O God, you will **not** despise.

19 Be favorable and gra**cious** to Zion,*
and rebuild the walls **of** Jerusalem.

20 Then you will be pleased with the appointed sacrifices,
with burnt-offerings **and** oblations;*
then shall they offer young bullocks up**on** your altar.

Antiphon A broken and a contrite **heart**, O God,*
you will **not** despise.

Silence for meditation

Almighty and merciful Father, you freely forgive those who, as David of old, acknowledge and confess their sins. Create in us pure hearts, and wash away all our sins in the blood of your dear Son, Jesus Christ our Lord. [MPES, LBW]

+

Stand

THE HYMN is sung. *Ein Lämmlein geht und trägt die Schuld*

A lamb goes un - com - lain - ing forth To
save a world of sin - ners. He bears the bur -
den all a - lone, Dies shorn of all his
hon - ors. He goes to slaugh - ter, weak and faint, Is
led to die with - out com - plaint; His spot - less life he
of - fers. He bears the shame, the stripes,
the wrath; His an - guish, mock - er - y, and
death For us he glad - ly suf - fers.

2 This Lamb is Christ, our greatest friend,
The Lamb of God, our Savior,
The one, his only Son, God sent
To win us rebels over.
"Go down, my child," the Father said,
"And free my children from their dread
Of death and condemnation.
The painful stripes are hard to bear,
But by your death they all can share
The joy of your salvation."

3 He answered from his tender heart
That he would take the burden:
"My Father's will is my command;
I'll do as I am bidden."
Oh, wondrous love! Oh, loving might!
To right what mortals cannot right
God sent his Son from heaven.
What love, O Love, who came to save
By loving even to the grave
Until the stone was riven.

4 Of death I am no more afraid;
His dying is my living.
He clothes me in his royal robes
That he is always giving.
His love is dress enough for me
To wear through all eternity
Before the highest Father,
Where we shall stand at Jesus' side,
His Church, the well-appointed bride,
When all the faithful gather. [TLH 142, LBW 105]

Text: Paul Gerhardt, 1607-1676; tr. LBW 1978
Tune: *An Wasserflüssen Babylon*, Wolfgang Dachstein, c. 1487-1553 PM

Sit

A LESSON is read.

Year 1

John 12:27-36

Now is the judgment of this world; now the ruler of this world will be driven out. And I, when I am lifted up from the earth, will draw all people to myself.

Year 2

Mark 12:1-11

This is the heir; come, let us kill him, and the inheritance will be ours.

Antiphon to the MAGNIFICAT

The teacher says, "My **time** is near;*
I will keep the Passover at your house with **my** disciples"

. [LH: Matt. 26:18]

The Paschal Triduum
of the Passion and Resurrection of the Lord

Maundy Thursday

Antiphon to PSALM 74 *Ut quid, Deus?*

Look upon your cove**nant**, O Lord;*
let not the oppressed turn a**way** ashamed.

74 *Lament on the destruction of the temple*

1 O God, why have you utterly **cast** us off?*
why is your wrath so hot against the sheep **of** your pasture?

2 Remember your congregation that you purchased **long** ago,*
the tribe you redeemed to be your inheritance,
and Mount Zion **where** you dwell.

3 Turn your steps toward the **end**less ruins;*
the enemy has laid waste everything **in** your sanctuary.

4 Your adversaries roared in your **ho**ly place;*
they set up their banners as to**kens** of victory.

5 They were like men coming up with axes to a **grove** of trees;*
they broke down all your carved work with hatch**ets**
and hammers.

6 They set fire to your **ho**ly place;*
they defiled the dwelling-place of your Name
and razed it **to** the ground.

7 They said to themselves. "Let us destroy them **al**together."*
They burned down all the meeting-places of God
in the land.

8 There are no signs for us to see;
there is no **proph**et left;*
there is not one among us who **knows** how long.

9 How long, O God, will the adver**sar**y scoff?*
will the enemy blaspheme your **Name** for ever?

10 Why do you draw **back** your hand?*
why is your right hand hidden **in** your bosom?

11 Yet God is my King from **an**cient times,*
victorious in the midst **of** the earth.

12 You divided the sea **by** your might*
and shattered the heads of the dragons up**on** the waters;

13 You crushed the heads **of** Leviathan*
and gave him to the people of the des**ert** for food.

14 You split open **spring** and torrent;*
you dried up ever-**flow**ing rivers.

15 Yours is the day, yours al**so** the night;*
you established the moon **and** the sun.

16 You fixed all the boundaries **of** the earth;*
you made both sum**mer** and winter.

17 Remember, O LORD, how the enemy scoffed,*
how a foolish people de**spised** your Name.

18 Do not hand over the life of your dove **to** wild beasts;*
never forget the lives **of** your poor.

19 Look up**on** your covenant;*
the dark places of the earth are **haunts** of violence.

20 Let not the oppressed turn a**way** ashamed;*
let the poor and needy **praise** your Name.

21 Arise, O God, main**tain** your cause;*
remember how fools revile you **all** day long.

22 Forget not the clamor of your **ad**versaries,*
the unending tumult of those who rise **up** against you.

Antiphon Look upon your cove**nant**, O Lord;*
let not the oppressed turn a**way** ashamed.

Silence for meditation

Lord our God, remember the covenant sealed with the blood of your Son. Make the Church your spiritual house and make us living stones built upon Christ, so that a full and true temple may be raised to your glory; for the sake of your Son, Jesus Christ our Lord. [LH, LBW]

+

Antiphon to PSALM 102 *Domine, exaudi orationem meum*

I said, "O my God, do not take **me** away*
in the midst **of** my days." [PBO]

102 *Prayer in misfortune: a penitential psalm*

1 LORD, hear my prayer, and let my cry **come** before you;*
hide not your face from me in the day **of** my trouble.

2 Incline your **ear** to me;*
when I call, make haste to **an**swer me,

3 For my days drift a**way** like smoke,*
and my bones are hot as **burn**ing coals.

4 My heart is smitten like **grass** and withered,*
so that I forget to **eat** my bread.

5 Because of the voice **of** my groaning*
I am but **skin** and bones.

6 I have become like a vulture **in** the wilderness,*
like an owl a**mong** the ruins.

7 I lie a**wake** and groan;*
I am like a sparrow, lonely **on** a house-top.

8 My enemies revile me **all** day long,*
and those who scoff at me have taken an **oath** against me.

9 For I have eaten ashes for bread*
and mingled my **drink** with weeping.

10 Because of your indigna**tion** and wrath*
you have lifted me up and thrown **me** away.

11 My days pass away **like** a shadow,*
and I wither **like** the grass.

12 But you, O LORD, en**dure** for ever,*
and your Name from **age** to age.

13 You will arise and have compassion on Zion,
for it is time to have mer**cy** upon her;*
indeed, the appointed **time** has come.

14 For your servants love her **ver**y rubble,*
and are moved to pity even **for** her dust.

15 The nations shall fear your **Name**, O LORD,*
and all the kings of the **earth** your glory.

16 For the LORD will **build** up Zion,*
and his glory **will** appear.

17 He will look with favor on the prayer **of** the homeless;*
he will not de**spise** their plea.

18 Let this be written for a future **gen**eration,*
so that a people yet unborn may **praise** the LORD.

19 For the LORD looked down from his holy **place** on high;*
from the heavens he be**held** the earth;

20 That he might hear the groan **of** the captive*
and set free those con**demned** to die;

21 That they may declare in Zion the Name **of** the LORD,*
and his praise **in** Jerusalem;

22 When the peoples are gath**ered** together,*
and the kingdoms also, to **serve** the LORD.

23 He has brought down my strength be**fore** my time;*
he has shortened the number **of** my days;

24 And I said, "O my God,
do not take me away in the midst **of** my days;*
your years endure throughout all **gen**erations.

25 In the beginning, O LORD, you laid the foundations **of** the earth,*
and the heavens are the work **of** your hands;

26 They shall perish, but you will endure;
they all shall wear out **like** a garment;*
as clothing you will change them,
and they **shall** be changed;

27 But you are al**ways** the same,*
and your years will **never** end.

28 The children of your servants **shall** continue,*
and their offspring shall stand fast **in** your sight."

Antiphon I said, "O my God, do not take **me** away*
in the midst **of** my days."

Silence for meditation

Lord, while our days vanish like shadows and our lives wear out like a garment, you remain undisturbed by change. Although our earthly lives come to an end, help us to live in Christ's endless life and at length attain our home, the heavenly Jerusalem, where he lives and reigns with you and the Holy Spirit, now and for ever. [LHd, LBW]

+

Stand

THE HYMN is sung.

2 Before the bitter scene began,
He took the bread, and blessed and broke.
What love through all his actions ran!
What wondrous words of grace he spoke!

3 "My body, broken for your sin,
Receive and eat as living food."
He took the cup and blest the wine:
"Share this new testament, my blood."

4 "Do this," he said, "till time shall end,
Remembering your dying friend;
Meet at my table and record
The full obedience of your Lord."

5 O Lord, your feast we celebrate;
We show your death; we sing your Name
Till you return, when we shall eat
The marriage supper of the Lamb. [LBW 127]

Text: Isaac Watts, 1674-1748, alt.
Tune: *Bourbon,* attr. Freeman Lewis, *1780-1859* LM

Sit

A LESSON is read.

Year 1	Year 2
John 17:1-11(12-26) Father, the hour has come; glorify your Son so that the Son may glorify you, since you have given him authority over all people, to give eternal life to all whom you have given him.	Mark 14:12-25 Truly I tell you, I will never again drink of the fruit of the vine until that day when I drink it new in the kingdom of God.

Silence for meditation follows the reading.

RESPONSORY

For our sake Christ **was** obedient,*
accepting **e**ven death. [LH: Phil. 2:8]

Antiphon to the MAGNIFICAT

While they were eating, Jesus took a **loaf** of bread,*
and after blessing it he broke it, and gave it
to **his** disciples. [LH, PBO: Matt. 26:26]

Good Friday

Antiphon to PSALM 54 *Deus, in nomine*

He was led like a lamb **to** the slaughter,*
and he did not o**pen** his mouth. [PBO; See Isa. 53:7]

54 *Plea for God's help*

1 Save me, O God, **by** your Name;*
in your might, de**fend** my cause.

2 Hear my **prayer**, O God;*
give ear to the words **of** my mouth.

3 For the arrogant have risen up against me,
and the ruthless have **sought** my life,*
those who have no re**gard** for God.

4 Behold, God **is** my helper;*
it is the Lord who sust**ains** my life.

5 Render evil to those who **spy** on me;*
in your faithful**ness**, destroy them.

6 I will offer you a **free**will sacrifice*
and praise your Name, O LORD, for **it** is good.

7 For you have rescued me from **ev**ery trouble,*
and my eye has seen the ruin **of** my foes.

Antiphon He was led like a lamb **to** the slaughter,*
and he did not o**pen** his mouth.

Silence for meditation

Father, hear our prayer and come to the aid of your Church. Mercifully deliver us from evil, so that from the rising of the sun to its setting we may offer you a pure sacrifice of praise; through your Son, Jesus Christ our Lord. [LHd, LBW]

+

Antiphon to PSALM 130 *De profundis*

I wait for the LORD; my soul **waits** for him;*
in his word **is** my hope. [PBO]

130 *From the depths: a penitential psalm*

1 Out of the depths have I called to you, O LORD;
LORD, **hear** my voice;*
let your ears consider well the voice of my **supp**lication.

2 If you, LORD, were to note what is **done** amiss,*
O Lord, **who** could stand?

3 For there is forgive**ness** with you;*
therefore you **shall** be feared.

4 I wait for the LORD; my soul **waits** for him;*
in his word **is** my hope.

5 My soul waits for the LORD,
more than watchmen **for** the morning,*
more than watchmen **for** the morning.

6 O Israel, wait **for** the LORD,*
for with the LORD **there** is mercy;

7 With him there is plente**ous** redemption,*
and he shall redeem Israel from **all** their sins.

Antiphon I wait for the LORD; my soul **waits** for him;*
in his word **is** my hope.

Silence for meditation

God of might and compassion, you sent your Word into the world to announce the dawn of salvation. Do not leave us in the depths of our sins, but listen to your Church pleading for the fullness of your redeeming grace; through Jesus Christ our Lord. [LHd, LBW]

+

Stand

THE HYMN is sung.

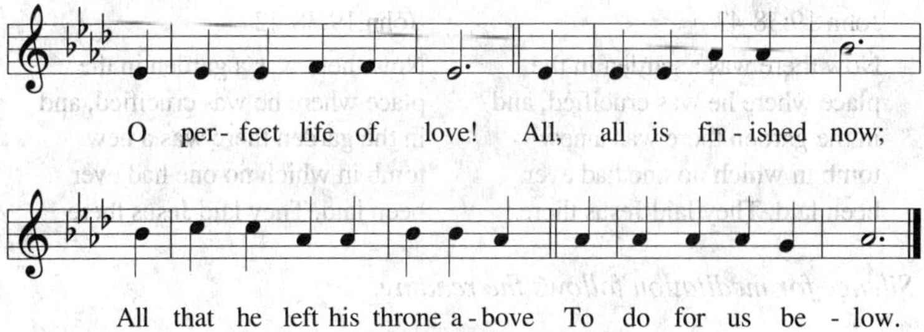

2 No work is left undone
Of all the Father willed;
His toil, his sorrows, one by one,
The Scripture have fulfilled.

3 No pain that we can share
But he has felt its smart;
All forms of human grief and care
Have pierced that tender heart.

4 In perfect love he dies;
For me he dies, for me;
O all-atoning Sacrifice,
I cling by faith to thee.

5 Work, then, O Lord in me,
As thou for me hast wrought;
And let my love the answer be
To grace thy love has brought. [CSB 103, SBH 89]

Text:Henry Williams Baker, 1821-1877

Tune: *Gorton,* arranged from Ludwig von Beethoven, 1807 SM

Sit

A LESSON is read.

Year 1

John 19:38-42

Now there was a garden in the place where he was crucified, and in the garden there was a new tomb in which no one had ever been laid. They laid Jesus there.

Year 2

John 19:38-42

Now there was a garden in the place where he was crucified, and in the garden there was a new tomb in which no one had ever been laid. They laid Jesus there.

Silence for meditation follows the reading.

RESPONSORY

For our sake Christ **was** obedient,*
accepting even death, death **on** a cross. [LH: Phil. 2:8]

Antiphon to the MAGNIFICAT

God did not withhold **his** own Son,*
but gave him up for **all** of us. [PBO: Rom. 8:32]

Holy Saturday

Antiphon to PSALM 3 *Domine, quid multiplicati*

You, O LORD, are a **shield** about me;*
you are the one who lifts **up** my head. [LH, PBO]

3 *Confidence under persecution*

1 LORD, how many adversar**ies** I have!*
how many there are who rise **up** against me!

2 How many there are who **say** of me,*
"There is no help for him **in** his God."

3 But you, O LORD, are a **shield** about me;*
you are my glory, the one who lifts **up** my head.

4 I call aloud up**on** the LORD,*
and he answers me from his **ho**ly hill;

5 I lie down and **go** to sleep;*
I wake again, because the **LORD** sustains me.

6 I do not fear the multi**tudes** of people*
who set themselves against me **all** around.

7 Rise up, O LORD; set me free, **O** my God;*
surely, you will strike all my enemies across the face,
you will break the teeth **of** the wicked.

8 Deliverance belongs **to** the LORD.*
Your blessing be up**on** your people!

Antiphon You, O LORD, are a **shield** about me;*
you are the one who lifts **up** my head

Silence for meditation

Lord God, you heard the cry of your Son when he was oppressed and delivered him from the sleep of death. Shield your Church so that it may hold up its head and radiate the glory of the resurrection; through Jesus Christ our Lord. [LH]

+

Antiphon to PSALM 27 *Dominus illuminatio*

I shall see the goodness **of** the LORD*
in the land **of** the living. [LH, PBO]

27 *Triumphant trust in God*

1 The LORD is my light and salvation;
whom then **shall** I fear?*
the LORD is the strength of my life;
of whom then shall I **be** afraid?

2 When evildoers came upon me to eat **up** my flesh,*
it was they, my foes and my adversaries, who
stum**bled** and fell.

3 Though an army should en**camp** against me,*
yet my heart shall not **be** afraid;

4 And though war should rise **up** against me,*
yet will I put my **trust** in him.

5 One thing have I asked of the LORD;
one **thing** I seek;*
that I may dwell in the house of the LORD all the days **of** my life;

6 To behold the fair beauty **of** the LORD*
and to seek him **in** his temple.

7 For in the day of trouble he shall keep me safe
in his shelter;*
he shall hide me in the secrecy of his dwelling
and set me high up**on** a rock.

8 Even now he lifts **up** my head*
above my enemies **round** about me.

9 Therefore I will offer in his dwelling an oblation
with sounds **of** great gladness;*
I will sing and make music **to** the LORD.

10 Hearken to my voice, O LORD, **when** I call;*
have mercy on me and **an**swer me.

11 You speak in my heart and say, "**Seek** my face."*
Your face, LORD, **will** I seek.

12 Hide not your **face** from me,*
nor turn away your servant **in** displeasure.

13 You have been my helper;
cast me **not** away;*
do not forsake me, O God of **my** salvation.

14 Though my father and my moth**er** forsake me,*
the LORD **will** sustain me.

15 Show me your **way**, O LORD;*
lead me on a level path, because **of** my enemies.

16 Deliver me not into the hand of my **ad**versaries,*
for false witnesses have risen up against me,
and also those **who** speak malice.

17 What if I had not believed
that I should see the goodness **of** the LORD*
in the land **of** the living!

18 O tarry and await the LORD's pleasure;
be strong, and he shall com**fort** your heart;*
wait patiently **for** the LORD.

Antiphon I shall see the goodness **of** the LORD*
in the land **of** the living.

Silence for meditation

Gracious Father, protector of those who hope in you: You heard the cry of your Son and kept him safe in your shelter in the day of evil. Grant that your servants who seek your face in times of trouble may see your goodness in the land of the living, through your Son, Jesus Christ our Lord. [LH, LBW]

+

Stand

THE HYMN is sung.

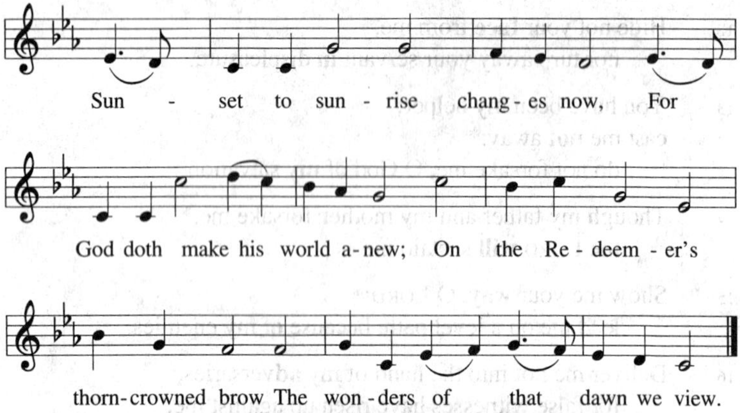

2 E'en though the sun withholds its light,
Lo! a more heavenly lamp shines here,
And from the cross on Calvary's height
Gleams of eternity appear.

3 Here in o'erwhelming final strife
The Lord of life hath victory;
And sin is slain, and death brings life,
And earth inherits heaven's key. [H82 163]

Text: St. Clement of Alexandria, c. 170-220; para. Howard Chandler Robbins, 1876-1952, alt.
Tune: *Kedron,* attrib. Elkanah Kelsay Dare, 1782-1826 LM

Sit

A LESSON is read.

Year 1

Romans 8:1-11

If the Spirit of him who raised Jesus from the dead dwells in you, he who raised Christ from the dead will give life to your mortal bodies also through his Spirit that dwells in you.

Year 2

Romans 8:1-11

If the Spirit of him who raised Jesus from the dead dwells in you, he who raised Christ from the dead will give life to your mortal bodies also through his Spirit that dwells in you.

Silence for meditation follows the reading.

RESPONSORY

For our sake Christ **was** obedient,*
accepting even death, death **on** a cross.
Therefore God has highly ex**alt**ed him,*
and bestowed on him the Name that is above **ev**ery name.
[LH: Phil. 2:8-9]

Antiphon to the MAGNIFICAT

O death, I will **be** your death;*
O grave, I will be **your** destruction. [PBO: see Hos. 13:14]

The transition to the fifty days of Easter takes place at the Easter Vigil. Daily Prayer for Easter begins with Morning Prayer of Easter Day.

MORNING PRAYER

Matins or Morning Praise during the Great and Holy Week

Stand

Leader

Congregation

Leader and Congregation

The Invitatory and Venite are omitted during Holy Week.

Sit

A Psalm is sung or said; an Old Testament canticle and an additional psalm may be sung or said also. Silence for meditation follows each psalm or canticle. The psalm prayer appropriate to each psalm or canticle follows the silence.

C Amen

Stand

THE HYMN is sung.

Sit

One or two LESSONS are read. Silence for meditation follows each reading.

The Responsory to the reading(s) follows the silence. After the Responsory the leader then continues:

L In many and various ways God spoke to his people of old by the prophets.

C But now in these last days he has spoken to us by his Son.

Stand

The GOSPEL CANTICLE, Benedictus Dominus Deus, *is sung or said. The proper Antiphon is given on pp. 1160-1223.*

The Antiphon is sung or said.

1 ✠ Blessed be the Lord,
the . . . . God of Israel; he has come
to his people and set them free.

3 Through his holy
prophets he promised
of old that he
would save us . . . . . . from our enemes, from the hands of all who hate us.

5 This was the oath
he swore to our . . . . fa - ther Abraham: to set us free
from the hands of our enemies,

2 He has raised up for
us a . . . . might - y Savior, born of the house of his ser -vant David.

4 He promised to show
mercy . . . . to our fathers and to remember his . . . ho - ly covenant.

6 free to worship him with - out fear, holy and righteous in
his sight all the days of our life.

7 You, my child, shall be
called the prophet of the most high, for you will
go before
the Lord to pre - pare his way,

9 In the tender
compassion . . . . of our God, the dawn
from on
high shall break up - on us.

11 Glory to the
Father and . . . . to the Son, and to the . . . . Ho - ly Spirit;

8 to give his people
knowledge . . . . of sal - vation by the forgiveness . . . . of their sins.

10 to shine on those
who dwell in darkness
and the shad - ow of death, and to guide
our feet into the . . . . . way of peace.

12 as it was in the
begin - ning, is now, and will be for ev - er. A - men.

The Antiphon is repeated.

I believe in God, the Father almighty,
creator of heaven and earth.
I believe in Jesus Christ, his only Son, our Lord,
He was conceived by the power of the Holy Spirit
and born of the Virgin Mary.
He suffered under Pontius Pilate,
was crucified, died, and was buried.
He descended to the dead [*or* He descended into hell].
On the third day he rose again.
He ascended into heaven,
and is seated at the right hand of the Father.
He will come again to judge the living and the dead.
I believe in the Holy Spirit,
the holy catholic Church,
the communion of saints,
the forgiveness of sins,
the resurrection of the body,
and the life everlasting. Amen.

Kneel or stand

The GREAT SUFFRAGES are said. [BR, Löhe, CB, CSB, SBH]

L Kyrie eleison.
C Lord, have mercy.
L Christe, eleison.
C Christ, have mercy.
L Kyrie, eleison.
C Lord, have mercy.

L	Our Father in heaven, hallowed be your Name, your kingdom come, your will be done, on earth as in heaven. Give us today our daily bread. Forgive us our sins as we forgive those who sin against us. Save us from the time of trial,	L	Our Father, who art in heaven, hallowed be thy Name, thy kingdom come, thy will be done, on earth as it is in heaven. Give us this day our daily bread; and forgive us our trespasses, as we forgive those who trespass against us; and lead us not into temptation,
C	and deliver us from evil.	C	but deliver us from evil.

L I said, "Lord, be merciful to me;
C Heal me, for I have sinned against you." [Ps. 41:4]

L Return, O Lord; how long will you tarry?
C Be gracious to your servants. [Ps. 90:13]

L Let your loving-kindness, O Lord, be upon us,
C As we have put our trust in you. [Ps. 33:22]

L O Lord, save our nation.
C And answer us when we call. [see Ps. 20:9]

L Let your priests be clothed with righteousness;
C Let your faithful people sing with joy. [Ps. 132:9]

L Save your people and bless your inheritance;
C Shepherd them and carry them for ever. [Ps. 28:11]

L Remember your congregation
C That you purchased long ago. [Ps. 74:2]

L Peace be within your walls
C And quietness within your towers. [Ps. 122:7]

L Let us remember the faithful departed.
C Rest eternal grant to them, O Lord,
and let light perpetual shine upon them

L May they rest in peace.
C Amen

L Let us pray for our absent brothers and sisters.
C Save your servants who put their trust in you. [Ps. 86:2]

L Let us pray for the afflicted and captives.
C Send them help from your holy place,
and strengthen them out of Zion. [Ps. 20:2]

L Restore us, O God of hosts;
C Show the light of your countenance, and we shall be saved. [Ps. 80:7]

L Arise, O Christ, for our help;
C And save us, for the sake of your steadfast love. [Ps. 44:26]

L Lord, hear my prayer,
C And let my prayer come before you. [Ps. 102:1]

L The Lord be with you.
C And also with you.

L Let us pray.

The PRAYER OF THE DAY is said.

The Sunday of the Passion

Almighty and everliving God, in your tender love for the human race you sent your Son our Savior Jesus Christ to take upon him our nature, and to suffer death upon the cross, giving us the example of his great humility: Mercifully grant that we may walk in the way of his suffering, and also share in his resurrection; through Jesus Christ our Lord, who lives and reigns with you and the Holy Spirit, one God, now and for ever.

[Gel., MR, RS, BCP, LBW]

Lord Jesus Christ, who for the redemption of the world ascended the wood of the cross, that you might enlighten the whole world which lay in darkness: Pour that light, we pray, into our souls and bodies, whereby we may be enabled to attain to the light eternal; who with the Father and the Holy Spirit, live and reign, God for ever. [Sarum, AC]

Monday in Holy Week

Grant, we beseech you, Almighty God, that we, who in our times of trial often grow weak and falter, may take heart again and find new strength, seeing that Christ in his Passion has offered for us the obedience we are too frail to offer you; through the same Jesus Christ our Lord, who lives and reigns with you and the Holy Spirit, one God, now and for ever.

[Greg., MR, RS, CB, CSB, SBH; tr. DvD]

Almighty God, whose most dear Son went not up to joy but first he suffered pain, and entered not into glory before he was crucified: Mercifully grant that we, walking in the way of the cross, may find it none other than the way of life and peace; through Jesus Christ your Son our Lord, who lives and reigns with you and the Holy Spirit, one God, for ever and ever. [William Reed Huntington, 1892, BCP]

Tuesday in Holy Week

Almighty and everlasting God, grant us grace so to contemplate the Passion of our Lord that we may find therein forgiveness for our sins; through Jesus Christ our Lord, who lives and reigns with you and the Holy Spirit, one God, now and for ever. [Greg., MR, RS, CB, CSB, SBH]

O God, by the passion of your blessed Son you made an instrument of shameful death to be for us the means of life: Grant us so to glory in the cross of Christ, that we may gladly suffer shame and loss for the sake of your Son our Savior Jesus Christ; who lives and reigns with you and the Holy Spirit, one God, for ever and ever. [BCPp, BCP]

Wednesday in Holy Week

Almighty and everlasting God, it was your will that your Son should bear for us the pains of the cross so that you might free us from the power of the enemy: Help us so to remember and give thanks for our Lord's Passion that we may obtain remission of sin and redemption from everlasting death; through your Son Jesus Christ our Lord, who lives and reigns with you and the Holy Spirit, one God, now and for ever.

[Greg., MR, RS, CB, CSB, SBH]

Lord God, whose blessed Son our Savior gave his body to be whipped and his face to be spit upon: Give us grace to accept joyfully the sufferings of the present time, confident of the glory that shall be revealed; through Jesus Christ your Son our Lord, who lives and reigns with you and the Holy Spirit, one God, for ever and ever. [1928 BCP]

Maundy Thursday

O Lord God, in a wonderful sacrament you have left us a memorial of your Passion: Deepen our reverence for the sacred mysteries of your Body and Blood, that we may ever perceive within ourselves the fruit of your redemption; who live and reign with the Father and the Holy Spirit, one God, now and for ever.

[Thomas Aquinas, MR, RS; CB, CSB, SBH, LBW; BCP]

Good Friday

Almighty God, we pray you graciously to behold this your family, for whom our Lord Jesus Christ was willing to be betrayed, and given into the hands of sinners, and to suffer death upon the cross; who now lives and reigns with you and the Holy Spirit, one God, now and for ever.

[Greg., Sarum, MG, LH; BCP; CB, CSB, SBH, LBW]

Holy Saturday

O God, Creator of heaven and earth: Grant that, as the crucified body of your dear Son was laid in the tomb and rested on this holy Sabbath, so we may await with him the coming of the third day, and rise with him to newness of life; who now lives and reigns with you and the Holy Spirit, one God, for ever and ever. [1979 BCP]

Additional prayers may be said.

The prayers conclude

O Lord God, whose blessed Son bore our sins in his own body on the tree: Give us, we pray, such true repentance and amendment of life, that we may never crucify him afresh, and put him to an open shame, by conscious and willful sin; through the same Jesus Christ our Lord.

[BCP Scotland]

We give thanks to you, heavenly Father, through Jesus Christ your dear Son, that you have protected us through the night from all danger and harm. We ask you to preserve and keep us, this day also, from all sin and evil, that in all our thoughts, words, and deeds, we may serve and please you. Into your hands we commend our bodies and souls and all that is ours. Let your holy angels have charge of us, that the wicked one have no power over us.

L Christ was wounded for our transgressions;
C He was crushed for our iniquities. [Isa. 53:5; CSB]

Almighty and everlasting God, you restore us by the Passion of your Christ: Preserve in us the works of your mercy, that by the celebration of this mystery our lives may be continually devoted to you; through the same Jesus Christ our Lord. [Leo., AC]

C Amen

Stand

The BENEDICTION concludes the service when there is no sermon or Paschal Blessing. On Sunday the Paschal Blessing (p. 990) may replace the benediction. A hymn may follow the benediction.

When there is a sermon, the order continues as on p. 20. On Sundays the Paschal Blessing may follow the prayer after the sermon.

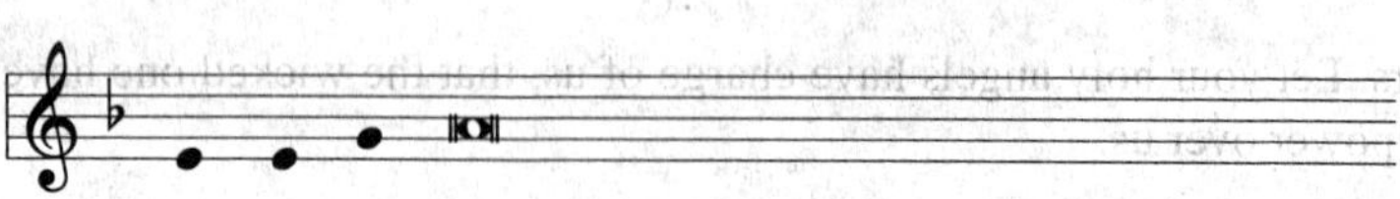

L The Lord al - mighty bless us, ✠ and direct our days and

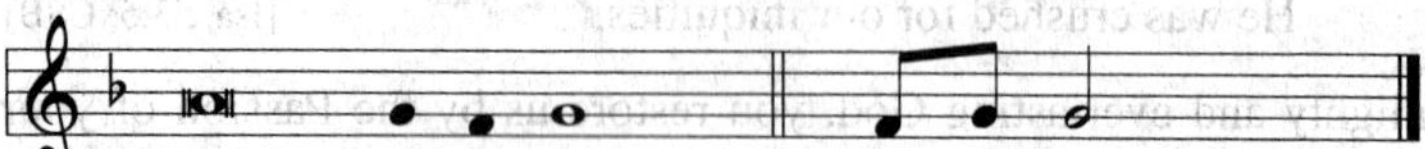

our deeds in his peace. C A - men

The Sunday of the Passion

Antiphon to PSALM 103 *Benedic, anima mea, Domino, et omnia*

The great crowd that had come to the festival cried out **to** the Lord,*
"Blessed is the one who comes in the Name of the Lord.
Hosanna **in** the highest." [LH: John 12:12-13; Mark 11:10]

103 *Praise of God's love*

1 Bless the LORD, **O** my soul,*
and all that is within me, bless his **ho**ly Name.

2 Bless the LORD, **O** my soul,*
and forget not **all** his benefits.

3 He forgives **all** your sins*
and heals all **your** infirmities;

4 He redeems your life **from** the grave*
and crowns you with mercy and **lov**ingkindness;

5 He satisfies you **with** good things,*
and your youth is renewed **like** an eagle's.

6 The LORD executes **right**eousness*
and judgment for all who **are** oppressed.

7 He made his ways **known** to Moses*
and his works to the chil**dren** of Israel.

8 The LORD is full of compas**sion** and mercy,*
slow to anger and **of** great kindness.

9 He will not al**ways** accuse us,*
nor will he keep his an**ger** forever.

10 He has not dealt with us according **to** our sins,*
nor rewarded us according **to** our wickedness.

11 For as the heavens are high a**bove** the earth,*
so is his mercy great upon **those** who fear him.

12 As far as the east is **from** the west,*
so far has he removed our **sins** from us.

13 As a father cares **for** his children,*
so does the LORD care for **those** who fear him.

14 For he himself knows whereof **we** are made;*
he remembers that we **are** but dust.

15 Our days are **like** the grass;*
we flourish like a flower **of** the field;

16 When the wind goes over it, **it** is gone,*
and its place shall know **it** no more.

17 But the merciful goodness of the LORD endures for ever on **those** who fear him,*
and his righteousness on **child**ren's children;

18 On those who **keep** his covenant*
and remember his command**ments** and do them.

19 The LORD has set his **throne** in heaven,*
and his kingship has dominion **o**ver all.

20 Bless the LORD, you angels of his,
you mighty ones who **do** his bidding,*
and hearken to the voice **of** his word.

21 Bless the LORD, all **you** his hosts,*
you ministers of his who **do** his will.

22 Bless the LORD, all you works of his,
in all places of **his** dominion;*
bless the LORD, **O** my soul.

Antiphon
The great crowd that had come to the festival cried out **to** the Lord,*
"Blessed is the one who comes in the Name of the Lord.
Hosanna **in** the highest."

Silence for meditation

Lord, you have compassion for the sinner, as a father has compassion for his children: Heal the weakness of your people and save us from everlasting death, that with the saints and angels we may praise and glorify you, Father, Son, and Holy Spirit, now and for ever. [LH, LBW]

+

Antiphon to the OLD TESTAMENT CANTICLE *Domine, audivi*

God grant that with the angels and the children we may be faithful and sing with them to the conquer**or** of death*
Hosanna **in** the highest. [LH: see Matt. 21:15]

A Song of Habakkuk Habakkuk 3:1-4, 6-10, 12-13, 15-16, 18-19

O LORD, I have heard of **your** renown;*
I am in awe, O LORD, **of** your work.
In our own **time** revive it;*
in our own time make it known,
in wrath re**mem**ber mercy.

God **came** from Teman,*
the Holy One from **Mount** Paran;
His radiance cov**ered** the skies,*
and his splendor **filled** the earth.
His brightness is **like** the dawn,*
rays flash from his hand where his pow**er** lay hidden.

He stopped and **shook** the earth,*
he looked and made the **na**tions tremble;
The eternal moun**tains** were shattered,*
along his ancient pathways
the everlasting **hills** sank low.
I saw the tents of Cu**shan** collapse,*
the tent curtains of **Mid**ian flutter.
Was your wrath against the rivers, O LORD,
or your rage **against** the sea*
when you drove your horses and chari**ots** to victory?
You brandished your **na**ked bow;*
sated were the arrows at **your** command.

You split the **earth** with rivers;*
the mountains saw you and **writhed** in fear.
A torrent of wat**er** swept by,*
and the deep sea thun**dered** aloud,
In fury you **trod** the earth;*
in anger you trampled **down** the nations.
You came forth to **save** your people;*
to save **your** anointed.

You trampled the sea **with** your horses,*
churning the **might**y waters.
I hear, and my **bod**y quakes;*
my lips quiver **at** the sound;
Trembling comes o**ver** my bones,*
and my feet tot**ter** beneath me.
Yet I will exult **in** the LORD*
and rejoice in the **God** who saves me.
God the LORD **is** my strength:*
he makes my feet nimble as the deer
and sets me up**on** the heights. [CSB, SBH, PHP]

Antiphon God grant that with the angels and the children we may be faithful and sing with them to the conquer**or** of death*
Hosanna **in** the highest.

Silence for meditation

God our Savior, when your Son went forth in lowly majesty to his last and fiercest struggle, the earth shook and all nature bowed in awe: Deepen our understanding of that cosmic battle, that by your mercy and strength we may rejoice in the magnitude of our salvation, which you have accomplished through your Son, Jesus Christ our Lord. [PHP]

+

Antiphon to PSALM 138 *Confitebor tibi*

Blessed is the King who comes in the Name **of** the Lord!*
Peace in heaven, and glory in the **high**est heaven!
[LH, PBO: Luke 19:38]

138 *Hymn of thanksgiving*

1 I will give thanks to you, O LORD, with **my** whole heart;*
before the gods I will **sing** your praise.

2 I will bow down toward your holy temple
and **praise** your name,*
because of your **love** and faithfulness;

3 For you have glori**fied** your Name*
and your word a**bove** all things.

4 When I called, you **an**swered me;*
you increased my **strength** within me.

5 All the kings of the earth will praise **you**, O LORD,*
when they have heard the words **of** your mouth.

6 They will sing of the ways **of** the LORD,*
that great is the glory **of** the LORD.

7 Though the LORD be high, he cares **for** the lowly;*
he perceives the haughty **from** afar.

8 Though I walk in the midst of trouble, you **keep** me safe;*
you stretch forth your hand against the fury of my enemies;
your right **hand** shall save me.

9 The LORD will make good his pur**pose** for me;*
O LORD, your love endures for ever;
do not abandon the works **of** your hands.

Antiphon Blessed is the King who comes in the Name **of** the Lord!*
Peace in heaven, and glory in the **high**est heaven!

Silence for meditation

Lord God, you keep the proud at a distance and look upon the lowly with favor: Stretch out your hand to us in our suffering, perfect in us the work of your love, and bring us to life in Jesus Christ our Lord.

[LH, LBW]

+

Stand

THE HYMN is sung. *Pange lingua gloriosi proelium*

2 Thirty years among us dwelling,
His appointed time fulfilled,
Born for this, he meets his passion,
This the Savior freely willed:
On the cross the Lamb is lifted,
Where his precious blood is spilled.

3 He endures the nails, the spitting,
Vinegar, and spear, and reed;
From that holy body broken
Blood and water forth proceed:
Earth, and stars, and sky, and ocean
By that blood from stain are freed.

4 Faithful cross! above all other,
One and only noble tree!
None in foliage, none in blossom,
None in fruit thy peer may be:
Sweetest wood and sweetest iron!
Sweetest weight is hung on thee.

5 Bend thy boughs, O tree of glory,
Thy relaxing sinews bend;
For a while the ancient rigor
That thy birth bestowed, suspend;
And the King of heavenly beauty
On thy bosom gently tend.

6 Praise and honor to the Father,
Praise and honor to the Son,
Praise and honor to the Spirit,
Ever Three and ever One:
One in might and one in glory
While eternal ages run. [H40 66, SBH 61, H82 166]

Text: Venantius Honorius Fortunatus, 530-609; tr. John Mason Neale, 1818-1866 alt.
Tune: *Pange lingua,* Plainsong, Mode 3, *Zisterzienser Hymnar,* 14th cent. Cologne, 1599
87 87 87

Sit

One or two LESSONS are read.

Silence for meditation follows each reading.

Year 1 and Year 2

Zechariah 9:9-12

Rejoice greatly, O daughter Zion! Shout aloud, O daughter Jerusalem! Lo, your king comes to you; triumphant and victorious is he, humble and riding on a donkey, on a colt, the foal of a donkey.

or Zechariah 12:9-11; 13:1, 7-9

On that day a fountain shall be opened for the house of David and the inhabitants of Jerusalem, to cleanse them from sin and impurity.

Silence for meditation

RESPONSORY

The great crowd heard that Jesus was coming **to** Jerusalem.*
They took branches of palm trees and went out to **meet** him saying,
  Hosanna to the **Son** of David!*
  Blessed is the one who comes in the Name **of** the Lord!
A very large crowd spread their cloaks on the road,
and others cut branches from the trees and spread them **on** the road.*
The crowds that went ahead of him and that fol**lowed** were shouting,
  Hosanna to the **Son** of David!*
  Blessed is the one who comes in the Name **of** the Lord!

[LH: John 12:12, 13; Matt. 21:8, 9]

1 Timothy 6:12-16

Keep the commandment without spot or blame until the manifestation of our Lord Jesus Christ.

Silence for meditation

RESPONSORY

Sacrifices and offerings you have not desired
but a body you have pre**pared** for me;*
I have come to do your **will**, O God.
Because it is impossible for the blood of bulls and goats
to take away sins,
when Christ came into the **world** he said,*
I have come to do your **will**, O God.
[LH: Hebrews 10:5, 6, 7, 4 (Ps. 40:7-8)]

Antiphon to the BENEDICTUS

Hosanna to the Son of David! Blessed is the one who comes in the Name **of** the Lord!*
O King of Israel, hosanna in the **high**est heaven!
[PBO: Matt 21:9; John 12:13]

Monday in Holy Week

Antiphon to PSALM 40 *Expectans, expectavi Dominum*

I love to do your will, **O** my God;*
your law is deep **in** my heart. [LH]

40 *Thanksgiving and plea for help*

1 I waited patiently up**on** the LORD;*
he stooped to me and **heard** my cry.

2 He lifted me out of the desolate pit, out of the **mire** and clay;*
he set my feet upon a high cliff and made my **foot**ing sure.

3 He put a new song in my mouth,
a song of praise **to** our God;*
many shall see, and stand in awe,
and put their trust **in** the Lord.

4 Happy are they who trust **in** the Lord!*
they do not resort to evil spirits or turn **to** false gods.

5 Great things are they that you have done, O LORD my God!
how great your wonders and your **plans** for us!*
there is none who can be com**pared** with you.

6 Oh, that I could make them **known** and tell them!*
but they are more than **I** can count.

7 In sacrifice and offering you **take** no pleasure;*
(you have given me **ears** to hear you);

8 Burnt-offering and sin-offering you have **not** required,*
and so I said, "Be**hold**, I come.

9 In the roll of the book it is written con**cern**ing me:*
'I love to do your will, O my God;
your law is deep **in** my heart.'"

10 I proclaimed righteousness in the great **con**gregation;*
behold, I did not restrain my lips;
and that, O **LORD**, you know.

11 Your righteousness have I not hidden in my heart;
I have spoken of your faithfulness and **your** deliverance;*
I have not concealed your love and faithfulness from
the great **con**gregation.

12 You are the LORD;
do not withhold your com**pas**sion from me;*
let your love and your faithfulness keep me **safe** for ever,

13 For innumerable troubles have crowded upon me;
my sins have overtaken me, and I **can**not see;*
they are more in number than the hairs of my head,
and **my** heart fails me.

14 Be pleased, O LORD, to de**li**ver me;*
O LORD, make **haste** to help me.

15 Let them be ashamed and altogether dismayed
who seek after my life **to** destroy it;*
let them draw back and be disgraced
who take pleasure in **my** misfortune.

16 Let those who say "Aha!" and gloat over me **be** confounded,*
because they **are** ashamed.

17 Let all who seek you rejoice in you **and** be glad;*
let those who love your salvation continually say,
"Great **is** the LORD!"

18 Though I am poor **and** afflicted,*
the Lord will have re**gard** for me.

19 You are my helper and **my** deliverer;*
do not tarry, **O** my God.

Antiphon I love to do your will, **O** my God;*
your law is deep **in** my heart.

Silence for meditation

Lord Jesus Christ, you became obedient to death and your Name was exalted above all others: Teach us always to do the Father's will, so that, made holy by your obedience and united to your sacrifice, we can know your great love in times of sorrow and sing a new song to our God now and for ever. [LH, LBW]

+

Antiphon to PSALM 42 *Quemadmodum desiderat cervus*

My soul is athirst for God, athirst for the **liv**ing God;*
when shall I come to appear before the pres**ence** of God?

[LH]

42 *The exile's nostalgia for God's temple*

1 As the deer longs **for** the water-brooks,*
so longs my soul for **you**, O God.

2 My soul is athirst for God, athirst for the **liv**ing God;*
when shall I come to appear before the pres**ence** of God?

3 My tears have been my food **day** and night,*
while all day long they say to me,
"Where now **is** your God?"

4 I pour out my soul when I think **on** these things;*
how I went with the multitude and led them into the
house of God,

5 With the voice of praise **and** thanksgiving,*
among those **who** keep holy-day.

6 Why are you so full of heaviness, **O** my soul?*
And why are you so disquiet**ed** within me?

7 Put your **trust** in God;*
for I will yet give thanks to him,
who is the help of my countenance, **and** my God.

8 My soul is heav**y** within me;*
therefore I will remember you from the land of Jordan,
and from the peak of Mizar among the **heights** of Hermon.

9 One deep calls to another in the noise **of** your cataracts;*
all your rapids and floods have gone **o**ver me.

10 The LORD grants his lovingkindness **in** the daytime;*
in the night season his song is with me,
a prayer to the God **of** my life.

11 I will say to the God of my strength,
"Why have you for**got**ten me,*
and why do I go so heavily while the enemy op**press**es me?"

12 While my bones are **be**ing broken,*
my enemies mock me **to** my face;

13 All day **long** they mock me*
and say to me, "Where now **is** your God?"

14 Why are you so full of heaviness, **O** my soul?*
And why are you so disquiet**ed** within me?

15 Put your **trust** in God;*
for I will yet give thanks to him,
who is the help of my countenance, **and** my God.

Antiphon My soul is athirst for God, athirst for the **liv**ing God;*
when shall I come to appear before the pres**ence** of God?

Silence for meditation

Lord God, never-failing fountain of life, through the saving waters of baptism you called us from the depth of sin to the depths of mercy. Do not forget the trials of our exile, but from the wellspring of the Word satisfy our thirst for you, so that we may come rejoicing to your holy mountain, where you live and reign now and for ever. [LHd, LBW]

+

Stand

THE HYMN is sung. *Jesu, deine Passion*

2 Make me see your great distress,
Anguish, and affliction,
Bonds and stripes and wretchedness
And your crucifixion;
Make me see how scourge and rod,
Spear and nails, did wound you,
How you died for those, O God,
Who with thorns had crowned you.

3 Yet, O Lord, not thus alone
Make me see your Passion.
But its cause to make me known
And its termination.
For I also and my sin
Wrought your deep affliction;
This the shameful cause has been
Of your crucifixion.

4 Let me view your pain and loss
With repentant grieving,
Nor prepare again your cross
By unholy living.
May I give you love for love!
Hear me, O my Savior,
That I may in heaven above
Sing your praise for ever. [TLH 140, LBW 115]

Text: Sigismund von Birken, 1626-1681; tr. August Crull, 1846-1923, alt.

Tune: *Jesu Kreutz, Leiden und Pein,* Melchior Vulpius, c. 1560-1615 76 76 D

Sit

One or two LESSONS are read.

Silence for meditation follows each reading.

Year 1

Jeremiah 11:18-20; 12:1-16 (17)

I was like a gentle lamb led to the slaughter.

Year 2

Lamentations 1:1-2, 6-12

It is nothing to you, all who pass by? Look and see if there is any sorrow like my sorrow.

Silence for meditation

RESPONSORY

Do not abandon your confidence; it brings a **great** reward.*
For you need endurance,
so that when you have done the will of God,
you may receive **what** was promised.
By your endurance you will **gain** your souls.*
For you need endurance,
so that when you have done the will of God,
you may receive **what** was promised.

[LH: Heb. 10:35-36; Luke 21:19]

Philippians 3:1-14

I want to know Christ and the power of his resurrection and the sharing of his sufferings.

2 Corinthians 1:1-7

For just as the sufferings of Christ are abundant for us, so also our consolation is abundant through Christ.

Silence for meditation

RESPONSORY

We worship your cross, O Lord;
we recall your glo**ri**ous Passion.*
Have mercy on us
for whose sake you en**dured** so much.
You have redeemed us with your precious blood;
hear the prayer of your servants and come **to** our help.*
Have mercy on us
for whose sake you en**dured** so much. [LH]

Antiphon to the BENEDICTUS

Righteous Father, the world does not know you, but **I** know you;*
and these know that **you** have sent me.

[LH, PBO: John 17:25]

Tuesday in Holy Week

Antiphon to PSALM 50 *Deus deorum*

Christ himself bore our sins in his body **on** the cross*
so that, free from sins, we might **live** for righteousness.
[1 Peter 2:24]

50 *Worship in spirit and truth*

1 The LORD, the God of **gods**, has spoken;*
he has called the earth from the rising of the sun **to** its setting.

2 Out of Zion, perfect **in** its beauty,*
God reveals him**self** in glory.

3 Our God will come and will **not** keep silence;*
before him there is a consuming flame,
and round about him a **rag**ing storm.

4 He calls the heavens and the earth **from** above*
to witness the judgment **of** his people.

5 "Gather before me my **loy**al followers,*
those who have made a covenant with me
and sealed **it** with sacrifice."

6 Let the heavens declare the rightness **of** his cause;*
for God him**self** is judge.

7 Hear, O my people, and I will speak:
"O Israel, I will bear wit**ness** against you;*
for I am **God**, your God.

8 I do not accuse you because **of** your sacrifices;*
your offerings are al**ways** before me.

9 I will take no bull-calf **from** your stalls,*
nor he-goats out **of** your pens;

10 For all the beasts of the for**est** are mine,*
the herds in their thousands up**on** the hills.

11 I know every bird **in** the sky,*
and the creatures of the fields are **in** my sight.

12 If I were hungry, I **would** not tell you,*
for the whole world is mine and all **that** is in it.

13 Do you think I eat the **flesh** of bulls,*
or drink the **blood** of goats?

14 Offer to God a sacrifice **of** thanksgiving*
and make good your vows to **the** Most High.

15 Call upon me in the **day** of trouble;*
I will deliver you, and you shall **hon**or me."

16 But to the wick**ed** God says:*
"Why do you recite my statutes,
and take my covenant up**on** your lips;

17 Since you **re**fuse discipline,*
and toss my words be**hind** your back?

18 When you see a thief, you make **him** your friend,*
and you cast in your lot **with** adulterers.

19 You have loosed your **lips** for evil,*
and harnessed your tongue **to** a lie.

20 You are always speaking evil **of** your brother*
and slandering your own **moth**er's son.

21 These things you have done, and **I** kept still,*
and you thought that I **am** like you."

22 I have made my **ac**cusation;*
I have put my case in order be**fore** your eyes.

23 Consider this well, you who **for**get God,*
lest I rend you and there be none to de**liv**er you.

24 Whoever offers me the sacrifice of thanksgiving **hon**ors me;*
but to those who keep in my way will I show the
salva**tion** of God."

Antiphon Christ himself bore our sins in his body **on** the cross*
so that, free from sins, we might **live** for righteousness.

Silence for meditation

Heavenly Father, because Jesus your servant became obedient to death, his sacrifice was greater than all the holocausts of old: Accept the sacrifice of praise we offer you through him, and help us show the effects of it in our lives by striving to do your will, until our whole life becomes adoration in spirit and truth; through your Son, Jesus Christ our Lord.

[LHd, LBW]

+

Antiphon to PSALM 120 *Ad Dominum*

I called to the LORD and he **an**swered me. [LH, PBO]

120 *Longing for peace*

1 When I was in trouble, I called **to** the LORD;*
I called to the LORD, and he **an**swered me.

2 Deliver me, O LORD, from **ly**ing lips*
and from the de**ceit**ful tongue.

3 What shall be done to you, and what **more** besides,*
O you de**ceit**ful tongue?

4 The sharpened arrows **of** a warrior,*
along with hot **glow**ing coals.

5 How hateful it is that I must **lodge** in Meshech*
and dwell among the **tents** of Kedar!

6 Too long have I **had** to live*
among the ene**mies** of peace.

7 I am on the **side** of peace,*
but when I speak of it, they **are** for war.

Antiphon I called to the Lord and he answered me.

Silence for meditation

Lord Jesus, you blessed the peacemakers and called them children of God: Give us that peace which the world cannot give, so that your Church may be freed from the schemes of the arrogant and, devoted to works of peace, may go forward joyfully to meet you, the Prince of Peace, our Savior and our Lord. [LH, LBW]

Stand

THE HYMN is sung.

2 He came from his blest throne,
Salvation to bestow;
But men made strange, and none
The longed-for Christ would know.
    But O my friend,
    My friend indeed,
    Who at my need
    His life did spend!

3 Sometimes they strew his way
And his sweet praises sing;
Resounding all the day
Hosannas to our King.
    Then "Crucify"
    Is all their breath,
    And for his death
    They thirst and cry.

4 Why, what hath my Lord done?
What makes this rage and spite?
He made the lame to run,
He gave the blind their sight.
    Sweet injuries!
    Yet they at these
    Themselves displease,
    And 'gainst him rise.

5 They rise, and needs will have
My dear Lord made away;
A murderer they save,
The prince of live they slay.
    Yet cheerful he
    To suffering goes,
    That he his foes
    From thence might free.

6 In life, no house, no home
My Lord on earth might have;
In death no friendly tomb
But what a stranger gave.
What may I say?
Heaven was his home,
But mine the tomb
Wherein he lay.

7 Here might I stay and sing—
No story so divine!
Never was love, dear King,
Never was grief like thine.
This is my friend
In whose sweet praise
I all my days
Could gladly spend! [LBW 94; H82 458]

Text: Samuel Crossman, c. 1624-1683

Tune: *Rhosydmedre,* John David Edwards, 1806-1885
or Love Unknown, John Ireland, 1879-1962 6666 4444

Sit

One or two LESSONS are read.

Year 1

Jeremiah 15:10-21

In your forbearance do not take me away; know that on your account I suffer insult.

Year 2

Lamentations 1:17-22

See, O LORD, how distressed I am; my stomach churns, my heart is wrung within me, because I have been very rebellious.

Silence for meditation

RESPONSORY

Jesus, the pioneer and perfector of our faith,
for the sake of the joy that was set before him, endured the cross,
disregard**ing** its shame.*
    He has taken his seat at the right hand of the **throne** of God.
He humbled himself and became obedient to the **point** of death.*
    He has taken his seat at the right hand of the **throne** of God.

[LH: Heb. 12:2; Phil 2:8]

Philippians 3:15-21

He will transform the body of our humiliation that it may be conformed to the body of his glory.

2 Corinthians 1:8-22

We felt that we had received the sentence of death so that we would rely not on ourselves but on God who raises the dead.

Silence for meditation

RESPONSORY

All of us who have been baptized into Christ Jesus
were baptized in**to** his death.*
    We have been united with him in a death like his;
    we will certainly be united with him in a resurrec**tion** like his.
We have been buried with him by baptism **in**to death.*

We have been united with him in a death like his;
we will certainly be united with him in a resurrec**tion** like his.

[LH: Rom. 6:3, 5, 4]

Antiphon to the BENEDICTUS

Father, glorify me in **your** own presence*
with the glory that I had in your presence before the **world** existed.

[LH, PBO: John 17:5]

Wednesday in Holy Week

Antiphon to PSALM 64 *Exaudi, Deus*

Protect my life from fear **of** the enemy;*
hide me from conspiracy **of** the wicked. [LH, PBO]

64 *Prayer for help against enemies*

1 Hear my voice, O God, when **I** complain;*
protect my life from fear **of** the enemy.

2 Hide me from the conspiracy **of** the wicked,*
from the mob of **e**vildoers.

3 They sharpen their tongue **like** a sword,*
and aim their bitter **words** like arrows,

4 That they may shoot down the blame**less** from ambush;*
they shoot without warning and are **not** afraid.

5 They hold fast to their **e**vil course;*
they plan how they may **hide** their snares.

6 They say, "Who will see us?
Who will find **out** our crimes?*
we have thought out a **per**fect plot."

7 The human mind and heart **are** a mystery;*
but God will loose an arrow at them,
and suddenly they **will** be wounded.

8 He will make them trip o**ver** their tongues,*
and all who see them will **shake** their heads.

9 Everyone will stand in awe and de**clare** God's deeds;*
they will recog**nize** his works.

10 The righteous will rejoice in the LORD and put their **trust** in him,*
and all who are true of **heart** will glory.

Antiphon Protect my life from fear **of** the enemy;*
hide me from the conspiracy **of** the wicked.

Silence for meditation

Heavenly Father, you gave your Son victory over those who plotted evil against him; when he cried to you in his agony, you delivered him from the fear of his enemies. May those who suffer with him in this life find refuge in you, for the sake of Jesus Christ our Lord. [LHd, LBW]

+

Antiphon to PSALM 109 *Deus, laudem*

Hold not your **tongue**, O God;*
they encompass me with **hate**ful words [DO]

109 *An appeal against enemies*

1 Hold not your tongue, O God **of** my praise;*
for the mouth of the wicked,
the mouth of the deceitful, is o**pened** against me.

2 They speak to me with a **ly**ing tongue;*
they encompass me with hateful words
and fight against me with**out** a cause.

3 Despite my love, **they** accuse me;*
but as for me, I **pray** for them.

4 They repay e**vil** for good,*
and hatred **for** my love.

5 Set a wicked **man** against him,*
and let an accuser stand at **his** right hand.

6 When he is judged, let him **be** found guilty,*
and let his appeal **be** in vain.

7 Let his **days** be few,*
and let another **take** his office.

8 Let his chil**dren** be fatherless,*
and his wife be**come** a widow.

9 Let his children be **waifs** and beggars;*
let them be driven from the ruins **of** their homes.

10 Let the creditor seize every**thing** he has;*
let strangers plun**der** his gains.

11 Let there be no one to **show** him kindness,*
and none to pity his fa**ther**less children.

12 Let his descendants **be** destroyed,*
and his name be blotted out in the next **gen**eration.

13 Let the wickedness of his fathers be remembered be**fore** the LORD,*
and his mother's sin not be **blot**ted out;

14 Let their sin be always be**fore** the LORD;*
but let him root out their names **from** the earth;

15 Because he did not remember **to** show mercy,*
but persecuted the poor and needy
and sought to kill the **bro**kenhearted.

16 He loved cursing;
let it **come** upon him;*
he took no delight in blessing;
let it de**part** from him.

17 He put on cursing **like** a garment;*
let it soak into his body like water
and into his **bones** like oil;

18 Let it be to him like the cloak which he wraps a**round** himself,*
and like the belt that he **wears** continually.

19 Let this be the recompense from the LORD to **my** accusers,*
and to those who speak e**vil** against me.

20 But you, O Lord my GOD,
oh, deal with me according **to** your Name;*
for your tender mercy's sake, de**liv**er me.

21 For I am **poor** and needy,*
and my heart is wound**ed** within me.

22 I have faded away like a shadow **when** it lengthens;*
I am shaken off **like** a locust.

23 My knees are **weak** through fasting,*
and my flesh is wast**ed** and gaunt.

24 I have become a re**proach** to them;*
they see and **shake** their heads.

25 Help me, O **LORD** my God;*
save me for your **mer**cy's sake.

26 Let them know that this **is** your hand,*
that you, O **LORD**, have done it.

27 They may curse, but **you** will bless;*
let those who rise up against me be put to shame,
and your servant **will** rejoice.

28 Let my accusers be clothed **with** disgrace*
and wrap themselves in their shame as **in** a cloak.

29 I will give great thanks to the LORD **with** my mouth;*
in the midst of the multitude **will** I praise him;

30 Because he stands at the right hand **of** the needy,*
to save his life from those who **would** condemn him.

Antiphon Hold not your **tongue**, O God;*
they encompass me with **hate**ful words.

Silence for meditation

Lord Jesus, on the cross you blessed those who cursed you and asked that the Father forgive those who nailed you there. Teach us to despise hatred and not those who hate, to detest the sin and not the sinner, and to forgive the offenses of others, as we have been forgiven by you, our Savior and our Lord. [LHd, LBW]

+

Stand

THE HYMN is sung. *Viva! Viva! Gesu! che per mio bene*

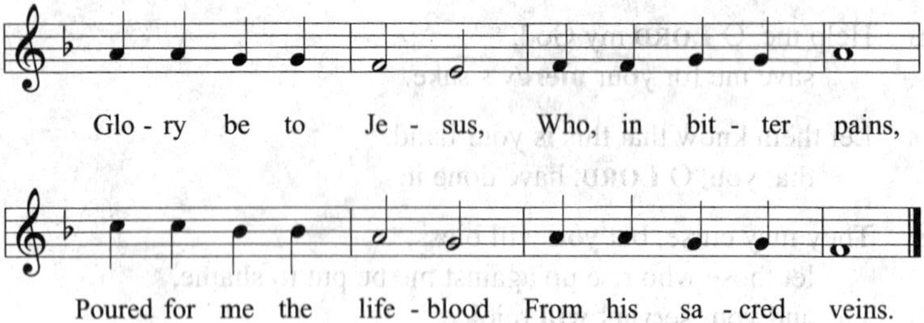

2 Grace and life eternal
In that blood I find;
Blest be his compassion,
Infinitely kind.

3 Blest through endless ages
Be the precious stream
Which from endless torment
Doth the world redeem.

4 Abel's blood for vengeance
Pleaded to the skies;
But the blood of Jesus
For our pardon cries.

5 Of as earth exulting
Wafts its praise on high,
Angel hosts rejoicing
Make their glad reply.

6 Lift ye then your voices,
Swell the mighty flood;
Louder still and louder
Praise the precious blood.

[SBH 76, LBW 95, H82 479]

Text: Italian, 18th century.; tr. Edward Caswall, 1814-1878
Tune: *Wem in Leidenstagen,* Friedrich Flitz, 1804-1876 65 65

Sit

One or two LESSONS are read.

Year 1

Jeremiah 17:5-10, 14-17 (18)

Heal me, O LORD, and I shall be healed; save me, and I shall be saved; for you are my praise.

Year 2

Lamentations 2:1-9

The Lord has thrown down from heaven to earth the splendor of Israel; he has not remembered his footstool in the day of his anger.

Silence for meditation

RESPONSORY

When you heard the voice out of the darkness,
while the mountain was burning with fire,
you approached **Mo**ses crying,*
The Lord our God has shown us his glo**ry** and greatness.
No you have come to Mount Zion and to the city of the living God,
the heaven**ly** Jerusalem.*
The Lord our God has shown us his glo**ry** and greatness.
[LH: Deut. 5:23-24; Heb. 12:22]

Philippians 4:1-13

I can do all things through him who strengthens me.

2 Corinthians 1:23-2:11

I wrote for this reason: to test you and to know whether you are obedient in everything.

Silence for meditation

RESPONSORY

God sent his only Son into the world so that we might **live** through him.*
Since God loved us so much,
we also ought to love **one** another.
In this is love, not that we loved God but that he loved us
and sent his Son to be the atoning sacrifice **for** our sins.*
Since God loved us so much,
we also ought to love **one** another.
[LH: 1 John 4:9, 11, 10]

Antiphon to the BENEDICTUS

Through the eternal Spirit,
Christ offered himself without blem**ish** to God.*
His blood purifies our conscience from dead works
to worship the **liv**ing God. [LH: Heb. 9:14]

Maundy Thursday

Antiphon to PSALM 57 *Miserere mei, Deus, miserere*

In the shadow of your wings will **I** take refuge*
until this time of trouble **has** gone by.

57 *In time of danger*

1 Be merciful to me, O God, be merciful,
for I have taken ref**uge** in you;*
in the shadow of your wings will I take refuge
until this time of trouble **has** gone by.

2 I will call upon the **Most** High God,*
the God who main**tains** my cause.

3 He will send from heaven and save me;
he will confound those who tram**ple** upon me;*
God will send forth his love **and** his faithfulness.

4 I lie in the midst of lions that de**vour** the people;*
their teeth are spears and arrows,
their tongue **a** sharp sword.

5 They have laid a net for my feet,
and I **am** bowed low;*
they have dug a pit before me,
but have fallen into **it** themselves.

6 Exalt yourself above the heav**ens**, O God,*
and your glory over **all** the earth.

7 My heart is firmly fixed, O God, my **heart** is fixed;*
I will sing **and** make melody.

8 Wake up, my spirit;
awake, **lute** and harp;*
I myself will wak**en** the dawn.

9 I will confess you among the peo**ples**, O LORD;*
I will sing praise to you a**mong** the nations.

10 For your lovingkindness is greater **than** the heavens,*
and your faithfulness reaches **to** the clouds.

11 Exalt yourself above the heav**ens**, O God,*
and your glory over **all** the earth.

Antiphon In the shadow of your wings will **I** take refuge*
until this time of trouble **has** gone by.

Silence for meditation

Lord, send your mercy and your truth to rescue us from the snares of the devil, and we will praise you among the peoples and proclaim you to the nations, happy to be known as companions of your Son, Jesus Christ our Lord. [LH, LBW]

+

Antiphon to PSALM 142 *Voce mea ad Dominum*

Listen to my cry for help, for I have been brought **ve**ry low;*
bring me out of prison, that I may give thanks **to** your Name.

142 *Prayer for help*

1 I cry to the LORD **with** my voice;*
to the LORD I make loud **supp**lication.

2 I pour out my com**plaint** before him*
and tell him **all** my trouble.

3 When my spirit languishes within me, you **know** my path;*
in the way wherein I walk they have hidden a **trap** for me.

4 I look to my right hand and find no **one** who knows me;*
I have no place to flee to, and no one **cares** for me.

5 I cry out to **you**, O LORD;*
I say, "You are my refuge,
my portion in the land **of** the living."

6 Listen to my cry for help, for I have been brought **ver**y low;*
save me from those who pursue me,
for they are too **strong** for me.

7 Bring me out of prison, that I may give thanks **to** your Name;*
when you have dealt bountifully with me,
the righteous will gath**er** around me.

Antiphon Listen to my cry for help, for I have been brought **ver**y low;*
bring me out of prison, that I may give thanks **to** your Name.

Silence for meditation

Lord Jesus, hanging on the cross and left alone by your disciples, you called on your Father with a mighty cry as you gave up your spirit. Deliver us from the prison of affliction, and be yourself our inheritance in the land of the living, where with the Father and the Holy Spirit you are blessed now and for ever. [LHd, LBW]

+

Stand

THE HYMN is sung. *Pange, Lingua, gloriosi corporis*

2 Given for us and condescending
   To be born for us below,
He with us in converse blending
   Dwelt, the seed of truth to sow
'Till he closed with wondrous ending
   His most patient life of woe.

3 That last night at supper lying,
   'Mid the twelve, his chosen band,
Jesus, with the Law complying,
   Keeps the feast its rites demand,
Then, more precious food supplying,
   Gives himself with his own hand.

4 Word made flesh, by word he maketh
   Very bread his flesh to be;
We in wine Christ's blood partaketh
   Through the senses fail to see;
Faith alone the true heart waketh
   To behold the mystery.

5 Therefore, we before him bending,
   This great sacrament revere;
Types and shadows have their ending,
   For the newer right is here;
Faith, our outward sense befriending,
   Makes our inward vision clear.

6 Glory let us give, and blessing
   To the Father and the Son:
Honor, thanks, and praise addressing,
   While eternal ages run;
Ever too his love confessing
   Who, from both, with both is one. Amen

[LBW 120; H82 329]

Text: Thomas Aquinas, 1227-1274; tr. composite
Tune: *Pange lingua,* Plainsong Mode 3, Vatican collection 87 87 87

Sit

One or two LESSONS are read.

Year 1

Jeremiah 20:7-11(12-13)14-18

The LORD is with me like a dread warrior; therefore my persecutors will stumble, and they will not prevail.

Year 2

Lamentations 2:10-18

The elders of the daughter of Zion sit on the ground in silence; they have thrown dust on their heads and put on sackcloth; the young girls of Jerusalem have bowed their heads to the ground.

Silence for meditation

RESPONSORY

Although he **was** a son, *
Christ learned obedience through **what** he suffered;
  and having **been** made perfect,*
  he became the source of eternal salvation for all **who** obey him.
In the days of his flesh, Jesus offered up prayers and supplications, with loud cries and tears, to the one who was able to save **him** from death,*
and he was heard because of his rever**ent** submission;
  and having **been** made perfect,*
  he became the source of eternal salvation for all **who** obey him.

[LH: Heb. 5:8, 9, 7]

1 Corinthians 10:14-17; 11:27-32

The cup of blessing that we bless, is it not a sharing in the blood of Christ? The bread that we break, is it not a sharing in the body of Christ?

1 Corinthians 10:14-17; 11:27-32

The cup of blessing that we bless, is it not a sharing in the blood of Christ? The bread that we break, is it not a sharing in the body of Christ?

Silence for meditation

RESPONSORY

All have sinned and fall short of the glo**ry** of God;*
we are now justified by his grace as a gift,
through the redemption that is **in** Christ Jesus
  whom God put forward as a sacrifice of atonement **by** his blood,*
  effec**tive** through faith.
Here is the **Lamb** of God*
who takes away the sin **of** the world,
  whom God put forward as a sacrifice of atonement **by** his blood,*
  effec**tive** through faith. [LH: Rom. 3:23-25; John 1:29]

Antiphon to the BENEDICTUS

  I have earnestly desired to eat this Passo**ver** with you*
    be**fore** I suffer. [LH, PBO: Luke 22:15]

Good Friday

Antiphon to PSALM 22 *Deus, Deus, meus*

God did not withold **his** own Son*
but gave him up for **all** of us. [LH: Rom. 8:32]

22 *God hears the suffering cry of his Holy One*

1 My God, my God, why have you for**sak**en me*
and are so far from my cry
and from the words of **my** distress?

2 O my God, I cry in the daytime, but you **do** not answer;*
by night as well, but I **find** no rest.

3 Yet you are the **Ho**ly One,*
enthroned upon the prais**es** of Israel.

4 Our forefathers put their **trust** in you;*
they trusted, and you de**liv**ered them.

5 They cried out to you and **were** delivered;*
they trusted in you and were not **put** to shame.

6 But as for me, I am a worm **and** no man,*
scorned by all and despised **by** the people.

7 All who see me laugh **me** to scorn;*
they curl their lips and wag **their** heads, saying,

8 "He trusted in the LORD; let him de**liv**er him;*
let him rescue him, if he de**lights** in him."

9 Yet you are he who took me out **of** the womb,*
and kept me safe upon my **moth**er's breast.

10 I have been entrusted to you ever since **I** was born;*
you were my God when I was still in my **moth**er's womb.

11 Be not far from me, for trou**ble** is near,*
and there is **none** to help.

12 Many young bulls en**cir**cle me;*
strong bulls of Ba**shan** surround me.

13 They open wide their **jaws** at me,*
like a ravening and a **roar**ing lion.

14 I am poured out like water;
all my bones are **out** of joint;*
my heart within my breast is **melt**ing wax.

15 My mouth is dried out like a pot-sherd;
my tongue sticks to the roof **of** my mouth;*
and you have laid me in the dust **of** the grave.

16 Packs of dogs close me in,
and gangs of evildoers cir**cle** around me;*
they pierce my hands and my feet;
I can count **all** my bones.

17 They stare and gloat **o**ver me;*
they divide my garments among them;
they cast lots **for** my clothing.

18 Be not far a**way**, O LORD;*
you are my strength; has**ten** to help me.

19 Save me **from** the sword,*
my life from the power **of** the dog.

20 Save me from the **li**on's mouth,*
my wretched body from the horns **of** wild bulls.

21 I will declare your Name **to** my brethren;*
in the midst of the congregation **I** will praise you.

22 Praise the LORD, **you** that fear him;*
stand in awe of him, O offspring of Israel;
all you of Jacob's **line**, give glory.

23 For he does not despise nor abhor the poor in their poverty;
neither does he hide his **face** from them;*
but when they cry to **him** he hears them.

24 My praise is of him in the **great** assembly;*
I will perform my vows in the presence of those
who **wor**ship him.

25 The poor shall eat and be satisfied,
and those who seek the **LORD** shall praise him:*
"May your heart **live** for ever!"

26 All the ends of the earth shall remember and turn **to** the LORD,*
and all the families of the nations shall **bow** before him.

27 For kingship belongs **to** the LORD;*
he rules o**ver** the nations.

28 To him alone all who sleep in the earth bow **down** in worship;*
all who go down to the dust **fall** before him.

29 My soul shall live for him;
my descend**ants** shall serve him;*
they shall be known as the **LORD**'s for ever.

30 They shall come and make known to a people **yet** unborn*
the saving deeds that **he** has done.

Antiphon God did not withold **his** own Son*
but gave him up for **all** of us.

Silence for meditation

Father, when your Son was handed over to torture and felt abandoned by you, he cried out from the cross. Then death was destroyed, and life was restored. By his death and resurrection save the poor, lift up the downtrodden, break the chains of the oppressed, that your Church may sing your praises; through your Son, Jesus Christ our Lord. [LH, LBW]

+

Antiphon to PSALM 69 *Salvum me fac, Deus*

Jesus **Christ** loved us*
and poured out his blood to wash a**way** our sins.
[LH: 1 John 1:7]

69 *Cry from the depths of sorrow*

1 Save **me**, O God,*
for the waters have risen up **to** my neck.

2 I am sinking **in** deep mire,*
and there is no firm ground **for** my feet.

3 I have come in**to** deep waters,*
and the torrent washes **o**ver me.

4 I have grown weary with my crying;
my throat **is** inflamed;*
my eyes have failed from looking **for** my God.

5 Those who hate me without a cause are more than the hairs of my head;
my lying foes who would destroy **me** are mighty.*
Must I then give back what I **nev**er stole?

6 O God, you **know** my foolishness,*
and my faults are not hid**den** from you.

7 Let not those who hope in you be put to shame through me, Lord **GOD** of hosts;*
let not those who seek you be disgraced because of me, O **God** of Israel.

8 Surely, for your sake have I suf**fered** reproach,*
and shame has cov**ered** my face.

9 I have become a stranger to **my** own kindred,*
an alien to my **moth**er's children.

10 Zeal for your house has eat**en** me up;*
the scorn of those who scorn you has fall**en** upon me.

11 I humbled my**self** with fasting,*
but that was turned to **my** reproach.

12 I put on **sack-**cloth also,*
and became a by**word** among them.

13 Those who sit at the gate mur**mur** against me,*
and the drunkards make **songs** about me.

14 But as for me, this is my **prayer** to you,*
at the time you have **set**, O LORD:

15 "In your great mer**cy**, O God,*
answer me with your un**fail**ing help.

16 Save me from the mire; do not **let** me sink;*
let me be rescued from those who hate me
and out of **the** deep waters.

17 Let not the torrent of waters wash over me,
neither let the deep swal**low** me up;*
do not let the Pit shut its **mouth** upon me.

18 Answer me, O LORD, for your **love** is kind;*
in your great compassion, **turn** to me.

19 Hide not your face **from** your servant;*
be swift and answer me, for I am **in** distress.

20 Draw near to me **and** redeem me;*
because of my enemies de**liv**er me.

21 You know my reproach, my shame, and **my** dishonor;*
my adversaries are all **in** your sight."

22 Reproach has broken my heart, and it can**not** be healed;*
I looked for sympathy, but there was none,
for comforters, but I **could** find no one.

23 They gave me **gall** to eat,*
and when I was thirsty, they gave me vine**gar** to drink.

24 Let the table before them **be** a trap*
and their sacred **feasts** a snare.

25 Let their eyes be darkened, that they **may** not see,*
and give them continual trembling **in** their loins.

26 Pour out your indigna**tion** upon them,*
and let the fierceness of your anger **o**vertake them.

27 Let their **camp** be desolate,*
and let there be none to dwell **in** their tents.

28 For they persecute him whom **you** have stricken*
and add to the pain of those whom **you** have pierced.

29 Lay to their charge guilt **up**on guilt,*
and let them not receive your **vin**dication.

30 Let them be wiped out of the book **of** the living*
and not be written a**mong** the righteous.

31 As for me, I am afflicted **and** in pain;*
your help, O God, will lift me **up** on high.

32 I will praise the Name of **God** in song;*
I will proclaim his greatness **with** thanksgiving.

33 This will please the LORD more than an offer**ing** of oxen,*
more than bullocks with **horns** and hoofs.

34 The afflicted shall see **and** be glad;*
you who seek God, your **heart** shall live.

35 For the LORD listens **to** the needy,*
and his prisoners he does **not** despise.

36 Let the heavens and **the** earth praise him,*
the seas and all that **moves** in them;

37 For God will save Zion and rebuild the cit**ies** of Judah;*
they shall live there and have it **in** possession.

38 The children of his servants will in**her**it it,*
and those who love his Name will **dwell** therein.

Antiphon Jesus **Christ** loved us*
and poured out his blood to wash a**way** our sins.

Silence for meditation

God our Father, you fulfilled the ancient prophecies in Christ's passover from death to life: Through the contemplation of his healing wounds, make us zealous for your Church and grateful for your love; through Jesus Christ our Lord. [LH, LBW]

+

Stand

THE HYMN is sung. *Solus ad victimam procedis*

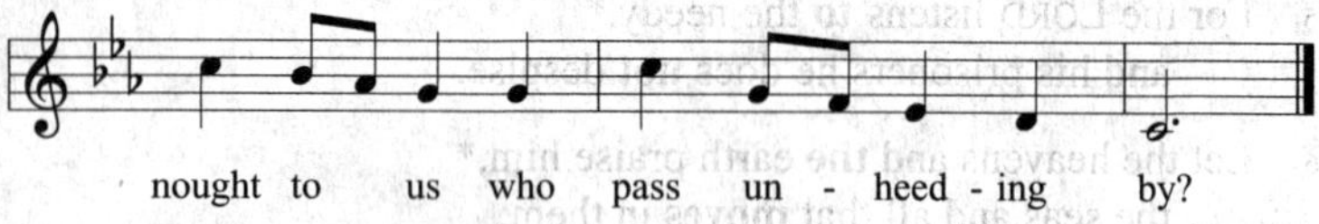

2 Our sins, not thine, thou bearest, Lord;
   Make us thy sorrow feel,
Till through our pity and our shame
   Love answers love's appeal.

3 This is earth's darkest hour, but thou
   Dost light and life restore;
Then let all praise be given thee
   Who livest evermore.

4 Grant us with thee to suffer pain,
   That, as we share this hour,
Thy cross may bring us to thy joy
   And resurrection power. [H82 164]

Text: Peter Abelard, 1079-1142; tr. F. Bland Tucker, 1895-1984

Tune: *Bangor* from *A Compleat Melody or Harmony of Zion,* 1734 CM

Sit

One or two LESSONS are read.

Year 1

Wisdom 1:16-2:1, 12-22

Let us lie in wait for the righteous man, because he is inconvenient to us and opposes our actions.
or Genesis 22:1-14

Year 2

Lamentations 3:1-9, 19-33

The Lord will not reject forever. Although he causes grief, he will have compassion according to the abundance of his steadfast love.

Silence for meditation

RESPONSORY

Like a lamb that is led to the slaughter
and like a sheep that before its shear**ers** is silent,*
so he did not **open** his mouth.
He was given **up** to death*
 to give his **peo**ple life.
He poured out himself to death and was numbered with **the** transgressors*
 to give his **peo**ple life. [CSB, SBH, LH: see Isa. 53:7, 12]

1 Peter 1:10-20

You know that you were ransomed from the futile ways inherited from your ancestors, not with perishable things like silver or gold, but with the precious blood of Christ, like that of a lamb without defect or blemish.

1 Peter 1:10-20

You know that you were ransomed from the futile ways inherited from your ancestors, not with perishable things like silver or gold, but with the precoius blood of Christ, like that of a lamb without defect or blemish.

Silence for meditation

RESPONSORY

You were ransomed not with perishable things like silver or gold,
but with the precious blood of Christ,
like that of a lamb **with**out blemish.*
Through him we have access in one Spirit **to** the Father.
The blood of Jesus cleanses us **from** all sin;*
Through him we have access in one Spirit **to** the Father.

[LH: 1 Peter 1:18-19; Eph. 2:18; 1 John 1:7]

Antiphon to the BENEDICTUS

Over his head they put the **charge** against him:*
Jesus of Nazareth, the King **of** the Jews.

[LH, PBO: Matt. 27:37; John 29:19]

Good Friday
Prayer during the Day

+ Mid-morning +

L Make haste, ✠ O God, to deliver me.
C Make haste to help me, O Lord. [Ps. 70:1]

Antiphon It was nine o'clock **in** the morning*
when they **cru**cified him. [LH: Mark 15:25]

40 *Thanksgiving and plea for help*

1 I waited patiently up**on** the LORD;*
he stooped to me and **heard** my cry.

2 He lifted me out of the desolate pit, out of the **mire** and clay;*
he set my feet upon a high cliff and made my **foot**ing sure.

3 He put a new song in my mouth,
a song of praise **to** our God;*
many shall see, and stand in awe,
and put their trust **in** the Lord.

4 Happy are they who trust **in** the Lord!*
they do not resort to evil spirits or turn **to** false gods.

5 Great things are they that you have done, O LORD my God!
how great your wonders and your **plans** for us!*
there is none who can be com**pared** with you.

6 Oh, that I could make them **known** and tell them!*
but they are more than **I** can count.

7 In sacrifice and offering you **take** no pleasure;*
(you have given me **ears** to hear you);

8 Burnt-offering and sin-offering you have **not** required,*
and so I said, "Be**hold**, I come.

9 In the roll of the book it is written con**cern**ing me:*
'I love to do your will, O my God;
your law is deep **in** my heart.'"

10 I proclaimed righteousness in the great **con**gregation;*
behold, I did not restrain my lips;
and that, O **LORD**, you know.

11 Your righteousness have I not hidden in my heart;
I have spoken of your faithfulness and **your** deliverance;*
I have not concealed your love and faithfulness from the great **con**gregation.

12 You are the LORD;
do not withhold your com**pass**ion from me;*
let your love and your faithfulness keep me **safe** for ever,

13 For innumerable troubles have crowded upon me;
my sins have overtaken me, and I **can**not see;*
they are more in number than the hairs of my head,
and **my** heart fails me.

14 Be pleased, O LORD, to de**liv**er me;*
O LORD, make **haste** to help me.

15 Let them be ashamed and altogether dismayed
who seek after my life **to** destroy it;*
let them draw back and be disgraced
who take pleasure in **my** misfortune.

16 Let those who say "Aha!" and gloat over me **be** confounded,*
because they **are** ashamed.

17 Let all who seek you rejoice in you **and** be glad;*
let those who love your salvation continually say,
"Great **is** the LORD!"

18 Though I am poor **and** afflicted,*
the Lord will have re**gard** for me.

19 You are my helper and **my** deliverer;*
do not tarry, **O** my God.

Antiphon It was nine o'clock **in** the morning*
when they **cru**cified him.

THE HYMN is sung. *Skriv dig, Jesus, paa mit Hjerte*

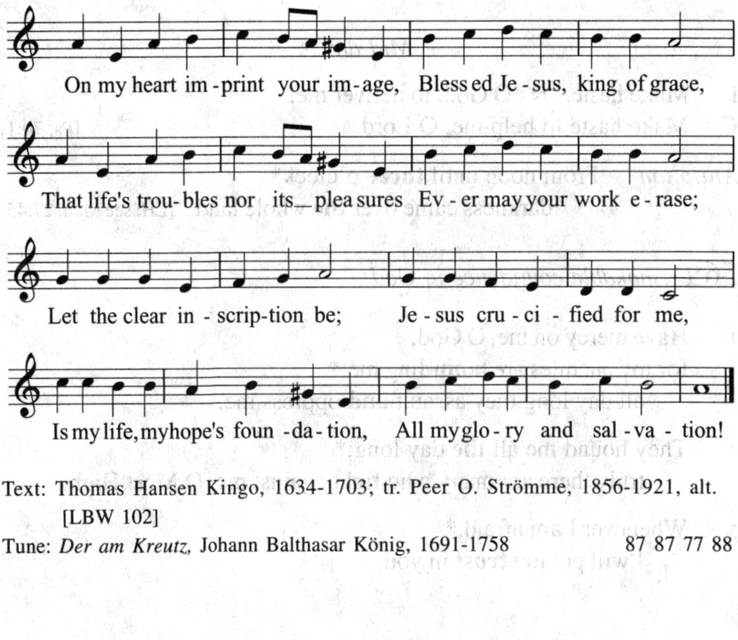

Text: Thomas Hansen Kingo, 1634-1703; tr. Peer O. Strömme, 1856-1921, alt.
[LBW 102]

Tune: *Der am Kreutz,* Johann Balthasar König, 1691-1758 87 87 77 88

Reading Isaiah 53:2-3

He grew up before him like a young plant, and like a root out of dry ground; he had no form or majesty that we should look at him, nothing in his appearance that we should desire him. He was despised and rejected by others; a man of suffering and acquainted with infirmity; and as one from whom others hide their faces he was despised, and we held him of no account.

L We adore you, O Christ, and we bless you,
C Because by your holy cross you have redeemed the world. [LH]

Concluding prayer p. 1214

+ *Mid-day* +

L Make haste, ✠ O God, to deliver me.
C Make haste to help me, O Lord. [Ps. 70:1]

Antiphon From noon until **three** o'clock*
darkness came over **the** whole land. [LH: see Matt. 27:45]

56 *Unshakable confidence in God*

1 Have mercy on me, O God,
for my enemies are **hound**ing me;*
all day long they assault **and** oppress me.

2 They hound me all **the** day long;*
truly there are many who fight against me, **O** Most High.

3 Whenever I **am** afraid,*
I will put my **trust** in you.

4 In God, whose word I praise,
in God I trust and will not **be** afraid,*
for what can flesh **do** to me?

5 All day long they dam**age** my cause;*
their only thought is to **do** me evil.

6 They band together; they **lie** in wait;*
they spy upon my footsteps; because they **seek** my life.

7 Shall they escape de**spite** their wickedness?*
O God, in your anger, cast **down** the peoples.

8 You have noted my lamentation;
put my tears in**to** your bottle;*
are they not recorded **in** your book?

9 Whenever I call upon you, my enemies will be **put** to flight;*
this I know, for God is **on** my side.

10 In God the LORD, whose word I praise,
in God I trust and will not **be** afraid,*
for what can mortals **do** to me?

11 I am bound by the vow I made to **you**, O God;*
I will present to **you** thank-offerings;

12 For you have rescued my soul from death and my **feet** from stumbling,*
that I may walk before God in the light **of** the living.

Antiphon From noon until **three** o'clock*
darkness came over **the** whole land.

THE HYMN is sung. ***Herzliebster Jesu***

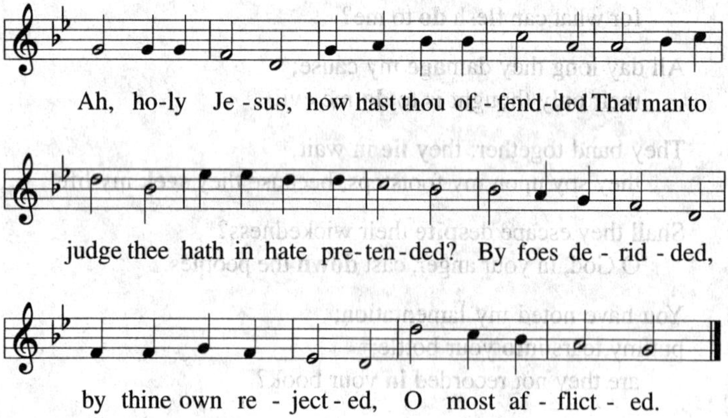

2 Who was the guilty? Who brought this upon thee?
Alas, my treason, Jesus, hath undone thee.
'Twas I, Lord Jesus, I it was denied thee;
I crucified thee.

3 Lo, the Good Shepherd for the sheep is offered;
The slave hath sinned, and the Son hath suffered
For man's atonement, while he nothing heedeth,
God intercedeth.

4 For me, kind Jesus, was thine incarnation,
Thy mortal sorrow, and thy life's oblation;
Thy death of anguish and thy bitter passion,
For my salvation.

5 Therefore, kind Jesus, sincc I cannot pay thee,
I do adore thee, and will ever pray thee;
Think on thy pity and thy love unswerving,
Not my deserving. [LBW 123]

Text: Johann Heermann, 1585-1647; tr. Robert Bridges, 1844-1930, alt.
Tune: Johann Crüger, 1598-1662 *Herzliebster Jesu* 11 11 11 5

Reading Isaiah 53:4-5

Surely he has borne our infirmities and carried our diseases; yet we accounted him stricken, struck down by God, and afflicted. But he was wounded for our transgressions, crushed for our iniquitites; upon him was the punishment that made us whole, and by his bruises we are healed.

L Jesus, remember me
C When you come into your kingdom. [LH: Luke 23:42]

Concluding prayer on p. 1214

+ *Mid-afternoon* +

L Make haste, ✠ O God, to deliver me.
C Make haste to help me, O Lord. [Ps. 70:1]

Antiphon At three o'clock Jesus cried out **with** a loud voice:*
My God, my God, why have you for**sak**en me? [LH]

143 *Prayer in distress: a penitential psalm*

1 Lord, hear my prayer,
and in your faithfulness, heed my **supp**lications;*
answer me **in** your righteousness.

2 Enter not into judgment **with** your servant,*
for in your sight shall no one liv**ing** be justified.

3 For my enemy has sought my life;
he has crushed me **to** the ground;*
he has made me live in dark places like those who **are** long dead.

4 My spirit **faints** within me;*
my heart within **me** is desolate.

5 I remember the time past;
I muse upon **all** your deeds;*
I consider the works **of** your hands.

6 I spread out my **hands** to you;*
my soul gasps to you like a **thirst**y land.

7 O LORD, make haste to answer me; my **spir**it fails me;*
do not hide your face from me
or I shall be like those who go down **to** the Pit.

8 Let me hear of your loving-kindness in the morning,
for I put my **trust** in you;*
show me the road that I must walk,
for I lift up my **soul** to you.

9 Deliver me from my ene**mies**, O LORD,*
for I flee to **you** for refuge.

10 Teach me to do what pleases you, for you **are** my God;*
let your good Spirit lead me on **lev**el ground.

11 Revive me, O LORD, for **your** Name's sake;*
for your righteousness' sake, bring me **out** of trouble.

12 Of your goodness, destroy my enemies
and bring all my **foes** to naught,*
for truly I **am** your servant.

Antiphon At three o'clock Jesus cried out **with** a loud voice:*
My God, my God, why have you for**sak**en me?

THE HYMN is sung. *O salutaris hostia*

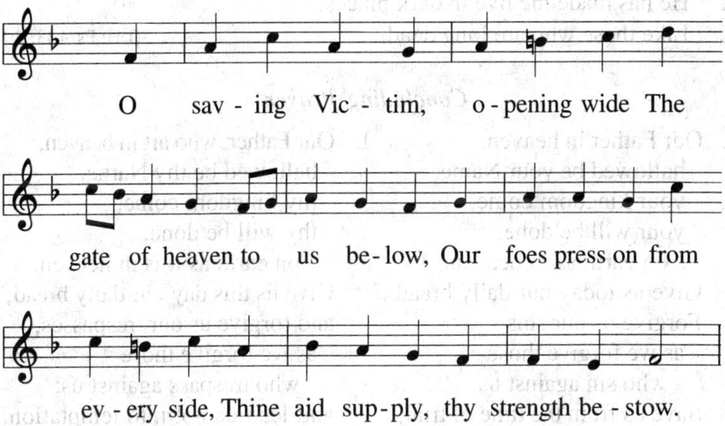

All praise and thanks to thee ascend
For evermore, blest One in Three;
O grant us life that shall not end
In our true native land with thee.

Text: Thomas Aquinas. 1227-1274; tr. Edward Caswall, 1814-1878, alt.
Tune: *Verbum supernum* Plainsong, mode 8 [H82 310, SBH 277]
LM

Reading Isaiah 53:6-7

All we like sheep have gone astray; we have all turned to our own way, and the LORD has laid on him the iniquity of us all. He was oppressed, and he was afflicted, yet he did not open his mouth; like a lamb that is led to the slaughter, and like a sheep that before its shearers is silent, so he did not open his mouth.

L He has made me live in dark places
C Like those who are long dead. [LH: Ps. 143:3b]

Concluding Prayer

L Our Father in heaven,
hallowed be your Name,
your kingdom come,
your will be done,
on earth as in heaven.
Give us today our daily bread.
Forgive us our sins
as we forgive those
who sin against us.
Save us from the time of trial,

C and deliver us from evil.

L Our Father, who art in heaven,
hallowed be thy Name,
thy kingdom come,
thy will be done,
on earth as it is in heaven.
Give us this day our daily bread;
and forgive us our trespasses,
as we forgive those
who trespass against us;
and lead us not into temptation,

C but deliver us from evil.

L Savior of the world,
   by your cross and precious blood you have redeemed us:
C Save us and help us, we humbly beseech you, O Lord.

Merciful and everlasting God, you did not spare your only Son but delivered him up for us all, that he might bear our sins on the Cross: Grant that our hearts may be so fixed with steadfast faith in him that we may not fear the power of any adversaries; through the same Jesus Christ our Lord.

[Saxon, 1540, CSB SBH]

L Let us bless the Lord.
C Thanks be to God.

Holy Saturday
The Great Sabbath

Antiphon to PSALM 88 *Domine, Deus*

I have become like one who **has** no strength,*
lost a**mong** the dead. [PBO]

88 *Prayer in desolation*

1 O LORD, my **God**, my Savior,*
by day and night I **cry** to you.

2 Let my prayer enter in**to** your presence;*
incline your ear to my **lam**entation.

3 For I am **full** of trouble;*
my life is at the brink **of** the grave.

4 I am counted among those who go down **to** the Pit;*
I have become like one who **has** no strength;

5 Lost a**mong** the dead,*
like the slain who lie **in** the grave,

6 Whom you remem**ber** no more,*
for they are cut off **from** your hand.

7 You have laid me in the depths **of** the Pit,*
in dark places, and in **the** abyss.

8 Your anger weighs up**on** me heavily,*
and all your great waves **o**verwhelm me.

9 You have put my friends far from me;
you have made me to be ab**horred** by them;*
I am in prison and can**not** get free.

10 My sight has failed me be**cause** of trouble;*
LORD, I have called upon you daily;
I have stretched out my **hands** to you.

11 Do you work wonders **for** the dead?*
will those who have died stand up and **give** you thanks?

12 Will your lovingkindness be declared **in** the grave,*
your faithfulness in the land **of** destruction?

13 Will your wonders be known **in** the dark*
or your righteousness in the country where all **is** forgotten?

14 But as for me, O LORD, I cry to **you** for help;*
in the morning my prayer **comes** before you.

15 LORD, why have you re**ject**ed me?*
why have you hidden your **face** from me?

16 Ever since my youth, I have been wretched and at the **point** of death;*
I have borne your terrors with a **trou**bled mind.

17 Your blazing anger has swept **o**ver me;*
your terrors **have** destroyed me;

18 They surround me all day long **like** a flood;*
they encompass me on **ev**ery side.

19 My friend and my neighbor you have put a**way** from me,*
and darkness is my on**ly** companion.

Antiphon I have become like one who **has** no strength,*
lost **among** the dead.

Silence for meditation

Lord Jesus, author of our salvation and redeemer of all, for us you descended to the dead and broke the grip of death: Hear the prayers of your family, and lift us from our slavery to evil, that we may be set free to see your Father's glory now and for ever. [LH, PHP]

+

Antiphon to PSALM 16 *Conserva me, Domine*

My body shall rest in hope [LH, PBO]

16 *The Lord is my heritage*

1 Protect me, O God, for I take ref**uge** in you;*
I have said to the LORD, "You are my Lord,
my good a**bove** all other."

2 All my delight is upon the godly that are **in** the land,*
upon those who are noble a**mong** the people.

3 But those who run after **oth**er gods*
shall have their troubles **mul**tiplied.

4 Their libations of blood I **will** not offer,*
nor take the names of their gods up**on** my lips.

5 O LORD, you are my portion **and** my cup;*
it is you who up**hold** my lot.

6 My boundaries enclose a **pleas**ant land;*
indeed, I have a **good**ly heritage.

7 I will bless the LORD who **gives** me counsel;*
my heart teaches me night **af**ter night.

8 I have set the LORD al**ways** before me;*
because he is at my right hand, I **shall** not fall.

9 My heart, therefore, is glad, and my spir**it** rejoices;*
my body also shall **rest** in hope.

10 For you will not abandon me **to** the grave,*
nor let your holy one **see** the Pit.

11 You will show me the **path** of life;*
in your presence there is fullness of joy,
and in your right hand are pleasures for **ev**ermore.

Antiphon My body shall rest in hope.

Silence for meditation

Lord Jesus, uphold those who hope in you, and give us your counsel, so that we may know the joy of your resurrection and share the pleasures of the saints at your right hand, where you live and reign with the Father and the Holy Spirit, one God, now and for ever. [LH, LBW]

+

Stand

THE HYMN is sung. *O Traurigkeit!*

2 O sorrow dread
Our God lies dead;
But his full expiation
Of our guilt, upon the cross,
Gained for us salvation.

3 O sinful race,
It was your place
In the tomb that brought him
Down to suffer for your sake
And such sorrow caused him.

4 Behold your Lord,
The Lamb of God,
Blood-sprinkled lies before you,
Pouring out his life, that he
May to life restore you.

5 O Ground of faith,
Laid low in death,
Sweet lips, now silent sleeping!
Surely all who live must mourn
Here with bitter weeping.

6 Blest shall they be
Eternally
Who oft in faith will ponder
Why the glorious Prince of Life
Should be buried yonder.

7 O Jesus blest,
My help and rest!
With tears I pray, Lord hear me,
Make me love you to the last,
And in death be near me. [TLH 167 alt.]

Text: st. 1 Friedrich von Spee, 1591-1635; tr. Charles Winfred Douglas, 1867-1944;
sts. 2-7 Johann Rist, 1607-1667, tr. Catherine Winkworth, 1829-1878, alt. PHP

Tune: *O Traurigkeit,* from *Würzburger Gesangbuch,* Mainz, 1628 44 776

Sit

One or two LESSONS are read.

Year 1

Job 19:21-27a

I know that my Redeemer lives, and that at the last he will stand upon the earth.

Year 2

Lamentations 3:37-58

You have taken up my cause, O Lord, you have redeemed my life.

Silence for meditation

RESPONSORY

They buried the Lord in a new tomb and rolled a great stone in **front** of it.*
They sealed the stone and stationed soldiers there to **guard** the tomb.
The chief priests asked Pilate **for** a guard.*
They sealed the stone and stationed soldiers there to **guard** the tomb.
[LH: see Matt. 27:66, 60, 62]

Year 1

Hebrews 4:1-16

So then, a sabbath rest still remains for the people of God; for those who enter God's rest also cease from their labors as God did from his. Let us therefore make every effort to enter that rest.

Year 2

Hebrews 4:1-16

So then, a sabbath rest still remains for the people of God, for those who enter God's rest also cease from their labors as God did from his. Let us therefore make every effort to enter that rest.

Silence for meditation

RESPONSORY

Our Shepherd, the fountain of living wa**ter**, has died.*
At his passing the **sun** was darkened;
but now humanity's captor **is** made captive.*
Today our Savior broke through the **gates** of death.
He has demolished the ramparts of hell
and overthrown the **de**vil's might.*
Today our Savior broke through the **gates** of death. [LH]

Antiphon to the BENEDICTUS

O Savior of the world, by your cross and precious blood
you **have** redeemed us:*
save us and help us, we humbly beseech **you**, O Lord. [LH, PBO]

Holy Saturday
Prayer during the Day

L Make haste, ✠ O God, to deliver me.
C Make haste to help me, O Lord. [Ps. 70:1]

Antiphon The earth was afraid **and** was still*
when God rose **up** to judgment. [PBO]

76 *Notus in Judæa*

1 In Judah **is** God known;*
his Name is **great** in Israel.

2 At Salem is his **tab**ernacle,*
and his dwelling **is** in Zion.

3 There he broke the **flash**ing arrows,*
the shield, the sword, and the weap**ons** of battle.

4 How glori**ous** you are!*
more splendid than the ever**last**ing mountains!

5 The strong of heart have been despoiled;
they sink **in**to sleep;*
none of the warriors can **lift** a hand.

6 At your rebuke, O **God** of Jacob,*
both horse and rid**er** lie stunned.

7 What terror **you** inspire!*
who can stand before you when **you** are angry?

8 From heaven you **pro**nounced judgment;*
the earth was afraid **and** was still,

9 When God rose **up** to judgment*
and to save all the oppressed **of** the earth.

10 Truly, wrathful Edom will **give** you thanks,*
and the remnant of Hamath will **keep** your feasts.

11 Make a vow to the LORD your **God** and keep it;*
let all around him bring gifts to him who is worthy
to be feared.

12 He breaks the spir**it** of princes,*
and strikes terror in the kings **of** the earth.

Antiphon The earth was afraid **and** was still*
when God rose **up** to judgment.

Silence for meditation

Mighty God, awesome in power and splendid in holiness, in your presence the earth both trembles and stands still, for you shattered death's power by the cross. Rise to help your people; give the light of your salvation to the meek of the earth, that they may praise your Name for ever; through your Son, Jesus Christ our Lord. [LH, LBW]

+

Stand

THE HYMN is sung. *O Traurigkeit!*

2 O sorrow dread
Our God lies dead;
But his full expiation
Of our guilt, upon the cross,
Gained for us salvation.

3 O sinful race,
It was your place
In the tomb that brought him
Down to suffer for your sake
And such sorrow caused him.

4 Behold your Lord,
The Lamb of God,
Blood-sprinkled lies before you,
Pouring out his life, that he
May to life restore you.

5 O Ground of faith,
Laid low in death,
Sweet lips, now silent sleeping!
Surely all who live must mourn
Here with bitter weeping.

6 Blest shall they be
Eternally
Who oft in faith will ponder
Why the glorious Prince of Life
Should be buried yonder.

7 O Jesus blest,
My help and rest!
With tears I pray, Lord hear me,
Make me love you to the last,
And in death be near me. [TLH 167 alt.]

Text: st. 1 Friedrich von Spee, 1591-1635; tr. Charles Winfred Douglas, 1867-1944; sts. 4-7 Johann Rist, 1607-1667; tr. Catherine Winkworth, 1829-1878, alt. PHP

Tune: *O Traurigkeit,* from *Wüerzburger Gesangbuch,,* Mainz, 1628 44 776

Sit

A LESSON is read Matthew 27:57-66

So they went with the guard and made the tomb secure
by sealing the stone.

L The gospel was proclaimed even to the dead,
C so that they might live in the spirit as God does. [1 Peter 4:6]

Kneel or stand

These prayers are sung or said.

In the midst of life we are in death;
from whom can **we** seek help?*
From you alone, O Lord,
who by our sins are **just**ly angered.

Holy God, holy and mighty,
*Holy and mer**ci**ful Savior,**
*deliver us not in the bitterness of e**ter**nal death.*

Lord, you know the secrets **of** our hearts;*
shut not your ears to our prayers,
but spare **us**, O Lord.

Holy God, holy and mighty,
*Holy and mer**ci**ful Savior,**
*deliver us not in the bitterness of e**ter**nal death.*

O worthy and e**ter**nal Judge,*
do not let the pains of death
turn us away from you at **our** last hour.

Holy God, holy and mighty,
*Holy and mer**ci**ful Savior,* *
*deliver us not in the bitterness of e**ter**nal death.* [Medieval, BCP]

Grant, O Lord, that as we are baptized into the death of your blessed Son, our Savior Jesus Christ, so by continual putting to death our corrupt desires we may be buried with him; and that through the grave and gate of death we may pass to our joyful resurrection; for his merits, who died, and was buried, and rose again for us, the same your Son Jesus Christ our Lord. [BCP 1662-1928]

L Our Father in heaven,
hallowed be your Name,
your kingdom come,
your will be done,
on earth as in heaven.
Give us today our daily bread.
Forgive us our sins
as we forgive those
who sin against us.
Save us from the time of trial,

C and deliver us from evil.

L Our Father, who art in heaven,
hallowed be thy Name,
thy kingdom come,
thy will be done,
on earth as it is in heaven.
Give us this day our daily bread;
and forgive us our trespasses,
as we forgive those
who trespass against us;
and lead us not into temptation,

C but deliver us from evil.

L Savior of the world,
by your cross and precious blood you have redeemed us:
C Save us and help us, we humbly beseech you, O Lord.

✠

EVENING PRAYER

Vespers or Evensong throughout Easter (Pascha)

The SERVICE OF LIGHT is appropriate for every day of the Fifty Days of Easter. The service may begin with a procession in which a large, lighted candle is carried to its stand in front of the congregation.

Stand

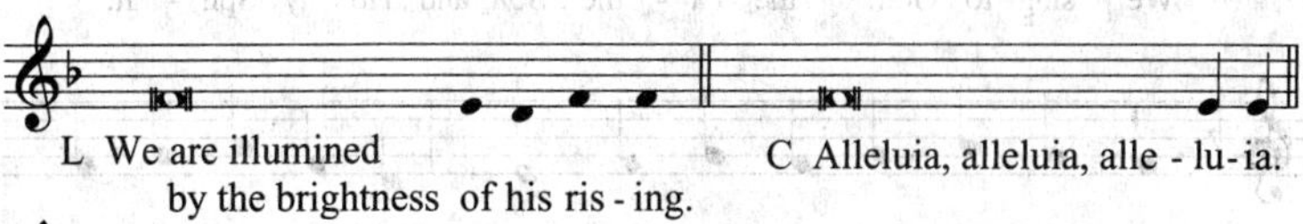

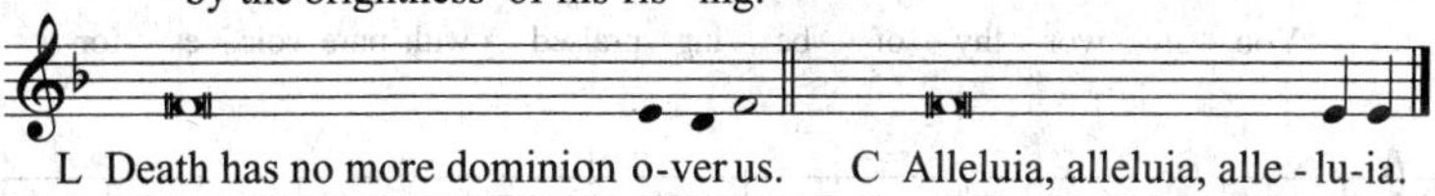

[Rom. 6:9a; Isa. 60:3; Rom. 6:9b]

As this ancient hymn, Phos hilaron, *is sung, the candles on and near the altar are lighted. When the large candle is used, the candles are lighted from its flame.*

Leader and Congregation

The thanksgiving from the Apostolic Tradition *(ca. 215) concludes the Service of Light.*

The PSALMODY begins with this song for forgiveness and protection, from Psalm 141, Domine clamavi.

Kneel or sit

C Let my prayer rise be - fore_ you as in - cense; the
lift - ing up of my hands as the eve - ning sac - ri - fice.
[I] O Lord, I call to you; come to me quick - ly; hear my voice when
I cry to you. [II] Let my prayer rise be - fore_ you as in - cense;
the lift - ing up of my hands as the eve - ning sac - ri - fice.
[I] Set a watch be - fore my mouth, O Lord, and guard the door of my lips.
[II] Let not my heart in - cline to an - y e - vil thing; let me
not be oc - cu - pied in wick - ed - ness with e - vil do - ers.

Silence for meditation.

L Let the incense of our repentant prayer ascend before you, O Lord, and let your lovingkindness descend upon us, that with purified minds we may sing your praises with the Church on earth and the whole heavenly host, and may glorify you for ever and ever.

C Amen

Sit

A second psalm is sung or said; additional psalms and a New Testament canticle may be sung or said also. Silence for meditation follows each psalm or canticle.

The psalm prayer appropriate to each psalm or canticle follows the silence.

C Amen

Stand

THE HYMN is sung.

Sit

One or two LESSONS are read. Silence for meditation follows each reading.

After this the leader continues:

L In many and various ways God spoke to his people of old by the prophets.

C But now in these last days he has spoken to us by his Son.

Stand

The GOSPEL CANTICLE, Magnificat, *is sung or said. The proper Antiphon is given on pp. 1257-1319.*

The Antiphon is sung or said.

C ✠ My soul pro-claims the great-ness of the Lord; my spir- it re -
joic-es in God my Sav- ior, for he has looked with fa -vor
on his low-ly ser - vant. From this day all gen-er -
a - tions will call me bless-ed. The Al-might-y has
done great things for me, and ho - ly is his Name. He has
mer-cy on those who fear_ him in ev-'ry gen-er - a-tion.
He has shown the strength of his arm; he has scat- tered the
proud in their con-ceit. He has cast down the might-y from their thrones,

The Antiphon is repeated.

The LITANY is sung or said. The complete litany may be sung to the alternative musical form.

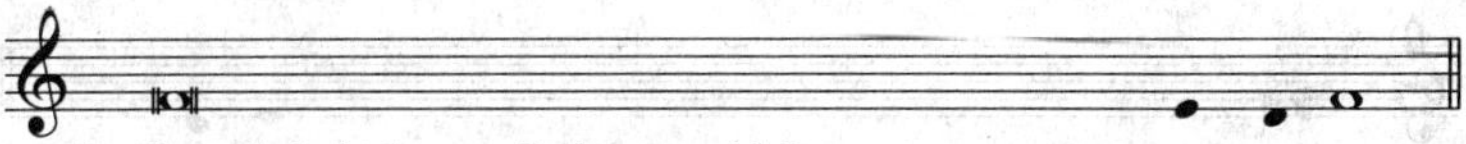

L For this holy house, [holy assembly],
and for all who offer here their worship and praise,
let us pray - - to the Lord.

C Lord, have mer - cy.

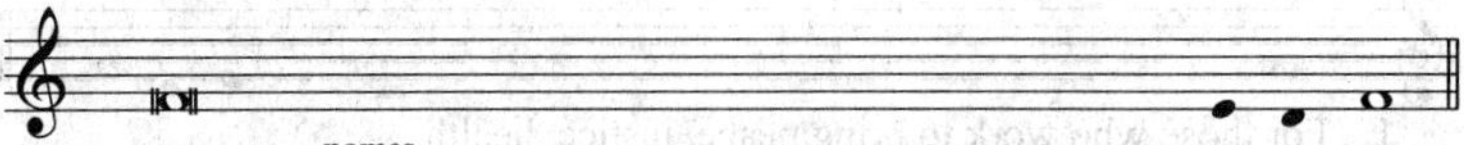

L For ______ names ______, for our *pastor /pastors* in Christ,
for all servants of the Church,
and for all the people, let us pray - - to the Lord.

C Lord, have mer - cy.

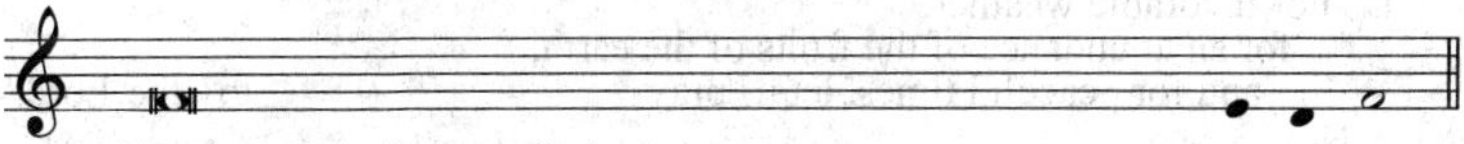

L For those who bring offerings,
those who do good works in this congregation,
those who toil, those who sing, and all the people
here present who await from the Lord
great and abundant mercy, let us pray - - to the Lord.

C Lord_ have mer cy.

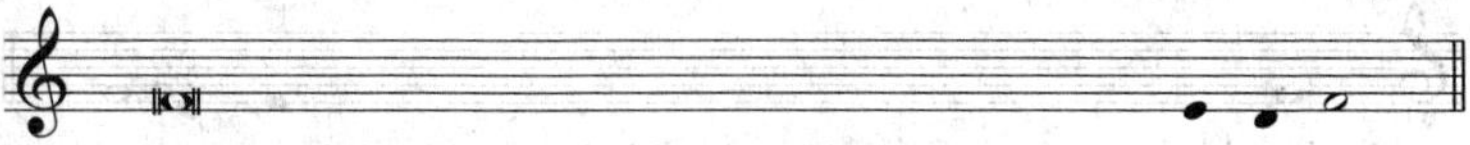

L For our public servants, for the government
and those who protect us, that they may be upheld
and strengthened in every good deed, let us pray to the Lord.

C Lord_ have mer- cy.

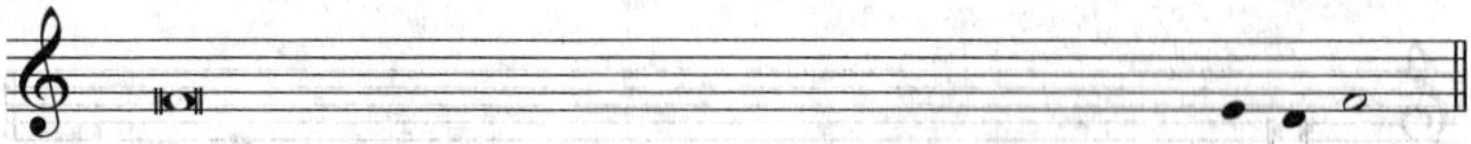

L For those who work to bring peace, justice, health,
and protection in this and every place, let us pray - to the Lord.

C Lord have mer - cy.

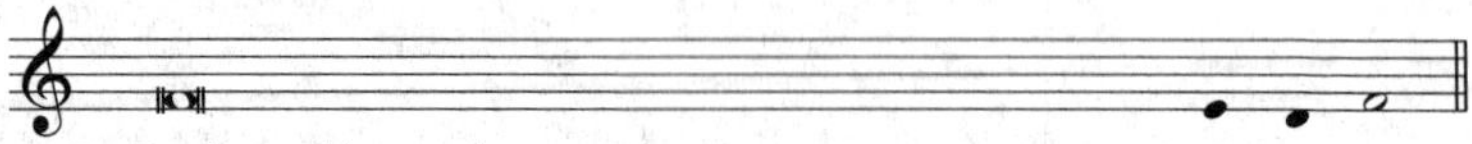

L For favorable weather,
for an abundance of the fruits of the earth,
and for peaceful times, let us pray - - to the Lord.

C Lord_ have mer- cy.

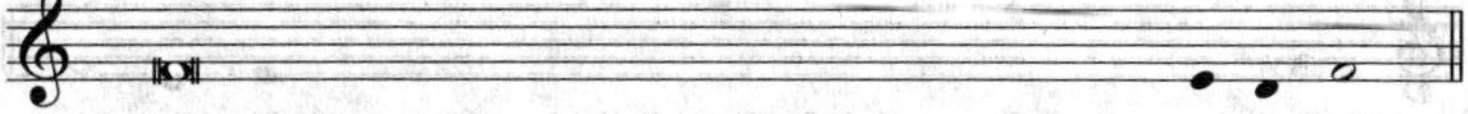
L For travellers, for the sick and suffering, for captives,
and for all who need our prayers, let us pray - to the Lord.

C Lord_ have mer - cy.

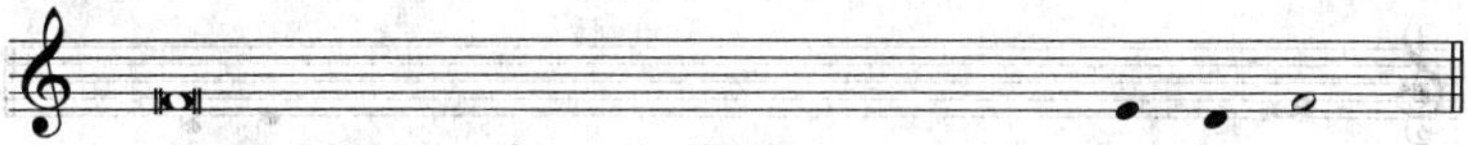
L For our deliverance from all affliction,
wrath, danger, and need, let us pray - to the Lord.

C Lord_ have mer - cy.

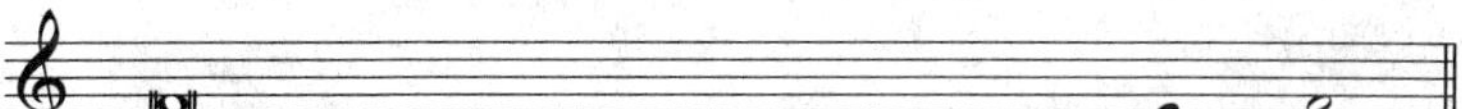
L For the faithful who have gone before us
and are at rest, let us pray [or give thanks] - to the Lord.

C Lord_ have mer - cy.

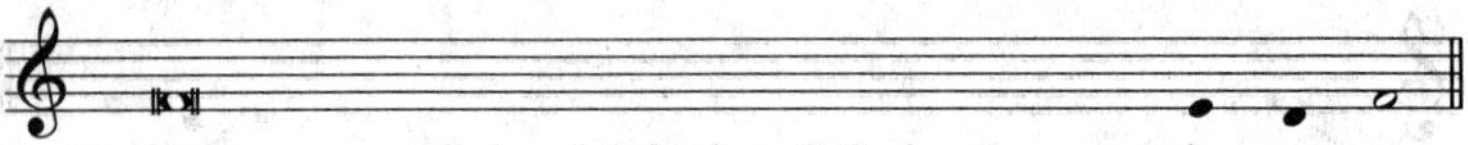

L Help, save, comfort, and defend us, O God - by your grace.

C Lord_ have mer - cy.

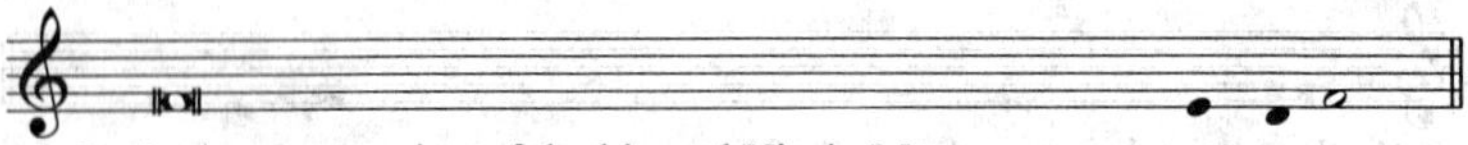

L In the communion of the blessed Virgin Mary,
the bearer of God, and all the saints, let us commend
ourselves, one another, and our whole life to Christ our God.

C To_ you, O_ Lord.

From Vespers of Easter Day until Ascension Day this prayer is said:

O God, you gladden our hearts by the annual celebration of the resurrection of our Lord: In your mercy grant that we, who celebrate these joyous days on earth, may at length attain to the eternal Easter in heaven; through your Son Jesus Christ our Lord, who lives and reigns with you and the Holy Spirit, one God, now and for ever.

[Gel., RS, Easter Wed., LBW Easter Evening; *Priest's Book of Private Devotion* (1884) rev. PHP]

From First Vespers of the Ascension until the Vigil of Pentecost this prayer is said:

O God, the King of glory, you have exalted your only Son Jesus Christ with great triumph to your kingdom in heaven: Do not leave us comfortless, but send to us your Holy Spirit to strengthen us and exalt us to that place where our Savior Christ has gone before; who lives and reigns with you and the Holy Spirit, one God, now and for ever.

[Antiphon to Magnificat; BCP Easter 7]

At First Vespers of Pentecost (the Vigil of Pentecost) this prayer is said:

Almighty and ever-living God, you fulfilled the promise of Easter by sending the Holy Spirit to unite the races and nations of earth to proclaim your glory: Look upon your people gathered in prayer, open to receive the Spirit's flame; let it come to rest in our hearts and heal the divisions of word and tongue, that with one voice we may praise your Name in joy and thanksgiving; through Jesus Christ our Lord, who lives and reigns with you and the Holy Spirit, one God, now and for ever.

[Gel., Greg., RS, LBW]

At Second Vespers of Pentecost this prayer is said:

O God, you gave your Holy Spirit to your apostles: Grant to your people the fulfillment of their desires, so that on us to whom you have given faith, you may also bestow peace; through your Son Jesus Christ our Lord, who lives and reigns with you and the Holy Spirit, one God, now and for ever. [Greg., MR, CB, CSB, SBH Mon. after Pentecost]

L Lord, remember us in your kingdom, and teach us to pray:

C Our Father in heaven,
hallowed be your Name
your kingdom come,
your will be done,
on earth as in heaven.
Give us this day our daily bread;
Forgive us our sins
as we forgive those
who sin against us.
Save us from the time of trial
and deliver us from evil.
For the kingdom, the power,
and the glory are yours,
now and for ever. Amen.

C Our Father who art in heaven,
hallowed be thy Name
thy kingdom come,
thy will be done,
on earth as it is in heaven.
Give us today our daily bread.
and forgive us our trespasses,
as we forgive those
who sin against us;
And lead us not into temptation
but deliver us from evil.
For thine is the kingdom,
and the power, and the glory,
for ever and ever. Amen.

L Let us bless the Lord.

C Thanks be to God.

The BENEDICTION concludes the service when there is no sermon. A hymn may follow the benediction.

When there is a sermon, this benediction is omitted, and the service continues as on p. 20.

L The almighty and merciful Lord,
the Father, the Son, and the Holy Spirit, bless and pre-serve us.

C A - men

Saturdays of Easter

Antiphon to PSALM 23 *Dominus regit me*

eve of Easter 2 — Christ, being raised from the dead,
will never **die** again,*
alleluia. [LH: Rom. 6:9]

eve of Easter 3 — The Lord has ris**en** indeed,*
and he has appeared to Simon,
alleluia. [Luke 24:34]

eve of Easter 4 — May the peace of Christ fill your **hearts** with joy,*
alleluia. [LH: see Col. 3:15]

eve of Easter 5 — The Lord has risen **from** the grave*
who hung upon the cross for us, **al**leluia. [LH]

eve of Easter 6 — Where, O death, is your **vic**tory?*
Where, O death, is your sting? **Al**leluia.
[1 Cor. 15:55]

eve of Easter 7 — God raised Jesus **from** the dead,*
and we are now his witnesses, **al**leluia.
[LH: see Acts 13:30-31]

eve of the Day of Pentecost — When the days of the Pentecost were
drawing **to** a close,*
they had all gathered together in
one place, **al**leluia. [LH: see Acts 2:1]

23 *The Good Shepherd*

1 The LORD **is** my shepherd;*
I shall not **be** in want.

2 He makes me lie down **in** green pastures*
and leads me be**side** still waters.

3 He re**vives** my soul*
and guides me along right pathways for **his** Name's sake.

4 Though I walk through the valley of the shadow of death,
I shall **fear** no evil;*
for you are with me;
your rod and your staff, they **com**fort me.

5 You spread a table before me in the presence of those
who **troub**le me;*
you have anointed my head with oil,
and my cup is **run**ning over.

6 Surely your goodness and mercy shall follow me all the days
of my life,*
and I will dwell in the house of the LORD for ever.

The Antiphon is repeated.

Silence for meditation

Lord Jesus Christ, shepherd of your Church, you give us new birth in the waters of baptism; you anoint us with oil, and call us to salvation at your table. Dispel the terrors of death and the darkness of error. Lead your people along safe paths, that they may rest securely in you and dwell in the house of the Lord now and for ever, for your Name's sake. [LH, LBW]

+

Antiphon to PSALM 114 *In exitu Israel*

eve of Easter 2 — Come, see the place where the **Lord** was buried,*
alleluia. [see Matt. 28:6]

eve of Easter 3 — Lord, you have broken the chains that
held me bound;*
I will offer you the sacrifice of
thanksgiving, **al**leluia. [LH: Ps. 116:14-15]

eve of Easter 4	By your blood you have ransomed **us** for God;* alleluia. [LH: Rev. 5:9]
eve of Easter 5	You have led me **forth** from prison* that I may give thanks to your Name, **al**leluia. [LH: Ps. 142:7]
eve of Easter 6	If you have been **raised** with Christ,* seek the things that are above, **al**leluia. [Col. 3:1]
eve of Easter 7	God has rescued us from the pow**er** of darkness* and transferred us into the kingdom of his beloved Son, **al**leluia. [LH, PBO: Col. 1:13]
eve of the Day of Pentecost	Tongues as of fire rested on each of **the** apostles.* All of them were filled with the Holy Spirit, **al**leluia. [LH: Acts 2:3-4]

114 *The wonders of the Exodus*

1 Hallelujah!
When Israel came **out** of Egypt,*
the house of Jacob from a people **of** strange speech,

2 Judah became God's **sanc**tuary*
and Israel **his** dominion.

3 The sea beheld **it** and fled;*
Jordan turned **and** went back.

4 The mountains **skipped** like rams,*
and the little hills **like** young sheep.

5 What ailed you, O sea, **that** you fled?*
O Jordan, that **you** turned back?

6 You mountains, that you **skipped** like rams?*
you little hills **like** young sheep?

7 Tremble, O earth, at the presence **of** the Lord,*
at the presence of the **God** of Jacob,

8 Who turned the hard rock into a **pool** of water*
and flint-stone into a **flow**ing spring.

The Antiphon is repeated.

Silence for meditation

Almighty God, you gave life to the new Israel by birth from water and the Spirit: Make all those whom you have called to walk in the splendor of the new light render you fitting service and adoration; through your Son, Jesus Christ our Lord. [LH, LBW]

+

Antiphon to the NEW TESTAMENT CANTICLE
Benedictus Deus et Pater Domini nostri

eve of Easter 2 — Jesus said, Do not be afraid; go and
tell my disciples to go to **Ga**lilee;*
there they will see me, **al**leluia.
[Matt. 28:10]

eve of Easter 3 — Even though you do not **see** him now,*
you believe in him and rejoice with
an indescribable and glorious joy,
alleluia. [1 Peter 1:8]

eve of Easter 4 — Christ has been raised **from** the dead,*
the first fruits of those who have
died, **al**leluia. [1 Cor. 15:20]

eve of Easter 5 — Jesus **died** for all,*
so that those who live might live no longer
for themselves, but for him who died and
was raised for them, **al**leluia. [2 Cor. 5:15]

eve of Easter 6	Even though we were dead through our trespasses, God made us alive togeth**er** with Christ* and raised us up with him in the heavenly places in Christ Jesus, **al**leluia. [Ephes. 2:5-6]
eve of Easter 7	Christ did not enter a sanctuary made by human hands, a mere copy of the true one, but he entered into heav**en** itself,* now to appear in the presence of God on our behalf, **al**leluia. [Heb. 9:24]
eve of the Day of Pentecost	The Spirit of truth who comes **from** the Father* will glorify me, al**le**luia. [John 15:26; 16:14]

A Song of Salvation 1 Peter 1:3-5

Bless**ed** be God,*
the Father **of** great mercy!

Through the resurrection of Jesus Christ **from** the dead*
he has given us new birth into a **liv**ing hope,

An inheritance, reserved in **hea**ven for you,*
which nothing can destroy or **spoil** or wither.

Through your faith God's pow**er** will guard you*
for a salvation even now prepared,
to be revealed at the **end** of time. [PHP]

The Antiphon is repeated.

Silence for meditation

Almighty and everlasting God, through the death and resurrection of your Son you have proclaimed to us the gospel of peace: Grant that by the power of his resurrection we may be born anew to a living hope and so overcome the world; through Jesus Christ our Lord. [*Gebete*, MPB]

+

Stand

THE HYMN is sung.

Through the Seventh Sunday of Easter

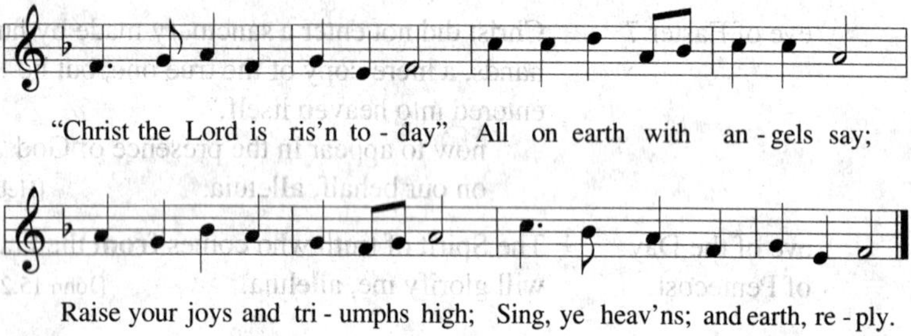

2 Love's redeeming work is done,
Fought the fight, the battle won;
Lo! The Sun's eclipse is o'er.
Lo! he sets in blood no more.

3 Vain the stone, the watch, the seal;
Christ has burst the gates of hell.
Death in vain forbids his rise;
Christ has opened paradise.

4 Lives again our glorious king!
Where, O death, is now thy sting?
Once he died our souls to save;
Where thy victory, O grave?

5 Soar we now where Christ hath led,
Following our exalted head.
Made like him, like him we rise;
Ours the cross, the grave, the skies.

6 Hail the Lord of earth and heav'n!
Praise to thee by both be giv'n.
Thee we greet triumphant now;
Hail, the resurrection thou!

7 King of glory, soul of bliss,
Everlasting life is this:
Thee to know, thy pow'r to prove,
Thus to sing, and thus to love!

[LBW 130; SBH 91; H82 188, 189]

Text: Charles Wesley, 1707-1788, alt.
Tune: *Orientis partibus*, French, 13th cent. 77 77

On the Eve (the Vigil) of the Day of Pentecost *Veni Creator Spiritus*

2 To you, the Comforter, we cry;
To you, the gift of God most high,
The fount of life, the fire of love,
The soul's anointing from above.

3 Your gracious gifts are sevenfold,
And we in them God's hand behold;
O promise of the Father, now
Our tongues with heavenly speech
endow.

4 Your light to every sense impart,
And shed your love in every heart;
Your own unfailing might supply
To strengthen our infirmity.

5 Drive far from us our wily foe,
And your abiding peace bestow;
If you be our protecting guide,
No evil can our steps betide.

6 To us make God the Father known;
Teach us th' eternal Son to own;
And you, whose Name we ever bless,
Of both the Spirit, to confess.

7 Praise we the Father and the Son
And Holy Spirit with them one;
And may the Son on us bestow
The gifts that from the Spirit flow.

[LBW 284 alt.]

Text: attr. Rhabanus Maurus, 776-856; tr. composite

Tune: *Komm, Gott Schöpfer*, J. Klug, *Geistliche Lieder*, 1533 LM

Sit

A LESSON is read.

Year 1	Year 2
eve of Easter 2	
John 16:16-33	Mark 12:18-27
I came from the Father and have come into the world; again, I am leaving the world and am going to the Father.	"I am the God of Abraham. the God Isaac, and the God Jacob." He is God not of the dead, but of the living.
eve of Easter 3	
Luke 4:1-13	John 16:16-33
Worship the Lord your God, and serve only him.	I came from the Father and have come into the world; again, I am leaving the world and am going to the Father.
eve of Easter 4	
Luke 5:27-39	Matthew 4:18-25
You cannot make wedding guests fast while the bridegroom is with them.	Jesus went throughout Galilee, teaching in their synagogues and proclaiming the good news of the kingdom and curing every disease and every sickness among the people.
eve of Easter 5	
Luke 7:18-28 (29-30) 31-35	Matthew 5:38-48
I tell you, among those born of women no one is greater than John; yet the least in the kingdom of God is greater than he.	Be perfect, therefore, as your heavenly Father is perfect.

eve of Easter 6

Lukc 9:1-17
Taking the five loaves and the two fish, Jesus looked up to heaven, and blessed and broke them, and gave them to the disciples to set before the crowd. And all ate and were filled.

Matthew 7:13-21
The gate is narrow and the road is hard that leads to life, and there are few who find it.

eve of Easter 7

Luke 9:37-50
Whoever welcomes this child in my name welcomes me, and who-ever welcomes me welcomes the one who sent me; for the least among all of you is the greatest.

Matthew 7:28-8:4
The crowds were astounded at his teaching, for he taught them as one having authority, and not as their scribes.

eve of the Day of Pentecost

Luke 11:14-23
If it is by the finger of God that I cast out the demons, then the kingdom of God has come to you.

Matthew 9:18-26
Take heart, daughter; your faith has made you well.

[BCP Exodus 19:3-8a, 16-20 | 1 Peter 2:4-10]

Silence for meditation follows the reading.

Antiphon to the MAGNIFICAT

eve of Easter 2 — A week later, although the **doors** were shut,*
Jesus come and stood among them and said,
Peace be with you, **al**leluia.

[LH, PBO:John 20:26]

eve of Easter 3 — Stay with us, because it is **al**most evening,*
and the day is nearly over, **al**leluia.

[LH, PBO: Luke 24:29]

eve of Easter 4	I am the gate, says the Lord; whoever enters by me **will** be saved,* and will come in and go out and find pasture, **all**eluia. [LH: John 10:9]
eve of Easter 5	I am the way, and the truth, **and** the life.* No one comes to the Father except through me, **all**eluia. [LH: John 14:6]
eve of Easter 6	I will **ask** the Father,* and he will give you another Advocate to be with you for ever, **all**eluia. [LH: John 14:16]
eve of Easter 7	I will not **leave** you orphaned;* I will see you again, and your hearts will rejoice, **all**eluia. [CSB, SBH, LH: John 14:18; 16:22]
eve of the Day of Pentecost	Come Holy Spirit, fill the hearts of the faithful and kindle in them the fire **of** your love.* Though they spoke many different languages, you made the nations one in professing the same faith, **all**eluia. [CSB, SBH, LH]

Sundays of Easter

Antiphon to PSALM 136 *Confitemini Domino*

Easter Day	Mary Magdalene and the other Mary went to **see** the tomb,* alleluia. [Matt. 28:1]
Easter 2	The Lord brought us out of Egypt with a mighty hand and an **out**stretched arm,* al**le**luia. [PBO: Deut. 26:8]
Easter 3	If anyone **is** in Christ,* there is a new creation, al**le**luia. [2 Cor. 5:17]
Easter 4	You were going a**stray** like sheep* but now you have returned to the shepherd and guardian of your souls, **al**leluia. [1 Peter 2:25]
Easter 5	The Lord **has** been raised* and is exalted at God's right hand, **al**leluia. [LH: see Acts 5:31]
Easter 6	God raised Christ **from** the dead* and seated him at his right hand in the heavenly places, **al**leluia. [LH: Eph. 1:20]
Easter 7	Seek the things that **are** above,* where Christ is, seated at the right hand of God, **al**leluia. [Col. 3:1]
The Day of Pentecost	The Spirit of the Lord has **filled** the world,* al**le**luia. [LH: Wisdom 1:7]

136 *Easter Hymn*

1 Give thanks to the LORD, for **he** is good,*
for his mercy en**dures** for ever.

2 Give thanks to the **God** of gods,*
for his mercy en**dures** for ever.

3 Give thanks to the **Lord** of lords,*
for his mercy en**dures** for ever.

4 Who only **does** great wonders,*
for his mercy en**dures** for ever;

5 Who by wisdom **made** the heavens,*
for his mercy en**dures** for ever;

6 Who spread out the earth up**on** the waters,*
for his mercy en**dures** for ever;

7 Who creat**ed** great lights,*
for his mercy en**dures** for ever;

8 The sun to **rule** the day,*
for his mercy en**dures** for ever;

9 The moon and the stars to gov**ern** the night,*
for his mercy en**dures** for ever.

10 Who struck down the first**born** of Egypt,*
for his mercy en**dures** for ever;

11 And brought out Israel **from** among them,*
for his mercy en**dures** for ever;

12 With a mighty hand and a **stretched**-out arm,*
for his mercy en**dures** for ever;

13 Who divided the Red **Sea** in two,*
for his mercy en**dures** for ever;

14 And made Israel to pass **through** the midst of it,*
for his mercy en**dures** for ever;

15 But swept Pharaoh and his army in**to** the Red Sea,*
for his mercy en**dures** for ever;

16 Who led his people **through** the wilderness,*
for his mercy en**dures** for ever.

17 Who struck **down** great kings,*
for his mercy en**dures** for ever;

18 And slew **might**y kings,*
for his mercy en**dures** for ever;

19 Sihon, king **of** the Amorites,*
for his mercy en**dures** for ever;

20 And Og, the **king** of Bashan,*
for his mercy en**dures** for ever;

21 And gave away their lands for **an** inheritance,*
for his mercy en**dures** for ever;

22 An inheritance for Isra**el** his servant,*
for his mercy en**dures** for ever.

23 Who remembered us in our **low** estate,*
for his mercy en**dures** for ever;

24 And delivered us **from** our enemies,*
for his mercy en**dures** for ever;

25 Who gives food **to** all creatures,*
for his mercy en**dures** for ever.

26 Give thanks to the **God** of heaven,*
for his mercy en**dures** for ever.

The Antiphon is repeated.

Silence for meditation

God of everlasting love, through your Word you made all things in heaven and on earth; you have opened to us the path from death to life: Listen to the song of the universe, the hymn of resurrection, sung by your Church, and give us your blessing; through Jesus Christ our Lord. [LHd, LBW]

+

Antiphon to PSALM 117 *Laudate Dominum*

Easter Day	Were not our hearts burning within us while he was talking to us **on** the road,* while he was opening the scriptures to us? **al**leluia. [Luke 24:32]
Easter 2	The kingdom of the world has become the kingdom of our Lord and of **his** Messiah,* al**le**luia. [PBO: Rev. 11:15]
Easter 3	The Lord has re**deemed** his people,* al**le**luia. [LH: see Luke 1:68]
Easter 4	Strong and steadfast is his **love** for us,* al**le**luia. [LH: see v. 2]
Easter 5	He has rescued us from the pow**er** of darkness* and transferred us into the kingdom of his beloved Son, **al**leluia. [LH: Col. 1:13]
Easter 6	You have been turned to **God** from idols* to serve a living and true God, **al**leluia. [LH: 1 Thess. 1:9]
Easter 7	The Gentiles will glorify God **for** his mercy,* al**le**luia. [LH: see Rom. 15:9]
The Day of Pentecost	Send your strength, O God, from your holy temple **in** Jerusalem,* and perfect your work in us, **al**leluia. [LH: see Ps. 68:28]

117 *Call to praise*

1 Praise the LORD, **all** you nations;*
laud him, **all** you peoples.

2 For his loving-kindness toward **us** is great,*
and the faithfulness of the LORD endures for ever.
Hallelujah!

The Antiphon is repeated.

Silence for meditation

Lord God, you have revealed your kindness to all people: Gather the nations into your Church, that in all the various tongues of this world one hymn of praise may be offered to you; through your Son, Jesus Christ our Lord. [LHd, LBW]

+

Antiphon to the NEW TESTAMENT CANTICLE *Salus et gloria*

Easter Day — Alleluia, **Christ** is risen.*
The Lord is risen indeed, **al**leluia.
[see Luke 24:34]

Easter 2 — Look at my hands and my feet;
see that it is **I** myself.*
Touch me and see, **al**leluia. [Luke 24:39]

Easter 3 — Alleluia, our **Lord** is king;*
let us rejoice and give glory to him,
alleluia. [LH: see Ps. 47:6-7; 98:6]

Easter 4 — Christ is risen from the dead,
trampling down **death** by death,*
and giving life to those who sleep in the tomb,
alleluia. [BCP]

Easter 5	Christ, being raised from the dead, will never **die** again;* death no longer has dominion over him, **al**leluia. [Rom. 6:9]
Easter 6	Seek the things that are a**bove**, where Christ is,* seated at the right hand of God, **al**leluia . [Col. 3:1]
Easter 7	When he ascended on high he made captivity it**self** a captive;* he gave gifts to his people, **al**leluia. [Eph. 4:8]
The Day of Pentecost	All of them were filled with the **Ho**ly Spirit,* and began to speak, **al**leluia. [Acts 2:4]

A Song of Heaven — Revelation 19:1-2, 5-7

Victory and glory and power **to** our God,*
for true and just **are** his judgments.

Praise our God, all **you** his servants,*
and all who fear him, both **small** and great.

The Lord our God, the Almighty, has be**gun** his reign;*
let us rejoice and exult and give **him** the glory.

The marriage feast of the **Lamb** has come,*
and his bride is prepared to **wel**come him. [LH; PHP]

The Antiphon is repeated.

Silence for meditation

Grant, we pray, almighty God, that we who celebrate with awe the Paschal feast may be found worthy to attain to everlasting joys; through Jesus Christ our Lord. [Greg., MGV, MG, BCP Easter Mon.]

+

Stand

THE HYMN is sung.

Through the Seventh Sunday of Easter 'Αναστασεως ημερα

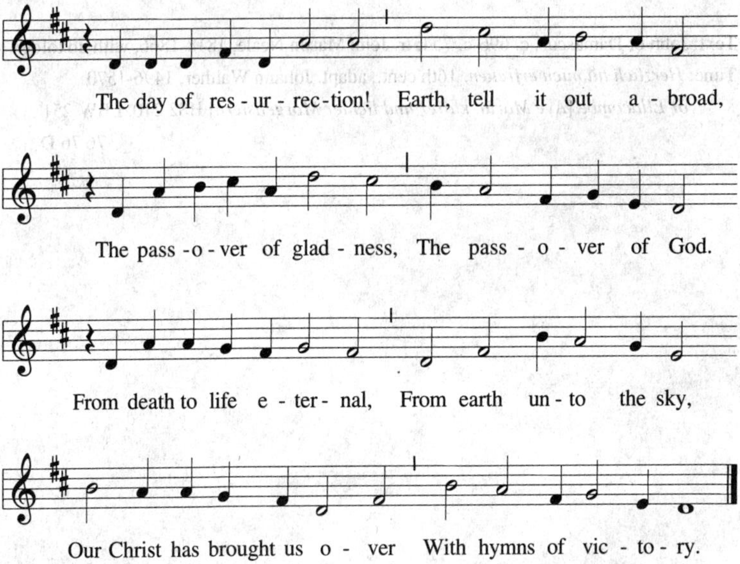

2 Our hearts be pure from evil,
That we may see aright
The Lord in rays eternal
Of resurrection light,
And list'ning to his accents,
May hear, so calm and plain,
His own "All hail!" and hearing,
May raise the victor strain.

3 Now let the heav'ns be joyful,
Let earth her song begin,
The round world keep high triumph
And all that is therein.
Let all things, seen and unseen,
Their notes together blend;
For Christ the Lord is risen,
Our joy that has no end!

4 Then praise we God the Father,
And praise we Christ his Son,
With them the Holy Spirit,
Eternal Three in One;

Till all the ransomed number
Fall down before the throne,
And honor, pow'r, and glory
Ascribe to God alone! [H82 210, LBW 141]

Text: John of Damascus, c. 696-c. 754; tr. John Mason Neale, 1818-1866, with doxology
Tune: *Herzlich tut mich erfreuen,* 16th cent., adapt. Johann Walther, 1496-1570
or Ellacombe [*Ave Maria, klarer und lichter Morgenstern*] H82 210, LBW 251
76 76 D

On the Day of Pentecost *Veni Creator Spiritus*

2 To you, the Comforter, we cry;
To you, the gift of God most high,
The fount of life, the fire of love,
The soul's anointing from above.

3 Your gracious gifts are sevenfold,
And we in them God's hand behold;
O promise of the Father, now
Our tongues with heavenly speech
endow.

4 Your light to every sense impart,
And shed your love in every heart;
Your own unfailing might supply
To strengthen our infirmity.

5 Drive far from us our wily foe,
And your abiding peace bestow;
If you be our protecting guide,
No evil can our steps betide.

6 To us make God the Father known;
Teach us th' eternal Son to own;
And you, whose Name we ever bless,
Of both the Spirit, to confess.

7 Praise we the Father and the Son
And Holy Spirit with them one;
And may the Son on us bestow
The gifts that from the Spirit flow.

[LBW 284 alt.]

Text: attr. Rhabanus Maurus, 776-856; tr. composite
Tune: *Komm, Gott Schöpfer*, J. Klug, *Geistliche Lieder*, 1533 LM

Sit

A LESSON is read.

Year 1	Year 2
Easter Day	
Luke 24:13-35	Luke 24:13-35
They told what had happened on the road, and how Jesus had been made known to them in the breaking of the bread.	They told what had happened on the road, and how Jesus had been made known to them in the breaking of the bread.
or John 20:19-23	*or* John 20:19-23
Jesus came and stood among them and said, "Peace be with you." After he said this, he showed them his hands and side.	Jesus came and stood among them and said, "Peace be with you." After he said this, he showed them his hands and side.
Easter 2	
John 14:1-7	John 14:1-7
If I go and prepare a place for you, I will come again and will take you to myself, so that where I am, there you may be also.	If I go and prepare a place for you, I will come again and will take you to myself, so that where I am, there you may be also.
Easter 3	
John 21:15-25	Mark 16:9-20
This is the disciple who is testifying to these things and has written them, and we know that his testimony is true.	Go into all the world and proclaim the good news to the whole creation.

Easter 4

Matthew 7:15-29

Beware of false prophets, who come to you in sheep's clothing but inwardly are ravenous wolves. You will know them by their fruits.

Mark 6:30-44

As Jesus went ashore, he saw a great crowd; and he had compassion for them, because they were like sheep without a shepherd; and he began to teach them many things.

Easter 5

Matthew 7:7-14

The gate is narrow and the road is hard that leads to life, and there are few who find it.

Luke 4:16-30

The Spirit of the Lord is upon me, because he has anointed me to bring good news to the poor.

Easter 6

Matthew 13:24-34a

Jesus told the crowds all these things in parables.

Luke 12:13-21

God said to him, "You fool! This very night your life is being demanded of you. And the things you have prepared, whose will they be?"

Easter 7

Matthew 10:24-33, 40-42

Whoever welcomes you welcomes me, and whoever welcomes me welcomes the one who sent me.

Luke 10:17-24

Blessed are the eyes that see what you see! For I tell you that many prophets and kings desired to see what you see, but did not see it, and to hear what you hear, and did not hear it.

The Day of Pentecost

John 14:21-29

The Advocate, the Holy Spirit, whom the Father will send in my name, will teach you everything, and remind you of all that I have said to you.

John 4:19-26

The hour is coming, and is now here, when the true worshipers will worship the Father in spirit and truth, for the Father seeks such as these to worship him.

Silence for meditation follows each reading.

Antiphon to the MAGNIFICAT

Easter Day

When it was evening on the first day of the week, and the doors of the house where the disciples had **met** were locked,*

Jesus came and stood among them and said, Peace be with you, **al**leluia. [John 20:19]

Easter 2

Have you believed because **you** have seen me?*

Blessed are those who have not seen and yet have come to believe, **al**leluia.

[LH, PBO: John 20:29]

Easter 3

Jesus said to his disciples, Bring some of the fish that you **have** just caught.*

So Simon Peter went aboard and hauled the net ashore, full of large fish, **al**leluia.

[LH: John 21:10-11]

Easter 4

My sheep **hear** my voice.*

I, their Lord, know them, **al**leluia.

[LH: see John 10:3,14]

Easter 5

I give you a **new** commandment,*

just as I have loved you, you should love one another, **al**leluia. [LH, PBO: John 13:34]

Easter 6

Those who love me will keep my word, and my Fa**ther** will love them,*

and we will come to them and make our home with them, **al**leluia. [LH: John 14:23]

Easter 7

I will send to you the spirit of truth who comes **from** the Father;*

he will testify on my behalf, **al**leluia.

[LH, PBO: John 15:26]

The Day of Pentecost: Today the Fifty Days have been completed, **al**leluia.*

The Holy Spirit gave the apostles spiritual gifts and sent them out to preach to the whole world and to proclaim that all who believe and are baptized shall be saved, **al**leluia. [LH, PBO]

The great Fifty Days of Easter conclude with Evening Prayer on the Day of Pentecost. General or ordinary (ordered) time, the time after Pentecost, begins the day following Pentecost with Morning Prayer for Monday of General Week I (pp. 599ff, 647.)

Antiphon to PSALM 124 *Nisi quia Dominus*

The **snare** is broken,*
and we have escaped, **al**leluia. [LH]

124 *The Savior of Israel*

1 If the LORD had not been **on** our side,*
let Isra**el** now say;

2 If the LORD had not been **on** our side,*
when enemies rose **up** against us;

3 Then would they have swallowed us **up** alive*
in their fierce **an**ger toward us;

4 Then would the waters have **o**verwhelmed us*
and the torrent gone **o**ver us;

5 Then would the **rag**ing waters*
have gone right **o**ver us.

6 Blessed **be** the LORD!*
he has not given us over to be a prey **for** their teeth.

7 We have escaped like a bird from the snare **of** the fowler;*
the snare is broken, and we **have** escaped.

8 Our help is in the Name **of** the LORD,*
the maker of heav**en** and earth.

Antiphon The **snare** is broken,*
and we have escaped, **al**leluia.

Silence for meditation

Lord Jesus, you foretold that your disciples would be despised on account of your Name, yet you number the very hairs of their heads: In times of persecution, defend and revive us by the power and comfort of the Holy Spirit, so that we can be freed from our enemies and praise your saving help now and for ever. [LH, LBW]

+

Antiphon to PSALM 115 *Non nobis, Domine*

We have been turned from the wor**ship** of idols*
to serve the living God, **al**leluia. [LH, PBO; see 1 Thess. 1:9]

115 *The one true God*

1 Not to us, O LORD, not to us,
but to your **Name** give glory;*
because of your love and because **of** your faithfulness.

2 Why should the **hea**then say,*
"Where then **is** their God?"

3 Our God **is** in heaven;*
whatever he wills to **do** he does.

4 Their idols are sil**ver** and gold,*
the work of **hu**man hands.

5 They have mouths, but they **can**not speak;*
eyes have they, but they **can**not see;

6 They have ears, but they **can**not hear;*
noses, but they **can**not smell;

7 They have hands, but they cannot feel;
feet, but they **can**not walk;*
they make no sound **with** their throat.

8 Those who make **them** are like them,*
and so are all who put their **trust** in them.

9 O Israel, trust **in** the LORD;*
he is their help **and** their shield.

10 O house of Aaron, trust **in** the LORD;*
he is their help **and** their shield.

11 You who fear the LORD, trust **in** the LORD;*
he is their help **and** their shield.

12 The LORD has been mindful of us, and **he** will bless us;*
he will bless the house of Israel;
he will bless the **house** of Aaron;

13 He will bless those who **fear** the LORD,*
both small and **great** together.

14 May the LORD increase you **more** and more,*
you and your children **af**ter you.

15 May you be blessed **by** the LORD,*
the maker of heav**en** and earth.

16 The heaven of heavens **is** the LORD's,*
but he entrusted the earth **to** its peoples.

17 The dead do not **praise** the LORD,*
nor all those who go down **in**to silence;

18 But we will **bless** the LORD,*
from this time forth for evermore.
Hallelujah!

Antiphon We have been turned from the wor**ship** of idols*
to serve the living God, **al**leluia.

Slence for meditation

Lord God, creator and ruler of the universe, you have entrusted the care of the earth to its peoples: Grant that your children, surrounded by signs of your presence, may live continually in Christ, praising you through him and with him, now and for ever. [LH, LBW]

+

Antiphon to the NEW TESTAMENT CANTICLE

Benedictus Deus et Pater

Through Christ you have come to **trust** in God,*
who raised him from the dead and gave him glory,
alleluia. [1 Peter 1:21]

A Song of God's Blessings in Christ Ephesians 1:3-12

Blessed be the God and Father of our Lord **Je**sus Christ;*
who has bestowed on us in Christ
every spiritual blessing **in** the heavens.

Before the world began God chose us in him
to be holy **in** his sight,*
without blemish and **full** of love.

He destined us to be adopted as his children
through **Je**sus Christ*
according to the purpose **of** his will,

That the glory of God's gracious gift,
freely bestowed on us in **the** Beloved,*
might redound **to** his praise.

In Christ we have redemption **through** his blood:*
the forgiveness of our sins
according to the riches of grace that he lav**ished** upon us.

He has made known to us the mystery **of** his will,*
the plan he was pleased to de**cree** in Christ,

A plan for the full**ness** of time,*
that all things in heaven and earth
might be unit**ed** in Christ,

In whom we have been given our share **in** the heritage,*
so that we might live for the praise **of** his glory. [PHP]

Antiphon Through Christ you have come to **trust** in God,*
who raised him from the dead and gave him glory,
alleluia.

Silence for meditation

Grant, we beseech you, almighty God, that we who celebrate the solemnities of the Lord's resurrection, may, by the renewal of your Holy Spirit, be raised from spiritual death; through Jesus Christ our Lord.
[Greg., CSB, SBH]

+

Stand

THE HYMN is sung. *Finita jam sunt praelia*

2 The pow'rs of death have done their worst,
But Christ their legions hath dispersed.
Let shouts of holy joy outburst.
Alleluia.

3 The three sad days are quickly sped,
He rises glorious from the dead;
All glory to our risen Head!
Alleluia.

4 He brake the age-bound chains of hell,
The bars from heav'n's high portals fell;
Let hymns of praise his triumph tell.
Alleluia.

5 Lord, by the stripes which wounded thee,
From death's dread sting thy servants free,
That we may live and sing to thee.
Alleluia. [H82 208, SBH 90; LBW 135]

Text: *Symphonia Sirenium*, Köln, 1695; tr. Francis Pott, 1832-1909
Tune: *Victory*, Giovanni Pierluigi da Palestrina, 1525-1594, adapt. 888 with alleluias

Sit

A LESSON is read.

Year 1

Monday in Easter [Bright] Week

John 14:1-14
If I go and prepare a place for you, I will come again and will take you to myself, so that where I am, there you may be also.

Year 2

Mark 16:1-8
He has been raised; he is not here. Look, there is the place they laid him.

Monday after Easter 2

John 17:1-11

This is eternal life, that they know you, the only true God, and Jesus Christ whom you have sent.

John 14:(1-7) 8-17

I will do whatever you ask in my name, so that the Father may be glorified in the Son.

Monday after Easter 3

Luke 4:14-30

Jesus, filled with the power of the Spirit, returned to Galilee, and a report about him spread through all the surrounding country.

Matthew (1:1-17) 3:1-6

They were baptized by John in the river Jordan, confessing their sins.

Monday after Easter 4

Luke 6:1-11

The Son of Man is lord of the sabbath.

Matthew 5:1-10

When Jesus saw the crowds, he went up the mountain; and after he sat down, his disciples came to him. Then he began to speak, and taught them.

Monday after Easter 5

Luke 7:36-50

Her sins, which were many, have been forgiven; hence she has shown great love. But the one to whom little is forgiven, loves little.

Matthew 6:1-6,16-18

Beware of practicing your piety before others in order to be seen by them; for then you have no reward from your Father in heaven.

Monday after Easter 6

Luke 9:18-27

Those who want to save their life will lose it, and those who lose their life for my sake will save it.

Matthew 13:1-16

To you it has been given to know the secrets of the kingdom of heaven, but to them it has not been given.

Monday after Easter 7

Luke 9:51-62

Go and proclaim the kingdom of God.

Matthew 8:5-17

That evening they brought to Jesus many who were possessed with demons; and he cast out the spirits with a word, and cured all who sick.

Silence for meditation follows each reading.

Antiphon to the MAGNIFICAT

Monday in Easter Week

Jesus met the women and **greet**ed them.*
They came to him, took hold of his feet, and worshiped him, **al**leluia. [LH; see Matt. 28:9]

Monday after Easter 2

What is born of the **flesh** is flesh,*
and what is born of the Spirit is spirit, **al**leluia. [LH: John 3:6]

Monday after Easter 3

This is the **work** of God:*
that you believe in him whom he has sent, **al**leluia. [LH: John 6:29]

Monday after Easter 4

I have other sheep that do not be**long** to this fold.*
I must bring them also, and they will listen **to** my voice.*
So there will be one **flock**, one shepherd,*
alleluia. [LH: John 10:16]

Monday after Easter 5

The Advocate, the Holy Spirit, whom the Father will send in my name, will teach you **e**verything*
and remind you of all that I have said to you, **al**leluia. [LH: John 14:26]

Monday after Easter 6

The Spirit of truth who comes from the Father will testify on **my** behalf.*
You also are to testify, **al**leluia. [LH: John 15:26-27]

Monday after Easter 7	The Spirit of truth a**bides** with you,* and he will be in you, **al**leluia. [LH: John 14:17]

Tuesdays of Easter

Antiphon to PSALM 66 *Jubilate Deo, omnis terra*

Bless our God, who holds our **souls** in life,*
alleluia. [LH, PBO]

66 *Corporate Thanksgiving*

1 Be joyful in God, **all** you lands;*
sing the glory of his Name;
sing the glory **of** his praise.

2 Say to God, "How awesome **are** your deeds!*
because of your great strength your enemies
cringe before you.

3 All the earth bows **down** before you,*
sings to you, sings **out** your Name."

4 Come now and see the **works** of God,*
how wonderful he is in his doing **toward** all people.

5 He turned the sea into dry land,
so that they went through the wa**ter** on foot,*
and there we re**joiced** in him.

6 In his might he rules for ever;
his eyes keep watch o**ver** the nations;*
let no rebel rise **up** against him.

7 Bless our **God**, you peoples;*
make the voice of his praise **to** be heard;

8 Who holds our **souls** in life,*
and will not allow our **feet** to slip.

9 For you, O **God**, have proved us;*
you have tried us just as sil**ver** is tried.

10 You brought us in**to** the snare;*
you laid heavy burdens up**on** our backs.

11 You let enemies ride over our heads;
we went through **fire** and water;*
but you brought us out into a place **of** refreshment.

12 I will enter your house with burnt-offerings
and will pay **you** my vows,*
which I promised with my lips
and spoke with my mouth when I **was** in trouble.

13 I will offer you sacrifices of fat beasts
with the **smoke** of rams;*
I will give you ox**en** and goats.

14 Come and listen, all you **who** fear God,*
and I will tell you what he has **done** for me.

15 I called out to him **with** my mouth,*
and his praise was **on** my tongue.

16 If I had found evil **in** my heart,*
the Lord would **not** have heard me;

17 But in truth **God** has heard me;*
he has attended to the voice **of** my prayer.

18 Blessed be God, who has not reject**ed** my prayer,*
nor withheld his **love** from me.

Antiphon Bless our God, who holds our **souls** in life,*
al**le**luia.

Silence for meditation

Almighty Father, you brought us through the waters of baptism to the shores of new life: Accept the sacrifice of our lives, and let us enter your house, there to praise your unfailing power and love; through your Son, Jesus Christ our Lord. [LH, LBW]

+

Antiphon to PSALM 116 *Dilexi, quoniam*

You have freed me from my **bonds**, O Lord;*
I will offer you the sacrifice of thanksgiving,
alleluia. [LH, PBO]

116 *Thanksgiving for deliverance from death*

1 I love the LORD, because he has heard the voice of
my **sup**plication,*
because he has inclined his ear to me whenever
I **called** upon him.

2 The cords of death entangled me;
the grip of the grave took **hold** of me;*
I came to **grief** and sorrow.

3 Then I called upon the Name **of** the LORD:*
"O LORD, I pray you, **save** my life."

4 Gracious is the **LORD** and righteous;*
our God is full **of** compassion.

5 The LORD watches **over** the innocent;*
I was brought very low, **and** he helped me.

6 Turn again to your rest, **O** my soul,*
for the LORD has treat**ed** you well.

7 For you have rescued my **life** from death,*
my eyes from tears, and my **feet** from stumbling.

8 I will walk in the presence **of** the LORD*
in the land **of** the living.

9 I believed, even when I said,
"I have been brought **ver**y low."*
In my distress I said, "No one **can** be trusted."

10 How shall I re**pay** the LORD*
for all the good things he has **done** for me?

11 I will lift up the cup **of** salvation*
and call upon the Name **of** the LORD.

12 I will fulfill my vows **to** the LORD*
in the presence of **all** his people.

13 Precious in the sight **of** the LORD*
is the death **of** his servants.

14 O LORD, I **am** your servant;*
I am your servant and the child of your handmaid;
you have freed me **from** my bonds.

15 I will offer you the sacrifice **of** thanksgiving*
and call upon the Name **of** the LORD.

16 I will fulfill my vows **to** the LORD*
in the presence of **all** his people,

17 In the courts **of** the LORD's house,*
in the midst of you, O Jerusalem.
Hallelujah!

Antiphon You have freed me from my **bonds**, O Lord;*
I will offer you the sacrifice of thanksgiving,
alleluia.

Silence for meditation

God of power and mercy, through the Passion and resurrection of your Son you have freed us from the bonds of death and the anguish of separation from you: Be with us on our pilgrimage, and help us offer you a sacrifice of praise, fulfill our vows, and glorify you in the presence of all your people; through Jesus Christ our Lord. [LH, LBW]

+

Antiphon to the NEW TESTAMENT CANTICLE *Dignus es*

Yours, O Lord, are the greatness, the power, the glory,
the victory, **and** the majesty,*
alleluia. [1 Chronicles 29:11; LH, PBO]

A Song to the Lamb Revelation 4:11; 5:9-10,13

Splendor and honor and **king**ly power*
are yours by right, O **Lord** our God,
For you created every**thing** that is,*
and by your will they were created and **have** their being.

And yours by right, O Lamb **that** was slain,*
for with your blood you have re**deemed** for God,
From every family, language, peo**ple**, and nation,*
a kingdom of priests to **serve** our God.

And so, to him who sits up**on** the throne,*
and to **Christ** the Lamb,
Be worship and praise, domin**ion** and splendor,*
for ever and for **ev**ermore. [BCP]

Antiphon Yours, O Lord, are the greatness, the power, the glory,
the victory, **and** the majesty,*
al**le**luia.

Silence for meditation

Grant, we implore you, almighty God, that we who celebrate your Paschal feast, inflamed with heavenly desires, may ever thirst for the fountain of life, Jesus Christ our Lord. [Greg., CSB, SBH]

+

Stand

THE HYMN is sung. *Jesus lebt, mit ihm auch ich*

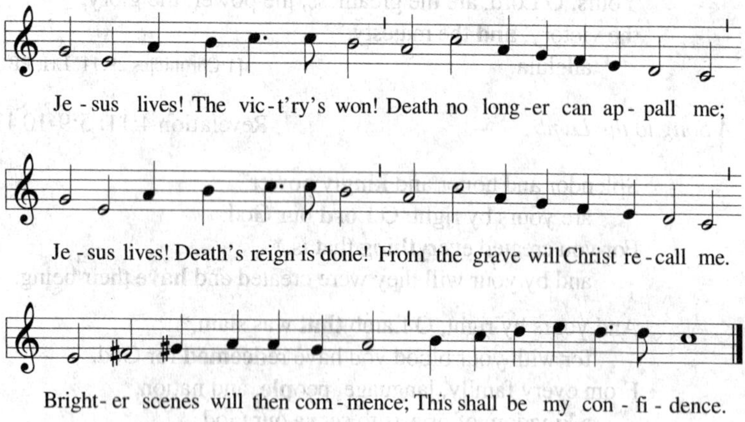

2 Jesus lives! To him the throne
High o'er heaven and earth is [given.
We shall go where he is gone,
Live and reign with him in heaven.
God is faithful; doubtings, hence!
This shall be my confidence!

3 Jesus lives! For me he died,
Hence will I, to Jesus living,
Pure in heart and act abide,
Praise to him and glory giving.
All I need God will dispense;
This shall be my confidence.

4 Jesus lives! And I am sure,
Neither life nor death shall sever
Me from him. I shall endure
In his love, through death, for ever.
God will be a sure defense;
This shall be my confidence.

5 Jesus lives! And now is death
But the gate of life immortal;
This shall calm my trembling breath
When I pass its gloomy portal.
Faith shall cry, as fails each sense:
Jesus is my confidence.

[TLH 201; LBW 133; see H82 194, 195]

Text: Christian Furchtegott Gellert, 1715-1769; tr. Frances Elizabeth Cox, 1812-1897, alt.
Tune: *Jesus, meine Zuversicht*, Johann Crüger, 1598-1662 78 78 77

Sit

A LESSON is read.

Year 1	Year 2
Tuesday in Easter [Bright] Week	
John 14:15-31 Because I live, you also will live.	Mark 16:9-20 Go into all the world and proclaim the good news to the whole creation.
Tuesday after Easter 2	
John 17:12-19 As you have sent me into the world, so I have sent them into the world.	John 14:18-31 Because I live, you also will live.
Tuesday after Easter 3	
Luke 4:31-37 What kind of utterance is this? For with authority and power he commands the unclean spirits, and out they come!	Matthew 3:7-12 Every tree that does not bear good fruit is cut down and thrown into the fire.
Tuesday after Easter 4	
Luke 6:12-26 All in the crowd were trying to touch him, for power came out from him and healed all of them.	Matthew 5:11-16 Let your light shine before others, so that they may see your good works and give glory to your Father in heaven.
Tuesday after Easter 5	
Luke 8:1-15 To you it has been given to know the secrets of the kingdom of God; but to others I speak in parables, so that 'looking they may not perceive, and listening they may not understand.'	Matthew 6:7-15 If you forgive others their trespasses, your heavenly Father will also forgive you.

Tuesday after Easter 6

Luke 11:1-13
If you then, who are evil, know how to give good gifts to your children, how much more will the heavenly Father give the Holy Spirit to those who ask him!

Matthew 13:18-23
As for what was sown on good soil, this is the one who hears the word and understands it, who indeed bears fruit and yields, in one case a hundredfold, in another sixty, and in another thirty.

Tuesday after Easter 7

Luke 10:1-17
The harvest is plentiful, but the laborers are few; therefore ask the Lord of harvest to send out laborers into his harvest.

Matthew 8:18-27
What sort of man is this, that even the winds and the sea obey him?

Silence for meditation

Antiphon to the MAGNIFICAT

Tuesday in Easter Week	While I was weeping at the tomb, I **saw** the Lord.* Al**le**luia. [LH: see John 20:11,14]
Tuesday after Easter 2	Were not our hearts burning within us while Jesus was talking to us **on** the road?* Al**le**luia. [LH: Luke 24:32]
Tuesday after Easter 3	The bread of God is that which comes **down** from heaven* and gives life to the world, **al**leluia. [LH: John 6:33]
Tuesday after Easter 4	I know my sheep and they **fol**low me;* I give them eternal life, **al**leluia. [LH: John 10:27-28]
Tuesday after Easter 5	If you loved me you would rejoice that I am going **to** the Father.* Al**le**luia. [LH: John 14:28]

Tuesday after Easter 6	I tell you the truth: it is to your advantage that I **go** away,* for if I do not go away, the Advocate will not come to you, **al**leluia. [LH: John 16:7]
Tuesday after Easter 7	You will receive power when the Holy Spirit has come upon you;* and you will be my witnesses to the end of the earth, **al**leluia. [LH: Acts 1:8]

Antiphon to PSALM 9 *Confitebor tibi*

You lifted me up from the **gate** of death,*
so that I may tell of all your praises
in the gates of the city of Zion, **al**leluia. [LH, PBO]

9 *Thanksgiving for victory*

1 I will give thanks to you, O LORD, with **my** whole heart;*
I will tell of all your mar**vel**ous works.

2 I will be glad and re**joice** in you;*
I will sing to your Name, **O** Most High.

3 When my enemies are **driv**en back,*
they will stumble and perish **at** your presence.

4 For you have maintained my right **and** my cause;*
you sit upon your throne **judg**ing right.

5 You have rebuked the ungodly and de**stroyed** the wicked;*
you have blotted out their name for ev**er** and ever.

6 As for the enemy, they are finished, in per**pet**ual ruin,*
their cities ploughed under, the memory **of** them perished;

7 But the LORD is en**throned** for ever;*
he has set up his **throne** for judgment.

8 It is he who rules the **world** with righteousness;*
he judges the peo**ples** with equity.

9 The LORD will be a refuge for **the** oppressed,*
a refuge in **time** of trouble.

10 Those who know your Name will put their **trust** in you,*
for you never forsake those who seek **you**, O LORD.

11 Sing praise to the LORD who **dwells** in Zion;*
proclaim to the peoples the things **he** has done.

12 The Avenger of blood will re**mem**ber them;*
he will not forget the cry of **the** afflicted.

13 Have pity on **me**, O LORD;*
see the misery I suffer from those who hate me,
O you who lift me up from the **gate** of death;

14 So that I may tell of all your praises
and rejoice in **your** salvation*
in the gates of the ci**ty** of Zion.

15 The ungodly have fallen into the **pit** they dug,*
and in the snare they set is their **own** foot caught.

16 The LORD is known by his **acts** of justice;*
the wicked are trapped in the works of **their** own hands.

17 The wicked shall be given over **to** the grave,*
and also all the peoples **that** forget God.

18 For the needy shall not always **be** forgotten,*
and the hope of the poor shall not per**ish** for ever.

19 Rise up, O LORD, let not the ungodly have the **up**per hand;*
let them be **judged** before you.

20 Put fear upon **them**, O LORD;*
let the ungodly know they **are** but mortal.

Antiphon You lifted me up from the **gate** of death,*
so that I may tell of all your praises
in the gates of the city of Zion, **al**leluia.

Silence for meditation

Lord God, righteous judge, hear the cries of your oppressed people. Rescue them from their oppressors, and save them from the gates of death, so that we may always rejoice in your help and speak your praise in the gates of Zion; through your Son, Jesus Christ our Lord. [LH, LBW]

+

Antiphon to PSALM 118 *Confitemini Domino*

I shall not **die**, but live;*
and declare the works of the LORD, **all**eluia. [LH]

118 *Processional song of praise*

1 Give thanks to the LORD, for **he** is good;*
his mercy en**dures** for ever.

2 Let Israel **now** proclaim,*
"His mercy en**dures** for ever."

3 Let the house of Aaron **now** proclaim,
"His mercy en**dures** for ever."

4 Let those who fear the LORD **now** proclaim,
"His mercy en**dures** for ever."

5 I called to the LORD in **my** distress;*
the LORD answered by set**ting** me free.

6 The LORD is at my side, therefore I **will** not fear;*
what can anyone **do** to me?

7 The LORD is at my **side** to help me;*
I will triumph over **those** who hate me.

8 It is better to rely **on** the LORD*
than to put any **trust** in flesh.

9 It is better to rely **on** the LORD*
than to put any **trust** in rulers.

10 All the ungodly en**com**pass me:*
in the name of the LORD I **will** repel them.

11 They hem me in, they hem me in on **ev**ery side;*
in the name of the LORD **I will** repel them.

12 They swarm about me like bees;
they blaze like a **fire** of thorns;*
in the name of the LORD **I will** repel them.

13 I was pressed so hard that I **al**most fell,*
but the LORD came **to** my help.

14 The LORD is my strength **and** my song,*
and he has become **my** salvation.

15 There is a sound of exulta**tion** and victory*
in the tents **of** the righteous:

16 "The right hand of the **LORD** has triumphed!*
the right hand of the LORD is exalted!
the right hand of the **LORD** has triumphed!"

17 I shall not **die**, but live,*
and declare the works **of** the LORD.

18 The LORD has pun**ished** me sorely,*
but he did not hand me o**ver** to death.

19 Open for me the **gates** of righteousness;*
I will enter them;
I will offer thanks **to** the LORD.

20 "This is the gate **of** the LORD;*
he who is right**eous** may enter."

21 I will give thanks to you, for you **an**swered me*
and have become **my** salvation.

22 The same stone which the buil**ders** rejected*
has become the chief **cor**nerstone.

23 This is **the** LORD's doing,*
and it is marvelous **in** our eyes.

24 On this day the **LORD** has acted;*
we will rejoice and be **glad** in it.

25 Hosannah, **LORD**, hosannah!*
LORD, send us **now** success.

26 Blessed is he who comes in the name **of** the Lord;*
we bless you from the house **of** the LORD.

27 God is the LORD; he has **shined** upon us;*
form a procession with branches up to the horns **of** the altar.

28 "You are my God, and **I** will thank you;*
you are my God, and I **will** exalt you."

29 Give thanks to the LORD, for **he** is good;*
his mercy en**dures** for ever.

Antiphon I shall not **die**, but live;*
and declare the works of the LORD, **al**leluia.

Silence for meditation

Lord God, your Son, rejected by the builders, has become the cornerstone of the Church. Shed rays of your glory upon your Church, that it may be seen as the gate of salvation open to all nations. Let cries of joy and exultation ring out from its courts to celebrate the wonder of Christ's resurrection, now and for ever. [LH, LBW]

+

Antiphon to the NEW TESTAMENT CANTICLE *Gratias agentes Deo Patri*

He is the first-born **of** the dead,*
supreme in all things, **al**leluia.

A Song of the Supremacy of Christ Colossians 1:12-20

Let us give thanks to **God** the Father,*
who has called us to share the inheritance
of the saints in the **realm** of light.

He rescued us from the do**main** of darkness*
and brought us into the kingdom of his beloved Son,
by whom we are set free and our **sins** forgiven.

He is the first-born of **all** creation;*
in him everything in heaven and on earth
was created, visible **and** invisible.

The whole universe has been created through him
and for him;*
he exists before all else that is;
in him everything is **held** together.

He is the head of the **Church**, his body,*
he is its origin, the first-born of the dead,
su**preme** in all things.

In him the fullness of God **came** to dwell;*
through him God chose to reconcile
the whole universe to himself,
making peace by the blood **of** his cross. [PHP]

Antiphon He is the first-born **of** the dead,*
supreme in all things, **al**leluia.

Silence for meditation

We thank you, heavenly Father, that you have delivered us from the dominion of sin and death and brought us into the kingdom of your Son; and we pray that, as by his death he has recalled us to life, so by his love he may raise us to eternal joys; who lives and reigns with you, in the unity of the Holy Spirit, one God, now and for ever. [Moz., AC, BCP Easter Sat.]

+

Stand

THE HYMN is sung.

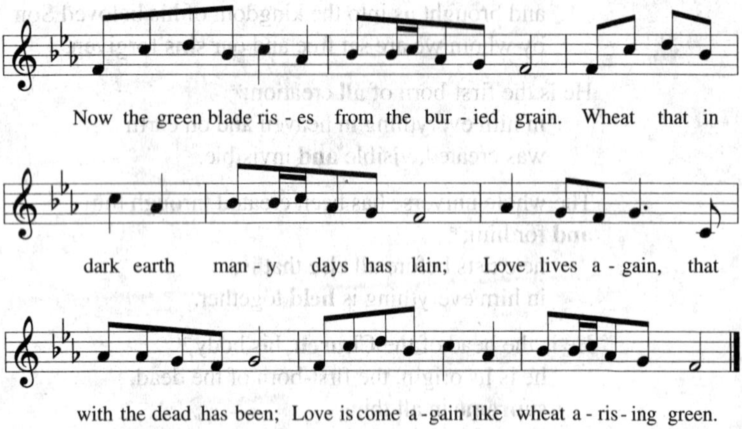

2 In the grave they laid him, love whom hate had slain,
Thinking that he would never wake again,
Laid in the earth like grain that sleeps unseen;
Love is come again like wheat arising green.

3 Forth he came at Easter, like the risen grain,
He that for three days in the grave had lain;
Raised from the dead, my living Lord is seen;
Love is come again like wheat arising green.

4 When our hearts are wintry, grieving, or in pain,
Your touch can call us back to life again,
Fields of our hearts that dead and bare have been;
Love is come again like wheat arising green. [H82 204, LBW 148]

Text: John Macleod Campbell Crum, 1872-1958, alt.
Tune: *Noël nouvelet*, French Carol 11 10 10 11

Sit

A LESSON is read.

Year 1	Year 2
Wednesday in Easter [Bright] Week	
John 15:1-11	Matthew 28:1-16
I have said these things to you so that my joy may be in you, and that your joy may be complete.	Go quickly and tell his disciples, 'He has been raised from the dead, and indeed he is going ahead of you to Galilee; there you will see him.'
Wednesday after Easter 2	
John 17:20-26	John 15:1-11
Father, I desire that those also, whom you have given me, may be with me where I am, to see my glory, which you have given me because you loved me before the foundation of the world.	I have said these things to you so that my joy may be in you, and that your joy may be complete.
Wednesday after Easter 3	
Luke 4:38-44	Matthew 3:13-17
As the sun was setting, all those who had any who were sick with various kinds of diseases brought them to Jesus; and he laid his	This is my Son, the Beloved, with whom I am well pleased.

hands on each of them and cured them.

Wednesday after Easter 4

Luke 6:27-38

Love your enemies, do good to those who hate you, bless those who curse you, pray for those who abuse you.

Matthew 5:17-20

Unless your righteousness exceeds that of the scribes and Pharisees, you will never enter the kingdom of heaven.

Wednesday after Easter 5

Luke 8:16-25

Who then is this, that he commands even the winds and the water, and they obey him?

Matthew 6:19-24

Where your treasure is, there your heart will be also.

Eve of Ascension Day

Luke 12:22-31

Life is more than food, and the body more than clothing.

Matthew 22:41-46

The Lord said to my Lord, Sit at my right hand, until I put your enemies under your feet.

Wednesday after Easter 7

Luke 10:17-24

Many prophets and kings desired to see what you see, but did not see it, and to hear what you hear, but did not hear it.

Matthew 8:28-34

Two demoniacs coming out of the tombs met Jesus. They were so fierce that no one could pass that way.

Silence for meditation follows each reading.

Antiphon to the MAGNIFICAT

Wednesday in Easter Week

Jesus went in to **stay** with them.*
While he was at the table with them, he took bread, blessed and broke it, and gave it to them, **al**leluia. [LH: Luke 24:29]

Wednesday after Easter 2	Those who do what is true come **to** the Light* so that it may be clearly seen that their deeds have been done in God, **all**eluia. [LH: see John 3:21]
Wednesday after Easter 3	Everything that the Father gives me will **come** to me,* and anyone who comes to me I will never drive away, **all**eluia. [LH: John 6:37]
Wednesday after Easter 4	God sent his Son not to judge the world but to **save** the world,* al**le**luia. [LH: John 12:47]
Wednesday after Easter 5	If you abide in me, and my words a**bide** in you,* ask whatever you wish, and it will be done for you, **all**eluia. [LH: John 15:7]
Wednesday after Easter 6, the Eve of Ascension Day	Father, I have made your name known to those whom you gave me **from** the world.* I am not asking on behalf of the world, but on behalf of those whom you gave me, because I am coming to you, **all**eluia. [LH: John 17:6,9,11]
Wednesday after Easter 7	Christ will baptize you with the Holy Spir**it** and fire,* al**le**luia. [LH: Luke 3:16]

Thursdays of Easter

Antiphon to Psalm 68 *Exsurgat Deus*

Sing to God, sing praises **to** his Name;*
exalt him who rides upon the heavens, **al**leluia. [LH]

68 *National song of triumph*

1 Let God arise, and let his ene**mies** be scattered;*
let those who hate him **flee** before him.

2 Let them vanish like smoke when the wind drives **it** away;*
as the wax melts at the fire, so let the wicked perish at
the pres**ence** of God.

3 But let the righteous be glad and rejoice **be**fore God;*
let them also be mer**ry** and joyful.

4 Sing to God, sing praises to his Name;
exalt him who rides up**on** the heavens;*
YAHWEH is his Name, re**joice** before him!

5 Father of orphans, defend**er** of widows,*
God in his holy **hab**itation!

6 God gives the solitary a home and brings forth prisoners
into freedom;*
but the rebels shall live **in** dry places.

7 O God, when you went forth be**fore** your people,*
when you marched **through** the wilderness,

8 The earth shook, and the skies poured down rain,
at the presence of God, the **God** of Sinai,*
at the presence of God, the **God** of Israel.

9 You sent a gracious rain, O God, upon **your** inheritance;*
you refreshed the land when **it** was weary.

10 Your people found their **home** in it;*
in your goodness, O God, you have made provision
for the poor.

11 The Lord **gave** the word;*
great was the company of women who **bore** the tidings:

12 "Kings with their armies are flee**ing** away;*
the women at home are divid**ing** the spoils."

13 Though you lingered a**mong** the sheepfolds,*
you shall be like a dove whose wings are covered with silver,
whose feathers are **like** green gold.

14 When the Almighty **scat**tered kings,*
it was like snow fall**ing** in Zalmon.

15 O mighty mountain, O **hill** of Bashan!*
O rugged mountain, O **hill** of Bashan!

16 Why do you look with envy, O rugged mountain,
at the hill which God chose for his **rest**ing place?*
truly, the LORD will dwell **there** for ever.

17 The chariots of God are twenty thousand,
even thous**ands** of thousands;*
the Lord comes in holi**ness** from Sinai.

18 You have gone up on high and led captivity captive;
you have received gifts even **from** your enemies,*
that the LORD God might **dwell** among them.

19 Blessed be the Lord **day** by day,*
the God of our salvation, who **bears** our burdens.

20 He is our God, the God of **our** salvation;*
God is the LORD, by whom we **es**cape death.

21 God shall crush the heads **of** his enemies,*
and the hairy scalp of those who go on still **in** their
wickedness.

22 The Lord has said, "I will bring them **back** from Bashan;*
I will bring them back from the depths **of** the sea;

23 That your foot may be **dipped** in blood,*
the tongues of your dogs in the blood **of** your enemies."

24 They see your proces**sion**, O God,*
your procession into the sanctuary, my God **and** my King.

25 The singers go before, musicians **fol**low after,*
in the midst of maidens playing up**on** the hand-drums.

26 Bless God in the **con**gregation;*
bless the LORD, you that are of the foun**tain** of Israel.

27 There is Benjamin, least of the tribes, at the head;
the princes of Judah **in** a company;*
and the princes of Zebulon **and** Naphtali.

28 Send forth your **strength**, O God;*
establish, O God, what you have **wrought** for us.

29 Kings shall bring **gifts** to you,*
for your temple's sake **at** Jerusalem.

30 Rebuke the wild beast **of** the reeds,*
and the peoples, a herd of wild bulls **with** its calves.

31 Trample down those who lust **af**ter silver;*
scatter the peoples that de**light** in war.

32 Let tribute be brought **out** of Egypt;*
let Ethiopia stretch out her **hands** to God.

33 Sing to God, O kingdoms **of** the earth;*
sing praises **to** the Lord.

34 He rides in the heavens, the **an**cient heavens;*
he sends forth his voice, his **migh**ty voice.

35 Ascribe pow**er** to God;*
his majesty is over Israel;
his strength is **in** the skies.

36 How wonderful is God in his **ho**ly places!*
the God of Israel giving strength and power to his people!
Bless**ed** be God!

Antiphon Sing to God, sing praises **to** his Name;*
exalt him who rides upon the heavens, **al**leluia.

Silence for meditation

Lord Jesus Christ, King of the universe, you have given us joy in your holy meal: Help us to understand the significance of your death and to acknowledge you as the conqueror of death, seated at the right hand of the Father, where you live and reign with him and the Holy Spirit, now and for ever. [LH, LBW]

+

Antiphon to Psalm 113 *Laudate, pueri*

The LORD is high a**bove** all nations.*
He takes up the weak out of the dust, **al**leluia. [LH, PBO]

113 *To the God of glory and compassion*

1 Hallelujah!
Give praise, you servants **of** the LORD;*
praise the Name **of** the LORD.

2 Let the Name of the **LORD** be blessed,*
from this time forth for **ev**ermore.

3 From the rising of the sun to its **go**ing down*
let the Name of the **LORD** be praised.

4 The LORD is high a**bove** all nations,*
and his glory a**bove** the heavens.

5 Who is like the LORD our God, who sits en**throned** on high,*
but stoops to behold the heavens **and** the earth?

6 He takes up the weak out **of** the dust*
and lifts up the poor **from** the ashes.

7 He sets them **with** the princes,*
with the princes **of** his people.

8 He makes the woman of a **child**less house*
to be a joyful moth**er** of children.

Antiphon The LORD is high a**bove** all nations.*
He takes up the weak out of the dust, **al**leluia.

Silence for meditation

Lord Jesus, surrendering the brightness of your glory, you become mortal so that we might be raised from the dust to share your very being: May the children of God always bless your Name from the rising of the sun to its going down, for you live and reign with the Father and the Holy Spirit, now and for ever. [LH, LBW]

+

Antiphon to the NEW TESTAMENT CANTICLE *Gratias agimus tibi*

Lord, who is like **you** in power?*
Who is your equal, majestic in holiness, awesome in splendor, doing wonders? **Al**leluia. [LH: Exodus 15:11]

A Song of the Judgment of God Revelation 11:17-18; 12:10b-12a

We give you thanks, Lord God almighty,
who are **and** who were,*
for you have taken your great power
and have be**gun** your reign.

The **na**tions raged,*
but your wrath has come
and the time to **judge** the dead,

The time to reward your servants, the prophets,
and the holy ones and all who **fear** your Name,*
great and **small** alike.

Now salvation and pow**er** have come,*
the Kingdom of our God
and the authority of **his** Messiah.

For the accuser of our companions
has **been** thrown down,*
who night and day accuses them **be**fore God.

They have conquered him by the sacrifice of the Lamb
and by the word of their **tes**timony,*
for they did not cling to life
even in the **face** of death.

Rejoice, **then**, you heavens,*
and all who **dwell** in them. [PHP]

Antiphon Lord, who is like **you** in power?*
Who is your equal, majestic in holiness, awesome in splendor, doing wonders? **Al**leluia.

Silence for meditation

Mighty God, you show us the depth of your love by freeing us from error and sin: Help us faithfully hold fast to your truth and make us part of your new creation in Jesus Christ our Lord. [PHP]

+

Stand

THE HYMN is sung. *Jesu, nostra redemptio*

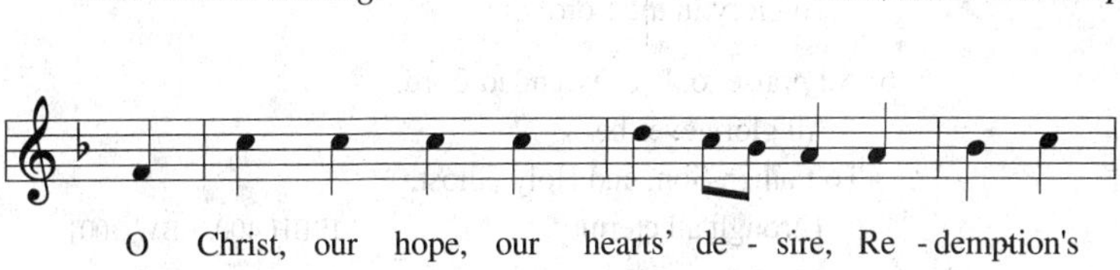

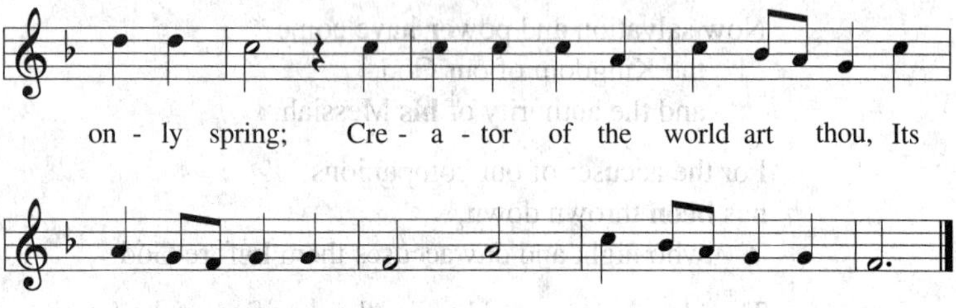

2 How vast the mercy and the love
Which laid our sins on thee:
And led thee to a cruel death
To set thy people free.

3 But now the bonds of death are burst,
The ransom has been paid;
And thou art on the Father's throne
In glorious robes arrayed.

4 O may thy mighty love prevail
Our sinful souls to spare
That we may come before thy throne
And find acceptance there.

5 O Christ, be thou our present joy,
Our future great reward;
Our only glory, may it be
To glory in the Lord!

6 All praise to thee, ascended Lord;
All glory ever be
To Father, Son, and Holy Ghost,
Through all eternity! [SBH 400, LBW 300]

Text: Latin hymn, c. 8th cent.; tr. John Chandler, 1806-1876
Tune: *Lobt Gott, ihr Christen*, Nikolaus Herman, c. 1480-1561 86 866

Sit

A LESSON is read.

Year 1	Year 2
Thursday in Easter [Bright] Week	
John 15:12-27	Matthew 28:16-20
This is my commandment, that you love one another as I have loved you.	I am with you always, to the end of the age.
Thursday after Easter 2	
Luke 3:1-14	John 15:12-27
John went into all the region around the Jordan, proclaiming a baptism of repentance for the forgiveness of sins.	This is my commandment, that you love one another as I have loved you.
Thursday after Easter 3	
Luke 5:1-11	Matthew 4:1-11
When they had brought their boats to shore, they left everything and followed him.	Jesus was led up by the Spirit into the wilderness to be tempted by the devil.
Thursday after Easter 4	
Luke 6:39-49	Matthew 5:21-26
Each tree is known by its own fruit.	First be reconciled to your brother and sister, and then come and offer your gift.
Thursday after Easter 5	
Luke 8:26-39	Matthew 6:25-34
Return to your home, and declare how much God has done for you.	Strive first for the kingdom of God and his righteousness, and

	all these things will be given to you as well.

Ascension Day

Matthew 28:16-20	Matthew 28:16-20
I am with you always, to the end of the age.	I am with you always, to the end of the age.

Thursday after Easter 7

Luke 10:25-37	Matthew 9:1-8
You shall love the Lord your God with all your heart, and with all your soul, and with all your srength, and with all your mind; and your neighbor as yourself.	So that you may know that the Son of Man has authority on earth to forgive sins—he then said to the paralytic—"Stand up, take your bed and go to your home."

Silence for meditation follows each reading.

Antiphon to the MAGNIFICAT

Thursday in Easter Week	Look at my **hands** and feet;* see that it is I myself, **al**leluia. [LH, PBO: Luke 24:39]
Thursday after Easter 2	Whoever believes in the Son has e**ter**nal life,* al**le**luia. [LH: see John 3:15]
Thursday after Easter 3	I am the living bread that came **down** from heaven.* Whoever eats of this bread will **live** for ever; and the bread that I will give for the life of the world **is** my flesh,* al**le**luia. [LH: John 6:51]
Thursday after Easter 4	I am **the** good shepherd.* I came that they may have life, and have it abundantly, **al**leluia. [LH: John 10:11, 10]
Thursday after Easter 5	I have said these things to you so that my joy may **be** in you,*

and that your joy may be complete, **all**eluia.
[LH: John 15:11]

Ascension Day	Victorious King, Lord of pow**er** and might,* today you have ascended in glory a**bove** the heavens. Do not **leave** us orphaned,* but send us the Father's promised gift, the Spirit of truth, **all**eluia. [LH: Eph. 4:10; John 14:18; Luke 24:49; John 16:13]
Thursday after Easter 7	When the Spirit of truth comes, he will guide you into **all** the truth;* and he will declare to you the things that are to come, **all**eluia. [LH: John 16:13]

Fridays of Easter

Antiphon to PSALM 8 *Domine, Dominus noster*

We see Jesus, who for a little while was made lower **than** the angels,*
now crowned with glory and honor, **al**leluia.

[PBO, LH: Heb. 2:9]

8 *The majesty of the Creator*

1 O LORD our Lord,* [BCP: O LORD our Governor*]
how exalted is your Name in **all** the world!

2 Out of the mouths of in**fants** and children*
your majesty is praised a**bove** the heavens.

3 You have set up a stronghold against your **ad**versaries,*
to quell the enemy and **the** avenger.

4 When I consider your heavens, the work **of** your fingers,*
the moon and the stars you have set **in** their courses,

5 What is man that you should be mind**ful** of him?*
the son of man that you should **seek** him out?

6 You have made him but little lower **than** the angels;*
you adorn him with glo**ry** and honor;

7 You give him mastery over the works **of** your hands;*
you put all things un**der** his feet:

8 All **sheep** and oxen,*
even the wild beasts **of** the field,

9 The birds of the air, the fish **of** the sea,*
and whatsoever walks in the paths **of** the sea.

10 O **LORD** our Lord,* [BCP: O Lord our Governor*]
how exalted is your Name in **all** the world!

Antiphon We see Jesus, who for a little while was made lower **than** the angels,*
now crowned with glory and honor, **al**leluia.

Silence for meditation

Almighty Lord, creator of all that exists, you made your Son one of us, but little lower than the angels; and when you crowned him with glory and honor you exalted the dignity of mortals beyond the skies: Enable us to give you worthy service, so that all creation may radiate the splendor of your Son, Jesus Christ our Lord. [LHd]

+

Antiphon to PSALM 105

Sing **to** the Lord,*
and remember the marvels he has done, **al**leluia. [LH, PBO]

105 *The faithfulness of God*

Part I *Confitemini Domino*

1 Give thanks to the LORD and call up**on** his Name;*
make known his deeds a**mong** the peoples.

2 Sing to him, sing prais**es** to him,*
and speak of all his **marvel**ous works.

3 Glory in his **ho**ly Name;*
let the hearts of those who seek the **LORD** rejoice.

4 Search for the LORD **and** his strength;*
continually **seek** his face.

5 Remember the marvels **he** has done,*
his wonders and the judgments **of** his mouth,

6 O offspring of Abra**ham** his servant,*
O children of Ja**cob** his chosen.

7 He is the **LORD** our God;*
his judgments prevail in **all** the world.

8 He has always been mindful **of** his covenant,*
the promise he made for a thousand **gen**erations:

9 The covenant he **made** with Abraham,*
the oath that he **swore** to Isaac,

10 Which he established as a stat**ute** for Jacob,*
an everlasting cove**nant** for Israel,

11 Saying, "To you will I give the **land** of Canaan*
to be your allott**ed** inheritance."

12 When they were **few** in number,*
of little account, and sojourners **in** the land,

13 Wandering from na**tion** to nation*
and from one kingdom **to** another,

14 He let no **one** oppress them*
and rebuked kings **for** their sake,

15 Saying, "Do not touch **my** anointed*
and do my proph**ets** no harm."

16 Then he called for a famine **in** the land*
and destroyed the sup**ply** of bread.

17 He sent a **man** before them,*
Joseph, who was sold **as** a slave.

18 They bruised his **feet** in fetters;*
his neck they put in an **i**ron collar.

19 Until his prediction **came** to pass,*
the word of the LORD **test**ed him.

20 The king sent **and** released him;*
the ruler of the peoples **set** him free.

21 He set him as a master o**ver** his household,*
as a ruler over all **his** possessions,

22 To instruct his princes according **to** his will*
and to teach his **eld**ers wisdom.

Antiphon Sing **to** the Lord,*
and remember the marvels he has done, **al**leluia.

105 Part II *Et intravit Israel*

Antiphon God remembered his **ho**ly word,*
and led forth his people with gladness, **al**leluia. [LH, PBO]

23 Israel came **in**to Egypt,*
and Jacob became a sojourner in the **land** of Ham.

24 The LORD made his people exceed**ing**ly fruitful;*
he made them stronger **than** their enemies;

25 Whose heart he turned, so that they hat**ed** his people,*
and dealt unjustly **with** his servants.

26 He sent Mos**es** his servant,*
and Aaron whom **he** had chosen.

27 They worked his **signs** among them,*
and portents in the **land** of Ham.

28 He sent darkness, and **it** grew dark;*
but the Egyptians rebelled a**gainst** his words.

29 He turned their waters **in**to blood*
and caused their **fish** to die.

30 Their land was over**run** by frogs,*
in the very chambers **of** their kings.

31 He spoke, and there came **swarms** of insects*
and gnats within **all** their borders.

32 He gave them hailstones in**stead** of rain,*
and flames of fire through**out** their land.

33 He blasted their vines **and** their fig trees*
and shattered every tree **in** their country.

34 He spoke, and the **lo**cust came,*
and young locusts **with**out number,

35 Which ate up all the green plants **in** their land*
and devoured the fruit **of** their soil.

36 He struck down the firstborn **of** their land,*
the firstfruits of **all** their strength.

37 He led out his people with sil**ver** and gold;*
in all their tribes there was not **one** that stumbled.

38 Egypt was glad **of** their going,*
because they were a**fraid** of them.

39 He spread out a cloud **for** a covering*
and a fire to give light in **the** night season.

40 They asked, and **quails** appeared,*
and he satisfied them with **bread** from heaven.

41 He opened the rock, and **wa**ter flowed,*
so the river ran in **the** dry places.

42 For God remembered his **ho**ly word*
and Abra**ham** his servant.

43 So he led forth his peo**ple** with gladness,*
his chosen with **shouts** of joy.

44 He gave his people the lands **of** the nations,*
and they took the fruit of **oth**ers' toil,

45 That they might **keep** his statutes*
and observe his laws.
Hallelujah!

Antiphon God remembered his **ho**ly word,*
and led forth his people with gladness, **al**leluia.

Silence for meditation

God our Father, through the death and resurrection of your Son, you have fulfilled the promise to Abraham, Joseph, and Moses to redeem the world from slavery and to lead us into the promised land: Grant us living water from the rock and bread from heaven, that we may survive our desert pilgrimage and praise you for ever; through Jesus Christ our Lord. [LH, LBW]

+

Antiphon to the NEW TESTAMENT CANTICLE *Magna et mirabilia*

I will sing to the LORD, for he has **tri**umphed gloriously.*
Al**le**luia. [LH: Exod. 15:1]

The Song of the Redeemed Revelation 15:3-4

O Ruler of the uni**verse**, Lord God,*
great are the deeds that you have done,*
surpassing human **un**derstanding.

Your ways are ways of righteous**ness** and truth,*
O King of all the nations,
O King of **all** the ages.

Who can fail to do you homage, Lord,
and sing the praises **of** your Name?*
For you alone are the **Ho**ly One.

All nations will draw near and bow **down** before you,*
because your just and holy works have **been** revealed.

[BCP alt. LBW 21]

Antiphon I will sing to the LORD, for he has **tri**umphed gloriously.*
Al**le**luia.

Silence for meditation

Holy God, ruler of the universe, you have vindicated your truth by raising your Son from death and exalting him to your right hand in glory: By the power of this love draw the nations of the world to you in whom alone we find perfect peace; through Jesus Christ our Lord. [PHP]

+

Stand

THE HYMN is sung. *Hallelujah! Jesus lebt!*

2 Jesus lives! Who do you weep?
Why that sad and frequent sigh?
He who died our brother here
Lives our brother still on high,
Lives for ever to bestow
Blessings on his Church below.

3 Jesus lives! And thus, my soul,
Life eternal waits for you;
Joined to him, your living head,
Where he is, you shall be too;
With the Lord, at his right hand,
As a victor you shall stand.

4 Jesus lives! Let all rejoice.
Praise him, ransomed of the earth.
Praise him in a nobler song,
Cherubim of heav'nly birth.
Praise the victor king, whose sway,
Sin and death and hell obey.

5 Hallelujah! Angels, sing!
Join us in our hymn of praise.
Let your chorus swell the strain
Which our feebler voices raise:
Glory to our God above
And on earth his peace and love!

[TLH 188, SBH 100, LBW 147]

Text: Carl Bernhard Garve, 1763-1841; tr. Jane Borthwick, 1813-1897, alt.
Tune: *Fred til Bod*, Ludwig M. Lindeman, 1812-1887 77 77 77

Sit

A LESSON is read.

Year 1	Year 2
Friday in Easter [Bright] Week	
John 16:1-15 When the Spirit of truth comes, he will guide you into all the truth.	Luke 24:1-12 Two men in dazzling clothes stood beside them. The women were terrified and bowed their faces to the ground, but the men said to them, "Why do you look for the living among the dead?"
Friday after Easter 2	
Luke 3:15-22 John answered all of them by saying, "I baptize you with water; but one who is more powerful than I is coming; I am not worthy to untie the thong of his sandals. He will baptize you with the Holy Spirit and fire."	John 16:1-15 When the Spirit of truth comes, he will guide you into all truth.
Friday after Easter 3	
Luke 5:12-26 Amazement seized all of them, and they glorified God and were filled with awe, saying, "We have seen strange things today."	Matthew 4:12-17 The people who sat in darkness have seen a great light, and for those who sat in the region and shadow of death light has dawned.
Friday after Easter 4	
Luke 7:1-17 Jesus said, "Young man, I say to you, rise!" The dead man sat up and began to speak, and Jesus gave him to his mother.	Matthew 5:27-37 I say to you, Do not swear at all, either by heaven, for it is the throne of God, or by the earth, for it is his footstool, or by Jerusalem, for it is the city of the great King.

Friday after Easter 5

Luke 8:40-56

Jesus took her by the hand and called out, "Child, get up!" Her spirit returned, and she got up at once. Then he directed them to give her something to eat.

Matthew 7:1-12

Ask, and it will given you; search, and you will find; knock, and the door will be opened for you.

Friday after Ascension Day

Luke 9:28-36

This is my Son, my Chosen; listen to him!

Matthew 7:22-27

That house did not fall, because it had been founded on rock.

Friday after Easter 7

Luke 10:38-42

Mary has chosen the better part, which will not be taken away from her.

Matthew 9:9-17

I have come to call not the righteous but sinners.

Silence for meditation follows each reading.

Antiphon to the MAGNIFICAT

Friday in Easter Week	The disciple whom Jesus loved said, It **is** the Lord!* Al**le**luia. [LH: John 21:7]
Friday after Easter 2	To destroy the power of hell Christ died **on** the cross;* clothed in strength and glory, he triumphed over death on the third day, **al**leluia. [LH]
Friday after Easter 3	Our crucified and risen Lord **has** redeemed us,* al**le**luia. [LH]
Friday after Easter 4	The good shepherd lays down his life **for** the sheep,* al**le**luia. [LH: John 10:11]

Friday after Easter 5	No one has greater **love** than this,* to lay down one's life for one's friends, **al**leluia. [LH: John 15:13]
Friday after Ascension Day	The heavenly Father will give the Holy Spirit to those who ask him,* al**le**luia. [LH: Luke 11:13]
Friday after Easter 7	The apostles were constantly devoting them**selves** to prayer,* together with certain women, including Mary the mother of Jesus, as well as his brothers, **al**leluia. [LH: Acts 1:14]

MORNING PRAYER
Matins or Morning Praise
throughout Easter (Pascha)

Stand

Leader

O Lord, open my lips,

Congregation

And my mouth shall de-clare your praise.

Leader and Congregation

Glo-ry to the Fa-ther, and to the Son and to the Ho-ly Spir-it;

as it was in the be-gin-ning, is now, and will be for ev-er. A-men

Al-le-lu-ia. Al-le-lu-ia.

The PSALMODY begins with this song of praise, Venite exultemus.

[I] In his hand are the cav - erns of the earth;
the heights of the hills are al - so his.
[II] The sea is his, for he made it;
and his hands have mold - ed the dry land.
[I] Oh, come, let us bow down and bend the knee,
and kneel be - fore the Lord, our Mak - er.
[II] For he is our God, and we are the peo-ple of his pas-ture
and the sheep of his hand.
C Glo - ry to the Fa - ther

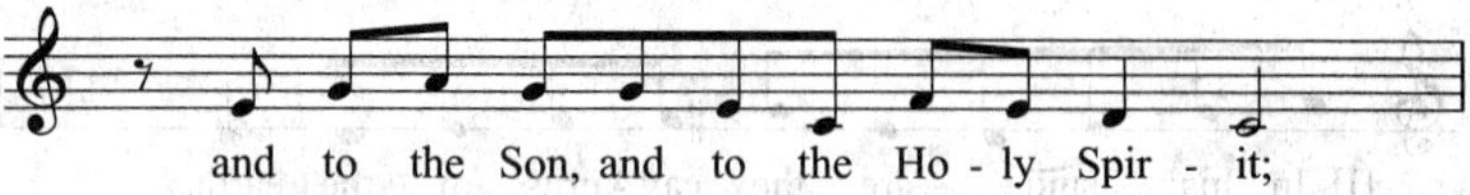

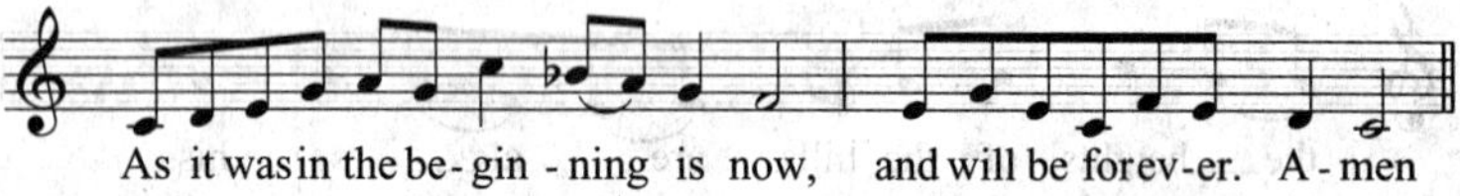

Until the Ascension:
Ascension Day:
The Day of Pentecost:

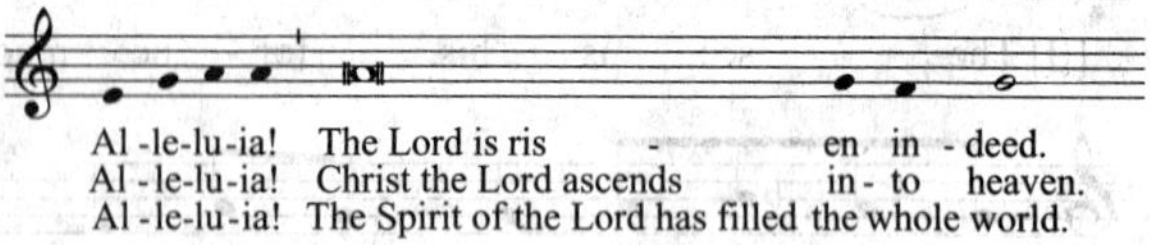

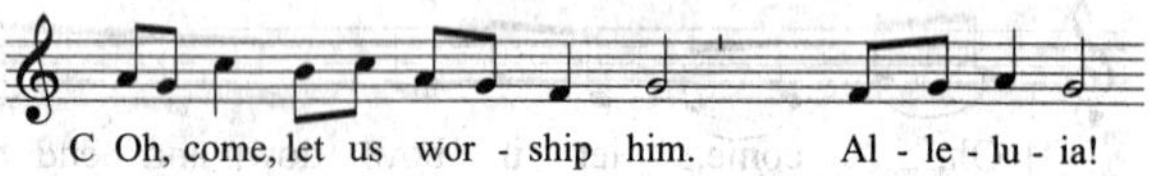

Sit

A second psalm is sung or said; additional psalms and an Old Testament canticle may be sung or said also. Silence for meditation follows each psalm or canticle.The psalm prayer appropriate to each psalm or canticle follows the silence.

C Amen

Stand

THE HYMN is sung.

Sit

One or two LESSONS are read. Silence for meditation follows each reading.

The Responsory to the reading(s) follows the silence. After the Responsory the leader then continues:

L In many and various ways God spoke to his people of old by the prophets.

C But now in these last days he has spoken to us by his Son.

Stand

The GOSPEL CANTICLE, Benedictus Dominus Deus, *is sung or said. The proper Antiphon is given on pages 1368-1444.*

The Antiphon is sung or said.

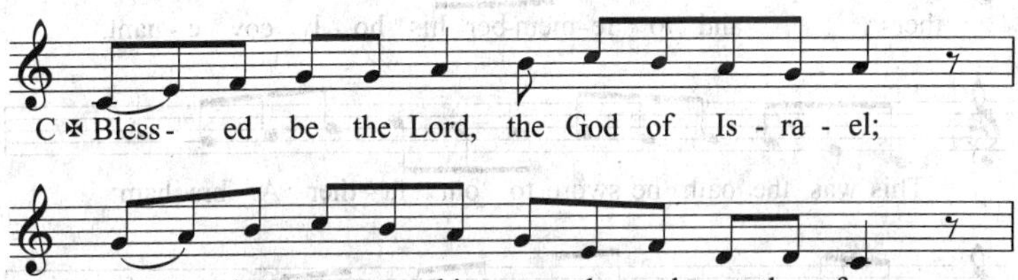

He has raised up for us a might - y Sav - ior,
born of the house of his ser - vant Da - vid. Through his
ho - ly proph - ets he prom - ised of old that he would
save us from our en - e - mies, from the hands of all who
hate us. He pro-mised to show mer - cy to our fa -
thers and to re-mem-ber his ho - ly cov - e - nant.
This was the oath he swore to our fa - ther A - bra - ham:
to set us free from the hands of our en - e - mies,

free to wor-ship him with-out fear, ho - ly and
right-eous in his sight all the days of our life.
L You, my child shall be called the pro - phet of the Most High,
for you will go be - fore the Lord to pre-pare his way,
to give his peo-ple know ledge of sal - va-tion by the for-give ness
of their sins. In the ten-der com-pas- sion of our God,
the dawn from on high shall break up - on us,
to shine on those who dwell in dark-ness and the shad-ow of death,

The Antiphon is repeated.

The PRAYER OF THE DAY is said.

EASTER DAY

Almighty God, who through your only-begotten Son Jesus Christ overcame death and opened to us the gate of everlasting life: Grant that we, who celebrate with joy the day of the Lord's resurrection, may be raised from the death of sin by your life-giving Spirit; through your Son Jesus Christ our Lord, who lives and reigns with you and the Holy Sprit, one God, now and for ever. [Gel., Sarum, RS, BCP]

Monday in Easter Week [Bright Monday]

O God, you continually increase your Church by the birth of new sons and daughters in Baptism: Grant that they may be obedient all the days of their life to the rule of faith which they received in that Sacrament;

through your Son Jesus Christ our Lord, who lives and reigns with you and the Holy Spirit, one God, now and for ever. [Gel., RS, LFF]

BCP: above, p. 1264

Tuesday in Easter Week [Bright Tuesday]

O God, through the paschal mystery you have healed the world: Continue to bless your people with heavenly gifts, so that may attain true liberty and enjoy the blessedness of heaven which we have begun to taste on earth; through your Son Jesus Christ our Lord, who lives and reigns with you and the Holy Spirit, one God, now and for ever.

[Greg., MR, RS, TLH, LFF rev. PHP]

BCP: below, p. 1351

Wednesday in Easter Week [Bright Wednesday]

O God, you gladden our hearts by the annual celebration of the resurrection of our Lord: In your mercy grant that we, who now celebrate these joyous days on earth, may at length attain to the eternal Easter in heaven; through your Son Jesus Christ our Lord, who lives and reigns with you and the Holy Spirit, one God, now and for ever.

[Gel., RS, LBW Easter evening, *Priest's Book of Private Devotion* (1884) rev. PHP]

Thursday in Easter Week [Bright Thursday]

O God, you have made many nations, peoples, and races one in the confession of your Name: Grant that all who have been born again in the waters of Baptism may be united in faith and in holiness of life; through your Son Jesus Christ our Lord, who lives and reigns with you and the Holy Spirit, one God, now and for ever. [Greg., RS, LFF rev. DvD, PHP]

BCP: see Friday in Easter Week

Friday in Easter Week [Bright Friday]

Almighty and everlasting God, in the paschal mystery you have established with all humanity the new covenant of reconciliation: Grant that all who have been reborn into the fellowship of Christ's body may show forth in their lives the faith they profess with their lips; through your Son Jesus Christ our Lord, who lives and reigns with you and the Holy Spirit, one God, now and for ever.

[Greg., RS, AC, TLH, BCP Easter Thursday, Easter 2]

Saturday in Easter Week [Bright Saturday]

O God, in the abundance of your grace you increase and multiply the number of those who believe in you: Mercifully look upon your chosen people, so that, having been reborn in the sacrament of Holy Baptism, they may be clothed in the garments of immortality; through your Son Jesus Christ our Lord, who lives and reigns with you and the Holy Spirit, one God, now and for ever. [Gel., Greg., RS tr. PHP]

BCP: above, p. 1296

THE SECOND SUNDAY OF EASTER

God of everlasting mercy, you renew the faith of your holy people by the yearly return of the paschal feast: Increase in us the grace you have bestowed, that we may comprehend more fully in whose font we have been cleansed, through whose Spirit we have been reborn, and by whose blood we have been redeemed; even your Son Jesus Christ our Lord, who lives and reigns with you and the Holy Spirit, one God, now and for ever. [MG, RS, LFF, tr. PHP]

BCP: above, Easter Friday

Monday in the Second Week of Easter

Almighty and everlasting God, with boldness and confidence we dare to call you Father: Fulfill and make perfect in our hearts the work of your Holy Spirit, through whom we have become your adopted children, so that we may be found worthy to enter upon the glorious inheritance you have promised to us in your Son, Jesus Christ our Lord; who lives and reigns with you and the Holy Spirit, one God, now and for ever.

[Berg., Ambrosian *Manuale*, RS also 19 Sun in Ordinary Time tr. DvD]

Tuesday in the Second Week of Easter

Almighty God, open our lips to proclaim the power of Christ our risen Lord; and grant that we, who have received this pledge of his love, may at the last attain the riches that it promises; through the same Jesus Christ our Lord, who lives and reigns with you and the Holy Spirit, one God, now and for ever. [Gel., RS tr., DvD]

Wednesday in the Second Week of Easter

O Lord, as year by year we recall the mysteries by which humanity was restored to its original dignity and granted the hope of resurrection, we humbly entreat your mercy that what we call to mind in faith we may take to heart in abiding love; through Jesus Christ our Lord, who lives and reigns with you and the Holy Spirit, one God, now and for ever.

[Gel., RS tr. DvD]

Thursday in the Second Week of Easter

Grant, Almighty God, that the commemoration of our Lord's death and resurrection may continually transform our lives and be manifested in our deeds; through Jesus Christ our Lord, who lives and reigns with you and the Holy Spirit, one God, now and for ever.

[Gel., RS tr. LFF; also Monday Easter 6]

Friday in the Second Week of Easter

For our sake, O God, you willed that your Son should undergo the shame of the Cross to drive from us the power of the enemy: Grant that we may come to share the grace and power of the resurrection of the same Jesus Christ our Lord; who lives and reigns with you and the Holy Spirit, one God, now and for ever. [Gel., RS tr. PHP]

Saturday in the Second Week of Easter

O God, you have redeemed us and adopted us into your family: Watch over your children with fatherly love, and grant to us, who believe in your Son Jesus Christ, both true freedom and an inheritance beyond change and decay; through the same Jesus Christ our Lord, who lives and reigns with you and the Holy Spirit, one God, now and for ever.

[Gel., Greg., RS tr. DvD, also Easter 5 and 23 Sun in Ordinary Time]

THE THIRD SUNDAY OF EASTER

God, who by the humiliation of your Son raised up the fallen world: Grant to your faithful people perpetual gladness, and make those whom you have delivered from the danger of everlasting death partakers of eternal joys; through your Son, Jesus Christ our Lord, who lives and reigns with you and the Holy Spirit, one God, now and for ever.

[Gel., Greg., MR, CB, CSB, SBH, LBW; RS Easter 4 Mon., 14th Sun. in Ordinary Time]

Monday in the Third Week of Easter

O God, by the abundance of your grace you unfailingly increase the number of your children: Look with favor upon those whom you have chosen to be members of your Church, that, having been born again in Baptism, they may be granted a glorious resurrection; through Jesus Christ our Lord, who lives and reigns with you and the Holy Spirit, one God, now and for ever. [RS tr. LFF; also Easter 4 and 15 Sun. in Ordinary Time]

Tuesday in the Third Week of Easter

O Lord, you open the gates of your kingdom to those who have been reborn by water and the Spirit: Increase the grace you have given to your children, that those who have been cleansed from sin may attain to all your promises; through Jesus Christ our Lord, who lives and reigns with you and the Holy Spirit, one God, now and for ever. [Gel., RS tr. LFF]

Wednesday in the Third Week of Easter

Almighty God, your blessed Son Jesus Christ came down from heaven to be the Bread of life that all who come to him may never hunger: Grant, we pray, that we may continually feed on him, our risen and living Lord, and so enjoy eternal life in this world and the next; through the same, your Son, Jesus Christ our Lord, who lives and reigns with you and the Holy Spirit, one God, now and for ever. [DvD]

Thursday in the Third Week of Easter

Almighty and everlasting God, who at this joyful Eastertide made known to us the depth of your love: Open wide our hearts to welcome your great love, and as you have delivered us from the night of error and sin, help us to cling more firmly to your word of truth, your Son Jesus Christ our Lord; who lives and reigns with you and the Holy Spirit, one God, now and for ever. [Gel., RS tr. DvD]

Friday in the Third Week of Easter

Grant, we beseech you, almighty God, that we, who have come to know the gift and the grace of our Lord's resurrection, may through your Holy Spirit of love rise to new life; through Jesus Christ our Lord, who lives and reigns with you and the Holy Spirit, one God, now and for ever.

[Berg., RS tr. DvD and LFF]

Saturday in the Third Week of Easter

O God, in the waters of Baptism you have given new birth to those who believe in you: Come to the help of all who have been reborn in Christ, that they may overcome the wiles of the devil, and faithfully keep hold of the gift they have received from you; through Jesus Christ our Lord, who lives and reigns with you and the Holy Spirit, one God, now and for ever. [Gel., Greg., RS tr. DvD; LFF]

THE FOURTH SUNDAY OF EASTER

Almighty God, you show to those who are in error the light of your truth, so that they may return into the way of righteousness: Grant to all those who are admitted into the fellowship of Christ's religion that they may resolutely reject those things that contradict the faith they profess and follow all those things that are in agreement with it; through your Son, Jesus Christ our Lord, who lives and reigns with you and the Holy Spirit, one God, now and for ever.

[Leo., MR, CB, CSB, SBH, LBW, LFF; RS Mon of Easter 3, 15 Sun. in Ordinary Time]

Monday in the Fourth Week of Easter

Almighty and everlasting God, you have given your Church the great joy of the resurrection of Jesus Christ: Give us also the greater joy of the kingdom of your elect, when the flock of your Son will share in the final victory of its Shepherd, Jesus Christ our Lord; who lives and reigns with you and the Holy Spirit, one God, now and for ever. [LFF]

RS: Easter 3

Tuesday in the Fourth Week of Easter

Grant, we pray you, Almighty God, that we who celebrate the mysteries of the Lord's resurrection may be filled with the joy of our redemption;

through the same Jesus Christ our Lord, who lives and reigns with you and the Holy Spirit, one God, now and for ever. [Greg., RS tr. DvD]

Wednesday in the Fourth Week of Easter

O Lord, the life of the faithful, the glory of the saints, and the delight of those who trust in you: Hear our supplications, that we who thirst for the life you promise may be filled to overflowing with your countless gifts; through Jesus Christ our Lord, who lives and reigns with you and the Holy Spirit, one God, now and for ever. [Gel., RS, LFF, rev. PHP]

Thursday in the Fourth Week of Easter

O God, you have restored our human nature and raised us to a dignity higher than we had at the beginning: Look with favor upon the wonderful mystery of your love, and preserve for ever the gifts of your grace and heavenly benediction in those who in Holy Baptism have been reborn through Jesus Christ our Lord; who lives and reigns with you and the Holy Spirit, one God, now and for ever. [Gel., RS tr. DvD]

Friday in the Fourth Week of Easter

O God, the author of our salvation and our freedom, you have redeemed us by the blood of your Son: Hear the voices of your people and grant that through you we may have life and in you find eternal refuge; through Jesus Christ our Lord, who lives and reigns with you and the Holy Spirit, one God, now and for ever. [Goth., RS tr. PHP]

Saturday in the Fourth Week of Easter

Almighty and everlasting God, keep alive within us the Paschal mysteries, that under your watchful eye we who have been renewed in the font of baptism may bear abundant fruit and attain the joys of eternal life;

through Jesus Christ our Lord, who lives and reigns with you and the Holy Spirit, one God, now and for ever. [Berg., RS tr. PHP]

THE FIFTH SUNDAY OF EASTER

O God, through whom redemption comes to us and our adoption is accomplished: Look in mercy on your children, and bestow upon all who believe in Christ perfect freedom and an eternal inheritance; through your Son, Jesus Christ our Lord, who lives and reigns with you and the Holy Spirit, one God, now and for ever.

[Gel., RS tr. DvD et al.; also used 23 Sun in Ordinary Time]

LBW: Proper 15

Monday in the Fifth Week of Easter

Almighty God, heavenly Father, your blessed Son Jesus Christ is the true Vine and your faithful people are the branches: Tend us, we pray, with loving care, and prune away our sins, that, always abiding in him, we may bear abundant fruit to your glory; through the same Jesus Christ our Lord, who lives and reigns with you and the Holy Spirit, one God, now and for ever. [DvD]

RS: Proper 16

Tuesday in the Fifth Week of Easter

O God, in the resurrection of your Son you restore your people to eternal life: Grant us a constant faith and a certain hope, that we may without wavering look forward to the fulfillment of your promises; through the same Jesus Christ our Lord, who lives and reigns with you and the Holy Spirit, one God, now and for ever. [Berg., RS tr. DvD et al.]

Wednesday in the Fifth Week of Easter

O God, lover and restorer of innocence: Direct the hearts of your family toward you that those you have freed from the night of unbelief may never abandon the light of your truth; through Jesus Christ our Lord, who lives and reigns with you and the Holy Spirit, one God, now and for ever. [Gel., RS tr. PHP]

Thursday in the Fifth Week of Easter

Lord God, we were sinners but your grace has made us righteous, we were without hope but you have made us glad: Establish in us your saving work, preserve in us your gifts of grace, and grant courage and perseverance to all whom you have called and justified by faith; through Jesus Christ our Lord, who lives and reigns with you and the Holy Spirit, one God, now and for ever. [Berg., RS tr. DvD, LFF]

Friday in the Fifth Week of Easter

Grant, O Lord, that we may worthily celebrate these mysteries of Christ's death and resurrection, so that as we observe them with joy, they may be our constant defense and salvation; through the same Jesus Christ our Lord, who lives and reigns with you and the Holy Spirit, one God, now and for ever. [Leo., Berg., RS tr. DvD; LFF]

Saturday in the Fifth Week in Easter

Almighty and eternal God, you deigned to confer upon us divine life by our rebirth in baptism: Grant that we who by your grace are called to immortality may through your continued care come to the fullness of glory; through Jesus Christ our Lord, who lives and reigns with you and the Holy Spirit, one God, now and for ever. [Berg., Leo., RS tr. PHP]

THE SIXTH SUNDAY OF EASTER

O God, you have prepared for those who love you such good things as surpass our understanding: Pour into our hearts such love toward you, that we, loving you [in all things and] above all things, may obtain your promises, which exceed all that we can desire; through your Son, Jesus Christ our Lord, who lives and reigns with you and the Holy Spirit, one God, now and for ever.

[1 Cor. 2:9; Gel., BCP; MR, CB, CSB, SBH Trinity 5; LBW 6 Pentecost]

The Monday, Tuesday, and Wednesday before Ascension Day are the traditional Rogation Days of prayer for fruitful fields and for human labor.

[Rogation] Monday in the Sixth Week of Easter

Almighty and everlasting God, you have given us a living hope by the resurrection of your Son Jesus Christ: we beseech you guard our faith, keep us joyful in our trials, and bring us unscathed to the inheritance of life eternal, which you have prepared for us in the same Jesus Christ our Lord; who lives and reigns with you and the Holy Spirit, one God, now and for ever. [1 Peter 1:3; DvD]

RS: Thursday of Easter 2 repeated

Almighty God, Lord of heaven and earth: We humbly pray that your gracious providence may give and preserve to our use the harvests of the land and of the seas, and may prosper all who labor to gather them, that we, who are constantly receiving good things from your hand, may always give you thanks; through your Son Jesus Christ our Lord, who lives and reigns with you and the Holy Spirit, one God, now and for ever.

[John Cosin, E. W. Benson, BCP (1928), LBW]

[Rogation] Tuesday in the Sixth Week of Easter

Let your people, O Lord, rejoice for ever that they have been renewed in spirit; and let the joy of our adoption as your sons and daughters strengthen the hope of our glorious resurrection in Jesus Christ our Lord; who lives and reigns with you and the Holy Spirit, one God, now and for ever. [Goth., RS, also Third Sunday of Easter, LFF]

Almighty God, whose Son Jesus Christ in his earthly life shared our toil and hallowed our labor: Be present with your people where they work; make those who carry on the industries and commerce of this land responsive to your will; and give to us all a pride in what we do, and a just return for our labor; through your Son, Jesus Christ our Lord, who lives and reigns with you and the Holy Spirit, one God, now and for ever. [BCP, LBW]

[Rogation] Wednesday in the Sixth Week of Easter

Grant to us, O Lord, we pray, that as we celebrate in faith the solemnity of the resurrection of your Son, so we may rejoice with all the saints when he comes again in glory; through the same Jesus Christ our Lord, who lives and reigns with you and the Holy Spirit, one God, now and for ever. [Goth., RS tr. PHP]

O merciful Creator, your hand is open wide to satisfy the needs of every living creature: Make us always thankful for your loving providence; and grant that we, remembering the account that we must one day give, may be faithful stewards of your good gifts; through your Son, Jesus Christ our Lord, who lives and reigns with you and the Holy Spirit, one God, now and for ever. [BCP (1928), LBW]

THE ASCENSION OF OUR LORD

Almighty God, on this day you took your only-begotten Son beyond our sight into heaven, exalting our human nature and promising us a share in your eternal splendor: Confirm our hope and lead us after him into the new creation, where he lives and reigns with you and the Holy Spirit, one God, now and for ever.

[Greg., sermon of Leo, RS tr.PHP; see LBW]

Friday after Ascension Day

O God, by the resurrection of your Son you have given us a new birth into eternal life: Lift our hearts to our Savior, who is seated at your right hand, so that, when he comes again, we who have been reborn in Baptism may be clothed in a glorious immortality; through Jesus Christ our Lord, who lives and reigns with you and the Holy Spirit, one God, now and for ever. [Gel., Berg., RS, LFF]

Saturday after Ascension Day

O Lord, when your Son ascended into heaven he sent down upon the Apostles the Holy Spirit, as he had promised, that they might comprehend the mysteries of the kingdom: Distribute among us also, we pray, the gifts of the selfsame Spirit; through Jesus Christ our Lord, who lives and reigns with you and the Holy Spirit, one God, now and for ever.

[Berg., RS, LFF]

THE SEVENTH SUNDAY OF EASTER

Almighty God, whose blessed Son our Savior Jesus Christ ascended far above all heavens so that he might fill all creation with his presence: Mercifully give us faith to perceive that, according to his promise, he abides with his Church on earth, even to the end of the ages; through the same Jesus Christ our Lord, who lives and reigns with you and the Holy Spirit, one God, now and for ever.

[Ephes. 4:10, Matt. 28:20; Leo., RS, LBW; BCP Ascension Day]

BCP: above p. 1245

Monday in the Seventh Week of Easter

Let the power of your Holy Spirit come upon us, O Lord, that we may be strengthened to keep your will faithfully in mind and to enact it in lives of loving obedience; through Jesus Christ our Lord, who lives and reigns with you and the Holy Spirit, one God, now and for ever. [RS tr. PHP]

Tuesday in the Seventh Week of Easter

Almighty and merciful God, send forth the Holy Spirit upon your Church to make us the temple where your glory dwells; through Jesus Christ our Lord, who lives and reigns with you and the Holy Spirit, one God, now and for ever. [RS]

Wednesday in the Seventh Week of Easter

O loving Father, grant that your Church, being gathered by your Holy Spirit, may be dedicated more fully to your service, and live united in love, according to your will; through Jesus Christ our Lord, who lives and reigns with you and the Holy Spirit, one God, now and for ever.

[Leo., RS tr. LFF]

Thursday in the Seventh Week of Easter

O Lord, we pray you, send upon the world your Spirit with power to fill us with every good gift, that our hearts may find favor in your sight and our wills be shaped according to your own; through Jesus Christ our Lord, who lives and reigns with you and the Holy Spirit, one God, now and for ever. [Gel., RS tr. PHP]

Friday in the Seventh Week of Easter

O God, by the glorification of Jesus Christ and the coming of the Holy Spirit you have opened for us the gates of your kingdom: Grant that we, who have received such great gifts, may dedicate ourselves more diligently to your service, and live more fully the riches of our faith; through Jesus Christ our Lord, who lives and reigns with you and the Holy Spirit, one God, now and for ever. [Leo., RS, LFF]

Saturday in the Seventh Week of Easter

Grant, we implore you, Almighty God, that we who celebrate the solemnity of the Lord's resurrection, may by the help of your grace bring forth its fruits in our lives and in our conduct; through the same Jesus Christ our Lord, who lives and reigns with you and the Holy Spirit, one God, now and for ever. [Greg., RS, SBH rev. DvD]

THE DAY OF PENTECOST. The Fiftieth Day of Easter

O God, who on this day taught the hearts of your faithful people by sending to them the light of your Holy Spirit: Grant us by the same Spirit to have a right judgment in all things, and evermore to rejoice in his holy comfort; through your Son, Jesus Christ our Lord, who lives and reigns with you and the Holy Spirit, one God, now and for ever.

[Greg., RM, CB, CSB, SBH, BCP; LBW]

After the Prayer of the Day, other prayers may be said by the leader with the congregation responding Amen *to each.*

The prayers conclude:

L The Lord is risen from the grave, alleluia,

C Who hung upon the cross for us, alleluia. [CSB, LH]

Almighty God, you gave your only Son to die for our sins and to rise for our justification: Give us grace so to put away the leaven of malice and wickedness, that we may always serve you in pureness of living and truth; through Jesus Christ your Son our Lord, who lives and reigns with you and the Holy Spirit, one God, now and for ever.

[1 Cor. 5:7-8; BCP (1549)]

C Amen

L Lord, remember us in your kingdom and teach us to pray.

C Our Father in heaven,
hallowed be your Name
your kingdom come,
your will be done,
on earth as in heaven.
Give us today our daily bread.
Forgive us our sins
as we forgive those
who sin against us.
Save us from the time of trial
and deliver us from evil.
For the kingdom, the power,
and the glory are yours,
now and for ever. Amen.

C Our Father who art in heaven,
hallowed be thy Name
thy kingdom come,
thy will be done,
on earth as it is in heaven.
Give us this day our daily bread;
and forgive us our trespasses,
as we forgive those
who sin against us;
And lead us not into temptation
but deliver us from evil.
For thine is the kingdom,
and the power, and the glory,
for ever and ever. Amen.

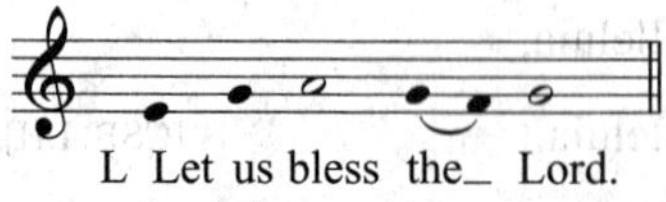

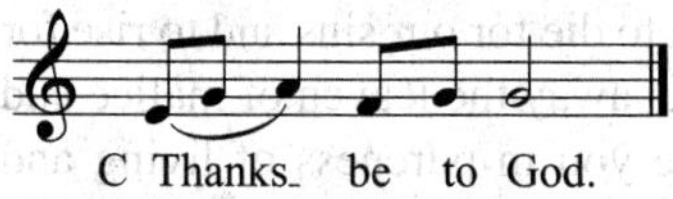

The BENEDICTION concludes the service when there is no sermon. A hymn may follow. The service may be concluded with the Paschal Blessing.

When there is a sermon, this benediction is omitted, and the service continues as on p. 20.

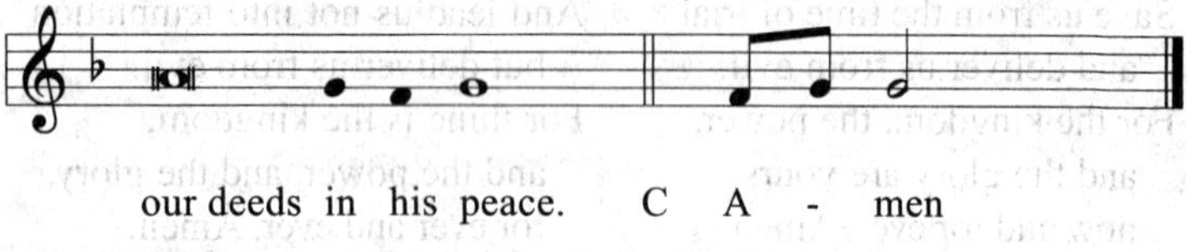

PASCHAL BLESSING

The Paschal Blessing may be used to conclude Morning Prayer. The service may be led from the font.

Stand

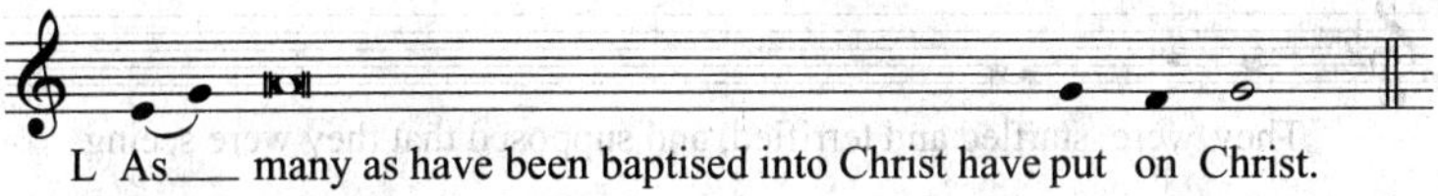

While the dis- ciples were talking about this, Jesus himself stood
among them and said to them, "Peace___ be with you."
They were startled and terrified, and supposed that they were seeing
a ghost. He said to them, "Why are you frightened, and why do doubts
arise in your hearts? Look at my hands and my feet; see that
it is I my - self. Touch me and see; for a ghost does not have flesh
and bones as you see that I have." And when he said this, he showed
them his hands and his feet. While in their joy they were disbelieving

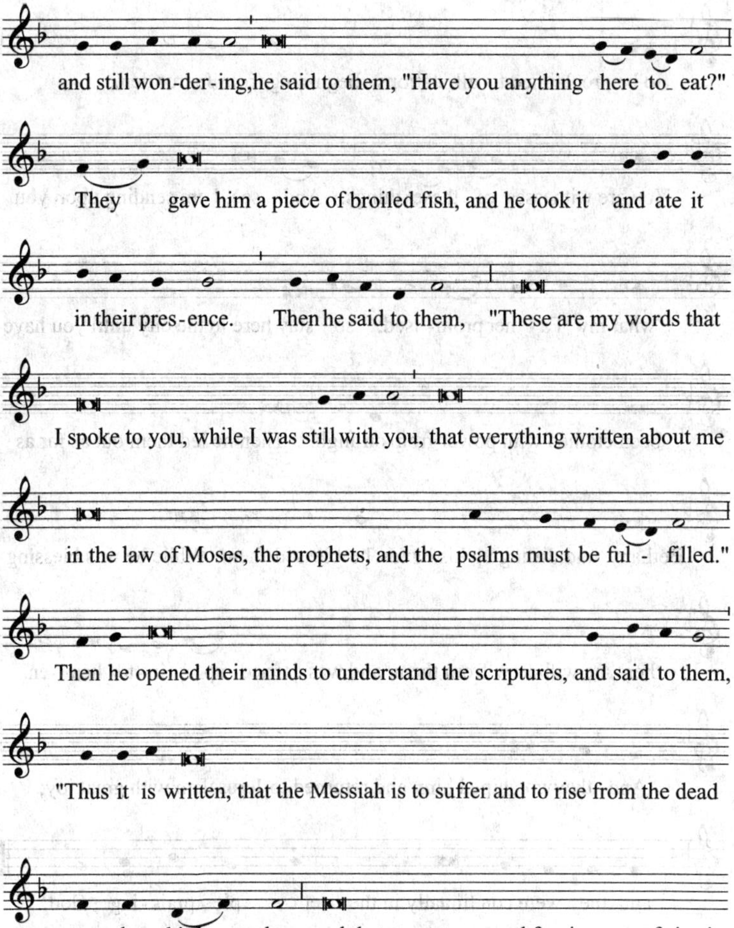
and still won-der-ing, he said to them, "Have you anything here to eat?"
They gave him a piece of broiled fish, and he took it and ate it
in their pres-ence. Then he said to them, "These are my words that
I spoke to you, while I was still with you, that everything written about me
in the law of Moses, the prophets, and the psalms must be ful - filled."
Then he opened their minds to understand the scriptures, and said to them,
"Thus it is written, that the Messiah is to suffer and to rise from the dead
on the third day, and that repentence and forgiveness of sins is

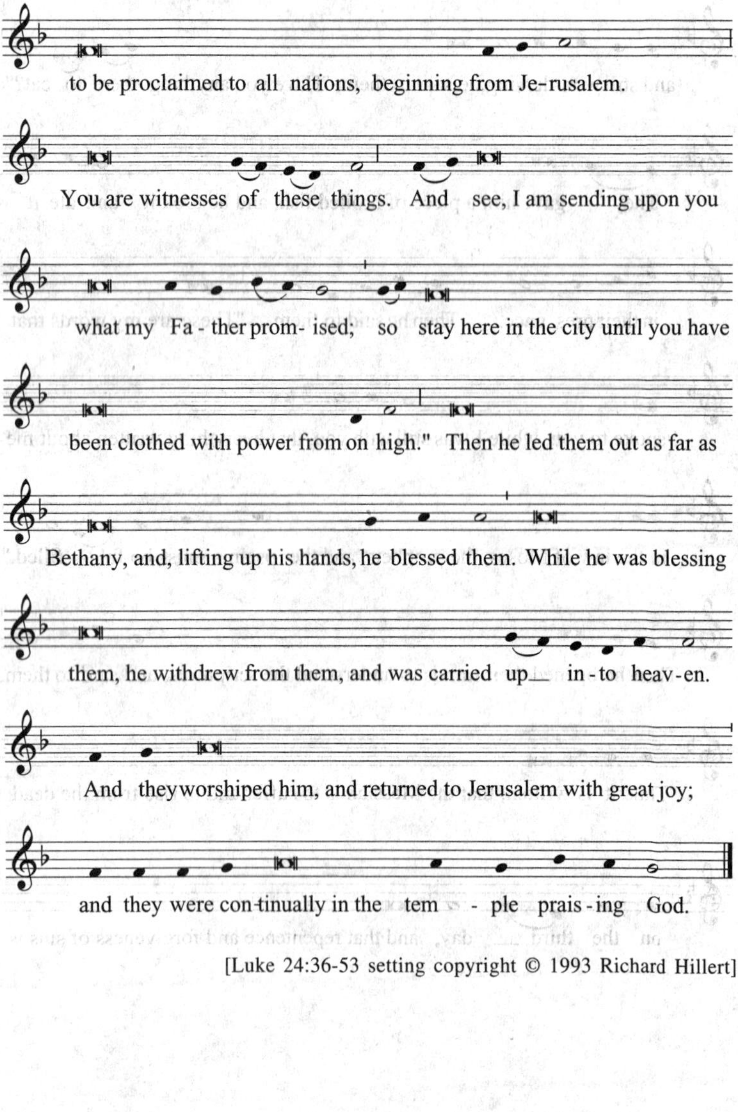
to be proclaimed to all nations, beginning from Je-rusalem.
You are witnesses of these things. And see, I am sending upon you
what my Fa - ther prom- ised; so stay here in the city until you have
been clothed with power from on high." Then he led them out as far as
Bethany, and, lifting up his hands, he blessed them. While he was blessing
them, he withdrew from them, and was carried up in - to heav - en.
And they worshiped him, and returned to Jerusalem with great joy;
and they were con-tinually in the tem - ple prais - ing God.

The Te Deum Laudamus is sung.

world the ho-ly Church ac-claims you: C Fa- ther, of maj-es-ty un-
bound-ed your true and on-ly Son, wor-thy of all wor-ship;
and the Ho-ly Spir-it, ad-vo-cate and guide. [I] You, Christ, are the
king of glo - ry, the e-ter-nal Son of the Fa - ther.
[II] When you be-came man to set us free, you did not spurn the
vir-gin's womb. [I] You o-ver came the sting of death,
and o-pened the king-dom of heav-en to all be-liev-ers.
[II] You are seat-ed at God's right hand in glo-ry.

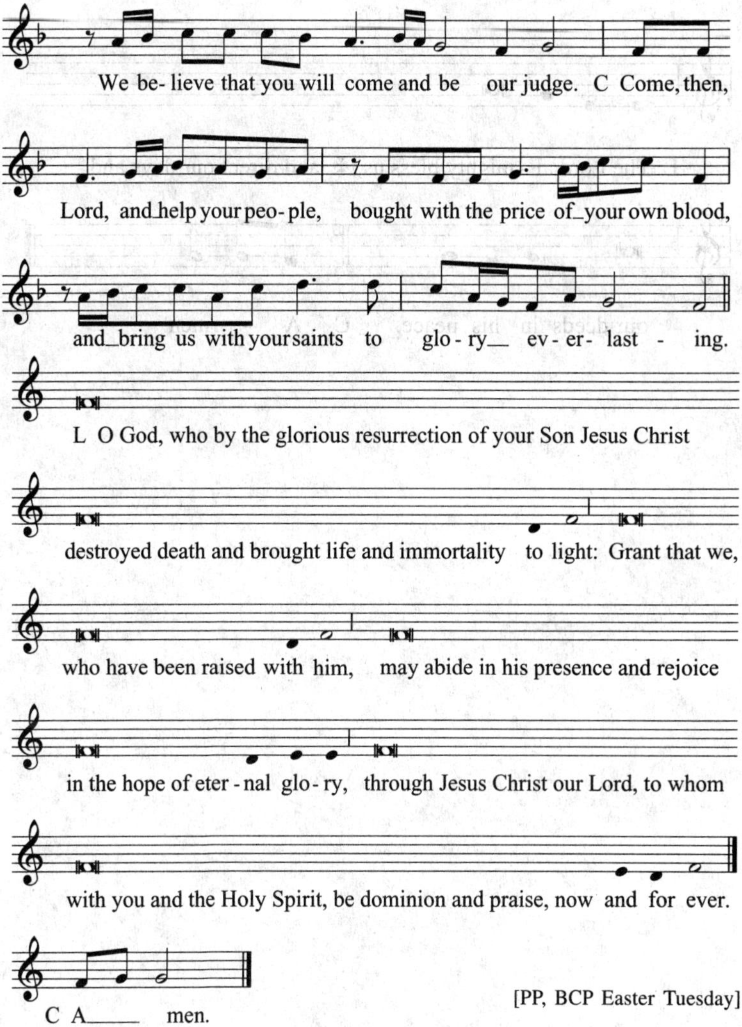

[PP, BCP Easter Tuesday]

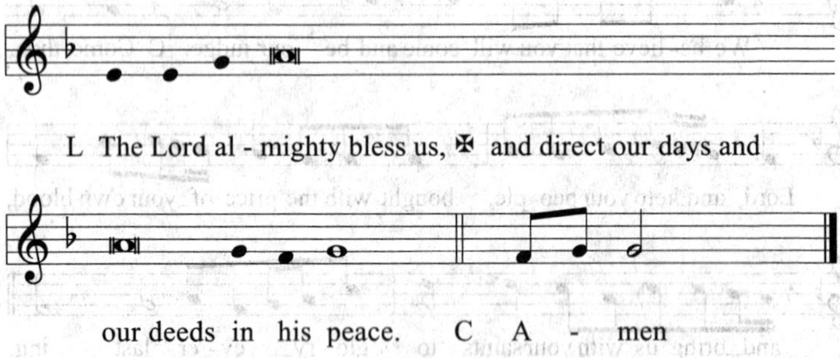
L The Lord al - mighty bless us, ✠ and direct our days and
our deeds in his peace. C A - men

Sundays of Easter

Antiphon to PSALM 93 *Dominus regnavit*
[BCP: *Deus ultionum*]

Easter Day — On this day the **Lord** has acted,*
we will rejoice and be glad in it, **al**leluia.
[Ps. 118:24, LBW]

Easter 2 — Death has been swallowed **up** in victory,*
al**le**luia. [1 Cor. 15:54]

Easter 3 — The Sun of Righteousness is **ris**en in glory*
giving light to those who sat in darkness
and the shadow of death, **al**leluia.
[LH: see Mal. 4:2; Luke 1:79]

Easter 4 — Mightier than the breakers of the sea
is the Lord who **dwells** on high,*
al**le**luia.

Easter 5 — The Lord our God, the Al**migh**ty, reigns.*
Let us rejoice and exult and give him the glory,
alleluia. [Rev. 19:6-7]

Easter 6 — The splendor of Christ risen from the dead has shined
on the people redeemed **by** his blood,*
alleluia. [LH]

Easter 7 — The **Lord** is king;*
he has put on splendid apparel, **al**leluia. [LH, PBO]

The Day of Pentecost	A sound like the rush of a violent wind filled the en**ti**re house.* Divided tongues, as of fire, appeared among them, and a tongue rested on **each** of them. All of them were filled with the Holy Spirit and be**gan** to speak.* al**le**luia. [LH: Acts 2:3]

93 *The splendor of God the creator*

1 The LORD is king;
he has put on splen**did** apparel;*
the LORD has put on his apparel
and girded him**self** with strength.

2 He has made the whole **world** so sure*
that it can**not** be moved;

3 Ever since the world began, your throne has **been** established;*
you are from **ev**erlasting.

4 The waters have lifted up, O LORD,
the waters have lifted **up** their voice;*
the waters have lifted up their **pound**ing waves.

5 Mightier than the sound of many waters,
mightier than the breakers **of** the sea,*
mightier is the LORD who **dwells** on high.

6 Your testimonies are **ver**y sure,*
and holiness adorns your house, O LORD,
for ever and for **ev**ermore.

The Antiphon is repeated.

Silence for meditation

Lord Jesus, king of glory, when you rose from the grave in the power of the Spirit, you firmly established your kingdom, never to be shaken or destroyed by death: May your will be done on earth as in heaven until the Church is made holy by your embrace, our Redeemer and our Lord.

[LHd, LBW]

+

Antiphon to the OLD TESTAMENT CANTICLE

Benedicite, omnia opera

Easter Day — Over your resurrec**tion**, O Christ,*
let heaven and earth rejoice,**al**leluia. [DO]

Easter 2 — Our Redeemer has risen **from** the tomb;*
let us sing a hymn of praise to the Lord
our God, **al**leluia. [LH]

Easter 3 — All creation **will** be freed;*
all peoples will know the glory and freedom of
God's children, **al**leluia. [LH: see Rom. 8:21]

Easter 4 — Bless the Lord, for he has rescued **us** from Hades*
and saved us from the power of death, **al**leluia.
[Song of the Three 66]

Easter 5 — Bless the Lord who made the heavens and the earth,*
springs of water and the mighty sea, **al**leluia. [LH]

Easter 6	Praise our God, all **you** his servants,* alleluia. [Rev. 19:5]
Easter 7	Give glory to the **King** of kings,* sing praise to God, **al**leluia. [LH]
The Day of Pentecost	You sent forth your Spirit, and they **are** created;* and so you renew the face of the earth, **al**leluia. [Ps. 104:31; CSB, SBH]

A Song of Creation — Song of the Three Young Men 35-65

All you works of the Lord, **bless** the Lord–*
praise him and magnify **him** for ever.

You angels of the Lord, **bless** the Lord;*
you heavens, **bless** the Lord;
All you powers of the Lord, **bless** the Lord–*
praise him and magnify **him** for ever.

You sun and moon, **bless** the Lord;*
you stars of heaven, **bless** the Lord;
You showers and dew, **bless** the Lord–*
praise him and magnify **him** for ever.

You winds of God, **bless** the Lord;*
you fire and heat **bless** the Lord;
You winter and summer, **bless** the Lord–*
praise him and magnify **him** for ever.

You dews and frost, **bless** the Lord;*
you frost and cold, **bless** the Lord;
You ice and snow, **bless** the Lord–*
praise him and magnify **him** for ever.

You nights and days, **bless** the Lord;*
you light and darkness, **bless** the Lord;
You lightnings and clouds, **bless** the Lord–*
praise him and magnify **him** for ever.

Let the earth **bless** the Lord;*
you mountains and hills, **bless** the Lord;
All you green things that grow on the earth, **bless** the Lord–*
praise him and magnify **him** for ever.

You wells and springs, **bless** the Lord;*
you rivers and seas, **bless** the Lord;
You whales and all who move in the waters, **bless** the Lord–*
praise him and magnify **him** for ever.

All you birds of the air, **bless** the Lord;*
all you beasts and cattle, **bless** the Lord;
All you children of mortals, **bless** the Lord–*
praise him and magnify **him** for ever.

You people of God, **bless** the Lord;*
you priests of the Lord, **bless** the Lord;
You servants of the Lord, **bless** the Lord–*
praise him and magnify **him** for ever.

You spirits and souls of righteous, **bless** the Lord;*
you pure and humble of heart, **bless** the Lord;
Let us bless the Father and the Son and the **Ho**ly Spirit–*
praise him and magnify **him** for ever. [LBW]

The Antiphon is repeated.

Silence for meditation

Lord God, creator of the cosmos, you have made the whole creation bright with the glory of Christ's resurrection: Breathe into us your Spirit that we may join the praises of all your creatures and magnify you for ever; through Jesus Christ our Lord. [PHP]

+

Antiphon to PSALM 150 *Laudate Dominum in sanctis ejus*

Easter Day — Alleluia, alleluia, alleluia.

Easter 2 — Al**le**luia.*
The Lord has been raised as he promised,
alleluia. [LH: Matt. 28:6]

Easter 3 — Let the Name of the LORD be praised in heaven **and** on earth,*
al**le**luia. [LH: see Ps. 113:3; 148:1,7]

Easter 4 — Give honor and **praise** to God;*
he is righteous in all his ways and loving in all his works, **al**leluia. [LH: Ps. 145:17]

Easter 5 — The Lion of the tribe of Judah,
the Root of Da**vid**, has conquered,*
al**le**luia. [Rev. 5:5]

Easter 6 — Worship God who is seated up**on** the throne;*
sing to him in praise: Amen, **al**leluia.
[LH: see Rev. 5:13]

Easter 7 — Sing to God, sing praises to his Name;*
exalt him who rides upon the heavens, **al**leluia.
[LH: Ps. 68:4]

The Day of Pentecost	The apostles preached in **dif**ferent tongues* and proclaimed the mighty works of God, **al**leluia. [LH: see Acts 2:11]

150 *The great alleluia*

1 Hallelujah!
Praise God in his **ho**ly temple;*
praise him in the firmament **of** his power.

2 Praise him for his **might**y acts;*
praise him for his ex**cel**lent greatness.

3 Praise him with the blast **of** the ram's horn;*
praise him with **lyre** and harp.

4 Praise him with tim**brel** and dance;*
praise him with **strings** and pipe.

5 Praise him with re**sound**ing cymbals;*
praise him with loud- **clang**ing cymbals.

6 Let everything **that** has breath*
praise the LORD.
Hallelujah!

The Antiphon is repeated.

Silence for meditation

God of surpassing greatness, enthroned upon the praises of your people, fill our hearts with your love and unite our voices with the praise of all creation so that you may be honored and glorified by everything that has breath; through Jesus Christ our Lord. [PHP]

+

Stand

THE HYMN is sung.

On the Sundays of Easter — *Αισωμεν παντες λαοι*

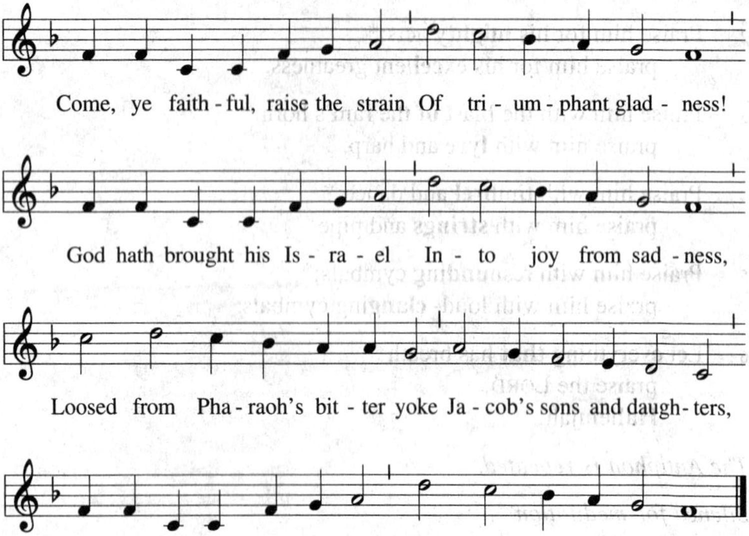

2 Tis the spring of souls today;
Christ hath burst his prison,
And from three days' sleep in death
As a sun hath risen;
All the winter of our sins,
Long and dark is flying
From his light, to whom we give
Laud and praise undying.

3 Now the queen of seasons, bright
With the day of splendor,
With the royal feast of feasts
Comes its joy to render;
Comes to glad Jerusalem,
Who with true affection
Welcomes in unwearied strains
Jesus' resurrection.

4 Neither might the gates of death,
Nor the tomb's dark portal,
Nor the watchers, nor the seal
Hold thee as a mortal.
But today amidst the twelve
Thou didst stand, bestowing
Thine own peace which evermore
Passeth human knowing.

5 Alleluia, now we cry
To our king immortal,
Who, triumphant, burst the bars
Of the tomb's dark portal.
Come, ye faithful, raise the strain
Of triumphant gladness;
God hath brought his Israel
Into joy from sadness. [LBW 132; H82, 199]

Text: John of Damascus, c. 696-c. 754; tr. John Mason Neale, 1818-1866 with doxology
Tune: *Gaudeamus pariter,* Johann Horn, c. 1490-1547 76 76 D

On the Day of Pentecost: *Beata nobis gaudia*

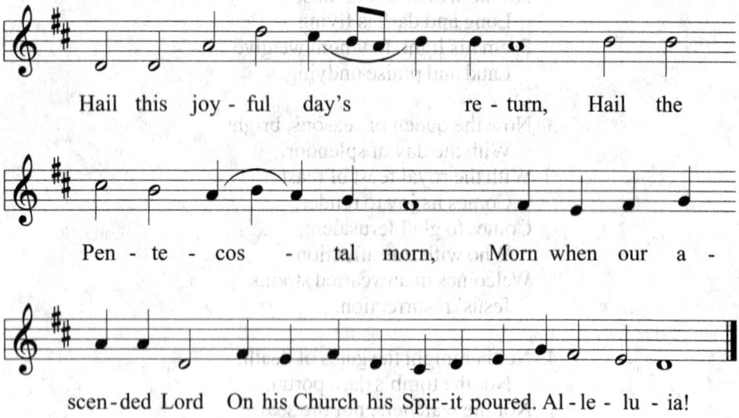

2 Like to cloven tongues of flame
On the twelve the Spirit came–
Tongues, that earth may hear their call,
Fire, that love may burn in all. Alleluia!

3 Bold in every tongue they spoke,
Wonder in the crowd awoke,
Mocking, as if drunk with wine,
Those who spoke with power divine. Alleluia!

4 Easter's days are now complete,
Symbols old and new now meet:
Fifty reached which once set free
Captives at the jubilee. Alleluia!

5 Lord, to you your people bend,
Unto us your Spirit send;
Blessings of this sacred day
Grant us, dearest Lord, we pray. Alleluia!

6 You who did our forebears guide,
With their children still abide;
Grant us pardon, grant us peace,
Till our earthly wanderings cease. Alleluia!

7 Praise the Father and the Son,
Holy Spirit with them one;
May the Son on us bestow
Gifts that from the Spirit flow. Alleluia! [H82 224]

Text: attr. Hilary of Potiers, 4th cent.; tr. Robert Campbell, 1824-1868 alt. PHP
Tune: *Sonne der Gerichtigkeit* Bohemian Brethren, *Kirchengeseng,* 1566 77 77 4

Sit

One or two LESSONS are read.

Year 1

Easter Day
Exodus 12:1-14

This day shall be a day of remembrance for you. You shall celebrate it as a festival to the LORD; throughout your generations you shall observe it as a perpetual ordinance.

Year 2

Exodus 12:1-14

This day shall be a day of remembrance for you. You shall celebrate it as a festival to the LORD; throughout your generations you shall observe it as a perpetual ordinance.
or Isaiah 51:9-11

Isaiah 51:9-11

The ransomed of the LORD shall return, and come to Zion with singing; everlasting joy shall be upon their heads; they shall obtain joy and gladness, and sorrow and sighing shall flee away. [BCP: John 1:1-18]

John 1:1-18

In him was life and the life was the light of all people.

Easter 2

Isaiah 43:8-13

I, I am the LORD, and besides me there is no savior.

Exodus 14:5-22

Moses said to the people, "Do not be afraid, stand firm, and see the deliverance that the LORD will accomplish for you today."

1 Peter 2:2-10

You are a chosen race, a royal priesthood, a holy nation, God's own people, in order that you may proclaim the mighty acts of him who called you out of darkness into his marvelous light.

1 John 1:1-7

This life was revealed, and we have seen it and testify to it, and declare to you the eternal life that was with the Father and was revealed to us.

Easter 3

Daniel 4:1-18

How great are his signs, how mighty his wonders! His kingdom is an everlasting kingdom, and his sovereignty is from generation to generation.

Exodus 18:1-12

Blessed be the LORD, who has delivered you from the Egyptians and from Pharaoh. Now I know that the LORD is greater than all gods.

1 Peter 4:7-11

Above all, maintain constant love for one another, for love covers a multitude of sins.

Easter 4
Wisdom 1:1-15

God did not make death, and he does not delight in the death of the living.
or Genesis 18:22-33

1 Peter 5:1-11

When the chief shepherd appears, you will win the crown of glory that never fades away.

Easter 5
Wisdom 7:22-8:1

Wisdom is a reflection of eternal light, a spotless mirror of the working of God, and an image of his goodness.
or Isaiah 32:1-8

2 Thessalonians 2:13-17

God called you through our proclamation of the good news, so

1 John 2:7-17

The world and its desire are passing away, but those who do the will of God live forever.

Exodus 28:1-4, 30-38

You shall make sacred vestments for the glorious adornment of your brother Aaron.

1 John 2:18-29

If what you heard from the beginning abides in you, then you will abide in the Son and in the Father. And this is what he has promised us, eternal life.

Leviticus 8:1-13, 30-36

Moses took some of the anointing oil and some of the blood that was on the altar and sprinkled them on Aaron and his vestments, and also on his sons and their vestments. Thus he consecrated Aaron and his vestments and also his sons and their vestments.

Hebrews 12:1-14

Jesus, the pioneer and perfecter of our faith, for the sake of the joy that

that you may obtain the glory of our Lord Jesus Christ.

was set before him, endured the cross, disregarding its shame, and has taken his seat at the right hand of the throne of God.

Easter 6

Sirach 43:1-12, 27-32

When you exalt the Lord, summon all your strength, and do not grow weary, for you cannot praise him enough.

or Deuteronomy 15:1-11

Leviticus 25:1-17

When you enter the land that I am giving you, the land shall observe a sabbath for the LORD.

1 Timothy 3:14-4:5

He was revealed in flesh, vindicated in spirit, seen by angels, proclaimed among Gentiles, believed in throughout the world, taken up in glory.

James 1:2-8, 16-18

Every generous act of giving, with every perfect gift, is from above, coming down from the Father of lights, with whom there is no variation or shadow due to change.

Easter 7

Ezekiel 3:16-27

Mortal, I have made you a sentinel for the house of Israel; whenever you hear a word from my mouth, you shall give them warning from me.

Exodus 3:1-12

I have observed the misery of my people who are in Egypt; I have heard their cry on account of their taskmasters. Indeed, I know their sufferings, and I have come down to deliver them.

Ephesians 2:1-10

God, who is rich in mercy, out of the

Hebrews 12:18-29

You have come to Mount Zion and to

great love with which he loved us even when we were dead through our trespasses, made us alive together with Christ–by grace you have been saved–and raised us up with him and seated us with him in the heavenly places in Christ Jesus.

the city of the living God, the heavenly Jerusalem, and to innumerable angels in festal gathering, and to the assembly of the first-born who are enrolled in heaven, and to God the judge of all, and to the spirits of the righteous made perfect, and to Jesus.

The Day of Pentecost

Isaiah 11:1-9

The spirit of the LORD shall rest on him, the spirit of wisdom and understanding, the spirit of counsel and might, the spirit of knowledge and the fear of the LORD.

Deuteronomy 16:9-12

You shall count seven weeks. Then you shall keep the festival of weeks for the LORD your God, contributing a freewill offering in proportion to the blessing that you have received from the LORD.

1 Corinthians 2:1-13

We have received the Spirit that is from God, so that we may understand the gifts bestowed on us by God.

Acts 4:18-21, 23-33

With great power the apostles gave their testimony to the resurrection of the Lord Jesus, and great grace was upon them all.

Silence for meditation follows each reading.

RESPONSORY

I heard a voice from heaven like the sound **of** loud thunder:*
The Lord our God **reigns** for ever.

If you have been **raised** with Christ,*
seek the things that are above,

Now have come the salvation and the power and the kingdom of **his** messiah,* al**le**luia.

From the throne came a voice saying, Praise our God, all **you** his servants,*
and all who fear him, **small** and great.

Now have come the salvation and the power and the kingdom of **his** messiah,* al**le**luia.

[LH: Revelation 14:2; 19:6; 12:10; 19:5]

where Christ is, seated at the right **hand** of God.

Set your minds on things that **are** above,*
not on things that are on earth, **al**leluia.

For **you** have died,*
and your life is hidden with **Christ** in God.

Set your minds on things that **are** above,*
not on things that are on earth, **al**leluia.

Glory to the Father, and **to** the Son,*
and to the **Ho**ly Spirit.

Set your minds on things that **are** above,*
not on things that are on earth, **al**leluia.

[LH: Colossians 3:1,2,3]

Antiphon to the BENEDICTUS

Easter Day

Very early on the first day of the week, when the sun had risen, they went **to** the tomb,*
al**le**luia. [LH: Mark 16:2]

Easter 2

With your hand touch the mark **of** the nails;*
do not be faithless, but believing, **al**leluia. [LH: see John 20:27]

Easter 3

It was necessary that the Messi**ah** should suffer,*
and then enter into his glory, **al**leluia. [LH: see Luke 24:26]

Easter 4

I am **the** Good Shepherd;*
I know my own and my own know me, **al**leluia [LH: John 10:14]

Easter 5

Those who abide in me and I in them **bear** much fruit,*
al**le**luia. [LH: John 15:5]

Easter 6

As the Father has loved me, so **I** have loved you;*
abide in my love, **al**leluia. [LH: John 15:9]

Easter 7

Father, I glorified you on earth by finishing the work that you gave **me** to do,*
al**le**luia. [LH: John 17:4]

The Day of Pentecost

Receive the **Ho**ly Spirit.*
If you forgive the sins of any, they are forgiven,
alleluia. [LH: John 20:22-23]

Mondays of Easter

Antiphon to PSALM 97 *Dominus regnavit, exultet*

Light has sprung up **for** the righteous,*
and joyful gladness for those who are truehearted,
alleluia. [LH, PBO]

97 *Earth rejoices in its king*

1 The LORD is king;
let the **earth** rejoice;*
let the multitude of the **isles** be glad.

2 Clouds and darkness are **round** about him,*
righteousness and justice are the foundations **of** his throne.

3 A fire **goes** before him*
and burns up his enemies on **ev**ery side.

4 His lightnings light **up** the world;*
the earth sees it and **is** afraid.

5 The mountains melt like wax at the presence **of** the LORD,*
at the presence of the Lord of **the** whole earth.

6 The heavens de**clare** his righteousness,*
and all the peoples **see** his glory.

7 Confounded be all who worship carved images
and delight **in** false gods!*
Bow down before him, **all** you gods.

8 Zion hears and is glad, and the cities of **Judah** rejoice,*
because of your judg**ments**, O LORD.

9 For you are the LORD,
most high over **all** the earth;*
you are exalted far a**bove** all gods.

10 The LORD loves those **who** hate evil;*
he preserves the lives of his saints
and delivers them from the hand **of** the wicked.

11 Light has sprung up **for** the righteous,*
and joyful gladness for those who **are** truehearted.

12 Rejoice in the **LORD**, you righteous,*
and give thanks to his **ho**ly Name.

Antiphon Light has sprung up **for** the righteous,*
and joyful gladness for those who are truehearted,
alleluia.

Silence for meditation

God our king, you clothe the sky with light and the depths of the ocean with darkness. Among the peoples you work wonders, and rain terror upon your enemies. Do not try your servants by fire, but bring us rejoicing to the shelter of your home, where with your Son and the Holy Spirit you live and reign, now and for ever. [LH, LBW]

+

Antiphon to the OLD TESTAMENT CANTICLE

Benedictus es, Domine

Great and amazing are your deeds, Lord God **the** Almighty!*
Just and true are your ways, King of the nations,
alleluia. [Rev. 15:3]

A Song of Praise Song of the Three Young Men 29-34

Blessed are you, O Lord, God **of** our ancestors:*
praised and exalt**ed** for ever.

Blessed are you for the radiance of your **ho**ly Name:*
praised and exalt**ed** for ever.

Blessed are you in the temple **of** your holiness:*
praised and exalt**ed** for ever.

Blessed are you beholding the depths
from your throne be**tween** the cherubim:*
praised and exalt**ed** for ever.

Blessed are you on the glorious throne **of** your kingdom:*
praised and exalt**ed** for ever.

Blessed are you in the firma**ment** of heaven:*
praised and exalt**ed** for ever. [BCP; NSRV alt.]

Antiphon Great and amazing are your deeds, Lord God **the** Almighty!*
Just and true are your ways, King of the nations,
alleluia.

Silence for meditation

God, our heavenly Father, send upon us the Holy Spirit which your Son promised, so that we may be taught to show forth your praise not only here on earth in weakness, since we know your power and glory only from afar, but also in power and glory on that day when, united with the choir of angels, we shall see you face to face; through Jesus Christ our Lord.

[*Gebete*, MPB rev.]

+

Antiphon to PSALM 145 *Exaltabo te, Deus*

God raised Christ from the dead and **gave** him glory,*
alleluia. [LH: 1 Peter 1:21]

145 *Praise of God's majesty*

1 I will exalt you, O **God** my King,*
and bless your Name for ev**er** and ever.

2 Every day **will** I bless you*
and praise your Name for ev**er** and ever.

3 Great is the LORD and greatly **to** be praised;*
there is no end **to** his greatness.

4 One generation shall praise your works **to** another*
and shall de**clare** your power.

5 I will ponder the glorious splendor **of** your majesty*
and all your **mar**velous works.

6 They shall speak of the might of your **won**drous acts,*
and I will tell **of** your greatness.

7 They shall publish the remembrance of **your** great goodness;*
they shall sing of your **right**eous deeds.

8 The LORD is gracious and full **of** compassion,*
slow to anger and **of** great kindness.

9 The LORD is loving to **e**veryone*
and his compassion is over **all** his works.

10 All your works praise **you**, O LORD,*
and your faithful **ser**vants bless you.

11 They make known the glory **of** your kingdom*
and speak **of** your power;

12 That the peoples may know **of** your power*
and the glorious splendor **of** your kingdom.

13 Your kingdom is an ever**last**ing kingdom;*
your dominion endures through**out** all ages.

14 The LORD is faithful in **all** his words*
and merciful in **all** his deeds.

15 The LORD upholds all **those** who fall;*
he lifts up those who **are** bowed down.

16 The eyes of all wait upon **you**, O LORD,*
and you give them their food **in** due season.

17 You open **wide** your hand*
and satisfy the needs of every **liv**ing creature.

18 The LORD is righteous in **all** his ways*
and loving in **all** his works.

19 The LORD is near to those who **call** upon him,*
to all who call up**on** him faithfully.

20 He fulfills the desire of **those** who fear him;*
he hears their **cry** and helps them.

21 The LORD preserves all **those** who love him,*
but he destroys **all** the wicked.

22 My mouth shall speak the praise **of** the LORD;*
let all flesh bless his holy Name for ev**er** and ever.

Antiphon God raised Christ from the dead and **gave** him glory,*
al**le**luia.

Silence for meditation

Loving Father, you are faithful in your promises and tender in your compassion: Listen to our hymn of joy, and continue to satisfy the needs of all your creatures, that all flesh may bless your Name in your everlasting kingdom, where with your Son and the Holy Spirit you live and reign, now and for ever. [LBW]

+

Stand

THE HYMN is sung. *Auf, auf, mein Herz, mit Freuden*

2 The Foe in triumph shouted
When Christ lay in the tomb;
But lo, he now is routed,
His boast is turned to gloom.
For Christ again is free;
In glorious victory
He who is strong to save
Has triumphed o'er the grave.

3 This is a sight that gladdens
Makes gloom and fear depart;
Now nothing ever saddens
The joy within my heart.
No cloud shall ever shake,
No foe shall ever take,
The hope which God's own Son
In love for me has won.

4 Now hell, its prince, the devil,
Of all their pow'r are shorn;
Now I am safe from evil,
And sin I laugh to scorn.
Grim death with all his might
Cannot my soul affright;
He is a pow'rless form,
Howe'er he rave and storm.

5 Now I will cling for ever
To Christ, my Savior true;
My Lord will leave me never,
Whate'er he passes through.
He rends death's iron chain;
He breaks through sin and pain;
He shatters hell's grim hall
And frees me from its thrall.

6 He brings me to the portal
That leads to bliss untold,
Whereon this rhyme immortal
Is found in script of gold:
"Who there my cross has shared
Finds here a crown prepared;
Who there with me has died
Shall here be glorified." [TLH 192, LBW 129 alt.]

Text: Paul Gerhardt, 1607-1676; tr. John Kelly, 1833-1890, alt.
Tune: *Auf, auf, mein Herz*, Johann Crüger, 1598-1662 76 76 66 66

Sit

One or two LESSONS are read.

Year 1

Monday in Easter [Bright]Week
Jonah 2:1-10

I called to the LORD out of my distress, and he answered me; out of the belly of Sheol I cried, and you heard my voice.

Acts 2:14, 22-32

This Jesus God raised up, and of that all of us are witnesses.

Monday after Easter 2
Daniel 1:1-21

To these four young men God gave knowledge and skill in every aspect of literature and wisdom; Daniel also had insight into all visions and dreams.

Year 2

Exodus 12:14-27

You shall observe this day throughout your generations as a perpetual ordinance.

1 Corinthians 15:1-11

I handed on to you as of first importance what I in turn had received: that Christ died for our sins in accordance with the scriptures, and that he was buried, and that he was raised on the third day in accordance with the scriptures, and that he appeared to Cephas, then to the twelve.

Exodus 14:21-31

The Israelites went into the sea on dry ground, the waters forming a wall for them on their right and on their left.

1 John 1:1-10

This life was revealed, and we have seen it and testify to it, and declare to you the eternal life that was with the Father and was revealed to us.

1 Peter 1:1-12

By God's great mercy he has given us a new birth into a living hope through the resurrection of Jesus Christ from the dead, and into an inheritance that is imperishable, undefiled, and unfading, kept in heaven for you.

Monday after Easter 3
Daniel 4:19-27

Atone for your sins with righteousness, and your iniquities with mercy to the oppressed.

Exodus 18:13-27

Moses chose able men from all Israel and appointed them as heads over the people, as officers over thousands, hundreds, fifties, and tens. And they judged the people at all times.

1 John 3:19-4:6

All who obey his commandments abide in him, and he abides in them.

1 Peter 5:1-14

After you have suffered for a little while, the God of all grace, who has called you to his eternal glory in Christ, will himself restore, support, strengthen, and establish you.

Monday after Easter 4
Wisdom 1:16; 2:11, 21-24

God created us for incorruption, and made us in the image of his own eternity.
or Jeremiah 30:1-9

Exodus 32:1-20

The people gathered around Aaron, and said to him, "Come, make gods for us, who shall go before us."

Colossians 1:1-14

God has rescued us from the power of darkness and transferred us into the kingdom of his beloved Son, in whom we have redemption, the forgiveness of sins.

Colossians 3:18-4:6(7-18)

Devote yourselves to prayer, keeping alert in it with thanksgiving.

Monday after Easter 5

Wisdom 9:1, 7-18

You have given command to build a temple on your holy mountain, and an altar in the city of your habitation, a copy of the holy tent that you prepared from the beginning.
or Jeremiah 32:1-15

Leviticus 16:1-19

Aaron shall sprinkle some of the blood on the altar with his finger seven times, and cleanse it and hallow it from the uncleannesses of the people of Israel.

Colossians 3:18-4:18

Devote yourselves to prayer, keeping alert in it with thanksgiving.

1 Thessalonians 4:13-18

Since we believe that Jesus died and rose again, even so, through Jesus, God will bring with him those who have died.

Monday after Easter 6 [Rogation Monday]

Deuteronomy 8:1-10

The LORD your God is bringing you into a good land.
or Deuteronomy 15:1-11

Leviticus 25:35-55

I am the LORD your God, who brought you out of the land of Egypt, to give you the land of Canaan, to be your God.

James 1:1-15

Let endurance have its full effect, so

Colossians 1:9b-14

God has rescued us from the power

that you may be mature and complete, lacking in nothing.

of darkness and transferred us into the kingdom of his beloved Son, in whom we have redemption, the forgiveness of sins.

Monday after Easter 7

Ezekiel 4:1-17

I am going to break the staff of bread in Jerusalem; they shall eat bread by weight and with fearfulness; and they shall drink water by measure and in dismay.

Joshua 1:1-9

Be strong and courageous; do not be frightened or dismayed, for the LORD your God is with you wherever you go.

Hebrews 6:1-12

It is impossible to restore again to repentance those who have once been enlightened, and have tasted the heavenly gift, and have shared in the Holy Spirit, and have tasted the goodness of the word of God and the powers of the age to come, and then have fallen away.

Ephesians 3:1-13

In Christ Jesus our Lord we have access to God in boldness and confidence through faith in him.

Silence for meditation follows each reading.

RESPONSORY

Cleanse out the old leaven **of** corruption,*
then you will be bread of
a new baking.

These new-born lambs sing alleluia as their **song** of praise.*
They have come to the streams of
living water;

Christ our Passover is sacri**ficed** for us,*
therefore let us keep the festival with joy in the Lord, **al**leluia.
He was put to death for our trespasses and raised for our jus**ti**fication.*
Therefore let us keep the festival with joy in the Lord, **al**leluia.
[LH: see 1 Cor. 5:7-8; Rom. 4:25]

now they are filled with **ra**diant beauty,*
al**le**luia.
Clothed in white robes and with palms **in** their hands,*
they stand in the presence **of** the Lamb.
Now they are filled with **ra**diant beauty,*
al**le**luia.
Glory to the Father and **to** the Son,*
and to the **Ho**ly Spirit.
Now they are filled with **ra**diant beauty,*
al**le**luia.
[LH: see Rev. 7:9; 22:1]

Antiphon to the BENEDICTUS

Monday in Easter Week

Go quickly and tell **his** disciples:*
the Lord has been raised, al**le**luia. [LH: Matthew 28:7, 6]

Monday after Easter 2

Very truly, **I** tell you,*
no one can see the kingdom of God without being born from above, **al**leluia. [LH: John 3:3]

Monday after Easter 3

Do not work for the **food** that perishes,*
but for the food that endures for eternal life,
alleluia. [LH: John 6:27]

Monday after Easter 4

I am the Good Shepherd. I know my own and my **own** know me.*
And I lay down my life for the sheep, **al**leluia [LH: John 10:14, 15]

Monday after Easter 5

Those who love me will be loved **by** my Father,*
and I will love them and reveal myself to them,
al**le**luia. [LH: John 14:21]

Monday after Easter 6

He has given us a new birth into a living hope
through the resurrection of Jesus Christ **from** the dead,*
and into an inheritance that is imperishable, **al**leluia.
[LH: 1 Peter 1:3-4]

Monday after Easter 7

In the world you will face persecution, **but** take courage;*
I have overcome the world, **al**leluia. [LH: John 16:33]

Tuesdays of Easter

Antiphon to PSALM 98 *Cantate Domino*

All the ends **of** the earth,*
have seen the victory of our God, **al**leluia. [LH, PBO]

98 *God, the ruler of the world*

1 Sing to the LORD **a** new song,*
for he has done **mar**velous things.

2 With his right hand and his **ho**ly arm*
has he won for him**self** the victory.

3 The LORD has made **known** his victory;*
his righteousness has he openly shown in the sight **of** the nations.

4 He remembers his mercy and faithfulness to the **house** of Israel,*
and all the ends of the earth have seen the victory **of** our God.

5 Shout with joy to the LORD, **all** you lands;*
lift up your voice, re**joice**, and sing.

6 Sing to the LORD **with** the harp,*
with the harp and the **voice** of song.

7 With trumpets and the sound **of** the horn*
shout with joy before the **King**, the LORD.

8 Let the sea make a noise and all **that** is in it,*
the lands and those who **dwell** therein.

9 Let the rivers **clap** their hands,*
and let the hills ring out with joy before the LORD,
when he comes to **judge** the earth.

10 In righteousness shall he **judge** the world*
and the peo**ples** with equity.

Antiphon All the ends **of** the earth,*
have seen the victory of our God, **al**leluia.

Silence for meditation

Lord, we sing to you a new song, for your victory is ever new. In the empty tomb you have given us a glimpse of your future, and in your victory over death you have shown us how we shall overcome the last enemy. As the seas roar and the hills sing together, we too will praise you for your great triumph, Father, Son, and Holy Spirit, now and for ever. [LBW]

+

Antiphon to the OLD TESTAMENT CANTICLE
Benedictus es, Domine, Deus Israel

Yours is the king**dom**, O LORD,*
and you are exalted as head above all, **al**leluia. [LH]

A Song of David 1 Chronicles 29:10-13

Blessed are you for ev**er** and ever,*
O LORD, God of our an**ces**tor Israel.

Yours, O LORD, are the greatness and the power and the glory and the victory **and** the majesty,*
for everything in the heavens and on **earth** is yours.

Yours is the king**dom**, O LORD,*
and you are exalted as head **a**bove all.

Riches and honor **come** from you;*
you have dominion **o**ver all.

In your hand are pow**er** and might;*
it is in your hand to make great and give **strength** to all.

Therefore our God, we **give** you thanks*
and praise your **glor**ious Name. [SBH, LH, PHP]

Antiphon Yours is the king**dom**, O LORD,*
and you are exalted as head above all, **all**eluia.

Silence for meditation

Almighty God, by the death of your Son you have destroyed sin and death, and by his resurrection you have restored innocence and everlasting life so that, delivered from the power of the evil one, we may live in your kingdom: Grant that we may believe this with our whole heart and, steadfast in this faith, may praise and thank you evermore; through Jesus Christ our Lord.
[Greg. adapt. Luther, CSB, MPB]

+

Antiphon to PSALM 146 *Lauda, anima mea*

O Zion, the LORD your God shall **reign** for ever,*
alleluia. [LH,PBO]

146 *Praise of God's faithfulness*

1 Hallelujah!
Praise the LORD, **O** my soul!*
I will praise the LORD as long as I live;
I will sing praises to my God while I **have** my being.

2 Put not your trust in rulers, nor in any **child** of earth,*
for there is no **help** in them.

3 When they breathe their last, they re**turn** to earth,*
and in that day **their** thoughts perish.

4 Happy are they who have the God of Jacob **for** their help,*
whose hope is in the **LORD** their God;

5 Who made heaven and earth, the seas, and all **that** is in them;*
who keeps his prom**ise** for ever;

6 Who gives justice to those who **are** oppressed,*
and food to **those** who hunger.

7 The LORD sets the prisoners free;
the LORD opens the eyes **of** the blind;*
the LORD lifts up those who **are** bowed down;

8 The LORD loves the righteous;
the LORD cares **for** the stranger;*
he sustains the orphan and widow,
but frustrates the way **of** the wicked.

9 The LORD shall **reign** for ever,*
your God, O Zion, throughout all generations.
Hallelujah!

Antiphon O Zion, the LORD your God shall **reign** for ever,*
al**le**luia.

Silence for meditation

God of glory and power, happy indeed are those who have put their trust in you. Shine the brightness of your light upon us, that we may love you always with a pure heart and praise you for ever; through your Son, Jesus Christ our Lord. [LH, LBW]

+

Stand

THE HYMN is sung. *Aurora lucis rutilat*

2 While he, the king of glorious might,
Treads down death's strength in death's despite,
And trampling hell by victor's right,
Brings forth his sleeping saints to light.

3 Fast barred beneath the stone of late,
In watch and ward where soldiers wait;
Now shining in triumphant state,
He rises victor from death's gate.

4 Th' apostles' hearts were full of pain,
For their dear Lord, so lately slain;
That Lord his servants' wicked train
With bitter scorn had dared arraign.

5 Hell's pains are loosed, and tears are fled;
Captivity is captive led;
The angel, crowned with light, hath said,
The Lord is risen from the dead.

6 We pray thee, king with glory decked,
In this our Paschal joy, protect
From all that death would fain effect,
Thy ransom'd flock, thine own elect.

7 To thee who dead again dost live,
All glory, Lord, thy people give;
All glory, as is ever meet,
To Father and to Paraclete. Amen. [HAM 142]

Text: Latin office hymn attr. St. Ambrose, 340-397; tr. John Mason Neale, 1818-1866
Tune: plainsong, mode viii

Sit

One or two LESSONS are read.

Year 1	Year 2
Tuesday in Easter [Bright]Week	
Isaiah 30: 18-26	Exodus 12:28-39
The light of the sun will be sevenfold, like the light of seven days, on the day when the LORD binds up the injuries of his people.	They baked unleavened cakes of the dough that they had brought out of Egypt; it was not leavened, because they were driven out of Egypt and could not wait.
Acts 2:36-41 (42-47)	1 Corinthians 15:12-28
The promise is for you, for your children, and for all who are far away, everyone whom the Lord our God calls to him.	As all die in Adam, so all will be made alive in Christ.
Tuesday after Easter 2	
Daniel 2:1-16	Exodus 15:1-21
Nebuchadnezzar said to them, "I have had such a dream that my spirit is troubled by the desire to understand it."	Miriam sang to them: "Sing to the LORD, for he has triumphed gloriously; horse and rider he has thrown into the sea."
1 John 2:1-11	1 Peter 1:13-25
The darkness is passing away and the true light is already shining.	Through Christ you have come to trust in God, who raised him from the dead and gave him glory.

Tuesday after Easter 3

Daniel 4:28-37

Now I, Nebuchadnezzar, praise and extol and honor the King of heaven, for all his works are truth, and his ways are justice; and he is able to bring low those who walk in pride.

Exodus 19:1-16

On the morning of the third day there was thunder and lightning, as well as a thick cloud upon the mountain, and a blast of a trumpet so loud that all the people who were in the camp trembled.

1 John 4:7-21

God's love was revealed among us in this way: God sent his only Son into the world so that we might live through him.

Colossians 1:1-14

He has rescued us from the power of darkness and transferred us into the kingdom of his beloved Son, in whom we have redemption, the forgiveness of sins.

Tuesday after Easter 4

Wisdom 3:1-9

The souls of the righteous are in the hand of God, and no torment will ever touch them.
or Jeremiah 30:10-17

Exodus 32:21-34

On the next day Moses said to the people, "You have sinned a great sin. But now I will go up to the LORD; perhaps I can make atonement for your sin."

Colossians 1:15-23

Christ is the head of the body, the church; he is the beginning, the first-born from the dead.

1 Thessalonians 1:1-10

You turned to God from idols, to serve a living and true God, and to wait for his Son from heaven, whom he raised from the dead–Jesus, who rescues us from the wrath that is coming.

Tuesday after Easter 5

Wisdom 10:1-4 (5-12) 13-21

A holy people and blameless race wisdom delivered from a nation of oppressors.
or Jeremiah 32:16-25

Romans 12:1-21

Present your bodies as a living sacrifice, holy and acceptable to God, which is your spiritual worship.

Leviticus 16:20-34

On this day atonement shall be made for you, to cleanse you; from all your sins you shall be clean before the LORD.

1 Thessalonians 5:1-11

Our Lord Jesus Christ died for us, so that whether we are awake or asleep we may live with him.

Tuesday after Easter 6 [Rogation Tuesday]

Deuteronomy 8:11-20

Take care that you do not forget the LORD your God, by failing to keep his commandments, his ordinances, and his statutes.
or Deuteronomy 18:9-24

James 1:16-27

Every generous act of giving, with every perfect gift, is from above, coming down from the Father of lights, with whom there is no variation or shadow due to change.

Leviticus 26:1-20

I will walk among you, and will be your God, and you shall be my people.

1 Timothy 2:1-6

God our Savior desires everyone to be saved and come to the knowledge of the truth.

Tuesday after Easter 7

Ezekiel 7:10-15, 23b-27

According to their way I will deal with them; according to their own judgments I will judge them. And they shall know that I am the LORD.

1 Samuel 16:1-13a

Samuel took the horn of oil, and anointed him in the presence of his brothers; and the spirit of the LORD came mightily upon David from that day forward.

Hebrews 6:13-20

We have this hope, a sure and steadfast anchor of the soul, a hope that enters the inner shrine behind the curtain, where Jesus, a forerunner on our behalf, has entered.

Ephesians 3:14-21

Now to him who by the power at work within us is able to accomplish far more than all we can ask or imagine, to him be glory in the church and in Christ Jesus to all generations, forever and ever.

Silence for meditation follows each reading.

RESPONSORY

In Christ **you** have died,*
and your life is hidden from with **him** in God.
When Christ who is your life **is** revealed,*
then you also will be revealed with him in glory, **al**leluia.
You must consider yourselves **dead** to sin*
and alive to God **in** Christ Jesus.

As Christ was raised from the dead by the glory **of** the Father,*
so we too must walk in new**ness** of life;
and we must love **one** another*
just as the Lord has commanded us, **al**leluia.
Let us sing the praises **of** the Lord;*
let us sing a new song **to** our God;

When Christ who is your life **is** revealed,*
then you also will be revealed with him in glory, **al**leluia.
[LH: Col. 3:3-4; Rom 6:11]

and we must love **one** another*
just as the Lord has commanded us, **al**leluia.
Glory to the Father and **to** the Son*
and to the **Ho**ly Spirit.
and we must love **one** another*
just as the Lord has commanded us, **al**leluia.
[LH: Col. 3:3-4; Rom. 6-11]

Antiphon to the BENEDICTUS

Tuesday in Easter Week

Jesus said to her, Mary! She turned and said to **him**, Rabboni.*
He said to her, Do not hold on to me, because I have not yet ascended to the Father, **al**leluia. [LH: John 20:16, 17]

Tuesday after Easter 2

I am the Alpha and the Omega, the beginning **and** the end.*
I am the root and the descendent of David,
the bright morning star, **al**leluia. [LH: Rev. 21:6; 22:16]

Tuesday after Easter 3

Truly I tell you,
it was not Moses who gave you the **bread** from heaven;*
but it is my Father who gives you the true bread from heaven, **al**leluia. [LH: John 6:32]

Tuesday after Easter 4

The works that I do in the Father's Name testi**fy** to me.*
alleluia [LH: John 10:25]

Tuesday after Easter 5

Peace I leave with you, **al**leluia*
my peace I give you, al**le**luia. [LH: John 14:27]

Tuesday after Easter 6

In a little while the world will no longer see me;
but **you** will see me.*
Because I live, you will also live, **al**leluia. [LH: John 14:19]

Tuesday after Easter 7

The Lord has been raised from the dead **as** he promised;*
let all the earth rejoice and be glad, for he shall reign for ever,
alleluia. [LH: Matt. 28:6; Ps. 97:1; Rev. 11:15]

Wednesdays of Easter

Antiphon to PSALM 99 *Dominus regnavit, irascantur*

The LORD is **great** in Zion;*
he is high above all peoples, **al**leluia. [LH, PBO]

99 *The power and holiness of God*

1 The LORD is King;
let the **peo**ple tremble;*
he is enthroned upon the cherubim;
let **the** earth shake.

2 The LORD is **great** in Zion;*
he is high a**bove** all peoples.

3 Let them confess his Name, which is **great** and awesome;*
he is the **Ho**ly One.

4 "O mighty King, lover of justice,
you have es**tab**lished equity;*
you have executed justice and righteous**ness** in Jacob."

5 Proclaim the greatness of the LORD our God
and fall down be**fore** his footstool;*
he is the **Ho**ly One.

6 Moses and Aaron among his priests,
and Samuel among those who call up**on** his Name,*
they called upon the LORD, and he **an**swered them.

7 He spoke to them out of the pil**lar** of cloud;*
they kept his testimonies and the decree **that** he gave them.

8 O LORD our God, you answered **them** indeed;*
you were a God who forgave them,
yet punished them for their **e**vil deeds.

9 Proclaim the greatness of the LORD our God
and worship him upon his **ho**ly hill;*
for the LORD our God is the **Ho**ly One.

Antiphon The LORD is **great** in Zion;*
he is high above all peoples, **al**leluia.

Silence for meditation

Most holy God, enthroned upon the cherubim, no one can look upon you and live: Forgive us our sins, and, through your life-giving Word, purify us to proclaim your praise; through Jesus Christ our Lord. [PHP]

+

Antiphon to the OLD TESTAMENT CANTICLE
Incipite Domino in tympanis [Hymnum cantabo Domino]

You send forth your Spir**it**, O Lord,*
and so you renew the face of the earth, **al**leluia. [LH: Ps. 104:31]

A Song of Judith Judith 16:1, 13-15

Strike up a song to my God with **tam**bourines,*
sing to the **Lord** with cymbals.

Raise a new psalm of **praise** to him,*
exalt him, and call up**on** his Name.

I will sing to my God **a** new song;*
O Lord, you are great and glorious,
wonderful in **strength**, invincible.

Let your whole creation serve you,*
for you spoke and all things **came** to be.

You sent forth your Spirit and it **gave** them form;*
there is none that can re**sist** your Word.

Mountains shall shake to their **depths** like water;*
before your glance the rocks shall **melt** like wax;

But to **those** who fear you*
you **still** show mercy. [LH; PHP]

Antiphon You send forth your Spir**it**, O Lord,*
and so you renew the face of the earth, **al**leluia.

Silence for meditation

Lord God almighty, every year you renew the face of the earth, and it is your will to renew the world fallen into sin and death: Grant that we may discern in your Son the dawning of true life and in him share in the new creation now and for ever. [*Gebete*, MPB]

+

Antiphon to PSALM 147 Part i *Laudate Dominum*

The LORD re**builds** Jerusalem;*
he heals the brokenhearted, **al**leluia. [LH]

147 *Praise of God who maintains the world*

1 Hallelujah!
How good it is to sing praises **to** our God!*
how pleasant it is to honor **him** with praise!

2 The LORD re**builds** Jerusalem;*
he gathers the ex**iles** of Israel.

3 He heals the **bro**kenhearted*
and binds **up** their wounds.

4 He counts the number **of** the stars*
and calls them all **by** their names.

5 Great is our LORD and might**y** in power;*
there is no limit **to** his wisdom.

6 The LORD lifts **up** the lowly,*
but casts the wicked **to** the ground.

7 Sing to the LORD **with** thanksgiving;*
make music to our God up**on** the harp.

8 He covers the heav**ens** with clouds*
and prepares rain **for** the earth;

9 He makes grass to grow up**on** the mountains*
and green plants to **serve** mankind.

10 He provides food for **flocks** and herds*
and for the young ravens **when** they cry.

11 He is not impressed by the might **of** a horse;*
he has no pleasure in the strength **of** a man;

12 But the LORD has pleasure in **those** who fear him,*
in those who await his **gra**cious favor.

Antiphon The LORD re**builds** Jerusalem;*
he heals the brokenhearted, **al**leluia.

Silence for meditation

God our Father, great builder of the heavenly Jerusalem, you know the number of the stars and call each of them by name: Heal hearts that are broken, gather those who have been scattered, and enrich us all from the plenitude of your eternal wisdom, Jesus Christ our Lord. [LH, LBW]

+

Stand

THE HYMN is sung. *Claro paschali gaudio*

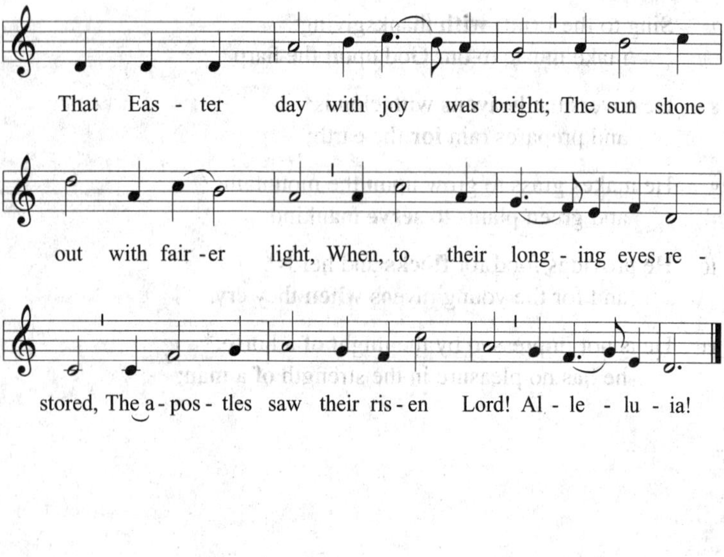

2 He bade them see his hands, his side,
Where yet the glorious wounds abide;
Those tokens true, which made it plain
Their Lord indeed was risen again.

3 O Jesus, king of gentleness,
With constant love our hearts possess;
To you our lips will ever raise
The tribute of our grateful praise.

4 O Lord of all, with us abide
In this our joyful Eastertide:
From every weapon death can wield
Your own redeemed for ever shield.

5 All praise be yours, O risen Lord,
From death to endless life restored;
All praise to God the Father be
With Holy Ghost eternally. [LBW 154 alt; H82 193]

Text: Latin hymn, 4th or 5th cent; tr. John Mason Neale, 1818-1866, alt.
Tune: *Erschienen ist der herrlich Tag*, Nikolaus Herman, c. 1480-1561 88 884

Sit

One or two LESSONS are read.

Year 1	Year 2
Wednesday in Easter [Bright] Week	
Micah 7:7-15	Exodus 12:40-51
As in the days when you came out of	That very day the LORD brought the

the land of Egypt, show us marvelous things.

Israelites out of the land of Egypt, company by company.

Acts 3:1-10

I have no silver or gold, but what I have I give you; in the name of Jesus Christ of Nazareth, stand up and walk.

1 Corinthians 15:(29) 30-41

What you sow does not come to life unless it dies.

Wednesday after Easter 2

Daniel 2:17-30

There is a God in heaven who reveals mysteries, and he has disclosed to King Nebuchadnezzar what will happen at the end of days.

Exodus 15:22-16:10

In the evening you shall know that it was the LORD who brought you out of the land of Egypt, and in the morning you shall see the glory of the LORD.

1 John 2:12-17

The world and its desire are passing away, but those who do the will of God live forever.

1 Peter 2:1-10

You are a chosen race, a royal priesthood, a holy nation, God's own people, in order that you may proclaim the mighty acts of him who called you out of darkness into his marvelous light.

Wednesday after Easter 3

Daniel 5:1-12

Immediately the fingers of a human hand appeared and began writing on the plaster of the wall of the royal palace, next to the lampstand. The king was watching the hand as it wrote.

Exodus 19:16-25

When the LORD descended upon Mount Sinai, to the top of the mountain, the LORD summoned Moses to the top of the mountain, and Moses went up.

1 John 5:1-12

This is the testimony: God gave us eternal life, and this life is in his Son.

Colossians 1:15-23

Christ is the head of the body, the church; he is the beginning, the firstborn from the dead, so that he might come to have first place in everything.

Wednesday after Easter 4

Wisdom 4:16-5:8

The righteous who have died will condemn the ungodly who are living.
or Jeremiah 30:18-22

Exodus 33:1-23

"I will make all my goodness pass before you, and will proclaim before you my name, 'The LORD'; and I will be gracious to whom I will be gracious, and will show mercy on whom I will show mercy. But," he said, "you cannot see my face."

Colossians 1:24-2:7

As you therefore have received Christ Jesus the Lord, continue to live your lives in him, rooted and built up in him and established in the faith, just as you were taught, abounding in thanksgiving.

1 Thessalonians 2:1-12

As you know, we dealt with each one of you like a father with his children, urging and encouraging you and pleading that you lead a life worthy of God, who calls you into his own kingdom and glory.

Wednesday after Easter 5

Wisdom 13:1-9

From the greatness and beauty of created things comes a corresponding perception of their Creator.
or Jeremiah 32:36-44

Leviticus 19:1-18

You shall be holy, for I the LORD your God am holy.

Romans 13:1-14

Love is the fulfilling of the law.

1 Thessalonians 5:12-28

Rejoice always, pray without ceasing, give thanks in all circumstances; for this is the will of God in Christ Jesus for you.

Wednesday after Easter 6 [Rogation Tuesday]

Baruch 3:24-37

O Israel, how great is the house of God, how vast the territory that he possesses!
or Deuteronomy 19:1-7

Leviticus 26:27-42

If they make amends for their iniquity, then will I remember my covenant with Jacob; I will remember also my covenant with Isaac and Abraham, and I will remember the land.

James 5:13-18

Confess your sins to one another, and pray for one another, so that you may be healed.

Ephesians 1:1-10

Blessed be the God and Father of our Lord Jesus Christ, who has blessed us in Christ with every spiritual blessing in the heavenly places.

Wednesday after Easter 7

Ezekiel 11:14-25

I will give them one heart, and put a new spirit within them.

Isaiah 4:2-6

On that day the branch of the LORD shall be beautiful and glorious.

Hebrews 7:1-17

You are a priest forever, according to the order of Melchizedek.

Ephesians 4:1-16

He who descended is the same one who ascended far above all the heavens, so that he might fill all things.

Silence for meditation follows each reading.

RESPONSORY

Your streets of **gold**, Jerusalem.*
will ring with **hymns** of joy;
throughout your length and breadth one great cry from the **lips** of all:*
al**le**luia.
You will shine in splendor **like** the sun;*
everyone on earth will **pay** you homage.
Throughout your length and breadth one great cry from the **lips** of all:*
al**le**luia.
[LH: see Rev. 21:21; see Tobit 13:16, 17, 11]

See, the home of God is among mortals. He will **dwell** with them*
and he will wipe every tear from their eyes, **al**leluia.
Death shall be no more, mourning and crying and pain will be no more, for the first things have **passed** away.*
And he will wipe every tear from their eyes, **al**leluia.
Glory to the Father and to the Son and to the **Ho**ly Spirit*
And he will wipe every tear from their eyes, **al**leluia.
[LH: Rev. 21:3, 4]

Antiphon to the BENEDICTUS

Wednesday in Easter [Bright] Week

Beginning with Moses and **all** the prophets,*
Jesus interpreted to them the things about himself in all the scriptures, **al**leluia. [LH: Luke 24:27]

Wednesday after Easter 2

God so loved the world that he gave his **on**ly Son*
so that everyone who believes in him may not perish but have eternal life, **al**leluia. [LH: John 3:16]

Wednesday after Easter 3

All who see the Son and believe in him will have e**ter**nal life,*
and I will raise them up on the last day, **al**leluia. [LH: John 6:40]

Wednesday after Easter 4

I am the light **of** the world;*
whoever follows me will never walk in darkness, **al**leluia [LH: John 16:12-13]

Wednesday after Easter 5

I am the vine, **al**leluia*
you are the branches, **al**leluia. [LH: John 15:5]

Wednesday after Easter 6

I still have many things to say to you, but you cannot **bear** them now.*
When the Spirit of truth comes, he will guide you into all the truth, **al**leluia. [LH: John 16:12-13]

Wednesday after Easter 7

Alleluia, thanks **be** to God,*
who gives us the victory through our Lord Jesus Christ, **al**leluia. [LH: John 14:19]

Thursdays of Easter

Antiphon to PSALM 47 *Omnes gentes, plaudite*

God is king of **all** the earth;*
sing praises with all your skill, **al**leluia. [LH, PBO]

47 *To God, King of the world*

1 Clap your hands, **all** you peoples;*
shout to God with a **cry** of joy.

2 For the LORD Most High is **to** be feared;*
he is the great King over **all** the earth.

3 He subdues the **peo**ples under us,*
and the nations **un**der our feet.

4 He chooses our inheri**tance** for us,*
the pride of Jacob **whom** he loves.

5 God has gone up **with** a shout,*
the LORD with the sound **of** the ram's horn.

6 Sing praises to **God**, sing praises;*
sing praises to our **King**, sing praises.

7 For God is King of **all** the earth;*
sing praises with **all** your skill.

8 God reigns o**ver** the nations;*
God sits upon his **ho**ly throne.

9 The nobles of the peoples have gath**ered** together*
with the people of the **God** of Abraham.

10 The rulers of the earth be**long** to God,*
and he is high**ly** exalted.

Antiphon God is king of **all** the earth;*
sing praises with all your skill, **al**leluia.

Silence for meditation

Lord Jesus, the dominion of the universe is yours, for you have ascended on high and are seated on the throne prepared for you by the Father: Gather all peoples into your Church and make them a holy nation, a royal priesthood, your chosen heritage, to praise and adore your divine majesty now and for ever. [LHd, LBW]

+

Antiphon to the OLD TESTAMENT CANTICLE
Audite verbum Domini

Our Lord Jesus died **and** was raised*
to gather into one all the dispersed children of God. **Al**leluia.
LH; see John 11:51-52

A Song of Jeremiah Jeremiah 31:10-14

Listen, you nations of the world;
listen to the word **of** the LORD;*
  announce it, make it known on the farthest coasts
  and to **dis**tant islands:

The LORD who scattered Israel will gather his peo**ple** again,*
  and will keep watch over them as a shepherd **guards** the flock.

For the LORD has **ran**somed Jacob*
  and has rescued them from hands too **strong** for them.

With shouts of joy **they** shall come*
  their faces radi**ant**ly happy;

For the LORD is so **gen**erous to them;*
  he showers his peo**ple** with gifts:

Grain and **wine** and oil,
  sheep and oxen of the **flock** and herd.

Like a garden refreshed **by** the rain,*
  they will never be in **want** again.

Young women will **dance** for joy,*
  and men young and old **will** make merry.

I will turn their mourning **in**to joy,*
  I will comfort them and give them glad**ness** for sorrow;

I will refresh the priests **with** rich foods*
  and my people shall be filled with my bounty, **says** the LORD.

[LBW, PHP]

Antiphon Our Lord Jesus died **and** was raised*
  to gather into one all the dispersed children of God.
  Alleluia.

Silence for meditation

God of all-embracing and everlasting love, you brought your people home from captivity in Babylon and redeemed us through Christ your Son: Refresh us evermore, we pray, with the grain and wine of the Eucharist, and gather into one your scattered children, that your people may sing you one song of praise; through Jesus Christ our Lord. [PHP]

+

Antiphon to PSALM 147 Part ii *Lauda, Jerusalem, Dominum*

Praise your **God**, O Zion,*
for he has established peace on your borders, **al**leluia. [LH,PBO]

147: 13-21 *Praise of God's care of Israel*

13 Worship the LORD, **O** Jerusalem;*
praise your **God**, O Zion;

14 For he has strengthened the bars **of** your gates;*
he has blessed your chil**dren** within you.

15 He has established peace **on** your borders;*
he satisfies you with the **fin**est wheat.

16 He sends out his command **to** the earth,*
and his word runs **ve**ry swiftly.

17 He gives **snow** like wool;*
he scatters hoar**frost** like ashes.

18 He scatters his **hail** like bread crumbs.*
Who can stand a**gainst** his cold?

19 He sends forth his **word** and melts them;*
he blows with his wind, and the **wa**ters flow.

20 He declares his **word** to Jacob,*
his statutes and his judg**ments** to Israel.

21 He has not done so to any **oth**er nation;*
to them he has not revealed his judgments. **Hal**lelujah!

Antiphon Praise your **God**, O Zion,*
for he has established peace on your borders,
alleluia.

Silence for meditation

Almighty God, through your Church, generously endowed with gifts of grace and fortified by the Holy Spirit, you send out your word to all nations. Strengthen your Church with heavenly food, make it dauntless in faith, and multiply its children, that with joy we may celebrate your love at the altar on high; through Jesus Christ our Lord. [LH, PHP]

+

Stand

THE HYMN is sung. *Ad regias Agni dapes*

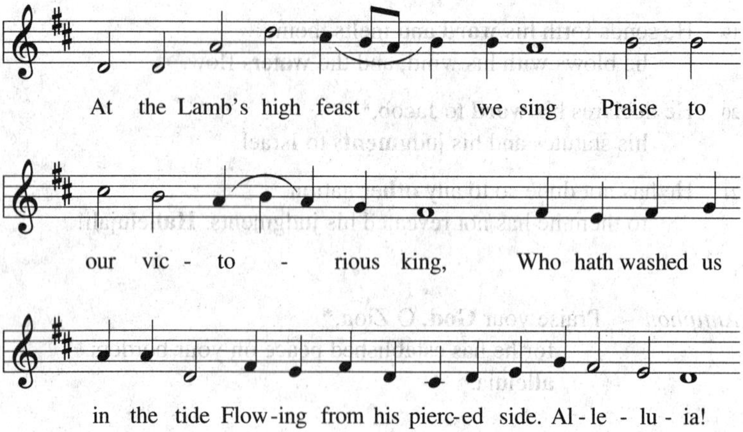

2 Praise we him, whose love divine
Gives his sacred blood for wine,
Gives his body for the feast,
Christ the victim, Christ the priest.
Alleluia!

3 Where the Paschal blood is poured
Death's dread angel sheathes the sword;
Israel's hosts triumphant go
Through the wave that drowns the foe.
Alleluia!

4 Praise we Christ, whose blood was shed,
Paschal victim, Paschal bread;
With sincerity and love
Eat we manna from above.
Alleluia!

5 Mighty victim from the sky,
Hell's fierce pow'rs beneath thee lie;
Thou hast conquered in the fight,
Thou hast brought us life and light.
Alleluia!

6 Now no more can death appal,
Now no more the grave enthrall;
Thou hast opened paradise,
And in thee thy saints shall rise.
Alleluia!

7 Easter triumph, Easter joy!
Only sin can these destroy;
From sin's power do thou set free
Souls newborn, O Lord, in thee.
Alleluia!

8 Father, who the crown shall give,
Savior, by whose death we live,
Spirit, guide through all our days,
Three in One, thy Name we praise.
Alleluia! [H82 174, LBW 210]

Text: office hymn, 17th cent.; tr. Robert Campbell, 1814-1868, alt.
Tune: *Sonne der Gerechtigkeit*, Bohemian Brethren, *Kirchenengeseng*, 1566 7 7 77 4

On Ascension Day "The head that once was crowned with thorns" page 395

Sit

One or two LESSONS are read.

Year 1

Thursday in Easter [Bright]Week
Ezekiel 37:1-14

You shall know that I am the LORD, when I open your graves, O my people. I will put my spirit within you, and you shall live.

Acts 3:11-26

The God of Abraham, the God of Isaac, and the God of Jacob, the God of our ancestors has glorified his servant Jesus, whom you handed over and rejcted.

Thursday after Easter 2
Daniel 2:31-49

In the days of those kings the God of heaven will set up a kingdom that shall never be destroyed, nor shall this kingdom be left to another people.

1 John 2:18-29

If what you heard from the beginning abides in you, then you will abide in

Year 2

Exodus 13:3-10

Remember this day, on which you came out of Egypt, out of the house of slavery, because the LORD brought you out from there by strength of hand.

1 Corinthians 15:41-50

Just as we have borne the image of the man of dust, we will also bear the image of the man of heaven.

Exodus 16:10-22

At twilight you shall eat meat, and in the morning you shall have your fill of bread; then you shall know that I am the LORD your God.

1 Peter 2:11-3:12

Christ himself bore our sins in his body on the cross, so that, free from

the Son and in the Father. And this is what he has promised us, eternal life.

sins, we might live for righteousness; by his wounds you have been healed.

Thursday after Easter 3
Daniel 5:13-30

God has numbered the days of your kingdom and brought it to an end.

Exodus 20:1-21

I am the LORD your God, who brought you out of the land of Egypt, out of the house of slavery.

1 John 5:13-20 (21)

I write these things to you who believe in the name of the Son of God, so that you may know that you have eternal life.

Colossians 1:24-2:7

As you therefore have received Christ Jesus the Lord, continue to live your lives in him, rooted and built up in him and established in the faith, just as you were taught, abounding in thanksgiving.

Thursday after Easter 4
Wisdom 5:9-23

The righteous live forever, and their reward is with the Lord; the Most High takes care of them.
or Jeremiah 31:1-14

Exodus 34:1-17

The LORD passed before Moses and proclaimed, "The LORD, the LORD, a God merciful and gracious, slow to anger, and abounding in steadfast love and faithfulness."

Colossians 2:8-23

When you were dead in trespasses and the uncircumcision of your flesh, God made you alive together with Christ, when he forgave us all our trespasses.

1 Thessalonians 2:13-20

When you received the word of God that you heard from us, you accepted it not as a human word but as what it really is, God's word, which is also at work in you believers.

Thursday after Easter 5
Wisdom 14:27-15:3

Our God, to know you is complete righteousness, and to know your power is the root of immortality.
or Jeremiah 33:1-13

Romans 14:1-12

To this end Christ died and lived again, so that he might be Lord of both the dead and the living.

Leviticus 19:26-37

You shall keep all my statutes and all my ordinances, and observe them: I am the LORD.

2 Thessalonians 1:1-12

We always pray for you, asking that our God will make you worthy of his call and will fulfill by his power every good resolve and work of faith, so that the name of our Lord Jesus may be glorified in you, and you in him.

Ascension Day
Ezekiel 1:1-14, 24-28b

Above the dome over their heads there was something like a throne, in appearance like sapphire; and seated above the likeness of a throne was something that seemed like a human form.

Hebrews 2:5-18

We see Jesus, who for a little while was made lower than the angels, now crowned with glory and honor because of the suffering of death.

Daniel 7:9-14

As I watched in the night visions, I saw one like a human being coming with the clouds of heaven. And he came to the Ancient One and was presented before him.

Hebrews 2:5-18

We see Jesus, who for a little while was made lower than the angels, now crowned with glory and honor because of the suffering of death.

Thursday after Easter 7

Ezekiel 18:1-4, 19-32

Cast away from you all the transgressions that you have committed against me, and get yourselves a new heart and a new spirit!

Zechariah 4:1-14

Not by might, nor by power, but by spirit, says the LORD of hosts.

Hebrews 7:18-28

He is able for all time to save those who approach God through him, since he always lives to make intercession for them.

Ephesians 4:17-32

You were taught to put away your former way of life, your old self, corrupt and deluded by its lusts, and, to be renewed in the spirit of your minds, and to clothe yourselves with the new self, created according to the likeness of God in true righteousness and holiness.

Silence for meditation follows each reading.

RESPONSORY

If you hear my voice
and **open** the door,*
  I will come in to you
  and eat with you
  and you with me, **al**leluia.
To everyone who conquers
I will give permission to eat from
the tree of life that is in the
paradi**se** of God.*

The Lord in all his beauty has
been raised a**bove** the stars,*
and his splendor shines forth
among the **clouds** of heaven,
  where his Name shall be
  praised for ever,*
  al**le**luia.
From the heights of heaven he
has come forth,*
and to those heights **he** returns,

I will come in to you*
and eat with you
and you with me, **al**leluia.
[LH: Rev. 3:20, 2:7]

where his Name shall be
praised for ever,*
al**le**luia.
Glory to the Father and **to** the Son*
and to the **Ho**ly Spirit.
Where his Name shall be
praised for ever,*
al**le**luia. [LH]

Antiphon to the BENEDICTUS

Thursday in Easter [Bright] Week

Jesus stood among his disciples and said, **Peace** be with you,*
al**le**luia. [LH: John 20:19]

Thursday after Easter 2

The Father loves the Son and has placed all things **in** his hands,*
al**le**luia. [LH: John 3:35]

Thursday after Easter 3

Truly, truly, I say to you, all who believe in me will have e**ter**nal life,*
alleluia. [LH: John 6:40]

Thursday after Easter 4

Servants are not greater **than** their master*
and should be glad to become like the master, **al**leluia
[LH: see John 13:16]

Thursday after Easter 5

If you keep **my** commandments,*
you will abide in my love, **al**leluia. [LH: John 15:10]

Ascension Day

I am ascending to my Father **and** your Father,*
to my God and your God, **al**leluia. [CSB, SBH, LH: John 20:17]

Thursday after Easter 7

Go therefore and make disciples **of** all nations,*
baptizing them in the Name of the Father, and of the Son, and of the Holy Spirit, **al**leluia. [LH: Matthew 28:19-20]

Fridays of Easter

Antiphon to PSALM 96 *Cantate Domino*

Tell it out a**mong** the nations:,*
The LORD is king, **al**leluia. [LH, PBO]

96 *The Lord, King and Judge of the world*

1 Sing to the LORD **a** new song;*
sing to the LORD, all **the** whole earth.

2 Sing to the LORD and **bless** his Name;*
proclaim the good news of his salvation from **day** to day.

3 Declare his glory a**mong** the nations*
and his wonders a**mong** all peoples.

4 For great is the LORD and greatly **to** be praised;*
he is more to be feared **than** all gods.

5 As for all the gods of the nations, they **are** but idols;*
but it is the LORD who **made** the heavens.

6 Oh, the majesty and magnificence **of** his presence!*
Oh, the power and the splendor of his **sanc**tuary!

7 Ascribe to the LORD, you families **of** the peoples;*
ascribe to the LORD hon**or** and power.

8 Ascribe to the LORD the honor **due** his Name;*
bring offerings and come in**to** his courts.

9 Worship the LORD in the beau**ty** of holiness;*
let the whole earth trem**ble** before him.

10 Tell it out among the nations: "The **LORD** is King!*
he has made the world so firm that it cannot be moved;
he will judge the peo**ples** with equity."

11 Let the heavens rejoice, and let the earth be glad;
let the sea thunder and all **that** is in it;*
let the field be joyful and all that **is** therein.

12 Then shall all the trees of the wood shout for joy
before the LORD **when** he comes,*
when he comes to **judge** the earth.

13 He will judge the **world** with righteousness*
and the peoples **with** his truth.

Antiphon Tell it out a**mong** the nations:
the LORD is king, **al**leluia.

Silence for meditation

Lord Jesus, the incarnate Word, when you consented to dwell with us, the heavens were glad and the earth rejoiced. In hope and love we await your return. Help us to proclaim your glory to those who do not know you, until the whole earth sings a new song to you and the Father and the Holy Spirit, one God, now and for ever. [LHd, LBW]

+

Antiphon to the OLD TESTAMENT CANTICLE

Miserere nostri, Deus universi

Fill Zion with your **prais**es, Lord,*
and let your wonders be proclaimed, **al**leluia. [LH]

A Song of Sirach [Ben Sira] Sirach 36:1-7, 13-19

Come to our aid, Lord God of the **un**iverse,*
strike fear into **ev**ery nation.

Raise up your hand a**gainst** the nations,*
and let them **see** your power.

As they have seen your holiness dis**played** among us,*
so let us see your greatness displayed **a**mong them.

Let them **learn** as we have*
that there is no **God** but you.

Give new signs and **work** new wonders;*
win glory for your mighty hand and **your** right arm.

Gather all the **tribes** of Jacob,*
and grant them their inheritance
as you did **long** ago.

Have mercy on the people called **by** your Name;*
on Israel, whom you **named** your first-born.

Show mercy to the city of your **sanc**tuary,*
Jerusalem, your **dwell**ing place.

Fill Zion with your praises of your **ma**jesty,*
and the temple **with** your glory. [LH; PHP]

Antiphon Fill Zion with your **prai**ses, Lord,*
and let your wonders be proclaimed, **al**leluia.

Silence for meditation

Almighty, everlasting God, prepare our hearts by your grace to receive your Holy Spirit; hear the prayers of your Church as it waits for you, and grant that the splendor of your glory may shine upon us and illumine the hearts of your reborn children; through Jesus Christ our Lord.

[*Gebete*, MPB rev.]

+

Antiphon to PSALM 148 *Laudate Dominum, de coelis*

The Name of the LORD **is** exalted*
above heaven and earth, **al**leluia. [LH, PBO]

148 *Cosmic praise*

1 Hallelujah!
Praise the LORD **from** the heavens;*
praise him **in** the heights.

2 Praise him, all you an**gels** of his;*
praise him, **all** his host.

3 Praise him, **sun** and moon;*
praise him, all you **shin**ing stars.

4 Praise him, heav**en** of heavens,*
and you waters a**bove** the heavens.

5 Let them praise the Name **of** the LORD;*
for he commanded, and they **were** created.

6 He made them stand fast for **ever** and ever;*
he gave them a law which shall not **pass** away.

7 Praise the LORD **from** the earth,*
you sea monsters **and** all deeps;

8 Fire and hail, **snow** and fog,*
tempestuous wind, do**ing** his will;

9 Mountains **and** all hills,*
fruit trees **and** all cedars;

10 Wild beasts **and** all cattle,*
creeping things and **wing**èd birds;

11 Kings of the earth **and** all peoples,*
princes and all rulers **of** the world;

12 Young **men** and maidens,*
old and **young** together.

13 Let them praise the Name **of** the LORD,*
for his name only is exalted,
his splendor is over **earth** and heaven.

14 He has raised up strength for his people
and praise for all his **loy**al servants,*
the children of Israel, a people who are near him.
Hallelujah!

Antiphon The Name of the LORD **is** exalted*
above heaven and earth, **al**leluia.

Silence for meditation

God Most High, by your Word you created a wondrous universe, and through your Spirit you breathed into it the breath of life. Accept creation's hymn of praise from our lips, and let the praise that is sung in heaven resound in the heart of every creature on earth to the glory of the Father, and the Son, and the Holy Spirit, now and for ever. [LHd, LBW]

+

Stand

THE HYMN is sung. *Upp, min tunga, att lovsjunga*
[Pange, lingua, gloriosi proelium]

2 Day of gladness, gone is sadness;
Christ hath bruised the serpent's head;
Death no longer is the stronger;
Hell itself is captive led.
Christ our Savior lives for ever;
O'er the tomb his light is shed.

3 Anthems glorious, hymns victorious,
Raise we to our Paschal King.
Bonds are broken, heaven is open;
Sing, ye ransomed mortals, sing!
Christ is risen from death's prison,
Healing in his wings to bring.

4 Earth rejoices, all its voices
Glory to the Father sing;
Praise the Savior, laud him ever,
Son of God, our Lord and King;
Praise the Spirit, through Christ's merit
Life eternal he doth bring! [SBH 104, LBW 155]

Text: Ventantius Honorius Fortunatus, 530-609; tr. *Service Book and Hymnal*, 1958
Tune: *Upp, min tunga*, from *Koralpsalmboken*, 1697

Sit

One or two LESSONS are read.

Year 1

Friday in Easter [Bright]Week
Daniel 12:1-4, 13

Many of those who sleep in the dust of the earth shall awake, some to everlasting life, and some to shame and everlasting contempt.

Acts 4:1-12

The apostles were teaching the people and proclaiming that in Jesus there is the resurrection of the dead.

Friday after Easter 2
Daniel 3:1-18

Our God whom we serve is able to deliver us from the furnace of blazing fire and out of your hand, O king.

1 John 3:1-10

See what love the Father has given us, that we should be called children of God; and that is what we are.

Friday after Easter 3
Daniel 6:1-15

The conspirators came and found Daniel praying and seeking mercy before his God.

Year 2

Exodus 13:1-2, 11-16

Consecrate to me all the firstborn; whatever is the first to open the womb among the Israelites, of human beings and of animals, is mine.

1 Corinthians 15:51-58

Thanks be to God, who gives us the victory through our Lord Jesus Christ.

Exodus 16:22-36

The Israelites ate manna forty years, until they came to a habitable land.

1 Peter 3:13-4:6

Christ also suffered for sins once for all, the righteous for the unrighteous, in order to bring you to God.

Exodus 24:1-18

The appearance of the glory of the LORD was like a devouring fire on the top of the mountain in the sight of the people of Israel. Moses

2 John 1-13

This is love, that we walk according to his commandments; this is the commandment just as you have heard it from the beginning–you must walk in it.

Friday after Easter 4
Wisdom 6:12-23

Wisdom is radiant and unfading, and she is easily discerned by those who love her, and is found by those who seek her.
or Jeremiah 31:15-22

Colossians 3:1-11

If you have been raised with Christ, seek the things that are above, where Christ is, seated at the right hand of God.

Friday after Easter 5
Wisdom 16:15-17:1

You gave your people food of angels, and without their toil you supplied them from heaven with bread ready to eat, providing every pleasure and suited to every taste.
or Deuteronomy 31:30-32:14

entered the cloud, and went up on the mountain.

Colossians 2:8-23

When you were dead in trespasses and the uncircumcision of your flesh, God made you alive together with him, when he forgave us all our trespasses.

Exodus 34:18-35

As he came down from the mountain with the two tablets of the covenant in his hand, Moses did not know that the skin of his face shone because he had been talking with God.

1 Thessalonians 3:1-13

May the Lord make you increase and abound in love for one another and for all.

Leviticus 23:1-22

These are the appointed festivals of the LORD that you shall proclaim as holy convocations, my appointed festivals.

Romans 14:13-23

Do not let what you eat cause the ruin of one for whom Christ died.

2 Thessalonians 2:1-17

Now may our Lord Jesus Christ himself and God our Father, who loved us and through grace gave us eternal comfort and good hope, comfort your hearts and strengthen them in every good work and word.

Friday after Ascension Day
Ezekiel 1:28-3:3

You shall say to them, "Thus says the Lord GOD." Whether they hear or refuse to hear (for they are a rebellious house), they shall know that there has been a prophet among them.

1 Samuel 2:1-10

The LORD will judge the ends of the earth; he will give strength to his king, and exalt the power of his annointed.

Hebrews 4:14-5:6

Since, then, we have a great high priest who has passed through the heavens, Jesus, the Son of God, let us hold fast to our confession.

Ephesians 2:1-10

God, who is rich in mercy, out of the great love with which he loved us even when we were dead through our trespasses, made us alive together with Christ–by grace you have been saved–and raised us up with him and seated us with him in the heavenly places in Christ Jesus.

Friday after Easter 7
Ezekiel 34:17-31

You are my sheep, the sheep of my pasture and I am your God, says the Lord GOD.

Jeremiah 31:27-34

I will put my law within them, and I will write it on their hearts; and I will be their God, and they shall be my people.

Hebrews 8:1-13

We have such a high priest, one who is seated at the right hand of the throne of the Majesty in the heavens.

Ephesians 5:1-32

Live in love, as Christ loved us and gave himself up for us, a fragrant offering and sacrifice to God.

Silence for meditation follows each reading.

RESPONSORY

Where, O death, is your victory?
Where, O death **is** your sting?*
The sting of death is sin, and the
power of sin **is** the law.
Thanks **be** to God,*
who gives us the victory
through our Lord Jesus Christ,
alleluia.
We have the same
spir**it** of faith*
because we know that the one
who raised the Lord Jesus will
raise us al**so** with Jesus.
Thanks **be** to God,*
who gives us the victory
through our Lord Jesus Christ,
alleluia.
[LH: 1 Cor. 15:55-56, 57; 2 Cor. 4:13, 14]

Christ suffered for sins, the
righteous for **the** unrighteous,*
in order to bring **you** to God.
He was put to death
in the flesh,*
but made alive in the spirit,
alleluia.
He is at the right **hand** of God,*
he died to make eternal **life** our
heritage.
He was put to death
in the flesh,*
but made alive in the spirit,
alleluia.
Glory to the Father and **to** the Son*
and to the **Ho**ly Spirit.
He was put to death
in the flesh,*
but made alive in the spirit,
alleluia.
[LH: 1 Peter 3:18, 22]

Antiphon to the BENEDICTUS

Friday in Easter [Bright] Week

This was the third time that Jesus appeared to the disciples
after he was raised **from** the dead,*
alleluia. [LH: John 21:14]

Friday after Easter 2

Jesus took the bread, blessed and broke it
and gave it to those who were at **ta**ble with him,*
al**le**luia. [LH: Luke 24:30]

Friday after Easter 3

Those who eat my flesh and drink my blood a**bide** in me,*
and I in them, **al**leluia. [LH: John 6:56]

Friday after Easter 4

I go and prepare a **place** for you,*
but I will come again and will take you to myself, so that
where I am, there you may be also, **al**leluia. [LH: John 14:3]

Friday after Easter 5

This is **my** commandment:*
love one another as I have loved you, **al**leluia. [LH: John 15:12]

Friday after Ascension Day

Because he **suf**fered death,*
we see Jesus crowned with glory and honor, **al**leluia.
[LH: see Hebrews 2:9]

Friday after Easter 7

Christ Jesus, who died and was raised, is at the right **hand** of God*
where he intercedes for us, **al**leluia. [LH: see Rom. 8:34]

Saturdays of Easter

Antiphon to PSALM 92 *Bonum est confiteri*

You have made me glad by your **acts**, O LORD*
and I shout for joy because of the works of your hands, **al**leluia.
[LH, PBO]

92 *Praise to God the Creator*

1 It is a good thing to give thanks **to** the LORD,*
and to sing praises to your Name, **O** Most High;

2 To tell of your loving-kindness early **in** the morning*
and of your faithfulness in **the** night season;

3 On the psaltery, and **on** the lyre,*
and to the melody **of** the harp.

4 For you have made me glad by your **acts**, O LORD;*
and I shout for joy because of the works **of** your hands.

5 LORD, how great **are** your works!*
your thoughts are **ver**y deep.

6 The dullard does not know,
nor does the fool **un**derstand,*
that though the wicked grow like weeds,
and all the workers of iniq**ui**ty flourish,

7 They flourish only to be des**troy**ed for ever;*
but you, O LORD, are exalted for **ev**ermore.

8 For lo, your enemies, O LORD,
lo, your ene**mies** shall perish,*
and all the workers of iniquity **shall** be scattered.

9 But my horn you have exalted like the horns **of** wild bulls;*
I am anointed **with** fresh oil.

10 My eyes also gloat o**ver** my enemies,*
and my ears rejoice to hear the doom of the wicked who rise **up** against me.

11 The righteous shall flourish **like** a palm tree,*
and shall spread abroad like a ce**dar** of Lebanon.

12 Those who are planted in the house **of** the LORD*
shall flourish in the courts **of** our God;

13 They shall still bear fruit **in** old age;*
they shall be **green** and succulent;

14 That they may show how up**right** the LORD is,*
my Rock, in whom there **is** no fault.

Antiphon You have made me glad by your **acts**, O LORD*
and I shout for joy because of the works
of your hands, **al**leluia.

Silence for meditation

Lord, take away our shame and make us rejoice in your saving acts, that we who have been redeemed by your Son may always abound in works of faith, hope, and love in your service; through Jesus Christ our Lord.

[LH, LBW]

+

Antiphon to the OLD TESTAMENT CANTICLE *Cantemus Domino*

Those who had conquered sang the song of Moses, the ser**vant** of God,*
and the song the Lamb, **al**leluia. [Rev. 15:3]

The Song of Miriam and Moses Exodus 15:1-2, 6, 11, 13, 17-18

I will sing to the Lord, for he has triumphed **glo**riously;*
horse and rider he has thrown in**to** the sea.

The Lord is my strength **and** my song;*
he has be**come** my savior.

This is my God and **I** will praise him,*
The God of my people and I **will** exalt him.

Your right hand, O Lord, glori**ous** in power,*
your right hand, O Lord, shat**ters** the enemy.

Who among the gods is like **you**, O Lord?*
Who is like you, majestic in holiness,
awesome in splendor, **do**ing wonders?

With your constant love you led forth the people whom **you** set free;*
you guided them in your strength to your holy **hab**itation.

You will bring them **in** and plant them*
on the mount that is **your** possession,

The place, O Lord , which your hands **have** prepared.
The Lord shall reign for ev**er** and ever. [BCP, RSV]

Antiphon Those who had conquered sang the song of Moses, the ser**vant** of God,*
and the song the Lamb, **al**leluia.

Silence for meditation

O God, whose wonderful deeds of old shine forth even to our own day, by the power of your mighty arm you once delivered your chosen people from slavery under Pharaoh, to be a sign for us of the salvation of all nations by the water of Baptism: Grant that all the peoples of the earth may be numbered among the offspring of Abraham, and rejoice in the inheritance of Israel; through Jesus Christ our Lord. [Gel., BCP, LBW]

+

Antiphon to PSALM 149 *Cantate Domino*

Let the faithful re**joice** in triumph,*
al**le**luia. [LH,PBO]

149 *Praise to the God of victories*

1 Hallelujah!
Sing to the LORD **a** new song;*
sing his praise in the congregation **of** the faithful.

2 Let Israel rejoice **in** his Maker;*
let the children of Zion be joyful **in** their King.

3 Let them praise his Name **in** the dance;*
let them sing praise to him with tim**brel** and harp.

4 For the LORD takes pleasure **in** his people*
and adorns the **poor** with victory.

5 Let the faithful re**joice** in triumph;*
let them be joyful **on** their beds.

6 Let the praises of God be **in** their throat*
and a two-edged sword **in** their hand;.

7 To wreak vengeance **on** the nations*
and punishment **on** the peoples;

8 To bind their **kings** in chains*
and their nobles with **links** of iron;

9 To inflict on them the judg**ment** decreed;*
this is glory for all his faithful people.
Hallelujah!

Antiphon Let the faithful re**joice** in triumph,*
al**le**luia.

Silence for meditation

Lord, let Israel rejoice in you and acknowledge you as creator and redeemer. In your lovingkindness embrace us now, that we may proclaim the wonderful truths of salvation with your saints in glory; through your Son, Jesus Christ our Lord. [LH, LBW]

+

Stand

THE HYMN is sung. *Salve festa dies*

2 Earth her joy confesses, clothing her for spring
All good gifts return with her returning King:
Bloom in every meadow, leaves on every bough,
Speak his sorrows ended, hail his triumph now.
"Hell today is vanquished, heaven is won today!"

3 Months in due succession, days of lengthening light,
Hours and passing moments praise thee in their flight.
Brightness of the morning, sky and fields and sea,
Vanquisher of darkness, bring their praise to thee.
"Welcome, happy morning!" age to age shall say.

4 Maker and Redeemer, life and health of all,
Thou from heaven beholding our abasing fall,
Of the eternal Father true and only Son,
Mortals to deliver, mortal flesh put on.
"Hell today is vanquished, heaven is won today!"

5 Thou, of life the author, death didst undergo,
Tread the path of darkness, saving strength to show;
Come, then, True and Faithful, now fulfill thy word,
'Tis thine own third morning; rise, O buried Lord!
"Welcome, happy morning!" age to age shall say.

6 Loose the souls long prisoned, bound with Satan's chain;
All that now is fallen raise to life again;
Show thy face in brightness, bid the nations see;
Bring again our daylight, day returns with thee,
"Hell today is vanquished, heaven is won today!"

[OAH 367, SBH 93; H82 179]

Text: Venantius Honorius Fortunatus, 530-609; tr. John Ellerton, 1826-1893
Tune: Arthur Seymour Sullivan, 1842-1900 *Fortunatus* 11 11 11 11 11

Sit

One or two LESSONS are read.

Year 1

Saturday in Easter [Bright]Week
Isaiah 25:1-9

It will be said that on that day, Lo, this is our God; we have waited for him, so that he might save us. This is

Year 2

Exodus 13:17-14:4

The LORD went in front of them in a pillar of cloud by day, to lead them along the way, and in a pillar of fire

the LORD for whom we have waited; let us be glad and rejoice in his salvation.

Acts 4:13-21 (22-31)

Whether it is right in God's sight to listen to you rather than to God, you must judge; for we cannot keep from speaking about what we have seen and heard.

Saturday after Easter 2
Daniel 3:19-30

I see four men unbound, walking in the middle of the fire, and they are not hurt; and the fourth has the appearance of a god.

1 John 3:11-18

We know that we have passed from death to life, because we love one another.

Saturday after Easter 3
Daniel 6:16-28

The God of Daniel is the living God, enduring forever. His kingdom shall never be destroyed, and his dominion has no end.

by night, to give them light, so that they might travel by day and by night.

2 Corinthians 4:16-5:10

This slight momentary affliction is preparing us for an eternal weight of glory beyond all measure, because we look not at what can be seen but at what cannot be seen; for what can be seen is temporary, but what cannot be seen is eternal.

Exodus 17:1-16

I will be standing there in front of you on the rock at Horeb. Strike the rock, and water will come out of it, so that the people may drink.

1 Peter 4:7-19

If you are reviled for the name of Christ, you are blessed, because the spirit of glory, which is the Spirit of God, is resting on you.

Exodus 25:1-22

There I will meet with you, and from above the mercy seat, from between the two cherubim that are on the ark of the covenant, I will deliver to you all my commands for the Israelites.

3 John 1-15

Beloved, do not imitate what is evil but imitate what is good.

Colossians 3:1-17

So if you have been raised with Christ, seek the things that are above, where Christ is, seated at the right hand of God.

Saturday after Easter 4
Wisdom 7:1-14

I prayed, and understanding was given me; I called on God, and the spirit of wisdom came to me.
or Jeremiah 31:23-25

Exodus 40:18-38

Moses was not able to enter the tent of meeting because the cloud settled upon it, and the glory of the LORD filled the tabernacle.

Colossians 3:12-17

Let the peace of Christ rule in your hearts, to which indeed you were called in one body. And be thankful.

1 Thessalonians 4:1-12

We ask and urge you in the Lord Jesus that, as you learned from us how you ought to live and to please God (as, in fact, you are doing), you should do so more and more.

Saturday after Easter 5
Wisdom 19:1-8, 18-22

In everything, O Lord, you have exalted and glorified your people, and you have not neglected to help them at all times and in all places.
or Deuteronomy 32:24-41 (42) 43

Leviticus 23:23-44

Thus Moses declared to the people of Israel the appointed festivals of the LORD.

Romans 15:1-13

May the God of hope fill you with all

2 Thessalonians 3:1-18

May the Lord direct your hearts to

joy and peace in believing, so that you may abound in hope by the power of the Holy Spirit.

the love of God and to the steadfastness of Christ.

Saturday after Ascension Day

Ezekiel 3:4-17

Mortal, all my words that I shall speak to you receive in your heart and hear with your ears; then go to the exiles, to your people, and speak to them. Say to them, "Thus says the Lord GOD"; whether they hear or refuse to hear.

Numbers 11:16-17, 24-29

The LORD came down in the cloud and spoke to Moses, and took some of the spirit that was on him and put it on the seventy elders; and when the spirit rested upon them, they prophesied.

Hebrews 5:7-14

Although he was a Son, he learned obedience through what he suffered; and having been made perfect, he became the source of eternal salvation for all who obey him.

Ephesians 2:11-22

Christ came and proclaimed peace to you who were far off and peace to those who were near; for through him both of us have access in one Spirit to the Father.

Saturday after Easter 7

Ezekiel 43:1-12

The glory of the God of Israel was coming from the east; the sound was like the sound of mighty waters; and the earth shone with his glory.

Ezekiel 36:22-27

I will put my spirit within you, and make you follow my statutes and be careful to observe my ordinances.

Hebrews 9:1-14

How much more will the blood of Christ, who through the eternal Spirit offered himself without blemish to

Ephesians 6:1-24

Grace be with all who have an undying love for our Lord Jesus Christ.

God, purify our conscience from dead works to worship the living God!

Silence for meditation follows each reading.

RESPONSORY

The kingdom of the world has become the kingdom of our Lord and of **his** Messiah,*
and he will reign for ever and ever, **al**leluia.
His kingdom shall be an everlasting kingdom, and all dominions shall serve **and** obey him;*
and he will reign for ever and ever, **al**leluia.
[LH:Rev. 11:15; Daniel 7:27]

You are worthy, Lord, to take the scroll and open its seals, for you were **slain** for us.*
By your blood you have purchased us for God, **al**leluia.
You have made us a kingdom of priests to **serve** our God;*
By your blood you have purchased us for God, **al**leluia.
Glory to the Father and to the Son and to the **Ho**ly Spirit;*
By your blood you have purchased us for God, **al**leluia.
[LH: see Rev. 5:9,10]

Antiphon to the BENEDICTUS

Saturday in Easter [Bright] Week

After Jesus rose early on the first day **of** the week,*
he appeared first to Mary Magdalene, **al**leluia. [LH: Mark 16:9]

Saturday after Easter 2

Peace be with you; it is I, **al**leluia.*
Do not be afraid, **al**leluia. [LH: John 20:19; 6:20]

Saturday after Easter 3

Lord, to whom can we go? You have the words of e**ter**nal life;*
we have come to believe and know that you are the Holy One of God, **al**leluia. [LH: John 6:68-69]

Saturday after Easter 4

When the chief shep**herd** appears,*
you will win the crown of unfading glory, **al**leluia [LH: 1 Peter 5:4]

Saturday after Easter 5

Christ died and **lived** again,*
so that he might be Lord of both the dead and the living, **al**leluia. [LH: John 14:27]

Saturday after Ascension Day

If you ask anything of the Father **in** my Name,*
he will give it to you, **al**leluia. [LH: John 16:23]

Saturday after Easter 7

I am **with** you always,*
to the end of the age, **al**leluia. [LH: Matt. 28:20]

Prayer for Mid-morning

Terce. Responsive Prayer 1

L Make haste, ✠ O God, to deliver me.

C O Lord, make haste to help me. [Ps. 70:1]

L Glory to the Father, and to the Son, and to the Holy Spirit;

C As it was in the beginning, is now, and will be for ever. Amen.

A portion of Psalm 119, Meditation on God's Law, *may be sung or said. The words in italics may be used as the antiphon.*

Sunday

Aleph *Beati immaculati*

1 *Happy are they* whose **way** is blameless,*
who walk in the law ***of*** *the* L*ORD!*

2 Happy are they who observe **his** decrees*
and seek him with **all** their hearts!

3 Who never do **an**y wrong,*
but always walk **in** his ways.

4 You laid down **your** commandments,*
that we should **ful**ly keep them.

5 Oh, that my ways were made **so** direct*
that I might **keep** your statutes!

6 Then I should not be **put** to shame,*
when I regard all **your** commandments.

7 I will thank you with an **un**feigned heart,*
when I have learned your **right**eous judgments.

8 I will **keep** your statutes;*
do not utter**ly** forsake me.

Most pure and mighty God, you call us to holiness and bless with happiness those whose lives are blameless: Make us seek your righteous ways with all our hearts, for the sake of Jesus Christ our Savior. [LH, PHP]

Monday

Daleth *Adhæsit pavimento*

25 My soul cleaves **to** the dust;*
give me life according **to** your word.

26 I have confessed my ways, and you **ans**wered me;*
instruct me **in** your statutes.

27 Make me understand the way of **your** commandments,*
that I may meditate on your **mar**velous works.

28 My soul melts a**way** for sorrow;*
strengthen me according **to** your word.

29 Take from me the **way** of lying;*
let me find grace **through** your law.

30 I have chosen the **way** of faithfulness;*
I have set your judg**ments** before me.

31 I hold fast to **your** decrees;*
O LORD, let me not be **put** to shame.

32 *I will run the way of* ***your*** *commandments,**
for you have set my ***heart*** *at liberty.*

God of strength and author of freedom, we are citizens of this earth and ask to be made citizens of heaven by your grace: Help us to run the way of your commandments and to set our hearts on you alone; through Jesus Christ our Lord. [LH, PHP]

Tuesday

Zayin *Memor esto verbi tui*

49 Remember your word **to** your servant,*
because you have giv**en** me hope.

50 This is my comfort **in** my trouble,*
that your promise **gives** me life.

51 The proud have derid**ed** me cruelly,*
but I have not turned **from** your law.

52 When I remember your judg**ments** of old,*
O LORD, I **take** great comfort.

53 I am filled with a **burn**ing rage,*
because of the wicked who for**sake** your law.

54 *Your statutes have been like* ***songs*** *to me**
wherever I have lived ***as*** *a stranger.*

55 I remember your Name in the **night**, O LORD,*
and dwell **upon** your law.

56 This is how it has **been** with me,*
because I have kept **your** commandments.

God of comfort and promise, you raise us up from our lowliness by giving us the hope of eternal life: Help us always to serve you in the our pilgrimage and come at last to enjoy the blessedness of our home with you; through Jesus Christ our Lord. [LH, PHP]

Wednesday

Kaph *Defecit in salutare [Defecit anima mea]*

81 My soul has longed for **your** salvation;*
I have put my hope ***in*** *your word.*

82 My eyes have failed from watching **for** your promise,*
and I say, "When will you **com**fort me?"

83 I have become like a leather flask **in** the smoke,*
but I have not forgot**ten** your statutes.

84 How much longer **must** I wait?*
when will you give judgment against those who
persecute me?

85 The proud have dug **pits** for me;*
they do not **keep** your law.

86 All your command**ments** are true;*
help me, for they persecute **me** with lies.

87 They had almost made an end of **me** on earth,*
but I have not forsaken **your** commandments.

88 In your loving-kind**ness**, revive me,*
that I may keep the decrees **of** your mouth.

God of steadfast love, when evil seems to triumph and our hope begins to fail, give us courage and perseverence in doing your will; for the sake of Jesus Christ our Lord. [LH, PHP]

Thursday

Nun *Lucerna pedibus meis*

105 *Your word is a lantern* ***to*** *my feet**
*and a light up****on*** *my path.*

106 I have sworn and **am** determined*
to keep your **right**eous judgments.

107 I am **deep**ly troubled;*
preserve my life, O LORD, according **to** your word.

108 Accept, O LORD, the willing tribute **of** my lips,*
and teach **me** your judgments.

109 My life is always **in** my hand,*
yet I do not for**get** your law.

110 The wicked have set a **trap** for me,*
but I have not strayed from **your** commandments.

111 Your decrees are my inheri**tance** for ever;*
truly, they are the joy **of** my heart.

112 I have applied my heart to ful**fill** your statutes*
for ever and **to** the end.

God, our teacher and guide, let your Word be a lantern to our feet and a light upon our path, so that we may understand what you teach us and follow the path you mark out for us; through Jesus Christ our Lord [LH, PHP]

Friday

Pe *Mirabilia testimonia tua*

129 Your de**crees** are wonderful;*
therefore I obey them with **all** my heart.

130 When your word goes forth **it** gives light;*
it gives understanding **to** the simple.

131 I open my **mouth** and pant;*
I long for **your** commandments.

132 Turn to **me** in mercy,*
as you always do to those who **love** your Name.

133 *Steady my footsteps* ***in*** *your word;**
let no iniquity have dominion **o**ver me.

134 Rescue me from those **who** oppress me,*
and I will keep **your** commandments.

135 Let your countenance shine up**on** your servant*
and teach **me** your statutes.

136 My eyes shed **streams** of tears,*
because people do not **keep** your law.

Holy God, you are just and righteous in your judgments: Deliver those who cry to you in their affliction, and give them peace and calmness to reflect on your commandments; through Jesus Christ our Lord. [LH, PHP]

Saturday

Resh *Vide humilitatem*

153 Behold my affliction and de**liv**er me,*
for I do not for**get** your law.

154 *Plead my cause* ***and*** *redeem me;**
according to your promise, **give** me life.

155 Deliverance is far **from** the wicked,*
for they do not stud**y** your statutes.

156 Great is your compas**sion**, O LORD;*
preserve my life, according **to** your judgments.

157 There are many who persecute **and** oppress me,*
yet I have not swerved from **your** decrees.

158 I look with loathing **at** the faithless,*
for they have not **kept** your word.

159 See how I love **your** commandments!*
O LORD, in your mer**cy**, preserve me.

160 The heart of your **word** is truth;*
all your righteous judgments endure for **ev**ermore.

Our creator and redeemer, help us always to rejoice in your promise and to praise the glory of your deeds. Keep us united in the love of your peace, for then we shall have little to fear from the threats of the enemy; through Jesus Christ our Lord.

[LH, PHP]

+

This hymn, Nunc, Sancte, nobis, Spiritus, *or another hymn such as* Breathe on me, breath of God *(H82 508; LBW 488) or* O Spirit of the living God *(H82 531; LBW 388), may be sung or read.*

Come, Holy Ghost, with God the Son
And God the Father ever one;
Shed forth your grace within our breast,
And dwell with us, a welcome Guest.

By every power, by heart and tongue,
By act and deed, your praise be sung;
Inflame with perfect love each sense,
That others' souls may kindle thence.

O Father, this we ask be done
Through Jesus Christ, your only Son,
Who with the Holy Ghost and you
Shall live and reign all ages through. Amen [see H82 19, 20]

[Ascribed to St. Ambrose; trans. John Mason Neale]

The verse from the appointed First Reading for the day given in the Proper for Morning Prayer may be read as a brief Lesson.

L Holy God, holy and mighty, holy and immortal,

C Have mercy on us.

C Our Father in heaven,
hallowed be your Name,
your kingdom come,
your will be done,
on earth as in heaven.
Give us today our daily bread.
Forgive us our sins
as we forgive those
who sin against us.
Save us from the time of trial
and deliver us from evil.
For the kingdom, the power,
and the glory are yours,
now and for ever. Amen.

C Our Father who art in heaven,
hallowed be thy Name,
thy kingdom come,
thy will be done,
on earth as it is in heaven.
Give us this day our daily bread;
and forgive us our trespasses,
as we forgive those
who trespass against us;
and lead us not into temptation,
but deliver us from evil.
For thine is the kingdom,
and the power, and the glory,
for ever and ever. Amen.

The Creed may be said.

I believe in God, the Father almighty,
creator of heaven and earth.

I believe in Jesus Christ, his only Son, our Lord.
He was conceived by the power of the Holy Spirit
and born of the virgin Mary.
He suffered under Pontius Pilate,
was crucified, died, and was buried.

He descended to the dead [*or* He descended into hell].
On the third day he rose again.
He ascended into heaven,
and is seated at the right hand of the Father.
He will come again to judge the living and the dead.

I believe in the Holy Spirit,
the holy catholic Church,
the communion of saints,
the forgiveness of sins,
the resurrection of the body,
and the life everlasting. Amen

L O Lord, I cry to you for help.

C In the morning my prayer comes before you. [Ps. 88:14; Prime]

L Give me the joy of your saving help again,

C And sustain me with your bountiful Spirit. [Ps. 51:13]

L Let my mouth be full of your praise

C And your glory all the day long. [Ps. 71:8; Prime]

L Every day will I bless you,

C And praise your Name for ever and ever. [Ps. 145:2; Prime]

L Bless the Lord, O my soul,

C And all that is within me, bless his holy Name.
[Ps. 103:1; Prime]

L He redeems your life from the grave

C And crowns you with mercy and lovingkindness.
[Ps. 103:4; Prime]

L Create in me a clean heart, O God;

C And renew a right spirit within me. [Ps. 51:10; Prime]

L Lord, hear my prayer.

C And let my cry come before you. [Ps. 102:1]

L The Lord be with you.

C And also with you.

L Let us pray.

The PRAYER OF THE DAY is said. Additional prayers may be said. The following prayers are always said.

Eternal God and Father, by whose power we are created and by whose love we are redeemed: Guide and strengthen us by your Spirit, poured out on your Apostles at this hour, that we too may give ourselves to your service, and live this day in love to one another and to you; through Jesus Christ our Lord.

[Joint Liturgical Group *Daily Office*, 1968; PHP]

We give thanks to you, heavenly Father, through Jesus Christ your dear Son, that you have protected us through the night from all danger and harm. We ask you to preserve and keep us, this day also, from all sin and evil, that in all our thoughts, words, and deeds we may serve and please you. Into your hands we commend our bodies and souls and all that is ours. Let your holy angels have charge of us that the wicked one have no power over us. [Luther, LBW]

C Amen.

The BENEDICAMUS and BENEDICTION conclude the service.

L Let us bless the Lord.

C Thanks be to God.

L The Lord almighty order our days and our deeds ✠ in his peace.

C Amen.

Prayer for Noon and Mid-afternoon

Sext and None. Responsive Prayer 2

L Make haste, ✠ O God, to deliver me.

C O Lord, make haste to help me. [Ps. 70:1]

L Glory to the Father, and to the Son, and to the Holy Spirit;

C As it was in the beginning, is now, and will be for ever.

A portion of Psalm 119, Meditation on God's Law, *may be sung or said. The words in italics may be used as the antiphon.*

Sunday Noon

Beth *In quo corrigit?*

9 How shall a young man **cleanse** his way?*
By keeping **to** your words.

10 With my whole **heart** I seek you;*
let me not stray from **your** commandments.

11 I treasure your promise **in** my heart,*
that I may not **sin** against you.

12 *Blessed are* ***you****, O* L*ORD;**
instruct me ***in*** *your statutes.*

13 With my lips will **I** recite*
all the judgments **of** your mouth.

14 I have taken greater delight in the way of **your** decrees*
than in all man**ner** of riches.

15 I will meditate on **your** commandments*
and give attention **to** your ways.

16 My delight is **in** your statutes;*
I will not for**get** your word.

God, our teacher and our delight, help us treasure your commandments as the greatest of all riches, and never let us fear that anything will be lacking to us while you are at our side; through Jesus Christ our Lord.
[LH, PHP]

Sunday Mid-afternoon

Gimel *Retribue servo tuo*

17 Deal bountifully **with** your servant,*
that I may live and **keep** your word.

18 *Open my eyes, that **I** may see**
*the wonders **of** your law.*

19 I am a stranger **here** on earth;*
do not hide your command**ments** from me.

20 My soul is consumed **at** all times*
with longing **for** your judgments.

21 You have re**buked** the insolent;*
cursed are they who stray from **your** commandments!

22 Turn from me shame **and** rebuke,*
for I have kept **your** decrees.

23 Even though rulers sit and **plot** against me,*
I will meditate **on** your statutes.

24 For your decrees are **my** delight,*
and they **are** my counselors.

Gracious God, giver of all gifts, do not let us go astray from your commands but help us to seek you with all our hearts; through Jesus Christ our Lord. [LH, PHP]

Monday Noon

He *Legem pone*

33 Teach me, O LORD, the way **of** your statutes,*
and I shall keep it **to** the end.

34 *Give me understanding, and I shall* ***keep*** *your law;**
I shall keep it with **all** my heart.

35 Make me go in the path of **your** commandments,*
for that is **my** desire.

36 Incline my heart to **your** decrees*
and not to **un**just gain.

37 Turn my eyes from watching **what** is worthless;*
give me life **in** your ways.

38 Fulfill your promise **to** your servant,*
which you make to **those** who fear you.

39 Turn away the reproach **which** I dread,*
because your judg**ments** are good.

40 Behold, I long for **your** commandments;*
in your righteousness pre**serve** my life.

Holy and wise God, do not allow greed to possess us but incline our hearts to your decrees. Give us understanding to know your law and direct us according to your will; through Jesus Christ our Lord. [LH, PHP]

Monday Mid-afternoon

Waw *Et veniat super me*

41 Let your loving-kindness come to **me**, O LORD,*
and your salvation, according **to** your promise.

42 Then shall I have a word for **those** who taunt me,*
because I trust **in** your words.

43 Do not take the word of truth out **of** my mouth,*
for *my hope is* ***in*** *your judgments.*

44 I shall continue to **keep** your law;*
I shall keep it for ev**er** and ever.

45 I will **walk** at liberty,*
because I study **your** commandments.

46 I will tell of your decrees **be**fore kings*
and will not **be** ashamed.

47 I delight in **your** commandments,*
which I have **al**ways loved.

48 I will lift up my hands to **your** commandments,*
and I will meditate **on** your statutes.

God of love, let your salvation come to us as you promised, that we may keep your law always and, taught by the Word of truth, find strength in his salvation; through Jesus Christ our Lord. [LH, PHP]

Tuesday Noon

Heth *Portio mea, Domine*

57 You only are my por**tion**, O LORD;*
I have promised to **keep** your words.

58 I entreat you with **all** my heart:*
be merciful to me according **to** your promise.

59 *I have consid**ered** my ways**
*and turned my feet toward **your** decrees.*

60 I hasten and **do** not tarry*
to keep **your** commandments.

61 Though the cords of the wicked en**tan**gle me,*
I do not for**get** your law.

62 At midnight I will rise to **give** you thanks,*
because of your **right**eous judgments.

63 I am a companion of **all** who fear you*
and of those who keep **your** commandments.

64 The earth, O LORD, is full **of** your love;*
instruct me **in** your statutes.

Lord, the earth is full of your love: Let the fulfillment of your law be our aim in life, so that you yourself may be our inheritance, and we your chosen portion for ever; through Jesus Christ our Lord. [LH, PHP]

Tuesday Mid-afternoon

Teth *Bonitatem fecisti*

65 O LORD, you have dealt graciously **with** your servant,*
according **to** your word.

66 Teach me discern**ment** and knowledge,*
for I have believed in **your** commandments.

67 Before I was afflicted I **went** astray,*
but now I **keep** your word.

68 You are good and you **bring** forth good;*
instruct me **in** your statutes.

69 The proud have smeared **me** with lies,*
but I will keep your commandments with **my** whole heart.

70 Their heart is **gross** and fat,*
but my delight is **in** your law.

71 It is good for me that I have **been** afflicted,*
that I might **learn** your statutes.

72 *The law of your mouth is deare**r** to me**
*than thousands in **gold** and silver.*

God of kindness and compassion, teach us goodness, discipline, and wisdom, that these gifts may keep us from becoming hardened by evil, weakened by laziness, or ignorant because of foolishness; through Jesus Christ our Lord. [LH, PHP]

Wednesday Noon

Lamedh *In æternum, Domine*

89 O LORD, your word is **e**verlasting;*
it stands firm **in** the heavens.

90 Your faithfulness remains from one generation **to** another;*
you established the earth, and **it** abides.

91 By your decree these continue **to** this day,*
for all things **are** your servants.

92 If my delight had not been **in** your law,*
I should have perished in **my** affliction.

93 *I will never forget **your** commandments,**
*because by them you **give** me life.*

94 I am yours; oh, that **you** would save me!*
for I study **your** commandments.

95 Though the wicked lie in wait for me **to** destroy me,*
I will apply my mind to **your** decrees.

96 I see that all things come **to** an end,*
but your commandment **has** no bounds.

Everlasting and ever-faithful God, your Word which stands firm for ever in heaven, dwells in your Church: Give lasting light to your temple by the abiding presence of Jesus Christ our Lord. [LH, PHP]

Wednesday Mid-afternoon

Mem *Quomodo dilexi!*

97 Oh, how I **love** your law!*
all the day long it is **in** my mind.

98 Your commandment has made me wiser **than** my enemies,*
and it is **al**ways with me.

99 I have more understanding than **all** my teachers,*
for your decrees **are** my study.

100 I am wiser **than** the elders,*
because I observe **your** commandments.

101 I restrain my feet from every **e**vil way,*
that I may **keep** your word.

102 I do not shrink **from** your judgments,*
because you your**self** have taught me.

103 *How sweet are your words **to** my taste!**
they are sweeter than honey **to** my mouth.

104 Through your commandments I gain **un**derstanding;*
therefore I hate every **ly**ing way.

Our God, source and center of our life, make us so love your law that we may ponder it continually in our hearts and bear fruit in works acceptable to you; through Jesus Christ our Lord. [LH, PHP]

Thursday Noon

Samekh *Iniquos odio habui*

113 I hate those who have a di**vi**ded heart,*
but your law **do** I love.

114 You are my ref**uge** and shield;*
my hope is **in** your word.

115 Away from **me**, you wicked!*
I will keep the commandments **of** my God.

116 *Sustain me according to your promise, that **I** may live,**
and let me not be disappointed **in** my hope.

117 Hold me up, and I **shall** be safe,*
and my delight shall be ever **in** your statutes.

118 You spurn all who stray **from** your statutes;*
their deceitfulness **is** in vain.

119 In your sight all the wicked of the earth **are** but dross;*
therefore I love **your** decrees.

120 My flesh trembles with **dread** of you;*
I am afraid **of** your judgments.

God, our refuge and our shield, help us and we shall be saved, for if you leave us we are doomed. Remain with us always so that the fullness of life may be ours in Jesus Christ our Lord. [LH, PHP]

Thursday Mid-afternoon

Ayin *Feci judicium*

121 I have done what is **just** and right;*
do not deliver me to **my** oppressors.

122 Be surety for your **ser**vant's good;*
let not the **proud** oppress me.

123 My eyes have failed from watching for **your** salvation*
and for your **right**eous promise.

124 Deal with your servant according to your **lov**ing-kindness,*
and teach **me** your statutes.

125 *I am your servant; grant me* ***un****derstanding,**
that I may know **your** decrees.

126 It is time for you to **act**, O LORD,*
for they have brok**en** your law.

127 Truly, I love **your** commandments*
more than gold and **pre**cious stones.

128 I hold all your commandments to be **right** for me;*
all paths of falsehood **I** abhor.

Lord God our defender, rise up to rescue us from our oppressors and give us your Holy Spirit that we may understand your decrees; through Jesus Christ our Lord. [PHP]

Friday Noon

Sadhe *Justus es, Domine*

137 You are righ**teous**, O LORD,*
and upright **are** your judgments.

138 You have issued **your** decrees*
with justice and in **per**fect faithfulness.

139 My indignation **has** consumed me,*
because my enemies for**get** your words.

140 Your word has been tested **to** the uttermost,*
and your servant **holds** it dear.

141 I am small and of lit**tle** account,*
yet I do not forget **your** commandments.

142 Your justice is an ever**lasting** justice*
and your law **is** the truth.

143 Trouble and distress have **come** upon me,*
yet your commandments are **my** delight.

144 *The righteousness of your decrees is* ***ev****erlasting;**
grant me understanding, that **I** may live.

Lord, our faithful God, you are just indeed and your commandments are eternal: Teach us to love you with all our hearts and to love our neighbor as ourselves; through Jesus Christ our Lord. [LH, PHP]

Friday Mid-afternoon

Qoph *Clamavi in toto corde meo*

145 I call with **my** whole heart;*
answer me, O LORD, that I may **keep** your statutes.

146 I call to you;
oh, that **you** would save me!*
I will keep **your** decrees.

147 Early in the morning I cry **out** to you,*
for *in your word* ***is*** *my trust.*

148 My eyes are open in **the** night watches,*
that I may meditate up**on** your promise.

149 Hear my voice, O LORD, according to your **lov**ing-kindness;*
according to your judgments, **give** me life.

150 They draw near who in malice **per**secute me;*
they are very far **from** your law.

151 You, O LORD, are **near** at hand,*
and all your command**ments** are true.

152 Long have I known from **your** decrees*
that you have established **them** for ever.

Ever-waking, ever-present God, save us by the power of your hand, for our enemies have ignored your words. By the fire of your Word consume our sins and by its brightness illumine our hearts; through Jesus Christ our Lord. [LH, PHP]

Saturday Noon

Shin *Principes persecuti sunt*

161 Rulers have persecuted me with**out** a cause,*
but my heart stands in awe **of** your word.

162 I am as glad because **of** your promise*
as one who **finds** great spoils.

163 As for lies, I hate **and** abhor them,*
but your law **is** my love.

164 Seven times a day **do** I praise you,*
because of your **right**eous judgments.

165 *Great peace have they who* ***love*** *your law;**
for them there is no **stum**bling block.

166 I have hoped for your salva**tion**, O LORD,*
and I have fulfilled **your** commandments.

167 I have kept **your** decrees*
and I have **loved** them deeply.

168 I have kept your commandments **and** decrees,*
for all my ways **are** before you.

God of our salvation, those who love your law have great peace and they never stumble: Grant that those who love you above all things may be undistrubed by thoughts of evil; through Jesus Christ our Lord.

[LH, PHP]

Saturday mid-afternoon

Taw *Appropinquet deprecatio*

169 Let my cry come before **you**, O LORD;*
give me understanding, according **to** your word.

170 Let my supplication **come** before you;*
deliver me, according **to** your promise.

171 My lips shall pour **forth** your praise,*
when you teach **me** your statutes.

172 My tongue shall sing **of** your promise,*
for all your command**ments** are righteous.

173 *Let your hand be ready to help me,**
for I have chosen ***your*** *commandments.*

174 I long for your salva**tion**, O LORD,*
and your law is **my** delight.

175 Let me live, and **I** will praise you,*
and let your **judg**ments help me.

176 I have gone astray like a sheep **that** is lost;*
search for your servant,
for I do not forget **your** commandments.

Good shepherd of your people, grant that we may never forget your commandments and always live to praise you, now and for ever.

[LH, PHP]

+

Noon

This hymn or another hymn such as Come, let us join our cheerful songs *(H82 374; LBW 254)* or Immortal Love, for ever full *(SBH 476, H40 360), may be sung or read.*

O God of truth, O Lord of might,
You order time and change aright,
And send the early morning ray
And light the glow of perfect day;

Extinguish now each sinful fire,
And banish every ill desire;
And while you keep the body whole,
Shed forth your peace upon the soul.

O Father, this we ask be done,
Through Jesus Christ, your only Son,
Who with the Holy Ghost and you
Shall live and reign all ages through.
Amen

[H82 21, 22]

[*Rector potens, verax Deus*, ascribed to St. Ambrose, trans. John Mason Neale]

Mid-afternoon

This hymn or another hymn such as O Master, let me walk with thee *(H82 374; LBW 254) or* Put thou thy trust in God *(SBH 579; CSB 399) may be sung or read.*

O God, creation's secret force,
Yourself unmoved, all motion's source,
Who from the morn till evening's ray
Through all its changes guide the day;

Grant us, when this short life is past,
The glorious evening that shall last;
That, by a holy death attained,
Eternal glory may be gained.

O Father, this we ask be done
Through Jesus Christ, your only Son,
Who with the Holy Ghost and you
Shall live and reign all ages through.
Amen

[H82 14]

[*Rerum Deus texax vigor*, ascribed to St. Ambrose, trans. John Mason Neale]

The verse from the appointed Second Reading for the day given in the Proper for Morning Prayer may be read as a brief Lesson.

L Holy God, holy and mighty, holy and immortal,

C Have mercy on us.

C Our Father in heaven,
hallowed be your Name,
your kingdom come,
your will be done,
on earth as in heaven.
Give us today our daily bread.
Forgive us our sins
as we forgive those
who sin against us.
Save us from the time of trial
and deliver us from evil.
For the kingdom, the power,
and the glory are yours,
now and for ever. Amen.

C Our Father who art in heaven,
hallowed be thy Name,
thy kingdom come,
thy will be done,
on earth as it is in heaven.
Give us this day our daily bread;
and forgive us our trespasses,
as we forgive those
who trespass against us;
and lead us not into temptation,
but deliver us from evil.
For thine is the kingdom,
and the power, and the glory,
for ever and ever. Amen.

The Creed may be said.

I believe in God, the Father almighty,
creator of heaven and earth.

I believe in Jesus Christ, his only Son, our Lord.
He was conceived by the power of the Holy Spirit
and born of the virgin Mary.
He suffered under Pontius Pilate,
was crucified, died, and was buried.
He descended to the dead [*or* He descended into hell].
On the third day he rose again.
He ascended into heaven,
and is seated at the right hand of the Father.
He will come again to judge the living and the dead.

I believe in the Holy Spirit,
the holy catholic Church,
the communion of saints,
the forgiveness of sins,
the resurrection of the body,
and the life everlasting. Amen

Noon

L Let your loving-kindness, O Lord, be upon us,
C As we have put our trust in you.
[Ps. 33:22]

L Remember your congregation, O God,
C Which you purchased and redeemed long ago.
[See Ps. 74:2]

Mid-afternoon

L In peace, let us pray to the Lord.
C Lord have mercy.

L For all the people in their daily life and work;
For our families friends, neighbors, and for those who

L Teach us, O Lord, the way of your statutes;
C Lead us in the path of your commandments.
[Ps. 119:33,35]

L Let your ways be known upon earth,
C Your saving health among all nations. [Ps. 67:2]

L Rule your people righteously
C And the poor with justice.
[Ps. 72:2]

L Pour out, O Lord, your Spirit upon all the people of the earth,
C That they may dwell in unity, peace, and concord.
[see Joel 2:28]

L Restore us, O God of hosts;
C Show us the light of your countenance, and we shall be saved. [Ps. 80:7]

are alone, let us pray to the Lord.
C Lord, have mercy.

L For this community, the nation, and the world; for all who work for justice, freedom, and peace, let us pray to the Lord.
C Lord have mercy.

L For the just and proper use of your creation; for the victims of hunger, fear, injustice, and oppression, let us pray to the Lord.
C Lord have mercy.

L For all who are in danger, sorrow, or any kind of trouble; for those who minister to the sick, the friendless, and the needy, let us pray to the Lord.
C Lord have mercy.

L For the peace and unity of the Church of God; for all who proclaim the Gospel, and all who seek the Truth, let us pray to the Lord.

C Lord have mercy.

L For our bishop(s); for all bishops and other ministers; for all who serve God in his Church, let us pray to the Lord.

C Lord have mercy.

L For the special needs and concerns of this congregation . . . [for those who have died . . .], let us pray to the Lord.

C Lord have mercy [BCP rev.]

The PRAYER OF THE DAY may be said. Additional prayers may be said. The prayers conclude

Noon

Gracious Jesus, our Lord and our God, at this hour you bore our sins in your own body on the tree so that we, being dead to sin, might live unto righteousness: Have mercy upon us now and at the hour of our death, and grant to us, your servants, with all others who devoutly remember your blessed Passion, a holy and peaceful life in

Mid-afternoon

Heavenly Father, in whom we live and move and have our being: We humbly pray you so to guide and govern us by your Holy Spirit, that in all the cares and occupations of our life we may not forget you, but remember that we are ever walking in your sight; through Jesus Christ our Lord. [*Chain*, BCP, LBW]

or

this world and, through your grace, eternal glory in the life to come; where with the Father and the Holy Spirit you live and reign, God for ever. [John Cosin, COB, LDP, LBW]

Lord Jesus Christ, at this hour on the cross you commended your spirit into the hands of the Father: Grant, we pray, that at the hour of our passing from this world, we too may commend ourselves to the Father, and be received into the Paradise of your everlasting kingdom; where, with the Father and the Holy Spirit, you live and reign, one God, now and for ever.
[medieval breviaries]

Before Travel

L Lord God our Father, you kept Abraham and Sarah in safety throughout the days of their pilgrimage, you led the children of Israel through the midst of the sea, and by a star you led the Wise Men to the infant Jesus. Protect and guide us now in this time as we set out to travel, make our ways safe and our homecomings joyful, and bring us at last to our heavenly home, where you dwell in glory with your Son and the Holy Spirit, God for ever. [Medieval Primers, LBW]

C Amen.

The BENEDICAMUS and BENEDICTION conclude the service.

L Let us bless the Lord.

C Thanks be to God.

L The Lord bless us ✠, defend us from all evil, and bring us to everlasting life.

C Amen.

Prayer at the Close of the Day

Compline. Night Prayer

The congregation assembles in silence.

Stand

L The Lord almighty grant us a qui - et night and peace at the last.

C A - men

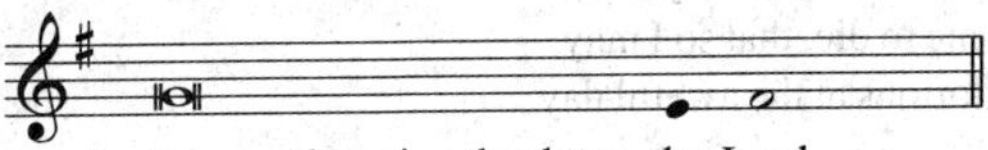

L It is good to give thanks to the Lord.

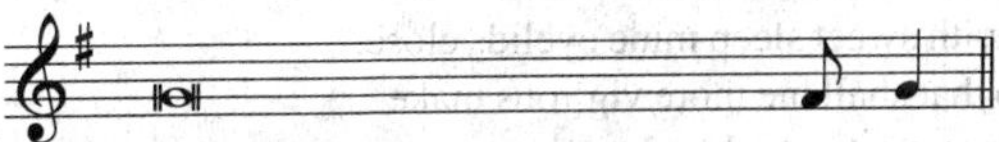

C To sing praise to your Name, O Most High:

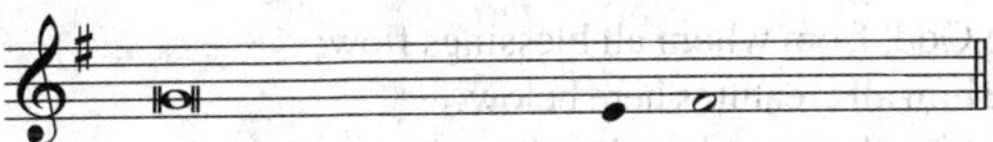

L To herald your love in the morning.

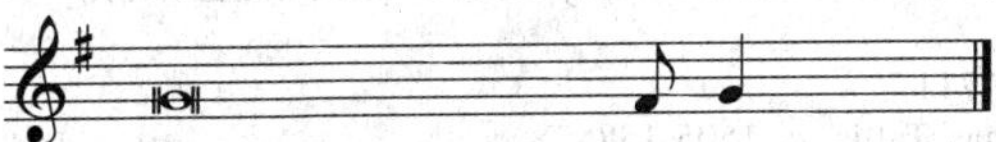

C Your truth at the close of the day.

[see Ps. 92:1-2]

One of these hymns, or another hymn appropriate for a night service, is sung.

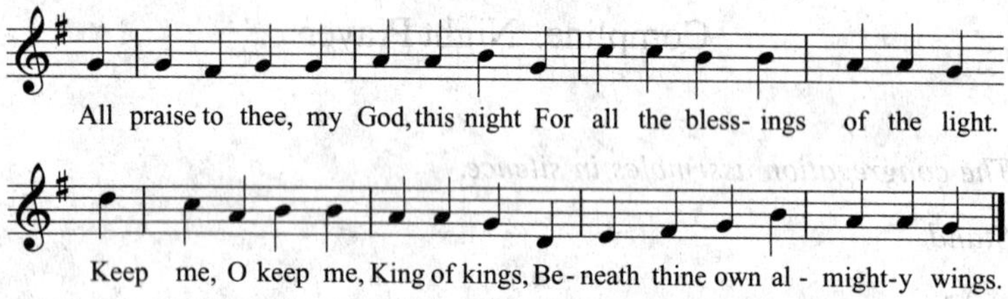

2 Forgive me, Lord, for thy dear Son,
The ill that I this day have done;
That with the world, myself, and thee,
I, ere I sleep, at peace may be.

3 Teach me to live, that I may dread
The grave as little as my bed.
Teach me to die, that so I may
Rise glorious at the aweful day.

4 Oh, may my soul in thee repose,
And with sweet sleep mine eyelids close,
Sleep that shall me more vig'rous make
To serve my God when I awake.

5 Praise God, from whom all blessings flow;
Praise him all creatures here below;
Praise him above, ye heav'nly host;
Praise Father, Son, and Holy Ghost [H82 43;LBW 278]

Text: Thomas Ken, 1637-1711
Tune: *Tallis' Canon*, Thomas Tallis, c. 1505-1585 LM

or

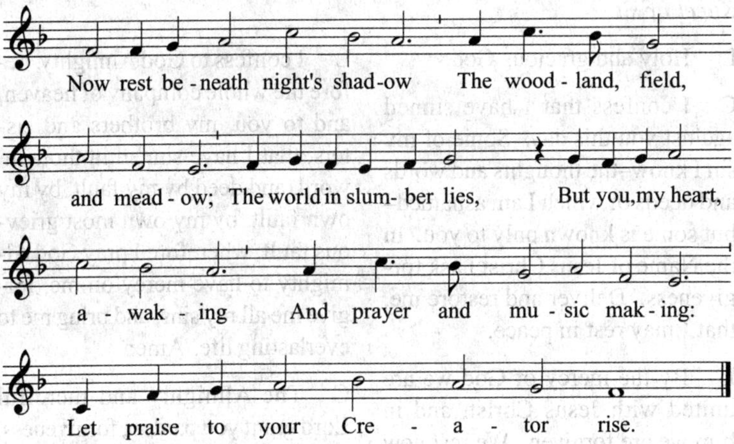

2 Lord, Jesus, since you love me,
Now spread your wings above me.
And shield me from alarm.
Though evil would assail me,
Your mercy will not fail me;
I rest in your protecting arm.

3 My loved ones, rest securely,
For God this night will surely
From peril guard your heads.
Sweet slumbers may he send you
And bid his hosts attend you
And through the night watch o'er your beds.

[CSB 469 LBW 282]

Text: Paul Gerhard, 1606-1676; st. 1 tr. Francis Elizabeth Cox, 1812-1897; sts. 2-3 tr. Catherine Winkworth, 1829-1878

Tune: *O Welt, Ich muss dich lassen*, Heinrich Isaac, ca. 1450-1517 776 778

Kneel or sit

L Holy and gracious God,

C I confess that I have sinned against you this day. Some of my sin I know–the thoughts and words and deeds of which I am ashamed–but some is known only to you. In the Name of Jesus Christ I ask forgiveness. Deliver and restore me, that I may rest in peace.

L By the mercy of God we are united with Jesus Christ, and in him we are forgiven. We rest now in his peace and rise in the morning to serve him.

L I confess to God Almighty, before the whole company of heaven, and to you, my brothers and sisters, that I have sinned in thought, word, and deed by my fault, by my own fault, by my own most grievous fault; wherefore I pray God Almighty to have mercy on me, forgive me all my sins, and bring me to everlasting life. Amen

C The Almighty and merciful Lord grant you pardon, forgiveness, and remission of all your sins.

L Amen

C I confess to God Almighty, before the whole company of heaven, and to you, my brothers and sisters, that I have sinned in thought, word, and deed by my fault, by my own fault, by my own most grievous fault; wherefore I pray God Almighty to have mercy on me, forgive me all my sins, and bring me to everlasting life. Amen.

L The almighty and merciful Lord grant you pardon, forgiveness, and remission of all your sins.

C Amen

Sit

The PSALMODY is sung or said. Silence for meditation follows each psalm. The psalm prayer is said following the silence.

Saturday

Antiphon to PSALM 4 *Cum invocarem*

Have mercy, Lord, and hear my prayer. [LH, PBO]

4 *Night prayer*

1 Answer me when I call, O God, defender **of** my cause;*
you set me free when I am hard-pressed;
have mercy on me and **hear** my prayer.

2 "You mortals, how long will you dishon**or** my glory;*
how long will you worship dumb idols
and run af**ter** false gods?"

3 Know that the LORD does wonders **for** the faithful;*
when I call upon the LORD, **he** will hear me.

4 Tremble, then, and **do** not sin;*
speak to your heart in silence up**on** your bed.

5 Offer the appointed **sa**crifices,*
and put your trust **in** the LORD.

6 Many are saying, "Oh, that we might see **bet**ter times!"*
Lift up the light of your countenance upon **us**, O LORD.

7 You have put gladness **in** my heart,*
more than when grain and wine and **oil** increase.

8 I lie down in peace; at once I **fall** asleep;*
for only you, LORD, make me **dwell** in safety.

Antiphon Have mercy, Lord, and hear my prayer.

Silence for meditation

Lord, you consoled your Son in his anguish and released him from the darkness of the grave: Turn your face toward us, that we may sleep in your peace and rise in your light; through your Son, Jesus Christ our Lord.
[LHd, LBW]

Antiphon to PSALM 134 *Ecce nunc*

In the silent hours of the night, bless the Lord. [LH]

134 *Evening prayer in the temple*

1 Behold now! Bless the LORD, all you servants **of** the LORD,*
you that stand by night in the house **of** the LORD.

2 Lift up your hands in the holy place and **bless** the LORD;*
the LORD who made heaven and earth bless you **out** of Zion.

Antiphon In the silent hours of the night, bless the Lord.

Silence for meditation

Lord, where two or three are gathered in your Name, you promised to be among them: Look down upon your family, lifting our hands in thanksgiving to you, and graciously pour out your blessing upon us; through Jesus Christ our Lord.
[LHd, PHP]

Sunday

Antiphon to PSALM 136 *Confitemini*

Great and wonderful **are** your deeds,*
Lord God **the** Almighty! [Rev. 15:3, LH, PBO]

136 *Litany of thanksgiving*

1 Give thanks to the LORD, for **he** is good,*
for his mercy en**dures** for ever.

2 Give thanks to the **God** of gods,*
for his mercy en**dures** for ever.

3 Give thanks to the **Lord** of lords,*
for his mercy en**dures** for ever;

4 Who only **does** great wonders,*
for his mercy en**dures** for ever;

5 Who by wisdom **made** the heavens,*
for his mercy en**dures** for ever;

6 Who spread out the earth up**on** the waters,*
for his mercy en**dures** for ever;

7 Who creat**ed** great lights,*
for his mercy en**dures** for ever;

8 The sun to **rule** the day,*
for his mercy en**dures** for ever;

9 The moon and the stars to gov**ern** the night,*
for his mercy en**dures** for ever;

10 Who struck down the first**born** of Egypt,*
for his mercy en**dures** for ever;

11 And brought out Israel **from** among them,*
for his mercy en**dures** for ever;

12 With a mighty hand and a **stretched**-out arm,*
for his mercy en**dures** for ever;

13 Who divided the Red **Sea** in two,*
for his mercy en**dures** for ever;

14 And made Israel to pass **through** the midst of it,*
for his mercy en**dures** for ever;

15 But swept Pharaoh and his army in**to** the Red Sea,*
for his mercy en**dures** for ever;

16 Who led his people **through** the wilderness,*
for his mercy en**dures** for ever;

17 Who struck **down** great kings,*
for his mercy en**dures** for ever;

18 And slew **migh**ty kings,*
for his mercy en**dures** for ever;

19 Sihon, king **of** the Amorites,*
for his mercy en**dures** for ever;

20 And Og, the **king** of Bashan,*
for his mercy en**dures** for ever;

21 And gave away their lands for **an** inheritance,*
for his mercy en**dures** for ever;

22 An inheritance for Isra**el** his servant,*
for his mercy en**dures** for ever;

23 Who remembered us in our **low** estate,*
for his mercy en**dures** for ever;

24 And delivered us **from** our enemies,*
for his mercy en**dures** for ever;

25 Who gives food **to** all creatures,*
for his mercy en**dures** for ever.

26 Give thanks to the **God** of heaven,*
for his mercy en**dures** for ever.

Antiphon Great and wonderful **are** your deeds,*
Lord God **the** Almighty!

Silence for meditation

God of everlasting love, through your Word you made all things in heaven and on earth; you have opened to us the path from death to life. Listen to the song of the universe, the hymn of resurrection, sung by your Church, and give us your blessing; through Jesus Christ our Lord.
[LHd, LBW]

Monday

Antiphon to PSALM 91 *Qui habitat*

Night holds no terrors for me sleeping under God's wings. [LH,]

91 *God's sheltering care*

1 He who dwells in the shelter of **the** Most High,*
abides under the shadow of **the** Almighty.

2 He shall say to the LORD,
"You are my refuge **and** my stronghold,*
my God in whom I **put** my trust."

3 He shall deliver you from the snare **of** the hunter*
and from the **dead**ly pestilence.

4 He shall cover you with his pinions,
and you shall find refuge un**der** his wings;*
his faithfulness shall be a **shield** and buckler.

5 You shall not be afraid of any ter**ror** by night,*
nor of the arrow that **flies** by day;

6 Of the plague that stalks **in** the darkness,*
nor of the sickness that lays **waste** at midday.

7 A thousand shall fall at your side
and ten thousand at **your** right hand,*
but it shall **not** come near you.

8 Your eyes have only **to** behold*
to see the reward **of** the wicked.

9 Because you have made the **LORD** your refuge,*
and the Most High your **hab**itation,

10 There shall no evil hap**pen** to you,*
neither shall any plague come **near** your dwelling.

11 For he shall give his angels charge **o**ver you,*
to keep you in **all** your ways.

12 They shall bear you **in** their hands,*
lest you dash your foot a**gainst** a stone.

13 You shall tread upon the li**on** and adder;*
you shall trample the young lion and the serpent **un**der your feet.

14 Because he is bound to me in love,
therefore will I de**li**ver him;*
I will protect him, because he **knows** my Name.

15 He shall call upon me, and I will **an**swer him;*
I am with him in trouble;
I will rescue him and bring **him** to honor.

16 With long life will I **sat**isfy him,*
and show him **my** salvation.

Antiphon Night holds no terrors for me sleeping under God's care.

Silence for meditation

Lord Jesus Christ, when tempted by the devil, you remained true to your Father, who commanded his angels to watch over you. Guard your Church from the plague of sin, so that we may remain faithful to you until the day when we enjoy the fullness of your salvation; for you live and reign with the Father and the Holy Spirit, now and for ever. [LHd, LBW]

Tuesday

Antiphon to PSALM 33 *Exultate, justi*

The loyal heart must praise the Lord. [LH]

33 *God's continual care*

1 Rejoice in the **LORD**, you righteous;*
it is good for the just **to** sing praises.

2 Praise the LORD **with** the harp;*
play to him upon the psaltery and lyre.

3 Sing for him **a** new song;*
sound a fanfare with all your skill up**on** the trumpet.

4 For the word of the **LORD** is right,*
and all his **works** are sure.

5 He loves righteous**ness** and justice;*
the lovingkindness of the LORD fills **the** whole earth.

6 By the word of the LORD were the **hea**vens made,*
by the breath of his mouth all the heav**en**ly hosts.

7 He gathers up the waters of the ocean as **in** a water-skin*
and stores up the depths **of** the sea.

8 Let all the earth **fear** the LORD;*
let all who dwell in the world stand in **awe** of him.

9 For he spoke, and it **came** to pass;*
he commanded, and **it** stood fast.

10 The LORD brings the will of the na**tions** to naught;*
he thwarts the designs **of** the peoples.

11 But the LORD's will stands **fast** for ever,*
and the designs of his heart from **age** to age.

12 Happy is the nation whose God **is** the LORD!*
happy the people he has chosen to **be** his own!

13 The LORD looks **down** from heaven,*
and beholds all the people **in** the world.

14 From where he sits enthroned he **turns** his gaze*
on all who dwell **on** the earth.

15 He fashions all the **hearts** of them*
and understands **all** their works.

16 There is no king that can be saved by a **mighty** army;*
a strong man is not delivered by **his** great strength.

17 The horse is a vain hope **for** deliverance;*
for all its strength it **can**not save.

18 Behold, the eye of the LORD is upon **those** who fear him,*
on those who wait up**on** his love,

19 To pluck their **lives** from death,*
and to feed them in **time** of famine.

20 Our soul waits **for** the LORD;*
he is our help **and** our shield.

21 Indeed, our heart rejoic**es** in him,*
for in his holy Name we **put** our trust.

22 Let your lovingkindness, O LORD, **be** upon us,*
as we have put our **trust** in you.

Silence for meditation

Lord God, through your Son you made the heavens and earth; through him you continue to accomplish the intentions of your heart. Make your chosen people witnesses of your truth among the nations and heralds of your glory in the heavens; for the sake of your Son, Jesus Christ our Lord. [LHd, LBW]

Wednesday

Antiphon to PSALM 31 *In te, Domine, speravi*

Incline your **ear** to me;*
make haste to de**liv**er me. [LH]

31 *Confident prayer in distress*

1 In you, O LORD, have I taken refuge;
let me never be **put** to shame;*
deliver me **in** your righteousness.

2 Incline your **ear** to me;*
make haste to de**liv**er me.

3 Be my strong rock, a castle to keep me safe,
for you are my crag **and** my stronghold;*
for the sake of your Name, lead **me** and guide me.

4 Take me out of the net that they have secretly **set** for me,*
for you are my tow**er** of strength.

5 Into your hands I com**mend** my spirit,*
for you have redeemed me,
O LORD, O **God** of truth.

6 I hate those who cling to **worth**less idols,*
and I put my trust **in** the LORD.

7 I will rejoice and be glad because **of** your mercy;*
for you have seen my affliction;
you know **my** distress.

8 You have not shut me up in the power **of** the enemy;*
you have set my feet in an **o**pen place.

9 Have mercy on me, O LORD, for I **am** in trouble;*
my eye is consumed with sorrow,
and also my throat **and** my belly.

10 For my life is wasted with grief,
and my **years** with sighing;*
my strength fails me because of affliction,
and my bones **are** consumed.

11 I have become a reproach to all my enemies and even to my neighbors,
a dismay to those of **my** acquaintance;*
when they see me in the street **they** avoid me.

12 I am forgotten like a dead man, **out** of mind;*
I am as useless as a **bro**ken pot.

13 For I have heard the whispering of the crowd;
fear is **all** around;*
they put their heads together against me;
they plot to **take** my life.

14 But as for me, I have trusted in **you**, O LORD.*
I have said, "You **are** my God.

15 My times are **in** your hand;*
rescue me from the hand of my enemies,
and from those who **per**secute me.

16 Make your face to shine up**on** your servant,*
and in your loving-**kind**ness save me."

17 LORD, let me not be ashamed for having **called** upon you;*
rather, let the wicked be put to shame;
let them be silent **in** the grave.

18 Let the lying lips be silenced which speak **against** the righteous,*
haughtily, disdainfully, and **with** contempt.

19 How great is your goodness, O LORD,
which you have laid up for **those** who fear you;*
which you have done in the sight of all
for those who put their **trust** in you.

20 You hide them in the covert of your presence from those who **slan**der them;*
you keep them in your shelter from the **strife** of tongues.

21 Blessed **be** the LORD!*
for he has shown me the wonders of his love in a **be**sieged city.

22 Yet I said in my alarm,
"I have been cut off from the sight **of** your eyes."*
Nevertheless, you heard the sound of my entreaty when I cried **out** to you.

23 Love the LORD, all you who **wor**ship him;*
the LORD protects the faithful,

but repays to the full those **who** act haughtily.

24 Be strong and let your **heart** take courage,*
all you who wait **for** the LORD.

Antiphon Incline your **ear** to me;*
make haste to de**li**ver me.

Silence for meditation

God of kindness and truth, you saved your chosen one, Jesus Christ, and you give your martyrs strength: Watch over your people who come to you now, and strengthen the hearts of those who hope in you, that they may proclaim your saving acts of kindness in the eternal city; through your Son, Jesus Christ our Lord. [LH, LBW]

Thursday

Antiphon to PSALM 34 *Benedicam Dominum*

Those who seek the LORD lack nothing that is good. [LH]

34 *In praise of God's justice*

1 I will bless the LORD **at** all times;*
his praise shall ever be **in** my mouth.

2 I will glory **in** the LORD;*
let the humble hear **and** rejoice.

3 Proclaim with me the greatness **of** the LORD;*
let us exalt his **Name** together.

4 I sought the Lord, and he **an**swered me*
and delivered me out of **all** my terror.

5 Look upon him **and** be radiant,*
and let not your faces **be** ashamed.

6 I called in my affliction, and **the** LORD heard me*
and saved me from **all** my troubles.

7 The angel of the LORD encompasses **those** who fear him,*
and he will de**liv**er them.

8 Taste and see that the **LORD** is good;*
happy are they who **trust** in him!

9 Fear the LORD, you that **are** his saints,*
for those who fear **him** lack nothing.

10 The young lions lack and **suf**fer hunger,*
but those who seek the LORD lack nothing **that** is good.

11 Come, children, and lis**ten** to me;*
I will teach you the fear **of** the LORD.

12 Who among **you** loves life*
and desires long life to en**joy** prosperity?

13 Keep your tongue from **e**vil-speaking*
and your lips from **ly**ing words.

14 Turn from evil **and** do good;*
seek peace **and** pursue it.

15 The eyes of the LORD are up**on** the righteous,*
and his ears are open **to** their cry.

16 The face of the LORD is against those **who** do evil,*
to root out the remembrance of them **from** the earth.

17 The righteous cry, and **the** LORD hears them*
and delivers them from **all** their troubles.

18 The LORD is near to the **bro**kenhearted*
and will save those whose spir**its** are crushed.

19 Many are the troubles **of** the righteous,*
but the LORD will deliver him out **of** them all.

20 He will keep safe **all** his bones;*
not one of them **shall** be broken.

21 Evil shall **slay** the wicked,*
and those who hate the righteous **will** be punished.

22 The LORD ransoms the life **of** his servants,*
and none will be punished who **trust** in him.

Antiphon Those who seek the LORD lack nothing that is good.

Silence for meditation

Lord, graciously hear us, for we seek you alone. Calm our bodies and minds with the peace which passes understanding, and make us radiant with joy; through your Son, Jesus Christ our Lord. [LH, LBW]

Friday

Antiphon to PSALM 86 *Inclina, Domine*

Gladden the soul **of** your servant,*
for to you, O LORD, I lift **up** my soul.

86 *Prayer in ordeal*

1 Bow down your ear, O LORD, and **an**swer me,*
for I am poor **and** in misery.

2 Keep watch over my life, for **I** am faithful;*
save your servant who puts his **trust** in you.

3 Be merciful to me, O LORD, for you **are** my God;*
I call upon you all **the** day long.

4 Gladden the soul **of** your servant,*
for to you, O LORD, I lift **up** my soul.

5 For you, O LORD, are good **and** forgiving,*
and great is your love toward all who **call** upon you.

6 Give ear, O LORD, **to** my prayer,*
and attend to the voice of my **sup**plications.

7 In the time of my trouble I will **call** upon you,*
for you will **an**swer me.

8 Among the gods there is none like **you**, O LORD,*
nor anything **like** your works.

9 All the nations you have made will come and worship **you**, O LORD,*
and glori**fy** your Name.

10 For you are great;
you do **won**drous things;*
and you a**lone** are God.

11 Teach me your way, O LORD,
and I will walk **in** your truth;*
knit my heart to you that I may **fear** your Name.

12 I will thank you, O LORD my God, with **all** my heart,*
and glorify your Name for **ev**ermore.

13 For great is your **love** toward me;*
you have delivered me from the neth**er**most Pit.

14 The arrogant rise up against me, O God,
and a band of violent men **seeks** my life;*
they have not set you be**fore** their eyes.

15 But you, O LORD, are gracious and full **of** compassion,*
slow to anger, and full of kind**ness** and truth.

16 Turn to me and have mer**cy** upon me;*
give your strength to your servant;
and save the child **of** your handmaid.

17 Show me a sign of your favor,
so that those who hate me may see it and **be** ashamed;*
because you, O LORD, have helped me and com**fort**ed me.

Antiphon Gladden the soul **of** your servant,*
for to you, O LORD, I lift **up** my soul.

Silence for meditation

God of mercy, when Christ called out to you in torment, you heard him and gave him victory over death. Fill us with the love of your Name and help us to proclaim you before the world, that all peoples may celebrate your glory in Jesus Christ our Lord. [LH, LBW]

+

A BRIEF LESSON is read.

on Saturday

I am convinced that neither death, nor life, nor angels, nor rulers, nor things present, nor things to come, nor powers, nor height, nor depth, nor anything else in all creation, will be able to separate us from the love of God in Christ Jesus our Lord. [Romans 8:38-39, LBW]

on Sunday

The servants of the Lamb will worship him; they will see his face, and his name will be on their foreheads. And there will be no more night; they will need no light of lamp or sun, for the Lord God will be their light, and they will reign for ever and ever. [Revelation 22:3c-5, LH]

on Monday

God has not destined us for wrath, but for obtaining salvation through our Lord Jesus Christ, who died for us, so that whether we are awake or asleep we may live with him. [1 Thessalonians 5:9-10, LH]

on Tuesday

[Humble yourselves under the mighty hand of God, so that he may exalt you in due time. Cast all your anxiety on him, because he cares for you.] Discipline yourselves, keep alert. Like a roaring lion your adversary the devil prowls around, looking for someone to devour. Resist him, steadfast in your faith. [1 Peter 5:6-9a, LH, BCP, LBW]

on Wednesday

Come to me, all you that are weary and are carrying heavy burdens, and I will give you rest. Take my yoke upon you, and learn from me; for I am gentile and humble in heart, and you will find rest for your souls. For my yoke is easy, and my burden is light. [Matthew 11:28-30, BCP, LBW]

on Thursday

Peace I leave with you; my peace I give to you. I do not give to you as the world gives. Do not let your hearts be troubled, and do not let them be afraid. [John 14:27, LBW]

on Friday

You, O LORD, are in the midst of us, and we are called by your name; do not forsake us, O LORD our God. [Jeremiah 14: 9, 22; LH, BCP, LBW]

The RESPONSORY follows the reading.

[PS. 31:5; LH, LBW]

Stand

THE HYMN is sung.

Te lucis ante terminum

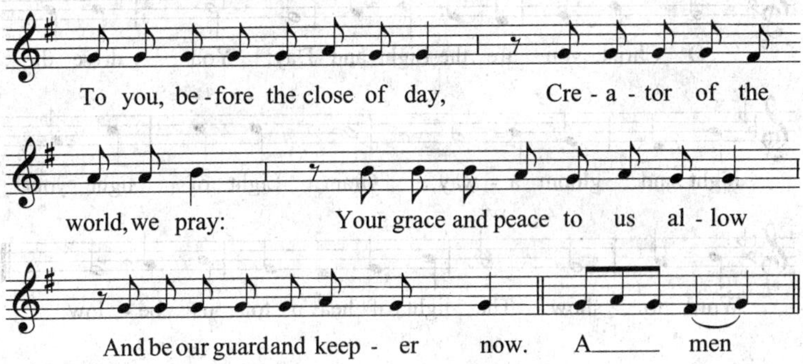

2 From evil dreams defend our sight,
From all the terrors of the night,
From all deluding thoughts that creep
On heedless minds disarmed by sleep.

3 O Father, this we ask be done
Through Jesus Christ our only Son,
Who with the Holy Ghost and you
Shall live and reign all ages through. Amen.

[LBW 277; H82 44]

Text: compline office hymn, c. 8th cent.; tr. John Mason Neale, 1818-1866, adapt.
Tune: *Jam lucis*, Benedictine plainsong, mode VI LM

or

Christe, qui lux es et dies

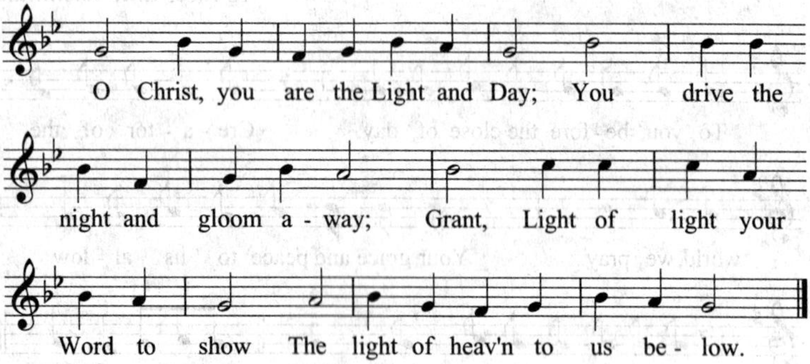

2 All-holy Lord, in humble prayer
We ask tonight your watchful care.
And pray that our repose may be
A quiet night, from perils free.

3 And while our eyes soft slumber take
Still be our heart to you awake;
Be your right hand outstretched above
Your servants resting in your love.

4 Arise, O God, our shield, repel
The crafts and subtleties of hell;
Direct your servants in all good.
Whom you have purchased with your blood.

5 O Lord, remember us who bear
The burden of the flesh we wear;
And with your strength our souls defend.
Be present with us to the end.

6 To God the Father and the Son
And Holy Spirit, three in one,
Be glory in the highest given
By all on earth and all in heaven.

[The English Hymnal 81; H82 40; LBW 273]

Text: Latin Hymn, 6th cent. Sts. 1-5 tr. William J. Copeland, 1804-1884, alt. *The English Hymnal*, PHP; st. 6 Isaac Watts, 1664-1748
Tune: *Christie, der du bist Tag und Licht*, J. Klug, *Geistliche Lieder*, 1533.

Kneel or stand

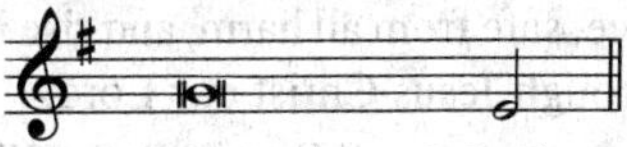

L Hear my prayer, O Lord;

C Listen to my cry.

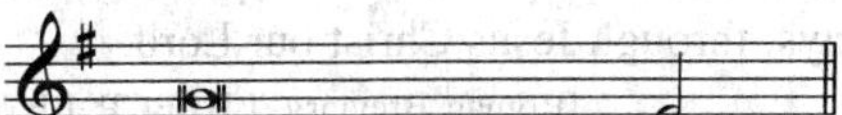

L Keep me as the apple of your eye;

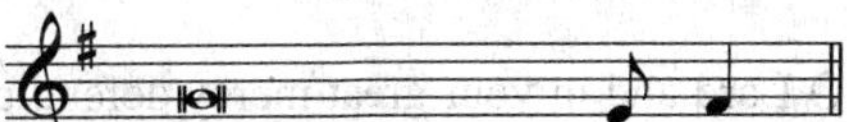

C Hide me in the shadow of your wings,

L In righteousness I shall see you;

C When I awake, your presence will give me joy.

[Ps. 71:1, 8, 16]

One of the following prayers is sung or said.

On Saturday

Be with us, Lord, through this night, so that rising in your strength at daybreak, we may rejoice in the resurrection of your Christ; who lives and reigns with you and the Holy Spirit, one God, now and for ever.

[LH trans. PHP]

On Sunday

Lord, we humbly pray that we who have this day celebrated the mystery of the Lord's resurrection may rest in peace, safe from all harm, and rise in the morning rejoicing in your praise; through Jesus Christ our Lord.

[LH trans. DvD, PHP]

On Monday

Visit our dwellings, O Lord, and drive from them all the snares of the enemy; let your holy angels dwell with us to preserve us in peace; and let your blessing be upon us always; through Jesus Christ our Lord.

[Roman Breviary, LH, BCP, LBW]

On Tuesday

Be our light in the darkness, O Lord and in your great mercy defend us from all perils and dangers of this night; for the love of your only Son, our Savior Jesus Christ [2 Sam. 22:29; Gel., Greg., Sarum, LH, BCP, CSB, SBH, LBW]

On Wednesday

Look down, O Lord, from your heavenly throne and illumine this night with your celestial brightness, and from the children of light banish the deeds of darkness, that by night as by day your people may glorify your holy Name; through Jesus Christ our Lord. [Ambrosian Breviary, DvD, BCP]

On Thursday

Be present, O merciful God, and protect us through the hours of this night, so that we who are wearied by the changes and chances of this life may rest in your eternal changelessness; through Jesus Christ our Lord.

[Leo., Greg., AC, BCP, LBW]

On Friday

O Lord, support us all the day long of this troublous life, until the shadows lengthen, and the busy world is hushed, the fever of life is over, and our work done. Then, O Lord, in your mercy, grant us safe lodging, a holy rest, and peace at the last; through Jesus Christ our Lord.

[John Henry Newman, BCP, LBW]

One of the following prayers may be added.

Keep watch, dear Lord, with those who wake or watch or weep this night, and give your angels charge over those who sleep. Tend the sick, Lord Christ; give rest to the weary, bless the dying, soothe the suffering, pity the afflicted, shield the joyous; and all for your love's sake.

[St. Augustine, *Chain*, PP, SBH, BCP, LBW]

or

Watch over us, O Lord, our heavenly Father; preserve us from all evil, and grant that we may this night rest secure beneath your care; bless your Church and our government; remember the sick and those who are in need or peril; have mercy on all your people; and when our last evening shall come, grant that we may fall asleep in your peace and awake in your glory; through Jesus Christ our Lord. [Church of Sweden, 1614; SBH]

or

Abide with us, O Lord, for it is toward evening and the day is far spent; abide with us and with your whole Church. Abide with us in the evening of the day, in the evening of life, in the evening of the world. Abide with us in your grace and mercy, in your holy Word and Sacrament, in your comfort and your blessing. Abide with us when we are overtaken by the night of disress and fear, by the night of doubt and temptation, by the night of bitter death. Abide with us and with all your faithful ones, O Lord, in time and in eternity; for the sake of Jesus Christ our Lord.

[Wilhelm Lohe; *The Church in Germany at Prayer*; F.B. Macnutt, *The Prayer Manual* (1951); *Venite Adoremus* (1951); *For all the Saints III*]

L Lord, remember us in your kingdom, and teach us to pray:

C Our Father in heaven,
hallowed be your Name
your kingdom come,
your will be done,
on earth as in heaven.
Give us today our daily bread.
Forgive us our sins
as we forgive those
who sin against us.
Save us from the time of trial
and deliver us from evil.
For the kingdom, the power,
and the glory are yours,
now and for ever. Amen.

C Our Father who art in heaven,
hallowed be thy Name
thy kingdom come,
thy will be done,
on earth as it is in heaven.
Give us this day our daily bread;
and forgive us our trespasses,
as we forgive those
who sin against us;
And lead us not into temptation
but deliver us from evil.
For thine is the kingdom,
and the power, and the glory,
for ever and ever. Amen.

Stand

The GOSPEL CANTICLE, Nunc Dimittis, *is sung or said.*

peo - ple Is - ra - el. Glo - ry to the Fa - ther, and
to the Son, and to the Ho - ly Spir - it as it
was in the be - gin - ning, is now, and will be for - ev - er. A - men.
Guide us wak - ing, O Lord, and guard us
sleep - ing; that a - wake we may watch with Christ
and a - sleep we may rest in peace.

The BENEDICTION concludes the service.

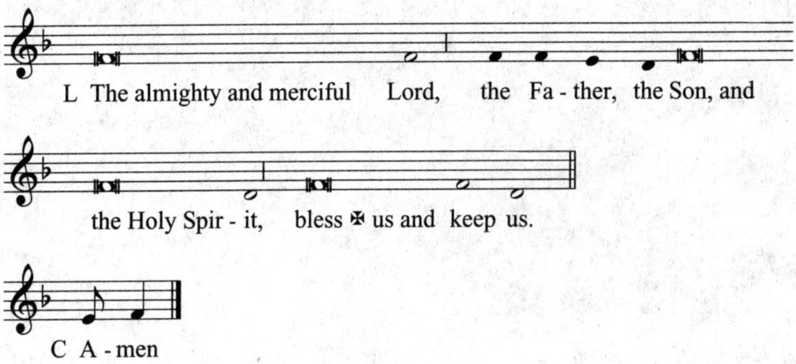

Collects (Prayers of the Day)
for
the Lesser Festivals and Commemorations

November 30 ST. ANDREW, Apostle

Almighty God, who gave such grace to your apostle Andrew that he readily obeyed the call of your Son Jesus Christ, and brought his brother with him: Give us, who are called by your Holy Word, grace to follow him without delay, and to bring those near to us into his gracious presence; who lives and reigns with you and the Holy Spirit, one God, now and for ever. [BCP (1552)]

December 1 *Nicholas Ferrar, deacon.* Common of Saints (3), p. XXXX

December 2 [*Channing Moore Williams, missionary bishop in China and Japan.* Common of Missionaries (1), p XXXX]

December 3 Francis Xavier, missionary to India and Asia. Missionaries (2),

December 4 John of Damascus, priest. Saints (1)

December 5 *Clement of Alexandria, priest.* Saints (2)

December 6 Nicholas, bishop of Myra. Pastors and Bishops (2) *or*

Almighty God, in your love you gave your servant Nicholas of Myra a perpetual name for deeds of kindness both on land and sea: Grant, we pray, that your Church may never cease to work for the happiness of children. the relief of the poor, and the protection of those tossed by tempests of doubt or grief; through Jesus Christ our Lord, who lives and reigns with you and the Holy Spirit, one God, now and for ever.

[LFF]

December 7 Ambrose, bishop of Milan. Pastors and Bishops (1)

December 11 [*Lars Olsen Skrefsrud, missionary to India.* Missionaries (1)]

December 13 *Lucy [Lucia].* Martyrs (2)

December 14 John of the Cross and Teresa of Avila. Renewers of the Church (2)

The prayers for St. Thomas' Day is given with Morning Prayer for Advent, p. XXXX; the prayers for St. Stephen, St. John the Holy Innocents, and the Holy Name of Jesus are given with Morning Prayer for Christmas, pp. XX-XXXX.

December 23 *Thorlak of Skalholt.* Renewers of the Church (2)

December 29 *Thomas Becket.* Martyrs (3)

January 2 *Wilhelm Löhe,pastor.* Renewers of the Church (1)

January 3 [*Charles Porterfield Krauth, teacher.* Theologians and Teachers (2)]

January 5 Kaj Munk. Martyrs (2)

January 6 THE EPIPHANY. Prayer given on page XXXIX

January 9 [*Julia Chester Emery.* Saints (3)]

January 10 [*William Laud, archbishop of Canterbury.* Pastors and Bishops (2)]

January 12 *Aelred, Abbot of Rievaulx.* Monastics

January 13 Hilary, bishop of Poitiers. Pastors and Bishops (1)

January 14 *Eivind Berggrav, bishop of Oslo.* Pastors and Bishops (1)

January 16 George Fox. Renewer of Society (2)

January 17 Antony, Abbot in Egypt. Monastics

January 18 THE CONFESSION OF ST. PETER.
The Week of Prayer for Christian Unity begins.

Almighty Father, who inspired Simon Peter, first among the apostles, to confess Jesus as Messiah and Son of the living God: Keep your Church steadfast upon the rock of this faith, so that in unity and peace we may proclaim the one truth and follow the one Lord, our Savior Jesus Christ, who lives and reigns with you and the Holy Spirit, one God, now and for ever. [BCP (1979), LBW]

During the Week of Prayer for Christian Unity (January 18-25):

Almighty Father, whose blessed Son before his passion prayed for his disciples that they might be one, as you and he are one: Grant that your Church, being bound together in love and obedience to you, may be united in one body by the one Spirit, that the world may believe in him whom you have sent, your Son, Jesus Christ our Lord, who lives and reigns with you and the Holy Spirit, one God, now and for ever.

[William Temple, PP, rev. BCP]

January 19 Henry, missionary to Finland. Missionaries (2)
Wulfstan, bishop of Worcester, Pastors and Bishops (1)

January 20 Fabian. Martyrs (1)

January 21 Agnes. Martyrs (2)

January 22 Vincent. Martyrs (1)

January 23 *Phillips Brooks.* Pastors and bishops (2)

January 24 Francis de Sales, Bishop of Geneva, 1622. Pastors and Bishops (1)
[*Ordination of Florence Li Tim-Oi.* Saints(2)]

January 25 THE CONVERSION OF ST. PAUL.
The Week of Prayer for Christian Unity ends

O God, by the preaching of your apostle Paul you have caused the light of the Gospel to shine throughout the world: Grant, we pray, that we, having his wonderful conversion in remembrance, may show ourselves thankful to you by following his holy teaching; through your Son Jesus Christ our Lord, who lives and reigns with you and the Holy Spirit, one God, now and for ever.

[Greg., RS, BCP, LBW]

January 26 Timothy, Titus, and Silas. Missionaries (2)

January 27 Lydia, Dorcas, and Phoebe. Saints (2)

January 28 Thomas Aquinas. Theologians and Teachers (1)

February 1 *Brigid [Bride].* Saints (2)

February 2 THE PRESENTATION OF OUR LORD

Almighty and everliving God, we humbly pray that, as your only-begotten Son was this day presented in the temple, so we may be presented to you with pure and clean hearts by Jesus Christ our Lord; who lives and reigns with you and the Holy Spirit, one God, now and for ever. [Greg., RS, BCP, CB, CSB, SBH]

February 3 Ansgar, missionary to Denmark and Sweden. Missionaries (1)

February 4 *Cornelius the Centurion.* Saints (3)

February 5 The Martyrs of Japan. Martyrs (1)

February 6 [*Philipp Jacob Spener.* Renewers of the Church (2)]

February 13 [*Absalom Jones.* Saints (2)]

February 14 Cyril and Methodius, Missionaries to the Slavs. Missionaries (1)

February 15 [*Thomas Bray.* Missionaries (2)]

February 17 [*Janani Luwum*, Martyrs (1)]

February 18 Martin Luther. Prayer at June 25, the Presentation of the Augsburg Confession

February 20 [*Rasmus Jensen.* Pastors and Bishops (2)]

February 23 Polycarp. Martyrs (3)

February 24 ST. MATTHIAS, Apostle

Almighty God, who in the place of Judas chose your faithful servant Matthias to be numbered among the Twelve: Grant that your Church, being delivered from false apostles, may always be guided by faithful and true pastors; through your Son Jesus Christ our Lord, who lives and reigns with you and the Holy Spirit, one God, now and for ever.

[BCP (1549)]

February 25 [*Elizabeth Fedde.* Renewers of society (2)]

February 26 [*Bartholmäus Ziegenbalg, missionary to India.* Missionaries (2)]

March 1 *David, bishop of Menevia.* Pastors and Bishops (1)
George Herbert. Pastors and Bishops (1)

March 2 *Chad, bishop of Lichfield.* Pastors and Bishops (1)
John and Charles Wesley. Renewers of the Church (2)

March 7 Perpetua and her companions. Martyrs (1)

March 12 Gregory the Great. Pastors and Bishops (1)

March 17 Patrick. bishop, missionary to Ireland. Missionaries (1)

March 18 Cyril of Jerusalem. Pastors and Bishops (2)

March 19 ST. JOSEPH

O God, who from the family of your servant David raised up Joseph to be the guardian of your incarnate Son and the spouse of his virgin mother: Give us grace to imitate the uprightness of his life and his obedience to your commands; through your Son, Jesus Christ our Lord, who lives and reigns with you and the Holy Spirit, one God, now and for ever. [BCP (1979)]

March 20 *Cuthbert, bishop of Lindisfarne.* Pastors and Bishops (2)

March 21 *Thomas Ken, bishop of Bath and Wells.* Pastors and Bishops (1)

March 22 Jonathan Edwards. Theologians and Teachers (2)
[*James De Koven.* Renewers of the Church (1)]

March 23 Gregory the Illuminator, bishop and Missionary of Armenia. Missionaries (2)

March 24 Oscar Arnulfo Romero. Martyrs (1)

March 25 THE ANNUNCIATION OF OUR LORD

Pour your grace into our hearts, O Lord, that we who have known the incarnation of your Son Jesus Christ, announced by an angel to the Virgin Mary, may by his cross and passion be brought to the glory of his resurrection; who lives and reigns with you and the Holy Spirit, one God, now and for ever.

[Greg., BCP, LBW; RS 4 Advent]

March 27	[*Charles Henry Brent, bishop.* Renewers of the Church (1)]
March 29	*John Keble, priest.* Renewers of the Church (2) [*Hans Nielsen Hauge.* Renewers of the Church (2)]
March 31	John Donne, priest. Saints (2)
April 1	*Amalie Sieveking.* Renewers of Society (1) *Frederick Denison Maurice.* Renewers of Society (1)
April 2	[*James Lloyd Breck.* Saints (3)]
April 3	Richard, bishop of Chichester. Pastors and Bishops (1)
April 4	Martin Luther King, Jr. Renewers of Society (2)
April 6	Albrecht Dürer and Michelangelo. Artists and Scientists (1)
April 8	*William Augustus Muhlenberg.* Renewers of the Church (1)
April 9	Dietrich Bonhöffer. Martyrs (1)
April 10	*Mikael Agricola.* Pastors and Bishops (2) *William Law, priest.* Pastors and Bishops (2) *or* Renewers of the Church (2)
April 11	[*George Augustus Seywyn.* Missionaries (1)]
April 19	*Alphege, archbishop of Canterbury.* Martyrs (1) *Olavus and Laurentius Petri.* Renewers of the Church (1)
April 21	Anselm, archbishop of Canterbury. Theologians and Teachers (2)
April 23	Toyohiko Kagawa. Renewers of Society (2)

April 25 ST. MARK, Evangelist

Almighty God, by the hand of Mark the evangelist you have given to your Church the Gospel of Jesus Christ the Son of God: We thank you for this witness, and pray that we may be firmly grounded in its truth; through your Son, Jesus Christ our Lord, who lives and reigns with you and the Holy Spirit, one God, now and for ever.

[Mark 1:1; BCP (1979), LBW]

April 29 Catherine of Siena. Theologians and Teachers (1)

May 1 ST. PHILIP AND ST. JAMES, Apostles

Almighty God, who gave to your apostles Philip and James grace and strength to bear witness to the truth: Grant that we, being mindful of their victory of faith, may glorify in life and death the Name of our Lord Jesus Christ; who lives and reigns with you and the Holy Spirit, one God, now and for ever. [BCP (1979); ~RS]

May 2 Athanasius, bishop of Alexandria. Theologians and Teachers (2)

May 8 Dame Julian of Norwich. Saints (2)

May 18 *Erik, King of Sweden.* Martyrs (1)

May 19 Dunstan, archbishop of Canterbury. Pastors and Bishops (1)

May 20 Alcuin, deacon and abbot of Tours. Monastics

May 21 John Eliot, missionary to Native Americans. Missionaries (1)

May 23 [*Ludwig Nommensen, missionary to Sumatra.* Missionaries (2)]

May 24 *Nicolaus Copernicus and Leonhard Euler.* Artists and Scientists (1)
[*Jackson Kemper.* Missionaries (1)]

May 25 Bede the Venerable. Monastics

May 26 Augustine, archbishop of Canterbury. Missionaries (1)

May 27 John Calvin. Renewers of the Church (1)

May 29 [*Jiri Tranovsky, hymnwriter.* Artists and Scientists (2)]

May 31 THE VISITATION

Almighty God, you have dealt wonderfully with your handmaiden the Virgin Mary, and in choosing her to be the mother of your Son you have made known that you graciously regard the poor and the lowly and the despised: Grant us grace to receive your Word in humility and with lively faith and so be made one with your Son, Jesus Christ our Lord; who lives and reigns with you and the Holy Spirit, one God, now and for ever.

[Strasbourg 1524; CB,CSB, SBH, LBW; ~AC, BCP]

June 1 Justin. Martyrs (2)

June 2 Blandina and companions at Lyons. Martyrs (1)

June 3 *The Martyrs of Uganda.* Martyrs (3)

June 4 John XXIII, bishop of Rome. Pastors and Bishops (2)

June 5 Boniface, bishop, missionary, martyr. Missionaries (1)

June 6 [*William A. Passavant.* Renewers of Society (1)]

June 7 Seattle. Saints (1)

June 9 Columba and Aidan. Saints (3)

June 10 Ephrem of Edessa. Saints (2)

June 11 ST. BARNABAS, Apostle

Grant, O God, that we may follow the example of your faithful servant Barnabas, who, seeking not his own renown but the well-being of your Church, gave generously of his life and substance for the relief of the poor and the spread of the Gospel; through your Son Jesus Christ our Lord, who lives and reigns with you and the Holy Spirit, one God, now and for ever.

[Acts 4:32-37, 9:19-30, 13:I-3; BCP (1979), LBW]

June 14 Macrina, Basil the Great, Gregory of Nazianzus, Gregory of Nyssa. Theologians and Teachers (2)

June 15 Evelyn Underhill. Saints (1)

June 16 [*Joseph Butler, bishop.* Theologians and Teachers (1)]

June 18 [*Bernard Mizeki.* Martyrs (3)]

June 21 [*Onesimos Nesib.* Missionaries (2)]

June 22 *Alban.* Martyrs (2)

June 24 THE NATIVITY OF ST. JOHN THE BAPTIST

Almighty God, your servant John the Baptist testified that Jesus Christ is the Lamb of God who takes away the sin of the world: Enlighten us by your Holy Spirit that we may at all times find joy and comfort in this testimony, and, walking steadfast in the way of life and peace, may at last with all believers come to him to whom John pointed, your Son Jesus Christ our Lord; who lives and reigns with you and the Holy Spirit, one God, now and for ever.

[Lüneburg 1564, CSB; ~Gel., RS, BCP]

June 25 *Presentation of the Augsburg Confession; Philipp Melanchthon*

Almighty God, through the preaching of your servants, the blessed Reformers, you have caused the light of the Gospel to shine forth: Grant, we pray, that, knowing its saving power, we may faithfully guard and defend it against all enemies and joyfully proclaim it to the salvation of souls and the glory of your holy Name; through Jesus Christ our Lord, who lives and reigns with you and the Holy Spirit, one God, now and for ever. [CSB, SBH]

June 28 Irenaeus. Pastors and Bishops (1)

June 29 ST. PETER AND ST. PAUL, Apostles

Almighty God, whose blessed apostles Peter and Paul glorified you by their martyrdom: Grant that your Church, instructed by their teaching and example, and knit together in unity by your Spirit, may ever stand firm upon the one foundation, which is your Son Jesus Christ our Lord; who lives and reigns with you in the unity of the Holy Spirit, one God, now and for ever. [Leo., Sarum, BCP, LBW]

June 30 [*Johann Olov Wallin, archbishop of Uppsala, hymnwriter.* Pastors and Bishops (2)]

July 1 Catherine Winkworth; John Mason Neale, hymnwriters. Artists and Scientists (2)

July 6 Jan Hus. Martyrs (2)

July 11 Benedict of Nursia; Scholastica. Monastics

July 12 Nathan Söderblom, archbishop, of Uppsala. Theologians and Teachers (1)

July 13 [Johannes Flierl. Missionaries (1)]

July 15 Olga and Vladimir. Saints (1)

July 17 Bartolome de Las Casas, missionary to the Indies. Renewers of Society (2) [*William White.* Pastors and Bishops (2)]

July 20 *Elizabeth Cady Stanton, Amelia Bloom, Sojourner Truth, Harriet Ross Tubman.* Renewers of Society (2)

July 22 ST. MARY MAGDALENE

Almighty God, whose blessed Son restored Mary Magdalene to health of body and of mind, and called her to be a witness of his resurrection: Mercifully grant that by his grace we may be healed from all our infirmities and know you in the power of his unending life; who with you and the Holy Spirit lives and reigns, one God, now and for ever. [BCPp, BCP, LBW]

July 23 Birgitta of Sweden. Saints (3)

July 24 *Thomas a Kempis.* Monastics

July 25 ST. JAMES THE ELDER, Apostle

O gracious God, we remember before you your servant and apostle James, first among the Twelve to suffer martyrdom for the Name of Jesus Christ; and we pray that you will pour out upon the leaders of your Church that spirit of self-denying service by which alone they may have true authority among your people; through Jesus Christ our Lord, who lives and reigns with you and the Holy Spirit, one God, now and for ever.

[Acts 11:27-12:3, Matt. 20:20-28; BCP (1979), LBW]

July 26 Parents of the Blessed Virgin Mary. Saints (3)

July 27 [*William Reed Huntington.* Renewers of the Church (1)]

July 28 J.S. Bach, Heinrich Schütz, G.F. Handel. Artists and Scientists (2)

July 29 Mary, Martha, and Lazarus. Saints (2)
Olav, king of Norway. Prayer for a sovereign, given at August 16

July 30 *William Wilberforce.* Renewers of Society (2)
July 31 Ignatius of Loyola. Renewers of the Church (2)

August 1 *Joseph of Arimathea.* Saints (1)

August 6 THE TRANSFIGURATION OF OUR LORD

O God, who on the holy mount revealed to chosen witnesses your well-beloved Son, wonderfully transfigured, in raiment white and glistening: Mercifully grant that we, being delivered from the disquietude of this world, may by faith behold the King in his beauty; who lives and reigns with you and the Holy Spirit, one God, now and for ever. [Isa. 33:17; William Reed Huntingdon, BCP (1892), LBW]

August 8 Dominic. Monastics

August 10 St. Lawrence.

Almighty God, you called your deacon Lawrence to serve you with deeds of love, and gave him the crown of martyrdom: Grant that we, following his example, may fulfill your commandments by defending and supporting the poor, and by loving you with all our hearts; through Jesus Christ our Lord, who lives and reigns with you and the Holy Spirit, one God, now and for ever. [RS, LFF]

August 11 Clare, abbess at Assisi. Monastics

August 13 Florence Nightingale and Clara Maas. Renewers of Society (1)
Jeremy Taylor. Pastors and Bishops (2) *or* p. XXXX no. 53

August 14 [*Jonathan Myrick Daniels.* Martyrs (1)]

August 15 ST. MARY THE VIRGIN, MOTHER OF OUR LORD

O God, you have taken to yourself the blessed Virgin Mary, mother of your incarnate Son: Grant that we, who have been redeemed by his blood, may share with her the glory of your eternal kingdom; through your Son Jesus Christ our Lord, who lives and reigns with you and the Holy Spirit, one God, now and for ever. [BCP (1979), LBW]

August 16 Stephen, King of Hungary

O God, you called your servant *Stephen* to an earthly throne that *he* might advance your heavenly kingdom, and gave *him* zeal for your Church and love for your people: Mercifully grant that we who commemorate *him* this day may be fruitful in good works, and attain to the glorious crown of your saints; through Jesus Christ our Lord, who lives and reigns with you and the Holy Spirit, one God, now and for ever.

[LFF August 25]

August 18 [*William Porcher DuBose.* Theologians and Teachers (2)]

August 20 Bernard of Clairvaux. Renewers of the Church (2)

August 24 ST. BARTHOLOMEW, Apostle

Almighty and everlasting God, who gave to your apostle Bartholomew grace truly to believe and to preach your Word: Grant that your Church may love what he believed and preach what he taught; through your Son Jesus Christ our Lord, who lives and reigns with you and the Holy Spirit, one God, now and for ever. [Leo., Greg., MG, BCP, LBW]

August 25 Louis, King of France. Prayer for a soverign, given at August 16

August 27 Monica, mother of Augustine. Saints (1)
[*Thomas Gallaudet and Henry Winter Syle.* Renewers of Society (1)]

August 28 Augustine, bishop of Hippo. Theologians and Teachers (2)

August 29 The Beheading of St. John the Baptist

O God, you called John the Baptist to be in birth and death the forerunner of your Son: Grant that as John gave his life in witness to truth and righteousness, so we may fearlessly contend for the right, even unto the end; through your Son Jesus Christ our Lord, who lives and reigns with you and the Holy Spirit, one God, now and for ever.

[Parisian Missal 1736, RS, PHP]

August 31 John Bunyan. Theologians and Teachers (1)

September 1 [*David Pendleton Oakerhater.* Missionaries (2)]

September 2 *Nikolai Frederik Severin Grundivig.* Renewers of the Church (1)
[*The Martyrs of New Guinea.* Martyrs (2)]

September 4 Albert Schweitzer. Missionaries (2)

September 5 [*Paul Jones.* Saints (2)]

September 8 The Nativity of the Blessed Virgin Mary

We pray you, O Lord, pour into our hearts the abundance of your heavenly grace, that as the childbearing of the blessed Virgin Mary was to us the dawn of salvation, so the devout celebration of her nativity may draw us closer to him who is our peace, Jesus Christ our Lord; who lives and reigns with you and the Holy Spirit, one God, now and for ever.

[Greg., *English Office,* RS]

September 9 Peter Claver. Missionaries (2)
[*Constance and her companions.* Martyrs (2)]

September 10 [*Alexander Crummell.* Saints (3)]

September 12 [*John Henry Hobart, bishop of New York.* Pastors and Bishops (2)]

September 13 John Chrysostom. Pastors and Bishops (1)

September 14 HOLY CROSS DAY

Almighty God, whose Son our Savior Jesus Christ was lifted high upon the cross that he might draw the whole world to himself: Mercifully grant that we, who glory in the mystery of our redemption, may have grace to take up our cross and follow him; who lives and reigns with you and the Holy Spirit, one God, now and for ever.

[John 3:14-15; Gal. 6:14; Matt. 16:24; BCP (1979), LBW]

September 16 *Cyprian, bishop and martyr.* Martyrs (1)
Ninian. Bishop in Galloway. Pastors and Bishops (1)

September 17 Hildegard of Bingen. Renewers of the Church (2)

September 18 Dag Hammarskjold, Peacemaker.

Almighty God, kindle, we pray, in every heart the true love of peace, and guide with your wisdom those who take counsel for the nations of the earth, that in tranquillity your dominion may increase until the earth is filled with the knowledge of your love; through Jesus Christ our Lord, who lives and reigns with you and the Holy Spirit, one God, now and for ever.

[John 3:14-15; Gal. 6:14; Matt. 16:24; BCPp, BCP (1979), LBW]

September 18 [*Edward Bouverie Pusey, priest.* Renewers of the Church (1)]

September 19 *Theodore of Tarsus, archbishop of Canterbury.* Pastors and Bishops (2)

September 20 [*John Coleridge Patteson, bishop, martyr.* Martyrs (2)]

September 21 ST. MATTHEW, Apostle, Evangelist

Almighty God, in your boundless mercy you chose Matthew, a tax collector, to share the dignity of your apostles: Enable us, sustained by his example, steadfastly to follow your Son Jesus Christ and to remain faithful in your service; through Jesus Christ our Lord, who lives and reigns with you and the Holy Spirit, one God, now and for ever. [Parisian Missal 1736, RS, PHP]

September 22 [*Justus Falckner*. Pastors and Bishops (2)]
[*Philander Chase*. Pastors and Bishops (2)]

September 25 Sergius of Radonezh, abbot of Holy Trinity. Monastics

September 26 *Lancelot Andrews*. Pastors and Bishops (1)

September 27 Vincent de Paul. Renewers of Society (1)

September 29 ST. MICHAEL AND ALL ANGELS.

Everlasting God, you have ordained and constituted in a wonderful order the ministries of angels and mortals: Mercifully grant that, as your holy angels always serve and worship you in heaven, so by your appointment they may help and defend us here on earth; through your Son Jesus Christ our Lord, who lives and reigns with you and the Holy Spirit, one God, now and for ever. [Greg., Sarum, RS, BCP, LBW]

September 30 Jerome, translator, teacher. Theologians and Teachers (1)

October 1 *Remigius, bishop of Rheims*. Pastors and Bishops (1)

October 4 Francis of Assisi. Renewers of the Church (1) or Monastics

October 5 *Frederike, Karolina, and Theodor Fliedner*. Renewers of Society (1)

October 6 William Tyndale, translator, martyr. Missionaries (1)

October 7 [*Henry Meichior Muhlenberg*. Missionary to America. Pastors and Bishops (2)]

October 9 *Robert Grosseteste, Bishop of Lincoln*. Pastors and Bishops (2)

October 11 *Philip the Deacon*. Missionaries (2)

October 13 Elizabeth Fry. Renewers of Society (2)

October 14 [*Samuel Isaac Schereschewsky, bishop of Shanghai.* Pastors and Bishops (2)]

October 15 Teresa of Avila. Renewers of the Church (2)

October 16 *Hugh Latimer, Nicholas Ridley, and Thomas Cranmer.* Martyrs (2)

October 17 Ignatius of Antioch, Martyrs (1)

October 18 ST. LUKE, Evangelist

Almighty God, who inspired your servant Luke the physician to set forth in the Gospel the love and healing power of your Son: Graciously continue in your Church this love and power to heal, to the praise and glory of your Name; through your Son Jesus Christ our Lord, who lives and reigns with you and the Holy Spirit, one God, now and for ever. [BCP (1928 rev. 1979), LBW]

October 19 [*Henry Martyn, missionary to India and Persia.* Missionaries (2)]

October 23 ST. JAMES OF JERUSALEM

Grant, O God, that, following the example of your servant James the Just, brother of our Lord, your Church may give itself continually to prayer and to the reconciliation of all who are at variance and enmity; through Jesus Christ our Lord, who lives and reigns with you and the Holy Spirit, one God, now and for ever. [BCP (1979), LBW]

October 24 [*Jehu Jones, pastor.* Renewers of Society (2)]

October 26 Philipp Nicolai, Johann Heermann, Paul Gerhardt. Artists (2)
Alfred the Great. Prayer for a Sovereign, given at August 16

October 28 ST. SIMON AND ST. JUDE, Apostles

O God, we thank you for the glorious company of the apostles, and especially on this day for Simon and Jude; and we pray that, as they were faithful and zealous in their mission, so we may with ardent devotion make known the love and mercy of our Lord and Savior Jesus Christ; who lives and reigns with you and the Holy Spirit, one God, now and for ever. [BCP (1979), LBW]

October 29 [*James Hannington and his companions.* Martyrs (1)]

October 31 Reformation Day

Almighty God, heavenly Father, pour out your Holy Spirit on your faithful people; keep them steadfast in your grace and truth, protect and comfort them in all temptation, defend them against all enemies of your Word, and bestow on Christ's Church militant your saving peace; through your Son Jesus Christ our Lord, who lives and reigns with you and the Holy Spirit, one God, now and for ever.

[Saxony (Duke Henry) 1539, CB, CSB, SBH, LBW]

November 1 ALL SAINTS' DAY

Almighty God, you have knit together your elect in one communion and fellowship in the mystical body of your Son Christ our Lord: Give us grace so to follow your saints in all virtuous and godly living, that we may come to those ineffable joys that you have prepared for those who truly love you; through your Son Jesus Christ our Lord, who lives and reigns with you and the Holy Spirit, one God, now and for ever. [BCP (1549), CB, CSB, SBH, LBW]

November 2 Commemoration of All the Faithful Departed

Almighty God, with whom still live the spirits of those who die in the Lord, and with whom the souls of the faithful, after they are delivered from the burden of the flesh, are in joy and felicity: We give you heartfelt thanks for the good examples of all your servants who, having finished their course in faith, now find rest and refreshment; and we pray that we, with all who have departed in the true faith of your holy Name, may have perfect fulfillment and bliss both in body and soul in your eternal and everlasting glory; through Jesus Christ our Lord, who lives and reigns with you and the Holy Spirit, one God, now and for ever. [medieval burial offices, BCP (1549), CSB, SBH, LBW]

November 3 [*Richard Hooker.* Theologians and Teachers (1)]

November 5 Elizabeth and Zechariah. Saints (2)

November 6 *William Temple*. Theologians and Teachers (2)

November 7 *Willibrord, missionary to Frisia.* Missionaries (2)

November 8 *John Frederick Christian Heyer,* Missionaries (2)

November 10 Leo the Great. Pastors and Bishops (2)

November 11 Martin of Tours. Pastors and Bishops (1)

November 12 [*Charles Simeon priest.* Saints (2)]
Soren Kierkegaard Theologians and Teachers (1)

November 14 [*Consecration of Samuel Seabury.* Pastors and Bishops (2)]

November 16 Margaret, Queen of Scotland. Prayer for a sovereign, given at August 16

November 17 Elizabeth of Thuringia Renewers of Society (1)
Hugh, Bishop of Lincoln. Pastors and Bishops (1)

November 18 Hilda, abbess of Whitby. Monastics

November 19 Mechtilde of Hageborn, Gertrude the Great, Mechtild of Magdeburg. Renewers of the Church (2)

November 20 *Edmund, king of East Anglia.* Prayer for a sovereign, given at August 16

November 22 C.S. Lewis. Theologians and Teachers (1)

November 23 Clement, Bishop of Rome. Pastors and Bishops (2)

November 24 Miguel Agustin Pro. Martyrs (3)

November 25 Isaac Watts, hymnwriter. Artists and Scientists (1)
[*James Otis Sargent Huntington.* Monastics]

November 28. [*Kamehameha and Emma, King and Queen of Hawaii.* Prayer for a sovereign, given on August 16]

Common Collects for the Commemorations

Martyrs

Almighty God, you gave to your servant *N.* boldness to confess the Name of our Savior Jesus Christ before the rulers of this world and courage to die for this faith: Grant that we may always be ready to give a reason for the hope that is in us, and to suffer gladly for the sake of our Lord Jesus Christ; who lives and reigns with you and the Holy Spirit, one God, now and for ever. [1 Peter 3:15; 4:16; BCP]

Almighty God, by whose grace and power your holy martyr *N.* triumphed over suffering and was faithful even to death: Grant us, who now remember *him/her* with thanksgiving, to be so faithful in our witness to you in this world, that we may receive with *him/her* the crown of life; through your Son Jesus Christ our Lord, who lives and reigns with you and the Holy Spirit, one God, now and for ever. [Rev. 2:10; BCP]

Almighty and everlasting God, who kindled the flame of your love in the heart of your holy martyr *N.*: Grant to us, your humble servants, a like faith and power of love, that we who rejoice in *his/her* triumph may profit by *his/her* example; through your Son Jesus Christ our Lord, who lives and reigns with you and the Holy Spirit, one God, now and for ever.

[MG, AC, BCP]

Missionaries

Almighty and everlasting God, we thank you for your servant *N.*, whom you called to preach the Gospel to the people of _________ (or to the ______ people): Raise up in this and every land evangelists and heralds of your kingdom, that your Church may proclaim the unsearchable riches of our Savior Jesus Christ; who lives and reigns with you and the Holy Spirit, one God, now and for ever. [Ephes. 3:8; Col 2:19; BCPp, BCP, LBW]

Almighty God, whose will it is to be glorified in your saints, and who raised up your servant *N.* to be a light in the world: Shine, we pray, in our hearts, that we also in our generation may show forth your praise, who called us out of darkness into your marvelous light; through your Son Jesus Christ our Lord, who lives and reigns with you and the Holy Spirit, one God, now and for ever. [Isa. 49:3; 2 Thes. 1:9-12; 1 Peter 2:9; BCPp, BCP]

Renewers of the Church

Almighty God, we praise you for the men and women you have sent to call the Church to its tasks and renew its life (particularly on this day your servant/servants ___________). Raise up in our day teachers and propehets inspired by your Spirit, whose voices will give strength to your Church and proclaim the reality of your kingdom; through your Son, Jesus Christ our Lord, who lives and reigns with you and the Holy Spirit, one God, now and for ever. [LBW]

O God, by whose grace your servant N., kindled with the flame of your love, became a burning and shining light in your Church: Grant that we also may be aflame with the spirit of love and discipline, and walk before you as children of light; through your Son, Jesus Christ our Lord, who lives and reigns with you and the Holy Spirit, one God, now and for ever. [Ephes. 5:8; BCP]

Monastics

O God, whose blessed Son became poor that we through his poverty might become rich: Deliver us from an inordinate love of this world, that we, inspired by the devotion of your servant *N.*, may serve you with singleness of heart, and attain to the riches of the age to come; through your Son, Jesus Christ our Lord, who lives and reigns with you and the Holy Spirit, one God, now and for ever. [2 Cor. 8:9; Ephes. 6:5; BCP]

Renewers of Society

Heavenly Father, whose blessed Son came not to be served but to serve: Bless all who, following in his steps, give themselves to the service of others; that with wisdom, patience, and courage, they [like your servant *N.*] may minister in his Name to the suffering, the friendliness, and the needy; for the love of him who laid down his life for us, your Son, Jesus Christ our Lord, who lives and reigns with you and the Holy Spirit, one God, now and for ever. [BCP (1928), LBW]

Almighty God, who created us in your own image: Grant us grace fearlessly to contend against evil and to make no peace with oppression; and, that we may reverently use our freedom, help us [like your servant ____] to employ it in the maintenance of justice in our communities and among the nations, to the glory of your Name; through your Son, Jesus Christ our Lord, who lives and reigns with you and the Holy Spirit, one God, now and for ever. [BCP (1928), LBW]

Pastors and Bishops

Heavenly Father, Shepherd of your people, we thank you for your servant *N.*, who was faithful in the care and nuture of your flock; and we pray that, following *his/her* example and the teaching of *his/her* holy life, we may by your grace grow into the stature and fullness of our Lord and Savior Jesus Christ; who lives and reigns with you and the Holy Spirit, one God, now and for ever. [Ephes. 4:11-13; CSI, BCP, LBW]

O God, our heavenly Father, who raised up your faithful servant *N.*, to be a [bishop and] pastor in your Church and to feed your flock: Give abundantly to all pastors the gifts of your Holy Spirit, that they may minister in your household as true servants of Christ and stewards of your divine mysteries; through your Son, Jesus Christ our Lord, who lives and reigns with you and the Holy Spirit, one God, now and for ever.

[1 Cor. 4:1; BCP]

Theologians and Teachers

O God, by your Holy Spirit you give to some the word of wisdom, to others the word of knowledge, and to others the word of faith: We praise your Name for the gifts of grace manifested in your servant *N.*, and we pray that your Church may never be destitute of such gifts; through your Son, Jesus Christ our Lord, who lives and reigns with you and the Holy Spirit, one God, now and for ever. [1 Cor. 12:4-11; BCP, alt. in LBW]

Almighty God, you gave to your servant *N.* special gifts of grace to understand and teach the truth as it is in Christ Jesus: Grant that by this teaching we may know you, the one true God, and Jesus Christ whom you have sent; who lives and reigns with you and the Holy Spirit, one God, now and for ever. [Ephes. 4:21; John 17:3; CSI, BCP]

Artists and Scientists

Almighty God, beautiful in majesty, majestic in holiness: You have shown us the splendor of creation in the work of your servant/servants _______. Teach us to drive from the world the ugliness of chaos and disorder, that our eyes may not be blind to your glory, and that at length everyone may know the inexhaustible richness of your new creation in Jesus Christ our Lord; who lives and reigns with you and the Holy Spirit, one God, now and for ever. [PHP, LBW]

O God, whom saints and angels delight to worship in heaven: Be ever present with your servants who seek through art and music to perfect the praises offered by your people on earth; and grant to them even now glimpses of your beauty, and make them [with *N.*] worthy at length to behold it unveiled for evermore; through your Son, Jesus Christ our Lord, who lives and reigns with you and the Holy Spirit, one God, now and for ever. [*Royal School of Church Music* rev., BCP]

Saints

Almighty God, you have surrounded us with a great cloud of witnesses: Grant that we, encouraged by the good example of your servant *N.*, may persevere in running the race that is set before us, until at last we may with *him/her* attain to your eternal joy; through your Son Jesus Christ our Lord, who lives and reigns with you and the Holy Spirit, one God, now and for ever. [Heb. 12:1-2; BCP (1928), LBW]

O God, you have brought us near to an innumerable company of angels and to the spirits of the righteous made perfect: Grant us during our earthly pilgrimage to abide in their fellowship, and in our heavenly country to become partakers of their joy; through your Son, Jesus Christ our Lord, who lives and reigns with you and the Holy Spirit, one God, now and for ever. [Heb. 11:13-16; 12:22-24; AC; BCP]

Almighty God, by your Holy Spirit you have made us one with your saints in heaven and on earth: Grant that in our earthly pilgrimage we may always be supported by this fellowship of love and prayer, and know ourselves to be surrounded by their witness to your power and mercy; through your Son, Jesus Christ our Lord, who lives and reigns with you and the Holy Spirit, one God, now and for ever. [BCP (1979)]

Occasions

The Anniversary of the Dedication of a Church

Almighty and most merciful God, from your chosen people, as from living stones, you build an eternal temple to your glory: Increase the spiritual gifts you have given to your Church, that your faithful people may continue to grow into the new Jerusalem; through your Son, Jesus Christ our Lord, who lives and reigns with you and the Holy Spirit, one God, now and for ever. [RS]

O God, year after year you return to us the day of the dedication of this holy temple to your service, and continually here you bring us into the presence of your holy mysteries: Hear the prayers of your people, and grant that all who worship before you in this place may find here your saving love and be filled with your joy and peace; through your Son, Jesus Christ our Lord, who lives and reigns with you and the Holy Spirit, one God, now and for ever. [Gel., SBH, RS; see BCP]

Thanksgiving Day

Almighty God, our heavenly Father, your mercies are new unto us every morning, and, although we have in no way deserved your goodness, you abundantly provide for all our needs of body and soul: Give us, we pray, your Holy Spirit that we may wholeheartedly acknowledge your merciful goodness toward us, give thanks for all your benefits, and serve you in willing obedience; through your Son, Jesus Christ our Lord, who lives and reigns with you and the Holy Spirit, one God, now and for ever. [CB, CSB, SBH]

Harvest

Almighty and gracious Father, we give you thanks for the fruits of the earth in their season and for the labors of those who harvest them. Make us, we pray, faithful stewards of your great bounty, for the provision of our necessities and the relief of all who are in need, to the glory of your Name; through your Son, Jesus Christ our Lord, who lives and reigns with you and the Holy Spirit, one God, now and for ever. [BCP (1789)]

For a National Holiday

Lord God almighty, you have made all the peoples of the earth for your glory, to serve you in freedom and in peace: Give to the people of our country a zeal for justice and the strength of forbearance, that we may use our liberty in accordancc with your gracious will; through Jesus Christ our Lord, who lives and reigns with you and the Holy Spirit, one God, now and for ever. [PP, BCP]

For Peace p. 1547 nos. 29, 30

Prayers and Intercessions

On Sunday (the Resurrection): For the Church

Week I

1. *For the Communion of Saints*

Eternal Father, of whom the whole family in heaven and earth is named: Unite us, as we worship you here, with all who in far-off places are lifting up their hands and hearts to you; that your Church may offer up one sacrifice of thanksgiving; through Jesus Christ our Lord. [DP]

2. *For the Church*

Gracious Father, we pray for your holy Catholic Church. Fill it with all truth, in all truth with all peace. Where it is corrupt, purify it; where it is in error, direct it; where in any thing it is amiss, reform it. Where it is right, strengthen it; where it is in want, provide for it; where it is divided, reunite it; for the sake of Jesus Christ our Savior.

[William Laud (1677), BCP (1928), SBH, LBW]

II

3. *For the Church*

O God of unchangeable power and eternal light: Look favorably on your whole Church, that wonderful and sacred mystery; and, by the effectual working of your perpetual providence, carry out the work of our salvation; let the whole world see and know that things which were cast down are being raised up, that things which had grown old are being made new, and that all things are being brought to their perfection by him through whom all things were made, your Son, Jesus Christ our Lord. [Gel., MR Holy Sat.; AC, SBH, BCP]

4. *For the Church*

Almighty and everlasting God, in Christ you have revealed your glory among the nations: Preserve the works of your mercy, that your Church throughout the world may persevere with steadfast faith in the confession of your Name; through Jesus Christ our Lord, who lives and reigns with you and the Holy Spirit, one God, now and for ever. [Gel., AC, BCP Proper 24; LBW 22 Pent.]

see also above, p. 20 Almighty, God grant to your Church

III

5. *For Grace to Receive the Word*

Blessed Lord, who caused all holy Scriptures to be written for our learning: Grant us so to hear them, read, mark, learn, and inwardly digest them, that we may embrace and ever hold fast the blessed hope of everlasting life, which you have given us in our Savior Jesus Christ; who lives and reigns with you and the Holy Spirit, one God, now and for ever. [Rom. 15:4, BCP (1549)Proper 28; SBH]

6. *For the Unity of the Church*

Lord Jesus Christ, before your passion you prayed that your disciples might be one, even as you are one with the Father: Draw us to yourself, that in love and obedience to you we may be united to one another by the one Spirit, that the world may believe and confess that you are Lord, to the glory of God the Father. [William Temple, PP]

IV

7. For the Unity of the Church

Eternal and merciful God, the God of peace and not of discord: Have mercy on your Church, divided in your service; and grant that we, seeking unity in Christ, and in the truth of your holy Word, and united by our baptism in one Spirit, may with one mind and one mouth glorify you, the Father of our Lord Jesus Christ.

[Lancelot Andrewes 1564, DP]

8. For the Parish

Almighty and everliving God, ruler of all things in heaven and earth, hear our prayers and grant to this parish all that is necessary for its spiritual health. Strengthen the faithful, visit and relieve the sick, rouse the careless, restore the penitent, remove all hindrances to the advancement of your truth, and bring us all to be of one heart and mind within the fold of your holy Church, to the honor and glory of your Name; through Jesus Christ our Lord.

[William J. Butler, MIP, SBH]

On Monday (the Holy Spirit): For the Ministry

I

9. For the Peace of God

Almighty Father, you have so formed us for yourself that our hearts are restless until they find rest in you: By the ministry of your Church and the lives of those who humbly love and serve you, convince the world that you are the sure refuge of all who are weary and distressed, the safe harbor of all who seek peace of heart, and the eternal salvation of every burdened soul; so that, coming to you, they may find and possess that peace which you give in your Son, Jesus Christ our Lord.

[Paul Zeller Strodach C&P, SBH]

10. For the Ministers of the Church

Almighty God, the giver of all good gifts, in your divine providence you have appointed the sacred ministry in your Church: Give your grace, we humbly pray, to all who are called to any office and ministry for your people; and so fill them with the truth of your doctrine and clothe them with holiness of life, that they may faithfully serve before you, to the glory of your great Name and for the benefit of your holy Church; through Jesus Christ our Lord. [BCP (1549) rev.]

II

11. For the Ministry of the Church

Almighty and everlasting God, from whom comes every good and perfect gift: Send down upon our bishops and other clergy and upon the congregations committed to their charge the healthful Spirit of your grace; and, that they may truly please you, pour upon them the continual dew of your blessing. Grant this, O Lord, for the honor of our Advocate and Mediator, Jesus Christ. [Gel., BCP (1559), SBH]

12. For the Ministry

O Lord, we implore you to raise up for the work of the ministry faithful and able servants who will count it all joy to give themselves for the sake of your dear Son and for the souls for whom he shed his most precious blood; and fit them for their holy office by your bountiful grace and heavenly benediction; through Jesus Christ our Lord. [Edward White Benson; SBH]

III

13. For Monastic Orders and Vocations

O Lord Jesus Christ, you became poor for our sake, that we might be made rich through your poverty: Guide and sanctify, we pray, those whom you call to follow you under the vows of poverty, chastity, and obedience, that by their prayer and service they may enrich your Church, and by their life and worship may glorify your Name; for you reign with the Father and the Holy Spirit, one God, now and for ever. [2 Cor. 8:9, BCP (1979)]

14. *For All Christians in Their Vocation*

Almighty and everlasting God, by whose Spirit the whole body of your faithful people is governed and sanctified: Receive our supplications and prayers, which we offer before you for all members of your holy Church, that in their vocation and ministry they may truly and devoutly serve you; through our Lord and Savior Jesus Christ. [Gel., BCP (1549)]

IV

15. *For Cheerful Confidence*

Teach us, O gracious Lord, to begin our works with fear, to go on with obedience, to finish them in love, and then to wait patiently in hope, with cheerful confidence looking up to you, whose promises are faithful and whose rewards infinite; through Jesus Christ our Lord.

[John Austin, PP]

16. *For Faithfulness in Vocation*

Remember, O Lord, what you have wrought in us and not what we deserve; and, as you have called us to your service, make us worthy of our calling; through Jesus Christ our Lord.

[Leo., BCPp, SBH; BCP Proper 1]

On Tuesday (the Holy Trinity): For All People in Society and Community

I

17. For the Holy Spirit

Lord God, you alone can satisfy the longing of our hearts: Let your Holy Spirit dwell in us, we pray, to enlighten us and to lead us into all truth, and evermore defend us from all adversities; through Jesus Christ our Lord. [Gel., MR. Pent. Ember Wed., CB, CSB]

18. For Trustfulness

Most loving Father, whose will it is for us to give thanks for all things, to fear nothing but the loss of you, and to cast all our care on you who care for us: Preserve us from faithless fears and worldly anxieties, that no clouds of this mortal life may hide from us the light of that love which is immortal, and which you have manifested to us in your Son, Jesus Christ our Lord, who lives and reigns with you and the Holy Spirit, one God, now and for ever.

[1 Tim. 2:11, Phil. 3:8, 1 Peter 5:7; AC, BCP 8 Epiph.]

II

19. For Guidance

Heavenly Father, in whom we live and move and have our being: We humbly pray you so to guide and govern us by your Holy Spirit, that in all the cares and occupations of our life we may not forget you, but may remember that we are ever walking in your sight; through Jesus Christ our Lord. [DFP, *Chain*, BCP, LBW]

20. For Trust in God's Strength

O God, the author of peace and lover of concord, to know you is eternal life and to serve you is perfect freedom: Defend us, your humble servants, in all assaults of our enemies; that we, surely trusting in your defense, may not fear the power of any adversaries; through the might of Jesus Christ our Lord. [Gel., BCP (1549)]

III

21. For Families Everywhere

Almighty God, our heavenly Father, you set the solitary in families. We commend to your continual care the homes in which your people dwell. Put far from them, we pray, every root of bitterness, the thirst for personal gain, and the pride of life. Fill them with faith, virtue, knowledge, moderation, patience, and godliness. Knit together in constant affection those who have been joined in marriage. Let children and parents have proper regard for one another; and kindle fervent love among us all; through Jesus Christ our Lord.

[BCP (1928) rev.]

22. For Children

Almighty and everlasting God, it is your will that none of your little ones should perish: Bless and guide children everywhere by your Holy Spirit, give them growth in grace and in knowledge of you, protect and defend them against all danger and harm, and give your holy angels charge of them; through Jesus Christ our Lord.

[Saxe-Coburg 1626; CB]

IV

23. For Catechumens

Almighty and everlasting God, with your light and grace you strengthen the hearts of those to whom you give new birth, confirming in them your covenant and faithfulness: Grant to all catechumens increase both of faith and knowledge, that they may rejoice in their

Baptism and gladly live in the strength of the covenant you make with them; through Jesus Christ our Lord.

[Gel., SBH; RS, LBW Good Friday]

24. *For Those We Love*

Almighty God, we entrust all who are dear to us to your never-failing care and love, for this life and the life to come, knowing that you are doing for them better things than we can desire or pray for; through Jesus Christ our Lord. [BCP (1928)]

On Wednesday (Creation and Providence): For the Civil Authority

I

25. *For Knowledge of God's Creation*

God of surpassing glory, you have called into being the universe in its tremendous majesty and uphold its fabric in a marvelous order and beauty: Give us, in whom you have planted the desire to know more of your creation, grace so to explore your work and wisdom, that we may more fully understand the beauty of what you have made and the wonder of your presence, and be led to thank you, adore you, and praise you for ever; through Jesus Christ our Lord.

[PHP after B.K. Cunningham and Milner-White, DP]

26. *For the Conservation of Natural Resources*

Almighty God, in giving us dominion over things on earth, you made us workers with you in your creation: Give us wisdom and reverence so to use the resources of nature, that no one may suffer from our abuse of them, and that generations yet to come may continue to praise you for your bounty; through Jesus Christ our Lord.

[BCP (1979) rev.]

II

27. For Protection Against the Perils of Abundance

O God, in your love you have bestowed upon us gifts such as our forebears neither knew nor dreamed of: Mercifully grant that we be not so occupied with material things that we forget the things which are spiritual; lest, having gained the whole world, we lose our own soul; for your mercy's sake. [DP, SBH]

28. For Those in Civil Authority

Almighty and everlasting God, we pray you graciously to regard all who hold civil authority among us; that they may be high in purpose, wise in counsel, and unwavering in duty, working always to insure freedom and justice for all our citizens, so that we may be a people at peace with ourselves and with one another, and a blessing to other nations of the earth; through Jesus Christ our Lord.

[PHP after Paul Zeller Strodach, CSB, SBH]

III

29. For Peace Among Nations

O God, the fountain of peace and source of all concord: Grant your mighty aid to all who work to establish peace among the nations of the world. Give strength of purpose to those who lead, and enlighten those who sit in council, that they may exalt peace above war, service above gain, justice above glory, and righteousness above all; through Jesus Christ our Lord. [Emil Fischer C&P, SBH rev. PHP]

30. For Peace

O God, it is your will to fold heaven and earth in a single peace: Let the design of your great love lighten upon the waste of our wraths and sorrows; and give peace in your Church, peace among nations, peace in our dwellings, and peace in our hearts; through your Son, our Savior, Jesus Christ. [MSO, SBH]

IV

31. For the Human Family

Our heavenly Father, in your wisdom you have made your children not in one mold, but all sharing a common likeness, which is your own: Take away from us, we pray, the pride of heart which strives to impress our image upon others, and give us the desire only to see in them the reflection of you; through Jesus Christ our Lord. [DP]

32. For Guidance

O God, by whom the humble are guided in judgment and light rises up in darkness for the righteous: Grant us, in all our doubts and uncertainties, the grace to ask what you would have us to do; that the Spirit of wisdom may save us from all false choices, and that in your light we may see light, and in your straight path may not stumble; through Jesus Christ our Lord.

[Ps. 25:9; 97:11; Isa. 11:2; Ps. 36:9; Jer. 31:9; William Bright AC, BCP rev. PHP]

On Thursday (the Sacraments): For Spiritual Gifts

I

33. For Rest in God

O God, the living God, you have put your own eternity in our hearts, and have made us to hunger and thirst after you: Satisfy, we pray, the need which you have implanted in us, that we may find you in life and find life in you; through Jesus Christ our Lord. [DP]

34. For Divine Assistance

Direct us, O Lord, in all our doings, with your most gracious favor, and further us with your continual help; that in all our works, begun, continued, and ended in you, we may glorify your holy Name; and finally, by your mercy, obtain everlasting life; through Jesus Christ, your Son, our Lord.

[Greg., BCP, CB, CSB, SBH, LBW; RS, LFF Thurs. after Ash Wed]

II

35. For the Gift of Love

O Lord, you have taught us that without love whatever we do is worth nothing: Send your Holy Spirit and pour into our hearts your greatest gift, which is love, the true bond of peace and of all virtue, without which whoever lives is accounted dead before you. Grant this for the sake of your only Son Jesus Christ, who lives and reigns with you and the Holy Spirit, one God, now and for ever.

[BCP (1549) 7 Epiphany]

36. For the Power of the Cross

O God, at our baptism you marked us with the sign of the holy cross: Grant us in the hour of temptation to be mindful of its might to vanquish the enemy; through Jesus Christ our Lord. [DP]

III

37. For Proper Regard for the Holy Communion

Lord God, in a wonderful Sacrament you have left us a memorial of your passion: Deepen our reverence for the sacred mysteries of your Body and Blood, that we may ever perceive within ourselves the fruit of your redemption; for you live and reign with the Father and the Holy Spirit, one God, for ever and ever.

[Thomas Aquinas, MR, RS, CB, CSB, SBH, LBW, BCP]

38. *For a Holy Life*

Almighty God, you have given your only Son to be for us a sacrifice for sin, and also an example of godly life: Give us grace to receive thankfully the fruits of his redeeming work, and to follow daily in the blessed steps of his most holy life; through Jesus Christ your Son our Lord, who lives and reigns with you and the Holy Spirit, one God, now and for ever. [BCP (1549) Proper 15; SBH, LBW]

IV

39. *For Humility*

Almighty and everlasting God, you resist the proud but give grace to the humble: Grant that we be not cast down from our chief happiness by the swellings of pride, but rather that we ascend into heaven by the steps of humility; through Jesus Christ our Lord

[Jas. 4:6, 1 Peter 5:5; Leo. and Moz., DP]

40. *General Thanksgving*

Almighty God, Father of all mercies, we your unworthy servants give you humble thanks for all your goodness and loving-kindness to us and to all whom you have made. We bless you for our creation, preservation, and all the blessings of this life; but above all for your immeasurable love in the redemption of the world by our Lord Jesus Christ; for the means of grace, and for the hope of glory. And, we pray, give us such an awareness of your mercies, that with truly thankful hearts we may show forth your praise, not only with our lips, but in our lives by giving up ourselves to your service, and by walking before you in holiness and righteousness all our days;

through Jesus Christ our Lord, to whom, with you and the Holy Spirit, be all honor and glory throughout all ages. [BCP (1662)]

On Friday (Redemption): For Missions

I

41. For Christian Witness

Lord Jesus, you stretched out your arms of love on the hard wood of the cross, that all nations might come within the reach of your saving embrace: Clothe us in your Spirit, that we, stretching forth our hands in loving concern for others, may bring those who do not know you to your knowledge and love; for you live and reign with the Father and the Holy Spirit, one God, now and for ever.

[Charles H. Brent, BCP (1979)]

42. For the Light of God

Dispel, O Lord of Light, all clouds of doubt and the darkness about our earthly course; that in your light we may see light, and come both to know you as we are known and to love you as we are loved; through Jesus Christ our Lord. [OPR]

II

43. For Faithful Witness

Almighty God, you have commanded us through your Son to go and make disciples of all nations, baptizing them into your Name: Grant that by the faithful and untiring witness of your Church, all the world, according to your will and promise, may come to know your Son and find its life and freedom in him to whom you have given all authority in heaven and on earth, Jesus Christ our Lord. [PHP]

44. *For the Mission of the Church*

O God of all the nations of the earth: Remember the multitudes who have been created in your image but have not known the redeeming work of our Savior Jesus Christ; and grant that, by the prayers and labors of your holy Church, they may be brought to know and worship you as you have been revealed in your Son; who lives and reigns with you and the Holy Spirit, one God, for ever and ever. [BCP]

III

45. *For the Mission of the Church*

Almighty God, heavenly Father, through your Son Jesus Christ you have commanded your people to go into all the world and preach the good news to the whole creation: Grant us a ready will to obey your Word; and as we have entered into the labors of others, help us so to serve you that others may enter into our labors; and that we with them and they with us may attain life everlasting; through Jesus Christ our Lord.

[Mark 16:15, John 4:37-38; Henry Eyster Jacobs, CSB, SBH]

46. *For the Mission of the Church*

O God, you have made of one blood all the peoples of the earth, and sent your blessed Son to preach peace to those who are far off and to those who are near: Grant that all people everywhere may seek after you and find you; bring the nations into your fold; and hasten the fulfillment of your promise to pour out your Spirit upon all flesh; through Jesus Christ our Lord.

[Acts 17:26-27 (AV); George Edward Lynch Cotton, BCP (1892), SBH]

IV

47. For the World

O God our protector, behold and look upon the face of your Anointed, who has given himself for the redemption of all, and grant that, from the rising of the sun to its setting, your Name may be great among the nations; and that in every place, sacrifice and a pure offering may be be made to your Name; through Jesus Christ our Lord.

[Mal. 1:11, MR For Propagation of the Faith, SBH]

48. For the New Creation

O God and Father of all, whom the whole heavens adore: Let the whole earth also worship you, all nations obey you, all tongues confess and bless you, and men and women everywhere love you and serve you in peace; through Jesus Christ our Lord. [MSO, BCP]

For Missionaries see pp. 1563 - 1584.

On Saturday (Death and the Judgment): The Needy, the Sick, the Aged, the Dying

I

49. For Watchfulness

Make us, we implore you, O Lord, our God, watchful and heedful in awaiting the coming of your Son Christ our Lord; that when he shall stand at the door and knock, he may find us, not sleeping in carelessness and sin, but awake and rejoicing in his praises; through Jesus Christ our Lord. [Gel., AC]

50. For Those in Need

O Lord, look down from heaven, behold, visit, and relieve your servants, for whom we offer our supplications; look upon them with the eyes of your mercy; give them comfort and sure confidence in you; defend them from the danger of the enemy, and keep them in perpetual peace and safety; through Jesus Christ, your Son, our Lord.

[Sarum, BCP (1928), SBH]

II

51. *For the Neglected*

Almighty and most merciful God, we remember before you all those whom it would be easy for us to forget: the homeless and the destitute, the old and the sick, and all who have none to care for them. Help us to heal those who are broken in body or spirit, and to turn their sorrow into joy. Grant this, Father, for the love of your Son, who for our sake became poor, Jesus Christ our Lord. [BCP (1928)]

52. *For Those Who Suffer*

Almighty and everlasting God, the consolation of the sorrowful and the strength of those who suffer: Let the prayers of your children who cry out in any tribulation come to you; and to every soul that is distressed grant mercy, grant relief, grant refreshment; through Jesus Christ our Lord. [Gel., OPR, SBH]

III

53. *For an Awareness of Mortality*

O God, whose days are without end, and whose mercies cannot be numbered: Make us, we pray, deeply aware of the shortness and uncertainty of human life; and let your Holy Spirit lead us in holiness and righteousness all our days; that, when we shall have served you in our generation, we may be gathered to our ancestors, having the testimony of a good conscience, in the communion of the Catholic

Church, in the confidence of a certain faith, in the comfort of a religious and holy hope, in favor with you, our God, and in perfect charity with the world. All this we ask through Jesus Christ our Lord.
[Jeremy Taylor, BCP (1789), SBH, LBW]

54. *For Fellowship with the Saints*

O God of the spirits of all flesh, we praise and magnify your holy Name for all your servants who have finished their course in your faith and fear, for the Blessed Virgin Mary, for the holy Patriarchs, Prophets, Apostles, and Martyrs and for all your righteous servants, known to us or unknown; and we pray you that, encouraged by their examples and strengthened by their fellowship, we also may be found worthy to be partakers of the inheritance of the saints in light; through the merits of your Son Jesus Christ our Lord. [BCPp]

IV

55. *For the Whole Church*

Eternal Lord God, you hold all souls in life: Give to your whole Church in paradise and on earth your light and your peace; and grant that we, following the good examples of those who served you here and are now at rest, may at last enter with them into your unending joy; through Jesus Christ our Lord. [WTT, BCP]

56. *For Mercy Upon All*

Lord Jesus Christ, Son of the living God, we pray you to set your passion, cross, and death between your judgment and our souls, now and in the hour of our death. Give mercy and grace to the living; pardon and rest to the dead; to your holy Church peace and concord; and to us sinners everlasting life and glory; for with the Father and the Holy Spirit you live and reign, one God, now and for ever.
[medieval primers, APP , BCP]

Devotional Prayers

O God of peace, you have taught us that in returning and rest we shall be saved, in quietness and confidence shall be our strength: By the might of your Spirit lift us, we pray, to your presence, where we may be still and know that you are God; through Jesus Christ our Lord.

[Isa. 35:15, Ps.46:10; William Bright AC; BCP (1928)]

Almighty God, from whom every good prayer comes, you pour out on all who desire it the spirit of grace and of supplication: Deliver us, when we draw near to you, from coldness of heart and wanderings of mind, that with steadfast thoughts and kindled affections we may worship you in spirit and in truth; through Jesus Christ our Lord. [William Bright AC, BCP]

Almighty God, fountain of all wisdom, you know our necessities before we ask and our ignorance in asking: Have compassion on our weakness, and mercifully give us those things which for our unworthiness we dare not, and for our blindness we cannot ask; through the worthiness of your Son, Jesus Christ our Lord, who lives and reigns with you and the Holy Spirit, one God, now and for ever.

[Sirach 1:5, Matt. 8:8, Rom. 8:26; BCP (1549) Proper 11]

O God, the sovereign good of the soul, you require the hearts of all your children: Deliver us from all sloth in your work and all coldness in your cause; and grant us by looking unto you to rekindle our love, and by waiting upon you to renew our strength; through Jesus Christ our Lord.

[William Bright AC, SBH]

Eternal God,
    the light of the minds that you know,
    the joy of the hearts that love you,
    the strength of the wills that serve you:
Help us to know you that we may truly love you,
    so to love you that we may gladly serve you,
        to the glory of your holy Name. [St. Augustine]

Christ be with me, Christ within me,
Christ behind me, Christ before me.
Christ beside me, Christ to win me,
Christ to comfort and restore me,
Christ beneath me, Christ above me,
Christ in quiet, Christ in danger,
Christ in hearts of all who love me,
Christ in mouth of friend and stranger.

[Attributed to St. Patrick (*c.* 372-466) H82 370]

Lord, make us instruments of your peace.
    Where there is hatred, let sow love;
    where there is injury, pardon;
    where there is discord, union;
    where there is doubt, faith;
    where there is despair, hope;
    where there is darkness, light;
    where there is sadness, joy.
Grant that we may not so much seek
    to be consoled as to console;
    to be understood as to understand;
    to be loved as to love.

For it is giving that we receive;
    it is in pardoning that we are pardoned;
    and it is in dying that we are born to eternal life.

[Attributed to St. Francis of Assisi, 1182-1226, BCP]

Thanks be to thee, my Lord Jesus Christ,
For all the benefits which thou hast given me,
For all the pains and insults which thou hast borne for me.
O most merciful Redeemer, Friend, and Brother,
May I know thee more clearly,
    love thee more dearly,
    follow thee more nearly:
for ever and ever.

[attributed St. Richard of Chichester (1244), PP]

Soul of Christ, sanctify me;
Body of Christ, save me;
Blood of Christ, refresh me;
Water from the side of Christ, wash me;
Passion of Christ, strengthen me;
O good Jesus, hear me;
Within thy wounds hide me;
Suffer me not to be separated from thee;
From the malicious enemy defend me;
In the hour of my death call me,
And bid me come to thee,
That with thy saints I may praise thee;
Through the ages of eternity.

[*Anima Christi,* 14th century]

Teach us, good Lord, to serve you as you deserve:
to give and not to count the cost;
to fight and not to heed the wounds;
to toil and not to seek for rest;
to labor and not to ask for any reward,
save that of knowing that we do your will;
through Jesus Christ our Lord.

[St. Ignatius Loyola (1491-1556)]

For the gift of his Spirit:
Blessed be Christ.
For the Catholic Church:
Blessed be Christ,
For the means of grace:
Blessed be Christ.
For the hope of glory:
Blessed be Christ.
For the triumphs of his gospel:
Blessed be Christ.
For the lives of his saints:
Blessed be Christ.
In joy and in sorrow:
Blessed be Christ.
In life and in death:
Blessed be Christ.
Now and unto the end of the ages:
Blessed be Christ.

[*Cambridge Prayers and Orisons*, 1921]

God, be in my head:
    and in mine understanding.
God be in mine eyes:
    and in my looking.
God be in my mouth:
    and in my speaking.
God be in my heart:
    and in my thinking.
God be at mine end:
    and at my departing. [Sarum Primer, 1558]

After Praying the Office

Almighty Father, mercifully accept these our unworthy prayers, which we have offered to your divine Majesty; look not, we pray, on our faltering lips but heal our infirmities and receive our prayers for your mercies' sake, in Jesus Christ our Lord, who lives and reigns with you and the Holy Spirit, one God, now and for ever.

+

Accept, most merciful God, through the merits of your only Son Jesus Christ, this our duty and service. Whatever has been offered aright, graciously regard; wherein we have been negligent, mercifully pardon; who in the perfect Trinity live and reign one God for ever.

✠

The Office of the Dead

for Use after a Death
and
on the One Month and One Year Anniversary of a Death

MORNING PRAYER. MATINS

L O Lord, open my lips.
C And my mouth shall declare your praise.

C Glory to the Father, and to the Son, and to the Holy Spirit; as it was in the beginning, is now, and will be for ever. Amen.

The alleluia is omitted during Lent.

C Alleluia, allelula.

L Come, let us wor**ship** the Lord
C to whom **all** things live. [LH: Luke 20:38]

Come, let us sing **to** the LORD;*
let us shout for joy to the Rock of **our** salvation.
Let us come before his presence **with** thanksgiving*
and raise a loud shout to **him** with psalms.

For the LORD **is** a great God,*
and a great King a**bove** all gods.

In his hand are the caverns **of** the earth,*
and the heights of the hills **are** his also.
The sea is his, **for** he made it,*
and his hands have molded **the** dry land.

Come, let us bow down, and **bend** the knee,*
and kneel before the **LORD** our Maker.
For he is our God,
and we are the people of his pasture and the **sheep of** his hand.*
Oh, that today you would hearken **to** his voice!

Glory to the Father, and to the Son, and to the **Ho**ly Spirit;*
as it was in the beginning, is now, and will be for **ev**er. Amen.

L Come, let us wor**ship** the Lord
C To whom **all** things live.

Antiphon to Psalm 40 *Expectans. expectavi*

Be pleased, O LORD, to de**li**ver me;*
O LORD, make **haste** to help me. [LH]

40 *Thanksgiving and plea for help*

1 I waited patiently up**on** the LORD;*
he stooped to me and **heard** my cry.

2 He lifted me out of the desolate pit, out of the **mire** and clay;*
he set my feet upon a high cliff and made my **foot**ing sure.

3 He put a new song in my mouth,
a song of praise **to** our God;*
many shall see, and stand in awe,

and put their trust **in** the LORD.

4 Happy are they who trust **in** the LORD!*
they do not resort to evil spirits or turn **to** false gods.

5 Great things are they that you have done, O LORD my God!
how great your wonders and your **plans** for us!*
there is none who can be com**pared** with you.

6 Oh, that I could make them **known** and tell them!*
but they are more than **I** can count.

7 In sacrifice and offering you **take** no pleasure;*
(you have given me **ears** to hear you);

8 Burnt-offering and sin-offering you have **not** required,*
and so I said, "Be**hold**, I come.

9 In the roll of the book it is written con**cern**ing me:*
'I love to do your will, O my God;
your law is deep **in** my heart.'"

10 I proclaimed righteousness in the great **con**gregation;*
behold, I did not restrain my lips;
and that, O **LORD**, you know.

11 Your righteousness have I not hidden in my heart;
I have spoken of your faithfulness and **your** deliverance;*
I have not concealed your love and faithfulness from
the great **con**gregation.

12 You are the LORD;
do not withhold your com**pas**sion from me;*
let your love and your faithfulness keep me **safe** for ever,

13 For innumerable troubles have crowded upon me;
my sins have overtaken me, and I **can**not see;*
they are more in number than the hairs of my head,
and **my** heart fails me.

14 Be pleased, O LORD, to de**liv**er me;*
O LORD, make **haste** to help me.

15 Let them be ashamed and altogether dismayed
who seek after my life **to** destroy it;*
let them draw back and be disgraced
who take pleasure in **my** misfortune.

16 Let those who say "Aha!" and gloat over me **be** confounded,*
because they **are** ashamed.

17 Let all who seek you rejoice in you **and** be glad;*
let those who love your salvation continually say,
"Great **is** the LORD!"

18 Though I am poor **and** afflicted,*
the Lord will have re**gard** for me.

19 You are my helper and **my** deliverer;*
do not tarry, **O** my God.

Antiphon Be pleased, O LORD, to de**liv**er me;*
O LORD, make **haste** to help me.

Silence for meditation

Lord Jesus Christ, you became obedient to death and your Name was exalted above all others: Teach us always to do the Father's will, so that, made holy by your obedience and united to your sacrifice, we can know your great love in times of sorrow and sing a new song to our God now and for ever. [LH, LBW]

Antiphon to the OLD TESTAMENT CANTICLE

Ego dixi: In dimidio dierum

At the very thresh**old** of death,*
rescue **me**, O Lord. [LH]

The Song of Hezekiah Isaiah 38:10-14,17-20; LH

I said: In the noontide of my days I **must** depart;*
for the rest of my years
I am consigned to the gates **of** the grave.

I said, I shall see the LORD no more in the land **of** the living;*
no longer shall I look upon mortals
among the inhabitants **of** the world.

My dwelling, like a **shep**herd's tent,*
is struck down and borne a**way** from me;
You have folded up my life, **like** a weaver*
who cuts **off** the last thread.

Day and night you **tor**ment me;*
I cry for help un**til** the dawn.

Like a lion he breaks **all** my bones;
day and night you **tor**ment me.

Like a swallow I ut**ter** shrill cries,*
I moan **like** a dove.

My eyes are weary with **look**ing upward.*
O Lord, I am oppressed; be **my** security!

You have preserved my life from the pit **of** destruction; *
for you have cast all my sins be**hind** your back.

For the grave cannot thank you;
death **can**not praise you;*
neither do those who go down to the abyss
a**wait** your kindness.

The living, the living give you thanks, as I **do** today;*
fathers make known to their children your **faith**fulness.

The Lord **is** our Savior;
therefore let the music of our praises resound all our life long
in the house **of** the Lord. [LH, SBH, NSRV]

Antiphon At the very thresh**old** of death,*
rescue **me**, O Lord.

Silence for meditation

God our Creator and Redeemer, you formed us from the earth and clothed us with flesh: In your mercy do not forget us or leave us in the dust but raise us up at the last day to live for ever in your sight; through Jesus Christ our Lord. [LH antiphon alt. PHP]

Antiphon to Psalm 42 *Quemadmodum*

My soul is athirst for the **li**ving God;*
when shall I come to appear before the pres**ence** of God?
[LH, PBO]

42 *The exile's nostalgia for God's Temple*

1 As the deer longs for the **wa**ter-brooks,*
so longs my soul for **you**, O God.

2 My soul is athirst for God, athirst for the **li**ving God;*
when shall I come to appear before the pres**ence** of God?

3 My tears have been my food **day** and night,*
while all day long they say to me,
"Where now **is** your God?"

4 I pour out my soul when I think **on** these things;*
how I went with the multitude and led them into the
house of God,

5 With the voice of praise **and** thanksgiving,*
among those **who** keep holy-day.

6 Why are you so full of heaviness, **O** my soul?*
And why are you so disquiet**ed** within me?

7 Put your **trust** in God;*
for I will yet give thanks to him,
who is the help of my countenance, **and** my God.

8 My soul is heav**y** within me;*
therefore I will remember you from the land of Jordan,
and from the peak of Mizar among the **heights** of Hermon.

9 One deep calls to another in the noise **of** your cataracts;*
all your rapids and floods have gone **o**ver me.

10 The LORD grants his lovingkindness **in** the daytime;*
in the night season his song is with me,
a prayer to the God **of** my life.

11 I will say to the God of my strength,
"Why have you for**got**ten me,*
and why do I go so heavily while the enemy op**press**es me?"

12 While my bones are **be**ing broken,*
my enemies mock me **to** my face;

13 All day **long** they mock me*
and say to me, "Where now **is** your God?"

14 Why are you so full of heaviness, **O** my soul?*
and why are you so disquiet**ed** within me?

15 Put your **trust** in God;*
for I will yet give thanks to him,
who is the help of my countenance, **and** my God.

Antiphon My soul is athirst for God, athirst for the **liv**ing God;
when shall I come to appear before the
pre**sence** of God?

Silence for meditation

Lord God, never-failing fountain of life, through the saving waters of baptism you called us from the depth of sin to the depths of mercy: Do not forget the trials of our exile, but from the wellspring of the Word satisfy our thirst for you, so that we may come rejoicing to your holy mountain, where you live and reign now and for ever. [LHd, LBW]

The HYMN is sung. *Jesus lebt, mit ihm auch ich*

Jesus lives! no longer now
Can thy terrors, Death, appall us;
Jesus lives! by this we know
From the grave he will recall us.
Brighter scenes will then commence;
This shall be our confidence.

Jesus lives! to him the throne
High o'er heaven and earth is given;
We shall go where he is gone,
Live and reign with him in heaven,
God is pledged; weak doubtings, hence!
This shall be our confidence.

Jesus lives! we know full well,
Nought from us his love shall sever;
Life, nor death, nor powers of hell,
Part us now from Christ for ever.
God will be a sure defence:
This shall be our confidence.

Jesus lives! henceforth is death
But the gate of life immortal;
This shall calm our trembling breath
When we pass its gloomy portal;
Faith shall cry as fails each sense:
"Lord, thou art our confidence!" [CSB 512]

Text: Christian Fürchtegott Gellert, 1715-1769; tr. Frances Elizabeth Cox, 1812-1897
Tune: *Jesus, meine Zuversicht*, Johann Crüger, 1598-1662 78 78 77
[given above, p. 1286]

READING: Job 14:1-20

A mortal, born of woman, few of days and full of trouble, comes up like a flower and withers, flees like a shadow and does not last.

RESPONSORY

I know that my Redeemer lives,
and that at the last he will stand up**on** the earth;*
then in my flesh I **shall** see God,
whom I shall see on my side,
and my eyes shall behold, and **not** another.*
Then in my flesh I **shall** see God. [CSB, SBH, LH: Job 19:25-27]

READING: 2 Corinthians 4:16-5:10 [BCP Burial]

We know that if the earthly tent we live in is destroyed, we have a building from God, a house not made with hands, eternal in the heavens.

RESPONSORY

Since we believe that Jesus died and **rose** again,*
even so, through Jesus, God will bring with him those **who** have died.
Therefore **do** not grieve*
as others do who **have** no hope.
For as all **die** in Adam,*
so all will be made a**live** in Christ
Therefore **do** not grieve*
as others do who **have** no hope.
[CSB, SBH, LH: 1 Thess. 4:14, 13; 1 Cor. 15:22]

The BENEDICTUS follows with this ANTIPHON:

I am the resurrection and the life;
those who believe in me, even though they **die** will live,*
and everyone who lives and believes in me
will **nev**er die. [CSB, SBH, LH, PBO: John 11:25-26]

✠ Blessed be the Lord, the **God** of Israel;*
he has come to his people and **set** them free.
He has raised up for us a **might**y Savior,*
born of the house of his **ser**vant David.
Through his holy prophets he promised of old
that he would save us **from** our enemies,*
from the hands of **all** who hate us.
He has promised to show mercy **to** our fathers*
and to remember his **ho**ly covenant.
This was the oath he swore to our **fa**ther Abraham,*
to set us free from the hands **of** our enemies,
Free to worship him **with**out fear,*
holy and righteous in his sight
all the days **of** our life.

You, my child shall be called the prophet of **the** Most High,*
for you will go before the Lord to pre**pare** his way,
To give his people knowledge **of** salvation*
by the forgiveness **of** their sins.
In the tender compassion **of** our God*
the dawn from on high shall **break** upon us,
To shine on those who dwell in darkness and the shad**ow** of death,*
and to guide our feet into the **way** of peace.

Glory to the Father, and to the Son, and to the **Ho**ly Spirit:*
as it was in the beginning, is now, and will be for ev**er**. Amen.

Antiphon I am the resurrection and the life;
those who believe in me, even though they **die** will live,*
and everyone who lives and be**lieves** in me will **nev**er die.

The PRAYERS are said

L O God, the Father in heaven:
C Have mercy on us.

L O God the Son, Redeemer of the world:
C Have mercy on us.

L O God the Holy Spirit, the Comforter:
C Grant us your peace.

O Lord God, before whose face the generations rise and pass away, the Strength of those who labor, and the Repose of the blessed dead: we bless you for all your saints who have witnessed in their lives a good confession, and especially for those dear to us who have fallen asleep in you. Grant us grace, so to follow their good example, that we may be one with them in spirit, and finally be partakers with them in your eternal rest; through Jesus Christ our Lord.

[Paul Zeller Strodach, FSB, C&P, SBH]

Most mighty and ever-living God, by raising your Son from the dead you have planted in us the hope of your final victory: Give us, we pray, the fulfillment of our faith that those who have fallen asleep in the peace of Christ, and all the departed whose faith only you can know, will share the resurrection of your Son, Jesus Christ our Lord. [LH, PHP]

O God, you have brought us near to an innumerable company of angels and to the spirits of the righteous made perfect: Grant us during our early pilgrimage to abide in their fellowship, and in our heavenly country to become partakers of their joy; through Jesus Christ our Lord. [Heb. 12:23; William Bright AC, SBH]

God of all grace, you sent your Son, our Savior Jesus Christ, to bring life and immortality to light. We give you thanks that by his death he has destroyed the power of death, and by his glorious resurrection has opened the kingdom of heaven to all believers. Grant that we may know with certainty that because he lives we shall live also, and that neither death nor life, nor things present nor things to come, shall be able to separate us from your love, which is in Christ Jesus our Lord, who lives and reigns with you and the Holy Spirit, one God, now and for ever.

[2 Tim. 1:10, Rom. 8:38-39 *Book of Common Order* (Scotland 1940), SBH, LBW]
See also Proper 20, p. 621 and p. 1555 no. 55

C Our Father . . . .

L Eternal rest grant to *him/her*, O Lord;
C And let light perpetual shine upon *him/her*.

L May *his/her* soul(s), and the souls of all the faithful departed, through the mercy of God, rest in peace.
C Amen.

EVENING PRAYER. VESPERS

L Make haste, ✠ O God, to deliver me.
C O Lord, make haste to help me.
L Glory to the Father and to the Son, and to the Holy Spirit;
C As it was in the beginning, is now, and will be for ever. Amen.

Except in Lent, add Alleluia.

Antiphon to Psalm 90 *Domine, refugium*

So teach us to num**ber** our days*
that we may apply our **hearts** to wisdom. [CSB, SBH]

90 *The brevity of life*

1 Lord, you have **been** our refuge*
from one generation **to** another.

2 Before the mountains were brought forth,
or the land and the **earth** were born,*
from age to age **you** are God.

3 You turn us back to the **dust** and say,*
"Go back, O **child** of earth."

4 For a thousand years in your sight are like yesterday
when **it** is past*
and like a watch **in** the night.

5 You sweep us away **like** a dream;*
we fade away suddenly **like** the grass.

6 In the morning it is **green** and flourishes;*
in the evening it is dried **up** and withered.

7 For we consume away in **your** displeasure;*
we are afraid because of your wrathful **in**dignation.

8 Our iniquities you have **set** before you,*
and our secret sins in the light **of** your countenance.

9 When you are angry, all our **days** are gone;*
we bring our years to an end **like** a sigh.

10 The span of our life is seventy years,
perhaps in strength **e**ven eighty;*
yet the sum of them is but labor and sorrow,
for they pass away quickly and **we** are gone.

11 Who regards the power **of** your wrath?*
who rightly fears your **in**dignation?

12 So teach us to num**ber** our days,*
that we may apply our **hearts** to wisdom.

13 Return, O LORD; how long **will** you tarry?*
be gracious **to** your servants.

14 Satisfy us by your lovingkindness **in** the morning;*
so shall we rejoice and be glad all the days **of** our life.

15 Make us glad by the measure of the days that you af**flict**ed us*
and the years in which we suf**fered** adversity.

16 Show your ser**vants** your works*
and your splendor **to** their children.

17 May the graciousness of the LORD our God **be** upon us;*
prosper the work of our hands;
pros**per** our handiwork.

Antiphon So teach us to num**ber** our days*
that we may apply our **hearts** to wisdom.

Silence for meditation.

Eternal Father of our mortal race, despite our sin you give us life and even add days and years to our lives to bring us to wisdom: Help us to consider the shortness of our life that we may acknowledge our dependence upon you until the day when we look upon the beauty of your face; through Jesus Christ our Lord. [LH, PHP]

Antiphon to Psalm 130 *De profundis*

If you, Lord, were to note what is **done** amiss,*
O Lord, **who** could stand? [CSB, SBH, LH]

130 *A cry from the depths*

1 Out of the depths have I called to you, O LORD;
LORD, **hear** my voice;*
let your ears consider well the voice of my **sup**plication.

2 If you, LORD, were to note what is **done** amiss,*
O LORD, **who** could stand?

3 For there is forgive**ness** with you;*
therefore you **shall** be feared.

4 I wait for the LORD; my soul **waits** for him;*
in his word is my hope.

5 My soul waits for the LORD,
more than watchmen **for** the morning,*
more than watchmen **for** the morning.

6 O Israel, wait **for** the LORD,*
for with the LORD **there** is mercy;

7 With him there is plen**te**ous redemption,*
and he shall redeem Israel from **all** their sins.

Antiphon If you, Lord were to note what is **done** amiss,*
O Lord, **who** could stand?

Silence for meditation

God of might and compassion, you sent your Word into the world as a watchman to announce the dawn of salvation: Do not leave us in the depths of our sins, but listen to your Church pleading for the fullness of your redeeming grace; through Jesus Christ our Lord. [LHd, LBW]

Antiphon to Psalm 121 *Levavi oculos*

The Lord shall preserve you **from** all evil;*
it is he who shall **keep** you safe. [LH, PBO]

121 *Guardian of God's people*

1 I lift up my eyes **to** the hills;*
from where is my **help** to come?

2 My help comes **from** the LORD,*
the maker of heav**en** and earth.

3 He will not let your **foot** be moved*
and he who watches over you will not **fall** asleep.

4 Behold, he who keeps watch **o**ver Israel*
shall neither slum**ber** nor sleep;

5 The LORD himself watches **o**ver you;*
the LORD is your shade at **your** right hand,

6 So that the sun shall not strike **you** by day,*
nor the **moon** by night.

7 The LORD shall preserve you **from** all evil;*
it is he who shall **keep** you safe.

8 The LORD shall watch over your going out and your **com**ing in,*
from this time forth for **ev**ermore.

Antiphon The Lord shall preserve you **from** all evil;*
it is he who shall **keep** you safe.

Silence for meditation

Lord Jesus Christ, you have prepared a quiet place for us in your Father's eternal home: Watch over our welfare on this perilous journey, shade us from the burning heat of day, and keep our lives free of evil now and for ever. [LH, LBW]

The HYMN is sung.

God of the living, in whose eyes
Unveiled thy whole creation lies,
All souls are thine; we must not say
That those are dead who pass away,
From this our world of flesh set free;
We know them living unto thee.

Released from earthly toil and stife,
With thee is hidden still their life;
Thine are their thoughts, their works, their powers,
All thine, and yet most truly ours;
For well we know where'er they be,
Our dead are living unto thee.

Not split like water on the ground,
Not wrapped in dreamless sleep profound,
Not wandering in unknown despair
Beyond thy voice, thine arm, thy care;
Not left to lie like fallen tree;
Not dead but living unto thee.

Thy Word is true, thy will is just,
To thee we leave them, Lord, in trust,
And bless thee for the love which gave
Thy Son to fill a human grave,
That none might fear that world to see
Where all are living unto thee.

O Breather into us our breath,
O Holder of the keys of death,
O Giver of the life within,
Save us from death, the death of sin;
That body, soul, and spirit be
For ever living unto the. [CSB 508]

Text: John Ellerton, 1826-1893
Tune: *David's Harp*, Robert King, *The Divine Companion* 1722 88 88 88

READING: John 14:1-6 [CSB, SBH, PBO]

If I go and prepare a place for you, I will come again and take you to myself, so that where I am, there you may be also.

RESPONSORY

I will lay me down in **peace** and sleep.*
We do not live to ourselves,
and we do not die **to** ourselves.*
Whether we live or whether we die,
we **are** the Lord's.*
We do not live to ourselves,
and we do not die **to** ourselves. [CSB, SBH: Romans 14:7-8]

The MAGNIFICAT follows with this ANTIPHON:

Everything that the Father gives me will **come** to me,*
and anyone who comes to me I will never **drive** away.
[LH, PBO: John 6:37]

✠ My soul proclaims the greatness of the Lord,
my spirit rejoices in **God** my savior;*
for he has looked with favor on his **low**ly servant.
From this day all generations will **call** me blessed:*
the Almighty has done great things for me,
and holy **is** his Name.
He has mercy on **those** who fear him*
in every **gen**eration.
He has shown the strength **of** his arm,*
he has scattered the proud in **their** conceit.
He has cast down the mighty **from** their thrones,*
and has lifted **up** the lowly.
He has filled the hungry **with** good things,*
and the rich he has sent **a**way empty.

He has come to the help of his **ser**vant Israel,*
for he has remembered his prom**ise** of mercy,
The promise he made **to** our fathers,*
to Abraham and his chil**dren** for ever.

Glory to the Father, and to the Son, and to the **Ho**ly Spirit:*
as it was in the beginning, is now, and will be for ev**er**. Amen.

Antiphon
Everything that the Father gives me will **come** to me,*
and anyone who comes to me I will never **drive** away.

The PRAYERS are said.

In the midst of life we are in death;
from whom we may seek for succor,
but from you, O Lord,
who for our sins are justly displeased?

Yet, O Lord God most holy, O Lord most mighty,
O holy and most merciful Savior,
deliver us not into the bitter pains of eternal death.

You know, Lord, the secrets of our hearts;
shut not your merciful ears to our prayer;
but spare us, Lord most holy, O God most mighty,
O holy and merciful Savior,
most worthy Judge eternal.
Suffer us not, at our last hour,
through any pains of death, to fall you.

[attrib. Notker A.D. 912; Luther; BCP]

Eternal Lord God, you hold all souls in life. We beseech you to shed forth upon your whole Church in paradise and on earth the bright beams of your light and heavenly comfort; and grant that we, following the good example of those who have loved and served you here and are now at rest, may at last enter with them into the fullness of your unending joy; through Jesus Christ our Lord.

[John Wordsworth, BCPp]

Our Father . . . .

L Eternal rest grant to *him/her*, O Lord;
C and let light perpetual shine upon *him/her*.

L May *his/her* soul, and the souls of all the faithful departed,
through the mercy of God, rest in peace.
C Amen.

ATHANASIAN CREED
Quicunque Vult

Whoever wants to be saved should above all cling to the cat**ho**lic faith.*
Whoever does not guard it whole and inviolable
will doubtless per**ish** eternally.

Now this is the cath**o**lic faith:*
We worship one God in trinity
and the Trini**ty** in unity,

neither confus**ing** the persons*
nor dividing the **di**vine being.

For the Father **is** one person,*
the Son is another,
and the Spirit is **still** another.

But the deity of the Father, Son, and Holy Spir**it** is one,*
equal in glory,
coeter**nal** in majesty.

What the **Fa**ther is,*
the Son is, and so is the **Ho**ly Spirit.

Uncreated **is** the Father;*
uncreated is the Son;
uncreated **is** the Spirit.

The Father is **in**finite;*
the Son is infinite;
the Holy Spir**it** is infinite.

Eternal **is** the Father;*
eternal is the Son;
eternal **is** the Spirit:

And yet there are not three e**ter**nal beings,*
but one who **is** eternal;

as there are not three uncreated and unlim**it**ed beings,*
but one who is uncreated **and** unlimited.

Almighty **is** the Father;*
almighty is the Son;
almighty **is** the Spirit:

And yet there are not three al**might**y beings,*
but one who **is** almighty.

Thus the Fa**ther** is God;*
the Son is God;
the Holy Spir**it** is God:

And yet there are **not** three gods,*
but one God.

Thus the Fa**ther** is Lord;*
the Son is Lord;
the Holy Spir**it** is Lord:

And yet there are **not** three lords,*
but one Lord.

As Christian truth compels us to acknowledge each distinct person as **God** and Lord,*
so catholic religion forbids us
to say that there are three **gods** or lords.

The Father was **nei**ther made*
    nor created **nor** begotten;

the Son was neither made **nor** created,*
    but was alone begotten **of** the Father;

the Spirit was neither made **nor** created,*
    but is proceeding from the Father **and** the Son.

Thus there is one Father, **not** three fathers;*
    one Son, not three sons;
    one Holy Spirit, **not** three spirits.

And in this Trinity, no one is be**fore** or after,*
    greater or less **than** the other;

but **all** three persons*
    are in themselves coeternal **and** coequal;

and so we must worship the Trini**ty** in unity*
    and the one God **in** three persons.

Whoever wants **to** be saved*
    should think thus a**bout** the Trinity.

It is necessary for eter**nal** salvation*
    that one also faithfully believe that our Lord Jesus Christ **be**came flesh.

For this is the true faith that we believe **and** confess:*
    That our Lord Jesus Christ, God's Son, is both **God** and man.

He is God, begotten before all worlds from the being **of** the Father,*
    and he is man, born in the world from the being **of** his mother—

existing fully as God and ful**ly** as man*
    with a rational soul and a **hu**man body;

equal to the Father **in** divinity,*
subordinate to the Father **in** humanity.

Although he is **God** and man,*
he is not divided, but **is** one Christ.

He is united because God has taken humanity in**to** himself;*
he does not transform deity in**to** humanity.

He is completely one in the unity **of** his person,*
without confus**ing** his natures.

For as the rational soul and body **are** one person,*
so the one Christ is **God** and man.

He suffered death for **our** salvation.*
He descended into hell and rose again **from** the dead.

He ascended **in**to heaven*
and is seated at the right hand **of** the Father.

He will come again to judge the living **and** the dead.*
At his coming all people shall rise bodily
to give an account of **their** own deeds.

Those who have done good will enter e**ter**nal life,*
those who have done evil will enter e**ter**nal fire.

This is the cath**o**lic faith.*
One cannot be saved without believing this firm**ly** and faithfully.

[tr. Ralph Quere, LBW]

Instead of silence for meditation, these anthems are said:

Blessed and glorious Trinity, Father, Son, and Holy Spirit,
thanks be to you, true and one Trinity,
one and perfect Godhead.

We confess you God the Father unbegotten,
you the only-begotten Son,
you the Holy Spirit the Paraclete.

Holy and undivided Trinity
we praise you with heart and voice;
to you be glory for ever. [Sarum, AC]

O God, you have made yourself known to us as Trinity in Unity and Unity in Trinity in order that we may be informed of your love and majesty: Mercifully grant that we may not be terrified by what you have revealed of your majesty, nor tempted to trespass upon your mercy by what we know of your love for us; but that by the power of your Holy Spirit we may be ever drawn to you in true adoration and worship; for you live and reign, one God, now and for ever.
[*Euchologium Anglicanum*]

Psalm Tones with Antiphons

Antiphon

1

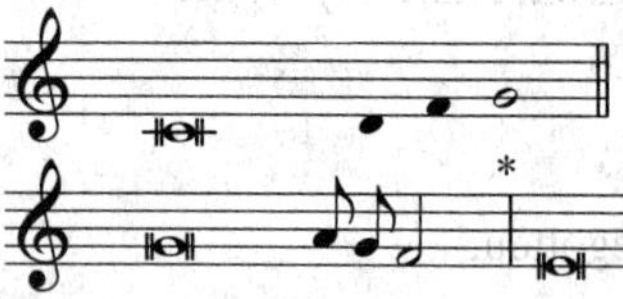

Antiphon

2

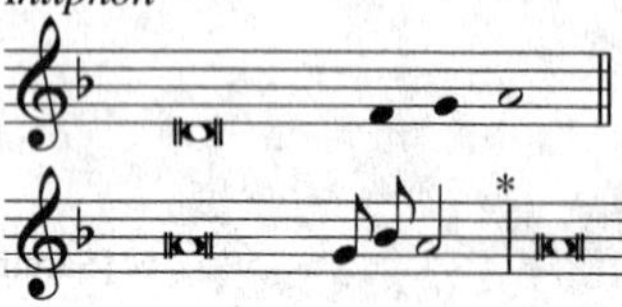

Antiphon

3

Antiphon

4

Antiphon

5

Antiphon

6

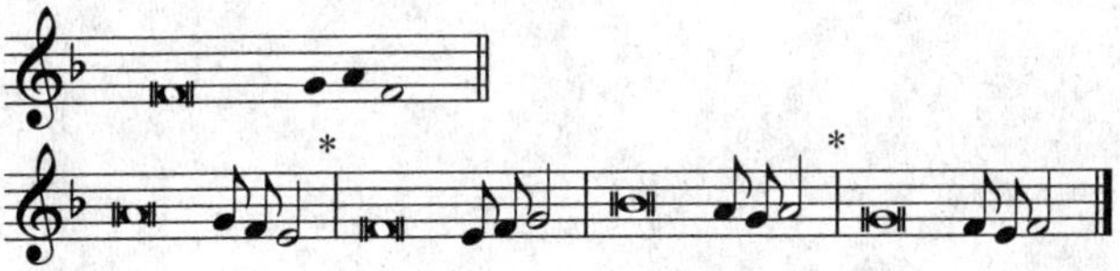

Antiphon

7

Antiphon

8

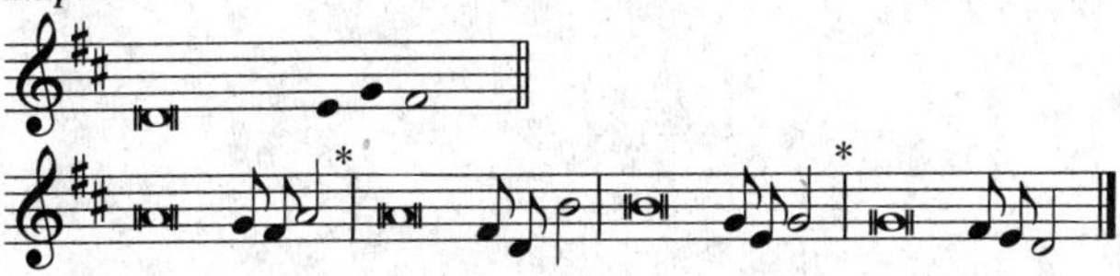

Antiphon

9

Antiphon

10

Additional Tones, for use with canticles and the Athanasian Creed, may be found on pp.11, 86-87, 89, 97.

Index of Psalms

Index of Canticles

a. alphabetical index of canticles

b. Biblical index of canticles

Index of Hymns
[English and Latin first lines]